| | | |
|---|---|---|
| computing | | |
| pejorative | *pej, péj* | péjoratif |
| philosophy | *Phil* | philosophie |
| photography | *Photo* | photographie |
| plural | *pl* | pluriel |
| politics | *Pol* | politique |
| possessive | *poss* | possessif |
| past participle | *pp* | participe passé |
| prefix | *pref, préf* | préfixe |
| preposition | *prep, prép* | préposition |
| present participle | *pres p* | participe présent |
| pronoun | *pron* | pronom |
| psychology | *Psych* | psychologie |
| past | *pt* | prétérit |
| something | *qch* | quelque chose |
| somebody | *qn* | quelqu'un |
| railway | *Rail* | chemin de fer |
| relative pronoun | *rel pron, pron rel* | pronom relatif |
| religion | *Relig* | religion |
| somebody | *sb* | quelqu'un |
| school | *School, Scol* | scolaire |
| sport | *Sport* | sport |
| something | *sth* | quelque chose |
| technology | *Tech* | technologie |
| theatre | *Theat, Théât* | théâtre |
| television | *TV* | télévision |
| university | *Univ* | université |
| American English | *US* | anglais américain |
| auxiliary verb | *v aux* | verbe auxiliaire |
| intransitive verb | *vi* | verbe intransitif |
| reflexive verb | *vpr* | verbe pronominal |
| transitive verb | *vt* | verbe transitif |
| transitive and intransitive verb | *vt/i* | verbe transitif et intransitif |
| approximate translation | ≈ | équivalent approximatif |
| trademark | ® | marque déposée |
| colloquial | ▣ | familier |
| slang | ▣ | argot |

# Oxford
# French
# Mini Dictionary

## FIFTH EDITION

French–English
English–French

Français–Anglais
Anglais–Français

OXFORD
UNIVERSITY PRESS

# OXFORD

UNIVERSITY PRESS

Great Clarendon Street, Oxford OX2 6DP

Oxford University Press is a department of the University of Oxford.
It furthers the University's objective of excellence in research, scholarship,
and education by publishing worldwide in

Oxford New York

Auckland Cape Town Dar es Salaam Hong Kong Karachi Kuala Lumpur
Madrid Melbourne Mexico City Nairobi New Delhi Shanghai Taipei
Toronto

With offices in
Argentina Austria Brazil Chile Czech Republic France Greece
Guatemala Hungary Italy Japan Poland Portugal
Singapore South Korea Switzerland Thailand Turkey Ukraine Vietnam

Oxford is a registered trade mark of Oxford University Press
in the UK and in certain other countries

Published in the United States
by Oxford University Press Inc., New York

© Oxford University Press 1986, 1993, 1999, 2005, 2009

British Library Cataloguing in Publication Data
Data available

Library of Congress Cataloging in Publication Data
Data available

ISBN 978-0-19-953436-4

10 9 8 7 6 5 4 3 2 1

Typeset by Interactive Sciences Ltd, Gloucester
Printed in Italy
by L.E.G.O. S.p.A., Lavis (TN)

# Contents/Table des matières

## Proprietary terms

This dictionary includes some words which are, or are asserted to be, proprietary terms or trademarks. The presence or absence of such assertions should not be regarded as affecting the legal status of any proprietary name or trademark. In cases where the editorial staff has evidence that a word is used as a proprietary name or trademark, this is indicated by the symbol ®. No judgement concerning the legal status of such words is made or implied thereby.

## Les marques déposées

Les mots qui, à notre connaissance, sont considérés comme des marques ou des noms déposés sont signalés dans cet ouvrage par ®. La présence ou l'absence de cette mention ne peut pas être considérée comme ayant valeur juridique.

# Contributors/Collaborateurs

### Fifth Edition/
### Cinquième édition

Joanna Rubery

Isabelle Stables-Lemoine

**Proofreader/Correcteur**

Amanda Leigh

### Fourth Edition/
### Quatrième édition

Nicholas Rollin

Jean Benoit Ormal-Grenon

**Data capture/
Saisie des données**

Susan Wilkin

**Proofreaders/Correcteurs**

Isabelle Stables-Lemoine

Meic Haines

Mary O'Neill

### Third Edition/
### Troisième édition

Isabelle Stables-Lemoine

Marianne Chalmers

Rosalind Combley

Catherine Roux

Laura Wedgeworth

**Phrasefinder/
Mini guide de conversation**

Hélène Haenen

Neil and Roswitha Morris

### First and Second Edition/
### Première et deuxième
### éditions

Michael Janes

Dora Latiri-Carpenter

Edwin Carpenter

# Introduction

This new edition of the *Oxford French Mini Dictionary* has been designed to be a practical reference tool for the student, adult learner, traveller and business professional. It provides user-friendly treatment of core vocabulary across a broad spectrum of written and spoken language.

## Enhanced coverage

The wordlist has been revised to reflect recent additions to both languages. The *Phrasefinder* has been expanded and enables the user to communicate in commonly encountered situations such as travel, shopping, eating out, and organizing leisure activities.

The more complex grammatical words, or *function words*, are given special treatment in highlighted entries to make them easily accessible. All verbs in the French-English section are cross-referenced to the verb tables at the end of the book. Here information is given on regular, irregular and reflexive verbs as well as the translation of French verb tenses.

## Easy reference

The dictionary layout has been designed to be clear, streamlined and easy to use. Bullet points separate each new part of speech within an entry. Nuances of meaning or usage are pinpointed by semantic indicators or by typical collocates with which the headword frequently occurs. Extra help is given with symbols to mark the register of language. A boxed exclamation mark ▣ indicates colloquial language and a cross ▣ indicates slang.

The pronunciation of French is given in the International Phonetic Alphabet. Irregular parts of French verbs appear as headwords with a cross-reference to the main entry of the verb.

# Pronunciation of French

| a | *as in* | patte | /pat/ | ɑ | *as in* | pâte | /pɑt/ |
|---|---|---|---|---|---|---|---|
| ã | | clan | /klã/ | e | | dé | /de/ |
| ɛ | | belle | /bɛl/ | ɛ̃ | | lin | /lɛ̃/ |
| ə | | demain | /dəmɛ̃/ | i | | gris | /gʀi/ |
| o | | gros | /gʀo/ | ɔ | | corps | /kɔʀ/ |
| ɔ̃ | | long | /lɔ̃/ | œ | | leur | /lœʀ/ |
| œ̃ | | brun | /bʀœ̃/ | ø | | deux | /dø/ |
| u | | fou | /fu/ | y | | pur | /pyʀ/ |

## Semi-Vowels

| j | *as in* | fille | /fij/ |
|---|---|---|---|
| ɥ | | huit | /ɥit/ |
| w | | oui | /wi/ |

## Consonants

Aspiration of 'h'
Where it is impossible to make a liaison this is indicated by /'/
immediately after the slash e.g. haine /'ɛn/.

| b | *as in* | bal | /bal/ | ŋ | *as in* | camping | /kãpiŋ/ |
|---|---|---|---|---|---|---|---|
| d | | dent | /dã/ | p | | porte | /pɔʀt/ |
| f | | foire | /fwaʀ/ | R | | rire | /ʀiʀ/ |
| g | | gomme | /gɔm/ | s | | sang | /sã/ |
| k | | clé | /kle/ | ʃ | | chien | /ʃjɛ̃/ |
| l | | lien | /ljɛ̃/ | t | | train | /tʀɛ̃/ |
| m | | mer | /mɛʀ/ | v | | voile | /vwal/ |
| n | | nage | /naʒ/ | z | | zèbre | /zɛbʀ/ |
| ɲ | | oignon | /ɲɔ̃/ | ʒ | | jeune | /ʒœn/ |

# Introduction

Cette nouvelle édition de l'*Oxford French Mini Dictionary* a été conçue comme un outil de référence practique destiné aux étudiants, aux touristes et aux professionnels. Il offre un traitement convivial du vocabulaire de base représentatif de la langue écrite et parlée.

### Une édition augmentée

La nomenclature a été revisée de façon à refléter les récents apports de vocabulaire dans les deux langues. La partie centrale intitulée *Mini guide de conversation* aidera l'utilisateur à communiquer dans les situations les plus courantes telles que le voyage, le shopping, les sorties au restaurant ou les loisirs.

Les mots grammaticaux, qui forment les structures de base des deux langues, font l'objet d'une présentation distincte qui les rend rapidement accessibles, les choix de traduction et les exemples étant clairement signalés. De courtes notes d'usage indiquent les pièges éventuels. Une liste de verbes irréguliers anglais se trouve à la fin de l'ouvrage.

### Une consultation facilitée

La présentation du dictionnaire a été conçue de façon à être claire, simplifiée et à faciliter la consultation de l'ouvrage. Des puces séparent chaque nouvelle partie du discours à l'intérieur d'une entrée, ce qui facilite leur repérage. Les nuances de sens ou d'usage sont marquées au moyen d'indicateurs sémantiques ou par des collocateurs types avec lesquels le mot s'emploie fréquemment, guidant ainsi rapidement l'utilisateur à la traduction appropriée. Un point d'exclamation 🗓 indique un niveau de langue familier et une croix 🗙 indique un niveau argotique.

Les symboles utilisés pour la prononciation sont ceux de l'Alphabet Phonétique International. Les pluriels irréguliers ainsi que les conjugaisons ou les formes du comparatif et du superlatif irrégulières anglaises sont indiqués entre parenthèses.

# La prononciation de l'anglais

Voyelles et diphtongues

| | | | | | | | |
|---|---|---|---|---|---|---|---|
| iː | see | ɔː | saw | eɪ | page | ɔɪ | join |
| ɪ | sit | ʊ | put | əʊ | home | ɪə | near |
| e | ten | uː | too | aɪ | five | eə | hair |
| æ | hat | ʌ | cup | aɪə | fire | ʊə | poor |
| ɑː | arm | ɜː | fur | aʊ | now | | |
| ɒ | got | ə | ago | aʊə | flour | | |

## Consonnes

| | | | | | | | |
|---|---|---|---|---|---|---|---|
| p | pen | tʃ | chin | s | so | n | no |
| b | bad | dʒ | June | z | zoo | ŋ | sing |
| t | tea | f | fall | ʃ | she | l | leg |
| d | dip | v | voice | ʒ | measure | r | red |
| k | cat | θ | thin | h | how | j | yes |
| g | got | ð | then | m | man | w | wet |

## L'accent d'intensité

L'accent d'intensité est indiqué au moyen du signe /'/, placé devant la syllabe qu'il affecte.

**a** /a/ ➞AVOIR **5**.

## à /a/

● **préposition**

à+le = **au**
à+les = **aux**

····▸ (avec verbe de mouvement) to.

····▸ (pour indiquer où l'on se trouve) ~ **la maison** at home; ~ **Nice** in Nice.

····▸ (âge, date, heure) ~ **l'âge de...** at the age of...; **au XIXe siècle** in the 19th century; ~ **deux heures** at two o'clock.

····▸ (description) with; **aux yeux verts** with green eyes.

····▸ (appartenance) ~ **qui est ce stylo?** whose pen is this?; **c'est ~ vous?** is this yours?

····▸ (avec nombre) ~ **90 km/h** at 90 km per hour; ~ **10 minutes d'ici** 10 minutes from here; **des tomates ~ 2 euros le kilo** tomatoes at 2 euros a kilo; **un timbre ~ 2 euros** a 2-euro stamp; **nous avons fait le travail ~ deux** two of us did the work; **mener 5 ~ 4** to lead 5 (to) 4.

····▸ (avec être) **c'est ~ moi** it's my turn; **je suis ~ vous tout de suite** I'll be with you in a minute; **c'est ~ toi de décider** it's up to you to decide.

····▸ (hypothèse) ~ **ce qu'il paraît** apparently; ~ **t'entendre** to hear you talk.

····▸ (exclamatif) ~ **ta santé!** cheers!; ~ **demain/bientôt!** see you tomorrow/soon!

····▸ (moyen) ~ **la main** by hand; ~ **vélo** by bike; ~ **pied** on foot; **chauffage au gaz** gas heating.

**abaissement** /abεsmɑ̃/ *nm* (de taux, de prix) cut; (de seuil) lowering.

**abaisser** /abese/ **1** *vt* lower; (*levier*) pull *ou* push down; (fig) humiliate. □ **s'~** *vpr* go down, drop; (fig) demean oneself; **s'~ à** to stoop to.

**abandon** /abɑ̃dɔ̃/ *nm* abandonment; (de personne) desertion; (de course) withdrawal; (naturel) abandon; **à l'~** in a state of neglect.

**abandonner** /abɑ̃dɔne/ **1** *vt* abandon; (épouse, cause) desert; (renoncer à) give up, abandon; (céder) give (à to); (course) withdraw from; (Ordinat) abort. □ **s'~** *vpr* give oneself up to.

**abasourdir** /abazuʀdiʀ/ **2** *vt* stun.

**abat-jour** /abaʒuʀ/ *nm inv* lampshade.

**abats** /aba/ *nmpl* offal.

**abattement** /abatmɑ̃/ *nm* dejection; (faiblesse) exhaustion; (Comm) reduction; ~ **fiscal** tax allowance.

**abattre** /abatʀ/ **11** *vt* knock down; (arbre) cut down; (animal) slaughter; (avion) shoot down; (affaiblir) weaken; (démoraliser) demoralize; **ne pas se laisser ~** not let things get one down. □ **s'~** *vpr* come down, fall (down).

**abbaye** /abei/ *nf* abbey.

**abbé** /abe/ *nm* priest; (supérieur d'une abbaye) abbot.

**abcès** /apsɛ/ *nm* abscess.

**abdiquer** /abdike/ **1** *vt/i* abdicate.

**abdomen** /abdɔmɛn/ *nm* abdomen.

**abdominal** (*pl* -aux) /abdɔminal/ *adj* abdominal. **abdominaux** *nmpl* (Sport) stomach exercises.

**abeille** /abɛj/ *nf* bee.

**aberrant,** ~e /abɛʀɑ̃, -t/ *adj* absurd.

**abêtir** /abetiʀ/ **2** *vt* turn into a moron.

**abîme** /abim/ *nm* abyss.

**abîmer** /abime/ **1** *vt* damage, spoil. □ s'~ *vpr* get damaged *ou* spoilt.

**ablation** /ablasjɔ̃/ *nf* removal.

**aboiement** /abwamɑ̃/ *nm* bark, barking; ~s barking.

**abolir** /abɔliʀ/ **2** *vt* abolish.

**abondance** /abɔ̃dɑ̃s/ *nf* abundance; (prospérité) affluence. **abondant,** ~e *adj* abundant, plentiful.

**abonder** /abɔ̃de/ **1** *vi* abound (en in); ~ dans le sens de qn agree wholeheartedly with sb.

**abonné,** ~e /abɔne/ *nm, f* (lecteur) subscriber; (voyageur, spectateur) season-ticket holder.

**abonnement** /abɔnmɑ̃/ *nm* (à un journal) subscription; (de bus, Théât) season-ticket; (au gaz) standing charge.

**abonner (s')** /(s)abɔne/ **1** *vpr* subscribe (à to).

**abord** /abɔʀ/ *nm* access; ~s surroundings; d'~ first.

**abordable** /abɔʀdabl/ *adj* (prix) affordable; (personne) approachable; (texte) accessible.

**aborder** /abɔʀde/ **1** *vt* approach; (lieu) reach; (problème) tackle. ● *vi* reach land.

**aborigène** /abɔʀiʒɛn/ *nm* aborigine.

**aboutir** /abutiʀ/ **2** *vi* succeed, achieve a result; ~ à end (up) in, lead to; n'~ à rien come to nothing.

**aboutissement** /abutismɑ̃/ *nm* outcome; (de carrière, d'évolution) culmination.

**aboyer** /abwaje/ **31** *vi* bark.

**abrégé** /abʀeʒe/ *nm* summary.

**abréger** /abʀeʒe/ **14 40** *vt* (texte) shorten, abridge; (mot) abbreviate, shorten; (visite) cut short.

**abreuver** /abʀœve/ **1** *vt* water; (fig) overwhelm (de with). □ s'~ *vpr* drink.

**abréviation** /abʀevjasjɔ̃/ *nf* abbreviation.

**abri** /abʀi/ *nm* shelter; à l'~ under cover; (en lieu sûr) safe; à l'~ de sheltered from; se mettre à l'~ take shelter.

**abricot** /abʀiko/ *nm* apricot.

**abriter** /abʀite/ **1** *vt* shelter; (recevoir) house. □ s'~ *vpr* (take) shelter.

**abrupt,** ~e /abʀypt/ *adj* steep, sheer; (fig) abrupt.

**abruti,** ~e /abʀyti/ *nm, f* 🎇 idiot.

**absence** /apsɑ̃s/ *nf* absence; il a des ~s sometimes his mind goes blank.

**absent,** ~e /apsɑ̃, -t/ *adj* (personne) absent, away; (chose) missing; il est toujours ~ he's still away; d'un air ~ absently. ● *nm, f* absentee.

**absenter (s')** /(s)apsɑ̃te/ **1** *vpr* go *ou* be away; (sortir) go out, leave.

**absolu,** ~e /apsɔly/ *adj* absolute.

**absorbant,** ~e /apsɔʀbɑ̃, -t/ *adj*

(*travail*) absorbing; (*matière*) absorbent.

**absorber** /apsɔʀbe/ **1** *vt* absorb; être absorbé par qch be engrossed in sth.

**abstenir (s')** /(s)apstəniʀ/ **58** *vpr* abstain; s'~ de refrain from.

**abstrait**, ~e /apstʀɛ, -t/ *adj & nm* abstract.

**absurde** /apsyʀd/ *adj* absurd.

**abus** /aby/ *nm* abuse, misuse; (*injustice*) abuse; ~ de confiance breach of trust.

**abuser** /abyze/ **1** *vt* deceive. ●*vi* go too far; ~ de abuse, misuse; (*profiter de*) take advantage of; (*alcool*) overindulge. □ s'~ *vpr* be mistaken.

**abusif**, **-ive** /abyzif, -v/ *adj* excessive; (*impropre*) wrong; (*injuste*) unfair.

**académie** /akademi/ *nf* academy; (*circonscription*) local education authority.

---

**Académie française** A  ***i***
scholarly body composed of 40 life members selected on the basis of their contribution to scholarship or literature. It monitors developments in the French language and rules on French usage, as encoded in the *Dictionnaire de l'Académie française* (which is not always taken seriously by the public at large).

---

**acajou** /akaʒu/ *nm* mahogany.

**accablant**, ~e /akablɑ̃, -t/ *adj* (*chaleur*) oppressive; (*fait, témoignage*) damning.

**accabler** /akable/ **1** *vt* overwhelm; ~ d'impôts burden with taxes; ~ d'injures heap insults upon.

**accéder** /aksede/ **14** *vi* ~ à (*lieu*)

reach; (*pouvoir, trône*) accede to; (*requête*) grant; (*Ordinat*) access; ~ à la propriété become a homeowner.

**accélérateur** /akseleʀatœʀ/ *nm* accelerator.

**accélérer** /akseleʀe/ **14** *vt*/*i* accelerate. □ s'~ *vpr* speed up.

**accent** /aksɑ̃/ *nm* accent; (sur une syllabe) stress, accent; mettre l'~ sur stress; ~ aigu/grave/circonflexe acute/grave/circumflex accent.

**accentuer** /aksɑ̃tɥe/ **1** *vt* (*lettre, syllabe*) accent; (fig) emphasize, accentuate. □ s'~ *vpr* become more pronounced, increase.

**accepter** /aksɛpte/ **1** *vt* accept; ~ de faire agree to do.

**accès** /aksɛ/ *nm* access; (porte) entrance; (de fièvre) bout; (de colère) fit; (d'enthousiasme) burst; (Ordinat) access; les ~ de (voies) the approaches to; facile d'~ easy to get to.

**accessoire** /akseswaʀ/ *adj* secondary, incidental. ●*nm* accessory; (Théât) prop.

**accident** /aksidɑ̃/ *nm* accident; ~ de train/d'avion train/plane crash; par ~ by accident. **accidenté**, ~e *adj* (*personne*) injured (in an accident); (voiture) damaged; (terrain) uneven, hilly. **accidentel**, ~le *adj* accidental.

**acclamer** /aklame/ **1** *vt* cheer, acclaim.

**accommoder** /akɔmɔde/ **1** *vt* adapt (à to); (cuisiner) prepare; (assaisonner) flavour. □ s'~ de *vpr* make the best of.

**accompagnateur**, **-trice** /akɔ̃paɲatœʀ, -tʀis/ *nm, f* (Mus) accompanist; (guide) guide; ~ d'enfants accompanying adult.

**a** **accompagner** /akɔ̃paɲe/ **1** vt accompany. □ s'~ de vpr be accompanied by.

**accomplir** /akɔ̃plir/ **2** vt carry out, fulfil. □ s'~ vpr take place, happen; (vœu) be fulfilled.

**accord** /akɔr/ nm agreement; (harmonie) harmony; (Mus) chord; être d'~ agree (pour to); se mettre d'~ come to an agreement, agree; d'~! all right ①, OK!

**accorder** /akɔrde/ **1** vt grant; (couleurs) match; (Mus) tune; (attribuer) (valeur, importance) assign. □ s'~ (se mettre d'accord) agree; (s'octroyer) allow oneself; s'~ avec (s'entendre avec) get on with.

**accotement** /akɔtmɑ̃/ nm verge; ~ non stabilisé soft verge.

**accouchement** /akuʃmɑ̃/ nm childbirth; (travail) labour.

**accoucher** /akuʃe/ **1** vi give birth (de to); (être en travail) be in labour. ● vt deliver. **accoucheur** nm médecin ~ obstetrician.

**accoudoir** /akudwar/ nm arm-rest.

**accoupler** /akuple/ **1** vt (Tech) couple. □ s'~ vpr mate.

**accourir** /akurir/ **20** vi run up.

**accoutumance** /akutymɑ̃s/ nf familiarization; (Méd) addiction.

**accoutumer** /akutyme/ **1** vt accustom. □ s'~ vpr get accustomed.

**accro** /akro/ nmf ① (drogué) addict; (amateur) fan.

**accroc** /akro/ nm tear, rip; (fig) hitch.

**accrochage** /akroʃaʒ/ nm hanging; hooking; (Auto) collision; (dispute) clash; (Mil) encounter.

**accrocher** /akroʃe/ **1** vt (suspendre) hang up; (attacher) hook, hitch; (déchirer) catch; (heurter) hit;

(attirer) attract. □ s'~ vpr cling, hang on (à to); (se disputer) clash.

**accroissement** /akrwasmɑ̃/ nm increase (de in).

**accroître** /akrwatr/ **24** vt increase. □ s'~ vpr increase.

**accroupir (s')** /(s)akrupir/ **2** vpr squat.

**accru**, ~e /akry/ adj increased, greater.

**accueil** /akœj/ nm reception, welcome.

**accueillant**, ~e /akœjɑ̃, -t/ adj friendly, welcoming.

**accueillir** /akœjir/ **23** vt receive, welcome; (film, livre) receive; (prendre en charge) (réfugiés, patients) take care of, cater for.

**accumuler** /akymyle/ **1** vt (énergie) store up; (capital) accumulate. □ s'~ vpr (neige, ordures) pile up; (dettes) accrue.

**accusation** /akyzasjɔ̃/ nf accusation; (Jur) charge; l'~ (magistrat) the prosecution.

**accusé**, ~e /akyze/ adj marked. ● nm, f defendant, accused.

**accuser** /akyze/ **1** vt accuse (of); (blâmer) blame (de for); (Jur) charge (de with); (fig) emphasize; ~ réception de acknowledge receipt of.

**acharné**, ~e /aʃarne/ adj relentless, ferocious. **acharnement** nm (énergie) furious energy; (ténacité) determination.

**acharner (s')** /(s)aʃarne/ **1** vpr persevere; s'~ sur set upon; (poursuivre) hound; s'~ à faire (s'évertuer) try desperately; (s'obstiner) keep on doing.

**achat** /aʃa/ nm purchase; ~s shopping; faire l'~ de buy; faire des ~s do some shopping.

**acheminer** /aʃ(ə)mine/ **1** vt dis-

patch, convey; (*courrier*) handle.
□ **s'~ vers** *vpr* head for.

**acheter** /aʃ(ə)te/ **6** *vt* buy; **~ qch
à qn** (*pour lui*) buy sth for sb; (*chez
lui*) buy sth from sb. **acheteur,
-euse** *nm, f* buyer; (*client de magasin*) shopper.

**achèvement** /aʃɛvmɑ̃/ *nm* completion.

**achever** /aʃ(ə)ve/ **6** *vt* finish (off).
□ **s'~** *vpr* end.

**acide** /asid/ *adj* acid, sharp.
● *nm* acid.

**acier** /asje/ *nm* steel.

**acné** /akne/ *nf* acne.

**acompte** /akɔ̃t/ *nm* deposit, part-
payment.

**à-côté** (*pl* **~s**) /akote/ *nm* side
issue; **~s** (*argent*) extras.

**acoustique** /akustik/ *nf* acoustics
(+ *sg*). ● *adj* acoustic.

**acquéreur** /akerœr/ *nm* purcha-
ser, buyer.

**acquérir** /akerir/ **7** *vt* acquire,
gain; (*biens*) purchase, acquire.

**acquis, ~e** /aki, -z/ *adj* acquired;
(*fait*) established; **tenir qch pour
~** take sth for granted. ● *nm* experience. **acquisition** *nf* acquisition;
purchase.

**acquitter** /akite/ **1** *vt* acquit;
(*dette*) settle. □ **s'~ de** *vpr* (*promesse*) fulfil; (*devoir*) discharge.

**âcre** /akr/ *adj* acrid.

**acrobatie** /akrɔbasi/ *nf* acrobatics
(+ *pl*). **~ aérienne** aerobatics (+ *pl*).

**acte** /akt/ *nm* act, action, deed;
(*Théât*) act; (*Jur*) deed; **~ de
naissance/mariage** birth/marriage
certificate; **~s** (*compte rendu*) proceedings; **prendre ~ de** note.

**acteur** /aktœr/ *nm* actor.

**actif, -ive** /aktif, -v/ *adj* active; (*population*) working. ● *nm* (*Comm*) as-
sets; **avoir à son ~** have to one's

**action** /aksjɔ̃/ *nf* action; (*Comm*)
share; (*Jur*) action; (*effet*) effect;
(*initiative*) initiative. **actionnaire**
*nmf* shareholder.

**activer** /aktive/ **1** *vt* speed up;
(*feu*) boost. □ **s'~** *vpr* hurry up;
(*s'affairer*) be very busy.

**activité** /aktivite/ *nf* activity; **en
~** (*volcan*) active; (*fonctionnaire*)
working; (*usine*) in operation.

**actrice** /aktris/ *nf* actress.

**actualité** /aktɥalite/ *nf* topicality;
**l'~** current affairs; **les ~s** news;
**d'~** topical.

**actuel, ~le** /aktɥɛl/ *adj* current,
present; (*d'actualité*) topical. **ac-
tuellement** *adv* currently, at the
present time.

**acupuncture** /akypɔ̃ktyr/ *nf* acupuncture.

**adaptateur** /adaptatœr/ *nm*
(*Électr*) adapter.

**adapter** /adapte/ **1** *vt* adapt;
(*fixer*) fit. □ **s'~** *vpr* adapt (oneself);
(*Tech*) fit.

**additif** /aditif/ *nm* (*note*) rider;
(*substance*) additive.

**addition** /adisjɔ̃/ *nf* addition; (*au
café*) bill; (US) check. **additionner**
**1** *vt* add; (*totaliser*) add (up).

**adepte** /adɛpt/ *nmf* follower; (*d'activité*) enthusiast.

**adéquat, ~e** /adekwa, -t/ *adj* suitable; (*suffisant*) adequate.

**adhérent, ~e** /aderɑ̃, -t/ *nm, f*
member.

**adhérer** /adere/ **14** *vi* adhere, stick
(à to); **~ à** (*club*) be a member of;
(*s'inscrire à*) join.

**adhésif, -ive** /adezif, -v/ *adj* adhesive; **ruban ~** sticky tape.

**adhésion** /adezjɔ̃/ *nf* membership;
(*soutien*) support.

**adieu** (*pl* **~x**) /adjø/ *interj* & *nm*

**a** goodbye, farewell.

**adjectif** /adʒɛktif/ nm adjective.

**adjoint, ~e** /adʒwɛ̃, -t/ nm, f assistant; ~ **au maire** deputy mayor. ●adj assistant.

**adjuger** /adʒyʒe/ 40 vt award; (aux enchères) auction. ▫ **s'~** vpr take (for oneself).

**ADM** abrév fpl (armes de destruction massive) WMD.

**admettre** /admɛtʀ/ 42 vt let in, admit; (tolérer) allow; (reconnaître) admit, acknowledge; (candidat) pass.

**administrateur, -trice** /administʀatœʀ, -tʀis/ nm, f administrator, director; (Jur) trustee; ~ **de site Internet** Webmaster.

**administratif, -ive** /administʀatif, -v/ adj administrative; (document) official. **administration** nf administration; (gestion) management; l'A~ Civil Service.

**administrer** /administʀe/ 1 vt run, manage; (justice, biens, antidote) administer.

**admirateur, -trice** /admiʀatœʀ, -tʀis/ nm, f admirer.

**admiration** /admiʀasjɔ̃/ nf admiration.

**admirer** /admiʀe/ 1 vt admire.

**admission** /admisjɔ̃/ nf admission.

**ADN** abrév m (acide désoxyribonucléique) DNA.

**adolescence** /adɔlesɑ̃s/ nf adolescence. **adolescent, ~e** nm, f adolescent, teenager.

**adopter** /adɔpte/ 1 vt adopt. **adoptif, -ive** adj (enfant) adopted; (parents) adoptive.

**adorer** /adɔʀe/ 1 vt love; (plus fort) adore; (Relig) worship, adore.

**adosser** /adose/ 1 vt lean (à, contre against). ▫ **s'~** vpr lean

back (à, contre against).

**adoucir** /adusiʀ/ 2 vt soften; (boisson) sweeten; (chagrin) ease. ▫ **s'~** vpr soften; (chagrin) ease; (temps) become milder. **adoucissant** nm (fabric) softener.

**adresse** /adʀɛs/ nf address; (habileté) skill; ~ **électronique** email address.

**adresser** /adʀese/ 1 vt send; (écrire l'adresse sur) address; (remarque) address; ~ **la parole à** speak to. ▫ **s'~ à** vpr address; (aller voir) (personne) go and ask ou see; (bureau) enquire at; (viser, intéresser) be directed at.

**adroit, ~e** /adʀwa, -t/ adj skilful, clever.

**ADSL** abrév m (asymmetrical digital subscriber line) ADSL.

**adulte** /adylt/ nmf adult. ●adj adult; (plante, animal) fully grown.

**adultère** /adyltɛʀ/ adj adulterous. ●nm adultery.

**adverbe** /advɛʀb/ nm adverb.

**adversaire** /advɛʀsɛʀ/ nmf opponent, adversary.

**aérer** /aeʀe/ 1 vt air; (texte) space out. ▫ **s'~** vpr get some air.

**aérien, ~ne** /aeʀjɛ̃, -jɛn/ adj air; (photo) aerial; (câble) overhead.

**aérobic** /aeʀɔbik/ nm aerobics (+ sg).

**aérogare** /aeʀogaʀ/ nf air terminal.

**aéroglisseur** /aeʀoɡlisœʀ/ nm hovercraft.

**aérogramme** /aeʀoɡʀam/ nm airmail letter; (US) aerogram.

**aéronautique** /aeʀonotik/ adj aeronautical. ●nf aeronautics (+ sg).

**aéroport** /aeʀopɔʀ/ nm airport.

**aérospatial, ~e** (mpl -iaux) /aeʀospasjal, -jo/ adj aerospace.

**affaiblir** /afeblir/ **2** vt weaken. □ s'~ vpr get weaker.

**affaire** /afɛʀ/ nf affair, matter; (Jur) case; (histoire, aventure) affair; (occasion) bargain; (entreprise) business; (transaction) deal; (question, problème) matter; ~s (Comm) business; (Pol) affairs; problèmes personnels business; (effets personnels) things; c'est mon ~ that's my business; avoir ~ à deal with; ça fera l'~ that will do the job; ça fera leur ~ that's just what they need; tirer qn d'~ help sb out of a tight spot; se tirer d'~ get out of trouble.

**affairé, ~e** /afeʀe/ adj busy.

**affaisser (s')** /(s)afese/ **1** vpr (terrain, route) sink, subside; (poutre) sag; (personne) collapse.

**affamé, ~e** /afame/ adj starving.

**affectation** /afɛktasjɔ̃/ nf (nomination) (à une fonction) appointment; (dans un lieu) posting; (de matériel, d'argent) allocation; (comportement) affectation.

**affecter** /afɛkte/ **1** vt (feindre) affect; (toucher, affliger) affect; (destiner) assign; (nommer) appoint, post.

**affectif, -ive** /afɛktif, -v/ adj emotional.

**affection** /afɛksjɔ̃/ nf affection; (maladie) complaint.

**affectueux, -euse** /afɛktɥø, -z/ adj affectionate.

**affichage** /afiʃaʒ/ nm billposting; (électronique) display.

**affiche** /afiʃ/ nf (public) notice; (publicité) poster; (Théât) bill; être à l'~ (film) be showing; (pièce) be on.

**afficher** /afiʃe/ **1** vt (annonce) put up; (événement) announce; (sentiment) display; (Ordinat) display.

**affirmatif, -ive** /afiʀmatif, -v/ adj affirmative. **affirmation** nf assertion.

**affirmer** /afiʀme/ **1** vt assert; (soutenir) maintain.

**affligé, ~e** /afliʒe/ adj distressed; ~ de afflicted with.

**affluer** /aflye/ **1** vi flood in; (sang) rush.

**affolant, ~e** /afɔlɑ̃, -t/ adj alarming.

**affoler** /afɔle/ **1** vt throw into a panic. □ s'~ vpr panic.

**affranchir** /afʀɑ̃ʃiʀ/ **2** vt stamp; (à la machine) frank; (esclave) emancipate; (fig) free. **affranchissement** nm (tarif) postage.

**affreux, -euse** /afʀø, -z/ adj (laid) hideous; (mauvais) awful.

**affrontement** /afʀɔ̃tmɑ̃/ nm confrontation.

**affronter** /afʀɔ̃te/ **1** vt confront. □ s'~ vpr confront each other.

**affûter** /afyte/ **1** vt sharpen.

**afin** /afɛ̃/ prép & conj ~ de faire in order to do; ~ que so that.

**africain, ~e** /afʀikɛ̃, -ɛn/ adj African. **A~, ~e** nm, f African.

**Afrique** /afʀik/ nf Africa; ~ du Sud South Africa.

**agacer** /agase/ **10** vt irritate, annoy.

**âge** /aʒ/ nm age; (vieillesse) (old) age; quel ~ avez-vous? how old are you?; ~ adulte adulthood; ~ mûr maturity; d'un certain ~ middle-aged.

**âgé, ~e** /aʒe/ adj elderly; ~ de cinq ans five years old.

**agence** /aʒɑ̃s/ nf agency, bureau, office; (succursale) branch; ~ d'interim employment agency; ~ de voyages travel agency; ~ publicitaire advertising agency.

**agenda** /aʒɛ̃da/ nm diary; ~ électronique electronic organizer.

**agent** /aʒɑ̃/ *nm* agent; (fonctionnaire) official; ~ (de police) policeman; ~ de change stockbroker; ~ commercial sales representative.

**agglomération** /aglɔmeʀasjɔ̃/ *nf* town, built-up area.

**aggraver** /agʀave/ **1** *vt* aggravate, make worse. □ s'~ *vpr* get worse.

**agile** /aʒil/ *adj* agile, nimble.

**agir** /aʒiʀ/ **2** *vi* act; (se comporter) behave; (avoir un effet) work, take effect. □ s'~ de *vpr* (être nécessaire) il s'agit de faire we/you *etc.* must do; (être question de) il s'agit de faire it is a matter of doing; dans ce livre il s'agit de this book is about; dont il s'agit in question; il s'agit de ton fils it's about your son; de quoi s'agit-il? what is it about?

**agitation** /aʒitasjɔ̃/ *nf* bustle; (trouble) agitation; (malaise social) unrest.

**agité**, ~e /aʒite/ *adj* restless, fidgety; (troublé) agitated; (mer) rough.

**agiter** /aʒite/ **1** *vt* (bras, mouchoir) wave; (liquide, boîte) shake; (troubler) agitate; (discuter) debate. □ s'~ *vpr* bustle about; (enfant) fidget; (foule, pensées) stir.

**agneau** (*pl* ~x) /aɲo/ *nm* lamb.

**agrafe** /agʀaf/ *nf* hook; (pour papiers) staple. **agrafeuse** *nf* stapler.

**agrandir** /agʀɑ̃diʀ/ **2** *vt* enlarge; (maison) extend. □ s'~ *vpr* expand, grow. **agrandissement** *nm* extension; (de photo) enlargement.

**agréable** /agʀeabl/ *adj* pleasant.

**agréé**, ~e /agʀee/ *adj* (agence) authorized; (nourrice, médecin) registered; (matériel) approved.

**agréer** /agʀee/ **15** *vt* accept; ~ à

please; veuillez ~, Monsieur, mes salutations distinguées (personne non nommée) yours faithfully; (personne nommée) yours sincerely.

**agrégation** /agʀegasjɔ̃/ *nf* highest examination for recruitment of teachers. **agrégé**, ~e *nm, f* teacher (who has passed the agrégation).

**agrément** /agʀemɑ̃/ *nm* charm; (plaisir) pleasure; (accord) assent.

**agresser** /agʀese/ **1** *vt* attack; (pour voler) mug.

**agressif**, -**ive** /agʀesif, -v/ *adj* aggressive. **agression** *nf* attack; (pour voler) mugging; (Mil) aggression.

**agricole** /agʀikɔl/ *adj* agricultural; (ouvrier, produit) farm. **agriculteur**, -**trice** *nm, f* farmer. **agriculture** *nf* agriculture, farming.

**agripper** /agʀipe/ **1** *vt* grab. □ s'~ *vpr* cling (à to).

**agroalimentaire** /agʀoalimɑ̃tɛʀ/ *nm* food industry.

**agrumes** /agʀym/ *nmpl* citrus fruit(s).

**ai** /e/ ⇒**avoir** **5**.

**aide** /ɛd/ *nf* help, assistance; (en agent) aid; à l'~ de with the help of; venir en ~ à help; ~ à domicile carer, home help; ~ familiale mother's help; ~ sociale social security; (US) welfare. ● *nmf* assistant. **aide-éducateur**, -**trice** *nm, f* classroom assistant. **aide-mémoire** *inv* handbook of key points.

**aider** /ede/ **1** *vt/i* help, assist; (subventionner) aid, give aid to; ~ à faire help to do. □ s'~ de *vpr* use.

**aïeul**, ~e /ajœl/ *nm, f* grandparent.

**aigle** /ɛgl/ *nm* eagle.

**aigre** /ɛgʀ/ *adj* sour, sharp; (fig) sharp.

**aigrir** /egʀiʀ/ **2** *vt* embitter. □ s'~ *vpr* turn sour; (personne) become embittered.

**aigu, ~ë** /egy/ adj (douleur, problème) acute; (objet) sharp; (voix) shrill; (Mus) high(-pitched); (accent) acute.

**aiguille** /eguij/ nf needle; (de montre) hand; (de balance) pointer; ~ à tricoter knitting needle.

**aiguilleur** /eguijœr/ nm pointsman; ~ du ciel air traffic controller.

**aiguiser** /eg(ɥ)ize/ **1** vt sharpen; (fig) stimulate.

**ail** (pl ~s ou **aulx**) /aj, o/ nm garlic.

**aile** /ɛl/ nf wing.

**ailier** /elje/ nm winger; (US) end.

**aille** /aj/ ➤ ALLER **8**.

**ailleurs** /ajœr/ adv elsewhere, somewhere else; **d'~** besides, moreover; **nulle part ~** nowhere else; **par ~** moreover, furthermore; **partout ~** everywhere else.

**aimable** /ɛmabl/ adj kind.

**aimant** /ɛmɑ̃/ nm magnet.

**aimer** /eme/ **1** vt like; (d'amour) love; **j'aimerais faire** I'd like to do; **~ bien** quite like; **~ mieux** ou **autant** prefer.

**aîné, ~e** /ene/ adj eldest; (de deux) elder. ● nm, f eldest (child); (premier de deux) elder (child); **~s** elders; **il est mon ~** he is older than me ou my senior.

**ainsi** /ɛ̃si/ adv like this, thus; (donc) so; **et ~ de suite** and so on; **pour ~ dire** so to speak, as it were; **~ que** as well as; (comme) as.

**air** /ɛr/ nm air; (mine) look, air; (mélodie) tune; **~ conditionné** air-conditioning; **avoir l'~** look, appear; **avoir de l'~** look like; **avoir l'~ de faire** appear to be doing; **en l'~** (up) in the air; (promesses) empty; **prendre l'~** get some fresh air.

**aire** /ɛr/ nf area; **~ d'atterrissage** landing-strip; **~ de pique-nique** picnic area; **~ de repas** rest area; **~ de services** (motorway) services.

**aisance** /ɛzɑ̃s/ nf ease; (richesse) affluence.

**aise** /ɛz/ nf joy; **à l'~** (sur un siège) comfortable; (pas gêné) at ease; (fortuné) comfortably off; **mal à l'~** uncomfortable; ill at ease; **aimer ses ~s** like one's creature comforts; **mettre qn à l'~** put sb at ease; **se mettre à l'~** make oneself comfortable.

**aisé, ~e** /eze/ adj easy; (fortuné) well-off.

**aisselle** /ɛsɛl/ nf armpit.

**ait** /ɛ/ ➤ AVOIR **5**.

**ajourner** /aʒurne/ **1** vt postpone; (débat, procès) adjourn.

**ajout** /aʒu/ nm addition.

**ajouter** /aʒute/ **1** vt add (à to); **~ foi à** lend credence to. □ s'~ vpr be added.

**ajuster** /aʒyste/ **1** vt adjust; (cible) aim at; (adapter) fit; **~ son coup** adjust one's aim.

**alarme** /alarm/ nf alarm; **donner l'~** raise the alarm.

**alarmer** /alarme/ **1** vt alarm. □ s'~ vpr become alarmed (de at).

**Albanie** /albani/ nf Albania.

**alcool** /alkɔl/ nm alcohol; (eau de vie) brandy; **~ à brûler** methylated spirit. **alcoolique** adj & nmf alcoholic. **alcoolisé, ~e** adj (boisson) alcoholic. **alcoolisme** nm alcoholism.

**alcootest** /alkɔtɛst/ nm breath test; (appareil) Breathalyser®.

**aléa** /alea/ nm hazard. **aléatoire** adj unpredictable, uncertain; (Ordinat) random.

**alentours** /alɑ̃tur/ nmpl surroundings; **aux ~ de** (de lieu) around; (de chiffre, date) about, around.

**alerte** /alɛrt/ adj (personne) alert;

**a**

(vif) lively. ● nf alert; ~ à la bombe bomb scare. **alerter 1** vt alert.

**algèbre** /alʒɛbʀ/ nf algebra.

**Algérie** /alʒeʀi/ nf Algeria.

**algue** /alg/ nf seaweed; les ~s (Bot) algae.

**aliéné, ~e** /aljene/ nm, f insane person.

**aliéner 14** vt alienate; (céder) give up. □ **s'~** vpr alienate.

**aligner** /aline/ **1** vt (objets) line up, make lines of; (chiffres) string together; ~ sur bring into line with. □ **s'~** vpr line up; **s'~ sur** align oneself on.

**aliment** /alimã/ nm food.

**alimentaire** /alimãtɛʀ/ adj (industrie) food; (habitudes) dietary; produits ~s foodstuffs.

**alimentation** /alimãtasjɔ̃/ nf feeding, supply(ing); (régime) diet; (aliments) food; magasin d'~ grocery shop ou store.

**alimenter** /alimãte/ **1** vt feed; (fournir) supply; (fig) sustain. □ **s'~** vpr eat.

**allaiter** /alete/ **1** vt (bébé) breast-feed; (US) nurse; (animal) suckle.

**allée** /ale/ nf path, lane; (menant à une maison) drive(way); (dans un cinéma, magasin) aisle; (rue) road; ~s et venues comings and goings.

**allégé, ~e** /aleʒe/ adj diet; (beurre, yaourt) low-fat.

**alléger 14 40** vt make lighter; (fardeau, chargement) lighten; (fig) (souffrance) alleviate.

**allégresse** /alegʀɛs/ nf gaiety, joy.

**alléguer 14** vt (exemple) invoke; (prétexter) allege.

**Allemagne** /almaɲ/ nf Germany.

**allemand, ~e** /almã, -d/ adj German. ● nm (Ling) German. **A~, ~e** nm, f German.

**aller** /ale/ **8**

● verbe auxiliaire

····▸ je vais l'appeler I'm going to call him; j'allais partir I was about to leave; va savoir! who knows?; ~ en s'améliorant be improving.

● verbe intransitif

····▸ (se déplacer) go; allons-y! let's go!; allez! come on!

····▸ (se porter) comment allez-vous?, comment ça va? how are you?; ça va (bien) I'm fine; qu'est-ce qui ne va pas? what's the matter?; ça ne va pas la tête? 🔲 are you mad? 🔲.

····▸ (mettre en valeur) ~ à qn suit sb; ça te va bien it really suits you.

····▸ (convenir) ça va ma coiffure? is my hair OK?; ça ne va pas du tout that's no good at all.

□ **s'en aller** verbe pronominal

····▸ go; va-t'en! go away!; ça ne s'en va pas (tache) it won't come out.

● nom masculin

····▸ outward journey; ~ (simple) single (ticket); (US) one-way (ticket); ~ retour return (ticket); (US) round trip (ticket); à l'~ on the way out.

**allergie** /alɛʀʒi/ nf allergy. **allergique** adj allergic (à to).

**alliance** /aljɑ̃s/ nf alliance; (bague) wedding-ring; (mariage) marriage.

**allier** /alje/ **45** vt combine; (Pol) ally. □ **s'~** vpr combine; (Pol) form an alliance; (famille) become related (à to).

**allô** /alo/ interj hallo, hello.

**allocation** /alɔkasjɔ̃/ nf allow-

**ance**; ~ **chômage** unemployment benefit; ~**s familiales** family allowance.

**allonger** /alɔ̃ʒe/ 40 vt lengthen; (bras, jambe) stretch (out); (coucher) lay down. □ s'~ vpr get longer; (s'étendre) lie down; (s'étirer) stretch (oneself) out.

**allouer** /alwe/ 1 vt allocate; (prêt) grant.

**allumer** /alyme/ 1 vt (bougie, gaz) light; (lampe, appareil) turn on; (pièce) switch the light(s) on in; (fig) arouse. □ s'~ vpr (lumière, appareil) come on.

**allumette** /alymɛt/ nf match.

**allure** /alyʀ/ nf speed, pace; (démarche) walk; (apparence) appearance; à toute ~ at full speed; avoir de l'~ have style; avoir des ~s de look like; avoir une drôle d'~ be funny-looking.

**allusion** /alyzjɔ̃/ nf allusion (à to); (implicite) hint (à at); faire ~ à allude to; hint at.

**alors** /alɔʀ/ adv (à ce moment-là) then; (de ce fait) so; (dans ce cas-là) then; ça ~! so what?; et ~? so what? ● conj ~ que (pendant que) while; (tandis que) whereas.

**alouette** /alwɛt/ nf lark.

**alourdir** /aluʀdiʀ/ 2 vt weigh down; (rendre plus important) increase.

**aloyau** (pl ~x) /alwajo/ nm sirloin.

**Alpes** /alp/ nfpl les ~ the Alps.

**alphabet** /alfabɛ/ nm alphabet. **alphabétique** /alfabetik/ adj alphabetical.

**alphabétiser** /alfabetize/ 1 vt teach to read and write.

**alpiniste** /alpinist/ nmf mountaineer.

**altérer** /alteʀe/ 14 vt (fait, texte) distort; (abîmer) spoil; (donner soif à) make thirsty. □ s'~ vpr de-

teriorate.

**alternance** /altɛʀnɑ̃s/ nf alternation; en ~ alternately.

**altitude** /altityd/ nf altitude, height.

**amabilité** /amabilite/ nf kindness.

**amaigrir** /amegʀiʀ/ 2 vt make thin(ner).

**amande** /amɑ̃d/ nf almond; (d'un fruit à noyau) kernel.

**amant** /amɑ̃/ nm lover.

**amarre** /amaʀ/ nf (mooring) rope; ~s moorings.

**amas** /amɑ/ nm heap, pile.

**amasser** /amɑse/ 1 vt amass, gather; (empiler) pile up. □ s'~ vpr pile up; (gens) gather.

**amateur** /amatœʀ/ nm amateur; ~ de lover of; d'~ amateur; (péj) amateurish.

**ambassade** /ɑ̃basad/ nf embassy. **ambassadeur, -drice** /ɑ̃basadœʀ, -dʀis/ nm, f ambassador.

**ambiance** /ɑ̃bjɑ̃s/ nf atmosphere. **ambiant, ~e** /ɑ̃bjɑ̃, -t/ adj surrounding.

**ambigu, -ë** /ɑ̃bigy/ adj ambiguous. **ambiguïté** /ɑ̃biguite/ nf ambiguity.

**ambitieux, -ieuse** /ɑ̃bisjø, -z/ adj ambitious. **ambition** /ɑ̃bisjɔ̃/ nf ambition.

**ambulance** /ɑ̃bylɑ̃s/ nf ambulance.

**ambulant, ~e** /ɑ̃bylɑ̃, -t/ adj itinerant, travelling.

**âme** /ɑm/ nf soul; ~ sœur soul mate.

**amélioration** /ameljɔʀasjɔ̃/ nf improvement.

**améliorer** /ameljɔʀe/ 1 vt improve. □ s'~ vpr improve.

**aménagement** /amenaʒmɑ̃/ nm (de magasin) fitting out; (de grenier) conversion; (de territoire) development; (de cuisine) equipping.

**a** **aménager** /amenaʒe/ 🔟 vt (*magasin*) fit out; (transformer) convert; (*territoire*) develop; (*cuisine*) equip.

**amende** /amɑ̃d/ nf fine; faire ~ honorable make amends.

**amener** /am(ə)ne/ 🔟 vt bring; (*causer*) bring about; ~ qn à faire cause sb to do. □ **s'~** vpr 🔟 turn up.

**amer, -ère** /amɛʀ/ adj bitter.

**américain, ~e** /amerikɛ̃, -ɛn/ adj American. **A~, ~e** nm, f American.

**Amérique** /amerik/ nf America; ~ centrale/latine Central/Latin America; ~ du Nord/Sud North/ South America.

**amertume** /amɛʀtym/ nf bitterness.

**ami, ~e** /ami/ nm, f friend; (*amateur*) lover; **un ~ des bêtes** an animal lover. ● adj friendly.

**amiable** /amjabl/ adj amicable; à l'~ (*divorcer*) by mutual consent; (se séparer) on friendly terms; (*séparation*) amicable.

**amical, ~e** (mpl -aux) /amikal, -o/ adj friendly.

**amiral** (pl -aux) /amiral, -o/ nm admiral.

**amitié** /amitje/ nf friendship; ~s (en fin de lettre) kind regards; prendre qn en ~ take a liking to sb.

**amnistie** /amnisti/ nf amnesty.

**amoindrir** /amwɛ̃dʀiʀ/ 🔟 vt reduce.

**amont:** en ~ /ɑ̃mɔ̃/ loc upstream.

**amorcer** /amɔʀse/ 🔟 vt start; (hameçon) bait; (pompe) prime; (arme à feu) arm.

**amortir** /amɔʀtiʀ/ 🔟 vt (choc) cushion; (bruit) deaden; (dette) pay off; ~ **un achat** make a purchase pay for itself.

**amortisseur** /amɔʀtisœʀ/ nm shock absorber.

**amour** /amuʀ/ nm love; pour l'~ de for the sake of.

**amoureux, -euse** /amuʀø, -z/ adj (*personne*) in love; (*relation, regard*) loving; (vie) love; ~ **de qn** in love with sb. ● nm, f lover.

**amour-propre** /amuʀpʀɔpʀ/ nm self-esteem.

**amphithéâtre** /ɑ̃fiteatʀ/ nm amphitheatre; (d'université) lecture hall.

**ampleur** /ɑ̃plœʀ/ nf extent, size; (de vêtement) fullness; **prendre de l'~** spread, grow.

**amplifier** /ɑ̃plifje/ 🔟 vt amplify; (fig) expand, develop. □ **s'~** vpr (son) grow; (scandale) intensify.

**ampoule** /ɑ̃pul/ nf (électrique) bulb; (sur la peau) blister; (Méd) phial, ampoule.

**amusant, ~e** /amyzɑ̃, -t/ adj (blague) funny; (soirée) enjoyable, entertaining.

**amuse-gueule** /amyzgœl/ nm inv cocktail snack.

**amusement** /amyzmɑ̃/ nm amusement; (passe-temps) entertainment.

**amuser** /amyze/ 🔟 vt amuse; (détourner l'attention de) distract. □ **s'~** vpr enjoy oneself; (jouer) play.

**amygdale** /amidal/ nf tonsil.

**an** /ɑ̃/ nm year; avoir dix ~s be ten years old; **un garçon de deux ~s** a two-year-old boy; à soixante ~s at the age of sixty; les moins de dix-huit ~s under eighteens.

**analogie** /analɔʒi/ nf analogy.

**analogue** /analɔg/ adj similar, analogous (à to).

**analphabète** /analfabɛt/ adj & nmf illiterate.

**analyse** /analiz/ nf analysis; (Méd) test. **analyser 🗹** vt analyse; (Méd) test.

**ananas** /anana(s)/ nm pineapple.

**anarchie** /anaʀʃi/ nf anarchy.

**anatomie** /anatɔmi/ nf anatomy.

**ancêtre** /ɑ̃sɛtʀ/ nm ancestor.

**anchois** /ɑ̃ʃwa/ nm anchovy.

**ancien, ~ne** /ɑ̃sjɛ̃, -jɛn/ adj old; (de jadis) ancient; (meuble) antique; (précédent) former, ex-, old; (dans une fonction) senior; **~ combattant** veteran. ● n f, senior; (par l'âge) elder. **anciennement** adv formerly. **ancienneté** nf age, seniority.

**ancre** /ɑ̃kʀ/ nf anchor; **jeter/lever l'~** cast/weigh anchor.

**andouille** /ɑ̃duj/ nf sausage (filled with chitterlings); (idiot 🗓) fool; **faire l'~** fool around.

**âne** /ɑn/ nm donkey, ass; (imbécile 🗓) dimwit 🗓.

**anéantir** /aneɑ̃tiʀ/ **🗹** vt destroy; (exterminer) annihilate; (accabler) overwhelm.

**anémie** /anemi/ nf anaemia.

**ânerie** /ɑnʀi/ nf stupid remark.

**anesthésie** /anɛstezi/ nf (opération) anaesthetic.

**ange** /ɑ̃ʒ/ nm angel; **aux ~s** in seventh heaven.

**angine** /ɑ̃ʒin/ nf throat infection.

**anglais, ~e** /ɑ̃glɛ, -z/ adj English. ● nm (Ling) English. **A~, ~e** nm, f Englishman, Englishwoman.

**angle** /ɑ̃gl/ nm angle; (coin) corner.

**Angleterre** /ɑ̃glətɛʀ/ nf England.

**anglophone** /ɑ̃glɔfɔn/ adj English-speaking. ● nmf English speaker.

**angoissant, ~e** /ɑ̃gwasɑ̃, -t/ adj alarming; (effrayant) harrowing.

**angoisse** /ɑ̃gwas/ nf anxiety. **angoissé, ~e** adj anxious. **angoisser**

**🗓** vi worry.

**animal** (pl **-aux**) /animal, -o/ nm animal; **~ familier, ~ de compagnie** pet. ● adj (pl **-aux**) animal.

**animateur, -trice** /animatœʀ, -tʀis/ nm, f organizer, leader; (TV) host, hostess.

**animation** /animasjɔ̃/ nf liveliness; (affairement) activity; (au cinéma) animation; (activité dirigée) organized activity.

**animé, ~e** /anime/ adj lively; (affairé) busy; (être) animate.

**animer** /anime/ **🗹** vt liven up; (débat, atelier) lead; (spectacle) host; (pousser) drive; (encourager) spur on. □ **s'~** vpr liven up.

**anis** /ani(s)/ nm (Culin) aniseed; (Bot) anise.

**anneau** (pl **~x**) /ano/ nm ring; (de chaîne) link.

**année** /ane/ nf year; **~ bissextile** leap year; **~ civile** calendar year.

**annexe** /anɛks/ adj (document) attached; (question) related; (bâtiment) adjoining. ● nf (bâtiment) annexe; (US) annex; (document) appendix; (électronique) attachment. **annexer 🗹** vt annex; (document) attach.

**anniversaire** /anivɛʀsɛʀ/ nm birthday; (d'un événement) anniversary. ● adj anniversary.

**annonce** /anɔ̃s/ nf announcement; (publicitaire) advertisement; (indice) sign.

**annoncer** /anɔ̃se/ **🔟** vt announce; (prédire) forecast; (être l'indice de) herald. □ **s'~** vpr (crise, tempête) be brewing; **s'~ bien/mal** look good/bad. **annonceur** nm advertiser.

**annuaire** /anɥɛʀ/ nm year-book; **~ (téléphonique)** (telephone) directory.

**annuel, ~le** /anɥɛl/ adj annual,

a

yearly.

**annulation** /anylasjɔ̃/ nf cancellation; (de sanction, loi) repeal; (de mesure) abolition.

**annuler** /anyle/ **1** vt cancel; (*contrat*) nullify; (*jugement*) quash; (*loi*) repeal. □ s'∼ vpr cancel each other out.

**anodin, ∼e** /anɔdɛ̃, -in/ adj insignificant; (*sans risques*) harmless, safe.

**anonymat** /anɔnima/ nm anonymity; garder l'∼ remain anonymous. **anonyme** adj anonymous.

**anorexie** /anɔrɛksi/ nf anorexia.

**anormal, ∼e** /anɔrmal/ (mpl **-aux**) adj abnormal.

**anse** /ɑ̃s/ nf handle; (baie) cove.

**Antarctique** /ɑ̃tarktik/ nm Antarctic.

**antenne** /ɑ̃tɛn/ nf aerial; (US) antenna; (d'insecte) antenna; (succursale) agency; (Mil) outpost; à l'∼ on the air; ∼ chirurgicale mobile emergency unit; ∼ parabolique satellite dish.

**antérieur, ∼e** /ɑ̃terjœr/ adj previous, earlier; (placé devant) front; ∼ à prior to.

**antiaérien, ∼ne** /ɑ̃tiaerjɛ̃, -ɛn/ adj anti-aircraft; abri ∼ air-raid shelter.

**antiatomique** /ɑ̃tiatɔmik/ adj abri ∼ nuclear fall-out shelter.

**antibiotique** /ɑ̃tibjɔtik/ nm antibiotic.

**anticipation** /ɑ̃tisipasjɔ̃/ nf d'∼ (*livre, film*) science fiction; par ∼ in advance.

**anticiper** /ɑ̃tisipe/ **1** vt ∼ (sur) anticipate; (effectuer à l'avance) bring forward.

**anticorps** /ɑ̃tikɔr/ nm antibody.

**antidater** /ɑ̃tidate/ **1** vt back-

date, antedate.

**antigel** /ɑ̃tiʒɛl/ nm antifreeze.

**Antilles** /ɑ̃tij/ nfpl les ∼ the West Indies.

**antipathique** /ɑ̃tipatik/ adj unpleasant.

**antiquaire** /ɑ̃tikɛr/ nmf antique dealer.

**antiquité** /ɑ̃tikite/ nf (objet) antique; l'A∼ antiquity.

**antisémite** /ɑ̃tisemit/ adj antiSemitic.

**antiseptique** /ɑ̃tisɛptik/ adj & nm antiseptic.

**antivirus** /ɑ̃tivirys/ nm inv (Ordinat) antivirus software.

**antivol** /ɑ̃tivɔl/ nm anti-theft device; (Auto) steering lock.

**anxiété** /ɑ̃ksjete/ nf anxiety.

**anxieux, -ieuse** /ɑ̃ksjø, -z/ adj anxious. ●nm, f worrier.

**août** /u(t)/ nm August.

**apaiser** /apeze/ **1** vt calm down; (colère, militant) appease; (douleur) soothe; (faim) satisfy. □ s'∼ vpr (tempête) die down.

**apathie** /apati/ nf apathy. **apathique** adj apathetic.

**apercevoir** /apɛrsəvwar/ **52** vt see. □ s'∼ de vpr notice; s'∼ que notice ou realize that.

**aperçu** /apɛrsy/ nm (échantillon) glimpse, taste; (intuition) insight.

**apéritif** /aperitif/ nm aperitif, drink.

**aphte** /aft/ nm mouth ulcer.

**apitoyer** /apitwaje/ **31** vt move (to pity). □ s'∼ vpr s'∼ sur (le sort de) ou feel sorry for sb.

**aplanir** /aplanir/ **2** vt level; (fig) iron out.

**aplatir** /aplatir/ **2** vt flatten (out). □ s'∼ vpr (s'immobiliser) flatten oneself.

**aplomb** /aplɔ̃/ nm balance; (fig) self-confidence; d'∼ (en équilibre) steady; je ne suis pas bien d'∼ 🔢 I don't feel very well.

**apogée** /apɔʒe/ nm peak.

**apologie** /apɔlɔʒi/ nf panegyric.

**apostrophe** /apɔstʁɔf/ nf apostrophe; (remarque) remark.

**apothéose** /apɔteoz/ nf high point; (d'événement) grand finale.

**apparaître** /apaʁɛtʁ/ 🔢 vi appear; **il apparaît que** it appears that.

**appareil** /apaʁɛj/ nm device; (électrique) appliance; (Anat) system; (téléphone) phone; (avion) plane; (Culin) mixture; (système administratif) apparatus; ∼ (dentaire) brace; (dentier) dentures; ∼ (photo) camera; **c'est Gabriel à l'**∼ it's Gabriel on the phone; ∼ auditif hearing aid; ∼ électroménager household electrical appliance.

**appareiller** /apaʁeje/ 🔢 vi (navire) cast off, put to sea.

**apparemment** /apaʁamɑ̃/ adv apparently.

**apparence** /apaʁɑ̃s/ nf appearance; **en** ∼ outwardly; (apparemment) apparently.

**apparent**, ∼e /apaʁɑ̃, -t/ adj apparent; (visible) conspicuous.

**apparenté**, ∼e /apaʁɑ̃te/ adj related; (semblable) similar.

**apparition** /apaʁisjɔ̃/ nf appearance; (spectre) apparition.

**appartement** /apaʁtəmɑ̃/ nm flat; (US) apartment.

**appartenir** /apaʁtəniʁ/ 🔢 vi belong (à to); **il lui appartient de** it is up to him to.

**appât** /apa/ nm bait; (fig) lure.

**appauvrir** /apovʁiʁ/ 🔢 vt impoverish. □ **s'**∼ vpr become

impoverished.

**appel** /apɛl/ nm call; (Jur) appeal; (supplique) appeal, plea; (Mil) callup; (US) draft; **faire** ∼ appeal; **faire** **à** (recourir à) call on; (invoquer) appeal to; (évoquer) call up; (exiger) call for; **faire l'**∼ (Scol) call the register; (Mil) take a roll-call; ∼ **d'offres** (Comm) invitation to tender; **faire un** ∼ **de phares** flash one's headlights.

**appeler** /aple/ 🔢 vt call; (téléphoner) phone; (nécessiter) call for; **en** ∼ **à** appeal to; **appelé à** (destiné) destined for. □ **s'**∼ vpr be called; **il s'appelle Tim** his name is Tim ou he is called Tim.

**appellation** /apelasjɔ̃/ nf name, designation.

**appendice** /apɛ̃dis/ nm appendix. **appendicite** nf appendicitis.

**appesantir** /apəzɑ̃tiʁ/ 🔢 vt weigh down. □ **s'**∼ vpr grow heavier; **s'**∼ **sur** dwell upon.

**appétissant**, ∼e /apetisɑ̃, -t/ adj appetizing.

**appétit** /apeti/ nm appetite; **bon** ∼! enjoy your meal!

**applaudir** /aplodiʁ/ 🔢 vt/i applaud. **applaudissements** nmpl applause.

**application** /aplikasjɔ̃/ nf (soin) care; (de loi) (respect) application; (mise en œuvre) implementation; (Ordinat) application program.

**appliqué**, ∼e /aplike/ adj (travail) painstaking; (sciences) applied; (élève) hard-working.

**appliquer** /aplike/ 🔢 vt apply; (loi) enforce. □ **s'**∼ vpr apply oneself (à to), take great care (à faire to do); **s'**∼ **à** (concerner) apply to.

**appoint** /apwɛ̃/ nm support; **d'**∼ extra; **faire l'**∼ give the correct money.

**apport** /apɔʀ/ nm contribution.

**apporter** /apɔʀte/ **1** vt bring; (aide, précision) give; (causer) bring about.

**appréciation** /apʀesjasjɔ̃/ nf estimate, evaluation; (de monnaie) appreciation; (jugement) assessment.

**apprécier** /apʀesje/ **45** vt appreciate; (évaluer) assess; (objet) value, appraise.

**appréhender** /apʀeɑ̃de/ **1** vt dread, fear; (arrêter) apprehend.

**apprendre** /apʀɑ̃dʀ/ **50** vt learn; (être informé de) hear, learn; (de façon indirecte) hear of; ~ qch à qn teach sb sth; (informer) tell sb sth; ~ à faire learn to do; ~ à qn à faire teach sb to do; ~ que learn that; (être informé) hear that.

**apprenti**, ~e /apʀɑ̃ti/ nm, f apprentice. **apprentissage** nm apprenticeship; (d'un sujet) learning.

**apprêter (s')** /apʀete/ **1** vt prepare; (bois) prime; (mur) size. □ s'~ à vpr prepare to.

**apprivoiser** /apʀivwaze/ **1** vt tame.

**approbation** /apʀɔbasjɔ̃/ nf approval.

**approchant**, ~e /apʀɔʃɑ̃, -t/ adj close, similar.

**approcher** /apʀɔʃe/ **1** vt (objet) move near (**de** to); (personne) approach; ~ **de** get nearer ou closer to. ● vi approach. □ s'~ **de** vpr approach, move near (de to).

**approfondir** /apʀɔfɔ̃diʀ/ **2** vt deepen; (sujet) go into sth in depth; (connaissances) improve.

**approprié**, ~e /apʀɔpʀije/ adj appropriate.

**approprier (s')** /(s)apʀɔpʀije/ **45** vt appropriate.

**approuver** /apʀuve/ **1** vt approve; (trouver louable) approve of; (soutenir) agree with.

**approvisionner** /apʀɔvizjɔne/ **1** vt supply (**en** with); (compte en banque) pay money into. □ s'~ vpr stock up.

**approximatif**, **-ive** /apʀɔksimatif, -v/ adj approximate.

**appui** /apɥi/ nm support; (de fenêtre) sill; (pour objet) rest; à l'~ **de** in support of; prendre ~ **sur** lean on.

**appui-tête** (pl **appuis-tête**) /apɥitɛt/ nm headrest.

**appuyer** /apɥije/ **31** vt lean, rest; (presser) press; (soutenir) support, back. ● vi ~ **sur** press (on); (fig) stress. □ s'~ **sur** vpr lean on; (compter sur) rely on.

**après** /apʀɛ/ prép after; (au-delà de) after, beyond; ~ **avoir fait** after doing; ~ **tout** after all; ~ **coup** after the event; **d'~** (selon) according to; (en imitant) from; (adapté de) based on. ● adv after (wards); (plus tard) later; **le bus d'~** the next bus. ● conj ~ **qu'il est parti** after he left. **après-demain** adv the day after tomorrow. **après-guerre** (pl ~s) nm ou f postwar period. **après-midi** nm ou f inv afternoon. **après-rasage** (pl ~s) nm aftershave. **après-shampooing** nm conditioner. **après-ski** nm inv moon boot. **après-vente** adj inv aftersales.

**a priori** /apʀijɔʀi/ adv (à première vue) offhand, on the face of it; (sans réfléchir) out of hand. ● nm preconception.

**à-propos** /apʀɔpo/ nm timing, timeliness; (fig) presence of mind.

**apte** /apt/ adj capable (**à** of); (ayant les qualités requises) suitable (**à** for); (en état) fit (**à** for).

**aptitude** /aptityd/ nf aptitude,

ability.

**aquarelle** /akwaʀɛl/ nf water-colour.

**aquatique** /akwatik/ adj aquatic; (Sport) water.

**arabe** /aʀab/ adj Arab; (Ling) Arabic; (désert) Arabian. ● nm (Ling) Arabic. A~ nmf Arab.

**Arabie** /aʀabi/ nf ~ Saoudite Saudi Arabia.

**arachide** /aʀaʃid/ nf groundnut; huile d'~ groundnut oil.

**araignée** /aʀɛɲe/ nf spider.

**arbitraire** /aʀbitʀɛʀ/ adj arbitrary.

**arbitre** /aʀbitʀ/ nm referee; (au cricket, tennis) umpire; (expert) arbiter; (Jur) arbitrator. **arbitrer** **1** vt (match) referee, umpire; (Jur) arbitrate in.

**arbre** /aʀbʀ/ nm tree; (Tech) shaft.

**arbuste** /aʀbyst/ nm shrub.

**arc** /aʀk/ nm (arme) bow; (courbe) curve; (voûte) arch; ~ de cercle arc of a circle.

**arc-en-ciel** ( pl **arcs-en-ciel**) /aʀkɑ̃sjɛl/ nm rainbow.

**arche** /aʀʃ/ nf arch; ~ de Noé Noah's ark.

**archéologie** /aʀkeɔlɔʒi/ nf archaeology.

**archevêque** /aʀʃəvɛk/ nm archbishop.

**architecte** /aʀʃitɛkt/ nmf architect. **architecture** nf architecture.

**Arctique** /aʀktik/ nm Arctic.

**ardent**, ~e /aʀdɑ̃, -t/ adj burning; (passionné) ardent; ( foi) fervent. **ardeur** nf ardour; (chaleur) heat.

**ardoise** /aʀdwaz/ nf slate; ~ électronique notepad computer.

**arène** /aʀɛn/ nf arena; ~s amphitheatre; (pour corridas) bullring.

**arête** /aʀɛt/ nf (de poisson) bone; (bord) ridge.

**argent** /aʀʒɑ̃/ nm money; (métal) silver; ~ comptant cash; prendre pour ~ comptant take at face value; ~ de poche pocket money.

**argenté**, ~e /aʀʒɑ̃te/ adj silver(y); (métal) (silver-)plated.

**argenterie** /aʀʒɑ̃tʀi/ nf silverware.

**Argentine** /aʀʒɑ̃tin/ nf Argentina.

**argile** /aʀʒil/ nf clay.

**argot** /aʀgo/ nm slang.

**argument** /aʀgymɑ̃/ nm argument; ~ de vente selling point. **argumenter** **1** vi argue.

**aristocratie** /aʀistɔkʀasi/ nf aristocracy.

**arithmétique** /aʀitmetik/ nf arithmetic. ● adj arithmetical.

**armature** /aʀmatyʀ/ nf framework; (de tente) frame.

**arme** /aʀm/ nf arm, weapon; ~ à feu firearm; ~s (blason) coat of arms; ~s de destruction massive weapons of mass destruction.

**armée** /aʀme/ nf army; ~ de l'air Air Force; ~ de terre Army.

**armer** /aʀme/ **1** vt arm; ( fusil) cock; (navire) equip; (renforcer) reinforce; (Photo) wind on. □ s'~ de vpr arm oneself with.

**armoire** /aʀmwaʀ/ nf cupboard; (penderie) wardrobe; (US) closet; ~ à pharmacie medicine cabinet.

**armure** /aʀmyʀ/ nf armour.

**arnaque** /aʀnak/ nf **1** swindling; c'est de l'~ it's a swindle **1**.

**arobas(e)** /aʀobas, aʀobaz/ nm at sign.

**aromate** /aʀomat/ nm herb, spice.

**aromatisé**, ~e /aʀomatize/ adj flavoured.

**arôme** /aʀom/ nm aroma; (additif) flavouring.

**arpenter** /aʀpɑ̃te/ **1** vt pace up and down; (terrain) survey.

**a**

**arqué, ~e** /aʀke/ *adj* arched; (*jambes*) bandy.

**arrache-pied:** d'~ /daʀaʃpje/ *loc* relentlessly.

**arracher** /aʀaʃe/ **1** *vt* pull out ou off; (*plante*) pull ou dig up; (*cheveux, page*) tear ou pull out; (*par une explosion*) blow off; ~ à (*enlever à*) snatch from; (*fig*) force ou wrest from. □ **s'~ qch** *vpr* fight over sth.

**arranger** /aʀɑ̃ʒe/ **40** *vt* arrange, fix up; (*réparer*) put right; (*régler*) sort out; (*convenir à*) suit. □ **s'~** *vpr* (se mettre d'accord) come to an arrangement; (se débrouiller) manage (pour).

**arrestation** /aʀɛstasjɔ̃/ *nf* arrest.

**arrêt** /aʀɛ/ *nm* stopping; (de combats) cessation; (de production) halt; (lieu) stop; (pause) pause; (Jur) ruling; aux ~s (Mil) under arrest; à l'~ (véhicule) stationary; (machine) idle; faire un ~ (make a) stop; sans ~ (sans escale) nonstop; (sans interruption) constantly; ~ maladie sick leave; ~ de travail (grève) stoppage; (Méd) sick leave.

**arrêté** /aʀete/ *nm* order; ~ municipal bylaw.

**arrêter** /aʀete/ **1** *vt* stop; (date) fix; (appareil) turn off; (renoncer à) give up; (appréhender) arrest. ● *vi* stop. □ **s'~** *vpr* stop; **s'~ de faire** stop doing.

**arrhes** /aʀ/ *nfpl* deposit; verser des ~ pay a deposit.

**arrière** /aʀjɛʀ/ *adj inv* back, rear. ● *nm* back, rear; (football) back; à l'~ in ou at the back; en ~ behind; (marcher, tomber) backwards; en ~ de behind. **arrière-boutique** (*pl* ~s) *nf* back room of the shop). **arrière-garde** (*pl* ~s) *nf* rearguard. **arrière-goût** (*pl* ~s) *nm* aftertaste. **arrière-grand-mère** (*pl* arrière-

grands-mères) *nf* great-grandmother. **arrière-grand-père** (*pl* arrière-grands-pères) *nm* great-grandfather. **arrière-pays** *nm inv* backcountry. **arrière-pensée** (*pl* ~s) *nf* ulterior motive. **arrière-plan** *nm* (*pl* ~s) background.

**arrimer** /aʀime/ **1** *vt* secure; (cargaison) stow.

**arrivage** /aʀivaʒ/ *nm* consignment.

**arrivée** /aʀive/ *nf* arrival; (Sport) finish.

**arriver** /aʀive/ **1** *vi* (aux être) arrive, come; (réussir) succeed; (se produire) happen; ~ à (atteindre) reach; ~ à faire manage to do; n'arrive pas à faire I can't do; en ~ à faire get to the stage of doing; il arrive que it happens that; il lui arrive de faire he (sometimes) does.

**arriviste** /aʀivist/ *nmf* go-getter, self-seeker.

**arrondir** /aʀɔ̃diʀ/ **2** *vt* (make) round; (somme) round off. □ **s'~** *vpr* become round(ed).

**arrondissement** /aʀɔ̃dismɑ̃/ *nm* district.

> **Arrondissement** A sub-division of a *département*. Each *arrondissement* has a *sous-préfet* representing the state administration at local level. In Paris, Lyons and Marseilles, an *arrondissement* is a sub-division of the commune, and has its own *maire* and local council.  *i*

**arroser** /aʀoze/ **1** *vt* water; (repas) wash down (with a drink); (rôti) baste; (victoire) drink to. **arrosoir** *nm* watering can.

**art** /aʀ/ *nm* art; (don) knack (de faire of doing); ~s et métiers arts and crafts; ∼s ménagers home economics (+ *sg*).

**artère** /artɛr/ *nf* artery; (grande) ∼ main road.

**arthrite** /artrit/ *nf* arthritis.

**arthrose** /artroz/ *nf* osteoarthritis.

**artichaut** /artiʃo/ *nm* artichoke.

**article** /artikl/ *nm* (Comm) item, article; à l'∼ de la mort at death's door; ∼ de fond feature (article); l'∼ de voyage travel goods.

**articulation** /artikylasjɔ̃/ *nf* articulation; (Anat) joint.

**articuler** /artikyle/ **1** *vt* articulate; (structurer) structure; (assembler) connect (sur to).

**artificiel**, ∼le /artifisjɛl/ *adj* artificial.

**artisan** /artizã/ *nm* artisan, craftsman; l'∼ de (fig) the architect of.

**artisanal**, ∼e (*mpl* ∼aux) /artizanal/ *adj* craft; (méthode) traditional; (amateur) home-made; de fabrication ∼e hand-made, hand-crafted.

**artiste** /artist/ *nmf* artist. **artistique** *adj* artistic.

**as**[1] /a/ ⇒AVOIR **5**.

**as**[2] /ɑs/ *nm* ace.

**ascenseur** /asɑ̃sœr/ *nm* lift; (US) elevator.

**ascension** /asɑ̃sjɔ̃/ *nf* ascent; l'A∼ Ascension.

**aseptiser** /asɛptize/ **1** *vt* disinfect; (stériliser) sterilize; (péj) sanitized.

**asiatique** /azjatik/ *adj* Asian. A∼ *nmf* Asian.

**Asie** /azi/ *nf* Asia.

**asile** /azil/ *nm* refuge; (Pol) asylum; (pour malades, vieillards) home; ∼ de nuit night shelter.

**aspect** /aspɛ/ *nm* appearance; (fa-

cettes) aspect; (perspective) side; à l'∼ de at the sight of.

**asperge** /aspɛrʒ/ *nf* asparagus.

**asperger** /aspɛrʒe/ **40** *vt* spray.

**asphyxier** /asfiksje/ **45** *vt* (*personne*) asphyxiate; (*entreprise, réseau*) paralyse. □ s'∼ *vpr* suffocate; gas oneself; (*entreprise, réseau*) become paralysed.

**aspirateur** /aspiratœr/ *nm* vacuum cleaner.

**aspirer** /aspire/ **1** *vt* inhale; (*liquide*) suck up. ●*vi* ∼ à aspire to.

**aspirine®** /aspirin/ *nf* aspirin.

**assainir** /asenir/ **2** *vt* clean up.

**assaisonnement** /asɛzɔnmã/ *nm* seasoning.

**assassin** /asasɛ̃/ *nm* murderer; (Pol) assassin. **assassiner** **1** *vt* murder; (Pol) assassinate.

**assaut** /aso/ *nm* assault, onslaught; donner l'∼ à, prendre d'∼ storm.

**assemblage** /asɑ̃blaʒ/ *nm* assembly; (combinaison) collection; (Tech) joint.

**assemblée** /asɑ̃ble/ *nf* meeting; (gens réunis) gathering; (Pol) assembly.

> **Assemblée nationale** The lower house of the French parliament, in which 577 *députés* are elected for a five-year term. *Députés* sit in parties in the semi-circular chamber, with the most left-wing to the extreme left and the most right-wing to the extreme right. The *Assemblée nationale* passes laws, votes on the Budget, and questions ministers.

**assembler** /asɑ̃ble/ **1** *vt* assemble, put together; (réunir) gather. □ s'∼ *vpr* gather, assemble.

**asseoir** /aswar/ **9** *vt* sit (down),

**seat**; (*bébé, malade*) sit up; (*affermir*) establish; (*baser*) base. □ s'~ vpr sit (down).

**assez** /ase/ adv (suffisamment) enough; (plutôt) quite, fairly; ~ grand/rapide big/fast enough (pour to); ~ de enough; j'en ai (~ de) I've had enough (of).

**assidu, ~e** /asidy/ adj (zélé) assiduous; (régulier) regular; ~ auprès de attentive to. **assiduité** nf assiduousness, regularity.

**assiéger** /asjeʒe/ [14] [40] vt besiege.

**assiette** /asjɛt/ nf plate; (équilibre) seat; ~ anglaise assorted cold meats; ~ creuse/plate soup-/dinner-plate; ne pas être dans son ~ feel out of sorts.

**assigner** /asiɲe/ [1] vt assign; (limite) fix.

**assimilation** /asimilasjɔ̃/ nf assimilation; (comparaison) likening, comparison.

**assimiler** /asimile/ [1] vt ~ à liken to; (classer) class as. □ s'~ vpr assimilate; (être comparable) be comparable (à to).

**assis, ~e** /asi, -z/ adj sitting (down), seated. ● ⇒ASSEOIR [9].

**assise** /asiz/ nf (base) foundation; ~s (tribunal) assizes; (congrès) conference, congress.

**assistance** /asistɑ̃s/ nf audience; (aide) assistance; l'A~ (publique) welfare services.

**assistant, ~e** /asistɑ̃, -t/ nm, f assistant; (Scol) foreign language assistant; ~s (spectateurs) members of the audience; ~e sociale social worker; ~ personnel numérique personal digital assistant, PDA.

**assister** /asiste/ [1] vt assist; ~ à attend, be (present) at; (accident) witness; **assisté par ordinateur** computer-assisted.

**association** /asɔsjasjɔ̃/ nf association.

**associé, ~e** /asɔsje/ nm, f partner, associate. ● adj associate.

**associer** /asɔsje/ [45] vt associate; (mêler) combine (à with); ~ qn à (projet) involve sb in; (bénéfices) give sb a share of. □ s'~ vpr (sociétés, personnes) become associated, join forces (à with); (s'harmoniser) combine (à with); s'~ à (joie, opinion de qn) share; (projet) take part in.

**assommer** /asɔme/ [1] vt knock out; (animal) stun; (fig) overwhelm; (ennuyer [1]) bore.

**Assomption** /asɔ̃psjɔ̃/ nf Assumption.

**assortiment** /asɔrtimɑ̃/ nm assortment.

**assortir** /asɔrtir/ [2] vt match (à with, to); ~ de accompany with. □ s'~ vpr match; s'~ à qch match sth.

**assoupir (s')** /(s)asupir/ [2] vpr doze off; (s'apaiser) subside.

**assouplir** /asuplir/ [2] vt make supple; (fig) make flexible.

**assourdir** /asurdir/ [2] vt (personne) deafen; (bruit) muffle.

**assouvir** /asuvir/ [2] vt satisfy.

**assujettir** /asyʒetir/ [2] vt subjugate, subdue; ~ à subject to.

**assumer** /asyme/ [1] vt assume; (coût) meet; (accepter) come to terms with, accept.

**assurance** /asyrɑ̃s/ nf (self-) surance; (garantie) assurance; (contrat) insurance; ~s sociales social insurance; ~ automobile/maladie car/health insurance.

**assuré, ~e** /asyre/ adj certain, assured; (sûr de soi) confident, assured. ● nm, f insured party.

**assurer** /asyre/ [1] vt ensure;

(fournir) provide; (exécuter) carry out; (Comm) insure; (stabiliser) steady; (*frontières*) make secure; ~ à qn que assure sb that; ~ qn de assure sb of; ~ la gestion/défense de manage/defend. □ **s'**~ vpr take out insurance; **s'**~ de/que make sure of/that; **s'**~ qch (se procurer) secure sth. **assureur** nm insurer.

**astérisque** /asterisk/ nm asterisk.

**asthmatique** /asmatik/ adj & nmf asthmatic.

**asthme** /asm/ nm asthma.

**asticot** /astiko/ nm maggot.

**astreindre** /astrɛ̃dʀ/ [22] vt ~ qn à qch force sth on sb; ~ qn à faire force sb to do.

**astrologie** /astʀɔlɔʒi/ nf astrology. **astrologue** nmf astrologer.

**astronaute** /astʀɔnot/ nmf astronaut.

**astronomie** /astʀɔnɔmi/ nf astronomy.

**astuce** /astys/ nf smartness; (truc) trick; (plaisanterie) wisecrack.

**astucieux, -ieuse** /astysjø, -z/ adj smart, clever.

**atelier** /atəlje/ nm (local) workshop; (de peintre) studio; (séance de travail) workshop.

**athée** /ate/ nmf atheist. ● adj atheistic.

**athlète** /atlɛt/ nmf athlete. **athlétisme** nm athletics.

**Atlantique** /atlɑ̃tik/ nm Atlantic (Ocean).

**atmosphère** /atmɔsfɛʀ/ nf atmosphere.

**atomique** /atɔmik/ adj atomic; (*énergie, centrale*) nuclear.

**atomiseur** /atɔmizœʀ/ nm spray.

**atout** /atu/ nm trump (card); (avantage) asset.

**atroce** /atʀɔs/ adj atrocious.

**attabler (s')** /(s)atable/ [1] vpr sit down at table.

**attachant, ~e** /ataʃɑ̃, -t/ adj charming.

**attache** /ataʃ/ nf (agrafe) fastener; (lien) tie.

**attaché, ~e** /ataʃe/ adj être ~ à (aimer) be attached to. ● nm, f (Pol) attaché.

**attacher** /ataʃe/ [1] vt tie (up); (ceinture, robe) fasten; (bicyclette) lock; ~ à (attribuer à) attach to. ● vi (Culin) stick. □ **s'**~ vpr fasten, do up; **s'**~ à (se tier à) become attached to; (se consacrer à) apply oneself to.

**attaquant, ~e** /atakɑ̃, -t/ nm, f attacker; (au football) striker; (au football américain) forward.

**attaque** /atak/ nf attack; ~ (cérébrale) stroke; il va en faire une ~ he'll have a fit; ~ à main armée armed attack.

**attaquer** /atake/ [1] vt attack; (banque) raid. ● vi attack. □ **s'**~ à vpr attack; (problème, sujet) tackle.

**attardé, ~e** /atarde/ adj backward; (idées) outdated; (en retard) late.

**attarder (s')** /(s)atarde/ [1] vpr linger.

**atteindre** /atɛ̃dʀ/ [22] vt reach; (blesser) hit; (affecter) affect.

**atteint, ~e** /atɛ̃, -t/ adj ~ de suffering from.

**atteinte** /atɛ̃t/ nf attack (on); porter ~ à attack; (droit) infringe.

**atteler** /atle/ [38] vt (cheval) harness; (remorque) couple. □ **s'**~ vpr get down to.

**attelle** /atɛl/ nf splint.

**attenant, ~e** /atnɑ̃, -t/ adj ~ (à) adjoining.

**attendant: en ~** /ɑ̃natɑ̃dɑ̃/ loc meanwhile.

**attendant**

**a** **attendre** /atɑ̃dʀ/ **3** vt wait for; (bébé) expect; (être le sort de) await; (escompter) expect; ~ que qn fasse wait for sb to do. ●vi wait; (au téléphone) hold. □ s'~ à vpr expect.

**attendrir** /atɑ̃dʀiʀ/ **2** vt move (to pity). □ s'~ vpr be moved to pity.

**attendu**[1] /atɑ̃dy/ prép given, considering; ~ que considering that.

**attendu**[2], ~e /atɑ̃dy/ adj (escompté) expected; (espéré) long-awaited.

**attentat** /atɑ̃ta/ nm assassination attempt; ~ (à la bombe) (bomb) attack.

**attente** /atɑ̃t/ nf wait(ing); (espoir) expectations (+ pl).

**attenter** /atɑ̃te/ **1** vi ~ à make an attempt on; (fig) violate.

**attentif, -ive** /atɑ̃tif, -v/ adj attentive; (scrupuleux) careful; ~ à mindful of; (soucieux) careful of.

**attention** /atɑ̃sjɔ̃/ nf attention; (soin) care; ~ (à) watch out (for)!; faire ~ à (écouter) pay attention to; (prendre garde à) watch out for; (prendre soin de) take care of; faire ~ à faire be careful to do. **attentionné, ~e** adj considerate.

**attentisme** /atɑ̃tism/ nm wait-and-see policy.

**atténuer** /atenɥe/ **1** vt (violence) reduce; (critique) tone down; (douleur) ease; (faute) mitigate. □ s'~ vpr subside.

**atterrir** /ateʀiʀ/ **2** vi land. **atterrissage** nm landing.

**attestation** /atɛstasjɔ̃/ nf certificate.

**attester** /atɛste/ **1** vt testify to; ~ que testify that.

**attirant, ~e** /atiʀɑ̃, -t/ adj attractive.

**attirer** /atiʀe/ **1** vt draw, attract;

(causer) bring. □ s'~ vpr bring upon oneself; (amis) win.

**attiser** /atize/ **1** vt (feu) poke; (sentiment) stir up.

**attitré, ~e** /atitʀe/ adj accredited; (habituel) usual, regular.

**attitude** /atityd/ nf attitude; (maintien) bearing.

**attraction** /atʀaksjɔ̃/ nf attraction.

**attrait** /atʀɛ/ nm attraction.

**attraper** /atʀape/ **1** vt catch; (corde, main) catch hold of; (habitude, accent) pick up; (maladie) catch; se faire ~ **1** get told off.

**attrayant, ~e** /atʀejɑ̃, -t/ adj attractive.

**attribuer** /atʀibɥe/ **1** vt allocate; (prix) award; (imputer) attribute. □ s'~ vpr claim (for oneself). **attribution** nf awarding, allocation.

**attrouper (s')** /(s)atʀupe/ **1** vpr gather.

**au** /o/ ➡**à**.

**aubaine** /obɛn/ nf godsend, opportunity.

**aube** /ob/ nf dawn, daybreak.

**auberge** /obɛʀʒ/ nf inn; ~ de jeunesse youth hostel.

**aubergine** /obɛʀʒin/ nf aubergine; (US) eggplant.

**aucun, ~e** /okœ̃, okyn/ adj (dans une phrase négative) no, not any; (positif) any. ●pron (dans une phrase négative) none, not any; (positif) any; ~ des deux neither of the two; d'~s some. **aucunement** adv not at all, in no way.

**audace** /odas/ nf daring; (impudence) audacity.

**audacieux, -ieuse** /odasjø, -z/ adj daring.

**au-delà** /od(ə)la/ adv beyond. ●prép ~ de beyond.

**au-dessous** /od(ə)su/ adv below.
● prép ~ de below; (couvert par) under.

**au-dessus** /od(ə)sy/ adv above.
● prép ~ de above.

**au-devant** /od(ə)vɑ̃/ prép aller ~ de qn go to meet sb; aller ~ des désirs de qn anticipate sb's wishes.

**audience** /odjɑ̃s/ nf audience; (d'un tribunal) hearing; (succès, attention) success.

**audimat®** /odimat/ nm l'~ the TV ratings.

**audiovisuel,** ~**le** /odjovizɥɛl/ adj audio-visual.

**auditeur, -trice** /oditœr, -tris/ nm, f listener.

**audition** /odisjɔ̃/ nf hearing; (Théât, Mus) audition.

**auditoire** /oditwar/ nm audience.

**augmentation** /ogmɑ̃tasjɔ̃/ nf increase; ~ (de salaire) (pay) rise; (US) raise.

**augmenter** /ogmɑ̃te/ **1** vt/i increase; (employé) give a pay rise ou raise to.

**augure** /ogyr/ nm (devin) oracle; être de bon/mauvais ~ be a good/ bad sign.

**aujourd'hui** /oʒurdɥi/ adv today.

**auparavant** /oparavɑ̃/ adv (avant) before; (précédemment) previously; (en premier lieu) beforehand.

**auprès** /oprɛ/ prép ~ de (à côté de) beside, next to; (comparé à) compared with; s'excuser/se plaindre ~ de apologize/complain to.

**auquel** /okɛl/ ➡LEQUEL.

**aura** /ora/, aurait /orɛ, orɛ/ ➡AVOIR **5**.

**aurore** /oror/ nf dawn.

**aussi** /osi/ adv (également) too, also, as well; (dans une comparaison) as; (si, tellement) so; ~ bien que as well as. ● conj (donc) so,

consequently.

**aussitôt** /osito/ adv immediately; ~ que as soon as, the moment; ~ arrivé as soon as he arrived.

**austère** /ostɛr/ adj austere.

**Australie** /ostrali/ nf Australia.

**australien,** ~**ne** /ostraljɛ̃, -ɛn/ adj Australian. A~, ~**ne** nm, f Australian.

**autant** /otɑ̃/ adv (travailler, manger) as much (que as); ~ (de) (quantité) as much (que as); (nombre) as many (que as); (tant) so much, so many; ~ faire one had better do; d'~ plus que all the more than; en faire ~ do the same; pour ~ for all that.

**autel** /otɛl/ nm altar.

**auteur** /otœr/ nm author; l'~ du crime the perpetrator of the crime.

**authentifier** /otɑ̃tifje/ **45** vt authenticate.

**authentique** /otɑ̃tik/ adj authentic.

**auto** /oto/ nf car; ~ tamponneuse dodgem, bumper car.

**autobus** /otobys/ nm bus.

**autocar** /otokar/ nm coach.

**autochtone** /otokton/ nmf native.

**autocollant,** ~**e** /otokolɑ̃, -t/ adj self-adhesive. ● nm sticker.

**autodidacte** /otodidakt/ nmf self-taught person.

**auto-école** (pl ~**s**) /otoekol/ nf driving school.

**automate** /otomat/ nm automaton, robot.

**automatique** /otomatik/ adj automatic.

**automatisation** /otomatizasjɔ̃/ nf automation.

**automne** /oton/ nm autumn; (US) fall.

**automobile** /otomobil/ adj

**a**

**motor, car; (US) automobile. ●** *nf* (motor) car; **l'~** the motor industry; (Sport) motoring. **automobiliste** *nmf* motorist.

**autonome** /otɔnɔm/ *adj* autonomous; (Ordinat) stand-alone.

**autoradio** /otɔʀadjo/ *nm* car radio.

**autorisation** /otɔʀizasjɔ̃/ *nf* permission, authorization; (permis) permit.

**autorisé, ~e** /otɔʀize/ *adj* (opinions) authoritative; (approuvé) authorized.

**autoriser** /otɔʀize/ **1** *vt* authorize, permit; (rendre possible) allow (of); (donner un droit) **~ qn à faire** entitle sb to do.

**autoritaire** /otɔʀitɛʀ/ *adj* authoritarian.

**autorité** /otɔʀite/ *nf* authority; **faire ~** be authoritative.

**autoroute** /otɔʀut/ *nf* motorway; (US) highway; **~ de l'information** (Ordinat) information superhighway.

**auto-stop** /otostɔp/ *nm* hitch-hiking; **faire de l'~** hitch-hike; **prendre qn en ~** give a lift to sb.

**autour** /otuʀ/ *adv* around; **tout ~** all around. **● prép ~ de** around.

**autre** /otʀ/ *adj* other; **un ~ jour/livre** another day/book; **~ chose/part** something/somewhere else; **quelqu'un/rien d'~** somebody/nothing else; **quoi d'~?** what else?; **d'~ part** on the other hand; (de plus) moreover, besides; **vous ~s Anglais** you English. **● pron un ~, une ~** another (one); **l'~** the other (one); **les ~s** the others; (autrui) others; **d'~s** (some) others; **l'un l'~** each other; **l'un et l'~** both of them; **d'un jour à l'~** (bientôt) any day now; **entre ~s** among other things.

**autrefois** /otʀəfwa/ *adv* in the past; (précédemment) formerly.

**autrement** /otʀəmã/ *adv* differently; (sinon) otherwise; (plus 🔲) far more; **~ dit** in other words.

**Autriche** /otʀiʃ/ *nf* Austria.

**autrichien, ~ne** /otʀiʃjɛ̃, -jɛn/ *adj* Austrian. **A~, ~ne** *nm, f* Austrian.

**autruche** /otʀyʃ/ *nf* ostrich.

**autrui** /otʀɥi/ *pron* others, other people.

**aux** /o/ **→À**.

**auxiliaire** /oksiljɛʀ/ *adj* auxiliary. **●** *nmf* (assistant) auxiliary. **●** *nm* (Gram) auxiliary.

**auxquels, -quelles** /okɛl/ **→LEQUEL**.

**aval**: **en ~** /ãnaval/ *loc* downstream.

**avaler** /avale/ **1** *vt* swallow.

**avance** /avãs/ *nf* advance; (sur un concurrent) lead; **~ (de fonds)** advance; **à l'~** in advance; **d'~** already; **en ~** early; (montre) fast; **en (~ sur)** (menant) ahead (of).

**avancement** /avãsmã/ *nm* promotion.

**avancé, ~e** /avãse/ *adj* advanced.

**avancer** /avãse/ **10** *vi* move forward, advance; (travail) make progress; (montre) be fast; (faire saillie) jut out. **●** *vt* move forward; (dans le temps) bring forward; (argent) advance; (montre) put forward. **□ s'~** *vpr* move forward, advance; (se hasarder) commit oneself.

**avant** /avã/ *nm* front; (Sport) forward. **●** *adj inv* front. **● prép** before; **~ de faire** before doing; **en ~ de** in front of; **~ peu** shortly; **~ tout** above all. **● adv** (dans le temps) before, beforehand; (d'abord) first; **en ~** (dans l'espace) forward(s); (dans le temps) ahead; **le bus d'~** the previous bus. ● *conj* ~ que before; ~ qu'il (ne) fasse before he does.

**avantage** /avɑ̃taʒ/ *nm* advantage; (Comm) benefit.

**avantager** /avɑ̃taʒe/ **40** *vt* favour; (embellir) show off to advantage.

**avantageux, -euse** /avɑ̃taʒø, -z/ *adj* advantageous, favourable; (*prix*) attractive.

**avant-bras** /avɑ̃bra/ *nm inv* forearm.

**avant-centre** (*pl* avants-centres) /avɑ̃sɑ̃tr/ *nm* centre forward.

**avant-coureur** (*pl* ~s) /avɑ̃kurœr/ *adj* precursory, foreshadowing.

**avant-dernier, -ière** (*pl* ~s) /avɑ̃dɛrnje, -jɛr/ *adj & nm, f* last but one.

**avant-goût** (*pl* ~s) /avɑ̃gu/ *nm* foretaste.

**avant-hier** /avɑ̃tjɛr/ *adv* the day before yesterday.

**avant-poste** (*pl* ~s) /avɑ̃post/ *nm* outpost.

**avant-première** (*pl* ~s) /avɑ̃prəmjɛr/ *nf* preview.

**avant-propos** /avɑ̃propo/ *nm inv* foreword.

**avare** /avar/ *adj* miserly; ~ de sparing with. ● *nmf* miser.

**avarié, ~e** /avarje/ *adj* (*aliment*) spoiled.

**avatar** /avatar/ *nm* misfortune.

**avec** /avɛk/ *prép* with. ● *adv* **1** with it ou them.

**avènement** /avɛnmɑ̃/ *nm* advent; (d'un roi) accession.

**avenir** /avnir/ *nm* future; à l'~ in future; d'~ with (future) prospects.

**aventure** /avɑ̃tyr/ *nf* adventure; (sentimentale) affair. **aventureux, -euse** *adj* adventurous; (hasardeux)

risky.

**avérer (s')** /(s)avere/ **14** *vpr* prove (to be).

**averse** /avɛrs/ *nf* shower.

**avertir** /avɛrtir/ **2** *vt* inform; (mettre en garde, menacer) warn. **avertissement** *nm* warning.

**avertisseur** /avɛrtisœr/ *nm* alarm; (Auto) horn; ~ d'incendie fire-alarm; ~ lumineux warning light.

**aveu** (*pl* ~x) /avø/ *nm* confession; de l'~ de by the admission of.

**aveugle** /avœgl/ *adj* blind. ● *nmf* blind man, blind woman.

**aviateur, -trice** /avjatœr, -tris/ *nm, f* aviator.

**aviation** /avjasjɔ̃/ *nf* flying; (industrie) aviation; (Mil) air force.

**avide** /avid/ *adj* greedy (de for); (anxieux) eager (de for); ~ de faire eager to do.

**avion** /avjɔ̃/ *nm* plane, aeroplane, aircraft; (US) airplane; ~ à réaction jet.

**aviron** /avirɔ̃/ *nm* oar; l'~ (Sport) rowing.

**avis** /avi/ *nm* opinion; (conseil) advice; (renseignement) notification; (Comm) advice; à mon ~ in my opinion; changer d'~ change one's mind; être d'~ que be of the opinion that; ~ au lecteur foreword.

**avisé, ~e** /avize/ *adj* sensible; être bien/mal ~ de be well-/ill-advised to.

**aviser** /avize/ **1** *vt* advise, notify. ● *vi* decide what to do. □ s'~ de *vpr* suddenly realize; s'~ de faire take it into one's head to do.

**avocat, ~e** /avɔka, -t/ *nm, f* barrister; (US) attorney; (fig) advocate; ~ de la défense counsel for the defence. ● *nm* (fruit) avocado (pear).

**avoine** /avwan/ *nf* oats (+ *pl*).

**a**

**b**

**avoir** /avwar/ **5**

● *verbe auxiliaire*

····➤ have; il nous a appelés hier he called us yesterday.

● *verbe transitif*

····➤ (possession) have (got).

····➤ (obtenir) get; (au téléphone) get through to.

····➤ (duper) 1 have; on m'a eu! I've been had!

····➤ ~ chaud/faim be hot/hungry.

····➤ ~ dix ans be ten years old.

● **avoir à** *verbe + préposition*

····➤ to have to; j'ai beaucoup à faire I have a lot to do; tu n'as qu'à leur écrire all you have to do is write to them.

● **en avoir pour** *verbe + préposition*

····➤ j'en ai pour une minute I will only be a minute; j'en ai eu pour 100 euros it cost me 100 euros.

● **il y a** *verbe impersonnel*

····➤ there is; (pluriel) there are; qu'est-ce qu'il y a? what's the matter?; il est venu il y a cinq ans he came here five years ago; il y a au moins 5 km jusqu'à la gare it's at least 5 km to the station.

● *nom masculin*

····➤ (dans un magasin) credit note.

····➤ (biens) asset (+ *pl*).

**avortement** /avɔrtəmɑ̃/ *nm* (Méd) abortion.

**avorter** /avɔrte/ **1** *vi* (*projet*) abort; (se faire) ~ have an abortion.

**avoué**, ~**e** /avwe/ *adj* avowed.

● *nm* solicitor; (US) attorney.

**avouer** /avwe/ **1** *vt* (*amour, ignorance*) confess; (*crime*) confess to, admit. ● *vi* confess.

**avril** /avril/ *nm* April.

**axe** /aks/ *nm* axis; (essieu) axle; (d'une politique) main line(s), basis; ~ (routier) main road.

**ayant** /ɛjɑ̃/ ➡AVOIR **5**.

**azote** /azɔt/ *nm* nitrogen.

**azur** /azyr/ *nm* sky-blue.

# Bb

**baba** /baba/ *nm* ~ (au rhum) (rum) baba; en rester ~ 1 be flabbergasted.

**babillard** /babijar/ *nm* ~ électronique (Internet) bulletin board system, BBS.

**babines** /babin/ *nfpl* se lécher les ~ lick one's chops.

**babiole** /babjɔl/ *nf* trinket.

**bâbord** /bɑbɔr/ *nm* port (side).

**baby-foot** /babifut/ *nm inv* table football.

**bac** /bak/ *nm* (Scol) ➡BACCALAURÉAT; (bateau) ferry; (récipient) tub; (plus petit) tray.

**baccalauréat** /bakalɔrea/ *nm* school leaving certificate.

**Baccalauréat** Known informally as *le bac*, the *Baccalauréat* is an examination taken in the final year of the *lycée* (*la terminale*). Students sit exams in a broad range of subjects in a particular category: the *bac S* emphasises science subjects, for example, while the *bac L* has a literary bias.

**bâche** /baʃ/ *nf* tarpaulin.

**bachelier, -ière** /baʃəlje, -jɛr, *f* holder of the *baccalauréat*.

**bachoter** /baʃɔte/ **1** *vi* cram (for an exam).

**bâcler** /bɑkle/ **1** *vt* botch (up).

**bactérie** /bakteri/ *nf* bacterium; ∼s bacteria.

**badaud, ∼e** /bado, -d/ *nm, f* onlooker.

**badigeonner** /badiʒɔne/ **1** *vt* whitewash; (barbouiller) daub.

**badiner** /badine/ **1** *vi* banter.

**baffe** /baf/ *nf* **①** slap.

**baffle** /bafl/ *nm* speaker.

**bafouiller** /bafuje/ **1** *vt/i* stammer.

**bagage** /bagaʒ/ *nm* bag; (connaissances) knowledge; ∼s luggage; à **main** hand luggage.

**bagarre** /bagar/ *nf* fight.

**bagatelle** /bagatɛl/ *nf* trifle; (somme) trifling amount.

**bagnard** /baɲar/ *nm* convict.

**bagnole** /baɲɔl/ *nf* **①** car.

**bague** /bag/ *nf* (bijou) ring.

**baguette** /bagɛt/ *nf* stick; (de chef d'orchestre) baton; (chinoise) chopstick; (pain) baguette; ∼ **magique** magic wand; ∼ **de tambour** drumstick.

**baie** /bɛ/ *nf* (Géog) bay; (fruit) berry; ∼ **(vitrée)** picture window; (Ordinat) bay.

**baignade** /bɛɲad/ *nf* swimming.

**baigner** /beɲe/ **1** *vt* bathe; (enfant) bath. ● *vi* ∼ **dans l'huile** swim in grease. □ **se** ∼ *vpr* have a swim. **baigneur, -euse** *nm, f*

swimmer.

**baignoire** /bɛɲwar/ *nf* bath(tub).

**bail** (*pl* **baux**) /baj, bo/ *nm* lease.

**bâiller** /baje/ **1** *vi* yawn; (être ouvert) gape.

**bailleur** /bajœr/ *nm* ∼ **de fonds** (Comm) sleeping partner.

**bain** /bɛ̃/ *nm* bath; (baignade) swim; prendre un ∼ **de soleil** sunbathe; ∼ **de bouche** mouthwash; être dans le ∼ (fig) be in the swing of things; se remettre dans le ∼ get back into the swing of things; prendre un ∼ **de foule** mingle with the crowd.

**bain-marie** (*pl* **bains-marie**) /bɛ̃mari/ *nm* double boiler.

**baiser** /beze/ **1** *vt* (main) kiss; **☒** screw **☒**. ● *nm* kiss.

**baisse** /bɛs/ *nf* fall, drop; être en ∼ be going down.

**baisser** /bese/ **1** *vt* lower; (radio, lampe) turn down. ● *vi* (niveau) go down, fall; (santé, forces) fail. □ **se** ∼ *vpr* bend down.

**bal** (*pl* ∼**s**) /bal/ *nm* dance; (habillé) ball; (lieu) dance-hall; ∼ **costumé** fancy-dress ball.

**balade** /balad/ *nf* stroll; (en auto) drive.

**balader** /balade/ **1** *vt* take for a stroll. □ **se** ∼ *vpr* (à pied) (go for a) stroll; (en voiture) go for a drive; (voyager) travel.

**baladeur** /baladœr/ *nm* personal stereo.

**balafre** /balafr/ *nf* gash; (cicatrice) scar.

**balai** /balɛ/ *nm* broom.

**balance** /balɑ̃s/ *nf* scales (+ *pl*); la B∼ Libra.

**balancer** /balɑ̃se/ **10** *vt* swing; (doucement) sway; (lancer **①**) chuck! (se débarrasser de **①**) chuck out **①**. ● *vi* sway. □ **se** ∼ *vpr* swing;

**b**

sway; **s'en** ~ ⓘ not to give a damn ⓘ.

**balancier** /balɑ̃sje/ *nm* (d'horloge) pendulum; (d'équilibriste) pole.

**balançoire** /balɑ̃swaʀ/ *nf* swing.

**balayage** /baleʒaʒ/ *nm* sweeping; (cheveux) highlights.

**balayer** /baleje/ ⒘ *vt* sweep (up); (*vent*) sweep away; (*se débarrasser de*) sweep aside.

**balbutiement** /balbysimɑ̃/ *nm* stammering; **les** ~**s** (fig) the first steps.

**balcon** /balkɔ̃/ *nm* balcony; (Théât) dress circle.

**baleine** /balɛn/ *nf* whale.

**balise** /baliz/ *nf* beacon; (bouée) buoy; (Auto) (road) sign. **baliser** ⓵ *vt* mark out (with beacons); (*route*) signpost; (*sentier*) mark out.

**balivernes** /balivɛʀn/ *nfpl* nonsense.

**ballant,** ~**e** /balɑ̃, -t/ *adj* dangling.

**balle** /bal/ *nf* (projectile) bullet; (Sport) ball; (paquet) bale.

**ballerine** /balʀin/ *nf* (danseuse) ballerina; (chaussure) ballet pump.

**ballet** /balɛ/ *nm* ballet.

**ballon** /balɔ̃/ *nm* (Sport) ball; ~ (de baudruche) balloon; ~ de football football.

**ballonné,** ~**e** /balɔne/ *adj* bloated.

**balnéaire** /balneɛʀ/ *adj* seaside.

**balourd,** ~**e** /baluʀ, -d/ *nm, f* oaf. ● *adj* uncouth.

**balustrade** /balystʀad/ *nf* railing.

**ban** /bɑ̃/ *nm* round of applause; ~**s** (de mariage) banns; **mettre au** ~ de cast out from.

**banal,** ~**e** (*mpl* ~**s**) /banal/ *adj* commonplace, banal.

**banane** /banan/ *nf* banana.

**banc** /bɑ̃/ *nm* bench; (de poissons)

shoal; ~ **des accusés** dock; ~ **d'essai** (test) testing ground.

**bancaire** /bɑ̃kɛʀ/ *adj* (secteur) banking; (chèque) bank.

**bancal,** ~**e** (*mpl* ~**s**) /bɑ̃kal/ *adj* wobbly; (solution) shaky.

**bande** /bɑ̃d/ *nf* (groupe) gang; (de papier) strip; (rayure) stripe; (de film) reel; (pansement) bandage; ~ **dessinée** comic strip; ~ (magnétique) tape; ~ **sonore** sound-track.

**Bande dessinée** More than just a comic book, this form of popular literature (known as the *neuvième art*) plays a significant cultural role in France and is celebrated annually at the Festival of Angoulême. Cartoon characters such as *Astérix*, *Lucky Luke* and *Tintin* are household names, and older *BD* are often collectors' items.

**bande-annonce** (*pl* **bandes-annonces**) /bɑ̃danɑ̃s/ *nf* trailer.

**bandeau** (*pl* ~**x**) /bɑ̃do/ *nm* headband; (sur les yeux) blindfold; ~ **publicitaire** (Ordinat) banner.

**bander** /bɑ̃de/ ⓵ *vt* bandage; (arc) bend; (muscle) tense; ~ **les yeux à** blindfold.

**banderole** /bɑ̃dʀɔl/ *nf* banner.

**bandit** /bɑ̃di/ *nm* bandit. **banditisme** *nm* crime.

**bandoulière** : **en** ~ /ɑ̃buduljɛʀ/ *loc* across one's shoulder.

**banlieue** /bɑ̃ljø/ *nf* suburbs; **de** ~ suburban. **banlieusard,** ~**e** *nm, f* (suburban) commuter.

**bannir** /baniʀ/ ⓶ *vt* banish.

**banque** /bɑ̃k/ *nf* bank; (activité) banking; ~ **de données** databank.

**banqueroute** /bɑ̃kʀut/ *nf* bankruptcy.

29 | banquet | basse

**banquet** /bɑ̃kɛ/ nm banquet.

**banquette** /bɑ̃kɛt/ nf seat.

**banquier, -ière** /bɑ̃kje, -jɛʀ/ nm, f banker.

**baptême** /batɛm/ nm baptism, christening. **baptiser** ■ vt baptize, christen; (nommer) call.

**bar** /baʀ/ nm (lieu) bar.

**baragouiner** /baʀaɡwine/ ■ vt/i gabble; (langue) speak a few words of.

**baraque** /baʀak/ nf hut, shed; (maison ■) house.

**baratin** /baʀatɛ̃/ nm ■ sweet ou smooth talk.

**barbare** /baʀbaʀ/ adj barbaric. ● nmf barbarian.

**barbe** /baʀb/ nf beard; ~ à papa candy-floss; (US) cotton candy; quelle ~! ■ what a drag! ■.

**barbelé** /baʀbəle/ adj fil ~ barbed wire.

**barber** /baʀbe/ ■ vt ■ bore.

**barboter** /baʀbote/ ■ vi (dans l'eau) paddle, splash. ● vt (voler ■) pinch.

**barbouiller** /baʀbuje/ ■ vt (souiller) smear (de with); tu es tout barbouillé your face is all dirty; être barbouillé feel queasy.

**barbu, ~e** /baʀby/ adj bearded.

**barème** /baʀɛm/ nm list, table; (échelle) scale.

**baril** /baʀil/ nm barrel.

**bariolé, ~e** /baʀjɔle/ adj multicoloured.

**baromètre** /baʀɔmɛtʀ/ nm barometer.

**baron, ~ne** /baʀɔ̃, -ɔn/ nm, f baron, baroness.

**barque** /baʀk/ nf (small) boat.

**barrage** /baʀaʒ/ nm dam; (sur route) roadblock.

**barre** /baʀ/ nf bar; (trait) line,

stroke; (Naut) helm; ~ de boutons (Ordinat) toolbar.

**barreau** (pl ~x) /baʀo/ nm bar; (d'échelle) rung; le ~ (Jur) the bar.

**barrer** /baʀe/ ■ vt block; (porte) bar; (rayer) cross out; (Naut) steer. □ se ~ vpr ■ leave.

**barrette** /baʀɛt/ nf (hair) slide.

**barrière** /baʀjɛʀ/ nf (porte) gate; (clôture) fence; (obstacle) barrier.

**bar-tabac** (pl bars-tabac) /baʀtaba/ nm café (selling stamps and cigarettes).

**bas, basse** /bɑ, bɑs/ adj (niveau, table) low; (action) base; au ~ mot at the lowest estimate; en ~ âge young; ~ morceaux (viande) cheap cuts. ● nm bottom; (chaussette) stocking; ~ de laine ■ nest-egg. ● adv low; en ~ down below; (dans une maison) downstairs; en ~ de la page at the bottom of the page; plus ~ further ou lower down; mettre ~ give birth (to). **bas de casse** nm inv lower case. **bas-côté** (pl ~s) nm (de route) verge; (US) shoulder.

**bascule** /baskyl/ nf (balance) scales (+ pl); **cheval/fauteuil à ~** rocking-horse/chair.

**basculer** /baskyle/ ■ vi topple over; (benne) tip up.

**base** /bɑz/ nf base; (fondement) basis; (Pol) rank and file; de ~ basic. **base de données** nf database.

**baser** /bɑze/ ■ vt base. □ se ~ sur vpr go by.

**bas-fonds** /bafɔ̃/ nmpl (eau) shallows; (fig) dregs.

**basilic** /bazilik/ nm basil.

**basilique** /bazilik/ nf basilica.

**basque** /bask/ adj Basque. **B~** nmf Basque.

**basse** /bɑs/ →BAS.

**basse-cour** (*pl* **basses-cours**) /baskuʀ/ *nf* farmyard.

**bassesse** /bɑsɛs/ *nf* baseness; (action) base act.

**bassin** /basɛ̃/ *nm* (pièce d'eau) pond; (de piscine) pool; (Géog) basin; (Anat) pelvis; (plat) bowl; ∼ houiller coalfield.

**bassine** /basin/ *nf* bowl.

**basson** /basɔ̃/ *nm* bassoon.

**bas-ventre** (*pl* ∼**s**) /bɑvɑ̃tʀ/ *nm* lower abdomen.

**bat** /ba/ →BATTRE **11**.

**bataille** /batɑj/ *nf* battle; (fig) fight.

**bâtard, ∼e** /bɑtaʀ, -d/ *adj* (solution) hybrid. ●*nm, f* bastard.

**bateau** (*pl* ∼**x**) /bato/ *nm* boat; pneumatique rubber dinghy. **bateau-mouche** (*pl* **bateaux-mouches**) *nm* sightseeing boat.

**bâti, ∼e** /bɑti/ *adj* bien ∼ well-built.

**bâtiment** /bɑtimɑ̃/ *nm* building; (industrie) building trade; (navire) vessel.

**bâtir** /bɑtiʀ/ **2** *vt* build.

**bâton** /bɑtɔ̃/ *nm* stick; conversation à ∼s rompus rambling conversation; ∼ de rouge lipstick.

**battant** /batɑ̃/ *nm* (vantail) flap; porte à deux ∼s double door.

**battement** /batmɑ̃/ *nm* (de cœur) beat(ing); (temps) interval; (Mus) beat.

**batterie** /batʀi/ *nf* (Mil, Électr) battery; (Mus) drums; ∼ de cuisine pots and pans.

**batteur** /batœʀ/ *nm* (Mus) drummer; (Culin) whisk.

**battre** /batʀ/ **11** *vt/i* beat; (cartes) shuffle; (Culin) whisk; (l'emporter sur) beat; ∼ des ailes flap its wings; ∼ des mains clap; ∼ des paupières blink; ∼ en retraite beat

a retreat; ∼ la semelle stamp one's feet; ∼ son plein be in full swing. □ **se** ∼ *vpr* fight.

**baume** /bom/ *nm* balm.

**bavard, ∼e** /bavaʀ, -d/ *adj* talkative. ●*nm, f* chatterbox.

**bavardage** /bavaʀdaʒ/ *nm* chatter, gossip. **bavarder 11** *vi* chat; (jacasser) chatter, gossip.

**bave** /bav/ *nf* dribble, slobber; (de limace) slime. **baver 11** *vi* dribble, slobber. **baveux, -euse** *adj* dribbling; (omelette) runny.

**bavoir** /bavwaʀ/ *nm* bib.

**bavure** /bavyʀ/ *nf* smudge; (erreur) blunder; ∼ policière police blunder.

**bazar** /bazaʀ/ *nm* bazaar; (objets **11**) clutter.

**BCBG** *abrév mf* (**bon chic bon genre**) posh.

**BD** *abrév f* (**bande dessinée**) comic strip.

**béant, ∼e** /beɑ̃, -t/ *adj* gaping.

**béat, ∼e** /bea, -t/ *adj* (hum) blissful; ∼ d'admiration wide-eyed with admiration.

**beau** (**bel** before vowel or mute h), **belle** (*mpl* ∼**x**) /bo, bɛl/ *adj* beautiful; (femme) beautiful; (homme) handsome; (temps) fine, nice. ●*nm* beauty; au ∼ fixe set fair. ●*adv* il fait ∼ the weather is nice; au ∼ milieu right in the middle; bel et bien well and truly; de plus belle more than ever; faire le ∼ sit up and beg; on a ∼ essayer/insister however much one tries/insists.

**beaucoup** /boku/ *adv* a lot, very much; ∼ de (nombre) many; (quantité) a lot of; pas ∼ (de) not many; (quantité) not much; ∼ plus/mieux much more/better; ∼ trop far too much; de ∼ by far.

**beau-fils** (*pl* **beaux-fils**) /bofis/

*nm* (remariage) stepson.
**beau-frère** (*pl* beaux-frères)
/bofʀɛʀ/ *nm* brother-in-law.
**beau-père** (*pl* beaux-pères)
/bopɛʀ/ *nm* father-in-law; (remariage) stepfather.
**beauté** /bote/ *nf* beauty; finir en
~ end magnificently.
**beaux-arts** /bozaʀ/ *nmpl* fine arts.
**beaux-parents** /boparɑ̃/ *nmpl*
parents-in-law.
**bébé** /bebe/ *nm* baby.
**bébé-éprouvette** (*pl*
bébés-éprouvette) *nm* test-
tube baby.
**bec** /bɛk/ *nm* beak; (de théière)
spout; (de casserole) lip; (bouche
🔢) mouth; ~ de gaz gas
street-lamp.
**bécane** /bekan/ *nf* 🔢 bike.
**bêche** /bɛʃ/ *nf* spade.
**bégayer** /begeje/ 🔢 *vt/i* stammer.
**bègue** /bɛg/ *nmf* stammerer. ● *adj*
être ~ stammer.
**bégueule** /begœl/ *adj* prudish.
**beige** /bɛʒ/ *adj* & *nm* beige.
**beignet** /bɛɲɛ/ *nm* fritter.
**bel** /bɛl/ ➡BEAU.
**bêler** /bele/ 🔢 *vi* bleat.
**belette** /bəlɛt/ *nf* weasel.
**belge** /bɛlʒ/ *adj* Belgian. B~ *nmf*
Belgian.
**Belgique** /bɛlʒik/ *nf* Belgium.
**bélier** /belje/ *nm* ram; le B~ Aries.
**belle** /bɛl/ ➡BEAU.
**belle-fille** (*pl* belles-filles)
/bɛlfij/ *nf* daughter-in-law; (remariage) stepdaughter.
**belle-mère** (*pl* belles-mères)
/bɛlmɛʀ/ *nf* mother-in-law; (remariage) stepmother.
**belle-sœur** (*pl* belles-sœurs)
/bɛlsœʀ/ *nf* sister-in-law.
**belliqueux**, -euse /belikø, -z/ *adj*

warlike.
**bémol** /bemɔl/ *nm* (Mus) flat.
**bénédiction** /benediksjɔ̃/ *nf*
blessing.
**bénéfice** /benefis/ *nm* (gain)
profit; (avantage) benefit.
**bénéficiaire** /benefisjɛʀ/ *nmf*
beneficiary.
**bénéficier** /benefisje/ 🔢 *vi* ~ de
benefit from; (jouir de) enjoy, have.
**bénéfique** /benefik/ *adj* beneficial.
**Bénélux** /benelyks/ *nm* Benelux.
**bénévole** /benevɔl/ *adj* voluntary.
**bénin**, -igne /benɛ̃, -iɲ/ *adj* minor;
(tumeur) benign.
**bénir** /beniʀ/ 🔢 *vt* bless. **bénit**,
~e *adj* (eau) holy; (pain) conse-
crated.
**benjamin**, ~e /bɛ̃ʒamɛ̃, -in/ *nm*, *f*
youngest child.
**benne** /bɛn/ *nf* (de grue) scoop; ~
à ordures (camion) waste disposal
truck; (conteneur) skip; ~ (bascu-
lante) dump truck.
**béquille** /bekij/ *nf* crutch; (de
moto) stand.
**berceau** (*pl* ~x) /bɛʀso/ *nm* (de
bébé, civilisation) cradle.
**bercer** /bɛʀse/ 🔢 *vt* (balancer)
rock; (apaiser) lull; (leurrer) delude.
**béret** /beʀe/ *nm* beret.
**berge** /bɛʀʒ/ *nf* (bord) bank.
**berger**, -ère /bɛʀʒe, -ɛʀ/ *nm*, *f*
shepherd; shepherdess.
**berne**: en ~ /âbɛʀn/ *loc* at
halfmast.
**berner** /bɛʀne/ 🔢 *vt* fool.
**besogne** /bəzɔɲ/ *nf* task, job.
**besoin** /bəzwɛ̃/ *nm* need; avoir ~
de need; au ~ if need be; dans le
~ in need.
**bestiole** /bɛstjɔl/ *nf* 🔢 bug.
**bétail** /betaj/ *nm* livestock.
**bête** /bɛt/ *adj* stupid. ● *nf* animal;

~ noire pet hate; ~ sauvage wild beast; chercher la petite ~ be overfussy.

**bêtise** /betiz/ nf stupidity; (action) stupid thing.

**béton** /betɔ̃/ nm concrete; ~ armé reinforced concrete; en ~ (mur) concrete; (argument 🔟) watertight. **bétonnière** nf concrete mixer.

**betterave** /bɛtʀav/ nf beet; ~ rouge beetroot.

**beugler** /bøgle/ 🔟 vi bellow; (radio) blare out.

**beur** /bœʀ/ nmf & adj 🔟 second-generation North African living in France.

**beurre** /bœʀ/ nm butter. **beurré, ~e** adj buttered; 🔟 drunk. **beurrier** nm butter-dish.

**bévue** /bevy/ nf blunder.

**biais** /bjɛ/ nm (moyen) way; par le ~ de by means of; de ~, en ~ at an angle.

**bibelot** /biblo/ nm ornament.

**biberon** /bibʀɔ̃/ nm (feeding) bottle; nourrir au ~ bottle-feed.

**bible** /bibl/ nf bible; la B~ the Bible.

**bibliographie** /biblijɔgʀafi/ nf bibliography.

**bibliothécaire** /biblijɔtekɛʀ/ nmf librarian.

**bibliothèque** /biblijɔtɛk/ nf library; (meuble) bookcase.

**bic®** /bik/ nm biro®.

**bicarbonate** /bikaʀbɔnat/ nm ~ (de soude) bicarbonate (of soda).

**biceps** /bisɛps/ nm biceps.

**biche** /biʃ/ nf doe; ma ~ darling.

**bichonner** /biʃɔne/ 🔟 vt pamper.

**bicyclette** /bisiklɛt/ nf bicycle.

**bide** /bid/ nm (ventre 🔟) paunch; (échec 🔟) flop.

**bidet** /bidɛ/ nm bidet.

**bidon** /bidɔ̃/ nm can; (plus grand) drum; (ventre 🔟) belly; c'est du ~! it's a load of hogwash! ● adj inv 🔟 phoney.

**bidonville** /bidɔ̃vil/ nm shanty town.

**bidule** /bidyl/ nm 🔟 thing.

**Biélorussie** /bjelɔʀysi/ nf Byelorussia.

**bien** /bjɛ̃/ adv well; (très) quite, very; ~ des (nombre) many; tu as ~ de la chance you are very lucky; j'aimerais ~ I would like to; ce n'est pas ~ de it is not nice to; ~ sûr of course. ● nm good; (patrimoine) possession; ~s de consommation consumer goods. ● adj inv good; (passable) all right; (en forme) well; (à l'aise) comfortable; (beau) attractive; (respectable) nice, respectable. ● conj ~ que (al-)though; ~ que ce soit although it is being. **bien-aimé, ~e** adj & nm, f beloved. **bien-être** nm wellbeing.

**bienfaisance** /bjɛ̃fəzɑ̃s/ nf charity; fête de ~ charity event. **bienfaisant, ~e** adj beneficial.

**bienfait** /bjɛ̃fɛ/ nm (kind) favour; (avantage) beneficial effect. **bienfaiteur, -trice** nm, f benefactor.

**bien-pensant, ~e** /bjɛ̃pɑ̃sɑ̃, -t/ adj right-thinking.

**bienséance** /bjɛ̃seɑ̃s/ nf propriety.

**bientôt** /bjɛ̃to/ adv soon; à ~ see you soon.

**bienveillance** /bjɛ̃vejɑ̃s/ nf kind-(li)ness.

**bienvenu, ~e** /bjɛ̃vny/ adj welcome. ● nm, f être le ~, être la ~e be welcome.

**bienvenue** /bjɛ̃vny/ nf welcome; souhaiter la ~ à welcome.

**bière** /bjɛʀ/ nf beer; (cercueil) coffin; ~ blonde lager; ~ brune ≈

stout; **~ pression** draught beer.

**bifteck** /biftɛk/ *nm* steak.

**bifurquer** /bifyʀke/ **1** *vi* branch off, fork.

**bigarré, ~e** /bigaʀe/ *adj* motley.

**bigoudi** /bigudi/ *nm* curler.

**bijou** (*pl* **~x**) /biʒu/ *nm* jewel; **~x en or** gold jewellery. **bijouterie** *nf* (boutique) jewellery shop; (Comm) jewellery. **bijoutier, -ière** *nm, f* jeweller.

**bilan** /bilɑ̃/ *nm* outcome; (d'une catastrophe) (casualty) toll; (Comm) balance sheet; **faire le ~ de** assess; **~ de santé** check-up.

**bile** /bil/ *nf* bile; **se faire de la ~** 🔢 worry.

**bilingue** /bilɛ̃g/ *adj* bilingual.

**billard** /bijaʀ/ *nm* billiards (+ *pl*); (table) billiard-table.

**bille** /bij/ *nf* (d'enfant) marble; (de billard) billiard-ball.

**billet** /bijɛ/ *nm* ticket; (lettre) note; (article) column; **~ (de banque)** (bank) note; **~ de 50 euros** 50-euro note.

**billetterie** /bijɛtʀi/ *nf* cash dispenser.

**billion** /biljɔ̃/ *nm* billion; (US) trillion.

**bimensuel, ~le** /bimɑ̃sɥɛl/ *adj* fortnightly, bimonthly.

**binette** /binɛt/ *nf* hoe; (visage) face; (Internet) smiley.

**biochimie** /bjoʃimi/ *nf* biochemistry.

**biodégradable** /bjodegʀadabl/ *adj* biodegradable.

**biographie** /bjɔgʀafi/ *nf* biography.

**biologie** /bjɔlɔʒi/ *nf* biology. **biologique** *adj* biological; (*produit*) organic.

**bioterrorisme** /bjotɛʀɔʀism/ *nm* bioterrorism.

**bis** /bis/ *nm & interj* encore.

**biscornu, ~e** /biskɔʀny/ *adj* crooked; (bizarre) cranky 🔢.

**biscotte** /biskɔt/ *nf* continental toast.

**biscuit** /biskɥi/ *nm* biscuit; (US) cookie; **~ salé** cracker; **~ de Savoie** sponge-cake.

**bise** /biz/ *nf* 🔢 kiss; (vent) north wind.

**bison** /bizɔ̃/ *nm* buffalo.

> **Bison Futé** Devised by the French traffic information service, *Bison Futé* reports on travel conditions nationally and recommends alternative routes (*les itinéraires 'bis'*) for travellers wishing to avoid traffic jams. *Bison Futé* traffic tips are made known through the media and appear on road signs in yellow on a green background.

**bisou** /bizu/ *nm* 🔢 kiss.

**bistro(t)** /bistʀo/ *nm* 🔢 café, bar.

**bit** /bit/ *nm* (Ordinat) bit.

**bitume** /bitym/ *nm* asphalt.

**bizarre** /bizaʀ/ *adj* odd, strange. **bizarrerie** *nf* peculiarity.

**blafard, ~e** /blafaʀ, -d/ *adj* pale.

**blague** /blag/ *nf* 🔢 joke; **sans ~!** no kidding! 🔢.

**blaguer** /blage/ **1** *vi* joke.

**blaireau** (*pl* **~x**) /blɛʀo/ *nm* shaving-brush; (animal) badger.

**blâmer** /blame/ **1** *vt* criticize.

**blanc, blanche** /blɑ̃, blɑ̃ʃ/ *adj* white; (*papier, page*) blank. ● *nm* white; (espace) blank; **~ d'œuf** egg white; **~ de poireau** white part of the leek; **~ (de poulet)** chicken breast; **le ~** (linge) whites; **laisser en ~** leave blank. **B~, Blanche** *nm,* *f* white man, white woman. **blanche** *nf* (Mus) minim.

**b** **blanchiment** /blɑ̃ʃimɑ̃/ *nm* (d'argent) laundering.

**blanchir** /blɑ̃ʃiʀ/ **2** *vt* whiten; (*personne*, fig) clear; (*argent*) launder; (Culin) blanch; ~ (à la chaux) whitewash. ● *vi* turn white.

**blanchisserie** /blɑ̃ʃisʀi/ *nf* laundry.

**blason** /blazɔ̃/ *nm* coat of arms.

**blasphème** /blasfɛm/ *nm* blasphemy.

**blé** /ble/ *nm* wheat.

**blême** /blɛm/ *adj* pallid.

**blessant, ~e** /blesɑ̃, -t/ *adj* hurtful.

**blessé, ~e** /blese/ *nm, f* casualty, injured person.

**blesser** /blese/ **1** *vt* injure, hurt; (*par balle*) wound; (*offenser*) hurt. □ se ~ *vpr* injure or hurt oneself. **blessure** *nf* wound.

**bleu, ~e** /blø/ *adj* blue; (Culin) very rare; ~ **marine/turquoise** navy blue/turquoise; **avoir une peur ~e** be scared stiff. ● *nm* blue; (*contusion*) bruise; ~ (**de travail**) overalls (+ pl).

**bleuet** /bløɛ/ *nm* cornflower.

**blindé, ~e** /blɛ̃de/ *adj* armoured; (fig) immune (**contre** to); **porte ~e** security car. ● *nm* armoured car, tank.

**blinder** /blɛ̃de/ **1** *vt* armour; (fig) harden.

**bloc** /blɔk/ *nm* block; (*de papier*) pad; **serrer à** ~ tighten hard; **en** ~ (*matériau*) in a block; (*nier*) outright.

**blocage** /blɔkaʒ/ *nm* (*des prix*) freeze, freezing; (*des roues*) locking; (Psych) block.

**bloc-notes** ( *pl* **blocs-notes**) /blɔknɔt/ *nm* note-pad.

**blocus** /blɔkys/ *nm* blockade.

**blond, ~e** /blɔ̃, -d/ *adj* fair, blond. ● *nm, f* fair-haired man, fairhaired woman.

**bloquer** /blɔke/ **1** *vt* block; (*porte, machine*) jam; (*roues*) lock; (*prix, crédits*) freeze. □ se ~ *vpr* jam; (*roues*) lock; ( *freins*) jam; (*ordinateur*) crash; **bloqué par la neige** snowbound.

**blottir (se)** /(sə)blɔtiʀ/ **2** *vpr* snuggle, huddle (**contre** against).

**blouse** /bluz/ *nf* overall. **blouse blanche** *nf* white coat.

**blouson** /bluzɔ̃/ *nm* jacket, blouson.

**bluffer** /blœfe/ **1** *vt/i* bluff.

**bobine** /bɔbin/ *nf* (*de fil, film*) reel; (Électr) coil.

**bobo** /bobo/ *nm* **1** sore, cut; **avoir** ~ have a pain.

**bocal** ( *pl* **-aux**) /bɔkal, -o/ *nm* jar.

**bœuf** ( *pl* **~s**) /bœf, bø/ *nm* bullock; (US) steer; (*viande*) beef; **~s** oxen.

**bogue** /bɔg/ *nm* (Ordinat) bug.

**bohème** /bɔɛm/ *adj & nmf* bohemian.

**boire** /bwaʀ/ **12** *vt/i* (*personne, plante*) drink; (*argile*) soak up; ~ **un coup** **1** have a drink.

**bois** /bwa/ ➤BOIRE **12**. ● *nm* (*matériau, forêt*) wood; **de** ~, **en** ~ wooden. ● *nmpl* (*de cerf*) antlers.

**boiseries** /bwazʀi/ *nfpl* panelling.

**boisson** /bwasɔ̃/ *nf* drink.

**boit** /bwa/ ➤BOIRE **12**.

**boîte** /bwat/ *nf* box; (*de conserves*) tin, can; (*entreprise* **1**) firm; **en** ~ tinned, canned; ~ **à gants** glove compartment; ~ **aux lettres** letterbox; ~ **aux lettres électronique** mailbox; ~ **de nuit** night-club; ~ **postale** post-office box; ~ **de vitesses** gear box.

**boiter** /bwate/ **1** vi limp. **boiteux, -euse** adj lame; (raisonnement) shaky.

**boîtier** /bwatje/ nm case.

**bol** /bɔl/ nm bowl; ~ **d'air** a breath of fresh air; **avoir du** ~! be lucky.

**bolide** /bɔlid/ nm racing car.

**Bolivie** /bɔlivi/ nf Bolivia.

**bombardement** /bɔ̃bardəmɑ̃/ nm bombing; shelling.

**bombarder** /bɔ̃barde/ **1** vt bomb; (par obus) shell; ~ **qn de** (fig) bombard sb with. **bombardier** nm (Aviat) bomber.

**bombe** /bɔ̃b/ nf bomb; (atomiseur) spray, aerosol.

**bombé, ~e** /bɔ̃be/ adj rounded; (route) cambered.

**bon, bonne** /bɔ̃, bɔn/ adj good; (qui convient) right; ~ **à/pour** (approprié) it to/for; bonne année happy New Year; ~ **anniversaire** happy birthday; ~ **appétit/voyage** enjoy your meal/trip; bonne chance/nuit good luck/night; ~ **sens** common sense; bonne femme (péj) woman; de bonne heure early; **à quoi** ~? what's the point? ● adv **sentir** ~ smell nice; **tenir** ~ stand firm; **il fait** ~ the weather is mild. ● interj right, well. ● nm (billet) voucher, coupon; ~ **de commande** order form; **pour de** ~ for good. **bonne** nf (domestique) maid.

**bonbon** /bɔ̃bɔ̃/ nm sweet; (US) candy.

**bonbonne** /bɔ̃bɔn/ nf demijohn; (de gaz) cylinder.

**bond** /bɔ̃/ nm leap; **faire un** ~ (de surprise) jump.

**bonde** /bɔ̃d/ nf plug; (trou) plughole.

**bondé, ~e** /bɔ̃de/ adj packed.

**bondir** /bɔ̃dir/ **2** vi leap; (de surprise) jump.

**bonheur** /bɔnœr/ nm happiness; (chance) (good) luck; **au petit** ~ haphazardly; **par** ~ luckily.

**bonhomme** (pl bonshommes) /bɔnɔm, bɔzɔm/ nm fellow; ~ **de neige** snowman. ● adj inv good hearted.

**bonifier (se)** /(sə)bɔnifje/ **45** vpr improve.

**bonjour** /bɔ̃ʒur/ nm & interj hallo, hello, good morning ou afternoon.

**bon marché** /bɔ̃marʃe/ adj inv cheap. ● adv cheap (ly)

**bonne** /bɔn/ →**BON**.

**bonne-maman** (pl bonnes-mamans) /bɔnmamɑ̃/ nf **1** granny.

**bonnement** /bɔnmɑ̃/ adv **tout** ~ quite simply.

**bonnet** /bɔnɛ/ nm hat; (de soutien-gorge) cup; ~ **de bain** swimming cap. **bonneterie** nf hosiery.

**bonsoir** /bɔ̃swar/ nm good evening; (en se couchant) good night.

**bonté** /bɔ̃te/ nf kindness.

**bonus** /bɔnys/ nm (Auto) no-claims bonus.

**boots** /buts/ nmpl ankle boots.

**bord** /bɔr/ nm edge; (rive) bank; **à** (~ **de**) on board; **au** ~ **de la mer** at the seaside; **au** ~ **des larmes** on the verge of tears; ~ **de la route** road-side.

**bordeaux** /bɔrdo/ adj inv maroon. ● nm inv Bordeaux.

**bordel** /bɔrdɛl/ nm brothel; (désordre **1**) shambles.

**border** /bɔrde/ **1** vt line, border; (tissu) edge; (personne, lit) tuck in.

**bordereau** (pl ~x) /bɔrdəro/ nm (document) slip.

**bordure** /bɔrdyr/ nf border; **en** ~

de on the edge of.

**borgne** /bɔrɲ/ adj one-eyed.

**borne** /bɔrn/ nf boundary marker; (pour barrer le passage) bollard; ∼ (kilométrique) ≈ milestone; ∼s limits.

**borné**, ∼e /bɔrne/ adj (esprit) narrow; ( personne) narrow minded.

**borner (se)** /(sə)bɔrne/ 1 vpr confine oneself (à to).

**bosniaque** /bɔsnjak/ adj Bosnian. B∼ nmf Bosnian.

**Bosnie** /bɔsni/ nf Bosnia.

**bosse** /bos/ nf bump; (de chameau) hump; avoir la ∼ de 1 have a gift for; avoir roulé sa ∼ have been around. **bosselé**, ∼e adj dented; (terrain) bumpy.

**bosser** /bose/ 1 vi 1 work (hard).

**bossu**, ∼e /bosy/ adj hunchbacked. ● nm, f hunchback.

**botanique** /bɔtanik/ nf botany. ● adj botanical.

**botte** /bɔt/ nf boot; (de fleurs, légumes) bunch; (de paille) bundle, bale; ∼s de caoutchouc wellingtons.

**botter** /bɔte/ 1 vt 1 ça me botte I like the idea.

**bottin®** /bɔtɛ̃/ nm phone book.

**bouc** /buk/ nm (billy-)goat; (barbe) goatee; ∼ émissaire scapegoat.

**boucan** /bukã/ nm 1 din.

**bouche** /buʃ/ nf mouth; (lèvres) lips; ∼ bée open-mouthed; ∼ d'égout manhole; ∼ d'incendie (fire)hydrant; ∼ de métro entrance to the underground or subway (US). **bouche-à-bouche** nm inv mouth-to-mouth resuscitation. **bouche-à-oreille** nm inv word of mouth.

**bouché**, ∼e /buʃe/ adj ( profession, avenir) oversubscribed; (stupide: péj) stupid.

**bouchée** /buʃe/ nf mouthful.

**boucher¹** /buʃe/ 1 vt block; (bouteille) cork. □ se ∼ vpr get blocked; se ∼ le nez hold one's nose.

**boucher²**, -ère /buʃe, -ɛr/ nm, f butcher. **boucherie** nf butcher's (shop); (carnage) butchery.

**bouchon** /buʃɔ̃/ nm stopper; (en liège) cork; (de stylo, tube) cap; (de pêcheur) float; (embouteillage) traffic jam; ∼ de cérumen plug of earwax.

**boucle** /bukl/ nf (de ceinture) buckle; (de cheveux) curl; (forme) loop; ∼ d'oreille earring. **bouclé**, ∼e adj (cheveux) curly.

**boucler** /bukle/ 1 vt fasten; (enfermer 1) shut up; (encercler) seal off; (budget) balance; (terminer) finish off. ● vi curl.

**bouclier** /buklije/ nm shield.

**bouddhiste** /budist/ adj & nmf Buddhist.

**bouder** /bude/ 1 vi sulk. ● vt stay away from.

**boudin** /budɛ̃/ nm black pudding.

**boue** /bu/ nf mud.

**bouée** /bwe/ nf buoy; ∼ de sauvetage lifebuoy.

**boueux**, -euse /buø, -z/ adj muddy.

**bouffe** /buf/ nf 1 food, grub.

**bouffée** /bufe/ nf puff, whiff; (d'orgueil) fit; ∼ de chaleur (Méd) hot flush.

**bouffi**, ∼e /bufi/ adj bloated.

**bouffon**, ∼ne /bufɔ̃, -ɔn/ adj farcical. ● nm buffoon.

**bougeoir** /buʒwar/ nm candlestick.

**bougeotte** /buʒɔt/ nf avoir la ∼ 1 have the fidgets.

**bouger** /buʒe/ 40 vt/i move. □ se ∼ vpr 1 move.

**bougie** /buʒi/ nf candle; (Auto)

spark(ing)-plug.
**bouillant,** ~e /bujɑ̃, -t/ adj boiling; (très chaud) boiling hot.

**bouillie** /buji/ nf (pour bébé) baby cereal; (péj) mush; **en** ~ crushed, mushy.

**bouillir** /bujir/ 🔟 vi boil; (fig) seethe; **faire** ~ boil.

**bouilloire** /bujwar/ nf kettle.

**bouillon** /bujɔ̃/ nm (de cuisson) stock; (potage) broth.

**bouillonner** /bujɔne/ 🔟 vi bubble.

**bouillotte** /bujɔt/ nf hot-water bottle.

**boulanger, -ère** /bulɑ̃ʒe, -ɛr/ nm, f baker. **boulangerie** nf bakery. **boulangerie-pâtisserie** nf bakery (selling cakes and pastries).

**boule** /bul/ nf ball; ~s (jeu) boules; **jouer aux** ~s play boules; **une** ~ **dans la gorge** a lump in one's throat; ~ **de neige** snowball.

> **Boules** A form of bowls, played on rough, dry ground with metal balls. The aim is to throw the balls to land as near as possible to a smaller target ball called the *co-chonnet*. In the South of France, *boules* is often called *pétanque*. ⓘ

**bouleau** (pl ~x) /bulo/ nm (silver) birch.

**boulet** /bulɛ/ nm (de forçat) ball and chain; ~ **(de canon)** cannonball; ~ **de charbon** coal nut.

**boulette** /bulɛt/ nf (de pain, papier) pellet; (bévue) blunder; ~ **de viande** meat ball.

**boulevard** /bulvar/ nm boulevard.

**bouleversant, ~e** /bulversɑ̃, -t/ adj deeply moving. **bouleverse-**

**ment** nm upheaval. **bouleverser** 🔟 vt turn upside down; (pays, plans) disrupt; (émouvoir) upset.

**boulimie** /bulimi/ nf bulimia.

**boulon** /bulɔ̃/ nm bolt.

**boulot, -te** /bulo, -ɔt/ adj (rond 🔟) dumpy. ●nm (travail 🔟) work.

**boum** /bum/ nm & interj bang. ●nf (fête 🔟) party.

**bouquet** /bukɛ/ nm (de fleurs) bunch, bouquet; (d'arbres) clump; **c'est le** ~! 🔟 that's the last straw!

**bouquin** /bukɛ̃/ nm 🔟 book. **bouquiner** 🔟 vt/i 🔟 read. **bouquiniste** nmf second-hand bookseller.

**bourbier** /burbje/ nm mire; (fig) tangle.

**bourde** /burd/ nf blunder.

**bourdon** /burdɔ̃/ nm bumble bee. **bourdonnement** nm buzzing.

**bourg** /bur/ nm (market) town (centre); village centre.

**bourgeois, ~e** /burʒwa, -z/ adj & nm,f middle-class (person); (péj) bourgeois. **bourgeoisie** nf middle class(es).

**bourgeon** /burʒɔ̃/ nm bud.

**bourgogne** /burgɔɲ/ nm Burgundy.

**bourlinguer** /burlɛ̃ge/ 🔟 vi 🔟 travel about.

**bourrage** /buraʒ/ nm ~ **de crâne** brainwashing.

**bourratif, -ive** /buratif, -v/ adj stodgy.

**bourreau** (pl ~x) /buro/ nm executioner; ~ **de travail** (fig) workaholic.

**bourrelet** /burlɛ/ nm weather strip, draught excluder; (de chair) roll of fat.

**bourrer** /bure/ 🔟 vt cram (de with); (pipe) fill; ~ **de** (nourriture) stuff with; ~ **de coups** thrash; ~

# bourrique | brasse

le crâne à qn brainwash sb.
**bourrique** /buʀik/ nf donkey; 🔢
pig-headed person.

**bourru, ~e** /buʀy/ adj gruff.

**bourse** /buʀs/ nf purse; (subvention) grant; **la B~** the Stock Exchange.

**boursier, -ière** /buʀsje, -jɛʀ/ adj
(valeurs) Stock Exchange. ● nm, f
grant holder.

**boursoufler** /buʀsufle/ 🔟 vt (visage) cause to swell; (peinture)
blister.

**bousculade** /buskylad/ nf crush;
(précipitation) rush. **bousculer** 🔟 vt
(pousser) jostle; (presser) rush; (renverser) knock over.

**bousiller** /buzije/ 🔟 vt 🔢 wreck.

**boussole** /busɔl/ nf compass.

**bout** /bu/ nm end; (de langue,
bâton) piece; (morceau) bit; à ~
exhausted; à ~ de souffle out of
breath; à ~ portant point-blank;
au ~ de (après) after; venir à ~
de (finir) manage to finish; d'un ~
à l'autre throughout; au ~ du
compte in the end; ~ filtre
filtertip.

**bouteille** /butɛj/ nf bottle; ~
d'oxygène oxygen cylinder.

**boutique** /butik/ nf shop; (de
mode) boutique.

**bouton** /butɔ̃/ nm button; (sur la
peau) spot, pimple; (pousse) bud;
(de porte, radio) knob; ~ de manchette cuff-link. **boutonner** 🔟 vt
button (up). **boutonnière** nf buttonhole. **bouton-pression** (pl
**boutons-pression**) nm press-stud;
(US) snap.

**bouture** /butyʀ/ nf cutting.

**bovin, ~e** /bɔvɛ̃, -in/ adj bovine.
**bovins** nmpl cattle (pl).

**box** (pl ~ ou **boxes**) /bɔks/ nm
lock-up garage; (de dortoir) cubicle;

(d'écurie) (loose) box; (Jur) dock.

**boxe** /bɔks/ nf boxing.

**boyau** (pl ~x) /bwajo/ nm gut;
(corde) catgut; (galerie) gallery; (de
bicyclette) tyre; (US) tire.

**boycotter** /bɔjkɔte/ 🔟 vt boycott.

**BP** abrév f (**boîte postale**) PO Box.

**bracelet** /bʀaslɛ/ nm bracelet; (de
montre) watchstrap.

**braconnier** /bʀakɔnje/ nm
poacher.

**brader** /bʀade/ 🔟 vt sell off. **braderie** nf clearance sale.

**braguette** /bʀagɛt/ nf fly.

**braille** /bʀaj/ nm & adj Braille.

**brailler** /bʀaje/ 🔟 vt/i bawl.

**braise** /bʀɛz/ nf embers (+ pl).

**braiser** /bʀeze/ 🔟 vt (Culin) braise.

**brancard** /bʀɑ̃kaʀ/ nm stretcher;
(de charrette) shaft.

**branche** /bʀɑ̃ʃ/ nf branch.

**branché, ~e** /bʀɑ̃ʃe/ adj 🔢
trendy.

**branchement** /bʀɑ̃ʃmɑ̃/ nm connection. **brancher** 🔟 vt (prise) plug
in; (à un réseau) connect.

**brandir** /bʀɑ̃diʀ/ 🔁 vt brandish.

**branler** /bʀɑ̃le/ 🔟 vi be shaky.

**braquer** /bʀake/ 🔟 vt (arme) aim;
(regard) fix; (roue) turn; (banque: 🔢)
hold up; ~ qn contre turn sb
against. ● vi (Auto) turn (the
wheel). □ **se ~** vpr dig one's
heels in.

**bras** /bʀa/ nm arm; (de rivière)
branch; (Tech) arm; ~ dessus ~
dessous arm in arm; ~ droit (fig)
right hand man; ~ de mer sound;
en ~ de chemise in one's shirtsleeves. ● nmpl (fig) labour, hands.

**brasier** /bʀazje/ nm blaze.

**brassard** /bʀasaʀ/ nm armband.

**brasse** /bʀas/ nf breast-stroke; ~
papillon butterfly (stroke).

**brasser** /bʀase/ **1** *vt* mix; (*bière*) brew; (*affaires*) handle a lot of.
**brasserie** *nf* brewery; (*café*) brasserie.

**brave** /bʀav/ *adj* (*bon*) good; (*valeureux*) brave. **braver 1** *vt* defy.

**bravo** /bʀavo/ *interj* bravo. ●*nm* cheer.

**bravoure** /bʀavuʀ/ *nf* bravery.

**break** /bʀɛk/ *nm* estate car; (US) station-wagon.

**brebis** /bʀəbi/ *nf* ewe.

**brèche** /bʀɛʃ/ *nf* gap, breach; être sur la ∼ be on the go.

**bredouille** /bʀəduj/ *adj* empty-handed.

**bredouiller** /bʀəduje/ **1** *vt/i* mumble.

**bref, brève** /bʀɛf, -v/ *adj* short, brief. ●*adv* in short; en ∼ in short.

**Brésil** /bʀezil/ *nm* Brazil.

**Bretagne** /bʀətaɲ/ *nf* Brittany.

**bretelle** /bʀətɛl/ *nf* (de sac, maillot) strap; (d'autoroute) access road; ∼s (pour pantalon) braces; (US) suspenders.

**breton, ∼ne** /bʀətɔ̃, -ɔn/ *adj & nm* (Ling) Breton. B∼, ∼ne *nm, f* Breton.

**breuvage** /bʀœvaʒ/ *nm* beverage.

**brève** /bʀɛv/ ➡**BREF.**

**brevet** /bʀəvɛ/ *nm* ∼ (d'invention) patent; (diplôme) diploma.

**breveté, ∼e** /bʀəvte/ *adj* patented.

**bribes** /bʀib/ *nfpl* scraps.

**bricolage** /bʀikɔlaʒ/ *nm* do-it-yourself (jobs).

**bricole** /bʀikɔl/ *nf* trifle.

**bricoler** /bʀikɔle/ **1** *vi* do DIY; (US) fix things, tinker with.

**bricoleur, -euse** /bʀikɔlœʀ, -øz/ *nm, f* handyman, handywoman.

**bride** /bʀid/ *nf* bridle.

**bridé, ∼e** /bʀide/ *adj* yeux ∼s slanting eyes.

**brider** /bʀide/ **1** *vt* (*cheval*) bridle; (fig) keep in check.

**brièvement** /bʀijɛvmã/ *adv* briefly.

**brigade** /bʀigad/ *nf* (de police) squad; (Mil) brigade; (fig) team.
**brigadier** *nm* (de gendarmerie) sergeant.

**brigand** /bʀigã/ *nm* robber.

**brillant, ∼e** /bʀijã, -t/ *adj* (couleur) bright; (luisant) shiny; (remarquable) brilliant. ●*nm* (éclat) shine; (diamant) diamond.

**briller** /bʀije/ **1** *vi* shine.

**brimade** /bʀimad/ *nf* vexation.

**brimer 1** *vt* bully, harass; se sentir brimé feel put down.

**brin** /bʀɛ̃/ *nm* (de muguet) sprig; (d'herbe) blade; (de paille) wisp; un ∼ de (un peu) a bit of.

**brindille** /bʀɛ̃dij/ *nf* twig.

**brioche** /bʀijɔʃ/ *nf* brioche, sweet bun; (ventre 🔲) paunch.

**brique** /bʀik/ *nf* brick.

**briquet** /bʀikɛ/ *nm* (cigarette-)lighter.

**brise** /bʀiz/ *nf* breeze.

**briser** /bʀize/ **1** *vt* break. □ se ∼ *vpr* break.

**britannique** /bʀitanik/ *adj* British. B∼ *nmf* Briton; les B∼s the British.

**brocante** /bʀɔkãt/ *nf* bric-à-brac trade; (marché) flea market.

**broche** /bʀɔʃ/ *nf* brooch; (Culin) spit; à la ∼ spit-roasted.

**broché, ∼e** /bʀɔʃe/ *adj* paperback.

**brochet** /bʀɔʃɛ/ *nm* pike.

**brochette** /bʀɔʃɛt/ *nf* skewer.

**brochure** /bʀɔʃyʀ/ *nf* brochure, booklet.

**broder** /bʀɔde/ **1** *vt/i* embroider.

**broderie** /bʀɔdʀi/ nf embroidery.

**broncher** /bʀɔ̃ʃe/ vi sans ~ without turning a hair.

**bronchite** /bʀɔ̃ʃit/ nf bronchitis.

**bronze** /bʀɔ̃z/ nm bronze.

**bronzé, ~e** /bʀɔ̃ze/ adj (sun-)tanned.

**bronzer** /bʀɔ̃ze/ ◉ vi (personne) get a (sun-)tan.

**brosse** /bʀɔs/ nf brush; ~ à dents toothbrush; ~ à habits clothes brush; en ~ (coiffure) in a crew cut.

**brosser** /bʀɔse/ ◉ vt brush; (fig) paint. □ se ~ vpr se ~ les dents/ les cheveux brush one's teeth/hair.

**brouette** /bʀuɛt/ nf wheelbarrow.

**brouhaha** /bʀuaa/ nm hubbub.

**brouillard** /bʀujaʀ/ nm fog.

**brouille** /bʀuj/ nf quarrel.

**brouiller** /bʀuje/ ◉ vt (vue) blur; (œufs) scramble; (amis) set at odds; ~ les pistes cloud the issue. □ se ~ vpr (ciel) cloud over; (amis) fall out.

**brouillon, ~ne** /bʀujɔ̃, -ɔn/ adj untidy. ● nm (rough) draft.

**brousse** /bʀus/ nf la ~ the bush.

**brouter** /bʀute/ vt/i graze.

**broyer** /bʀwaje/ ◉ vt crush; (moudre) grind.

**bru** /bʀy/ nf daughter-in-law.

**bruine** /bʀɥin/ nf drizzle.

**bruissement** /bʀɥismɑ̃/ nm rustling.

**bruit** /bʀɥi/ nm noise; ~ de couloir (fig) rumour.

**bruitage** /bʀɥitaʒ/ nm sound effects.

**brûlant, ~e** /bʀylɑ̃, -t/ adj burning (hot); (sujet) red-hot; (passion) fiery.

**brûlé /bʀyle/ nm burning; ça sent le ~ I can smell something burning. ● ➡BRÛLER ◉.

**brûler** /bʀyle/ ◉ vt/i burn; (es-

sence) use (up); (cierge) light (à to); ~ un feu (rouge) jump the lights; ~ d'envie de faire be longing to do. □ se ~ vpr burn oneself.

**brûlure** /bʀylyʀ/ nf burn; ~s d'estomac heartburn.

**brume** /bʀym/ nf mist. **brumeux, -euse** adj misty; (esprit) hazy.

**brun, ~e** /bʀœ̃, -yn/ adj brown, dark. ● nm brown. ● nm, f dark-haired person. **brunir** ◉ vi turn brown; (bronzer) get a tan.

**brushing** /bʀœʃiŋ/ nm blow-dry.

**brusque** /bʀysk/ adj (personne) abrupt; (geste) violent; (soudain) sudden.

**brusquer** /bʀyske/ ◉ vt be abrupt with; (précipiter) rush.

**brut, ~e** /bʀyt/ adj (diamant) rough; (champagne) dry; (pétrole) crude; (Comm) gross.

**brutal, ~e** (mpl -aux) /bʀytal, -o/ adj brutal. **brutalité** nf brutality.

**brute** /bʀyt/ nf brute.

**Bruxelles** /bʀysɛl/ npr Brussels.

**bruyant, ~e** /bʀɥijɑ̃, -t/ adj noisy.

**bruyère** /bʀyjɛʀ/ nf heather.

**bu** /by/ ➡BOIRE 12.

**bûche** /byʃ/ nf log; ~ de Noël Christmas log; ramasser une ◉ fall.

**bûcher** /byʃe/ ◉ vt/i slog away (at) ◉. ● nm (supplice) stake.

**bûcheron** /byʃʀɔ̃/ nm lumberjack.

**budget** /bydʒɛ/ nm budget. **budgétaire** adj budgetary.

**buée** /bɥe/ nf condensation.

**buffet** /byfɛ/ nm sideboard; (table garnie) buffet.

**buffle** /byfl/ nm buffalo.

**buisson** /bɥisɔ̃/ nm bush.

**buissonnière** /bɥisɔnjɛʀ/ adj faire l'école ~ play truant.

**bulbe** /bylb/ nm bulb.

**bulgare** /bylgaʀ/ adj & nm Bulgarian. **B~** nmf Bulgarian.

**Bulgarie** /bylgaʀi/ nf Bulgaria.

**bulldozer** /byldozɛʀ/ nm bulldozer.

**bulle** /byl/ nf bubble.

**bulletin** /byltɛ̃/ nm bulletin, report; (Scol) report; **~ d'information** news bulletin; **~ météorologique** weather report; **~ (de vote)** ballot-paper; **~ de salaire** pay-slip.

**buraliste** /byʀalist/ nmf tobacconist.

**bureau** (pl ~x) /byʀo/ nm office; (meuble) desk; (comité) board; **~ d'études** design office; **~ de poste** post office; **~ de tabac** tobacconist's (shop); **~ de vote** polling station.

**bureaucrate** /byʀokʀat/ nmf bureaucrat. **bureaucratie** nf bureaucracy. **bureaucratique** adj bureaucratic.

**bureautique** /byʀotik/ nf office automation.

**burlesque** /byʀlɛsk/ adj (histoire) ludicrous; (film) farcical.

**bus** /bys/ nm bus.

**business** /biznɛs/ nm inv (affaires commerciales) business; (affaires privées) affairs.

**buste** /byst/ nm bust.

**but** /by(t)/ nm target; (dessein) aim, goal; (football) goal; **avoir pour ~ de** aim to; **de ~ en blanc** point-blank; **dans le ~ de** with the intention of; **aller droit au ~** go straight to the point.

**butane** /bytan/ nm butane, Calor gas®.

**buté,** **~e** /byte/ adj obstinate.

**buter** /byte/ **1** vi **~ contre** knock against; (trébucher) come up against. ● vt antagonize. □ **se ~** vpr (s'entêter) become obstinate.

**buteur** /bytœʀ/ nm (au football) striker.

**butin** /bytɛ̃/ nm booty, loot.

**butte** /byt/ nf mound; **en ~ à** exposed to.

**buvard** /byvaʀ/ nm blotting-paper.

**buvette** /byvɛt/ nf (refreshment) bar.

**buveur, -euse** /byvœʀ, -øz/ nm, f drinker.

. . . . . . . . . . . . . . . . . . . . . . . . . . . . . .

# Cc

. . . . . . . . . . . . . . . . . . . . . . . . . . . . . .

**c'** /s/ ➡CE.

**ça** /sa/

● pronom démonstratif

····▸ (sujet) it; that; **~ flotte** it floats; **~ suffit!** that's enough!; **~ y est!** that's it!; **~ sent le brûlé** there's a smell of burning; **~ va?** how are things?

····▸ (objet) (proche) this; (plus éloigné) that; **c'est ~** that's right.

····▸ (dans expressions) **où ~?** where?; **quand ~?** when?; **et avec ~?** anything else?

**çà** /sa/ adv **~ et là** here and there.

**cabane** /kaban/ nf hut; (à outils) shed.

**cabaret** /kabaʀɛ/ nm cabaret.

**cabillaud** /kabijo/ nm cod.

**cabine** /kabin/ nf (à la piscine) cubicle; (de bateau) cabin; (de camion) cab; (d'ascenseur) cage; **~ d'essayage** fitting room; **~ de pilotage** cockpit; **~ de plage** beach hut; ~ (téléphonique) phone booth, phone box.

**cabinet** /kabinɛ/ nm (de médecin) surgery; (US) office; (d'avocat) office; (clientèle) practice; (cabinet collectif) firm; (Pol) Cabinet; (pièce) room; ~s (toilettes) toilet; (US) bathroom; ~ de toilette bathroom.

**câble** /kɑbl/ nm cable; (corde) rope; (TV) cable TV. **câbler** vt cable; (TV) install cable television in.

**cabosser** /kabɔse/ ❶ vt dent.

**cabotage** /kabotaʒ/ nm coastal navigation.

**cabrer (se)** /(sə)kabʀe/ ❶ vpr (cheval) rear; se ~ contre rebel against.

**cabriole** /kabʀijɔl/ nf faire des ~s caper about.

**cacahuète** /kakawɛt/ nf peanut.

**cacao** /kakao/ nm cocoa.

**cachalot** /kaʃalo/ nm sperm whale.

**cache** /kaʃ/ nm mask. ● nf hiding place; ~ d'armes arms cache.

**cache-cache** /kaʃkaʃ/ nm inv hide-and-seek.

**cache-nez** /kaʃne/ nm inv scarf.

**cacher** /kaʃe/ ❶ vt hide, conceal (à from). □ se ~ vpr hide; (se trouver caché) be hidden.

**cachet** /kaʃɛ/ nm (de cire) seal; (à l'encre) stamp; (de la poste) postmark; (comprimé) tablet; (d'artiste) fee; (chic) style, cachet.

**cachette** /kaʃɛt/ nf hiding-place; en ~ in secret.

**cachot** /kaʃo/ nm dungeon.

**cachottier, -ière** /kaʃɔtje, -jɛʀ/ adj secretive.

**cacophonie** /kakɔfɔni/ nf cacophony.

**cactus** /kaktys/ nm cactus.

**cadavérique** /kadaveʀik/ adj (teint) deathly pale.

**cadavre** /kadavʀ/ nm corpse; (de victime) body.

**caddie** /kadi/ nm (de supermarché®) trolley; (au golf) caddie.

**cadeau** (pl ~x) /kado/ nm present, gift; faire un ~ à qn give sb a present.

**cadenas** /kadna/ nm padlock.

**cadence** /kadɑ̃s/ nf rhythm, cadence; (de travail) rate; en ~ in time; (marcher) in step.

**cadet, -te** /kadɛ, -t/ adj youngest; (entre deux) younger. ● nm, f youngest (child); younger (child).

**cadran** /kadʀɑ̃/ nm dial; ~ solaire sundial.

**cadre** /kadʀ/ nm frame; (lieu) setting; (milieu) surroundings; (limites) scope; (contexte) framework; dans le ~ de (à l'occasion de) on the occasion of; (dans le contexte de) in the framework of. ● nm (personne) executive; les ~s the managerial staff.

**cadrer** /kadʀe/ ❶ vi ~ avec tally with. ● vt (photo) centre.

**cafard** /kafaʀ/ nm (insecte) cockroach; avoir le ❶ be down in the dumps.

**café** /kafe/ nm coffee; (bar) café; ~ crème espresso with milk; ~ en grains coffee beans; ~ au lait white coffee.

**cafetière** /kaftjɛʀ/ nf coffee-pot; ~ électrique coffee machine.

**cage** /kaʒ/ nf cage; ~ d'ascenseur lift shaft; ~ d'escalier stairwell; ~ thoracique rib cage.

**cageot** /kaʒo/ nm crate.

**cagibi** /kaʒibi/ nm storage room.

**cagneux, -euse** /kaɲø, -z/ adj avoir les genoux ~ be knock-kneed.

**cagnotte** /kaɲɔt/ nf kitty.

**cagoule** /kagul/ nf hood; (passe-montagne) balaclava.

**cahier** /kaje/ nm notebook; (Scol) exercise book; ~ de textes homework notebook; ~ des charges (Tech) specifications (+ pl).

**cahot** /kao/ nm bump, jolt. **cahoteux, -euse** adj bumpy.

**caïd** /kaid/ nm 1 big shot.

**caille** /kɑj/ nf quail.

**cailler** /kɑje/ 1 vi curdle; ça caille 1 it's freezing. □ se ~ vpr (sang) clot; (lait) curdle. **caillot** nm (blood) clot.

**caillou** (pl ~x) /kaju/ nm stone; (galet) pebble.

**caisse** /kɛs/ nf crate, case; (tiroir, machine) till; (guichet) cash desk; (au supermarché) check-out; (bureau) office; (Mus) drum; ~ enregistreuse cash register; ~ d'épargne savings bank; ~ de retraite pension fund. **caissier, -ière** nm, f cashier.

**cajoler** /kaʒɔle/ 1 vt coax.

**calcaire** /kalkɛR/ adj (sol) chalky; (eau) hard.

**calciné, ~e** /kalsine/ adj charred.

**calcul** /kalkyl/ nm calculation; (Scol) arithmetic; (différentiel) calculus; ~ biliaire gallstone.

**calculatrice** /kalkylatRis/ nf calculator. **calculer** 1 vt calculate. **calculette** nf (pocket) calculator.

**cale** /kal/ nf wedge; (pour roue) chock; (de navire) hold; ~ sèche dry dock.

**calé, ~e** /kale/ adj 1 clever.

**caleçon** /kalsɔ̃/ nm boxer shorts (+ pl); underpants (+ pl); (de femme) leggings.

**calembour** /kalãbuR/ nm pun.

**calendrier** /kalãdRije/ nm calendar; (fig) schedule, timetable.

**calepin** /kalpɛ̃/ nm notebook.

**caler** /kale/ 1 vt wedge. ● vi stall; (abandonner 1) give up.

**calfeutrer** /kalføtRe/ 1 vt (fissure) stop up; (porte) draught proof.

**calibre** /kalibR/ nm calibre; (d'un œuf, fruit) grade.

**calice** /kalis/ nm (Relig) chalice; (Bot) calyx.

**califourchon: à ~** /akalifuRʃɔ̃/ loc astride.

**câlin, ~in** /kɑlɛ̃, -in/ adj (regard, ton) affectionate; (personne) cuddly.

**calmant** /kalmã/ nm sedative.

**calme** /kalm/ adj calm. ● nm peace; calm; (maîtrise de soi) composure; du ~! calm down!

**calmer** /kalme/ 1 vt (personne) calm down; (situation) defuse; (douleur) ease; (soif) quench. □ se ~ vpr (personne, situation) calm down; (agitation, tempête) die down; (douleur) ease.

**calomnie** /kalɔmni/ nf (orale) slander; (écrite) libel. **calomnier** 45 vt slander; libel. **calomnieux, -ieuse** adj slanderous; libellous.

**calorie** /kalɔRi/ nf calorie.

**calque** /kalk/ nm tracing; (papier) ~ tracing paper; (fig) exact copy. **calquer** /kalke/ 1 vt trace; (fig) copy; ~ qch sur model sth on.

**calvaire** /kalvɛR/ nm (croix) Calvary; (fig) suffering.

**calvitie** /kalvisi/ nf baldness.

**camarade** /kamaRad/ nmf friend; (Pol) comrade; ~ de jeu playmate. **camaraderie** nf friendship.

**cambouis** /kãbwi/ nm dirty oil.

**cambrer** /kãbRe/ 1 vt arch. □ se ~ vpr straighten one's back.

**cambriolage** /kãbRijɔlaʒ/ nm burglary. **cambrioler** 1 vt burgle.

**cambrioleur, -euse** nm, f burglar.
**camelot** /kamlo/ nm ① street vendor.
**camelote** /kamlɔt/ nf ① junk.
**caméra** /kamera/ nf (cinéma, télévision) camera.
**caméscope®** /kameskɔp/ nm camcorder.
**camion** /kamjɔ̃/ nm lorry, truck.
**camion-citerne** (pl **camions-citernes**) nm tanker. **camionnage** nm haulage. **camionnette** nf van. **camionneur** nm lorry ou truck driver; (entrepreneur) haulage contractor.
**camisole** /kamizɔl/ nf ~ (de force) straitjacket.
**camoufler** /kamufle/ ① vt camouflage.
**camp** /kɑ̃/ nm camp; (Sport, Pol) side.
**campagnard, ~e** /kɑ̃paɲar, -d/ adj country. ● nm, f countryman, countrywoman.
**campagne** /kɑ̃paɲ/ nf country; countryside; (Mil, Pol) campaign.
**campement** /kɑ̃pmɑ̃/ nm camp, encampment.
**camper** /kɑ̃pe/ ① vi camp. ● vt (esquisser) sketch. □ **se** ~ vpr plant oneself. **campeur, -euse** nf, f camper.
**camping** /kɑ̃piŋ/ nm camping; **faire du** ~ go camping; (terrain de) ~ campsite. **camping-car** (pl ~**s**) nm camper-van; (US) motorhome. **camping-gaz®** nm inv (réchaud) camping stove.
**Canada** /kanada/ nm Canada.
**canadien, ~ne** /kanadjɛ̃, -ɛn/ adj Canadian. **C~, ~ne** nm, f Canadian. **canadienne** nf (veste) fur-lined jacket; (tente) ridge tent.
**canaille** /kanɑj/ nf rogue.
**canal** (pl -**aux**) /kanal, -o/ nm (artificiel) canal; (bras de mer) channel; (Tech, TV) channel; (moyen) channel; **par le** ~ **de** through. **canalisation** nf (tuyaux) mains (+ pl). **canaliser** ① vt (eau) canalize; (fig) channel.
**canapé** /kanape/ nm sofa.
**canard** /kanar/ nm duck; (journal ①) rag.
**canari** /kanari/ nm canary.
**cancans** /kɑ̃kɑ̃/ nmpl ① gossip.
**cancer** /kɑ̃ser/ nm cancer; **le C~** Cancer. **cancéreux, -euse** adj cancerous. **cancérigène** adj carcinogenic.
**cancre** /kɑ̃kr/ nm dunce.
**candeur** /kɑ̃dœr/ nf ingenuousness.
**candidat, ~e** /kɑ̃dida, -t/ nm, f (à un examen, Pol) candidate; (à un poste) applicant, candidate (à for). **candidature** /kɑ̃didatyr/ nf application; (Pol) candidacy; **poser sa** ~ **à un poste** apply for a job.
**candide** /kɑ̃did/ adj ingenuous.
**cane** /kan/ nf (female) duck. **caneton** nm duckling.
**canette** /kanet/ nf (bouteille) bottle; (boîte) can.
**canevas** /kanva/ nm canvas; (ouvrage) tapestry; (plan) framework, outline.
**caniche** /kaniʃ/ nm poodle.
**canicule** /kanikyl/ nf scorching heat; (vague de chaleur) heatwave.
**canif** /kanif/ nm penknife.
**canine** /kanin/ nf canine (tooth).
**caniveau** (pl ~**x**) /kanivo/ nm gutter.
**cannabis** /kanabis/ nm cannabis.
**canne** /kan/ nf (walking) stick; ~ **à pêche** fishing rod; ~ **à sucre** sugar cane.
**cannelle** /kanel/ nf cinnamon.

**cannibale** /kanibal/ adj & nmf cannibal.

**canoë** /kanɔe/ nm canoe; (Sport) canoeing.

**canon** /kanɔ̃/ nm (big) gun; (ancien) cannon; (d'une arme) barrel; (principe, règle) canon.

**canot** /kano/ nm dinghy, (small) boat; ~ de sauvetage lifeboat; ~ pneumatique rubber dinghy. **canotier** nm boater.

**cantatrice** /kɑ̃tatris/ nf opera singer.

**cantine** /kɑ̃tin/ nf canteen.

**cantique** /kɑ̃tik/ nm hymn.

**cantonner** /kɑ̃tɔne/ **1** vt (Mil) billet. □ **se** ~ **dans** vpr confine oneself to.

**canular** /kanylar/ nm hoax.

**caoutchouc** /kautʃu/ nm rubber; (élastique) rubber band; ~ **mousse** foam rubber.

**cap** /kap/ nm cape, headland; (direction) course; (obstacle) hurdle; **franchir le** ~ **de la cinquantaine** pass the fifty mark; **mettre le** ~ **sur** steer a course for.

**capable** /kapabl/ adj capable (of); ~ **de faire** able to do, capable of doing.

**capacité** /kapasite/ nf ability; (contenance, potentiel) capacity.

**cape** /kap/ nf cape; **rire sous** ~ laugh up one's sleeve.

**capillaire** /kapilɛr/ adj (lotion, soins) hair; (vaisseau) capillary.

**capitaine** /kapitɛn/ nm captain.

**capital**, ~**e** (mpl -**aux**) /kapital,-o/ adj key, crucial, fundamental; (peine, lettre) capital. ●nm (pl -**aux**) (Comm) capital; (fig) stock; **capitaux** (Comm) capital; ~-**risque** venture capital; ~-**risqueur** venture capitalist. **capitale** nf (ville, lettre) capital.

**capitalisme** /kapitalism/ nm capitalism.

**capitonné**, ~**e** /kapitɔne/ adj padded.

**capituler** /kapityle/ **1** vi capitulate.

**caporal** (pl -**aux**) /kapɔral, -o/ nm corporal.

**capot** /kapo/ nm (Auto) bonnet; (US) hood.

**capote** /kapɔt/ nf (Auto) hood; (US) top; (préservatif 🔢) condom.

**capoter** /kapɔte/ **1** vi overturn; (fig) collapse.

**câpre** /kɑpr/ nf (Culin) caper.

**caprice** /kapris/ nm whim; (colère) tantrum; **faire un** ~ throw a tantrum. **capricieux, -ieuse** adj capricious; (appareil) temperamental.

**Capricorne** /kaprikɔrn/ nm **le** ~ Capricorn.

**capsule** /kapsyl/ nf capsule; (de bouteille) cap.

**capter** /kapte/ **1** vt (eau) collect; (émission) get; (signal) pick up; (fig) win, capture.

**captif, -ive** /kaptif, -v/ adj & nm, f captive.

**captiver** /kaptive/ **1** vt captivate.

**capturer** /kaptyre/ **1** vt capture.

**capuche** /kapyʃ/ nf hood. **capuchon** nm hood; (de stylo) cap.

**car** /kar/ conj because, for. ●nm coach; (US) bus.

**carabine** /karabin/ nf rifle.

**caractère** /karaktɛr/ nm (lettre) character; (nature) nature; ~**s d'imprimerie** block letters; **avoir bon/mauvais** ~ be good-natured/bad-tempered; **avoir du** ~ have character.

**caractériel**, ~**le** /karakterjɛl/ adj (trait) character; (enfant) disturbed.

**caractériser** /karakterize/ **1** vt

characterize. □ **se ~ par** *vpr* be characterized by. **caractéristique** *adj & nf* characteristic.

**carafe** /kaʀaf/ *nf* carafe.

**Caraïbes** /kaʀaib/ *nfpl* **les ~** the Caribbean.

**carambolage** /kaʀɑ̃bɔlaʒ/ *nm* pile-up.

**caramel** /kaʀamɛl/ *nm* caramel; (bonbon) toffee.

**carapace** /kaʀapas/ *nf* shell.

**caravane** /kaʀavan/ *nf* (Auto) caravan; (US) trailer; (convoi) caravan.

**carbone** /kaʀbɔn/ *nm* carbon; (papier) ~ carbon (paper). **carboniser** **1** *vt* burn to ashes.

**carburant** /kaʀbyʀɑ̃/ *nm* (motor) fuel.

**carburateur** /kaʀbyʀatœʀ/ *nm* carburettor; (US) carburetor.

**carcan** /kaʀkɑ̃/ *nm* constraints (+ *pl*).

**carcasse** /kaʀkas/ *nf* (squelette) carcass; (armature) frame; (de voiture) shell.

**cardiaque** /kaʀdjak/ *adj* heart. ● *nmf* heart patient.

**cardinal, ~e** /kaʀdinal, -o/ (*mpl* **-aux**) *adj & nm* cardinal.

**Carême** /kaʀɛm/ *nm* **le ~** Lent.

**carence** /kaʀɑ̃s/ *nf* shortcomings (+ *pl*); inadequacy; (Méd) deficiency; (absence) lack.

**caresse** /kaʀɛs/ *nf* caress; (à un animal) stroke. **caresser** **1** *vt* caress, stroke; (espoir) cherish.

**cargaison** /kaʀɡɛzɔ̃/ *nf* cargo.

**cargo** /kaʀɡo/ *nm* cargo boat.

**caricature** /kaʀikatyʀ/ *nf* caricature.

**carie** /kaʀi/ *nf* (trou) cavity; **la ~** (dentaire) tooth decay.

**carillon** /kaʀijɔ̃/ *nm* chimes (+ *pl*);

(horloge) chiming clock.

**caritatif, -ive** /kaʀitatif, -v/ *adj* **association caritative** charity.

**carnage** /kaʀnaʒ/ *nm* carnage.

**carnassier, -ière** /kaʀnasje, -jɛʀ/ *adj* carnivorous.

**carnaval** (*pl* **~s**) /kaʀnaval/ *nm* carnival.

**carnet** /kaʀnɛ/ *nm* notebook; (de tickets, timbres) book; ~ **d'adresses** address book; ~ **de chèques** chequebook.

**carotte** /kaʀɔt/ *nf* carrot.

**carpe** /kaʀp/ *nf* carp.

**carré, ~e** /kaʀe/ *adj* (forme, mesure) quare; (fig) straightforward; **un mètre ~** one square metre. ● *nm* square; (de terrain) patch.

**carreau** (*pl* **~x**) /kaʀo/ *nm* (window) pane; (par terre, au mur) tile; (dessin) check; (aux cartes) diamonds (+ *pl*); **à ~x** (tissu) check(ed); (papier) squared.

**carrefour** /kaʀfuʀ/ *nm* crossroads (+ *sg*).

**carrelage** /kaʀlaʒ/ *nm* tiling; (sol) tiles.

**carrément** /kaʀemɑ̃/ *adv* (complètement) completely; (stupide, dangereux) downright; (dire) straight out; **elle a ~ démissionné** she went straight ahead and resigned.

**carrière** /kaʀjɛʀ/ *nf* career; (terrain) quarry.

**carrossable** /kaʀosabl/ *adj* suitable for vehicles.

**carrosse** /kaʀos/ *nm* (horse-drawn) coach.

**carrosserie** /kaʀosʀi/ *nf* (Auto) body(work).

**carrure** /kaʀyʀ/ *nf* shoulders; (fig) necessary qualities, calibre.

**cartable** /kaʀtabl/ *nm* satchel.

**carte** /kaʀt/ *nf* card; (Géog) map;

(Naut) chart; (au restaurant) menu; **~s** (jeu) cards; **à la ~** (manger) à la carte; (horaire) personalized; **donner ~ blanche à** to give a free hand to; **~ bleue®** credit card; **~ de crédit** credit card; **~ de fidélité** loyalty card; **~ grise** (car) registration document; **~ d'identité** identity card; **~ magnétique** swipe card; **~ de paiement** debit card; **~ postale** postcard; **~ à puce** smart card; **~ de séjour** resident's permit; **~ SIM** SIM card; **~ des vins** wine list; **~ de visite** (business) card; **~ vitale** social insurance smart card.

> **Carte d'identité** Not to be confused with a passport, this is a proof of identity carried by French citizens. It is issued by the *préfecture* and is valid for ten years. Though not compulsory, it is used to guarantee payments by cheque and is accepted as a travel document within the EU.

**cartilage** /kaʀtilaʒ/ nm cartilage.

**carton** /kaʀtɔ̃/ nm cardboard; (boîte) (cardboard) box; **~ à dessin** portfolio; **faire un ~** 🔢 do well.

**cartonné, ~e** /kaʀtone/ adj **livre ~** hardback.

**cartouche** /kaʀtuʃ/ nf cartridge; (de cigarettes) carton. **cartouchière** nf cartridge-belt.

**cas** /kɑ/ nm case; **au ~ où** in case; **~ urgent** emergency; **en aucun ~** on no account; **en ~ de** in the event of, in case of; **en tout ~** in any case; (du moins) at least; **faire ~ de** to set great store by; **~ de conscience** moral dilemma.

**casanier, -ière** /kazanje, -jɛʀ/ adj home-loving.

**cascade** /kaskad/ nf waterfall; (au cinéma) stunt; (fig) spate, series (+ sg).

**cascadeur, -euse** /kaskadœʀ, -øz/ nm, f stuntman, stuntwoman.

**case** /kɑz/ nf hut; (de damier) square; (compartiment) pigeon-hole; (sur un formulaire) box.

**caser** /kaze/ **1** vt 🔢 (mettre) put; (loger) put up; (dans un travail) find a job for; (marier: péj) marry off.

**caserne** /kazɛʀn/ nf barracks; **~ de sapeurs-pompiers** fire station.

**casier** /kazje/ nm pigeon-hole, compartment; (à chaussures) rack; **~ judiciaire** criminal record.

**casque** /kask/ nm (de motard) crash helmet; (de cycliste) cycle helmet; (chez le coiffeur) (hair-)drier; **~ (à écouteurs)** headphones; **~ anti-bruit** ear defenders; **~ de protection** safety helmet.

**casquette** /kaskɛt/ nf cap.

**cassant, ~e** /kasɑ̃, -t/ adj brittle; (brusque) curt.

**cassation** /kasasjɔ̃/ nf **cour de ~** appeal court.

**casse** /kɑs/ nf (objets) breakages; (lieu) breaker's yard; **mettre à la ~** scrap.

**casse-cou** /kasku/ nmf inv daredevil.

**casse-croûte** /kɑskʀut/ nm inv snack.

**casse-noix** /kɑsnwa/ nm inv nutcrackers (+ pl).

**casse-pieds** /kɑspje/ nmf inv 🔢 pain (in the neck) 🔢.

**casser** /kɑse/ **1** vt break; (annuler) annul; **~ les pieds à qn** 🔢 annoy sb. ●vi break. □ **se ~** vpr break; (partir) 🔢 be off 🔢.

**casserole** /kɑsʀɔl/ nf saucepan.

**casse-tête** /kɑstɛt/ nm inv (problème) headache; (jeu) brain teaser.

**cassette** /kasɛt/ nf casket; (de magnétophone) cassette, tape; (de vidéo) video tape; ~ audio numérique ~ digital audio tape.

**cassis** /kasi(s)/ nm inv blackcurrant.

**cassure** /kasyʀ/ nf break.

**castor** /kastɔʀ/ nm beaver.

**castration** /kastʀasjɔ̃/ nf castration.

**catalogue** /katalɔg/ nm catalogue.

**catalyseur** /katalizœʀ/ nm catalyst; (Auto) catalytic convertor.

**catastrophe** /katastʀɔf/ nf disaster, catastrophe. **catastrophique** adj catastrophic.

**catch** /katʃ/ nm (all-in) wrestling.

**catéchisme** /kateʃism/ nm catechism.

**catégorie** /kategɔʀi/ nf category. **catégorique** adj categorical.

**cathédrale** /katedʀal/ nf cathedral.

**catholique** /katɔlik/ adj Catholic; pas très ~ a bit fishy.

**catimini** : en ~ /ɑ̃katimini/ loc on the sly.

**cauchemar** /koʃmaʀ/ nm nightmare.

**cause** /koz/ nf cause; (raison) reason; (Jur) case; à ~ de because of; en ~ (en jeu, concerné) involved; pour ~ de on account of; mettre en ~ implicate; remettre en ~ call into question.

**causer** /koze/ **1** vt cause; (discuter de **1**) ~ travail talk shop; ~ de talk about. ● vi chat. **causerie** nf talk.

**causette** /kozɛt/ nf (Internet) chat; faire la ~ have a chat.

**caution** /kosjɔ̃/ nf surety; (Jur) bail; (appui) backing; (garantie) deposit; libéré sous ~ released on bail. **cautionner** vt guarantee; (soutenir) back.

**cavalcade** /kavalkad/ nf stampede, rush.

**cavalier**, -ière /kavalje, -jɛʀ/ adj offhand; allée cavalière bridle path. ● nm, f rider; (pour danser) partner. ● nm (aux échecs) knight.

**cave** /kav/ nf cellar. ● adj sunken.

**caveau** (pl ~x) /kavo/ nm vault.

**caverne** /kavɛʀn/ nf cave.

**CCP** abrév m (compte chèque postal) post office account.

**CD** abrév m (compact disc) CD.

**CD-ROM** abrév m inv (compact disc read only memory) CD-ROM.

---

**ce, c', cet, cette** (pl ces)
/sə, s, sɛt, se/

c' before e. cet before vowel or
mute h.

● **ce, cet, cette** (pl ces) adjectif
démonstratif

····▸ this; (plus éloigné) that; ces these; (plus éloigné) those; cette nuit (passée) last night; (à venir) tonight.

● **ce, c'** pronom démonstratif

····▸ c'est it's ou it is; c'est un policier he's a policeman; ~ sont eux qui l'ont fait they did it; qui est- ~? who is it?

····▸ ce que/qui what; ~ que je ne comprends pas what I don't understand; elle est venue, ~ qui est étonnant she came, which is surprising; ~ que tu as de la chance! how lucky you are! tout ~ qu'elle trouve/peut everything she finds/can

---

**CE** abrév f (Communauté européenne) EC.

**CEAM** abrév f (Carte européenne d'assurance maladie) EHIC.

**ceci** /səsi/ pron this.

**cécité** /sesite/ nf blindness.

**céder** /sede/ **14** vt give up; ~ **le passage** give way; (vendre) sell. ● vi (se rompre) give way; (se soumettre) give in.

**cédérom** /sederɔm/ nm CD-ROM.

**cédille** /sedij/ nf cedilla.

**cèdre** /sɛdʀ/ nm cedar.

**CEI** abrév f (**Communauté des États indépendants**) CIS.

**ceinture** /sɛtyʀ/ nf belt; (taille) waist; ~ **de sauvetage** lifebelt; ~ **de sécurité** seatbelt.

**cela** /səla/ pron it, that; (pour désigner) that; ~ **va de soi** it is obvious; ~ **dit/fait** having said/done that.

**célèbre** /selɛbʀ/ adj famous. **célébrer** **14** vt celebrate. **célébrité** nf fame; (personne) celebrity.

**céleri** /sɛlʀi/ nm (en branches) celery. **céleri-rave** (pl **célerisraves**) nm celeriac.

**célibat** /seliba/ nm celibacy; (état) single status.

**célibataire** /selibatɛʀ/ adj single. ● nm bachelor. ● nf single woman.

**celle, celles** /sɛl/ ⇒CELUI.

**cellulaire** /selylɛʀ/ adj cell; emprisonnement ~ solitary confinement; fourgon ou voiture ~ prison van; téléphone ~ cellular phone.

**cellule** /selyl/ nf cell; ~ **souche** stem cell.

**celui, celle** (pl **ceux, celles**) /səlɥi, sɛl, sø/ pron the one; ~ **de mon ami** my friend's; ~**-ci** this (one); ~**-là** that (one); **ceux-ci** these (ones); **ceux-là** those (ones).

**cendre** /sɑdʀ/ nf ash.

**cendrier** /sɑdʀije/ nm ashtray.

**censé, ~e** /sɑse/ adj être ~ **faire** be supposed to do.

**censeur** /sɑsœʀ/ nm censor; (Scol)

administrator in charge of discipline.

**censure** /sɑsyʀ/ nf censorship. **censurer** **1** vt censor; (critiquer) censure.

**cent** /sɑ/ adj (a) hundred; 20 pour ~ 20 per cent. ● n (quantité) hundred; ~ **un** a hundred and one; )**centième d'euro**) cent.

**centaine** /sɑtɛn/ nf hundred; une ~ (de) (about) a hundred.

**centenaire** /sɑtnɛʀ/ nm (anniversaire) centenary.

**centième** /sɑtjɛm/ adj & nmf hundredth.

**centimètre** /sɑtimɛtʀ/ nm centimetre; (ruban) tape-measure.

**central, ~e** (mpl **-aux**) /sɑtʀal,-o/ adj central. ● nm (pl **-aux**) ~ (téléphonique) (telephone) exchange. **centrale** nf power-station.

**centre** /sɑtʀ/ nm centre; ~ **commercial** shopping centre; (US) mall; ~ **d'appels** call centre; ~ **de formation** training centre; ~ **hospitalier** hospital. **centrer** **1** vt centre. **centre-ville** (pl **centres-villes**) nm town centre.

**centuple** /sɑtypl/ nm **le** ~ **de** a hundred times; **au** ~ **a** hundredfold.

**cep** /sɛp/ nm vine stock.

**cépage** /sepaʒ/ nm grape variety.

**cèpe** /sɛp/ nm cep.

**cependant** /səpɑdɑ/ adv however.

**céramique** /seramik/ nf ceramic; (art) ceramics (+ sg).

**cercle** /sɛʀkl/ nm circle; (cerceau) hoop; (association) society, club; ~ **vicieux** vicious circle.

**cercueil** /sɛʀkœj/ nm coffin.

**céréale** /seʀeal/ nf cereal; ~**s** (Culin) (breakfast) cereal.

**cérébral, ~e** (mpl **-aux**) /seʀebʀal, -o/ adj cerebral.

**cérémonie** /seʀemɔni/ nf ceremony; sans ~s (repas) informal; (recevoir) informally.

**cet, cette** /sɛt/ ➡CE.

**ceux** /sø/ ➡CELUI.

**cerf** /sɛʀ/ nm stag.

**cerfeuil** /sɛʀfœj/ nm chervil.

**cerf-volant** (pl **cerfs-volants**) /sɛʀvɔlɑ̃/ nm kite.

**chacun, ~e** /ʃakœ̃, -yn/ pron each (one), every one; (tout le monde) everyone; ~ d'entre nous each (one) of us.

**cerise** /s(ə)ʀiz/ nf cherry. **cerisier** nm cherry tree.

**chagrin** /ʃagʀɛ̃/ nm sorrow; avoir du ~ be sad.

**cerner** /sɛʀne/ **1** vt surround; (question) define; avoir les yeux cernés have rings under one's eyes.

**chahut** /ʃay/ nm row, din.

**chahuter** /ʃayte/ **1** vi make a row. ●vt (enseignant) be rowdy with; (orateur) heckle.

**certain, ~e** /sɛʀtɛ̃, -ɛn/ adj certain; (sûr) certain, sure (de of; que that); d'un ~ âge no longer young; un ~ temps some time. **certainement** adv (probablement) most probably; (avec certitude) certainly. **certains, -es** pron some people.

**chaîne** /ʃɛn/ nf chain; (de télévision) channel; ~ (d'assemblage) assembly line; ~s (Auto) snow chains; ~ de montagnes mountain range; ~ de montage/fabrication assembly/production line; ~ hi-fi hi-fi system; ~ laser CD player; en ~ (accidents) multiple; (réaction) chain. **chaînette** nf (small) chain. **chaînon** nm link.

**certes** /sɛʀt/ adv (sans doute) admittedly; (bien sûr) of course.

**certificat** /sɛʀtifika/ nm certificate.

**certifier** /sɛʀtifje/ **45** vt certify; ~ qch à qn assure sb of sth; copie certifiée conforme certified true copy.

**chair** /ʃɛʀ/ nf flesh; bien en ~ plump; en ~ et en os in the flesh; ~ à saucisses sausage meat; la ~ de poule goose pimples. ●adj inv (couleur) ~ flesh-coloured.

**certitude** /sɛʀtityd/ nf certainty.

**cerveau** (pl ~x) /sɛʀvo/ nm brain.

**cervelle** /sɛʀvɛl/ nf (Anat) brain; (Culin) brains.

**chaire** /ʃɛʀ/ nf (d'église) pulpit; (Univ) chair.

**chaise** /ʃɛz/ nf chair; ~ longue deckchair.

**ces** /se/ ➡CE.

**châle** /ʃɑl/ nm shawl.

**césarienne** /sezaʀjɛn/ nf Caesarean (section).

**chaleur** /ʃalœʀ/ nf heat; (moins intense) warmth; (d'un accueil, d'une couleur) warmth. **chaleureux, -euse** adj warm.

**cesse** /sɛs/ nf n'avoir de ~ que have no rest until; sans ~ constantly, incessantly.

**cesser** /sese/ **1** vt stop; ~ de faire stop doing. ●vi cease; faire ~ put an end to.

**chalumeau** (pl ~x) /ʃalymo/ nm blowtorch.

**cessez-le-feu** /seselfø/ nm inv ceasefire.

**chalutier** /ʃalytje/ nm trawler.

**chamailler (se)** /(sə)ʃamaje/ **1** vpr squabble.

**cession** /sesjɔ̃/ nf transfer.

**c'est-à-dire** /setadiʀ/ conj that is (to say).

**chambre** /ʃɑ̃bʀ/ nf (bed) room; (Pol, Jur) chamber; faire ~ à part sleep in separate rooms; ~ à air inner tube; ~ **d'amis** spare ou guest room; ~ **de commerce (et d'industrie)** Chamber of Commerce; ~ **à coucher** bedroom; ~ **à un lit/deux lits** single/twin/double room; ~ **pour deux personnes** double room; ~ **forte** strong-room; ~ **d'hôte** bed and breakfast. **chambrer 1** vt (vin) bring to room temperature.

**chameau** /ʃamo/ (pl ~x) nm camel.

**chamois** /ʃamwa/ nm chamois.

**champ** /ʃã/ nm field; ~ **de bataille** battlefield; ~ **de courses** racecourse; ~ **de tir** firing range.

**champêtre** /ʃãpɛtʁ/ adj rural.

**champignon** /ʃãpiɲɔ̃/ nm mushroom; (moisissure) fungus; ~ **de Paris** button mushroom.

**champion, -ne** /ʃãpjɔ̃, -ɔn/ nm, f champion. **championnat** nm championship.

**chance** /ʃãs/ nf (good) luck; (possibilité) chance; **avoir de la** ~ **be lucky; quelle** ~! what luck!

**chanceler** /ʃãsle/ 38 vi stagger; (fig) falter, waver.

**chancelier** /ʃãsalje/ nm chancellor.

**chanceux, -euse** /ʃãsø, -z/ adj lucky.

**chandail** /ʃãdaj/ nm sweater.

**chandelier** /ʃãdalje/ nm candlestick.

**chandelle** /ʃãdɛl/ nf candle; **dîner aux** ~**s** candlelight dinner.

**change** /ʃãʒ/ nm (foreign) exchange; (taux) exchange rate.

**changement** /ʃãʒmã/ nm change; ~ **climatique** climate change; ~ **de vitesse** (dispositif) ears.

**changer** /ʃãʒe/ 40 vt change; ~ **qch de place** move sth; (échanger) change (pour, contre for); ~ **de**

**nom/voiture** change one's name/ car; ~ **de place/train** change places/trains; ~ **de direction** change direction; ~ **d'avis** ou **d'idée** change one's mind; ~ **de vitesse** change gear. □ **se** ~ vpr change, get changed.

**chanson** /ʃãsɔ̃/ nf song.

**chant** /ʃã/ nm singing; (chanson) song; (Relig) hymn.

**chantage** /ʃãtaʒ/ nm blackmail.

**chanter** /ʃãte/ 1 vt sing; **si cela vous chante** 1 if you feel like it. ● vi sing; **faire** ~ (délit) blackmail. **chanteur, -euse** nm, f singer.

**chantier** /ʃãtje/ nm building site; ~ **naval** shipyard; **mettre en** ~ get under way, start.

**chaos** /kao/ nm chaos.

**chaparder** /ʃapaʁde/ 1 vt 1 pinch 1, filch.

**chapeau** /ʃapo/ (pl ~x) nm hat; ~! well done!

**chapelet** /ʃaplɛ/ nm rosary; (fig) string.

**chapelle** /ʃapɛl/ nf chapel.

**chapelure** /ʃaplyʁ/ nf (Culin) breadcrumbs.

**chaperonner** /ʃapʁɔne/ 1 vt chaperone.

**chapiteau** /ʃapito/ (pl ~x) nm marquee; (de cirque) big top; (de colonne) capital.

**chapitre** /ʃapitʁ/ nm chapter; (fig) subject.

**chaque** /ʃak/ adj every, each.

**char** /ʃaʁ/ nm (Mil) tank; (de carnaval) float; (charrette) cart; (dans l'antiquité) chariot.

**charabia** /ʃaʁabja/ nm 1 gibberish.

**charade** /ʃaʁad/ nf riddle.

**charbon** /ʃaʁbɔ̃/ nm coal; (Méd) anthrax; ~ **de bois** charcoal.

**charcuterie** /ʃaʁkytʁi/ nf pork

butcher's shop; (aliments) (cooked) pork meats. **charcutier, -ière** *nm, f* pork butcher.

**chardon** /ʃaʁdɔ̃/ *nm* thistle.

**charge** /ʃaʁʒ/ *nf* load, burden; (Mil, Élect, Jur) charge; (responsabilité) responsibility; avoir qn à ~ be responsible for; ~s expenses; (de locataire) service charges; être à la ~ de (personne) be the responsibility of; (frais) be payable by; ~s sociales social security contributions; prendre en ~ take charge of.

**chargé, ~e** /ʃaʁʒe/ *adj* (véhicule) loaded; (journée, emploi du temps) busy; (langue) coated. ● *nm, f* ~ de mission head of mission; ~ d'affaires chargé d'affaires; ~ de cours lecturer.

**chargement** /ʃaʁʒəmɑ̃/ *nm* loading; (objets) load.

**charger** /ʃaʁʒe/ [40] *vt* load; (Ordinat, Photo) load; (attaquer) charge; (batterie) charge; ~ qn à (fardeau) weigh sb down with; (tâche) entrust sb with; ~ qn de faire make sb responsible for doing. ● *vi* (attaquer) charge. □ se ~ de *vpr* take charge ou care of.

**chariot** /ʃaʁjo/ *nm* (à roulettes) trolley; (US) cart; (charrette) cart.

**charitable** /ʃaʁitabl/ *adj* charitable.

**charité** /ʃaʁite/ *nf* charity; faire la ~ à give (money) to.

**charlatan** /ʃaʁlatɑ̃/ *nm* charlatan.

**charmant, ~e** /ʃaʁmɑ̃, -t/ *adj* charming.

**charme** /ʃaʁm/ *nm* charm; (qui envoûte) spell. **charmer** [1] *vt* charm. **charmeur, -euse** *nm, f* charmer.

**charnel, ~le** /ʃaʁnɛl/ *adj* carnal.

**charnière** /ʃaʁnjɛʁ/ *nf* hinge; à la ~ de at the meeting point between.

**charnu, ~e** /ʃaʁny/ *adj* plump, fleshy.

**charpente** /ʃaʁpɑ̃t/ *nf* framework; (carrure) build.

**charpentier** /ʃaʁpɑ̃tje/ *nm* carpenter.

**charrette** /ʃaʁɛt/ *nf* cart.

**charrue** /ʃaʁy/ *nf* plough.

**chasse** /ʃas/ *nf* hunting; (au fusil) shooting; (poursuite) chase; (recherche) hunt(ing); ~ (d'eau) (toilet) flush; ~ sous-marine harpoon fishing.

**chasse-neige** /ʃasnɛʒ/ *nm inv* snowplough.

**chasser** /ʃase/ [1] *vt* hunt; (au fusil) shoot; (faire partir) chase away; (odeur, employé) get rid of. ● *vi* go hunting; (au fusil) go shooting.

**chasseur, -euse** /ʃasœʁ, -øz/ *nm, f* hunter. ● *nm* bellboy; (US) bellhop; (avion) fighter plane.

**châssis** /ʃasi/ *nm* frame; (Auto) chassis.

**chasteté** /ʃastəte/ *nf* chastity.

**chat¹** /ʃa/ *nm* cat; (mâle) tomcat.

**chat²** /tʃat/ *nm* (Internet) chat.

**châtaigne** /ʃatɛɲ/ *nf* chestnut. **châtaignier** *nm* chestnut tree. **châtain** *adj inv* chestnut (brown).

**château** (*pl* ~x) /ʃato/ *nm* castle; (manoir) manor; ~ d'eau water tower; ~ fort fortified castle.

**châtiment** /ʃatimɑ̃/ *nm* punishment.

**chaton** /ʃatɔ̃/ *nm* (chat) kitten.

**chatouillement** /ʃatujmɑ̃/ *nm* tickling. **chatouiller** [1] *vt* tickle. **chatouilleux, -euse** *adj* ticklish; (susceptible) touchy.

**châtrer** /ʃatʁe/ [1] *vt* castrate; (chat) neuter.

**chatte** /ʃat/ *nf* female cat.

**chaud,** ∼e /ʃo, -d/ adj warm; (brûlant) hot; (vif: fig) warm. ●nm heat; **au** ∼ in the warm(th); **avoir** ∼ be warm; be hot; **il fait** ∼ it is warm; it is hot; **pour te tenir** ∼ to keep you warm. **chaudement** adv warmly; (disputé) hotly.

**chaudière** /ʃodjɛr/ nf boiler.

**chaudron** /ʃodrɔ̃/ nm cauldron.

**chauffage** /ʃofaʒ/ nm heating; ∼ **central** central heating.

**chauffard** /ʃofar/ nm (péj) reckless driver.

**chauffer** /ʃofe/ **1** vt/i heat (up); (moteur, appareil) overheat. □ se ∼ vpr warm oneself (up).

**chauffeur** /ʃofœr/ nm driver; (aux gages de qn) chauffeur.

**chaume** /ʃom/ nm (de toit) thatch.

**chaussée** /ʃose/ nf road (way).

**chausse-pied** /ʃospje/ (pl ∼s) /ʃospje/ nm shoehorn.

**chausser** /ʃose/ **1** vt (chaussures) put on; (enfant) put shoes on (to). ●vi ∼ **bien** (aller) fit well; ∼ **du 35** take a size 35 shoe. □ se ∼ vpr put one's shoes on.

**chaussette** /ʃosɛt/ nf sock.

**chausson** /ʃosɔ̃/ nm slipper; (de bébé) bootee; ∼ **de danse** ballet shoe; ∼ **aux pommes** apple turnover.

**chaussure** /ʃosyr/ nf shoe; ∼ **de ski** ski boot; ∼ **de marche** hiking boot.

**chauve** /ʃov/ adj bald.

**chauve-souris** (pl **chauves-souris**) /ʃovsuri/ nf bat.

**chauvin,** ∼e /ʃovɛ̃, -in/ adj chauvinistic. ●nm, f chauvinist.

**chavirer** /ʃavire/ **1** vt (bateau) capsize; (objets) tip over.

**chef** /ʃɛf/ nm leader, head; (supérieur) boss, superior; (Culin) chef; (de tribu) chief; **architecte en** ∼

chief ou head architect; ∼ **d'accusation** (Jur) charge; ∼ **d'équipe** foreman; (Sport) captain; ∼ **d'État** head of State; ∼ **de famille** head of the family; ∼ **de file** (Pol) leader; ∼ **de gare** stationmaster; ∼ **d'orchestre** conductor; ∼ **de service** department head; ∼ **de train** guard; (US) conductor.

**chef-d'œuvre** (pl **chefs-d'œuvre**) /ʃedœvr/ nm masterpiece.

**chef-lieu** (pl **chefs-lieux**) /ʃefljø/ nm county town, administrative centre.

**chemin** /ʃəmɛ̃/ nm road; (étroit) lane; (de terre) track; (pour piétons) path; (passage) way; (direction, trajet) way; **avoir du** ∼ **à faire** have a long way to go; ∼ **de fer** railway; **par** ∼ **de fer** by rail; ∼ **de halage** towpath; ∼ **vicinal** country lane.

**cheminée** /ʃəmine/ nf chimney; (intérieure) fireplace; (encadrement) mantelpiece; (de bateau) funnel.

**cheminot** /ʃəmino/ nm railwayman; (US) railroad man.

**chemise** /ʃəmiz/ nf shirt; (dossier) folder; (de livre) jacket; ∼ **de nuit** nightdress. **chemisette** nf shortsleeved shirt. **chemisier** nm blouse.

**chêne** /ʃɛn/ nm oak.

**chenil** /ʃəni(l)/ nm (pension) kennels (+ sg).

**chenille** /ʃənij/ nf caterpillar; **véhicule à** ∼s tracked vehicle.

**cheptel** /ʃɛptɛl/ nm livestock.

**chèque** /ʃɛk/ nm cheque; ∼ **sans provision** bad cheque; ∼ **de voyage** traveller's cheque. **chéquier** nm chequebook.

**cher, chère** /ʃɛr/ adj (coûteux) dear, expensive; (aimé) dear; (dans la correspondance) dear. ●adv (coûter, payer) a lot (of money); (en importance) dearly. ● nm, f mon ~, ma chère my dear.

**chercher** /ʃɛrʃe/ **1** vt look for; (aide, paix, gloire) seek; aller ~ go and get ou fetch, go for; ~ à faire attempt to do; ~ la petite bête be finicky.

**chercheur, -euse** /ʃɛrʃœr, -øz/ nm, f research worker.

**chèrement** /ʃɛrmɑ̃/ adv dearly.

**chéri, ~e** /ʃeri/ adj beloved. ● nm, f darling.

**chérir** /ʃerir/ **2** vt cherish.

**chétif, -ive** /ʃetif, -v/ adj puny.

**cheval** (pl -aux) /ʃəval, -o/ nm horse; à ~ on horseback; à ~ sur astride, straddling; faire du ~ ride, go horse-riding.

**chevalerie** /ʃəvalri/ nf chivalry.

**chevalet** /ʃəvalɛ/ nm easel; (de menuisier) trestle.

**chevalier** /ʃəvalje/ nm knight.

**chevalière** /ʃəvaljɛr/ nf signet ring.

**cheval-vapeur** (pl chevaux-vapeur) /ʃəvalvapœr/ nm horsepower.

**chevaucher** /ʃəvoʃe/ **1** vt sit astride. □ se ~ vpr overlap.

**chevelu, ~e** /ʃəvly/ adj (péj) long-haired; (Bot) hairy.

**chevelure** /ʃəvlyr/ nf hair.

**chevet** /ʃəvɛ/ nm au ~ de at the bedside of; livre de ~ bedside book.

**cheveu** (pl ~x) /ʃəvø/ nm (poil) air; ~x (chevelure) hair; avoir les ~x longs have long hair.

**cheville** /ʃəvij/ nf ankle; (fiche) peg, pin; (pour mur) (wall) plug.

**chèvre** /ʃɛvr/ nf goat.

**chevreuil** /ʃəvrœj/ nm roe (deer); (Culin) venison.

**chevron** /ʃəvrɔ̃/ nm (poutre)

rafter; à ~s herringbone.

**chez** /ʃe/ prép (au domicile de) at the house of; (parmi) among; (dans le caractère ou l'œuvre de) in; aller ~ qn go to sb's house; ~ le boucher at ou to the butcher's; ~ soi at home; rentrer ~ soi go home. **chez-soi** nm inv home.

**chic** /ʃik/ adj inv smart; (gentil) kind. ● nm style; avoir le ~ pour have a knack for; ~ (alors)! great!

**chicane** /ʃikan/ nf double bend; chercher ~ à qn pick a quarrel with sb.

**chiche** /ʃiʃ/ adj mean (de with); ~ que je le fais! **1** I bet you I can do it.

**chichis** /ʃiʃi/ nmpl **1** fuss.

**chicorée** /ʃikɔre/ nf (frisée) endive; (à café) chicory.

**chien** /ʃjɛ̃/ nm dog; ~ d'aveugle guide dog; ~ de garde watch-dog. **chienne** nf dog, bitch.

**chiffon** /ʃifɔ̃/ nm rag; (pour nettoyer) duster; ~ humide damp cloth. **chiffonner** **1** vt crumple; (préoccuper **1**) bother.

**chiffre** /ʃifr/ nm figure; (numéro) number; (code) code; ~s arabes/romains Arabic/Roman numerals; ~s (statistiques) statistics; ~ d'affaires turnover.

**chiffrer** /ʃifre/ **1** vt put a value on, assess; (texte) encode. □ se ~ à vpr come to.

**chignon** /ʃiɲɔ̃/ nm bun, chignon.

**Chili** /ʃili/ nm Chile.

**chimère** /ʃimɛr/ nf fantasy. **chimique** adj chemical. **chimiste** nmf chemist.

**chimie** /ʃimi/ nf chemistry. chimique adj chemical. chimiste nmf chemist.

**chimpanzé** /ʃɛ̃pɑ̃ze/ nm chimpanzee.

**Chine** /ʃin/ nf China.

**chinois**, ~e /ʃinwa, -z/ adj Chinese. ●nm (Ling) Chinese. C~, ~e nm, f Chinese.

**chiot** /ʃjo/ nm pup(py).

**chipoter** /ʃipote/ **1** vi (manger) pick at one's food; (discuter) quibble.

**chips** /ʃips/ nf inv crisp; (US) chip.

**chirurgie** /ʃiryrʒi/ nf surgery; ~ esthétique plastic surgery. **chirurgien** nm surgeon.

**chlore** /klɔr/ nm chlorine.

**choc** /ʃɔk/ nm (heurt) impact, shock; (émotion) shock; (collision) crash; (affrontement) clash; (Méd) shock; **sous le ~** in shock.

**chocolat** /ʃɔkɔla/ nm chocolate; (à boire) drinking chocolate; ~ au lait milk chocolate; ~ chaud hot chocolate; ~ noir plain ou dark chocolate.

**chœur** /kœr/ nm (antique) chorus; (chanteurs, nef) choir; **en ~** in chorus.

**choisir** /ʃwazir/ **2** vt choose, select.

**choix** /ʃwa/ nm choice, selection; **fromage ou dessert au ~** a choice of cheese or dessert; **de ~** choice; **de premier ~** top quality.

**chômage** /ʃomaʒ/ nm unemployment; **au ~,** ~ unemployed; **mettre en ~ technique** lay off.

**chômeur**, -euse /ʃomœr, -øz/ nm, f unemployed person; **les ~s** the unemployed.

**choquer** /ʃɔke/ **1** vt shock; (commotionner) shake.

**choral**, ~e (mpl ~s) /kɔral/ adj choral. **chorale** nf choir, choral society.

**chorégraphie** /kɔregrafi/ nf choreography.

**choriste** /kɔrist/ nmf (à l'église) chorister; (à l'opéra) member of the chorus ou choir.

**chose** /ʃoz/ nf thing; (très) peu de ~ nothing much; pas grand ~ not much.

**chou** (pl ~x) /ʃu/ nm cabbage; ~ (à la crème) cream puff; ~ de Bruxelles Brussels sprout; **mon petit ~** **1** my dear.

**chouchou**, ~te /ʃuʃu, -t/ nm, f (de professeur) pet; (du public) darling.

**choucroute** /ʃukrut/ nf sauerkraut.

**chouette** /ʃwɛt/ nf owl. ●adj **1** super.

**chou-fleur** (pl **choux-fleurs**) /ʃuflœr/ nm cauliflower.

**choyer** /ʃwaje/ **31** vt pamper.

**chrétien**, ~ne /kretjɛ̃, -jɛn/ adj & nm, f Christian.

**Christ** /krist/ nm **le ~** Christ.

**chrome** /krom/ nm chromium, chrome.

**chromosome** /krɔmozom/ nm chromosome.

**chronique** /krɔnik/ adj chronic. ●nf (rubrique) column; (nouvelles) news; (annales) chronicle.

**chronologique** /krɔnɔlɔʒik/ adj chronological.

**chronomètre** /krɔnɔmɛtr/ nm stopwatch. **chronométrer** **14** vt time.

**chrysanthème** /krizɑ̃tɛm/ nm chrysanthemum.

**chuchoter** /ʃyʃɔte/ **1** vt/i whisper.

**chut** /ʃyt/ interj shh, hush.

**chute** /ʃyt/ nf fall; (déchet) offcut; ~ (d'eau) waterfall; ~ de pluie rainfall; ~ des cheveux hair loss; ~ des ventes ~ drop in sales; ~ de 5% 5% drop. **chuter** **1** vi fall.

**Chypre** /ʃipʀ/ nf Cyprus.

**ci** /si/ adv here; ~-gît here lies; cet homme-~ this man; ces maisons-~ these houses.

**ci-après** /siapʀɛ/ adv below.

**cible** /sibl/ nf target.

**ciboulette** /sibulɛt/ nf (Culin) chives (+ pl).

**cicatrice** /sikatʀis/ nf scar.

**cicatriser** /sikatʀize/ **1** vt heal. □ se ~ vpr heal.

**ci-dessous** /sidəsu/ adv below.

**ci-dessus** /sidəsy/ adv above.

**cidre** /sidʀ/ nm cider.

**ciel** (pl cieux, ciels) /sjɛl, sjø/ nm sky; (Relig) heaven; cieux (Relig) heaven.

**clerge** /sjɛʀ/ nm (church) candle.

**cigale** /sigal/ nf cicada.

**cigare** /sigaʀ/ nm cigar.

**cigarette** /sigaʀɛt/ nf cigarette.

**cigogne** /sigɔɲ/ nf stork.

**ci-joint** /siǰwɛ̃/ adv enclosed.

**cil** /sil/ nm eyelash.

**cime** /sim/ nf peak, tip.

**ciment** /simɑ̃/ nm cement.

**cimetière** /simtjɛʀ/ nm cemetery, graveyard; ~ de voitures breaker's yard.

**cinéaste** /sineast/ nmf film-maker.

**cinéma** /sinema/ nm cinema; (US) movie theater. **cinémathèque** nf film archive; (salle) film theatre. **cinématographique** adj cinema.

**cinéphile** /sinefil/ nmf film lover.

**cinglant,** ~e /sɛ̃glɑ̃, -t/ adj (vent) biting; (remarque) scathing.

**cinglé,** ~e /sɛ̃gle/ adj **1** crazy.

**cinq** /sɛ̃k/ adj & nm five.

**cinquante** /sɛ̃kɑ̃t/ adj & nm fifty.

**cinquième** /sɛ̃kjɛm/ adj & nmf fifth.

**Cinquième République** ℹ️
As established by the constitution of 1958 and still in force today, the *Cinquième République* refers to the system of government established by Charles de Gaulle, enshrining a strong executive and institutions to guarantee stability.

**cintre** /sɛ̃tʀ/ nm coat-hanger; (Archit) curve.

**cirage** /siʀaʒ/ nm polish.

**circoncision** /siʀkɔ̃sizjɔ̃/ nf circumcision.

**circonflexe** /siʀkɔ̃flɛks/ adj circumflex.

**circonscription** /siʀkɔ̃skʀipsjɔ̃/ nf district; ~ électorale constituency; (US) district; (de conseiller, maire) ward.

**circonscrire** /siʀkɔ̃skʀiʀ/ **30** vt (incendie, épidémie) contain; (sujet) define.

**circonspect,** ~e /siʀkɔ̃spɛkt/ adj circumspect.

**circonstance** /siʀkɔ̃stɑ̃s/ nf circumstance; (situation) situation; (occasion) occasion; ~s atténuantes mitigating circumstances.

**circuit** /siʀkɥi/ nm circuit; (trajet) tour, trip.

**circulaire** /siʀkylɛʀ/ adj & nf circular.

**circulation** /siʀkylasjɔ̃/ nf circulation; (de véhicules) traffic.

**circuler** /siʀkyle/ **1** vi (se répandre, être distribué) circulate; (aller d'un lieu à un autre) get around; (en voiture) travel; (piéton) walk; (être en service) (bus, train) run; faire ~ (badauds) move on; (rumeur) spread.

**cire** /siʀ/ nf wax.

**ciré** /siʀe/ nm oilskin.

**cirer** /siʀe/ **1** vt polish.

**cirque** /siʀk/ nm circus; (arène) amphitheatre; (désordre: fig) chaos; **faire le** ~! make a racket 🗓.

**ciseau** (pl ~x) /sizo/ nm chisel; ~x scissors.

**ciseler** /sizle/ **6** vt chisel.

**citadelle** /sitadɛl/ nf citadel.

**citadin**, ~e /sitadɛ̃, -in/ nm, f city-dweller. ● adj city.

**citation** /sitasjɔ̃/ nf quotation; (Jur) summons.

**cité** /site/ nf city; (logements) housing estate; ~ **universitaire** (university) halls of residence.

**citer** /site/ **1** vt quote, cite; (Jur) summon.

**citerne** /sitɛʀn/ nf tank.

**citoyen**, ~ne /sitwajɛ̃, -ɛn/ nm, f citizen.

**citron** /sitʀɔ̃/ nm lemon; ~ **vert** lime. **citronnade** nf lemon squash, (still) lemonade.

**citrouille** /sitʀuj/ nf pumpkin.

**civet** /sive/ nm stew; ~ **de lièvre** jugged hare.

**civière** /sivjɛʀ/ nf stretcher.

**civil**, ~e /sivil/ adj civil; (non militaire) civilian; (poli) civil. ● nm civilian; **dans le** ~ in civilian life; **en** ~ in plain clothes.

**civilisation** /sivilizasjɔ̃/ nf civilization.

**civiliser** /sivilize/ **1** vt civilize. □ **se** ~ vpr become civilized.

**civique** /sivik/ adj civic.

**clair**, ~e /klɛʀ/ adj clear; (éclairé) light, bright; (couleur) light; **le plus** ~ **de** most of. ● adv clearly; **il faisait** ~ it was already light. ● nm ~ **de lune** moonlight; **tirer une histoire au** ~ get to the bottom of things. **clairement** adv clearly.

**clairière** /klɛʀjɛʀ/ nf clearing.

**clairsemé**, ~e /klɛʀsame/ adj sparse.

**clamer** /klame/ **1** vt proclaim.

**clameur** /klamœʀ/ nf clamour.

**clan** /klɑ̃/ nm clan.

**clandestin**, ~e /klɑ̃dɛstɛ̃, -in/ adj secret; (journal) underground; (immigration, travail) illegal; **passager** ~ stowaway.

**clapier** /klapje/ nm (rabbit) utch.

**clapoter** /klapɔte/ **1** vi lap.

**claquage** /klakaʒ/ nm strained muscle; **se faire un** ~ pull a muscle.

**claque** /klak/ nf slap.

**claquer** /klake/ **1** vi bang; (porte) slam, bang; (fouet) crack; (se casser 🗓) conk out; (mourir 🗓) snuff it!; ~ **des doigts** snap one's fingers; ~ **des mains** clap one's hands; **il claque des dents** his teeth are chattering. ● vt (porte) slam, bang; (dépenser 🗓) blow; (fatiguer 🗓) tire out.

**claquettes** /klakɛt/ nfpl tap-dancing.

**clarifier** /klaʀifje/ **45** vt clarify.

**clarinette** /klaʀinɛt/ nf clarinet.

**clarté** /klaʀte/ nf light, brightness; (netteté) clarity.

**classe** /klas/ nf class; (salle: Scol) classroom; (cours) class, lesson; **aller en** ~ go to school; **faire la** ~ teach; ~ **ouvrière/moyenne** working/middle class.

**classement** /klasmɑ̃/ nm classification; (d'élèves) grading; (de documents) filing; (rang) place, grade; (de coureur) placing.

**classer** /klase/ **1** vt classify; (par mérite) grade; (papiers) file; (Jur) (affaire) close. □ **se** ~ vpr rank.

**classeur** /klasœʀ/ nm (meuble) filing cabinet; (chemise) file; (à anneaux) ring binder.

**classification** /klasifikasjɔ̃/ nf

classification.

**classique** /klasik/ *adj* classical; (de qualité) classic; (habituel) classic, standard. ●*nm* classic; (auteur) classical author.

**clavecin** /klavsɛ̃/ *nm* harpsichord.

**clavicule** /klavikyl/ *nf* collarbone.

**clavier** /klavje/ *nm* keyboard; ~ numérique keypad.

**clé, clef** /kle/ *nf* key; (outil) spanner; (Mus) clef; ~ anglaise (monkey-)wrench; ~ de contact ignition key; ~ à molette adjustable spanner; ~ de voûte keystone. ●*adj inv* key.

**clémence** /klemãs/ *nf* (de climat) mildness; (indulgence) leniency.

**clergé** /klɛʀʒe/ *nm* clergy.

**clérical, ~e** /klerikal, -o/ *adj* clerical.

**clic** /klik/ *nm* (Ordinat) click.

**cliché** /kliʃe/ *nm* cliché; (Photo) negative.

**client, ~e** /klijã, -t/ *nm, f* customer; (d'un avocat) client; (d'un médecin) patient; (d'hôtel) guest; (de taxi) passenger.

**clientèle** /klijãtɛl/ *nf* customers, clientele; (d'un avocat) clients, practice; (d'un médecin) patients, practice; (soutien) custom.

**cligner** /kliɲe/ **1** *vi* ~ des yeux blink; ~ de l'œil wink.

**clignotant** /kliɲɔtã/ *nm* (Auto) indicator, turn.

**clignoter** /kliɲɔte/ **1** *vi* blink; (lumière) flicker; (comme signal) flash.

**climat** /klima/ *nm* climate.

**climatisation** /klimatizasjɔ̃/ *nf* air-conditioning.

**clin d'œil** /klɛ̃dœj/ *nm* wink; en un ~ in a flash.

**clinique** /klinik/ *adj* clinical. ●*nf* (private) clinic.

**clinquant, ~e** /klɛ̃kã, -t/ *adj* showy.

**clip** /klip/ *nm* video.

**cliquer** /klike/ **1** *vi* (Ordinat) click (sur on).

**cliqueter** /klikte/ **38** *vi* (couverts) clink; (clés, monnaie) jingle; (ferraille) rattle. **cliquetis** *nm* clink(ing), jingle, rattle.

**clivage** /klivaʒ/ *nm* divide.

**clochard, ~e** /klɔʃaʀ, -d/ *nm, f* tramp.

**cloche** /klɔʃ/ *nf* bell; (imbécile ⊞) idiot; ~ à fromage cheese-cover.

**cloche-pied: à ~** /aklɔʃpje/ *loc* sauter à ~ hop on one leg.

**clocher** /klɔʃe/ *nm* bell-tower; (pointu) steeple; de ~ parochial.

**cloison** /klwazɔ̃/ *nf* partition; (fig) barrier.

**cloître** /klwatʀ/ *nm* cloister. **cloîtrer (se)** /klwatʀe/ **1** *vpr* shut oneself away.

**clonage** /klɔnaʒ/ *nm* clonage.

**cloner** /klɔne/ **1** *vt* clone.

**cloque** /klɔk/ *nf* blister.

**clos, ~e** /klo, -z/ *adj* closed.

**clôture** /klotyʀ/ *nf* fence; (fermeture) closure; (de magasin, bureau) closing; (de débat, liste) close; (en Bourse) close of trading. **clôturer** **1** *vt* enclose, fence in; (festival, séance) close.

**clou** /klu/ *nm* nail; (furoncle) boil; (de spectacle) star attraction; les ~s (passage) pedestrian crossing; (US) crosswalk.

**clouer** /klue/ **1** *vt* nail down; (fig) pin down; être cloué au lit be confined to one's bed; ~ le bec à qn shut sb up.

**clouté, ~e** /klute/ *adj* studded; passage ~ pedestrian crossing; (US) crosswalk.

**CMU** *abrév f* free health care for

*people on low incomes.*

**coaliser (se)** /(sə)kɔalize/ **1** *vpr* join forces.

**coalition** /kɔalisjɔ̃/ *nf* coalition.

**cobaye** /kɔbaj/ *nm* guinea-pig.

**cocaïne** /kɔkain/ *nf* cocaine.

**cocasse** /kɔkas/ *adj* comical.

**coccinelle** /kɔksinɛl/ *nf* ladybird; (US) ladybug.

**cocher** /kɔʃe/ **1** *vt* tick (off), check. ● *nm* coachman.

**cochon**, ~**ne** /kɔʃɔ̃, -ɔn/ *nm, f* (*personne* **1**) pig. ● *adj* **1** filthy. ● *nm* pig. **cochonnerie** *nf* (saleté **1**) filth; (*marchandise* **1**) rubbish, junk.

**cocon** /kɔkɔ̃/ *nm* cocoon.

**cocorico** /kɔkɔriko/ *nm* cock-a-doodle-doo.

**cocotier** /kɔkɔtje/ *nm* coconut palm.

**cocotte** /kɔkɔt/ *nf* (marmite) casserole; ~ **minute®** pressure-cooker; **ma** ~ **1** my dear.

**cocu**, ~**e** /kɔky/ *nm, f* **1** deceived husband, deceived wife.

**code** /kɔd/ *nm* code; ~**s** dipped headlights; **se mettre en** ~**s** dip one's headlights; ~ **(à) barre** bar code; ~ **confidentiel (d'identification)** PIN number; ~ **postal** post code; (US) zip code; ~ **de la route** Highway Code. **coder 1** *vt* code, encode.

**coéquipier**, -**ière** /kɔekipje, -jɛr/ *nm, f* team mate.

**cœur** /kœr/ *nm* heart; (aux cartes) hearts (+ *pl*); ~ **d'artichaut** artichoke heart; ~ **de palmier** palm heart; **à** ~ **ouvert** (*opération*) open-heart; (*parler*) freely; **avoir bon** ~ be kind-hearted; **de bon** ~ willingly; (*rire*) heartily; **par** ~ by heart; **avoir mal au** ~ feel sick *ou* nauseous; **je veux en avoir le** ~

**net** I want to be clear in my own mind (about it).

**coffre** /kɔfr/ *nm* chest; (*pour argent*) safe; (Auto) boot; (US) trunk. **coffre-fort** (*pl* **coffres-forts**) *nm* safe.

**coffret** /kɔfrɛ/ *nm* casket, box; (*de livres, cassettes*) boxed set.

**cogner** /kɔɲe/ **1** *vt/i* knock. □ **se** ~ *vpr* knock oneself; **se** ~ **la tête** bump one's head.

**cohabiter** /kɔabite/ **1** *vi* live together.

**cohérent**, ~**e** /kɔerɑ̃, -t/ *adj* coherent; (*homogène*) consistent.

**cohue** /kɔy/ *nf* crowd.

**coi**, ~**te** /kwa, -t/ *adj* silent.

**coiffe** /kwaf/ *nf* headgear.

**coiffer** /kwafe/ **1** *vt* do the hair of; (*chapeau*) put on; (*surmonter*) cap; ~ **qn d'un chapeau** put a hat on sb; **coiffé de** wearing; **être bien/mal coiffé** have tidy/untidy hair. □ **se** ~ *vpr* do one's hair.

**coiffeur**, -**euse** /kwafœr, -øz/ *nm, f* hairdresser. **coiffeuse** *nf* dressing-table.

**coiffure** /kwafyr/ *nf* hairstyle; (*métier*) hairdressing; (*chapeau*) hat.

**coin** /kwɛ̃/ *nm* corner; (*endroit*) spot; (*cale*) wedge; **au** ~ **du feu** by the fireside; **dans le** ~ locally; **du** ~ local.

**coincer** /kwɛ̃se/ **10** *vt* jam; (*caler*) wedge; (*attraper* **1**) catch. □ **se** ~ *vpr* get jammed.

**coïncidence** /kɔɛ̃sidɑ̃s/ *nf* coincidence.

**coing** /kwɛ̃/ *nm* quince.

**coït** /kɔit/ *nm* intercourse.

**col** /kɔl/ *nm* collar; (*de bouteille*) neck; (*de montagne*) pass; ~ **blanc** white-collar worker; ~ **roulé** polo-neck; (US) turtle-neck; ~ **de l'utérus** cervix; **se casser le** ~ **du**

fémur break one's hip.

**colère** /kɔlɛʀ/ nf anger; (accès) fit of anger; **en ~** angry; **se mettre en ~** lose one's temper; **faire un ~** throw a tantrum.

**coléreux, -euse** /kɔleʀø, -z/ adj quick-tempered.

**colin** /kɔlɛ̃/ nm (merlu) hake; (lieu noir) coley.

**colique** /kɔlik/ nf diarrhoea; (Méd) colic.

**colis** /kɔli/ nm parcel.

**collaborateur, -trice** /kɔlabɔʀatœʀ, -tʀis/ nm, f collaborator; (journaliste) contributor; (collègue) colleague.

**collaboration** /kɔlabɔʀasjɔ̃/ nf collaboration (à on); (à ouvrage, projet) contribution (à to).

**collaborer** /kɔlabɔʀe/ **1** vi collaborate (à on); **~ à** (journal) contribute to.

**collant, ~e** /kɔlɑ̃, -t/ adj (moulant) kin-tight; (poisseux) sticky. ●nm (bas) tights; (US) panty hose.

**colle** /kɔl/ nf glue; (en pâte) paste; (problème **1**) poser; (Scol **1**) detention.

**collecter** /kɔlɛkte/ **1** vt collect.

**collectif, -ive** /kɔlɛktif, -v/ adj collective; (billet, voyage) group.

**collection** /kɔlɛksjɔ̃/ nf collection; (ouvrages) series (+ sg); (du même auteur) set. **collectionner** **1** vt collect. **collectionneur, -euse** nm, f collector.

**collectivité** /kɔlɛktivite/ nf community; **~ locale** local authority.

**collège** /kɔlɛʒ/ nm secondary school (up to age 15); (US) junior high school; (assemblée) college. **collégien, ~ne** nm, f schoolboy, schoolgirl.

**collègue** /kɔlɛg/ nmf colleague.

**coller** /kɔle/ **1** vt stick; (avec colle liquide) glue; (affiche) stick up; (mettre **1**) stick; (par une question **1**) stump; (Scol **1**) se faire **~** get a detention; **je me suis fait ~ en maths** I failed ou flunked maths. ●vi stick (à to); (être collant) be sticky; **~ à** (convenir à) fit, correspond to.

**collet** /kɔlɛ/ nm (piège) snare; **~ monté** prim and proper; **mettre la main au ~ de qn** collar sb.

**collier** /kɔlje/ nm necklace; (de chien) collar.

**colline** /kɔlin/ nf hill.

**collision** /kɔlizjɔ̃/ nf (choc) collision; (lutte) clash; **entrer en ~ (avec)** collide (with).

**collyre** /kɔliʀ/ nm eye drops (+ pl).

**colmater** /kɔlmate/ **1** vt plug, seal.

**colombe** /kɔlɔ̃b/ nf dove.

**Colombie** /kɔlɔ̃bi/ nf Colombia.

**colon** /kɔlɔ̃/ nm settler.

**colonel** /kɔlɔnɛl/ nm colonel.

**colonie** /kɔlɔni/ nf colony; **~ de vacances** children's holiday camp.

---

**Colonie de vacances** A holiday village or summer camp where children take part in a variety of outdoor activities. Originally set up to give poorer children a means of getting out into the countryside, they are still largely state-subsidized. Colloquially they are referred to as *la/une* **colo**.

---

**colonne** /kɔlɔn/ nf column; **~ vertébrale** spine; **en ~ par deux** in double file.

**colorant** /kɔlɔʀɑ̃/ nm colouring.

**colorier** /kɔlɔʀje/ **45** vt colour (in).

**colosse** /kɔlɔs/ nm giant.

**colza** /kɔlza/ nm rape(-seed).

**coma** /kɔma/ *nm* coma; **dans le** ~ in a coma.

**combat** /kɔba/ *nm* fight; (Sport) match; ~**s** fighting. **combatif, -ive** *adj* eager to fight; (*esprit*) fighting.

**combattre** /kɔbatʀ/ 🟊 *vt/i* fight.

**combien** /kɔbjɛ̃/ *adv* ~ (**de**) (*quantité*) how much; (*nombre*) how many; (*temps*) how long; ~ **il a changé!** (comme) how he has changed!; ~ **y a-t-il d'ici à…?** how far is it to…?; **on est le** ~ **aujourd'hui?** what's the date today?

**combinaison** /kɔbinɛzɔ̃/ *nf* combination; (*de femme*) slip; (*bleu de travail*) boiler suit; (US) overalls; ~ **d'aviateur** flying-suit; ~ **de plongée** wetsuit.

**combine** /kɔbin/ *nf* trick; (*fraude*) fiddle; (*intrigue*) scheme.

**combiné** /kɔbine/ *nm* (*de téléphone*) receiver, handset.

**combiner** /kɔbine/ 🟊 *vt* (*réunir*) combine; (*calculer*) devise; ~ **de faire** plan to do.

**comble** /kɔbl/ *adj* packed. ●*nm* height; ~**s** (*mansarde*) attic, loft; **c'est le** ~! that's the (absolute) limit!

**combler** /kɔble/ 🟊 *vt* fill; (*perte, déficit*) make good; (*désir*) fulfil; ~ **qn de cadeaux** lavish gifts on sb.

**combustible** /kɔbystibl/ *nm* fuel.

**comédie** /kɔmedi/ *nf* comedy; (*histoire*) fuss; ~ **musicale** musical; **jouer la** ~ put on an act. **comédien, ~ne** *nm, f* actor, actress.

**comestible** /kɔmɛstibl/ *adj* edible.

**comète** /kɔmɛt/ *nf* comet.

**comique** /kɔmik/ *adj* comical, funny; (*genre*) comic. ●*nm* (*acteur*) comic; (*comédie*) comedy; (*côté*) drôle) comical aspect.

**commandant** /kɔmɑ̃dɑ̃/ *nm*

commander; (dans l'armée de terre) major; ~ (**de bord**) captain; ~ **en chef** Commander-in-Chief.

**commande** /kɔmɑ̃d/ *nf* (Comm) order; (Tech) control; ~**s** (d'avion) controls.

**commandement** /kɔmɑ̃dmɑ̃/ *nm* command; (Relig) commandment.

**commander** /kɔmɑ̃de/ 🟊 *vt* command; (*acheter*) order; (*étude, œuvre d'art*) commission; ~ **à** (*maîtriser*) control; ~ **à qn de faire** command sb to. ●*vi* be in command.

**comme** /kɔm/ *adv* ~ **c'est bon!** it's so good!; ~ **il est mignon!** isn't he sweet! ●*conj* (dans une comparaison) as; (dans une équivalence, illustration) like; (en tant que) as; (puisque) as, since; (au moment où) as; *vif* ~ **l'éclair** as quick as a flash; **travailler** ~ **sage-femme** work as a midwife; ~ **ci** ~ **ça** so-so; **il faut** properly; ~ **pour faire** as if to do; **jolie** ~ **tout** as pretty as anything; **qu'est-ce qu'il y a** ~ **légumes?** what is there in the way of vegetables?

**commencer** /kɔmɑ̃se/ 🔟 *vt/i* begin, start; ~ **à faire** begin or start to do.

**comment** /kɔmɑ̃/ *adv* how; ~? (*répétition*) pardon?; (*surprise*) what?; ~ **est-il?** what is he like?; **le** ~ **et le pourquoi** the whys and wherefores.

**commentaire** /kɔmɑ̃tɛʀ/ *nm* comment; (d'un texte, événement) commentary. **commentateur, -trice** *nm, f* commentator.

**commenter** /kɔmɑ̃te/ 🟊 *vt* comment on; (*film, visite*) provide a commentary for; (radio, TV) commentate.

**commérages** /kɔmeʀaʒ/ *nmpl*

gossip.

**commerçant,** -e /kɔmɛʁsɑ̃, -t/ adj (rue) shopping; (personne) business-minded. ● nm, f shopkeeper.

**commerce** /kɔmɛʁs/ nm trade, commerce; (magasin) business; faire du ~ be in business; ~ électrique e-commerce; ~ équitable fair trade.

**commercial,** -e (mpl -iaux) /kɔmɛʁsjal, -jo/ adj commercial. **commercialiser** 🔟 vt market.

**commettre** /kɔmɛtʁ/ 🔁 vt commit.

**commis** /kɔmi/ nm (de magasin) assistant; (de bureau) clerk.

**commissaire** /kɔmisɛʁ/ nm commissioner; (Sport) steward; ~ (de police) (police) superintendent. **commissaire-priseur** (pl commissaires-priseurs) nm auctioneer.

**commissariat** /kɔmisaʁja/ nm ~ (de police) police station.

**commission** /kɔmisjɔ̃/ nf commission; (course) errand; (message) message; ~s shopping.

**commode** /kɔmɔd/ adj handy; (facile) easy; il n'est pas ~ he's a difficult customer. ● nf chest of drawers. **commodité** nf convenience.

**commotion** /kɔmosjɔ̃/ nf ~ (cérébrale) concussion.

**commun,** -e /kɔmœ̃, -yn/ adj common; (effort, action) joint; (frais, pièce) shared; en ~ jointly; avoir ou mettre en ~ share; le ~ des mortels ordinary mortals.

**communal,** -e (mpl -aux) adj of the commune, local.

**communauté** /kɔmynote/ nf community.

**commune** /kɔmyn/ nf (circonscription, collectivité) commune.

**communicatif,** -ive /kɔmynikatif, -v/ adj (personne) talkative; (gaieté) infectious.

**communication** /kɔmynikasjɔ̃/ nf communication; (téléphonique) call; ~s (relations) communications (+ pl); voies ou moyens de ~ communications (+ pl).

**communier** /kɔmynje/ 🔁 vi (Relig) receive communion; (fig) commune.

**communiqué** /kɔmynike/ nm statement; (de presse) communiqué.

**communiquer** /kɔmynike/ 🔟 vt pass on, communicate; (date, décision) announce. ● vi communicate. □ se ~ à vpr spread to.

**communiste** /kɔmynist/ adj & nmf communist.

**commutateur** /kɔmytatœʁ/ nm (Électr) switch.

**compagne** /kɔ̃paɲ/ nf companion.

**compagnie** /kɔ̃paɲi/ nf company; tenir ~ à keep company; en ~ de together with; ~ aérienne airline.

**compagnon** /kɔ̃paɲɔ̃/ nm companion.

**comparable** /kɔ̃paʁabl/ adj comparable (à to). **comparaison** nf comparison; (littéraire) simile.

**comparaître** /kɔ̃paʁɛtʁ/ 🔞 vi (Jur) appear (devant before).

**comparatif,** -ive /kɔ̃paʁatif, -v/ adj & nm comparative.

**comparer** /kɔ̃paʁe/ 🔟 vt com-

**pare** (à with). □ **se** ~ *vpr* compare oneself; (être comparable) be comparable.

**compartiment** /kɔ̃paʀtimɑ̃/ *nm* compartment.

**comparution** /kɔ̃paʀysjɔ̃/ *nf* (Jur) appearance.

**compas** /kɔ̃pa/ *nm* (pair of) compasses; (boussole) compass.

**compassion** /kɔ̃pasjɔ̃/ *nf* compassion.

**compatible** /kɔ̃patibl/ *adj* compatible.

**compatir** /kɔ̃patiʀ/ ②  *vi* sympathize; ~ à share in.

**compatriote** /kɔ̃patʀijɔt/ *nmf* compatriot.

**compensation** /kɔ̃pɑ̃sasjɔ̃/ *nf* compensation. **compenser** ①  *vt* compensate for, make up for.

**compère** /kɔ̃pɛʀ/ *nm* accomplice.

**compétence** /kɔ̃petɑ̃s/ *nf* competence; (fonction) domain, sphere; **entrer dans les** ~**s de qn** be in sb's domain. **compétent, ~e** *adj* competent.

**compétition** /kɔ̃petisjɔ̃/ *nf* competition; (sportive) event; **de** ~ competitive.

**complaire (se)** /(sə)kɔ̃plɛʀ/ ④⑦  *vpr* **se** ~ **dans** delight in.

**complaisance** /kɔ̃plɛzɑ̃s/ *nf* kindness; (indulgence) indulgence.

**complément** /kɔ̃plemɑ̃/ *nm* supplement; (Gram) complement; ~ **(d'objet)** (Gram) object; ~ **d'information** further information. **complémentaire** *adj* complementary; (renseignements) supplementary.

**complet, -ète** /kɔ̃plɛ, -t/ *adj* complete; (train, hôtel) full. ●*nm* suit.

**compléter** /kɔ̃plete/ ⑭  *vt* complete; (agrémenter) complement. □ **se** ~ *vpr* complement each other.

**complexe** /kɔ̃plɛks/ *adj* com-

plex. ● *nm* (sentiment, bâtiments) complex.

**complexé, ~e** /kɔ̃plɛkse/ *adj* **être** ~ have a lot of hang-ups.

**complice** /kɔ̃plis/ *nm* accomplice.

**compliment** /kɔ̃plimɑ̃/ *nm* compliment; ~**s** (félicitations) compliments, congratulations.

**compliquer** /kɔ̃plike/ ①  *vt* complicate. □ **se** ~ *vpr* become complicated.

**complot** /kɔ̃plo/ *nm* plot.

**comportement** /kɔ̃pɔʀtəmɑ̃/ *nm* behaviour; (de joueur, voiture) performance.

**comporter** /kɔ̃pɔʀte/ ①  *vt* (être composé de) comprise; (inclure) include; (risque) entail. □ **se** ~ *vpr* behave; (joueur, voiture) perform.

**composant** /kɔ̃pozɑ̃/ *nm* component.

**composé, ~e** /kɔ̃poze/ *adj* composite; (salade) mixed; (guindé) affected. ●*nm* compound.

**composer** /kɔ̃poze/ ①  *vt* make up, compose; (chanson, visage) compose; (numéro) dial; (page) typeset. ●*vi* (transiger) compromise. □ **se** ~ **de** *vpr* be made up *ou* composed of. **compositeur, -trice** *nm, f* (Mus) composer.

**composter** /kɔ̃pɔste/ ①  *vt* (billet) punch.

**compote** /kɔ̃pɔt/ *nf* stewed fruit; ~ **de pommes** stewed apples.

**compréhensible** /kɔ̃pʀeɑ̃sibl/ *adj* understandable; (intelligible) comprehensible.

**compréhensif, -ive** /kɔ̃pʀeɑ̃sif, -v/ *adj* understanding.

**compréhension** /kɔ̃pʀeɑ̃sjɔ̃/ *nf* understanding, comprehension.

**comprendre** /kɔ̃pʀɑ̃dʀ/ ⑤  *vt* understand; (comporter) comprise, be made up of. □ **se** ~

*vpr* (*personnes*) understand each other; **ça se comprend** that is understandable.

**compresse** /kɔ̃pʀɛs/ *nf* compress.

**comprimé** /kɔ̃pʀime/ *nm* tablet.

**comprimer** /kɔ̃pʀime/ **1** *vt* compress; (*réduire*) reduce.

**compris, ~e** /kɔ̃pʀi, -z/ *adj* included; (*d'accord*) agreed; **~ entre** (*contenu*) between; **service (non) ~** service (not) included; **tout ~** (all) inclusive; **y ~** including.

**compromettre** /kɔ̃pʀɔmɛtʀ/ **42** *vt* compromise. **compromis** *nm* compromise.

**comptabilité** /kɔ̃tabilite/ *nf* accountancy; (*comptes*) accounts; (*service*) accounts department.

**comptable** /kɔ̃tabl/ *adj* accounting. ● *nmf* accountant.

**comptant** /kɔ̃tɑ̃/ *adv* (*payer*) (in) cash; (*acheter*) for cash.

**compte** /kɔ̃t/ *nm* count; (*facture, comptabilité*) account; (*nombre exact*) right number; **~ bancaire, ~ en banque** bank account; **prendre qch en ~, tenir ~ de qch** take sth into account; **se rendre ~ de** realize; **demander/rendre des ~s** ask for/give an explanation; **à bon ~** cheaply; **s'en tirer à bon ~** get off lightly; **travailler à son ~** be self-employed; **faire le ~ de** count; **pour le ~ de** on behalf of; **sur le ~ de** about; **au bout du ~** all things considered; **~ à rebours** countdown.

**compte-gouttes** /kɔ̃tgut/ *nm inv* (*Méd*) dropper; **au ~** (*fig*) in dribs and drabs.

**compter** /kɔ̃te/ **1** *vt* count; (*prévoir*) allow, reckon on; (*facturer*) charge for; (*avoir*) have; (*classer*) consider; **~ faire** intend to do. ● *vi* (*calculer, importer*) count; **~ avec** reckon with; **~ parmi** (*figurer*) be

considered among; **~ sur** rely on, count on.

**compte(-)rendu** /kɔ̃tʀɑ̃dy/ *nm* report; (*de film, livre*) review.

**compteur** /kɔ̃tœʀ/ *nm* meter; **~ de vitesse** speedometer.

**comptine** /kɔ̃tin/ *nf* nursery rhyme.

**comptoir** /kɔ̃twaʀ/ *nm* counter; (*de café*) bar.

**comte** /kɔ̃t/ *nm* count.

**comté** /kɔ̃te/ *nm* county.

**comtesse** /kɔ̃tɛs/ *nf* countess.

**con, ~ne** /kɔ̃, kɔn/ *adj* ✗ bloody stupid ✗. ● *nm, f* ✗ bloody fool ✗.

**concentrer** /kɔ̃sɑ̃tʀe/ **1** *vt* concentrate. □ **se ~** *vpr* be concentrated.

**concept** /kɔ̃sɛpt/ *nm* concept.

**concerner** /kɔ̃sɛʀne/ **1** *vt* concern; **en ce qui me concerne** as far as I am concerned.

**concert** /kɔ̃sɛʀ/ *nm* concert; **de ~** in unison.

**concerter** /kɔ̃sɛʀte/ **1** *vt* organize, prepare. □ **se ~** *vpr* confer.

**concession** /kɔ̃sesjɔ̃/ *nf* concession; (*terrain*) plot.

**concevoir** /kɔ̃svwaʀ/ **52** *vt* (*imaginer, engendrer*) conceive; (*comprendre*) understand; (*élaborer*) design.

**concierge** /kɔ̃sjɛʀʒ/ *nmf* caretaker.

**concilier** /kɔ̃silje/ **45** *vt* reconcile. □ **se ~** *vpr* (*s'attirer*) win (over).

**concis, ~e** /kɔ̃si, -z/ *adj* concise.

**conclure** /kɔ̃klyʀ/ **16** *vt* conclude; **~ à** conclude in favour of. ● *vi* **~ en faveur de/contre** find in favour of/against. **conclusion** *nf* conclusion.

**concombre** /kɔ̃kɔ̃bʀ/ *nm* cucumber.

**concordance** /kɔ̃kɔʀdɑ̃s/ *nf* agreement.

**concourir** /kɔ̃kuʀiʀ/ 20 *vi* compete. ● *vt* ~ à contribute towards.

**concours** /kɔ̃kuʀ/ *nm* competition; (*examen*) competitive examination; (*aide*) help; (*de circonstances*) combination.

**concret, -ète** /kɔ̃kʀɛ, -t/ *adj* concrete.

**concrétiser** /kɔ̃kʀetize/ 1 *vt* give concrete form to. □ se ~ *vpr* materialize.

**conçu,** ~e /kɔ̃sy/ *adj* bien/mal ~ well/badly designed.

**concubinage** /kɔ̃kybinaʒ/ *nm* cohabitation; vivre en ~ live together, cohabit.

**concurrence** /kɔ̃kyʀɑ̃s/ *nf* competition; faire ~ à compete with; jusqu'à ~ de up to a limit of.

**concurrencer** /kɔ̃kyʀɑ̃se/ 10 *vt* compete with.

**concurrent,** ~e /kɔ̃kyʀɑ̃, -t/ *nm, f* competitor; (*Scol*) candidate. ● *adj* rival.

**condamnation** /kɔ̃danasjɔ̃/ *nf* condemnation; (*peine*) sentence; ~ centralisée des portières central locking. **condamné,** ~e *nm, f* condemned man, condemned woman. **condamner** 1 *vt* (*censurer, obliger*) condemn; (*Jur*) sentence; (*porte*) block up.

**condition** /kɔ̃disjɔ̃/ *nf* condition; ~s (*prix*) terms; à ~ de ou que provided (that); sans ~ unconditional(ly); sous ~ conditionally.

**conditionnel,** ~le /kɔ̃disjɔnɛl/ *adj* conditional. ● *nm* conditional (tense).

**conditionnement** /kɔ̃disjɔnmɑ̃/ *nm* conditioning; (*emballage*) packaging.

**condoléances** /kɔ̃dɔleɑ̃s/ *nfpl* condolences.

**conducteur, -trice** /kɔ̃dyktœʀ,

-tʀis/ *nm, f* driver.

**conduire** /kɔ̃dɥiʀ/ 17 *vt* take (à to); (*guider*) lead; (*Auto*) drive; (*affaire*) conduct; ~ à (*faire aboutir*) lead to. ● *vi* drive. □ se ~ *vpr* behave.

**conduit** /kɔ̃dɥi/ *nm* duct.

**conduite** /kɔ̃dɥit/ *nf* conduct, behaviour; (*Auto*) driving; (*tuyau*) pipe; voiture avec ~ à droite right-hand drive car.

**confection** /kɔ̃fɛksjɔ̃/ *nf* making; de ~ ready-made; la ~ the clothing industry.

**conférence** /kɔ̃feʀɑ̃s/ *nf* conference; (*exposé*) lecture; ~ au sommet summit meeting. **conférencier, -ière** *nm, f* lecturer.

**confesser** /kɔ̃fese/ 1 *vt* confess. □ se ~ *vpr* go to confession.

**confiance** /kɔ̃fjɑ̃s/ *nf* trust; avoir ~ en trust.

**confiant,** ~e /kɔ̃fjɑ̃, -t/ *adj* (*assuré*) confident; (*sans défiance*) trusting.

**confidence** /kɔ̃fidɑ̃s/ *nf* confidence.

**confidentiel,** ~le /kɔ̃fidɑ̃sjɛl/ *adj* confidential.

**confier** /kɔ̃fje/ 45 *vt* ~ à qn entrust sb with; ~ un secret à qn tell sb a secret. □ se ~ à *vpr* confide in.

**configuration** /kɔ̃figyʀasjɔ̃/ *nf* configuration.

**configurer** /kɔ̃figyʀe/ *vt* configure.

**confiner** /kɔ̃fine/ 1 *vt* confine; ~ à border on. □ se ~ *vpr* confine oneself (à, dans to).

**confirmation** /kɔ̃fiʀmasjɔ̃/ *nf* confirmation. **confirmer** 1 *vt* confirm.

**confiserie** /kɔ̃fizʀi/ *nf* sweet shop; ~s confectionery.

**confisquer** /kɔ̃fiske/ 1 *vt* confiscate.

**confit,** ~e /kɔ̃fi, -t/ adj candied; (fruits) crystallized. ●nm ~ de canard confit of duck.

**confiture** /kɔ̃fityR/ nf jam.

**conflit** /kɔ̃fli/ nm conflict.

**confondre** /kɔ̃fɔ̃dR/ 🖪 vt confuse, mix up; (étonner) confound. □ se ~ vpr merge; se ~ en excuses apologize profusely.

**conforme** /kɔ̃fɔRm/ adj être ~ à comply with; (être en accord) be in keeping with.

**conformer** /kɔ̃fɔRme/ 🖪 vt adapt. □ se ~ à vpr conform to.

**conformité** /kɔ̃fɔRmite/ nf compliance, conformity; agir en ~ avec act in accordance with.

**confort** /kɔ̃fɔR/ nm comfort; tout ~ with all mod cons. **confortable** adj comfortable.

**confrère** /kɔ̃fRεR/ nm colleague.

**confronter** /kɔ̃fRɔ̃te/ 🖪 vt confront; (textes) compare. □ se ~ à vpr be confronted with.

**confus,** ~e /kɔ̃fy, -z/ adj confused; (gêné) embarrassed.

**congé** /kɔ̃ʒe/ nm holiday; (arrêt momentané) time off, leave; (avis de départ) notice; en ~ on holiday ou sick leave; ~ de maladie/maternité sick/maternity leave; jour de ~ day off; prendre ~ de take one's leave of.

**congédier** /kɔ̃ʒedje/ 🔠 vt dismiss.

**congélateur** /kɔ̃ʒelatœR/ nm freezer.

**congeler** /kɔ̃ʒle/ 🖪 vt freeze.

**congère** /kɔ̃ʒεR/ nf snowdrift.

**congrès** /kɔ̃gRε/ nm conference; (Pol) congress.

**conjoint,** ~e /kɔ̃ʒwɛ̃, -t/ nm, f spouse. ●adj joint.

**conjonctivite** /kɔ̃ʒɔ̃ktivit/ nf conjunctivitis.

**conjoncture** /kɔ̃ʒɔ̃ktyR/ nf situation; (économique) economic climate.

**conjugaison** /kɔ̃ʒygεzɔ̃/ nf conjugation.

**conjugal,** ~e (mpl -aux) /kɔ̃ʒygal, -o/ adj conjugal, married.

**conjuguer** /kɔ̃ʒyge/ 🖪 vt (Gram) conjugate; (efforts) combine. □ se ~ vpr (Gram) be conjugated; (facteurs) be combined.

**conjurer** /kɔ̃ʒyRe/ 🖪 vt (éviter) avert; (implorer) beg.

**connaissance** /kɔnεsɑ̃s/ nf knowledge; (personne) acquaintance; ~s (science) knowledge; faire la ~ de meet; (apprécier une personne) get to know; perdre/reprendre ~ lose/regain consciousness; sans ~ unconscious.

**connaisseur** /kɔnεsœR/ nm expert, connoisseur.

**connaître** /kɔnεtR/ 🔢 vt know; (difficultés, faim, succès) experience; faire ~ make known. □ se ~ vpr (se rencontrer) meet; s'y ~ en know (all) about.

**connecter** /kɔnεkte/ 🖪 vt connect; être/ne pas être connecté be on/off-line. □ se ~ à vpr (Ordinat) log on to.

**connerie** /kɔnRi/ 🗵 nf faire une ~ do something stupid; dire des ~s talk rubbish.

**connexion** /kɔnεksjɔ̃/ nf (Ordinat) connection.

**connu,** ~e /kɔny/ adj well-known.

**conquérant,** ~e /kɔ̃keRɑ̃, -t/ nm, f conqueror.

**conquête** /kɔ̃kεt/ nf conquest.

**consacrer** /kɔ̃sakRe/ 🖪 vt devote; (Relig) consecrate; (sanctionner) sanction. □ se ~ à vpr devote oneself to.

**conscience** /kɔ̃sjɑ̃s/ nf conscience; (perception) awareness; (de collectivité) consciousness; avoir/ prendre ~ de be/become aware of; perdre/reprendre ~ lose/regain consciousness; avoir bonne/ mauvaise ~ have a clear/guilty conscience.

**conscient, ~e** /kɔ̃sjɑ̃, -t/ *adj* conscious; ~ **de** aware *ou* conscious of.

**conseil** /kɔ̃sɛj/ *nm* (piece of) advice; (assemblée) council, committee; (séance) meeting; (personne) consultant; ~ **d'administration** board of directors; ~ **en gestion** management consultant; ~ **des ministres** Cabinet; ~ **municipal** town council.

**conseiller**[1] /kɔ̃seje/ **1** *vt* advise; ~ **à qn de** advise sb to; ~ **qch à qn** recommend sth to sb.

**conseiller,**[2] **-ère** /kɔ̃seje, -jɛʀ/ *nm, f* adviser, counsellor; ~ **municipal** town councillor; ~ **d'orientation** careers adviser.

**consentement** /kɔ̃sɑ̃tmɑ̃/ *nm* consent.

**conséquence** /kɔ̃sekɑ̃s/ *nf* consequence; **en** ~ (comme il convient) accordingly; **en** ~ (**de quoi**) as a result of which.

**conséquent, ~e** /kɔ̃sekɑ̃, -t/ *adj* consistent, logical; (important) substantial; **par** ~ consequently, therefore.

**conservateur, -trice** /kɔ̃sɛʀvatœʀ, -tʀis/ *adj* conservative; (de musée) curator. ●*nm* preservative.

**conservation** /kɔ̃sɛʀvasjɔ̃/ *nf* preservation; (d'espèce, patrimoine) conservation.

**conservatoire** /kɔ̃sɛʀvatwaʀ/ *nm* academy.

**conserve** /kɔ̃sɛʀv/ *nf* tinned *ou* canned food; **en** ~ tinned, canned; **boîte de** ~ tin, can.

**conserver** /kɔ̃sɛʀve/ **1** *vt* keep; (en bon état) preserve; (Culin) preserve. □ **se** ~ *vpr* (Culin) keep.

**considérer** /kɔ̃sideʀe/ **14** *vt* consider; (respecter) esteem; ~ **comme** consider to be.

**consigne** /kɔ̃siɲ/ *nf* (de gare) left-luggage office; (US) baggage checkroom; (somme) deposit; (ordres) orders; ~ **automatique** left-luggage lockers; (US) baggage lockers.

**consistance** /kɔ̃sistɑ̃s/ *nf* consistency; (fig) substance, weight. **consistant, ~e** *adj* solid; (épais) thick.

**consister** /kɔ̃siste/ **1** *vi* ~ **en/dans** consist of/in; ~ **à faire** consist in doing.

**consoler** /kɔ̃sɔle/ **1** *vt* console. □ **se** ~ *vpr* find consolation; **se** ~ **de qch** get over sth.

**consolider** /kɔ̃sɔlide/ **1** *vt* strengthen; (fig) consolidate.

**consommateur, -trice** /kɔ̃sɔmatœʀ, -tʀis/ *nm, f* (Comm) consumer; (dans un café) customer.

**consommation** /kɔ̃sɔmasjɔ̃/ *nf* consumption; (accomplissement) consummation; (boisson) drink; **de** ~ (Comm) consumer.

**consommer** /kɔ̃sɔme/ **1** *vt* consume, use; (manger) eat; (boire) drink; (mariage) consummate. □ **se** ~ *vpr* (être mangé) be eaten; (être utilisé) be used.

**consonne** /kɔ̃sɔn/ *nf* consonant.

**constat** /kɔ̃sta/ *nm* (official) report; ~ (**à l'**)**amiable** accident report drawn up by those involved.

**constatation** /kɔ̃statasjɔ̃/ *nf* observation, statement of fact. **constater** **1** *vt* note, notice; (certifier) certify.

**consternation** /kɔ̃stɛʀnasjɔ̃/ *nf* dismay.

**constipé,** ~e /kɔ̃stipe/ adj constipated; (fig) uptight.

**constituer** /kɔ̃stitɥe/ **1** vt (composer) make up, constitute; (organiser) form; (être) constitute; constitué de made up of. □ se ~ ~ prisonnier give oneself up.

**constitution** /kɔ̃stitysjɔ̃/ nf formation, setting up; (Pol, Méd) constitution.

**constructeur** /kɔ̃stryktœr/ nm manufacturer, builder.

**construction** /kɔ̃stryksjɔ̃/ nf building; (structure, secteur) construction; (fabrication) manufacture.

**construire** /kɔ̃strɥir/ **17** vt build; (système, phrase) construct.

**consulat** /kɔ̃syla/ nm consulate.

**consultation** /kɔ̃syltasjɔ̃/ nf consultation; (réception: Méd) surgery; (US) office; **heures de** ~ surgery ou office (US) hours.

**consulter** /kɔ̃sylte/ **1** vt consult. ● vi (médecin) hold surgery, see patients. □ se ~ vpr consult together.

**contact** /kɔ̃takt/ nm contact; (toucher) touch; **au** ~ **de** on contact with; (personne) by contact with, by seeing; **mettre/couper le** ~ (Auto) switch on/off the ignition; **prendre** ~ **avec** get in touch with. **contacter** **1** vt contact.

**contagieux, -ieuse** /kɔ̃taʒjø, -z/ adj contagious.

**conte** /kɔ̃t/ nm tale; ~ **de fées** fairy tale.

**contempler** /kɔ̃tɑ̃ple/ **1** vt contemplate.

**contemporain,** ~e /kɔ̃tɑ̃pɔrɛ̃, -ɛn/ adj & nm,f contemporary.

**contenance** /kɔ̃t(ə)nɑ̃s/ nf (volume) capacity; (allure) bearing; **perdre** ~ lose one's composure.

**contenir** /kɔ̃t(ə)nir/ **58** vt contain; (avoir une capacité de) hold. □ se

~ vpr contain oneself.

**content,** ~e /kɔ̃tɑ̃, -t/ adj pleased, happy (de with); ~ **de faire** pleased ou happy to do.

**contenter** /kɔ̃tɑ̃te/ **1** vt satisfy. □ se ~ **de** vpr content oneself with.

**contenu** /kɔ̃t(ə)ny/ nm (de récipient) contents (+ pl); (de texte) content.

**conter** /kɔ̃te/ **1** vt tell, relate.

**contestation** /kɔ̃testasjɔ̃/ nf dispute; (opposition) protest.

**contester** /kɔ̃teste/ **1** vt question, dispute; (s'opposer) protest against. ● vi protest.

**conteur, -euse** /kɔ̃tœr, -øz/ nm, f storyteller.

**contigu,** ~ë /kɔ̃tigy/ adj adjacent (à to).

**continent** /kɔ̃tinɑ̃/ nm continent.

**continu,** ~e /kɔ̃tiny/ adj continuous.

**continuer** /kɔ̃tinɥe/ **1** vt continue. ● vi continue, go on; ~ **à** ou **de faire** carry on ou go on ou continue doing.

**contorsionner (se)** /(sə) kɔ̃tɔrsjɔne/ **1** vpr wriggle.

**contour** /kɔ̃tur/ nm outline, contour; ~s (d'une route) twists and turns, bends.

**contourner** /kɔ̃turne/ **1** vt go round, by-pass; (difficulté) get round.

**contraceptif, -ive** /kɔ̃trasɛptif, -v/ adj contraceptive. ● nm contraceptive. **contraception** nf contraception.

**contracter** /kɔ̃trakte/ **1** vt (maladie) contract; (dette) incur; (muscle) tense; (assurance) take out. □ se ~ vpr contract.

**contractuel,** ~le /kɔ̃traktɥel/ nm, f (agent) traffic warden.

**contradictoire** /kɔ̃tradiktwar/

*adj* contradictory; (*débat*) open.

**contraignant, ~e** /kɔ̃tʀɛɲɑ̃, -t/ *adj* restricting.

**contraindre** /kɔ̃tʀɛ̃dʀ/ **22** *vt* force, compel (**à faire** to do).

**contrainte** /kɔ̃tʀɛ̃t/ *nf* constraint.

**contraire** /kɔ̃tʀɛʀ/ *adj* opposite; **~ à** contrary to. ●*nm* opposite; **au ~** on the contrary; **au ~ de** unlike.

**contrarier** /kɔ̃tʀaʀje/ **45** *vt* annoy; (*projet, volonté*) frustrate; (*chagriner*) upset.

**contraste** /kɔ̃tʀast/ *nm* contrast.

**contrat** /kɔ̃tʀa/ *nm* contract.

**contravention** /kɔ̃tʀavɑ̃sjɔ̃/ *nf* (parking) ticket; **en ~** in breach (à of).

**contre** /kɔ̃tʀ(ə)/ *prép* against; (*en échange de*) for; **par ~** on the other hand; **tout ~** close by.

**contreattaque** (*pl* **~s**) *nf* counterattack. **contre-attaquer** **1** *vt* counter-attack. **contre-balancer** **10** *vt* counterbalance.

**contrebande** /kɔ̃tʀabɑ̃d/ *nf* contraband; **faire la ~ de** smuggle.

**contrebas: en ~** /ɑ̃kɔ̃tʀəba/ *loc* below.

**contrebasse** /kɔ̃tʀabas/ *nf* double bass.

**contrecœur: à ~** /akɔ̃tʀəkœʀ/ *loc* reluctantly.

**contrecoup** /kɔ̃tʀaku/ *nm* effects, repercussions.

**contredire** /kɔ̃tʀadiʀ/ **37** *vt* contradict. ▫ **se ~** *vpr* contradict oneself.

**contrée** /kɔ̃tʀe/ *nf* region; (*pays*) land.

**contrefaçon** /kɔ̃tʀafasɔ̃/ *nf* (*objet imité, action*) forgery.

**contre-indiqué, ~e** /kɔ̃tʀɛ̃dike/ *adj* (Méd) contra-indicated; (*déconseillé*) not recommended.

**contre-jour: à ~** /akɔ̃tʀəʒuʀ/ *loc* against the light.

**contrepartie** /kɔ̃tʀaparti/ *nf* compensation; **en ~** in exchange, in return.

**contreplaqué** /kɔ̃tʀaplake/ *nm* plywood.

**contresens** /kɔ̃tʀasɑ̃s/ *nm* misinterpretation; (*absurdité*) nonsense; **à ~** the wrong way.

**contretemps** /kɔ̃tʀatɑ̃/ *nm* hitch; **à ~** (fig) at the wrong time.

**contribuable** /kɔ̃tʀibɥabl/ *nmf* taxpayer.

**contribuer** /kɔ̃tʀibɥe/ **1** *vt* contribute (à to, towards).

**contrôle** /kɔ̃tʀol/ *nm* (maîtrise) control; (vérification) check; (des prix) control; (poinçon) hallmark; (Scol) test; **~ continu** continuous assessment; **~ des changes** exchange control; **~ des naissances** birth control; **~ de soi-même** self-control; **~ technique** (des véhicules) MOT (test).

**contrôler** /kɔ̃tʀole/ **1** *vt* (vérifier) check; (surveiller, maîtriser) control. ▫ **se ~** *vpr* control oneself.

**contrôleur, -euse** /kɔ̃tʀolœʀ, -øz/ *nm, f* inspector.

**convaincre** /kɔ̃vɛ̃kʀ/ **59** *vt* convince; **~ qn de faire** persuade sb to do.

**convalescence** /kɔ̃valesɑ̃s/ *nf* convalescence; **être en ~** be convalescing.

**convenable** /kɔ̃vnabl/ *adj* (correct) decent, proper; (approprié) suitable; (acceptable) reasonable, acceptable.

**convenance** /kɔ̃vnɑ̃s/ *nf* **à ma ~** to my satisfaction; **les ~s** convention.

**convenir** /kɔ̃vniʀ/ **58** *vt/i* be suitable; **~ à** suit; **~ que** admit that;

~ de qch (avouer) admit sth; (s'accorder sur) agree on sth; ~ de faire agree to do; il convient de it is advisable to; (selon les bienséances) it would be right to.

**convention** /kɔ̃vɑ̃sjɔ̃/ nf agreement, convention; (clause) article, clause; ~s (convenances) convention; de ~ conventional; ~ collective industrial agreement.

**convenu, ~e** /kɔ̃vny/ adj agreed.

**conversation** /kɔ̃vɛʀsasjɔ̃/ nf conversation.

**convertir** /kɔ̃vɛʀtiʀ/ 2 vt convert (à to; en into). □ se ~ vpr be converted, convert.

**conviction** /kɔ̃viksjɔ̃/ nf conviction; avoir la ~ que be convinced that.

**convivial, ~e** (mpl -iaux) /kɔ̃vivjal, -jo/ adj convivial; (Ordinat) user-friendly.

**convocation** /kɔ̃vɔkasjɔ̃/ nf (Jur) summons; (d'une assemblée) convening; (document) notification to attend.

**convoi** /kɔ̃vwa/ nm convoy; (train) train; ~ (funèbre) funeral procession.

**convoquer** /kɔ̃vɔke/ 1 vt (assemblée) convene; (personne) summon; être convoqué pour un entretien be called for interview.

**coopération** /kooperasjɔ̃/ nf cooperation; (Mil) civilian national service abroad.

**coordination** /kɔɔʀdinasjɔ̃/ nf coordination. **coordonnées** nfpl coordinates; (adresse) address and telephone number.

**copain** /kɔpɛ̃/ nm friend; (petit ami) boyfriend.

**copie** /kɔpi/ nf copy; (Scol) paper; ~ d'examen exam paper ou script; ~ de sauvegarde back-up copy.

**copier** /kɔpje/ 45 vt/i copy; ~ sur (Scol) copy ou crib from.

**copieux, -ieuse** /kɔpjø, -z/ adj copious.

**copine** /kɔpin/ nf friend; (petite amie) girlfriend.

**coq** /kɔk/ nm cockerel.

**coque** /kɔk/ nf shell; (de bateau) hull.

**coquelicot** /kɔkliko/ nm poppy.

**coqueluche** /kɔklyʃ/ nf whooping cough.

**coquet, ~te** /kɔkɛ, -t/ adj flirtatious; (élégant) pretty; (somme 1) tidy.

**coquetier** /kɔktje/ nm eggcup.

**coquillage** /kɔkijaʒ/ nm shellfish; (coquille) shell.

**coquille** /kɔkij/ nf shell; (faute) misprint; ~ Saint-Jacques scallop.

**coquin, ~e** /kɔkɛ̃, -in/ adj mischievous. ● nm, f rascal.

**cor** /kɔʀ/ nm (Mus) horn; (au pied) corn.

**corail** (pl -aux) /kɔʀaj, -o/ nm coral.

**corbeau** (pl ~x) /kɔʀbo/ nm (oiseau) crow.

**corbeille** /kɔʀbɛj/ nf basket; ~ à papier waste-paper basket.

**corbillard** /kɔʀbijaʀ/ nm hearse.

**cordage** /kɔʀdaʒ/ nm rope; ~s (Naut) rigging.

**corde** /kɔʀd/ nf rope; (d'arc, de violon) string; ~ à linge washing line; ~ à sauter skipping-rope; ~ raide tightrope; ~s vocales vocal cords.

**cordon** /kɔʀdɔ̃/ nm string, cord; ~ de police police cordon.

**cordonnier** /kɔʀdɔnje/ nm cobbler.

**Corée** /kɔʀe/ nf Korea.

**coriace** /kɔʀjas/ adj tough.

**corne** /kɔʀn/ *nf* horn.

**corneille** /kɔʀnɛj/ *nf* crow.

**cornemuse** /kɔʀnəmyz/ *nf* bag-pipes (+ *pl*).

**corner** /kɔʀne/ **1** *vt* (*page*) turn down the corner of; **page cornée** dog-eared page. ● *vi* (Auto) hoot, honk.

**cornet** /kɔʀnɛ/ *nm* (paper) cone; (crème glacée) cornet, cone.

**corniche** /kɔʀniʃ/ *nf* cornice; (*route*) cliff road.

**cornichon** /kɔʀniʃɔ̃/ *nm* gherkin.

**corporel,** ∼le /kɔʀpɔʀɛl/ *adj* bodily; (*châtiment*) corporal.

**corps** /kɔʀ/ *nm* body; (Mil) corps; **combat à** ∼ hand-to-hand combat; ∼ **électoral** electorate; ∼ **enseignant** teaching profession.

**correct,** ∼e /kɔʀɛkt/ *adj* proper, correct; (*exact*) correct.

**correcteur, -trice** /kɔʀɛktœʀ, -tʀis/ *nm, f* (d'épreuves) proof-reader; (Scol) examiner; ∼ **liquide** correction fluid; ∼ **d'orthographe** spell-checker.

**correction** /kɔʀɛksjɔ̃/ *nf* correction; (d'examen) marking, grading; (punition) beating.

**correspondance** /kɔʀɛspɔ̃dɑ̃s/ *nf* correspondence; (de train, d'autobus) connection; **vente par** ∼ mail order; **faire des études par** ∼ do a correspondence course.

**correspondant,** ∼e /kɔʀɛspɔ̃dɑ̃, -t/ *adj* corresponding. ● *nm, f* correspondent; penfriend; (au téléphone) **votre** ∼ the person you are calling.

**correspondre** /kɔʀɛspɔ̃dʀ/ **3** *vi* (s'accorder, écrire) correspond; (*chambres*) communicate. ● *v + prép* ∼ **à** (être approprié à) match, suit; (équivaloir à) correspond to. □ **se** ∼ *vpr* correspond.

**corrida** /kɔʀida/ *nf* bullfight.

**corriger** /kɔʀiʒe/ **40** *vt* correct; (*devoir*) mark, grade, correct; (*punir*) beat; (*guérir*) cure.

**corsage** /kɔʀsaʒ/ *nm* bodice; (chemisier) blouse.

**corsaire** /kɔʀsɛʀ/ *nm* pirate.

**Corse** /kɔʀs/ *nf* Corsica. ● *nmf* Corsican. **corse** *adj* Corsican.

**corsé,** ∼e /kɔʀse/ *adj* (*vin*) full-bodied; (*café*) strong; (*scabreux*) racy; (*problème*) tough.

**cortège** /kɔʀtɛʒ/ *nm* procession; ∼ **funèbre** funeral procession.

**corvée** /kɔʀve/ *nf* chore.

**cosmonaute** /kɔsmɔnot/ *nmf* cosmonaut.

**cosmopolite** /kɔsmɔpɔlit/ *adj* cosmopolitan.

**cosse** /kɔs/ *nf* (de pois) pod.

**cossu,** ∼e /kɔsy/ *adj* (gens) well-to-do; (demeure) opulent.

**costaud,** ∼e /kɔsto, -d/ **1** *adj* strong. ● *nm* strong man.

**costume** /kɔstym/ *nm* suit; (Théât) costume.

**cote** /kɔt/ *nf* (classification) mark; (en Bourse) quotation; (de cheval) odds (de on); (de candidat, acteur) rating; ∼ **d'alerte** danger level; **avoir la** ∼ be popular.

**côte** /kot/ *nf* (littoral) coast; (pente) hill; (Anat) rib; (Culin) chop; ∼ **à** ∼ side by side; **la C**∼ **d'Azur** the (French) Riviera.

**côté** /kote/ *nm* side; (direction) way; **à** ∼ nearby; **voisin d'à** ∼ next-door neighbour; **à** ∼ **de** next to; (comparé à) compared to; **à** ∼ **de la cible** wide of the target; **aux** ∼s **de** by the side of; **de** ∼ (regarder) sideways; (sauter) to one side; **mettre de** ∼ put aside; **de ce** ∼ this way; **de chaque** ∼ on each side; **de tous les** ∼s on every side;

(partout) everywhere; **du ~ de** (vers) towards; (proche de) near.

**côtelette** /kotlɛt/ nf chop.

**coter** /kɔte/ **1** vt (Comm) quote; **coté en Bourse** listed on the Stock Exchange; **très coté** highly rated.

**cotiser** /kɔtize/ **1** vi pay one's contributions (à to); (à un club) pay one's subscription. □ **se ~** vpr club together.

**coton** /kɔtɔ̃/ nm cotton; **~ hydrophile** cotton wool.

**cou** /ku/ nm neck.

**couchant** /kuʃɑ̃/ nm sunset.

**couche** /kuʃ/ nf layer; (de peinture) coat; (de bébé) nappy; (US) diaper; **~s** (Méd) childbirth; **~s sociales** social strata.

**coucher** /kuʃe/ **1** vt put to bed; (loger) put up; (étendre) lay down; **~ (par écrit)** set down. ● vi sleep. □ **se ~** vpr go to bed; (s'étendre) lie down; (soleil) set. ● nm **~ de soleil** sunset.

**couchette** /kuʃɛt/ nf (de train) couchette; (Naut) berth.

**coude** /kud/ nm elbow; (de rivière, chemin) bend; **~ à ~** side by side.

**cou-de-pied** ( pl **cous-de-pied**) /kudpje/ nm instep.

**coudre** /kudʀ/ **19** vt/i sew.

**couette** /kwɛt/ nf duvet, quilt.

**couler** /kule/ **1** vi flow, run; (fromage, nez) run; (fuir) leak; (bateau) sink; (entreprise) go under; **faire ~ un bain** run a bath. ● vt (bateau) sink; (sculpture, métal) cast. □ **se ~** vpr slip (dans into).

**couleur** /kulœʀ/ nf colour; (peinture) paint; (aux cartes) suit; **~s** (teint) colour; **de ~** (homme, femme) coloured; **en ~s** (télévision, film) colour.

**couleuvre** /kulœvʀ/ nf grass snake.

**coulisse** /kulis/ nf (de tiroir) runner; **à ~** ( porte, fenêtre) sliding; **~s** (Théât) wings; **dans les ~s** (fig) behind the scenes.

**couloir** /kulwaʀ/ nm corridor; (Sport) lane; **~ de bus** bus lane.

**coup** /ku/ nm blow; (choc) knock; (Sport) stroke; (de crayon, craie, cloche) stroke; (de fusil, pistolet) shot; (fois) time; (aux échecs) move; **donner un ~ de pied/poing à qn** kick/punch; **à ~ sûr** definitely; **après ~** after the event; **boire un ~** **1** have a drink; **~ sur ~** in rapid succession; **du ~** as a result; **d'un seul ~** in one go; **du premier ~** first go; **sale ~** dirty trick; **sous le ~ de la fatigue/colère** out of tiredness/anger; **sur le ~** instantly; **tenir le ~** hold out; **manquer son ~** **1** blow it!; **~ de chiffon** wipe (with a rag); **~ de coude** nudge; **~ de couteau** stab; **~ d'envoi** kick-off; **~ d'État** (Pol) coup; **~ franc** free kick; **~ de main** helping hand; **~ d'œil** glance; **~ de soleil** sunburn; **~ de téléphone** telephone call; **~ de vent** gust of wind.

**coupable** /kupabl/ adj guilty.

**coupe** /kup/ nf cup; (de champagne) goblet; (à fruits) dish; (de vêtement) cut; (dessin) section; **~ de cheveux** haircut.

**couper** /kupe/ **1** vt cut; (arbre) cut down; (arrêter) cut off; (voyage) break up; (appétit) take away; (vin) water down; **~ par** take a short cut via; **~ la parole à qn** cut sb short. ● vi cut. □ **se ~** vpr cut oneself; **se ~ le doigt** cut one's finger; (routes) intersect; **se ~** cut oneself off from.

**couple** /kupl/ nm couple; (d'animaux) pair.

**coupure** /kupyʀ/ nf cut; (billet de banque) note; (de presse) cutting;

(pause, rupture) break; (~ de courant) power cut.

**cour** /kuʁ/ nf (court) yard; (du roi) court; (tribunal) court; (~ de récréation) playground; ~ martiale court-martial; faire la ~ à court.

**courageux, -euse** /kuʁaʒø, -z/ adj courageous.

**couramment** /kuʁamã/ adv frequently; (parler) fluently.

**courant, ~e** /kuʁã, -t/ adj standard, ordinary; (en cours) current. ● nm current; (de mode, d'idées) trend; ~ d'air draught; dans le ~ de in the course of; être/mettre au ~ de know/tell about; (à jour) be/bring up to date on.

**courbature** /kuʁbatyʁ/ nf ache; avoir des ~s be stiff, ache.

**courber** /kuʁbe/ **1** vt bend.

**coureur, -euse** /kuʁœʁ, -øz/ nm, f (Sport) runner; ~ automobile racing driver; ~ cycliste racing cyclist. ● nm womanizer.

**courgette** /kuʁʒet/ nf courgette; (US) zucchini.

**courir** /kuʁiʁ/ **20** vi run; (se hâter) rush; (nouvelles) go round; ~ après qn/qch chase after sb/ sth. ● vt (risque) run; (danger) face; (épreuve sportive) run ou compete in; (fréquenter) do the rounds of; (filles) chase (after).

**couronne** /kuʁɔn/ nf crown; (de fleurs) wreath.

**couronnement** /kuʁɔnmã/ nm coronation, crowning; (fig) crowning achievement.

**courriel** /kuʁjel/ nm email.

**courrier** /kuʁje/ nm post, mail; (à écrire) letters; ~ du cœur problem page; ~ électronique email.

**cours** /kuʁ/ nm (leçon) class; (série de leçons) course; (prix) price; (cote) (de valeur, denrée) price; (de

devises) exchange rate; (déroulement, d'une rivière) course; (allée) avenue; au ~ de in the course of; avoir ~ (monnaie) be legal tender; (fig) be current; (Scol) have a lesson; ~ d'eau river, stream; ~ du soir evening class; ~ particulier private lesson; ~ magistral (Univ) lecture; en ~ current; (travail) in progress; en ~ de route along the way.

**course** /kuʁs/ nf running; (épreuve de vitesse) race; (activité) racing; (entre rivaux: fig) race; (de projectile) flight; (voyage) journey; (commission) errand; ~s (achats) shopping; (de chevaux) races; faire la ~ avec qn race sb.

**coursier, -ière** /kuʁsje, -jeʁ, f messenger.

**court, ~e** /kuʁ, -t/ adj short. ● adv short; à ~ de short of; pris de ~ caught unawares. ● nm ~ (de tennis) (tennis) court.

**courtier, -ière** /kuʁtje, -jeʁ/ nm, f broker.

**courtiser** /kuʁtize/ **1** vt woo, court.

**courtois, ~e** /kuʁtwa, -z/ adj courteous. **courtoisie** nf courtesy.

**cousin, ~e** /kuzɛ̃, -in/ nm, f cousin; ~ germain first cousin.

**coussin** /kusɛ̃/ nm cushion.

**coût** /ku/ nm cost; le ~ de la vie the cost of living.

**couteau** (pl ~x) /kuto/ nm knife; ~ à cran d'arrêt flick knife.

**coûter** /kute/ **1** vt/i cost; coûte que coûte at all costs; au prix coûtant at cost price.

**coutume** /kutym/ nf custom.

**couture** /kutyʁ/ nf sewing; (métier) dressmaking; (points) seam. **couturier** nm fashion designer. **couturière** nf dressmaker.

**couvée** /kuve/ nf brood.

**couvent** /kuvɑ̃/ nm convent.

**couver** /kuve/ ◼ vt (œufs) hatch; (personne) overprotect, pamper; (maladie) be coming down with, be sickening for. ● vi (feu) smoulder; (mal) be brewing.

**couvercle** /kuvɛʀkl/ nm (de marmite, boîte) lid; (qui se visse) screwtop.

**couvert, ~e** /kuvɛʀ, -t/ adj covered (de with); (habillé) covered up; (ciel) overcast. ● nm (à table) place setting; (prix) cover charge; ~s (couteaux etc.) cutlery; mettre le ~ lay the table; (abri) cover; à ~ (Mil) under cover; à ~ de (fig) safe from.

**couverture** /kuvɛʀtyʀ/ nf cover; (de lit) blanket; (toit) roofing; (dans la presse) coverage; ~ chauffante electric blanket.

**couvre-feu** (pl ~x) /kuvʀəfø/ nm curfew.

**couvre-lit** (pl ~s) /kuvʀəli/ nm bedspread.

**couvrir** /kuvʀiʀ/ ◼ vt cover. □ se ~ vpr (s'habiller) wrap up; (se coiffer) put one's hat on; (ciel) become overcast.

**covoiturage** /kɔvwatyʀaʒ/ nm car sharing.

**cracher** /kʀaʃe/ ◼ vi spit; (radio) crackle. ● vt spit (out); (fumée) belch out.

**crachin** /kʀaʃɛ̃/ nm drizzle.

**craie** /kʀɛ/ nf chalk.

**craindre** /kʀɛ̃dʀ/ ◼ vt be afraid of, fear; (être sensible à) be easily damaged by.

**crainte** /kʀɛ̃t/ nf fear (pour for); de ~ de/que for fear of/that.

**craintif, -ive** adj timid.

**crampon** /kʀɑ̃pɔ̃/ nm (de chaussure) stud.

**cramponner (se)** /(sə)kʀɑ̃pɔne/ ◼ vpr se ~ à cling to.

**cran** /kʀɑ̃/ nm (entaille) notch; (trou) hole; (courage 🔢) guts 🔢, courage; ~ de sûreté safety catch.

**crâne** /kʀɑn/ nm skull.

**crapaud** /kʀapo/ nm toad.

**craquer** /kʀake/ ◼ vi crack, snap; (plancher) creak; (couture) split; (fig) (personne) break down; (céder) give in. ● vt (allumette) strike; (vêtement) split.

**crasse** /kʀas/ nf grime.

**cravache** /kʀavaʃ/ nf (horse) whip.

**cravate** /kʀavat/ nf tie.

**crayon** /kʀejɔ̃/ nm pencil; ~ de couleur coloured pencil; ~ à bille ballpoint pen; ~ optique light pen.

**créateur, -trice** /kʀeatœʀ, -tʀis/ adj creative. ● nm, f creator, designer.

**crèche** /kʀɛʃ/ nf day nursery, crèche; (Relig) crib.

**crédit** /kʀedi/ nm credit; (somme allouée) funds; à ~ on credit; faire ~ give credit (à to).

**créer** /kʀee/ 🔢 vt create; (produit) design; (société) set up.

**crémaillère** /kʀemajɛʀ/ nf pendre la ~ have a housewarming party.

**crème** /kʀɛm/ adj inv cream. ● nm (café) espresso with milk. ● nf cream; (dessert) cream dessert; ~ anglaise egg custard; ~ fouettée whipped cream; ~ pâtissière confectioner's custard. **crémerie** nf dairy. **crémeux, -euse** adj creamy. **crémier, -ière** nm, f dairyman; dairywoman.

**créneau** (pl ~x) /kʀeno/ nm (trou, moment) slot, window; (dans le marché) gap; faire un ~ to parallel-park.

**crêpe** /kʀɛp/ nf (galette) pancake. ● nm (tissu) crêpe; (matière) crêpe (rubber).

**crépitement** /kʀepitmɑ̃/ nm crackling; (d'huile) sizzling.

**crépuscule** /kʀepyskyl/ nm twilight, dusk.

**cresson** /kʀɑsɔ̃/ nm (water) cress.

**crête** /kʀɛt/ nf crest; (de coq) comb.

**crétin, ~e** /kʀetɛ̃, -in/ nm, f T moron T.

**creuser** /kʀøze/ **1** vt dig; (évider) hollow out; (fig) go into in depth. □ se ~ vpr (écart) widen; se ~ (la cervelle) T rack one's brains.

**creux, -euse** /kʀø, -z/ adj hollow; (heures) off-peak. ● nm hollow; (de l'estomac) pit; **dans le ~ de la main** in the palm of the hand.

**crevaison** /kʀəvɛzɔ̃/ nf puncture.

**crevasse** /kʀəvas/ nf crack; (de glacier) crevasse; (de la peau) chap.

**crevé, ~e** /kʀəve/ adj T worn out.

**crever** /kʀəve/ **1** vt burst; (pneu) puncture, burst; (exténuer T) exhaust; (œil) put out. ● vi (pneu, sac) burst; (mourir T) die.

**crevette** /kʀəvɛt/ nf ~ **grise** shrimp; ~ **rose** prawn.

**cri** /kʀi/ nm cry; (de douleur) scream, cry; **pousser un ~** cry out, scream.

**criard, ~e** /kʀijaʀ, -d/ adj (couleur) garish; (voix) shrill.

**crier** /kʀije/ **45** vi (fort) shout, cry (out); (de douleur) scream; (grincer) creak. ● vt (ordre) shout (out).

**crime** /kʀim/ nm crime; (meurtre) murder.

**criminel, ~le** /kʀiminɛl/ adj criminal. ● nm, f criminal; (assassin) murderer.

**crinière** /kʀinjɛʀ/ nf mane.

**crise** /kʀiz/ nf crisis; (Méd) attack; (de colère) fit; ~ **cardiaque** heart attack; ~ **de foie** bilious attack; ~ **de nerfs** hysterics (+ pl).

**crisper** /kʀispe/ **1** vt tense; (énerver T) irritate. □ se ~ vpr tense; (mains) clench.

**critère** /kʀitɛʀ/ nm criterion.

**critique** /kʀitik/ adj critical. ● nf criticism; (article) review; (commentateur) critic; **la ~** (personnes) the critics. **critiquer** **1** vt criticize.

**Croate** /kʀɔat/ adj Croatian. **C~** nmf Croatian.

**Croatie** /kʀɔasi/ nf Croatia.

**croche** /kʀɔʃ/ nf quaver.

**croche-pied** (pl ~**s**) /kʀɔʃpje/ nm **faire un ~ à** trip up.

**crochet** /kʀɔʃɛ/ nm hook; (détour) detour; (signe) (square) bracket; (tricot) crochet; **faire au ~** crochet.

**crochu, ~e** /kʀɔʃy/ adj hooked.

**crocodile** /kʀɔkɔdil/ nm crocodile.

**croire** /kʀwaʀ/ **23** vt believe (à, en in); (estimer) think, believe (que that). ● vi believe.

**croisade** /kʀwazad/ nf crusade.

**croisement** /kʀwazmɑ̃/ nm crossing; (fait de passer à côté de) passing; (carrefour) crossroads.

**croiser** /kʀwaze/ **1** vi (bateau) cruise. ● vt cross; (passant, véhicule) pass; ~ **les bras** fold one's arms; ~ **les jambes** cross one's legs; (animaux) crossbreed. ● se ~ vpr (véhicules, piétons) pass each other; (lignes) cross. **croisière** nf cruise.

**croissance** /kʀwasɑ̃s/ nf growth.

**croissant, ~e** /kʀwasɑ̃, -t/ adj growing. ● nm crescent; (pâtisserie) croissant.

**croix** /kʀwa/ nf cross; ~ **gammée** swastika; **C~-Rouge** Red Cross.

**croquant, ~e** /kʀɔkɑ̃, -t/ adj crunchy.

**croque-monsieur** /kʀɔkməsjø/ nm inv toasted ham and cheese sandwich.

**croque-mort** (pl ∼s) /kʀɔkmɔʀ/ nm ① undertaker.

**croquer** /kʀɔke/ ① vt crunch; (dessiner) sketch; **chocolat à** ∼ plain chocolate. ● vi be crunchy.

**croquis** /kʀɔki/ nm sketch.

**crotte** /kʀɔt/ nf dropping.

**crotté,** ∼e /kʀɔte/ adj muddy.

**crottin** /kʀɔtɛ̃/ nm (horse) dropping.

**croupir** /kʀupiʀ/ ② vi stagnate.

**croustillant,** ∼e /kʀustijɑ̃, -t/ adj crispy; (pain) crusty; (fig) spicy.

**croûte** /kʀut/ nf crust; (de fromage) rind; (de plaie) scab; **en** ∼ (Culin) in pastry.

**croûton** /kʀutɔ̃/ nm (bout de pain) crust; (avec potage) croûton.

**CRS** abrév m (**Compagnie républicaine de sécurité**) French riot police; **un** ∼ a member of the French riot police.

**cru**[1] /kʀy/ ⇒**CROIRE** ㉓.

**cru**[2], ∼e /kʀy/ adj raw; (lumière) harsh; (propos) crude. ● nm vineyard; (vin) vintage wine.

**crû** /kʀy/ ⇒**CROÎTRE** ㉔.

**cruauté** /kʀyote/ nf cruelty.

**cruche** /kʀyʃ/ nf jug, pitcher.

**crucial,** ∼e (mpl **-iaux**) /kʀysjal, -jo/ adj crucial.

**crudité** /kʀydite/ nf (de langage) crudeness; ∼s (Culin) raw vegetables.

**crue** /kʀy/ nf rise in water level; **en** ∼ in spate.

**crustacé** /kʀystase/ nm shellfish.

**cube** /kyb/ nm cube. ● adj (mètre) cubic.

**cueillir** /kœjiʀ/ ㉕ vt pick, gather; (personne ①) pick up.

**cuiller,** **cuillère** /kɥijɛʀ/ nf spoon; ∼ **à soupe** soup spoon; (mesure) tablespoonful.

**cuir** /kɥiʀ/ nm leather; ∼ **chevelu** scalp.

**cuire** /kɥiʀ/ ⑰ vt cook; ∼ **(au four)** bake. ● vi cook; **faire** ∼ cook.

**cuisine** /kɥizin/ nf kitchen; (art) cookery, cooking; (aliments) food; **faire la** ∼ cook.

**cuisiner** /kɥizine/ ① vt cook; (interroger ①) grill. ● vi cook.

**cuisinier,** **-ière** /kɥizinje, -jɛʀ/ nm, f cook. **cuisinière** nf (appareil) cooker, stove.

**cuisse** /kɥis/ nf thigh; (de poulet) thigh; (de grenouille) leg.

**cuisson** /kɥisɔ̃/ nf cooking.

**cuit,** ∼e /kɥi, -t/ adj cooked; **bien** ∼ well done ou cooked; **trop** ∼ overdone.

**cuivre** /kɥivʀ/ nm copper; ∼ **(jaune)** brass; ∼s (Mus) brass.

**cul** /ky/ nm (derrière 🅇) backside, bottom, arse 🅇.

**culbuter** /kylbyte/ ① vi (personne) tumble; (objet) topple (over). ● vt knock over.

**culminer** /kylmine/ ① vi reach its highest point ou peak.

**culot** /kylo/ nm (audace ①) nerve, cheek; (Tech) base.

**culotte** /kylɔt/ nf (de femme) pants (+ pl), knickers (+ pl); (US) panties (+ pl); ∼ **de cheval** riding breeches; **en** ∼ **courte** in short trousers.

**culpabilité** /kylpabilite/ nf guilt.

**culte** /kylt/ nm cult, worship; (religion) religion; (office protestant) service.

**cultivateur,** **-trice** /kyltivatœʀ, -tʀis/ nm, f farmer.

**cultiver** /kyltive/ ① vt cultivate; (plantes) grow.

**culture** /kyltyʀ/ nf cultivation; (de plantes) growing; (agriculture) farming; (éducation) culture; (connaissances) knowledge; ∼s (terrains) lands under cultivation; ∼ physique physical training.

**culturel, ∼le** /kyltyʀɛl/ adj cultural.

**cumuler** /kymyle/ **1** vt accumulate; (fonctions) hold concurrently.

**cure** /kyʀ/ nf (course of) treatment.

**curé** /kyʀe/ nm (parish) priest.

**cure-dent** (pl ∼s) /kyʀdɑ̃/ nm toothpick.

**curer** /kyʀe/ **1** vt clean. □ se ∼ vpr se ∼ les dents/ongles clean one's teeth/nails.

**curieux, -ieuse** /kyʀjø, -z/ adj curious. ● nm, f (badaud) onlooker.

**curiosité** /kyʀjozite/ nf curiosity; (objet) curio; (spectacle) unusual sight.

**curriculum vitae** /kyʀikylɔm vite/ nm inv curriculum vitae; (US) résumé.

**curseur** /kyʀsœʀ/ nm cursor.

**cutané, ∼e** /kytane/ adj skin.

**cuve** /kyv/ nf vat; (à mazout, eau) tank.

**cuvée** /kyve/ nf (de vin) vintage.

**cuvette** /kyvɛt/ nf bowl; (de lavabo) (wash) basin; (des cabinets) pan, bowl.

**CV** abrév m (curriculum vitae) CV.

**cyberbranché, ∼e** /sibɛʀbʀɑ̃ʃe/ adj cyberwired.

**cybercafé** /sibɛʀkafe/ nm cybercafe.

**cyberespace** /sibɛʀsepas/ nm cyberspace.

**cybernaute** /sibɛʀnot/ nmf Netsurfer.

**cybernétique** /sibɛʀnetik/ nf cybernetics (+ pl).

**cyclisme** /siklism/ nm cycling.

**cycliste** /siklist/ nmf cyclist. ● nm cycling shorts. ● adj cycle.

**cyclone** /siklon/ nm cyclone.

**cygne** /siɲ/ nm swan.

**cynique** /sinik/ adj cynical. ● nm cynic.

c
d

# Dd

**d'** /d/ ⇒DE.

**d'abord** /dabɔʀ/ adv first; (au début) at first.

**dactylo** /daktilo/ nf typist. **dactylographier** 45 vt type.

**dada** /dada/ nm hobby-horse.

**daim** /dɛ̃/ nm (fallow) deer; (cuir) suede.

**dallage** /dalaʒ/ nm paving. **dalle** nf slab.

**daltonien, ∼ne** /daltɔnjɛ̃, -ɛn/ adj colour-blind.

**dame** /dam/ nf lady; (cartes, échecs) queen; ∼s (jeu) draughts; (US) checkers.

**damier** /damje/ nm draught board; (US) checker-board; à ∼ chequered.

**damner** /dane/ **1** vt damn.

**dandiner (se)** /(sə)dɑ̃dine/ **1** vpr waddle.

**Danemark** /danmaʀk/ nm Denmark.

**danger** /dɑ̃ʒe/ nm danger; en ∼ in danger; mettre en ∼ endanger.

**dangereux, -euse** /dɑ̃ʒ(ə)ʀø, -z/ adj dangerous.

**danois, ∼e** /danwa, -z/ adj Danish. ● nm (Ling) Danish. D∼, ∼e nm, f Dane.

**dans** /dã/ *prep* in; (mouvement) into; (à l'intérieur de) inside, in; être ~ un avion be on a plane; ~ dix jours in ten days' time; boire ~ un verre drink out of a glass; ~ les 10 euros about 10 euros.

**danse** /dãs/ *nf* dance; (art) dancing.

**danser** /dãse/ *vt/i* dance. **danseur, -euse** *nm, f* dancer.

**darne** /daʀn/ *nf* steak (of fish).

**date** /dat/ *nf* date; ~ limite deadline; ~ limite de vente sell-by date; ~ de péremption use-by date.

**dater** /date/ **1** *vt/i* date; à ~ de as from.

**datte** /dat/ *nf* (fruit) date.

**daube** /dob/ *nf* casserole.

**dauphin** /dofɛ̃/ *nm* (animal) dolphin.

**davantage** /davãtaʒ/ *adv* more; (plus longtemps) longer; ~ de more; je n'en sais pas ~ that's as much as I know.

**de,** d' /də, d/

d' before vowel or mute h.

● **préposition**
····▸ of; le livre ~ mon ami my friend's book; un pont ~ fer an iron bridge.
····▸ (provenance) from.
····▸ (temporel) from; ~ 8 heures à 10 heures from 8 till 10.
····▸ (mesure, manière) dix mètres ~ haut ten metres high; pleurer ~ rage cry with rage.
····▸ (agent) by; un livre ~ Marcel Aymé a book by Marcel Aymé.

● **de, de l', de la, du,** (*pl* **des**) *déterminant*

····▸ some; du pain (some) bread; des fleurs (some) flowers; je ne bois jamais ~ vin I never drink wine.

de + le = du
de + les = des

**dé** /de/ *nm* (à jouer) dice; (à coudre) thimble; ~s (jeu) dice.

**débâcle** /debakl/ *nf* (Géog) breaking up; (Mil) rout.

**déballer** /debale/ **1** *vt* unpack; (révéler) spill out.

**débarbouiller** /debaʀbuje/ *vt* wash the face of. □ **se** ~ *vpr* wash one's face.

**débarcadère** /debaʀkadɛʀ/ *nm* landing-stage.

**débardeur** /debaʀdœʀ/ *nm* (vêtement) tank top.

**débarquement** /debaʀkəmã/ *nm* disembarkation. **débarquer** **1** *vt/i* disembark, land; (arriver **1**) turn up.

**débarras** /debaʀa/ *nm* junk room; bon ~! good riddance!

**débarrasser** /debaʀase/ **1** *vt* clear (de of); ~ qn de relieve sb of; (défaut, ennemi) rid sb of. □ **se** ~ **de** *vpr* get rid of.

**débat** /deba/ *nm* debate.

**débattre** /debatʀ/ **11** *vt* debate. ● *vi* ~ **de** discuss. □ **se** ~ *vpr* struggle (to get free).

**débauche** /deboʃ/ *nf* debauchery; (fig) profusion.

**débaucher** /deboʃe/ **1** *vt* (licencier) lay off; (distraire) tempt away.

**débile** /debil/ *adj* weak; (**1**) stupid. ● *nmf* moron.

**débit** /debi/ *nm* (rate of) flow; (élocution) delivery; (de compte) debit; ~ de tabac tobacconist's shop; ~ de boissons bar; haut ~

broadband.

**débiter** /debite/ **1** *vt* (*compte*) debit; (fournir) produce; (vendre) sell; (dire: péj) spout; (couper) cut up.

**débiteur, -trice** /debitœʀ, -tʀis/ *nm, f* debtor. ● *adj* (*compte*) in debit.

**déblayer** /debleje/ **31** *vt* clear.

**déblocage** /deblɔkaʒ/ *nm* (de prix) deregulating. **débloquer** **1** *vt* (*prix, salaires*) unfreeze.

**déboiser** /debwaze/ **1** *vt* clear (of trees).

**déboîter** /debwate/ **1** *vi* (*véhicule*) pull out. ● *vt* (*membre*) dislocate.

**débordement** /debɔʀdəmɑ̃/ *nm* (de joie) excess.

**déborder** /debɔʀde/ **1** *vi* overflow. ● *vt* (*dépasser*) extend beyond; ∼ de (*joie etc.*) be brimming over with.

**débouché** /debuʃe/ *nm* opening; (carrière) prospect; (Comm) outlet; (sortie) end, exit.

**déboucher** /debuʃe/ **1** *vt* (*bouteille*) uncork; (*évier*) unblock. ● *vi* come out (de from); ∼ sur (*rue*) lead into.

**débourser** /debuʀse/ **1** *vt* pay out.

**debout** /dəbu/ *adv* standing; (levé, éveillé) up; être ∼, se tenir ∼ be standing, stand; se mettre ∼ stand up.

**déboutonner** /debutɔne/ **1** *vt* unbutton. □ **se** ∼ *vpr* unbutton oneself; (*vêtement*) come undone.

**débrancher** /debʀɑ̃ʃe/ **1** *vt* (*prise*) unplug; (*système*) disconnect.

**débrayer** /debʀeje/ **31** *vi* (Auto) declutch; (faire grève) stop work.

**débris** /debʀi/ *nmpl* fragments; (détritus) rubbish (+ *sg*); debris.

**débrouillard, -e** /debʀujaʀ, -d/ *adj* 🛈 resourceful.

**débrouiller** /debʀuje/ **1** *vt* disentangle; (*problème*) solve. □ **se** ∼ *vpr* manage.

**début** /deby/ *nm* beginning; faire ses ∼s (en public) make one's début; à mes ∼s when I started out. **débutant, -e** *nm, f* beginner. **débuter** **1** *vi* begin; (dans un métier etc.) start out.

**déca** /deka/ *nm* 🛈 decaf.

**décacheter** /dekaʃte/ **6** *vt* open.

**décade** /dekad/ *nf* ten days; (décennie) decade.

**décadent, -e** /dekadɑ̃, -t/ *adj* decadent.

**décalage** /dekalaʒ/ *nm* (écart) gap; ∼ horaire time difference. **décaler** **1** *vt* shift.

**décalquer** /dekalke/ **1** *vt* trace.

**décamper** /dekɑ̃pe/ **1** *vi* clear off.

**décanter** /dekɑ̃te/ *vt* allow to settle. □ **se** ∼ *vpr* settle.

**décapant** /dekapɑ̃/ *nm* chemical agent; (pour peinture) paint stripper. ● *adj* (humour) caustic.

**décapotable** /dekapɔtabl/ *adj* convertible.

**décapsuleur** /dekapsylœʀ/ *nm* bottle-opener.

**décédé, -e** /desede/ *adj* deceased. **décéder** **14** *vi* die.

**déceler** /desle/ **6** *vt* detect; (démontrer) reveal.

**décembre** /desɑ̃bʀ/ *nm* December.

**décemment** /desamɑ̃/ *adv* decently. **décence** *nf* decency. **décent, -e** *adj* decent.

**décennie** /deseni/ *nf* decade.

**décentralisation** /desɑ̃tʀalizasjɔ̃/ *nf* decentralization. **décentraliser** **1** *vt* decentralize.

**déception** /desɛpsjɔ̃/ *nf* disappointment.

**décerner** /desɛʀne/ **1** *vt* award.

**décès** /desɛ/ *nm* death.

**décevant,** ~e /des(ə)vɑ̃, -t/ *adj* disappointing. **décevoir** 52 *vt* disappoint.

**déchaîner** /deʃene/ **1** *vt* (*enthousiasme*) rouse. □ **se** ~ *vpr* go wild.

**décharge** /deʃaʀʒ/ *nf* (*de fusil*) discharge; ~ **électrique** electric shock; ~ **publique** municipal dump.

**décharger** /deʃaʀʒe/ 40 *vt* unload; ~ **qn de** relieve sb from. □ **se** ~ *vpr* (*batterie, pile*) go flat.

**déchausser (se)** /(sə)deʃose/ **1** *vpr* take off one's shoes; (*dent*) work loose.

**dèche** /dɛʃ/ *nf* **1** **dans la** ~ broke.

**déchéance** /deʃeɑ̃s/ *nf* decay.

**déchet** /deʃɛ/ *nm* (*reste*) scrap; (*perte*) waste; ~**s** (*ordures*) refuse.

**déchiffrer** /deʃifʀe/ **1** *vt* decipher.

**déchiqueter** /deʃikte/ 38 *vt* tear to shreds.

**déchirement** /deʃiʀmɑ̃/ *nm* heartbreak; (*conflit*) split.

**déchirer** /deʃiʀe/ **1** *vt* (*par accident*) tear; (*lacérer*) tear up; (*arracher*) tear off *ou* out; (*diviser*) tear apart. □ **se** ~ *vpr* tear. **déchirure** *nf* tear.

**décibel** /desibɛl/ *nm* decibel.

**décidément** /desidemɑ̃/ *adv* really.

**décider** /deside/ **1** *vt* decide on; (*persuader*) persuade; ~ **que/de** decide that/to; ~ **de qch** decide on sth. □ **se** ~ *vpr* make up one's mind. ●

**décimal,** ~e (*mpl* ~**aux**) /desimal, -o/ *adj* & *nf* decimal.

**décisif,** **-ive** /desizif, -v/ *adj* decisive.

**décision** /desizjɔ̃/ *nf* decision.

**déclaration** /deklaʀasjɔ̃/ *nf* declaration; (*commentaire politique*) statement; ~ **d'impôts** tax return.

**déclarer** /deklaʀe/ **1** *vt* declare; (*naissance*) register; **déclaré coupable** found guilty; **déclaré forfait** (Sport) withdraw. □ **se** ~ *vpr* (*feu*) break out.

**déclencher** /deklɑ̃ʃe/ **1** *vt* (Tech) set off; (*conflit*) spark off; (*avalanche*) start; (*rire*) provoke. □ **se** ~ *vpr* (Tech) go off. **déclencheur** *nm* (Photo) shutter release.

**déclic** /deklik/ *nm* click.

**déclin** /deklɛ̃/ *nm* decline.

**déclinaison** /deklinɛzɔ̃/ *nf* (Ling) declension.

**décliner** /dekline/ **1** *vt* (*refuser*) decline; (*dire*) state; (Ling) decline.

**décocher** /dekɔʃe/ **1** *vt* (*coup*) fling; (*regard*) shoot.

**décollage** /dekɔlaʒ/ *nm* take-off.

**décoller** /dekɔle/ **1** *vt* unstick. ● *vi* (*avion*) take off. □ **se** ~ *vpr* come off.

**décolleté,** ~e /dekɔlte/ *adj* low-cut. ● *nm* low neckline.

**décolorer** /dekɔlɔʀe/ **1** *vt* fade; (*cheveux*) bleach. □ **se** ~ *vpr* fade.

**décombres** /dekɔ̃bʀ/ *nmpl* rubble.

**décommander** /dekɔmɑ̃de/ **1** *vt* cancel.

**décomposer** /dekɔ̃poze/ **1** *vt* break up; (*substance*) decompose. □ **se** ~ *vpr* (*pourrir*) decompose.

**décompte** /dekɔ̃t/ *nm* deduction; (*détail*) breakdown.

**décongeler** /dekɔ̃ʒle/ 6 *vt* thaw.

**déconseillé,** ~e /dekɔ̃seje/ *adj* not recommended, inadvisable.

**déconseiller** /dekɔ̃seje/ **1** *vt* ~

81

qch à qn advise sb against sth.
**décontracté**, **~e** /dekɔ̃trakte/ *adj* relaxed.
**déconvenue** /dekɔ̃vny/ *nf* disappointment.
**décor** /dekɔr/ *nm* (paysage) scenery; (de cinéma, théâtre) set; (cadre) setting; (de maison) décor.
**décoratif**, **-ive** /dekɔratif, -v/ *adj* decorative.
**décorateur**, **-trice** /dekɔratœr, -tris/ *nm, f* (de cinéma) set designer. **décoration** *nf* decoration. **décorer** **1** *vt* decorate.
**décortiquer** /dekɔrtike/ **1** *vt* shell; (fig) dissect.
**découdre (se)** /(sə)dekudr/ **19** *vpr* come unstitched.
**découler** /dekule/ **1** *vi* ~ de follow from.
**découper** /dekupe/ **1** *vt* cut up; (viande) carve; (détacher) cut out.
**découragement** /dekuraʒmɑ̃/ *nm* discouragement.
**décourager** /dekuraʒe/ **40** *vt* discourage. □ **se ~** *vpr* become discouraged.
**décousu**, **~e** /dekuzy/ *adj* (vêtement) which has come unstitched; (idées) disjointed.
**découvert**, **~e** /dekuver, -t/ *adj* (tête) bare; (terrain) open. ● *nm* (de compte) overdraft; à ~ exposed; (fig) openly.
**découverte** /dekuvert/ *nf* discovery; à la ~ de in search of.
**découvrir** /dekuvrir/ **21** *vt* discover; (voir) see; (montrer) reveal. □ **se ~** *vpr* (se décoiffer) take one's hat off; (ciel) clear.
**décrasser** /dekrase/ **1** *vt* clean.
**décrépit**, **~e** /dekrepi, -t/ *adj* decrepit. **décrépitude** *nf* decay.
**décret** /dekre/ *nm* decree. **décréter** **14** *vt* order; (dire) declare.

**décrié**, **~e** /dekrije/ *adj* criticized.
**décrire** /dekrir/ **30** *vt* describe.
**décrocher** /dekrɔʃe/ *adj* (téléphone) off the hook.
**décrocher** /dekrɔʃe/ **1** *vt* unhook; (obtenir **1**) get. ● *vi* (abandonner **1**) give up; ~ (le téléphone) pick up the phone.
**décroître** /dekrwatr/ **24** *vi* decrease.
**déçu**, **~e** /desy/ *adj* disappointed.
**décupler** /dekyple/ **1** *vt/i* increase tenfold.
**dédaigner** /dedeɲe/ **1** *vt* scorn.
**dédain** /dedɛ̃/ *nm* scorn.
**dédale** /dedal/ *nm* maze.
**dedans** /dədɑ̃/ *adv* & *nm* inside; en ~ on the inside.
**dédicacer** /dedikase/ **10** *vt* dedicate; (signer) sign.
**dédier** /dedje/ **45** *vt* dedicate.
**dédommagement** /dedɔmaʒmɑ̃/ *nm* compensation. **dédommager** **40** *vt* compensate (de for).
**déduction** /dedyksjɔ̃/ *nf* deduction; ~ d'impôts tax deduction.
**déduire** /dedɥir/ **17** *vt* deduct; (conclure) deduce.
**déesse** /dees/ *nf* goddess.
**défaillance** /defajɑ̃s/ *nf* (panne) failure; (évanouissement) blackout. **défaillant**, **~e** /defajɑ̃, -t/ *adj* (système) faulty; (personne) faint.
**défaire** /defer/ **33** *vt* undo; (valise) unpack; (démonter) take down. □ **se ~** *vpr* come undone; se ~ de rid oneself of.
**défait**, **~e** /defε, -t/ *adj* (cheveux) ruffled; (visage) haggard; (nœud) undone. **défaite** *nf* defeat.
**défaitiste** /defetist/ *adj* & *nmf* defeatist.
**défalquer** /defalke/ **1** *vt* (somme)

deduct.

**défaut** /defo/ nm fault, defect; (d'un verre, diamant, etc.) flaw; (pénurie) shortage; à ~ de for lack of; pris en ~ caught out; faire ~ (argent etc.) be lacking; par ~ (Jur) in one's absence; ~ de paiement non-payment.

**défavorable** /defavɔrabl/ adj unfavourable.

**défavoriser** /defavɔrize/ **1** vt discriminate against.

**défectueux, -euse** /defɛktɥø, -z/ adj faulty, defective.

**défendre** /defɑ̃dr/ **3** vt defend; (interdire) forbid; ~ à qn de forbid sb to. □ se ~ vpr defend oneself; (se protéger) protect oneself; (se débrouiller) manage; se ~ de (refuser) refrain from.

**défense** /defɑ̃s/ nf defence; ~ de fumer no smoking; (d'éléphant) tusk. **défenseur** nm defender. **défensif, -ive** adj defensive.

**déferler** /defɛrle/ **1** vi (vagues) break; (violence) erupt.

**défi** /defi/ nm challenge; (provocation) defiance; mettre au ~ challenge.

**déficience** /defisjɑ̃s/ nf deficiency. **déficient, ~e** adj deficient.

**déficit** /defisit/ nm deficit. **déficitaire** adj in deficit.

**défier** /defje/ **45** vt challenge; (braver) defy.

**défilé** /defile/ nm procession; (Mil) parade; (fig) (continual) stream; (Géog) gorge; ~ de mode fashion parade.

**défiler** /defile/ **1** vi march; (visiteurs) stream; (images) flash by; (chiffres, minutes) add up. □ se ~ vpr **1** sneak off.

**défini, ~e** /defini/ adj (Ling) definite.

**définir** /definir/ **2** vt define.

**définitif, -ive** /definitif, -v/ adj final, definitive; **en définitive** in the end.

**définition** /definisjɔ̃/ nf definition; (de mots croisés) clue.

**définitivement** /definitivmɑ̃/ adv definitively, permanently.

**déflagration** /deflagrasjɔ̃/ nf explosion.

**déflation** /deflasjɔ̃/ nf deflation. **déflationniste** adj deflationary.

**défoncé, ~e** /defɔ̃se/ adj (terrain) full of potholes; (siège) broken; (drogué: **1**) high.

**défoncer** /defɔ̃se/ **10** vt (porte) break down; (mâchoire) break. □ se ~ vpr **1** to give one's all.

**déformation** /defɔrmasjɔ̃/ nf distortion. **déformer** **1** vt put out of shape; (faits, pensée) distort.

**défouler (se)** /(sə)defule/ **1** vpr let off steam.

**défrayer** /defreje/ **31** vt (payer) pay the expenses of; ~ la chronique be the talk of the town.

**défricher** /defrije/ **1** vt clear.

**défroisser** /defrwase/ **1** vt smooth out.

**défunt, ~e** /defœ̃, -t/ adj (mort) late. ● nm, f deceased.

**dégagé, ~e** /degaʒe/ adj (ciel) clear; (front) bare; **d'un ton ~** casually.

**dégagement** /degaʒmɑ̃/ nm clearing; (football) clearance.

**dégager** /degaʒe/ **40** vt (exhaler) give off; (désencombrer) clear; (faire ressortir) bring out; (ballon) clear. □ se ~ vpr free oneself; (ciel, rue) clear; (odeur) emanate.

**dégarnir (se)** /(sə)degarnir/ **2** vpr clear, empty; (personne) be going bald.

**dégâts** /dega/ nmpl damage (+ sg).

**dégel** /deʒɛl/ *nm* thaw. **dégeler** 6 *vi* thaw (out).

**dégénéré**, ~e /deʒenere/ *adj & nm,f* degenerate.

**dégivrer** /deʒivre/ 1 *vt* (Auto) de-ice; (*réfrigérateur*) defrost.

**déglinguer** /deglɛ̃ge/ 1 1 *vt* bust. □ se ~ *vpr* break down.

**dégonflé**, ~e /degɔ̃fle/ *adj* (*pneu*) flat; (*lâche* 1) yellow.

**dégonfler** /degɔ̃fle/ 1 *vt* deflate. ● *vi* (*blessure*) go down. □ se ~ *vpr* 1 chicken out.

**dégouliner** /deguline/ 1 *vi* trickle.

**dégourdi**, ~e /degurdi/ *adj* smart.

**dégourdir** /degurdir/ 2 *vt* (*membre, liquide*) warm up. □ se ~ *vpr* se ~ les jambes stretch one's legs.

**dégoût** /degu/ *nm* disgust.

**dégoûtant**, ~e /degutɑ̃, -t/ *adj* disgusting.

**dégoûter** /degute/ 1 *vt* disgust; ~ qn de qch put sb off sth.

**dégradant**, ~e /degradɑ̃, -t/ *adj* degrading.

**dégradation** /degradasjɔ̃/ *nf* damage; **commettre des** ~s cause damage.

**dégrader** /degrade/ 1 *vt* (*abîmer*) damage. □ se ~ *vpr* (se détériorer) deteriorate.

**dégrafer** /degrafe/ 1 *vt* unhook.

**degré** /dəgre/ *nm* degree; (d'escalier) step.

**dégressif, -ive** /degresif, -v/ *adj* graded; **tarif** ~ tapering charge.

**dégrèvement** /degrɛvmɑ̃/ *nm* ~ fiscal *ou* d'impôts tax reduction.

**dégringolade** /degrɛ̃gɔlad/ *nf* tumble.

**dégrossir** /degrosir/ 2 *vt* (*bois*)

trim; (*projet*) rough out.

**déguerpir** /degɛrpir/ 2 *vi* clear off.

**dégueulasse** /degœlas/ *adj* 🗙 disgusting, lousy.

**dégueuler** /degœle/ 1 *vt* 🗙 throw up.

**déguisement** /degizmɑ̃/ *nm* (de carnaval) fancy dress; (pour duper) disguise.

**déguiser** /degize/ 1 *vt* dress up; (pour duper) disguise. □ se ~ *vpr* (au carnaval) dress up; (pour duper) disguise oneself.

**déguster** /degyste/ 1 *vt* taste, sample; (savourer) enjoy.

**dehors** /dəɔr/ *adv* en ~ de outside; (hormis) apart from; jeter/ mettre ~ throw/put out. ● *nm* outside. ● *nmpl* (aspect de qn) exterior.

**déjà** /deʒa/ *adv* already; (avant) before, already.

**déjeuner** /deʒœne/ 1 *vi* have lunch; (le matin) have breakfast. ● *nm* lunch; petit ~ breakfast.

**delà** /dəla/ *adv & prép* au ~ (de) par ~ beyond.

**délai** /delɛ/ *nm* time-limit; (attente) wait; (sursis) extension (of time); sans ~ immediately; dans un ~ de 2 jours within 2 days; finir dans les ~s finish within the deadline; dans les plus brefs ~s as soon as possible.

**délaisser** /delese/ 1 *vt* (négliger) neglect.

**délassement** /delasmɑ̃/ *nm* relaxation.

**délation** /delasjɔ̃/ *nf* informing.

**délavé**, ~e /delave/ *adj* faded.

**délayer** /deleje/ 31 *vt* mix (with liquid); (idée) drag out.

**délecter (se)** /(sə)delɛkte/ 1 *vpr* se ~ de delight in.

**délégué**, ~e /delege/ *nm, f*

delegate.

**délibéré, ~e** /delibere/ adj deliberate; (résolu) determined.

**délicat, ~e** /delika, -t/ adj delicate; (plein de tact) tactful. **délicatesse** nf delicacy; (tact) tact. **délicatesses** nfpl (kind) attentions.

**délice** /delis/ nm delight. **délicieux, -ieuse** adj (au goût) delicious; (charmant) delightful.

**délier** /delje/ 45 vt untie; (délivrer) free. □ **se ~** vpr come untied.

**délimiter** /delimite/ 1 vt determine, demarcate.

**délinquance** /delēkɑ̃s/ nf delinquency. **délinquant, ~e** adj & nm, f delinquent.

**délirant, ~e** /delirɑ̃, -t/ adj delirious; (frénétique) frenzied; 1 wild.

**délire** /delir/ nm delirium; (fig) frenzy. **délirer** 1 vi be delirious (de with); 1 be off one's rocker 1.

**délit** /deli/ nm offence.

**délivrance** /delivrɑ̃s/ nf release; (soulagement) relief; (remise) issue. **délivrer** 1 vt free, release; (pays) liberate; (remettre) issue.

**déloyal, ~e** (mpl **-aux**) /delwajal, -jo/ adj disloyal; (procédé) unfair.

**deltaplane** /dɛltaplan/ nm hangglider.

**déluge** /delyʒ/ nm downpour; le D~ the Flood.

**démagogie** /demagɔʒi/ nf demagogy. **démagogue** nmf demagogue.

**demain** /dəmɛ̃/ adv tomorrow.

**demande** /dəmɑ̃d/ nf request; ~ d'emploi job application; ~ en mariage marriage proposal.

**demander** /dəmɑ̃de/ 1 vt ask for; (chemin, heure) ask; (nécessiter) require; ~ que/si ask that/if; ~ qch à qn ask sb for sth; ~ à qn de faire ask sb to; ~ en mariage propose to. □ se ~ vpr se ~ si/où wonder if/where.

**demandeur, -euse** /dəmɑ̃dœr, -øz/ nm, f ~ d'emploi job seeker; ~ d'asile asylum-seeker.

**démangeaison** /demɑ̃ʒɛzɔ̃/ nf itch(ing).

**démanteler** /demɑ̃tle/ 6 vt break up.

**démaquillant** /demakijɑ̃/ nm make-up remover. **démaquiller (se)** 1 vpr remove one's make-up.

**démarchage** /demarʃaʒ/ nm door-to-door selling.

**démarche** /demarʃ/ nf walk, gait; (procédé) step.

**démarcheur, -euse** /demarʃœr, -øz/ nm, f (door-to-door) canvasser.

**démarrage** /demaraʒ/ nm start.

**démarrer** /demare/ 1 vi (moteur) start (up); (partir) move off; (fig) get moving. ● vt 1 get moving.

**démarreur** /demarœr/ nm starter.

**démêlant** /demelɑ̃/ nm conditioner. **démêler** 1 vt disentangle.

**déménagement** /demenaʒmɑ̃/ nm move; (transport) removal.

**déménager** /demenaʒe/ 40 vi move (house). ● vt (meubles) remove.

**déménageur** /demenaʒœr/ nm removal man.

**démence** /demɑ̃s/ nf insanity.

**démener (se)** /(sə)demne/ 6 vpr move about wildly; (fig) put oneself out.

**dément, ~e** /demɑ̃, -t/ adj insane. ● nm, f lunatic.

**démenti** /demɑ̃ti/ nm denial.

**démentir** /demɑ̃tir/ 42 vt deny; (contredire) refute; ~ que deny that.

**démerder (se)** /(sə)demɛrde/ 1 vpr ✗ manage.

**démettre** /demɛtʀ/ 42 vt (*poignet etc.*) dislocate; ~ qn de relieve sb of. □ se ~ vpr resign (de from).

**demeure** /dəmœʀ/ nf residence; mettre en ~ de order to.

**demeurer** /dəmœʀe/ 1 vi live; (*rester*) remain.

**demi**, ~e /dəmi/ adj half(-). ● nm, f half. ● nm (*bière*) (half-pint) glass of beer; (*football*) half-back. ● adv à ~ half; (*ouvrir, fermer*) halfway; à la ~e at half past; une heure et ~e an hour and a half; (à l'horloge) half past one; une ~-journée/-livre half a day/pound. **demi-cercle** (*pl* ~s) nm semicircle. **demi-finale** (*pl* ~s) nf semifinal. **demi-frère** (*pl* ~s) nm half-brother, stepbrother. **demi-heure** (*pl* ~s) nf half-hour, half an hour. **demi-litre** (*pl* ~s) nm half a litre. **demi-mesure** (*pl* ~s) nf half-measure. **à demi mot** adv without having to express every word. **demi-pension** (*pl* ~s) nf half-board. **demi-queue** nm boudoir grand piano.

**demi-sel** adj inv slightly salted.

**demi-sœur** (*pl* ~s) nf half-sister, stepsister.

**démission** /demisjɔ̃/ nf resignation.

**demi-tarif** (*pl* ~s) /dəmitaʀif/ nm half-fare.

**demi-tour** (*pl* ~s) /dəmituʀ/ nm about turn; (Auto) U-turn; faire ~ turn back.

**démocrate** /demɔkʀat/ nmf democrat. ● adj democratic. **démocratie** /demɔkʀasi/ nf democracy.

**démodé**, ~e /demode/ adj old-fashioned.

**demoiselle** /dəmwazɛl/ nf young lady; (*célibataire*) single lady; ~ d'honneur bridesmaid.

**démolir** /demɔliʀ/ 2 vt demolish.

**démon** /demɔ̃/ nm demon; le D~

the Devil. **démoniaque** adj fiendish.

**démonstration** /demɔ̃stʀasjɔ̃/ nf demonstration; (de force) show.

**démonter** /demɔ̃te/ 1 vt take apart, dismantle; (*installation*) take down; (fig) disconcert. □ se ~ vpr come apart.

**démontrer** /demɔ̃tʀe/ 1 vt demonstrate; (*indiquer*) show.

**démoraliser** /demɔʀalize/ 1 vt demoralize.

**démuni**, ~e /demyni/ adj impoverished; ~ de without.

**démunir** /demyniʀ/ 2 vt ~ de deprive of. □ se ~ de vpr part with.

**dénaturer** /denatyʀe/ 1 vt (*faits*) distort.

**dénigrement** /denigʀəmɑ̃/ nm denigration.

**dénivellation** /denivelasjɔ̃/ nf (pente) slope.

**dénombrer** /denɔ̃bʀe/ 1 vt count.

**dénomination** /denɔminasjɔ̃/ nf designation.

**dénommé**, ~e /denɔme/ nm, f le ~ X the said X.

**dénoncer** /denɔ̃se/ 10 vt denounce. □ se ~ vpr give oneself up. **dénonciateur, -trice** nm, f informer.

**dénouement** /denumɑ̃/ nm outcome; (Théât) denouement.

**dénouer** /denwe/ 1 vt undo. □ se ~ vpr (*nœud*) come undone.

**dénoyauter** /denwajote/ 1 vt stone.

**denrée** /dɑ̃ʀe/ nf ~ alimentaire foodstuff.

**dense** /dɑ̃s/ adj dense. **densité** nf density.

**dent** /dɑ̃/ nf tooth; faire ses ~s teethe; ~ de lait milk tooth; ~ de sagesse wisdom tooth; (de roue) cog. **dentaire** *adj* dental.

**denté**, ~e /dɑ̃te/ *adj* (*roue*) toothed.

**dentelé**, ~e /dɑ̃tle/ *adj* jagged.

**dentelle** /dɑ̃tɛl/ *nf* lace.

**dentier** /dɑ̃tje/ *nm* dentures (+ *pl*), false teeth (+ *pl*).

**dentifrice** /dɑ̃tifʀis/ *nm* toothpaste.

**dentiste** /dɑ̃tist/ *nmf* dentist.

**dentition** /dɑ̃tisjɔ̃/ *nf* teeth, dentition.

**dénudé**, ~e /denyde/ *adj* bare.

**dénué**, ~e /denɥe/ *adj* ~ de devoid of.

**dénuement** /denymɑ̃/ *nm* destitution.

**déodorant** /deɔdɔʀɑ̃/ *nm* deodorant.

**dépannage** /depanaʒ/ *nm* repair; (Ordinat) troubleshooting. **dépanner** **1** *vt* repair; (fig) help out. **dépanneuse** *nf* breakdown lorry.

**dépareillé**, ~e /depaʀeje/ *adj* odd, not matching.

**départ** /depaʀ/ *nm* departure; (Sport) start; au ~ de Nice from Nice; au ~ (d'abord) at first.

**département** /depaʀtəmɑ̃/ *nm* department.

> **Département** An administrative unit, of which there are 96 in Metropolitan France, most are named after rivers or mountains within their borders. Each *département* has a number which appears as the first two digits in postcodes for addresses within the *département* and as the final two-digit number in vehicle registration numbers. See ▸ RÉGION.

**dépassé**, ~e /depase/ *adj* outdated.

**dépasser** /depase/ **1** *vt* go past, pass; (*véhicule*) overtake; (*excéder*) exceed; (*rival*) surpass; ça me dépasse **I** it's beyond me. ● *vi* stick out.

**dépaysement** /depeizmɑ̃/ *nm* change of scenery; (désagréable) disorientation.

**dépêche** /depɛʃ/ *nf* dispatch.

**dépêcher** /depeʃe/ **1** *vt* dispatch. □ se ~ *vpr* hurry up.

**dépendance** /depɑ̃dɑ̃s/ *nf* dependence; (à une drogue) dependency; (bâtiment) outbuilding.

**dépendre** /depɑ̃dʀ/ **3** *vt* take down. ● *vi* depend (~ de on); ~ de (appartenir à) belong to.

**dépens** /depɑ̃/ *nmpl* aux ~ de at the expense of.

**dépense** /depɑ̃s/ *nf* expense; expenditure.

**dépenser** /depɑ̃se/ **1** *vt/i* spend; (énergie etc.) use up. □ se ~ *vpr* get some exercise.

**dépérir** /depeʀiʀ/ **2** *vi* wither.

**dépêtrer (se)** /(sə)depetʀe/ **1** *vpr* get oneself out (de of).

**dépeupler** /depœple/ **1** *vt* depopulate. □ se ~ *vpr* become depopulated.

**déphasé**, ~e /defaze/ *adj* **I** out of step.

**dépilatoire** /depilatwaʀ/ *adj & nm* depilatory.

**dépistage** /depistaʒ/ *nm* screening. **dépister** **1** *vt* detect; (criminel) track down.

**dépit** /depi/ *nm* resentment; par ~ out of pique; en ~ de despite; en ~ du bon sens in a very illogical way. **dépité**, ~e *adj* vexed.

**déplacé**, ~e /deplase/ *adj* (remarque) uncalled for.

**déplacement** /deplasmɑ̃/ *nm*

(voyage) trip.

**déplacer** /deplase/ **10** vt move. □ se ~ vpr move.

**déplaire** /deplɛʀ/ **47** vi ~ à (irriter) displease; ça me déplaît I don't like it.

**déplaisant**, ~e /deplɛzɑ̃, -t/ adj unpleasant, disagreeable.

**dépliant** /deplijɑ̃/ nm leaflet.

**déplier** /deplije/ **45** vt unfold.

**déploiement** /deplwamɑ̃/ nm (démonstration) display; (militaire) deployment.

**déplorable** /deplɔʀabl/ adj deplorable. **déplorer** **1** vt (trouver regrettable) deplore; (mort) lament.

**déployer** /deplwaje/ **31** vt (ailes, carte) spread; (courage) display; (armée) deploy.

**déportation** /depɔʀtasjɔ̃/ nf (en 1940) internment in a concentration camp.

**déposer** /depoze/ **1** vt put down; (laisser) leave; (passager) drop; (argent) deposit; (plainte) lodge; (armes) lay down. ● vi (Jur) testify. □ se ~ vpr settle.

**dépositaire** /depozitɛʀ/ nmf (Comm) agent.

**déposition** /depozisjɔ̃/ nf (Jur) statement.

**dépôt** /depo/ nm (entrepôt) warehouse; (d'autobus) depot; (particules) deposit; (garantie) deposit; laisser en ~ give for safe keeping; ~ légal formal deposit of a publication with an institution.

**dépouille** /depuj/ nf skin, hide; (~ mortelle) mortal remains.

**dépouiller** /depuje/ **1** vt (courrier) open; (scrutin) count; (écorcher) skin; ~ qn de strip sb of.

**dépourvu**, ~e /depuʀvy/ adj ~ de devoid of; prendre au ~ catch unawares.

**déprécier** /depʀesje/ **45** vt depreciate. □ se ~ vpr depreciate.

**déprédations** /depʀedasjɔ̃/ nfpl damage (+ sg).

**dépression** /depʀesjɔ̃/ nf depression; ~ nerveuse nervous breakdown.

**déprimer** /depʀime/ **1** vt depress.

**depuis** /dəpɥi/

● *préposition*

┄┄▸ (point de départ) since; ~ quand attendez-vous? how long have you been waiting?

┄┄▸ (durée) for; ~ toujours always; ~ peu recently.

● *adverbe*

┄┄▸ since; il a eu une attaque le mois dernier, ~ nous sommes inquiets he had a stroke last month and we've been worried ever since.

● **depuis que** *conjunction*

┄┄▸ since, ever since; Sophie a beaucoup changé depuis que Camille est née Sophie has changed a lot since Camille was born.

**député** /depyte/ nm ≈ Member of Parliament.

**déraciné**, -e /deʀasine/ nm, f rootless person.

**déraillement** /deʀajmɑ̃/ nm derailment.

**dérailler** /deʀaje/ **1** vi be derailed; (fig **1**) be talking nonsense; faire ~ derail. **dérailleur** nm (de vélo) derailleur.

**déraisonnable** /deʀezɔnabl/ adj unreasonable.

**dérangement** /deʀɑ̃ʒmɑ̃/ nm bother; (désordre) disorder, upset;

d

en ~ out of order; les ~s the fault
reporting service.

**déranger** /deʀɑʒe/ 40 vt (gêner)
bother, disturb; (déréger) upset,
disrupt. □ se ~ vpr (aller) go; (fig)
put oneself out; ça te dérangerait
de…? would you mind…?

**dérapage** /deʀapaʒ/ nm skid. **déraper** 1 vi skid; (fig) (prix) get out
of control.

**déréglé**, ~e /deʀegle/ adj (vie)
dissolute; (estomac) upset; (mécanisme) (that is) not running
properly.

**dérégler** /deʀegle/ 14 vt make go
wrong. □ se ~ vpr go wrong.

**dérision** /deʀizjɔ̃/ nf mockery;
tourner en ~ ridicule.

**dérive** /deʀiv/ nf aller à la ~ drift.

**dérivé** /deʀive/ nm by-product.

**dériver** /deʀive/ 1 vi (bateau)
drift; ~ de stem from.

**dermatologie** /dɛʀmatɔlɔʒi/ nf
dermatology.

**dernier**, -ière /dɛʀnje, -jɛʀ/ adj
last; (nouvelles, mode) latest; (étage)
top. ● nm, f last (one); ce ~ the latter; le ~ de mes soucis the least
of my worries.

**dernièrement** /dɛʀnjɛʀmɑ̃/ adv
recently.

**dérober** /deʀɔbe/ 1 vt steal. □ se
~ vpr slip away; se ~ à (obligation)
shy away from.

**dérogation** /deʀɔgasjɔ̃/ nf special
authorization.

**déroger** /deʀɔʒe/ 40 vi ~ à depart from.

**déroulement** /deʀulmɑ̃/ nm
(d'une action) development.

**dérouler** /deʀule/ 1 vt (fil etc.)
unwind. □ se ~ vpr unwind; (avoir
lieu) take place; (récit, paysage)
unfold.

**déroute** /deʀut/ nf (Mil) rout.

**dérouter** /deʀute/ 1 vt disconcert.

**derrière** /dɛʀjɛʀ/ prép & adv behind. ● nm back, rear; (postérieur
⟨⟨) behind ⟨⟨; de ~ (fenêtre) back,
rear; (pattes) hind.

**des** /de/ ⇒DE.

**dès** /dɛ/ prép (right) from; ~ lors
from then on; ~ que as soon as.

**désabusé**, ~e /dezabyze/ adj dis-
illusioned.

**désaccord** /dezakɔʀ/ nm disagreement.

**désaffecté**, ~e /dezafɛkte/ adj
disused.

**désagréable** /dezagʀeabl/ adj unpleasant.

**désagrément** /dezagʀemɑ̃/ nm
annoyance, inconvenience.

**désaltérer (se)** /(sə)dezaltere/
14 vpr quench one's thirst.

**désamorcer** /dezamɔʀse/ 10 vt
(situation, obus) defuse.

**désapprobation** /dezapʀɔbasjɔ̃/
nf disapproval. **désapprouver** 1 vt
disapprove of.

**désarçonner** /dezaʀsɔne/ 1 vt
throw.

**désarmement** /dezaʀməmɑ̃/ nm
(Pol) disarmament.

**désarroi** /dezaʀwa/ nm distress.

**désastre** /dezastʀ/ nm disaster.
**désastreux**, -euse adj disastrous.

**désavantage** /dezavɑ̃taʒ/ nm disadvantage. **désavantager** 40 vt put
at a disadvantage.

**désaveu** (pl ~x) /dezavø/ nm denial. **désavouer** 1 vt deny.

**descendance** /desɑ̃dɑ̃s/ nf descent; (enfants) descendants (+ pl).
**descendant**, ~e nm, f descendant.

**descendre** /desɑ̃dʀ/ 3 vi (aux
être) go down; (venir) come down;
(passager) get off ou out; (nuit) fall;

~ à pied walk down; ~ par l'ascenseur take the lift down; ~ de (être issu de) be descended from; ~ à l'hôtel go to a hotel; ~ dans la rue (Pol) take to the streets. ● vt (aux avoir) (escalier etc.) go ou come down; (objet) take down; (abattre 🔟) shoot down.

**descente** /desãt/ nf descent; (à ski) downhill; (raid) raid; **dans la** ~ going downhill; ~ **de lit** bedside rug.

**descriptif, -ive** /dɛskʀiptif, -v/ adj descriptive. **description** nf description.

**désemparé, ~e** /dezãpaʀe/ adj distraught.

**désendettement** /dezãdɛtmã/ nm reduction of the debt.

**déséquilibré, ~e** /dezekilibʀe/ adj unbalanced; 🔟 crazy. ● nm, f lunatic. **déséquilibrer** 🔟 vt throw off balance.

**désert, ~e** /dezɛʀ, -t/ adj deserted. ● nm desert.

**déserter** /dezɛʀte/ 🔟 vt/i desert. **déserteur** nm deserter.

**désertique** /dezɛʀtik/ adj desert.

**désespérant, ~e** /dezɛspeʀã, -t/ adj utterly disheartening.

**désespéré, ~e** /dezɛspeʀe/ adj in despair; (état, cas) hopeless; (effort) desperate.

**désespérer** /dezɛspeʀe/ 🔢 vt drive to despair. ● vi despair, lose hope; ~ **de** despair of. ▫ se ~ vpr despair.

**désespoir** /dezɛspwaʀ/ nm despair; **en** ~ **de cause** as a last resort.

**déshabillé, ~e** /dezabije/ adj undressed. ● nm négligee.

**déshabiller** /dezabije/ 🔟 vt undress. ▫ se ~ vpr get undressed.

**désherbant** /dezɛʀbã/ nm

weedkiller.

**déshérité, ~e** /dezeʀite/ adj (région) deprived; (personne) the underprivileged.

**déshériter** /dezeʀite/ 🔟 vt disinherit.

**déshonneur** /dezɔnœʀ/ nm disgrace.

**déshonorer** /dezɔnɔʀe/ 🔟 vt dishonour.

**déshydrater** /dezidʀate/ 🔟 vt dehydrate. ▫ se ~ vpr get dehydrated.

**désigner** /dezine/ 🔟 vt (montrer) point to ou out; (élire) appoint; (signifier) designate.

**désillusion** /dezilyzjɔ̃/ nf disillusionment.

**désinence** /dezinãs/ nf (Gram) ending.

**désinfectant** /dezɛ̃fɛktã/ nm disinfectant. **désinfecter** 🔟 vt disinfect.

**désintéressé, ~e** /dezɛ̃teʀese/ adj (personne, acte) selfless.

**désintéresser (se)** /(sa)dezɛ̃teʀese/ 🔟 vpr se ~ de lose interest in.

**désintoxiquer** /dezɛ̃tɔksike/ 🔟 vt detoxify; se faire ~ to undergo detoxification.

**désinvolte** /dezɛ̃vɔlt/ adj casual. **désinvolture** nf casualness.

**désir** /deziʀ/ nm wish, desire; (convoitise) desire.

**désirer** /deziʀe/ 🔟 vt want; (sexuellement) desire; **vous désirez?** what would you like?

**désireux, -euse** /deziʀø, -z/ adj ~ **de faire** anxious to do.

**désistement** /dezistəmã/ nm withdrawal.

**désobéir** /dezɔbeiʀ/ 🔢 vi (~ à) disobey. **désobéissant, ~e** adj disobedient.

**désobligeant,** ~e /dezɔbliʒɑ̃, -t/ *adj* disagreeable, unkind.

**désodorisant** /dezɔdɔrizɑ̃/ *nm* air freshener.

**désodoriser** /dezɔdɔrize/ **1** *vt* freshen up.

**désœuvré,** ~e /dezœvre/ *adj* at a loose end. **désœuvrement** *nm* lack of anything to do.

**désolation** /dezɔlasjɔ̃/ *nf* distress.

**désolé,** ~e /dezɔle/ *adj* (au regret) sorry; (*région*) desolate.

**désoler** /dezɔle/ **1** *vt* distress.
□ **se** ~ *vpr* be upset (de qch about sth).

**désopilant,** ~e /dezɔpilɑ̃, -t/ *adj* hilarious.

**désordonné,** ~e /dezɔrdɔne/ *adj* untidy; (*mouvements*) uncoordinated.

**désordre** /dezɔrdr/ *nm* untidiness; (Pol) disorder; en ~ untidy.

**désorganiser** /dezɔrganize/ **1** *vt* disorganize.

**désorienter** /dezɔrjɑ̃te/ **1** *vt* disorient.

**désormais** /dezɔrmɛ/ *adv* from now on.

**desquels, desquelles** /dekɛl/ →LEQUEL.

**dessécher** /deseʃe/ **1** *vt* dry out.
□ **se** ~ *vpr* dry out, become dry; (*plante*) wither.

**dessein** /desɛ̃/ *nm* intention; à ~ intentionally.

**desserrer** /desere/ **1** *vt* loosen; il n'a pas desserré les dents he never once opened his mouth. □ **se** ~ *vpr* come loose.

**dessert** /desɛr/ *nm* dessert; en ~ for dessert.

**desservir** /deservir/ **46** *vt/i* (débarrasser) clear away; (*autobus*) serve.

**dessin** /desɛ̃/ *nm* drawing; (motif)

design; (discipline) art; (contour) outline; professeur de ~ art teacher; ~ animé (cinéma) cartoon; ~ humoristique cartoon.

**dessinateur, -trice** /desinatœr, -tris/ *nm, f* artist; (industriel) draughtsman.

**dessiner** /desine/ **1** *vt/i* draw; (fig) outline. □ **se** ~ *vpr* appear, take shape.

**dessoûler** /desule/ **1** *vt/i* sober up.

**dessous** /dəsu/ *adv* underneath.
● *nm* underside, underneath. ● *nmpl* underwear; les ~ d'une histoire what is behind a story; du ~ bottom; (*voisins*) downstairs; en ~, par-~ underneath. **dessous-de-plat** *nm inv* (heat resistant) table-mat. **dessous-de-table** *nm inv* backhander. **dessous-de-verre** *nm inv* coaster.

**dessus** /dəsy/ *adv* on top (of it), on it. ● *nm* top; du ~ top; (*voisins*) upstairs; avoir le ~ get the upper hand. **dessus-de-lit** *nm inv* bedspread.

**destabiliser** /destabilize/ **1** *vt* destabilize, unsettle.

**destin** /destɛ̃/ *nm* (sort) fate; (avenir) destiny.

**destinataire** /destinatɛr/ *nmf* addressee.

**destination** /destinasjɔ̃/ *nf* destination; (fonction) purpose; vol à ~ de flight to.

**destinée** /destine/ *nf* destiny.

**destiner** /destine/ **1** *vt* ~ à intend for; (vouer) destine for; le commentaire m'est destiné this comment is aimed at me; être destiné à faire be intended to do; (obligé) destined to do. □ **se** ~ à *vpr* (carrière) intend to take up.

**destituer** /destitɥe/ **1** *vt* discharge.

**destructeur, -trice** /dεstryktœr, -tris/ adj destructive. **destruction** nf destruction.

**désuet, -ète** /dezyε, -t/ adj outdated.

**détachant** /detaʃɑ̃/ nm stain remover.

**détacher** /detaʃe/ **1** vt untie; (ôter) remove, detach; (déléguer) second. □ **se ~** vpr come off, break away; (nœud etc.) come undone; (ressortir) stand out.

**détail** /detaj/ nm detail; (de compte) breakdown; (Comm) retail; **au ~** (vendre etc.) retail; **de ~** (prix etc.) retail; **en ~** in detail; **entrer dans les ~s** go into detail.

**détaillant, ~e** /detajɑ̃, -t/ nm, f retailer.

**détaillé** /detaje/ adj detailed.

**détailler** /detaje/ **1** vt (rapport) detail; **~ ce que qn fait** scrutinize what sb does.

**détaler** /detale/ **1** vi 🔟 bolt.

**détartrant** /detartrɑ̃/ nm descaler.

**détecter** /detεkte/ **1** vt detect. **détecteur** nm detector.

**détective** /detεktiv/ nm detective.

**déteindre** /detɛ̃dr/ **1** vi (dans l'eau) run (sur on to); (au soleil) fade; **~ sur** (fig) rub off on.

**détendre** /detɑ̃dr/ **1** vt slacken; (ressort) release; (personne) relax. □ **se ~** vpr slacken (ressort); (personne) relax. **détendu, ~e** adj (calme) relaxed.

**détenir** /det(ə)nir/ **58** vt hold; (secret, fortune) possess.

**détente** /detɑ̃t/ nf relaxation; (Pol) détente; (saut) spring; (gâchette) trigger; **être lent à la ~** 🔟 be slow on the uptake.

**détenteur, -trice** /detɑ̃tœr, -tris/ nm, f holder.

**détention** /detɑ̃sjɔ̃/ nf detention; **~ provisoire** custody.

**détenu, ~e** /det(ə)ny/ nm, f prisoner.

**détergent** /detεrʒɑ̃/ nm detergent.

**détérioration** /deterjɔrasjɔ̃/ nf deterioration; (dégât) damage.

**détériorer** /deterjɔre/ **1** vt damage. □ **se ~** vpr deteriorate.

**détermination** /determinasjɔ̃/ nf determination. **déterminé, ~e** adj (résolu) determined; (précis) definite. **déterminer** **1** vt determine.

**déterrer** /detere/ **1** vt dig up.

**détestable** /detεstabl/ adj (caractère, temps) foul.

**détester** /detεste/ **1** vt hate. □ **se ~** vpr hate each other.

**détonation** /detɔnasjɔ̃/ nf explosion, detonation.

**détour** /detur/ nm (crochet) detour; (fig) roundabout means; (virage) bend.

**détournement** /deturnəmɑ̃/ nm hijack(ing); (de fonds) embezzlement.

**détourner** /deturne/ **1** vt (attention) divert; (tête, yeux) turn away; (avion) hijack; (argent) embezzle. □ **se ~ de** vpr stray from.

**détraquer** /detrake/ **1** vt make go wrong; (estomac) upset. □ **se ~** vpr (machine) go wrong.

**détresse** /detrεs/ nf distress; **dans la ~,** **en ~** in distress.

**détritus** /detrity(s)/ nmpl rubbish (+ sg).

**détroit** /detrwa/ nm strait.

**détromper** /detrɔ̃pe/ **1** vt set straight. □ **se ~** vpr **détrompe-toi!** you'd better think again!

**détruire** /detrɥir/ **17** vt destroy.

**dette** /dεt/ nf debt.

**deuil** /dœj/ nm (période) mourning; (décès) bereavement; **porter le ~**

be in mourning; **faire son ~ de qch** give sth up as lost.

**deux** /dø/ *adj* & *nm* two; **~ fois** twice; **tous (les ~)** both.

**deuxième** *adj* & *nmf* second. **deux-pièces** *nm inv* (maillot de bain) two-piece; (logement) two-room flat.
**deux-points** *nm inv* (Gram) colon.
**deux-roues** *nm inv* two-wheeled vehicle.

**dévaliser** /devalize/ **1** *vt* rob, clean out.

**dévalorisant, ~e** /devalɔʀizɑ̃, -t/ *adj* demeaning.

**dévaloriser** /devalɔʀize/ **1** *vt* (monnaie) devalue. □ **se ~** *vpr* (personne) put oneself down.

**dévaluation** /devaluasjɔ̃/ *nf* devaluation.

**dévaluer** /devalɥe/ **1** *vt* devalue. □ **se ~** *vpr* devalue.

**devancer** /dəvɑ̃se/ **10** *vt* be ou go ahead of; (arriver) arrive ahead of; (prévenir) anticipate.

**devant** /d(ə)vɑ̃/ *prép* in front of; (distance) ahead of; (avec mouvement) past; (en présence de) in front of; (face à) in the face of; **avoir du temps ~ soi** have plenty of time. ● *adv* in front; (à distance) ahead; **de ~** front. ● *nm* front; **prendre les ~s** take the initiative.

**devanture** /dəvɑ̃tyʀ/ *nf* shop front; (vitrine) shop window.

**développement** /devlɔpmɑ̃/ *nm* development; (de photos) developing.

**développer** /devlɔpe/ **1** *vt* develop. □ **se ~** *vpr* (corps, talent) develop; (entreprise) grow, expand.

**devenir** /dəvniʀ/ **58** *vi* (aux être) become; **qu'est-il devenu?** what has become of him?

**dévergondé, ~e** /devɛʀɡɔ̃de/ *adj* & *nm,f* shameless (person).

**déverser** /devɛʀse/ **1** *vt* (liquide)

pour; (ordures, pétrole) dump. □ **se ~** *vpr* (rivière) flow; (égout, foule) pour.

**dévêtir** /devetiʀ/ **61** *vt* undress. □ **se ~** *vpr* get undressed.

**déviation** /devjasjɔ̃/ *nf* diversion.

**dévier** /devje/ **45** *vt* divert; (coup) deflect. ● *vi* (ballon, balle) veer; (personne) deviate.

**devin** /dəvɛ̃/ *nm* soothsayer.

**deviner** /dəvine/ **1** *vt* guess; (apercevoir) distinguish.

**devinette** /dəvinɛt/ *nf* riddle.

**devis** /dəvi/ *nm* estimate, quote.

**dévisager** /devizaʒe/ **40** *vt* stare at.

**devise** /dəviz/ *nf* motto; **~s** (monnaie) (foreign) currency.

**dévisser** /devise/ **1** *vt* unscrew.

**dévitaliser** /devitalize/ **1** *vt* (dent) carry out root canal treatment on.

**dévoiler** /devwale/ **1** *vt* reveal.

---

**devoir** /dəvwaʀ/ **28**

● *verbe auxiliaire*

····▸ **~ faire** (obligation, hypothèse) must do; (nécessité) have got to do; **je dois dire que...** I have to say that...; **il a dû partir** (nécessité) he had to leave; (hypothèse) he must have left.

····▸ **~** (prévision) **je devais lui dire** I was to tell her; **elle doit rentrer bientôt** she's due back soon.

····▸ **~** (conseil) **tu devrais** you should.

● *verbe transitif*

····▸ **~** (argent, excuses) owe; **combien je vous dois?** (en achetant) how much is it?

□ **se devoir** *verbe pronominal*

d

···▶ je me dois de le faire it's my duty to do it.
● **nom masculin**
···▶ duty; faire son ∼ do one's duty.
···▶ (Scol) ∼ (surveillé) test; les ∼s homework (+ sg); faire ses ∼s do one's homework.

**dévorer** /devɔʀe/ **1** vt devour.

**dévot**, ∼e /devo, -ɔt/ adj devout.

**dévoué**, ∼e /devwe/ adj devoted. **dévouement** nm devotion.

**dévouer (se)** /(sə)devwe/ **1** vpr devote oneself (à to); (se sacrifier) sacrifice oneself.

**dextérité** /dɛksteʀite/ nf skill.

**diabète** /djabɛt/ nm diabetes. **diabétique** adj & nmf diabetic.

**diable** /djabl/ nm devil.

**diagnostic** /djagnɔstik/ nm diagnosis. **diagnostiquer** **1** vt diagnose.

**diagonal**, ∼e (mpl -aux) /djagɔnal, -o/ adj diagonal. **diagonale** nf diagonal; en ∼e diagonally.

**diagramme** /djagʀam/ nm diagram; (graphique) graph.

**dialecte** /djalɛkt/ nm dialect.

**dialogue** /djalɔg/ nm dialogue. **dialoguer** **1** vi have talks, enter into a dialogue.

**diamant** /djamã/ nm diamond.

**diamètre** /djamɛtʀ/ nm diameter.

**diapositive** /djapozitiv/ nf slide.

**diarrhée** /djaʀe/ nf diarrhoea.

**dictateur** /diktatœʀ/ nm dictator.

**dicter** /dikte/ **1** vt dictate. **dictée** nf dictation.

**dictionnaire** /diksjɔnɛʀ/ nm dictionary.

**dicton** /diktõ/ nm saying.

**dièse** /djɛz/ nm (Mus) sharp.

**diesel** /djezɛl/ nm & adj inv diesel.

**diète** /djɛt/ nf restricted diet.

**diététicien**, ∼ne /djetetisjɛ̃, -ɛn/ nm, f dietician.

**diététique** /djetetik/ nf dietetics.
● adj produit ou aliment ∼ dietary product; magasin ∼ health food shop ou store.

**dieu** (pl ∼x) /djø/ nm god; D∼ God.

**diffamation** /difamasjõ/ nf slander; (par écrit) libel. **diffamer** **1** vt slander; (par écrit) libel.

**différé**: en ∼ /ãdifeʀe/ loc (émission) pre-recorded.

**différemment** /difeʀamã/ adv differently.

**différence** /difeʀãs/ nf difference; à la ∼ de unlike.

**différencier** /difeʀãsje/ **45** vt differentiate. ● □ se ∼ vpr differentiate oneself; se ∼ de (différer de) differ from.

**différend** /difeʀã/ nm difference (of opinion).

**différent**, ∼e /difeʀã, -t/ adj different (from).

**différer** /difeʀe/ **14** vt postpone.
● vi differ (de from).

**difficile** /difisil/ adj difficult; (exigeant) fussy. **difficilement** adv with difficulty.

**difficulté** /difikylte/ nf difficulty; faire des ∼s raise objections.

**diffus**, ∼e /dify, -z/ adj diffuse.

**diffuser** /difyze/ **1** vt (émission) broadcast; (nouvelle) spread; (lumière, chaleur) diffuse; (Comm) distribute. **diffusion** nf broadcasting; diffusion; distribution.

**digérer** /diʒeʀe/ **14** vt digest; (endurer **1**) stomach. **digeste** adj digestible.

**digestif**, **-ive** /diʒɛstif, -v/ adj digestive. ● nm after-dinner liqueur.

**digital**, ∼e (mpl -aux) /diʒital, -o/

*adj* digital.

**digne** /diɲ/ *adj* (noble) dignified; (*approprié*) worthy; ~ worthy of; ~ de foi trustworthy.

**digue** /dig/ *nf* dyke; (US) dike.

**dilater** /dilate/ **1** *vt* dilate. □ se ~ *vpr* dilate; (*estomac*) distend.

**dilemme** /dilɛm/ *nm* dilemma.

**dilettante** /diletɑ̃t/ *nmf* amateur.

**diluant** /dilɥɑ̃/ *nm* thinner.

**diluer** /dilɥe/ **1** *vt* dilute.

**dimanche** /dimɑ̃ʃ/ *nm* Sunday.

**dimension** /dimɑ̃sjɔ̃/ *nf* (*taille*) size; (*mesure*) dimension; (*aspect*) dimension.

**diminuer** /diminɥe/ **1** *vt* reduce, decrease; (*plaisir, courage*) dampen; (*dénigrer*) diminish. ● *vi* (*se réduire*) decrease; (*faiblir*) (*bruit, flamme*) die down; (*ardeur*) cool. **diminutif** *nm* diminutive; (*surnom*) pet name. **diminution** *nf* decrease (de in); (*réduction*) reduction; (*affaiblissement*) diminishing.

**dinde** /dɛ̃d/ *nf* turkey.

**dîner** /dine/ **1** *vi* have dinner. ● *nm* dinner.

**dingue** /dɛ̃g/ *adj* **1** crazy.

**dinosaure** /dinozɔʀ/ *nm* dinosaur.

**diphtongue** /diftɔ̃g/ *nf* diphthong.

**diplomate** /diplɔmat/ *nmf* diplomat. ● *adj* diplomatic. **diplomatique** *adj* diplomatic.

**diplôme** /diplom/ *nm* certificate, diploma; (Univ) degree. **diplômé, ~e** *adj* qualified.

**dire** /diʀ/ **27** *vt* say; (*secret, vérité, heure*) tell; (*penser*) think; ~ que say that; ~ à qn que tell sb that; ~ à qn de tell sb to; ça me dit de faire I feel like doing; on dirait que it would seem that, it seems that; dis/dites donc! hey! □ se ~ *vpr* (*mot*) be said; (*penser*) tell oneself;

(*se prétendre*) claim to be. ● *nm* au ~ de, selon les ~s de according to.

**direct, ~e** /diʀɛkt/ *adj* direct. ● *nm* (*train*) express train; en ~ (*émission*) live.

**directeur, -trice** /diʀɛktœʀ, -tʀis/ *nm, f* director; (*chef de service*) manager, manageress; (*de journal*) editor; (*d'école*) headteacher; (US) principal; ~ de banque bank manager; ~ commercial sales manager; ~ des ressources humaines human resources manager.

**direction** /diʀɛksjɔ̃/ *nf* (*sens*) direction; (*de société*) management; (Auto) steering; en ~ de (*going*) to.

**dirigeant, ~e** /diʀiʒɑ̃, -t/ *nm, f* (Pol) leader; (Comm) manager. ● *adj* (*classe*) ruling.

**diriger** /diʀiʒe/ **40** *vt* (*service, école, parti, pays*) run; (*entreprise, usine*) manage; (*travaux*) supervise; (*véhicule*) steer; (*orchestre*) conduct; (*braquer*) aim; (*tourner*) turn. □ se ~ *vpr* (*s'orienter*) find one's way; se ~ vers head for, make for.

**dis** /di/ ➡DIRE **27**.

**discernement** /disɛʀnəmɑ̃/ *nm* discernment.

**disciplinaire** /disiplinɛʀ/ *adj* disciplinary. **discipline** *nf* discipline.

**discontinu, ~e** /diskɔ̃tiny/ *adj* intermittent.

**discordant, ~e** /diskɔʀdɑ̃, -t/ *adj* discordant.

**discothèque** /diskɔtɛk/ *nf* record library; (*boîte de nuit*) disco- (thèque).

**discours** /diskuʀ/ *nm* speech; (*propos*) views.

**discret, -ète** /diskʀɛ, -t/ *adj* discreet.

**discrétion** /diskʀesjɔ̃/ *nf* discretion; à ∼ (*vin*) unlimited; (*manger, boire*) as much as one desires.

**discrimination** /diskʀiminasjɔ̃/ *nf* discrimination. **discriminatoire** *adj* discriminatory.

**disculper** /diskylpe/ **1** *vt* exonerate. □ se ∼ *vpr* vindicate oneself.

**discussion** /diskysjɔ̃/ *nf* discussion; (*querelle*) argument.

**discutable** /diskytabl/ *adj* debatable; (*critiquable*) questionable.

**discuter** /diskyte/ **1** *vt* discuss; (*contester*) question. ● *vi* (*parler*) talk; (*répliquer*) argue; ∼ de discuss.

**disette** /dizɛt/ *nf* food shortage.

**disgrâce** /disgʀɑs/ *nf* disgrace.

**disgracieux**, -ieuse /disgʀasjø, -z/ *adj* ugly, unsightly.

**disjoindre** /disʒwɛ̃dʀ/ **22** *vt* take apart. □ se ∼ *vpr* come apart.

**disloquer** /dislɔke/ **1** *vt* (*membre*) dislocate; (*machine*) break (apart). □ se ∼ *vpr* (*parti, cortège*) break up; (*meuble*) come apart.

**disparaître** /dispaʀɛtʀ/ **18** *vi* disappear; (*mourir*) die; faire ∼ get rid of. **disparition** *nf* disappearance; (*mort*) death.

**disparate** /dispaʀat/ *adj* ill-assorted.

**disparu**, ∼e /dispaʀy/ *adj* missing. ● *nm, f* missing person; (*mort*) dead person.

**dispensaire** /dispɑ̃sɛʀ/ *nm* clinic.

**dispense** /dispɑ̃s/ *nf* exemption.

**dispenser** /dispɑ̃se/ **1** *vt* exempt (de from). □ se ∼ de *vpr* avoid.

**disperser** /dispɛʀse/ **1** *vt* (*éparpiller*) scatter; (*répartir*) disperse. □ se ∼ *vpr* disperse.

**disponibilité** /disponibilite/ *nf* availability. **disponible** *adj* available.

**dispos**, ∼e /dispo, -z/ *adj* frais et

∼ fresh and alert.

**disposé**, ∼e /dispoze/ *adj* bien/ mal ∼ in a good/bad mood; ∼ à prepared to; ∼ envers disposed towards.

**disposer** /dispoze/ **1** *vt* arrange; ∼ à (engager à) incline to. ● *vi* ∼ de have at one's disposal. □ se ∼ à *vpr* prepare to.

**dispositif** /dispozitif/ *nm* device; (ensemble de mesures) operation.

**disposition** /dispozisjɔ̃/ *nf* arrangement, layout; (tendance) tendency; ∼s (humeur) mood; (préparatifs) arrangements; (mesures) measures; (aptitude) aptitude; mettre à la ∼ de place ou put at the disposal of.

**disproportionné**, ∼e /dis pʀopɔʀsjɔne/ *adj* disproportionate; ∼ à out of proportion with.

**dispute** /dispyt/ *nf* quarrel.

**disputer** /dispyte/ **1** *vt* (*match*) play; (*course*) run in; (*prix*) fight for; (*gronder* ☺) tell off. □ se ∼ *vpr* quarrel; (se battre pour) fight over; (*match*) be played.

**disquaire** /diskɛʀ/ *nmf* record dealer.

**disque** /disk/ *nm* (Mus) record; (Sport) discus; (*cercle*) disc, disk; (Ordinat) disk; ∼ compact compact disc; ∼ dur hard disk; ∼ optique compact CD-ROM; ∼ souple floppy disk.

**disquette** /diskɛt/ *nf* floppy disk, diskette; ∼ de sauvegarde backup disk.

**disséminer** /disemine/ **1** *vt* spread, scatter.

**dissertation** /disɛʀtasjɔ̃/ *nf* essay, paper.

**disserter** /disɛʀte/ **1** *vi* ∼ sur speak about; (par écrit) write about.

**dissident**, ∼e /disidɑ̃, -t/ *adj &*

d

*nm, f* dissident.

**dissimulation** /disimylasjɔ̃/ *nf* concealment; (fig) deceit.

**dissimuler** /disimyle/ **1** *vt* conceal (à from). □ se ∼ *vpr* conceal oneself.

**dissipé,** ∼e /disipe/ *adj* (élève) unruly.

**dissiper** /disipe/ **1** *vt* (fumée, crainte) dispel; (fortune) squander; (personne) distract. □ se ∼ *vpr* disappear; (élève) grow restless.

**dissolvant** /disɔlvɑ̃/ *nm* solvent; (pour ongles) nail polish remover.

**dissoudre** /disudʀ/ **53** *vt* dissolve. □ se ∼ *vpr* dissolve.

**dissuader** /disɥade/ **1** *vt* dissuade (de from).

**dissuasion** /disɥazjɔ̃/ *nf* dissuasion; force de ∼ deterrent force.

**distance** /distɑ̃s/ *nf* distance; (écart) gap; à ∼ at ou from a distance.

**distancer** /distɑ̃se/ **10** *vt* outdistance.

**distendre** /distɑ̃dʀ/ **3** *vt* (estomac) distend; (corde) stretch.

**distinct,** ∼e /distɛ̃(kt) , -ɛ̃kt/ *adj* distinct.

**distinctif,** -ive /distɛ̃ktif, -v/ *adj* (trait) distinctive; (signe, caractère) distinguishing.

**distinction** /distɛ̃ksjɔ̃/ *nf* distinction; (récompense) honour.

**distinguer** /distɛ̃ge/ **1** *vt* distinguish.

**distraction** /distʀaksjɔ̃/ *nf* absent-mindedness; (passe-temps) entertainment, leisure; (détente) recreation.

**distraire** /distʀɛʀ/ **29** *vt* amuse; (rendre inattentif) distract; ∼ qn de qch take sb's mind off sth. □ se ∼ *vpr* amuse oneself.

**distrait,** ∼e /distʀɛ, -t/ *adj* absent-

minded; (élève) inattentive.

**distrayant,** ∼e /distʀɛjɑ̃, -t/ *adj* entertaining.

**distribuer** /distʀibɥe/ **1** *vt* hand out, distribute; (répartir) distribute; (tâches, rôles) allocate; (cartes) deal; (courrier) deliver.

**distributeur** /distʀibytœʀ/ *nm* (Auto, Comm) distributor; ∼ (automatique) vending-machine; ∼ de billets (de banque) cash dispenser.

**distribution** *nf* distribution; (du courrier) delivery; (acteurs) cast; (secteur) retailing.

**district** /distʀikt/ *nm* district.

**dit¹, dites** /di, dit/ ➡DIRE **27**.

**dit²,** ∼e /di, dit/ *adj* (décidé) agreed; (surnommé) known as.

**diurne** /djyʀn/ *adj* diurnal; (activité) daytime.

**divagations** /divagasjɔ̃/ *nfpl* ravings.

**divergence** /divɛʀʒɑ̃s/ *nf* divergence. **divergent,** ∼e *adj* divergent. **diverger** **40** *vi* diverge.

**divers,** ∼e /divɛʀ, -s/ *adj* (varié) diverse; (différent) various; (frais) miscellaneous; dépenses ∼es sundries. **diversifier** **45** *vt* diversify.

**diversité** /divɛʀsite/ *nf* diversity, variety.

**divertir** /divɛʀtiʀ/ **2** *vt* amuse, entertain. □ se ∼ *vpr* amuse oneself; (passer du bon temps) enjoy oneself. **divertissement** *nm* amusement, entertainment.

**dividende** /dividɑ̃d/ *nm* dividend.

**divin,** ∼e /divɛ̃, -in/ *adj* divine. **divinité** *nf* divinity.

**diviser** /divize/ **1** *vt* divide. □ se ∼ *vpr* become divided; se ∼ par sept be divisible by seven. **division** *nf* division.

**divorce** /divɔʀs/ *nm* divorce.

**divorcé,** ∼e /divɔʀse/ *adj*

divorced. ● nm, f divorcee.

**divorcer** /divɔʀse/ **10** vi (d'avec) divorce.

**dix** /dis/ (/di/ before consonant, /diz/ before vowel) adj & nm ten.

**dix-huit** /dizɥit/ adj & nm eighteen.

**dixième** /dizjɛm/ adj & nmf tenth.

**dix-neuf** /diznœf/ adj & nm nineteen.

**dix-sept** /disɛt/ adj & nm seventeen.

**docile** /dɔsil/ adj docile.

**docteur** /dɔktœʀ/ nm doctor.

**doctorat** /dɔktɔʀa/ nm doctorate, PhD.

**document** /dɔkymã/ nm document. **documentaire** adj & nm documentary.

**documentaliste** /dɔkymãtalist/ nmf information officer; (Scol) librarian.

**documentation** /dɔkymãtasjɔ̃/ nf information, literature; centre de ∼ resource centre.

**documenté**, ∼e /dɔkymãte/ adj well-documented.

**documenter** /dɔkymãte/ **1** vt provide with information. □ se ∼ vpr collect information.

**dodo** /dodo/ nm faire ∼ (langage enfantin) sleep.

**dodu**, ∼e /dody/ adj plump.

**dogmatique** /dɔgmatik/ adj dogmatic. **dogme** nm dogma.

**doigt** /dwa/ nm finger; un ∼ de a drop of; montrer qch du ∼ point at sth; à deux ∼s de a hair's breadth away from; ∼ de pied toe. **doigté** nm (Mus) fingering, touch; (diplomatie) tact.

**dois**, **doit** /dwa/ →DEVOIR **26**.

**doléances** /dɔleãs/ nfpl grievances.

**dollar** /dɔlaʀ/ nm dollar.

**domaine** /dɔmɛn/ nm estate, domain; (fig) domain, field.

**domestique** /dɔmɛstik/ adj domestic. ● nmf servant. **domestiquer** **1** vt domesticate.

**domicile** /dɔmisil/ nm home; à ∼ at home; (livrer) to the home.

**domicilié**, ∼e /dɔmisilje/ adj resident; être ∼ à Paris live ou be resident in Paris.

**dominant**, ∼e /dɔminã, -t/ adj dominant. **dominante** nf dominant feature.

**dominer** /dɔmine/ **1** vt dominate; (surplomber) tower over, dominate; (sujet) master; (peur) overcome. ● vi dominate; (équipe) be in the lead; (prévaloir) stand out.

**domino** /dɔmino/ nm domino.

**dommage** /dɔmaʒ/ nm (tort) harm; (∼s) (dégâts) damage; c'est ∼ it's a pity ou shame; quel ∼ what a pity ou shame. **dommages-intérêts** nmpl (Jur) damages.

**dompter** /dõte/ **1** vt tame. **dompteur**, **-euse** nm, f tamer.

**DOM-TOM** /dɔmtɔm/ abrév mpl (**départements et territoires d'outre-mer**) French overseas departments and territories.

**don** /dõ/ nm (cadeau, aptitude) gift. **donateur**, **-trice** nm, f donor. **donation** nf donation.

**donc** /dõk/ conj so, then; (par conséquent) so, therefore; (avec) quoi ∼? what did you say?; tiens ∼! fancy that!

**donjon** /dõʒõ/ nm (tour) keep.

**donné**, ∼e /dɔne/ adj (fixé) given; (pas cher **1**) dirt cheap; étant ∼ que given that.

**donnée** /dɔne/ nf (élément d'information) fact; ∼s data.

**donner** /dɔne/ **1** vt give; (vieilles

*affaires*) give away; (*distribuer*) give out; (*fruits, résultats*) produce; (*film*) show; (*pièce*) put on; ça donne soif/faim it makes one thirsty/hungry; ~ qch à réparer take sth to be repaired; ~ lieu à give rise to. ● *vi* ~ sur look out on to; ~ dans tend towards. □ se ~ à *vpr* devote oneself to; se ~ du mal go to a lot of trouble (pour faire to do).

---

**dont** /dɔ̃/

● *pronom*

····▸ (*personne*) la fille ~ je te parlais the girl I was telling you about; l'homme ~ la fille a dit... the man whose daughter said...

····▸ (*chose*) which, l'affaire ~ il parle the matter which he is referring to; la manière ~ elle parle the way she speaks; ce ~ il parle what he's talking about

····▸ (*provenance*) from which.

····▸ (*parmi lesquels*) deux personnes ~ toi two people, one of whom is you; plusieurs thèmes ~ l'identité et le racisme several topics including identity and racism.

---

**dopage** /dɔpaʒ/ *nm* (*de cheval*) doping; (*d'athlète*) illegal drug-use.

**doper** /dɔpe/ **1** *vt* dope. □ se ~ *vpr* take drugs.

**doré, ~e** /dɔʀe/ *adj* (*couleur d'or*) golden; (*qui rappelle de l'or*) gold; (*avec de l'or*) gilt; la jeunesse ~e gilded youth.

**dorénavant** /dɔʀenavɑ̃/ *adv* henceforth.

**dorer** /dɔʀe/ **1** *vt* gild; (*Culin*) brown.

**dormir** /dɔʀmiʀ/ **46** *vi* sleep; (*être endormi*) be asleep; ~ debout be asleep on one's feet; une histoire à ~ debout a cock-and-bull story.

**dortoir** /dɔʀtwaʀ/ *nm* dormitory.

**dorure** /dɔʀyʀ/ *nf* gilding.

**dos** /do/ *nm* back; (*de livre*) spine; à ~ de riding on; au ~ de (*chèque*) on the back of; de ~ from behind; ~ crawlé backstroke.

**dosage** /dozaʒ/ *nm* (*mélange*) mixture; (*quantité*) amount, proportions. **dose** *nf* dose. **doser** **1** *vt* measure out; (*contrôler*) use in a controlled way.

**dossier** /dɔsje/ *nm* (*documents*) file; (*Jur*) case; (*de chaise*) back; (TV, presse) special feature.

**dot** /dɔt/ *nf* dowry.

**douane** /dwan/ *nf* customs.

**douanier, -ière** /dwanje, -jɛʀ/ *adj* customs. ● *nm* customs officer.

**double** /dubl/ *adj & adv* double. ● *nm* (*copie*) duplicate; (*sosie*) double; le ~ (de) twice as much *ou* as many (as); le ~ messieurs the men's doubles.

**double-cliquer** /dublklike/ **1** *vi* double-click.

**doubler** /duble/ **1** *vt* double; (*dépasser*) overtake; (*vêtement*) line; (*film*) dub; (*classe*) repeat; (*cap*) round. ● *vi* double.

**doublure** /dublyʀ/ *nf* (*étoffe*) lining; (*acteur*) understudy.

**douce** /dus/ ➝DOUX.

**doucement** /dusmɑ̃/ *adv* gently; (*sans bruit*) quietly; (*lentement*) slowly.

**douceur** /dusœʀ/ *nf* (*mollesse*) softness; (*de climat*) mildness; (*de personne*) gentleness; (*friandise*) sweet; (US) candy; en ~ smoothly.

**douche** /duʃ/ *nf* shower.

**doucher (se)** /duʃe/ **1** *vpr* have

*ou* take a shower.

**doudoune** /dudun/ *nf* 🔲 down jacket.

**doué**, ~e /dwe/ *adj* gifted; ~ de endowed with.

**douille** /duj/ *nf* (Électr) socket.

**douillet**, ~te /dujɛ, -t/ *adj* cosy, comfortable; (*personne*) péj) soft.

**douleur** /dulœʀ/ *nf* pain; (*chagrin*) sorrow, grief. **douloureux, -euse** *adj* painful.

**doute** /dut/ *nm* doubt; sans ~ no doubt; sans aucun ~ without doubt.

**douter** /dute/ 🔳 *vt* ~ de doubt; ~ que doubt that. ● *vi* doubt. □ se ~ de *vpr* suspect; je m'en doutais ! thought so.

**douteux, -euse** /dutø, -z/ *adj* dubious, doubtful.

**Douvres** /duvʀ/ *npr* Dover.

**doux, douce** /du, dus/ *adj* (*moelleux*) soft; (*sucré*) sweet; (*clément, pas fort*) mild; (*pas brusque, bienveillant*) gentle.

**douzaine** /duzɛn/ *nf* about twelve; (*douze*) dozen; une ~ d'œufs a dozen eggs.

**douze** /duz/ *adj & nm* twelve. **douzième** *adj & nmf* twelfth.

**doyen**, ~ne /dwajɛ̃, -ɛn/ *nm, f* dean; (en âge) most senior person.

**dragée** /dʀaʒe/ *nf* sugared almond.

**draguer** /dʀage/ 🔳 *vt* (*rivière*) dredge; (*filles* 🔲) chat up.

**drainer** /dʀene/ 🔳 *vt* drain.

**dramatique** /dʀamatik/ *adj* dramatic; (*tragique*) tragic. ● *nf* (television) drama.

**dramatiser** /dʀamatize/ 🔳 *vt* dramatize.

**dramaturge** /dʀamatyʀʒ/ *nmf* dramatist.

**drame** /dʀam/ *nm* (genre) drama;

(*pièce*) play; (*événement tragique*) tragedy.

**drap** /dʀa/ *nm* sheet; (*tissu*) (woollen) cloth.

**drapeau** (*pl* ~x) /dʀapo/ *nm* flag.

**drap-housse** (*pl* draps-housses) /dʀaus/ *nm* fitted sheet.

**dressage** /dʀesaʒ/ *nm* training; (*compétition équestre*) dressage.

**dresser** /dʀese/ 🔳 *vt* put up, erect; (*tête*) raise; (*animal*) train; (*liste, plan*) draw up; ~ l'oreille prick up one's ears. □ se ~ *vpr* (*bâtiment*) stand; (*personne*) draw oneself up. **dresseur, -euse** *nm, f* trainer.

**dribbler** /dʀible/ 🔳 *vi* (Sport) dribble.

**drive** /dʀajv/ *nm* (Ordinat) drive.

**drogue** /dʀɔg/ *nf* drug; la ~ drugs.

**drogué**, ~e /dʀɔge/ *nm, f* drug addict.

**droguer** /dʀɔge/ 🔳 *vt* (*malade*) drug heavily; (*victime*) drug. □ se ~ *vpr* take drugs.

**droguerie** /dʀɔgʀi/ *nf* hardware shop. **droguiste** *nmf* owner of a hardware shop.

**droit**, ~e /dʀwa, -t/ *adj* (contraire de gauche) right; (non courbe) straight; (loyal) upright; angle ~ right angle. ● *adv* straight. ● *nm* right; ~(s) (*taxe*) duty; le ~ (Jur) law; avoir ~ à be entitled to; avoir le ~ de be allowed to; être dans son ~ be in the right; ~ d'auteur copyright; ~ d'inscription registration fee; ~s d'auteur royalties.

**droite** /dʀwat/ *nf* (contraire de gauche) right; à ~ on the right; (direction) (to) the right; la ~ the right (side); (Pol) the right (wing); (*ligne*) straight line. **droitier, -ière** *adj* right-handed.

**drôle** /dʀol/ adj (amusant) funny; (bizarre) funny, odd. **drôlement** adv funnily; (très 🔳) really.

**dru**, ∼e /dʀy/ adj thick; tomber ∼ fall thick and fast.

**drugstore** /dʀœgstɔʀ/ nm drugstore.

**DTD** abrév m (document type definition) DTD.

**du** /dy/ →DE.

**dû**, **due** /dy/ adj due. ● nm due; (argent) dues; ∼ à due to. ● →DEVOIR 🔟.

**duc**, **duchesse** /dyk, dyʃɛs/ nm, f duke, duchess.

**duo** /dɥo/ nm (Mus) duet; (fig) duo.

**dupe** /dyp/ nf dupe.

**duplex** /dyplɛks/ nm split-level apartment; (US) duplex; (émission) link-up.

**duplicata** /dyplikata/ nm inv duplicate.

**duquel** /dykɛl/ →LEQUEL.

**dur**, ∼e /dyʀ/ adj hard; (sévère) harsh, hard; (viande) tough; (col, brosse) stiff; ∼ d'oreille hard of hearing. ● adv hard. ● nm, f tough nut 🔳; (Pol) hardliner.

**durable** /dyʀabl/ adj lasting.

**durant** /dyʀɑ̃/ prép (au cours de) during; (avec mesure de temps) for; ∼ des heures for hours; des heures ∼ for hours and hours.

**durcir** /dyʀsiʀ/ 🔲 vt harden. ● vi (terre) harden; (ciment) set; (pain) go hard. □ se ∼ vpr harden.

**durée** /dyʀe/ nf length; (période) duration; de courte ∼ short-lived; pile longue ∼ long-life battery.

**durer** /dyʀe/ 🔳 vi last.

**dureté** /dyʀte/ nf hardness; (sévérité) harshness.

**duvet** /dyvɛ/ nm down; (sac) sleeping-bag.

**DVD** abrév m (digital versatile disc) DVD.

**dynamique** /dinamik/ adj dynamic.

**dynamite** /dinamit/ nf dynamite.

**dynamo** /dinamo/ nf dynamo.

. . . . . . . . . . . . . . . . . . . . . . . . . .

# Ee

. . . . . . . . . . . . . . . . . . . . . . . . . .

**eau** (pl ∼x) /o/ nf water; ∼ courante running water; ∼ de mer seawater; ∼ de source spring water; ∼ douce/salée fresh/salt water; ∼ de pluie rainwater; ∼ potable drinking water; ∼ de Javel bleach; ∼ minérale mineral water; ∼ gazeuse sparkling water; ∼ plate still water; ∼ de toilette eau de toilette; ∼x usées dirty water; ∼x et forêts forestry commission (+ sg); tomber à l'∼ (fig) fall through; prendre l'∼ take in water. **eau-de-vie** (pl eaux-de-vie) nf brandy.

**ébahi**, ∼e /ebai/ adj dumbfounded.

**ébauche** /eboʃ/ nf (dessin) sketch; (fig) attempt.

**ébéniste** /ebenist/ nm cabinetmaker.

**éblouir** /ebluiʀ/ 🔲 vt dazzle.

**éboueur** /ebwœʀ/ nm dustman.

**ébouillanter** /ebujɑ̃te/ 🔳 vt scald.

**éboulement** /ebulmɑ̃/ nm landslide.

**ébouriffé**, ∼e /eburife/ adj dishevelled.

**ébrécher** /ebreʃe/ 🔢 vt chip.

**ébruiter** /ebruite/ 🔳 vt spread

about. □ **s'~** vpr get out.

**ébullition** /ebylisjɔ̃/ nf boiling; en ~ boiling.

**écaille** /ekaj/ nf (de poisson) scale; (de peinture, roc) flake; (matière) tortoiseshell.

**écarlate** /ekarlat/ adj scarlet.

**écarquiller** /ekarkije/ **1** vt ~ les yeux open one's eyes wide.

**écart** /ekar/ nm gap; (de prix) difference; (embardée) swerve; ~ de conduite lapse in behaviour; être à l'~ be isolated; se tenir à l'~ stand apart from; (fig) keep out of the way of.

**écarté, ~e** /ekarte/ adj (lieu) remote; les jambes ~es (with) legs apart; les bras ~s with one's arms out.

**écarter** /ekarte/ **1** vt (séparer) move apart; (membres) spread; (branches) part; (éliminer) dismiss; ~ qch de move sth away from; ~ qn de keep sb away from. □ **s'~** vpr (s'éloigner) move away; (quitter son chemin) move aside; s'~ de stray from.

**ecchymose** /ekimoz/ nf bruise.

**écervelé, ~e** /eservale/ adj scatterbrained. ● nm, f scatterbrain.

**échafaudage** /eʃafodaʒ/ nm scaffolding; (amas) heap.

**échalote** /eʃalɔt/ nf shallot.

**échancré, ~e** /eʃɑ̃kre/ adj lowcut.

**échange** /eʃɑ̃ʒ/ nm exchange; en ~ (de) in exchange (for). **échanger** **40** vt exchange (contre for).

**échangeur** /eʃɑ̃ʒœr/ nm (Auto) interchange.

**échantillon** /eʃɑ̃tijɔ̃/ nm sample.

**échappatoire** /eʃapatwar/ nf way out.

**échappement** /eʃapmɑ̃/ nm exhaust.

**échapper** /eʃape/ **1** vi ~ à escape; (en fuyant) escape (from); ~ des mains de slip out of the hands of; ça m'a échappé (fig) it just slipped out; l'~ belle have a narrow ou lucky escape. □ **s'~** vpr escape.

**écharde** /eʃard/ nf splinter.

**écharpe** /eʃarp/ nf scarf; (de maire) sash; (en ~ bras) in a sling.

**échasse** /eʃas/ nf stilt.

**échauffement** /eʃofmɑ̃/ nm (Sport) warm-up.

**échauffer** /eʃofe/ **1** vt heat; (fig) excite. □ **s'~** vpr warm up.

**échéance** /eʃeɑ̃s/ nf due date (for payment); (délai) deadline; (obligation) (financial) commitment.

**échéant** /eʃeɑ̃/ le cas ~ /ləkazeʃeɑ̃/ loc if need be.

**échec** /eʃɛk/ nm failure; ~s (jeu) chess; ~ et mat checkmate.

**échelle** /eʃɛl/ nf ladder; (dimension) scale.

**échelon** /eʃlɔ̃/ nm rung; (hiérarchique) grade; (niveau) level.

**échevelé, ~e** /eʃavle/ adj dishevelled.

**écho** /eko/ nm echo; ~s (dans la presse) gossip.

**échographie** /ekɔgrafi/ nf (ultrasound) scan.

**échouer** /eʃwe/ **1** vi (bateau) run aground; (ne pas réussir) fail; ~ à un examen fail an exam. ● vt (bateau) ground. □ **s'~** vpr run aground.

**échu, ~e** /eʃy/ adj (délai) expired.

**éclabousser** /eklabuse/ **1** vt splash.

**éclair** /eklɛr/ nm (flash of) lightning; (fig) flash; (gâteau) éclair. ● adj inv (visite) brief.

**éclairage** /eklɛraʒ/ nm lighting.

**éclaircie** /eklɛʀsi/ nf sunny interval.

**éclaircir** /eklɛʀsiʀ/ [2] vt lighten; (mystère) clear up. □ s'~ vpr (ciel) clear; (mystère) become clearer. **éclaircissement** nm clarification.

**éclairer** /eklere/ [1] vt light (up); (personne) (fig) enlighten; (situation) throw light on. ● vi give light. □ s'~ vpr become clearer.

**éclaireur, -euse** /eklɛʀœʀ, -øz/ nm, f (boy) scout, (girl) guide.

**éclat** /ekla/ nm fragment; (de lumière) brightness; (splendeur) brilliance; ~ de rire burst of laughter.

**éclatant, ~e** /eklatã, -t/ adj brilliant; (soleil) dazzling.

**éclater** /eklate/ [1] vi burst; (explosier) go off; (verre) shatter; (guerre) break out; (groupe) split up; ~ de rire burst out laughing.

**éclipse** /eklips/ nf eclipse.

**éclosion** /eklozjõ/ nf hatching, opening.

**écluse** /eklyz/ nf (de canal) lock.

**écœurant, ~e** /ekœʀã, -t/ adj (gâteau) sickly; (fig) disgusting. **écœurer** [1] vt sicken.

**éco-guerrier, -ière** /ekogeʀje, jɛʀ/ nmf eco-warrior.

**école** /ekɔl/ nf school; ~ maternelle/primaire/secondaire nursery/primary/secondary school; ~ normale teachers' training college. **écolier, -ière** nm, f schoolboy, schoolgirl.

**écologie** /ekɔlɔʒi/ nf ecology. **écologique** adj ecological, green. **écologiste** nmf (chercheur) ecologist; (dans l'âme) environmentalist; (Pol) Green.

**économie** /ekɔnɔmi/ nf economy; (discipline) economics; ~s (argent) savings; une ~ de (gain) a saving of. **économique** adj (Pol) economic;

(bon marché) economical.

**économiser** /ekɔnɔmize/ [1] vt/i save.

**écorce** /ekɔʀs/ nf bark; (de fruit) peel.

**écorcher** /ekɔʀʃe/ [1] vt (genou) graze; (animal) skin. □ s'~ vpr graze oneself. **écorchure** nf graze.

**écossais, ~e** /ekɔsɛ, -z/ adj Scottish. **É.~, ~e** nm, f Scot.

**Écosse** /ekɔs/ nf Scotland.

**écoulement** /ekulmã/ nm flow.

**écouler** /ekule/ [1] vt dispose of, sell. □ s'~ vpr (liquide) flow; (temps) pass.

**écourter** /ekuʀte/ [1] vt shorten.

**écoute** /ekut/ nf listening; à l'~ (de) listening in (to); heures de grande ~ prime time; ~s téléphoniques phone tapping.

**écouter** /ekute/ [1] vt listen to. ● vi listen; ~ aux portes eavesdrop. **écouteur** nm earphones (+ pl); (de téléphone) receiver.

**écran** /ekʀã/ nm screen; ~ total sun-block.

**écraser** /ekʀaze/ [1] vt crush; (piéton) run over; (cigarette) stub out. □ s'~ vpr crash (contre into).

**écrémé, ~e** /ekʀeme/ adj skimmed; demi-~ semi-skimmed.

**écrevisse** /ekʀəvis/ nf crayfish.

**écrier (s')** /(s)ekʀije/ [45] vpr exclaim.

**écrin** /ekʀɛ̃/ nm case.

**écrire** /ekʀiʀ/ [30] vt/i write; (orthographier) spell. □ s'~ vpr (mot) be spelt.

**écrit** /ekʀi/ nm document; (examen) written paper; par ~ in writing.

**écriteau** (pl ~x) /ekʀito/ nm notice.

**écriture** /ekʀityʀ/ nf writing; ~s

(Comm) accounts.

**écrivain** /ekʀivɛ̃/ nm writer.

**écrou** /ekʀu/ nm (Tech) nut.

**écrouler (s')** /(s)ekʀule/ **1** vpr collapse.

**écru,** ~e /ekʀy/ adj (couleur) natural; (tissu) raw.

**écueil** /ekœj/ nm reef; (fig) danger.

**éculé,** ~e /ekyle/ adj (soulier) worn at the heel; (fig) well-worn.

**écume** /ekym/ nf foam; (Culin) scum.

**écumer** /ekyme/ **1** vt skim. ● vi foam.

**écureuil** /ekyʀœj/ nm squirrel.

**écurie** /ekyʀi/ nf stable.

**écuyer, -ère** /ekɥije, -jɛʀ/ nm, f (horse) rider.

**eczéma** /ɛgzema/ nm eczema.

**EDF** abrév f (**Électricité de France**) French electricity board.

**édifice** /edifis/ nm building.

**édifier** /edifje/ **45** vt construct; (porter à la vertu) edify.

**Édimbourg** /edɛ̃buʀ/ npr Edinburgh.

**édit** /edi/ nm edict.

**éditer** /edite/ **1** vt publish; (annoter) edit. **éditeur, -trice** nm, f publisher; (réviseur) editor.

**édition** /edisjɔ̃/ nf (activité) publishing; (livre, disque) edition.

**éditique** /editik/ nf electronic publishing.

**éditorial,** ~e (pl -iaux) /editoʀjal, -jo/ adj & nm editorial.

**édredon** /edʀədɔ̃/ nm eiderdown.

**éducateur, -trice** /edykatœʀ, -tʀis/ nm, f youth worker.

**éducatif, -ive** /edykatif, -v/ adj educational.

**éducation** /edykasjɔ̃/ nf (façon d'élever) upbringing; (enseignement) education; (manières) manners; ~ **physique** physical education.

**éduquer** /edyke/ **1** vt (élever) bring up; (former) educate.

**effacé,** ~e /efase/ adj (modeste) unassuming.

**effacer** /efase/ **10** vt (gommer) rub out; (à l'écran) delete; (souvenir) erase. □ **s'**~ vpr fade; (s'écarter) step aside.

**effarer** /efaʀe/ **1** vt alarm; **être effaré** be astounded.

**effaroucher** /efaʀuʃe/ **1** vt scare away.

**effectif, -ive** /efɛktif, -v/ adj effective. ● nm (d'école) number of pupils; ~s numbers. **effectivement** adv effectively; (en effet) indeed.

**effectuer** /efɛktɥe/ **1** vt carry out, make.

**efféminé,** ~e /efemine/ adj effeminate.

**effervescent,** ~e /efɛʀvesɑ̃, -t/ adj **comprimé** ~ effervescent tablet.

**effet** /efɛ/ nm effect; (impression) impression; ~s (habits) clothes, things; **sous l'**~ **d'une drogue** under the influence of drugs; **en** ~ indeed; **faire de l'**~ have an effect, be effective; **faire bon/ mauvais** ~ make a good/bad impression; **ça fait un drôle d'**~ it feels strange.

**efficace** /efikas/ adj effective; (personne) efficient. **efficacité** nf effectiveness; (de personne) efficiency.

**effleurer** /eflœʀe/ **1** vt touch lightly; (sujet) touch on; **ça ne m'a pas effleuré** it did not cross my mind.

**effondrement** /efɔ̃dʀəmɑ̃/ nm collapse. **effondrer (s')** **1** vpr collapse.

**efforcer (s')** /(s)efɔʀse/ **10** vpr try (hard) (de to).

**effort** /efɔʀ/ nm effort.

**effraction** /efʀaksjɔ̃/ nf entrer par ~ break in.

**effrayant**, ~e /efʀejã, -t/ adj frightening; (fig) frightful.

**effrayer** /efʀeje/ 31 vt frighten; (décourager) put off. □ **s'~** vpr be frightened.

**effréné**, ~e /efʀene/ adj wild.

**effriter (s')** /(s)efʀite/ 1 vpr crumble.

**effroi** /efʀwa/ nm dread.

**effronté**, ~e /efʀɔ̃te/ adj cheeky. ●nm, f cheeky boy, cheeky girl.

**effroyable** /efʀwajabl/ adj dreadful.

**égal**, ~e (mpl -aux) /egal, -o/ adj equal; (surface, vitesse) even. ●nm, f equal; ça m'est/lui est ~ it is all the same to me/him; sans ~ matchless; d'~ à ~ between equals. **également** adv equally; (aussi) as well. **égaler** 1 vt equal.

**égaliser** /egalize/ 1 vt/i (Sport) equalize; (niveler) level out; (cheveux) trim.

**égalitaire** /egalitɛʀ/ adj egalitarian.

**égalité** /egalite/ nf equality; (de surface) evenness; être à ~ be level.

**égard** /egaʀ/ nm consideration; ~s respect (+ sg); par ~ pour out of consideration for; à cet ~ in this respect; à l'~ de with regard to; (envers) towards.

**égarer** /egaʀe/ 1 vt mislay; (tromper) lead astray. □ **s'~** vpr get lost; (se tromper) go astray.

**égayer** /egeje/ 31 vt (personne) cheer up; (pièce) brighten up.

**église** /egliz/ nf church.

**égoïsme** /egɔism/ nm selfishness, egoism.

**égoïste** /egɔist/ adj selfish. ●nmf egoist.

**égorger** /egɔʀʒe/ 40 vt slit the throat of.

**égout** /egu/ nm sewer.

**égoutter** /egute/ 1 vt drain. □ **s'~** vpr (vaisselle) drain; (lessive) drip dry. **égouttoir** nm draining-board.

**égratigner** /egʀatiɲe/ 1 vt scratch. **égratignure** nf scratch.

**Égypte** /eʒipt/ nf Egypt.

**éjecter** /eʒɛkte/ 1 vt eject.

**élaboration** /elabɔʀasjɔ̃/ nf elaboration. **élaborer** 1 vt elaborate.

**élan** /elɑ̃/ nm (animal) moose; (Sport) run-up; (vitesse) momentum; (fig) surge.

**élancé**, ~e /elɑ̃se/ adj slender.

**élancement** /elɑ̃smɑ̃/ nm twinge.

**élancer (s')** /(s)elɑ̃se/ 10 vpr leap forward, dash; (arbre, édifice) soar.

**élargir** /elaʀʒiʀ/ 2 vt (route) widen; (connaissances) broaden. □ **s'~** vpr (famille) expand; (route) widen; (écart) increase; (vêtement) stretch.

**élastique** /elastik/ adj elastic. ●nm elastic band; (tissu) elastic.

**électeur**, -trice /elɛktœʀ, -tʀis/ nm, f voter. **élection** nf election. **électoral**, ~e (mpl -aux) adj (réunion) election. **électorat** nm electorate, voters (+ pl).

**électricien**, ~ne /elɛktʀisjɛ̃, ɛn/ nm, f electrician. **électricité** nf electricity.

**électrifier** /elɛktʀifje/ 45 vt electrify.

**électrique** /elɛktʀik/ adj electric; (installation) electrical.

**électrocuter** /elɛktʀɔkyte/ 1 vt electrocute.

**électroménager** /elɛktʀɔmenaʒe/ nm l'~ household

appliances (+ *pl*).

**électron** /elɛktʁɔ̃/ *nm* electron. **électronicien**, **~ne** *nm, f* electronics engineer.

**électronique** /elɛktʁɔnik/ *adj* electronic. ● *nf* electronics.

**élégance** /elegɑ̃s/ *nf* elegance. **élégant**, **~e** *adj* elegant.

**élément** /elemɑ̃/ *nm* element; (*meuble*) unit. **élémentaire** *adj* elementary.

**éléphant** /elefɑ̃/ *nm* elephant.

**élevage** /ɛlvaʒ/ *nm* (stock-) breeding.

**élévation** /elevasjɔ̃/ *nf* rise; (*hausse*) rise; (*plan*) elevation; **~ de terrain** rise in the ground.

**élève** /elɛv/ *nmf* pupil.

**élevé**, **~e** /ɛlve/ *adj* high; (*noble*) elevated; **bien ~** well-mannered.

**élever** /ɛlve/ [6] *vt* (*lever*) raise; (*enfants*) bring up, raise; (*animal*) breed. □ **s'~** *vpr* rise; (*dans le ciel*) soar up; **s'~ à** amount to. **éleveur**, **-euse** *nm, f* (stock-)breeder.

**éligible** /eliʒibl/ *adj* eligible.

**élimination** /eliminasjɔ̃/ *nf* elimination.

**éliminatoire** /eliminatwaʁ/ *adj* qualifying. ● *nf* (Sport) heat.

**éliminer** /elimine/ [1] *vt* eliminate.

**élire** /eliʁ/ [39] *vt* elect.

**elle** /ɛl/ *pron* she; (*complément*) her; (*chose*) it. **elle-même** *pron* herself; itself. **elles** *pron* they; (*complément*) them. **elles-mêmes** *pron* themselves.

**élocution** /elɔkysjɔ̃/ *nf* diction.

**éloge** /elɔʒ/ *nm* praise; **faire l'~ de** praise; **~s** praise (+ *sg*).

**éloigné**, **~e** /elwaɲe/ *adj* distant; **~ de** far away from; **parent ~** distant relative.

**éloigner** /elwaɲe/ [1] *vt* take away

ou remove (de from); (*danger*) ward off; (*visite*) put off. □ **s'~** *vpr* go ou move away (de from); (*affectivement*) become estranged (de from).

**élongation** /elɔ̃gasjɔ̃/ *nf* strained muscle.

**éloquent**, **~e** /elɔkɑ̃, -t/ *adj* eloquent.

**élu**, **~e** /ely/ *adj* elected. ● *nm, f* (Pol) elected representative.

**élucider** /elyside/ [1] *vt* elucidate.

**éluder** /elyde/ [1] *vt* evade.

> **Élysée** The *palais de l'Élysée* is the official residence of the *Président de la République*, not far from the *Champs Élysées* in central Paris. The word *Élysée* is often used to refer to the president's office. See ▷ **MATIGNON**.

**émacié**, **~e** /emasje/ *adj* emaciated.

**e-mail** /imɛl/ *nm* email; **envoyer un ~ à qn** email sb.

**émail** (*pl* **-aux**) /emaj, -o/ *nm* enamel.

**émanciper** /emɑ̃sipe/ [1] *vt* emancipate. □ **s'~** *vpr* become emancipated.

**émaner** /emane/ [1] *vi* emanate.

**emballage** /ɑ̃balaʒ/ *nm* (dur) packaging; (souple) wrapping.

**emballer** /ɑ̃bale/ [1] *vt* pack; (en papier) wrap; **ça ne m'emballe pas** [1] I'm not really taken by it. □ **s'~** *vpr* (moteur) race; (cheval) bolt; (personne) get carried away; (prices) shoot up.

**embarcadère** /ɑ̃baʁkadɛʁ/ *nm* landing-stage.

**embarcation** /ɑ̃baʁkasjɔ̃/ *nf* boat.

**embardée** /ɑ̃baʁde/ *nf* swerve.

**embarquement** /ɑ̃baʀkəmɑ̃/ nm (de passagers) boarding; (de fret) loading.

**embarquer** /ɑ̃baʀke/ **1** vt take on board; (fret) load; (emporter 🖅) cart off. ● vi board. □ s'~ vpr board; s'~ dans embark upon.

**embarras** /ɑ̃baʀa/ nm (gêne) embarrassment; (difficulté) difficulty.

**embarrasser** /ɑ̃baʀase/ **1** vt (encombrer) clutter (up); (fig) embarrass. □ s'~ de vpr burden oneself with.

**embauche** /ɑ̃boʃ/ nf hiring. **embaucher** **1** vt hire, take on.

**embaumer** /ɑ̃bome/ **1** vt (pièce) fill; (cadavre) embalm. ● vi be fragrant.

**embellir** /ɑ̃beliʀ/ **2** vt make more attractive; (récit) embellish.

**embêtant, ~e** /ɑ̃bɛtɑ̃, -t/ adj annoying.

**embêter** /ɑ̃bete/ **1** vt bother. □ s'~ vpr be bored.

**emblée: d'~** /dɑ̃ble/ loc right away.

**emblème** /ɑ̃blɛm/ nm emblem.

**emboîter** /ɑ̃bwate/ **1** vt fit together; ~ le pas à qn (imiter) follow suit. □ s'~ vpr fit together; (s')~ dans fit into.

**embonpoint** /ɑ̃bɔ̃pwɛ̃/ nm stoutness.

**embourber (s')** /(s)ɑ̃buʀbe/ vpr get stuck in the mud; (fig) get bogged down.

**embouteillage** /ɑ̃butɛjaʒ/ nm traffic jam.

**emboutir** /ɑ̃butiʀ/ **2** vt (Auto) crash into.

**embraser (s')** /(s)ɑ̃bʀaze/ vpr catch fire.

**embrasser** /ɑ̃bʀase/ **1** vt kiss; (adopter, contenir) embrace. □ s'~ vpr kiss.

**embrayage** /ɑ̃bʀɛjaʒ/ nm clutch. **embrayer** **31** vi engage the clutch.

**embrouiller** /ɑ̃bʀuje/ **1** vt confuse; (fils) tangle. □ s'~ vpr become confused.

**embryon** /ɑ̃bʀijɔ̃/ nm embryo.

**embûches** /ɑ̃byʃ/ nfpl traps.

**embuer(s')** /(s)ɑ̃bɥe/ **1** vpr mist up.

**embuscade** /ɑ̃byskad/ nf ambush.

**émeraude** /ɛmʀod/ nf emerald.

**émerger** /emɛʀʒe/ **40** vi emerge; (fig) stand out.

**émeri** /ɛmʀi/ nm emery.

**émerveillement** /emɛʀvɛjmɑ̃/ nm amazement, wonder.

**émerveiller** /emɛʀveje/ **1** vt fill with wonder. □ s'~ vpr marvel at.

**émetteur** /emetœʀ/ nm transmitter.

**émettre** /emɛtʀ/ **42** vt (son) produce; (message) send out; (timbre, billet) issue; (opinion) express.

**émeute** /emøt/ nf riot.

**émietter** /emjete/ **1** vt crumble. □ s'~ vpr crumble.

**émigrant, ~e** /emigʀɑ̃, -t/ nm, f emigrant. **émigration** nf emigration. **émigrer** **1** vi emigrate.

**émincer** /emɛ̃se/ **10** vt cut into thin slices.

**éminent, ~e** /eminɑ̃, -t/ adj eminent.

**émissaire** /emisɛʀ/ nm emissary.

**émission** /emisjɔ̃/ nf (programme) programme; (de chaleur, gaz) emission; (de timbre) issue.

**emmagasiner** /ɑ̃magazine/ **1** vt store.

**emmanchure** /ɑ̃mɑ̃ʃyʀ/ nf armhole.

**emmêler** /ɑ̃mele/ **1** vt tangle. □ s'~ vpr get mixed up.

**emménager** /ɑmenaʒe/ 40 vi move in; ~ dans move into.

**emmener** /ɑmne/ 6 vt take; (comme prisonnier) take away.

**emmerder** /ɑmɛʁde/ 1 ✖ vt ~ qn get on sb's nerves. □ s'~ vpr be bored.

**emmitoufler** /ɑmitufle/ 1 vt wrap up warmly. □ s'~ vpr wrap oneself up warmly.

**émoi** /emwa/ nm turmoil; (plaisir) excitement.

**émotif, -ive** /emotif, -v/ adj emotional. **émotion** nf emotion; (peur) fright. **émotionnel, ~le** adj emotional.

**émousser** /emuse/ 1 vt blunt.

**émouvant, ~e** /emuvɑ̃, -t/ adj moving.

**empailler** /ɑpaje/ 1 vt stuff.

**empaqueter** /ɑpakte/ 38 vt package.

**emparer (s')** /(s)ɑpaʁe/ 1 vpr s'~ de get hold of.

**empêchement** /ɑpɛʃmɑ̃/ nm avoir un ~ to be held up.

**empêcher** /ɑpeʃe/ 1 vt prevent; ~ de faire prevent ou stop (from) doing; (il) n'empêche que... □ s'~ vpr il ne peut pas s'en ~ he cannot help it.

**empereur** /ɑpʁɛʁ/ nm emperor.

**empester** /ɑpɛste/ 1 vt stink out; (essence) stink of. ● vi stink.

**empêtrer (s')** /(s)ɑpetʁe/ 1 vpr become entangled.

**empiéter** /ɑpjete/ 14 vi ~ sur encroach upon.

**empiffrer (s')** /(s)ɑpifʁe/ 1 vpr 1 stuff oneself.

**empiler** /ɑpile/ 1 vt pile up. □ s'~ vpr pile up.

**empire** /ɑpiʁ/ nm empire.

**emplacement** /ɑplasmɑ̃/ nm site.

**emplâtre** /ɑplɑtʁ/ nm (Méd) plaster.

**emploi** /ɑplwa/ nm (travail) job; (embauche) employment; (utilisation) use; un ~ de chauffeur a job as a driver; ~ du temps timetable. **employé, ~e** nm, f employee.

**employer** /ɑplwaje/ 31 vt (personne) employ; (utiliser) use. □ s'~ vpr be used; s'~ à devote oneself to. **employeur, -euse** nm, f employer.

**empoigner** /ɑpwaɲe/ 1 vt grab. □ s'~ vpr come to blows.

**empoisonnement** /ɑpwazɔnmɑ̃/ nm poisoning.

**empoisonner** /ɑpwazɔne/ 1 vt poison; (embêter 1) annoy. □ s'~ vpr to poison oneself.

**emporter** /ɑpɔʁte/ 1 vt take (away); (entraîner) sweep away; (arracher) tear off. ~ le ~ lose one's temper; l'~ get the upper hand (sur of); plat à ~ take-away.

**empote, ~e** /ɑpote/ adj clumsy.

**empreinte** /ɑpʁɛ̃t/ nf mark; ~ (digitale) fingerprint; ~ écologique carbon footprint; ~ de pas footprint.

**empressé, ~e** /ɑpʁese/ adj attentive.

**empresser (s')** /(s)ɑpʁese/ 1 vpr s'~ de hasten to; s'~ auprès de be attentive to.

**emprise** /ɑpʁiz/ nf influence.

**emprisonnement** /ɑpʁizɔnmɑ̃/ nm imprisonment. **emprisonner** 1 vt imprison.

**emprunt** /ɑpʁœ̃/ nm loan; faire un ~ take out a loan.

**emprunté, ~e** /ɑpʁœ̃te/ adj awkward.

**emprunter** /ɑpʁœ̃te/ 1 vt borrow (à from); (route) take; (fig) assume. **emprunteur, -euse** nm, f borrower.

**ému**, ~e /emy/ adj moved; (intimidé) nervous.

**émule** /emyl/ nmf imitator.

**en** /ɑ̃/

Pour les expressions comme en principe, en train de, s'en aller, etc. ➡prin-cipe, train, aller, etc.

● préposition
····▸ (lieu) in.
····▸ (avec mouvement) to.
····▸ (temps) in.
····▸ (manière, état) in; ~ faisant by ou while doing; je t'appelle ~ rentrant I will call you when I get back.
····▸ (en qualité de) as.
····▸ (transport) by.
····▸ (composition) made of; table ~ bois wooden table.

● pronom
····▸ en avoir/vouloir have/want some; ne pas ~ avoir/vouloir not have/want any; j'~ ai deux I've got two; prends-~ plusieurs take several; il m'~ reste un I have one left; j'~ suis content I am pleased with him/her/it/them; je m'~ souviens I remember it.
····▸ ~ êtes-vous sûr? are you sure?

**encadrement** /ɑ̃kadʀəmɑ̃/ nm framing; (de porte) frame. **encadrer** 1 vt frame; (entourer d'un trait) circle; (superviser) supervise.

**encaisser** /ɑ̃kese/ vt (argent) collect; (chèque) cash; (coups 1) take.

**encart** /ɑ̃kaʀ/ nm ~ publicitaire (advertising) insert.

**en-cas** /ɑ̃kɑ/ nm (stand-by) snack.

**encastré**, ~e /ɑ̃kastʀe/ adj built-in.

**encaustique** /ɑ̃kɔstik/ nf wax polish.

**enceinte** /ɑ̃sɛ̃t/ adj f pregnant; ~ de 3 mois 3 months pregnant. ● nf enclosure; ~ (acoustique) speaker.

**encens** /ɑ̃sɑ̃/ nm incense.

**encercler** /ɑ̃seʀkle/ 1 vt surround.

**enchaînement** /ɑ̃ʃɛnmɑ̃/ nm (suite) chain; (d'idées) sequence.

**enchaîner** /ɑ̃ʃene/ 1 vt chain (up); (phrases) link (up). ● vi continue. □ s'~ vpr follow on.

**enchanté**, ~e /ɑ̃ʃɑ̃te/ adj (ravi) delighted. **enchanter** 1 vt delight; (ensorceler) enchant.

**enchère** /ɑ̃ʃɛʀ/ nf bid; mettre ou vendre aux ~s sell by auction.

**enchevêtrer** /ɑ̃ʃəvetʀe/ 1 vt tangle. □ s'~ vpr become tangled.

**enclave** /ɑ̃klav/ nf enclave.

**enclencher** /ɑ̃klɑ̃ʃe/ 1 vt engage.

**enclin**, ~e /ɑ̃klɛ̃, -in/ adj ~ à inclined to.

**enclos** /ɑ̃klo/ nm enclosure.

**enclume** /ɑ̃klym/ nf anvil.

**encoche** /ɑ̃kɔʃ/ nf notch.

**encolure** /ɑ̃kɔlyʀ/ nf neck.

**encombrant**, ~e /ɑ̃kɔ̃bʀɑ̃, -t/ adj cumbersome.

**encombre** /ɑ̃kɔ̃bʀ/ nm sans ~ without any problems.

**encombrement** /ɑ̃kɔ̃bʀəmɑ̃/ nm (Auto) traffic congestion; (volume) bulk.

**encombrer** /ɑ̃kɔ̃bʀe/ 1 vt clutter (up); (obstruer) obstruct. □ s'~ de vpr burden oneself with.

**encontre:** à l'~ de /alɑ̃kɔ̃tʀədə/ loc against.

**encore** /ɑ̃kɔʀ/ adv (toujours) still; (de nouveau) again; (de plus) more;

(aussi) also; ~ **plus grand** even larger; ~ **un café** another coffee; **pas** ~ not yet; **si** ~ if only; **et puis quoi** ~? 🛈 what next?

**encouragement** /ãkuraʒmã/ nm encouragement. **encourager** 40 vt encourage.

**encourir** /ãkuRiR/ 20 vt incur.

**encrasser** /ãkRase/ 1 vt clog up (with dirt).

**encre** /ãkR/ nf ink. **encrier** nm ink-well.

**encyclopédie** /ãsiklɔpedi/ nf encyclopaedia.

**endettement** /ãdɛtmã/ nm debt.

**endetter** /ãdete/ 1 vt put into debt. □ **s'~** vpr get into debt.

**endiguer** /ãdige/ 1 vt dam; (fig) curb.

**endimanché, ~e** /ãdimãʃe/ adj in one's Sunday best.

**endive** /ãdiv/ nf chicory.

**endoctriner** /ãdɔktRine/ 1 vt indoctrinate.

**endommager** /ãdɔmaʒe/ 40 vt damage.

**endormi, ~e** /ãdɔRmi/ adj asleep; (apathique) sleepy.

**endormir** /ãdɔRmiR/ 46 vt send to sleep; (médicalement) put to sleep; (duper) dupe (**avec** with). □ **s'~** vpr fall asleep.

**endosser** /ãdose/ 1 vt (vêtement) put on; (assumer) take on; (Comm) endorse.

**endroit** /ãdRwa/ nm place; (de tissu) right side; **à l'~** the right way round; **par ~s** in places.

**enduire** /ãduiR/ 17 vt coat. **enduit** nm coating.

**endurance** /ãdyRãs/ nf endurance. **endurant, ~e** adj tough.

**endurcir** /ãdyRsiR/ 2 vt strengthen. □ **s'~** vpr become

hard (hardened).

**endurer** /ãdyRe/ 1 vt endure.

**énergétique** /enɛRʒetik/ adj energy; (food) high-calorie. **énergie** nf energy; (Tech) power. **énergique** adj energetic.

**énervant, ~e** /enɛRvã, -t/ adj irritating, annoying.

**énerver** /enɛRve/ 1 vt irritate. □ **s'~** vpr get worked up.

**enfance** /ãfãs/ nf childhood; **la petite** ~ infancy.

**enfant** /ãfã/ nmf child. **enfantillage** nm childishness. **enfantin, ~e** adj simple, easy; (puéril) childish; (jeu, langage) children's.

**enfer** /ãfɛR/ nm (Relig) Hell; (fig) hell.

**enfermer** /ãfɛRme/ 1 vt shut up. □ **s'~** vpr shut oneself up.

**enfiler** /ãfile/ 1 vt (aiguille) thread; (vêtement) slip on; (rue) take.

**enfin** /ãfɛ̃/ adv (de soulagement) at last; (en dernier lieu) finally; (résignation, conclusion) well; ~ **presque** well nearly.

**enflammé, ~e** /ãflame/ adj (Méd) inflamed; (discours) fiery; (lettre) passionate.

**enflammer** /ãflame/ 1 vt set fire to. □ **s'~** vpr catch fire.

**enfler** /ãfle/ 1 vt (histoire) exaggerate. ● vi (partie du corps) swell (up); (mer) swell; (rumeur, colère) spread. □ **s'~** vpr (colère) mount; (rumeur) grow.

**enfoncer** /ãfõse/ 10 vt (épingle) push ou drive in; (chapeau) push down; (porte) break down. ● vi sink. □ **s'~** vpr sink (**dans** into).

**enfouir** /ãfwiR/ 2 vt bury.

**enfourcher** /ãfuRʃe/ 1 vt mount.

**enfreindre** /ãfRɛdR/ 22 vt infringe, break.

**enfuir (s')** /(s)ãfчir/ 35 vpr run away.

**enfumé,** ~e /ãfyme/ adj filled with smoke.

**engagé,** ~e /ãgaʒe/ adj committed.

**engagement** /ãgaʒmã/ nm (promesse) promise; (Pol, Comm) commitment.

**engager** /ãgaʒe/ 40 vt (lier) bind, commit; (embaucher) take on; (commencer) start; (introduire) insert; (investir) invest. □ **s'~** vpr (promettre) commit oneself; (commencer) start; (soldat) enlist; (concurrent) enter; **s'~ à faire** undertake to do; **s'~ dans** (voie) enter.

**engelure** /ãʒlyr/ nf chilblain.

**engendrer** /ãʒãdre/ 1 vt (causer) generate.

**engin** /ãʒɛ̃/ nm device; (véhicule) vehicle; (missile) missile.

**engloutir** /ãglutir/ 2 vt swallow (up).

**engouement** /ãgumã/ nm passion.

**engouffrer** /ãgufre/ 1 vt 1 gobble up. □ **s'~** vpr rush in.

**engourdir** /ãgurdir/ 2 vt numb. □ **s'~** vpr go numb.

**engrais** /ãgrɛ/ nm manure; (chimique) fertilizer.

**engrenage** /ãgrənaʒ/ nm gears (+ pl); (fig) spiral.

**engueuler** /ãgœle/ 1 ✗ vt shout at. □ **s'~** vpr have a row.

**enhardir (s')** /(s)ãardir/ 2 vpr become bolder.

**énième** /ɛnjɛm/ adj umpteenth.

**énigmatique** /enigmatik/ adj enigmatic. **énigme** nf enigma; (devinette) riddle.

**enivrer (s')** /ãnivre/ 1 vt intoxicate. □ **s'~** vpr get intoxicated.

**enjambée** /ãʒãbe/ nf stride. **enjamber** 1 vt step over; (pont) span.

**enjeu** (pl ~x) /ãʒø/ nm stake.

**enjoué,** ~e /ãʒwe/ adj cheerful.

**enlacer** /ãlase/ 10 vt entwine.

**enlèvement** /ãlɛvmã/ nm (de colis) removal; (d'ordures) collection; (rapt) kidnapping.

**enlever** /ãlve/ 6 vt remove (à from); (vêtement) take off; (tache, organe) take out; remove; (kidnapper) kidnap; (gagner) win.

**enliser (s')** /(s)ãlize/ 1 vpr get bogged down.

**enneigé,** ~e /ãneʒe/ adj snowcovered.

**ennemi,** ~e /ɛnmi/ adj & nm enemy; ~ **de** (fig) hostile to.

**ennui** /ãnqi/ nm problem; (tracas) boredom; **s'attirer des ~s** run into trouble.

**ennuyer** /ãnqije/ 31 vt bore; (irriter) annoy; (préoccuper) worry; **si cela ne t'ennuie pas** if you don't mind. □ **s'~** vpr get bored.

**ennuyeux, -euse** /ãnqijø, -z/ adj boring; (fâcheux) annoying.

**énoncé** /enõse/ nm wording, text; (Gram) utterance.

**énoncer** /enõse/ 10 vt express, state.

**enorgueillir (s')** /(s)ãnorgœjir/ 2 vpr **s'~ de** pride oneself on.

**énorme** /enɔrm/ adj enormous.

**enquête** /ãkɛt/ nf (Jur) investigation, inquiry; (sondage) survey; **mener l'~** lead the inquiry. **enquêter** 1 vi ~ **(sur)** investigate. **enquêteur, -euse** nm, f investigator.

**enquiquinant,** ~e /ãkikinã, -t/ adj 1 irritating.

**enraciné,** ~e /ãrasine/ adj deeprooted.

**enragé**, ~e /ɑ̃ʀaʒe/ adj furious; (chien) rabid; (fig) fanatical.

**enrager** /ɑ̃ʀaʒe/ **40** vi be furious; faire ~ qn annoy sb.

**enregistrement** /ɑ̃ʀ(ə)ʒistʀəmɑ̃/ nm recording; (des bagages) check-in. **enregistrer** **1** vt (Mus, TV) record; (mémoriser) take in; (bagages) check in.

**enrhumer (s')** /(s)ɑ̃ʀyme/ **1** vpr catch a cold.

**enrichir** /ɑ̃ʀiʃiʀ/ **2** vt enrich. □ s'~ vpr grow rich(er). **enrichissant**, ~e adj (expérience) rewarding.

**enrober** /ɑ̃ʀɔbe/ **1** vt coat (de with).

**enrôler** /ɑ̃ʀole/ **1** vt recruit. □ s'~ vpr enlist, enrol.

**enroué**, ~e /ɑ̃ʀwe/ adj hoarse.

**enrouler** /ɑ̃ʀule/ **1** vt wind, wrap. □ s'~ vpr wind; s'~ dans une couverture roll oneself up in a blanket.

**ensanglanté**, ~e /ɑ̃sɑ̃glɑ̃te/ adj bloodstained.

**enseignant**, ~e /ɑ̃sɛɲɑ̃, -t/ nm, f teacher. ● adj teaching.

**enseigne** /ɑ̃sɛɲ/ nf sign.

**enseignement** /ɑ̃sɛɲəmɑ̃/ nm (profession) teaching; (instruction) education.

**enseigner** /ɑ̃sɛɲe/ **1** vt/i teach; ~ qch à qn teach sb sth.

**ensemble** /ɑ̃sɑ̃bl/ adv together. ● nm group; (Mus) ensemble; (vêtements) outfit; (cohésion) unity; (maths) set; dans l'~ on the whole; d'~ (idée) general; l'~ de (totalité) all of, the whole of.

**ensevelir** /ɑ̃səvliʀ/ **2** vt bury.

**ensoleillé**, ~e /ɑ̃sɔleje/ adj sunny.

**ensorceler** /ɑ̃sɔʀsəle/ **38** vt bewitch.

**ensuite** /ɑ̃sɥit/ adv next, then; (plus tard) later.

**ensuivre (s')** /(s)ɑ̃sɥivʀ/ **57** vpr follow; et tout ce qui s'ensuit and all the rest of it.

**entaille** /ɑ̃tɑj/ nf cut; (profonde) gash; (encoche) notch.

**entamer** /ɑ̃tame/ **1** vt start; (inciser) cut into; (ébranler) shake.

**entasser** /ɑ̃tase/ **1** vt (livres) pile; (argent) hoard; (personnes) cram (dans into). □ s'~ vpr (objets) pile up (dans into); (personnes) squeeze (dans into).

**entendement** /ɑ̃tɑ̃dmɑ̃/ nm understanding; ça dépasse l'~ it's beyond belief.

**entendre** /ɑ̃tɑ̃dʀ/ **3** vt hear; (comprendre) understand; (vouloir dire) mean; ~ parler de hear of; ~ dire que hear that. □ s'~ vpr (être d'accord) agree; (bien) get on (avec with); cela s'entend of course.

**entendu**, ~e /ɑ̃tɑ̃dy/ adj (convenu) agreed; (sourire, air) knowing; bien ~ of course; (c'est) ~! all right!

**entente** /ɑ̃tɑ̃t/ nf understanding; bonne ~ good relationship.

**enterrement** /ɑ̃tɛʀmɑ̃/ nm funeral.

**enterrer** /ɑ̃teʀe/ **1** vt bury.

**en-tête** /ɑ̃tɛt/ nm heading; à ~ headed.

**entêté**, ~e /ɑ̃tete/ adj stubborn. **entêtement** nm stubbornness. **entêter (s')** **1** vpr persist (à, dans in).

**enthousiasme** /ɑ̃tuzjasm/ nm enthusiasm. **enthousiasmer** **1** vt fill with enthusiasm. **enthousiaste** adj enthusiastic.

**enticher (s')** /(s)ɑ̃tiʃe/ **1** vpr s'~ de become infatuated with.

**entier**, -ière /ɑ̃tje, -jɛʀ/ adj whole; (absolu) absolute; (entêté) unyielding. ● nm whole; en ~ entirely.

**entonnoir** /ɑ̃tɔnwaʀ/ nm funnel; (trou) crater.

**entorse** /ɑ̃tɔʀs/ nf sprain; (fig) ~ à (loi) infringement of.

**entortiller** /ɑ̃tɔʀtije/ **1** vt wind, wrap (autour around); (duper 🔢) get round.

**entourage** /ɑ̃tuʀaʒ/ nm circle of family and friends; (bordure) surround.

**entouré**, ~e /ɑ̃tuʀe/ adj (personne) supported.

**entourer** /ɑ̃tuʀe/ **1** vt surround (de with); (réconforter) rally round; ~ qch de mystère shroud sth in mystery.

**entracte** /ɑ̃tʀakt/ nm interval.

**entraide** /ɑ̃tʀɛd/ nf mutual aid. **entraider (s')** **1** vpr help each other.

**entrain** /ɑ̃tʀɛ̃/ nm zest, spirit.

**entraînement** /ɑ̃tʀɛnmɑ̃/ nm (Sport) training.

**entraîner** /ɑ̃tʀene/ **1** vt (emporter) carry away; (provoquer) lead to; (Sport) train; (actionner) drive. □ s'~ vpr train. **entraîneur** nm trainer.

**entrave** /ɑ̃tʀav/ nf hindrance. **entraver** **1** vt hinder.

**entre** /ɑ̃tʀ(ə)/ prép between; (parmi) among(st); ~ autres among other things; l'un d'~ nous/eux one of us/them.

**entrebâillé**, ~e /ɑ̃tʀəbɑje/ adj ajar, half-open.

**entrechoquer (s')** /(s)ɑ̃tʀə ʃɔke/ **1** vpr knock against each other.

**entrecôte** /ɑ̃tʀəkot/ nf rib steak.

**entrecouper** /ɑ̃tʀəkupe/ **1** vt ~ de intersperse with.

**entrecroiser (s')** /(s)ɑ̃tʀə kʀwaze/ **1** vpr (routes) intertwine.

**entrée** /ɑ̃tʀe/ nf entrance; (vesti-

bule) hall; (accès) admission, entry; (billet) ticket; (Culin) starter; (Ordinat) tapez sur E~ press Enter; '~ interdite' 'no entry'.

**entrejambes** /ɑ̃tʀəʒɑ̃b/ nm crotch.

**entremets** /ɑ̃tʀəmɛ/ nm dessert.

**entremise** /ɑ̃tʀəmiz/ nf intervention; par l'~ de through.

**entreposer** /ɑ̃tʀəpoze/ **1** vt store.

**entrepôt** /ɑ̃tʀəpo/ nm warehouse.

**entreprenant**, ~e /ɑ̃tʀəpʀənɑ̃, -t/ adj (actif) enterprising; (séducteur) forward.

**entreprendre** /ɑ̃tʀəpʀɑ̃dʀ/ **50** vt start on, undertake; (personne) buttonhole; ~ de faire undertake to do.

**entrepreneur** /ɑ̃tʀəpʀənœʀ/ nm (de bâtiment) contractor; (chef d'entreprise) firm manager.

**entreprise** /ɑ̃tʀəpʀiz/ nf (projet) undertaking; (société) firm, business, company.

**entrer** /ɑ̃tʀe/ **1** vi (aux être) go in, enter; (venir) come in, enter; ~ dans go ou come into, enter; (club) join; ~ en collision collide (avec with); faire ~ (personne) show in; laisser ~ let in; ~ en guerre go to war. ● vt (données) enter.

**entre-temps** /ɑ̃tʀətɑ̃/ adv meanwhile.

**entretenir** /ɑ̃tʀət(ə)niʀ/ **58** vt (appareil) maintain; (vêtement) look after; (alimenter) (feu) keep going; (amitié) keep alive; ~ qn de converse with sb about. □ s'~ vpr speak (de about; avec to). **entretien** nm maintenance; (discussion) talk; (pour un emploi) interview.

**entrevoir** /ɑ̃tʀəvwaʀ/ **63** vt make out; (brièvement) glimpse.

**entrevue** /ɑ̃tʀəvy/ nf meeting.

**entrouvert**, ~e /ɑ̃tʀuvɛʀ, -t/ adj ajar, half-open.

**énumération** /enymeʀasjɔ̃/ nf enumeration. **énumérer** 14 vt enumerate.

**envahir** /ɑ̃vaiʀ/ 2 vt invade, overrun; (douleur, peur) overcome.

**enveloppe** /ɑ̃vlɔp/ nf envelope; (emballage) wrapping; ~ budgétaire budget. **envelopper** 1 vt wrap (up); (fig) envelop.

**envergure** /ɑ̃vɛʀgyʀ/ nf wingspan; (importance) scope; (qualité) calibre.

**envers** /ɑ̃vɛʀ/ prép toward(s), to. ● nm (de tissu) wrong side; à l'~ (tableau) upside down; (devant derrière) back to front; (chaussette) inside out.

**envie** /ɑ̃vi/ nf urge; (jalousie) envy; avoir ~ de qch feel like sth; avoir ~ de faire want to do; (moins urgent) feel like doing; faire ~ à qn make sb envious.

**envier** /ɑ̃vje/ 45 vt envy. **envieux, -ieuse** adj envious.

**environ** /ɑ̃viʀɔ̃/ adv about.

**environnant**, ~e /ɑ̃viʀɔnɑ̃, -t/ adj surrounding.

**environnement** /ɑ̃viʀɔnmɑ̃/ nm environment.

**environs** /ɑ̃viʀɔ̃/ nmpl vicinity; aux ~ de (lieu) in the vicinity of; (heure) round about.

**envisager** /ɑ̃vizaʒe/ 40 vt consider; (imaginer) envisage; ~ de faire consider doing.

**envoi** /ɑ̃vwa/ nm dispatch; (paquet) consignment; faire un ~ send; coup d'~ (Sport) kick-off.

**envoler (s')** /(s)ɑ̃vɔle/ 1 vpr fly away; (avion) take off; (papiers) blow away.

**envoyé**, ~e /ɑ̃vwaje/ nm, f envoy; ~ spécial special correspondent.

**envoyer** /ɑ̃vwaje/ 32 vt send; (lancer) throw.

**éolienne** /eɔljɛn/ nf windmill; ferme d'~s wind farm.

**épais**, ~se /epɛ, -s/ adj thick. **épaisseur** nf thickness.

**épaissir** /epesiʀ/ 2 vt/i thicken. □ s'~ vpr thicken; (mystère) deepen.

**épanoui**, ~e /epanwi/ adj (personne) beaming, radiant.

**épanouir (s')** /(s)epanwiʀ/ 2 vpr (fleur) open out; (visage) beam; (personne) blossom. **épanouissement** nm (éclat) blossoming, full bloom.

**épargne** /epaʀɲ/ nf savings.

**épargner** /epaʀɲe/ 1 vt/i save; (ne pas tuer) spare; ~ qch à qn spare sb sth.

**éparpiller** /epaʀpije/ 1 vt scatter. □ s'~ vpr scatter; (fig) dissipate one's efforts.

**épars**, ~e /epaʀ, -s/ adj scattered.

**épatant**, ~e /epatɑ̃, -t/ adj 1 amazing.

**épaule** /epol/ nf shoulder.

**épave** /epav/ nf wreck.

**épée** /epe/ nf sword.

**épeler** /ɛple/ 6 vt spell.

**éperdu**, ~e /epɛʀdy/ adj wild, frantic.

**éperon** /epʀɔ̃/ nm spur.

**éphémère** /efemɛʀ/ adj ephemeral.

**épi** /epi/ nm (de blé) ear; (mèche) tuft of hair; ~ de maïs corn cob.

**épice** /epis/ nf spice. **épicé**, ~e adj spicy.

**épicerie** /episʀi/ nf grocery shop; (produits) groceries. **épicier, -ière** nm, f grocer.

**épidémie** /epidemi/ nf epidemic.

**épiderme** /epidɛʀm/ nm skin.

**épier** /epje/ 45 vt spy on.

**épilepsie** /epilɛpsi/ *nf* epilepsy. **épileptique** *adj* & *nmf* epileptic.

**épiler** /epile/ **1** *vt* remove unwanted hair from; (*sourcils*) pluck.

**épilogue** /epilɔg/ *nm* epilogue; (fig) outcome.

**épinard** /epinar/ *nm* ~s spinach (+ *sg*).

**épine** /epin/ *nf* thorn, prickle; (d'animal) prickle, spine; ~ dorsale backbone. **épineux, -euse** *adj* thorny.

**épingle** /epɛ̃gl/ *nf* pin; ~ de nourrice, ~ de sûreté safety-pin.

**épisode** /epizɔd/ *nm* episode; à ~s serialized.

**épitaphe** /epitaf/ *nf* epitaph.

**épluche-légumes** /eplyʃlegym/ *nm inv* (potato) peeler.

**éplucher** /eplyʃe/ **1** *vt* peel; (examiner: fig) scrutinize.

**épluchure** /eplyʃyr/ *nf* ~s peelings.

**éponge** /epɔ̃ʒ/ *nf* sponge. **éponger** **40** *vt* (*liquide*) mop up; (*surface, front*) mop; (fig) (*dettes*) wipe out.

**épopée** /epɔpe/ *nf* epic.

**époque** /epɔk/ *nf* time, period; à l'~ at the time; d'~ period.

**épouse** /epuz/ *nf* wife.

**épouser** /epuze/ **1** *vt* marry; (*forme, idée*) adopt.

**épousseter** /epuste/ **38** *vt* dust.

**épouvantable** /epuvɑ̃tabl/ *adj* appalling.

**épouvantail** /epuvɑ̃taj/ *nm* scarecrow.

**épouvante** /epuvɑ̃t/ *nf* terror. **épouvanter** **1** *vt* terrify.

**époux** /epu/ *nm* husband; les ~ the married couple.

**éprendre (s')** /(s)eprɑ̃dr/ **50** *vpr* s'~ de fall in love with.

**épreuve** /eprœv/ *nf* test; (Sport)

event; (*malheur*) ordeal; (Photo, d'imprimerie) proof; mettre à l'~ put to the test.

**éprouver** /epruve/ **1** *vt* (ressentir) experience; (*affliger*) distress; (tester) test.

**éprouvette** /epruvɛt/ *nf* test tube.

**EPS** *abrév f* (**éducation physique et sportive**) PE.

**épuisé, ~e** /epɥize/ *adj* exhausted; (*livre*) out of print. **épuisement** *nm* exhaustion.

**épuiser** /epɥize/ **1** *vt* (fatiguer, user) exhaust. □ **s'~** *vpr* become exhausted.

**épuration** /epyrasjɔ̃/ *nf* purification; (Pol) purge. **épurer** **1** *vt* purify; (Pol) purge.

**équateur** /ekwatœr/ *nm* equator.

**équilibre** /ekilibr/ *nm* balance; être *ou* se tenir en ~ (*personne*) balance; (*objet*) be balanced. **équilibré, ~e** *adj* well-balanced.

**équilibrer** /ekilibre/ **1** *vt* balance. □ **s'~** *vpr* balance each other.

**équilibriste** /ekilibrist/ *nmf* acrobat.

**équipage** /ekipaʒ/ *nm* crew.

**équipe** /ekip/ *nf* team; ~ de nuit/jour night/day shift.

**équipé, ~e** /ekipe/ *adj* equipped; cuisine ~e fitted kitchen.

**équipement** /ekipmɑ̃/ *nm* equipment; ~s (installations) amenities, facilities.

**équiper** /ekipe/ **1** *vt* equip (de with). □ **s'~** *vpr* equip oneself.

**équipier, -ière** /ekipje, -jɛr/ *nm, f* team member.

**équitable** /ekitabl/ *adj* fair.

**équitation** /ekitasjɔ̃/ *nf* (horse-)riding.

**équivalence** /ekivalɑ̃s/ *nf* equivalence. **équivalent**, ∼e *adj* equivalent.

**équivaloir** /ekivalwaʀ/ 60 *vi* ∼ à be equivalent to.

**équivoque** /ekivɔk/ *adj* equivocal; (louche) questionable. ● *nf* ambiguity.

**érable** /eʀabl/ *nm* maple.

**érafler** /eʀafle/ 1 *vt* scratch. **éraflure** *nf* scratch.

**éraillé**, ∼e /eʀaje/ *adj* (*voix*) raucous.

**ère** /eʀ/ *nf* era.

**éreintant**, ∼e /eʀɛ̃tɑ̃, -t/ *adj* exhausting. **éreinter (s')** 1 *vpr* wear oneself out.

**ériger** /eʀiʒe/ 40 *vt* erect. □ **s'∼ en** *vpr* set (oneself) up as.

**éroder** /eʀɔde/ 1 *vt* erode. **érosion** *nf* erosion.

**errer** /eʀe/ 1 *vi* wander.

**erreur** /eʀœʀ/ *nf* mistake, error; dans l'∼ mistaken; par ∼ by mistake; ∼ judiciaire miscarriage of justice.

**erroné**, ∼e /eʀɔne/ *adj* erroneous.

**érudit**, ∼e /eʀydi, -t/ *adj* scholarly. ● *nm, f* scholar.

**éruption** /eʀypsjɔ̃/ *nf* eruption; (Méd) rash.

**es** /ɛ/ ➡ÊTRE 4.

**escabeau** (*pl* ∼x) /ɛskabo/ *nm* step-ladder.

**escadron** /ɛskadʀɔ̃/ *nm* (Mil) company.

**escalade** /ɛskalad/ *nf* climbing; (Pol, Comm) escalation. **escalader** 1 *vt* climb.

**escale** /ɛskal/ *nf* (d'avion) stopover; (port) port of call; faire ∼ à (*avion, passager*) stop over at; (*navire, passager*) put in at.

**escalier** /ɛskalje/ *nm* stairs (+ *pl*); ∼ mécanique *ou* roulant escalator.

**escalope** /ɛskalɔp/ *nf* escalope.

**escargot** /ɛskaʀgo/ *nm* snail.

**escarpé**, ∼e /ɛskaʀpe/ *adj* steep.

**escarpin** /ɛskaʀpɛ̃/ *nm* court shoe; (US) pump.

**escient**: à bon ∼ /abɔnesjɑ̃/ *loc* wisely.

**esclandre** /ɛsklɑ̃dʀ/ *nm* scene.

**esclavage** /ɛsklavaʒ/ *nm* slavery. **esclave** *nmf* slave.

**escompte** /ɛskɔ̃t/ *nm* discount. **escompter** 1 *vt* expect; (Comm) discount.

**escorte** /ɛskɔʀt/ *nf* escort.

**escrime** /ɛskʀim/ *nf* fencing.

**escroc** /ɛskʀo/ *nm* swindler.

**escroquer** /ɛskʀɔke/ 1 *vt* swindle; ∼ qch à qn swindle sb out of sth. **escroquerie** *nf* swindle.

**espace** /ɛspas/ *nm* space; ∼s verts gardens and parks.

**espacer** /ɛspase/ 10 *vt* space out. □ **s'∼** *vpr* become less frequent.

**espadrille** /ɛspadʀij/ *nf* rope sandal.

**Espagne** /ɛspaɲ/ *nf* Spain.

**espagnol**, ∼e /ɛspaɲɔl/ *adj* Spanish. ● *nm* (Ling) Spanish. **E∼**, ∼e *nm, f* Spaniard.

**espèce** /ɛspɛs/ *nf* kind, sort; (race) species; en ∼s (*argent*) in cash; ∼ d'idiot! 🅸 you idiot! 🅸.

**espérance** /ɛspeʀɑ̃s/ *nf* hope.

**espérer** /ɛspeʀe/ 14 *vt* hope for; ∼ faire/que hope to do/that. ● *vi* hope.

**espiègle** /ɛspjɛgl/ *adj* mischievous.

**espion**, ∼ne /ɛspjɔ̃, -ɔn/ *nm, f* spy. **espionnage** *nm* espionage, spying. **espionner** 1 *vt* spy (on).

**espoir** /ɛspwaʀ/ *nm* hope; reprendre ∼ feel hopeful again.

**esprit** /ɛspʀi/ *nm* (intellect) mind; (humour) wit; (fantôme) spirit; (ambiance) atmosphere; **perdre l'~** lose one's mind; **reprendre ses ~s** come to; **faire de l'~** try to be witty.

**esquimau**, ~de (mpl ~x) /ɛskimo, -d/ nm, f Eskimo.

**esquinter** /ɛskɛ̃te/ **1** vt ruin.

**esquisse** /ɛskis/ nf sketch; (fig) outline.

**esquiver** /ɛskive/ **1** vt dodge. □ **s'~** vpr slip away.

**essai** /esɛ/ nm (épreuve) test, trial; (tentative) (article) essay; (au rugby) try; ~s (Auto) qualifying round (+ sg); **à l'~** on trial.

**essaim** /esɛ̃/ nm swarm.

**essayage** /esɛjaʒ/ nm fitting; **salon d'~** fitting room.

**essayer** /eseje/ **31** vt/i try; (vêtement) try (on); (voiture) try (out); ~ **de faire** try to do.

**essence** /esɑ̃s/ nf (carburant) petrol; (nature, extrait) essence; ~ **sans plomb** unleaded petrol.

**essentiel**, ~le /esɑ̃sjɛl/ adj essential. ● nm **l'~** the main thing; (quantité) the main part.

**essieu** (pl ~x) /esjø/ nm axle.

**essor** /esɔʀ/ nm expansion; **prendre son ~** expand.

**essorage** /esɔʀaʒ/ nm spin drying.

**essorer** /esɔʀe/ **1** vt (linge) spin-dry; (en tordant) wring.

**essoreuse** /esɔʀøz/ nf spin-drier; ~ **à salade** salad spinner.

**essoufflé**, ~e /esufle/ adj out of breath.

**essuie-glace** /esɥiglas/ nm inv windscreen wiper.

**essuie-mains** /esɥimɛ̃/ nm inv hand-towel.

**essuie-tout** /esɥitu/ nm inv kitchen paper.

**essuyer** /esɥije/ **31** vt wipe; (subir) suffer. □ **s'~** vpr dry ou wipe oneself.

**est¹** /ɛ/ ⇒**ÊTRE** **4**.

**est²** /ɛst/ nm east. ● adj inv east; (partie) eastern; (direction) easterly.

**estampe** /ɛstɑ̃p/ nf print.

**esthète** /ɛstɛt/ nmf aesthete.

**esthéticienne** /ɛstetisjɛn/ nf beautician.

**esthétique** /ɛstetik/ adj aesthetic.

**estimation** /ɛstimasjɔ̃/ nf (de coûts) estimate; (valeur) valuation.

**estime** /ɛstim/ nf esteem.

**estimer** /ɛstime/ **1** vt (tableau) value; (calculer) estimate; (respecter) esteem; (considérer) consider (que that).

**estival**, ~e (mpl ~aux) /ɛstival, -o/ adj summer. **estivant**, ~e nm, f summer visitor.

**estomac** /ɛstɔma/ nm stomach.

**estomaqué**, ~e /ɛstɔmake/ adj **1** stunned.

**Estonie** /ɛstɔni/ nf Estonia.

**estrade** /ɛstʀad/ nf platform.

**estragon** /ɛstʀagɔ̃/ nm tarragon.

**estropié**, ~e /ɛstʀɔpje/ nm, f cripple. ● adj crippled.

**estuaire** /ɛstɥɛʀ/ nm estuary.

**et** /e/ conj and; ~ **moi?** what about me?; ~ **alors?** so what?

**étable** /etabl/ nf cow-shed.

**établi**, ~e /etabli/ adj established; **un fait bien ~** a well-established fact. ● nm work-bench.

**établir** /etabliʀ/ **2** vt establish; (liste, facture) draw up; (personne, camp, record) set up. □ **s'~** vpr (personne) settle; **s'~ à son compte** set up on one's own.

**établissement** /etablismɑ̃/ nm (entreprise) organization; (institution) establishment; ~ **scolaire** school.

**étage** /etaʒ/ nm floor, storey; (de fusée) stage; à l'~ upstairs; au premier ~ on the first floor.

**étagère** /etaʒɛʀ/ nf shelf; (meuble) shelving unit.

**étain** /etɛ̃/ nm pewter.

**étais, était** /etɛ/ ⇒ÊTRE 4.

**étalage** /etalaʒ/ nm display; (vitrine) shop-window; faire ~ de flaunt. **étalagiste** nmf window-dresser.

**étaler** /etale/ 1 vt spread out; (journal) spread (out); (pâte) roll out; (exposer) display; (richesse) flaunt. □ s'~ vpr (prendre de la place) spread out; (tomber 🗓) fall flat; s'~ sur (paiement) be spread over.

**étalon** /etalɔ̃/ nm (cheval) stallion; (modèle) standard.

**étanche** /etɑ̃ʃ/ adj watertight; (montre) waterproof.

**étancher** /etɑ̃ʃe/ 1 vt (soif) quench.

**étang** /etɑ̃/ nm pond.

**étant** /etɑ̃/ ⇒ÊTRE 4.

**étape** /etap/ nf stage; (lieu d'arrêt) stopover; (fig) stage.

**état** /eta/ nm state; (liste) statement; (métier) profession; en bon/mauvais ~ in good/bad condition; en ~ de in a position to; en ~ de marche in working order; faire ~ de (citer) mention; être dans tous ses ~s be in a state; ~ civil civil status; ~ des lieux inventory of fixtures. **État** nm State.

**état-major** (pl **états-majors**) /etamaʒɔʀ/ nm (officiers) staff (+ pl).

**États-Unis** /etazyni/ nmpl ~ (d'Amérique) United States (of America).

**étau** (pl ~x) /eto/ nm vice.

**étayer** /eteje/ 51 vt prop up.

**été¹** /ete/ ⇒ÊTRE 4.

**été²** /ete/ nm summer.

**éteindre** /etɛ̃dʀ/ 22 vt (feu) put out; (lumière, radio) turn off. □ s'~ vpr (feu, lumière) go out; (appareil) go off; (mourir) die. **éteint, ~e** adj (feu) out; (volcan) extinct.

**étendard** /etɑ̃daʀ/ nm standard.

**étendre** /etɑ̃dʀ/ 3 vt (nappe) spread (out); (bras, jambes) stretch (out); (linge) hang out; (agrandir) extend. □ s'~ vpr (s'allonger) lie down; (se propager) spread; (plaine) stretch; s'~ sur (sujet) dwell on.

**étendu, ~e** /etɑ̃dy/ adj extensive. **étendue** nf area; (d'eau) stretch; (importance) extent.

**éternel, ~le** /etɛʀnɛl/ adj (vie) eternal; (fig) endless.

**éterniser (s')** /(s)etɛʀnize/ 1 vpr (durer) drag on.

**éternité** /etɛʀnite/ nf eternity.

**éternuement** /etɛʀnymɑ̃/ nm sneeze. **éternuer** /etɛʀnɥe/ 1 vi sneeze.

**êtes** /ɛt/ ⇒ÊTRE 4.

**éthique** /etik/ adj ethical. ●nf ethics (+ sg).

**ethnie** /ɛtni/ nf ethnic group. **ethnique** adj ethnic.

**étincelant, ~e** /etɛ̃slɑ̃, -t/ adj sparkling. **étinceler** 38 vi sparkle. **étincelle** nf spark.

**étiqueter** /etikte/ 38 vt label. **étiquette** nf label; (protocole) etiquette.

**étirer** /etire/ 1 vt stretch. □ s'~ vpr stretch.

**étoffe** /etɔf/ nf fabric.

**étoffer** /etɔfe/ 1 vt expand. □ s'~ vpr fill out.

**étoile** /etwal/ nf star; à la belle ~ in the open; ~ filante shooting star; ~ de mer starfish.

**étonnant, ~e** /etɔnɑ̃, -t/ adj (curieux) surprising; (formidable) amazing. **étonnement** nm surprise; (plus fort) amazement.

e

**étonner** /etɔne/ **1** vt amaze.
□ **s'~** vpr be amazed (de at).

**étouffant, ~e** /etufɑ̃, -t/ adj
stifling.

**étouffer** /etufe/ **1** vt/i suffocate;
(sentiment, révolte) stifle; (feu)
smother; (bruit) muffle; **on étouffe**
it is stifling. □ **s'~** vpr suffocate; (en
mangeant) choke.

**étourderie** /eturdɛri/ nf thoughtlessness; (acte) careless mistake.

**étourdi, ~e** /eturdi/ adj absent-
minded. ● nm, f scatterbrain.

**étourdir** /eturdir/ **2** vt stun; (fatiguer) make sb's head spin. **étour-
dissant, ~e** adj stunning.

**étourneau** (pl ~x) /eturno/ nm
starling.

**étrange** /etrɑ̃ʒ/ adj strange.

**étranger, -ère** /etrɑ̃ʒe, -ɛr/ adj
(inconnu) strange, unfamiliar; (d'un
autre pays) foreign. ● nm, f foreigner; (inconnu) stranger; **à l'~**
abroad; **de l'~** from abroad.

**étrangler** /etrɑ̃gle/ **1** vt strangle;
(col) throttle. □ **s'~** vpr choke.

**être** /ɛtr/ **4**
● **verbe auxiliaire**
••••► (du passé) have; **elle est
partie/venue hier** she left/came
yesterday.
••••► (de la voix passive) be.
● **verbe intransitif** (aux avoir)
••••► be; **~ médecin** be a doctor;
**je suis à vous** I'm all yours; **j'en
suis à me demander si...** I'm
beginning to wonder whether...;
**qu'en est-il de...?** what's the
news about...?
••••► (appartenance) belong to.
••••► (heure, date) be; **nous sommes le 3 mars** it's March 3.

••••► (aller) be; **je n'y ai jamais
été** I've never been; **il a été le
voir** he went to see him.
••••► **c'est** it is or it's; **c'est moi
qui l'ai fait** I did it; **est-ce que
tu veux du thé?** do you want
some tea?
● **nom masculin**
••••► being; **~ humain** human
being.
••••► (personne) person; **un ~
cher** a loved one.

**étreindre** /etrɛ̃dr/ **22** vt embrace.

**étreinte** /etrɛ̃t/ nf embrace.

**étrennes** /etrɛn/ nfpl (New Year's)
gift (+ sg); (argent) money.

**étrier** /etrije/ nm stirrup.

**étriqué, ~e** /etrike/ adj tight.

**étroit, ~e** /etrwa, -t/ adj narrow;
(vêtement) tight; (liens, surveillance)
close; **à l'~** cramped. **étroitement**
adv closely. **étroitesse** nf nar-
rowness.

**étude** /etyd/ nf study; (enquête)
survey; (bureau) office; (salle d')~
(Scol) prep room; **à l'~** under consideration; **faire des ~s (de)** study;
**il n'a pas fait d'~s** he didn't go to
university; **~ de marché** market research.

**étudiant, ~e** /etydjɑ̃, -t/ nm, f
student.

**étudier** /etydje/ **45** vt/i study.

**étui** /etɥi/ nm case.

**étuve** /etyv/ nf steam room.

**eu, ~e** /y/ ⇒AVOIR **5**.

**euro** /øro/ nm euro.

**Europe** /ørɔp/ nf Europe.

**européen, ~ne** /øropeɛ̃, -eɛn/ adj
European. **E~, ~ne** nm, f European.

**euthanasie** /øtanazi/ nf euthanasia.

**eux** /ø/ pron they; (complément)
them. **eux-mêmes** pron themselves.

**évacuation** /evakɥasjɔ̃/ nf evacuation; (d'eaux usées) discharge. **évacuer 1** vt evacuate.

**évadé**, ~e /evade/ adj escaped. ●nm, f escaped prisoner. **évader (s') 1** vpr escape.

**évaluation** /evalɥasjɔ̃/ nf assessment. **évaluer 1** vt assess.

**évangile** /evɑ̃ʒil/ nm gospel; l'É~ the Gospel.

**évanouir (s')** /(s)evanwiʀ/ 2 vpr faint; (disparaître) vanish.

**évaporation** /evapɔʀasjɔ̃/ nf evaporation. **évaporer (s') 1** vpr evaporate.

**évasif**, -ive /evazif, -v/ adj evasive.

**évasion** /evazjɔ̃/ nf escape.

**éveil** /evɛj/ nm awakening; en ~ alert.

**éveillé**, ~e /eveje/ adj awake; (intelligent) alert.

**éveiller** /eveje/ 1 vt awake(n); (susciter) arouse. □ s'~ vpr awake.

**événement** /evɛnmɑ̃/ nm event.

**éventail** /evɑ̃taj/ nm fan; (gamme) range.

**éventrer** /evɑ̃tʀe/ 1 vt (sac) rip open.

**éventualité** /evɑ̃tɥalite/ nf possibility; dans cette ~ in that event.

**éventuel**, ~le /evɑ̃tɥɛl/ adj possible. **éventuellement** adv possibly.

**évêque** /evɛk/ nm bishop.

**évertuer (s')** /(s)evɛʀtɥe/ 1 vpr s'~ à struggle hard to.

**éviction** /eviksjɔ̃/ nf eviction.

**évidemment** /evidamɑ̃/ adv obviously; (bien sûr) of course.

**évidence** /evidɑ̃s/ nf obviousness; (fait) obvious fact; être en ~ be conspicuous; mettre en ~ (fait) highlight. **évident**, ~e adj obvious, evident.

**évier** /evje/ nm sink.

**évincer** /evɛ̃se/ 10 vt oust.

**éviter** /evite/ 1 vt avoid (de faire doing); ~ qch à qn (dérangement) save sb sth.

**évocateur**, -trice /evɔkatœʀ, -tʀis/ adj evocative. **évocation** nf evocation.

**évolué**, ~e /evɔlɥe/ adj highly developed.

**évoluer** /evɔlɥe/ 1 vi evolve; (situation) develop; (se déplacer) glide. **évolution** nf evolution; (d'une situation) development.

**évoquer** /evɔke/ 1 vt call to mind, evoke.

**exacerber** /ɛgzasɛʀbe/ 1 vt exacerbate.

**exact**, ~e /ɛgza(kt), -akt/ adj (précis) exact, accurate; (juste) correct; (personne) punctual. **exactement** adv exactly. **exactitude** nf exactness; punctuality.

**ex æquo** /ɛgzeko/ adv être ~ tie (avec qn with sb).

**exagération** /ɛgzaʒeʀasjɔ̃/ nf exaggeration. **exagéré**, ~e adj excessive.

**exagérer** /ɛgzaʒeʀe/ 14 vt/i exaggerate; (abuser) go too far.

**exalté**, ~e /ɛgzalte/ nm, f fanatic. **exalter 1** vt excite; (glorifier) exalt.

**examen** /ɛgzamɛ̃/ nm examination; (Scol) exam. **examinateur**, -trice nm, f examiner. **examiner 1** vt examine.

**exaspération** /ɛgzaspeʀasjɔ̃/ nf exasperation. **exaspérer 14** vt exasperate.

**exaucer** /ɛgzose/ 10 vt grant; (personne) grant the wish(es) of.

**excédent** /ɛksedɑ̃/ nm surplus; ~ de bagages excess luggage; ~ de la balance commerciale trade surplus. **excédentaire** adj excess, surplus.

**excéder** /ɛksede/ [14] vt (dépasser) exceed; (agacer) irritate.

**excellence** /ɛksɛlɑ̃s/ nf excellence. **excellent, ~e** adj excellent. **exceller** [1] vi excel (dans in).

**excentricité** /ɛksɑ̃trisite/ nf eccentricity. **excentrique** adj & nmf eccentric.

**excepté, ~e** /ɛksɛpte/ adj & prép except.

**excepter** /ɛksɛpte/ [1] vt except.

**exception** /ɛksɛpsjɔ̃/ nf exception; **à l'~** de except for; **d'~** exceptional; **faire ~** be an exception. **exceptionnel, ~le** adj exceptional. **exceptionnellement** adv exceptionally.

**excès** /ɛksɛ/ nm excess; **~ de vitesse** speeding.

**excessif, -ive** /ɛksesif, -v/ adj excessive.

**excitant, ~e** /ɛksitɑ̃, -t/ adj stimulating; (palpitant) exciting. ● nm stimulant.

**exciter** /ɛksite/ [1] vt excite; (irriter) get excited. □ **s'~** vpr get excited.

**exclamer (s')** /(s)ɛksklame/ [1] vpr exclaim.

**exclure** /ɛksklyʀ/ [16] vt exclude; (expulser) expel; (empêcher) preclude.

**exclusif, -ive** /ɛksklyzif, -v/ adj exclusive.

**exclusion** /ɛksklyzjɔ̃/ nf exclusion.

**exclusivité** /ɛksklyzivite/ nf (Comm) exclusive rights (+ pl); **projeter en ~** show exclusively.

**excursion** /ɛkskyʀsjɔ̃/ nf excursion; (à pied) hike.

**excuse** /ɛkskyz/ nf excuse; **~s** apology (+ sg); **faire des ~s** apologize.

**excuser** /ɛkskyze/ [1] vt excuse; **excusez-moi** excuse me. □ **s'~** vpr

apologize (de for).

**exécrable** /ɛgzekʀabl/ adj dreadful. **exécrer** [14] vt loathe.

**exécuter** /ɛgzekyte/ [1] vt carry out, execute; (Mus) perform; (tuer) execute.

**exécutif, -ive** /ɛgzekytif, -v/ adj & nm (Pol) executive.

**exécution** /ɛgzekysjɔ̃/ nf execution; (Mus) performance.

**exemplaire** /ɛgzɑ̃plɛʀ/ adj exemplary. ● nm copy.

**exemple** /ɛgzɑ̃pl/ nm example; **par ~** for example; **donner l'~** set an example.

**exempt, ~e** /ɛgzɑ̃, -t/ adj **~ de** exempt (de from).

**exempter** /ɛgzɑ̃te/ [1] vt exempt (de from). **exemption** nf exemption.

**exercer** /ɛgzɛʀse/ [10] vt exercise; (influence, contrôle) exert; (former) train, exercise; **~ un métier** have a job; **~ le métier de...** work as a... □ **s'~** vpr practise.

**exercice** /ɛgzɛʀsis/ nm exercise; (de métier) practice; **en ~** in office; (médecin) in practice.

**exhaler** /ɛgzale/ [1] vt emit.

**exhaustif, -ive** /ɛgzostif, -v/ adj exhaustive.

**exhiber** /ɛgzibe/ [1] vt exhibit.

**exhorter** /ɛgzɔʀte/ [1] vt exhort (à to).

**exigeant, ~e** /ɛgziʒɑ̃, -t/ adj demanding; **être ~ avec qn** demand a lot of sb. **exigence** nf demand. **exiger** [40] vt demand.

**exigu, ~ë** /ɛgzigy/ adj tiny.

**exil** /ɛgzil/ nm exile. **exilé, ~e** nm, f exile.

**exiler** /ɛgzile/ [1] vt exile. □ **s'~** vpr go into exile.

**existence** /ɛgzistɑ̃s/ nf existence.

**exister** /ɛgziste/ **1** vi exist.

**exode** /ɛgzɔd/ nm exodus.

**exonérer** /ɛgzɔneʀe/ **14** vt exempt (de from).

**exorbitant, ~e** /ɛgzɔʀbitɑ̃, -t/ adj exorbitant.

**exorciser** /ɛgzɔʀsize/ **1** vt exorcize.

**exotique** /ɛgzɔtik/ adj exotic.

**expansé, ~e** /ɛkspɑ̃se/ adj (Tech) expanded.

**expansif, -ive** /ɛkspɑ̃sif, -v/ adj expansive. **expansion** nf expansion.

**expatrié, ~e** /ɛkspatʀije/ nm, f expatriate.

**expectative** /ɛkspɛktativ/ nf être dans l'~ wait and see.

**expédient** /ɛkspedjɑ̃/ nm expedient; vivre d'~s live by one's wits; user d'~s resort to expedients.

**expédier** /ɛkspedje/ **45** vt send, dispatch; (tâche **1**) polish off. **expéditeur, -trice** nm, f sender. **expéditif, -ive** /ɛkspeditif, -v/ adj quick.

**expédition** /ɛkspedisjɔ̃/ nf (envoi) dispatching; (voyage) expedition.

**expérience** /ɛkspeʀjɑ̃s/ nf experience; (scientifique) experiment.

**expérimental, ~e** (mpl -aux) /ɛkspeʀimɑ̃tal, o/ adj experimental. **expérimentation** nf experimentation. **expérimenté, ~e** adj experienced. **expérimenter 1** vt test, experiment with.

**expert, ~e** /ɛkspɛʀ, -t/ adj expert. ●nm expert; (d'assurances) adjuster. **expert-comptable** (pl **experts-comptables**) nm accountant.

**expertise** /ɛkspɛʀtiz/ nf valuation; (de dégâts) assessment. **expertiser 1** vt value; (dégâts) assess.

**expier** /ɛkspje/ **45** vt atone for.

**expiration** /ɛkspiʀasjɔ̃/ nf expiry.

**expirer** /ɛkspiʀe/ **1** vi breathe out; (finir, mourir) expire.

**explicatif, -ive** /ɛksplikatif, -v/ adj explanatory.

**explication** /ɛksplikasjɔ̃/ nf explanation; (fig) discussion; ~ de texte (Scol) literary commentary.

**explicite** /ɛksplisit/ adj explicit.

**expliquer** /ɛksplike/ **1** vt explain. □ **s'~** vpr explain oneself; (discuter) discuss things; (être explicable) be understandable.

**exploit** /ɛksplwa/ nm exploit.

**exploitant, ~e** /ɛksplwatɑ̃, -t/ nm, f ~ (agricole) farmer.

**exploitation** /ɛksplwatasjɔ̃/ nf exploitation; (d'entreprise) running; (ferme) farm.

**exploiter** /ɛksplwate/ **1** vt exploit; (ferme) run; (mine) work.

**explorateur, -trice** /ɛksplɔʀatœʀ, -tʀis/ nm, f explorer. **exploration** nf exploration. **explorer 1** vt explore.

**exploser** /ɛksploze/ **1** vi explode; faire ~ explode; (bâtiment) blow up.

**explosif, -ive** /ɛksplozif, -v/ adj & nm explosive. **explosion** nf explosion.

**exportateur, -trice** /ɛkspɔʀtatœʀ, -tʀis/ nm, f exporter. ● adj exporting. **exportation** nf export. **exporter 1** vt export.

**exposant, ~e** /ɛkspozɑ̃, -t/ nm, f exhibitor.

**exposé, ~e** /ɛkspoze/ nm talk (sur on); (d'une action) account; faire l'~ de la situation give an account of the situation. ● adj ~ au nord facing north.

**exposer** /ɛkspoze/ **1** vt display, show; (expliquer) explain; (soumettre, mettre en danger) expose (à to); (vie) endanger. □ s'∼ à vpr expose oneself to.

**exposition** /ɛkspozisjɔ̃/ nf (d'art) exhibition; (de faits) exposition; (géographique) aspect.

**exprès¹** /ɛksprɛ/ adv specially; (délibérément) on purpose.

**exprès², -esse** /ɛksprɛs/ adj express.

**express** /ɛksprɛs/ adj & nm inv (café) ∼ espresso; (train) ∼ fast train.

**expressif, -ive** /ɛkspresif, -v/ adj expressive. **expression** nf expression.

**exprimer** /ɛksprime/ **1** vt express. □ s'∼ vpr express oneself.

**expulser** /ɛkspylse/ **1** vt expel; (locataire) evict; ( joueur) send off. **expulsion** nf (d'élève) expulsion; (de locataire) eviction; (d'immigré) deportation.

**exquis, ∼e** /ɛkski, -z/ adj exquisite.

**extase** /ɛkstaz/ nf ecstasy.

**extasier (s')** /(s)ɛkstazje/ **45** vpr s'∼ sur be ecstatic about.

**extensible** /ɛkstɑ̃sibl/ adj (tissu) stretch.

**extension** /ɛkstɑ̃sjɔ̃/ nf extension; (expansion) expansion.

**exténuer** /ɛkstenɥe/ **1** vt exhaust.

**extérieur, ∼e** /ɛksterjœr/ adj outside; (signe, gaieté) outward; ( politique) foreign. ● nm outside, exterior; (de personne) exterior; à l'∼ (de) outside. **extérioriser** **1** vt show, externalize.

**extermination** /ɛkstɛrminasjɔ̃/ nf extermination. **exterminer** **1** vt exterminate.

**externe** /ɛkstɛrn/ adj external. ● nmf (Scol) day pupil.

**extincteur** /ɛkstɛ̃ktœr/ nm fire extinguisher.

**extinction** /ɛkstɛ̃ksjɔ̃/ nf extinction; avoir une ∼ de voix have lost one's voice.

**extorquer** /ɛkstɔrke/ **1** vt extort.

**extra** /ɛkstra/ adj inv first-rate. ● nm inv (repas) (special) treat.

**extraction** /ɛkstraksjɔ̃/ nf extraction.

**extrader** /ɛkstrade/ **1** vt extradite.

**extraire** /ɛkstrɛr/ **29** vt extract. **extrait** nm extract.

**extraordinaire** /ɛkstraɔrdinɛr/ adj extraordinary.

**extravagance** /ɛkstravagɑ̃s/ nf extravagance. **extravagant, ∼e** adj extravagant.

**extraverti, ∼e** /ɛkstravɛrti/ nm, f extrovert.

**extrême** /ɛkstrɛm/ adj & nm extreme. **extrêmement** adv extremely.

**Extrême-Orient** /ɛkstrɛmɔrjɑ̃/ nm Far East.

**extrémiste** /ɛkstremist/ nmf extremist.

**extrémité** /ɛkstremite/ nf end; (mains, pieds) extremity.

**exubérance** /ɛgzyberɑ̃s/ nf exuberance. **exubérant, ∼e** adj exuberant.

# Ff

**F** abrév f (franc, francs) franc, francs.

**fabricant, ∼e** /fabrikɑ̃, -t/ nm, f manufacturer. **fabrication** nf making; manufacture.

**fabrique** /fabrik/ nf factory. **fabriquer** **1** vt make; (industriellement)

manufacture; (fig) make up.
**fabuler** /fabyle/ 🔳 vi fantasize.
**fabuleux**, **-euse** /fabylø, -z/ adj fabulous.

**fac** /fak/ nf 🔲 university.

**façade** /fasad/ nf front; (fig) façade.

**face** /fas/ nf face; (d'un objet) side; en (∼ de), d'en ∼ opposite; en ∼ de (fig) faced with; ∼ à facing; (fig) faced with; **faire** ∼ à face. **face-à-face** nm inv (débat) one-to-one debate.

**fâcher** /fɑʃe/ 🔳 vt anger; fâché angry; (désolé) sorry. □ **se** ∼ vpr get angry; (se brouiller) fall out.

**facile** /fasil/ adj easy; (caractère) easygoing.

**facilité** /fasilite/ nf easiness; (aisance) ease; (aptitude) ability; ∼s (possibilités) facilities, opportunities; ∼s d'importation import opportunities; ∼s de paiement easy terms.

**faciliter** /fasilite/ 🔳 vt facilitate, make easier.

**façon** /fasɔ̃/ nf way; (de vêtement) cut; de cette ∼ in this way; de ∼ à so as to; de toute ∼ anyway; ∼s (chichis) fuss; **faire des** ∼ stand on ceremony; **sans** ∼ (repas) informal; (personne) unpretentious. **façonner** 🔳 vt shape; (faire) make.

**fac-similé** (pl ∼s) /faksimile/ nm facsimile.

**facteur**, **-trice** /faktœr, -tris/ nm, f postman, postwoman. ● nm (élément) factor.

**facture** /faktyr/ nf bill; (Comm) invoice; ∼ détaillée itemized bill. **facturer** 🔳 vt invoice. **facturette** nf credit card slip.

**facultatif**, **-ive** /fakyltatif, -v/ adj optional.

**faculté** /fakylte/ nf faculty; (possi-bilité) power; (Univ) faculty.

**fade** /fad/ adj insipid.

**faible** /fɛbl/ adj weak; (espoir, quantité, écart) slight; (revenu, intensité) low; ∼ d'esprit feeble-minded. ● nm (personne) weakling; (penchant) weakness. **faiblesse** nf weakness. **faiblir** 🔲 vi weaken.

**faïence** /fajɑ̃s/ nf earthenware.

**faillir** /fajir/ 🔲 vi j'ai failli acheter I almost bought.

**faillite** /fajit/ nf bankruptcy; (fig) collapse.

**faim** /fɛ̃/ nf hunger; **avoir** ∼ be hungry; **rester sur sa** ∼ (fig) be left wanting more.

**fainéant**, ∼**e** /feneɑ̃, -t/ adj idle. ● nm, f idler.

**faire** /fɛr/ 🔳

⟹ Pour les expressions comme faire attention, faire la cuisine, etc. ➡ attention, cuisine etc.

● verbe transitif

····▸ (préparer, créer) make; ∼ une tarte/une erreur make a tart/a mistake.

····▸ (se livrer à une activité) do; ∼ du droit do law; ∼ du foot/du violon play football/the violin; qu'est-ce qu'elle fait? (dans la vie) what does she do?; (en ce moment précis) what is she doing?

····▸ (dans les calculs, mesures, etc.) 10 et 10 font 20 10 and 10 make 20; ça fait 25 euros that's 25 euros; ∼ 60 kilos weigh 60 kilos; il fait 1,75 m he's 1.75 m tall.

····▸ (dans les expressions de temps) ça fait une heure que

j'attends I have been waiting for an hour.

····▶ (imiter) ∼ le clown act the clown; **faire le malade** pretend to be ill.

····▶ (parcourir) ∼ **10 km** do ou cover 10 km; ∼ **les musées** go round the museums.

····▶ (entraîner, causer) **ça ne fait rien** it doesn't matter; **l'accident a fait 8 morts** 8 people died in the accident.

····▶ (dire) say; **'excusez-moi', fit-elle** 'excuse me', she said.

● verbe auxiliaire

····▶ (faire + infinitif + qn) make; ∼ **pleurer qn** make sb cry.

····▶ (faire + infinitif + qch) have, get; ∼ **réparer sa voiture** have ou get one's car mended.

····▶ (ne faire que + infinitif) (continuellement) **ne** ∼ **que pleurer** do nothing but cry; (seulement) **je ne fais qu'obéir** I'm only following orders.

● verbe intransitif

····▶ (agir) do, act; ∼ **vite** act quickly; **fais comme tu veux** do as you please; **fais comme chez toi** make yourself at home.

····▶ (paraître) look; ∼ **joli** look pretty; **ça fait cher** it's expensive.

····▶ (en parlant du temps) **il fait chaud/gris** it's hot/overcast.

□ **se faire** verbe pronominal

····▶ (obtenir, confectionner) make; **se** ∼ **des amis** make friends; **se** ∼ **un thé** make (oneself) a cup of tea.

····▶ (se faire + infinitif) **se** ∼ **gronder** be scolded; **se** ∼ **couper les cheveux** have one's hair cut.

····▶ (devenir) **il se fait tard** it's getting late.

····▶ (être d'usage) **ça ne se fait pas** it's not the done thing.

····▶ (emploi impersonnel) **comment se fait-il que tu sois ici?** how come you're here?

····▶ □ **se faire à** get used to; **je ne m'y fais pas** I can't get used to it.

····▶ □ **s'en faire** worry; **ne t'en fais pas** don't worry.

🔟 Lorsque **faire** remplace un verbe plus précis, on traduira quelquefois par ce dernier: **faire une visite** pay a visit, **faire un nid** build a nest.

**faire-part** /fɛʀpaʀ/ nm inv announcement.

**fais** /fɛ/ ➡FAIRE 33.

**faisan** /fəzɑ̃/ nm pheasant.

**faisceau** (pl ∼**x**) /fɛso/ nm (rayon) beam; (fagot) bundle.

**fait, ∼e** /fɛ, fɛt/ adj done; (fromage) ripe; **pour** made for; **tout** ∼ ready made; **c'est bien** ∼ **pour toi** it serves you right. ● nm fact; (événement) event; **au** ∼ **(de)** informed (of); **de ce** ∼ therefore; **du** ∼ **de** on account of; ∼ **divers** (trivial) news item; ∼ **nouveau** new development; **prendre qn sur le** ∼ catch sb in the act. ● ➡FAIRE 33.

**faîte** /fɛt/ nm top; (fig) peak.

**faites** /fɛt/ ➡FAIRE 33.

**falaise** /falɛz/ nf cliff.

**falloir** /falwaʀ/ 34 vi **il faut qch/qn** we/you etc. need sth/sb; **il lui faut du pain** he needs bread; **il faut rester** we/you must stay; **il faut que j'y aille** I have to ou must go; **il faut que tu partes** you should leave; **il aurait fallu le faire** we/you etc. should have

**falsifier** /falsifje/ 49 vt falsify; (signature, monnaie) forge.

**famé**, ~e /fame/ adj mal ~ disreputable, seedy.

**fameux**, -euse /famø, -z/ adj famous; (excellent 🗆) first-rate.

**familial**, ~e (mpl -iaux) /familjal, -jo/ adj family.

**familiale** /familjal/ nf estate car; (US) station wagon.

**familiariser** /familjarize/ 🗓 vt familiarize (avec with). □ se ~ vpr familiarize oneself.

**familier**, -ière /familje, -jɛʀ/ adj familiar; (amical) informal.

**famille** /famij/ nf family; en ~ with one's family.

**famine** /famin/ nf famine.

**fanatique** /fanatik/ adj fanatical. ● nmf fanatic.

**fanfare** /fɑ̃faʀ/ nf brass band; (musique) fanfare.

**fantaisie** /fɑ̃tezi/ nf imagination, fantasy; (caprice) whim; (de) ~ (boutons etc.) fancy. **fantaisiste** adj unorthodox; (personne) eccentric.

**fantasme** /fɑ̃tasm/ nm fantasy.

**fantastique** /fɑ̃tastik/ adj fantastic.

**fantôme** /fɑ̃tom/ nm ghost; cabinet(-) ~ (Pol) shadow cabinet.

**faon** /fɑ̃/ nm fawn.

**FAQ** abrév f (**Foire aux questions**) (Internet) FAQ, Frequently Asked Questions.

**farce** /faʀs/ nf (practical) joke; (Théât) farce; (hachis) stuffing.

**farcir** /faʀsiʀ/ 🛿 vt stuff.

**fard** /faʀ/ nm make-up; ~ à paupières eye-shadow; piquer un ~ blush.

**fardeau** (pl ~x) /faʀdo/ nm burden.

**farfelu**, ~e /faʀfaly/ adj & nm,f eccentric.

**farine** /faʀin/ nf flour. **farineux**, -euse adj floury. **farineux** nmpl starchy food.

**farouche** /faʀuʃ/ adj shy; (peu sociable) unsociable; (violent) fierce.

**fascicule** /fasikyl/ nm (brochure) booklet; (partie d'un ouvrage) fascicule.

**fasciner** /fasine/ 🗓 vt fascinate.

**fascisme** /faʃism/ nm fascism.

**fasse** /fas/ ➡FAIRE 33.

**fast-food** /fastfud/ nm fast-food place.

**fastidieux**, -ieuse /fastidjø, -z/ adj tedious.

**fatal**, ~e (mpl ~s) /fatal/ adj inevitable; (mortel) fatal. **fatalité** nf (destin) fate.

**fatigant**, ~e /fatigɑ̃, -t/ adj tiring; (ennuyeux) tiresome.

**fatigue** /fatig/ nf fatigue, tiredness.

**fatigué**, ~e /fatige/ adj tired.

**fatiguer** /fatige/ 🗓 vt tire; (yeux, moteur) strain. ● vi (moteur) labour. □ se ~ vpr get tired, tire (de of).

**faubourg** /fobuʀ/ nm suburb.

**faucher** /foʃe/ 🗓 vt (herbe) mow; (voler 🗆) pinch; ~ qn (véhicule, tir) mow sb down.

**faucon** /fokɔ̃/ nm falcon, hawk.

**faudra**, faudrait /fodʀa, fodʀe/ ➡FALLOIR 34.

**faufiler (se)** /(sə)fofile/ 🗓 vpr edge one's way, squeeze.

**faune** /fon/ nf wildlife, fauna.

**faussaire** /fosɛʀ/ nmf forger.

**fausse** /fos/ →FAUX².

**fausser** /fose/ **1** vt buckle; (fig) distort; ~ compagnie à qn give sb the slip.

**faut** /fo/ →FALLOIR 34.

**faute** /fot/ nf mistake; (responsabilité) fault; (délit) offence; (péché) sin; en ~ at fault; ~ de for want of; ~ de quoi failing which; sans ~ without fail; ~ de frappe typing error; ~ de goût bad taste; ~ professionnelle professional misconduct.

**fauteuil** /fotœj/ nm armchair; (de président) chair; (Théât) seat; ~ roulant wheelchair.

**fautif, -ive** /fotif, -v/ adj guilty; (faux) faulty. ● nm, f guilty party.

**fauve** /fov/ adj (couleur) fawn, tawny. ● nm wild cat.

**faux¹** /fo/ nf scythe.

**faux²**, **fausse** /fo, fos/ adj false; (falsifié) fake, forged; (numéro, calcul) wrong; (voix) out of tune; c'est ~! that is wrong!; ~ témoignage perjury; faire ~ bond à qn stand sb up; fausse couche miscarriage; ~ frais incidental expenses. ● adv (chanter) out of tune. ● nm forgery. **faux-filet** (pl ~s) nm sirloin.

**faveur** /favœʀ/ nf favour; de ~ (régime) preferential; en ~ de in favour of.

**favorable** /favɔʀabl/ adj favourable.

**favori**, ~te /favɔʀi, -t/ adj & nm,f favourite. **favoriser** **1** vt favour.

**fax** /faks/ nm fax. **faxer** **1** vt fax.

**fébrile** /febʀil/ adj feverish.

**fécond**, ~e /fekɔ̃, -d/ adj fertile. **féconder** **1** vt fertilize. **fécondité** nf fertility.

**fédéral**, ~e (mpl -aux) /fedeʀal, -o/ adj federal. **fédération** nf federation.

**fée** /fe/ nf fairy. **féerie** nf magical spectacle. **féerique** adj magical.

**feindre** /fɛ̃dʀ/ 22 vt feign; ~ de pretend to.

**fêler** /fele/ **1** vt crack. □ se ~ vpr crack.

**félicitations** /felisitasjɔ̃/ nfpl congratulations (pour on). **féliciter** **1** vt congratulate (de on).

**félin**, ~e /felɛ̃, -in/ adj & nm feline.

**femelle** /fəmɛl/ adj & nf female.

**féminin**, ~e /feminɛ̃, -in/ adj feminine; (sexe) female; (mode, équipe) women's. ● nm feminine. **féministe** nmf feminist.

**femme** /fam/ nf woman; (épouse) wife; ~ au foyer housewife; ~ de chambre chambermaid; ~ de ménage cleaning lady.

**fémur** /femyʀ/ nm thigh-bone.

**fendre** /fɑ̃dʀ/ **3** vt (couper) split; (fissurer) crack. □ se ~ vpr crack.

**fenêtre** /fənɛtʀ/ nf window.

**fenouil** /fənuj/ nm fennel.

**fente** /fɑ̃t/ nf (ouverture) slit, slot; (fissure) crack.

**féodal**, ~e (mpl -aux) /feɔdal, -o/ adj feudal.

**fer** /fɛʀ/ nm iron; ~ (à repasser) iron; ~ à cheval horseshoe; ~ de lance spearhead; ~ forgé wrought iron.

**fera**, **ferait** /fəʀa, fəʀɛ/ →FAIRE 33.

**férié**, ~e /feʀje/ adj jour ~ public holiday.

**ferme** /fɛʀm/ nf farm; (maison) farm(house); ~ éolienne wind farm. ● adj firm. ● adv (travailler) hard.

**fermé**, ~e /fɛʀme/ adj closed; (gaz, radio) off.

**fermenter** /fɛʀmɑ̃te/ **1** vi ferment.

**fermer** /fɛʀme/ **1** vt/i close, shut;

(cesser d'exploiter) close ou shut down; (gaz, robinet) turn off. □ se ~ vpr close, shut.

**fermeté** /fɛrməte/ nf firmness.

**fermeture** /fɛrmətyr/ nf closing; (dispositif) catch; ~ **annuelle** annual closure; ~ **éclair®** zip(-fastener); (US) zipper.

**fermier, -ière** /fɛrmje, -jɛr/ adj farm. ●nm farmer. **fermière** nf farmer's wife.

**féroce** /feros/ adj ferocious.

**ferraille** /fɛrɑj/ nf scrap-iron.

**ferrer** /fɛre/ 🔟 vt (cheval) shoe.

**ferroviaire** /fɛrɔvjɛr/ adj rail(way).

**ferry** /feri/ nm ferry.

**fertile** /fɛrtil/ adj fertile; ~ **en** (fig) rich in. **fertiliser** 🔟 vt fertilize. **fertilité** nf fertility.

**fervent, ~e** /fɛrvɑ̃, -t/ adj fervent. ●nm, f enthusiast (de of).

**fesse** /fɛs/ nf buttock. **fessée** nf spanking, smack.

**festin** /fɛstɛ̃/ nm feast.

**festival** (pl ~s) /fɛstival/ nm festival.

**fêtard, ~e** /fɛtar, -d/ nm, f 🔟 party animal.

**fête** /fɛt/ nf holiday; (religieuse) feast; (du nom) name-day; (réception) party; (en famille) celebration; (foire) fair; (folklorique) festival; ~ **des Mères** Mother's Day; ~ **foraine** fun-fair; **faire la** ~ live it up; **les ~s (de fin d'année)** the Christmas season. **fêter** 🔟 vt celebrate; (personne) give a celebration for.

**fétiche** /fetiʃ/ nm fetish; (fig) mascot.

**feu¹** (pl ~x) /fø/ nm fire; (lumière) light; (de réchaud) burner; **à** ~ **doux/vif** on a low/high heat; ~ **rouge/vert/orange** red/green/amber light; **aux** ~x, **tournez à**

**droite** turn right at the traffic lights; **avez-vous du** ~? (pour cigarette) have you got a light?; **au** ~! fire!; **mettre le** ~ **à** set fire to; **prendre** ~ catch fire; **jouer avec le** ~ play with fire; **ne pas faire long** ~ not last; ~ **d'artifice** firework display; ~ **de joie** bonfire; ~ **de position** sidelight.

**feu²** /fø/ adj inv (mort) late.

**feuillage** /fœjaʒ/ nm foliage.

**feuille** /fœj/ nf leaf; (de papier) sheet; (formulaire) form; ~ **d'impôts** tax return; ~ **de paie** payslip.

**feuilleté, ~e** /fœjte/ adj pâte ~e puff pastry. ●nm savoury pasty.

**feuilleter** /fœjte/ 🔟 vt leaf through.

**feuilleton** /fœjtɔ̃/ nm (à suivre) serial; (histoire complète) series.

**feutre** /føtr/ nm felt; (chapeau) felt hat; (crayon) felt-tip (pen).

**fève** /fɛv/ nf broad bean.

**février** /fevrije/ nm February.

**fiable** /fjabl/ adj reliable.

**fiançailles** /fjɑ̃sɑj/ nfpl engagement.

**fiancé, ~e** /fjɑ̃se/ adj engaged. ●nm fiancé. **fiancée** nf fiancée. **fiancer (se)** 🔟 vpr become engaged (avec to).

**fibre** /fibr/ nf fibre; ~ **de verre** fibreglass.

**ficeler** /fisle/ 🔟 vt tie up.

**ficelle** /fisɛl/ nf string.

**fiche** /fiʃ/ nf (index) card; (formulaire) form, slip; (Électr) plug.

**ficher¹** /fiʃe/ 🔟 vt (enfoncer) drive (dans into).

**ficher²** /fiʃe/ 🔟 vt (faire) do; (donner) give; (mettre) put; ~ **le camp** clear off. □ se ~ **de** vpr make fun of; **il s'en fiche** he couldn't care less.

**fichier** /fiʃje/ nm file.

**fichu, ~e** /fiʃy/ adj 🅵 (mauvais) rotten; (raté) done for; **mal ~** terrible.

**fictif, -ive** /fiktif, -v/ adj fictitious. **fiction** nf fiction.

**fidèle** /fidɛl/ adj faithful. ● nmf (client) regular; (Relig) believer; **~s** (à l'église) congregation. **fidélité** nf fidelity.

**fier¹, fière** /fjɛʀ/ adj proud (de of).

**fier²(se)** /(sə)fje/ 🔢 vpr **se ~ à** trust.

**fierté** /fjɛʀte/ nf pride.

**fièvre** /fjɛvʀ/ nf fever; **avoir de la ~** have a temperature; **~ aphteuse** foot-and-mouth disease. **fiévreux, -euse** adj feverish.

**figer** /fiʒe/ 🔢 vi (graisse) congeal; (sang) clot; **figé sur place** frozen to the spot. □ **se ~** vpr (personne, sourire) freeze; (graisse) congeal; (sang) clot.

**figue** /fig/ nf fig.

**figurant, ~e** /figyʀɑ̃, -t/ nm, f (au cinéma) extra.

**figure** /figyʀ/ nf face; (forme, personnage) figure; (illustration) picture.

**figuré, ~e** /figyʀe/ adj (sens) figurative.

**figurer** /figyʀe/ 🔢 vi appear. ● vt represent. □ **se ~** vpr imagine.

**fil** /fil/ nm thread; (métallique, électrique) wire; (de couteau) edge; (à coudre) cotton; **au ~ de** with the passing of; **au ~ de l'eau** with the current; **~ de fer** wire; **au bout du ~** 🅵 on the phone.

**file** /fil/ nf line; (voie: Auto) lane; **~** (d'attente) queue; (US) line; **en ~ indienne** in single file.

**filer** /file/ 🔢 vt spin; (suivre) shadow; **~ qch à qn** 🅵 slip sb sth. ● vi (bas) ladder, run; (liquide) run;

(aller vite 🅵) speed along, fly by; (partir 🅵) dash off; (disparaître 🅵) **~ entre les mains** slip through one's fingers; **~ doux** do as one's told.

**filet** /filɛ/ nm net; (d'eau) trickle; (de viande) fillet; **~** (à bagages) (luggage) rack; **~ à provisions** string bag ( for shopping).

**filiale** /filjal/ nf subsidiary (company).

**filière** /filjɛʀ/ nf (official) channels; (de trafiquants) network; **passer par** ou **suivre la ~** (employé) work one's way up.

**fille** /fij/ nf girl; (opposé à fils) daughter. **fillette** nf little girl.

**filleul** /fijœl/ nm godson.

**filleule** /fijœl/ nf god-daughter.

**film** /film/ nm film; **~** d'épouvante/muet/parlant horror/silent/talking film; **~ dramatique** drama. **filmer** 🔢 vt film.

**filon** /filɔ̃/ nm (Géol) seam; (travail lucratif 🅵) money spinner; **avoir trouvé le bon ~** be onto a good thing.

**fils** /fis/ nm son.

**filtre** /filtʀ/ nm filter. **filtrer** 🔢 vt/i filter; (personne) screen.

**fin¹** /fɛ̃/ nf end; **à la ~** finally; **en ~ de compte** all things considered; **~ de semaine** weekend; **mettre ~ à** put an end to; **prendre ~** come to an end.

**fin², ~e** /fɛ̃, fin/ adj fine; (tranche, couche) thin; (taille) slim; (plat) exquisite; (esprit, vue) sharp; **~es herbes** mixed herbs. ● adv (couper) finely.

**final, ~e** (mpl -**aux**) /final, -o/ adj final.

**finale** /final/ nm (Mus) finale. ● nf (Sport) final; (Gram) final syllable.

**finalement** adv finally; (somme

toute) after all. **finaliste** *nmf* finalist.

**finance** /finãs/ *nf* finance. **financer** ⑩ *vt* finance.

**financier, -ière** /finãsje, -jɛR/ *adj* financial. ● *nm* financier.

**finesse** /finɛs/ *nf* fineness; (de taille) slimness; (acuité) sharpness; ~s (de langue) niceties.

**finir** /finiR/ ② *vt* | ① finish, end; (arrêter) stop; (manger) finish (up); en ~ avec have done with; ~ par faire end up doing; ça va mal ~ it will turn out badly.

**finlandais, ~e** /fēlãdɛ, -z/ *adj* Finnish. F~, ~e *nm, f* Finn.

**Finlande** /fēlãd/ *nf* Finland.

**finnois, ~e** /finwa/ *adj* Finnish. ● *nm* (Ling) Finnish.

**firme** /fiRm/ *nf* firm.

**fisc** /fisk/ *nm* tax authorities. **fiscal, ~e** (*mpl* **-aux**) *adj* tax, fiscal. **fiscalité** *nf* tax system.

**fissure** /fisyR/ *nf* crack.

**FIV** *abrév f* (**fécondation in vitro**) IVF.

**fixe** /fiks/ *adj* fixed; (stable) steady; à heure ~ at a set time; menu à prix ~ set menu. ● *nm* basic pay.

**fixer** /fikse/ ① *vt* fix; ~ (du regard) stare at; être fixé (personne) have made up one's mind. □ se ~ *vpr* (s'attacher) be attached; (s'installer) settle down.

**flacon** /flakõ/ *nm* bottle.

**flagrant, ~e** /flagRã, -t/ *adj* flagrant, blatant; en ~ délit in the act.

**flair** /flɛR/ *nm* (sense of) smell; (fig) intuition.

**flamand, ~e** /flamã, -d/ *adj* Flemish. ~e *nm* (Ling) Flemish. F~, ~e *nm, f* Fleming.

**flamant** /flamã/ *nm* flamingo.

**flambeau** (*pl* ~**x**) /flãbo/ *nm* torch.

**flambée** /flãbe/ *nf* blaze; (fig) explosion.

**flamber** /flãbe/ ① *vi* blaze; (prix) shoot up. ● *vt* (aiguille) sterilize; (volaille) singe.

**flamme** /flam/ *nf* flame; (fig) ardour; en ~s ablaze.

**flan** /flã/ *nm* custard tart.

**flanc** /flã/ *nm* side; (d'animal, d'armée) flank.

**flâner** /flane/ ① *vi* stroll. **flânerie** *nf* stroll.

**flanquer** /flãke/ ① *vt* flank; (jeter 🔟) chuck; (donner 🔟) give; ~ à la porte kick out.

**flaque** /flak/ *nf* (d'eau) puddle; (de sang) pool.

**flash** (*pl* ~**es**) /flaʃ/ *nm* (Photo) flash; (information) news flash; ~ publicitaire commercial.

**flatter** /flate/ ① *vt* flatter. □ se ~ de *vpr* pride oneself on.

**flatteur, -euse** /flatœR, -øz/ *adj* flattering. ● *nm, f* flatterer.

**fléau** (*pl* ~**x**) /fleo/ *nm* (désastre) scourge; (personne) pest.

**flèche** /flɛʃ/ *nf* arrow; (de clocher) spire; monter en ~ spiral; partir en ~ shoot off.

**flécher** /fleʃe/ ⑭ *vt* mark *ou* signpost (with arrows). **fléchette** *nf* dart.

**fléchir** /fleʃiR/ ② *vt* bend; (personne) move, sway. ● *vi* (faiblir) weaken; (prix) fall; (poutre) sag, bend.

**flemme** /flɛm/ *nf* 🔟 laziness; j'ai la ~ de faire I can't be bothered doing.

**flétrir (se)** /(sa)fletRiR/ ② *vpr* (plante) wither; (fruit) shrivel; (beauté) fade.

**fleur** /flœR/ *nf* flower; à ~ de terre/d'eau just above the ground/

water; à ~s flowery; ~ de l'âge
prime of life; en ~s in flower.
**fleurir** /flœʀiʀ/ **2** vi flower; (arbre)
blossom; (fig) flourish. • vt decorate
with flowers. **fleuriste** nmf florist.
**fleuve** /flœv/ nm river.
**flic** /flik/ nm 🔲 cop.
**flipper** /flipœʀ/ nm pinball
(machine).
**flirter** /flœʀte/ **1** vi flirt.
**flocon** /flɔkɔ̃/ nm flake.
**flore** /flɔʀ/ nf flora.
**florissant,** ~e /flɔʀisɑ̃, -t/ adj
flourishing.
**flot** /flo/ nm flood, stream; être à
~ be afloat; les ~s the waves.
**flottant,** ~e /flɔtɑ̃, -t/ adj (vêtement) loose; (indécis) indecisive.
**flotte** /flɔt/ nf fleet; (pluie 🔲) rain;
(eau 🔲) water.
**flottement** /flɔtmɑ̃/ nm (incertitude) indecision.
**flotter** /flɔte/ **1** vi float; (drapeau)
flutter; (nuage, parfum, pensées)
drift; (pleuvoir 🔲) rain. **flotteur** nm
float.
**flou,** ~e /flu/ adj out of focus; (fig)
vague.
**fluctuer** /flyktɥe/ **1** vi fluctuate.
**fluet,** ~te /flɥɛ, -t/ adj thin.
**fluide** /flɥid/ adj & nm fluid.
**fluor** /flyɔʀ/ nm (pour les dents)
fluoride.
**fluorescent,** ~e /flyɔʀesɑ̃, -t/ adj
fluorescent.
**flûte** /flyt/ nf flute; (verre) champagne glass.
**fluvial,** ~e (mpl -iaux) /flyvjal,
-jo/ adj river.
**flux** /fly/ nm flow; ~ et reflux ebb
and flow.
**FM** abrév f (frequency modula-
tion) FM.
**fœtus** /fetys/ nm foetus.

**foi** /fwa/ nf faith; être de bonne/
mauvaise ~ be acting in good/bad
faith; ma ~! well (indeed)!
**foie** /fwa/ nm liver.
**foin** /fwɛ̃/ nm hay.
**foire** /fwaʀ/ nf fair; faire la ~ 🔲
live it up.
**fois** /fwa/ nf time; une ~ once;
deux ~ twice; à la ~ at the same
time; des ~ (parfois) sometimes;
une ~ pour toutes once and
for all.
**fol** /fɔl/ ➡FOU.
**folie** /fɔli/ nf madness; (bêtise)
foolish thing, folly; faire une ~,
faire des ~s be extravagant.
**folklore** /fɔlklɔʀ/ nm folklore. **folklorique** adj folk; 🔲 eccentric.
**folle** /fɔl/ ➡FOU.
**foncé,** ~e /fɔ̃se/ adj dark.
**foncer** /fɔ̃se/ **1** vt darken. • vi
(s'assombrir) darken; (aller vite 🔲)
dash along; ~ sur 🔲 charge at.
**foncier,** -ière /fɔ̃sje, -jɛʀ/ adj fundamental; (Comm) real estate.
**fonction** /fɔ̃ksjɔ̃/ nf function; (emploi) position; ~s (obligations)
duties; en ~ de according to; ~
publique civil service; voiture de
~ company car. **fonctionnaire** nmf
civil servant. **fonctionnement** nm
working.
**fonctionner** /fɔ̃ksjɔne/ **1** vi
work; faire ~ work.
**fond** /fɔ̃/ nm bottom; (de salle, magasin, etc.) back; (essentiel) basis;
(contenu) content; (plan) background; (Sport) long-distance running; à ~ thoroughly; au ~ basically; de ~ (bruit) background; de ~
en comble from top to bottom; au
ou dans le ~ really; ~ de teint
foundation, make-up base.
**fondamental,** ~e (mpl -aux)
/fɔ̃damɑ̃tal, -o/ adj fundamental.

**fondateur**, **-trice** /fɔ̃datœʀ, -tʀis/ nm, f founder. **fondation** nf foundation.

**fonder** /fɔ̃de/ **1** vt found; (baser) base (sur on); (bien) fondé wellfounded. □ se ~ sur vpr be guided by, be based on.

**fonderie** /fɔ̃dʀi/ nf foundry.

**fondre** /fɔ̃dʀ/ **3** vt/i melt; (dans l'eau) dissolve; (mélanger) merge; faire ~ melt; dissolve; ~ en larmes burst into tears; ~ sur swoop on. □ se ~ vpr merge.

**fonds** /fɔ̃/ nm fund; ~ de commerce business. ● nmpl (capitaux) funds.

**fondu**, ~e /fɔ̃dy/ adj melted; (métal) molten.

**font** /fɔ̃/ →FAIRE 33.

**fontaine** /fɔ̃tɛn/ nf fountain; (source) spring.

**fonte** /fɔ̃t/ nf melting; (fer) cast iron; ~ des neiges thaw.

**foot** /fut/ nm **1** football.

**football** /futbol/ nm football.

**footing** /futiŋ/ nm jogging.

**forain**, ~e /fɔʀɛ̃/ nm fairground entertainer; marchand ~ stallholder.

**forçat** /fɔʀsa/ nm convict.

**force** /fɔʀs/ nf force; (physique) strength; (hydraulique etc.) power; ~s (physiques) strength; à ~ de by sheer force of; de ~, par la ~ by force; ~ de dissuasion deterrent; ~ de frappe strike force, deterrent; ~ de l'âge prime of life; ~ de l'ordre police (force) ; ~s de marché market forces.

**forcé**, ~e /fɔʀse/ adj forced; (inévitable) inevitable; c'est ~ qu'il fasse **1** he's bound to do. **forcément** adv necessarily; (évidemment) obviously.

**forcené**, ~e /fɔʀsəne/ adj frenzied. ● nm, f maniac.

**forcer** /fɔʀse/ **10** vt force (à faire to do); (voix) strain; ~ la dose **1** overdo it. ● vi force; (exagérer) overdo it. □ se ~ vpr force oneself.

**forer** /fɔʀe/ **1** vt drill.

**forestier**, **-ière** /fɔʀɛstje, -jɛʀ/ adj forest. ● nm, f forestry worker.

**forêt** /fɔʀɛ/ nf forest.

**forfait** /fɔʀfɛ/ nm (Comm) (prix fixe) fixed price; (offre promotionnelle) package. **forfaitaire** adj (prix) fixed.

**forger** /fɔʀʒe/ **40** vt forge; (inventer) make up.

**forgeron** /fɔʀʒəʀɔ̃/ nm blacksmith.

**formaliser (se)** /(sə)fɔʀmalize/ **1** vpr take offence (de at).

**formalité** /fɔʀmalite/ nf formality.

**format** /fɔʀma/ nm format. **formater** **1** vt (Ordinat) format.

**formation** /fɔʀmasjɔ̃/ nf formation; (professionnelle) training; (culture) education; ~ permanente ou continue continuing education.

**forme** /fɔʀm/ nf form; (contour) shape, form; ~s (de femme) figure; être en ~ be in good shape, be on form; en ~ de in the shape of; en bonne et due ~ in due form.

**formel**, ~le /fɔʀmɛl/ adj formal; (catégorique) positive.

**former** /fɔʀme/ **1** vt form; (instruire) train. □ se ~ vpr form.

**formidable** /fɔʀmidabl/ adj fantastic.

**formulaire** /fɔʀmylɛʀ/ nm form.

**formule** /fɔʀmyl/ nf formula; (expression) expression; (feuille) form; ~ de politesse polite phrase, letter ending. **formuler** **1** vt formulate.

**fort**, ~e /fɔʀ, -t/ adj strong; (grand) big; (pluie) heavy; (bruit) loud; (pente) steep; (élève) clever; au plus ~ de at the height of; c'est une ~e tête she/he's headstrong. ● adv

( *frapper*) hard; ( *parler*) loud; (très) very; (beaucoup) very much. ● nm (atout) strong point; (Mil) fort.

**fortifiant** /fɔʀtifjɑ̃/ nm tonic. **fortifier** 45 vt fortify.

**fortune** /fɔʀtyn/ nf fortune; de ~ (improvisé) makeshift; faire ~ make one's fortune.

**forum** /fɔʀɔm/ nm forum; ~ de discussion (Internet) newsgroup.

**fosse** /fos/ nf pit; (tombe) grave; ~ d'orchestre orchestra pit; ~ septique septic tank.

**fossé** /fose/ nm ditch; (fig) gulf; ~ numérique digital divide.

**fossette** /fosɛt/ nf dimple.

**fossile** /fɔsil/ nm fossil.

**fou** (fol *before vowel or mute* h ), **folle** /fu, fɔl/ adj mad; (course, regard) wild; (énorme 🇮) tremendous; ~ de crazy about; le ~ rire the giggles. ● nm madman; (bouffon) jester. **folle** nf madwoman.

**foudre** /fudʀ/ nf lightning.

**foudroyant, ~e** /fudʀwajɑ̃, -t/ adj (mort, maladie) violent.

**foudroyer** 31 vt (orage) strike; (maladie etc.) strike down; ~ qn du regard look daggers at sb.

**fouet** /fwɛ/ nm whip; (Culin) whisk.

**fougère** /fuʒɛʀ/ nf fern.

**fougue** /fug/ nf ardour. **fougueux, -euse** adj ardent.

**fouille** /fuj/ nf search; (Archéol) excavation.

**fouiller** /fuje/ 1 vt/i search; (creuser) dig; ~ dans (tiroir) rummage through.

**fouillis** /fuji/ nm jumble.

**foulard** /fulaʀ/ nm scarf.

**foule** /ful/ nf crowd; une ~ de (fig) a mass of.

**foulée** /fule/ nf stride; il l'a fait

dans la ~ he did it while he was at ou about it.

**fouler** /fule/ 1 vt (raisin) press; (sol) set foot on; ~ qch aux pieds trample sth underfoot; (fig) ride roughshod over sth. □ se ~ ~ le poignet/le pied sprain one's wrist/foot; ne pas se ~ 🇮 not strain oneself.

**four** /fuʀ/ nm oven; (de potier) kiln; (Théât) flop; ~ à micro-ondes microwave oven; ~ crématoire crematorium.

**fourbe** /fuʀb/ adj deceitful.

**fourche** /fuʀʃ/ nf fork; (à foin) pitchfork. **fourchette** nf fork; (Comm) bracket, range.

**fourgon** /fuʀgɔ̃/ nm van.

**fourmi** /fuʀmi/ nf ant; avoir des ~s have pins and needles.

**fourmiller** /fuʀmije/ 1 vi swarm (with).

**fourneau** (pl ~x) /fuʀno/ nm stove.

**fourni, ~e** /fuʀni/ adj (épais) thick.

**fournir** /fuʀniʀ/ 2 vt supply, provide; (client) supply; (effort) put in; ~ à qn supply sb with. □ se ~ chez vpr shop at.

**fournisseur** /fuʀnisœʀ/ nm supplier; ~ d'accès à l'Internet Internet service provider.

**fourniture** /fuʀnityʀ/ nf supply.

**fourrage** /fuʀaʒ/ nm fodder.

**fourré, ~e** /fuʀe/ adj (vêtement) fur-lined; (gâteau etc.) filled (with jam, cream, etc.). ● nm thicket.

**fourre-tout** /fuʀtu/ nm inv (sac) holdall.

**fourreur** /fuʀœʀ/ nm furrier.

**fourrière** /fuʀjɛʀ/ nf (lieu) pound.

**fourrure** /fuʀyʀ/ nf fur.

**foutre** /futʀ/ 3 vt ⚠ = ficher² 1.

**foutu,** ~e /futy/ adj 🖾 = fichu.

**foyer** /fwaje/ nm home; (âtre) hearth; (club) club; (d'étudiants) hostel; (Théât) foyer; (Photo) focus; (centre) centre.

**fracas** /fraka/ nm din; (de train) roar; (d'objet qui tombe) crash. **fracassant,** ~e adj (bruyant) deafening; (violent) shattering.

**fraction** /fraksjɔ̃/ nf fraction.

**fracture** /fraktyr/ nf fracture; ~ du poignet fractured wrist.

**fragile** /fraʒil/ adj fragile; (peau) sensitive; (cœur) weak. **fragilité** nf fragility.

**fragment** /fragmã/ nm bit, fragment. **fragmenter** 🚹 vt split, fragment.

**fraîchement** /frɛʃmã/ adv (récemment) freshly; (avec froideur) coolly. **fraîcheur** nf coolness; (nouveauté) freshness. **fraîchir** 🛾 vi freshen, become colder.

**frais¹,** fraîche /frɛ, -ʃ/ adj fresh; (temps, accueil) cool; (peinture) wet; ~ et dispos fresh; **il fait** ~ it is cool. ●adv (récemment) newly, freshly. ●nm **mettre au** ~ put in a cool place; **prendre le** ~ get some fresh air.

**frais²** /frɛ/ nmpl expenses; (droits) fees; **aux** ~ **de** at the expense of; **faire des** ~ spend a lot of money; ~ **généraux** (Comm) overheads, running expenses; ~ **de scolarité** school fees.

**fraise** /frɛz/ nf strawberry. **fraisier** nm strawberry plant; (gâteau) strawberry gateau.

**framboise** /frɑ̃bwaz/ nf raspberry. **framboisier** nm raspberry bush.

**franc,** franche /frɑ̃, -ʃ/ adj frank; (regard) frank, candid; (cassure) clean; (net) clear; (libre) free; (véritable) downright. ●nm franc.

**français,** ~e /frɑ̃sɛ, -z/ adj French. ●nm (Ling) French. F~, ~e nm, f Frenchman, Frenchwoman.

**France** /frɑ̃s/ nf France.

**franchement** /frɑ̃ʃmã/ adv frankly; (nettement) clearly; (tout à fait) really.

**franchir** /frɑ̃ʃir/ 🛾 vt (obstacle) get over; (distance) cover; (limite) exceed; (traverser) cross.

**franchise** /frɑ̃ʃiz/ nf (qualité) frankness; (Comm) franchise; (exemption) exemption; ~ **douanière** exemption from duties.

**franc-maçon** (pl **francs-maçons**) /frɑ̃masɔ̃/ nm Freemason. **franc-maçonnerie** nf Freemasonry.

**franco** /frɑ̃ko/ adv postage paid.

**francophone** /frɑ̃kɔfɔn/ adj French-speaking. ●nmf French speaker.

**franc-parler** /frɑ̃parle/ nm inv outspokenness.

**frange** /frɑ̃ʒ/ nf fringe.

**frappe** /frap/ nf (de texte) typing.

**frappé,** ~e /frape/ adj chilled.

**frapper** /frape/ 🚹 vt/i strike; (battre) hit, strike; (monnaie) print; (à la porte) knock, bang; **frappé de panique** panic-stricken.

**fraternel,** ~le /fraternɛl/ adj brotherly. **fraternité** nf brotherhood.

**fraude** /frod/ nf fraud; (à un examen) cheating; **passer qch en** ~ smuggle sth in. **frauder** 🚹 vt/i cheat. **frauduleux, -euse** adj fraudulent.

**frayer** /freje/ 🛐 vt open up. □ **se** ~ vpr **se** ~ **un passage** force one's way (à travers, dans through).

**frayeur** /frejœr/ nf fright.

**fredonner** /frədɔne/ 🚹 vt hum.

**free-lance** /frilɑ̃s/ adj & nmf freelance.

**freezer** /fʀizœʀ/ nm freezer.

**frein** /fʀɛ̃/ nm brake; mettre un ~ à qch; ~ à main hand brake.

**freiner** /fʀene/ **1** vt slow down; (modérer, enrayer) curb. ● vi (Auto) brake.

**frêle** /fʀɛl/ adj frail.

**frelon** /fʀəlɔ̃/ nm hornet.

**frémir** /fʀemiʀ/ **2** vi shudder, shake; (feuille, eau) quiver.

**frêne** /fʀɛn/ nm ash.

**frénésie** /fʀenezi/ nf frenzy. **frénétique** adj frenzied.

**fréquemment** /fʀekamɑ̃/ adv frequently. **fréquence** nf frequency. **fréquent, ~e** adj frequent. **fréquentation** nf frequenting.

**fréquentations** /fʀekɑ̃tasjɔ̃/ nfpl acquaintances; avoir de mauvaises ~ keep bad company.

**fréquenter** /fʀekɑ̃te/ **1** vt frequent; (école) attend; (personne) see.

**frère** /fʀɛʀ/ nm brother.

**fret** /fʀɛt/ nm freight.

**friand, ~e** /fʀijɑ̃, -d/ adj ~ de very fond of.

**friandise** /fʀijɑ̃diz/ nf sweet; (US) candy; (gâteau) cake.

**fric** /fʀik/ nm **1** money.

**friction** /fʀiksjɔ̃/ nf friction; (massage) rub-down.

**frigidaire** ® /fʀiʒidɛʀ/ nm refrigerator.

**frigo** /fʀigo/ nm **1** fridge. **frigorifique** adj (vitrine etc.) refrigerated.

**frileux, -euse** /fʀilø, -z/ adj sensitive to cold.

**frime** /fʀim/ nf **1** c'est de la ~ it's all pretence; pour la ~ for show.

**frimousse** /fʀimus/ nf face.

**fringale** /fʀɛ̃gal/ nf **1** ravenous appetite.

**fringant, ~e** /fʀɛ̃gɑ̃, -t/ adj dashing.

**fringues** /fʀɛ̃g/ nfpl **1** gear.

**friper** /fʀipe/ **1** vt crumple, crease. □ se ~ vpr crumple, crease.

**fripon, ~ne** /fʀipɔ̃, -ɔn/ nm, f rascal. ● adj mischievous.

**fripouille** /fʀipuj/ nf rogue.

**frire** /fʀiʀ/ **58** vt/i fry; faire ~ fry.

**frise** /fʀiz/ nf frieze.

**friser** /fʀize/ **1** vt/i (cheveux) curl; (personne) curl the hair of; frisé curly.

**frisson** /fʀisɔ̃/ nm (de froid) shiver; (de peur) shudder. **frissonner** **1** vi shiver; shudder.

**frit, ~e** /fʀi, -t/ adj fried.

**frite** /fʀit/ nf chip; avoir la ~ **1** feel good.

**friteuse** /fʀitøz/ nf chip pan; (électrique) (deep) fryer.

**friture** /fʀityʀ/ nf fried fish; (huile) (frying) oil ou fat.

**frivole** /fʀivɔl/ adj frivolous.

**froid, ~e** /fʀwa, -d/ adj & nm cold; avoir/prendre ~ be/catch cold; il fait ~ it is cold. **froidement** adv coldly; (calculer) coolly. **froideur** nf coldness.

**froisser** /fʀwase/ **1** vt crumple; (fig) offend. □ se ~ vpr crumple; (fig) take offence; se ~ un muscle strain a muscle.

**frôler** /fʀole/ **1** vt brush against, skim; (fig) come close to.

**fromage** /fʀɔmaʒ/ nm cheese.

**fromager, -ère** /fʀɔmaʒe, -ɛʀ/ adj cheese. ● nm, f (fabricant) cheese-maker; (marchand) cheesemonger.

**froment** /fʀɔmɑ̃/ nm wheat.

**froncer** /fʀɔ̃se/ **10** vt gather; ~ les sourcils frown.

**front** /fʀɔ̃/ nm forehead; (Mil, Pol) front; de ~ at the same time; (de

face) head-on; (côte à côte)
abreast; faire ~ à face up to. **fron-
tal, ~e** (*mpl* **-aux**) */fʀɔ̃tal/ adj* frontal; (Ordinat) front-end.

**frontalier, -ière** /fʀɔ̃talje, -jɛʀ/ *adj*
border; travailleur ~ commuter
from across the border.

**frontière** /fʀɔ̃tjɛʀ/ *nf* border,
frontier.

**frottement** /fʀɔtmɑ̃/ *nm* rubbing;
(Tech) friction. **frotter 1** */vt/i* rub;
(*allumette*) strike.

**frottis** /fʀɔti/ *nm* ~ vaginal cer-
vical smear.

**frousse** /fʀus/ *nf* 1 fear; avoir la
~ 1 be scared.

**fructifier** /fʀyktifje, 45 *vi* faire ~
put to work.

**fructueux, -euse** /fʀyktɥø, -z/ *adj*
fruitful.

**frugal, ~e** (*mpl* **-aux**) /fʀygal, -o/
*adj* frugal.

**fruit** /fʀɥi/ *nm* fruit; des ~s (some)
fruit; ~s de mer seafood. **fruité,
~e** *adj* fruity.

**frustrant, ~e** /fʀystʀɑ̃, -t / *adj*
frustrating. **frustrer 1** *vt* frustrate.

**fuel** /fjul/ *nm* fuel oil.

**fugitif, -ive** /fyʒitif, -v/ *adj* (*passager*) fleeting. ● *nm, f* fugitive.

**fugue** /fyg/ *nf* (Mus) fugue; faire
une ~ run away.

**fuir** /fɥiʀ/ 35 *vi* flee, run away; (*eau,
robinet, etc.*) leak. ● *vt* (quitter) flee;
(éviter) shun.

**fuite** /fɥit/ *nf* flight; (de liquide,
d'une nouvelle) leak; en ~ on the
run; mettre en ~ put to flight;
prendre la ~ take flight.

**fulgurant, ~e** /fylgyʀɑ̃, -t/ *adj*
(*vitesse*) lightning.

**fumé, ~e** /fyme/ *adj* (*poisson,
verre*) smoked.

**fumée** /fyme/ *nf* smoke; (vapeur)
steam.

**fumer** /fyme/ 1 *vt/i* smoke.

**fumeur, -euse** /fymœʀ, -øz/ *nm, f*
smoker; zone non-~s no smok-
ing area.

**fumier** /fymje/ *nm* manure.

**funambule** /fynɑ̃byl/ *nmf* tightrope walker.

**funèbre** /fynɛbʀ/ *adj* funeral; (fig)
gloomy.

**funérailles** /fyneʀɑj/ *nfpl* funeral.

**funéraire** /fyneʀɛʀ/ *adj* funeral.

**funeste** /fynɛst/ *adj* fatal.

**fur:** au ~ et à mesure /ofyʀea-
mɑzyʀ/ *loc* as one goes along, pro-
gressively; au ~ et à mesure
que as.

**furet** /fyʀɛ/ *nm* ferret.

**fureur** /fyʀœʀ/ *nf* fury; (passion)
passion; avec ~ furiously; passion-
ately; mettre en ~ infuriate; faire
~ be all the rage.

**furieux, -ieuse** /fyʀjø, -z/ *adj*
furious.

**furoncle** /fyʀɔ̃kl/ *nm* boil.

**furtif, -ive** /fyʀtif, -v/ *adj* furtive.

**fuseau** (*pl* **~x**) /fyzo/ *nm* ski trousers; (pour filer) spindle; ~ horaire
time zone.

**fusée** /fyze/ *nf* rocket.

**fusible** /fyzibl/ *nm* fuse.

**fusil** /fyzi/ *nm* rifle, gun; (de chasse)
shotgun; ~ mitrailleur
machine-gun.

**fusion** /fyzjɔ̃/ *nf* fusion; (Comm)
merger. **fusionner 1** *vt/i* merge.

**fut** /fy/ ⇒**ÊTRE 5**.

**fût** /fy/ *nm* (tonneau) barrel; (d'arbre) trunk.

**futé, ~e** /fyte/ *adj* cunning.

**futile** /fytil/ *adj* futile.

**futur, ~e** /fytyʀ/ *adj* future; ~e
femme/maman wife-/mother-
to-be. ● *nm* future.

**fuyant, ~e** /fɥijɑ̃, -t/ *adj* (*front,*

*ligne*) receding; (*personne*) evasive.
**fuyard, ~e** /fɥijaʀ, -d/ *nm, f* runaway.

# Gg

**gabardine** /gabaʀdin/ *nf* raincoat.
**gabarit** /gabaʀi/ *nm* size; (patron) template; (fig) calibre.
**gâcher** /gɑʃe/ **1** *vt* (gâter) spoil; (gaspiller) waste.
**gâchette** /gɑʃɛt/ *nf* trigger.
**gâchis** /gɑʃi/ *nm* waste.
**gaffe** /gaf/ *nf* Ⓘ blunder; **faire ~** be careful (à of).
**gage** /gaʒ/ *nm* security; (de bonne foi) pledge; (de jeu) forfeit; **~s** (salaire) wages; **en ~ de** as a token of; **mettre en ~** pawn; **tueur à ~s** hired killer.
**gageure** /gaʒyʀ/ *nf* challenge.
**gagnant, ~e** /gaɲɑ̃, -t/ *adj* winning. ● *nm, f* winner.
**gagne-pain** /gaɲpɛ̃/ *nm inv* job.
**gagner** /gaɲe/ **1** *vt* (*match, prix*) win; (*argent, pain*) earn; (*terrain*) gain; (*temps*) save; (atteindre) reach; (convaincre) win over; **~ sa vie** earn one's living. ● *vi* win; (fig) gain.
**gai, ~e** /ge/ *adj* cheerful; (ivre) merry. **gaiement** *adv* cheerfully. **gaieté** *nf* cheerfulness.
**gain** /gɛ̃/ *nm* (salaire) earnings; (avantage) gain; (économie) saving; **~s** (Comm) profits; (au jeu) winnings.
**gaine** /gɛn/ *nf* (corset) girdle; (étui) sheath.
**galant, ~e** /galɑ̃, -t/ *adj* courteous; (amoureux) romantic.
**galaxie** /galaksi/ *nf* galaxy.
**gale** /gal/ *nf* (de chat etc.) mange.
**galère** /galɛʀ/ *nf* (navire) galley; **c'est la ~!** Ⓘ what an ordeal!
**galérer** /galeʀe/ **14** *vi* Ⓘ (peiner) have a hard time.
**galerie** /galʀi/ *nf* gallery; (Théât) circle; (de voiture) roof-rack; **~ marchande** shopping arcade.
**galet** /galɛ/ *nm* pebble.
**galette** /galɛt/ *nf* flat cake; **~ des Rois** Twelfth Night cake.
**Galles** /gal/ *nfpl* **le pays de ~** Wales.
**gallois, ~e** /galwa, -z/ *adj* Welsh. ● *nm* (Ling) Welsh. **G~, ~e** *nm, f* Welshman, Welshwoman.
**galon** /galɔ̃/ *nm* braid; (Mil) stripe; **prendre du ~** be promoted.
**galop** /galo/ *nm* canter; **aller au ~** canter; **grand ~** gallop; **~ d'essai** trial run. **galoper** **1** *vi* (*cheval*) canter; (au grand galop) gallop; (*personne*) run.
**galopin** /galɔpɛ̃/ *nm* Ⓘ rascal.
**gambader** /gɑ̃bade/ **1** *vi* leap about.
**gamelle** /gamɛl/ *nf* (de soldat) mess kit; (d'ouvrier) lunch-box.
**gamin, ~e** /gamɛ̃, -in/ *adj* childish; (*air*) youthful. ● *nm, f* Ⓘ kid.
**gamme** /gam/ *nf* (Mus) scale; (série) range; **haut de ~** up-market, top of the range; **bas de ~** down-market, bottom of the range.
**gang** /gɑ̃g/ *nm* Ⓘ gang.
**ganglion** /gɑ̃glijɔ̃/ *nm* ganglion.
**gangster** /gɑ̃gstɛʀ/ *nm* gangster; (escroc) crook.
**gant** /gɑ̃/ *nm* glove; **~ de ménage** rubber glove; **~ de toilette** face-flannel, face-cloth.

**garage** /gaʀaʒ/ nm garage. **garagiste** nmf garage owner; (employé) car mechanic.

**garant, ~e** /gaʀɑ̃, -t/ nm, f guarantor. ● adj se porter ~ de vouch for.

**garanti, ~e** /gaʀɑ̃ti/ adj guaranteed.

**garantie** /gaʀɑ̃ti/ nf guarantee; ~s (de police d'assurance) cover. **garantir** ❷ vt guarantee; (protéger) protect (de from).

**garçon** /gaʀsɔ̃/ nm boy; (jeune homme) young man; (célibataire) bachelor; ~ (de café) waiter; ~ d'honneur best man. **garçonnière** nf bachelor flat.

**garde**[1] /gaʀd/ nf guard; (d'enfants, de bagages) care; (service) guard (duty); (infirmière) nurse; de ~ on duty; ~ à vue (police) custody; mettre en ~ warn; prendre ~ be careful (à of); (droit de) ~ custody (of).

**garde**[2] /gaʀd/ nm guard; (de propriété, parc) warden; ~ champêtre village policeman; ~ du corps bodyguard.

**garde-à-vous** /gaʀdavu/ nm inv (Mil) se mettre au ~ stand to attention.

**garde-chasse** (pl ~s) /gaʀdəʃas/ nm gamekeeper.

**garde-manger** /gaʀdəmɑ̃ʒe/ nm inv meat safe; (placard) larder.

**garder** /gaʀde/ ❶ vt (conserver, maintenir) keep; (vêtement) keep on; (surveiller) look after; (défendre) guard; ~ le lit stay in bed. □ se ~ vpr (denrée) keep; se ~ de faire be careful not to do.

**garderie** /gaʀdəʀi/ nf day nursery.

**garde-robe** (pl ~s) /gaʀdəʀɔb/ nf wardrobe.

**gardien, ~ne** /gaʀdjɛ̃, -ɛn/ nm, f (de locaux) security guard; (de pri-

son, réserve) warden; (d'immeuble) caretaker; (de musée) attendant; (de zoo) keeper; (de traditions) guardian; ~ de but goalkeeper; ~ de la paix policeman; ~ de nuit night watchman; **gardienne d'enfants** childminder.

**gare** /gaʀ/ nf (Rail) station; ~ routière coach station; (US) bus station. ● interj ~ (à toi) watch out!

**garer** /gaʀe/ ❶ vt park. □ se ~ vpr park; (s'écarter) move out of the way.

**gargouille** /gaʀguj/ nf waterspout; (sculptée) gargoyle. **gargouiller** ❶ vi gurgle; (stomach) rumble.

**garni, ~e** /gaʀni/ adj (plat) served with vegetables; **bien ~** (rempli) well-filled.

**garnir** /gaʀniʀ/ ❷ vt (remplir) fill; (décorer) decorate; (couvrir) cover; (doubler) line; (Culin) garnish. **garniture** nf (légumes) vegetables; (ornement) trimming; (de voiture) trim.

**gars** /ga/ nm 🗓 lad; (adulte) guy, bloke.

**gas-oil** /gazwal/ nm diesel (oil).

**gaspillage** /gaspijaʒ/ nm waste. **gaspiller** ❶ vt waste.

**gastrique** /gastʀik/ adj gastric.

**gastronome** /gastʀɔnɔm/ nmf gourmet.

**gâteau** (pl ~x) /gato/ nm cake; ~ sec biscuit; (US) cookie; **un papa ~** a doting dad.

**gâter** /gate/ ❶ vt spoil. □ se ~ vpr (viande) go bad; (dent) rot; (temps) get worse.

**gâterie** /gatʀi/ nf little treat.

**gâteux, -euse** /gatø, -z/ adj senile.

**gauche** /goʃ/ adj left; (maladroit) awkward. ● nf left; à ~ on the left; (direction) (to the) left; **la ~** the left (side); (Pol) the left (wing).

**gaucher**, -ère /goʃe, -ɛʀ/ adj left handed.

**gaufre** /gofʀ/ nf waffle. **gaufrette** nf wafer.

**gaulois**, ~e /golwa, -z/ adj Gallic; (fig) bawdy. **G~**, ~e nm, f Gaul.

**gaver** /gave/ **1** vt force-feed; (fig) cram. □ **se** ~ **de** vpr gorge oneself with; (fig) devour.

**gaz** /gaz/ nm inv gas; ~ **d'échappement** exhaust fumes; ~ **lacrymogène** tear-gas.

**gaze** /gaz/ nf gauze.

**gazer** /gaze/ **1** vi **1** ça gaze? how's things?

**gazette** /gazɛt/ nf newspaper.

**gazeux**, -euse /gazø, -z/ adj (boisson) fizzy; (eau) sparkling.

**gazoduc** /gazɔdyk/ nm gas pipeline.

**gazon** /gazɔ̃/ nm lawn, grass.

**gazouiller** /gazuje/ **1** vi (oiseau) chirp; (bébé) babble.

**GDF** abrév m (**Gaz de France**) French gas board.

**géant**, ~e /ʒeɑ̃, -t/ adj giant. ● nm giant. **géante** nf giantess.

**geindre** /ʒɛ̃dʀ/ **22** vi groan, moan.

**gel** /ʒɛl/ nm frost; (produit) gel; (Comm) freeze; ~ **coiffant** hair gel.

**gelée** /ʒ(ə)le/ nf frost; (Culin) jelly; ~ **blanche** hoarfrost.

**geler** /ʒəle/ **6** vt/i freeze; on gèle (on a froid) it's freezing; il ou ça gèle (il fait froid) it's freezing.

**gélule** /ʒelyl/ nf (Méd) capsule.

**Gémeaux** /ʒemo/ nmpl Gemini.

**gémir** /ʒemiʀ/ **2** vi groan.

**gênant**, ~e /ʒɛnɑ̃, -t/ adj embarrassing; (irritant) annoying; (incommode) cumbersome.

**gencive** /ʒɑ̃siv/ nf gum.

**gendarme** /ʒɑ̃daʀm/ nm police-

man, gendarme. **gendarmerie** nf police force; (local) police station.

**gendre** /ʒɑ̃dʀ/ nm son-in-law.

**gène** /ʒɛn/ nm gene.

**gêne** /ʒɛn/ nf discomfort; (confusion) embarrassment; (dérangement) trouble, inconvenience; (pauvreté) poverty.

**gêné**, ~e /ʒene/ adj embarrassed; (désargenté) short of money.

**généalogie** /ʒenealɔʒi/ nf genealogy.

**gêner** /ʒene/ **1** vt bother, disturb; (troubler) embarrass; (entraver) block; (faire mal) hurt.

**général**, ~e /ʒeneʀal/ adj general; en ~ in general. ● nm (pl **-aux**) general.

**généralement** /ʒeneʀalmɑ̃/ adv generally.

**généraliser** /ʒeneʀalize/ **1** vt make general. ● vi generalize. □ **se** ~ vpr become widespread ou general.

**généraliste** /ʒeneʀalist/ nmf general practitioner, GP.

**généralité** /ʒeneʀalite/ nf general point.

**génération** /ʒeneʀasjɔ̃/ nf generation.

**généreux**, ~euse /ʒeneʀø, -z/ adj generous.

**générique** /ʒeneʀik/ nm (au cinéma) credits. ● adj generic.

**générosité** /ʒeneʀozite/ nf generosity.

**génétique** /ʒenetik/ adj genetic. ● nf genetics.

**Genève** /ʒanɛv/ npr Geneva.

g

**génial, ∼e** /ʒenjal, -jo/ (mpl **-iaux**) adj brilliant; (fantastique 🗊) fantastic.

**génie** /ʒeni/ nm genius; ∼ civil civil engineering.

**génital, ∼e** /ʒenital, -o/ (mpl **-aux**) adj genital.

**génocide** /ʒenosid/ nm genocide.

**génoise** /ʒenwaz/ nf sponge (cake).

**génome** /ʒenom/ nm genome.

**génothèque** /ʒenotɛk/ nf gene bank.

**genou** /ʒənu/ (pl **∼x**) nm knee; **être à ∼x** be kneeling.

**genre** /ʒɑ̃r/ nm sort, kind; (Gram) gender; (allure) **avoir bon/mauvais ∼** to look nice/disreputable; (comportement) **c'est bien son ∼** it's just like him/her.

**gens** /ʒɑ̃/ nmpl people.

**gentil, ∼le** /ʒɑ̃ti, -j/ adj kind, nice; (sage) good. **gentillesse** nf kindness. **gentiment** adv kindly.

**géographie** /ʒeografi/ nf geography.

**geôlier, -ière** /ʒolje, -jɛr/ nm, f gaoler, jailer.

**géologie** /ʒeoloʒi/ nf geology.

**géomètre** /ʒeomɛtr/ nm surveyor.

**géométrie** /ʒeometri/ nf geometry. **géométrique** adj geometric.

**gérance** /ʒerɑ̃s/ nf management.

**gérant, ∼e** /ʒerɑ̃, -t/ nm, f manager, manageress; ∼ **d'immeuble** landlord's agent.

**gerbe** /ʒɛrb/ nf (de fleurs) bunch, bouquet; (d'eau) spray; (de blé) sheaf.

**gercer** /ʒɛrse/ 🔟 vt chap; **avoir les lèvres gercées** have chapped lips. ● vi become chapped. **gerçure** nf crack, chap.

**gérer** /ʒere/ 🔢 vt manage, run;

(traiter: fig) (crise, situation) handle.

**germe** /ʒɛrm/ nm germ; ∼**s de soja** bean sprouts.

**germer** /ʒɛrme/ 🔳 vi germinate.

**gestation** /ʒɛstasjɔ̃/ nf gestation.

**geste** /ʒɛst/ nm gesture.

**gesticuler** /ʒɛstikyle/ 🔳 vi gesticulate.

**gestion** /ʒɛstjɔ̃/ nf management. **gestionnaire** nmf administrator.

**ghetto** /ɡeto/ nm ghetto.

**gibier** /ʒibje/ nm (animaux) game.

**giboulée** /ʒibule/ nf shower.

**gicler** /ʒikle/ 🔳 vi squirt; **faire ∼** squirt.

**gifle** /ʒifl/ nf slap in the face. **gifler** 🔳 vt slap.

**gigantesque** /ʒiɡɑ̃tɛsk/ adj gigantic.

**gigot** /ʒiɡo/ nm leg (of lamb).

**gigoter** /ʒiɡote/ 🔳 vi wriggle; (nerveusement) fidget.

**gilet** /ʒile/ nm waistcoat; (cardigan) cardigan; ∼ **de sauvetage** life jacket.

**gingembre** /ʒɛ̃ʒɑ̃br/ nm ginger.

**girafe** /ʒiraf/ nf giraffe.

**giratoire** /ʒiratwar/ adj **sens ∼** roundabout.

**girofle** /ʒirofl/ nm **clou de ∼** clove.

**girouette** /ʒirwɛt/ nf weathercock, weathervane.

**gisement** /ʒizmɑ̃/ nm deposit.

**gitan, ∼e** /ʒitɑ̃, -an/ nm, f gypsy.

**gîte** /ʒit/ nm (maison) home; (abri) shelter; ∼ **rural** holiday cottage.

**givre** /ʒivr/ nm frost; (sur parebrise) ice.

**givré, ∼e** /ʒivre/ adj 🗊 crazy.

**glace** /ɡlas/ nf ice; (crème) icecream; (vitre) window; (miroir) mirror; (verre) glass.

g

**glacé**, ~e /glase/ adj (vent, accueil) icy; (hands) frozen; (gâteau) iced.

**glacer** /glase/ 🔟 vt freeze; (gâteau, boisson) chill; (pétrifier) chill. □ se ~ vpr freeze.

**glacier** /glasje/ nm (Géog) glacier; (vendeur) ice-cream seller. **glacière** nf coolbox. **glaçon** nm ice-cube.

**glaïeul** /glajœl/ nm gladiolus.

**glaise** /glɛz/ nf clay.

**gland** /glɑ̃/ nm acorn; (ornement) tassel.

**glande** /glɑ̃d/ nf gland.

**glander** /glɑ̃de/ 🔟 vi 🗍 laze around.

**glaner** /glane/ 🔟 vt glean.

**glauque** /glok/ adj (fig) murky; (street) squalid.

**glissade** /glisad/ nf (jeu) slide; (dérapage) skid.

**glissant**, ~e /glisɑ̃, -t/ adj slippery.

**glissement** /glismɑ̃/ nm sliding; gliding; (fig) shift; ~ de terrain landslide.

**glisser** /glise/ 🔟 vi slide; (être glissant) be slippery; (sur l'eau) glide; (déraper) slip; (véhicule) skid. ● vt (objet) slide; (dans dans) slip in. □ se ~ vpr slip (dans into).

**glissière** /glisjɛʀ/ nf slide; porte à ~ sliding door; ~ de sécurité (Auto) crash-barrier; fermeture à ~ zip.

**global**, ~e (mpl -aux) /glɔbal, -o/ adj (entier, général) overall. **globalement** adv as a whole.

**globe** /glɔb/ nm globe; ~ oculaire eyeball; ~ terrestre globe.

**globule** /glɔbyl/ nm (du sang) corpuscle.

**gloire** /glwaʀ/ nf glory, fame. **glorieux, -ieuse** adj glorious. **glorifier** 🔢 vt glorify.

**glose** /gloz/ nf gloss.

**glossaire** /glɔsɛʀ/ nm glossary.

**gloussement** /glusmɑ̃/ nm chuckle; (de poule) cluck.

**glouton**, ~ne /glutɔ̃, -ɔn/ adj gluttonous. ● nm, f glutton.

**gluant**, ~e /glyɑ̃, -t/ adj sticky.

**glucose** /glykoz/ nm glucose.

**glycérine** /gliseʀin/ nf glycerin(e).

**GO** abrév fpl **(grandes ondes)** long wave.

**goal** /gol/ nm 🗍 goalkeeper.

**gobelet** /gɔblɛ/ nm cup; (en verre) tumbler.

**gober** /gɔbe/ 🔟 vt swallow (whole); je ne peux pas le ~ 🗍 I can't stand him.

**goéland** /gɔelɑ̃/ nm (sea)gull.

**gogo:** à ~ /agogo/ loc 🗍 galore, in abundance.

**goinfre** /gwɛ̃fʀ/ nm (glouton 🗍) pig. **goinfrer (se)** 🔟 vpr 🗍 stuff oneself (with de with).

**golf** /gɔlf/ nm golf; (terrain) golf course.

**golfe** /gɔlf/ nm gulf.

**gomme** /gɔm/ nf rubber; (US) eraser; (résine) gum. **gommer** 🔟 vt rub out.

**gond** /gɔ̃/ nm hinge; sortir de ses ~s 🗍 go mad.

**gondoler (se)** /(sə)gɔ̃dɔle/ 🔟 vpr (bois) warp; (métal) buckle.

**gonflé**, ~e /gɔ̃fle/ adj swollen; il est ~ 🗍 he's got a nerve.

**gonflement** /gɔ̃flmɑ̃/ nm swelling.

**gonfler** /gɔ̃fle/ 🔟 vt (ballon, pneu) pump up, blow up; (augmenter) increase; (exagérer) inflate. ● vi swell.

**gorge** /gɔʀʒ/ nf throat; (poitrine) breast; (vallée) gorge.

**gorgée** /gɔʀʒe/ nf sip, gulp.

**gorger** /gɔrʒe/ 40 *vt* fill (de with); **gorgé de** full of. □ **se ~** *vpr* gorge oneself (de with).

**gorille** /gɔrij/ *nm* gorilla; (garde 1) bodyguard.

**gosier** /gozje/ *nm* throat.

**gosse** /gɔs/ *nmf* 1 kid.

**gothique** /gɔtik/ *adj* Gothic.

**goudron** /gudrɔ̃/ *nm* tar. **goudronner** 1 *vt* tarmac.

**gouffre** /gufr/ *nm* abyss, gulf.

**goujat** /guʒa/ *nm* lout, boor.

**goulot** /gulo/ *nm* neck; **boire au ~** drink from the bottle.

**goulu, ~e** /guly/ *adj* gluttonous. ● *nm, f* glutton.

**gourde** /gurd/ *nf* (à eau) flask; (idiot 1) fool.

**gourer (se)** /(sə)gure/ 1 *vpr* 1 make a mistake.

**gourmand, ~e** /gurmɑ̃, -d/ *adj* greedy. ● *nm, f* glutton.

**gourmandise** /gurmɑ̃diz/ *nf* greed; ~s sweets.

**gourmet** /gurmɛ/ *nm* gourmet.

**gourmette** /gurmɛt/ *nf* chain bracelet.

**gousse** /gus/ *nf* ~ **d'ail** clove of garlic.

**goût** /gu/ *nm* taste; (gré) liking; **prendre ~ à** develop a taste for; **avoir bon ~** (aliment) taste nice; (personne) have good taste; **donner du ~ à** give flavour.

**goûter** /gute/ 1 *vt* taste; (apprécier) enjoy; ~ **à** ou **de** taste. ● *vi* have tea. ● *nm* tea, snack.

**goutte** /gut/ *nf* drop; (Méd) gout. **goutte-à-goutte** *nm inv* drip. **goutter** 1 *vi* drip.

**gouttière** /gutjɛr/ *nf* gutter.

**gouvernail** /guvɛrnaj/ *nm* rudder; (barre) helm.

**gouvernement** /guvɛrnəmɑ̃/ *nm* government.

**gouverner** /guvɛrne/ 1 *vt/i* govern; (dominer) control. **gouverneur** *nm* governor.

**GPS** *abrév m* (global positioning system) GPS.

**grâce** /grɑs/ *nf* (charme) grace; (faveur) favour; (volonté) grace; (Jur) pardon; (Relig) grace; ~ **à** thanks to; **rendre** (~s) **à** give thanks to.

**gracier** /grasje/ 45 *vt* pardon.

**gracieusement** /grasjøzmɑ̃/ *adv* gracefully; (gratuitement) free (of charge).

**gracieux, -ieuse** /grasjø, -z/ *adj* graceful.

**grade** /grad/ *nm* rank; **monter en ~** be promoted.

**gradin** /gradɛ̃/ *nm* tier, step; **en ~s** terraced; **les ~s** terraces.

**gradué, ~e** /gradɥe/ *adj* graded, graduated; **verre ~** measuring jug.

**graffiti** /grafiti/ *nmpl* graffiti.

**grain** /grɛ̃/ *nm* grain; (Naut) squall; ~ **de beauté** beauty spot; ~ **de café** coffee bean; ~ **de poivre** pepper corn; ~ **de raisin** grape.

**graine** /grɛn/ *nf* seed.

**graisse** /grɛs/ *nf* fat; (lubrifiant) grease. **graisser** 1 *vt* grease. **graisseux, -euse** *adj* greasy.

**grammaire** /gram(m)ɛr/ *nf* grammar.

**gramme** /gram/ *nm* gram.

**grand, ~e** /grɑ̃, -d/ *adj* big, large; (haut) tall; (intense, fort) great; (brillant) great; (principal) main; (plus âgé) big, elder; (adulte) grown-up; **au ~ air** in the open air; **au ~ jour** in broad daylight; (fig) in the open; **en ~e partie** largely; ~**e banlieue** outer suburbs; ~ **ensemble** housing estate; ~**es lignes** (Rail) main lines; ~ **magasin** department store; ~**e personne**

grown-up; ~ **public** general public; ~e **surface** hypermarket; ~es **vacances summer** holidays. ● adv (ouvrir) wide; ~ **ouvert** wide open; **voir** ~ think big. ● nm, f (adulte) grown-up; (enfant) big boy, big girl; (Scol) senior.

**grand-chose** /gʁɑ̃ʃoz/ pron pas ~ not much, not a lot.

**Grande-Bretagne** /gʁɑ̃dbʁətaɲ/ nf Great Britain.

> **Grande école** A prestigious tertiary education institution to which admission is usually by competitive examination or concours. Places are much sought after as they generally guarantee more promising career prospects than the standard universities. Many grandes écoles specialize in particular disciplines or fields of study, e.g. ENA (public administration), Sciences Po (political science), etc.

**grandeur** /gʁɑ̃dœʁ/ nf greatness; (dimension) size; **folie des** ~s delusions of grandeur.

**grandir** /gʁɑ̃diʁ/ ② vi grow; (bruit) grow louder. ● vt (talons) make taller; (loupe) magnify.

**grand-mère** (pl **grands-mères**) /gʁɑ̃mɛʁ/ nf grandmother.

**grand-père** (pl **grands-pères**) /gʁɑ̃pɛʁ/ nm grandfather.

**grands-parents** /gʁɑ̃paʁɑ̃/ nmpl grandparents.

**grange** /gʁɑ̃ʒ/ nf barn.

**granulé** /gʁanyle/ nm granule.

**graphique** /gʁafik/ adj graphic; (Ordinat) graphics; **informatique** ~ computer graphics. ● nm graph.

**graphologie** /gʁafɔlɔʒi/ nf graphology.

**grappe** /gʁap/ nf cluster; ~ de

raisin bunch of grapes.

**gras, ~se** /gʁɑ, -s/ adj (gros) fat; (aliment) fatty; (surface, peau, cheveux) greasy; (épais) thick; (caractères) bold; **faire la** ~se **matinée** sleep late. ● nm (Culin) fat.

**gratifiant, ~e** /gʁatifjɑ̃, -t/ adj gratifying; (travail) rewarding.

**gratifier** /gʁatifje/ ⏵ vt favour, reward (de with).

**gratin** /gʁatɛ̃/ nm gratin (baked dish with cheese topping); (élite ▯) upper crust.

**gratis** /gʁatis/ adv free.

**gratitude** /gʁatityd/ nf gratitude.

**gratte-ciel** /gʁatsjɛl/ nm inv skyscraper.

**gratter** /gʁate/ ▯ vt/i scratch; (avec un outil) scrape; **ça me gratte** ▯ it itches. □ **se** ~ vpr scratch oneself; **se** ~ **la tête** scratch one's head.

**gratuiciel** /gʁatɥisjɛl/ nm (Internet) freeware.

**gratuit, ~e** /gʁatɥi, -t/ adj free; (acte) gratuitous. **gratuitement** adv free (of charge).

**grave** /gʁav/ adj (maladie, accident, problème) serious; (solennel) grave; (voix) deep; (accent) grave. **gravement** adv seriously; gravely.

**graver** /gʁave/ ▯ vt engrave; (sur bois) carve; (Ordinat) burn.

**graveur** /gʁavœʁ/ nm (Ordinat) burner.

**gravier** /gʁavje/ nm **du** ~ gravel.

**gravité** /gʁavite/ nf gravity.

**graviter** /gʁavite/ ▯ vi revolve.

**gravure** /gʁavyʁ/ nf engraving; (de tableau, photo) print, plate.

**gré** /gʁe/ nm willing will; (goût) taste; **à son** ~ (agir) as one likes; **de bon** ~ willingly; **bon** ~ **mal** ~ like it or not; **je vous en saurais** ~ I'd be grateful for that.

**grec**, ~que /gʀɛk/ adj Greek. ●nm (Ling) Greek. **G~**, ~que nm, f Greek.

**Grèce** nf /gʀɛs/ Greece.

**greffe** /gʀɛf/ nf graft; (d'organe) transplant. **greffer 1** vt graft; transplant.

**greffier**, -ière /gʀefje, -jɛʀ/ nm, f clerk of the court.

**grêle** /gʀɛl/ adj (maigre) spindly; (voix) shrill. ●nf hail.

**grêler** /gʀele/ **1** vi hail; **il grêle** it's hailing. **grêlon** nm hailstone.

**grelot** /gʀəlo/ nm (little) bell.

**grelotter** /gʀəlɔte/ **1** vi shiver.

**grenade** /gʀənad/ nf (fruit) pomegranate; (explosif) grenade.

**grenat** /gʀəna/ adj inv dark red.

**grenier** /gʀənje/ nm attic; (pour grain) loft.

**grenouille** /gʀənuj/ nf frog.

**grès** /gʀɛ/ nm sandstone; (poterie) stoneware.

**grésiller** /gʀezije/ **1** vi sizzle; (radio) crackle.

**grève** /gʀɛv/ nf (rivage) shore; (cessation de travail) strike; **faire ~**, **être en ~** be on strike; **se mettre en ~** go on strike. **gréviste** nmf striker.

**gribouiller** /gʀibuje/ **1** vt/i scribble.

**grief** /gʀijɛf/ nm grievance.

**grièvement** /gʀijɛvmã/ adv seriously.

**griffe** /gʀif/ nf claw; (de couturier) label; **coup de ~** scratch.

**griffé**, ~e /gʀife/ adj (vêtement, article) designer.

**griffer** /gʀife/ **1** vt scratch, claw.

**grignoter** /gʀiɲɔte/ **1** vt/i nibble.

**gril** /gʀil/ nm (de cuisinière) grill; (plaque) grill pan.

**grillade** /gʀijad/ nf (viande) grill.

**grillage** /gʀijaʒ/ nm wire netting.

**grille** /gʀij/ nf railings; (portail) (metal) gate; (de fenêtre) bars; (de cheminée) grate; (fig) grid. **grille-pain** nm inv toaster.

**griller** /gʀije/ **1** vt (pain) toast; (viande) grill; (ampoule) blow; (feu rouge) go through; (appareil) burn out. ●vi (ampoule) blow; (Culin) **faire ~** (viande) grill; (pain) toast.

**grillon** /gʀijõ/ nm cricket.

**grimace** /gʀimas/ nf (funny) face; (de douleur, dégoût) grimace; **faire des ~s** make faces; **faire la ~** pull a face, grimace.

**grimper** /gʀɛ̃pe/ **1** vt climb. ●vi climb; **~ sur ou dans un arbre** climb a tree.

**grincement** /gʀɛ̃smã/ nm creak(ing).

**grincer** /gʀɛ̃se/ **10** vi creak; **~ des dents** grind one's teeth.

**grincheux**, -euse /gʀɛ̃ʃø, -z/ adj grumpy.

**grippe** /gʀip/ nf influenza, flu.

**grippé**, ~e /gʀipe/ adj **être ~** have (the) flu; (mécanisme) be seized up ou jammed.

**gris**, ~e /gʀi, -z/ adj grey; (saoul) tipsy.

**grivois**, ~e /gʀivwa, -z/ adj bawdy.

**grog** /gʀɔg/ nm hot toddy.

**grogner** /gʀɔɲe/ **1** vi (animal) growl; (personne) grumble.

**grognon** /gʀɔɲõ/ adj grumpy.

**groin** /gʀwɛ̃/ nm snout.

**gronder** /gʀõde/ **1** vi (tonnerre, volcan) rumble; (chien) growl; (conflit) be brewing. ●vt scold.

**groom** /gʀum/ nm bellboy.

**gros**, ~se /gʀo, -s/ adj big, large; (gras) fat; (important) big; (épais) thick; (lourd) heavy; (buveur, fu-

*meur*) heavy; ~ **bonnet** 🖼 bigwig; ~ **lot** jackpot; ~ **mot** swear word; ~ **plan** close-up; ~**se caisse** bass drum; ~ **titre** headline. ● *nm, f* fat man, fat woman. ● *adv* (*écrire*) big; (*risquer, gagner*) a lot. ● *nm* **le** ~ **de** the bulk of; **de** ~ (Comm) wholesale; **en** ~ roughly; (Comm) wholesale.

**groseille** /gRozɛj/ *nf* redcurrant; ~ **à maquereau** gooseberry.

**grossesse** /gRosɛs/ *nf* pregnancy.

**grosseur** /gRosœR/ *nf* (*volume*) size; (*enflure*) lump.

**grossier, -ière** /gRosje, -jɛR/ *adj* (*sans finesse*) coarse, rough; (*rudimentaire*) crude; (*vulgaire*) coarse; (*impoli*) rude; (*erreur*) gross. **grossièrement** *adv* (*sommairement*) roughly; (*vulgairement*) coarsely.

**grossièreté** *nf* coarseness; crudeness; rudeness; (*mot*) rude word.

**grossir** /gRosiR/ 🔁 *vt* (*faire augmenter*) increase, boost; (*agrandir*) enlarge; (*exagérer*) exaggerate; ~ **les rangs** *ou* **la foule** swell the ranks. ● *vi* (*personne*) put on weight; (*augmenter*) grow.

**grossiste** /gRosist/ *nmf* wholesaler.

**grosso modo** /gRosomodo/ *adv* roughly.

**grotesque** /gRotɛsk/ *adj* grotesque; (*ridicule*) ludicrous.

**grotte** /gRot/ *nf* cave; grotto.

**grouiller** /gRuje/ 🔁 *vi* swarm; ~ **de** be swarming with.

**groupe** /gRup/ *nm* group; (Mus) group, band; ~ **électrogène** generating set; ~ **scolaire** school; ~ **de travail** working party.

**groupement** /gRupmɑ̃/ *nm* grouping.

**grouper** /gRupe/ 🔁 *vt* put together. □ **se** ~ *vpr* group (together).

**grue** /gRy/ *nf* (*machine, oiseau*) crane.

**gruyère** /gRyjɛR/ *nm* gruyère (cheese).

**gué** /ge/ *nm* ford; **passer** *ou* **traverser à** ~ ford.

**guenon** /gənɔ̃/ *nf* female monkey.

**guépard** /gepaR/ *nm* cheetah.

**guêpe** /gɛp/ *nf* wasp.

**guère** /gɛR/ *adv* **ne** ~ hardly; **il n'y a** ~ **d'espoir** there is no hope; **elle n'a** ~ **dormi** she didn't sleep much, she hardly slept.

**guérilla** /geRija/ *nf* guerrilla warfare; (*groupe*) guerillas.

**guérir** /geRiR/ 🔁 *vt* (*personne, maladie, mal*) cure (**de** of); (*plaie, membre*) heal. ● *vi* get better; (*blessure*) heal; ~ **de** recover from. **guérison** *nf* curing; healing; (*de personne*) recovery.

**guerre** /gɛR/ *nf* war; **en** ~ at war; **faire la** ~ wage war (**à** against); ~ **civile** civil war; ~ **mondiale** world war.

**guerrier, -ière** /geRje, -jɛR/ *adj* warlike. ● *nm, f* warrior.

**guet** /gɛ/ *nm* watch; **faire le** ~ **be** on the watch. **guet-apens** (*pl* **guets-apens**) *nm* ambush.

**guetter** /gete/ 🔁 *vt* watch; (*attendre*) watch out for.

**gueule** /gœl/ *nf* mouth; (figure 🖼) face; **ta** ~! shut up!; ~ **de bois** 🖼 hangover.

**gueuleton** /gœltɔ̃/ *nm* 🖼 blowout, slap-up meal.

**gui** /gi/ *nm* mistletoe.

**guichet** /giʃɛ/ *nm* window, counter; (*de gare*) ticket-office; (Théât) box-office; **jouer à** ~**s fermés** (*pièce*) be sold out; ~ **automatique** cash dispenser.

**guide** /gid/ *nm* guide. ● *nf* (*fille scout*) girl guide.

**guider** /gide/ **1** vt guide.

**guidon** /gidɔ̃/ nm handlebars.

**guignol** /giɲɔl/ nm puppet; (personne) clown; (spectacle) puppet-show.

**guillemets** /gijmɛ/ nmpl quotation marks, inverted commas; entre ~ in inverted commas.

**guillotine** /gijɔtin/ nf guillotine.

**guimauve** /gimov/ nf marshmallow; c'est de la ~ **1** it's slushy ou schmaltzy **1**.

**guindé**, ~e /gɛ̃de/ adj stiff, formal; (style) stilted.

**guirlande** /giʀlɑ̃d/ nf garland, tinsel.

**guitare** /gitaʀ/ nf guitar.

**gym** /ʒim/ nf gymnastics; (Scol) physical education, PE.

**gymnase** /ʒimnaz/ nm gym(nasium). **gymnastique** nf gymnastics.

**gynécologie** /ʒinekɔlɔʒi/ nf gynaecology.

# Hh

**habile** /abil/ adj skilful, clever.

**habillé**, ~e /abije/ adj (vêtement) smart; (soirée) formal.

**habillement** /abijmɑ̃/ nm clothing.

**habiller** /abije/ **1** vt dress (de in); (équiper) clothe; (recouvrir) cover (de with). □ s'~ vpr get dressed; (élégamment) dress up.

**habit** /abi/ nm (de personnage) outfit; (de cérémonie) tails; ~s clothes.

**habitant**, ~e /abitɑ̃, -t/ nm, f (de maison, quartier) resident; (de pays) inhabitant.

**habitat** /abita/ nm (mode de peuplement) settlement; (conditions) housing.

**habitation** /abitasjɔ̃/ nf (logement) house.

**habité**, ~e /abite/ adj (terre) inhabited.

**habiter** /abite/ **1** vi live. ● vt live in.

**habitude** /abityd/ nf habit; avoir l'~ de be used to; d'~ usually; comme d'~ as usual.

**habitué**, ~e /abitye/ nm, f (client) regular.

**habituel**, ~le /abitɥɛl/ adj usual. **habituellement** adv usually.

**habituer** /abitye/ **1** vt ~ qn à get sb used to. □ s'~ à vpr get used to.

**hache** /'aʃ/ nf axe.

**haché**, ~e /'aʃe/ adj (viande) minced; (phrases) jerky.

**hacher** /'aʃe/ **1** vt mince; (au couteau) chop.

**hachis** /'aʃi/ nm minced meat; (US) ground meat; ~ Parmentier ≈ shepherd's pie.

**hachisch** /'aʃiʃ/ nm hashish.

**hachoir** /'aʃwaʀ/ nm (appareil) mincer; (couteau) chopper; (planche) chopping board.

**haie** /'ɛ/ nf hedge; course de ~s hurdle race.

**haillon** /'ajɔ̃/ nm rag.

**haine** /'ɛn/ nf hatred.

**haïr** /'aiʀ/ **38** vt hate.

**hâlé**, ~e /'ɑle/ adj (sun-)tanned.

**haleine** /alɛn/ nf breath; travail de longue ~ long job.

**haleter** /'alte/ **6** vi pant.

**hall** /'ol/ nm hall; (de gare) concourse.

**halle** /'al/ nf market hall; ∼s covered market.

**halte** /'alt/ nf stop; faire ∼ stop. ● interj stop; (Mil) halt.

**haltère** /altɛʀ/ nm dumbbell; faire des ∼s to do weightlifting.

**hameau** (pl ∼x) /'amo/ nm hamlet.

**hameçon** /amsɔ̃/ nm hook.

**hanche** /'ɑ̃ʃ/ nf hip.

**handicap** /'ɑ̃dikap/ nm handicap. **handicapé, ∼e** adj & nm, f disabled (person).

**hangar** /'ɑ̃gaʀ/ nm shed; (pour avions) hangar.

**hanter** /'ɑ̃te/ **1** vt haunt.

**hantise** /'ɑ̃tiz/ nf dread; avoir la ∼ de dread.

**haras** /'aʀa/ nm stud-farm.

**harasser** /'aʀase/ **1** vt exhaust.

**harcèlement** /aʀsɛlmɑ̃/ nm ∼ sexuel sexual harassment.

**harceler** /aʀsəle/ **6** vt harass.

**hardi, ∼e** /aʀdi/ adj bold.

**hareng** /'aʀɑ̃/ nm herring.

**hargne** /'aʀɲ/ nf (aggressive) bad temper.

**haricot** /'aʀiko/ nm bean; ∼ vert French bean; (US) green bean.

**harmonie** /aʀmɔni/ nf harmony. **harmonieux, -ieuse** adj harmonious.

**harmoniser** /aʀmɔnize/ **1** vt harmonize. □ s'∼ vpr harmonize.

**harnacher** /'aʀnaʃe/ **1** vt harness.

**harnais** /'aʀnɛ/ nm harness.

**harpe** /'aʀp/ nf harp.

**harpon** /'aʀpɔ̃/ nm harpoon.

**hasard** /'azaʀ/ nm chance; (coïncidence) coincidence; les ∼s de the fortunes of; au ∼ (choisir etc.) at random; (flâner) aimlessly. **hasardeux, -euse** adj risky.

**hasarder** /'azaʀde/ **1** vt risk; (remarque) venture.

**hâte** /'ɑt/ nf haste; à la ∼, en ∼ hurriedly; avoir ∼ de look forward to.

**hâter** /'ɑte/ **1** vt hasten. □ se ∼ vpr hurry (de to).

**hâtif, -ive** /'ɑtif, -v/ adj hasty; (précoce) early.

**hausse** /'os/ nf rise (de in); ∼ des prix price rise; en ∼ rising.

**hausser** /'ose/ **1** vt raise; (épaules) shrug.

**haut, ∼e** /'o, 'ot/ adj high; (de taille) tall; à voix ∼e aloud; ∼ en couleur colourful; plus ∼ higher up; (dans un texte) above; en ∼ lieu in high places. ● adv high; tout ∼ out loud. ● nm top; des ∼s et des bas ups and downs; en ∼ (regarder) up; (à l'étage) upstairs; en ∼ de) at the top (of).

**hautbois** /'obwa/ nm oboe.

**haut-de-forme** /'odfɔʀm/ (pl hauts-de-forme) nm top hat.

**hauteur** /'otœʀ/ nf height; (colline) hill; (arrogance) haughtiness; être à la ∼ be up to it; à la ∼ de (ville) near; être à la ∼ de la situation be equal to the situation.

**haut-le-cœur** /'olkœʀ/ nm inv nausea.

**haut-parleur** (pl ∼s) /'opaʀlœʀ/ nm loudspeaker.

**havre** /'ɑvʀ/ nm haven (de of).

**hayon** /'ajɔ̃/ nm (Auto) hatchback.

**hebdomadaire** /ɛbdɔmadɛʀ/ adj & nm weekly.

**hébergement** /ebɛʀʒəmɑ̃/ nm accommodation.

**héberger** /ebɛʀʒe/ **40** vt (ami) put up; (réfugiés) take in.

**hébreu** (pl ∼x) /ebʀø/ am Hebrew. ● nm (Ling) Hebrew; c'est de l'∼! it's all Greek to me!

**Hébreu** (*pl* ~x) /ebʀø/ *nm* Hebrew; les ~x the Hebrews.

**hécatombe** /ekatɔ̃b/ *nf* slaughter.

**hectare** /ɛktaʀ/ *nm* hectare (= 10,000 square metres).

**hélas** /'elɑs/ *interj* alas. ● *adv* sadly.

**hélice** /elis/ *nf* propeller.

**hélicoptère** /elikɔptɛʀ/ *nm* helicopter.

**helvétique** /ɛlvetik/ *adj* Swiss.

**hématome** /ematɔm/ *nm* bruise.

**hémorragie** /emɔʀaʒi/ *nf* haemorrhage.

**hémorroïdes** /emɔʀɔid/ *nfpl* piles, haemorrhoids.

**hennir** /'eniʀ/ ② *vi* neigh.

**hépatite** /epatit/ *nf* hepatitis.

**herbe** /ɛʀb/ *nf* grass; (Méd, Culin) herb; en ~ in the blade; (fig) budding.

**héréditaire** /eʀeditɛʀ/ *adj* hereditary.

**hérédité** /eʀedite/ *nf* heredity.

**hérisser** /eʀise/ ① *vt* bristle; ~ qn (fig) ruffle sb. □ se ~ *vpr* bristle.

**hérisson** /eʀisɔ̃/ *nm* hedgehog.

**héritage** /eʀitaʒ/ *nm* inheritance; (spirituel) heritage.

**hériter** /eʀite/ ① *vt/i* inherit (de from); ~ de qch inherit sth. **héritier, -ière** *nm, f* heir, heiress.

**hermétique** /ɛʀmetik/ *adj* airtight; (fig) unfathomable.

**hernie** /'ɛʀni/ *nf* hernia.

**héroïne** /eʀɔin/ *nf* (femme) heroine; (drogue) heroin.

**héroïque** /eʀɔik/ *adj* heroic.

**héros** /'eʀo/ *nm* hero.

**hésiter** /ezite/ ① *vi* hesitate (à to); j'hésite I'm not sure.

**hétérogène** /eteʀɔʒɛn/ *adj* heterogeneous.

**hétérosexuel, ~le** /eteʀɔsɛksɥɛl/ *nm/ f* & *adj* heterosexual.

**hêtre** /'ɛtʀ/ *nm* beech.

**heure** /œʀ/ *nf* time; (soixante minutes) hour; quelle ~ est-il? what time is it? il est dix ~s it is ten o'clock; à l'~ (venir, être) on time; d'~ en ~ by the hour; toutes les deux ~s every two hours; ~ de pointe rush-hour; ~ de cours (Scol) period; ~ indue ungodly hour; ~s creuses off peak periods; ~s supplémentaires overtime.

**heureusement** /œʀøzmɑ̃/ *adv* fortunately, luckily.

**heureux, -euse** /œʀø, -z/ *adj* happy; (chanceux) lucky, fortunate.

**heurt** /'œʀ/ *nm* collision; (conflit) clash; sans ~ smoothly.

**heurter** /'œʀte/ ① *vt* (cogner) hit; (mur) bump into, hit; (choquer) offend. □ se ~ à *vpr* bump into, hit; (fig) come up against.

**hexagone** /ɛgzagɔn/ *nm* hexagon; l'~ France.

**hiberner** /ibɛʀne/ ① *vi* hibernate.

**hibou** (*pl* ~x) /'ibu/ *nm* owl.

**hier** /jɛʀ/ *adv* yesterday; ~ soir last night, yesterday evening.

**hiérarchie** /'jeʀaʀʃi/ *nf* hierarchy.

**hilare** /ilaʀ/ *adj* (visage) merry; être ~ be laughing.

**hindou, ~e** /ɛ̃du/ *adj* & *nm, f* Hindu. H~, ~e *nm, f* Hindu.

**hippique** /ipik/ *adj* equestrian; le concours ~ showjumping.

**hippodrome** /ipɔdʀom/ *nm* racecourse.

**hippopotame** /ipɔpɔtam/ *nm* hippopotamus.

**hirondelle** /iʀɔ̃dɛl/ *nf* swallow.

**hisser** /'ise/ ① *vt* hoist, haul. □ se ~ *vpr* heave oneself up.

**histoire** /istwaʀ/ *nf* (récit) story; (étude) history; (affaire) business;

h

~(s) (chichis) fuss; (ennuis) trouble.

**historique** /istɔrik/ adj historical.

**hiver** /ivɛr/ nm winter. **hivernal,
~e** (mpl -aux) adj winter; (glacial)
wintry.

**H.L.M.** abbrév m ou f (**habitation à
loyer modéré**) block of council
flats; (US) low-rent apartment
building.

**hocher** /ɔʃe/ **1** vt ~ la tête (pour
dire oui) nod; (pour dire non) shake
one's head.

**hochet** /ɔʃɛ/ nm rattle.

**hockey** /ɔkɛ/ nm hockey; ~ sur
glace ice hockey.

**hollandais, ~e** /ɔlɑ̃dɛ, -z/ adj
Dutch. ● nm (Ling) Dutch. H~, ~e
nm, f Dutchman, Dutchwoman.

**Hollande** /ɔlɑ̃d/ nf Holland.

**homard** /ɔmar/ nm lobster.

**homéopathie** /ɔmeɔpati/ nf
homoeopathy.

**homicide** /ɔmisid/ nm homicide;
~ involontaire manslaughter.

**hommage** /ɔmaʒ/ nm tribute; ~s
(salutations) respects; rendre ~ à
pay tribute to.

**homme** /ɔm/ nm man; (espèce)
man (kind); ~ d'affaires business-
man; ~ de la rue man in the
street; ~ d'État statesman; ~ politique politician.

**homogène** /ɔmɔʒɛn/ adj homo-
geneous.

**homonyme** /ɔmɔnim/ nm (personne) namesake.

**homosexualité** /ɔmɔsɛksɥalite/
nf homosexuality.

**homosexuel, ~le** /ɔmɔsɛksɥɛl/
adj & nm, f homosexual.

**Hongrie** /ɔ̃gri/ nf Hungary.

**hongrois, ~e** /ɔ̃grwa, -z/ adj
Hungarian. ● nm (Ling) Hungarian.
H~, ~e nm, f Hungarian.

**honnête** /ɔnɛt/ adj honest; (juste)
fair. **honnêteté** nf honesty.

**honneur** /ɔnœr/ nm honour; (mérite) credit; d'~ (invité, place) of
honour; en l'~ de in honour of; en
quel ~? **1** why?; faire ~ à
(équipe, famille) bring credit to.

**honorable** /ɔnɔrabl/ adj honour-
able; (convenable) respectable.

**honoraire** /ɔnɔrɛr/ adj honorary.
**honoraires** nmpl fees.

**honorer** /ɔnɔre/ **1** vt honour;
(faire honneur à) do credit to.

**honte** /ɔ̃t/ nf shame; avoir ~ be
ashamed (de of); faire ~ à make
ashamed. **honteux, -euse** adj (personne) ashamed (de of); (action)
shameful.

**hôpital** (pl -aux) /ɔpital, -o/ nm
hospital.

**hoquet** /ɔkɛ/ nm le ~ (the)
hiccups.

**horaire** /ɔrɛr/ adj hourly. ● nm
timetable; ~s libres flexitime.

**horizon** /ɔrizɔ̃/ nm horizon; (Fig)
outlook.

**horizontal, ~e** (mpl -aux) /ɔri-
zɔ̃tal, -o/ adj horizontal.

**horloge** /ɔrlɔʒ/ nf clock.

**hormis** /ɔrmi/ prép save.

**hormonal, ~e** (mpl -aux)
/ɔrmɔnal, -o/ adj hormonal,
hormone.

**hormone** /ɔrmɔn/ nf hormone.

**horreur** /ɔrœr/ nf horror; avoir ~
de hate.

**horrible** /ɔribl/ adj horrible.

**horrifier** /ɔrifje/ **45** vt horrify.

**hors** /ɔr/ prép ~ de outside, (avec
mouvement) out of; ~ d'atteinte
out of reach; ~ d'haleine out of
breath; ~ de prix extremely expensive; ~ pair outstanding; ~ de soi
beside oneself. **hors-bord** nm inv
speedboat. **hors-d'œuvre** nm inv

hors-d'œuvre. **hors-jeu** adj inv off-side. **hors-la-loi** nm inv outlaw. **hors-piste** nm off-piste skiing. **hors-taxe** adj inv duty-free.

**horticulteur, -trice** /ɔʀtikyltœʀ, -tʀis/ nm, f horticulturist.

**hospice** /ɔspis/ nm home.

**hospitalier, -ière** /ɔspitalje, -jɛʀ/ adj hospitable; (Méd) hospital. **hospitaliser** 1 vt to hospital. **hospitalité** nf hospitality.

**hostile** /ɔstil/ adj hostile. **hostilité** nf hostility.

**hôte** /ot/ nm (maître) host; (invité) guest.

**hôtel** /otɛl/ nm hotel; ∼ (particulier) (private) mansion; ∼ de ville town hall.

**hôtelier, -ière** /otalje, -jɛʀ/ adj hotel. ● nm, f hotel keeper. **hôtellerie** nf hotel business.

**hôtesse** /otɛs/ nf hostess; ∼ de l'air stewardess.

**hotte** /'ɔt/ nf basket; ∼ aspirante extractor (hood), (US) ventilator.

**houblon** /'ublɔ̃/ nm le ∼ hops.

**houille** /'uj/ nf coal; ∼ blanche hydroelectric power.

**houle** /'ul/ nf swell. **houleux, -euse** adj (mer) rough; (débat) stormy.

**housse** /'us/ nf cover; ∼ de siège seat cover.

**houx** /'u/ nm holly.

**huées** /'ɥe/ nfpl boos. **huer** 1 vt boo.

**huile** /ɥil/ nf oil; (personne 1) big-wig. **huiler** 1 vt oil. **huileux, -euse** adj oily.

**huis** /'ɥi/ nm à ∼ clos in camera.

**huissier** /ɥisje/ nm (Jur) bailiff; (portier) usher.

**huit** /'ɥi(t) / adj eight; ∼ jours a week; lundi en ∼ a week on Mon-

day. ● nm eight. **huitième** adj & nmf eighth.

**huître** /ɥitʀ/ nf oyster.

**humain, -e** /ymɛ̃, -ɛn/ adj human; (compatissant) humane. **humanitaire** adj humanitarian. **humanité** nf humanity.

**humble** /œbl/ adj humble.

**humeur** /ymœʀ/ nf mood; (tempérament) temper; **de bonne/mauvaise** ∼ in a good/bad mood.

**humide** /ymid/ adj damp; (chaleur, climat) humid; (lèvres, yeux) moist. **humidité** nf humidity.

**humilier** /ymilje/ 45 vt humiliate.

**humoristique** /ymɔʀistik/ adj humorous.

**humour** /ymuʀ/ nm humour; **avoir de l'∼** have a sense of humour.

**hurlement** /'yʀlǝmɑ̃/ nm howl (ing). **hurler** 1 vt/i howl.

**hutte** /'yt/ nf hut.

**hydratant, -e** /idʀatɑ̃, -t/ adj (lotion) moisturizing.

**hydravion** /idʀavjɔ̃/ nm seaplane.

**hydroélectrique** /idʀɔelɛktʀik/ adj hydroelectric.

**hydrogène** /idʀɔʒɛn/ nm hydrogen.

**hygiène** /iʒjɛn/ nf hygiene. **hygiénique** adj hygienic.

**hymne** /imn/ nm hymn; ∼ national national anthem.

**hyperlien** /ipɛʀljɛ̃/ nm (Internet) hyperlink.

**hypermarché** /ipɛʀmaʀʃe/ nm (supermarché) hypermarket.

**hypertension** /ipɛʀtɑ̃sjɔ̃/ nf high blood-pressure.

**hypertexte** /ipɛʀtɛkst/ nm (Internet) hypertext.

**hypnotiser** /ipnotize/ 1 vt hypnotize.

h

**hypocrisie** /ipɔkrizi/ *nf* hypocrisy.
**hypocrite** /ipɔkʀit/ *adj* hypocritical. ● *nmf* hypocrite.
**hypothèque** /ipɔtɛk/ *nf* mortgage.
**hypothèse** /ipɔtɛz/ *nf* hypothesis.
**hystérie** /isteʀi/ *nf* hysteria.

. . . . . . . . . . . . . . . . . . . . . . . . . .

# I i

. . . . . . . . . . . . . . . . . . . . . . . . . .

**ici** /isi/ *adv* (dans l'espace) here; (dans le temps) now; d'~ demain by tomorrow; d'~ là in the meantime; d'~ peu shortly; ~ même in this very place; jusqu'~ until now; (dans le passé) until then.

**idéal**, ~e *(mpl* -aux*)* /ideal, -o/ *adj & nm* ideal. **idéaliser** 1 *vt* idealize.

**idée** /ide/ *nf* idea; (esprit) mind; avoir dans l'~ de faire plan to do; il ne me viendrait jamais à l'~ de faire it would never occur to me to do; ~ fixe obsession; ~ reçue conventional opinion.

**identification** /idātifikasjɔ̃/ *nf* identification. **identifier** 45 *vt*, s'identifier *vpr* identify (à with).

**identique** /idātik/ *adj* identical.

**identité** /idātite/ *nf* identity.

**idéologie** /ideɔlɔʒi/ *nf* ideology.

**idiome** /idjom/ *nm* idiom.

**idiot**, ~e /idjo, -ɔt/ *adj* idiotic. ● *nm, f* idiot. **idiotie** /idjɔsi/ *nf* idiocy; (acte, parole) idiotic thing.

**idole** /idɔl/ *nf* idol.

**if** /if/ *nm* yew.

**ignare** /iɲaʀ/ *adj* ignorant. ● *nmf* ignoramus.

**ignoble** /iɲɔbl/ *adj* vile.

**ignorance** /iɲɔʀɑ̃s/ *nf* ignorance.

**ignorant**, ~e /iɲɔʀɑ̃, -t/ *adj* ignorant. ● *nm, f* ignoramus.

**ignorer** /iɲɔʀe/ 1 *vt* not know; je l'ignore I don't know; (personne) ignore.

**il** /il/ *pron* (personne, animal familier) he; (chose, animal) it; (impersonnel) it; ~ est vrai que it is true that; ~ neige/pleut it is snowing/raining; ~ y a there is; (pluriel) there are; (temps) ago; (durée) for; ~ y a 2 ans 2 years ago; ~ y a plus d'une heure que j'attends I've been waiting for over an hour.

**île** /il/ *nf* island; ~ déserte desert island; ~s anglo-normandes Channel Islands; ~s Britanniques British Isles.

**illégal**, ~e *(mpl* -aux*)* /ilegal, -o/ *adj* illegal.

**illégitime** /ileʒitim/ *adj* illegitimate.

**illettré**, ~e /iletʀe/ *adj & nm, f* illiterate.

**illicite** /ilisit/ *adj* illicit; (Jur) unlawful.

**illimité**, ~e /ilimite/ *adj* unlimited.

**illisible** /ilizibl/ *adj* illegible; (livre) unreadable.

**illogique** /ilɔʒik/ *adj* illogical.

**illuminé**, ~e /ilymine/ *adj* lit up; (monument) floodlit.

**illusion** /ilyzjɔ̃/ *nf* illusion; se faire des ~ delude oneself. **illusoire** *adj* illusory.

**illustre** /ilystʀ/ *adj* illustrious.

**illustré**, ~e /ilystʀe/ *adj* illustrated. ● *nm* comic.

**illustrer** /ilystʀe/ 1 *vt* illustrate. □ s'~ *vpr* become famous.

**îlot** /ilo/ *nm* islet; (de maisons) block.

**ils** /il/ *pron* they.

**image** /imaʒ/ *nf* picture; (méta-

phore) image; (reflet) reflection.
**imagé, ~e** adj full of imagery.
**imaginaire** /imaʒinɛʀ/ adj imaginary. **imaginatif, -ive** adj imaginative. **imagination** nf imagination.
**imaginer** /imaʒine/ **1** vt imagine; (inventer) think up. □ **s'~** vpr (se représenter) imagine (que that); (croire) think (que that).
**imbécile** /ɛbesil/ adj idiotic. ● nmf idiot.
**imbiber** /ɛbibe/ **1** vt soak (de with). □ **s'~** vpr become soaked (de with).
**imbriqué, ~e** /ɛbʀike/ adj (lié) interlinked; (tuiles) overlapping.
**imbu, ~e** /ɛby/ adj ~ de full of.
**IMC** abrév m (**indice de masse corporelle**) BMI.
**imitateur, -trice** /imitatœʀ, -tʀis/ nm, f imitator; (comédien) impersonator. **imiter** **1** vt imitate; (personnage) impersonate; (signature) forge; (faire comme) do the same as.
**immatriculation** /imatʀikylasjɔ̃/ nf registration.
**immatriculer** /imatʀikyle/ **1** vt register; **se faire ~** register; **faire ~ une voiture** have a car registered.
**immédiat, ~e** /imedja, -t/ adj immediate. ● nm **dans l'~** for the time being.
**immense** /imɑ̃s/ adj huge.
**immerger** /imɛʀʒe/ **40** vt immerse. □ **s'~** vpr immerse oneself (dans in).
**immeuble** /imœbl/ nm block of flats, building; **~ de bureaux** office building ou block.
**immigrant, ~e** /imigʀɑ̃, -t/ adj & nm, f immigrant. **immigration** nf immigration. **immigré, ~e** adj &

nm, f immigrant. **immigrer** **1** vi immigrate.
**imminent, ~e** /iminɑ̃, -t/ adj imminent.
**immobile** /imɔbil/ adj still, motionless.
**immobilier, -ière** /imɔbilje, -jɛʀ/ adj property; **agence immobilière** estate agent's office; (US) real estate office; **agent ~** estate agent; (US) real estate agent. ● nm **l'~** property; (US) real estate.
**immobiliser** /imɔbilize/ **1** vt immobilize; (stopper) stop. □ **s'~** vpr stop.
**immonde** /imɔ̃d/ adj filthy.
**immoral, ~e** (mpl -**aux**) /imɔʀal, -o/ adj immoral.
**immortel, ~le** /imɔʀtɛl/ adj immortal.
**immuable** /imɥabl/ adj unchanging.
**immuniser** /imynize/ **1** vt immunize; **immunisé contre (à l'abri de) immune to. **immunité** nf immunity.
**impact** /ɛpakt/ nm impact.
**impair, ~e** /ɛpɛʀ/ adj (numéro) odd. ● nm blunder, faux pas.
**imparfait, ~e** /ɛpaʀfɛ, -t/ adj & nm imperfect.
**impasse** /ɛpas/ nf (rue) dead end; (situation) deadlock.
**impatient, ~e** /ɛpasjɑ̃, -t/ adj impatient.
**impatienter** /ɛpasjɑ̃te/ **1** vt annoy. □ **s'~** vpr get impatient (contre qn with sb).
**impayé, ~e** /ɛpeje/ adj unpaid.
**impeccable** /ɛpekabl/ adj (propre) impeccable, spotless; (soigné) perfect.
**impensable** /ɛpɑ̃sabl/ adj unthinkable.

**impératif, -ive** /ɛ̃peʀatif, -v/ adj imperative. ● nm (Gram) imperative; (contrainte) imperative; ~s (exigences) requirements, demands (de of).

**impératrice** /ɛ̃peʀatʀis/ nf empress.

**impérial, ~e** (mpl -iaux) /ɛ̃peʀjal, -jo/ adj imperial.

**impérieux, -ieuse** /ɛ̃peʀjø, -z/ adj imperious; (pressant) pressing.

**imperméable** /ɛ̃pɛʀmeabl/ adj impervious (à to); (manteau, tissu) waterproof. ● nm raincoat.

**impersonnel, ~le** /ɛ̃pɛʀsɔnɛl/ adj impersonal.

**impertinent, ~e** /ɛ̃pɛʀtinɑ̃, -t/ adj impertinent.

**imperturbable** /ɛ̃pɛʀtyʀbabl/ adj unshakeable, unruffled.

**impétueux, -euse** /ɛ̃petɥø, -z/ adj impetuous.

**impitoyable** /ɛ̃pitwajabl/ adj merciless.

**implant** /ɛ̃plɑ̃/ nm implant.

**implanter** /ɛ̃plɑ̃te/ **1** vt establish, set up. □ s'~ vpr become established.

**implication** /ɛ̃plikasjɔ̃/ nf (conséquence) implication; (participation) involvement.

**impliquer** /ɛ̃plike/ **1** vt (mêler) implicate (dans in); (signifier) imply, mean (que that); (nécessiter) involve (de faire doing).

**implorer** /ɛ̃plɔʀe/ **1** vt implore, beg for.

**impoli, ~e** /ɛ̃pɔli/ adj impolite, rude.

**importance** /ɛ̃pɔʀtɑ̃s/ nf importance; (taille) size; (ampleur) extent; sans ~ unimportant.

**important, ~e** /ɛ̃pɔʀtɑ̃, -t/ adj important; (en quantité) considerable, sizeable, big; (air) self-

important. ● nm l'~ the important thing.

**importateur, -trice** /ɛ̃pɔʀtatœʀ, -tʀis/ nm, f importer. ● adj importing. **importation** nf import.

**importer** /ɛ̃pɔʀte/ **1** vt (Comm) import. ● vi matter, be important (à to); **il importe que** it is important that; **n'importe, peu importe** it does not matter; **n'importe comment** anyhow; **n'importe où** anywhere; **n'importe qui** anybody; **n'importe quoi** anything.

**importun, ~e** /ɛ̃pɔʀtœ̃, -yn/ adj troublesome. ● nm, f nuisance.

**imposer** /ɛ̃poze/ **1** vt impose (à on); (taxer) tax; **en ~ à qn** impress sb. □ s'~ vpr (action) be essential; (se faire reconnaître) stand out; (s'astreindre à) s'~ de faire force oneself to do.

**imposition** /ɛ̃pozisjɔ̃/ nf taxation; ~ des mains laying-on of hands.

**impossible** /ɛ̃posibl/ adj impossible. ● nm faire l'~ do one's utmost.

**impôt** /ɛ̃po/ nm tax; ~s (contributions) tax(ation); taxes; ~ sur le revenu income tax.

**impotent, ~e** /ɛ̃potɑ̃, -t/ adj disabled.

**imprécis, ~e** /ɛ̃presi, -z/ adj imprecise.

**imprégner** /ɛ̃pʀeɲe/ **14** vt fill (de with); (imbiber) impregnate (de with). □ s'~ de vpr (fig) immerse oneself in.

**impression** /ɛ̃pʀesjɔ̃/ nf impression; (de livre) printing. **impressionnant, ~e** adj impressive; (choquant) disturbing. **impressionner** **1** vt impress; (choquer) disturb.

**imprévisible** /ɛ̃pʀevizibl/ adj unpredictable.

**imprévu, ~e** /ɛ̃pʀevy/ adj unexpected. ● *nm* unexpected incident; **sauf ~** unless anything unexpected happens.

**imprimante** /ɛ̃pʀimɑ̃t/ *nf* (Ordinat) printer; **~ à jet d'encre** ink-jet printer; **~ (à) laser** laser printer.

**imprimé**, **~e** /ɛ̃pʀime/ *adj* printed. ● *nm* printed form.

**imprimer** /ɛ̃pʀime/ **1** *vt* print; (marquer) imprint. **imprimerie** *nf* (art) printing; (lieu) printing works. **imprimeur** *nm* printer.

**improbable** /ɛ̃pʀɔbabl/ *adj* unlikely, improbable.

**impropre** /ɛ̃pʀɔpʀ/ *adj* incorrect; **~ à** unfit for.

**improviste: à l'~** /alɛ̃pʀɔvist/ *loc* unexpectedly.

**imprudence** /ɛ̃pʀydɑ̃s/ *nf* carelessness; (acte) careless action.

**imprudent**, **~e** /ɛ̃pʀydɑ̃, -t/ *adj* careless; **il est ~ de** it is unwise to.

**impudent**, **~e** /ɛ̃pydɑ̃, -t/ *adj* impudent.

**impuissant**, **~e** /ɛ̃pɥisɑ̃, -t/ *adj* helpless; (Méd) impotent; **~ à faire** powerless to do.

**impulsif**, **-ive** /ɛ̃pylsif, -v/ *adj* impulsive. **impulsion** *nf* (poussée, influence) impetus; (instinct, mouvement) impulse.

**impur**, **~e** /ɛ̃pyʀ/ *adj* impure.

**imputer** /ɛ̃pyte/ **1** *vt* **~ à** attribute to, impute to.

**inabordable** /inabɔʀdabl/ *adj* (prix) prohibitive.

**inacceptable** /inaksɛptabl/ *adj* unacceptable.

**inactif**, **-ive** /inaktif, -v/ *adj* inactive.

**inadapté**, **~e** /inadapte/ *adj* maladjusted. ● *nm*, *f* (Psych) maladjusted person.

**inadmissible** /inadmisibl/ *adj* unacceptable.

**inadvertance** /inadvɛʀtɑ̃s/ *nf* **par ~** by mistake.

**inanimé**, **~e** /inanime/ *adj* (évanoui) unconscious; (mort) lifeless; (matière) inanimate.

**inaperçu**, **~e** /inapɛʀsy/ *adj* unnoticed.

**inapte** /inapt/ *adj* unsuited (à to); **~ à faire** incapable of doing; **~ au service militaire** unfit for military service.

**inattendu**, **~e** /inatɑ̃dy/ *adj* unexpected.

**inaugurer** /inogyʀe/ **1** *vt* inaugurate.

**incapable** /ɛ̃kapabl/ *adj* incapable (de qch of sth); **~ de faire** unable to do, incapable of doing. ● *nmf* incompetent.

**incapacité** /ɛ̃kapasite/ *nf* inability, incapacity; **être dans l'~ de faire** be unable to do.

**incarcérer** /ɛ̃kaʀseʀe/ **14** *vt* imprison, incarcerate.

**incarnation** /ɛ̃kaʀnasjɔ̃/ *nf* embodiment, incarnation. **incarné**, **~e** *adj* (ongle) ingrowing.

**incassable** /ɛ̃kɑsabl/ *adj* unbreakable.

**incendiaire** /ɛ̃sɑ̃djɛʀ/ *adj* incendiary; (propos) inflammatory. ● *nmf* arsonist.

**incendie** /ɛ̃sɑ̃di/ *nm* fire; **~ criminel** arson. **incendier** **45** *vt* set fire to.

**incertain**, **~e** /ɛ̃sɛʀtɛ̃, -ɛn/ *adj* uncertain; (contour) vague; (temps) unsettled. **incertitude** *nf* uncertainty.

**inceste** /ɛ̃sɛst/ *nm* incest.

**incidence** /ɛ̃sidɑ̃s/ *nf* effect.

**incident** /ɛ̃sidɑ̃/ *nm* incident; **~ technique** technical hitch.

**incinérer** /ɛ̃sineʀe/ **14** *vt* incinerate; (mort) cremate.

**inciser** /ɛ̃size/ **1** *vt* make an incision in; (*abcès*) lance. **incisif, -ive** *adj* incisive. **incision** *nf* incision; (*d'abcès*) lancing.

**incitation** /ɛ̃sitasjɔ̃/ *nf* (Jur) incitement (à to); (encouragement) incentive. **inciter** 1 *vt* incite (à to); (encourager) encourage.

**inclinaison** /ɛ̃klinɛzɔ̃/ *nf* incline; (de la tête) tilt.

**inclination** /ɛ̃klinasjɔ̃/ *nf* (penchant) inclination; (geste) (du buste) bow; (de la tête) nod.

**incliner** /ɛ̃kline/ 1 *vt* tilt, lean; (courber) bend; (inciter) encourage (à to); **la tête** (approuver) nod; (révérence) bow. ● *vi* **à** **être** inclined to. □ s'~ *vpr* lean forward; (se courber) bow down (devant before); (céder) give in, yield (devant to); (chemin) slope.

**inclure** /ɛ̃klyr/ 18 *vt* include; (enfermer) enclose; **jusqu'au lundi inclus** up to and including Monday.

**incohérence** /ɛ̃kɔerɑ̃s/ *nf* incoherence; (contradiction) discrepancy. **incohérent, ~e** *adj* incoherent, inconsistent.

**incolore** /ɛ̃kɔlɔr/ *adj* colourless; (verre) clear.

**incommoder** /ɛ̃kɔmɔde/ 1 *vt* inconvenience, bother.

**incompatible** /ɛ̃kɔ̃patibl/ *adj* incompatible.

**incompétent, ~e** /ɛ̃kɔ̃petɑ̃, -t/ *adj* incompetent.

**incomplet, -ète** /ɛ̃kɔ̃plɛ, -t/ *adj* incomplete.

**incompréhension** /ɛ̃kɔ̃preɑ̃sjɔ̃/ *nf* lack of understanding.

**incompris, ~e** /ɛ̃kɔ̃pri, -z/ *adj* misunderstood.

**inconcevable** /ɛ̃kɔ̃svabl/ *adj* inconceivable.

**incongru, ~e** /ɛ̃kɔ̃gry/ *adj* unseemly.

**inconnu, ~e** /ɛ̃kɔny/ *adj* unknown (à to). ● *nm, f* stranger. ● *nm* **l'~** the unknown.

**inconscience** /ɛ̃kɔ̃sjɑ̃s/ *nf* unconsciousness; (folie) madness.

**inconscient, ~e** /ɛ̃kɔ̃sjɑ̃, -t/ *adj* unconscious (de of); (fou) mad. ● *nm* (Psych) subconscious.

**incontestable** /ɛ̃kɔ̃tɛstabl/ *adj* indisputable.

**incontrôlable** /ɛ̃kɔ̃trolabl/ *adj* unverifiable; (non maîtrisé) uncontrollable.

**inconvenant, ~e** /ɛ̃kɔ̃vnɑ̃, -t/ *adj* improper.

**inconvénient** /ɛ̃kɔ̃venjɑ̃/ *nm* disadvantage, drawback; (objection) objection.

**incorporer** /ɛ̃kɔrpɔre/ 1 *vt* incorporate; (Culin) blend (à into); (Mil) enlist.

**incorrect, ~e** /ɛ̃kɔrɛkt/ *adj* (faux) incorrect; (malséant) improper; (impoli) impolite; (déloyal) unfair.

**incrédule** /ɛ̃kredyl/ *adj* incredulous.

**incriminer** /ɛ̃krimine/ 1 *vt* (personne) incriminate; (conduite, action) attack.

**incroyable** /ɛ̃krwajabl/ *adj* incredible.

**incruster** /ɛ̃kryste/ 1 *vt* inlay (de with).

**incubateur** /ɛ̃kybatœr/ *nm* incubator.

**inculpation** /ɛ̃kylpasjɔ̃/ *nf* charge (de, pour of). **inculpé, ~e** *nm, f* accused. **inculper** 1 *vt* charge (de with).

**inculquer** /ɛ̃kylke/ 1 *vt* instil (à into).

**inculte** /ɛ̃kylt/ *adj* uncultivated; (personne) uneducated.

**incurver** /ɛ̃kyrve/ 1 *vt* curve, bend. □ s'~ *vpr* curve, bend.

**Inde** /ɛ̃d/ *nf* India.

**indécent, ~e** /ɛ̃desɑ̃, -t/ *adj* indecent.

**indécis, ~e** /ɛ̃desi, -z/ *adj* (de nature) indecisive; (temporairement) undecided.

**indéfini, ~e** /ɛ̃defini/ *adj* (Gram) indefinite; (vague) undefined; (sans limites) indeterminate.

**indemne** /ɛ̃dɛmn/ *adj* unharmed.

**indemniser** /ɛ̃dɛmnize/ **1** *vt* compensate (de for).

**indemnité** /ɛ̃dɛmnite/ *nf* indemnity, compensation; (allocation) allowance; **~s de licenciement** redundancy payment.

**indépendance** /ɛ̃depɑ̃dɑ̃s/ *nf* independence. **indépendant, ~e** /ɛ̃depɑ̃dɑ̃/ *adj* independent.

**indéterminé, ~e** /ɛ̃detɛrmine/ *adj* unspecified.

**index** /ɛ̃dɛks/ *nm* forefinger; (liste) index.

**indicateur, -trice** /ɛ̃dikatœr, -tris/ *nm, f* (police) informer. ●*nm* (livre) guide; (Tech) indicator.

**indicatif, -ve** /ɛ̃dikatif, -v/ *adj* indicative (de of). ●*nm* (à la radio) signature tune; (téléphonique) dialling code; (Gram) indicative.

**indication** /ɛ̃dikasjɔ̃/ *nf* indication; (renseignement) information; (directive) instruction.

**indice** /ɛ̃dis/ *nm* sign; (dans une enquête) clue; (des prix) index; (évaluation) rating; **~ d'écoute** audience ratings.

**indifférence** /ɛ̃diferɑ̃s/ *nf* indifference.

**indifférent, ~e** /ɛ̃diferɑ̃, -t/ *adj* indifferent (à to); **ça m'est ~** it makes no difference to me.

**indigène** /ɛ̃diʒɛn/ *adj & nmf* native, indigenous; (du pays) local. ●*nmf* native.

**indigent, ~e** /ɛ̃diʒɑ̃, -t/ *adj* destitute.

**indigeste** /ɛ̃diʒɛst/ *adj* indigestible. **indigestion** *nf* indigestion.

**indigne** /ɛ̃diɲ/ *adj* unworthy (de of); (*acte*) vile. **indigner (s')** **1** *vpr* become indignant (de at).

**indiquer** /ɛ̃dike/ **1** *vt* (montrer) show, indicate; (renseigner sur) point out, tell; (déterminer) give, state, appoint; **~ du doigt** point to *ou* out *ou* at.

**indirect, ~e** /ɛ̃dirɛkt/ *adj* indirect.

**indiscipliné, ~e** /ɛ̃disipline/ *adj* unruly.

**indiscret, -ète** /ɛ̃diskrɛ, -t/ *adj* (*personne*) inquisitive; (*question*) indiscreet.

**indiscutable** /ɛ̃diskytabl/ *adj* unquestionable.

**indispensable** /ɛ̃dispɑ̃sabl/ *adj* indispensable; **il est ~ qu'il vienne** it is essential that he comes.

**individu** /ɛ̃dividy/ *nm* individual.

**individuel, ~le** /ɛ̃dividɥɛl/ *adj* (pour une personne) individual; (qui concerne l'individu) personal; **chambre ~le** single room; **maison ~le** detached house.

**indolore** /ɛ̃dɔlɔr/ *adj* painless.

**Indonésie** /ɛ̃dɔnezi/ *nf* Indonesia.

**indu, ~e** /ɛ̃dy/ *adj* **à une heure ~e** at some ungodly hour.

**induire** /ɛ̃dɥir/ **17** *vt* infer (de from); (inciter) induce (à faire to do); **~ en erreur** mislead.

**indulgence** /ɛ̃dylʒɑ̃s/ *nf* indulgence; (de jury) leniency. **indulgent, ~e** *adj* indulgent; (clément) lenient.

**industrialisé, ~e** /ɛ̃dystrijalize/

*adj* industrialized.

**industrie** /ɛ̃dystʀi/ *nf* industry.

**industriel, ~le** /ɛ̃dystʀijɛl/ *adj* industrial. ● *nm* industrialist.

**inédit, ~e** /inedi, -t/ *adj* unpublished; (fig) original.

**inefficace** /inefikas/ *adj* (*remède, mesure*) ineffective; (*appareil, système*) inefficient.

**inégal, ~e** /inegal/ *adj* (*mpl -aux*) /inegal, -o/ unequal; (*irrégulier*) uneven. **inégalable** *adj* matchless. **inégalité** *nf* (*injustice*) inequality; (*irrégularité*) unevenness; (*disproportion*) disparity.

**inéluctable** /inelyktabl/ *adj* inescapable.

**inepte** /inɛpt/ *adj* inept, absurd.

**inerte** /inɛʀt/ *adj* inert; (*immobile*) lifeless; (*sans énergie*) apathetic. **inertie** /inɛʀsi/ *nf* inertia; (fig) apathy.

**inespéré, ~e** /inɛspeʀe/ *adj* unhoped for.

**inestimable** /inɛstimabl/ *adj* priceless; (*aide*) invaluable.

**inexact, ~e** /inɛgza(kt), -kt/ *adj* (*imprécis*) inaccurate; (*incorrect*) incorrect.

**in extremis** /inɛkstʀemis/ *adv* (*par nécessité*) as a last resort; (*au dernier moment*) at the last minute. ● *adj* last-minute.

**infaillible** /ɛ̃fajibl/ *adj* infallible.

**infâme** /ɛ̃fam/ *adj* vile.

**infantile** /ɛ̃fɑ̃til/ *adj* (*puéril*) infantile; (*maladie*) childhood; (*mortalité*) infant.

**infarctus** /ɛ̃faʀktys/ *nm* coronary, heart attack.

**infatigable** /ɛ̃fatigabl/ *adj* tireless.

**infect, ~e** /ɛ̃fɛkt/ *adj* revolting.

**infecter** /ɛ̃fɛkte/ **1** *vt* infect. □ **s'~** *vpr* become infected. **infectieux, -ieuse** *adj* infectious.

**infection** *nf* infection.

**inférieur, ~e** /ɛ̃feʀjœʀ/ *adj* (plus bas) lower; (moins bon) inferior (à to); ~ à (plus petit que) smaller than; (plus bas que) lower than. ● *nm, f* inferior. **infériorité** *nf* inferiority.

**infernal, ~e** /ɛ̃fɛʀnal, -o/ *adj* (*mpl -aux*) infernal.

**infester** /ɛ̃fɛste/ **1** *vt* infest.

**infidèle** /ɛ̃fidɛl/ *adj* unfaithful (à to). **infidélité** *nf* unfaithfulness; (*acte*) infidelity.

**infiltrer (s')** /sɛ̃filtʀe/ **1** *vpr* **s'~** (dans) (*personnes, idées*) infiltrate; (*liquide*) seep through.

**infime** /ɛ̃fim/ *adj* tiny, minute.

**infini, ~e** /ɛ̃fini/ *adj* infinite. ● *nm* infinity; à l'~ endlessly.

**infinité** /ɛ̃finite/ *nf* l'~ infinity; une ~ de an endless number of.

**infinitif** /ɛ̃finitif/ *nm* infinitive.

**infirme** /ɛ̃fiʀm/ *adj* disabled. ● *nmf* disabled person. **infirmerie** *nf* sickbay, infirmary. **infirmier** *nm* (male) nurse. **infirmière** *nf* nurse. **infirmité** *nf* disability.

**inflammable** /ɛ̃flamabl/ *adj* inflammable.

**inflation** /ɛ̃flasjõ/ *nf* inflation.

**infliger** /ɛ̃fliʒe/ **40** *vt* inflict; (*sanction*) impose.

**influence** /ɛ̃flyɑ̃s/ *nf* influence. **influencer** **10** *vt* influence. **influent, ~e** *adj* influential.

**influer** /ɛ̃flye/ **1** *vi* ~ sur influence.

**informateur, -trice** /ɛ̃fɔʀmatœʀ, -tʀis/ *nm, f* informant; (pour la police) informer.

**informaticien, ~ne** /ɛ̃fɔʀmatisjɛ̃, -ɛn/ *nm, f* computer scientist.

**information** /ɛ̃fɔʀmasjõ/ *nf* information; (Jur) inquiry; une ~ (some) information; (nouvelle) (some) news; les ~s the news.

**informatique** /ɛ̃fɔʀmatik/ nf computer science; (techniques) information technology. **Informatiser** 1 vt computerize.

**informer** /ɛ̃fɔʀme/ 1 vt inform (de about, of). □ s'~ vpr enquire (de about).

**inforoute** /ɛ̃fɔʀut/ nf (Ordinat) information highway.

**infortune** /ɛ̃fɔʀtyn/ nf misfortune.

**infraction** /ɛ̃fʀaksjɔ̃/ nf offence; ~ à (loi, règlement) breach of.

**infrastructure** /ɛ̃fʀastʀyktyʀ/ nf infrastructure; (équipements) facilities.

**infructueux, -euse** /ɛ̃fʀyktɥø, -z/ adj fruitless.

**infuser** /ɛ̃fyze/ 1 vt/i infuse, brew. **infusion** nf herbal tea, infusion.

**ingénier (s')** /(s)ɛ̃ʒenje/ 45 vpr s'~ à strive to.

**ingénieur** /ɛ̃ʒenjœʀ/ nm engineer.

**ingénieux, -ieuse** /ɛ̃ʒenjø, -z/ adj ingenious. **ingéniosité** nf ingenuity.

**ingénu, ~e** /ɛ̃ʒeny/ adj naïve.

**ingérence** /ɛ̃ʒeʀɑ̃s/ nf interference.

**ingérer (s')** /(s)ɛ̃ʒeʀe/ 14 vpr s'~ dans interfere in.

**ingrat, ~e** /ɛ̃gʀa, -t/ adj (personne) ungrateful; (travail) unrewarding, thankless; (visage) unattractive.

**ingrédient** /ɛ̃gʀedjɑ̃/ nm ingredient.

**ingurgiter** /ɛ̃gyʀʒite/ 1 vt swallow.

**inhabité, ~e** /inabite/ adj uninhabited.

**inhabituel, ~le** /inabitɥɛl/ adj unusual.

**inhumain, ~e** /inymɛ̃, -ɛn/ adj inhuman.

**inhumation** /inymasjɔ̃/ nf burial.

**initial, ~e** (mpl **-iaux**) /inisjal, -jo/ adj initial. **initiale** nf initial.

**initialisation** /inisjalizasjɔ̃/ nf (Ordinat) formatting. **initialiser** 1 vt format.

**initiation** /inisjasjɔ̃/ nf initiation; (formation) introduction (à to); cours d'~ introductory course.

**initiative** /inisjativ/ nf initiative.

**initier** /inisje/ 45 vt initiate (à into); (faire découvrir) introduce (à to). □ s'~ vpr s'~ à qch learn sth.

**injecter** /ɛ̃ʒekte/ 1 vt inject; injecté de sang bloodshot. **injection** nf injection.

**injure** /ɛ̃ʒyʀ/ nf insult. **injurier** 45 vt insult. **injurieux, -ieuse** adj insulting.

**injuste** /ɛ̃ʒyst/ adj unjust, unfair. **injustice** nf injustice.

**inné, ~e** /inne/ adj innate, inborn.

**innocence** /inɔsɑ̃s/ nf innocence. **innocent, ~e** adj & nm, f innocent. **innocenter** 1 vt clear, prove innocent.

**innombrable** /inɔ̃bʀabl/ adj countless.

**innovateur, -trice** /inɔvatœʀ, -tʀis/ nm, f innovator. **innovation** nf innovation. **innover** 1 vt innovate.

**inodore** /inɔdɔʀ/ adj odourless.

**inoffensif, -ive** /inɔfɑ̃sif, -v/ adj harmless.

**inondation** /inɔ̃dasjɔ̃/ nf flood; (action) flooding.

**inonder** /inɔ̃de/ 1 vt flood; (mouiller) soak; (envahir) inundate (de with); inondé de soleil bathed in sunlight.

**inopiné, ~e** /inɔpine/ adj unexpected; (mort) sudden.

**inopportun, ~e** /inɔpɔʀtœ̃, -yn/ adj inopportune, ill-timed.

**inoubliable** /inublijabl/ *adj* unforgettable.

**inouï**, ~e /inwi/ *adj* incredible; (*événement*) unprecedented.

**inox®** /inɔks/ *nm* stainless steel.

**inoxydable** /inɔksidabl/ *adj* acier ~ stainless steel.

**inqualifiable** /ɛ̃kalifjabl/ *adj* unspeakable.

**inquiet**, -iète /ɛ̃kjɛ, -t/ *adj* worried. **inquiétant**, ~e *adj* worrying.

**inquiéter** /ɛ̃kjete/ [14] *vt* worry. □ s'~ *vpr* worry (de about). **inquiétude** *nf* anxiety, worry.

**insaisissable** /ɛ̃sezisabl/ *adj* (*personne*) elusive; (*nuance*) indefinable.

**insalubre** /ɛ̃salybʁ/ *adj* unhealthy.

**insatisfaisant**, ~e /ɛ̃satisfəzɑ̃, -t/ *adj* unsatisfactory. **insatisfait**, ~e *adj* (*mécontent*) dissatisfied; (*frustré*) unfulfilled.

**inscription** /ɛ̃skʁipsjɔ̃/ *nf* inscription; (*immatriculation*) enrolment.

**inscrire** /ɛ̃skʁiʁ/ [30] *vt* write (down); (*graver, tracer*) inscribe; (*personne*) enrol; (*sur une liste*) put down. □ s'~ *vpr* put one's name down; s'~ à (*école*) enrol at; (*club, parti*) join; (*examen*) enter for.

**insecte** /ɛ̃sɛkt/ *nm* insect.

**insécurité** /ɛ̃sekyʁite/ *nf* insecurity.

**insensé**, ~e /ɛ̃sɑ̃se/ *adj* mad.

**insensibilité** /ɛ̃sɑ̃sibilite/ *nf* insensitivity. **insensible** *adj* insensitive (à to); (*graduel*) imperceptible.

**insérer** /ɛ̃seʁe/ [14] *vt* insert. □ s'~ *vpr* be inserted; s'~ dans be part of.

**insigne** /ɛ̃siɲ/ *nm* badge; ~s (d'une fonction) insignia.

**insignifiant**, ~e /ɛ̃siɲifjɑ̃, -t/ *adj* insignificant.

**insinuation** /ɛ̃sinɥasjɔ̃/ *nf* insinuation.

**insinuer** /ɛ̃sinɥe/ [1] *vt* insinuate. □ s'~ *vpr* (socialement) ingratiate oneself (auprès de qn with sb); s'~ dans (se glisser) slip into; (*idée, nuance*) creep into.

**insipide** /ɛ̃sipid/ *adj* insipid.

**insistance** /ɛ̃sistɑ̃s/ *nf* insistence. **insistant**, ~e *adj* insistent.

**insister** /ɛ̃siste/ [1] *vi* insist (pour faire on doing); ~ sur stress.

**insolation** /ɛ̃sɔlasjɔ̃/ *nf* (Méd) sunstroke.

**insolent**, ~e /ɛ̃sɔlɑ̃, -t/ *adj* insolent.

**insolite** /ɛ̃sɔlit/ *adj* unusual.

**insolvable** /ɛ̃sɔlvabl/ *adj* insolvent.

**insomnie** /ɛ̃sɔmni/ *nf* insomnia.

**insonoriser** /ɛ̃sɔnɔʁize/ [1] *vt* soundproof.

**insouciance** /ɛ̃susjɑ̃s/ *nf* lack of concern. **insouciant**, ~e *adj* carefree.

**insoutenable** /ɛ̃sutnabl/ *adj* unbearable; (*argument*) untenable.

**inspecter** /ɛ̃spɛkte/ [1] *vt* inspect. **inspecteur**, -trice *nm, f* inspector. **inspection** *nf* inspection.

**inspiration** /ɛ̃spiʁasjɔ̃/ *nf* inspiration; (*respiration*) breath.

**inspirer** /ɛ̃spiʁe/ [1] *vt* inspire; ~ la méfiance à qn inspire distrust in sb. ●*vi* breathe in. □ s'~ de *vpr* be inspired by.

**instabilité** /ɛ̃stabilite/ *nf* instability; unsteadiness. **instable** *adj* unstable; (*temps*) unsettled.

**installation** /ɛ̃stalasjɔ̃/ *nf* installation; (de local) fitting out; (de locataire) settling in. **installations** *nfpl* facilities.

**installer** /ɛ̃stale/ [1] *vt* install; (*meuble*) put in; (*étagère*) put up; (*gaz, téléphone*) connect; (*équiper*) fit out. □ **s'~** *vpr* settle (down); (emménager) settle in; **s'~ comme** set oneself up as.

**instance** /ɛ̃stɑ̃s/ *nf* authority; (prière) entreaty; **avec ~** with insistence; **en ~** pending; **en ~ de** in the course of, on the point of.

**instant** /ɛ̃stɑ̃/ *nm* moment, instant; **à l'~** this instant.

**instantané, ~e** /ɛ̃stɑ̃tane/ *adj* instantaneous; (*café*) instant.

**instar**: **à l'~ de** /alɛstaʀdə/ *loc* like.

**instaurer** /ɛ̃stɔʀe/ **1** *vt* institute.

**instigateur, -trice** /ɛ̃stigatœʀ, -tʀis/ *nm, f* instigator.

**instinct** /ɛ̃stɛ̃/ *nm* instinct; **d'~** instinctively. **instinctif, -ive** *adj* instinctive.

**instituer** /ɛ̃stitɥe/ **1** *vt* establish.

**institut** /ɛ̃stity/ *nm* institute; **~ de beauté** beauty parlour.

**instituteur, -trice** /ɛ̃stitytœʀ, -tʀis/ *nm, f* primary-school teacher.

**institution** /ɛ̃stitysjɔ̃/ *nf* institution; (école) private school.

**instructif, -ive** /ɛ̃stʀyktif, -v/ *adj* instructive.

**instruction** /ɛ̃stʀyksjɔ̃/ *nf* (formation) education; (Mil) training; (document) directive; **~s** (ordres, mode d'emploi) instructions; (Ordinat) (énoncé) instruction; (pas de séquence) statement.

**instruire** /ɛ̃stʀɥiʀ/ **17** *vt* teach, educate; **~ de** inform of. □ **s'~** learn, educate oneself; **s'~ de** enquire about. **instruit, ~e** *adj* educated.

**instrument** /ɛ̃stʀymɑ̃/ *nm* instrument; (outil) tool; (moyen: fig) instrument; **~ de gestion** management tool; **~s de bord** (Aviat) controls.

**insu**: **à l'~ de** /alɛsyda/ *loc* with-

out the knowledge of.

**insuffisance** /ɛ̃syfizɑ̃s/ *nf* (pénurie) shortage; (médiocrité) inadequacy. **insuffisant, ~e** *adj* inadequate; (en nombre) insufficient.

**insulaire** /ɛ̃sylɛʀ/ *adj* island. ● *nmf* islander.

**insuline** /ɛ̃sylin/ *nf* insulin.

**insulte** /ɛ̃sylt/ *nf* insult. **insulter** **1** *vt* insult.

**insupportable** /ɛ̃sypɔʀtabl/ *adj* unbearable.

**insurger (s')** /(s)ɛ̃syʀʒe/ **40** *vpr* rebel.

**intact, ~e** /ɛ̃takt/ *adj* intact.

**intangible** /ɛ̃tɑ̃ʒibl/ *adj* intangible; (principe) inviolable.

**intarissable** /ɛ̃taʀisabl/ *adj* inexhaustible.

**intégral, ~e** /ɛ̃tegʀal, -o/ *adj* complete; (texte, édition) unabridged; (paiement) full, in full. **intégralement** *adv* in full. **intégralité** *nf* whole.

**intègre** /ɛ̃tɛgʀ/ *adj* upright.

**intégrer** /ɛ̃tegʀe/ **14** *vt* integrate. □ **s'~** *vpr* (personne) integrate; (maison) fit in.

**intégriste** /ɛ̃tegʀist/ *nmf* fundamentalist.

**intégrité** /ɛ̃tegʀite/ *nf* integrity.

**intellect** /ɛ̃telɛkt/ *nm* intellect. **intellectuel, ~le** *adj* & *nm, f* intellectual.

**intelligence** /ɛ̃teliʒɑ̃s/ *nf* intelligence; (compréhension) understanding; (complicité) agreement; **agir d'~ avec qn** act in agreement with sb. **intelligent, ~e** *adj* intelligent.

**intempéries** /ɛ̃tɑ̃peʀi/ *nfpl* severe weather.

**intempestif, -ive** /ɛ̃tɑ̃pɛstif, -v/ *adj* untimely.

**intenable** /ɛ̃tnabl/ adj unbearable; (enfant) impossible.

**intendance** /ɛ̃tɑ̃dɑ̃s/ nf (Scol) bursar's office.

**intendant, ~e** /ɛ̃tɑ̃dɑ̃, -t/ nm (Mil) quartermaster. ● nm, f (Scol) bursar.

**intense** /ɛ̃tɑ̃s/ adj intense; (circulation) heavy. **intensif, -ive** adj intensive. **intensité** nf intensity.

**intenter** /ɛ̃tɑ̃te/ **1** vt ~ un procès ou une action institute proceedings (à, contre against).

**intention** /ɛ̃tɑ̃sjɔ̃/ nf intention (de faire of doing); à l'~ de qn for sb. **intentionnel, ~le** adj intentional.

**interactif, -ive** /ɛ̃tɛʀaktif, -v/ adj (TV, vidéo) interactive.

**interaction** /ɛ̃tɛʀaksjɔ̃/ nf interaction.

**intercaler** /ɛ̃tɛʀkale/ **1** vt insert.

**intercéder** /ɛ̃tɛʀsede/ **14** vi intercede (en faveur de on behalf of).

**intercepter** /ɛ̃tɛʀsepte/ **1** vt intercept.

**interdiction** /ɛ̃tɛʀdiksjɔ̃/ nf ban; ~ de fumer no smoking.

**interdire** /ɛ̃tɛʀdiʀ/ **37** vt forbid; (officiellement) ban, prohibit; ~ à qn de faire forbid sb to do.

**interdit, ~e** /ɛ̃tɛʀdi, -t/ adj prohibited, forbidden; (étonné) dumbfounded.

**intéressant, ~e** /ɛ̃teʀesɑ̃, -t/ adj interesting; (avantageux) attractive.

**intéressé, ~e** /ɛ̃teʀese/ adj (en cause) concerned; (pour profiter) self-interested. ● nm, f person concerned.

**intéresser** /ɛ̃teʀese/ **1** vt interest; (concerner) concern. □ s'~ à vpr be interested in.

**intérêt** /ɛ̃teʀɛ/ nm interest; (égoïsme) self-interest; (~s) (Comm) interest; vous avez ~ à il is in your interest to.

**interface** /ɛ̃teʀfas/ nf (Ordinat) interface.

**intérieur, ~e** /ɛ̃teʀjœʀ/ adj inner, inside; (mur, escalier) internal; (vol, politique) domestic; (vie, calme) inner. ● nm interior; (de boîte, tiroir) inside; à l'~ (de) inside; (fig) within. **intérieurement** adv inwardly.

**intérim** /ɛ̃teʀim/ nm interim; assurer l'~ deputize (de for); par ~ on an interim basis; **président par ~** acting president; **faire de l'~** temp.

**intérimaire** /ɛ̃teʀimɛʀ/ adj temporary, interim. ● nmf (secrétaire) temp; (médecin) locum.

**interjection** /ɛ̃tɛʀʒɛksjɔ̃/ nf interjection.

**interlocuteur, -trice** /ɛ̃tɛʀlɔkytɔʀ, -tʀis/ nm, f son ~ the person one is speaking to.

**interloqué, ~e** /ɛ̃tɛʀlɔke/ adj être ~ be taken aback.

**intermède** /ɛ̃tɛʀmɛd/ nm interlude.

**intermédiaire** /ɛ̃tɛʀmedjɛʀ/ adj intermediate. ● nmf intermediary. ● nm sans ~ without an intermediary, direct; par l'~ de through.

**interminable** /ɛ̃tɛʀminabl/ adj endless.

**intermittence** /ɛ̃tɛʀmitɑ̃s/ nf par ~ intermittently.

**internat** /ɛ̃tɛʀna/ nm boarding-school.

**international, ~e** (mpl -aux) /ɛ̃tɛʀnasjɔnal, -o/ adj international.

**internaute** /ɛ̃tɛʀnot/ nmf (Ordinat) Netsurfer, Internet user.

**interne** /ɛ̃tɛʀn/ adj internal; (cours, formation) in-house. ● nmf (Scol) boarder; (Méd) house officer; (US) intern.

**internement** /ɛ̃tɛʀnəmɑ̃/ nm (Pol) internment. **interner 1** vt

(Pol) intern; (Méd) commit.
**Internet** /ɛ̃tɛʀnɛt/ nm Internet; sur
~ on the Internet.
**interpellation** /ɛ̃tɛʀpelasjɔ̃/ nf
(Pol) questioning. **interpeller** ❶ vt
shout to; (apostropher) shout at;
(interroger) question.
**interphone** /ɛ̃tɛʀfɔn/ nm intercom; (d'immeuble) entry phone.
**interposer (s')** /(s)ɛ̃tɛʀpoze/ ❶
vpr intervene.
**interprétariat** /ɛ̃tɛʀpʀetaʀja/ nm
interpreting. **interprétation** nf interpretation; (d'artiste) performance. **interprète** nmf interpreter;
(artiste) performer. **interpréter** ⓯
vt interpret; (jouer) play; (chanter) sing.
**interrogateur, -trice**
/ɛ̃tɛʀɔgatœʀ, -tʀis/ adj questioning.
**interrogatif, -ive** adj interrogative. **interrogation** nf question; (action)
questioning; (épreuve) test. **interrogatoire** nm interrogation. **interroger** ⓵ vt question; (élève) test.
**interrompre** /ɛ̃teʀɔ̃pʀ/ ❸ vt
break off, interrupt; (personne)
interrupt. □ s'~ vpr break off. **interrupteur** nm switch. **interruption** nf interruption; (arrêt) break.
**interurbain, ~e** /ɛ̃tɛʀyʀbɛ̃, -ɛn/
adj long-distance, trunk.
**intervalle** /ɛ̃tɛʀval/ nm space;
(temps) interval; dans l'~ in the
meantime.
**intervenir** /ɛ̃tɛʀvəniʀ/ ⓹ vi (agir)
intervene (auprès de qn with sb);
(survenir) occur, take place; (Méd)
operate. **intervention** nf intervention; (Méd) operation.
**intervertir** /ɛ̃tɛʀvɛʀtiʀ/ ❷ vt invert; (rôles) reverse.
**interview** /ɛ̃tɛʀvju/ nf interview.
**interviewer** ❶ vt interview.
**intestin** /ɛ̃tɛstɛ̃/ nm intestine.

**intime** /ɛ̃tim/ adj intimate; ( fête,
vie) private; (dîner) quiet. ● nmf intimate friend.
**intimider** /ɛ̃timide/ ❶ vt intimidate.
**intimité** /ɛ̃timite/ nf intimacy; (vie
privée) privacy.
**intituler** /ɛ̃tityle/ ❶ vt call, entitle. □ s'~ vpr be called ou entitled.
**intolérable** /ɛ̃tɔleʀabl/ adj intolerable. **intolérance** nf intolerance. **intolérant, ~e** adj intolerant.
**intonation** /ɛ̃tɔnasjɔ̃/ nf intonation.
**intox** /ɛ̃tɔks/ nf ⓵ brainwashing.
**intoxication** /ɛ̃tɔksikasjɔ̃/ nf poisoning; (fig) brainwashing; ~ alimentaire food poisoning. **intoxiquer** ❶ vt poison; (fig) brainwash.
**intraitable** /ɛ̃tʀɛtabl/ adj inflexible.
**Intranet** /ɛ̃tʀanɛt/ nm Intranet.
**intransigeant, ~e** /ɛ̃tʀɑ̃ziʒɑ̃, -t/
adj intransigent.
**intransitif, -ive** /ɛ̃tʀɑ̃zitif, -v/ adj
intransitive.
**intraveineux, -euse** /ɛ̃tʀavɛnø,
-z/ adj intravenous.
**intrépide** /ɛ̃tʀepid/ adj fearless.
**intrigue** /ɛ̃tʀig/ nf intrigue; (scénario) plot.
**intrinsèque** /ɛ̃tʀɛ̃sɛk/ adj intrinsic.
**introduction** /ɛ̃tʀɔdyksjɔ̃/ nf
introduction; (insertion) insertion.
**introduire** /ɛ̃tʀɔduiʀ/ ⓱ vt introduce, bring in; (insérer) put in, insert; ~ qn show sb in. □ s'~ vpr
get in; s'~ dans get into, enter.
**introuvable** /ɛ̃tʀuvabl/ adj that
cannot be found.
**introverti, ~e** /ɛ̃tʀɔvɛʀti/ nm, f
introvert. ● adj introverted.

**intrus**, ~e /ɛ̃try, -z/ nm, f intruder. **intrusion** nf intrusion.

**intuitif, -ive** /ɛ̃tɥitif, -iv/ adj intuitive. **intuition** nf intuition.

**inusable** /inyzabl/ adj hard-wearing.

**inusité**, ~e /inyzite/ adj little used.

**inutile** /inytil/ adj useless; (vain) needless. **inutilement** adv needlessly. **inutilisable** adj unusable.

**invalide** /ɛ̃valid/ adj & nmf disabled (person).

**invariable** /ɛ̃varjabl/ adj invariable.

**invasion** /ɛ̃vazjɔ̃/ nf invasion.

**invectiver** /ɛ̃vɛktive/ **1** vt abuse.

**inventaire** /ɛ̃vɑ̃tɛr/ nm inventory; (Comm) stocklist; faire l'~ draw up an inventory; (Comm) do a stocktake.

**inventer** /ɛ̃vɑ̃te/ **1** vt invent. **inventeur, -trice** nm, f inventor. **inventif, -ive** adj inventive. **invention** nf invention.

**inverse** /ɛ̃vɛrs/ adj opposite; (ordre) reverse; en sens ~ in ou from the opposite direction. • nm reverse; c'est l'~ it's the other way round. **inversement** adv conversely. **inverser 1** vt reverse, invert.

**investir** /ɛ̃vɛstir/ **2** vt invest. **investissement** nm investment.

**investiture** /ɛ̃vɛstityr/ nf (de candidat) nomination; (de président) investiture.

**invétéré**, ~e /ɛ̃vetere/ adj inveterate; (menteur) compulsive; (enraciné) deep-rooted.

**invisible** /ɛ̃vizibl/ adj invisible.

**invitation** /ɛ̃vitasjɔ̃/ nf invitation. **invité**, ~e nm, f guest. **inviter 1** vt invite (à to).

**involontaire** /ɛ̃vɔlɔ̃tɛr/ adj involuntary; (témoin, héros) unwitting.

**invoquer** /ɛ̃vɔke/ **1** vt call upon, invoke.

**invraisemblable** /ɛ̃vrɛsɑ̃blabl/ adj improbable, unlikely; (incroyable) incredible. **invraisemblance** nf improbability.

**iode** /jɔd/ nm iodine.

**ira, irait** /ira, irɛ/ ➡ALLER **8**.

**Irak** /irak/ nm Iraq.

**Iran** /irɑ̃/ nm Iran.

**iris** /iris/ nm iris.

**irlandais**, ~e /irlɑ̃dɛ, -z/ adj Irish. I~, ~e nm, f Irishman, Irishwoman.

**Irlande** /irlɑ̃d/ nf Ireland.

**IRM** abrév m (imagerie par résonance magnétique) magnetic resonance imaging.

**ironie** /irɔni/ nf irony. **ironique** adj ironic.

**irrationnel, ~le** /irasjɔnɛl/ adj irrational.

**irréalisable** /irealizabl/ adj (idée, rêve) unachievable; (projet) unworkable.

**irrécupérable** /irekyperabl/ adj irretrievable; (capital) irrecoverable.

**irréel, ~le** /ireɛl/ adj unreal.

**irréfléchi**, ~e /irefleʃi/ adj thoughtless.

**irrégulier, -ière** /iregylje, -jɛr/ adj irregular.

**irrémédiable** /iremedjabl/ adj irreparable.

**irremplaçable** /irɑ̃plasabl/ adj irreplaceable.

**irréparable** /ireparabl/ adj (objet) beyond repair; (tort, dégâts) irreparable.

**irréprochable** /ireprɔʃabl/ adj flawless.

**irrésistible** /irezistibl/ adj irresistible; (drôle) hilarious.

**irrésolu**, ~e /irezɔly/ adj indecisive; (problème) unsolved.

**irrespirable** /iʀɛspiʀabl/ *adj* stifling.

**irresponsable** /iʀɛspɔ̃sabl/ *adj* irresponsible.

**irrigation** /iʀigasjɔ̃/ *nf* irrigation. **irriguer** ① *vt* irrigate.

**irritable** /iʀitabl/ *adj* irritable.

**irriter** /iʀite/ ① *vt* irritate. □ **s'~** *vpr* get annoyed (de at).

**irruption** /iʀypsjɔ̃/ *nf* faire ~ dans burst into.

**Islam** /islam/ *nm* Islam. **islamique** *adj* Islamic.

**islamiste** /islamist/ *adj* Islamist, Islamic; *n m,f* Islamist.

**islandais**, ~e /islɑ̃dɛ, -z/ *adj* Icelandic. ●*nm* (Ling) Icelandic. **I~**, ~e *nm, f* Icelander.

**Islande** /islɑ̃d/ *nf* Iceland.

**isolant**, ~e /izolɑ̃/ *nm* insulating material. **isolation** *nf* insulation.

**isolé**, ~e /izole/ *adj* isolated. **isolement** *nm* isolation.

**isoler** /izole/ ① *vt* isolate; (Électr) insulate. □ **s'~** *vpr* isolate oneself.

**isoloir** /izolwaʀ/ *nm* polling booth.

**Isorel** ® /izoʀɛl/ *nm* hardboard.

**Israël** /israɛl/ *nm* Israel. **israélien**, ~ne *adj* Israeli.

**israélite** /israelit/ *adj* Jewish. ●*nmf* Jew.

**issu**, ~e /isy/ *adj* être ~ de (*personne*) come from; (*résulter de*) result ou stem from.

**issue** /isy/ *nf* (sortie) exit; (résultat) outcome; (fig) solution; à l'~ de at the conclusion of; ~ de secours emergency exit; **rue** ou **voie sans** ~ dead end.

**Italie** /itali/ *nf* Italy.

**italien**, ~ne /italjɛ̃, -ɛn/ *adj* Italian. ●*nm* (Ling) Italian. **I~**, ~ne *nm, f* Italian.

**italique** /italik/ *nm* italics.

**itinéraire** /itineʀɛʀ/ *nm* itinerary, route.

**I.U.T.** *abrév m* (**Institut universitaire de technologie**) university institute of technology.

**I.V.G.** *abrév f* (**interruption volontaire de grossesse**) abortion.

**ivoire** /ivwaʀ/ *nm* ivory.

**ivre** /ivʀ/ *adj* drunk. **ivresse** *nf* drunkenness; (fig) exhilaration. **ivrogne** *nmf* drunk(ard).

**j'** /ʒ/ ➡**JE**.

**jacinthe** /ʒasɛ̃t/ *nf* hyacinth.

**jadis** /ʒadis/ *adv* long ago.

**jaillir** /ʒajiʀ/ ② *vi* (*liquide*) spurt (out); (*lumière*) stream out; (*apparaître*) burst forth, spring out.

**jalonner** /ʒalone/ ① *vt* mark (out).

**jalousie** /ʒaluzi/ *nf* jealousy; (store) (venetian) blind. **jaloux**, **-ouse** *adj* jealous.

**jamais** /ʒamɛ/ *adv* ever; ne ~ never; **il ne boit** ~ he never drinks; **à** ~ for ever; **si** ~ if ever.

**jambe** /ʒɑ̃b/ *nf* leg.

**jambon** /ʒɑ̃bɔ̃/ *nm* ham. **jambonneau** (*pl* ~x) *nm* knuckle of ham.

**janvier** /ʒɑ̃vje/ *nm* January.

**Japon** /ʒapɔ̃/ *nm* Japan.

**japonais**, ~e /ʒaponɛ, -z/ *adj* Japanese. ●*nm* (Ling) Japanese. **J~**, ~e *nm, f* Japanese.

**japper** /ʒape/ ① *vi* yap.

**jaquette** /ʒakɛt/ *nf* (de livre, femme) jacket; (d'homme) morning coat.

**jardin** /ʒaʀdɛ̃/ nm garden; ~ **d'enfants** nursery (school); ~ **public** public park. **jardinage** nm gardening. **jardiner 🔟** vi do some gardening, garden. **jardinier, -ière** nm, f gardener.

**jardinière** /ʒaʀdinjɛʀ/ nf (meuble) plant-stand; ~ **de légumes** mixed vegetables.

**jarretelle** /ʒaʀtɛl/ nf suspender; (US) garter.

**jarretière** /ʒaʀtjɛʀ/ nf garter.

**jatte** /ʒat/ nf bowl.

**jauge** /ʒoʒ/ nf capacity; (de navire) tonnage; (compteur) gauge; ~ **d'huile** dipstick.

**jaune** /ʒon/ adj & nm yellow; (péj) scab; ~ **d'œuf** (egg) yolk; **rire** ~ give a forced laugh. **jaunir 🔁** vt/i turn yellow. **jaunisse** nf jaundice.

**javelot** /ʒavlo/ nm javelin.

**jazz** /dʒaz/ nm jazz.

**J.C.** abrév m (Jésus-Christ) 500 **avant/après** ~ 500 B.C./A.D.

**je, j'** /ʒə, ʒ/ pron I.

**jean** /dʒin/ nm jeans; **un** ~ a pair of jeans.

**jet¹** /ʒɛ/ nm throw; (de liquide, vapeur) jet; ~ **d'eau** fountain.

**jet²** /dʒɛt/ nm (avion) jet.

**jetable** /ʒətabl/ adj disposable.

**jetée** /ʒəte/ nf pier.

**jeter** /ʒəte/ 🔢 vt throw; (au rebut) throw away; (regard, ancre, lumière) cast; (cri) utter; (bases) lay; ~ **un coup d'œil** have ou take a look (à at). □ **se** ~ vpr **se** ~ **contre** crash ou bash into; **se** ~ **dans** (fleuve) flow into; **se** ~ **sur** (se ruer sur) rush at.

**jeton** /ʒətɔ̃/ nm token; (pour compter) counter; (au casino) chip.

**jeu** (pl ~x) /ʒø/ nm game; (amusement) play; (au casino) gambling; (Théât) acting; (série) set; (de lu-

mière, ressort) play; **en** ~ (honneur) at stake; (forces) at work; ~ **de cartes** (paquet) pack of cards; ~ **d'échecs** (boîte) chess set; ~ **de mots** pun; ~ **télévisé** tv game show; ~ **vidéo** video game; ~x **de grattage** scratch cards; **les** ~x **olympiques/paralympiques** the Olympic Games/Paralympic Games.

**jeudi** /ʒødi/ nm Thursday.

**jeun: à** ~ /aʒœ/ loc on an empty stomach.

**jeune** /ʒœn/ adj young; ~ **fille** girl; ~ **pousse** (Comm) start-up; ~s **mariés** newlyweds. ● nmf young person; **les** ~s young people.

**jeûne** /ʒøn/ nm fast.

**jeunesse** /ʒœnɛs/ nf youth; (apparence) youthfulness; **la** ~ (jeunes) the young.

**joaillerie** /ʒɔajʀi/ nf jewellery; (magasin) jeweller's shop.

**joie** /ʒwa/ nf joy.

**joindre** /ʒwɛ̃dʀ/ 🔢 vt join (à to); (mains, pieds) put together; (efforts) combine; (contacter) contact; (dans une enveloppe) enclose. □ **se** ~ **à** vpr join.

**joint, ~e** /ʒwɛ̃, -t/ adj (efforts) joint; (pieds) together. ● nm joint; (de robinet) washer.

**joli, ~e** /ʒɔli/ adj pretty, nice; (somme, profit) nice; **c'est du** ~! (ironique) charming! **c'est bien** ~ **mais** that is all very well but.

**joncher** /ʒɔ̃ʃe/ 🔟 vt litter, be strewn over; **jonché de** littered with.

**jonction** /ʒɔ̃ksjɔ̃/ nf junction.

**jongleur, -euse** /ʒɔ̃glœʀ, øz/ nm, f juggler.

**jonquille** /ʒɔ̃kij/ nf daffodil.

**joue** /ʒu/ nf cheek.

**jouer** /ʒwe/ 🔟 vt/i play; (Théât) act; (au casino) gamble; (fonctionner) work; (*film, pièce*) put on; (*cheval*) back; (*être important*) count; ~ à (*jeu, Sport*) play; ~ de (*Mus*) play; ~ **la comédie** put on an act; **bien joué!** well done!

**jouet** /ʒwɛ/ *nm* toy; (*personne*: fig) plaything; (*victime*) victim.

**joueur, -euse** /ʒwœʀ, -øz/ *nm, f* player; (*parieur*) gambler.

**joufflu, ~e** /ʒufly/ *adj* chubby-cheeked; (*visage*) chubby.

**jouir** /ʒwiʀ/ **2** *vi* (sexe) come; ~ de (*droit, avantage*) enjoy; (*bien, concession*) enjoy the use of. **jouissance** *nf* pleasure; (*usage*) use (de qch of sth).

**joujou** (pl ~x) /ʒuʒu/ *nm* **1** toy.

**jour** /ʒuʀ/ *nm* day; (*opposé à nuit*) day (time); (*lumière*) daylight; (*aspect*) light; (*ouverture*) gap; **de nos ~s** nowadays; **du ~ au lendemain** overnight; **il fait ~** it is daylight; ~ **chômé** *ou* **férié** public holiday; ~ **de fête** holiday; ~ **ouvrable**, ~ **de travail** working day; **mettre à ~** update; **mettre au ~** uncover; **au grand ~** in the open; **donner le ~** give birth; **voir le ~** be born; **vivre au ~ le jour** live from day to day.

**journal** (pl **-aux**) /ʒuʀnal, -o/ *nm* (news)paper; (*spécialisé*) journal; (*intime*) diary; (*à la radio*) news; ~ **de bord** log-book.

**journalier, -ière** /ʒuʀnalje, -jɛʀ/ *adj* daily.

**journalisme** /ʒuʀnalism/ *nm* journalism. **journaliste** *nmf* journalist.

**journée** /ʒuʀne/ *nf* day.

**jovial, ~e** (mpl **-iaux**) /ʒɔvjal, -jo/ *adj* jovial.

**joyau** (pl ~x) /ʒwajo/ *nm* gem.

**joyeux, -euse** /ʒwajø, -z/ *adj* merry, joyful; ~ **anniversaire** happy birthday.

**jubiler** /ʒybile/ **1** *vi* be jubilant.

**jucher** /ʒyʃe/ **1** *vt* perch. □ **se ~** *vpr* perch.

**judaïsme** /ʒydaism/ *nm* Judaism.

**judiciaire** /ʒydisjɛʀ/ *adj* judicial.

**judicieux, -ieuse** /ʒydisjø, -z/ *adj* judicious.

**judo** /ʒydo/ *nm* judo.

**juge** /ʒyʒ/ *nm* judge; (*arbitre*) referee; ~ **de paix** Justice of the Peace; ~ **de touche** linesman.

**jugé: au ~** /oʒyʒe/ *loc* by guesswork.

**jugement** /ʒyʒmã/ *nm* judgement; (*criminel*) sentence.

**juger** /ʒyʒe/ **40** *vt/i* judge; (*estimer*) consider (que that); ~ **de** judge.

**juguler** /ʒygyle/ **1** *vt* stamp out; curb.

**juif, -ive** /ʒɥif, -v/ *adj* Jewish. ● *nm, f* Jew.

**juillet** /ʒɥijɛ/ *nm* July.

**juin** /ʒɥɛ̃/ *nm* June.

**jumeau, -elle** (mpl ~x) /ʒymo, -ɛl/ *adj & nm, f* twin. **jumeler** **38** *vt* (*villes*) twin.

**jumelles** /ʒymɛl/ *nfpl* binoculars.

**jument** /ʒymã/ *nf* mare.

**junior** /ʒynjɔʀ/ *adj & nmf* junior.

**jupe** /ʒyp/ *nf* skirt.

**jupon** /ʒypõ/ *nm* slip, petticoat.

**juré, ~e** /ʒyʀe/ *nm, f* juror. ● *adj* sworn.

**jurer** /ʒyʀe/ **1** *vt* swear (que that). ● *vi* (*pester*) swear; (*contraster*) clash (avec with).

**juridiction** /ʒyʀidiksjõ/ *nf* jurisdiction; (*tribunal*) court of law.

**juridique** /ʒyʀidik/ *adj* legal.

**juriste** /ʒyʀist/ *nmf* legal expert.

**juron** /ʒyʀõ/ *nm* swearword.

**jury** /ʒyʀi/ *nm* (Jur) jury; (examinateurs) panel of judges.

**jus** /ʒy/ *nm* juice; (de viande) gravy; ∼ de fruit fruit juice.

**jusque** /ʒysk(ə)/ *prép* jusqu'à (up) to, as far as; (temps) until, till; (limite) up to; (y compris) even; jusqu'à ce que until; jusqu'à présent until now; jusqu'en until; jusqu'où? how far?; ∼ dans, ∼ sur as far as.

**juste** /ʒyst/ *adj* fair, just; (légitime) just; (correct, exact) right; (vrai) true; (vêtement) tight; (quantité) on the short side; le ∼ milieu the happy medium. ● *adv* rightly, correctly; (chanter) in tune; (seulement, exactement) just; (un peu) ∼ (calculer, mesurer) a bit fine ou close; au ∼ exactly; c'était ∼ (presque raté) it was a close thing. **justement** *adv* (précisément) precisely; (à l'instant) just; (avec justesse) correctly; (légitimement) justifiably.

**justesse** /ʒystɛs/ *nf* accuracy; de ∼ just, narrowly.

**justice** /ʒystis/ *nf* justice; (autorités) law; (tribunal) court.

**justifier** /ʒystifje/ [45] *vt* justify. ● *vi* ∼ de prove. □ **se** ∼ *vpr* justify oneself.

**juteux, -euse** /ʒytø, -z/ *adj* juicy.

**juvénile** /ʒyvenil/ *adj* youthful; (délinquance, mortalité) juvenile.

· · · · · · · · · · · · · · · · · · · · · ·

# Kk

· · · · · · · · · · · · · · · · · · · · · ·

**kaki** /kaki/ *adj inv & nm* khaki.

**kangourou** /kɑ̃guʁu/ *nm* kangaroo.

**karaté** /kaʁate/ *nm* karate.

**kart** /kaʁt/ *nm* go-cart.

**kascher** /kaʃɛʁ/ *adj inv* kosher.

**kayak** /kajak/ *nm* kayak.

**képi** /kepi/ *nm* kepi.

**kermesse** /kɛʁmɛs/ *nf* fête.

**kidnapper** /kidnape/ [1] *vt* kidnap.

**kilo** /kilo/ *nm* kilo.

**kilogramme** /kilɔgʁam/ *nm* kilogram.

**kilométrage** /kilɔmetʁaʒ/ *nm* ≈ mileage. **kilomètre** *nm* kilometre.

**kinésithérapeute** /kineziteʁapø t/ *nmf* physiotherapist. **kinésithérapie** *nf* physiotherapy.

**kiosque** /kjɔsk/ *nm* kiosk; ∼ à musique bandstand.

**kit** /kit/ *nm* kit; ∼ mains libres conducteur hands-free kit.

**klaxon®** /klaksɔn/ *nm* (Auto) horn. **klaxonner** [1] *vi* sound one's horn.

**Ko** *abrév m* (**kilo-octet**) (Ordinat) KB.

**KO** *abrév m* (**knock-out**) KO [1].

**K-way®** /kawɛ/ *nm inv* windcheater.

**kyste** /kist/ *nm* cyst.

· · · · · · · · · · · · · · · · · · · · · ·

# Ll

· · · · · · · · · · · · · · · · · · · · · ·

**l', la** /l/, /la/, ➡**le.**

**là** /la/
● *adverbe*
····▶ (dans ce lieu) there; (ici) here; (chez soi) in; c'est ∼ que this is where; ∼ où where; par ∼ (dans cette direction) this

way; (dans cette zone) around there; de ∼ hence.

····▸ (à ce moment) then; c'est ∼ que that's when.

····▸ cet homme-∼ that man; ces maisons-∼ those houses.

● interjection

····▸ ∼ ! c'est fini there (now), it's all over!

**là-bas** /labɑ/ adv there; (à l'endroit que l'on indique) over there.

**label** /label/ nm seal, label.

**laboratoire** /labɔratwar/ nm laboratory.

**laborieux, -ieuse** /labɔrjø, -z/ adj laborious; (personne) industrious; **classes laborieuses** working classes.

**labour** /labur/ nm ploughing; (US) plowing. **labourer** ❶ vt plough; (US) plow; (déchirer) rip at.

**labyrinthe** /labirɛ̃t/ nm maze, labyrinth.

**lac** /lak/ nm lake.

**lacer** /lase/ ❿ vt lace up.

**lacet** /lasɛ/ nm (de chaussure) (shoe-)lace; (de route) sharp bend.

**lâche** /lɑʃ/ adj cowardly; (détendu) loose; (sans rigueur) lax. ● nmf coward.

**lâcher** /lɑʃe/ ❶ vt let go of; (laisser tomber) drop; (abandonner) give up; (laisser) leave; (libérer) release; (flèche, balle) fire; (juron, phrase) come out with; (desserrer) loosen; ∼ **prise** let go. ● vi give way.

**lâcheté** /lɑʃte/ nf cowardice.

**lacrymogène** /lakrimɔʒɛn/ adj **gaz ∼** tear gas.

**lacune** /lakyn/ nf gap.

**là-dedans** /lad(ə)dɑ̃/ adv (près) in here; (plus loin) in there.

**là-dessous** /lad(ə)su/ adv (près)

under here; (plus loin) under there.

**là-dessus** /lad(ə)sy/ adv (sur une surface) on here; (plus loin) on there; (sur ce) with that; (quelque temps après) after that; **qu'avez-vous à dire ∼?** what have you got to say about it?

**ladite** /ladit/ ⇒**ledit**.

**lagune** /lagyn/ nf lagoon.

**là-haut** /lao/ adv (en hauteur) up here; (plus loin) up there; (à l'étage) upstairs.

**laïc** /laik/ nm layman.

**laid, -e** /lɛ, lɛd/ adj ugly; (action) vile. **laideur** nf ugliness.

**lainage** /lɛnaʒ/ nm woollen garment.

**laine** /lɛn/ nf wool; **de ∼** woollen.

**laïque** /laik/ adj (état, loi) secular; (habit, personne) lay; (école) nondenominational. ● nmf layman, laywoman.

**laisse** /lɛs/ nf lead, leash; **tenir en ∼** keep on a lead.

**laisser** /lese/ ❶ vt (déposer) leave, drop off; (confier) leave (à qn with sb); (abandonner) leave; (rendre) ∼ **qn perplexe/froid** leave sb puzzled/cold; ∼ **qch à qn** (céder, prêter) let sb have sth; (donner) (choix, temps) give sb sth. □ **se ∼** vpr **se ∼ persuader/insulter** let oneself be persuaded/insulted; **elle ne se laisse pas faire** she won't be pushed around; **laisse-le faire** leave it to him/her etc.; **se ∼ aller** let oneself go. ● v aux ∼ **qn/qch faire** let sb/sth do; **laisse-moi faire** (ne m'aide pas) let me do it; (je m'en occupe) leave it to me; **laisse faire!** so what! **laisser-aller** nm inv carelessness; (dans la tenue) scruffiness. **laissez-passer** nm inv pass.

**lait** /lɛ/ nm milk; ∼ **longue conser-**

vation long-life *ou* UHT milk; **frère/ sœur ~** foster-brother/-sister.
**laitage** *nm* milk product. **laiterie** *nf* dairy. **laiteux, -euse** *adj* milky.
**laitier, -ière** /letje, -jɛʀ/ *adj* dairy.
● *nm, f* (livreur) milkman, milkwoman.
**laiton** /lɛtɔ̃/ *nm* brass.
**laitue** /lety/ *nf* lettuce.
**lama** /lama/ *nm* llama.
**lambeau** (*pl* ~x) /lɑ̃bo/ *nm* shred; **en ~x** in shreds.
**lame** /lam/ *nf* blade; (lamelle) strip; (vague) wave; **~ de fond** ground swell; **~ de rasoir** razor blade.
**lamentable** /lamɑ̃tabl/ *adj* deplorable. **lamenter (se)** 🔟 *vpr* moan (sur about, over).
**lampadaire** /lɑ̃padɛʀ/ *nm* standard lamp; (de rue) street lamp.
**lampe** /lɑ̃p/ *nf* lamp; (ampoule) bulb; (de radio) valve; **~ (de poche)** torch; (US) flashlight; **~ à souder** blowlamp; **~ de chevet** bedside lamp; **~ solaire, ~ à bronzer** sunlamp.
**lance** /lɑ̃s/ *nf* spear; (de tournoi) lance; (tuyau) hose; **~ d'incendie** fire hose.
**lancement** /lɑ̃smɑ̃/ *nm* throwing; (de navire, de missile, mise sur le marché) launch.
**lance-missiles** /lɑ̃smisil/ *nm inv* missile launcher.
**lance-pierres** /lɑ̃spjɛʀ/ *nm inv* catapult.
**lancer** /lɑ̃se/ 🔟 *vt* throw; (avec force) hurl; (navire, idée, artiste) launch; (émettre) give out; (regard) cast; (moteur) start. □ **se ~** *vpr* (Sport) gain momentum; (se précipiter) rush; **se ~ dans** (explication) launch into; (passetemps) take up.
● *nm* throw; (action) throwing.
**lancinant, ~e** /lɑ̃sinɑ̃, -t/ *adj*

(douleur) shooting; (problème) nagging.
**landau** /lɑ̃do/ *nm* pram; (US) baby carriage.
**lande** /lɑ̃d/ *nf* heath, moor.
**langage** /lɑ̃gaʒ/ *nm* language; **~ machine/de programmation** machine/programming language.
**langouste** /lɑ̃gust/ *nf* spiny lobster. **langoustine** *nf* Dublin Bay prawn.
**langue** /lɑ̃g/ *nf* (Anat) tongue; (Ling) language; **il m'a tiré la ~** he stuck his tongue out at me; **de ~ anglaise** English-speaking; (journal) English-language; **~ maternelle** mother tongue; **~ vivante** modern language.
**lanière** /lanjɛʀ/ *nf* strap.
**lanterne** /lɑ̃tɛʀn/ *nf* lantern; (électrique) lamp; (de voiture) sidelight.
**lapin** /lapɛ̃/ *nm* rabbit; **poser un ~ à qn** 🆃 stand sb up; **le coup du ~** rabbit punch; (en voiture) whiplash injury.
**lapsus** /lapsys/ *nm* slip (of the tongue).
**laque** /lak/ *nf* lacquer; (pour cheveux) hairspray; (peinture) gloss paint.
**laquelle** /lakɛl/ ➡LEQUEL.
**lard** /laʀ/ *nm* streaky bacon.
**large** /laʀʒ/ *adj* wide, broad; (grand) large; (généreux) generous; **avoir les idées ~s** be broad-minded; **~ d'esprit** broad-minded.
● *adv* (calculer, mesurer) on the generous side; **voir ~** think big. ● *nm* **faire 10 cm de ~** be 10 cm wide; **le ~** (mer) the open sea; **au ~ de** (Naut) off. **largement** *adv* widely; (ouvrir) wide; (amplement) amply; (généreusement) generously; (au moins) easily.
**largesse** /laʀʒɛs/ *nf* generous gift.

**largeur** /laʀʒœʀ/ nf width, breadth; ~ **d'esprit** broad-mindedness.
**larguer** /laʀge/ **1** vt drop; ~ **les amarres** cast off.
**larme** /laʀm/ nf tear; (goutte 🔢) drop; **en ~s** in tears.
**larmoyant,** ~e /laʀmwajɑ̃, -t/ adj full of tears. **larmoyer** **31** vi (yeux) water; (pleurnicher) whine.
**larynx** /laʀɛ̃ks/ nm larynx.
**las,** ~se /lɑ, lɑs/ adj weary.
**lasagnes** /lazaɲ/ nfpl lasagna.
**laser** /lazɛʀ/ nm laser.
**lasser** /lɑse/ **1** vt weary. □ se ~ vpr grow tired, tire. se ~ **de** (of).
**latéral,** ~e (mpl **-aux**) /lateʀal, -o/ adj lateral.
**latin,** ~e /latɛ̃, -in/ adj Latin. ● nm (Ling) Latin.
**latte** /lat/ nf lath; (de plancher) board; (de siège) slat; (de mur, plafond) lath.
**lauréat,** ~e /loʀea, -t/ adj prize-winning. ● nm, f prize-winner.
**laurier** /loʀje/ nm (Bot) laurel; (Culin) bay-leaves.
**lavable** /lavabl/ adj washable.
**lavabo** /lavabo/ nm wash-basin; ~s toilet(s).
**lavage** /lavaʒ/ nm washing; ~ **de cerveau** brainwashing.
**lavande** /lavɑ̃d/ nf lavender.
**lave** /lav/ nf lava.
**lave-glace** (pl ~s) /lavglas/ nm windscreen washer.
**lave-linge** /lavlɛ̃ʒ/ nm inv washing machine.
**laver** /lave/ **1** vt wash; ~ **qn de** (fig) clear sb of. □ se ~ vpr wash (oneself); se ~ **les mains** wash one's hands.
**laverie** /lavʀi/ nf ~ (**automatique**) launderette; (US) laundromat.

**lave-vaisselle** /lavvɛsɛl/ nm inv dishwasher.
**laxatif, -ive** /laksatif, -v/ adj & nm laxative.
**layette** /lɛjɛt/ nf baby clothes.

---

**le, la, l'** (pl **les**) /lə, la, l, le/

> l' before vowel or mute h.

● **déterminant**
····▸ the.
····▸ (notion générale) **aimer la musique** like music; **l'amour** love.
····▸ (possession) **avoir les yeux verts** have green eyes; **il s'est cassé la jambe** he broke his leg.
····▸ (prix) **10 euros ~ kilo** 10 euros a kilo.
····▸ (temps) ~ **lundi** on Mondays; **tous les mardis** every Tuesday.
····▸ (avec nom propre) **les Dury** the Durys; **la reine Margot** Queen Margot; **la Belgique** Belgium.
····▸ (avec adjectif) the; **je veux la rouge** I want the red one; **les riches** the rich.
● **pronom**
····▸ (homme) him; (femme) her; (chose, animal) it; (au pluriel) them.
····▸ (remplaçant une phrase) **je te l'avais bien dit** I told you so; **je ~ croyais aussi** I thought so too.

---

**lécher** /leʃe/ **14** vt lick; (flamme) lick; (mer) lap.
**lèche-vitrines** /lɛʃvitʀin/ nm inv **faire du ~** go window-shopping.
**leçon** /ləsɔ̃/ nf lesson; **faire la ~ à** lecture sb; ~ **particulière** private lesson; ~s **de conduite**

driving lessons.

**lecteur, -trice** /lɛktœʀ, -tʀis/ *nm, f* reader; (Univ) foreign language assistant; ~ de cassettes cassette player; ~ de disquettes (disk) drive; ~ laser CD player; ~ optique optical scanner.

**lecture** /lɛktyʀ/ *nf* reading.

**ledit, ladite** (*pl* lesdit(e)s) /lədi, ladit, ledi(t)/ *adj* the aforementioned.

**légal, ~e** (*mpl* -aux) /legal, -o/ *adj* legal. **légaliser** 🔢 *vt* legalize. **légalité** *nf* legality; (loi) law.

**légendaire** /leʒɑ̃dɛʀ/ *adj* legendary. **légende** *nf* (histoire, inscription) legend; (de carte) key; (d'illustration) caption.

**léger, -ère** /leʒe, -ɛʀ/ *adj* light; (bruit, faute, maladie) slight; (café, argument) weak; (imprudent) thoughtless; (frivole) fickle; à la légère thoughtlessly. **légèrement** *adv* lightly; (agir) thoughtlessly; (un peu) slightly. **légèreté** *nf* lightness; thoughtlessness.

**légion** /leʒjɔ̃/ *nf* legion.

**Légion d'honneur** The system of honours awarded by the state for meritorious achievement. The *Président de la République* is the *Grand maître*. The basic rank is *Chevalier*. Holders of the *Légion d'honneur* are entitled to wear *une rosette* (a small red lapel ribbon).

**légionellose** /leʒjɔnɛloz/ *nf* (Méd) legionnaire's disease.

**législatif, -ive** /leʒislatif, -v/ *adj* legislative; **élections législatives** general election.

**législature** /leʒislatyʀ/ *nf* term of office.

**légitime** /leʒitim/ *adj* (Jur) legitim-

ate; (fig) rightful; **agir en état de** ~ **défense** act in self-defence. **légitimité** *nf* legitimacy.

**legs** /lɛg/ *nm* legacy; (d'effets personnels) bequest.

**léguer** /lege/ 🔢 *vt* bequeath.

**légume** /legym/ *nm* vegetable.

**lendemain** /lɑ̃dmɛ̃/ *nm* le ~ the next day; (fig) the future; le ~ de the day after; le ~ matin/soir the next morning/evening; du jour au ~ from one day to the next.

**lent, ~e** /lɑ̃, -t/ *adj* slow. **lentement** *adv* slowly. **lenteur** *nf* slowness.

**lentille** /lɑ̃tij/ *nf* (Culin) lentil; (verre) lens; ~s de contact contact lenses.

**léopard** /leɔpaʀ/ *nm* leopard.

**lèpre** /lɛpʀ/ *nf* leprosy.

**lequel, laquelle** (*pl* lesquel(le)s, auquel (*pl* auxquel(le)s), duquel (*pl* desquel(le)s) /lakɛl, lakɛl, lekɛl, okɛl, dykɛl, dekɛl/

> à + lequel = auquel,
> à + lesquel(le)s = auxquel(le)s;
> de + lequel = duquel,
> de + lesquel(le)s = desquel(le)s

● *pronom*
····▸ (relatif) (personne) who; (complément indirect) whom; (autres cas) which; **l'ami auquel tu as écrit** the friend to whom you wrote; **les voisins chez lesquels Sophie est allée** the neighbours whose house Sophie went to.
····▸ (interrogatif) which; ~ **tu veux?** which one do you want?
● *adjectif*
····▸ **auquel cas** in which case.

**les** /le/ ➡ **le.**

**lesbienne** /lɛsbjɛn/ nf lesbian.

**léser** /leze/ **14** vt wrong.

**lésiner** /lezine/ **1** vi ne pas ∼ sur not stint on.

**lesquels, lesquelles** /lekɛl/ ➡ **lequel.**

**lessive** /lesiv/ nf (poudre) washing-powder; (liquide) washing liquid; (linge, action) washing.

**leste** /lɛst/ adj agile, nimble; (grivois) coarse.

**Lettonie** /lɛtɔni/ nf Latvia.

**lettre** /lɛtʀ/ nf letter; à la ∼, au pied de la ∼ literally; en toutes ∼s in full; les ∼s (Univ) (the) arts.

**leucémie** /løsemi/ nf leukaemia.

---

**leur** (pl ∼s) /lœʀ/

● pronom personnel invariable

····▸ them; **donne-le** ∼ give it to them; **je** ∼ **fais confiance** I trust them.

● adjectif possessif

····▸ their; ∼s enfants their children; à ∼ arrivée when they arrived.

● le leur, la leur, (pl les leurs) pronom possessif

····▸ theirs; chacun le ∼ one each; je suis des ∼s I am one of them.

---

**levain** /ləvɛ̃/ nm leaven.

**levé, ∼e** /ləve/ adj (debout) up.

**levée** /ləve/ nf (de peine, de sanctions) lifting; (de courrier) collection; (de troupes, d'impôts) levying.

**lever** /ləve/ **6** vt lift up, raise; (interdiction) lift; (séance) close; (armée, impôts) levy. ● vi (pâte) rise. □ se ∼ vpr get up; (soleil, rideau) rise; (jour) break. ● nm au ∼ on getting up; ∼ du jour daybreak; ∼

**de rideau** (Théât) curtain (up); ∼ **du soleil** sunrise.

**levier** /ləvje/ nm lever; ∼ de changement de vitesse gear lever.

**lèvre** /lɛvʀ/ nf lip.

**lévrier** /levʀije/ nm greyhound.

**levure** /ləvyʀ/ nf yeast; ∼ chimique baking powder.

**lexique** /lɛksik/ nm vocabulary; (glossaire) lexicon.

**lézard** /lezaʀ/ nm lizard.

**lézarde** /lezaʀd/ nf crack.

**liaison** /ljɛzɔ̃/ nf connection; (transport, Ordinat) link; (contact) contact; (Gram, Mil) liaison; (amoureuse) affair; être en ∼ avec be in contact with; assurer la ∼ entre liaise between.

**liane** /ljan/ nf creeper.

**Liban** /libɑ̃/ nm Lebanon.

**libeller** /libele/ **1** vt (chèque) write; (contrat) draw up; **libellé à l'ordre de** made out to.

**libellule** /libelyl/ nf dragonfly.

**libéral, ∼e** (mpl -aux) /liberal, -o/ adj liberal; **les professions** ∼**es** the professions.

**libérateur, -trice** /liberatœʀ, -tʀis/ adj liberating. ● nm, f liberator.

**libération** nf release; (de pays) liberation.

**libérer** /libere/ **14** vt (personne) free, release; (pays) liberate, free; (bureau, lieux) vacate; (gaz) release. □ se ∼ vpr free oneself.

**liberté** /libɛʀte/ nf freedom, liberty; (loisir) free time; être/mettre en ∼ be/set free; ∼ conditionnelle parole; ∼ provisoire provisional release (pending trial); ∼ surveillée probation; ∼s publiques civil liberties.

**Libertel** /libɛʀtɛl/ nm (Internet) Freenet.

**libraire** /libʀɛʀ/ nmf bookseller.

**librairie** nf bookshop.

**libre** /libʀ/ adj free; (place, pièce) vacant, free; (passage) clear; (école) private (usually religious); ~ **de qch**/ **de faire** free from sth/to do.

**libre-échange** nm free trade. **libre-service** (pl **libres-services**) nm (magasin) self-service shop; (restaurant) self-service restaurant.

**licence** /lisɑ̃s/ nf licence; (Univ) degree.

**licencié**, ~e /lisɑ̃sje/ nm, f graduate; ~ **ès lettres**/**sciences** Bachelor of Arts/Science.

**licenciements** /lisɑ̃simɑ̃/ nm redundancy; (pour faute) dismissal. **licencier** 45 vt make redundant; (pour faute) dismiss.

**licorne** /likɔʀn/ nf unicorn.

**liège** /liɛʒ/ nm cork.

**lien** /ljɛ̃/ nm (rapport) link; (attache) bond, tie; (corde) rope; ~**s affectifs**/**de parenté** emotional/ family ties.

**lier** /lje/ 45 vt tie (up), bind; (relier) link; (engager, unir) bind; ~ **conversation** strike up a conversation; **ils sont très liés** they are very close. □ **se** ~ **avec** vpr make friends with.

**lierre** /ljɛʀ/ nm ivy.

**lieu** (pl ~**x**) /ljø/ nm place; ~**x** (locaux) premises; (d'un accident) scene; **sur les** ~**x** at the scene; **au** ~ **de** instead of; **avoir** ~ take place; **donner** ~ **à** to give rise to; **tenir** ~ **de** serve as; **s'il y a** ~ if necessary; **en premier** ~ firstly; **en dernier** ~ lastly; ~ **commun** commonplace; ~ **de rencontre** meeting place.

**lièvre** /ljɛvʀ/ nm hare.

**lifting** /liftiŋ/ nm face-lift.

**ligne** /liɲ/ nf line; (trajet) route; (de métro, train) line; (formes) lines;

(de femme) figure; **en** ~ (joueurs) lined up; (au téléphone) on the phone; (Ordinat) on line; ~ **spécialisée** (Internet) dedicated line.

**ligoter** /ligɔte/ 1 vt tie up.

**ligue** /lig/ nf league. **liguer (se)** 1 vpr join forces (contre against).

**lilas** /lila/ nm & a inv lilac.

**limace** /limas/ nf slug.

**limande** /limɑ̃d/ nf (poisson) dab.

**lime** /lim/ nf file; ~ **à ongles** nail file.

**limitation** /limitasjɔ̃/ nf limitation; ~ **de vitesse** speed limit.

**limite** /limit/ nf limit; (de jardin, champ) boundary; **à la** ~ **de** (fig) verging on, bordering on; **à la** ~ if it comes to it, at a pinch; **dans une certaine** ~ up to a point; **dans la** ~ **du possible** as far as possible. ● adj (vitesse, âge) maximum; **cas** ~ borderline case; **date** ~ deadline; **date** ~ **de vente** sell-by date.

**limiter** /limite/ 1 vt limit; (délimiter) form the border of. □ **se** ~ vpr limit oneself (à to).

**limonade** /limɔnad/ nf lemonade.

**limpide** /lɛ̃pid/ adj limpid, clear.

**lin** /lɛ̃/ nm (tissu) linen.

**linge** /lɛ̃ʒ/ nm linen; (lessive) washing; (torchon) cloth; ~ **(de corps)** underwear. **lingerie** nf underwear. **lingette** nf wipe.

**lingot** /lɛ̃go/ nm ingot.

**linguistique** /lɛ̃gɥistik/ adj linguistic. ● nf linguistics.

**lion** /ljɔ̃/ nm lion; **le L**~ Leo. **lionceau** (pl ~**x**) nm lion cub. **lionne** nf lioness.

**liquidation** /likidasjɔ̃/ nf liquidation; (vente) (clearance) sale; **entrer en** ~ go into liquidation.

**liquide** /likid/ adj liquid. ● nm (argent) ~ ready money; **payer en** ~ pay cash; ~ **de frein** brake fluid.

**liquider** /likide/ **1** vt liquidate; (vendre) sell.

**lire** /liʀ/ **39** vt/i read. ● nf lira.

**lis¹** /li/ ➡ LIRE **39**.

**lis²** /lis/ nm (fleur) lily.

**lisible** /lizibl/ adj legible; (roman) readable.

**lisière** /lizjɛʀ/ nf edge.

**lisse** /lis/ adj smooth.

**liste** /list/ nf list; ~ d'attente waiting list; ~ électorale register of voters; être sur (la) ~ rouge be ex-directory.

**listing** /listiŋ/ nm printout.

**lit** /li/ nm bed; se mettre au ~ get into bed; ~ de camp camp-bed; ~ d'enfant cot; ~ d'une personne single bed; ~ de deux personnes, grand ~ double bed.

**literie** /litʀi/ nf bedding.

**litière** /litjɛʀ/ nf litter.

**litige** /litiʒ/ nm dispute.

**litre** /litʀ/ nm litre.

**littéraire** /liteʀɛʀ/ adj literary; (études, formation) arts.

**littéral, ~e** (mpl -aux) /liteʀal, -o/ adj literal.

**littérature** /liteʀatyʀ/ nf literature.

**littoral** (pl -aux) /litɔʀal, -o/ nm coast.

**Lituanie** /lituani/ nf Lithuania.

**livide** /livid/ adj deathly pale.

**livraison** /livʀɛzɔ̃/ nf delivery.

**livre** /livʀ/ nf (monnaie, poids) pound. ● nm book; ~ de bord logbook; ~ de compte books; ~ de poche paperback.

**livrer** /livʀe/ **1** vt (Comm) deliver; (abandonner) give over (à to); (remettre) (coupable, document) hand over (à to); livré à soi-même left to oneself. □ se ~ vpr (se rendre)

give oneself up (à to); se ~ à (boisson, actes) indulge in; (ami) confide in.

**livret** /livʀɛ/ nm book; (Mus) libretto; ~ de caisse d'épargne savings book; ~ scolaire school report (book).

**livreur, -euse** /livʀœʀ, -øz/ nm, f delivery man, delivery woman.

**local¹, ~e** (mpl -aux) /lɔkal, -o/ adj local.

**local²** (pl -aux) /lɔkal, -o/ nm premises; locaux premises.

**localement** /lɔkalmɑ̃/ adv locally.

**localisation** /lɔkalizasjɔ̃/ nf localization.

**localiser** /lɔkalize/ **1** vt (repérer) locate; (circonscrire) localize.

**locataire** /lɔkatɛʀ/ nmf tenant; (de chambre) lodger.

**location** /lɔkasjɔ̃/ nf (de maison) renting; (de voiture, de matériel) hire, rental; (de place) booking, reservation; (par propriétaire) renting out; hiring out; en ~ (voiture) on hire, rented; (habiter) in rented accommodation.

**locomotive** /lɔkɔmɔtiv/ nf engine, locomotive.

**locution** /lɔkysjɔ̃/ nf phrase.

**loft** /lɔft/ nm loft (apartment).

**loge** /lɔʒ/ nf (de concierge, de franc-maçons) lodge; (d'acteur) dressing-room; (de spectateur) box.

**logement** /lɔʒmɑ̃/ nm accommodation; (appartement) flat; (habitat) housing.

**loger** /lɔʒe/ **40** vt (réfugié, famille) house; (ami) put up; (client) accommodate. ● vi live. □ se ~ vpr live; trouver à se ~ find accommodation; se ~ dans (balle) lodge itself in.

**logiciel** /lɔʒisjɛl/ nm software; ~

**contributif** shareware; ~ **d'application** application software; ~ **de groupe** groupware; ~ **de jeux** games software; ~ **de navigation** browser; ~ **public** freeware.

**logique** /lɔʒik/ *adj* logical. ●*nf* logic.

**logis** /lɔʒi/ *nm* dwelling.

**logistique** /lɔʒistik/ *nf* logistics.

**loi** /lwa/ *nf* law.

**loin** /lwɛ̃/ *adv* far (away); **au** ~ far away; **de** ~ from far away; (de beaucoup) by far; ~ **de là** far from it; **plus** ~ further; **il revient de** ~ (fig) he had a close shave.

**lointain**, ~e /lwɛ̃tɛ̃, -ɛn/ *adj* distant. ●*nm* distance; **dans le** ~ in the distance.

**loisir** /lwazir/ *nm* (spare) time; ~s (temps libre) leisure, spare time; (distractions) leisure activities; **à** ~ at one's leisure; **avoir le** ~ **de faire** have time to do.

**londonien**, ~ne /lɔ̃dɔnjɛ̃, -ɛn/ *adj* London. **L~**, ~e **n**, f Londoner.

**Londres** /lɔ̃dʀ/ *npr* London.

**long**, **longue** /lɔ̃, lɔ̃g/ *adj* long; **à** ~ **terme** long-term; **être** ~ **à faire** be a long time doing. ●*nm* **de** ~ (mesure) long; **de** ~ **en large** back and forth; (tout) **le** ~ **de** (all) along. ●*adv* **en dire** ~ **sur** qn/qch say a lot about sb/sth; **en savoir plus** ~ **sur** know more about.

**longer** /lɔ̃ʒe/ **40** *vt* go along; (limiter) border.

**longitude** /lɔ̃ʒityd/ *nf* longitude.

**longtemps** /lɔ̃tɑ̃/ *adv* a long time; **avant** ~ before long; **trop** ~ too long; **ça prendra** ~ it will take a long time; **prendre plus** ~ **que prévu** take longer than anticipated.

**longuement** /lɔ̃gmɑ̃/ *adv* (longtemps) for a long time; (en

détail) at length.

**longueur** /lɔ̃gœʀ/ *nf* length; ~s (de texte) over-long parts; **à** ~ **de journée** all day long; **en** ~ lengthwise; ~ **d'onde** wavelength.

**lopin** /lɔpɛ̃/ *nm* ~ **de terre** patch of land.

**loque** /lɔk/ *nf* ~s rags; ~ (humaine) (human) wreck.

**loquet** /lɔkɛ/ *nm* latch.

**lors de** /lɔʀdə/ *prép* (au moment de) at the time of; (pendant) during.

**lorsque** /lɔʀsk(ə)/ *conj* when.

**losange** /lɔzɑ̃ʒ/ *nm* diamond.

**lot** /lo/ *nm* (portion) share; (aux enchères) lot; (Ordinat) batch; (destin) lot; **gagner le gros** ~ hit the jackpot.

**loterie** /lɔtʀi/ *nf* lottery.

**lotion** /lɔsjɔ̃/ *nf* lotion.

**lotissement** /lɔtismɑ̃/ *nm* (à construire) building plot; (construit) (housing) development.

**louable** /luabl/ *adj* praiseworthy.

**louange** *nf* praise.

**louche** /luʃ/ *adj* shady, dubious. ●*nf* ladle.

**loucher** /luʃe/ **1** *vi* squint.

**louer** /lwe/ **1** *vt* (approuver) praise (de for); (prendre en location) (maison) rent; (voiture, matériel) hire, rent; (place) book, reserve; (donner en location) (maison) rent out; (matériel) rent out, hire out; **à** ~ to let, for rent (US).

**loufoque** /lufɔk/ *adj* **1** crazy.

**loup** /lu/ *nm* wolf.

**loupe** /lup/ *nf* magnifying glass.

**louper** /lupe/ **1** *vt* **1** miss; (examen) flunk **1**.

**lourd**, ~e /luʀ, -d/ *adj* heavy; (faute) serious; ~ **de dangers**

fraught with danger; **il fait ~** it's close ou muggy.

**loutre** /lutʀ/ *nf* otter.

**louveteau** (*pl* **~x**) /luvto/ *nm* wolf cub; (scout) Cub (Scout).

**loyal, ~e** (*mpl* **-aux**) /lwajal, -o/ *adj* loyal, faithful; (honnête) fair.

**loyauté** /lwajote/ *nf* loyalty; fairness.

**loyer** /lwaje/ *nm* rent.

**lu** /ly/ →LIRE 39.

**lubrifiant** /lybʀifjɑ̃/ *nm* lubricant.

**lucide** /lysid/ *adj* lucid. **lucidité** *nf* lucidity.

**lucratif, -ive** /lykʀatif, -v/ *adj* lucrative; **à but non ~** non-profitmaking.

**ludiciel** /lydisjɛl/ *nm* (Ordinat) games software.

**lueur** /lɥœʀ/ *nf* (faint) light, glimmer; (fig) glimmer, gleam.

**luge** /lyʒ/ *nf* toboggan.

**lugubre** /lygybʀ/ *adj* gloomy.

---

**lui** /lɥi/

● *pronom*

····▸ (masculin) (sujet) he; **~, il est à l'étranger** he's abroad; **c'est ~!** it's him!; (objet) him; (animal) it; **c'est à ~** it's his; **elle conduit mieux que ~** she's a better driver than he is.

····▸ (féminin) her; **je ~ ai annoncé** I told her.

····▸ (masculin/féminin) donne-le-~ give it to him/her.

---

**lui-même** /lɥimɛm/ *pron* himself; (animal) itself.

**luire** /lɥiʀ/ 17 *vi* shine; (reflet humide) glisten; (reflet chaud, faible) glow.

**lumière** /lymjɛʀ/ *nf* light; **~s** (connaissances) knowledge; **faire** **(toute) la ~ sur une affaire** clear a matter up.

**luminaire** /lyminɛʀ/ *nm* lamp.

**lumineux, -euse** /lyminø, -z/ *adj* luminous; (éclairé) illuminated; (rayon) of light; (radieux) radiant; **source lumineuse** light source.

**lunaire** /lynɛʀ/ *adj* lunar.

**lunatique** /lynatik/ *adj* temperamental.

**lunch** /lœnʃ/ *nm* buffet lunch.

**lundi** /lœdi/ *nm* Monday.

**lune** /lyn/ *nf* moon; **~ de miel** honeymoon.

**lunettes** /lynɛt/ *nfpl* glasses; (de protection) goggles; **~ de ski/ natation** ski/swimming goggles; **~ noires** dark glasses; **~ de soleil** sun-glasses.

**lustre** /lystʀ/ *nm* (éclat) lustre; (objet) chandelier.

**lutin** /lytɛ̃/ *nm* goblin.

**lutte** /lyt/ *nf* fight, struggle; (Sport) wrestling. **lutter** 1 *vi* fight, struggle; (Sport) wrestle. **lutteur, -euse** *nm, f* fighter; (Sport) wrestler.

**luxe** /lyks/ *nm* luxury; **de ~** luxury; (produit) de luxe.

**Luxembourg** /lyksɑ̃buʀ/ *nm* Luxemburg.

**luxer (se)** /(sə)lykse/ 1 *vpr* **se ~ le genou** dislocate one's knee.

**luxueux, -euse** /lyksɥø, -z/ *adj* luxurious.

**lycée** /lise/ *nm* (secondary) school. **lycéen, ~ne** *nm, f* pupil (at secondary school).

**lyophilisé, ~e** /ljɔfilize/ *adj* freeze-dried.

**lyrique** /liʀik/ *adj* (poésie) lyric; (passionné) lyrical; **artiste/théâtre ~** opera singer/house.

**lys** /lis/ *nm* lily.

# Mm

**m'** /m/ →ME.

**ma** /ma/ →MON.

**macabre** /makabʀ/ adj macabre.

**macadam** /makadam/ nm Tarmac®.

**macaron** /makaʀɔ̃/ nm (gâteau) macaroon; (insigne) badge.

**macédoine** /masedwan/ nf mixed diced vegetables; ∼ de fruits fruit salad.

**macérer** /maseʀe/ 14 vt/i soak; (dans du vinaigre) pickle.

**mâcher** /maʃe/ 1 vt chew; ne pas ∼ ses mots not mince one's words.

**machin** /maʃɛ̃/ nm 1 (chose) thing; (dont on ne trouve pas le nom) whatsit 1.

**machinal, ∼e** (mpl **-aux**) /maʃinal, -o/ adj automatic. **machinalement** adv mechanically, automatically.

**machination** /maʃinasjɔ̃/ nf plot; des ∼s machinations.

**machine** /maʃin/ nf machine; (d'un train, navire) engine; ∼ à écrire typewriter; ∼ à laver/coudre washing-/sewing-machine; ∼ à sous fruit machine; (US) slot machine. **machine-outil** (pl **machines-outils**) nf machine tool. **machinerie** nf machinery.

**machiniste** /maʃinist/ nm (Théât) stage-hand; (conducteur) driver.

**mâchoire** /maʃwaʀ/ nf jaw.

**mâchonner** /maʃɔne/ 1 vt chew.

**maçon** /masɔ̃/ nm (entrepreneur) builder; (poseur de briques) bricklayer; (qui construit en pierre)

mason. **maçonnerie** nf (briques) brickwork; (pierres) stonework, masonry; (travaux) building.

**madame** (pl **mesdames**) /madam, medam/ nf (à une inconnue) (dans une lettre) M∼ Dear Madam; bonjour, ∼ good morning; mesdames et messieurs ladies and gentlemen; (à une femme dont on connaît le nom) (dans une lettre) Chère M∼ Dear Mrs ou Ms X; bonjour, ∼ good morning Mrs ou Ms X; oui M∼ le Ministre yes Minister; (formule de respect) oui M∼ yes madam.

**mademoiselle** (pl **mesdemoiselles**) /madmwazɛl, medmwazɛl/ nf (à une inconnue) (dans une lettre) M∼ Dear Madam; bonjour, ∼ good morning; entrez mesdemoiselles come in (ladies); (à une jeune fille dont on connaît le nom) (dans une lettre) Chère M∼ Dear Ms ou Miss X; bonjour, ∼ good morning Miss ou Ms X.

**magasin** /magazɛ̃/ nm shop, store; (entrepôt) warehouse; (d'une arme) magazine; en ∼ in stock.

**magazine** /magazin/ nm magazine; (émission) programme.

**Maghreb** /magʀɛb/ nm North Africa.

**magicien, ∼ne** /maʒisjɛ̃, -ɛn/ nm, f magician.

**magie** /maʒi/ nf magic. **magique** adj magic; (mystérieux) magical.

**magistral, ∼e** (mpl **-aux**) /maʒistʀal, -o/ adj masterly; (grand-hum) tremendous; cours ∼ lecture.

**magistrat** /maʒistʀa/ nm magistrate.

**magistrature** /maʒistʀatyʀ/ nf judiciary; (fonction) public office.

**magner (se)** /(sə)maɲe/ 1 vpr ✗ get a move on.

**magnétique** /maɲetik/ adj magnetic. **magnétiser** 🔟 vt magnetize. **magnétisme** nm magnetism.

**magnétophone** /maɲetɔfɔn/ nm tape recorder; (à cassettes) cassette recorder.

**magnétoscope** /maɲetɔskɔp/ nm video recorder.

**magnificence** /maɲifisãs/ nf magnificence. **magnifique** adj magnificent.

**magot** /mago/ nm 🔟 hoard (of money).

**magouille** /maguj/ nf 🔟 scheming, skulduggery.

**magret** /magʀɛ/ nm ~ de canard duck breast.

**mai** /mɛ/ nm May.

**maigre** /mɛgʀ/ adj thin; (viande) lean; (yaourt) low-fat; (fig) poor, meagre; **faire** ~ abstain from meat. **maigreur** nf thinness; leanness; (fig) meagreness.

**maigrir** /megʀiʀ/ 🖸 vi get thin(ner); (en suivant un régime) slim. ● vt make thin(ner).

**maille** /maj/ nf stitch; (de filet) mesh; ~ qui file ladder, run; **avoir** ~ **à partir avec qn** have a brush with sb.

**maillet** /majɛ/ nm mallet.

**maillon** /majɔ̃/ nm link.

**maillot** /majo/ nm (Sport) shirt, jersey; (~ de corps) vest; (US) undershirt; (~ de bain) (swimming) costume.

**main** /mɛ̃/ nf hand; **donner la** ~ **à qn** hold sb's hand; **se donner la** ~ hold hands; **en** ~**s propres** in person; **en bonnes** ~**s** in good hands; ~ **courante** handrail; **se faire la** ~ get the hang of it; **perdre la** ~ lose one's touch; **sous la** ~ to hand; **vol à** ~ **armée** armed robbery; **fait (à la)** ~ handmade; **haut**

**les** ~**s!** hands up! **main-d'œuvre** (pl **mains-d'œuvre**) nf labour; (ouvriers) labour force.

**main-forte** /mɛ̃fɔʀt/ nf inv **prêter** ~ **à qn** come to sb's aid.

**maint**, ~**e** /mɛ̃, mɛ̃t/ adj many a (+ sg); ~**s** many; **à** ~**es reprises** many times.

**maintenant** /mɛ̃t(ə)nã/ adv now; (de nos jours) nowadays; (l'époque actuelle) today.

**maintenir** /mɛ̃t(ə)niʀ/ 🖘 vt keep, maintain; (soutenir) support, hold up; (affirmer) maintain; (decision) stand by. □ **se** ~ vpr (tendance) persist; (prix, malade) remain stable.

**maintien** /mɛ̃tjɛ̃/ nm (attitude) bearing; (conservation) maintenance.

**maire** /mɛʀ/ nm mayor.

**mairie** /meʀi/ nf town hall; (administration) town council.

**mais** /mɛ/ conj but; ~ **oui** of course; ~ **non** of course not.

**maïs** /mais/ nm maize, corn; (Culin) sweetcorn.

**maison** /mɛzɔ̃/ nf house; (foyer) home; (immeuble) building; (~ de commerce) firm; **à la** ~ at home; **rentrer** ou **aller à la** ~ go home; ~ **des jeunes** youth club; ~ **de repos** rest home; ~ **de convalescence** convalescent home; ~ **de retraite** old people's home; ~ **mère** parent company. ● adj inv (Culin) home-made.

> **Maison des jeunes et de la culture** The Maison des jeunes et de la culture (MJC) is an organization which provides community arts, sports and leisure activities for young people. Attached to the Ministry of Sport, the MJC was founded in 1964 to

enable young people in rural communities to take part in cultural activities in winter.

**maître, -esse** /mɛtʀ, -ɛs/ adj (qui contrôle) être ∼ de soi be one's own master; ∼ de la situation in control of the situation; (principal) (idée, qualité) key, main. ● nm, f (Scol) teacher; (d'animal) owner, master. ● nm (expert, guide) master; (dirigeant) leader; ∼ de conférences senior lecturer; ∼ d'hôtel head waiter; (domestique) butler.

**maître-assistant**, ∼ **e** (pl **maîtres-assistants**) nm, f lecturer.

**maître-chanteur** (pl **maîtres-chanteurs**) nm blackmailer. **maître-nageur** (pl **maîtres-nageurs**) nm swimming instructor. **maîtresse** nf (amante) mistress.

**maîtrise** /mɛtʀiz/ nf mastery; (contrôle) control; (Mil) supremacy; (Univ) master's degree; (∼ de soi) self-control.

**maîtriser** /mɛtʀize/ **1** vt (sujet, technique) master; (incendie, sentiment, personne) control. □ **se** ∼ vpr have self-control.

**maïzena®** /maizena/ nf cornflour.

**majesté** /maʒɛste/ nf majesty.

**majestueux, -euse** /maʒɛstɥø, z/ adj majestic.

**majeur, ∼e** /maʒœʀ/ adj major, main; (Jur) of age; en ∼e partie mostly; la ∼e partie de most of. ● nm middle finger.

**majoration** /maʒɔʀasjɔ̃/ nf increase (de in). **majorer** **1** vt increase.

**majoritaire** /maʒɔʀitɛʀ/ adj majority; être ∼ be in the majority. **majorité** nf majority; en ∼ chiefly.

**Majorque** /maʒɔʀk/ nf Majorca.

**majuscule** /maʒyskyl/ adj capital.

● nf capital letter.

**mal¹** /mal/ adv badly; (incorrectement) wrong(ly); aller ∼ (personne) be unwell; (affaires) go badly; ∼ entendre/comprendre not hear/understand properly; ∼ en point in a bad state; pas ∼ quite a lot. ● adj inv bad, wrong; c'est ∼ de it is wrong ou bad to; ce n'est pas ∼ 🄸 it's not bad; Nick n'est pas ∼ 🄸 Nick is not bad-looking.

**mal²** (pl **maux**) /mal, mo/ nm evil; (douleur) pain, ache; (maladie) disease; (effort) trouble; (dommage) harm; (malheur) misfortune; avoir ∼ à la tête/à la gorge have a headache/a sore throat; avoir le ∼ de mer/du pays be seasick/ homesick; faire ∼ hurt; se faire ∼ hurt oneself; j'ai ∼ it hurts; faire du ∼ à hurt, harm; se donner du ∼ pour faire qch go to a lot of trouble to do sth.

**malade** /malad/ adj sick, ill; (bras, œil) bad; (plante, poumons, côlon) diseased; tomber ∼ fall ill; (fou 🄸) mad. ● nmf sick person; (d'un médecin) patient; ∼ mental mentally ill person.

**maladie** /maladi/ nf illness, disease; (manie 🄸) mania.

**maladif, -ive** /maladif, -v/ adj sickly; (jalousie, peur) pathological.

**maladresse** /maladʀɛs/ nf clumsiness; (erreur) blunder.

**maladroit, ∼e** /maladʀwa, -t/ adj clumsy; (sans tact) tactless.

**malaise** /malɛz/ nm feeling of faintness; (gêne) uneasiness; (état de crise) unrest.

**malaisé, ∼e** /maleze/ adj difficult.

**Malaisie** /malɛzi/ nf Malaysia.

**malaria** /malaʀja/ nf malaria.

**malaxer** /malakse/ **1** vt (pétrir) knead; (mêler) mix.

'm

**malchance** /malʃɑ̃s/ nf misfortune. **malchanceux, -euse** adj unlucky.

**mâle** /mɑl/ adj male; (viril) manly. ● nm male.

**malédiction** /malediksjɔ̃/ nf curse.

**maléfice** /malefis/ nm evil spell. **maléfique** adj evil.

**malentendant, ~e** /malɑ̃tɑ̃dɑ̃, -t/ adj hard of hearing.

**malentendu** /malɑ̃tɑ̃dy/ nm misunderstanding.

**malfaçon** /malfasɔ̃/ nf defect.

**malfaisant, ~e** /malfəzɑ̃, -t/ adj harmful; (personne) evil.

**malfaiteur** /malfɛtœʀ/ nm criminal.

**malformation** /malfɔʀmasjɔ̃/ nf malformation.

**malgré** /malgʀe/ prép in spite of, despite; ~ tout nevertheless.

**malheur** /malœʀ/ nm misfortune; (accident) accident; par ~ unfortunately; faire un ~ 🗉 be a big hit; porter ~ ou bring bad luck.

**malheureusement** /malœʀøzmɑ̃/ adv unfortunately.

**malheureux, -euse** /malœʀø, -z/ adj unhappy; (regrettable) unfortunate; (sans succès) unlucky; (insignifiant) paltry, pathetic. ● nm, f (poor) wretch.

**malhonnête** /malɔnɛt/ adj dishonest. **malhonnêteté** nf dishonesty.

**malice** /malis/ nf mischief; sans ~ harmless; avec ~ mischievously. **malicieux, -ieuse** adj mischievous.

**malignité** /maliɲite/ nf malignancy. **malin, -igne** adj clever, smart; (méchant) malicious; (tumeur) malignant; (difficile 🗉) difficult.

**malingre** /malɛ̃gʀ/ adj puny.

**malle** /mal/ nf (valise) trunk; (Auto) boot; (US) trunk.

**mallette** /malɛt/ nf (small) suitcase; (pour le bureau) briefcase.

**malmener** /malməne/ 🖪 vt manhandle; (fig) give a rough ride to.

**malnutrition** /malnytʀisjɔ̃/ nf malnutrition.

**malodorant, ~e** /malɔdɔʀɑ̃, -t/ adj smelly, foul-smelling.

**malpoli, ~e** /malpɔli/ adj rude, impolite.

**malpropre** /malpʀɔpʀ/ adj dirty.

**malsain, ~e** /malsɛ̃, -ɛn/ adj unhealthy.

**malt** /malt/ nm malt.

**Malte** /malt/ nf Malta.

**maltraiter** /maltʀete/ 🗉 vt illtreat.

**malveillance** /malvɛjɑ̃s/ nf malice. **malveillant, ~e** adj malicious.

**maman** /mamɑ̃/ nf mum(my), mother; (US) mom(my).

**mamelle** /mamɛl/ nf teat.

**mamelon** /mamlɔ̃/ nm (Anat) nipple; (colline) hillock.

**mamie** /mami/ nf 🗉 granny.

**mammifère** /mamifɛʀ/ nm mammal.

**manche** /mɑ̃ʃ/ nf sleeve; (Sport, Pol) round. ● nm (d'un instrument) handle; ~ à balai broomstick; (Aviat) joystick. M~ nf la M~ the Channel; le tunnel sous la M~ the Channel tunnel.

**manchette** /mɑ̃ʃɛt/ nf cuff; (de journal) headline.

**manchot, ~te** /mɑ̃ʃo, -ɔt/ nm, f one-armed person; (sans bras) armless person. ● nm (oiseau) penguin.

**mandarine** /mɑ̃daʀin/ nf tangerine, mandarin (orange).

**mandat** /mɑ̃da/ nm (postal) money order; (Pol) mandate; (procuration) proxy; (de police) warrant; ~ d'arrêt arrest warrant.

**mandataire** /mɑ̃datɛʀ/ nm representative; (Jul) proxy.

**manège** /manɛʒ/ nm riding school; (à la foire) merry-go-round; (manœuvre) trick, ploy.

**manette** /manɛt/ nf lever; (de jeu) joystick.

**mangeable** /mɑ̃ʒabl/ adj edible.

**mangeoire** /mɑ̃ʒwaʀ/ nf trough; (pour oiseaux) feeder.

**manger** /mɑ̃ʒe/ **40** vt eat; (fortune) go through; (profits) eat away at; (économies) use up; (ronger) eat into. ● vi eat; **donner à ~** à feed. ● nm food.

**mangue** /mɑ̃g/ nf mango.

**maniable** /manjabl/ adj easy to handle.

**maniaque** /manjak/ adj fussy. ● nmf fusspot; (fou) maniac; (fanatique) fanatic; **un ~ de l'ordre** a stickler for tidiness.

**manie** /mani/ nf habit; (marotte) obsession.

**maniement** /manimɑ̃/ nm handling. **manier** **45** vt handle.

**manière** /manjɛʀ/ nf way, manner; ~s (politesse) manners; (chichis) fuss; **à la ~ de** in the style of; **de ~ à** so as to; **de toute ~** anyway, in any case.

**maniéré,** ~**e** /manjeʀe/ adj affected.

**manif** /manif/ nf **1** demo.

**manifestant,** ~**e** /manifɛstɑ̃, -t/ nm, f demonstrator.

**manifestation** /manifɛstasjɔ̃/ nf expression, manifestation; (de maladie, phénomène) appearance; (Pol) demonstration; (événement) event; ~ **culturelle** cultural event.

**manifeste** /manifɛst/ adj obvious. ● nm manifesto.

**manifester** /manifɛste/ **1** vt show, manifest; (désir, crainte) express. ● vi (Pol) demonstrate. □ **se ~** vpr (sentiment) show itself; (apparaître) appear; (répondre à un appel) come forward.

**manigance** /manigɑ̃s/ nf little plot. **manigancer** **10** vt plot.

**manipulation** /manipylasjɔ̃/ nf handling; (péj) manipulation.

**manivelle** /manivɛl/ nf handle, crank.

**mannequin** /mankɛ̃/ nm (personne) model; (statue) dummy.

**manœuvrer** /manœvʀe/ **1** vt manoeuvre; (machine) operate. ● vi manoeuvre.

**manoir** /manwaʀ/ nm manor.

**manque** /mɑ̃k/ nm lack (de of); (lacune) gap; ~ **à gagner** loss of earnings; **en (état de) ~** having withdrawal symptoms.

**manqué,** ~**e** /mɑ̃ke/ adj (écrivain) failed; **garçon ~** tomboy.

**manquement** /mɑ̃kmɑ̃/ nm ~ **à** breach of.

**manquer** /mɑ̃ke/ **1** vt miss; (gâcher) spoil; ~ **à** (devoir) fail in; ~ **de** be short of, lack; **il/ça lui manque** he misses him/it; ~ **(de) faire** (faillir) nearly do; **ne manquez pas de** be sure to; ~ **à sa parole** break one's word. ● vi be short ou lacking; (être absent) be absent; (en moins, disparu) be missing; **il manque 20 euros** I'm 20 euros short.

**mansarde** /mɑ̃saʀd/ nf attic (room).

**manteau** (pl ~**x**) /mɑ̃to/ nm coat.

**manucure** /manykyʀ/ nmf manicurist. ● nf (soins) manicure.

**manuel,** ~**le** /manɥɛl/ adj manual. ● nm (livre) manual; (Scol) textbook.

**manufacture** /manyfaktyʀ/ nf factory; (fabrication) manufacture.
**manufacturer** ❶ vt manufacture.

**manuscrit**, ~e /manyskʀi, -t/ adj handwritten. ● nm manuscript.

**mappemonde** /mapmɔ̃d/ nf world map; (sphère) globe.

**maquereau** (pl ~x) /makʀo/ nm (poisson) mackerel; ▣ pimp.

**maquette** /makɛt/ nf (scale) model; ~ (de mise en page) paste-up.

**maquillage** /makijaʒ/ nm make-up.

**maquiller** /makije/ ❶ vt make up; (truquer) doctor, fake. ▢ se ~ vpr make (oneself) up.

**maquis** /maki/ nm (paysage) scrub; (Mil) Maquis, underground.

**marais** /maʀɛ/ nm marsh.

**marasme** /maʀasm/ nm slump, stagnation; dans le ~ in the doldrums.

**marbre** /maʀbʀ/ nm marble.

**marc** /maʀ/ nm (eau-de-vie) marc; ~ de café coffee grounds.

**marchand**, ~e /maʀʃɑ̃, -d/ adj (valeur) market. ● nm, f trader; (de charbon, vins) merchant; ~ de couleurs ironmonger; (US) hardware merchant; ~ de journaux newsagent; ~ de légumes greengrocer; ~ de poissons fishmonger.

**marchander** /maʀʃɑ̃de/ ❶ vt haggle over. ● vi haggle.

**marchandise** /maʀʃɑ̃diz/ nf goods.

**marche** /maʀʃ/ nf (démarche, trajet) walk; (rythme) pace; (Mil, Mus, Pol) march; (d'escalier) step; (Sport) walking; (de machine) operation, working; (de véhicule) running; en ~ (train) moving; (moteur, machine) running; faire ~ arrière (véhicule) reverse; mettre en ~ start (up); se mettre en ~ start moving.

**marché** /maʀʃe/ nm market; (contrat) deal; faire son ~ do one's shopping; ~ aux puces flea market; ~ noir black market.

**marchepied** /maʀʃəpje/ nm (de train, camion) step.

**marcher** /maʀʃe/ ❶ vi walk; (poser le pied) tread (sur on); (aller) go; (fonctionner) work, run; (prospérer) go well; ( film, livre) do well; (consentir ▣) agree; faire ~ qn ▣ pull sb's leg.

**mardi** /maʀdi/ nm Tuesday; M ~ gras Shrove Tuesday.

**mare** /maʀ/ nf (étang) pond; (flaque) pool.

**marécage** /maʀekaʒ/ nm marsh; (sous les tropiques) swamp.

**maréchal** (pl -aux) /maʀeʃal, -o/ nm field marshal.

**maréchal-ferrant** (pl -aux-ferrants /maʀeʃalferɑ̃/ nm blacksmith.

**marée** /maʀe/ nf tide; (poissons) fresh fish; ~ haute/basse high/ low tide; ~ noire oil slick.

**marelle** /maʀɛl/ nf hopscotch.

**margarine** /maʀgaʀin/ nf margarine.

**marge** /maʀʒ/ nf margin; en ~ (à l'écart de) on the fringe(s) of; ~ bénéficiaire profit margin.

**marginal**, ~e (mpl -aux) /maʀʒinal, -o/ adj marginal. ● nm, f drop-out.

**marguerite** /maʀgøʀit/ nf daisy; (qui imprime) daisy-wheel.

**mari** /maʀi/ nm husband.

**mariage** /maʀjaʒ/ nm marriage; (cérémonie) wedding.

**marié**, ~e /maʀje/ adj married.

● *nm, f* (bride) groom, bride; les ~s the bride and groom.

**Marianne** The symbolic female figure often used to represent the French Republic. There are statues of her in public places all over France, always wearing the Phrygian bonnet, a pointed cap which became a symbol of liberty as represented by the 1789 Revolution. She also appears on the standard French postage stamp.

**marier** /marje/ 45 *vt* marry. □ **se ~ vpr** get married, marry; **se ~ avec** marry, get married to.

**marin, ~e** /marɛ̃, -in/ *adj* sea. ● *nm* sailor.

**marine** /marin/ *nf* navy; ~ **marchande** merchant navy. ● *adj inv* navy (blue).

**marionnette** /marjɔnɛt/ *nf* puppet; (à fils) marionette.

**maritalement** /maritalmɑ̃/ *adv* (vivre) as husband and wife.

**maritime** /maritim/ *adj* maritime, coastal; (agent, compagnie) shipping.

**marmaille** /marmaj/ *nf* brats.

**marmelade** /marməlad/ *nf* stewed fruit; ~ **d'oranges** (orange) marmalade.

**marmite** /marmit/ *nf* (cooking-)pot.

**marmonner** /marmɔne/ 1 *vt* mumble.

**marmot** /marmo/ *nm* 🔟 kid.

**Maroc** /marɔk/ *nm* Morocco.

**maroquinerie** /marɔkinri/ *nf* (magasin) leather goods shop.

**marquant, ~e** /markɑ̃, -t/ *adj* (remarquable) outstanding; (qu'on n'oublie pas) memorable.

**marque** /mark/ *nf* mark; (de produits) brand, make; (décompte) score; à vos ~s! (Sport) on your marks!; de ~ (Comm) brand name; (fig) important; ~ de fabrique trademark; ~ déposée registered trademark.

**marquer** /marke/ 1 *vt* mark; (indiquer) show, say; (écrire) note down; (point, but) score; (joueur) mark; (influencer) leave its mark on; (exprimer) (volonté, sentiment) show. ● *vi* (laisser une trace) leave a mark; (événement) stand out; (Sport) score.

**marquis, ~e** /marki, -z/ *nm, f* marquis, marchioness.

**marraine** /marɛn/ *nf* godmother.

**marrant, ~e** /marɑ̃, -t/ *adj* 🔟 funny.

**marre** /mar/ *adv* en avoir ~ 🔟 be fed up (de with).

**marrer (se)** /(sə)mare/ 1 *vpr* 🔟 laugh, have a (good) laugh.

**marron** /marɔ̃/ *nm* chestnut; (couleur) brown; (coup 🔟) thump; ~ **d'Inde** horse chestnut. ● *adj inv* brown.

**mars** /mars/ *nm* March.

**Marseillaise, la** The popular name of the French national anthem, composed by Claude-Joseph Rouget de Lisle in 1792. It was adopted as a marching song by a group of Republican volunteers from Marseilles and became famous as they sang it on entering Paris.

**marteau** (*pl* ~x) /marto/ *nm* hammer; ~ **(de porte)** (door) knocker; ~ **piqueur** ou **pneumatique** pneumatic drill; être ~ 🔟 be mad.

**marteler** /martəle/ 6 *vt* hammer;

(*poings, talons*) pound; (*scander*) rap out.

**martial**, ∼e (*mpl* -iaux) /maʀsjal, -jo/ *adj* military; (*art*) martial.

**martien**, ∼ne /maʀsjɛ̃, -ɛn/ *adj & nm, f* Martian.

**martyr**, ∼e /maʀtiʀ/ *nm, f* martyr. ● *adj* martyred; (*enfant*) battered.

**martyre** /maʀtiʀ/ *nm* (Relig) martyrdom; (*fig*) agony, suffering.

**martyriser** /maʀtiʀize/ **1** *vt* (Relig) martyr; (*torturer*) torture; (*enfant*) batter.

**marxisme** /maʀksism/ *nm* Marxism. **marxiste** *adj & nmf* Marxist.

**masculin**, ∼e /maskylɛ̃, -in/ *adj* masculine; (*sexe*) male; (*mode, équipe*) men's. ● *nm* masculine.

**masochisme** /mazoʃism/ *nm* masochism.

**masochiste** /mazoʃist/ *nmf* masochist. ● *adj* masochistic.

**masque** /mask/ *nm* mask; ∼ de beauté face pack. **masquer** **1** *vt* (*cacher*) hide, conceal (à from); (*lumière*) block (off).

**massacre** /masakʀ/ *nm* massacre. **massacrer** **1** *vt* massacre; (*abîmer* **1**) ruin.

**massage** /masaʒ/ *nm* massage.

**masse** /mas/ *nf* (volume) mass; (*gros morceau*) lump, mass; (*outil*) sledge-hammer; en ∼ (*vendre*) in bulk; (*venir*) in force; **produire en** ∼ mass-produce; **la** ∼ (*foule*) the masses; **une** ∼ **de** **1** masses of; **la** ∼ **de** the majority of.

**masser** /mase/ **1** *vt* (*assembler*) assemble; (*pétrir*) massage. □ **se** ∼ *vpr* (*gens, foule*) mass.

**massif**, -ive /masif, -v/ *adj* massive; (*or, argent*) solid. ● *nm* (de fleurs) clump; (*parterre*) bed; (Géog) massif. **massivement** *adv* (*en masse*) in large numbers.

**massue** /masy/ *nf* club, bludgeon.

**mastic** /mastik/ *nm* putty; (*pour trous*) filler.

**mastiquer** /mastike/ **1** *vt* (mâcher) chew.

**mat** /mat/ *adj* (*couleur*) matt; (*bruit*) dull; (*teint*) olive; **être** ∼ (aux échecs) be in checkmate.

**mât** /mɑ/ *nm* mast; (pylône) pole; ∼ de drapeau flagpole.

**match** /matʃ/ *nm* match; (US) game; **faire** ∼ **nul** tie, draw; ∼ **aller** first leg; ∼ **retour** return match.

**matelas** /matla/ *nm* mattress; ∼ pneumatique air bed.

**matelassé**, ∼e /matlase/ *adj* padded; (*tissu*) quilted.

**matelot** /matlo/ *nm* sailor.

**mater** /mate/ **1** *vt* (*révolte*) put down; (*personne*) bring into line.

**matérialiser (se)** /(sa)mateʀjalize/ **1** *vpr* materialize.

**matérialiste** /mateʀjalist/ *adj* materialistic. ● *nmf* materialist.

**matériau** (*pl* ∼x) /mateʀjo/ *nm* material.

**matériel**, ∼le /mateʀjɛl/ *adj* material. ● *nm* equipment, materials; ∼ informatique hardware.

**maternel**, ∼le /matɛʀnɛl/ *adj* maternal; (*comme d'une mère*) motherly. **maternelle** *nf* nursery school.

**maternité** /matɛʀnite/ *nf* maternity hospital; (*état de mère*) motherhood; **de** ∼ maternity.

**mathématicien**, ∼ne /matematisjɛ̃, -ɛn/ *nm, f* mathematician.

**mathématique** /matematik/ *adj* mathematical. **mathématiques** *nfpl* mathematics (+ *sg*).

**maths** /mat/ *nfpl* **1** maths (+ *sg*).

**Matignon** The *Hôtel Matignon* is the official residence and office of the French prime minister, situated in the *rue de Varenne*, Paris. The word *Matignon* is often used to refer to the prime minister's office. See ▷ÉLYSÉE

**matière** /matjɛʀ/ nf matter; (produit) material; (sujet) subject; **en ~ de** as regards; **~ plastique** plastic; **~s grasses** fat content; **~s premières** raw materials.

**matin** /matɛ̃/ nm morning; **de bon ~** early in the morning.

**matinal, ~e** (mpl **-aux**) /matinal, -o/ adj morning; (de bonne heure) early; **être ~** be up early; (d'habitude) be an early riser.

**matinée** /matine/ nf morning; (spectacle) matinée.

**matou** /matu/ nm tomcat.

**matraque** /matʀak/ nf (de police) truncheon; (pour frapper) club. **matraquer** ▌1▐ vt club, beat; (produit, chanson) plug.

**matrimonial, ~e** (mpl **-iaux**) /matʀimɔnjal, -jo/ adj matrimonial; **agence ~e** marriage bureau.

**maturité** /matyʀite/ nf maturity.

**maudire** /modiʀ/ ▌41▐ vt curse.

**maudit, ~e** /modi, -t/ adj ▐1▐ blasted, damned.

**maugréer** /mogʀee/ ▌15▐ vi grumble.

**mausolée** /mozole/ nm mausoleum.

**maussade** /mosad/ adj gloomy.

**mauvais, ~e** /movɛ, -z/ adj bad; (erroné) wrong; (malveillant) evil; (désagréable) nasty, bad; (mer) rough; **le ~ moment** the wrong time; **~e herbe** weed; **~e langue** gossip; **~e passe** tight spot; **~**

**traitements** ill-treatment. ●adv (sentir) bad; **il fait ~** the weather is bad. ●nm **le bon et le ~** the good and the bad.

**mauve** /mov/ adj & nm mauve.

**mauviette** /movjɛt/ nf weakling, wimp.

**maux** /mo/ ⟶MAL².

**maximal, ~e** (mpl **-aux**) /maksimal, -o/ adj maximum.

**maxime** /maksim/ nf maxim.

**maximum** /maksimɔm/ adj maximum. ●nm maximum; **au ~** as much as possible; (tout au plus) at most; **faire le ~** do one's utmost.

**mazout** /mazut/ nm (fuel) oil.

**me, m'** /mə, m/ pron me; (indirect) (to) me; (réfléchi) myself.

**méandre** /meɑ̃dʀ/ nm meander.

**mec** /mɛk/ nm ▐1▐ bloke, guy.

**mécanicien, ~ne** /mekanisjɛ̃, -jɛn/ nm, f mechanic. ●nm train driver.

**mécanique** /mekanik/ adj mechanical; (jouet) clockwork; **problème ~** engine trouble. ●nf mechanics (+ sg); (mécanisme) mechanism. **mécaniser** ▌1▐ vt mechanize.

**mécanisme** /mekanism/ nm mechanism.

**méchamment** /meʃamɑ̃/ adv spitefully. **méchanceté** nf nastiness; (action) wicked action.

**méchant, ~e** /meʃɑ̃, -t/ adj (cruel) wicked; (désagréable, grave) nasty; (enfant) naughty; (chien) vicious; (sensationnel ▐1▐) terrific. ●nm, f (enfant) naughty child.

**mèche** /mɛʃ/ nf (de cheveux) lock; (de bougie) wick; (d'explosif) fuse; (outil) drill bit; **de ~ avec** in league with.

**méconnaissable** /mekɔnɛsabl/ adj unrecognizable.

**méconnaître** /mekɔnɛtʀ/ ▌18▐ vt

misunderstand, misread; (*mésestimer*) underestimate.

**méconnu**, ~e /mekɔny/ *adj* unrecognized; (*artiste*) neglected.

**mécontent**, ~e /mekɔ̃tɑ̃, -t/ *adj* dissatisfied (de with); (*irrité*) annoyed (de at, with). **mécontentement** *nm* dissatisfaction; annoyance. **mécontenter** ➊ *vt* dissatisfy; (*irriter*) annoy.

**médaille** /medaj/ *nf* medal; (*insigne*) badge; (*bijou*) medallion. **médaillé**, ~e *nm, f* medallist.

**médaillon** /medajɔ̃/ *nm* medallion; (*bijou*) locket.

**médecin** /medsɛ̃/ *nm* doctor.

**médecine** /mɛdsin/ *nf* medicine.

**média** /medja/ *nm* medium; les ~s the media.

**médiateur, -trice** /medjatœʀ, -tʀis/ *nm, f* mediator.

**médiatique** /medjatik/ *adj* (*événement, personnalité*) media.

**médical**, ~e (*mpl* -**aux**) /medikal, -o/ *adj* medical.

**médicament** /medikamɑ̃/ *nm* medicine, drug.

**médico-légal**, ~e (*mpl* -**aux**) /medikolegal, -o/ *adj* forensic.

**médiéval**, ~e (*mpl* -**aux**) /medjeval, -o/ *adj* medieval.

**médiocre** /medjɔkʀ/ *adj* mediocre, poor. **médiocrité** *nf* mediocrity.

**médire** /mediʀ/ 🔁 *vi* ~ de speak ill of, malign.

**médisance** /medizɑ̃s/ *nf* ~(s) malicious gossip.

**méditer** /medite/ ➊ *vi* meditate (sur on). ● *vt* contemplate; (*paroles, conseils*) mull over; ~ de plan to.

**Méditerranée** /mediteʀane/ *nf* la ~ the Mediterranean.

**méditerranéen, ~ne**

**méditerranée**, -ɛn/ *adj* Mediterranean.

**médium** /medjom/ *nm* (*personne*) medium.

**méduse** /medyz/ *nf* jellyfish.

**meeting** /mitiŋ/ *nm* meeting.

**méfait** /mefɛ/ *nm* misdeed; les ~s de (*conséquences*) the ravages of.

**méfiance** /mefjɑ̃s/ *nf* suspicion, distrust. **méfiant**, ~e *adj* suspicious, distrustful.

**méfier (se)** /(sə)mefje/ 🔢 *vpr* be wary ou careful; se ~ de distrust, be wary of.

**mégaoctet** /megaɔktɛ/ *nm* (*Ordinat*) megabyte.

**mégère** /meʒɛʀ/ *nf* (*femme*) shrew.

**mégot** /mego/ *nm* cigarette end.

**meilleur**, ~e /mɛjœʀ/ *adj* (*comparatif*) better (que than); (*superlatif*) best; le ~ **livre** the best book; mon ~ ami my best friend; ~ marché cheaper. ● *nm, f* le ~, la ~e the best (one). ● *adv* (*sentir*) better; il fait ~ the weather is better.

**mél** /mel/ *nm* email; envoyer un ~ send an email.

**mélancolie** /melɑ̃kɔli/ *nf* melancholy.

**mélange** /melɑ̃ʒ/ *nm* mixture, blend.

**mélanger** /melɑ̃ʒe/ 🔢 *vt* mix; (*thés, parfums*) blend. □ se ~ *vpr* mix; (*thés, parfums*) blend; (*idées*) get mixed up.

**mélasse** /melas/ *nf* black treacle; (US) molasses.

**mêlée** /mele/ *nf* free for all; (au rugby) scrum.

**mêler** /mele/ ➊ *vt* mix (à with); (*qualités*) combine; (*embrouiller*) mix up; ~ qn à (*impliquer dans*) involve sb in. □ se ~ *vpr* mix; com-

**m**

bine; se ~ à (se joindre à) mingle with; (participer à) join in; se ~ de meddle in; mêle-toi de ce qui te regarde mind your own business.

**méli-mélo** /melimelo/ (pl **mélis-mélos**) nm jumble.

**mélo** /melo/ 🔟 nm melodrama. ● adj inv slushy, schmaltzy 🔟.

**mélodie** /melɔdi/ nf melody. **mélodieux, -ieuse** adj melodious. **mélodique** adj melodic.

**mélodramatique** /melɔdʀamatik/ adj melodramatic. **mélodrame** nm melodrama.

**mélomane** /melɔman/ nmf music lover.

**melon** /məlɔ̃/ nm melon; (chapeau) ~ bowler (hat).

**membrane** /mãbʀan/ nf membrane.

**membre** /mãbʀ/ nm (Anat) limb; (adhérent) member.

**m** **même** /mɛm/ adj same; ce livre ~ this very book; la bonté ~ kindness itself; en ~ temps at the same time. ● pron le ~, la ~ the same (one). ● adv even; à ~ (sur) directly on; à ~ de in a position to; de ~ (aussi) too; (de la même façon) likewise; de ~ que just as; ~ si even if.

**mémé** /meme/ nf 🔟 granny.

**mémo** /memo/ nm note, memo.

**mémoire** /memwaʀ/ nm (rapport) memorandum, (Univ) dissertation; ~s (souvenirs écrits) memoirs. ● nf memory; à la ~ de to the memory of; de ~ from memory; ~ morte/vive (Ordinat) ROM/RAM.

**mémorable** /memɔʀabl/ adj memorable.

**menace** /mənas/ nf threat. **menacer** 🔟 vt threaten (de faire to do).

**ménage** /menaʒ/ nm (couple) couple; (travail) housework; (fa-

mille) household; se mettre en ~ set up house.

**ménagement** /menaʒmã/ nm avec ~s gently; sans ~s (dire) bluntly; (jeter, pousser) roughly.

**ménager¹, -ère** /menaʒe, -ɛʀ/ adj household, domestic; travaux ~s housework.

**ménager²** /menaʒe/ 🔟 vt be gentle with, handle carefully; (utiliser) be careful with; (organiser) prepare (carefully); ne pas ~ ses efforts spare no effort.

**ménagère** /menaʒɛʀ/ nf housewife.

**ménagerie** /menaʒʀi/ nf menagerie.

**mendiant, ~e** /mãdjã, -t/ nm, f beggar.

**mendier** /mãdje/ 🔟 vt beg for. ● vi beg.

**mener** /məne/ 🔟 vt lead; (entreprise, pays) run; (étude, enquête) carry out; (politique) pursue; ~ à (accompagner à) take to; (faire aboutir à) lead to; ~ à bien see through. ● vi lead.

**méningite** /menɛ̃ʒit/ nf meningitis.

**menotte** /mənɔt/ nf 🔟 hand; ~s handcuffs.

**mensonge** /mãsɔ̃ʒ/ nm lie; (action) lying. **mensonger, -ère** adj untrue, false.

**mensualité** /mãsɥalite/ nf monthly payment.

**mensuel, ~le** /mãsɥɛl/ adj monthly. ● nm monthly (magazine). **mensuellement** adv monthly.

**mensurations** /mãsyʀasjɔ̃/ nfpl measurements.

**mental, ~e** (mpl **-aux**) /mãtal, -o/ adj mental; malade ~ mentally ill person; handicapé ~ mentally handicapped person.

187

**mentalité** /mɑ̃talite/ nf mentality.

**menteur, -euse** /mɑ̃tœr, -øz/ nm, f liar. ● adj untruthful.

**menthe** /mɑ̃t/ nf mint.

**mention** /mɑ̃sjɔ̃/ nf mention; (annotation) note; (Scol) grade; **rayer la ~ inutile** delete as appropriate. **mentionner 1** vt mention.

**mentir** /mɑ̃tir/ 46 vi lie.

**menton** /mɑ̃tɔ̃/ nm chin.

**menu, ~e** /məny/ adj (petit) tiny; (fin) fine; (insignifiant) minor. ● adv (couper) fine. ● nm (carte) menu; (repas) meal; (Ordinat) menu; **~ déroulant** pull-down menu.

**menuiserie** /mənɥizri/ nf carpentry, joinery. **menuisier** nm carpenter, joiner.

**méprendre (se)** /(sə)meprɑ̃dr/ 50 vpr **se ~ sur** be mistaken about.

**mépris** /mepri/ nm contempt, scorn (de for); **au ~ de** regardless of.

**méprisable** /meprizabl/ adj contemptible, despicable.

**méprise** /mepriz/ nf mistake.

**méprisant, ~e** /meprizɑ̃, -t/ adj scornful. **mépriser 1** vt scorn, despise.

**mer** /mɛr/ nf sea; (marée) tide; **en pleine ~** out at sea.

**mercenaire** /mɛrsənɛr/ nm & a mercenary.

**mercerie** /mɛrs(ə)ri/ nf haberdashery; (US) notions store. **mercier, -ière** nm, f haberdasher; (US) notions seller.

**merci** /mɛrsi/ interj thank you, thanks (de, pour for); **~ beaucoup, ~ bien** thank you very much. ● nm thank you. ● nf mercy.

**mercredi** /mɛrkrədi/ nm Wednesday; **~ des Cendres** Ash Wednesday.

**merde** /mɛrd/ nf 🗙 shit 🗙.

**mère** /mɛr/ nf mother; **~ de famille** mother.

**méridional, ~e** (mpl **-aux**) /meridjɔnal, -o/ adj southern. ● nm, f Southerner.

**mérite** /merit/ nm merit; **avoir du ~ à faire** deserve credit for doing.

**mériter** /merite/ 1 vt deserve; **~ d'être lu** be worth reading.

**méritoire** /meritwar/ adj commendable.

**merlan** /mɛrlɑ̃/ nm whiting.

**merle** /mɛrl/ nm blackbird.

**merveille** /mɛrvɛj/ nf wonder, marvel; **à ~** wonderfully; **faire des ~s** work wonders.

**merveilleux, -euse** /mɛrvɛjø, -z/ adj wonderful, marvellous.

**mes** /me/ ➡MON.

**mésange** /mezɑ̃ʒ/ nf tit(mouse).

**mésaventure** /mezavɑ̃tyr/ nf misadventure; **par ~** by some misfortune.

**mesdames** /medam/ ➡MADAME.

**mesdemoiselles** /medmwazɛl/ ➡MADEMOISELLE.

**mésentente** /mezɑ̃tɑ̃t/ nf disagreement.

**mesquin, ~e** /mɛskɛ̃, -in/ adj mean-minded, petty; (chiche) mean. **mesquinerie** nf meanness.

**message** /mesaʒ/ nm message; **un ~ électronique** an email; **~ texte** text message.

**messager, -ère** /mesaʒe, -ɛr/ nm, f messenger. ● nm **~ de poche** pager.

**messagerie** /mesaʒri/ nf (transports) freight forwarding; (télécommunications) messaging; **~ électronique** electronic mail; **~ vocale** voice mail.

**messe** /mɛs/ nf (Relig) mass.

**messieurs** /mesjø/ ➡MONSIEUR.

m

**mesure** /məzyʀ/ nf measurement; (quantité, unité) measure; (disposition) measure, step; (cadence) time; **en ~** in time; (modération) moderation; **à ~ que** as; **dans la ~ où** in so far as; **dans une certaine ~** to some extent; **en ~ de** in a position to; **sans ~** to excess; **(fait) sur ~** made-to-measure.

**mesuré**, **~e** /məzyʀe/ adj measured; (atttitude) moderate.

**mesurer** /məzyʀe/ **1** vt measure; (juger) assess; (argent, temps) ration. ● vi **~ 15 mètres de long** be 15 metres long. □ **se ~ avec** vpr pit oneself against.

**met** /me/ ►**METTRE 42**.

**métal** (pl **-aux**) /metal, -o/ nm metal. **métallique** adj (objet) metal; (éclat) metallic.

**métallurgie** /metalyʀʒi/ nf (industrie) metalworking industry.

**métamorphoser** /metamɔʀfoze/ **1** vt transform. □ **se ~** vpr be transformed; **se ~ en** metamorphose into.

**métaphore** /metafɔʀ/ nf metaphor.

**météo** /meteo/ nf (bulletin) weather forecast.

**météore** /meteɔʀ/ nm meteor.

**météorologie** /meteɔʀɔlɔʒi/ nf meteorology.

**météorologique** /meteɔʀɔlɔʒik/ adj meteorological; **conditions ~s** weather conditions.

**méthode** /metɔd/ nf method; (ouvrage) course, manual. **méthodique** adj methodical.

**méticuleux**, **-euse** /metikylø, -z/ adj meticulous.

**métier** /metje/ nm job; (manuel) trade; (intellectuel) profession; (expérience) experience, skill; **~ (à tisser)** loom; **remettre qch sur le ~** rework sth.

**métis**, **~se** /metis/ adj mixed race. ● nm, f person of mixed race.

**métrage** /metʀaʒ/ nm length; **court ~** short (film); **long ~** feature-length film.

**mètre** /mɛtʀ/ nm metre; (règle) rule; **~ à ruban** tape-measure.

**métreur**, **-euse** /metʀœʀ, -øz/ nm, f quantity surveyor.

**métrique** /metʀik/ adj metric.

**métro** /metʀo/ nm underground; (US) subway.

**métropole** /metʀɔpɔl/ nf metropolis; (pays) mother country. **métropolitain**, **~e** adj metropolitan.

**mets** /me/ nm dish. ● ►**METTRE 42**.

**mettable** /mɛtabl/ adj wearable.

**metteur** /mɛtœʀ/ nm **~ en scène** director.

**mettre** /mɛtʀ/ **42** vt put; (radio, chauffage) put ou switch on; (réveil) set; (installer) put in; (revêtir) put on; (porter habituellement) (vêtement, lunettes) wear; (prendre) take; (investir, dépenser) put; (écrire) write, say; **elle a mis deux heures** it took her two hours; **~ la table** lay the table; **~ en question** question; **~ en valeur** highlight; (terrain) develop; **mettons que** let's suppose that. ● vi **~ bas** (animal) give birth. □ **se ~** vpr (vêtement, maquillage) put on; (se placer) (objet) go; (personne) stand; (assis) sit; (couché) lie; **se ~ en short** put shorts on; **se ~ debout** stand up; **se ~ au lit** go to bed; **se ~ à table** sit down at table; **se ~ en ligne** line up; **se ~ du sable dans les yeux** get sand in one's eyes; **se ~ au chinois/tennis** take up Chinese/tennis; **se ~ au travail** set to work; **se ~ à faire** start to do.

**meuble** /mœbl/ nm piece of furniture; ~s furniture.

**meublé** /møble/ nm furnished flat.

**meubler** /møble/ **1** vt furnish; (fig) fill. □ se ~ vpr buy furniture.

**meugler** /møgle/ **1** vi moo.

**meule** /møl/ nf millstone; ~ de foin haystack.

**meunier, -ière** /mønje, -jɛʀ/ nm, f miller.

**meurs, meurt** /mœʀ/ ➡MOURIR 43.

**meurtre** /mœʀtʀ/ nm murder.

**meurtrier, -ière** /mœʀtʀije, -jɛʀ/ adj deadly. ● nm murderer.

**meurtrir** /mœʀtʀiʀ/ **2** vt bruise.

**meute** /møt/ nf pack of hounds.

**Mexique** /mɛksik/ nm Mexico.

**mi-** /mi/ préf mid-, half-; à mi-chemin half-way; à mi-pente half-way up the hill; à la mi-juin in mid-June.

**miauler** /mjole/ **1** vi miaow.

**micro** /mikʀo/ nm microphone, mike; (Ordinat) micro.

**microbe** /mikʀob/ nm germ.

**microfilm** /mikʀofilm/ nm microfilm.

**micro-onde** /mikʀoɔ̃d/ nf microwave; un four à ~s microwave (oven). **micro-ondes** nm inv microwave (oven).

**micro-ordinateur** (pl ~s) /mikʀoɔʀdinatœʀ/ nm personal computer.

**microphone** /mikʀofɔn/ nm microphone.

**microprocesseur** /mikʀopʀosesœʀ/ nm microprocessor.

**microscope** /mikʀoskɔp/ nm microscope.

**midi** /midi/ nm twelve o'clock, midday, noon; (déjeuner) lunch-time;

(sud) south. Midi nm le M~ the South of France.

**mie** /mi/ nf soft part (of the loaf); un pain de ~ a sandwich loaf.

**miel** /mjɛl/ nm honey.

**mielleux, -euse** /mjɛlø, -z/ adj unctuous.

**mien, ~ne** /mjɛ̃, -ɛn/ pron le ~, la ~ne, les ~(ne)s mine.

**miette** /mjɛt/ nf crumb; (fig) scrap; en ~s in pieces.

**mieux** /mjø/ adj inv better (que than); le ou la ou les ~ (the) best. ● nm best; (progrès) improvement; faire de son ~ do one's best; le ~ serait de the best thing would be to. ● adv better; le ou la ou les ~ (de deux) the better; (de plusieurs) the best; elle va ~ she is better; j'aime ~ rester I'd rather stay; il vaudrait ~ partir it would be best to leave; tu ferais ~ de faire you would be best to do.

**mièvre** /mjɛvʀ/ adj insipid.

**mignon, ~ne** /miɲɔ̃, -ɔn/ adj cute; (gentil) kind.

**migraine** /migʀɛn/ nf headache; (plus fort) migraine.

**migrant, ~e** /migʀɑ̃, -t/ nm, f migrant.

**migration** /migʀasjɔ̃/ nf migration.

**mijoter** /miʒote/ **1** vt/i simmer; (tramer 1) cook up.

**mil** /mil/ nm a thousand.

**milice** /milis/ nf militia.

**milieu** (pl ~x) /miljø/ nm middle; (environnement) environment; (appartenance sociale) background; (groupe) circle; (voie) middle way; (criminel) underworld; au ~ de in the middle of; en plein ou au beau ~ de right in the middle (of).

**militaire** /militɛʀ/ adj military. ● nm soldier, serviceman.

**militant, ~e** /militɑ̃, -t/ nm, f

militant.

**militer** /milite/ **1** vi be a militant; ~ **pour** militate in favour of.

**mille**[1] /mil/ adj & nm inv a thousand; **deux** ~ two thousand; **mettre dans le** ~ (fig) hit the nail on the head.

**mille**[2] /mil/ nm ~ (marin) (nautical) mile.

**millénaire** /milenɛʀ/ nm millennium. ● adj a thousand years old.

**mille-pattes** /milpat/ nm inv centipede.

**millésime** /milezim/ nm date; (de vin) vintage.

**millet** /mijɛ/ nm millet.

**milliard** /miljaʀ/ nm thousand million, billion. **milliardaire** nmf multimillionaire.

**millième** /miljɛm/ adj & nmf thousandth.

**millier** /milje/ nm thousand; **un** ~ **(de)** about a thousand.

**millimètre** /milimɛtʀ/ nm millimetre.

**million** /miljɔ̃/ nm million; **deux** ~s **(de)** two million. **millionnaire** nmf millionaire.

**mime** /mim/ nmf mime-artist. ● nm (art) mime. **mimer** **1** vt mime; (imiter) mimic.

**mimique** /mimik/ nf expressions and gestures.

**minable** /minabl/ adj **1** (logement) shabby; (médiocre) pathetic, crummy.

**minauder** /minode/ **1** vi simper.

**mince** /mɛ̃s/ adj thin; (svelte) slim; (faible) (espoir, majorité) slim. ● interj **1** blast **1**, darn it **1**. **minceur** nf thinness; slimness.

**mincir** /mɛ̃siʀ/ **2** vi get slimmer; **ça te mincit** it makes you look slimmer.

**mine** /min/ nf expression; (allure) appearance; **avoir bonne** ~ look well; **faire** ~ **de** make as if to; (exploitation, explosif) mine; (de crayon) lead; ~ **de charbon** coalmine.

**miner** /mine/ **1** vt (saper) undermine; (garnir d'explosifs) mine.

**minerai** /minʀɛ/ nm ore.

**minéral, ~e** /mineʀal/ (mpl -aux), -o/ adj mineral. ● nm (pl -aux) mineral.

**minéralogique** /mineʀalɔʒik/ adj plaque ~ numberplate; (US) license plate.

**minet, ~te** /minɛ, -t/ nm, f (chat **1**) pussy(cat).

**mineur, ~e** /minœʀ/ adj minor; (Jur) under age. ● nm, f (Jur) minor. ● nm (ouvrier) miner.

**miniature** /minjatyʀ/ nf & adj miniature.

**minier, -ière** /minje, -jɛʀ/ adj mining.

**minimal, ~e** /minimal/ (mpl -aux) /minimal, o/ adj minimal, minimum.

**minime** /minim/ adj minimal, minor. ● nmf (Sport) junior.

**minimum** /minimɔm/ adj minimum. ● nm minimum; **au** ~ (pour le moins) at the very least; **en faire un** ~ do as little as possible.

**ministère** /ministɛʀ/ nm ministry; (gouvernement) government; ~ **public** public prosecutor's office. **ministériel, ~le** adj ministerial, government.

**ministre** /ministʀ/ nm minister; (au Royaume-Uni) Secretary of State; (US) Secretary.

**Minitel®** /minitɛl/ nm Minitel (telephone videotext system).

**minorer** /minɔʀe/ **1** vt reduce.

**minoritaire** /minɔʀitɛʀ/ adj minority; être ~ be in the minority. **minorité** nf minority.

**minuit** /minɥi/ nm midnight.

**minuscule** /minyskyl/ adj minute. ● nf (lettre) ~ lower case.

**minute** /minyt/ nf minute; 'talons ~' 'heels repaired while you wait'.

**minuterie** /minytRi/ nf time-switch.

**minutie** /minysi/ nf meticulousness.

**minutieux, -ieuse** /minysjø, -z/ adj meticulous.

**mioche** /mjɔʃ/ nm, f 🔳 kid.

**mirabelle** /miRabɛl/ nf (mirabelle) plum.

**miracle** /miRakl/ nm miracle; par ~ miraculously.

**miraculeux, -euse** /miRakylø, -z/ adj miraculous.

**mirage** /miRaʒ/ nm mirage.

**mire** /miR/ nf (fig) centre of attraction; (TV) test card.

**mirobolant, ~e** /miRɔbɔlɑ̃, -t/ adj 🔳 marvellous.

**miroir** /miRwaR/ nm mirror.

**miroiter** /miRwate/ 🔟 vi shimmer, sparkle.

**mis, ~e** /mi, miz/ adj bien ~ well-dressed. ● →METTRE 42.

**mise** /miz/ nf (argent) stake; (tenue) attire; ~ à feu blast-off; ~ au point adjustment; (fig) clarification; ~ de fonds capital outlay; ~ en garde warning; ~ en plis set; ~ en scène direction.

**miser** /mize/ 🔟 vt (argent) bet, stake (sur e). ● vi ~ sur (parier) place a bet on; (compter sur) bank on.

**misérable** /mizeRabl/ adj miserable, wretched; (indigent) destitute; (minable) seedy, squalid.

**misère** /mizɛR/ nf destitution;

(malheur) trouble, woe. **miséreux, -euse** nm, f destitute person.

**miséricorde** /mizeRikɔRd/ nf mercy.

**missel** /misɛl/ nm missal.

**missile** /misil/ nm missile.

**mission** /misjɔ̃/ nf mission. **missionnaire** nmf missionary.

**missive** /misiv/ nf missive.

**mistral** /mistRal/ nm (vent) mistral.

**mitaine** /mitɛn/ nf fingerless mitt.

**mite** /mit/ nf (clothes-)moth.

**mi-temps** /mitɑ̃/ nf inv (arrêt) half-time; (période) half. ● nm inv part-time work; à ~ part-time.

**miteux, -euse** /mitø, -z/ adj shabby.

**mitigé, ~e** /mitiʒe/ adj (modéré) lukewarm; (succès) qualified.

**mitonner** /mitɔne/ 🔟 vt cook slowly with care; (fig) cook up.

**mitoyen, ~ne** /mitwajɛ̃, -ɛn/ adj mur ~ party wall.

**mitrailler** /mitRaje/ 🔟 vt machine-gun; (fig) bombard. **mitraillette** /mitRajɛt/ nf sub-machine gun. **mitrailleuse** nf machine gun.

**mi-voix: à ~** /amivwa/ loc in a low voice.

**mixeur** /miksœR/ nm liquidizer, blender; (batteur) mixer.

**mixte** /mikst/ adj mixed; (commission) joint; (école) coeducational; (peau) combination.

**mobile** /mɔbil/ adj mobile; (pièce) moving; (feuillet) loose. ● nm (art) mobile; (raison) motive.

**mobilier** /mɔbilje/ nm furniture.

**mobilisation** /mɔbilizasjɔ̃/ nf mobilization. **mobiliser** 🔟 vt mobilize.

**mobilité** /mɔbilite/ nf mobility.

m

**mobylette®** /mɔbilɛt/ *nf* moped.

**moche** /mɔʃ/ *adj* ① (laid) ugly; (mauvais) lousy.

**modalités** /mɔdalite/ *nfpl* (conditions) terms; (façon de fonctionner) practical details.

**mode** /mɔd/ *nf* fashion; (coutume) custom; à la ~ fashionable. ● *nm* method, mode; (genre) way; ~ d'emploi directions (for use).

**modèle** /mɔdɛl/ *adj* model. ● *nm* model; (exemple) example; (Comm) (type) model; (taille) size; (style) style; ~ familial family size; ~ réduit (small-scale) model.

**modeler** /mɔdle/ ⑥ *vt* model (sur on). □ se ~ sur *vpr* model oneself on.

**modem** /mɔdɛm/ *nm* modem.

**modérateur, -trice** /mɔderatœr, -tris/ *adj* moderating. **modération** *nf* moderation.

**modéré, ~e** /mɔdere/ *adj & nm, f* moderate.

**modérer** /mɔdere/ ⑭ *vt* (propos) moderate; (désirs, sentiments) curb. □ se ~ *vpr* restrain oneself.

**moderne** /mɔdɛrn/ *adj* modern. **moderniser** ① *vt* modernize.

**modeste** /mɔdɛst/ *adj* modest. **modestie** *nf* modesty.

**modification** /mɔdifikasjɔ̃/ *nf* modification.

**modifier** /mɔdifje/ ㊺ *vt* change, modify. □ se ~ *vpr* change, alter.

**modique** /mɔdik/ *adj* modest.

**modiste** /mɔdist/ *nf* milliner.

**moduler** /mɔdyle/ ① *vt* modulate; (adapter) adjust.

**moelle** /mwal/ *nf* marrow; ~ épinière spinal cord; ~ osseuse bone marrow.

**moelleux, -euse** /mwalø, -z/ *adj* soft; (onctueux) smooth.

**mœurs** /mœr(s)/ *nfpl* (morale) morals; (usages) customs; (manières) habits, ways.

**moi** /mwa/ *pron* me; (indirect) (to) me; (sujet) I. ● *nm* self.

**moignon** /mwaɲɔ̃/ *nm* stump.

**moi-même** /mwamɛm/ *pron* myself.

**moindre** /mwɛ̃dr/ *adj* (moins grand) lesser; le ou la ~, les ~s the slightest, the least.

**moine** /mwan/ *nm* monk.

**moineau** (*pl* ~x) /mwano/ *nm* sparrow.

**moins** /mwɛ̃/ *prép* minus; (pour dire l'heure) to; une heure ~ dix ten to one. ● *adv* less (que than); le ou la ou les ~ the least; le ~ grand/haut the smallest/lowest; ~ de (avec un nom non dénombrable) less (que than); ~ de dix euros less than ten euros; ~ de livres fewer books; au ~, du ~ at least; à ~ que unless; de ~ less; de en ~ less and less; en ~ less; (manquant) missing.

**mois** /mwa/ *nm* month.

**moisi, ~e** /mwazi/ *adj* mouldy. ● *nm* mould; de ~ (odeur) musty. **moisir** ② *vi* go mouldy. **moisissure** *nf* mould.

**moisson** /mwasɔ̃/ *nf* harvest.

**moissonner** /mwasɔne/ ① *vt* harvest, reap. **moissonneur, -euse** *nm, f* harvester.

**moite** /mwat/ *adj* sticky, clammy.

**moitié** /mwatje/ *nf* half; (milieu) halfway mark; s'arrêter à la ~ stop halfway through; à ~ vide half empty; à ~ prix (at) half-price; la ~ de half (of). **moitié-moitié** *adv* half-and-half.

**mol** /mɔl/ →MOU.

**molaire** /mɔlɛr/ *nf* molar.

**molécule** /mɔlekyl/ *nf* molecule.

**molester** /mɔlɛste/ ■ *vt* man-handle, rough up.

**molle** /mɔl/ →MOU.

**mollement** /mɔlmɑ̃/ *adv* softly; (faiblement) feebly. **mollesse** *nf* softness; (faiblesse) feebleness; (apathie) listlessness.

**mollet** /mɔlɛ/ *nm* (de jambe) calf.

**mollir** /mɔliʀ/ ② *vi* soften; (céder) yield.

**môme** /mom/ *nmf* 🗓 kid.

**moment** /mɔmɑ̃/ *nm* moment; (période) time; (petit) ~ short while; **au** ~ **où** when; **par** ~s now and then; **du** ~ **où** ou **que** (pourvu que) as long as, provided that; (puisque) since; **en ce** ~ at the moment.

**momentané, ~e** /mɔmɑ̃tane/ *adj* momentary. **momentanément** *adv* momentarily; (en ce moment) at present.

**momie** /mɔmi/ *nf* mummy.

**mon, ma** (**mon** before vowel or mute h) (*pl* **mes**) /mɔ̃, ma, mɔ̃, me/ *adj* my.

**Monaco** /mɔnako/ *npr* Monaco.

**monarchie** /mɔnaʀʃi/ *nf* monarchy.

**monarque** /mɔnaʀk/ *nm* monarch.

**monastère** /mɔnastɛʀ/ *nm* monastery.

**monceau** (*pl* ~x) /mɔ̃so/ *nm* heap, pile.

**mondain, ~e** /mɔ̃dɛ̃, -ɛn/ *adj* society, social.

**monde** /mɔ̃d/ *nm* world; **du** ~ (a lot of) people; (quelqu'un) somebody; **le** (**grand**) ~ (high) society; **se faire** (**tout**) **un** ~ **de qch** make a great deal of fuss about sth; **pas le moins du** ~ not in the least.

**mondial, ~e** (*mpl* **-iaux**) /mɔ̃djal, -jo/ *adj* world; (influence) worldwide.

**mondialement** *adv* the world over.

**mondialisation** /mɔ̃djalizasjɔ̃/ *nf* globalisation.

**monétaire** /mɔnetɛʀ/ *adj* monetary.

**moniteur, -trice** /mɔnitœʀ, -tʀis/ *nm, f* instructor; (de colonie de vacances) group leader; (US) (camp) counselor.

**monnaie** /mɔnɛ/ *nf* currency; (pièce) coin; (appoint) change; **faire la** ~ **de** get change for; **faire de la** ~ **à qn** give sb change; **menue** ou **petite** ~ small change.

**monnayer** /mɔneje/ ③ *vt* convert into cash.

**monologue** /mɔnɔlɔg/ *nm* monologue.

**monoparental, ~e** /mɔnɔpaʀɑ̃tal/ *adj* **famille** ~**e** single-parent family.

**monopole** /mɔnɔpɔl/ *nm* monopoly. **monopoliser** ■ *vt* monopolize.

**monospace** /mɔnɔspas/ *nm* (Auto) people carrier.

**monotone** /mɔnɔtɔn/ *adj* monotonous. **monotonie** *nf* monotony.

**Monseigneur** (*pl* **Messeigneurs**) /mɔsɛɲœʀ/ *nm* (à un duc, archevêque) Your Grace; (à un prince) Your Highness.

**monsieur** (*pl* **messieurs**) /masjø, mesjø/ *nm* (à un inconnu) (dans une lettre) M~ Dear Sir; **bonjour,** ~ good morning; **mesdames et messieurs** ladies and gentlemen; (à un homme dont on connaît le nom) (dans une lettre) **Cher M~** Dear Mr X; **bonjour,** ~ good morning Mr X; **M~ le curé** Father X; **oui M~ le ministre** yes Minister; (homme) man; (formule de respect) sir.

**monstre** /mɔstʀ/ *nm* monster.
● *adj* 🗓 colossal.

**monstrueux, -euse** /mɔstʀyø, -z/

*adj* monstrous. **monstruosité** *nf* monstrosity.

**mont** /mɔ̃/ *nm* mountain; le ~ Everest Mount Everest; être toujours par ~s et par vaux be always on the move.

**montage** /mɔ̃taʒ/ *nm* (assemblage) assembly; (au cinéma) editing.

**montagne** /mɔ̃taɲ/ *nf* mountain; (région) mountains; ~s russes roller-coaster. **montagneux, -euse** *adj* mountainous.

**montant, ~e** /mɔ̃tɑ̃, -t/ *adj* rising; (col) high; (chemin) uphill. ● *nm* amount; (pièce de bois) upright.

**mont-de-piété** /mɔ̃dpjete/ (*pl* **monts-de-piété**) *nm* pawnshop.

**monte-charge** /mɔ̃tʃaʀʒ/ *nm inv* goods lift.

**montée** /mɔ̃te/ *nf* ascent, climb; (de prix) rise; (de coûts, risques) increase; (côte) hill.

**monter** /mɔ̃te/ **1** *vt* (aux. avoir) take up; (à l'étage) take upstairs; (escalier, rue, pente) go up; (assembler) assemble; (tente, échafaudage) put up; (col, manche) set in; (organiser) (pièce) stage; (société) set up; (attaque, garde) mount. ● *vi* (aux. être) go *ou* come up; (à l'étage) go *ou* come upstairs; (avion) climb; (route) go uphill, climb; (augmenter) rise; (marée) come up; ~ sur (trottoir, toit) get up on; (cheval, bicyclette) get on; ~ à l'échelle/ l'arbre climb the ladder/tree; ~ dans (voiture) get in; (train, bus, avion) get on; ~ à bord climb on board; ~ (à cheval) ride; ~ à bicyclette/moto ride a bike/ motorbike.

**monteur, -euse** /mɔ̃tœʀ, -øz/ *nm, f* (Tech) fitter; (au cinéma) editor.

**montre** /mɔ̃tʀ/ *nf* watch; faire ~ de show.

**montrer** /mɔ̃tʀe/ **1** *vt* show (à to); ~ du doigt point to. □ **se** ~ *vpr* show oneself; (être) be; (s'avérer) prove to be.

**monture** /mɔ̃tyʀ/ *nf* (cheval) mount; (de lunettes) frames (+ *pl*); (de bijou) setting.

**monument** /mɔnymɑ̃/ *nm* monument; ~ aux morts war memorial. **monumental** (*mpl* **-aux**) *adj* monumental.

**moquer (se)** /(sə)mɔke/ **1** *vpr* se ~ de make fun of; je m'en moque **1** I couldn't care less. **moquerie** *nf* mockery. **moqueur, -euse** *adj* mocking.

**moquette** /mɔkɛt/ *nf* fitted carpet; (US) wall-to-wall carpeting.

**moral, ~e** (*mpl* **-aux**) /mɔʀal, -o/ *adj* moral. ● *nm* (*pl* **-aux**) morale; ne pas avoir le ~ feel down; avoir le ~ be in good spirits; ça m'a remonté le ~ it gave me a boost.

**morale** /mɔʀal/ *nf* moral code; (mœurs) morals; (de fable) moral; faire la ~ à lecture. **moralité** *nf* (de personne) morals (+ *pl*); (d'action, œuvre) morality; (de fable) moral.

**moralisateur, -trice** /mɔʀalizatœʀ, -tʀis/ *adj* moralizing.

**morbide** /mɔʀbid/ *adj* morbid.

**morceau** (*pl* ~x) /mɔʀso/ *nm* piece, bit; (de sucre) lump; (de viande) cut; (passage) passage; manger un ~ **1** have a bite to eat; mettre en ~x smash *ou* tear to bits.

**morceler** /mɔʀsəle/ **6** *vt* divide up.

**mordant, ~e** /mɔʀdɑ̃, -t/ *adj* scathing; (froid) biting. ● *nm* vigour, energy.

**mordiller** /mɔʀdije/ **1** *vt* nibble at.

**mordre** /mɔrdr/ **3** *vi* bite (dans into); ~ sur (ligne) go over; (territoire) encroach on; ~ à l'hameçon bite. ● *vt* bite.

**mordu**, ~e /mɔrdy/ **1** *nm, f* fan. ● *adj* smitten; ~ de crazy about.

**morfondre (se)** /(sə)mɔrfɔdr/ **3** *vpr* wait anxiously; (languir) mope.

**morgue** /mɔrg/ *nf* morgue, mortuary; (attitude) arrogance.

**moribond**, ~e /mɔribɔ̃, -d/ *adj* dying.

**morne** /mɔrn/ *adj* dull.

**morphine** /mɔrfin/ *nf* morphine.

**mors** /mɔr/ *nm* (de cheval) bit.

**morse** /mɔrs/ *nm* (animal) walrus; (code) Morse code.

**morsure** /mɔrsyr/ *nf* bite.

**mort**[1] /mɔr/ *nf* death.

**mort**[2], ~e /mɔr, -t/ *adj* dead; ~ de fatigue dead tired. ● *nm, f* dead man, dead woman; les ~s the dead.

**mortalité** /mɔrtalite/ *nf* mortality; (taux de) ~ death rate.

**mortel**, ~le /mɔrtɛl/ *adj* mortal; (accident) fatal; ( poison, silence) deadly. ● *nm, f* mortal. **mortellement** *adv* mortally.

**mortifié**, ~e /mɔrtifje/ *adj* mortified.

**mort-né**, ~e /mɔrne/ *adj* stillborn.

**mortuaire** /mɔrtɥer/ *adj* (cérémonie) funeral.

**morue** /mɔry/ *nf* cod.

**mosaïque** /mɔzaik/ *nf* mosaic.

**mosquée** /mɔske/ *nf* mosque.

**mot** /mo/ *nm* word; (lettre, message) note; ~ d'ordre watchword; ~ de passe password; ~s croisés crossword (puzzle).

**motard** /mɔtar/ *nm* biker; (policier) police motorcyclist.

**moteur**, -trice /mɔtœr, -tris/ *adj* (Méd) motor; ( force) driving; à 4 roues motrices 4-wheel drive. ● *nm* engine, motor; barque à ~ motor launch; ~ de recherche (Internet) search engine.

**motif** /mɔtif/ *nm* (raisons) grounds (+ pl); (cause) reason; (Jur) motive; (dessin) pattern.

**motion** /mosjɔ̃/ *nf* motion.

**motivation** /mɔtivasjɔ̃/ *nf* motivation. **motiver** **1** *vt* motivate.

**moto** /mɔto/ *nf* motor cycle. **motocycliste** *nmf* motorcyclist.

**motorisé**, ~e /mɔtɔrize/ *adj* motorized.

**motrice** /mɔtris/ ➡**MOTEUR**.

**motte** /mɔt/ *nf* lump; (de beurre) slab; (de terre) clod; ~ de gazon turf.

**mou** (**mol** before vowel or mute h), **molle** /mu, mɔl/ *adj* soft; (ventre) flabby; (sans conviction) feeble; (apathique) sluggish, listless. ● *nm* slack; avoir du ~ be slack.

**mouchard**, ~e /muʃar, -d/ *nm, f* informer; (Scol) sneak.

**mouche** /muʃ/ *nf* fly; (de cible) bull's eye.

**moucher (se)** /(sə)muʃe/ **1** *vpr* blow one's nose.

**moucheron** /muʃrɔ̃/ *nm* midge.

**moucheté**, ~e /muʃte/ *adj* speckled.

**mouchoir** /muʃwar/ *nm* handkerchief, hanky; ~ en papier tissue.

**moue** /mu/ *nf* pout; faire la ~ pout.

**mouette** /mwet/ *nf* (sea)gull.

**moufle** /mufl/ *nf* (gant) mitten.

**mouillé**, ~e /muje/ *adj* wet.

**mouiller** /muje/ **1** *vt* wet, make wet; ~ l'ancre drop anchor.

m

□ se ~ *vpr* get (oneself) wet.

**moulage** /mulaʒ/ *nm* cast.

**moule** /mul/ *nf* (coquillage) mussel. ●*nm* mould; ~ à gâteau cake tin; ~ à tarte flan dish. **mouler** **1** *vt* mould; (statue) cast.

**moulin** /mulɛ̃/ *nm* mill; ~ à café coffee grinder; ~ à poivre pepper mill; ~ à vent windmill.

**moulinet** /mulinɛ/ *nm* (de canne à pêche) reel; **faire des** ~**s avec qch** twirl sth around.

**moulinette**® /mulinɛt/ *nf* vegetable mill.

**moulu**, ~**e** /muly/ *adj* ground; (fatigué 🗓) worn out.

**moulure** /mulyʀ/ *nf* moulding.

**mourant**, ~**e** /muʀɑ̃, -t/ *adj* dying. ●*nm, f* dying person.

**mourir** /muʀiʀ/ **43** *vi* (aux. être) die; ~ **d'envie de** be dying to; ~ **de faim** be starving; ~ **d'ennui** be dead bored.

**mousquetaire** /muskətɛʀ/ *nm* musketeer.

**mousse** /mus/ *nf* moss; (écume) froth, foam; (de savon) lather; (dessert) mousse; ~ **à raser** shaving foam. ●*nm* ship's boy.

**mousseline** /muslin/ *nf* muslin; (de soie) chiffon.

**mousser** /muse/ **1** *vi* froth, foam; (savon) lather.

**mousseux**, -**euse** /musø, -z/ *adj* frothy. ●*nm* sparkling wine.

**mousson** /musɔ̃/ *nf* monsoon.

**moustache** /mustaʃ/ *nf* moustache; ~**s** (d'animal) whiskers.

**moustique** /mustik/ *nm* mosquito.

**moutarde** /mutaʀd/ *nf* mustard.

**mouton** /mutɔ̃/ *nm* sheep; (peau) sheepskin; (viande) mutton.

**mouvant**, ~**e** /muvɑ̃, -t/ *adj* chan-

ging; (terrain) shifting, unstable.

**mouvement** /muvmɑ̃/ *nm* movement; (agitation) bustle; (en gymnastique) exercise; (impulsion) impulse; (tendance) tend, tendency; **en** ~ in motion.

**mouvementé**, ~**e** /muvmɑ̃te/ *adj* eventful.

**moyen**, ~**ne** /mwajɛ̃, -ɛn/ *adj* average; (médiocre) poor; **de taille moyenne** medium-sized. ●*nm* means, way; ~**s** means; (dons) ability; **au** ~ **de** by means of; **il n'y a pas** ~ it is not possible to. **Moyen Âge** *nm* Middle Ages (+ *pl*).

**moyennant** /mwajɛnɑ̃/ *prép* (pour) for; (grâce à) with.

**moyenne** /mwajɛn/ *nf* average; (Scol) pass-mark; **en** ~ on average; ~ **d'âge** average age. **moyennement** *adv* moderately.

**Moyen-Orient** /mwajɛnɔʀjɑ̃/ *nm* Middle East.

**moyeu** (*pl* ~**x**) /mwajø/ *nm* hub.

**mû**, **mue** /my/ *adj* driven (par by).

**mucoviscidose** /mykɔvisidoz/ *nf* cystic fibrosis.

**mue** /my/ *nf* moulting; (de voix) breaking of the voice.

**muer** /mɥe/ **1** *vi* moult; (voix) break. □ se ~ **en** *vpr* change into.

**muet**, ~**te** /mɥɛ, -t/ *adj* (Méd) dumb; (fig) speechless (de with); (silencieux) silent. ●*nm, f* mute.

**mufle** /myfl/ *nm* nose, muzzle; (personne 🗓) boor, lout.

**mugir** /myʒiʀ/ **2** *vi* (vache) moo; (bœuf) bellow; (fig) howl.

**muguet** /mygɛ/ *nm* lily of the valley.

**mule** /myl/ *nf* (female) mule; (pantoufle) mule.

**mulet** /mylɛ/ *nm* (male) mule.

**multicolore** /myltikɔlɔʀ/ *adj* multicoloured.

**multimédia** /myltimedja/ adj &
nm multimedia.

**multinational,** ~e (mpl -aux)
/myltinasjɔnal, -o/ adj multinational. **multinationale** nf multinational (company).

**multiple** /myltipl/ nm multiple.
●adj numerous, many; (naissances)
multiple.

**multiplication** /myltiplikasjɔ̃/ nf
multiplication.

**multiplicité** /myltiplisite/ nf
multiplicity.

**multiplier** /myltiplije/ [45] vt
multiply; (risques) increase. □ se ~
vpr multiply; (accidents) be on the
increase; (difficultés) increase.

**multitude** /myltityd/ nf multitude, mass.

**municipal,** ~e (mpl -aux)
/mynisipal, -o/ adj municipal; conseil ~ town council. **municipalité**
nf (ville) municipality; (conseil) town
council.

**munir** /mynir/ [2] vt ~ de provide
with. □ se ~ de vpr (apporter)
bring; (emporter) take.

**munitions** /mynisjɔ̃/ nfpl ammunition.

**mur** /myr/ nm wall; ~ du son
sound barrier.

**mûr,** ~e /myr/ adj ripe; (personne)
mature.

**muraille** /myrɑj/ nf (high) wall.

**mural,** ~e (mpl -aux) /myral, -o/
adj wall; peinture ~e mural.

**mûre** /myr/ nf blackberry.

**mûrir** /myrir/ [2] vi ripen; (abcès)
come to a head; (personne, projet)
mature. ●vt (fruit) ripen; (personne)
mature.

**murmure** /myrmyr/ nm murmur.

**muscade** /myskad/ nf noix ~
nutmeg.

**muscle** /myskl/ nm muscle. **mus-**

**clé,** ~e adj muscular. **musculaire**
adj muscular.

**musculation** /myskylasjɔ̃/ nf
bodybuilding.

**musculature** /myskylatyr/ nf
muscles (+ pl).

**museau** (pl ~x) /myzo/ nm muzzle; (de porc) snout.

**musée** /myze/ nm museum; (de
peinture) art gallery.

**muselière** /myzəljɛr/ nf muzzle.

**musette** /myzɛt/ nf haversack.

**muséum** /myzeɔm/ nm natural
history museum.

**musical,** ~e (mpl -aux) /myzikal,
-o/ adj musical.

**musicien,** ~ne /myzisjɛ̃, -ɛn/ adj
musical. ●nm, f musician.

**musique** /myzik/ nf music; (orchestre) band.

**must** /myst/ nm [1] must.

**musulman,** ~e /myzylmɑ̃, -an/
adj & nm, f Muslim.

**mutation** /mytasjɔ̃/ nf change;
(biologique) mutation; (d'un employé) transfer.

**muter** /myte/ [1] vt transfer. ●vi
mutate.

**mutilation** /mytilasjɔ̃/ nf mutilation. **mutiler** [1] vt mutilate. **mu-**
**tilé,** ~e nm, f disabled person.

**mutin,** ~e /mytɛ̃, -in/ adj mischievous. ●nm mutineer; (prisonnier) rioter.

**mutinerie** /mytinri/ nf mutiny;
(de prisonniers) riot.

**mutisme** /mytism/ nm silence.

**mutuel,** ~le /mytɥɛl/ adj mutual.
**mutuelle** nf mutual insurance company. **mutuellement** adv mutually;
(l'un l'autre) each other.

**myope** /mjɔp/ adj short-sighted.
**myopie** nf short-sightedness.

**myosotis** /mjozɔtis/ nm

m

forget-me-not.

**myrtille** /miʀtij/ *nf* bilberry, blueberry.

**mystère** /mistɛʀ/ *nm* mystery.

**mystérieux, -ieuse** /misteʀjø, -z/ *adj* mysterious.

**mystification** /mistifikasjɔ̃/ *nf* hoax.

**mysticisme** /mistisism/ *nm* mysticism.

**mystique** /mistik/ *adj* mystic(al). ● *nmf* mystic. ● *nf* mystique.

**mythe** /mit/ *nm* myth. **mythique** *adj* mythical.

**mythologie** /mitɔlɔʒi/ *nf* mythology.

····························

# Nn

**n'** /n/ ⇒NE.

**nacre** /nakʀ/ *nf* mother-of-pearl.

**nage** /naʒ/ *nf* swimming; (manière) stroke; **traverser à la ~** swim across; **en ~** sweating.

**nageoire** /naʒwaʀ/ *nf* fin; (de mammifère) flipper.

**nager** /naʒe/ 40 *vt/i* swim. **nageur, -euse** *nm, f* swimmer.

**naguère** /nagɛʀ/ *adv* (autrefois) formerly.

**naïf, -ive** /naif, -v/ *adj* naïve.

**nain, ~e** /nɛ̃, nɛn/ *nm, f & adj* dwarf.

**naissance** /nɛsɑ̃s/ *nf* birth; **donner ~ à** give birth to; (fig) give rise to.

**naître** /nɛtʀ/ 44 *vi* be born; (résulter) arise (de from); **faire ~** (susciter) give rise to.

**naïveté** /naivte/ *nf* naïvety.

**nappe** /nap/ *nf* tablecloth; (de pétrole, gaz) layer; **~ phréatique** ground water.

**napperon** /napʀɔ̃/ *nm* (cloth) tablemat.

**narco-dollars** /naʀkodɔlaʀ/ *nmpl* drug money.

**narcotique** /naʀkɔtik/ *adj & nm* narcotic. **narco(-)trafiquant, ~e** (*pl* **~s**) *nm, f* drug trafficker.

**narguer** /naʀge/ 1 *vt* taunt; (autorité) flout.

**narine** /naʀin/ *nf* nostril.

**nasal, ~e** (*mpl* **-aux**) /nazal, -o/ *adj* nasal.

**naseau** (*pl* **~x**) /nazo/ *nm* nostril.

**natal, ~e** (*mpl* **~s**) /natal/ *adj* native.

**natalité** /natalite/ *nf* birth rate.

**natation** /natasjɔ̃/ *nf* swimming.

**natif, -ive** /natif, -v/ *adj* native.

**nation** /nasjɔ̃/ *nf* nation.

**national, ~e** (*mpl* **-aux**) /nasjonal, -o/ *adj* national. **nationale** *nf* A road; (US) highway. **nationaliser** 1 *vt* nationalize.

**nationalité** /nasjonalite/ *nf* nationality.

**natte** /nat/ *nf* (de cheveux) plait; (US) braid; (tapis de paille) mat.

**nature** /natyʀ/ *nf* nature; **~ morte** still life; **de ~ à** likely to; **payer en ~** pay in kind. ● *adj inv* plain; (*yaourt*) natural; (*thé*) black.

**naturel, ~le** /natyʀɛl/ *adj* natural. ● *nm* nature; (simplicité) naturalness; (Culin) **au ~** plain; (*thon*) in brine. **naturellement** *adv* (naturally); (bien sûr) of course.

**naufrage** /nofʀaʒ/ *nm* shipwreck; **faire ~** be shipwrecked; (*bateau*) be wrecked.

**nauséabond, ~e** /nozeabɔ̃, -d/ *adj* nauseating.

**nausée** /noze/ *nf* nausea.

**nautique** /notik/ *adj* nautical; **sports** ~s water sports.

**naval**, ~e *(mpl* ~s) /naval/ *adj* naval; **chantier** ~ shipyard.

**navet** /navε/ *nm* turnip; (film: péj) flop; (US) turkey.

**navette** /navεt/ *nf* shuttle (service); **faire la** ~ shuttle back and forth.

**navigateur**, **-trice** /navigatœR, -tRis/ *nm, f* sailor; (qui guide) navigator; (Internet) browser. **navigation** *nf* navigation; (trafic) shipping; (Internet) browsing.

**naviguer** /navige/ **1** *vi* sail; (piloter) navigate; (Internet) browse; ~ **dans l'Internet** surf the Internet.

**navire** /naviR/ *nm* ship.

**navré**, ~e /navRe/ *adj* sorry (de to).

---

**ne**, **n'** /nə, n/

n' before vowel or mute h.

● *adverbe*

····▸ **je n'ai que 10 euros** I've only got 10 euros.

····▸ **tu n'avais qu'à le dire!** you only had to say so!

····▸ **je crains qu'il ~ parte !** I am afraid he will leave.

➡   Pour les expressions comme **ne... guère**, **ne... jamais**, **ne... pas**, **ne... plus**, etc. ➡**guère, jamais, pas, plus**, etc.

---

**né**, ~e /ne/ *adj* born; ~e **Martin** née Martin; (dans composés) **dernier**-~ last-born. ●●▸**NAÎTRE** 44.

**néanmoins** /neãmwἓ/ *adv* nevertheless.

**néant** /neã/ *nm* nothingness; **réduire à** ~ *(effet, efforts)* negate, nullify; *(espoir)* dash; **'revenus: ~'** 'income: nil'.

**nécessaire** /neseseR/ *adj* necessary. ●*nm* (sac) bag; (trousse) kit; **le** ~ (l'indispensable) the necessities *ou* essentials; **faire le** ~ do what is necessary.

**nécessité** /nesesite/ *nf* necessity; **de première** ~ vital.

**nécessiter** /nesesite/ **1** *vt* necessitate.

**néerlandais**, ~e /neεRlãdε, -z/ *adj* Dutch. ●*nm* (Ling) Dutch. **N**~, ~e *nm, f* Dutchman, Dutchwoman.

**néfaste** /nefast/ *adj* harmful (à to).

**négatif**, **-ive** /negatif, -v/ *adj & nm* negative.

**négligé**, ~e /negliʒe/ *adj* (travail) careless; (tenue) scruffy. ●*nm* (tenue) negligee.

**négligent**, ~e /negliʒã, -t/ *adj* careless, negligent.

**négliger** /negliʒe/ **40** *vt* neglect; (ne pas tenir compte de) ignore, disregard; ~ **de faire** fail to do. □ **se** ~ *vpr* neglect oneself.

**négoce** /negɔs/ *nm* business, trade. **négociant**, ~e *nm, f* merchant.

**négociation** /negɔsjasjɔ̃/ *nf* negotiation. **négocier** 45 *vt/i* negotiate.

**nègre** /nεgR/ *adj* (musique, art) Negro. ●*nm* (écrivain) ghost writer.

**neige** /nεʒ/ *nf* snow. **neiger** 40 *vi* snow.

**nénuphar** /nenyfaR/ *nm* waterlily.

**nerf** /nεR/ *nm* nerve; (vigueur) stamina; **être sur les** ~s be on edge.

**nerveux**, **-euse** /nεRvø, -z/ *adj* nervous; (irritable) nervy; (centre, cellule) nerve; (voiture) responsive.

**nervosité** *nf* nervousness; (irritabilité) touchiness.

**net,** ~te /nɛt/ adj (clair, distinct) clear; (propre) clean; (notable) marked; (soigné) neat; (prix, poids) net. ● **N**~ nm (Ordinat) Int. ● adv (s'arrêter) dead; (refuser) flatly; (parler) plainly; (se casser) cleanly; (tuer) outright. **nettement** adv (expliquer) clearly; (augmenter, se détériorer) markedly; (indiscutablement) distinctly, decidedly. **netteté** nf clearness.

**netéconomie** /nɛtekɔnɔmi/ nf e-economy.

**nétiquette** /netikɛt/ nf netiquette.

**nettoyage** /nɛtwajaʒ/ nm cleaning; ~ à sec dry-cleaning; produit de ~ cleaner; ~ ethnique ethnic cleansing.

**nettoyer** /nɛtwaje/ 31 vt clean.

**neuf**[1] /nœf/ (/nœv/ before vowels and mute h) adj inv & nm nine.

**neuf**[2], **-euve** /nœf, -v/ adj new; tout ~ brand new. ● nm new; remettre à ~ brighten up; du ~ a new development; quoi de ~? what's new?

**neutre** /nøtʀ/ adj neutral; (Gram) neuter. ● nm (Gram) neuter.

**neuve** /nœv/ →NEUF[2].

**neuvième** /nœvjɛm/ adj & nm, f ninth.

**neveu** (pl ~x) /nəvø/ nm nephew.

**névrose** /nevʀoz/ nf neurosis. **névrosé,** ~e adj & nm, f neurotic.

**nez** /ne/ nm nose; ~ à ~ face to face; ~ retroussé turned-up nose.

**ni** /ni/ conj neither, nor; ~ grand ~ petit neither big nor small; ~ l'un ~ l'autre ne fument neither (one nor the other) smokes; sortir sans manteau ~ chapeau go without a coat or hat; elle n'a dit ~ oui ~ non she didn't say either yes or no.

**niais,** ~e /njɛ, -z/ adj silly.

**niche** /niʃ/ nf (de chien) kennel; (cavité) niche.

**nicher** /niʃe/ 1 vi nest. □ se ~ vpr nest; (se cacher) hide.

**nicotine** /nikɔtin/ nf nicotine.

**nid** /ni/ nm nest; faire un ~ build a nest. **nid-de-poule** (pl **nids-de-poule**) nm pot-hole.

**nièce** /njɛs/ nf niece.

**nier** /nje/ 45 vt deny.

**nigaud,** ~e /nigo, -d/ nm, f fool.

**nippon,** ~e /nipɔ̃, -ɔn/ adj Japanese. **N**~, ~e nm, f Japanese.

**niveau** (pl ~x) /nivo/ nm level; (compétence) standard; (étage) storey; (US) story; au ~ up to standard; mettre à ~ (Ordinat) upgrade; ~ à bulle (d'air) spirit level; ~ de vie standard of living.

**niveler** /nivle/ 6 vt level.

**noble** /nɔbl/ adj noble. ● nm, f nobleman, noblewoman. **noblesse** nf nobility.

**noce** /nɔs/ nf (fête Int) party; (invités) wedding guests; ~s wedding; faire la ~ [1] live it up.

**nocif,** **-ive** /nɔsif, -v/ adj harmful.

**nocturne** /nɔktyʀn/ adj nocturnal. ● nm (Mus) nocturne. ● nf (Sport) evening fixture; (de magasin) late-night opening.

**Noël** /nɔɛl/ nm Christmas.

**nœud** /nø/ nm (Naut) knot; (pour lier) knot; (pour orner) bow; ~s (fig) ties; ~ coulant slipknot, noose; ~ papillon bow-tie.

**noir,** ~e /nwaʀ/ adj black; (obscur, sombre) dark; (triste) gloomy. ● nm black; (obscurité) dark; travail au ~ moonlighting. ● nm, f (personne) Black.

**noircir** /nwaʀsiʀ/ 2 vt blacken; ~ la situation paint a black picture of the situation. ● vi (banane) go black; (*mur*) get dirty; (*métal*) tarnish. □ **se ~** *vpr* (*ciel*) darken.

**noire** /nwar/ *nf* (Mus) crotchet.

**noisette** /nwazɛt/ *nf* hazelnut; (de beurre) knob.

**noix** /nwa/ *nf* nut; (du noyer) walnut; (de beurre) knob; **~ de cajou** cashew nut; **~ de coco** coconut; **à la ~** 🔟 useless.

**nom** /nõ/ *nm* name; (Gram) noun; **au ~ de** on behalf of; **~ et prénom** full name; **~ déposé** registered trademark; **~ de famille** surname; **~ de jeune fille** maiden name; **~ de plume** pen name; **~ propre** proper noun; **~ d'utilisateur** username.

**nomade** /nɔmad/ *adj* nomadic; (worker) mobile. ● *nmf* nomad.

**nombre** /nõbr/ *nm* number; **au ~ de** (parmi) among; (l'un de) one of; **en (grand) ~** in large numbers; **sans ~** countless.

**nombreux, -euse** /nõbrø, -z/ *adj* (en grand nombre) many, numerous; (important) large; **de ~ enfants** many children; **nous étions très ~** there were a great many of us.

**nombril** /nõbril/ *nm* navel.

**nomination** /nɔminasjõ/ *nf* appointment.

**nommer** /nɔme/ 🔟 *vt* name; (élire) (à un poste) appoint; (à un lieu) post. □ **se ~** *vpr* (s'appeler) be called.

**non** /nõ/ *adv* no; (pas) not; **~ (pas) que** not that; **il vient, ~?** he is coming, isn't he? **moi ~ plus** neither am/do/can/etc. I. ● *nm inv* no.

**non-** /nõ/ *préf* non-; **~-fumeur** non-smoker.

**nonante** /nɔnãt/ *adj & nm* ninety.

**non-sens** /nõsãs/ *nm inv* absurdity.

**nord** /nɔr/ *nm & adj inv* (façade, côte)

north; (frontière, zone) northern. ● *nm* north; **le ~** the ~ de l'Europe northern Europe; **vent de ~** northerly (wind); **aller vers le ~** go north; **le Nord** the North; **du Nord** northern; **le nord-est** *nm* north-east.

**nordique** /nɔrdik/ *adj* Scandinavian.

**nord-ouest** /nɔrwɛst/ *nm* north-west.

**normal, -e** (*mpl* **-aux**) /nɔrmal, -o/ *adj* normal. **normale** *nf* normality; (norme) norm; (moyenne) average.

**normand, ~e** /nɔrmã, -d/ *adj* Norman. **N~, ~e** *nm, f* Norman.

**Normandie** /nɔrmãdi/ *nf* Normandy.

**norme** /nɔrm/ *nf* norm; (de production) standard; **~s de sécurité** safety standards.

**Norvège** /nɔrvɛʒ/ *nf* Norway.

**norvégien, ~ne** /nɔrveʒjɛ̃, -ɛn/ *adj* Norwegian. **N~, ~ne** *nm, f* Norwegian.

**nos** /no/ ➡**NOTRE**.

**nostalgie** /nɔstalʒi/ *nf* nostalgia; **avoir la ~ de son pays** be homesick. **nostalgique** *adj* nostalgic.

**notaire** /nɔtɛr/ *nm* notary public.

**notamment** /nɔtamã/ *adv* notably.

**note** /nɔt/ *nf* (remarque) note; (chiffrée) mark, grade; (facture) bill; (Mus) note; **~ (de service)** memorandum.

**noter** /nɔte/ 🔟 *vt* note, notice; (écrire) note (down); (devoir) mark; (US) grade; **bien/mal noté** (employé) highly/poorly rated.

**notice** /nɔtis/ *nf* note; (mode d'emploi) instructions, directions.

**notifier** /nɔtifje/ 45 *vt* notify (à to).

**notion** /nɔsjõ/ *nf* notion; **avoir des**

n

∼s de have a basic knowledge of.
**notoire** /nɔtwaʀ/ adj well-known;
(criminel) notorious.

**notre** (pl nos) /nɔtʀ, no/ adj our.

**nôtre** /notʀ/ pron le ou la ∼, les
∼s ours.

**nouer** /nwe/ **1** vt tie, knot; (relations) strike up.

**nouille** /nuj/ nf (Culin) noodle; des
∼s noodles, pasta; (idiot 🛈) idiot.

**nounours** /nunuʀs/ nm 🛈
teddy bear.

**nourri,** ∼e /nuʀi/ adj être logé ∼
have bed and board; ∼ au sein
breastfed.

**nourrice** /nuʀis/ nf childminder.

**nourrir** /nuʀiʀ/ **2** vt feed; (espoir,
crainte) harbour; (projet) nurture;
(passion) fuel. ● vi be nourishing.
□ se ∼ vpr eat; se ∼ de feed on.

**nourrissant,** ∼e adj nourishing.

**nourrisson** /nuʀisɔ̃/ nm infant.

**nourriture** /nuʀityʀ/ nf food.

**nous** /nu/ pron (sujet) we; (complément) us; (indirect) (to) us; (réfléchi) ourselves; (l'un l'autre) each
other; la voiture est à ∼ the car is
ours. **nous-mêmes** pron ourselves.

**nouveau** (nouvel before vowel or
mute h), **nouvelle** (mpl ∼x) /nuvo,
nuvɛl/ adj new; nouvel an new
year; ∼x mariés newly-weds; ∼
venu, nouvelle venue newcomer.
● nm, f (élève) new boy, new girl.
● nm du ∼ (fait nouveau) a new
development; de ∼, à ∼ again.
**nouveau-né** (pl ∼s) nm newborn baby.

**nouveauté** /nuvote/ nf novelty;
(chose) new thing; (livre) new publication; (disque) new release.

**nouvelle** /nuvɛl/ nf (piece of)
news; (récit) short story; ∼s news.

**Nouvelle-Zélande** /nuvɛlzelɑ̃d/
nf New Zealand.

**novembre** /nɔvɑ̃bʀ/ nm November.

**noyade** /nwajad/ nf drowning.

**noyau** (pl ∼x) /nwajo/ nm (de
fruit) stone; (TV) pit; (de cellule)
nucleus; (groupe) group; (centre;
fig) core.

**noyer** /nwaje/ **31** vt drown; (inonder) flood. □ se ∼ vpr drown; (volontairement) drown oneself; se ∼
dans un verre d'eau make a
mountain out of a molehill. ● nm
walnut-tree.

**nu,** ∼e /ny/ adj (corps, personne)
naked; (mains, mur, fil) bare; à l'œil
∼ to the naked eye. ● nm nude;
mettre à ∼ expose.

**nuage** /nyaʒ/ nm cloud.

**nuance** /nyɑ̃s/ nf shade; (de sens)
nuance; (différence) difference.
**nuancer** **10** vt (opinion) qualify.

**nucléaire** /nykleɛʀ/ adj nuclear.
● nm le ∼ nuclear energy.

**nudisme** /nydism/ nm nudism.

**nudité** /nydite/ nf nudity; (de lieu)
bareness.

**nuée** /nɥe/ nf swarm, host.

**nues** /ny/ nfpl tomber des ∼ be
amazed; porter qn aux ∼ praise sb
to the skies.

**nuire** /nɥiʀ/ **17** vi ∼ à harm.

**nuisible** /nɥizibl/ adj harmful
(à to).

**nuit** /nɥi/ nf night; cette ∼ tonight; (hier) last night; il fait ∼ it is
dark; ∼ blanche sleepless night; la
∼, de ∼ at night; ∼ de noces
wedding night.

**nul,** ∼le /nyl/ adj (aucun) no;
(zéro) nil; (qui ne vaut rien) useless;
(non valable) null; (contrat) void;
(testament) invalid; match ∼ draw;
∼ en sciences no good at science;
nulle part nowhere; ∼ autre no
one else. ● pron no one. **nullement**

*adv* not at all. **nullité** *nf* uselessness; (personne) nonentity.

**numérique** /nymerik/ *adj* numerical; (*montre, horloge*) digital.

**numériser** /nymerize/ *vt* digitize.

**numéro** /nymero/ *nm* number; (de journal) issue; (spectacle) act; ~ de téléphone telephone number; ~ vert freephone number. **numéroter** 1 *vt* number.

**nuque** /nyk/ *nf* nape (of the neck).

**nurse** /nœrs/ *nf* nanny.

**nutritif, -ive** /nytritif, -v/ *adj* nutritious; (*valeur*) nutritional.

.........................................

# Oo

.........................................

**oasis** /ɔazis/ *nf* oasis.

**obéir** /ɔbeir/ 2 *vt* ~ à obey. • *vi* obey. **obéissance** *nf* obedience. **obéissant, ~e** *adj* obedient.

**obèse** /ɔbɛz/ *adj* obese.

**objecter** /ɔbʒɛkte/ 1 *vt* object.

**objectif, -ive** /ɔbʒɛktif, -v/ *adj* objective. • *nm* objective; (Photo) lens.

**objection** /ɔbʒɛksjɔ̃/ *nf* objection; soulever des ~s raise objections.

**objet** /ɔbʒɛ/ *nm* (chose) object; (sujet) subject; (but) purpose, object; être ou faire l'~ de be the subject of; ~ d'art objet d'art; ~s trouvés lost property; (US) lost and found.

**obligation** /ɔbligasjɔ̃/ *nf* obligation; (Comm) bond; être dans l'~ de be under obligation to.

**obligatoire** /ɔbligatwar/ *adj* compulsory. **obligatoirement** *adv* (par règlement) of necessity; (inévitablement) inevitably.

**obligeance** /ɔbliʒɑ̃s/ *nf* avoir l'~ de faire be kind enough to do.

**obliger** /ɔbliʒe/ 40 *vt* compel, force (à faire to do); (aider) oblige; être obligé de have to (de for).

**oblique** /ɔblik/ *adj* oblique; regard ~ sidelong glance; en ~ at an angle.

**oblitérer** /ɔblitere/ 14 *vt* (timbre) cancel.

**obnubilé, ~e** /ɔbnybile/ *adj* obsessed.

**obscène** /ɔpsɛn/ *adj* obscene.

**obscur, ~e** /ɔpskyr/ *adj* dark; (confus, humble) obscure; (vague) vague.

**obscurcir** /ɔpskyrsir/ 2 *vt* make dark; (fig) obscure. □ s'~ *vpr* (ciel) darken.

**obscurité** /ɔpskyrite/ *nf* dark(-ness); (de passage, situation) obscurity.

**obsédant, ~e** /ɔpsedɑ̃, -t/ *adj* (problème) nagging; (musique, souvenir) haunting.

**obsédé, ~e** /ɔpsede/ *nm, f* ~ (sexuel) sex maniac; ~ du ski/jazz ski/jazz freak.

**obséder** /ɔpsede/ 14 *vt* obsess.

**obsèques** /ɔpsɛk/ *nfpl* funeral.

**observateur, -trice** /ɔpservatœr, -tris/ *adj* observant. • *nm, f* observer.

**observation** /ɔpservasjɔ̃/ *nf* observation; (remarque) remark, comment; (reproche) criticism; (obéissance) observance; en ~ under observation.

**observer** /ɔpserve/ 1 *vt* (regarder) observe; (surveiller) watch, observe; (remarquer) notice, observe; faire ~ qch point sth out (à to).

**obsession** /ɔpsesjɔ̃/ *nf* obsession.

**obstacle** /ɔpstakl/ *nm* obstacle; (pour cheval) fence, jump; (pour

n
o

athlète) hurdle; **faire ~ à** stand in the way of, obstruct.

**obstétrique** /ɔpstetʀik/ *nf* obstetrics (+ *sg*).

**obstiné**, **~e** /ɔpstine/ *adj* obstinate.

**obstiner (s')** /(s)ɔpstine/ **1** *vpr* persist (**à** in).

**obstruction** /ɔpstʀyksjɔ̃/ *nf* obstruction; (de conduit) blockage.

**obstruer** /ɔpstʀye/ **1** *vt* obstruct.

**obtenir** /ɔptəniʀ/ **58** *vt* get, obtain. **obtention** *nf* obtaining.

**obus** /ɔby/ *nm* shell.

**occasion** /ɔkazjɔ̃/ *nf* opportunity (de faire of doing); (circonstance) occasion; (achat) bargain; (article non neuf) second-hand buy; **à l'~** sometimes; **d'~** second-hand. **occasionnel**, **~le** *adj* occasional.

**occasionner** /ɔkazjone/ **1** *vt* cause.

**occident** /ɔksidɑ̃/ *nm* (direction) west; **l'O~** the West.

**occidental**, **~e** (*mpl* **-aux**) /ɔksidɑ̃tal, -o/ *adj* western. **O~**, **~e** (*mpl* **-aux**) *nm*, *f* westerner.

**occulte** /ɔkylt/ *adj* occult.

**occupant**, **~e** /ɔkypɑ̃, -t/ *nm*, *f* occupant. ● *nm* (Mil) forces of occupation.

**occupation** /ɔkypasjɔ̃/ *nf* occupation.

**occupé**, **~e** /ɔkype/ *adj* busy; ( *place*, *pays*) occupied; ( *téléphone*) engaged, busy; ( *toilettes*) engaged.

**occuper** /ɔkype/ **1** *vt* occupy; ( *poste*) hold; ( *espace*, *temps*) take up. □ **s'~ de** ( *personne*, *problème*) take care of; ( *bureau*, *firme*) be in charge of; ( *se mêler*) **occupe-toi de tes affaires** mind your own business.

**occurrence:** **en l'~** /ãlɔkyʀɑ̃s/

loc in this case.

**océan** /ɔseɑ̃/ *nm* ocean.

**Océanie** /ɔseani/ *nf* Oceania.

**ocre** /ɔkʀ/ *adj inv* ochre.

**octante** /ɔktɑ̃t/ *adj* eighty.

**octet** /ɔktɛ/ *nm* byte.

**octobre** /ɔktɔbʀ/ *nm* October.

**octogone** /ɔktɔgɔn/ *nm* octagon.

**octroyer** /ɔktʀwaje/ **31** *vt* grant.

**oculaire** /ɔkyleʀ/ *adj* **témoin** **~** eye-witness; **troubles ~s** eye trouble.

**oculiste** /ɔkylist/ *nmf* ophthalmologist.

**odeur** /ɔdœʀ/ *nf* smell.

**odieux**, **-ieuse** /ɔdjø, -z/ *adj* odious.

**odorant**, **~e** /ɔdɔʀɑ̃, -t/ *adj* sweet-smelling.

**odorat** /ɔdɔʀa/ *nm* sense of smell.

**œil** ( *pl* **yeux**) /œj, jø/ *nm* eye; **à l'~** **1** for free; **à mes yeux** in my view; **faire de l'~ à** make eyes at; **faire les gros yeux à** glare at; **ouvrir l'~** keep one's eyes open; **~ poché** black eye; **fermer les yeux** shut one's eyes; (fig) turn a blind eye.

**œillères** /œjeʀ/ *nfpl* blinkers.

**œillet** /œje/ *nm* (plante) carnation; (trou) eyelet.

**œuf** ( *pl* **~s**) /œf, ø/ *nm* egg; **~ à la coque/dur/sur le plat** boiled/hard-boiled/fried egg.

**œuvre** /œvʀ/ *nf* (ouvrage, travail) work; **~ d'art** work of art; **~ de bienfaisance** charity; **être à l'~** be at work; **mettre en ~** ( *réforme*, *moyens*) implement; **mise en ~** implementation. ● *nm* (ensemble spécifié) **l'~ entier de Beethoven** the complete works of Beethoven.

**œuvrer** /œvʀe/ **1** *vi* work.

**offense** /ɔfɑ̃s/ *nf* insult.

**offenser** /ɔfɑ̃se/ **1** *vt* offend.

□ **s'~** *vpr* take offence (de at).

**offensive** /ɔfɑ̃siv/ *nf* offensive.

**offert, ~e** /ɔfɛʀ, -t/ ➡OFFRIR 21.

**office** /ɔfis/ *nm* office; (Relig) service; (de cuisine) pantry; **faire ~ de** act as; **d'~** without consultation, automatically; **~ du tourisme** tourist information office.

**officiel, ~le** /ɔfisjɛl/ *adj* official. ●*nm* official.

**officier** /ɔfisje/ 45 *vi* (Relig) officiate. ●*nm* officer.

**officieux, -ieuse** /ɔfisjø, -z/ *adj* unofficial.

**offre** /ɔfʀ/ *nf* offer; (aux enchères) bid; **l'~ et la demande** supply and demand; **'~s d'emploi** 'situations vacant'.

**offrir** /ɔfʀiʀ/ 21 *vt* offer (de faire to do); (cadeau) give; (acheter) buy; **~ à boire à** (chez soi) give a drink to; (au café) buy a drink for. □ **s'~** *vpr* (se proposer) offer oneself (comme as); (solution) present itself; (s'acheter) treat oneself to.

**ogive** /ɔʒiv/ *nf* **~ nucléaire** nuclear warhead.

**OGM (organisation génétique ment modifié)** genetically modified organism.

**oie** /wa/ *nf* goose.

**oignon** /ɔɲɔ̃/ *nm* (légume) onion; (de fleur) bulb.

**oiseau** (pl **~x**) /wazo/ *nm* bird.

**oisif, -ive** /wazif, -v/ *adj* idle.

**olive** /ɔliv/ *nf & adj* olive. **olivier** *nm* olive tree.

**olympique** /ɔlɛ̃pik/ *adj* Olympic.

**ombrage** /ɔ̃bʀaʒ/ *nm* shade; **prendre ~ de** take offence at. **ombragé, ~e** *adj* shady.

**ombre** /ɔ̃bʀ/ *nf* (pénombre) shade; (contour) shadow; (soupçon: fig) hint, shadow; **dans l'~** (agir, rester) behind the scenes; **faire de l'~ à**

qn be in sb's light.

**ombrelle** /ɔ̃bʀɛl/ *nf* parasol.

**omelette** /ɔmlɛt/ *nf* omelette.

**omettre** /ɔmɛtʀ/ 42 *vt* omit, leave out.

**omnibus** /ɔmnibys/ *nm* stopping ou local train.

**omoplate** /ɔmɔplat/ *nf* shoulder blade.

**on** /ɔ̃/ *pron* (tu, vous) you; (nous) we; (ils, elles) they; (les gens) people, they; (quelqu'un) someone; (indéterminé) one, you; **~ dit** people say, they say, it is said; **~ m'a demandé mon avis** I was asked for my opinion.

**oncle** /ɔ̃kl/ *nm* uncle.

**onctueux, -euse** /ɔktɥø, -z/ *adj* smooth.

**onde** /ɔ̃d/ *nf* wave; **~s courtes/ longues** short/long wave; **sur les ~s** on the air.

**on-dit** /ɔ̃di/ *nm inv* les **~** hearsay.

**onduler** /ɔ̃dyle/ 1 *vi* undulate; (cheveux) be wavy.

**onéreux, -euse** /ɔneʀø, -z/ *adj* costly.

**ONG** *abrév f* (**organisation non gouvernementale**) NGO, non-governmental organization.

**ongle** /ɔ̃gl/ *nm* (finger) nail; **~ de pied** toenail; **se faire les ~s** do one's nails.

**ont** /ɔ̃/ ➡AVOIR 5.

**ONU** *abrév f* (**Organisation des Nations unies**) UN.

**onze** /ɔ̃z/ *adj & nm* eleven. **onzième** *adj & nmf* eleventh.

**OPA** *abrév f* (**offre publique d'achat**) takeover bid.

**opéra** /ɔpeʀa/ *nm* opera; (édifice) opera house. **opéra-comique** (pl **opéras-comiques**) *nm* light opera.

**opérateur, -trice** /ɔpeʀatœʀ,

**o**

-tris/ *nm, f* operator.

**opération** /ɔperasjɔ̃/ *nf* operation; (Comm) deal; (calcul) calculation; ~ escargot slow-moving protest convoy.

**opératoire** /ɔperatwar/ *adj* (Méd) surgical; **bloc** ~ operating suite.

**opérer** /ɔpere/ **14** *vt* (*personne*) operate on; (*exécuter*) carry out, make; ~ **qn d'une tumeur** operate on sb to remove a tumour; **se faire** ~ have surgery ou an operation. ● *vi* (Méd) operate; (*faire effet*) work. □ **s'~** *vpr* (*se produire*) occur.

**opiniâtre** /ɔpinjɑtr/ *adj* tenacious.

**opinion** /ɔpinjɔ̃/ *nf* opinion.

**opportuniste** /ɔpɔrtynist/ *nmf* opportunist.

**opposant,** ~**e** /ɔpozɑ̃, -t/ *nm, f* opponent.

**opposé,** ~**e** /ɔpoze/ *adj* (*sens, angle, avis*) opposite; (*factions*) opposing; (*intérêts*) conflicting; **être** ~ **à** be opposed to. ● *nm* opposite; **à l'~ de** (*contrairement à*) contrary to, unlike.

**opposer** /ɔpoze/ **1** *vt* (*objets*) place opposite each other; (*personnes*) match, oppose; (*contraster*) contrast; (*résistance, argument*) put up. □ **s'~** *vpr* (*personnes*) confront each other; (*styles*) contrast; **s'~ à** oppose.

**opposition** /ɔpozisjɔ̃/ *nf* opposition; **par** ~ **à** in contrast with; **entrer en** ~ **avec** come into conflict with; **faire** ~ **à un chèque** stop a cheque.

**oppressant,** ~**e** /ɔpresɑ̃, -t/ *adj* oppressive.

**opprimer** /ɔprime/ **1** *vt* oppress.

**opter** /ɔpte/ **1** *vi* ~ **pour** opt for.

**opticien,** ~**ne** /ɔptisjɛ̃, -ɛn/ *nm, f* optician.

**optimisme** /ɔptimism/ *nm* optimism.

**optimiste** /ɔptimist/ *nmf* optimist. ● *adj* optimistic.

**option** /ɔpsjɔ̃/ *nf* option.

**optique** /ɔptik/ *adj* (*verre*) optical. ● *nf* (*science*) optics (+ *sg*); (*perspective*) perspective.

**or**[1] /ɔr/ *nm* gold; **d'**~ golden; **en** ~ gold; (*occasion*) golden.

**or**[2] /ɔr/ *conj* now; well; (*indiquant une supposition*) and yet.

**orage** /ɔraʒ/ *nm* (thunder)storm.

**orageux, -euse** *adj* stormy.

**oral,** ~**e** (*mpl* -**aux**) /ɔral, -o/ *adj* oral. ● *nm* (*pl* -**aux**) oral.

**orange** /ɔrɑ̃ʒ/ *adj inv* orange; (Aut) (*feu*) amber; (US) yellow. ● *nf* orange. **orangeade** *nf* orangeade. **oranger** *nm* orange tree.

**orateur, -trice** /ɔratœr, -tris/ *nm, f* speaker.

**orbite** /ɔrbit/ *nf* orbit; (*d'œil*) socket.

**orchestre** /ɔrkɛstr/ *nm* orchestra; (*de jazz*) band; (*parterre*) stalls.

**ordinaire** /ɔrdinɛr/ *adj* ordinary; (*habituel*) usual; (*qualité*) standard; (*médiocre*) very average. ● *nm* **l'**~ the ordinary; (*nourriture*) the standard fare; **d'**~, **à l'**~ usually. **ordinairement** *adv* usually.

**ordinateur** /ɔrdinatœr/ *nm* computer; ~ **personnel/de bureau** personal/desktop computer; ~ **portable** laptop (computer); ~ **hôte** (Internet) host.

**ordonnance** /ɔrdɔnɑ̃s/ *nf* (*ordre, décret*) order; (*de médecin*) prescription.

**ordonné,** ~**e** /ɔrdɔne/ *adj* tidy.

**ordonner** /ɔrdɔne/ **1** *vt* order (**à qn de** sb to); (*agencer*) arrange; (Méd) prescribe; (*prêtre*) ordain.

**ordre** /ɔrdr/ *nm* order; (*propreté*) tidiness; **aux** ~**s de qn** at sb's disposal; **avoir de l'~** be tidy; **en ~** tidy, in order; **de premier ~** first-rate; **d'~ officiel** of an official nature; **l'~ du jour** (*programme*) agenda; **mettre de l'~ dans** tidy up; **jusqu'à nouvel ~** until further notice; **un ~ de grandeur** an approximate idea.

**ordure** /ɔʀdyʀ/ *nf* filth; **~s** (*détritus*) rubbish; (US) garbage; **~s ménagères** household refuse.

**oreille** /ɔʀɛj/ *nf* ear.

**oreiller** /ɔʀeje/ *nm* pillow.

**oreillons** /ɔʀɛjɔ̃/ *nmpl* mumps.

**orfèvre** /ɔʀfɛvʀ/ *nm* goldsmith.

**organe** /ɔʀgan/ *nm* organ.

**organigramme** /ɔʀganigʀam/ *nm* organization chart; (Ordinat) flowchart.

**organique** /ɔʀganik/ *adj* organic.

**organisateur, -trice** /ɔʀganizatœʀ, -tʀis/ *nm, f* organizer.

**organisation** /ɔʀganizasjɔ̃/ *nf* organization.

**organiser** /ɔʀganize/ **1** *vt* organize. □ **s'~** *vpr* organize oneself, get organized.

**organisme** /ɔʀganism/ *nm* body, organism.

**orge** /ɔʀʒ/ *nf* barley.

**orgelet** /ɔʀʒəlɛ/ *nm* sty.

**orgue** /ɔʀg/ *nm* organ; **~ de Barbarie** barrel-organ. **orgues** *nfpl* organ.

**orgueil** /ɔʀgœj/ *nm* pride. **orgueilleux, -euse** *adj* proud.

**orient** /ɔʀjɑ̃/ *nm* (*direction*) east; **l'O~** the Orient.

**oriental, ~e** (*mpl* **-aux**) /ɔʀjɑ̃tal, -o/ *adj* eastern; (*de l'Orient*) oriental. **O~, ~e** (*mpl* **-aux**) *nm, f* Asian.

**orientation** /ɔʀjɑ̃tasjɔ̃/ *nf* direction; (*tendance politique*) leanings (+ *pl*); (*de maison*) aspect; (Sport)

orienteering; **~ professionnelle** careers advice; **~ scolaire** curriculum counselling.

**orienter** /ɔʀjɑ̃te/ **1** *vt* position; (*personne*) direct. □ **s'~** *vpr* (se repérer) find one's bearings; **s'~ vers** turn towards.

**origan** /ɔʀigɑ̃/ *nm* oregano.

**originaire** /ɔʀiʒinɛʀ/ *adj* **être ~ de** be a native of.

**original, ~e** (*mpl* **-aux**) /ɔʀiʒinal, -o/ *adj* original; (*curieux*) eccentric. ●*nm* (*œuvre*) original. ●*nf* eccentric. **originalité** *nf* originality; eccentricity.

**origine** /ɔʀiʒin/ *nf* origin; **à l'~** originally; **d'~** (*pièce, pneu*) original; **être d'~ noble** come from a noble background.

**originel, ~le** /ɔʀiʒinɛl/ *adj* original.

**orme** /ɔʀm/ *nm* elm.

**ornement** /ɔʀnəmɑ̃/ *nm* ornament.

**orner** /ɔʀne/ **1** *vt* decorate.

**orphelin, ~e** /ɔʀfəlɛ̃, -in/ *nm, f* orphan. ●*adj* orphaned. **orphelinat** *nm* orphanage.

**orteil** /ɔʀtɛj/ *nm* toe.

**orthodoxe** /ɔʀtɔdɔks/ *adj* orthodox.

**orthographe** /ɔʀtɔgʀaf/ *nf* spelling.

**ortie** /ɔʀti/ *nf* nettle.

**os** /ɔs, o/ *nm inv* bone.

**OS** *abrév m* ►**OUVRIER SPÉCIALISÉ.**

**osciller** /ɔsile/ **1** *vi* sway; (Tech) oscillate; (hésiter) waver; (fluctuer) fluctuate.

**osé, ~e** /oze/ *adj* daring.

**oseille** /ozɛj/ *nf* (*plante*) sorrel.

**oser** /oze/ **1** *vi* dare.

**osier** /ozje/ *nm* wicker.

**ossature** /ɔsatyʀ/ *nf* skeleton,

o

frame.

**ossements** /ɔsmã/ nmpl bones, remains.

**osseux, -euse** /ɔsø, -z/ adj bony; (Méd) bone.

**otage** /ɔtaʒ/ nm hostage.

**OTAN** /ɔtã/ abrév f (**Organisation du traité de l'Atlantique Nord**) NATO.

**otarie** /ɔtari/ nf eared seal.

**ôter** /ote/ **1** vt remove (à qn from sb); (déduire) take away.

**otite** /ɔtit/ nf ear infection.

**ou** /u/ conj or; ~ **bien** or else; ~ (**bien**)... ~ (**bien**)... either... or...; **vous** ~ **moi** either you or me.

**où** /u/ pron where; (dans lequel) in which; (sur lequel) on which; (auquel) at which; **d'**~ from which; (pour cette raison) hence; **par** ~ through which; ~ **qu'il soit** wherever he may be; **juste au moment** ~ just as; **le jour** ~ the day when. ● adv where; **d'**~? where from?

**ouate** /wat/ nf cotton wool; (US) absorbent cotton.

**oubli** /ubli/ nm forgetfulness; (trou de mémoire) lapse of memory; (négligence) oversight; **tomber dans l'**~ sink into oblivion.

**oublier** /ublije/ **45** vt forget; (omettre) leave out, forget. □ **s'**~ vpr (chose) be forgotten.

**ouest** /wɛst/ adj inv ( façade, côte) west; ( frontière, zone) western. ● nm west; **l'**~ **de l'Europe** western Europe; **vent d'**~ westerly (wind); **aller vers l'**~ go west; **l'O**~ the West; **de l'O**~ western.

**oui** /wi/ adv & nm inv yes.

**ouï-dire** /parwidir/ loc by hearsay.

**ouïe** /wi/ nf hearing; (de poisson) gill.

**ouragan** /uragã/ nm hurricane.

**ourlet** /urlɛ/ nm hem.

**ours** /urs/ nm bear; ~ **blanc** polar bear; ~ **en peluche** teddy bear.

**outil** /uti/ nm tool. **outillage** nm tools (+ pl). **outiller 1** vt equip.

**outrage** /utraʒ/ nm (grave) insult.

**outrance** /utrãs/ nf **à** ~ excessively. **outrancier, -ière** adj extreme.

**outre** /utr/ prép besides. ● adv passer ~ pay no heed; ~ **mesure** unduly; **en** ~ in addition. **outre-mer** adv overseas.

**outrepasser** /utrapase/ **1** vt exceed.

**outrer** /utre/ **1** vt exaggerate; (indigner) incense.

**ouvert, -e** /uvɛr, -t/ adj open; (gaz, radio) on. ●→OUVRIR **21**.

**ouverture** /uvɛrtyr/ nf opening; (Mus) overture; (Photo) aperture; ~**s** (offres) overtures; ~ **d'esprit** open-mindedness.

**ouvrable** /uvrabl/ adj jour ~ working day; **aux heures** ~**s** during business hours.

**ouvrage** /uvraʒ/ nm (travail, livre) work; (couture) (piece of) needlework.

**ouvre-boîtes** /uvrabwat/ nm inv tin-opener.

**ouvre-bouteilles** /uvrabutɛj/ nm inv bottle-opener.

**ouvreur, -euse** /uvrœr, -øz/ nm, f usherette.

**ouvrier, -ière** /uvrije, -jɛr/ nm, f worker; ~ **qualifié/spécialisé** skilled/unskilled worker. ● adj working-class; (conflit) industrial; **syndicat** ~ trade union.

**ouvrir** /uvrir/ **21** vt open (up); (gaz, robinet) turn on. ● vi open (up). □ **s'**~ vpr open (up); **s'**~ **à** open one's heart to sb.

**ovaire** /ɔvɛr/ nm ovary.

**ovale** /ɔval/ adj & nm oval.

**ovni** /ɔvni/ abrév m (**objet volant non-identifié**) UFO.

**ovule** /ɔvyl/ nm (à féconder) ovum; (gynécologique) pessary.

**oxygène** /ɔksiʒɛn/ nm oxygen.

**oxygéner (s')** /(s)ɔksiʒene/ [14] vpr get some fresh air.

**ozone** /ozon/ nf ozone; **la couche d'~** the ozone layer.

## Pp

**pacifique** /pasifik/ adj peaceful; (personne) peaceable; (Géog) Pacific. **P~** nm **le P~** the Pacific.

**pacotille** /pakɔtij/ nf junk, rubbish.

**PACS** abrév nm (**pacte de solidarité**) contract of civil union.

**pacser (se)** /səpakse/ [1] vpr sign a contract of civil union (PACS).

**pagaie** /pagɛ/ nf paddle.

**pagaille** /pagaj/ nf [1] mess, shambles (+ sg).

**page** /paʒ/ nf page; **mise en ~** layout; **tourner la ~** turn over a new leaf; **être à la ~** be up to date; **~ d'accueil** (Internet) home page.

**paie** /pɛ/ nf pay.

**paiement** /pɛmã/ nm payment.

**païen, ~ne** /pajɛ̃, -ɛn/ adj & nm, f pagan.

**paillasson** /pajasɔ̃/ nm doormat.

**paille** /paj/ nf straw. ● adj (cheveux) straw-coloured.

**paillette** /pajɛt/ nf (sur robe) sequin; (de savon) flake.

**pain** /pɛ̃/ nm bread; (miche) loaf (of bread); (de savon, cire) bar; **~ d'é-**

pices gingerbread; **~ grillé** toast.

**pair, ~e** /pɛr/ adj (nombre) even.
● nm (personne) peer; **aller de ~** go together (**avec** with); **au ~** (jeune fille) au pair. **paire** nf pair.

**paisible** /pezibl/ adj peaceful.

**paître** /pɛtr/ [44] vi graze.

**paix** /pɛ/ nf peace; **fiche-moi la ~!** [1] leave me alone!

**Pakistan** /pakistã/ nm Pakistan.

**palace** /palas/ nm luxury hotel.

**palais** /palɛ/ nm palace; (Anat) palate; **~ de justice** law courts; **~ des sports** sports stadium.

**pâle** /pɑl/ adj pale.

**Palestine** /palɛstin/ nf Palestine.

**palier** /palje/ nm (d'escalier) landing; (étape) stage.

**pâlir** /pɑlir/ [2] vt/i (turn) pale.

**palissade** /palisad/ nf fence.

**pallier** /palje/ [45] vt compensate for.

**palmarès** /palmarɛs/ nm list of prize-winners.

**palme** /palm/ nf palm leaf; (de nageur) flipper. **palmé, ~e** adj (patte) webbed.

**palmier** /palmje/ nm palm (tree).

**palper** /palpe/ [1] vt feel.

**palpiter** /palpite/ [1] vi (battre) pound; (frémir) quiver.

**paludisme** /palydism/ nm malaria.

**pamplemousse** /pãpləmus/ nm grapefruit.

**panaché, ~e** /panaʃe/ adj (bariolé, mélangé) motley; **glace ~e** mixed-flavour ice cream. ● nm shandy.

**pancarte** /pãkart/ nf sign; (de manifestant) placard.

**pané, ~e** /pane/ adj breaded.

**panier** /panje/ nm basket; (de basket-ball) basket; **mettre au ~** [1]

throw out; ~ à salade salad shaker; (fourgon 🔢) police van.

**panique** /panik/ nf panic. **paniquer 🔢** vi panic.

**panne** /pan/ nf breakdown; être en ~ have broken down; être en ~ sèche have run out of petrol; ~ d'électricité ou de courant power failure.

**panneau** (pl ~x) /pano/ nm sign; (publicitaire) hoarding; (de porte) panel; (d'affichage) notice board; (~ de signalisation) road sign.

**panoplie** /panɔpli/ nf (jouet) outfit; (gamme) range.

**pansement** /pɑ̃smɑ̃/ nm dressing; ~ adhésif plaster. **panser 🔢** vt (plaie) dress; (personne) dress the wound(s) of; (cheval) groom.

**pantalon** /pɑ̃talɔ̃/ nm trousers (+ pl).

**panthère** /pɑ̃tɛr/ nf panther.

**pantin** /pɑ̃tɛ̃/ nm puppet.

**pantomime** /pɑ̃tɔmim/ nf mime; (spectacle) mime show.

**pantoufle** /pɑ̃tufl/ nf slipper.

**paon** /pɑ̃/ nm peacock.

**papa** /papa/ nm dad(dy).

**pape** /pap/ nm pope.

**paperasse** /papras/ nf (péj) bumf.

**papeterie** /papetri/ nf (magasin) stationer's shop.

**papier** /papje/ nm paper; (formulaire) form; ~s (d'identité) (identity) papers; ~ absorbant kitchen paper; ~ aluminium tin foil; ~ buvard blotting paper; ~ cadeau wrapping paper; ~ calque tracing paper; ~ carbone carbon paper; ~ collant adhesive tape; ~ hygiénique toilet paper; ~ journal newspaper; ~ à lettres writing paper; ~ mâché papier mâché; ~ peint wallpaper; ~ de verre sandpaper.

**papillon** /papijɔ̃/ nm butterfly; (contravention 🔢) parking-ticket; ~ de nuit moth.

**papoter** /papɔte/ 🔢 vi 🔢 chatter.

**paquebot** /pakbo/ nm liner.

**pâquerette** /pakrɛt/ nf daisy.

**Pâques** /pak/ nfpl & nm Easter.

**paquet** /pakɛ/ nm packet; (de cartes) pack; (colis) parcel; un ~ de (beaucoup 🔢) a mass of.

**par** /par/ prép by; (à travers) through; (motif) out of, from; (provenance) from; commencer/finir ~ qch begin/end with sth; commencer/finir ~ faire begin by/ end up (by) doing; ~ an/mois a ou per year/month; ~ jour a day; ~ personne each, per person; ~ avion (lettre) (by) airmail; ~-ci, ~-là here and there; ~ contre on the other hand; ~ ici/là this/ that way.

**parachute** /paraʃyt/ nm parachute. **parachutiste** nmf parachutist; (Mil) paratrooper.

**parade** /parad/ 🔢 vi show off.

**paradis** /paradi/ nm (Relig) heaven; (lieu idéal) paradise; ~ fiscal tax haven.

**paradoxal**, ~e (mpl -aux) /paradɔksal, -o/ adj paradoxical.

**paraffine** /parafin/ nf paraffin wax.

**parages** /paraʒ/ nmpl dans les ~ around.

**paragraphe** /paragraf/ nm paragraph.

**paraître** /parɛtr/ 🔢 vi (se montrer) appear; (sembler) seem, appear; (ouvrage) be published, come out; faire ~ (ouvrage) bring out; il paraît qu'ils... apparently they...; oui, il paraît so I hear.

**parallèle** /paralɛl/ adj parallel; (illégal) unofficial. ● nm parallel; faire le ~ make a connection. ● *nf* parallel (line).

**paralyser** /paralize/ **1** *vt* paralyse. **paralysie** *nf* paralysis.

**paramètre** /parametr/ *nm* parameter.

**parapente** /parapɑ̃t/ *nm* paraglider; (*activité*) paragliding.

**parapharmacie** /parafarmasi/ *nf* toiletries and vitamins (*pl.*).

**parapher** /parafe/ **1** *vi* initial; (*signer*) sign.

**parapluie** /paraplɥi/ *nm* umbrella.

**parasite** /parazit/ *nm* parasite; ~s (*radio*) interference (+ *sg*).

**parasol** /parasɔl/ *nm* sunshade.

**paratonnerre** /paratɔnɛr/ *nm* lightning conductor *ou* rod.

**paravent** /paravɑ̃/ *nm* screen.

**parc** /park/ *nm* park; (*de bétail*) pen; (*de bébé*) play-pen; (*entrepôt*) depot; ~ **de loisirs** theme park; ~ **relais** park and ride; ~ **de stationnement** car park.

**parce que** /parsk(ə)/ *conj* because.

**parchemin** /parʃəmɛ̃/ *nm* parchment.

**parcmètre** /parkmɛtr/ *nm* parking meter.

**parcourir** /parkurir/ **20** *vt* travel *ou* go through; (*distance*) travel; (*des yeux*) glance at *ou* over.

**parcours** /parkur/ *nm* route; (*voyage*) journey.

**par-delà** /pardəla/ *prép* beyond.

**par-derrière** /pardɛrjɛr/ *adv* (*attaquer*) from behind; (*critiquer*) behind sb's back.

**par-dessous** /pardəsu/ *prép & adv* under (neath).

**pardessus** /pardəsy/ *nm* overcoat.

**par-dessus** /pardəsy/ *prép & adv* over; ~ **bord** overboard; ~ **le marché** 🗓 into the bargain; ~ **tout** above all.

**par-devant** /pardəvɑ̃/ *adv* (*passer*) by the front.

**pardon** /pardɔ̃/ *nm* forgiveness; (*je vous demande*) ~! (I am) sorry!; (*pour demander qch*) excuse me.

**pardonner** /pardɔne/ **1** *vt* forgive; ~ **qch à qn** forgive sb for sth.

**pare-brise** /parbriz/ *nm inv* windscreen.

**pare-chocs** /parʃɔk/ *nm inv* bumper.

**pareil**, ~le /parɛj/ *adj* similar (à to); (*tel*) such (a); **c'est** ~ it's the same; **ce n'est pas** ~ it's not the same thing. ● *nm, f* equal. ● *adv* 🗓 the same.

**parent**, ~e /parɑ̃, -t/ *adj* related (de to). ● *nm, f* relative, relation; ~s (*père et mère*) parents; ~ **isolé** single parent; **réunion de** ~s **d'élèves** parents' evening.

**parenté** /parɑ̃te/ *nf* relationship.

**parenthèse** /parɑ̃tɛz/ *nf* bracket, parenthesis; (*fig*) digression.

**parer** /pare/ **1** *vt* (*esquiver*) parry; (*orner*) adorn. ● *vi* ~ **à** deal with; ~ **au plus pressé** tackle the most urgent things first.

**paresse** /parɛs/ *nf* laziness.

**paresseux**, -euse /parɛso, -z/ *adj* lazy. ● *nm, f* lazy person.

**parfait**, ~e /parfɛ, -t/ *adj* perfect. **parfaitement** *adv* perfectly; (*bien sûr*) absolutely.

**parfois** /parfwa/ *adv* sometimes.

**parfum** /parfœ̃/ *nm* (*senteur*) scent; (*substance*) perfume, scent; (*goût*) flavour. **parfumé**, ~e *adj* fragrant; (*savon*) scented; (*thé*) flavoured.

**parfumer** /parfyme/ **1** *vt* (*embaumer*) scent; (*gâteau*) flavour.

p

□ **se ~** *vpr* put on one's perfume.
**parfumerie** *nf* (produits) perfumes; (boutique) perfume shop.

**pari** /paʀi/ *nm* bet.

**Paris** /paʀi/ *npr* Paris.

**parisien**, **~ne** /paʀizjɛ̃, -ɛn/ *adj* Parisian; (banlieue) Paris. **P~**, **~ne** *nm*, *f* Parisian.

**parking** /paʀkiŋ/ *nm* car park.

**parlement** /paʀləmɑ̃/ *nm* parliament.

**parlementaire** /paʀləmɑ̃tɛʀ/ *adj* parliamentary. ● *nmf* Member of Parliament.

**parlementer** /paʀləmɑ̃te/ **1** *vi* negotiate.

**parler** /paʀle/ **1** *vi* talk (à to); **~ de** talk about; **tu parles d'un avantage!** call that a benefit!; **de quoi ça parle?** what is it about? ● *vt* (langue) speak; (politique, affaires) talk. □ **se ~** *vpr* (personnes) talk (to each other); (langue) be spoken. ● *nm* speech; (dialecte) dialect.

**parmi** /paʀmi/ *prép* among(st).

**paroi** /paʀwa/ *nf* wall; **~ rocheuse** rock face.

**paroisse** /paʀwas/ *nf* parish.

**parole** /paʀɔl/ *nf* (mot, promesse) word; (langage) speech; **demander la ~** ask to speak; **prendre la ~** (begin to) speak; **tenir ~** keep one's word; **croire qn sur ~** take sb's word for it.

**parquet** /paʀkɛ/ *nm* (parquet) floor; **lame de ~** floorboard; **le ~** (Jur) prosecution.

**parrain** /paʀɛ̃/ *nm* godfather; (fig) sponsor.

**parsemer** /paʀsəme/ **6** *vt* strew (de with).

**part** /paʀ/ *nf* share, part; **à ~** (de côté) aside; (séparément) separate; (excepté) apart from; **d'une ~** on the one hand; **d'autre ~** on the

other hand; (de plus) moreover; **de la ~ de** from; **de toutes ~s** from all sides; **de ~ et d'autre** on both sides; **faire ~ à qn** inform sb (de of); **faire la ~ des choses** make allowances; **prendre ~ à** take part in; (joie, douleur) share; **pour ma ~** as for me.

**partage** /paʀtaʒ/ *nm* (division) dividing; (répartition) sharing out; **recevoir qch en ~** be left sth in a will.

**partager** /paʀtaʒe/ **40** *vt* divide; (distribuer) share out; (avoir en commun) share. □ **se ~ qch** *vpr* share sth.

**partenaire** /paʀtənɛʀ/ *nmf* partner.

**parterre** /paʀtɛʀ/ *nm* flower bed; (Théât) stalls.

**parti** /paʀti/ *nm* (Pol) party; (décision) decision; (en mariage) match; **~ pris** bias; **prendre ~** get involved; **prendre ~ pour qn** side with sb; **j'en ai pris mon ~** I've come to terms with that.

**partial**, **~e** (*mpl* **-iaux**) /paʀsjal, -jo/ *adj* biased.

**participe** /paʀtisip/ *nm* (Gram) participle.

**participant**, **~e** /paʀtisipɑ̃, -t/ *nm*, *f* participant (à in).

**participation** /paʀtisipasjɔ̃/ *nf* participation; (financière) contribution; (d'un artiste) appearance.

**participer** /paʀtisipe/ **1** *vi* **~ à** take part in, participate in; (profits, frais) share.

**particule** /paʀtikyl/ *nf* particle.

**particulier**, **-ière** /paʀtikylje, -jɛʀ/ *adj* (spécifique) particular; (bizarre) unusual; (privé) private; **rien de ~** nothing special. ● *nm* private individual; **en ~** in particular, particularly. **particulièrement** *adv* particularly.

**partie** /paʀti/ nf part; (cartes, Sport) game; (Jur) party; **une ~ de pêche** a fishing trip; **en ~** partly, in part; **en grande ~** largely; **faire ~ de** be part of; (adhérer à) be a member of; **faire ~ intégrante de** be an integral part of.

**partiel, ~le** /paʀsjɛl/ adj partial. ●nm (Univ) exam based on a module.

**partir** /paʀtiʀ/ 46 vi (aux être) go; (quitter un lieu) leave, go; (tache) come out; (bouton) come off; (coup de feu) go off; (commencer) start; **~ pour le Brésil** leave for Brazil; **~ du principe que** work on the assumption that; **à ~de** from; **à ~ de maintenant** from now on.

**partisan, ~e** /paʀtizɑ̃, -an/ nm, f supporter. ●nm (Mil) partisan; **être ~ de** be in favour of.

**partition** /paʀtisjɔ̃/ nf (Mus) score.

**partout** /paʀtu/ adv everywhere; **~ où** wherever.

**paru** /paʀy/ →**PARAÎTRE** 18.

**parure** /paʀyʀ/ nf finery; (bijoux) set of jewels; (de draps) set.

**parution** /paʀysjɔ̃/ nf publication.

**parvenir** /paʀvəniʀ/ 58 vi (aux être) **~ à** reach; **~ à faire** manage to do; **faire ~** send.

**parvenu, ~e** /paʀvəny/ nm, f upstart.

**pas¹** /pɑ/

➡ Pour les expressions comme **pas encore, pas mal,** etc. ➡**encore, mal** etc.

●adverbe

••••▸ not; **ne ~** not; **je ne sais ~** I don't know; **je ne pense ~** I

don't think so; **il a aimé, moi ~** he liked it, I don't; **~ cher/poli** cheap/impolite.

••••▸ **~ du tout** not at all; **~ de chance!** tough luck!

••••▸ **on a bien ri, ~ vrai?** 🄸 we had a good laugh, didn't we?

❗ In spoken colloquial French **ne… ~** is often shortened to **pas.** You will hear **j'ai pas compris** instead of **je n'ai pas compris** (I didn't understand). NB This is not correct written French.

**pas²** /pɑ/ nm step; (bruit) footstep; (trace) footprint; (vitesse) pace; **à deux ~ (de)** a step away (from); **marcher au ~** march; **rouler au ~** move very slowly; **à ~ de loup** stealthily; **faire les cent ~** walk up and down; **faire le premier ~** make the first move; **~ de porte** doorstep; **~ de vis** (Tech) thread.

**passage** /pɑsaʒ/ nm (traversée) crossing; (visite) visit; (chemin) way, passage; (d'une œuvre) passage; **de ~** (voyageur) visiting; (amant) casual; **la tempête a tout emporté sur son ~** the storm swept everything away; **~ clouté** pedestrian crossing; **~ interdit** (voyageur) no thoroughfare; **~ à niveau** level crossing; **~ souterrain** subway.

**passager, -ère** /pɑsaʒe, -ɛʀ/ adj temporary. ●nm, f passenger; **~ clandestin** stowaway.

**passant, ~e** /pɑsɑ̃, -t/ adj (rue) busy. ●nm, f passer-by. ●nm (anneau) loop.

**passe** /pɑs/ nf pass; **bonne/ mauvaise ~** good/bad patch; **en ~ de** on the road to.

**passé, ~e** /pɑse/ adj (révolu) past; (dernier) last; (fané) faded; **~ de**

mode out of fashion. ● nm past.
● prép after.

**passe-partout** /pɑspaʀtu/ nm inv
master-key. ● adj inv for all occasions.

**passeport** /pɑspɔʀ/ nm passport.

**passer** /pɑse/ **1** vi (aux être ou
avoir) go past, pass; (aller) go;
(venir) come; (temps, douleur) pass;
(film) be on; (couleur) fade; laisser
~ let through; (occasion) miss; ~
devant (à pied) walk past; (en voiture) drive past; ~ par go through;
où est-il passé? where did he get
to?; ~ outre take no notice; passons! let's forget about it!; passons
aux choses sérieuses let's turn to
serious matters; ~ dans la classe
supérieure go up a year; ~ pour
un idiot look a fool. ● vt (aux avoir)
(franchir) pass, cross; (donner) pass,
hand; (temps) spend; (enfiler) slip
on; (vidéo, disque) put on; (examen)
take, sit; (commande) place; (faire)
~ le temps while away the time;
~ l'aspirateur hoover; ~ un coup
de fil à qn give sb a ring; je vous
passe Mme X (par le standard) I'll
put you through to Mrs X; (en donnant l'appareil) I'll pass you over to
Mrs X; ~ qch en fraude smuggle
sth. □ se ~ vpr happen, take place;
(s'écouler) go by; se ~ de go ou
do without.

**passerelle** /pɑsʀɛl/ nf footbridge;
(de navire) gangway; (d'avion) (passenger) footbridge; (Internet)
gateway.

**passe-temps** /pɑstɑ̃/ nm inv
pastime.

**passif, -ive** /pasif, -v/ adj passive.
● nm (Comm) liabilities.

**passion** /pɑsjɔ̃/ nf passion. **passionnant, ~e** adj fascinating.

**passionné, ~e** /pɑsjɔne/ adj passionate; être ~ de have a

passion for.

**passionner** /pɑsjɔne/ **1** vt fascinate. □ se ~ **pour** vpr have a passion for.

**passoire** /pɑswaʀ/ nf (à thé)
strainer; (à légumes) colander.

**pastèque** /pɑstɛk/ nf watermelon.

**pasteur** /pɑstœʀ/ nm (Relig)
minister.

**pastille** /pɑstij/ nf (médicament)
pastille, lozenge.

**patate** /patat/ nf 🗉 spud; ~
(douce) sweet potato.

**patauger** /patoʒe/ 🗐 vi splash
about.

**pâte** /pɑt/ nf paste; (à gâteau)
dough; (à tarte) pastry; (à frire) batter; ~s (alimentaires) pasta (+ sg;)
~ à modeler Plasticine®; ~ d'amandes marzipan.

**pâté** /pɑte/ nm (Culin) pâté; (d'encre) blot; (de sable) sandpie; ~ en
croûte ≈ pie; ~ de maisons block
(of houses).

**pâtée** /pɑte/ nf feed, mash.

**patente** /patɑ̃t/ nf trade licence.

**paternel, ~le** /patɛʀnɛl/ adj paternal. **paternité** nf paternity.

**pathétique** /patetik/ adj moving.

**patience** /pasjɑ̃s/ nf patience. **patient, ~e** adj & nm, f patient. **patienter** **1** vi wait.

**patin** /patɛ̃/ nm skate; ~ à roulettes roller-skate.

**patinage** /patinaʒ/ nm skating.
**patiner** **1** vi skate; (roue) spin. **patinoire** nf ice rink.

**pâtisserie** /pɑtisʀi/ nf cake shop;
(gâteau) pastry; (secteur) cake making. **pâtissier, -ière** nm, f confectioner, pastry-cook.

**patrie** /patʀi/ nf homeland.

**patrimoine** /patʀimwan/ nm
heritage.

**patriote** /patʀijɔt/ adj patriotic. ●nm patriot.

**patron**, ∼ne /patʀɔ̃, -ɔn/ nm, f employer, boss; (propriétaire) owner, boss; (saint) patron saint. ●nm (couture) pattern. **patronal**, ∼e /e (mpl -aux) adj employers'. **patronat** nm employers (+ pl).

**patrouille** /patʀuj/ nf patrol.

**patte** /pat/ nf leg; (pied) foot; (de chat) paw; ∼s (favoris) sideburns; marcher à quatre ∼s walk on all fours; (bébé) crawl; ∼s de derrière hind legs.

**paume** /pom/ nf (de main) palm.

**paumé**, ∼e /pome/ nm, f 🛈 misfit.

**paupière** /popjɛʀ/ nf eyelid.

**pause** /poz/ nf pause; (halte) break.

**pauvre** /povʀ/ adj poor. ●nmf poor man, poor woman. **pauvreté** nf poverty.

**pavé** /pave/ nm cobblestone.

**pavillon** /pavijɔ̃/ nm (maison) house; (drapeau) flag.

**payant**, ∼e /pejɑ̃, -t/ adj (hôte) paying; c'est ∼ you have to pay to get in.

**payer** /peje/ 31 vt/i pay; (service, travail) pay for; ∼ qch à qn buy sb sth; faire ∼ qn charge sb; il me le paiera he'll pay for this. □ se ∼ vpr se ∼ qch buy oneself sth; se ∼ la tête de make fun of.

**pays** /pei/ nm country; (région) region; du ∼ local.

**paysage** /peizaʒ/ nm landscape.

**paysan**, ∼ne /peizɑ̃, -an/ nm, f farmer, country person; (péj) peasant. ●adj (agricole) farming; (rural) country.

**Pays-Bas** /peiba/ nmpl les ∼ the Netherlands.

**PCV** abrév m (**paiement contre vérification**) téléphoner en ∼ reverse the charges.

**PDG** abrév m (**président-directeur général**) chairman and managing director.

**péage** /peaʒ/ nm toll; (lieu) tollgate.

**peau** (pl ∼x) /po/ nf skin; (cuir) hide; ∼ de chamois shammy (leather); ∼ de mouton sheepskin; être bien/mal dans sa ∼ be/not be at ease with oneself.

**pêche** /pɛʃ/ nf (fruit) peach; (activité) fishing; (poissons) catch; ∼ à la ligne angling.

**péché** /peʃe/ nm sin.

**pêcher** /peʃe/ vt (poisson) catch; (dénicher 🛈) dig up. ●vi fish. **pêcheur** nm fisherman; (à la ligne) angler.

**pécuniaire** /pekynjɛʀ/ adj financial.

**pédagogie** /pedagɔʒi/ nf education.

**pédale** /pedal/ nf pedal.

**pédalo** ® /pedalo/ nm pedal boat.

**pédant**, ∼e /pedɑ̃, -t/ adj pedantic.

**pédestre** /pedɛstʀ/ adj faire de la randonnée ∼ go walking ou hiking.

**pédiatre** /pedjatʀ/ nmf paediatrician.

**pédicure** /pedikyʀ/ nmf chiropodist.

**peigne** /pɛɲ/ nm comb.

**peigner** /peɲe/ 1 vt comb; (personne) comb the hair of. □ se ∼ vpr comb one's hair.

**peignoir** /peɲwaʀ/ nm dressing gown.

**peindre** /pɛ̃dʀ/ 22 vt paint.

**peine** /pɛn/ nf sadness, sorrow; (effort, difficulté) trouble; (Jur) sentence; avoir de la ∼ feel sad; faire de la ∼ à hurt; ce n'est pas la ∼ de sonner you don't need to ring the bell; **j'ai de la ~ à le croire** I find it hard to believe; **se donner ou prendre la ~ de faire** go to the trouble of doing; **~ de mort** death penalty. ● adv **à ~** hardly.

**peiner** /pene/ **1** vi struggle. ● vt sadden.

**peintre** /pɛtʀ/ nm painter; **~ en bâtiment** house painter.

**peinture** /pɛtyʀ/ nf painting; (matière) paint; **~ à l'huile** oil painting.

**péjoratif, -ive** /peʒɔʀatif, -v/ adj pejorative.

**pelage** /pəlaʒ/ nm coat, fur.

**pêle-mêle** /pɛlmɛl/ adv in a jumble.

**peler** /pəle/ **6** vt/i peel.

**pèlerinage** /pɛlʀinaʒ/ nm pilgrimage.

**pelle** /pɛl/ nf shovel; (d'enfant) spade.

**pellicule** /pelikyl/ nf film; **~s** (cheveux) dandruff.

**pelote** /pəlɔt/ nf (of wool) ball.

**peloton** /p(ə)lɔtɔ̃/ nm platoon; (Sport) pack; **~ d'exécution** firing squad.

**pelotonner (se)** /(sə)plɔtɔne/ **1** vpr curl up.

**pelouse** /p(ə)luz/ nf lawn.

**peluche** /p(ə)lyʃ/ nf (matière) plush; (jouet) cuddly toy; **en ~** (lapin, chien) fluffy.

**pénal, ~e** /penal/ (mpl **-aux**) /penal, -o/ adj penal. **pénaliser** **1** vt penalize. **pénalité** nf penalty.

**penchant** /pɑ̃ʃɑ̃/ nm inclination; (goût) liking (**pour** for).

**pencher** /pɑ̃ʃe/ **1** vt tilt; **~ pour** favour. ● vi lean (over), tilt. □ **se ~** vpr lean (forward); **se ~ sur** (problème) examine.

**pendaison** /pɑ̃dɛzɔ̃/ nf hanging.

**pendant¹** /pɑ̃dɑ̃/ prép (au cours

de) during; (durée) for; **~ que** while.

**pendant², ~e** /pɑ̃dɑ̃, -t/ adj hanging; **jambes ~es** with one's legs dangling. ● nm (contrepartie) matching piece (**de** to); **~ d'oreille** drop earring.

**pendentif** /pɑ̃dɑ̃tif/ nm pendant.

**penderie** /pɑ̃dʀi/ nf wardrobe.

**pendre** /pɑ̃dʀ/ **3** vt/i hang. □ **se ~** vpr hang (**à** from); (se tuer) hang oneself.

**pendule** /pɑ̃dyl/ nf clock. ● nm pendulum.

**pénétrer** /penetʀe/ **14** vi **~ (dans)** enter; **faire ~ une crème** rub a cream in. ● vt penetrate.

**pénible** /penibl/ adj (travail) hard; (nouvelle) painful; (enfant) tiresome.

**péniche** /peniʃ/ nf barge.

**pénitence** /penitɑ̃s/ nf (Relig) penance; (punition) punishment; **faire ~** repent.

**pénitentiaire** /penitɑ̃sjɛʀ/ adj (établissement) penal.

**pénombre** /penɔ̃bʀ/ nf half-light.

**pensée** /pɑ̃se/ nf (idée) thought; (fleur) pansy.

**penser** /pɑ̃se/ **1** vt/i think; **~ à** (réfléchir à) think about; (se souvenir de, prévoir) think of; **~ faire** think of doing; **faire ~ à** remind one of.

**pensif, -ive** /pɑ̃sif, -v/ adj pensive.

**pension** /pɑ̃sjɔ̃/ nf (Scol) boarding school; (repas, somme) board; (allocation) pension; (**~ de famille**) guest house; **~ alimentaire** (Jur) alimony. **pensionnaire** nmf (Scol) boarder; (d'hôtel) guest. **pensionnat** nm boarding school.

**pente** /pɑ̃t/ nf slope; **en ~** sloping.

**Pentecôte** /pɑ̃tkot/ nf **la ~** Whitsun.

**pénurie** /penyʀi/ nf shortage.

**pépin** /pepɛ̃/ nm (graine) pip; (ennui ⓘ) hitch.

**pépinière** /pepinjɛʀ/ nf (tree) nursery.

**perçant, ~e** /pɛʀsɑ̃, -t/ adj (cri) shrill; (regard) piercing.

**perce-neige** /pɛʀsənɛʒ/ nm or f inv snowdrop.

**percepteur** /pɛʀsɛptœʀ/ nm tax inspector.

**percer** /pɛʀse/ ⑩ vt pierce; (avec perceuse) drill; (mystère) penetrate. ● vi break through; (dent) come through. **perceuse** nf drill.

**percevoir** /pɛʀsəvwaʀ/ ⓾ vt perceive; (impôt) collect.

**perche** /pɛʀʃ/ nf (bâton) pole.

**percher (se)** /(sə)pɛʀʃe/ ⓵ vpr perch.

**percolateur** /pɛʀkɔlatœʀ/ nm coffee machine.

**percuter** /pɛʀkyte/ ⓵ vt (véhicule) crash into.

**perdant, ~e** /pɛʀdɑ̃, -t/ adj losing. ● nm, f loser.

**perdre** /pɛʀdʀ/ ⓷ vt/i lose; (gaspiller) waste; ~ **ses poils** (chat) moult. □ **se** ~ vpr get lost; (rester inutilisé) go to waste.

**perdrix** /pɛʀdʀi/ nf partridge.

**perdu, ~e** /pɛʀdy/ adj lost; (endroit) isolated; (balle) stray; **c'est du temps** ~ it's a waste of time.

**père** /pɛʀ/ nm father; ~ **de famille** father, family man; ~ **spirituel** father figure; **le** ~ **Noël** Santa Claus.

**perfection** /pɛʀfɛksjɔ̃/ nf perfection.

**perfectionner** /pɛʀfɛksjɔne/ ⓵ vt (technique) perfect; (art) refine. □ **se** ~ vpr improve; **se** ~ **en anglais** improve one's English.

**perforer** /pɛʀfɔʀe/ ⓵ vt perforate; (billet, bande) punch.

**performance** /pɛʀfɔʀmɑ̃s/ nf performance.

**perfusion** /pɛʀfyzjɔ̃/ nf drip; **sous** ~ on a drip.

**péridurale** /peʀidyʀal/ nf epidural.

**péril** /peʀil/ nm peril; **à tes risques et** ~**s** at your own risk.

**périlleux, -euse** /peʀijø, -z/ adj perilous.

**périmé, ~e** /peʀime/ adj (produit) past its use-by date; (désuet) outdated.

**période** /peʀjɔd/ nf period.

**périodique** /peʀjɔdik/ adj periodic(al). ● nm (journal) periodical.

**péripétie** /peʀipesi/ nf (unexpected) event, adventure.

**périphérique** /peʀifeʀik/ adj peripheral. ● nm (boulevard) ~ ring road.

**périple** /peʀipl/ nm journey.

**périr** /peʀiʀ/ ⓶ vi perish, die.

**perle** /pɛʀl/ nf (d'huître) pearl; (de verre) bead.

**permanence** /pɛʀmanɑ̃s/ nf permanence; (Scol) study room; **de** ~ on duty; **en** ~ permanently; **assurer une** ~ keep the office open.

**permanent, ~e** /pɛʀmanɑ̃, -t/ adj permanent; (constant) constant; **formation** ~**e** continuous education. **permanente** nf (coiffure) perm.

**permettre** /pɛʀmɛtʀ/ ⓾ vt allow; ~ **à qn de allow sb to** ~; **se** ~ vpr (achat) afford; **se** ~ **de faire** take the liberty of doing.

**permis, ~e** /pɛʀmi, -z/ adj allowed. ● nm licence, permit; ~ **(de conduire)** driving licence.

**permission** /pɛʀmisjɔ̃/ nf permission; **en** ~ (Mil) on leave.

**Pérou** /peʀu/ nm Peru.

**perpendiculaire** /pɛʀpɑ̃dikylɛʀ/
adj & nf perpendicular.

**perpétuité** /pɛʀpetɥite/ nf à ~
for life.

**perplexe** /pɛʀplɛks/ adj perplexed.

**perquisition** /pɛʀkizisjɔ̃/ nf (police) search.

**perron** /peʀɔ̃/ nm (front) steps.

**perroquet** /peʀɔkɛ/ nm parrot.

**perruche** /peʀyʃ/ nf budgerigar.

**perruque** /peʀyk/ nf wig.

**persécuter** /pɛʀsekyte/ [1] vt persecute.

**persévérance** /pɛʀseveʀɑ̃s/ nf
perseverance. **persévérer** [14] vi persevere.

**persienne** /pɛʀsjɛn/ nf (outside)
shutter.

**persil** /pɛʀsi/ nm parsley.

**persistance** /pɛʀsistɑ̃s/ nf persistence. **persistant, ~e** adj persistent;
(feuillage) evergreen.

**persister** /pɛʀsiste/ [1] vi persist
(à faire in doing).

**personnage** /pɛʀsɔnaʒ/ nm character; (personne célèbre) personality.

**personnalité** /pɛʀsɔnalite/ nf
personality.

**personne** /pɛʀsɔn/ nf person; ~s
people. ● pron nobody, no-one; je
n'ai vu ~ I didn't see anybody.

**personnel, ~le** /pɛʀsɔnɛl/ adj
personal; (égoïste) selfish. ● nm
staff.

**perspective** /pɛʀspɛktiv/ nf (art,
point de vue) perspective; (vue)
view; (éventualité) prospect.

**perspicace** /pɛʀspikas/ adj
shrewd. **perspicacité** nf
shrewdness.

**persuader** /pɛʀsɥade/ [1] vt persuade (de faire to do).

**persuasif, -ive** /pɛʀsɥazif, -v/ adj

persuasive.

**perte** /pɛʀt/ nf loss; (ruine) ruin; à
~ de vue as far as the eye can see;
~ de (temps, argent) waste of; ~
sèche total loss; ~s (Méd) discharge.

**pertinent, ~e** /pɛʀtinɑ̃, -t/ adj
pertinent.

**perturbateur, -trice** /pɛʀtyʀbatœʀ, -tʀis/ nm, f disruptive element. **perturbation** nf disruption.
**perturber** [1] vt disrupt; (personne)
perturb.

**pervers, ~e** /pɛʀvɛʀ, -s/ adj (dépravé) perverted; (méchant) wicked.

**pervertir** /pɛʀvɛʀtiʀ/ [2] vt
pervert.

**pesant, ~e** /pəzɑ̃, -t/ adj heavy.

**pesanteur** /pəzɑ̃tœʀ/ nf heaviness; la ~ (force) gravity.

**pesée** /pəze/ nf weighing; (effort)
pressure.

**pèse-personne** (pl ~s) /pɛzpɛʀsɔn/ nm (bathroom) scales.

**peser** /pəze/ [6] vt/i weigh; ~ sur
bear upon.

**pessimisme** /pesimist/ adj pessimistic. ● nmf pessimist.

**peste** /pɛst/ nf plague; (personne
[!]) pest.

**pet** /pɛ/ nm [!] fart [!].

**pétale** /petal/ nm petal.

---

**Pétanque** See ▷ **BOULES.**    *i*

---

**pétard** /petaʀ/ nm banger.

**péter** /pete/ [14] vi [!] fart [!], go
bang; (casser) snap.

**pétillant, ~e** /petijɑ̃, -t/ adj (boisson) sparkling; (personne) bubbly.

**pétiller** /petije/ [1] vi (feu) crackle;
(champagne, yeux) sparkle; ~ d'intelligence sparkle with intelligence.

**petit, ~e** /p(ə)ti, -t/ adj small;

(avec nuance affective) little; (jeune) young, small; (défaut) minor; (mesquin) petty; en ∼ in miniature; ∼ à ∼ little by little; un ∼ peu a little bit; ∼ ami boyfriend; ∼e amie girlfriend; ∼es annonces small ads; ∼e cuillère teaspoon; ∼ déjeuner breakfast; ∼ pois garden pea. ●nm, f little child; (Scol) junior; ∼s (de chat) kittens; (de chien) pups. **petite-fille** (pl **petites-filles**) nf granddaughter. **petit-fils** (pl **petits-fils**) nm grandson.

**pétition** /petisjɔ̃/ nf petition.

**petits-enfants** /pətizɑ̃fɑ̃/ nmpl grandchildren.

**pétrin** /petrɛ̃/ nm dans le ∼ 🔢 in a fix 🔢.

**pétrir** /petriʀ/ 🔢 vt knead.

**pétrole** /petʀɔl/ nm oil; ∼ brut crude oil.

**pétrolier, -ière** /petʀɔlje, -jɛʀ/ adj oil. ●nm (navire) oil-tanker.

**peu** /pø/ adv (∼ de) (quantité) little, not much; (nombre) few, not many; ∼ intéressant not very interesting; il mange ∼ he doesn't eat very much. ●pron few. ●nm little; un ∼ (de) a little; à ∼ près more or less; de ∼ only just; ∼ à ∼ gradually; ∼ après/avant shortly after/before; ∼ de chose not much; ∼ nombreux few; ∼ souvent seldom; pour ∼ que if.

**peuple** /pœpl/ nm people. **peupler** 🔢 vt populate.

**peuplier** /pøplije/ nm poplar.

**peur** /pœʀ/ nf fear; avoir ∼ be afraid (de of); de ∼ de for fear of; faire ∼ à frighten. **peureux, -euse** adj fearful.

**peut** /pø/ ⇒POUVOIR 🔢.

**peut-être** /pøtɛtʀ/ adv perhaps, maybe; ∼ qu'il viendra he might come.

**peux** /pø/ ⇒POUVOIR 🔢.

**phare** /faʀ/ nm (tour) lighthouse; (de véhicule) headlight; ∼ antibrouillard fog lamp.

**pharmacie** /faʀmasi/ nf (magasin) chemist's (shop), pharmacy; (science) pharmacy; (armoire) medicine cabinet. **pharmacien, ∼ne** nm, f chemist, pharmacist.

**phénomène** /fenɔmɛn/ nm phenomenon; (personne 🔢) eccentric.

**philosophe** /filozɔf/ nmf philosopher. ●adj philosophical. **philosophie** nf philosophy. **philosophique** adj philosophical.

**phobie** /fɔbi/ nf phobia.

**phonétique** /fɔnetik/ adj phonetic. ●nf phonetics.

**phoque** /fɔk/ nm (animal) seal.

**photo** /fɔto/ nf (cliché); (art) photography; prendre en ∼ take a photo of; ∼ d'identité passport photograph.

**photocopie** /fɔtokɔpi/ nf photocopy. **photocopier** 🔢 vt photocopy.

**photographe** /fɔtograf/ nmf photographer. **photographie** nf photograph; (art) photography. **photographier** 🔢 vt take a photo of.

**phrase** /fʀaz/ nf sentence.

**physicien, ∼ne** /fizisjɛ̃, -ɛn/ nm, f physicist.

**physique** /fizik/ adj physical. ●nm physique; au ∼ physically. ●nf physics (+ sg.).

**piano** /pjano/ nm piano.

**pianoter** /pjanote/ 🔢 vi tinkle; ∼ sur (ordinateur) tap at.

**PIB** abrév m (**produit intérieur brut**) GDP.

**pic** /pik/ nm (outil) pickaxe; (sommet) peak; (oiseau) woodpecker; à ∼ (falaise) sheer; (couler) straight to the bottom; tomber à ∼ 🔢 come just at the right time.

**pichet** /piʃɛ/ nm jug.

**picorer** /pikɔʀe/ **1** vt/i peck.

**picotement** /pikɔtmɑ̃/ nm tingling. **picoter 1** vt sting; (yeux) sting.

**pie** /pi/ nf magpie.

**pièce** /pjɛs/ nf (d'habitation) room; (de monnaie) coin; (Théât) play; (pour raccommoder) patch; (écrit) document; (morceau) piece; (~ de théâtre) play; **dix euros (la ~)** ten euros each; **~ détachée** part; **~ d'identité** identity paper; **~s jointes** enclosures; (courrier électronique) attachments; **~s justificatives** written proof; **~ montée** tiered cake; **~ de rechange** spare part; **un deux-~s** a twooroom flat.

**pied** /pje/ nm foot; (de meuble) leg; (de lampe) base; (de verre) stem; (d'appareil photo) stand; **être ~s nus** be barefoot; **à ~** on foot; **au ~ de la lettre** literally; **avoir ~** be able to touch the bottom; **jouer au tennis comme un □** be hopeless at tennis; **mettre sur ~** set up; **sur un ~ d'égalité** on an equal footing; **mettre les ~s dans le plat □** put one's foot in it; **c'est le ~ □** it's great. **pied-bot** (pl **pieds-bots**) nm club-foot.

**piédestal** /pjedɛstal/ nm pedestal.

**piège** /pjɛʒ/ nm trap.

**piéger** /pjeʒe/ **14 40** vt trap; lettre/voiture piégée letter/car bomb.

**piercing** /piʀsiŋ/ nm body piercing.

**pierre** /pjɛʀ/ nf stone; **~ précieuse** precious stone; **~ tombale** tombstone.

**piétiner** /pjetine/ **1** vi (avancer lentement) shuffle along; (fig) make no headway; **~ d'impatience** hop up and down with impatience. ● vt trample (on).

**piéton** /pjetɔ̃/ nm pedestrian.

**pieu** (pl **~x**) /pjø/ nm post, stake.

**pieuvre** /pjœvʀ/ nf octopus.

**pieux, -ieuse** /pjø, -z/ adj pious.

**pigeon** /piʒɔ̃/ nm pigeon.

**piger** /piʒe/ **40** vt/i understand, get (it).

**pile** /pil/ nf (tas) pile; (Électr) battery; **~ ou face?** heads or tails? ● adv (s'arrêter □) dead; **à dix heures ~ □** at ten on the dot.

**pilier** /pilje/ nm pillar.

**pillage** /pijaʒ/ nm looting. **pillard, ~e** nm, f looter. **piller 1** vt loot.

**pilote** /pilɔt/ nm (Aviat, Naut) pilot; (Auto) driver. ● adj pilot. **piloter 1** vt (Aviat, Naut) pilot; (Auto) drive.

**pilule** /pilyl/ nf pill; **la ~** the pill.

**piment** /pimɑ̃/ nm hot pepper; (fig) spice. **pimenté, ~e** adj spicy.

**pin** /pɛ̃/ nm pine.

**pinard** /pinaʀ/ nm □ plonk □, cheap wine.

**pince** /pɛ̃s/ nf (outil) pliers (+ pl); (levier) crowbar; (de crabe) pincer; (à sucre) tongs (+ pl); **~ à épiler** tweezers (+ pl); **~ à linge** clothes peg.

**pinceau** (pl **~x**) /pɛ̃so/ nm paintbrush.

**pincée** /pɛ̃se/ nf pinch (de of).

**pincer** /pɛ̃se/ **10** vt pinch; (attraper □) catch. □ **se ~** vpr catch oneself; **se ~ le doigt** catch one's finger.

**pince-sans-rire** /pɛ̃ssɑ̃ʀiʀ/ nmf inv **c'est un ~** he has a deadpan sense of humour.

**pingouin** /pɛ̃gwɛ̃/ nm penguin.

**pingre** /pɛ̃gʀ/ adj □ stingy.

**pintade** /pɛ̃tad/ nf guinea fowl.

**piocher** /pjɔʃe/ **1** vt/i dig; (étudier □) study hard, slog away (at).

**pion** /pjɔ̃/ nm (de jeu) counter; (aux échecs) pawn; (Scol □) supervisor.

**pipe** /pip/ nf pipe; **fumer la ~** smoke a pipe.

**piquant, ~e** /pikɑ̃, -t/ adj (barbe) prickly; (goût) pungent; (remarque) cutting. ● nm picturesque.

**pique** /pik/ nm (aux cartes) spades. ● nf pique.

**pique-nique** (pl ~s) /piknik/ nm picnic.

**piquer** /pike/ **1** vt (épine) prick; (épice) burn, sting; (abeille, ortie) sting; (serpent, moustique) bite; (enfoncer) stick; (coudre) (machine-) stitch; (curiosité) excite; (voler 1) pinch. ● vi (avion) dive; (goût) be hot. □ **se ~** vpr prick oneself.

**piquet** /pike/ nm stake; (de tente) peg; (de parasol) pole; **~ de grève** (strike) picket.

**piqûre** /pikyʀ/ nf prick; (d'abeille) sting; (de serpent) bite; (point) stitch; (Méd) injection, jab; **faire une ~ à qn** give sb an injection.

**pirate** /piʀat/ nm pirate; **~ informatique** computer hacker; **~ de l'air** hijacker.

**pire** /piʀ/ adj worse (que than); **les ~s mensonges** the most wicked lies. ● nm **le ~** the worst; **au ~** at worst.

**pis** /pi/ nm (de vache) udder. ● adj inv & adv worse; **aller de mal en ~** go from bad to worse.

**piscine** /pisin/ nf swimming pool; **~ couverte** indoor swimming-pool.

**pissenlit** /pisɑ̃li/ nm dandelion.

**pistache** /pistaʃ/ nf pistachio.

**piste** /pist/ nf track; (de personne, d'animal) track, trail; (Aviat) runway; (de cirque) ring; (de ski) slope; (de danse) floor; (Sport) racetrack; **~ cyclable** cycle lane.

**pistolet** /pistolɛ/ nm gun, pistol; (de peintre) spray-gun.

**piteux, -euse** /pitø, -z/ adj pitiful.

**pitié** /pitje/ nf pity; **il me fait ~ I**

feel sorry for him.

**piton** /pitɔ̃/ nm (à crochet) hook; (sommet pointu) peak.

**pitoyable** /pitwajabl/ adj pitiful.

**pitre** /pitʀ/ nm clown; **faire le ~** clown around.

**pittoresque** /pitɔʀɛsk/ adj picturesque.

**pivot** /pivo/ nm pivot. **pivoter 1** vi revolve; (personne) swing round.

**placard** /plakaʀ/ nm cupboard; (affiche) poster. **placarder 1** vt (affiche) post up; (mur) cover with posters.

**place** /plas/ nf place; (espace libre) room, space; (siège) seat, place; (prix d'un trajet) fare; (esplanade) square; (emploi) position; (de parking) space; **à la ~ de** instead of; **en ~, à sa ~** in its place; **faire ~ à** give way to; **sur ~** on the spot; **remettre qn à sa ~** put sb in his place; **ça prend de la ~** it takes up a lot of room; **se mettre à la ~ de qn** put oneself in sb's shoes ou place.

**placement** /plasmɑ̃/ nm (d'argent) investment.

**placer** /plase/ **10** vt place; (invité, spectateur) seat; (argent) invest. □ **se ~** vpr (personne) take up a position.

**plafond** /plafɔ̃/ nm ceiling.

**plage** /plaʒ/ nf beach; **~ horaire** time slot.

**plagiat** /plaʒja/ nm plagiarism.

**plaider** /plede/ **1** vt/i plead. **plaidoirie** nf (defence) speech. **plaidoyer** nm plea.

**plaie** /plɛ/ nf wound; (personne 1) nuisance.

**plaignant, ~e** /plɛɲɑ̃, -t/ nm, f plaintiff.

**plaindre** /plɛ̃dʀ/ **22** vt pity. □ **se ~** vpr complain (de about); **se ~**

de (souffrir de) complain of.
**plaine** /plɛn/ nf plain.
**plainte** /plɛ̃t/ nf complaint; (gémissement) groan. **plaintif, -ive** adj plaintive.
**plaire** /plɛʀ/ 47 vi ~ à please; ça lui plaît he likes it; elle lui plaît he likes her; ça me plaît de faire I like ou enjoy doing; s'il vous plaît please. □ se ~ vpr il se plaît ici he likes it here.
**plaisance** /plɛzɑ̃s/ nf la (navigation de) ~ boating.
**plaisant, ~e** /plɛzɑ̃, -t/ adj pleasant; (drôle) amusing.
**plaisanter** /plɛzɑ̃te/ 1 vi joke. **plaisanterie** nf joke. **plaisantin** nm joker.
**plaisir** /plɛziʀ/ nm pleasure; faire ~ à please; pour le ~ for fun ou pleasure.
**plan** /plɑ̃/ nm plan; (de ville) map; (de livre) outline; ~ d'eau artificial lake; ~ social planned redundancy programme; **premier** ~ foreground.
**planche** /plɑ̃ʃ/ nf board, plank; (gravure) plate; ~ à repasser ironing-board; ~ à voile windsurfing board; (Sport) windsurfing.
**plancher** /plɑ̃ʃe/ nm floor.
**planer** /plane/ 1 vi glide; ~ sur (mystère, danger) hang over.
**planète** /planɛt/ nf planet.
**planeur** /planœʀ/ nm glider.
**planifier** /planifje/ 45 vt plan.
**plant** /plɑ̃/ nm seedling; (de légumes) patch.
**plante** /plɑ̃t/ nf plant; ~ d'appartement houseplant; ~ des pieds sole of the foot.
**planter** /plɑ̃te/ 1 vt (plante) plant; (enfoncer) drive in; (tente) put up; **rester planté** 1 stand still.
**plaque** /plak/ nf plate; (de marbre) slab; (insigne) badge; ~ **chauffante** hotplate; ~ **commémorative** plaque; ~ **minéralogique** numberplate; ~ **de verglas** patch of ice.
**plaquer** /plake/ 1 vt (bois) veneer; (aplatir) flatten; (rugby) tackle; (abandonner 1) ditch 1; **tout** ~ chuck it all.
**plastique** /plastik/ adj & nm plastic; **en** ~ plastic.
**plastiquer** /plastike/ 1 vt blow up.
**plat, ~e** /pla, -t/ adj flat. ● nm (Culin) dish; (partie de repas) course; (de la main) flat. ● **à plat** adv (poser) flat; (batterie, pneu) flat; **à** ~ **ventre** flat on one's face.
**platane** /platan/ nm plane tree.
**plateau** (pl ~x) /plato/ nm tray; (de cinéma) set; (de balance) pan; (Géog) plateau; ~ **de fromages** cheeseboard; ~ **de fruits de mer** seafood platter. **plate-bande** (pl **plates-bandes**) nf flower bed.
**platine** /platin/ nm platinum. ● nf (tourne-disque) turntable; ~ **laser** compact disc player.
**plâtre** /plɑtʀ/ nm plaster; (Méd) (plaster) cast.
**plein, ~e** /plɛ̃, -ɛn/ adj full (de of); (total) complete. ● nm faire le ~ (d'essence) fill up (the tank); **à** ~ fully; **à** ~ **temps** full-time; **en** ~ air in the open air; **en** ~ **milieu/ visage** right in the middle/the face; **en** ~ **nuit** in the middle of the night. ● adv avoir des idées ~ la tête be full of ideas. **pleinement** adv fully.
**pleurer** /plœʀe/ 1 vi cry, weep (sur over); (yeux) water. ● vt mourn.
**pleurnicher** /plœʀniʃe/ 1 vi snivel.

**pleurs** /plœʀ/ *nmpl* tears; **en ~** in tears.

**pleuvoir** /pløvwaʀ/ 48 *vi* rain; (fig) rain *ou* shower down; **il pleut** it is raining; **il pleut à verse** *ou* **des cordes** it is pouring.

**pli** /pli/ *nm* fold; (de jupe) pleat; (de pantalon) crease; (lettre) letter; (habitude) habit; (**faux ~**) crease.

**pliant, ~e** /plijɑ̃, -t/ *adj* folding. ●*nm* folding stool, camp-stool.

**plier** /plije/ 45 *vt* fold; (courber) bend; (soumettre) submit (**à** to). ●*vi* bend. □ **se ~** *vpr* fold; **se ~ à** submit to.

**plinthe** /plɛ̃t/ *nf* skirting-board.

**plissé, ~e** /plise/ *adj* (*jupe*) pleated.

**plisser** /plise/ 1 *vt* crease; (*yeux*) screw up.

**plomb** /plɔ̃/ *nm* lead; (fusible) fuse; **~s** (de chasse) lead shot; **de** *ou* **en ~** lead. **plombage** *nm* filling.

**plomberie** /plɔ̃bʀi/ *nf* plumbing. **plombier** *nm* plumber.

**plongée** /plɔ̃ʒe/ *nf* diving; **en ~** (*sous-marin*) submerged.

**plongeoir** /plɔ̃ʒwaʀ/ *nm* diving board.

**plonger** /plɔ̃ʒe/ 40 *vi* dive; (*route*) plunge. ●*vt* plunge. □ **se ~** *vpr* plunge into; **se ~ dans** (fig) (*lecture*) bury oneself in. **plongeur, -euse** *nm, f* diver; (de restaurant) dishwasher.

**plu** /ply/ ➡PLAIRE 47, PLEUVOIR 48.

**pluie** /plɥi/ *nf* rain; (averse) shower; **~ battante/diluvienne** driving/torrential rain.

**plume** /plym/ *nf* feather; (pointe) nib.

**plumeau** (*pl* **~x**) /plymo/ *nm* feather duster.

**plumier** /plymje/ *nm* pencil box.

**plupart: la ~** /laplypaʀ/ *loc* **la ~ des** (*gens, cas*) most; **la ~ du temps** most of the time; **pour la ~** for the most part.

**pluriel, ~le** /plyʀjɛl/ *adj & nm* plural.

**plus** /ply, plys, plyz/

●*adverbe de comparaison*

····▸more (**que** than); **~ âgé/tard** older/later; **~ beau** more beautiful; **~ j'y pense...** the more I think about it...; **deux fois ~** twice as much; **deux fois ~ cher** twice as expensive.

····▸**le ~** the most; **le ~ grand** the biggest; (de deux) the bigger.

····▸**~ de** (*pain*) more; (*dix jours*) more than; **il est ~ de 8 heures** it is after 8 o'clock.

····▸**de ~** more (**que** than); (en outre) moreover; **les enfants de ~ de 10 ans** children over 10 years old; **de ~ en ~** more and more.

····▸**en ~** on top of that; **c'est en ~** it's extra; **en ~ de** in addition to.

····▸**~ ou moins** more or less.

····▸**au ~ tard** at the latest.

●*adverbe de négation*

····▸**ne ~** (*temps*) no longer, not any more; **je n'y vais ~** I don't go there any longer *ou* any more.

····▸**ne ~ de** (quantité) no more; **il n'y a ~ de pain** there is no more bread.

····▸**~ que deux jours!** only two days left!

●*préposition & nom masculin*

····▸(maths) plus.

P

**plusieurs** /plyzjœr/ *adj & pron* several.

**plus-value** (*pl* ~s) /plyvaly/ *nf* (bénéfice) profit.

**plutôt** /plyto/ *adv* rather (que than).

**pluvieux, -ieuse** /plyvjø, -z/ *adj* rainy.

**PME** *abrév f* (petites et moyennes entreprises) SME.

**PNB** *abrév m* (produit national brut) GNP.

**pneu** (*pl* ~s) /pnø/ *nm* tyre. **pneumatique** *adj* inflatable.

**pneumonie** /pnømɔni/ *nf* pneumonia; ~ **atypique** severe acute respiratory syndrome.

**poche** /pɔʃ/ *nf* pocket; (sac) bag; ~s (sous les yeux) bags.

**pocher** /pɔʃe/ ① *vt* (œuf) poach.

**pochette** /pɔʃɛt/ *nf* (de documents) folder; (sac) bag, pouch; (d'allumettes) book; (de disque) sleeve; (mouchoir) pocket handkerchief.

**poêle** /pwal/ *nf* (~ à frire) frying-pan. ● *nm* stove.

**poème** /pɔɛm/ *nm* poem. **poésie** *nf* poetry; (poème) poem. **poète** *nm* poet. **poétique** *adj* poetic.

**poids** /pwa/ *nm* weight; ~ **coq/lourd/plume** bantamweight/heavyweight/featherweight; ~ **lourd** (camion) lorry, juggernaut; (US) truck.

**poignard** /pwaɲar/ *nm* dagger. **poignarder** ① *vt* stab.

**poigne** /pwaɲ/ *nf* avoir de la ~ have a strong grip.

**poignée** /pwaɲe/ *nf* (de porte) handle; (quantité) handful; ~ **de main** handshake.

**poignet** /pwaɲɛ/ *nm* wrist; (de chemise) cuff.

**poil** /pwal/ *nm* hair; (pelage) fur;

(de brosse) bristle; ~s (de tapis) pile; à ~ ☐ naked; ~ à **gratter** itching powder. **poilu, ~e** *adj* hairy.

**poinçon** /pwɛsɔ̃/ *nm* awl; (marque) hallmark. **poinçonner** ① *vt* (billet) punch.

**poing** /pwɛ̃/ *nm* fist.

**point** /pwɛ̃/ *nm* (endroit, Sport) point; (marque visible) spot, dot; (de couture) stitch; (pour évaluer) mark; **enlever un ~ par faute** take a mark off for each mistake; **à ~** (Culin) medium; (arriver) at the right time; **faire le ~** take stock; **mettre au ~** (photo) focus; (technique) develop; **mettre les choses au ~** get things clear; **Camille n'est pas encore au ~ pour ses examens** Camille is not ready for her exams; **sur le ~ de** about to; **au ~ que** to the extent that; (~ **final**) full stop, period; **deux ~s** colon; ~ **d'interrogation/d'exclamation** question/exclamation mark; ~s **de suspension** suspension points; ~ **virgule** semicolon; ~ **culminant** peak; ~ **du jour** daybreak; ~ **mort** (Auto) neutral; ~ **de repère** landmark; ~ **de suture** (Méd) stitch; ~ **de vente** point of sale; ~ **de vue** point of view. ● *adv* (ne) ~ not.

**pointe** /pwɛt/ *nf* point, tip; (clou) tack; (de grille) spike; (fig) touch (de of); **de** ~ (industrie) high-tech; **en** ~ pointed; **heure de** ~ peak hour; **sur la** ~ **des pieds** on tiptoe.

**pointer** /pwɛte/ ① *vt* (cocher) tick off; (diriger) point, aim. ● *vi* (employé) (en arrivant) clock in; (en sortant) clock out. ☐ **se** ~ *vpr* ☐ turn up.

**pointillé** /pwɛtije/ *nm* dotted line.

**pointilleux, -euse** /pwɛtijø, -z/ *adj* fastidious, particular.

**pointu, ~e** /pwɛty/ *adj* pointed; (aiguisé) sharp.

**pointure** /pwɛ̃tyʀ/ *nf* size.

**poire** /pwaʀ/ *nf* pear.

**poireau** (*pl* ~x) /pwaʀo/ *nm* leek.

**poirier** /pwaʀje/ *nm* pear tree.

**pois** /pwa/ *nm* pea; (*motif*) dot; robe à ~ polka dot dress.

**poison** /pwazɔ̃/ *nm* poison.

**poisseux, -euse** /pwasø, -z/ *adj* sticky.

**poisson** /pwasɔ̃/ *nm* fish; ~ rouge goldfish; ~ d'avril April fool; les P~s Pisces. **poissonnerie** *nf* fish shop. **poissonnier, -ière** *nm, f* fishmonger.

**poitrine** /pwatʀin/ *nf* chest; (*seins*) bosom.

**poivre** /pwavʀ/ *nm* pepper. **poivré, ~e** *adj* peppery. **poivrière** *nf* pepper-pot.

**poivron** /pwavʀɔ̃/ *nm* sweet pepper.

**polaire** /polɛʀ/ *adj* polar. ● *nf* (*veste*) fleece.

**pôle** /pol/ *nm* pole.

**polémique** /polemik/ *nf* debate. ● *adj* controversial.

**poli, ~e** /poli/ *adj* (*personne*) polite.

**police** /polis/ *nf* (*force*) police (+ *pl*); (*discipline*) (law and) order; (*d'assurance*) policy.

**policier, -ière** /polisje, -jɛʀ/ *adj* police; (*roman*) detective. ● *nm* policeman.

**polir** /poliʀ/ [2] *vt* polish.

**politesse** /polites/ *nf* politeness; (*parole*) polite remark.

**politicien, ~ne** /politisjɛ̃, -ɛn/ *nm, f* (*péj*) politician.

**politique** /politik/ *adj* political; homme ~ politician. ● *nf* politics; (*ligne de conduite*) policy.

**pollen** /polɛn/ *nm* pollen.

**polluant, ~e** /polɥɑ̃, -t/ *adj* polluting. ● *nm* pollutant.

**polluer** /polɥe/ [1] *vt* pollute. **pollution** *nf* pollution.

**polo** /polo/ *nm* (Sport) polo; (*vêtement*) polo shirt.

**Pologne** /polɔɲ/ *nf* Poland.

**polonais, -e** /polonɛ, -z/ *adj* Polish. ● *nm* (Ling) Polish. **P~, ~e** *nm, f* Pole.

**poltron, ~ne** /poltʀɔ̃, -ɔn/ *adj* cowardly. ● *nm, f* coward.

**polygame** /poligam/ *nmf* polygamist.

**polyvalent, ~e** /polivalɑ̃, -t/ *adj* varied; (*personne*) versatile.

**pommade** /pomad/ *nf* ointment.

**pomme** /pom/ *nf* apple; (*d'arrosoir*) rose; ~ d'Adam Adam's apple; ~ de pin pine cone; ~ de terre potato; ~s frites chips; (US) French fries; tomber dans les ~s [1] pass out.

**pommette** /pomɛt/ *nf* cheekbone.

**pommier** /pomje/ *nm* apple tree.

**pompe** /pɔ̃p/ *nf* pump; (*splendeur*) pomp; ~ à incendie fire engine; ~s funèbres undertaker's (+ *sg*).

**pomper** /pɔ̃pe/ [1] *vt* pump; (*copier* [1]) copy, crib; ~ l'air à qn [1] get on sb's nerves.

**pompier** /pɔ̃pje/ *nm* fireman.

**pomponner (se)** /(sə)pɔ̃pone/ [1] *vpr* get dolled up.

**poncer** /pɔ̃se/ [10] *vt* sand.

**ponctuation** /pɔ̃ktɥasjɔ̃/ *nf* punctuation.

**ponctuel, ~le** /pɔ̃ktɥel/ *adj* punctual.

**pondre** /pɔ̃dʀ/ [3] *vt/i* lay.

**poney** /ponɛ/ *nm* pony.

**pont** /pɔ̃/ *nm* bridge; (*de navire*) deck; (*de graissage*) ramp; faire le ~ get an extended weekend; ~ aérien airlift. **pont-levis** (*pl* **ponts-**

levis /ləvi/ nm drawbridge.

**populaire** /pɔpylɛʀ/ adj popular; (expression) colloquial; (quartier, origine) working-class. **popularité** nf popularity.

**population** /pɔpylasjɔ̃/ nf population.

**porc** /pɔʀ/ nm pig; (viande) pork.

**porcelaine** /pɔʀsəlɛn/ nf china, porcelain.

**porc-épic** (pl **porcs-épics**) /pɔʀkepik/ nm porcupine.

**porcherie** /pɔʀʃəʀi/ nf pigsty.

**pornographie** /pɔʀnɔgʀafi/ nf pornography.

**port** /pɔʀ/ nm port, harbour; à bon ∼ safely; ∼ maritime seaport; (transport) carriage; (d'armes) carrying; (de barbe) wearing.

**portable** /pɔʀtabl/ nm (Ordinat) laptop (computer); (telephone) mobile (phone).

**portail** /pɔʀtaj/ nm gate.

**portatif, -ive** /pɔʀtatif, -v/ adj portable.

**porte** /pɔʀt/ nf door; (passage) doorway; (de jardin, d'embarquement) gate; mettre à la ∼ throw out; ∼ d'entrée front door.

**porté, ~e** /pɔʀte/ adj ∼ à inclined to; ∼ sur keen on.

**porte-avions** /pɔʀtavjɔ̃/ nm inv aircraft carrier.

**porte-bagages** /pɔʀtbagaʒ/ nm inv (de vélo) carrier.

**porte-bonheur** /pɔʀtbɔnœʀ/ nm inv lucky charm.

**porte-clefs** /pɔʀtəkle/ nm inv key ring.

**porte-documents** /pɔʀtdɔkymɑ̃/ nm inv briefcase.

**portée** /pɔʀte/ nf (d'une arme) range; (de voûte) span; (d'animaux) litter; (impact) significance; (Mus)

stave; à ∼ de (la) main within (arm's) reach; hors de ∼ (de) out of reach (of); à la ∼ de qn at sb's level.

**porte-fenêtre** (pl **portes-fenêtres**) /pɔʀtfənɛtʀ/ nf French window.

**portefeuille** /pɔʀtəfœj/ nm wallet; (de ministre) portfolio.

**porte-jarretelles** /pɔʀtʒaʀtɛl/ nm inv suspender belt.

**portemanteau** (pl ∼x) /pɔʀtmɑ̃to/ nm coat ou hat stand.

**porte-monnaie** /pɔʀtmɔnɛ/ nm purse.

**porte-parole** /pɔʀtpaʀɔl/ nm inv spokesperson.

**porter** /pɔʀte/ **1** vt carry; (vêtement, bague) wear; (fruits, responsabilité, nom) bear; (coup) strike; (amener) bring; (inscrire) enter. ●vi (bruit) carry; (coup) hit home; ∼ sur rest on; (concerner) be about. □ se ∼ vpr bien se ∼ be ou feel well; se ∼ candidat stand as a candidate.

**porteur, -euse** /pɔʀtœʀ, -øz/ nm, f (de nouvelles) bearer; (Méd) carrier. ●nm (Rail) porter.

**portier** /pɔʀtje/ nm doorman.

**portière** /pɔʀtjɛʀ/ nf door.

**porto** /pɔʀto/ nm port (wine).

**portrait** /pɔʀtʀɛ/ nm portrait. **portrait-robot** (pl **portraits-robots**) nm identikit®, photofit®.

**portuaire** /pɔʀtɥɛʀ/ adj port.

**portugais, ~e** /pɔʀtygɛ, -z/ adj Portuguese. ●nm (Ling) Portuguese. **P∼, ~e** nm, f Portuguese.

**Portugal** /pɔʀtygal/ nm Portugal.

**pose** /poz/ nf installation; (attitude) pose; (Photo) exposure.

**posé, ~e** /poze/ adj calm, serious.

**poser** /poze/ **1** vt put (down); (installer) install, put in; (fondations) lay; (*question*) ask; (*problème*) pose; ~ sa candidature apply (à for). ●*vi* (*modèle*) pose. □ se ~ *vpr* (*avion, oiseau*) land; (*regard*) fall; (se présenter) arise.

**positif, -ive** /pozitif, -v/ *adj* positive.

**position** /pozisjɔ̃/ *nf* position; prendre ~ take a stand.

**posologie** /pozolɔʒi/ *nf* dosage.

**posséder** /posede/ [14] *vt* (*propriété*) own, possess; (*diplôme*) have.

**possessif, -ive** /posesif, -v/ *adj* possessive.

**possession** /posesjɔ̃/ *nf* possession; prendre ~ de take possession of.

**possibilité** /posibilite/ *nf* possibility.

**possible** /posibl/ *adj* possible; dès que ~ as soon as possible; le plus tard ~ as late as possible. ●*nm* le ~ what is possible; faire son ~ do one's utmost.

**postal** /postal, -o/ (*mpl* **-aux**) *adj* postal.

**poste**¹ /post/ *nf* (service) post; (bureau) post office; (~ aérienne airmail; mettre à la ~ post; ~ restante poste restante. ●*nm* (lieu, emploi) post; (de radio, télévision) set; (téléphone) extension (number); ~ d'essence petrol station; ~ d'incendie fire point; ~ de pilotage cockpit; ~ de police police station; ~ de secours first-aid post.

**poster**¹ /poste/ [1] *vt* (*lettre, personne*) post.

**poster**² /pɔstɛʀ/ *nm* poster.

**postérieur, -e** /posterjœʀ/ *adj* later; (*partie*) back; ~ à after. ●*nm* [1] posterior.

**posthume** /postym/ *adj* posthumous.

**postiche** /postiʃ/ *adj* false.

**postier, -ière** /postje, -jɛʀ/ *nm, f* postal worker.

**post-scriptum** /pɔstskʀiptɔm/ *nm inv* postscript.

**postuler** /postyle/ [1] *vt/i* apply (à for); (*principe*) postulate.

**pot** /po/ *nm* pot; (en plastique) carton; (en verre) jar; (chance [1]) luck; (boisson [1]) drink; ~ catalytique catalytic converter; ~ d'échappement exhaust pipe.

**potable** /potabl/ *adj* eau ~ drinking water.

**potage** /potaʒ/ *nm* soup.

**potager, -ère** /potaʒe, -ɛʀ/ *adj* vegetable. ●*nm* vegetable garden.

**pot-au-feu** /pɔtofø/ *nm inv* (plat) stew.

**pot-de-vin** (*pl* **pots-de-vin**) /podvɛ̃/ *nm* bribe.

**poteau** (*pl* **~x**) /poto/ *nm* post; (télégraphique) pole; ~ indicateur signpost.

**potelé, -e** /potle/ *adj* plump.

**potentiel, -le** /potɑ̃sjɛl/ *adj & nm* potential.

**poterie** /potʀi/ *nf* pottery; (objet) piece of pottery. **potier** *nm* potter.

**potins** /potɛ̃/ *nmpl* gossip (+ *sg*).

**potiron** /potiʀɔ̃/ *nm* pumpkin.

**pou** (*pl* **~x**) /pu/ *nm* louse.

**poubelle** /pubɛl/ *nf* dustbin.

**pouce** /pus/ *nm* thumb; (de pied) big toe; (mesure) inch.

**poudre** /pudʀ/ *nf* powder; (~ à canon) gunpowder; en (*lait*) powdered; (*chocolat*) drinking.

**poudrier** /pudʀije/ *nm* (powder) compact.

**pouf** /puf/ *nm* pouffe.

**poulailler** /pulaje/ *nm* henhouse.

**poulain** /pulɛ̃/ *nm* foal; (protégé) protégé.

**poule** /pul/ *nf* hen; (Culin) fowl;

(femme ⊠) tart.

**poulet** /pulɛ/ nm chicken.

**pouliche** /puliʃ/ nf filly.

**poulie** /puli/ nf pulley.

**pouls** /pu/ nm pulse.

**poumon** /pumɔ̃/ nm lung.

**poupe** /pup/ nf stern.

**poupée** /pupe/ nf doll.

**pour** /puʀ/ prép for; (envers) to; (à la place de) on behalf of; (comme) as; ~ cela for that reason; ~ cent per cent; ~ de bon for good; ~ faire (in order) to do; ~ que so that; ~ moi (à mon avis) as for me; trop poli ~ too polite to; ~ ce qui est de as for; être ~ be in favour. ● nm inv le ~ et le contre the pros and cons.

**pourboire** /puʀbwaʀ/ nm tip.

**pourcentage** /puʀsɑ̃taʒ/ nm percentage.

**pourparlers** /puʀpaʀle/ nmpl talks.

**pourpre** /puʀpʀ/ adj & nm crimson; (violet) purple.

**pourquoi** /puʀkwa/ conj & adv why. ● nm inv le ~ et le comment the why and the wherefore.

**pourra, pourrait** /puʀa, puʀɛ/ →POUVOIR 49.

**pourri**, ~e /puʀi/ adj rotten.

**pourrir** 2 vt/i rot. **pourriture** nf rot.

**poursuite** /puʀsɥit/ nf pursuit (de of); ~s (Jur) legal action (+ sg).

**poursuivre** /puʀsɥivʀ/ 57 vt pursue; (continuer) continue (with); ~ (en justice) take to court; (droit civil) sue. ● vi continue. □ se ~ vpr continue.

**pourtant** /puʀtɑ̃/ adv yet.

**pourvoir** /puʀvwaʀ/ 63 vi ~ à provide for; **pourvu de** supplied with.

**pourvu que** /puʀvyk(ə)/ conj (condition) provided (that); (souhait) let us hope (that).

**pousse** /pus/ nf growth; (bourgeon) shoot.

**poussé**, ~e /puse/ adj (études) advanced; (enquête) thorough.

**poussée** /puse/ nf pressure; (coup) push; (de prix) upsurge; (Méd) attack.

**pousser** /puse/ ① vt push; (cri) let out; (soupir) heave; (continuer) continue; (exhorter) urge (à to); (forcer) drive (à to). ● vi push; (grandir) grow; faire ~ (cheveux) let grow; (plante) grow. □ se ~ vpr move over ou up; pousse-toi! move over!

**poussette** /pusɛt/ nf pushchair.

**poussière** /pusjɛʀ/ nf dust. **poussiéreux**, -euse adj dusty.

**poussin** /pusɛ̃/ nm chick.

**poutre** /putʀ/ nf beam; (en métal) girder.

**pouvoir** /puvwaʀ/ 49 v aux (possibilité) can, be able; (permission, éventualité) may, can; il peut/pouvait/pourrait venir he can/could/might come; je n'ai pas pu I couldn't; j'ai pu faire (réussi à) I managed to do; je n'en peux plus I am exhausted; il se peut que it may be that. ● nm power; (gouvernement) government; au ~ in power; ~s publics authorities.

**prairie** /pʀeʀi/ nf meadow.

**praticien**, ~ne /pʀatisjɛ̃, -ɛn/ nm, f practitioner.

**pratiquant**, ~e /pʀatikɑ̃, -t/ adj practising. ● nm, f churchgoer.

**pratique** /pʀatik/ adj practical. ● nf practice; (expérience) experience; la ~ du golf/du cheval golfing/riding. **pratiquement** adv (en pratique) in practice; (presque) practically.

**pratiquer** /pʀatike/ **1** vt/i practise; (Sport) play; (faire) make.

**pré** /pʀe/ nm meadow.

**pré-affranchi, ~e** /pʀeafʀɑ̃ʃi/ adj postage-paid.

**préalable** /pʀealabl/ adj preliminary, prior. ● nm precondition; au ~ first.

**préambule** /pʀeɑ̃byl/ nm preamble.

**préavis** /pʀeavi/ nm notice.

**précaire** /pʀekɛʀ/ adj precarious. **précarité** nf (d'emploi) insecurity.

**précaution** /pʀekosjɔ̃/ nf (mesure) precaution; (prudence) caution.

**précédent, ~e** /pʀesedɑ̃, -t/ adj previous. ● nm precedent.

**précéder** /pʀesede/ **14** vt/i precede.

**précepteur, -trice** /pʀesɛptœʀ, -tʀis/ nm,f (private) tutor.

**prêcher** /pʀeʃe/ **1** vt/i preach.

**précieux, -ieuse** /pʀesjø, -z/ adj precious.

**précipitamment** /pʀesipitamɑ̃/ adv hastily. **précipitation** nf haste.

**précipiter** /pʀesipite/ **1** vt throw, precipitate; (hâter) hasten. □ se ~ vpr (se dépêcher) rush (sur at, on to); (se jeter) throw oneself; (s'accélérer) speed up.

**précis, ~e** /pʀesi, -z/ adj precise, specific; (mécanisme) accurate; **dix heures ~es** ten o'clock sharp. ● nm summary.

**préciser** /pʀesize/ **1** vt specify; **précisez votre pensée** could you be more specific. □ se ~ vpr become clear(er). **précision** nf precision; (détail) detail.

**précoce** /pʀekɔs/ adj (enfant) precocious.

**préconiser** /pʀekɔnize/ **1** vt advocate.

**précurseur** /pʀekyʀsœʀ/ nm forerunner.

**prédicateur** /pʀedikatœʀ/ nm preacher.

**prédilection** /pʀedilɛksjɔ̃/ nf preference.

**prédire** /pʀediʀ/ **37** vt predict.

**prédominer** /pʀedɔmine/ **1** vi predominate.

**préface** /pʀefas/ nf preface.

**préfecture** /pʀefɛktyʀ/ nf préfecture; ~ de police police headquarters.

**préféré, ~e** /pʀefeʀe/ adj & nm, f favourite.

**préférence** /pʀefeʀɑ̃s/ nf preference; de ~ preferably.

**préférentiel, ~le** /pʀefeʀɑ̃sjɛl/ adj preferential.

**préférer** /pʀefeʀe/ **14** vt prefer (à to); ~ **faire** prefer to do; **je ne préfère pas** I'd rather not; **j'aurais préféré ne pas savoir** I wish I hadn't found out.

**préfet** /pʀefɛ/ nm prefect; ~ de police prefect ou chief of police.

**préfixe** /pʀefiks/ nm prefix.

**préhistorique** /pʀeistɔʀik/ adj prehistoric.

**préjudice** /pʀeʒydis/ nm harm, prejudice; **porter** ~ à harm.

**préjugé** /pʀeʒyʒe/ nm prejudice; **être plein de ~s** be very prejudiced.

**prélasser (se)** /(sə)pʀelɑse/ **1** vpr loll (about).

**prélèvement** /pʀelɛvmɑ̃/ nm deduction; (de sang) sample. **prélever** **6** vt deduct (sur from); (sang) take.

**préliminaire** /pʀeliminɛʀ/ adj & nm preliminary; ~s (sexuels) foreplay.

**prématuré, ~e** /pʀematyʀe/ adj

**p**

premature. ● *nm* premature baby.

**premier, -ière** /prəmje, -jɛr/ *adj* first; (*rang*) front, first; (*enfance*) early; (*nécessité, souci*) prime; (*qualité*) top, prime; **de ~ ordre** first-rate; **~ ministre** Prime Minister. ● *nm, f* first (one). ● *nm* (*date*) first; (*étage*) first floor; **en ~** first. **première** *nf* (Rail) first class; (*exploit jamais vu*) first; (*cinéma, Théât*) première; (Aut) (*vitesse*) first (gear). **premièrement** *adv* firstly.

**prémunir** /prɛmynir/ [2] *vt* protect (**contre** against).

**prenant, ~e** /prənã, -t/ *adj* (*activité*) engrossing; (*enfant*) demanding.

**prénatal, ~e** (*mpl* **~s**) /prɛnatal/ *adj* antenatal.

**prendre** /prãdr/ [50] *vt* take; (*attraper*) catch, get; (*acheter*) get; (*repas*) have; (*engager, adopter*) take on; (*poids*) put on; (*chercher*) pick up; **qu'est-ce qui te prend?** what's the matter with you? ● *vi* (*liquide*) set; (*feu*) catch; (*vaccin*) take. □ **se ~** *vpr* **se ~ pour** think one is; **s'en ~ à** attack; (*rendre responsable*) blame; **s'y ~** set about (it).

**preneur, -euse** /prənœr, -øz/ *nm, f* buyer; **être ~** be willing to buy; **trouver ~** find a buyer.

**prénom** /prɛnɔ̃/ *nm* first name.

**prénommer** /prɛnɔme/ [1] *vt* call. □ **se ~** *vpr* be called.

**préoccupation** /prɛɔkypasjɔ̃/ *nf* (*souci*) worry; (*idée fixe*) preoccupation.

**préoccuper** /prɛɔkype/ [1] *vt* worry; (*absorber*) preoccupy. □ **se ~ de** *vpr* think about.

**préparation** /prɛparasjɔ̃/ *nf* preparation. **préparatoire** *adj* preparatory.

**préparer** /prɛpare/ [1] *vt* prepare;

(*repas, café*) make; **plats préparés** ready-cooked meals. □ **se ~** *vpr* prepare oneself (**à** for); (*s'apprêter*) get ready; (*être proche*) be brewing.

**préposé, ~e** /prɛpoze/ *nm, f* employee; (*des postes*) postman, postwoman.

**préposition** /prɛpozisjɔ̃/ *nf* preposition.

**préretraite** /prɛrətrɛt/ *nf* early retirement.

**près** /prɛ/ *adv* near, close; **~ de** near (to), close to; (*presque*) nearly; **à cela ~** except that; **de ~** closely.

**présage** /prɛzaʒ/ *nm* omen.

**presbyte** /prɛsbit/ *adj* long-sighted, far-sighted.

**prescrire** /prɛskrir/ [30] *vt* prescribe.

**préséance** /prɛseãs/ *nf* precedence.

**présence** /prɛzãs/ *nf* presence; (Scol) attendance.

**présent, ~e** /prɛzã, -t/ *adj* present. ● *nm* (*temps, cadeau*) present; **à ~** now.

**présentateur, -trice** /prɛzãtatœr, -tris/ *nm, f* presenter.

**présentation** /prɛzãtasjɔ̃/ *nf* (*de personne*) introduction; (*exposé*) presentation.

**présenter** /prɛzãte/ [1] *vt* present; (*personne*) introduce (**à** to); (*montrer*) show. ● *vi* **~ bien** have a pleasing appearance. □ **se ~** *vpr* introduce oneself (**à** to); (*aller*) go; (*apparaître*) appear; (*candidat*) come forward; (*occasion*) arise; **se ~ à** (*examen*) sit for; (*élection*) stand for; **se ~ bien** look good.

**préservatif** /prɛzɛrvatif/ *nm* condom.

**préserver** /prɛzɛrve/ [1] *vt* protect.

**présidence** /pʀezidɑ̃s/ nf (d'État) presidency; (de société) chairmanship.

**président, ~e** /pʀezidɑ̃, -t/ nm, f president; (de société, comité) chairman, chairwoman; **~-directeur général** managing director.

**présidentiel, ~le** /pʀezidɑ̃sjɛl/ adj presidential.

**présider** /pʀezide/ **1** vt preside.

**présomptueux, -euse** /pʀezɔ̃ptɥø, -z/ adj presumptuous.

**presque** /pʀɛsk(ə)/ adv almost, nearly; **~ jamais** hardly ever; **~ rien** hardly anything; **~ pas (de)** hardly any.

**presqu'île** /pʀɛskil/ nf peninsula.

**pressant, ~e** /pʀesɑ̃, -t/ adj pressing, urgent.

**presse** /pʀɛs/ nf (journaux, appareil) press.

**pressentiment** /pʀesɑ̃timɑ̃/ nm premonition. **pressentir** 46 vt have a premonition of.

**pressé, ~e** /pʀese/ adj in a hurry; (orange, citron) freshly squeezed.

**presser** /pʀese/ **1** vt squeeze, press; (appuyer sur, harceler) press; (hâter) hasten; (inciter) urge (de to). ● vi (temps) press; (affaire) be pressing. □ **se ~** vpr (se hâter) hurry; (se grouper) crowd.

**pressing** /pʀesiŋ/ nm (teinturerie) dry-cleaner's.

**pression** /pʀesjɔ̃/ nf pressure; (bouton) press-stud.

**prestance** /pʀɛstɑ̃s/ nf (imposing) presence.

**prestation** /pʀɛstasjɔ̃/ nf allowance; (d'artiste) performance.

**prestidigitation** /pʀɛstidiʒitasjɔ̃/ nf conjuring.

**prestige** /pʀɛstiʒ/ nm prestige.

**prestigieux, -ieuse** adj prestigious.

**présumé, e** /pʀezyme/ adj alleged.

**présumer** /pʀezyme/ **1** vt presume; **~ que** assume that; **~ de** overrate.

**prêt, ~e** /pʀɛ, -t/ adj ready (à qch for sth, à faire to do). ● nm loan.

**prêt-à-porter** nm inv ready-to-wear clothes.

**prétendre** /pʀetɑ̃dʀ/ **3** vt claim (que that); (vouloir) intend; on le prétend riche he is said to be very rich. **prétendu, ~e** adj so-called. **prétendument** adv supposedly, allegedly.

**prétentieux, -ieuse** /pʀetɑ̃sjø, -z/ adj pretentious.

**prêter** /pʀete/ **1** vt lend (à to); (attribuer) attribute; **~ son aide à qn** give sb some help; **~ attention** pay attention; **~ serment** take an oath. ● vi **~ à** lead to.

**prêteur, -euse** /pʀetœʀ, -øz/ nm, f (money-)lender; **~ sur gages** pawnbroker.

**prétexte** /pʀetɛkst/ nm pretext, excuse.

**prêtre** /pʀɛtʀ/ nm priest.

**preuve** /pʀœv/ nf proof; des **~s** evidence (+ sg); **faire ~ de** show; **faire ses ~s** prove oneself.

**prévaloir** /pʀevalwaʀ/ 60 vi prevail.

**prévenant, ~e** /pʀevnɑ̃, -t/ adj thoughtful.

**prévenir** /pʀevniʀ/ 58 vt (menacer) warn; (informer) tell; (médecin) call; (éviter, anticiper) prevent.

**préventif, -ive** /pʀevɑ̃tif, -v/ adj preventive.

**prévention** /pʀevɑ̃sjɔ̃/ nf prevention; **faire de la ~** take preventive action; **~ routière** road safety.

**prévenu, ~e** /pʀevny/ nm, f defendant.

P

**prévisible** /pʀevizibl/ adj predict-able. **prévision** nf prediction; (météorologique) forecast.

**prévoir** /pʀevwaʀ/ [63] vt foresee; (temps) forecast; (organiser) plan (for); (envisager) allow (for); **prévu pour** (jouet) designed for; **comme prévu** as planned.

**prévoyance** /pʀevwajɑ̃s/ nf foresight. **prévoyant, ~e** adj farsighted.

**prier** /pʀije/ [45] vi pray. ● vt pray to; (demander à) ask (de to); **je vous en prie** please; (il n'y a pas de quoi) don't mention it.

**prière** /pʀijɛʀ/ nf prayer; (demande) request; **~ de** (vous êtes prié de) will you please.

**primaire** /pʀimɛʀ/ adj primary.

**prime** /pʀim/ nf free gift; (d'employé) bonus; (subvention) subsidy; (d'assurance) premium.

**primé, ~e** /pʀime/ adj prize-winning.

**primeurs** /pʀimœʀ/ nfpl early fruit and vegetables.

**primevère** /pʀimvɛʀ/ nf primrose.

**primitif, -ive** /pʀimitif, -v/ adj primitive; (d'origine) original. ● nm, f primitive.

**primordial, ~e** (mpl **-iaux**) /pʀimɔʀdjal, -jo/ adj essential.

**prince** /pʀɛ̃s/ nm prince. **princesse** nf princess.

**principal, ~e** (mpl **-aux**) /pʀɛ̃sipal, -o/ adj main, principal. ● nm headmaster; (chose) main thing.

**principe** /pʀɛ̃sip/ nm principle; **en ~** in theory; (d'habitude) as a rule.

**printanier, -ière** /pʀɛ̃tanje, -jɛʀ/ adj spring(-like).

**printemps** /pʀɛ̃tɑ̃/ nm spring.

**prioritaire** /pʀijɔʀitɛʀ/ adj prior-

ity; **être ~** have priority. **priorité** nf priority; (Auto) right of way.

> **Priorité à droite** Except at roundabouts, and unless there are other indications or regulations in force, French drivers must always give way to traffic approaching from the right.

**pris, ~e** /pʀi, -z/ adj (place) taken; (personne, journée) busy; (nez) stuffed up; **~ de** (peur, fièvre) stricken with; **~ de panique** panic-stricken. ● ⇒PRENDRE [50].

**prise** /pʀiz/ nf hold, grip; (animal attrapé) catch; (Mil) capture; (~ de courant) (mâle) plug; (femelle) socket; **~ multiple** multiplug adapter; **avoir ~ sur qn** have a hold over sb; **aux ~s avec** to grapple with; **~ de conscience** awareness; **~ de contact** first contact, initial meeting; **~ de position** stand; **~ de sang** blood test.

**prisé, ~e** /pʀize/ adj popular.

**prison** /pʀizɔ̃/ nf prison, jail; (réclusion) imprisonment. **prisonnier, -ière** nm, f prisoner.

**privation** /pʀivasjɔ̃/ nf deprivation; (sacrifice) hardship.

**privatiser** /pʀivatize/ [1] vt privatize.

**privé** /pʀive/ adj private. ● nm (Comm) private sector; (Scol) private schools (+ pl); **en ~** in private.

**priver** /pʀive/ [1] vt **~ de** deprive of. □ **se ~ (de)** vpr go without.

**privilège** /pʀivilɛʒ/ nm privilege. **privilégié, ~e** nm, f privileged person.

**prix** /pʀi/ nm price; (récompense) prize; **à tout ~** at all costs; **au ~ de** (fig) at the expense of; **~ coûtant, ~ de revient** cost price; **à ~ fixe** set price.

**probabilité** /pʀɔbabilite/ nf probability. **probable** adj probable, likely. **probablement** adv probably.

**probant**, ~e /pʀɔbɑ̃, -t/ adj convincing, conclusive.

**problème** /pʀɔblɛm/ nm problem.

**procédé** /pʀɔsede/ nm process; (manière d'agir) practice.

**procéder** /pʀɔsede/ 14 vi proceed; ~ à carry out.

**procès** /pʀɔsɛ/ nm (criminel) trial; (civil) lawsuit, proceedings (+ pl).

**processus** /pʀɔsesys/ nm process; ~ de paix peace process.

**procès-verbal** (pl **procès-verbaux**) /pʀɔsɛvɛʀbal, -o/ nm minutes (+ pl); (contravention) ticket.

**prochain**, ~e /pʀɔʃɛ̃, -ɛn/ adj (suivant) next; (proche) imminent; (avenir) near. ● nm fellow man. **prochainement** adv soon.

**proche** /pʀɔʃ/ adj near, close; (avoisinant) neighbouring; (parent, ami) close; ~ de close ou near to; de ~ en ~ gradually; dans un ~ avenir in the near future; être ~ (imminent) to be approaching. ● nm close relative; (ami) close friend.

**Proche-Orient** /pʀɔʃɔʀjɑ̃/ nm Near East.

**proclamation** /pʀɔklamasjɔ̃/ nf declaration, proclamation. **proclamer** 1 vt declare, proclaim.

**procuration** /pʀɔkyʀasjɔ̃/ nf proxy.

**procurer** /pʀɔkyʀe/ 1 vt bring (à to). □ se ~ vpr obtain.

**procureur** /pʀɔkyʀœʀ/ nm public prosecutor.

**prodige** /pʀɔdiʒ/ nm (fait) marvel; (personne) prodigy; enfant/musicien ~ child/musical prodigy. **prodigieux**, **-ieuse** adj tremendous, prodigious.

**prodigue** /pʀɔdig/ adj wasteful;

fils ~ prodigal son.

**producteur**, **-trice** /pʀɔdyktœʀ, -tʀis/ adj producing. ● nm, f producer. **productif**, **-ive** adj productive. **production** nf production; (produit) product. **productivité** nf productivity.

**produire** /pʀɔdɥiʀ/ 17 vt produce. □ se ~ vpr (survenir) happen; (acteur) perform.

**produit** /pʀɔdɥi/ nm product; ~s (de la terre) produce (+ sg) ; ~ chimique chemical; ~s alimentaires foodstuffs; ~ de consommation consumer goods; ~ intérieur brut gross domestic product; ~ national brut gross national product.

**proéminent**, ~e /pʀɔeminɑ̃, -t/ adj prominent.

**profane** /pʀɔfan/ adj secular. ● nmf lay person.

**proférer** /pʀɔfeʀe/ 14 vt utter.

**professeur** /pʀɔfesœʀ/ nm teacher; (Univ) lecturer; (avec chaire) professor.

**profession** /pʀɔfesjɔ̃/ nf occupation; ~ libérale profession.

**professionnel**, **-le** /pʀɔfesjɔnɛl/ adj professional; (école) vocational. ● nm, f professional.

**profil** /pʀɔfil/ nm profile.

**profit** /pʀɔfi/ nm profit; au ~ de in aid of. **profitable** adj profitable.

**profiter** /pʀɔfite/ 1 vi ~ à benefit; ~ de take advantage of.

**profond**, ~e /pʀɔfɔ̃, -d/ adj deep; (sentiment, intérêt) profound; (causes) underlying; au plus ~ de in the depths of. **profondément** adv deeply; (différent, triste) profoundly; (dormir) soundly. **profondeur** nf depth.

**progéniture** /pʀɔʒenityʀ/ nf offspring.

**progiciel** /pʀɔʒisjɛl/ nm (Ordinat)

P

package.

**programmation** /pʀɔgʀamasjɔ̃/ nf programming.

**programme** /pʀɔgʀam/ nm programme; (Scol) (d'une matière) syllabus; (général) curriculum; (Ordinat) program. **programmer 1** vt (ordinateur, appareil) program; (émission) schedule. **programmeur, -euse** nm, f computer programmer.

**progrès** /pʀɔgʀɛ/ nm & nmpl progress; faire des ~ make progress. **progresser 1** vi progress. **progressif, -ive** adj progressive. **progression** nf progression.

**prohibitif, -ive** /pʀɔibitif, -v/ adj prohibitive.

**proie** /pʀwa/ nf prey; en ~ à tormented by.

**projecteur** /pʀɔʒɛktœʀ/ nm floodlight; (Mil) searchlight; (cinéma) projector.

**projectile** /pʀɔʒɛktil/ nm missile.

**projection** /pʀɔʒɛksjɔ̃/ nf projection; (séance) show.

**projet** /pʀɔʒɛ/ nm plan; (ébauche) draft; ~ de loi bill.

**projeter** /pʀɔʒte/ 38 vt (prévoir) plan (de to); (film) project, show; (jeter) hurl, project.

**prolétaire** /pʀɔletɛʀ/ nmf proletarian.

**prologue** /pʀɔlɔg/ nm prologue.

**prolongation** /pʀɔlɔ̃gasjɔ̃/ nf extension; ~s (football) extra time.

**prolonger** /pʀɔlɔ̃ʒe/ 40 vt extend. □ se ~ vpr go on.

**promenade** /pʀɔmnad/ nf walk; (à bicyclette, à cheval) ride; (en auto) drive, ride; faire une ~ go for a walk.

**promener** /pʀɔmne/ 6 vt take for a walk; ~ son regard sur cast an eye over. □ se ~ vpr walk; (aller) se ~ go for a walk. **prome-**

**neur, -euse** nm, f walker.

**promesse** /pʀɔmɛs/ nf promise.

**prometteur, -euse** /pʀɔmɛtœʀ, -øz/ adj promising.

**promettre** /pʀɔmɛtʀ/ 42 vt/i promise. ● vi be promising. □ se ~ de vpr resolve to.

**promoteur** /pʀɔmɔtœʀ/ nm (immobilier) property developer.

**promotion** /pʀɔmɔsjɔ̃/ nf promotion; (Univ) year; (Comm) special offer.

**prompt,** ~e /pʀɔ̃, -t/ adj swift.

**promu,** ~e /pʀɔmy/ adj être ~ be promoted.

**prôner** /pʀone/ 1 vt extol.

**pronom** /pʀɔnɔ̃/ nm pronoun. **pronominal,** ~e (mpl -aux) adj pronominal.

**prononcé,** ~e /pʀɔnɔ̃se/ adj strong.

**prononcer** /pʀɔnɔ̃se/ 10 vt pronounce; (discours) make. □ se ~ vpr (mot) be pronounced; (personne) make a decision (pour in favour of). **prononciation** nf pronunciation.

**pronostic** /pʀɔnɔstik/ nm forecast; (Méd) prognosis.

**propagande** /pʀɔpagɑ̃d/ nf propaganda.

**propager** /pʀɔpaʒe/ 40 vt spread. □ se ~ vpr spread.

**prophète** /pʀɔfɛt/ nm prophet. **prophétie** nf prophecy.

**propice** /pʀɔpis/ adj favourable.

**proportion** /pʀɔpɔʀsjɔ̃/ nf proportion; (en mathématiques) ratio; toutes ~s gardées relatively speaking. **proportionné,** ~e adj proportionate (à to). **proportionnel, ~le** adj proportional. **proportionnellement** adv proportionately.

**propos** /pʀɔpo/ nm intention; (sujet) subject; à ~ at the right time; (dans un dialogue) by the way; à ~ de about; à tout ~ at every possible occasion. ● nmpl (paroles) remarks.

**proposer** /pʀɔpoze/ **1** vt suggest, propose; (offrir) offer. □ se ~ vpr volunteer (pour to). **proposition** nf proposal; (affirmation) proposition; (Gram) clause.

**propre** /pʀɔpʀ/ adj (non sali) clean; (soigné) neat; (honnête) decent; (à soi) own; (sens) literal; ~ à (qui convient) suited to; (spécifique) particular to. ● nm mettre au ~ write out again neatly; c'est du ~! (ironique) well done!

**proprement** /pʀɔpʀəmɑ̃/ adv (avec soin) neatly; (au sens strict) strictly; le bureau ~ dit the office itself.

**propreté** /pʀɔpʀəte/ nf cleanliness.

**propriétaire** /pʀɔpʀijetɛʀ/ nmf owner; (Comm) proprietor; (qui loue) landlord, landlady.

**propriété** /pʀɔpʀijete/ nf property; (droit) ownership.

**propulser** /pʀɔpylse/ **1** vt propel.

**proroger** /pʀɔʀɔʒe/ **40** vt (contrat) defer; (passeport) extend.

**proscrire** /pʀɔskʀiʀ/ **30** vt proscribe.

**proscrit**, ~e /pʀɔskʀi, -t/ adj proscribed. ● nm, f (exilé) exile.

**prose** /pʀoz/ nf prose.

**prospectus** /pʀɔspɛktys/ nm leaflet.

**prospère** /pʀɔspɛʀ/ adj flourishing, thriving. **prospérer** **14** vi thrive, prosper. **prospérité** nf prosperity.

**prosterner (se)** /(sə)pʀɔstɛʀne/ **1** vpr prostrate oneself; prosterné devant prostrate before.

**prostituée** /pʀɔstitɥe/ nf prostitute. **prostitution** nf prostitution.

**protecteur, -trice** /pʀɔtɛktœʀ,

-tʀis/ nm, f protector. ● adj protective.

**protection** /pʀɔtɛksjɔ̃/ nf protection.

**protégé**, ~e /pʀɔteʒe/ nm, f protégé.

**protéger** /pʀɔteʒe/ **40** vt protect. □ se ~ vpr protect oneself.

**protéine** /pʀɔtein/ nf protein.

**protestant**, ~e /pʀɔtɛstɑ̃, -t/ adj & nm, f Protestant.

**protestation** /pʀɔtɛstasjɔ̃/ nf protest. **protester** **1** vt/i protest.

**protocole** /pʀɔtɔkɔl/ nm protocol.

**protubérant**, ~e /pʀɔtybeʀɑ̃/ adj protruding.

**proue** /pʀu/ nf bow, prow.

**prouesse** /pʀuɛs/ nf feat, exploit.

**prouver** /pʀuve/ **1** vt prove.

**provenance** /pʀɔvnɑ̃s/ nf origin; en ~ de from.

**provençal**, ~e (mpl -aux) /pʀɔvɑ̃sal, -o/ adj & nm, f Provençal.

**provenir** /pʀɔvniʀ/ **58** vi ~ de come from.

**proverbe** /pʀɔvɛʀb/ nm proverb.

**province** /pʀɔvɛ̃s/ nf province; de ~ provincial; la ~ the provinces (+ pl). **provincial**, ~e (mpl -iaux) adj & nm, f provincial.

**proviseur** /pʀɔvizœʀ/ nm headmaster, principal.

**provision** /pʀɔvizjɔ̃/ nf supply, store; (sur un compte) credit (balance); (acompte) deposit; ~s (vivres) food shopping.

**provisoire** /pʀɔvizwaʀ/ adj provisional.

**provocant**, ~e /pʀɔvɔkɑ̃, -t/ adj provocative. **provocation** nf provocation. **provoquer** **1** vt cause; (sexuellement) arouse; (défier) provoke.

P

**proxénète** /pʀɔksenɛt/ nm pimp, procurer.

**proximité** /pʀɔksimite/ nf proximity; à ~ de close to.

**prude** /pʀyd/ adj prudish.

**prudemment** /pʀydamɑ̃/ adv (conduire) carefully; (attendre) cautiously. **prudence** nf caution. **prudent**, ~e adj (au volant) careful; (à agir) cautious; (sage) wise.

**prune** /pʀyn/ nf plum.

**pruneau** (pl ~x) /pʀyno/ nm prune.

**prunelle** /pʀynɛl/ nf (pupille) pupil; (fruit) sloe.

**prunier** /pʀynje/ nm plum tree.

**psaume** /psom/ nm psalm.

**pseudonyme** /psødɔnim/ nm pseudonym.

**psychanalyse** /psikanaliz/ nf psychoanalysis. **psychanalyste** nmf psychoanalyst.

**psychiatre** /psikjatʀ/ nmf psychiatrist. **psychiatrie** nf psychiatry. **psychiatrique** adj psychiatric.

**psychique** /psiʃik/ adj mental, psychological.

**psychologie** /psikɔlɔʒi/ nf psychology. **psychologique** adj psychological. **psychologue** nmf psychologist.

**pu** /py/ ➡POUVOIR 49.

**puant**, ~e /pɥɑ̃, -t/ adj stinking.

**pub** /pyb/ nf 1 la ~ advertising; une ~ an advert.

**puberté** /pybɛʀte/ nf puberty.

**public**, -que /pyblik/ adj public. • nm public; (assistance) audience; (Scol) state schools (+ pl); en ~ in public.

**publication** /pyblikasjɔ̃/ nf publication.

**publicitaire** /pyblisitɛʀ/ adj pub-

licity. **publicité** nf publicity, advertising; (annonce) advertisement.

**publier** /pyblije/ 45 vt publish.

**publiquement** /pyblikmɑ̃/ adv publicly.

**puce** /pys/ nf flea; (électronique) chip; marché aux ~s flea market.

**pudeur** /pydœʀ/ nf modesty.

**pudibond**, ~e /pydibɔ̃, -d/ adj prudish.

**pudique** /pydik/ adj modest.

**puer** /pɥe/ 1 vi stink. • vt stink of.

**puéricultrice** /pɥeʀikyltʀis/ nf pediatric nurse.

**puéril**, ~e /pɥeʀil/ adj puerile.

**puis** /pɥi/ adv then.

**puiser** /pɥize/ 1 vt draw (dans from). • vi ~ dans qch dip into sth.

**puisque** /pɥisk(ə)/ conj since, as.

**puissance** /pɥisɑ̃s/ nf power; en ~ potential.

**puissant**, ~e /pɥisɑ̃, -t/ adj powerful.

**puits** /pɥi/ nm well; (de mine) shaft.

**pull(-over)** /pyl(ɔvɛʀ)/ nm pullover, jumper.

**pulpe** /pylp/ nf pulp.

**pulsation** /pylsasjɔ̃/ nf (heart-) beat.

**pulvériser** /pylveʀize/ 1 vt pulverize; (liquide) spray.

**punaise** /pynɛz/ nf (insecte) bug; (clou) drawing pin.

**punch¹** /pɔ̃ʃ/ nm (boisson) punch.

**punch²** /pœnʃ/ nm avoir du ~ have drive.

**punir** /pyniʀ/ 2 vt punish. **punition** nf punishment.

**pupille** /pypij/ nf (de l'œil) pupil. • nmf (enfant) ward.

**pupitre** /pypitʀ/ nm (Scol) desk; ~ à musique music stand.

**pur** /pyʀ/ adj pure; (whisky) neat.

**purée** /pyʀe/ nf purée; (de pommes de terre) mashed potatoes (+ pl).

**pureté** /pyʀte/ nf purity.

**purgatoire** /pyʀgatwaʀ/ nm purgatory.

**purge** /pyʀʒ/ nf purge. **purger** 🔟 vt (Pol, Méd) purge; (peine: Jur) serve.

**purifier** /pyʀifje/ 🔢 vt purify.

**puritain**, ~e /pyʀitɛ̃, -ɛn/ nm, f puritan. ● adj puritanical.

**pur-sang** /pyʀsɑ̃/ nm inv (cheval) thoroughbred.

**pus** /py/ nm pus.

**putain** /pytɛ̃/ nf p whore.

**puzzle** /pœzl/ nm jigsaw (puzzle).

**P-V** abrév m (**procès-verbal**) ticket, traffic fine.

**pyjama** /piʒama/ nm pyjamas (+ pl); un ~ a pair of pyjamas.

**pylône** /pilon/ nm pylon.

**Pyrénées** /piʀene/ nfpl les ~ the Pyrenees.

**pyromane** /piʀɔman/ nmf arsonist.

........................

# Qq

........................

**QG** abrév m (**quartier général**) HQ.

**QI** abrév m (**quotient intellectuel**) IQ.

**qu'** /k/ ➞QUE.

**quadriller** /kadʀije/ 🔟 vt (armée) take control of; (police) spread one's net over; **papier quadrillé** squared paper.

**quadrupède** /kadʀypɛd/ nm quadruped.

**quadruple** /kadʀypl/ adj quadruple. ● nm le ~ de four times. **quadrupler** 🔟 vt/i quadruple.

**quai** /ke/ nm (de gare) platform; (de port) quay; (de rivière) bank.

**qualification** /kalifikasjõ/ nf qualification; (compétence pratique) skills (+ pl).

**qualifié**, ~e /kalifje/ adj (diplomé) qualified; (main-d'œuvre) skilled.

**qualifier** /kalifje/ 🔢 vt qualify; (décrire) describe (de as). □ se ~ vpr qualify (pour for).

**qualité** /kalite/ nf quality; (titre) occupation; (fonction) position; en sa ~ de in his ou her capacity as.

**quand** /kɑ̃/ adv when; ~ même all the same. ● conj when; (toutes les fois que) whenever; ~ bien même even if.

**quant à** /kɑ̃ta/ prép as for.

**quantité** /kɑ̃tite/ nf quantity; une ~ de a lot of; des ~s (de) masses ou lots (of).

**quarantaine** /kaʀɑ̃tɛn/ nf (Méd) quarantine; une ~ (de) about forty; avoir la ~ be in one's forties.

**quarante** /kaʀɑ̃t/ adj & nm forty.

**quart** /kaʀ/ nm quarter; (Naut) watch; **onze heures moins le** ~ quarter to eleven; ~ (de litre) quarter litre; ~ de finale quarterfinal; ~ d'heure quarter of an hour; ~ de tour ninety-degree turn.

**quartier** /kaʀtje/ nm area, district; (zone ethnique) quarter; (de lune, pomme, bœuf) quarter; (d'une orange) segment; ~s (Mil) quarters; de ~, du ~ local; ~ général headquarters; avoir ~

**P**
**q**

libre be free.

**quasiment** /kazimɑ̃/ adv almost, practically.

**quatorze** /katɔʀz/ adj & nm fourteen.

**quatre** /katʀ(ə)/ adj & nm four. **quatre-vingt(s)** adj & nm eighty. **quatre-vingt-dix** adj & nm ninety.

**quatre-quatre** /katʀkatʀ/ nm four-wheel drive.

**quatrième** /katʀijɛm/ adj & nmf fourth. ●nf (Auto) fourth gear.

**quatuor** /kwatɥɔʀ/ nm quartet.

**que,** qu' /kə, k/

qu' before vowel or mute h.

● conjonction

‥‥▸ that; je crains ∼… I'm worried that…

‥‥▸ (souhait, volonté) je veux ∼ tu viennes I want you to come; ∼ tu viennes ou non whether you come or not; qu'il entre let him come in.

‥‥▸ (comparaison) than; plus grand ∼ toi taller than you.

● pronom interrogatif

‥‥▸ what; ∼ voulez-vous manger? what would you like to eat?

● pronom relatif

‥‥▸ (personne) whom, that; l'homme ∼ j'ai rencontré the man (whom) I met.

‥‥▸ (chose) that, which; le cheval ∼ Nick m'a offert the horse (which) Nick gave me.

● adverbe

‥‥▸ que c'est joli! it's so pretty!; ∼ de monde! what a lot of people!

**Québec** /kebɛk/ nm Quebec.

**quel,** quelle (pl **quel(le)s**) /kɛl/

● adjectif interrogatif

‥‥▸ which, what; ∼ auteur a écrit…? which writer wrote…?; ∼ jour sommes-nous? what day is it today?

● adjectif exclamatif

‥‥▸ what; ∼ idiot! what an idiot!; quelle horreur! that's horrible!

● adjectif relatif

‥‥▸ ∼ que soit son âge whatever his age; quelles que soient tes raisons whatever your reasons; ∼ que se le gagnant whoever the winner is.

**quelconque** /kɛlkɔ̃k/ adj any, some; (banal) ordinary; (médiocre) poor, second rate.

**quelque** /kɛlkə/ adj some; ∼s a few, some. ●adv (environ) about, some; et ∼ 🅣 and a bit; ∼ chose something; (dans les phrases interrogatives) anything; ∼ part somewhere; ∼ peu somewhat.

**quelquefois** /kɛlkəfwa/ adv sometimes.

**quelques-uns,** -unes /kɛlkəzœ̃, -yn/ pron some, a few.

**quelqu'un** /kɛlkœ̃/ pron someone, somebody; (dans les phrases interrogatives) anyone, anybody.

**querelle** /kəʀɛl/ nf quarrel. **quereller (se)** 🃁 vpr quarrel. **querelleur, -euse** adj quarrelsome.

**question** /kɛstjɔ̃/ nf question; (affaire) matter, question; poser une ∼ ask a question; en ∼ in question; il est ∼ de (l'affaire concerne) it is about; (on parle de) there is talk of; il n'en est pas ∼ it is out of the question; pas ∼! no way!

**questionnaire** /kɛstjɔnɛʀ/ nm questionnaire.

**questionner** /kɛstjɔne/ **1** vt question.

**quête** /kɛt/ nf (Relig) collection; (recherche) search; en ~ de in search of.

**queue** /kø/ nf tail; (de poêle) handle; (de fruit) stalk; (de fleur) stem; (file) queue; (US) line; (de train) rear; faire la ~ queue (up); (US) line up; ~ de cheval ponytail; faire une ~ de poisson à qn (Auto) cut in front of sb.

**qui** /ki/

● *pronom interrogatif*

····▸ (sujet) who; ~ a fait ça? who did that?

····▸ (complément) whom; à ~ est ce livre? whose book is this?

● *pronom relatif*

····▸ (personne sujet) who; c'est Isabelle qui vient d'appeler it's Isabelle who's just called.

····▸ (autres cas) that, which; qu'est-ce ~ te prend? what is the matter with you?; invite ~ tu veux invite whoever you want; ~ que ce soit whoever it is, anybody.

**quiche** /kiʃ/ nf quiche.

**quiconque** /kikɔ̃k/ pron whoever; (n'importe qui) anyone.

**quille** /kij/ nf (de bateau) keel; (jouet) skittle.

**quincaillerie** /kɛ̃kɑjʀi/ nf hardware; (magasin) hardware shop. **quincaillier, -ière** nm, f hardware dealer.

**quintal** (pl **-aux**) /kɛ̃tal, -o/ nm quintal, one hundred kilos.

**quinte** /kɛ̃t/ nf ~ de toux coughing fit.

**quintuple** /kɛ̃typl/ adj quintuple. ● nm le ~ de five times. **quintupler** **1** vt/i quintuple, increase fivefold.

**quinzaine** /kɛ̃zɛn/ nf une ~ (de) about fifteen.

**quinze** /kɛ̃z/ adj & nm inv fifteen; ~ jours two weeks.

**quiproquo** /kipʀɔko/ nm misunderstanding.

**quittance** /kitɑ̃s/ nf receipt.

**quitte** /kit/ adj quits (envers with); ~ à faire even if it means doing.

**quitter** /kite/ **1** vt leave; (vêtement) take off; ne quittez pas! hold the line, please! □ se ~ vpr part.

**qui-vive** /kiviv/ nm inv être sur le ~ be alert.

**quoi** /kwa/ pron what; (après une préposition) which; de ~ vivre (assez) enough to live on; de ~ écrire something to write with; ~ qu'il dise whatever he says; ~ que ce soit anything; il n'y a pas de ~ my pleasure; il n'y a pas de ~ s'inquiéter there's nothing to worry about.

**quoique** /kwak(ə)/ conj although, though.

**quota** /kɔta/ nm quota.

**quote-part** (pl **quotes-parts**) /kɔtpaʀ/ nf share.

**quotidien, ~ne** /kɔtidjɛ̃, -ɛn/ adj daily; (banal) everyday. ● nm daily (paper); (vie quotidienne) everyday life. **quotidiennement** adv daily.

**q**

# Rr

**rabâcher** /ʀabaʃe/ **1** *vt* keep repeating.

**rabais** /ʀabɛ/ *nm* reduction, discount. **rabaisser** **1** *vt* (déprécier) belittle; (réduire) reduce.

**rabat-joie** /ʀabaʒwa/ *nm inv* killjoy.

**rabattre** /ʀabatʀ/ **11** *vt* (chapeau, visière) pull down; (fermer) shut; (diminuer) reduce; (déduire) take off; (col, drap) turn down. □ se ~ *vpr* (se refermer) close; (véhicule) cut back in; se ~ sur make do with.

**rabot** /ʀabo/ *nm* plane.

**rabougri**, ~e /ʀabugʀi/ *adj* stunted.

**racaille** /ʀakaj/ *nf* rabble.

**raccommoder** /ʀakɔmɔde/ **1** *vt* mend; (personnes **1**) reconcile.

**raccompagner** /ʀakɔ̃paɲe/ **1** *vt* see *ou* take back (home).

**raccord** /ʀakɔʀ/ *nm* (de papier peint) join; (retouche) touch-up. **raccorder** **1** *vt* connect, join.

**raccourci** /ʀakuʀsi/ *nm* short cut; en ~ in short.

**raccourcir** /ʀakuʀsiʀ/ **2** *vt* shorten. ● *vi* get shorter.

**raccrocher** /ʀakʀɔʃe/ **1** *vt* hang back up; (passant) grab hold of; (relier) connect; ~ le combiné *or* le téléphone hang up. ● *vi* hang up. □ se ~ à *vpr* cling to; (se relier à) be connected to *ou* with.

**race** /ʀas/ *nf* race; (animale) breed; de ~ (chien) pedigree; (cheval) thoroughbred.

**racheter** /ʀaʃte/ **6** *vt* buy (back); (acheter encore) buy more; (nouvel objet) buy another; (société) buy

out; ~ des chaussettes buy new socks. □ se ~ *vpr* make amends.

**racial**, ~e (*mpl* -iaux) /ʀasjal, -o/ *adj* racial.

**racine** /ʀasin/ *nf* root; ~ carrée/ cubique square/cube root.

**racisme** /ʀasism/ *nm* racism. **raciste** *adj & nmf* racist.

**racket** /ʀakɛt/ *nm* racketeering.

**raclée** /ʀɑkle/ *nf* **1** thrashing.

**racler** /ʀɑkle/ **1** *vt* scrape. □ se ~ *vpr* se ~ la gorge clear one's throat.

**racolage** /ʀakɔlaʒ/ *nm* soliciting.

**raconter** /ʀakɔ̃te/ **1** *vt* (histoire) tell; (vacances) tell about; (vie, épisode) describe; ~ à qn que tell sb that, say to sb that; qu'est-ce que tu racontes? what are you talking about?

**radar** /ʀadaʀ/ *nm* radar; (automatique) speed camera.

**radeau** (*pl* ~x) /ʀado/ *nm* raft.

**radiateur** /ʀadjatœʀ/ *nm* radiator; (électrique) heater.

**radiation** /ʀadjasjɔ̃/ *nf* radiation.

**radical**, ~e (*mpl* -aux) /ʀadikal, -o/ *adj* radical. ● *nm* (*pl* -aux) radical.

**radieux**, -ieuse /ʀadjø, -z/ *adj* radiant.

**radin**, ~e /ʀadɛ̃, -in/ *adj* **1** stingy **1**.

**radio** /ʀadjo/ *nf* radio; à la ~ on the radio; (radiographie) X-ray.

**radioactif**, -ive /ʀadjoaktif, -v/ *adj* radioactive. **radioactivité** *nf* radioactivity.

**radiocassette** /ʀadjokaset/ *nf* radio cassette player.

**radiodiffuser** /ʀadjodifyze/ **1** *vt* broadcast.

**radiographie** /ʀadjɔgʀafi/ *nf* (photographie) X-ray.

**radiomessageur** /ʀadjɔmesa-ʒœʀ/ *nm* pager.

**radis** /ʀadi/ *nm* radish; ne pas avoir un ∼ 🔲 be broke.

**radoter** /ʀadɔte/ 🔢 *vi* 🔲 talk drivel.

**radoucir (se)** /(sə)ʀadusiʀ/ 🔢 *vpr* (*humeur*) improve; (*temps*) become milder.

**rafale** /ʀafal/ *nf* (de vent) gust; (de mitraillette) burst.

**raffermir** /ʀafɛʀmiʀ/ 🔢 *vt* strengthen. □ se ∼ *vpr* become stronger.

**raffiné, ∼e** /ʀafine/ *adj* refined. **raffinement** *nm* refinement.

**raffiner** /ʀafine/ 🔢 *vt* refine. **raffinerie** *nf* refinery.

**raffoler** /ʀafɔle/ 🔢 *vi* 🔲 ∼ de be crazy about.

**raffut** /ʀafy/ *nm* 🔲 din.

**rafle** /ʀafl/ *nf* (police) raid.

**rafraîchir** /ʀafʀeʃiʀ/ 🔢 *vt* cool (down); (*mur*) give a fresh coat of paint to; (*personne, mémoire*) refresh. □ se ∼ *vpr* (*boire*) refresh oneself; (*temps*) get cooler. **rafraîchissant, ∼e** *adj* refreshing.

**rafraîchissement** /ʀafʀeʃismɑ̃/ *nm* (boisson) cold drink; ∼s refreshments.

**ragaillardir** /ʀagajaʀdiʀ/ 🔢 *vt* 🔲 cheer up.

**rage** /ʀaʒ/ *nf* rage; (maladie) rabies; faire ∼ (bataille, incendie) rage; (maladie) be rife; ∼ de dents raging toothache. **rageant, ∼e** *adj* infuriating.

**ragots** /ʀago/ *nmpl* 🔲 gossip.

**ragoût** /ʀagu/ *nm* stew.

**raid** /ʀɛd/ *nm* (Mil) raid; (Sport) trek.

**raide** /ʀɛd/ *adj* stiff; (côte) steep; (corde) tight; (cheveux) straight.
● *adv* (monter, descendre) steeply.

**raideur** *nf* stiffness; steepness.

**raidir** /ʀediʀ/ 🔢 *vt* (corps) tense. □ se ∼ *vpr* tense up; (position) harden; (corde) tighten.

**raie** /ʀɛ/ *nf* (ligne) line; (bande) strip; (de cheveux) parting; (poisson) skate.

**raifort** /ʀɛfɔʀ/ *nm* horseradish.

**rail** /ʀɑj/ *nm* rail, track; le ∼ (transport) rail.

**raisin** /ʀɛzɛ̃/ *nm* le ∼ grapes; ∼ sec raisin; un grain de ∼ a grape.

**raison** /ʀɛzɔ̃/ *nf* reason; à ∼ de at the rate of; avec ∼ rightly; avoir ∼ be right (de faire to do); avoir ∼ de qn get the better of sb; donner ∼ à qn prove right; en ∼ de because of; ∼ de plus all the more reason; perdre la ∼ lose one's mind.

**raisonnable** /ʀɛzɔnabl/ *adj* reasonable, sensible.

**raisonnement** /ʀɛzɔnmɑ̃/ *nm* reasoning; (propositions) argument.

**raisonner** /ʀɛzɔne/ 🔢 *vi* think.
● *vt* (personne) reason with.

**rajeunir** /ʀaʒœniʀ/ 🔢 *vt* ∼ qn make sb (look) younger; (moderniser) modernize; (Méd) rejuvenate.
● *vi* (personne) look younger.

**rajuster** /ʀaʒyste/ 🔢 *vt* straighten; (salaires) (re)adjust.

**ralenti, ∼e** /ʀalɑ̃ti/ *adj* slow. ● *nm* (au cinéma) slow motion; tourner au ∼ tick over, idle.

**ralentir** /ʀalɑ̃tiʀ/ 🔢 *vt/i* slow down. □ se ∼ *vpr* slow down.

**ralentisseur** /ʀalɑ̃tisœʀ/ *nm* speed ramp.

**râler** /ʀɑle/ 🔢 *vi* groan; (protester 🔲) moan.

**rallier** /ʀalje/ 45 *vt* rally; (rejoindre) rejoin. □ se ∼ *vpr* ∼ à (avis) come round to; (parti) join.

**rallonge** /ʀalɔ̃ʒ/ *nf* (de table) leaf; (de fil électrique) extension lead.

**rallonger** 40 vt lengthen; (*séjour, fil, table*) extend.

**rallumer** /Ralyme/ 1 vt (*feu*) relight; (*lampe*) switch on again; (*ranimer: fig*) revive.

**rallye** /Rali/ nm rally.

**ramassage** /Ramasaʒ/ nm (*cueillette*) gathering; (*d'ordures*) collection; ~ **scolaire** school bus service.

**ramasser** /Ramase/ 1 vt pick up; (*récolter*) gather; (*recueillir, rassembler*) collect. □ **se** ~ vpr huddle up, curl up.

**rame** /Ram/ nf (*aviron*) oar; (*train*) train.

**ramener** /Ramne/ 1 vt (*rapporter, faire revenir*) bring back; (*reconduire*) take back; ~ **à** (*réduire à*) reduce to. □ **se** ~ vpr 1 turn up; **se** ~ **à** (*problème*) come down to.

**ramer** /Rame/ 1 vi row.

**ramollir** /Ramɔlir/ 2 vt soften. □ **se** ~ vpr become soft.

**ramoneur** /Ramɔnœʀ/ nm (chimney) sweep.

**rampe** /Rɑ̃p/ nf banisters; (*pente*) ramp; ~ **d'accès** (*Auto*) slip road; ~ **de lancement** launching pad.

**ramper** /Rɑ̃pe/ 1 vi crawl.

**rancard** /Rɑ̃kaʀ/ nm 1 date.

**rancart** /Rɑ̃kaʀ/ nm **mettre** ou **jeter au** ~ 1 scrap.

**rance** /Rɑ̃s/ adj rancid.

**rancœur** /Rɑ̃kœʀ/ nf resentment.

**rançon** /Rɑ̃sɔ̃/ nf ransom. **rançonner** 1 vt rob, extort money from.

**rancune** /Rɑ̃kyn/ nf grudge; **sans** ~! no hard feelings! **rancunier, -ière** adj vindictive.

**randonnée** /Rɑ̃dɔne/ nf walk, ramble; **la** ~ **à cheval** pony trekking; **faire une** ~ go walking ou rambling.

**rang** /Rɑ̃/ nm row; (*hiérarchie, condition*) rank; **se mettre en** ~ line up; **au premier** ~ in the first row; (*fig*) at the forefront; **de second** ~ (*péj*) second-rate.

**rangée** /Rɑ̃ʒe/ nf row.

**rangement** /Rɑ̃ʒmɑ̃/ nm (*de pièce*) tidying (up); (*espace*) storage space.

**ranger** /Rɑ̃ʒe/ 40 vt put away; (*chambre*) tidy (up); (*disposer*) place. □ **se** ~ vpr (*véhicule*) park; (*s'écarter*) stand aside; (*conducteur*) pull over; (*s'assagir*) settle down; **se** ~ **à** (*avis*) accept.

**ranimer** /Ranime/ 1 vt revive; (*Méd*) resuscitate. □ **se** ~ vpr come round.

**rapace** /Rapas/ nm bird of prey. ● adj grasping.

**rapatriement** /Rapatrimɑ̃/ nm repatriation. **rapatrier** 45 vt repatriate.

**rap** /Rap/ nm rap (music).

**râpe** /Rɑp/ nf (*Culin*) grater; (*lime*) rasp.

**râpé, ~e** /Rɑpe/ adj (*vêtement*) threadbare; (*fromage*) grated.

**râper** /Rɑpe/ 1 vt grate; (*bois*) rasp.

**rapide** /Rapid/ adj fast, rapid. ● nm (*train*) express (train); (*cours d'eau*) rapids (+ pl). **rapidement** adv fast, rapidly. **rapidité** nf speed.

**rappel** /Rapɛl/ nm recall; (*deuxième avis*) reminder; (*de salaire*) back pay; (*Méd*) booster; (*de réservistes*) call-up; (*Théât*) curtain call.

**rappeler** /Raple/ 38 vt (*par téléphone*) call back; (*réserviste*) call up; (*diplomate*) recall; (*évoquer*) recall; ~ **qch à qn** remind sb of sth. □ **se** ~ vpr remember, recall.

**rappeur, -euse** /Rapœœːr, -øz/

*nmf* rapper.

**rapport** /ʀapɔʀ/ *nm* connection; (compte-rendu) report; (profit) yield; ∼s (relations) relations; **en** ∼ **avec** (accord) in keeping with; **mettre/se mettre en** ∼ **avec** put/ get in touch with; **par** ∼ **à** (comparé à) compared with; (vis-à-vis de) with regard to; ∼s (sexuels) intercourse.

**rapporter** /ʀapɔʀte/ **1** *vt* (ici) bring back; (là-bas) take back, return; (profit) bring in; (dire, répéter) report. ●*vi* (Comm) bring in a good return; (moucharder 🗊) tell tales. □ **se** ∼ **à** *vpr* relate to.

**rapporteur, -euse** /ʀapɔʀtœʀ, -øz/ *nm, f* (mouchard) tell-tale. ●*nm* protractor.

**rapprochement** /ʀapʀɔʃmɑ̃/ *nm* reconciliation; (Pol) rapprochement; (rapport) connection; (comparaison) parallel.

**rapprocher** /ʀapʀɔʃe/ *vt* move closer (de to); (réconcilier) bring together; (comparer) compare; (date, rendez-vous) bring forward. □ **se** ∼ *vpr* get *ou* come closer (de to); (personnes, pays) come together; (s'apparenter) be close (de to).

**rapt** /ʀapt/ *nm* abduction.

**raquette** /ʀakɛt/ *nf* (de tennis) racket; (de ping-pong) bat.

**rare** /ʀaʀ/ *adj* rare; (insuffisant) scarce. **rarement** *adv* rarely, seldom. **rareté** *nf* rarity; scarcity.

**ras, ∼e** /ʀa, ʀaz/ *adj* coupé ∼ cut short. ●*adj* (herbe, poil) short; **à** ∼ **de terre** very close to the ground; **en avoir** ∼ **le bol 🗊** be really fed up; ∼**e campagne** open country; **à** ∼ **bord** to the brim.

**raser** /ʀaze/ **1** *vt* shave; (cheveux, barbe) shave off; (frôler) skim; (abattre) raze. □ **se** ∼ *vpr* shave.

**rasoir** /ʀazwaʀ/ *nm* razor. ●*adj inv* 🗊 boring.

**rassasier** /ʀasazje/ **45** *vt* satisfy, fill up; **être rassasié de** have had enough of.

**rassemblement** /ʀasɑ̃bləmɑ̃/ *nm* gathering; (manifestation) rally.

**rassembler** /ʀasɑ̃ble/ **1** *vt* gather; (forces, courage) summon up; (idées) collect. □ **se** ∼ *vpr* gather.

**rassis, ∼e** /ʀasi, -z/ *adj* (pain) stale.

**rassurer** /ʀasyʀe/ **1** *vt* reassure. □ **se** ∼ *vpr* reassure oneself; **rassure-toi** don't worry.

**rat** /ʀa/ *nm* rat.

**rate** /ʀat/ *nf* spleen.

**raté, -e** /ʀate/ *nm, f* (personne) failure. ●*nm* **avoir des** ∼**s** (voiture) backfire.

**râteau** (*pl* ∼**x**) /ʀato/ *nm* rake.

**râtelier** /ʀatəlje/ *nm* hayrack; (dentier 🗊) dentures.

**rater** /ʀate/ **1** *vt* (train, rendez-vous, cible) miss; (gâcher) make a mess of, spoil; (examen) fail. ●*vi* fail.

**ratio** /ʀasjo/ *nm* ratio.

**rationaliser** /ʀasjonalize/ **1** *vt* rationalize.

**rationnel, ∼le** /ʀasjonɛl/ *adj* rational.

**rationnement** /ʀasjonmɑ̃/ *nm* rationing.

**ratisser** /ʀatise/ **1** *vt* rake; (fouiller) comb.

**rattacher** /ʀataʃe/ **1** *vt* (lacets) tie up again; (ceinture de sécurité, collier) refasten; (relier) link; (incorporer) join.

**rattrapage** /ʀatʀapaʒ/ *nm* (Comm) adjustment; **cours de** ∼ remedial lesson.

**rattraper** /ʀatʀape/ **1** *vt* catch;

r

(rejoindre) catch up with; (retard, erreur) make up for. □ se ~ vpr catch up; (se dédommager) make up for it; se ~ à catch hold of.

**rature** /ʀatyʀ/ nf deletion.

**rauque** /ʀok/ adj raucous, harsh.

**ravager** /ʀavaʒe/ [40] vt devastate, ravage.

**ravages** /ʀavaʒ/ nmpl faire des ~ wreak havoc.

**ravaler** /ʀavale/ [1] vt (façade) clean; (colère) swallow.

**ravi**, ~e /ʀavi/ adj delighted (que that).

**ravin** /ʀavɛ̃/ nm ravine.

**ravir** /ʀaviʀ/ [2] vt delight; ~ qch à qn rob sb of sth.

**ravissant**, ~e /ʀavisɑ̃, -t/ adj beautiful.

**ravisseur**, -euse /ʀavisœʀ, -øz/ nm, f kidnapper.

**ravitaillement** /ʀavitajmɑ̃/ nm provision of supplies (de to); (denrées) supplies; ~ en essence refuelling.

**ravitailler** /ʀavitaje/ [1] vt provide with supplies; (avion) refuel. □ se ~ vpr stock up.

**raviver** /ʀavive/ [1] vt revive; (feu, colère) rekindle.

**rayé**, ~e /ʀeje/ adj striped.

**rayer** /ʀeje/ [31] vt scratch; (biffer) cross out; '~ la mention inutile' 'delete as appropriate'.

**rayon** /ʀejɔ̃/ nm ray; (étagère) shelf; (de magasin) department; (de roue) spoke; (de cercle) radius; ~ d'action range; ~ de miel honeycomb; ~ X X-ray; en connaître un ~ [1] know one's stuff [1].

**rayonnement** /ʀejɔnmɑ̃/ nm (éclat) radiance; (influence) influence; (radiations) radiation. **rayonner** /ʀejɔne/ [1] vi radiate; (de joie) beam; (se déplacer) tour around (from a

central point).

**rayure** /ʀejyʀ/ nf scratch; (dessin) stripe; à ~s striped.

**raz-de-marée** /ʀɑdmaʀe/ nm inv tidal wave; ~ électoral electoral landslide.

**réacteur** /ʀeaktœʀ/ nm jet engine; (nucléaire) reactor.

**réaction** /ʀeaksjɔ̃/ nf reaction; ~ en chaîne chain reaction; moteur à ~ jet engine.

**réagir** /ʀeaʒiʀ/ [2] vi react; ~ sur have an effect on.

**réalisateur**, -trice /ʀealizatœʀ, -tʀis/ nm, f (au cinéma) director; (TV) producer.

**réalisation** /ʀealizasjɔ̃/ nf (de rêve) fulfilment; (œuvre) achievement; (TV, cinéma) production; projet en ~ project in progress.

**réaliser** /ʀealize/ [1] vt carry out; (effort, bénéfice, achat) make; (rêve) fulfil; (film) direct; (capital) realize; (se rendre compte de) realize. □ se ~ vpr be fulfilled.

**réalisme** /ʀealism/ nm realism.

**réaliste** /ʀealist/ adj realistic. ● nmf realist.

**réalité** /ʀealite/ nf reality.

**réanimation** /ʀeanimasjɔ̃/ nf resuscitation; service de ~ intensive care. **réanimer** [1] vt resuscitate.

**réarmement** /ʀeaʀməmɑ̃/ nm rearmament.

**rébarbatif**, -ive /ʀebaʀbatif, -v/ adj forbidding, off-putting.

**rebelle** /ʀəbɛl/ adj rebellious; (soldat) rebel; ~ à resistant to. ● nmf rebel.

**rébellion** /ʀebeljɔ̃/ nf rebellion.

**rebondir** /ʀəbɔ̃diʀ/ [2] vi bounce; rebound; (fig) get moving again.

**rebondissement** /ʀəbɔ̃dismɑ̃/ nm (new) development.

**rebord** /ʀəbɔʀ/ nm edge; ~ de la fenêtre window ledge ou sill.

**rebours**: à ~ /aʀabuʀ/ loc (compter, marcher) backwards.

**rebrousse-poil**: à ~ /aʀabʀuspwal/ loc the wrong way; (fig) prendre qn à ~ rub sb up the wrong way.

**rebrousser** /ʀəbʀuse/ 🔢 vt ~ chemin turn back.

**rebut** /ʀəby/ nm mettre ou jeter au ~ scrap.

**rebutant, ~e** /ʀəbytɑ̃, -t/ adj offputting.

**recaler** /ʀəkale/ 🔢 vt 🔢 fail; se faire ~, être recalé fail.

**recel** /ʀəsɛl/ nm receiving. **receler** 🔢 vt (objet volé) receive; (cacher) conceal.

**récemment** /ʀesamɑ̃/ adv recently.

**recensement** /ʀəsɑ̃smɑ̃/ nm census; (inventaire) inventory. **recenser** 🔢 vt (population) take a census of; (objets) list.

**récent, ~e** /ʀesɑ̃, -t/ adj recent.

**récépissé** /ʀesepise/ nm receipt.

**récepteur** /ʀesɛptœʀ/ nm receiver.

**réception** /ʀesɛpsjɔ̃/ nf reception; (de courrier) receipt. **réceptionniste** nmf receptionist.

**récession** /ʀesesjɔ̃/ nf recession.

**recette** /ʀəsɛt/ nf (Culin) recipe; (argent) takings; ~s (Comm) receipts.

**receveur, -euse** /ʀəs(ə)vœʀ, -øz/ nm, f (de bus) conductor; ~ des contributions tax collector.

**recevoir** /ʀəs(ə)vwaʀ/ 🔢 vt receive, get; (client, malade) see; (invités) welcome, receive; être reçu à un examen pass an exam.

**rechange**: de ~ /dəʀəʃɑ̃ʒ/ loc (roue, vêtements) spare; (solution) alternative.

**réchapper** /ʀeʃape/ 🔢 vt/i ~ de come through, survive.

**recharge** /ʀəʃaʀʒ/ nf (de stylo) refill.

**réchaud** /ʀeʃo/ nm stove.

**réchauffement** /ʀeʃofmɑ̃/ nm (de température) rise (de in); le ~ de la planète global warming.

**réchauffer** /ʀeʃofe/ 🔢 vt warm up. □ se ~ vpr warm oneself up; (temps) get warmer.

**rêche** /ʀɛʃ/ adj rough.

**recherche** /ʀəʃɛʀʃ/ nf search (de for); (raffinement) meticulousness; ~(s) (Univ) research; ~s (enquête) investigations; ~ d'emploi jobhunting.

**recherché, ~e** /ʀəʃɛʀʃe/ adj in great demand; (style) original, recherché (péj); ~ pour meurtre wanted for murder.

**rechercher** /ʀəʃɛʀʃe/ 🔢 vt search for.

**rechute** /ʀəʃyt/ nf (Méd) relapse; faire une ~ have a relapse.

**récidiver** /ʀesidive/ 🔢 vi commit a second offence.

**récif** /ʀesif/ nm reef.

**récipient** /ʀesipjɑ̃/ nm container.

**réciproque** /ʀesipʀɔk/ adj mutual, reciprocal.

**réciproquement** /ʀesipʀɔkmɑ̃/ adv each other; et ~ and vice versa.

**récit** /ʀesi/ nm (compte-rendu) account, story; (histoire) story.

**réciter** /ʀesite/ 🔢 vt recite.

**réclamation** /ʀeklamasjɔ̃/ nf complaint; (demande) claim.

**réclame** /ʀeklam/ nf advertisement; faire de la ~ advertise; en ~ on offer.

**réclamer** /ʀeklame/ 🔢 vt call for, demand. ● vi complain.

**reclus, ~e** /ʀəkly, -z/ nm, f recluse.

●*adj* reclusive.

**réclusion** /ʀeklyzjɔ̃/ *nf* imprisonment.

**récolte** /ʀekɔlt/ *nf* (action) harvest; (produits) crop, harvest; (fig) crop. **récolter** ▯ *vt* harvest, gather; (fig) collect, get.

**recommandation** /ʀəkɔmɑ̃dasjɔ̃/ *nf* recommendation.

**recommandé** /ʀəkɔmɑ̃de/ *nm* registered letter; envoyer en ~ send by registered post.

**recommander** /ʀəkɔmɑ̃de/ ▯ *vt* recommend.

**recommencer** /ʀəkɔmɑ̃se/ ⑩ *vt* (reprendre) begin ou start again; (refaire) repeat. ●*vi* start ou begin again; ne recommence pas don't do it again.

**récompense** /ʀekɔ̃pɑ̃s/ *nf* reward; (prix) award. **récompenser** ▯ *vt* reward (de for).

**réconcilier** /ʀekɔ̃silje/ ⑬ *vt* reconcile. □ **se** ~ *vpr* become reconciled (avec with).

**reconduire** /ʀəkɔ̃dɥiʀ/ ⑰ *vt* see home; (à la porte) show out; (renouveler) renew.

**réconfort** /ʀekɔ̃fɔʀ/ *nm* comfort.

**reconnaissance** /ʀəkɔnɛsɑ̃s/ *nf* gratitude; (fait de reconnaître) recognition; (Mil) reconnaissance. **reconnaissant**, ~**e** *adj* grateful (de for).

**reconnaître** /ʀəkɔnɛtʀ/ ⑱ *vt* recognize; (admettre) admit (que that); (Mil) reconnoitre; (enfant, tort) acknowledge. □ **se** ~ *vpr* (s'orienter) know where one is; (l'un l'autre) recognize each other.

**reconstituer** /ʀəkɔ̃stitɥe/ ▯ *vt* reconstitute; (crime) reconstruct; (époque) recreate.

**reconversion** /ʀəkɔ̃vɛʀsjɔ̃/ *nf* (de main-d'œuvre) redeployment.

**recopier** /ʀəkɔpje/ ㊺ *vt* copy out.

**record** /ʀəkɔʀ/ *nm & a inv* record.

**recoupe** /ʀəkupe/ ▯ *vt* confirm. □ **se** ~ *vpr* check, tally, match up.

**recourbé** /ʀəkuʀbe/ *adj* curved; (nez) hooked.

**recourir** /ʀəkuʀiʀ/ ⑳ *vi* ~ à (expédient, violence) resort to; (remède, méthode) have recourse to.

**recours** /ʀəkuʀ/ *nm* resort; avoir ~ à have recourse to, resort to; avoir ~ à qn turn to sb.

**recouvrer** /ʀəkuvʀe/ ▯ *vt* recover.

**recouvrir** /ʀəkuvʀiʀ/ ㉑ *vt* cover.

**récréation** /ʀekʀeasjɔ̃/ *nf* recreation; (Scol) break; (US) recess.

**recroqueviller (se)** /(sə)ʀakʀɔkvije/ ▯ *vpr* curl up.

**recrudescence** /ʀəkʀydesɑ̃s/ *nf* new outbreak.

**recrue** /ʀəkʀy/ *nf* recruit.

**recrutement** /ʀəkʀytmɑ̃/ *nm* recruitment. **recruter** ▯ *vt* recruit.

**rectangle** /ʀɛktɑ̃gl/ *nm* rectangle. **rectangulaire** *adj* rectangular.

**rectifier** /ʀɛktifje/ ㊺ *vt* correct, rectify.

**recto** /ʀɛkto/ *nm* au ~ on the front of the page.

**reçu**, ~**e** /ʀəsy/ *adj* accepted; (candidat) successful. ●*nm* receipt.
●→**RECEVOIR** ㊼.

**recueil** /ʀəkœj/ *nm* collection.

**recueillement** /ʀəkœjmɑ̃/ *nm* meditation.

**recueillir** /ʀəkœjiʀ/ ㉕ *vt* collect; (prendre chez soi) take in. □ **se** ~ *vpr* meditate.

**recul** /ʀəkyl/ *nm* retreat; (éloignement) distance; (déclin) decline; avoir un mouvement de ~ recoil; être en ~ be on the decline; avec le ~ with hindsight.

**reculé**, ~e /Rəkyle/ *adj* (région) remote.

**reculer** /Rəkyle/ **1** *vt* move back; (véhicule) reverse; (différer) postpone. ● *vi* move back; (voiture) reverse; (armée) retreat; (régresser) fall; (céder) back down; ~ devant (fig) shrink from. □ **se** ~ *vpr* move back.

**récupération** /Rekypeʀasjɔ̃/ *nf* (de l'organisme, de dette) recovery; (d'objets) salvage.

**récupérer** /Rekypeʀe/ **14** *vt* recover; (vieux objets) salvage. ● *vi* recover.

**récurer** /Rekyʀe/ **1** *vt* scour; poudre à ~ scouring powder.

**récuser** /Rekyze/ **1** *vt* challenge. □ **se** ~ *vpr* state that one is not qualified to judge.

**recyclage** /Rəsiklaʒ/ *nm* (de personnel) retraining; (de matériau) recycling.

**recycler** /Rəsikle/ **1** *vt* (personne) retrain; (chose) recycle. □ **se** ~ *vpr* retrain.

**rédacteur, -trice** /Redaktœʀ, -tʀis/ *nm, f* author, writer; (de journal, magazine) editor.

**rédaction** /Redaksjɔ̃/ *nf* writing; (Scol) essay, composition; (personnel) editorial staff.

**redevable** /Rədvabl/ *adj* être ~ à qn de (argent) owe sb; (fig) be indebted to sb for.

**redevance** /Rədvɑ̃s/ *nf* (de télévision) licence fee; (de téléphone) rental charge.

**rédiger** /Rediʒe/ **40** *vt* write; (contrat) draw up.

**redire** /Rədiʀ/ **27** *vt* repeat; avoir ou trouver à ~ à find fault with.

**redondant**, ~e /Rədɔ̃dɑ̃, -t/ *adj* superfluous.

**redonner** /Rədɔne/ **1** *vt* (rendre) give back; (donner davantage) give more; (donner de nouveau) give again.

**redoubler** /Rəduble/ **1** *vt* increase; (classe) repeat; ~ de prudence be even more careful. ● *vi* (Scol) repeat a year; (s'intensifier) intensify.

**redoutable** /Rədutabl/ *adj* formidable.

**redouter** /Rədute/ **1** *vt* dread.

**redressement** /RədʀɛsmÃ/ *nm* (reprise) recovery; ~ judiciaire receivership.

**redresser** /Rədʀese/ **1** *vt* straighten (out ou up); (situation) right, redress; (économie, entreprise) turn around. □ **se** ~ *vpr* (personne) straighten (oneself) up; (se remettre debout) stand up; (pays, économie) recover.

**réduction** /Redyksjɔ̃/ *nf* reduction.

**réduire** /Reduiʀ/ **17** *vt* reduce (à to). □ **se** ~ *vpr* be reduced ou cut; se ~ à (revenir à) come down to.

**réduit**, ~e /Redui, -t/ *adj* (objet) small-scale; (limité) limited. ● *nm* cubbyhole.

**rééducation** /Reedykasjɔ̃/ *nf* (de handicapé) rehabilitation; (Méd) physiotherapy. **rééduquer** **1** *vt* (personne) rehabilitate; (membre) restore normal movement to.

**réel**, ~le /Reɛl/ *adj* real. ● *nm* reality. **réellement** *adv* really.

**réexpédier** /Reɛkspedje/ **45** *vt* forward; (retourner) send back.

**refaire** /RəfɛR/ **33** *vt* do again; (erreur, voyage) make again; (réparer) do up, redo.

**réfectoire** /Refɛktwaʀ/ *nm* refectory.

**référence** /ʀefeʀɑ̃s/ nf reference.

**référendum** /ʀefeʀɛ̃dɔm/ nm referendum.

**référer** /ʀefeʀe/ 🔟 vi en ~ à consult. □ se ~ à vpr refer to, consult.

**refermer** /ʀəfɛʀme/ 🔟 vt close (again). □ se ~ vpr close (again).

**réfléchi**, ~e /ʀefleʃi/ adj (personne) thoughtful; (verbe) reflexive.

**réfléchir** /ʀefleʃiʀ/ 🔟 vi think (à, sur about). ● vt reflect. □ se ~ vpr be reflected.

**reflet** /ʀəflɛ/ nm reflection; (nuance) sheen.

**refléter** /ʀəflete/ 🔟 vt reflect. □ se ~ vpr be reflected.

**réflexe** /ʀeflɛks/ adj reflex. ● nm reflex; (réaction) reaction.

**réflexion** /ʀeflɛksjɔ̃/ nf (pensée) thought, reflection; (remarque) remark, comment; à la ~ on second thoughts.

**refluer** /ʀəflye/ 🔟 vi flow back; (foule) retreat; (inflation) go down.

**reflux** /ʀəfly/ nm (marée) ebb, tide.

**réforme** /ʀefɔʀm/ nf reform. **réformer** 🔟 vt reform; (soldat) invalid out.

**refouler** /ʀəfule/ 🔟 vt (larmes) hold back; (désir) repress; (souvenir) suppress.

**refrain** /ʀəfʀɛ̃/ nm chorus; le même ~ the same old story.

**refréner** /ʀəfʀene/ 🔟 vt curb, check.

**réfrigérateur** /ʀefʀiʒeʀatœʀ/ nm refrigerator.

**refroidir** /ʀəfʀwadiʀ/ 🔟 vt/i cool (down). □ se ~ vpr (personne, temps) get cold. **refroidissement** nm cooling; (rhume) chill.

**refuge** /ʀəfyʒ/ nm refuge; (chalet) mountain hut.

**réfugié**, ~e /ʀefyʒje/ nm, f refugee. **réfugier (se)** 🔟 vpr take refuge.

**refus** /ʀəfy/ nm refusal; ce n'est pas de ~ 🔟 wouldn't say no.

**refuser** /ʀəfyze/ 🔟 vt refuse (de to); (client, spectateur) turn away; (recaler) fail; (à un poste) turn down. □ se ~ à vpr (évidence) reject; se ~ à faire refuse to do.

**regain** /ʀəgɛ̃/ nm ~ de renewal ou revival of; (Comm) rise.

**régal** (pl ~s) /ʀegal/ nm treat, delight.

**régaler** /ʀegale/ 🔟 vt ~ qn de treat sb to. □ se ~ vpr (de nourriture) je me régale it's delicious.

**regard** /ʀəgaʀ/ nm (expression, coup d'œil) look; (vue) eye; (yeux) eyes; ~ fixe stare; au ~ de with regard to; en ~ de compared with.

**regardant**, ~e /ʀəgaʀdɑ̃, -t/ adj ~ avec son argent careful with money; peu ~ (sur) not fussy (about).

**regarder** /ʀəgaʀde/ 🔟 vt look at; (observer) watch; (considérer) consider; (concerner) concern; ~ fixement stare at; ~ à think about, pay attention to. ● vi look. □ se ~ vpr (soi-même) look at oneself; (personnes) look at each other.

**régate** /ʀegat/ nf regatta.

**régie** /ʀeʒi/ nf ~ d'État public corporation; (radio, TV) control room; (au cinéma) production; (Théât) stage management.

**régime** /ʀeʒim/ nm (organisation) system; (Pol) regime; (Méd) diet; (de moteur) speed; (de bananes) bunch; se mettre au ~ go on a diet; à ce ~ at this rate.

**régiment** /ʀeʒimɑ̃/ nm regiment.

**région** /ʀeʒjɔ̃/ nf region. **régional**, ~e (mpl -aux) adj regional.

**Région** The largest administrative unit in France, consisting of a number of *départements*. Each has its own *Conseil régional* (regional council) which has responsibilities in education and economic planning. ▷ **DÉPARTEMENT.**

**régir** / reʒiʀ/ **2** vt govern.

**régisseur** /reʒisœʀ/ nm (Théât) stage manager; ~ **de plateau** (TV) floor manager; (au cinéma) studio manager.

**registre** /ʀɘʒistʀ/ nm register.

**réglage** /ʀeɡlaʒ/ nm adjustment; (de moteur) tuning.

**règle** /ʀɛɡl/ nf rule; (instrument) ruler; ~**s** (de femme) period; **en** ~ in order.

**réglé**, ~**e** /ʀeɡle/ adj (vie) ordered; (arrangé) settled; (papier) ruled.

**règlement** /ʀɛɡləmɑ̃/ nm (règles) regulations; (solution) settlement; (paiement) payment. **réglementaire** adj (uniforme) regulation. **réglementation** nf regulation, rules. **réglementer** **1** vt regulate, control.

**régler** /ʀeɡle/ **14** vt settle; (machine) adjust; (programmer) set; (facture) settle; (personne) set up with; ~ **son compte à** **1** settle a score with.

**réglisse** /ʀeɡlis/ nf liquorice.

**règne** /ʀɛɲ/ nm reign; (végétal, animal, minéral) kingdom.

**regret** /ʀɘɡʀɛ/ nm regret; **à** ~ with regret.

**regretter** /ʀɘɡʀete/ **1** vt regret; (personne) miss; (pour s'excuser) be sorry.

**regrouper** /ʀɘɡʀupe/ **1** vt group *ou* bring together. □ **se** ~ vpr gather *ou* group together.

**régularité** /ʀeɡylaʀite/ nf regularity; (de rythme, progrès) steadiness; (de surface, écriture) evenness.

**régulier**, -**ière** /ʀeɡylje, -jɛʀ/ adj regular; (qualité, vitesse) steady, even; (ligne, paysage) even; (légal) legal; (honnête) honest.

**rehausser** /ʀɘose/ **1** vt raise; (faire valoir) enhance.

**rein** /ʀɛ̃/ nm kidney; ~**s** (dos) small of the back.

**reine** /ʀɛn/ nf queen.

**réinsertion** /ʀeɛ̃sɛʀsjɔ̃/ nf reintegration.

**réintégrer** /ʀeɛ̃teɡʀe/ **14** vt (lieu) return to; (Jur) reinstate; (personne) reintegrate.

**réitérer** /ʀeiteʀe/ **14** vt repeat.

**rejaillir** /ʀɘʒajiʀ/ **2** vi ~ **sur** splash back onto; ~ **sur qn** (succès) reflect on sb.

**rejet** /ʀɘʒɛ/ nm rejection; ~**s** (déchets) waste.

**rejeter** /ʀɘʒte/ **38** vt throw back; (refuser) reject; (déverser) discharge; ~ **une faute sur qn** shift the blame for a mistake onto sb.

**rejoindre** /ʀɘʒwɛ̃dʀ/ **22** vt go back to, rejoin; (rattraper) catch up with; (rencontrer) join, meet up with. □ **se** ~ vpr (personnes) meet up; (routes) join, meet.

**réjoui**, ~**e** /ʀeʒwi/ adj joyful.

**réjouir** /ʀeʒwiʀ/ **2** vt delight. □ **se** ~ vpr be delighted (de at). **réjouissances** nfpl festivities. **réjouissant**, ~**e** adj cheering.

**relâche** /ʀɘlɑʃ/ nm (repos) break, rest; **faire** ~ (Théât) be closed.

**relâcher** /ʀɘlɑʃe/ **1** vt slacken; (personne) release; (discipline) relax. □ **se** ~ vpr slacken.

**relais** /ʀɘlɛ/ nm (Sport) relay; (hôtel) hotel; (intermédiaire) intermediary; **prendre le ~ de** take over from.

**relancer** /rəlɑ̃se/ 10 vt boost, revive; (renvoyer) throw back.

**relatif, -ive** /rəlatif, -v/ adj relative; **~ à** relating to.

**relation** /rəlasjɔ̃/ nf relationship; (ami) acquaintance; (personne puissante) connection; **~s** relations; **~s extérieures** foreign affairs; **en ~ avec qn** in touch with sb.

**relativement** /rəlativmɑ̃/ adv relatively; **~ à** in relation to.

**relativité** /rəlativite/ nf relativity.

**relax** /rəlaks/ adj inv 🔟 laid-back.

**relaxer (se)** /(sə)rəlakse/ 1 vpr relax.

**relayer** /rəleje/ 31 vt relieve; (émission) relay. □ **se ~** vpr take over from one another.

**reléguer** /rəlege/ 14 vt relegate.

**relent** /rəlɑ̃/ nm stink; (fig) whiff.

**relève** /rəlɛv/ nf relief; **prendre ou assurer la ~** take over (de from).

**relevé, -e** /rəlve/ adj spicy. ● nm (de compteur) reading; (facture) bill; **~ bancaire,** **~ de compte** bank statement; **faire le ~ de** list.

**relever** /rəlve/ 6 vt pick up; (personne tombée) help up; (remonter) raise; (col) turn up; (compteur) read; (défi) accept; (relayer) relieve; (remarquer, noter) note; (plat) spice up; (rebâtir) rebuild; **~ de** come within the competence of; (Méd) recover from. □ **se ~** vpr (personne) get up (again); (pays, économie) recover.

**relief** /rəljɛf/ nm relief; **mettre en ~** highlight.

**relier** /rəlje/ 45 vt link (up) (à to); (livre) bind.

**religieux, -ieuse** /rəliʒjø, -z/ adj religious. ● nm, f monk, nun.

**religion** /rəliʒjɔ̃/ nf religion.

**reliure** /rəljyr/ nf binding.

**reluire** /rəlɥir/ 17 vi shine.

**remaniement** /rəmanimɑ̃/ nm revision; **~ ministériel** cabinet reshuffle.

**remarquable** /rəmarkabl/ adj remarkable.

**remarque** /rəmark/ nf remark; (par écrit) comment.

**remarquer** /rəmarke/ 1 vt notice; (dire) say; **faire ~ point out (à to);** **se faire ~** draw attention to oneself; **remarque(z)** mind you.

**remblai** /rɑ̃blɛ/ nm embankment.

**remboursement** /rɑ̃bursəmɑ̃/ nm (d'emprunt, dette) repayment; (Comm) refund.

**rembourser** /rɑ̃burse/ 1 vt (dette, emprunt) repay; (billet, frais) refund; (client) give a refund to; (ami) pay back.

**remède** /rəmɛd/ nm remedy; (médicament) medicine.

**remédier** /rəmedje/ 45 vi **~ à** remedy.

**remerciements** /rəmɛrsimɑ̃/ nmpl thanks. **remercier** 45 vt thank (de for); (licencier) dismiss.

**remettre** /rəmɛtr/ 42 vt put back; (vêtement) put back on; (donner) hand over; (devoir, démission) hand in; (faire fonctionner) switch back on; (restituer) give back; (différer) put off; (ajouter) add; (se rappeler) remember; **~ en cause ou en question** call into question. □ **se ~** vpr (guérir) recover; **se ~ au tennis** take up tennis again; **se ~ au travail** get back to work; **se ~ à faire** start doing again; **s'en ~ à** leave it to.

**remise** /rəmiz/ nf (abri) shed; (rabais) discount; (transmission) handing over; (ajournement) postponement; **~ en cause ou en question**

calling into question; ~ des prix prizegiving; ~ des médailles medals ceremony; ~ de peine remission.

**remontant** /rəmɔ̃tɑ̃/ *nm* tonic.

**remontée** /rəmɔ̃te/ *nf* ascent; (d'eau, de prix) rise; ~ mécanique ski lift.

**remonte-pente** (*pl* ~s) /rəmɔ̃tpɑ̃t/ *nm* ski tow.

**remonter** /rəmɔ̃te/ **1** *vi* go ou come (back) up; (*prix, niveau*) rise (again); (revenir) go back (à to); ~ dans le temps go back in time. ● *vt* (*rue, escalier*) go ou come (back) up; (relever) raise; (*montre*) wind up; (*objet démonté*) put together again; (*personne*) buck up.

**remontoir** /rəmɔ̃twaR/ *nm* winder.

**remords** /rəmɔR/ *nm* remorse; avoir du ou des ~ feel remorse.

**remorque** /rəmɔRk/ *nf* trailer; en ~ on tow. **remorquer** **1** *vt* tow.

**remous** /rəmu/ *nm* eddy; (de bateau) backwash; (fig) turmoil.

**rempart** /rɑ̃paR/ *nm* rampart.

**remplaçant**, ~e /rɑ̃plasɑ̃, -t/ *nm, f* replacement; (joueur) reserve, substitute.

**remplacement** /rɑ̃plasmɑ̃/ *nm* replacement; faire des ~s do supply teaching. **remplacer** **10** *vt* replace.

**rempli**, ~e /rɑ̃pli/ *adj* full (de of); (journée) busy.

**remplir** /rɑ̃pliR/ **2** *vt* fill (up); (*formulaire*) fill in ou out; (*condition*) fulfil; (*devoir, tâche, rôle*) carry out. □ se ~ *vpr* fill (up). **remplissage** *nm* filling; (de texte) padding.

**remporter** /rɑ̃pɔRte/ **1** *vt* take back; (*victoire*) win.

**remuant**, ~e /rəmɥɑ̃, -t/ *adj* boisterous.

**remue-ménage** /rəmymenaʒ/ *nm inv* commotion, bustle.

**remuer** /rəmɥe/ **1** *vt* move; (*thé, café*) stir; (*passé*) rake up. ● *vi* move; (*gigoter*) fidget. □ se ~ *vpr* move.

**rémunération** /remyneRasjɔ̃/ *nf* payment.

**renaissance** /Rənɛsɑ̃s/ *nf* rebirth.

**renard** /RənaR/ *nm* fox.

**renchérir** /Rɑ̃ʃeRiR/ **2** *vi* (dans une vente) raise the bidding; ~ sur go one better than. ● *vt* increase, put up.

**rencontre** /Rɑ̃kɔ̃tR/ *nf* meeting; (de routes) junction; (Mil) encounter; (match) match; (US) game.

**rencontrer** /Rɑ̃kɔ̃tRe/ **1** *vt* meet; (heurter) hit; (trouver) find. □ se ~ *vpr* meet.

**rendement** /Rɑ̃dmɑ̃/ *nm* yield; (travail) output.

**rendez-vous** /Rɑ̃devu/ *nm* appointment; (d'amoureux) date; (lieu) meeting-place; prendre ~ (avec) make an appointment (with).

**rendormir (se)** /(sə)Rɑ̃dɔRmiR/ **46** *vpr* go back to sleep.

**rendre** /Rɑ̃dR/ **3** *vt* give back, return; (donner en retour) return; (monnaie) give; (justice) dispense; (jugement) pronounce; ~ heureux/possible make happy/possible; (vomir **1**) vomit; ~ compte de report on; ~ service (à) help; ~ visite à visit. ● *vi* (terres) yield; (activité) be profitable. □ se ~ *vpr* (capituler) surrender; (aller) go (à to); se ~ utile make oneself useful.

**rêne** /Rɛn/ *nf* rein.

**renfermé**, ~e /Rɑ̃fɛRme/ *adj* withdrawn. ● *nm* sentir le ~ smell musty.

**renflé**, ~e /Rɑ̃fle/ *adj* bulging.

**renforcer** /Rɑ̃fɔRse/ **10** *vt*

reinforce.

**renfort** /ʀɑ̃fɔʀ/ *nm* reinforcement; **à grand ~ de** with a great deal of.

**renier** /ʀənje/ **45** *vt* (*personne, œuvre*) disown; (*foi*) renounce.

**renifler** /ʀənifle/ **1** *vt/i* sniff.

**renne** /ʀɛn/ *nm* reindeer.

**renom** /ʀənɔ̃/ *nm* renown; (*réputation*) reputation. **renommé, ~e** *adj* famous. **renommée** *nf* (*célébrité*) fame; (*réputation*) reputation.

**renoncement** /ʀənɔ̃smɑ̃/ *nm* renunciation.

**renoncer** /ʀənɔ̃se/ **10** *vi* ~ **à** (*habitude, ami*) give up, renounce; (*projet*) abandon; **~ à faire** abandon the idea of doing.

**renouer** /ʀənwe/ **1** *vt* tie up (again); (*amitié*) renew; **~ avec qn** get back in touch with sb; (*après une dispute*) make up with sb.

**renouveau** (*pl* **~x**) /ʀənuvo/ *nm* revival.

**renouveler** /ʀənuvle/ **38** *vt* renew; (*réitérer*) repeat; (*remplacer*) replace. □ **se ~** *vpr* be renewed; (*incident*) recur, happen again.

**renouvellement** /ʀənuvɛlmɑ̃/ *nm* renewal.

**rénovation** /ʀenɔvasjɔ̃/ *nf* (*d'édifice*) renovation; (*d'institution*) reform.

**renseignement** /ʀɑ̃sɛɲ(ə)mɑ̃/ *nm* ~(s) information; (**bureau des**) ~**s** information desk; (**service des**) ~**s téléphoniques** directory enquiries.

**renseigner** /ʀɑ̃seɲe/ **1** *vt* inform, give information to. □ **se ~** *vpr* enquire, make enquiries, find out.

**rentabilité** /ʀɑ̃tabilite/ *nf* profitability. **rentable** *adj* profitable.

**rente** /ʀɑ̃t/ *nf* (*private*) income; (*pension*) annuity. **rentier, -ière** *nm, f* person of private means.

**rentrée** /ʀɑ̃tʀe/ *nf* return; (*revenu*) income; **la ~ (des classes)** the start of the new school year; **faire sa ~** make a comeback.

**rentrer** /ʀɑ̃tʀe/ **1** *vi* (*aux être*) go *ou* come back home, return home; (*entrer*) go *ou* come in; (*entrer à nouveau*) go *ou* come back in; (*revenu*) come in; (*élèves*) go back (to school); **~ dans** (*heurter*) smash into; **tout est rentré dans l'ordre** everything is back to normal; **~ dans ses frais** break even. ● *vt* (*aux avoir*) bring in; (*griffes*) draw in; (*vêtement*) tuck in.

**renverser** /ʀɑ̃vɛʀse/ **1** *vt* knock over *ou* down; (*piéton*) knock down; (*liquide*) upset, spill; (*mettre à l'envers*) turn upside down; (*gouvernement*) overthrow; (*inverser*) reverse. □ **se ~** *vpr* (*véhicule*) overturn; (*verre, vase*) fall over.

**renvoi** /ʀɑ̃vwa/ *nm* return; (*d'employé*) dismissal; (*d'élève*) expulsion; (*report*) postponement; (*dans un livre, fichier*) cross-reference; (*rot*) burp.

**renvoyer** /ʀɑ̃vwaje/ **32** *vt* send back, return; (*employé*) dismiss; (*élève*) expel; (*ajourner*) postpone; (*référer*) refer; (*réfléchir*) reflect.

**repaire** /ʀəpɛʀ/ *nm* den.

**répandre** /repɑ̃dʀ/ **3** vt (liquide) spill; (étendre, diffuser) spread; (odeur) give off. □ se ~ vpr spread; (liquide) spill; se ~ **en injures** let out a stream of abuse.

**répandu, ~e** /repɑ̃dy/ adj widespread.

**réparateur, -trice** /repaʀatœʀ, -tʀis/ nm engineer. **réparation** nf repair; (compensation) compensation. **réparer** **1** vt repair, mend; (faute) make amends for; (remédier à) put right.

**repartie** /repaʀti/ nf retort; avoir de la ~ always have a ready reply.

**repartir** /repaʀtiʀ/ **46** vi start again; (voyageur) set off again; (s'en retourner) go back; (secteur économique) pick up again.

**répartir** /repaʀtiʀ/ **2** vt distribute; (partager) share out; (étaler) spread. **répartition** nf distribution.

**repas** /repɑ/ nm meal.

**repassage** /repasaʒ/ nm ironing.

**repasser** /repase/ **1** vi come ou go back; ~ **devant qch** go past sth again. ● vt (linge) iron; (examen) retake, resit; (film) show again.

**repêcher** /repeʃe/ **1** vt recover, fish out; (candidat) allow to pass.

**repentir** [1] /repɑ̃tiʀ/ nm repentance.

**repentir** [2] (se) /(sə)repɑ̃tiʀ/ **2** vpr (Relig) repent (de of); se ~ de (regretter) regret.

**répercuter** /repeʀkyte/ **1** vt (bruit) send back. □ se ~ echo; se ~ sur have repercussions on.

**repère** /repeʀ/ nm mark; (jalon) marker; (événement) landmark; (référence) reference point.

**repérer** /repeʀe/ **14** vt locate, spot. □ se ~ vpr get one's bearings.

**répertoire** /repeʀtwaʀ/ nm (artistique) repertoire; (liste) directory;

~ **téléphonique** telephone directory; (personnel) telephone book.

**répertorier** **45** vt index.

**répéter** /repete/ **14** vt repeat; (Théât) rehearse. ● vi rehearse. □ se ~ vpr be repeated; (personne) repeat oneself.

**répétition** /repetisjɔ̃/ nf repetition; (Théât) rehearsal.

**répit** /repi/ nm respite, break.

**replier** /rəplije/ **45** vt fold (up); (ailes, jambes) tuck in. □ se ~ vpr withdraw (sur **soi-même** into oneself).

**réplique** /replik/ nf reply; (riposte) retort; (objection) objection; (Théât) line; (copie) replica. **répliquer** **1** vt/i reply; (riposter) retort; (objecter) answer back.

**répondeur** /repɔ̃dœʀ/ nm answering machine.

**répondre** /repɔ̃dʀ/ **3** vt (injure, bêtise) reply with; ~ **que** answer ou reply that; ~ **à** (être conforme à) answer; (affection, sourire) return; (avances, appel, critique) respond to; ~ **de** answer for. ● vi answer, reply; (être insolent) answer back; (réagir) respond (à to).

**réponse** /repɔ̃s/ nf answer, reply; (fig) response.

**report** /rəpɔʀ/ nm (transcription) transfer; (renvoi) postponement.

**reportage** /rəpɔʀtaʒ/ nm report; (par écrit) article.

**reporter** [1] /rəpɔʀte/ **1** vt take back; (ajourner) put off; (transcrire) transfer. □ se ~ **à** ou refer to.

**reporter** [2] /rəpɔʀtɛʀ/ nm reporter.

**repos** /rəpo/ nm rest; (paix) peace. **reposant, ~e** adj restful.

**reposer** /rəpoze/ **1** vt put down again; (délasser) rest. ● vi rest (**sur** on); laisser ~ (pâte) leave to stand. □ se ~ vpr rest;

**r**

**se ~ sur** rely on.

**repousser** /ʁəpuse/ **1** *vt* push back; (*écarter*) push away; (*dégoûter*) repel; (*décliner*) reject; (*ajourner*) postpone, put back. ● *vi* grow again.

**reprendre** /ʁəpʁɑ̃dʁ/ **50** *vt* take back; (*confiance, conscience*) regain; (*souffle*) get back; (*évadé*) recapture; (*recommencer*) resume; (*redire*) repeat; (*modifier*) alter; (*blâmer*) reprimand; **~ du pain** take some more bread; **on ne m'y reprendra pas** I won't be caught out again. ● *vi* (*recommencer*) resume; (*affaires*) pick up. □ **se ~** *vpr* (se ressaisir) pull oneself together; (se corriger) correct oneself.

**représailles** /ʁəpʁezaj/ *nfpl* reprisals.

**représentant, ~e** /ʁəpʁezɑ̃tɑ̃, -t/ *nm, f* representative.

**représentation** /ʁəpʁezɑ̃tasjɔ̃/ *nf* representation; (Théât) performance.

**représenter** /ʁəpʁezɑ̃te/ **1** *vt* represent; (*figures*) depict, show; (*pièce de théâtre*) perform. □ **se ~** *vpr* (s'imaginer) imagine.

**répression** /ʁepʁesjɔ̃/ *nf* repression; (d'élan) suppression.

**réprimande** /ʁepʁimɑ̃d/ *nf* reprimand.

**réprimer** /ʁepʁime/ **1** *vt* (*peuple*) repress; (*sentiment*) suppress; (*fraude*) crack down on.

**reprise** /ʁəpʁiz/ *nf* resumption; (Théât) revival; (TV) repeat; (de tissu) darn, mend; (essor) recovery; (Comm) part-exchange, trade-in; **à plusieurs ~s** on several occasions.

**repriser** /ʁəpʁize/ **1** *vt* darn, mend.

**reproche** /ʁəpʁɔʃ/ *nm* reproach; **faire des ~s à** find fault with.

**reprocher** /ʁəpʁɔʃe/ **1** *vt* **~ qch à qn** reproach *ou* criticize sb for sth.

**reproducteur, -trice** /ʁəpʁɔdyktœʁ, -tʁis/ *adj* reproductive.

**reproduire** /ʁəpʁɔdɥiʁ/ **17** *vt* reproduce; (*répéter*) repeat. □ **se ~** *vpr* reproduce; (se répéter) recur.

**reptile** /ʁɛptil/ *nm* reptile.

**repu, ~e** /ʁəpy/ *adj* satiated, replete.

**républicain, ~e** /ʁepyblikɛ̃, -ɛn/ *adj & nm, f* republican.

**république** /ʁepyblik/ *nf* republic; **~ populaire** people's republic.

**répudier** /ʁepydje/ **45** *vt* repudiate; (*droit*) renounce.

**répugnance** /ʁepyɲɑ̃s/ *nf* repugnance; (*hésitation*) reluctance; **avoir de la ~ pour** loathe. **répugnant, ~e** *adj* repulsive.

**répugner** /ʁepyɲe/ **1** *vt* be repugnant to, disgust; **~ à** (*effort, violence*) be averse to; **~ à faire** be reluctant to do.

**répulsion** /ʁepylsjɔ̃/ *nf* repulsion.

**réputation** /ʁepytasjɔ̃/ *nf* reputation.

**réputé, ~e** /ʁepyte/ *adj* renowned (*pour for*); (*école, compagnie*) reputable; **~ pour être** reputed to be.

**requérir** /ʁəkeʁiʁ/ **7** *vt* require, demand.

**requête** /ʁəkɛt/ *nf* request; (Jur) petition.

**requin** /ʁəkɛ̃/ *nm* shark.

**requis, ~e** /ʁəki, -z/ *adj* (*exigé*) required; (*nécessaire*) necessary.

**RER** *abrév m* (*réseau express régional*) Parisian rapid transit rail system.

**rescapé, ~e** /ʁɛskape/ *nm, f* survivor. ● *adj* surviving.

**rescousse** /ʁɛskus/ *nf* **à la ~** to

**réseau | ressembler**

the rescue.

**réseau** /plʌx/ (pl ~x) /Rezo/ nm network; ~ **local** local area network, LAN; le ~ **des** ~x (Ordinat) Internet.

**réservation** /RezERvasjɔ̃/ nf reservation, booking.

**réserve** /RezERv/ nf reserve; (restriction) reservation, reserve; (indienne) reservation; (entrepôt) store-room; en ~ in reserve; les ~s (Mil) the reserves.

**réserver** /RezERve/ ▣ vt reserve; (place) book, reserve. □ se ~ vpr ~ qch save sth for oneself; se ~ pour save oneself for; se ~ le droit de reserve the right to.

**réservoir** /RezERvwaR/ nm tank; (lac) reservoir.

**résidence** /Rezidɑ̃s/ nf residence; ~ **secondaire** second home; ~ **universitaire** hall of residence.

**résident**, ~e /Rezidɑ̃, -t/ nm, f resident; (étranger) foreign resident.

**résider** /Rezide/ ▣ vi reside; ~ **dans qch** (difficulté) lie in.

**résigner (se)** /(sə)Rezine/ ▣ vpr se ~ à faire resign oneself to doing.

**résilier** /Rezilje/ 45 vt terminate.

**résine** /Rezin/ nf resin.

**résistance** /Rezistɑ̃s/ nf resistance; (fil électrique) element. **résistant**, ~e adj tough.

**résister** /Reziste/ ▣ vi resist; ~ à (agresseur, assaut, influence, tentation) resist; (corrosion, chaleur) withstand.

**résolu**, ~e /Rezɔly/ adj resolute; ~ à faire determined to do.
● ➡RÉSOUDRE 58.

**résolution** /Rezɔlysjɔ̃/ nf (fermeté) resolution; (d'un problème) solving.

**résonner** /Rezɔne/ ▣ vi resound.

**résorber** /RezɔRbe/ ▣ vt reduce.

□ se ~ vpr be reduced.

**résoudre** /RezudR/ 58 vt solve; (crise, conflit) resolve. □ se ~ vpr (se décider) resolve to; (se résigner) resign oneself to.

**respect** /RespE/ nm respect. **respectabilité** nf respectability.

**respecter** /RespEkte/ ▣ vt respect; faire ~ (loi, décision) enforce.

**respectueux**, -euse /RespEktɥø, -z/ adj respectful; ~ de l'environnement environmentally friendly.

**respiration** /RespiRasjɔ̃/ nf breathing; (haleine) breath. **respiratoire** adj respiratory, breathing.

**respirer** /RespiRe/ ▣ vi breathe; (se reposer) catch one's breath. ● vt breathe (in); (exprimer) radiate.

**resplendir** /Resplɑ̃diR/ ② vi shine (de with). **resplendissant**, ~e adj brilliant, radiant.

**responsabilité** /RespɔsabilitE/ nf responsibility; (légale) liability.

**responsable** /Respɔsablə/ adj responsible (de for); ~ de (chargé de) in charge of. ● nmf person in charge; (coupable) person responsible.

**resquiller** /Reskije/ ▣ vi ▣ (dans le train) fare-dodge; (au spectacle) get in without paying; (dans la queue) jump the queue.

**ressaisir (se)** /(sə)RəseziR/ ② vpr pull oneself together; (équipe sportive, valeurs boursières) make a recovery.

**ressemblance** /Rəsɑ̃blɑ̃s/ nf resemblance.

**ressemblant**, ~e /Rəsɑ̃blɑ̃, -t/ adj être ~ (portrait) be a good likeness.

**ressembler** /Rəsɑ̃ble/ ▣ vi ~ à resemble, look like. □ se ~ vpr be alike; (physiquement) look alike.

**ressentiment** /Rəsɑ̃timɑ̃/ nm resentment.

**ressentir** /Rəsɑ̃tiR/ 46 vt feel. □ se ~ de vpr feel the effects of.

**resserrer** /RəseRe/ 1 vt tighten; (contracter) compress; (vêtement) take in. □ se ~ vpr tighten; (route) narrow; (se regrouper) move closer together.

**ressort** /RəsɔR/ nm (objet) spring; (fig) energy; être du ~ de be the province of; (Jur) be within the jurisdiction of; en dernier ~ as a last resort.

**ressortir** /RəsɔRtiR/ 46 vi go ou come back out; (se voir) stand out; (film, disque) be re-released; faire ~ bring out; il ressort que it emerges that. ●vt take out again; (redire) come out with again; (disque, film) re-release.

**ressortissant**, ~e /RəsɔRtisɑ̃, -t/ nm, f national.

**ressource** /RəsuRs/ nf resource; ~s resources; à bout de ~ at one's wits' end.

**ressusciter** /Resysite/ 1 vi come back to life. ●vt bring back to life; (fig) revive.

**restant**, ~e /Restɑ̃, -t/ adj remaining. ●nm remainder.

**restaurant** /RestɔRɑ̃/ nm restaurant.

**restauration** /RestɔRasjɔ̃/ nf restoration; (hôtellerie) catering.

**restaurer** /RestɔRe/ 1 vt restore. □ se ~ vpr eat.

**reste** /Rest/ nm rest; (d'une soustraction) remainder; ~s remains (de of); (nourriture) leftovers; un ~ de poulet some left-over chicken; au ~, du ~ moreover, besides.

**rester** /Reste/ 1 vi (aux être) stay, remain; (subsister) be left, remain; il reste du pain there is some

bread left (over); il me reste du pain I have some bread left (over); il me reste à it remains for me to; en ~ à go no further than; en ~ là stop there.

**restituer** /Restitɥe/ 1 vt (rendre) return; (recréer) reproduce; (rétablir) reconstruct.

**restreindre** /RestRɛ̃dR/ 22 vt restrict. □ se ~ vpr (dans les dépenses) cut back.

**restriction** /RestRiksjɔ̃/ nf restriction.

**résultat** /Rezylta/ nm result.

**résulter** /Rezylte/ 1 vi ~ de result from, be the result of.

**résumé** /Rezyme/ nm summary; en ~ in short; (pour finir) to sum up.

**résumer** 1 vt summarize.

**résurrection** /RezyReksjɔ̃/ nf resurrection; (renouveau) revival.

**rétablir** /Retablir/ 2 vt restore; (personne) restore to health. □ se ~ vpr (ordre, silence) be restored; (guérir) recover. **rétablissement** nm restoration; (de malade, monnaie) recovery.

**retard** /RətaR/ nm lateness; (sur un programme) delay; (infériorité) backwardness; avoir du ~ be late; (montre) be slow; en ~ late; (retardé) behind; en ~ sur l'emploi du temps behind schedule; rattraper ou combler son ~ catch up; prendre du ~ fall behind.

**retardataire** /RətaRdatɛR/ nmf latecomer. ●adj late.

**retarder** /RətaRde/ 1 vt ~ qn/ qch delay sb/sth, hold sb/sth up; (par rapport à une heure convenue) make sb/sth late; (montre) put back. ●vi (montre) be slow; (personne) be out of touch.

**retenir** /RətniR/ 58 vt hold back; (souffle, attention, prisonnier) hold;

(*eau, chaleur*) retain, hold; (*larmes*) hold back; (*garder*) keep; (*retarder*) detain, hold up; (*réserver*) book; (*se rappeler*) remember; (*déduire*) deduct; (*accepter*) accept. □ **se ~** *vpr* (*se contenir*) restrain oneself; se ~ à qch to hold on to; se ~ de faire stop oneself from doing.

**rétention** /retɑ̃sjɔ̃/ *nf* retention.

**retentir** /rətɑ̃tiR/ **2** *vi* ring out, resound; ~ **sur** have an impact on. **retentissant, ~e** *adj* resounding. **retentissement** *nm* (*effet*) effect.

**retenue** /rətny/ *nf* restraint; (*somme*) deduction; (*Scol*) detention.

**réticent, ~e** /retisɑ̃, -t/ *adj* (*hésitant*) hesitant; (*qui rechigne*) reluctant; (*réservé*) reticent.

**rétine** /retin/ *nf* retina.

**retiré, ~e** /rətiRe/ *adj* (*vie*) secluded; (*lieu*) remote.

**retirer** /rətiRe/ **1** *vt* (*sortir*) take out; (*ôter*) take off; (*argent, offre, candidature*) withdraw; (*écarter*) (*main, pied*) withdraw; (*billet, bagages*) collect, pick up; (*avantage*) derive; ~ **à qn** take sth away from sb. □ **se ~** *vpr* withdraw, retire.

**retombées** /rətɔ̃be/ *nfpl* (*conséquences*) effects; ~ **radioactives** nuclear fall-out.

**retomber** /rətɔ̃be/ **1** *vi* (*faire une chute*) fall again; (*retourner au sol*) land, come down; ~ **dans** (*erreur*) fall back into.

**retouche** /rətuʃ/ *nf* alteration; (*de photo, tableau*) retouch.

**retour** /rətuR/ *nm* return; être de ~ be back (de from); ~ **en arrière** flashback; **par** ~ **du courrier** by return of post; ~ **en** return.

**retourner** /rətuRne/ **1** *vt* (*aux avoir*) turn over; (*vêtement*) turn inside out; (*maison*) turn upside down; (*lettre, compliment*) return; (*émouvoir* [1]) shake, upset. ● *vi* (*aux être*) go back, return. □ **se ~** *vpr* turn round; (*dans son lit*) twist and turn; **s'en** ~ go back; **se ~ contre** turn against.

**retrait** /rətRɛ/ *nm* withdrawal; (*des eaux*) receding; être (*situé*) **en ~** (*de*) be set back (from).

**retraite** /rətRɛt/ *nf* retirement; (*pension*) (*retirement*) pension; (*fuite, refuge*) retreat; **mettre à la ~** pension off; **prendre sa ~** retire.

**retraité, ~e** /rətRɛte/ *adj* retired. ● *nm, f* (*old-age*) pensioner.

**retrancher** /rətRɑ̃ʃe/ **1** *vt* remove; (*soustraire*) deduct, subtract. □ **se ~** *vpr* (*Mil*) entrench oneself; **se ~ derrière** take refuge behind.

**retransmettre** /rətRɑ̃smɛtR/ **42** *vt* broadcast.

**rétrécir** /retResiR/ **2** *vt* make narrower; (*vêtement*) take in. ● *vi* (*tissu*) shrink. □ **se ~** *vpr* (*rue*) narrow.

**rétribution** /retRibysjɔ̃/ *nf* payment.

**rétroactif, -ive** /retRoaktif, -v/ *adj* retrospective; **augmentation à effet ~** backdated pay rise.

**retrousser** /rətRuse/ **1** *vt* pull up; (*manche*) roll up.

**retrouvailles** /rətRuvaj/ *nfpl* reunion.

**retrouver** /rətRuve/ **1** *vt* find (again); (*rejoindre*) meet (again); (*forces, calme*) regain; (*lieu*) be back in; (*se rappeler*) remember. □ **se ~** *vpr* find oneself (back); (*se réunir*) meet (again); (*être présent*) be found; **s'y ~** (*s'orienter, comprendre*) find one's way; (*rentrer dans ses frais* [1]) break even.

**rétroviseur** /retRovizœR/ *nm* (*Auto*) (rear-view) mirror.

**réunion** /Reynjɔ̃/ *nf* meeting; (*ren-*

r

contre) gathering; (après une séparation) réunion; (d'objets) collection.

**réunir** /ʁeyniʁ/ [2] vt gather, collect; (rapprocher) bring together; (convoquer) call together; (raccorder) join; (qualités) combine. □ se ~ vpr meet.

**réussi**, ~e /ʁeysi/ adj successful.

**réussir** /ʁeysiʁ/ [2] vi succeed, be successful; ~ à faire succeed in doing, manage to do; ~ à un examen pass an exam; ~ à qn (méthode) work well for sb; (climat, mode de vie) agree with sb. ● vt (vie) make a success of.

**réussite** /ʁeysit/ nf success; (jeu) patience.

**revaloir** /ʁəvalwaʁ/ [60] vt je vous revaudrai cela (en mal) I'll pay you back for this; (en bien) I'll repay you some day.

**revanche** /ʁəvãʃ/ nf revenge; (Sport) return ou revenge match; en ~ on the other hand.

**rêvasser** /ʁevase/ [1] vi daydream.

**rêve** /ʁɛv/ nm dream; faire un ~ have a dream.

**réveil** /ʁevɛj/ nm waking up, (fig) awakening; (pendule) alarm clock.

**réveillé**, ~e /ʁeveje/ adj awake.

**réveille-matin** /ʁevɛjmatɛ̃/ nm inv alarm clock.

**réveiller** /ʁeveje/ [1] vt wake (up); (sentiment, souvenir) awaken; (curiosité) arouse. □ se ~ vpr wake up.

**réveillon** /ʁevɛjɔ̃/ nm (Noël) Christmas Eve; (nouvel an) New Year's Eve. **réveillonner** [1] vi see Christmas ou the New Year in.

**révéler** /ʁevele/ [14] vt reveal. □ se ~ vpr be revealed; se ~ facile turn out to be easy, prove easy.

**revendeur**, -euse /ʁəvãdœʁ, -øz/ nm, f dealer, stockist; ~ de drogue

drug dealer.

**revendication** /ʁəvãdikasjɔ̃/ nf claim. **revendiquer** [1] vt claim.

**revendre** /ʁəvãdʁ/ [3] vt sell (again); avoir de l'énergie à ~ have energy to spare.

**revenir** /ʁəvniʁ/ [58] vi (aux être) come back, return (à to); ~ à (activité) go back to; (se résumer à) come down to; (échoir à) fall to; ~ à 100 euros cost 100 euros; ~ de (maladie, surprise) get over; ~ sur ses pas retrace one's steps; faire ~ (Culin) brown; ça me revient! now I remember!; je n'en reviens pas! I can't get over it!

**revenu** /ʁəvny/ nm income; (de l'État) revenue.

**rêver** /ʁeve/ [1] vt/i dream (à of; de faire of doing).

**réverbère** /ʁevɛʁbɛʁ/ nm street lamp.

**révérence** /ʁeveʁãs/ nf reverence; (salut d'homme) bow; (salut de femme) curtsy.

**rêverie** /ʁevʁi/ nf daydream; (activité) daydreaming.

**revers** /ʁəvɛʁ/ nm reverse; (de main) back; (d'étoffe) wrong side; (de veste) lapel; (de pantalon) turn-up; (de manche) cuff; (tennis) backhand; (fig) set-back.

**revêtement** /ʁəvɛtmã/ nm covering; (de route) surface; ~ de sol floor covering. **revêtir** [61] vt cover; (habit) put on; (prendre, avoir) assume.

**rêveur**, -euse /ʁevœʁ, -øz/ adj dreamy. ● nm, f dreamer.

**réviser** /ʁevize/ [1] vt revise; (machine, véhicule) service. **révision** nf revision; service.

**revivre** /ʁəvivʁ/ [62] vi come alive again. ● vt relive.

**révocation** /ʁevɔkasjɔ̃/ nf repeal;

(d'un fonctionnaire) dismissal.

**revoir**¹ /ʀəvwaʀ/ [63] vt see (again); (réviser) revise.

**revoir**² /ʀəvwaʀ/ nm au ∼ goodbye.

**révolte** /ʀevɔlt/ nf revolt. **révolté, ∼e** nm, f rebel.

**révolter** /ʀevɔlte/ [1] vt appal, revolt. □ **se** ∼ vpr revolt.

**révolu, ∼e** /ʀevɔly/ adj past; avoir 21 ans ∼s be over 21 years of age.

**révolution** /ʀevɔlysjɔ̃/ nf revolution. **révolutionnaire** adj & nmf revolutionary. **révolutionner** [1] vt revolutionize.

**revolver** /ʀevɔlvɛʀ/ nm revolver, gun.

**révoquer** /ʀevɔke/ [1] vt repeal; (fonctionnaire) dismiss.

**revue** /ʀəvy/ nf (examen, défilé) review; (magazine) magazine; (spectacle) variety show.

**rez-de-chaussée** /ʀedʃose/ nm inv ground floor; (US) first floor.

**RF** abrév f (**République Française**) French Republic.

**rhinocéros** /ʀinɔseʀɔs/ nm rhinoceros.

**rhubarbe** /ʀybaʀb/ nf rhubarb.

**rhum** /ʀɔm/ nm rum.

**rhumatisme** /ʀymatism/ nm rheumatism.

**rhume** /ʀym/ nm cold; ∼ des foins hay fever.

**ri** /ʀi/ ➡**RIRE** [54].

**ricaner** /ʀikane/ [1] vi snigger.

**riche** /ʀiʃ/ adj rich (en in). ● nmf rich man, rich woman.

**richesse** /ʀiʃɛs/ nf wealth; (de sol, décor) richness; ∼s wealth; (ressources) resources.

**ride** /ʀid/ nf wrinkle; (sur l'eau) ripple.

**rideau** (pl ∼x) /ʀido/ nm curtain;

(métallique) shutter; (fig) screen.

**ridicule** /ʀidikyl/ adj ridiculous. ● nm (d'une situation) absurdity; (le grotesque) le ∼ ridicule. **ridiculiser** [1] vt ridicule.

**rien** /ʀjɛ̃/ pron nothing; (quoi que ce soit) anything; de ∼! don't mention it!; ∼ de bon nothing good; elle n'a ∼ dit she didn't say anything; ∼ d'autre/de plus nothing else/more; ∼ du tout nothing at all; ∼ que (seulement) just, only; trois fois ∼ next to nothing; il n'y est pour ∼ he has nothing to do with it; ∼ à faire! (c'est impossible) it's no good!; (refus) no way! [I]. ● nm un ∼ a touch of; être puni pour un ∼ be punished for the slightest thing; se disputer pour un ∼ fight over nothing; en un ∼ de temps in next to no time.

**rieur, -euse** /ʀijœʀ, -øz/ adj cheerful; (yeux) laughing.

**rigide** /ʀiʒid/ adj rigid.

**rigolade** /ʀigɔlad/ nf fun.

**rigoler** /ʀigɔle/ [1] vi laugh; (s'amuser) have some fun; (plaisanter) joke.

**rigolo, ∼te** /ʀigɔlo, -ɔt/ adj [I] funny. ● nm, f [I] joker.

**rigoureux, -euse** /ʀiguʀø, -z/ adj rigorous; (hiver) harsh; (sévère) strict; (travail, recherches) meticulous.

**rigueur** /ʀigœʀ/ nf rigour; à la ∼ at a pinch; être de ∼ be obligatory; tenir ∼ à qn de qch bear sb a grudge for sth.

**rime** /ʀim/ nf rhyme.

**rimer** /ʀime/ [1] vi rhyme (avec with); cela ne rime à rien it makes no sense.

**rinçage** /ʀɛ̃saʒ/ nm rinse; (action) rinsing.

**rincer** /ʀɛ̃se/ [10] vt rinse.

**riposte** /ʀipɔst/ nf retort.

**riposter** /ʀipɔste/ **1** vi retaliate; ~ à (attaque) counter; (insulte) reply to. ● vt retort (que that).

**rire** /ʀiʀ/ **52** vi laugh de at; (plaisanter) joke; (s'amuser) have fun; c'était pour ~ it was a joke. ● nm laugh; des ~s laughter.

**risée** /ʀize/ nf la ~ de the laughing stock of.

**risque** /ʀisk/ nm risk. **risqué, ~e** adj risky; (osé) daring.

**risquer** /ʀiske/ **1** vt risk (de faire of doing); (être passible de) face; il risque de pleuvoir it might rain; tu risques de te faire mal you might hurt yourself. □ **se** ~ **à/ dans** vpr venture to/into.

**ristourne** /ʀistuʀn/ nf discount.

**rite** /ʀit/ nm rite; (habitude) ritual. **rituel, ~le** adj & nm ritual.

**rivage** /ʀivaʒ/ nm shore.

**rival, ~e** (mpl **-aux**) /ʀival, -o/ adj & nm, f rival. **rivaliser** **1** vi compete (avec with). **rivalité** nf rivalry.

**rive** /ʀiv/ nf (de fleuve) bank; (de lac) shore.

**riverain, ~e** /ʀivʀɛ̃, -ɛn/ adj riverside. ● nm, f riverside resident; (d'une rue) resident.

**rivière** /ʀivjɛʀ/ nf river.

**riz** /ʀi/ nm rice. **rizière** nf paddy field.

**robe** /ʀɔb/ nf (de femme) dress; (de juge) robe; (de cheval) coat; ~ de chambre dressing-gown.

**robinet** /ʀɔbinɛ/ nm tap; (US) faucet.

**robot** /ʀɔbo/ nm robot; ~ ménager food processor.

**robuste** /ʀɔbyst/ adj robust.

**roche** /ʀɔʃ/ nf rock.

**rocher** /ʀɔʃe/ nm rock.

**rock** /ʀɔk/ nm (Mus) rock.

**rodage** /ʀɔdaʒ/ nm en ~ (Auto) running in.

**roder** /ʀɔde/ **1** vt (Auto) run in; être rodé (personne) have got the hang of things.

**rôder** /ʀode/ **1** vi roam; (suspect) prowl.

**rogne** /ʀɔɲ/ nf **1** anger; en ~ in a temper.

**rogner** /ʀɔɲe/ **1** vt trim; ~ **sur** cut down on.

**rognon** /ʀɔɲɔ̃/ nm (Culin) kidney.

**roi** /ʀwa/ nm king; les R~ mages the Magi; la fête des R~ Twelfth Night.

**rôle** /ʀol/ nm role, part.

**roller** /ʀɔlɛʀ/ nm (patin) rollerblade®; (activité) rollerblading.

**romain, ~e** /ʀɔmɛ̃, -ɛn/ adj Roman. R~, ~e nm, f Roman. **romaine** nf (laitue) cos.

**roman** /ʀɔmɑ̃/ nm novel; (genre) fiction.

**romance** /ʀɔmɑ̃s/ nf ballad.

**romancier, -ière** /ʀɔmɑ̃sje, -jɛʀ/ nm, f novelist.

**romanesque** /ʀɔmanɛsk/ adj romantic; (fantastique) fantastic; (récit) fictional; œuvres ~s novels, fiction.

**romantique** /ʀɔmɑ̃tik/ adj & nmf romantic. **romantisme** nm romanticism.

**rompre** /ʀɔ̃pʀ/ **3** vt break; (relations) break off. ● vi (se séparer) break up; ~ **avec** (fiancé) break up with; (parti) break away from; (tradition) break with. □ **se** ~ vpr break.

**ronce** /ʀɔ̃s/ nf bramble.

**rond, ~e** /ʀɔ̃, -d/ adj round; (gras) plump; (ivre **1**) drunk. ● nm (cercle) ring; (tranche) slice; en ~ in a circle; il n'a pas un ~ **1** he hasn't got a penny.

**ronde** /ʀɔ̃d/ nf (de policier) beat; (de soldat, gardien) watch; (Mus) semibreve.

**rondelle** /ʀɔ̃dɛl/ nf (Tech) washer; (tranche) slice.

**rondement** /ʀɔ̃dmɑ̃/ adv promptly; (franchement) frankly.

**rondeur** /ʀɔ̃dœʀ/ nf roundness; (franchise) frankness; (embonpoint) plumpness.

**rondin** /ʀɔ̃dɛ̃/ nm log.

**rond-point** (pl ronds-points) /ʀɔ̃pwɛ̃/ nm roundabout; (US) traffic circle.

**ronfler** /ʀɔ̃fle/ **1** vi snore; (moteur) purr.

**ronger** /ʀɔ̃ʒe/ **40** vt gnaw (at); (vers, acide) eat into. □ se ~ les ongles bite one's nails.

**rongeur** /ʀɔ̃ʒœʀ/ nm rodent.

**ronronner** /ʀɔ̃ʀɔne/ **1** vi purr.

**rosbif** /ʀɔsbif/ nm roast beef.

**rose** /ʀoz/ nf rose. ● adj & nm pink.

**rosé**, ~e /ʀoze/ adj pinkish. ● nm rosé.

**roseau** (pl ~x) /ʀozo/ nm reed.

**rosée** /ʀoze/ nf dew.

**rosier** /ʀozje/ nm rose bush.

**rossignol** /ʀɔsiɲɔl/ nm nightingale.

**rotatif**, -ive /ʀɔtatif, -v/ adj rotary.

**roter** /ʀɔte/ **1** vi **11** burp.

**rôti** /ʀoti/ nm joint; (cuit) roast; ~ de porc roast pork.

**rotin** /ʀotɛ̃/ nm (rattan) cane.

**rôtir** /ʀotiʀ/ **2** vt roast.

**rôtissoire** /ʀotiswaʀ/ nf roasting spit.

**rotule** /ʀotyl/ nf kneecap.

**rouage** /ʀwaʒ/ nm (Tech) wheel; les ~s the works; (d'une organisation: fig) wheels.

**roucouler** /ʀukule/ **1** vi coo.

**roue** /ʀu/ nf wheel; ~ dentée cog

(wheel); ~ de secours spare wheel.

**rouer** /ʀwe/ **1** vt ~ de coups thrash.

**rouge** /ʀuʒ/ adj red; (fer) red-hot. ● nm red; (vin) red wine; (fard) blusher; ~ à lèvres lipstick. ● nmf (Pol) red. **rouge-gorge** (pl rouges-gorges) nm robin.

**rougeole** /ʀuʒɔl/ nf measles (+ sg). **rouget** /ʀuʒɛ/ nm red mullet.

**rougeur** /ʀuʒœʀ/ nf redness; (tache) red blotch.

**rougir** /ʀuʒiʀ/ **2** vi turn red; (de honte) blush.

**rouille** /ʀuj/ nf rust. **rouillé**, ~e adj rusty.

**rouiller** /ʀuje/ **1** vi rust. □ se ~ vpr get rusty.

**rouleau** (pl ~x) /ʀulo/ nm roll; (outil, vague) roller; ~ à pâtisserie rolling pin; ~ compresseur steam-roller.

**roulement** /ʀulmɑ̃/ nm rotation; (bruit) rumble; (alternance) rotation; (de tambour) roll; ~ à billes ballbearing; travailler par ~ work in shifts.

**rouler** /ʀule/ **1** vt roll up; (ficelle, manches) roll up; (pâte) roll out; (duper **11**) cheat. ● vi (véhicule, train) go, travel; (conducteur) drive. □ se ~ dans vpr (herbe) roll in; (couverture) roll oneself up in.

**roulette** /ʀulɛt/ nf (de meuble) castor; (de dentiste) drill; (jeu) roulette; comme sur des ~s very smoothly.

**roulotte** /ʀulɔt/ nf caravan.

**roumain**, ~e /ʀumɛ̃, -ɛn/ adj Romanian. R~, ~e nm, f Romanian.

**Roumanie** /ʀumani/ nf Romania.

**rouquin**, ~e /ʀukɛ̃, -in/ **11** adj redhaired. ● nm, f redhead.

**rouspéter** /ʀuspete/ **14** vi **11** grumble, moan.

r

**rousse** /Rus/ →ROUX.

**roussir** /RusiR/ [2] vt scorch. ● vi turn brown.

**route** /Rut/ nf road; (Naut, Aviat) route; (direction) way; (voyage) journey; (chemin: fig) path; en ~ on the way; en ~! let's go!; mettre en ~ start; ~ nationale trunk road, main road; se mettre en ~ set out.

**routier, -ière** /Rutje, -jɛR/ adj road. ● nm long-distance lorry ou truck driver; (restaurant) transport café; (US) truck stop.

**routine** /Rutin/ nf routine.

**roux, rousse** /Ru, Rus/ adj red, russet; (personne) red-haired; (chat) ginger. ● nm, f redhead.

**royal, ~e** (mpl -aux) /Rwajal, -jo/ adj royal; (cadeau) fit for a king.

**royaume** /Rwajom/ nm kingdom.

**Royaume-Uni** /Rwajomyni/ nm United Kingdom.

**royauté** /Rwajote/ nf royalty.

**RTT** abrév f (réduction du temps de travail) reduction in working hours.

**ruban** /Rybɑ̃/ nm ribbon; (de chapeau) band; ~ adhésif sticky tape; ~ magnétique magnetic tape.

**rubéole** /Rybeɔl/ nf German measles (+ sg).

**rubis** /Rybi/ nm ruby.

**rubrique** /RybRik/ nf heading; (article) column.

**ruche** /Ryʃ/ nf beehive.

**rude** /Ryd/ adj (au toucher) rough; (pénible) tough; (grossier) coarse; (fameux [1]) tremendous.

**rudement** /Rydmɑ̃/ adv (frapper) hard; (traiter) harshly; (très [1]) really.

**rudimentaire** /Rydimɑ̃tɛR/ adj rudimentary.

**rue** /Ry/ nf street.

**ruée** /Rɥe/ nf rush.

**ruer** /Rɥe/ [1] vi (cheval) buck. □ se ~ vpr rush (dans into; vers towards); se ~ sur pounce on.

**rugby** /Rygbi/ nm rugby.

**rugir** /RyʒiR/ [2] vi roar.

**rugueux, -euse** /Rygø, -z/ adj rough.

**ruine** /Rɥin/ nf ruin; en (~s) in ruins. **ruiner** [1] vt ruin.

**ruisseau** (pl ~x) /Rɥiso/ nm stream; (rigole) gutter.

**rumeur** /RymœR/ nf (nouvelle) rumour; (son) murmur, hum.

**ruminer** /Rymine/ [1] vi (animal) ruminate; (méditer) meditate.

**rupture** /RyptyR/ nf break; (action) breaking; (de contrat) breach; (de pourparlers) breakdown; (de relations) breaking off; (de couple, coalition) break-up.

**rural, ~e** (mpl -aux) /RyRal, -o/ adj rural.

**ruse** /Ryz/ nf cunning; une ~ a trick, a ruse. **rusé, ~e** adj cunning.

**russe** /Rys/ adj Russian. ● nm (Ling) Russian. **R~** nmf Russian.

**Russie** /Rysi/ nf Russia.

**rustique** /Rystik/ adj rustic.

**rythme** /Ritm/ nm rhythm; (vitesse) rate; (de la vie) pace. **rythmique** adj rhythmical.

. . . . . . . . . . . . . . . . . . . . . . . . . . . . . . .

# Ss

. . . . . . . . . . . . . . . . . . . . . . . . . . . . . . .

**s'** /s/ →SE.

**sa** /sa/ →SON[1].

**SA** abrév f (société anonyme) PLC.

**sabbatique** /sabatik/ adj (année) sabbatical year.

**sable** /sabl/ nm sand; ~s mouvants quicksands. **sabler** vt **1** grit.

**sablier** /sablije/ nm (Culin) eggtimer.

**sablonneux, -euse** /sablɔnø, -z/ adj sandy.

**sabot** /sabo/ nm (de cheval) hoof; (chaussure) clog; (de frein) shoe; ~ de Denver® (wheel) clamp.

**saboter** /sabɔte/ **1** vt sabotage; (bâcler) botch.

**sac** /sak/ nm bag; (grand, en toile) sack; mettre à ~ (maison) ransack; (ville) sack; ~ à dos rucksack; ~ à main handbag; ~ de couchage sleeping-bag; mettre dans le même ~ lump together.

**saccadé, -e** /sakade/ adj jerky.

**saccager** /sakaʒe/ **40** vt (abîmer) wreck; (maison) ransack; (ville, pays) sack.

**saccharine** /sakarin/ nf saccharin.

**sachet** /saʃɛ/ nm (small) bag; (d'aromates) sachet; ~ de thé teabag.

**sacoche** /sakɔʃ/ nf bag; (de vélo) saddlebag.

**sacre** /sakr/ nm (de roi) coronation; (d'évêque) consecration.

**sacré, -e** adj sacred; (maudit **!**) damned. **sacrement** nm sacrament. **sacrer** **1** vt crown; consecrate.

**sacrifice** /sakrifis/ nm sacrifice.

**sacrifier** /sakrifje/ **45** vt sacrifice; ~ à conform to. □ se ~ vpr sacrifice oneself.

**sacrilège** /sakrilɛʒ/ nm sacrilege. ● adj sacrilegious.

**sadique** /sadik/ adj sadistic. ● nmf sadist.

**sage** /saʒ/ adj wise; (docile) good, well behaved. ● nm wise man. **sage-femme** (pl **sages-femmes**) /saʒfam/ nf midwife.

**sagesse** /saʒɛs/ nf wisdom.

**Sagittaire** /saʒitɛr/ nm le ~ Sagittarius.

**saignant, ~e** /sɛɲɑ̃, -t/ adj (Culin) rare.

**saigner** /seɲe/ **1** vt/i bleed; ~ du nez have a nosebleed.

**saillant, ~e** /sajɑ̃, -t/ adj prominent.

**sain, ~e** /sɛ̃, sɛn/ adj healthy; (moralement) sane; ~ et sauf safe and sound.

**saindoux** /sɛ̃du/ nm lard.

**saint, ~e** /sɛ̃, -t/ adj holy; (bon, juste) saintly. ● nm, f saint. **Saint-Esprit** nm Holy Spirit. **sainteté** nf holiness; (d'un lieu) sanctity. **Sainte Vierge** nf Blessed Virgin. **Saint-Sylvestre** nf New Year's Eve.

**sais** /sɛ/ ➡SAVOIR **55**.

**saisie** /sezi/ nf (Jur) seizure; (Comput) keyboarding; ~ de données data capture.

**saisir** /sezir/ **2** vt grab (hold of); (proie) seize; (occasion, biens) seize; (comprendre) grasp; (frapper) strike; (Ordinat) keyboard, capture; saisi de (peur) stricken by, overcome by. □ se ~ de vpr seize. **saisissant, ~e** adj (spectacle) gripping.

**saison** /sezɔ̃/ nf season; la morte ~ the off season. **saisonnier, -ière** adj seasonal.

**sait** /sɛ/ ➡SAVOIR **55**.

**salade** /salad/ nf (plat) salad; (plante) lettuce. **saladier** nm salad bowl.

**salaire** /salɛr/ nm wages (+ pl); salary.

**salarié, ~e** /salarje/ adj wage-earning. ● nm, f wage earner.

**sale** /sal/ adj dirty; (mauvais) nasty.

**salé, ~e** /sale/ adj (goût) salty; (plat) salted; (opposé à sucré) savoury; (grivois **!**) spicy; (excessif

① steep. **saler** ① *vt* salt.

**saleté** /salte/ *nf* dirtiness; (crasse) dirt; (obscénité) obscenity; ~(s) (camelote) rubbish; (détritus) mess.

**salir** /saliʀ/ ② *vt* (make) dirty; (réputation) tarnish. □ **se ~** *vpr* get dirty. **salissant, ~e** *adj* dirty; (étoffe) easily dirtied.

**salive** /saliv/ *nf* saliva.

**salle** /sal/ *nf* room; (grande, publique) hall; (de restaurant) dining room; (Théât, cinéma) auditorium; **cinéma à trois ~s** three-screen cinema; ~ **à manger** dining room; ~ **d'attente** waiting room; ~ **de bains** bathroom; ~ **de causette** chatroom; ~ **de séjour** living room; ~ **de classe** classroom; ~ **d'embarquement** departure lounge; ~ **d'opération** operating theatre; ~ **des ventes** saleroom.

**salon** /salɔ̃/ *nm* lounge; (de coiffure, beauté) salon; (exposition) show; ~ **de thé** tea-room; ~ **virtuel** chatroom.

**salopette** /salɔpɛt/ *nf* dungarees (+ *pl*); (d'ouvrier) overalls (+ *pl*).

**saltimbanque** /saltẽbãk/ *nmf* (street) acrobat.

**salubre** /salybʀ/ *adj* healthy.

**saluer** /salɥe/ ① *vt* greet; (en partant) take one's leave of; (de la tête) nod to; (de la main) wave to; (Mil) salute; (accueillir favorablement) welcome.

**salut** /saly/ *nm* greeting; (de la tête) nod; (de la main) wave; (Mil) salute; (rachat) salvation. ●*interj* (bonjour ①) hello; (au revoir ①) bye.

**salutation** /salytasjɔ̃/ *nf* greeting.

**samedi** /samdi/ *nm* Saturday.

**SAMU** /samy/ *abrév m* (**Service d'assistance médicale d'urgence**) ≈ mobile accident unit.

**sanction** /sãksjɔ̃/ *nf* sanction. **sanctionner** ① *vt* sanction; (punir) punish.

**sandale** /sãdal/ *nf* sandal.

**sang** /sã/ *nm* blood; **se faire du mauvais** ~ **ou un** ~ **d'encre** be worried stiff. **sang-froid** *nm inv* self-control. **sanglant, ~e** *adj* bloody.

**sangle** /sãgl/ *nf* strap.

**sanglier** /sãglije/ *nm* wild boar.

**sanglot** /sãglo/ *nm* sob. **sangloter** ① *vi* sob.

**sanguin, ~e** /sãgɛ̃, -in/ *adj* (groupe) blood.

**sanguinaire** /sãginɛʀ/ *adj* bloodthirsty.

**sanitaire** /sanitɛʀ/ *adj* (directives) health; (conditions) sanitary; (appareils, installations) bathroom, sanitary. **sanitaires** *nmpl* bathroom.

**sans** /sã/ *prép* without; ~ **ça,** ~ **quoi** otherwise; ~ **arrêt** nonstop; ~ **encombre/faute/tarder** without incident/fail/delay; ~ **fin/goût/limite** endless/tasteless/limitless; ~ **importance/pareil/précédent/travail** unimportant/unparalleled/unprecedented/unemployed; **j'ai aimé mais** ~ **plus** it was good, it wasn't great.

**sans-abri** /sãzabʀi/ *nmf inv* homeless person.

**sans-gêne** /sãʒɛn/ *adj inv* inconsiderate, thoughtless. ●*nm inv* thoughtlessness.

**sans-papiers** /sãpapje/ *nm inv* illegal immigrant.

**santé** /sãte/ *nf* health; **à ta ou**

votre ~! cheers!

**saoul**, ~e /su, sul/ ➡SOUL.

**sapin** /sapɛ̃/ nm fir (tree); ~ de Noël Christmas tree.

**sarcasme** /saʀkasm/ nm sarcasm. **sarcastique** adj sarcastic.

**sardine** /saʀdin/ nf sardine.

**sas** /sɑs/ nm (Naut, Aviat) airlock.

**satané**, ~e /satane/ adj ① damned.

**satellite** /satelit/ nm satellite.

**satin** /satɛ̃/ nm satin.

**satire** /satiʀ/ nf satire.

**satisfaction** /satisfaksjɔ̃/ nf satisfaction.

**satisfaire** /satisfɛʀ/ 33 vt satisfy. ● vi ~ à fulfil. **satisfaisant**, ~e adj (acceptable) satisfactory. **satisfait**, ~e adj satisfied (de with).

**saturer** /satyʀe/ ① vt saturate.

**sauce** /sos/ nf sauce; ~ tartare tartar sauce. **saucière** nf sauceboat.

**saucisse** /sosis/ nf sausage.

**saucisson** /sosisɔ̃/ nm (slicing) sausage.

**sauf**[1] /sof/ prép except; ~ erreur if I'm not mistaken; ~ imprévu unless anything unforeseen happens; ~ avis contraire unless otherwise stated.

**sauf**[2], **-ve** /sof, sov/ adj safe, unharmed.

**sauge** /soʒ/ nf (Culin) sage.

**saule** /sol/ nm willow; ~ pleureur weeping willow.

**saumon** /somɔ̃/ nm salmon. ● adj inv salmon-(pink).

**sauna** /sona/ nm sauna.

**saupoudrer** /sopudʀe/ ① vt sprinkle (de with).

**saut** /so/ nm jump; faire un ~ chez qn pop round to sb's (place); le ~ (Sport) jumping; ~ en hauteur/longueur high/long jump;

~ périlleux somersault; au ~ du lit on getting up.

**sauté**, ~e /sote/ adj & nm (Culin) sauté.

**saute-mouton** /sotmutɔ̃/ nm inv leap-frog.

**sauter** /sote/ ① vi jump; (exploser) blow up; (fusible) blow; (se détacher) come off; faire ~ (détruire) blow up; (fusible) blow; (casser) break; ~ à la corde skip; ~ aux yeux be obvious; ~ au cou de qn fling one's arms round sb; ~ sur une occasion jump at an opportunity. ● vt jump (over); (page, classe) skip.

**sauterelle** /sotʀɛl/ nf grasshopper.

**sautiller** /sotije/ ① vi hop.

**sauvage** /sovaʒ/ adj wild; (primitif, cruel) savage; (farouche) unsociable; (illégal) unauthorized. ● nmf unsociable person; (brute) savage.

**sauve** /sov/ ➡SAUF.[2]

**sauvegarder** /sovgaʀde/ ① vt safeguard; (Ordinat) back up.

**sauver** /sove/ ① vt save; (d'un danger) rescue, save; (matériel) salvage. □ **se** ~ vpr (fuir) run away; (partir ①) be off. **sauvetage** nm rescue. **sauveteur** nm rescuer. **sauveur** nm saviour.

**savamment** /savamɑ̃/ adv learnedly; (habilement) cleverly.

**savant**, ~e /savɑ̃, -t/ adj learned; (habile) skilful. ● nm scientist.

**saveur** /savœʀ/ nf flavour; (fig) savour.

**savoir** /savwaʀ/ 65 vt know; elle sait conduire/nager she can drive/swim; faire ~ à qn que inform sb that; (pas) que je sache (not) as far as I know; à ~ namely. ● nm learning.

**savon** /savɔ̃/ nm soap; passer un ~ à qn ① give sb a telling-off. **savonnette** nf bar of soap.

**savourer** /savuʀe/ ① vt savour. **savoureux**, **-euse** adj tasty;

**s**

(fig) spicy.

**scandale** /skãdal/ nm scandal; (tapage) uproar; (en public) noisy scene; faire ~ shock people; faire un ~ make a scene. **scandaleux, -euse** adj scandalous. **scandaliser** 1 vt scandalize, shock.

**scander** /skãde/ 1 vt (vers) scan; (slogan) chant.

**scandinave** /skãdinav/ adj Scandinavian. S~ nmf Scandinavian.

**Scandinavie** /skãdinavi/ nf Scandinavia.

**scarabée** /skaʀabe/ nm beetle.

**sceau** (pl ~x) /so/ nm seal.

**scélérat** /selera/ nm scoundrel.

**sceller** /sele/ 1 vt seal.

**scène** /sɛn/ nf scene; (estrade, art dramatique) stage; mettre en ~ (pièce) stage; (film) direct; mise en ~ direction; ~ de ménage domestic dispute.

**scepticisme** /sɛptisism/ nm scepticism.

**sceptique** /sɛptik/ adj sceptical. ● nmf sceptic.

**schéma** /ʃema/ nm diagram. **schématique** adj schematic; (sommaire) sketchy. **schématiser** 1 vt simplify.

**schizophrène** /skizɔfʀɛn/ adj & nmf schizophrenic.

**sciatique** /sjatik/ adj (nerf) sciatic. ● nf sciatica.

**scie** /si/ nf saw.

**sciemment** /sjamã/ adv knowingly.

**science** /sjãs/ nf science; (savoir) knowledge.

**science-fiction** /sjãsfiksjõ/ nf science fiction.

**scientifique** /sjãtifik/ adj scientific. ● nmf scientist.

**scier** /sje/ 45 vt saw.

**scintiller** /sɛ̃tije/ 1 vi glitter; (étoile) twinkle.

**scission** /sisjõ/ nf split.

**sclérose** /skleʀoz/ nf sclerosis; ~ en plaques multiple sclerosis.

**scolaire** /skɔlɛʀ/ adj school. **scolarisé, ~e** adj going to school. **scolarité** nf schooling.

**score** /skɔʀ/ nm score.

**scorpion** /skɔʀpjõ/ nm scorpion; le S~ Scorpio.

**scotch** /skɔtʃ/ nm (boisson) Scotch (whisky); (ruban adhésif)® Sellotape®.

**scout, ~e** /skut/ nm & adj scout.

**scrupule** /skʀypyl/ nm scruple. **scrupuleux, -euse** adj scrupulous.

**scruter** /skʀyte/ 1 vt examine, scrutinize.

**scrutin** /skʀytɛ̃/ nm (vote) ballot; (élections) polls (+ pl).

**sculpter** /skylte/ 1 vt sculpt, carve. **sculpteur** nm sculptor. **sculpture** nf sculpture.

**SDF** abrév m (sans domicile fixe) homeless person.

**se,** s' /sə, s/

s' before vowel or mute h.

● pronom
····▸ himself, (féminin) herself; (indéfini) oneself; (non humain) itself; (au pluriel) themselves; ~ laver les mains wash one's hands; (réciproque) each other, one another; ils se détestent they hate each other.

❗ The translation of se will vary according to which verb it is associated with. You should therefore refer to the verb to find it. For example, se promener, se taire will be treated respectively under promener and taire.

**séance** /seɑ̃s/ nf session; (Théât, cinéma) show; ~ de pose sitting; ~ tenante forthwith.

**seau** (pl ~x) /so/ nm bucket, pail.

**sec**, **sèche** /sɛk, sɛʃ/ adj dry; (fruits) dried; (coup, bruit) sharp; (cœur) hard; (whisky) neat. ● nm à ~ (sans eau) dry; (sans argent) broke; au ~ in a dry place.

**sèche-cheveux** /sɛʃʃəvø/ nm inv hairdrier.

**sèchement** /sɛʃmɑ̃/ adv drily.

**sécher** /seʃe/ [14] vt/i dry; (cours [1]) skip; (ne pas savoir [1]) be stumped. □ **se** ~ vpr dry oneself. **sécheresse** nf (de climat) dryness; (temps sec) drought. **séchoir** nm drier.

**second**, ~e /səgɔ̃, -d/ adj & nm, f second. ● nm (adjoint) second in command; (étage) second floor. **secondaire** adj secondary. **seconde** nf (instant) second; (vitesse) second gear.

**seconder** /səgɔ̃de/ [1] vt assist.

**secouer** /sakwe/ [1] vt shake; (poussière, torpeur) shake off. □ **se** ~ vpr [1] (se dépêcher) get a move on; (réagir) shake oneself up.

**secourir** /səkuʀiʀ/ [20] vt assist, help. **secouriste** nmf first-aid worker.

**secours** /səkuʀ/ nm assistance, help; au ~! help!; de ~ (sortie) emergency; (équipe, opération) rescue. ● nmpl (Méd) first aid.

**secousse** /səkus/ nf jolt, jerk; (séisme) tremor.

**secret**, **-ète** /səkʀɛ, -t/ adj secret. ● nm secret; (discrétion) secrecy; le ~ professionnel professional confidentiality; ~ de Polichinelle open secret; en ~ in secret, secretly.

**secrétaire** /səkʀetɛʀ/ nmf secretary; ~ de direction personal as-

sistant. ● nm (meuble) writing desk; ~ d'État junior minister.

**secrétariat** /səkʀetaʀja/ nm secretarial work; (bureau) secretariat.

**sectaire** /sɛktɛʀ/ adj sectarian.

**secte** /sɛkt/ nf sect.

**secteur** /sɛktœʀ/ nm area; (Comm) sector; (circuit: Électr) mains (+ pl).

**section** /sɛksjɔ̃/ nf section; (Scol) stream; (Mil) platoon. **sectionner** [1] vt sever.

**sécuriser** /sekyʀize/ [1] vt reassure.

**sécurisé**, **e** /sekyʀize/ adj (Ordinat) secure; une ligne ~e a secure line.

**sécurité** /sekyʀite/ nf security; (absence de danger) safety; en ~ safe, secure; **Sécurité sociale** nf social services, social security services; ~ des frontières homeland security.

**sédatif** /sedatif/ nm sedative.

**sédentaire** /sedɑ̃tɛʀ/ adj sedentary.

**séducteur**, **-trice** /sedyktœʀ, -tʀis/ adj seductive. ● nm, f seducer. **séduction** nf seduction; (charme) charm.

**séduire** /sedɥiʀ/ [17] vt charm; (plaire à) appeal to; (sexuellement) seduce. **séduisant**, ~e adj (personne) attractive.

**ségrégation** /segʀegasjɔ̃/ nf segregation.

**seigle** /sɛgl/ nm rye.

**seigneur** /sɛɲœʀ/ nm lord; le S~ the Lord.

**sein** /sɛ̃/ nm breast; au ~ de within.

**séisme** /seism/ nm earthquake.

**seize** /sɛz/ adj & nm sixteen.

**séjour** /seʒuʀ/ nm stay; (pièce) living room. **séjourner** [1] vi stay.

s

**sel** /sɛl/ nm salt; (piquant) spice.

**sélectif, -ive** /selɛktif, -v/ adj selective.

**sélection** /selɛksjɔ̃/ nf selection. **sélectionner** ① vt select.

**selle** /sɛl/ nf saddle; ~s (Méd) stools.

**sellette** /sɛlɛt/ nf sur la ~ (personne) in the hot seat.

**selon** /səlɔ̃/ prép according to; ~ que depending on whether.

**semaine** /səmɛn/ nf week; en ~ during the week.

**sémantique** /semãtik/ adj semantic. ● nf semantics.

**semblable** /sãblabl/ adj similar (à to). ● nm fellow (creature).

**semblant** /sãblã/ nm faire ~ de pretend to; un ~ de a semblance of.

**sembler** /sãble/ ① vi seem (à to; que that); il me semble que it seems to me that.

**semelle** /səmɛl/ nf sole; ~ compensée wedge heel.

**semence** /s(ə)mãs/ nf seed.

**semer** /s(ə)me/ ⑥ vt (graine, doute) sow; (jeter, parsemer) strew; (personne ①) lose; ~ la panique spread panic.

**semestre** /səmɛstʀ/ nm half year; (Univ) semester. **semestriel, ~le** adj (revue) biannual; (examen) end-of-semester.

**séminaire** /seminɛʀ/ nm (Relig) seminary; (Univ) seminar.

**semi-remorque** /s(ə)miʀ(ə)mɔʀk/ nm articulated lorry.

**semis** /s(ə)mi/ nm seedling.

**semoule** /s(ə)mul/ nf semolina.

**sénat** /sena/ nm senate. **sénateur** nm senator.

**sénile** /senil/ adj senile.

**senior** /senjɔʀ/ adj (âgé) senior; (mode, publication) for senior citizens. ● nmf senior citizen.

**sens** /sãs/ nm (Méd) sense; (signification) meaning, sense; (direction) direction; à mon ~ to my mind; à ~ unique (rue) one-way; ça n'a pas de ~ it doesn't make sense; ~ commun common sense; ~ giratoire roundabout; ~ interdit no-entry sign; (rue) one-way street; dans le ~ des aiguilles d'une montre clockwise; dans le ~ inverse des aiguilles d'une montre anticlockwise; ~ dessus dessous upside down; ~ devant derrière back to front.

**sensation** /sãsasjɔ̃/ nf feeling, sensation; faire ~ create a sensation. **sensationnel, ~le** adj sensational.

**sensé, ~e** /sãse/ adj sensible.

**sensibiliser** /sãsibilize/ ① vt ~ l'opinion increase people's awareness (à qch to sth).

**sensibilité** /sãsibilite/ nf sensitivity. **sensible** adj sensitive (à to); (appréciable) noticeable. **sensiblement** adv noticeably.

**sensoriel, ~le** /sãsɔʀjɛl/ adj sensory.

**sensualité** /sãsɥalite/ nf sensuousness; sensuality. **sensuel, ~le** adj sensual.

**sentence** /sãtãs/ nf sentence.

**senteur** /sãtœʀ/ nf scent.

**sentier** /sãtje/ nm path.

**sentiment** /sãtimã/ nm feeling; faire du ~ sentimentalize; j'ai le ~ que... I get the feeling that... **sentimental, ~e** (mpl -aux) adj sentimental.

**sentir** /sãtiʀ/ ㊻ vt feel; (odeur) smell; (pressentir) sense; ~ la lavande smell of lavender; je ne peux pas le ∼ ①I can't stand him. ● vi smell. □ se ∼ vpr se ∼ fier/ mieux feel proud/better.

**séparation** /separasjɔ̃/ nf separation.

**séparatiste** /separatist/ adj & nmf separatist.

**séparé,** ∼e /separe/ adj separate; (conjoints) separated.

**séparer** /separe/ ❶ vt separate; (en deux) split. □ se ∼ vpr separate, part (de from); (se détacher) split; se ∼ de (se défaire de) part with.

**sept** /set/ adj & nm seven.

**septante** /septɑ̃t/ adj & nm seventy.

**septembre** /septɑ̃bʀ/ nm September.

**septentrional,** ∼e (mpl -aux) /septɑ̃tʀijɔnal, -o/ adj northern.

**septième** /setjɛm/ adj & nmf seventh.

**sépulture** /sepyltyʀ/ nf burial; (lieu) burial place.

**séquelles** /sekɛl/ nfpl (maladie) after-effects; (fig) aftermath.

**séquence** /sekɑ̃s/ nf sequence.

**séquestrer** /sekɛstʀe/ ❶ vt confine (illegally).

**sera, serait** /səʀa, sərɛ/ ➡ÊTRE ❹.

**serbe** /sɛʀb/ adj Serbian. S∼ nmf Serbian.

**Serbie** /sɛʀbi/ nf Serbia.

**serein,** ∼e /sərɛ̃, -ɛn/ adj serene.

**sérénité** /serenite/ nf serenity.

**sergent** /sɛʀʒɑ̃/ nm sergeant.

**série** /seʀi/ nf series (+ sg) ; (d'objets) set; de ∼ (véhicule etc.) standard; fabrication ou production en ∼ mass production.

**sérieusement** /serjøzmɑ̃/ adv seriously.

**sérieux, -ieuse** /serjø, -z/ adj serious; (digne de confiance) reliable;

(chances, raison) good. ● nm seriousness; garder son ∼ keep a straight face; prendre au ∼ take seriously.

**serin** /səʀɛ̃/ nm canary.

**seringue** /səʀɛ̃g/ nf syringe.

**serment** /sɛʀmɑ̃/ nm oath; (promesse) vow.

**sermon** /sɛʀmɔ̃/ nm sermon. **sermonner** ❶ vt lecture.

**séropositif, -ive** /seʀopozitif, -v/ adj HIV positive.

**serpent** /sɛʀpɑ̃/ nm snake; ∼ à sonnettes rattlesnake.

**serpillière** /sɛʀpijɛʀ/ nf floorcloth.

**serre** /sɛʀ/ nf (de jardin) greenhouse; (griffe) claw.

**serré,** ∼e /seʀe/ adj (habit, nœud, écrou) tight; (personnes) packed, crowded; (lutte, mailles) close; (écriture) cramped; (cœur) heavy.

**serrer** /seʀe/ ❶ vt (saisir) grip; (presser) squeeze; (vis, corde, ceinture) tighten; (poing, dents) clench; ∼ qn dans ses bras hug sb; ∼ les rangs close ranks; ∼ qn (vêtement) be tight on sb; ∼ qn de près follow sb closely; ∼ la main à shake hands with. ● vi ∼ à droite keep over to the right. □ se ∼ vpr (se rapprocher) squeeze (up).

**serrure** /seʀyʀ/ nf lock. **serrurier** nm locksmith.

**servante** /sɛʀvɑ̃t/ nf (maid) servant.

**serveur, -euse** /sɛʀvœʀ, -øz/ nm, f (homme) waiter; (femme) waitress. ● nm (Ordinat) server.

**serviable** /sɛʀvjabl/ adj helpful.

**service** /sɛʀvis/ nm service; (fonction, temps de travail) duty; (pourboire) service (charge); (dans une société) department; (∼ non) compris service (not) included; être de ∼ be on duty; pendant le ∼

(when) on duty; rendre ~ à qn be a help to sb; ~ d'ordre stewards (+ pl); ~ après-vente after-sales service; ~ militaire military service; les ~s secrets the secret service (+ sg).

**serviette** /sɛʀvjɛt/ nf (de toilette) towel; (cartable) briefcase; (~ de table) serviette, napkin; ~ hygiénique sanitary towel.

**servir** /sɛʀviʀ/ 46 vt/i serve; (être utile) be of use, serve; ~ qn (à table) wait on sb; ça sert à (outil, récipient) it is used for; ça me sert à/de I use it to/as; ça ne sert à rien (action) it's pointless; ~ de serve as, be used as; ~ à qn de guide act as a guide for sb. □ se ~ vpr (à table) help oneself (de); se ~ de use. **serviteur** nm servant.

**ses** /se/ →SON.[^1]

**session** /sesjɔ̃/ nf session.

**seuil** /sœj/ nm doorstep; (entrée) doorway; (fig) threshold.

**seul, ~e** /sœl/ adj alone, on one's own; (unique) only; un ~ exemple only one example; pas un ~ ami not a single friend; lui ~ le sait only he knows; dans le ~ but de with the sole aim of; parler tout ~ talk to oneself; faire qch tout ~ do sth on one's own. ● nm, f le ~ la ~e the only one. **seulement** adv only.

**sève** /sɛv/ nf sap.

**sévère** /sevɛʀ/ adj severe. **sévérité** nf severity.

**sévices** /sevis/ nmpl physical abuse.

**sévir** /seviʀ/ 2 vi (fléau) rage; ~ contre punish.

**sevrer** /səvʀe/ 6 vt wean.

**sexe** /sɛks/ nm sex; (organes) genitals (+ pl). **sexiste** adj sexist. **sexualité** nf sexuality. **sexuel, ~le** adj sexual.

**shampooing** /ʃɑ̃pwɛ̃/ nm

shampoo.

**shérif** /ʃeʀif/ nm sheriff.

**short** /ʃɔʀt/ nm shorts (+ pl).

**si** (s' before il, ils) /si, s/ conj if; (interrogation indirecte) if, whether; ~ on allait se promener? what about a walk?; s'il vous ou te plaît please; ~ oui if so; ~ seulement if only. ● adv (tellement) so; (oui) yes; un ~ bon repas such a good meal; ~ habile qu'il soit however skilful he may be; ~ bien que with the result that.

**sida** /sida/ nm (Méd) Aids.

**sidérurgie** /sideʀyʀʒi/ nf steel industry.

**siècle** /sjɛkl/ nm century; (époque) age.

**siège** /sjɛʒ/ nm seat; (Mil) siege; ~ éjectable ejector seat; ~ social head office, headquarters (+ pl). **siéger** 14 40 vi (assemblée) sit.

**sien, ~ne** /sjɛ̃, -ɛn/ pron le ~, la ~ne, les (~ne)s (homme) his; (femme) hers; (chose) its; les ~s (famille) one's family.

**sieste** /sjɛst/ nf nap, siesta.

**sifflement** /sifləmɑ̃/ nm whistling; un ~ a whistle.

**siffler** /sifle/ 1 vi whistle; (avec un sifflet) blow one's whistle; (serpent, gaz) hiss. ● vt (air) whistle; (chien) whistle to ou for; (acteur) hiss.

**sifflet** /sifle/ nm whistle; ~s (huées) boos.

**sigle** /sigl/ nm acronym.

**signal** (pl -aux) /siɲal, -o/ nm signal; ~ sonore (de répondeur) tone.

**signalement** /siɲalmɑ̃/ nm description.

**signaler** /siɲale/ 1 vt indicate; (par une sonnerie, un écriteau) signal; (dénoncer, mentionner) report; (faire remarquer) point out.

**signalisation** /siɲalizasjɔ̃/ nf sig-

[^1]: 5

nalling, signposting; (signaux) signals (+ pl).

**signataire** /siɲatɛʀ/ nmf signatory.

**signature** /siɲatyʀ/ nf signature; (action) signing; ~ électronique digital signature.

**signe** /siɲ/ nm sign; (de ponctuation) mark; faire ~ à qn wave at sb; (contacter) contact; faire ~ à qn de beckon sb to; faire ~ que non shake one's head; faire ~ que oui nod.

**signer** /siɲe/ **1** vt sign. □ se ~ vpr (Relig) cross oneself.

**signet** /siɲɛ/ nm (pour livre, Internet) bookmark; ~s favoris (Internet) hotlist.

**significatif, -ive** /siɲifikatif, -v/ adj significant.

**signification** /siɲifikasjɔ̃/ nf meaning. **signifier** **45** vt mean, signify; (faire connaître) make known (à to).

**silence** /silɑ̃s/ nm silence; (Mus) rest; garder le ~ keep silent.

**silencieux, -ieuse** /silɑ̃sjø, -z/ adj silent. ● nm silencer.

**silex** /silɛks/ nm inv flint.

**silhouette** /silwɛt/ nf outline, silhouette.

**sillon** /sijɔ̃/ nm furrow; (de disque) groove.

**sillonner** /sijɔne/ **1** vt crisscross.

**similaire** /similɛʀ/ adj similar. **similitude** nf similarity.

**simple** /sɛ̃pl/ adj simple; (non double) single. ● nm ~ dames/ messieurs ladies'/men's singles (+ pl). **simple d'esprit** nmf simpleton. **simplement** adv simply. **simplicité** nf simplicity; (naïveté) simpleness.

**simplification** /sɛ̃plifikasjɔ̃/ nf simplification. **simplifier** **45** vt simplify.

**simpliste** /sɛ̃plist/ adj simplistic.

**simulacre** /simylakʀ/ nm pretence, sham.

**simulation** /simylasjɔ̃/ nf simulation. **simuler** **1** vt simulate.

**simultané, -e** /simyltane/ adj simultaneous.

**sincère** /sɛ̃sɛʀ/ adj sincere. **sincérité** nf sincerity.

**singe** /sɛ̃ʒ/ nm monkey; (grand) ape. **singer** **40** vt mimic, ape.

**singulier, -ière** /sɛ̃gylje, -jɛʀ/ adj peculiar, remarkable; (Gram) singular. ● nm (Gram) singular.

**sinistre** /sinistʀ/ adj sinister. ● nm disaster; (incendie) blaze; (dommages) damage.

**sinistré, -e** /sinistʀe/ adj stricken. ● nm, f disaster victim.

**sinon** /sinɔ̃/ conj (autrement) otherwise; (sauf) except (que that); difficile ~ impossible difficult if not impossible.

**sinueux, -euse** /sinɥø, -z/ adj winding; (fig) tortuous.

**sirène** /siʀɛn/ nf (appareil) siren; (femme) mermaid.

**sirop** /siʀo/ nm (de fruits, Méd) syrup; (boisson) cordial.

**sismique** /sismik/ adj seismic.

**site** /sit/ nm site; ~ touristique place of interest; ~ Internet or Web site web site.

**sitôt** /sito/ adv ~ entré immediately after coming in; ~ que as soon as; pas de ~ not for a while.

**situation** /situasjɔ̃/ nf situation; (emploi) job, position; ~ de famille marital status.

**situé, -e** /situe/ adj situated.

**situer** /situe/ **1** vt situate, locate. □ se ~ vpr (se trouver) to be situated.

**six** /sis/ (/si/ before consonant, /siz/ before vowel) adj & nm six. **sixième**

adj & nmf sixth.

**sketch** (pl ∼es) /skɛtʃ/ nm (Théât) sketch.

**ski** /ski/ nm (matériel) ski; (Sport) skiing; **faire du** ∼ ski; ∼ **de fond** cross-country skiing; ∼ **nautique** water skiing. **skier** 45 vi ski.

**slave** /slav/ adj Slav; (Ling) Slavonic.

**slip** /slip/ nm (d'homme) underpants (+ pl); (de femme) knickers (+ pl); ∼ **de bain** (swimming) trunks (+ pl); (du bikini) bikini bottom.

**slogan** /slɔgã/ nm slogan.

**Slovaquie** /slɔvaki/ nf Slovakia.

**Slovénie** /slɔveni/ nf Slovenia.

**smoking** /smɔkiŋ/ nm dinner jacket.

**SNCF** abrév f (**Société nationale des Chemins de fer français**) French national railway company.

**snob** /snɔb/ nmf snob. ● adj snobbish. **snobisme** nm snobbery.

**sobre** /sɔbʀ/ adj sober.

**social** /e (mpl -iaux) /sɔsjal, -jo/ adj social.

**socialisme** /sɔsjalism/ nm socialism. **socialiste** nmf & a socialist.

**société** /sɔsjete/ nf society; (entreprise) company; ∼ **point com** dot-com.

**socle** /sɔkl/ nm (de colonne, statue) plinth; (de lampe) base.

**socquette** /sɔkɛt/ nf ankle sock.

**soda** /sɔda/ nm fizzy drink.

**sœur** /sœʀ/ nf sister.

**soi** /swa/ pron oneself; **derrière** ∼ behind one; **en** ∼ in itself; **aller de** ∼ be obvious.

**soi-disant** /swadizã/ adj inv so-called. ● adv supposedly.

**soie** /swa/ nf silk.

**soif** /swaf/ nf thirst; **avoir** ∼ be thirsty; **donner** ∼ make one thirsty.

**soigné**, ∼e /swaɲe/ adj (apparence) tidy, neat; (travail) carefully done.

**soigner** /swaɲe/ 1 vt (s'occuper de) look after, take care of; (tenue, style) take care over; (maladie) treat. □ **se** ∼ vpr look after oneself.

**soigneusement** /swaɲøzmã/ adv carefully. **soigneux, -euse** adj careful (de about); (ordonné) tidy.

**soi-même** /swamɛm/ pron oneself.

**soin** /swɛ̃/ nm (ordre) tidiness; ∼**s** care; (Méd) treatment; **avec** ∼ carefully; **avoir** ou **prendre** ∼ **de** qn/de faire take care of sb/to do; **premiers** ∼**s** first aid (+ sg).

**soir** /swaʀ/ nm evening; **à ce** ∼ see you tonight.

**soirée** /sware/ nf evening; (réception) party.

**soit** /swa/ conj (à savoir) that is to say; ∼... ∼ either... or.
● →ÊTRE 4.

**soixante** /swasãt/ adj & nm sixty. **soixante-dix** adj & nm seventy.

**soja** /sɔʒa/ nm (graines) soya beans (+ pl); (plante) soya.

**sol** /sɔl/ nm ground; (de maison) floor; (terrain agricole) soil.

**solaire** /sɔlɛʀ/ adj solar; (huile, filtre) sun.

**soldat** /sɔlda/ nm soldier.

**solde**[1] /sɔld/ nf (salaire) pay.

**solde**[2] /sɔld/ nm (Comm) balance; **les** ∼**s** the sales; ∼**s** (écrit en vitrine) sale; **en** ∼ (acheter) at sale price.

**solder** /sɔlde/ 1 vt sell off at sale price; (compte) settle. □ **se** ∼ **par** vpr (aboutir à) end in.

**sole** /sɔl/ nf (poisson) sole.

**soleil** /sɔlɛj/ nm sun; (fleur) sunflower; **il y a du** ∼ it's sunny.

273

**solennel,** ~le /sɔlanɛl/ adj solemn.

**solfège** /sɔlfɛʒ/ nm musical theory.

**solidaire** /sɔlidɛʀ/ adj (mécanismes) interdependent; (collègues) (mutually) supportive; être ~ de qn support sb. **solidarité** nf solidarity.

**solide** /sɔlid/ adj solid; (personne) strong. ● nm solid.

**solidifier** /sɔlidifje/ 45 vt solidify. □ se ~ vpr solidify.

**solitaire** /sɔlitɛʀ/ adj solitary. ● nmf (personne) loner. **solitude** nf solitude.

**solliciter** /sɔlisite/ 1 vt seek; (faire appel à) call upon; être très **sollicité** be very much in demand.

**sollicitude** /sɔlisityd/ nf concern.

**solo** /sɔlo/ nm & a inv (Mus) solo.

**solution** /sɔlysjɔ̃/ nf solution.

**solvable** /sɔlvabl/ adj solvent.

**solvant** /sɔlvɑ̃/ nm solvent.

**sombre** /sɔ̃bʀ/ adj dark; (triste) sombre.

**sombrer** /sɔ̃bʀe/ 1 vi sink (dans into).

**sommaire** /sɔmɛʀ/ adj (exécution) summary; (description) rough. ● nm contents (+ pl); **au** ~ **on** the programme.

**sommation** /sɔmasjɔ̃/ nf (Mil) warning; (Jur) notice.

**somme** /sɔm/ nf sum; **en** ~, ~ **toute** in short; **faire la** ~ **de** add (up), total (up). ● nm nap.

**sommeil** /sɔmɛj/ nm sleep; **avoir** ~ **be** ou feel sleepy; **en** ~ (projet) put on ice. **sommeiller** 1 vi doze; (fig) lie dormant.

**sommelier** /sɔməlje/ nm wine steward.

**sommer** /sɔme/ 1 vt summon.

**sommes** /sɔm/ →ÊTRE 4.

**sommet** /sɔmɛ/ nm top; (de montagne) summit; (de triangle) apex; (gloire) height.

**sommier** /sɔmje/ nm bed base.

**somnambule** /sɔmnɑ̃byl/ nm sleepwalker.

**somnifère** /sɔmnifɛʀ/ nm sleeping pill.

**somnolent,** ~e /sɔmnɔlɑ̃, -t/ adj drowsy. **somnoler** 1 vi doze.

**somptueux,** -euse /sɔ̃ptɥø, -z/ adj sumptuous.

**son¹, sa** (**son** before vowel or mute h) (pl **ses**) /sɔ̃, sa, sɔ̃, se/ adj (homme) his; (femme) her; (chose) its; (indéfini) one's.

**son²** /sɔ̃/ nm (bruit) sound; (de blé) bran; **baisser le** ~ turn the volume down.

**sondage** /sɔ̃daʒ/ nm ~ (**d'opinion**) (opinion) poll.

**sonde** /sɔ̃d/ nf (de forage) drill; (Méd) (d'évacuation) catheter; (d'examen) probe.

**sonder** /sɔ̃de/ 1 vt (population) poll; (explorer) sound; (terrain) drill; (intentions) sound out.

**songe** /sɔ̃ʒ/ nm dream.

**songer** /sɔ̃ʒe/ 40 vt ~ que think that; ~ à think about. **songeur, -euse** adj pensive.

**sonné,** ~e /sɔne/ adj (étourdi) groggy; 1 crazy.

**sonner** /sɔne/ 1 vt/i ring; (clairon, glas) sound; (heure) strike; (domestique) ring for; **midi sonné** well past noon; ~ **de** (clairon) sound, blow.

**sonnerie** /sɔnʀi/ nf ringing; (de clairon) sounding; (sonnette) bell; (téléphone portable) ringtone.

**sonnette** /sɔnɛt/ nf bell.

**sonore** /sɔnɔʀ/ adj resonant; (onde, effets) sound; (rire) resounding.

**sonorisation** /sɔnɔʀizasjɔ̃/ nf

s

(matériel) public address system.

**sonorité** /sɔnɔʀite/ nf resonance; (d'un instrument) tone.

**sont** /sɔ̃/ ⇒ÊTRE 4.

**sophistiqué**, ~e /sɔfistike/ adj sophisticated.

**sorcellerie** /sɔʀsɛlʀi/ nf witchcraft. **sorcier** nm (guérisseur) witch doctor; (maléfique) sorcerer. **sorcière** nf witch.

**sordide** /sɔʀdid/ adj sordid; (lieu) squalid.

**sort** /sɔʀ/ nm (destin, hasard) fate; (condition) lot; (maléfice) spell; tirer (qch) au ~ draw lots (for sth).

**sortant**, ~e /sɔʀtɑ̃, -t/ adj (président etc.) outgoing.

**sorte** /sɔʀt/ nf sort, kind; de ~ que so that; en quelque ~ in a way; de la ~ in this way; faire en ~ que make sure that.

**sortie** /sɔʀti/ nf exit; (promenade, dîner) outing; (déclaration [I]) remark; (parution) publication; (de disque, film) release; (d'un ordinateur) output; ~s (argent) outgoings.

**sortilège** /sɔʀtilɛʒ/ nm (magic) spell.

**sortir** /sɔʀtiʀ/ 46 vi (aux être) go out, leave; (venir) come out; (aller au spectacle) go out; (livre, film) come out; (plante) come up; ~ de (pièce) leave; (milieu social) come from; (limites) go beyond; ~ du commun ou de l'ordinaire be out of the ordinary. ● vt (aux avoir) take out; (livre, modèle) bring out; (dire [I]) come out with; ~ qn de get sb out of; (être sorti d'affaire be in the clear. □ s'en ~ vpr cope, manage.

**sosie** /sozi/ nm double.

**sot**, ~te /so, sɔt/ adj silly.

**sottise** /sotiz/ nf silliness; (action,

remarque) foolish thing; faire des ~s be naughty.

**sou** /su/ nm [I] ~s money; sans le ~ without a penny; près de ses ~s tight-fisted.

**soubresaut** /subʀəso/ nm (sudden) start.

**souche** /suʃ/ nf (d'arbre) stump; (de famille) stock; (de carnet) counterfoil.

**souci** /susi/ nm (inquiétude) worry; (préoccupation) concern; (plante) marigold; se faire du ~ worry.

**soucier (se)** /(sə)susje/ 45 vpr se ~ de care about. **soucieux, -ieuse** adj concerned (about).

**soucoupe** /sukup/ nf saucer; ~ volante flying saucer.

**soudain**, ~e /sudɛ̃, -ɛn/ adj sudden. ● adv suddenly.

**soude** /sud/ nf soda.

**souder** /sude/ 1 vt weld, solder; famille très soudée close-knit family. □ se ~ vpr (os) knit (together).

**soudoyer** /sudwaje/ 31 vt bribe.

**souffle** /sufl/ nm (haleine) breath; (respiration) breathing; (explosion) blast; (vent) breath of air; le ~ coupé out of breath; à couper le ~ breathtaking.

**souffler** /sufle/ 1 vi blow; (haleter) puff. ● vt (bougie) blow out; (poussière, fumée) blow; (verre) blow; (par explosion) destroy; (chuchoter) whisper; ~ la réplique à prompt. **souffleur, -euse** nm, f (Théât) prompter.

**souffrance** /sufʀɑ̃s/ nf suffering; en ~ (affaire) pending. **souffrant**, ~e adj unwell.

**souffrir** /sufʀiʀ/ 21 vi suffer (de from). ● vt (endurer) suffer; il ne peut pas le ~ he cannot stand ou bear him.

**soufre** /sufʀ/ nm sulphur.

**souhait** /swɛ/ nm wish; **à tes ~s!** bless you!; **paisible à ~** incredibly peaceful. **souhaitable** adj desirable.

**souhaiter** /swete/ **1** vt ~ **qch à qn** wish sb sth; ~ **que/faire** hope that/to do; ~ **la bienvenue à qn** welcome sb.

**soûl,** ~**e** /su, sul/ adj drunk. ● nm **tout son ~** as much as one can.

**soulagement** /sulaʒmɑ̃/ nm relief. **soulager** 40 vt relieve.

**soûler** /sule/ **1** vt make drunk. □ **se ~** vpr get drunk.

**soulèvement** /sulɛvmɑ̃/ nm uprising.

**soulever** /sulve/ 6 vt lift, raise; (question, poussière) raise; (enthousiasme) arouse; (foule) stir up. □ **se ~** vpr lift ou raise oneself up; (se révolter) rise up.

**soulier** /sulje/ nm shoe.

**souligner** /suliɲe/ **1** vt underline; (yeux) outline; (taille) emphasize.

**soumettre** /sumɛtʀ/ 42 vt (assujettir) subject (à to); (présenter) submit (à to). □ **se ~** vpr submit (à to). **soumis,** ~**e** adj submissive. **soumission** nf submission.

**soupape** /supap/ nf valve.

**soupçon** /supsɔ̃/ nm suspicion; **un ~ de** (un peu de) a touch of. **soupçonner** 1 vt suspect. **soupçonneux, -euse** adj suspicious.

**soupe** /sup/ nf soup.

**souper** /supe/ 6 vi have supper. ● nm supper.

**soupeser** /supəze/ **1** vt judge the weight of; (fig) weigh up.

**soupière** /supjɛʀ/ nf (soup) tureen.

**soupir** /supiʀ/ nm sigh; **pousser un ~** heave a sigh.

**soupirer** /supiʀe/ **1** vi sigh.

**souple** /supl/ adj supple; (règlement, caractère) flexible. **souplesse**

nf suppleness; (de règlement) flexibility.

**source** /suʀs/ nf (de rivière, origine) source; (eau) spring; **prendre sa ~ à** rise in; **de ~ sûre** from a reliable source; ~ **thermale** hot spring.

**sourcil** /suʀsi/ nm eyebrow.

**sourciller** /suʀsije/ **1** vi **sans ~** without batting an eyelid.

**sourd,** ~**e** /suʀ, -d/ adj deaf; (bruit, douleur) dull; **faire la ~e oreille** turn a deaf ear. ● nm, f deaf person.

**sourd-muet** (pl **sourds-muets**), **sourde-muette** (pl **sourdes-muettes**) /suʀmɥe, suʀdmɥet/ adj deaf and dumb. ● nm, f deafmute.

**souricière** /suʀisjɛʀ/ nf mousetrap; (fig) trap.

**sourire** /suʀiʀ/ 54 vi smile (à at); ~ **à** (fortune) smile on. ● nm smile; **garder le ~** keep smiling.

**souris** /suʀi/ nf mouse; **des ~ mice**.

**sournois,** ~**e** /suʀnwa, -z/ adj sly, underhand.

**sous** /su/ prép under, beneath; ~ **la main** handy; ~ **la pluie** in the rain; ~ **peu** shortly; ~ **terre** underground.

**sous-alimenté,** ~**e** /suzalimɑ̃te/ adj undernourished.

**souscription** /suskʀipsjɔ̃/ nf subscription. **souscrire** 30 vi ~ **à** subscribe to.

**sous-entendre** /suzɑ̃tɑ̃dʀ/ 3 vt imply. **sous-entendu** nm innuendo, insinuation.

**sous-estimer** /suzɛstime/ **1** vt underestimate.

**sous-jacent,** ~**e** /suʒasɑ̃, -t/ adj underlying.

**sous-marin,** ~**e** /sumaʀɛ̃, -in/ adj underwater; (plongée) deep-sea. ● nm submarine.

s

**soussigné**, ~e /susiɲe/ adj & nm, f undersigned.

**sous-sol** /susɔl/ nm (cave) basement.

**sous-titre** /sutitʀ/ nm subtitle.

**soustraction** /sustʀaksjɔ̃/ nf (déduction) subtraction.

**soustraire** /sustʀɛʀ/ 29 vt (déduire) subtract; (retirer) take away (à from). □ se ~ à vpr escape from.

**sous-traitant** /sutʀɛtɑ̃/ nm subcontractor.

**sous-verre** /suvɛʀ/ nm inv glass mount.

**sous-vêtement** /suvɛtmɑ̃/ nm underwear.

**soute** /sut/ nf (de bateau) hold; ~ à charbon coal-bunker.

**soutenir** /sutniʀ/ 59 vt support; (effort, rythme) sustain; (résister à) withstand; ~ que maintain that.

**soutenu**, ~e /sutny/ adj (constant) sustained; (style) formal.

**souterrain**, ~e /sutɛʀɛ̃, -ɛn/ adj underground. ● nm underground passage.

**soutien** /sutjɛ̃/ nm support.

**soutien-gorge** (pl soutiens-gorge) /sutjɛ̃ɡɔʀʒ/ nm bra.

**soutirer** /sutiʀe/ 1 vt ~ à qn extract from sb.

**souvenir**[1] /suvniʀ/ nm memory, recollection; (objet) memento; (cadeau) souvenir; en ~ de in memory of.

**souvenir**[2] (se) /(sə)suvniʀ/ 59 vpr se ~ de remember; se ~ que remember that.

**souvent** /suvɑ̃/ adv often.

**souverain**, ~e /suvʀɛ̃, -ɛn/ adj sovereign. ● nm,f sovereign.

**soviétique** /sɔvjetik/ adj Soviet.

**soyeux**, -euse /swajø, -z/ adj silky.

**spacieux**, -ieuse /spasjø, -z/ adj

spacious.

**sparadrap** /spaʀadʀa/ nm (sticking) plaster.

**spatial**, ~e (mpl -iaux) /spasjal, -jo/ adj space.

**speaker**, ~ine /spikœʀ, -kʀin/ nm,f announcer.

**spécial**, ~e (mpl -iaux) /spesjal, -jo/ adj special; (bizarre) odd. **spécialement** adv (exprès) specially; (très) especially.

**spécialiser (se)** /səspesjalize/ 1 vpr specialize (dans in). **spécialiste** nmf specialist. **spécialité** nf speciality; (US) specialty.

**spécifier** /spesifje/ 45 vt specify.

**spécifique** /spesifik/ adj specific.

**spécimen** /spesimɛn/ nm specimen.

**spectacle** /spɛktakl/ nm show; (vue) sight, spectacle.

**spectaculaire** /spɛktakylɛʀ/ adj spectacular.

**spectateur**, -trice /spɛktatœʀ, -tʀis/ nm,f (Sport) spectator; (témoin oculaire) onlooker; les ~s (Théât) the audience (+ sg).

**spectre** /spɛktʀ/ nm (revenant) spectre; (images) spectrum.

**spéculateur**, -trice /spekylatœʀ, -tʀis/ nm,f speculator. **spéculation** nf speculation. **spéculer** 1 vi speculate.

**spéléologie** /speleolɔʒi/ nf cave exploration, pot-holing.

**spermatozoïde** /spɛʀmatozoid/ nm spermatozoon. **sperme** nm sperm.

**sphère** /sfɛʀ/ nf sphere.

**spirale** /spiʀal/ nf spiral.

**spirituel**, ~le /spiʀityɛl/ adj spiritual; (amusant) witty.

**spiritueux** /spiʀityø/ nm (alcool) spirit.

**splendeur** /splɑ̃dœʀ/ nf splendour. **splendide** adj splendid.

**sponsoriser** /spɔ̃sɔʀize/ **1** vt sponsor.

**spontané, ~e** /spɔ̃tane/ adj spontaneous. **spontanéité** nf spontaneity.

**sport** /spɔʀ/ adj inv (vêtements) casual. ●nm sport; veste/voiture de ~ sports jacket/car.

**sportif, -ive** /spɔʀtif, -v/ adj (personne) sporty; (physique) athletic; (résultats) sports. ●nm, f sportsman, sportswoman.

**spot** /spɔt/ nm spotlight; (~ publicitaire) ad.

**square** /skwaʀ/ nm small public garden.

**squatter** /skwate/ **1** vt squat in.

**squelette** /skəlɛt/ nm skeleton. **squelettique** adj skeletal.

**SRAS** abrév m (**syndrome respiratoire aigu sévère**) SARS.

**SSII** abrév f (**société de services et d'ingénierie informatiques**) computer services company

**stabiliser** /stabilize/ **1** vt stabilize. **stable** adj stable.

**stade** /stad/ nm (Sport) stadium; (phase) stage.

**stage** /staʒ/ nm (cours) course; (professionnel) placement. **stagiaire** nmf course member; (apprenti) trainee.

**stagner** /stagne/ **1** vi stagnate.

**stand** /stɑ̃d/ nm stand; (de fête foraine) stall.

**standard** /stɑ̃daʀ/ nm switchboard. ●adj inv standard. **standardiser** **1** vt standardize.

**standardiste** /stɑ̃daʀdist/ nmf switchboard operator.

**standing** /stɑ̃diŋ/ nm status, standing; de ~ (hôtel) luxury.

**starter** /staʀtɛʀ/ nm (Auto) choke.

**station** /stasjɔ̃/ nf station; (halte) stop; ~ **debout** standing position; ~ **de taxis** taxi rank; ~ **balnéaire**/de ski seaside/ski resort; ~ **thermale** spa.

**stationnaire** /stasjɔnɛʀ/ adj stationary.

**stationnement** /stasjɔnmɑ̃/ nm parking. **stationner** **1** vi park.

**station-service** (pl **stations-service**) /stasjɔ̃sɛʀvis/ nf service station.

**statique** /statik/ adj static.

**statistique** /statistik/ nf statistic; (science) statistics (+ sg.). ●adj statistical.

**statue** /staty/ nf statue.

**statuer** /statɥe/ **1** vi ~ **sur** give a ruling on.

**statut** /staty/ nm status. **statutaire** adj statutory.

**sténo** /steno/ nf (sténographie) shorthand. **sténodactylo** nf shorthand typist. **sténographie** nf shorthand.

**stéréo** /stereo/ nf & adj inv stereo.

**stéréotype** /stereɔtip/ nm stereotype.

**stérile** /steʀil/ adj sterile.

**stérilet** /steʀilɛ/ nm coil, IUD.

**stérilisation** /steʀilizasjɔ̃/ nf sterilization. **stériliser** **1** vt sterilize.

**stéroïde** /steʀɔid/ adj & nm steroid.

**stimulant** /stimylɑ̃/ nm stimulus; (médicament) stimulant.

**stimulateur** /stimylatœʀ/ nm ~ **cardiaque** (Méd) pacemaker.

**stimuler** /stimyle/ **1** vt stimulate.

**stipuler** /stipyle/ **1** vt stipulate.

**stock** /stɔk/ nm stock. **stocker** **1** vt stock.

**stoïque** /stɔik/ adj stoical. ●nmf stoic.

**stop** /stɔp/ *interj* stop. ● *nm* stop sign; (feu arrière) brake light; faire du ∼ ⬛ hitch-hike. **stopper** ⬛ *vt/i* stop.

**store** /stɔʀ/ *nm* blind; (de magasin) awning.

**strapontin** /stʀapɔ̃tɛ̃/ *nm* folding seat, jump seat.

**stratégie** /stʀateʒi/ *nf* strategy. **stratégique** *adj* strategic.

**stress** /stʀɛs/ *nm* stress. **stressant,** ∼e *adj* stressful. **stressé,** ∼e *adj* stressed. **stresser** ⬛ *vt* put under stress.

**strict** /stʀikt/ *adj* strict; (tenue, vérité) plain; le ∼ minimum the bare minimum. **strictement** *adv* strictly.

**strident,** ∼e /stʀidɑ̃, -t/ *adj* shrill.

**strophe** /stʀɔf/ *nf* stanza, verse.

**structure** /stʀyktyʀ/ *nf* structure.

**studieux, -ieuse** /stydjø, -z/ *adj* studious.

**studio** /stydjo/ *nm* (d'artiste, de télévision) studio; (logement) studio flat.

**stupéfaction** /stypefaksjɔ̃/ *nf* amazement. **stupéfait,** ∼e *adj* amazed.

**stupéfiant,** ∼e /stypefjɑ̃, -t/ *adj* astounding. ● *nm* drug, narcotic. **stupéfier** 45 *vt* amaze.

**stupeur** /stypœʀ/ *nf* amazement; (Méd) stupor.

**stupide** /stypid/ *adj* stupid. **stupidité** *nf* stupidity.

**style** /stil/ *nm* style.

**styliste** /stilist/ *nmf* fashion designer.

**stylo** /stilo/ *nm* pen; ∼ (à) bille ballpoint pen; ∼ (à) encre fountain pen.

**su** /sy/ →**SAVOIR** 55.

**suave** /sɥav/ *adj* sweet.

**subalterne** /sybaltɛʀn/ *adj & nmf*

subordinate.

**subconscient** /sypkɔ̃sjɑ̃/ *nm* subconscious.

**subir** /sybiʀ/ 2 *vt* be subjected to; (traitement, opération) undergo.

**subit,** ∼e /sybi, -t/ *adj* sudden.

**subjectif, -ive** /sybʒɛktif, -v/ *adj* subjective.

**subjonctif** /sybʒɔ̃ktif/ *nm* subjunctive.

**subjuguer** /sybʒyge/ ⬛ *vt* (charmer) captivate.

**sublime** /syblim/ *adj* sublime.

**submerger** /sybmɛʀʒe/ 40 *vt* submerge; (fig) overwhelm.

**subordonné,** ∼e /sybɔʀdɔne/ *adj & nm, f* subordinate.

**subside** /sybzid/ *nm* grant.

**subsidiaire** /sybzidjɛʀ/ *adj* subsidiary; question ∼ tiebreaker.

**subsistance** /sybzistɑ̃s/ *nf* subsistence. **subsister** ⬛ *vi* subsist; (durer, persister) exist.

**substance** /sypstɑ̃s/ *nf* substance.

**substantiel,** ∼le /sypstɑ̃sjɛl/ *adj* substantial.

**substantif** /sypstɑ̃tif/ *nm* noun.

**substituer** /sypstitɥe/ ⬛ *vt* substitute (à for). □ **se** ∼ **à** *vpr* (remplacer) substitute for. **substitut** *nm* substitute; (Jur) deputy public prosecutor.

**subtil,** ∼e /syptil/ *adj* subtle.

**subtiliser** /syptilize/ ⬛ *vt* ∼ qch (à qn) steal sth (from sb).

**subvenir** /sybvəniʀ/ 59 *vi* ∼ à provide for.

**subvention** /sybvɑ̃sjɔ̃/ *nf* subsidy. **subventionner** ⬛ *vt* subsidize.

**subversif, -ive** /sybvɛʀsif, -v/ *adj* subversive.

**suc** /syk/ *nm* juice.

**succédané** /syksedane/ *nm* substitute (de for).

**succéder** /syksede/ [14] *vi* ~ à succeed. □ **se** ~ *vpr* succeed one another.

**succès** /syksε/ *nm* success; à ~ (film, livre) successful; avoir du ~ be a success.

**successeur** /syksεsœʀ/ *nm* successor. **successif, -ive** *adj* successive. **succession** *nf* succession; (Jur) inheritance.

**succinct, ~e** /syksε̃, -t/ *adj* succinct.

**succomber** /sykɔ̃be/ [1] *vi* die; ~ à succumb to.

**succulent, ~e** /sykylã, -t/ *adj* delicious.

**succursale** /sykyʀsal/ *nf* (Comm) branch.

**sucer** /syse/ [10] *vt* suck.

**sucette** /sysεt/ *nf* (bonbon) lollipop; (tétine) dummy; (US) pacifier.

**sucre** /sykʀ/ *nm* sugar; ~ d'orge barley sugar; ~ en poudre caster sugar; ~ glace icing sugar; ~ roux brown sugar.

**sucré** /sykʀe/ *adj* sweet; (additionné de sucre) sweetened. **sucrer** [1] *vt* sugar, sweeten. **sucreries** *nfpl* sweets.

**sucrier, -ière** /sykʀije, -jεʀ/ *adj* sugar. ● *nm* (récipient) sugar-bowl.

**sud** /syd/ *nm* south. ● *adj inv* south; (partie) southern.

**sud-est** /sydεst/ *nm* south-east.

**sud-ouest** /sydwεst/ *nm* southwest.

**Suède** /sɥεd/ *nf* Sweden.

**suédois, ~e** /sɥedwa, -z/ *adj* Swedish. ● *nm* (Ling) Swedish. **S~, ~e** *nm, f* Swede.

**suer** /sɥe/ [1] *vi* sweat; faire ~ qn [1] get on sb's nerves.

**sueur** /sɥœʀ/ *nf* sweat; en ~ covered in sweat.

**suffire** /syfiʀ/ [57] *vi* be enough (à qn for sb); **il suffit de compter** all you have to do is count; **une goutte suffit** a drop is enough; ~ à (besoin) satisfy. □ **se** ~ *vpr* se à soi-même be self-sufficient.

**suffisamment** /syfizamã/ *adv* sufficiently; ~ **de** qch enough of sth. **suffisance** *nf* (vanité) conceit. **suffisant, ~e** *adj* sufficient; (vaniteux) conceited.

**suffixe** /syfiks/ *nm* suffix.

**suffoquer** /syfɔke/ [1] *vt/i* choke, suffocate.

**suffrage** /syfʀaʒ/ *nm* (voix: Pol) vote; (système) suffrage.

**suggérer** /sygʒeʀe/ [14] *vt* suggest. **suggestion** *nf* suggestion.

**suicidaire** /sɥisidεʀ/ *adj* suicidal. **suicide** *nm* suicide. **suicider (se)** [1] *vpr* commit suicide.

**suinter** /sɥɛ̃te/ [1] *vi* ooze.

**suis** /sɥi/ ⇒**ÊTRE** [4]. ⇒**SUIVRE** [57].

**Suisse** /sɥis/ *nf* Switzerland. ● *nmf* Swiss. **suisse** *adj* Swiss.

**suite** /sɥit/ *nf* continuation, rest; (d'un film) sequel; (série) series; (appartement, escorte) suite; (résultat) consequence; **à la** ~, **de** ~ (successivement) in a row; **à la** ~ **de** (derrière) behind; **à la** ~ **de**, **par** ~ **de** (en conséquence) as a result of; **faire** ~ (**à**) follow; **par la** ~ afterwards; ~ **à votre lettre du** further to your letter of the; **des** ~**s de** as a result of.

**suivant[1], ~e** /sɥivã, -t/ *adj* following, next. ● *nm, f* following *ou* next person.

**suivant[2]** /sɥivã/ *prép* (selon) according to.

**suivi, ~e** /sɥivi/ *adj* (effort) steady, sustained; (cohérent) consistent; **peu/très** ~ (cours) poorly/well attended.

**s**

**suivre** /sɥivʀ/ 57 vt/i follow; (comprendre) follow; faire ∼ (courrier) forward. □ se ∼ vpr follow each other.

**sujet**, ∼te /syʒɛ, -t/ adj ∼ à liable ou subject to. ● nm (d'un royaume) subject; (question) subject; (motif) cause; (Gram) subject; au ∼ de about.

**super** /sypɛʀ/ nm (essence) fourstar. ● adj inv 1 (très) great. ● adv 1 ultra, really.

**superbe** /sypɛʀb/ adj superb.

**supérette** /sypeʀɛt/ nf minimarket.

**superficie** /sypɛʀfisi/ nf area.

**superficiel**, ∼le /sypɛʀfisjɛl/ adj superficial.

**superflu** /sypɛʀfly/ adj superfluous. ● nm (excédent) surplus.

**supérieur**, ∼e /sypeʀjœʀ/ adj (plus haut) upper; (quantité, nombre) greater (à than); (études, principe) higher (à than); (meilleur, hautain) superior (à to). ● nm, f superior. **supériorité** nf superiority.

**superlatif**, -ive /sypɛʀlatif, -v/ adj & nm superlative.

**supermarché** /sypɛʀmaʀʃe/ nm supermarket.

**superposer** /sypɛʀpoze/ 1 vt superimpose; lits superposés bunk beds.

**superproduction** /sypɛʀpʀɔdyksjɔ̃/ nf (film) blockbuster.

**superpuissance** /sypɛʀpɥisɑ̃s/ nf superpower.

**superstitieux**, -ieuse /sypɛʀstisjø, -z/ adj superstitious.

**superviser** /sypɛʀvize/ 1 vt supervise.

**suppléant**, ∼e /sypleɑ̃, -t/ nmf & adj (professeur ∼) supply teacher; (juge) ∼ deputy (judge).

**suppléer** /syplee/ 15 vt (remplacer) fill in for. ● vi ∼ à (compenser) make up for.

**supplément** /syplemɑ̃/ nm (argent) extra charge; (de frites, légumes) extra portion; en ∼ extra; un ∼ de (travail) additional; payer un ∼ pay a supplement. **supplémentaire** adj extra, additional.

**supplice** /syplis/ nm torture.

**supplier** /syplije/ 45 vt beg, beseech (de to).

**support** /sypɔʀ/ nm support; (Ordinat) medium.

**supportable** /sypɔʀtabl/ adj bearable.

**supporter**¹ /sypɔʀte/ 1 vt (privations) bear; (personne) put up with; (structure: Ordinat) support; il ne supporte pas les enfants/de perdre he can't stand children/losing.

**supporter**² /sypɔʀtɛʀ/ nm (Sport) supporter.

**supposer** /sypoze/ 1 vt suppose; (impliquer) imply; à ∼ que supposing that.

**suppression** /sypʀesjɔ̃/ nf (de taxe) abolition; (de sanction) lifting; (de mot) deletion. **supprimer** 1 vt (allocation) withdraw; (contrôle) lift; (train) cancel; (preuve) suppress.

**suprématie** /sypʀemasi/ nf supremacy.

**suprême** /sypʀɛm/ adj supreme.

**sur** /syʀ/ prép on, upon; (pardessus) over; (au sujet de) about, on; (proportion) out of; (mesure) by; ∼ la photo in the photograph; mettre/jeter ∼ put/throw on to; ∼ mesure made to measure; ∼ place on the spot; ∼ ce, je pars with that, I must go; ∼ le moment at the time.

**sûr** /syʀ/ adj certain, sure; (sans danger) safe; (digne de confiance) reliable; (main) steady; (jugement) sound; **être ~ de soi** be self-confident; **j'en étais ~!** I knew it!

**surabondance** /syʀabɔ̃dɑ̃s/ nf overabundance.

**surcharge** /syʀʃaʀʒ/ nf overloading; (poids) excess load. **surcharger** **1** vt overload; (texte) alter.

**surchauffer** /syʀʃofe/ **1** vt overheat.

**surcroît** /syʀkʀwa/ nm increase (de in); **de ~** in addition.

**surdité** /syʀdite/ nf deafness.

**surélever** /syʀelve/ **6** vt raise.

**sûrement** /syʀmɑ̃/ adv certainly; (sans danger) safely; **il a ~ oublié** he must have forgotten.

**surenchère** /syʀɑ̃ʃɛʀ/ nf higher bid. **surenchérir** **2** vi bid higher (sur than).

**surestimer** /syʀɛstime/ **1** vt overestimate.

**sûreté** /syʀte/ nf safety; (de pays) security; (d'un geste) steadiness; **être en ~** be safe; **S~ (nationale)** police (+ pl).

**surexcité, ~e** /syʀɛksite/ adj very excited.

**surf** /sœʀf/ nm surfing.

**surface** /syʀfas/ nf surface; **faire ~** (sous-marin, fig) surface; **en ~** on the surface.

**surfait, ~e** /syʀfɛ, -t/ adj overrated.

**surfer** /sœʀfe/ **1** vi go surfing; **~ sur l'Internet** surf the Internet.

**surgelé, ~e** /syʀʒəle/ adj (deep-)frozen; **aliments ~s** frozen food.

**surgir** /syʀʒiʀ/ **2** vi appear (suddenly); (difficulté) crop up.

**sur-le-champ** /syʀ ləʃɑ̃/ adv right away.

**surlendemain** /syʀlɑ̃dmɛ̃/ nm **le ~** two days later; **le ~ de** two days after.

**surligneur** /syʀliɲœʀ/ nm highlighter (pen).

**surmenage** /syʀmənaʒ/ nm overwork.

**surmonter** /syʀmɔ̃te/ **1** vt (vaincre) overcome, surmount; (être au-dessus de) surmount, top.

**surnaturel, ~le** /syʀnatyʀɛl/ adj supernatural.

**surnom** /syʀnɔ̃/ nm nickname. **surnommer** **1** vt nickname.

**surpeuplé, ~e** /syʀpœple/ adj overpopulated.

**surplomber** /syʀplɔ̃be/ **1** vt/i overhang.

**surplus** /syʀply/ nm surplus.

**suprenant, ~e** /syʀpʀənɑ̃, -t/ adj surprising. **surprendre** **50** vt (étonner) surprise; (prendre au dépourvu) catch, surprise; (entendre) overhear. **surpris, ~e** adj surprised (de at).

**surprise** /syʀpʀiz/ nf surprise.

**surréaliste** /syʀʀealist/ adj & nmf surrealist.

**sursaut** /syʀso/ nm start, jump; **en ~** with a start; **~ de (regain)** burst of. **sursauter** **1** vi start, jump.

**sursis** /syʀsi/ nm reprieve; (Mil) deferment; **deux ans (de prison) avec ~** a two-year suspended sentence.

**surtaxe** /syʀtaks/ nf surcharge.

**surtout** /syʀtu/ adv especially; (avant tout) above all; **~ pas** certainly not.

**surveillance** /syʀvejɑ̃s/ nf watch; (d'examen) supervision; (de la police) surveillance. **surveillant, ~e** nm, f (de prison) warder; (au lycée) supervisor (in charge of discipline). **surveiller** **1** vt watch; (travaux, élèves) supervise.

**survenir** /syʀvəniʀ/ **59** vi occur, take place; (personne) turn up.

s

**survêtement** /syʀvɛtmɑ̃/ *nm* (Sport) tracksuit.

**survie** /syʀvi/ *nf* survival.

**survivant**, ~e /syʀvivɑ̃, -t/ *adj* surviving. ● *nm, f* survivor.

**survivre** /syʀvivʀ/ [58] *vi* survive; ~ à (conflit) survive; (personne) outlive.

**survoler** /syʀvɔle/ [1] *vt* fly over; (livre) skim through.

**sus**: en ~ /ɑ̃sys/ *loc* in addition.

**susceptible** /syseptibl/ *adj* touchy; ~ de faire likely to do.

**susciter** /sysite/ [1] *vt* (éveiller) arouse; (occasionner) create.

**suspect**, ~e /syspɛ, -ɛkt/ *adj* (individu, faits) suspicious; (témoignage) suspect; ~ de suspected of. ● *nm, f* suspect. **suspecter** [1] *vt* suspect.

**suspendre** /syspɑ̃dʀ/ [3] *vt* (accrocher) hang (up); (interrompre, destituer) suspend; suspendu à hanging from. □ **se** ~ à *vpr* hang from.

**suspens**: en ~ /ɑ̃syspɑ̃/ *loc* (affaire) outstanding; (dans l'indécision) in suspense.

**suspense** /syspɛns/ *nm* suspense.

**suture** /sytyʀ/ *nf* point de ~ stitch.

**svelte** /svɛlt/ *adj* slender.

**S.V.P.** *abrév* (s'il vous plaît) please.

**syllabe** /silab/ *nf* syllable.

**symbole** /sɛ̃bɔl/ *nm* symbol. **symboliser** [1] *vt* symbolize.

**symétrie** /simetʀi/ *nf* symmetry.

**sympa** /sɛ̃pa/ *adj inv* être ~ nice; sois ~ be a pal.

**sympathie** /sɛ̃pati/ *nf* (goût) liking; (compassion) sympathy; avoir de la ~ pour like. **sympathique** *adj* nice, pleasant. **sympathisant**, ~e *nm, f* sympathizer. **sympathiser** [1] *vi* get on well (avec with).

**symphonie** /sɛ̃fɔni/ *nf* symphony.

**symptôme** /sɛ̃ptom/ *nm* symptom.

**synagogue** /sinagɔg/ *nf* synagogue.

**synchroniser** /sɛ̃kʀɔnize/ [1] *vt* synchronize.

**syncope** /sɛ̃kɔp/ *nf* (Méd) blackout.

**syndic** /sɛ̃dik/ *nm* ~ (d'immeuble) property manager.

**syndicaliste** /sɛ̃dikalist/ *nmf* (trade-)unionist. ● *adj* (trade-) union.

**syndicat** /sɛ̃dika/ *nm* (trade) union; ~ d'initiative tourist office.

**syndiqué**, ~e /sɛ̃dike/ *adj* être ~ be a (trade-)union member.

**synonyme** /sinɔnim/ *adj* synonymous. ● *nm* synonym.

**syntaxe** /sɛ̃taks/ *nf* syntax.

**synthèse** /sɛ̃tɛz/ *nf* synthesis. **synthétique** *adj* synthetic.

**synthé(tiseur)** /sɛ̃te(tizœʀ)/ *nm* synthesizer.

**systématique** /sistematik/ *adj* systematic.

**système** /sistɛm/ *nm* system; le ~ D [1] resourcefulness.

...........................................

# Tt

**t'** /t/ ➡TE.

**ta** /ta/ ➡TON¹.

**tabac** /taba/ *nm* tobacco; (magasin) tobacconist's shop.

**table** /tabl/ *nf* table; à ~! dinner is ready!; ~ de nuit bedside table; ~ des matières table of contents; ~ à repasser ironing board; ~ roulante (tea-)trolley; (US) (serving) cart.

**tableau** ( pl ∼x) /tablo/ nm picture; (peinture) painting; (panneau) board; (graphique) chart; (Scol) blackboard; ∼ d'affichage noticeboard; ∼ de bord dashboard.

**tablette** /tablɛt/ nf shelf; ∼ de chocolat bar of chocolate.

**tableur** /tablœʀ/ nm spreadsheet.

**tablier** /tablije/ nm apron; (de pont) platform; (de magasin) shutter.

**tabou** /tabu/ nm & adj taboo.

**tabouret** /tabuʀɛ/ nm stool.

**tache** /taʃ/ nf mark, spot; (salissure) stain; faire ∼ d'huile spread; ∼ de rousseur freckle.

**tâche** /taʃ/ nf task, job.

**tacher** /taʃe/ **1** vt stain. □ se ∼ vpr ( personne) get oneself dirty.

**tâcher** /taʃe/ **1** vi ∼ de faire try to do.

**tacheté, ∼e** /taʃte/ adj spotted.

**tact** /takt/ nm tact.

**tactique** /taktik/ adj tactical. ● nf (Mil) tactics; une ∼ a tactic.

**taie** /tɛ/ nf ∼ (d'oreiller) pillowcase.

**taille** /taj/ nf (milieu du corps) waist; (hauteur) height; (grandeur) size; de ∼ sizeable; être de ∼ à faire be up to doing.

**taille-crayons** /tajkʀɛjɔ̃/ nm inv pencil-sharpener.

**tailler** /taje/ **1** vt cut; (arbre) prune; (crayon) sharpen; (vêtement) cut out. □ se ∼ vpr **1** clear off.

**tailleur** /tajœʀ/ nm (costume) woman's suit; (couturier) tailor; en ∼ cross-legged; ∼ de pierre stonecutter.

**taire** /tɛʀ/ **47** vt not to reveal; faire ∼ silence. □ se ∼ vpr be silent ou quiet; (devenir silencieux) fall silent.

**talc** /talk/ nm talcum powder.

**talent** /talɑ̃/ nm talent. **talentueux, -euse** adj talented, gifted.

**talon** /talɔ̃/ nm heel; (de chèque) stub.

**tambour** /tɑ̃buʀ/ nm drum; (d'église) vestibule.

**Tamise** /tamiz/ nf Thames.

**tampon** /tɑ̃pɔ̃/ nm (de bureau) stamp; (ouate) wad, pad; (∼ hygiénique) tampon.

**tamponner** /tɑ̃pɔne/ **1** vt (document) stamp; (véhicule) crash into; ( plaie) swab.

**tandem** /tɑ̃dɛm/ nm (vélo) tandem; (personnes: fig) duo.

**tandis que** /tɑ̃di(s)/ conj while.

**tanière** /tanjɛʀ/ nf den.

**tant** /tɑ̃/ adv (travailler, manger) so much; ∼ de (quantité) so much; (nombre) so many; ∼ que as long as; en ∼ que as; ∼ mieux! all the better!; ∼ pis! too bad!

**tante** /tɑ̃t/ nf aunt.

**tantôt** /tɑ̃to/ adv sometimes.

**tapage** /tapaʒ/ nm din.

**tape** /tap/ nf slap. **tape-à-l'œil** adj inv flashy, tawdry.

**taper** /tape/ **1** vt hit; (prendre **1**) scrounge; ∼ (à la machine) type. ● vi (cogner) bang; (soleil) beat down; ∼ dans (puiser dans) dig into; ∼ sur hit; ∼ sur l'épaule de qn tap sb on the shoulder. □ se ∼ vpr (corvée **1**) get stuck with **1**.

**tapis** /tapi/ nm carpet; (petit) rug; ∼ de bain bathmat; ∼ roulant (pour objets) conveyor belt; (pour piétons) moving walkway.

**tapisser** /tapise/ **1** vt (wall) paper; (fig) cover (de with). **tapisserie** nf tapestry; (papier peint) wallpaper.

**taquin, ∼e** /takɛ̃, -in/ adj fond of teasing. ● nm, f tease(r).

**tard** /taʀ/ adv late; au plus ~ at the latest; plus ~ later; sur le ~ late in life.

**tarder** /taʀde/ **1** vi (être lent à venir) be a long time coming; ~ (à faire) take a long time (doing); sans (plus) ~ without (further) delay; il me tarde de I'm longing to.

**tardif, -ive** /taʀdif, -v/ adj late.

**tare** /taʀ/ nf (défaut) defect.

**tarif** /taʀif/ nm rate; (de train, taxi) fare; plein ~ full price.

**tarir** /taʀiʀ/ **2** vt/i dry up. □ se ~ vpr dry up.

**tarte** /taʀt/ nf tart. ● adj inv (ridicule ☐) ridiculous.

**tartine** /taʀtin/ nf slice of bread; ~ de beurre slice of bread and butter. **tartiner 1** vt spread.

**tartre** /taʀtʀ/ nm (de bouilloire) fur, scale; (sur les dents) tartar.

**tas** /tɑ/ nm pile, heap; un ou des ~ de ☐ lots of.

**tasse** /tɑs/ nf cup; ~ à thé teacup.

**tasser** /tɑse/ **1** vt pack, squeeze; (terre) pack (down). □ se ~ vpr (terrain) sink; (se serrer) squeeze up.

**tâter** /tɑte/ **1** vt feel; (opinion: fig) sound out. ● vi ~ de try out.

**tatillon, -ne** /tatijɔ̃, -jɔn/ adj finicky.

**tâtonnements** /tɑtɔnmɑ̃/ nmpl (essais) trial and error (+ sg). **tâtons: à ~** /atatɔ̃/ loc avancer à ~ grope one's way along.

**tatouage** /tatwaʒ/ nm (dessin) tattoo.

**taupe** /top/ nf mole.

**taureau** (pl ~x) /tɔʀo/ nm bull; le T~ Taurus.

**taux** /to/ nm rate.

**taxe** /taks/ nf tax.

**taxi** /taksi/ nm taxi(-cab); (personne ☐) taxi driver.

**taxiphone** ® /taksifɔn/ nm pay phone.

**Tchécoslovaquie** /tʃekɔslɔvaki/ nf Czechoslovakia.

**tchèque** /tʃɛk/ adj Czech; République ~ Czech Republic. **T~** nmf Czech.

**te, t'** /tə, t/ pron you; (indirect) (to) you; (réfléchi) yourself.

**technicien, ~ne** /tɛknisjɛ̃, -ɛn/ nm, f technician.

**technique** /tɛknik/ adj technical. ● nf technique.

**techno** /tɛkno/ nf (Mus) techno.

**technologie** /tɛknɔlɔʒi/ nf technology.

**teindre** /tɛ̃dʀ/ **22** vt dye. □ se ~ vpr se ~ les cheveux dye one's hair.

**teint** /tɛ̃/ nm complexion.

**teinte** /tɛ̃t/ nf shade. **teinter 1** vt (verre) tint; (bois) stain.

**teinture** /tɛ̃tyʀ/ nf (produit) dye.

**teinturier, -ière** /tɛ̃tyʀje, -jɛʀ/ nm, f dry-cleaner.

**tel, ~le** /tɛl/ adj such; un ~ livre such a book; ~ que such as, like; (ainsi que) (just) as; ~ ou ~ such-and-such; ~ quel (just) as it is.

**télé** /tele/ nf ☐ TV; ~ réalité nf reality TV.

**télécharger** /teleʃaʀʒe/ **40** vt (Ordinat) download.

**télécommande** /telekɔmɑ̃d/ nf remote control.

**télécommunications** /telekɔmynikasjɔ̃/ nfpl telecommunications.

**téléconférence** /telekɔ̃feʀɑ̃s/ nf teleconferencing.

**télécopie** /telekɔpi/ nf fax. **télécopieur** nm fax machine.

**téléfilm** /telefilm/ nm TV film.

**télégramme** /telegram/ nm telegram.

**télégraphier** /telegrafje/ **45** vt/i ~ (à) cable.

**téléguidé**, ~e /telegide/ adj radiocontrolled.

**télématique** /telematik/ nf telematics (+ sg).

**téléphérique** /teleferik/ nm cable car.

**téléphone** /telefɔn/ nm (tele)phone; ~ à carte cardphone. **téléphoner** **1** vt/i ~ (à) (tele)phone.

**téléphonie** /telefɔni/ nf telephony; ~ mobile mobile telephony. **téléphonique** adj (tele)phone.

**télé-réalité** /telerealite/ nf reality TV.

**téléserveur** /teleservœr/ nm (Internet) remote server.

**télésiège** /telesjeʒ/ nm chairlift.

**téléski** /teleski/ nm ski tow.

**téléspectateur**, **-trice** /telespɛktatœr, -tris/ nm, f (tv) viewer.

**télévente** /televãt/ nf telesales (+ pl).

**télévisé**, ~e /televize/ adj (débat) televised; **émission** ~e television programme. **télévision** nf television.

**télex** /telɛks/ nm telex.

**tellement** /telmã/ adv (tant) so much; (si) so; ~ de (quantité) so much; (nombre) so many.

**téméraire** /temerɛr/ adj (personne) reckless.

**témoignage** /temwaɲaʒ/ nm testimony, evidence; (récit) account; ~ de (marque) token of.

**témoigner** /temwaɲe/ **1** vi testify (de to). ●vt (montrer) show; ~ que testify that.

**témoin** /temwɛ̃/ nm witness; (Sport) baton; être ~ de witness;

~ oculaire eyewitness.

**tempe** /tãp/ nf (Anat) temple.

**tempérament** /tãperamã/ nm temperament, disposition.

**température** /tãperatyr/ nf temperature.

**tempête** /tãpɛt/ nf storm; ~ de neige snowstorm.

**temple** /tãpl/ nm temple; (protestant) church.

**temporaire** /tãporɛr/ adj temporary.

**temps** /tã/ nm (notion) time; (Gram) tense; (étape) stage; à ~ partiel/plein part-/full-time; ces derniers ~ lately; dans le ~ at one time; dans quelque ~ in a while; de ~ en ~ from time to time; ~ d'arrêt pause; avoir tout son ~ have plenty of time; (météo) weather; ~ de chien filthy weather; quel ~ fait-il? what's the weather like?

**tenace** /tɔnas/ adj stubborn.

**tenaille** /tɔnaj/ nf pincers (+ pl).

**tendance** /tãdãs/ nf tendency; (évolution) trend; avoir ~ à tend to.

**tendon** /tãdɔ̃/ nm tendon.

**tendre**¹ /tãdr/ **3** vt stretch; (piège) set; (bras) stretch out; (main) hold out; (cou) crane; ~ à qn hold sth out to sb; ~ l'oreille prick up one's ears. ●vi ~ à tend to.

**tendre**² /tãdr/ adj tender; (couleur, bois) soft. **tendresse** nf tenderness.

**tendu**, ~e /tãdy/ adj (corde) tight; (personne, situation) tense.

**ténèbres** /tenɛbr/ nfpl darkness.

**teneur** /tɔnœr/ nf content.

**tenir** /tɔnir/ **59** vt hold; (pari, promesse, hôtel) keep; (place) take up; (propos) utter; (rôle) play; ~ de (avoir reçu de) have got from; ~

**t**

pour regard as; ~ chaud keep warm; ~ compte de take into account; ~ le coup hold out; ~ tête à stand up to. ● *vi* hold; ~ à be attached to; ~ à faire be anxious to do; ~ bon stand firm; ~ dans fit into; ~ de qn take after sb; tiens! (surprise) hey! □ se ~ *vpr* (debout) stand; (avoir lieu) be held; se ~ à hold on to; s'en ~ à (se limiter à) confine oneself to.

**tennis** /tenis/ *nm* tennis; ~ de table table tennis. ● *nmpl* (chaussures) sneakers.

**ténor** /tenɔʀ/ *nm* tenor.

**tension** /tɑ̃sjɔ̃/ *nf* tension; avoir de la ~ have high blood pressure.

**tentation** /tɑ̃tasjɔ̃/ *nf* temptation.

**tentative** /tɑ̃tativ/ *nf* attempt.

**tente** /tɑ̃t/ *nf* tent.

**tenter** /tɑ̃te/ **1** *vt* (allécher) tempt; (essayer) try (**de** faire to do).

**tenture** /tɑ̃tyʀ/ *nf* curtain; ~s draperies.

**tenu**, ~e /təny/ *adj* bien ~ well kept; ~ de required. ● →TENIR 58.

**tenue** /təny/ *nf* (habillement) dress; (de maison) upkeep; (conduite) (good) behaviour; (maintien) posture; ~ de soirée evening dress.

**Tergal** ® /tɛʀgal/ *nm* Terylene®.

**terme** /tɛʀm/ *nm* (mot) term; (date limite) time-limit; (fin) end; né avant ~ premature; à long/court ~ long-/short-term; en bons ~s on good terms (avec with).

**terminaison** /tɛʀminɛzɔ̃/ *nf* (Gram) ending.

**terminal**, ~e *(mpl* -aux) /tɛʀminal, -o/ *adj* terminal. ● *nm* terminal. **terminale** *nf* (Scol) ≈ sixth form; (US) twelfth grade.

**terminer** /tɛʀmine/ **1** *vt/i* finish; (discours) end, finish. □ se ~ *vpr* end (par with).

**terne** /tɛʀn/ *adj* dull, drab.

**ternir** /tɛʀniʀ/ **2** *vt/i* tarnish. □ se ~ *vpr* tarnish.

**terrain** /teʀɛ̃/ *nm* ground; (parcelle) piece of land; (à bâtir) plot; ~ d'aviation airfield; ~ de camping campsite; ~ de golf golf course; ~ de jeu playground; ~ vague waste ground.

**terrasse** /teʀas/ *nf* terrace; à la ~ (d'un café) outside (a café).

**terrasser** /teʀase/ **1** *vt* (adversaire) knock down; (maladie) strike down.

**terre** /tɛʀ/ *nf* (planète, matière) earth; (étendue, pays) land; (sol) ground; à ~ (Naut) ashore; par ~ (dehors) on the ground; (dedans) on the floor; ~ (cuite) terracotta; la ~ ferme dry land; ~ glaise clay.

**terreau** *(pl* ~x) *nm* compost.

**terre-plein** *(pl* terre-pleins) *nm* platform; (de route) central reservation.

**terrestre** /teʀɛstʀ/ *adj* (animaux) land; (de notre planète) of the Earth.

**terreur** /teʀœʀ/ *nf* terror.

**terrible** /teʀibl/ *adj* terrible; (formidable □) terrific.

**terrier** /teʀje/ *nm* (trou) burrow; (chien) terrier.

**terrifier** /teʀifje/ 45 *vt* terrify.

**territoire** /teʀitwaʀ/ *nm* territory.

**terroir** /teʀwaʀ/ *nm* land; du ~ local.

**terroriser** /teʀɔʀize/ **1** *vt* terrorize.

**terrorisme** /teʀɔʀism/ *nm* terrorism. **terroriste** *nmf* terrorist.

**tertiaire** /tɛʀsjɛʀ/ *adj* (secteur) service.

**tes** /te/ →TON¹.

**test** /tɛst/ *nm* test.

**testament** /tɛstamɑ̃/ *nm* (Jur) will;

(politique, artistique) testament; Ancien/Nouveau T∼ Old/New Testament.

**tétanos** /tetanos/ nm tetanus.

**têtard** /tɛtaʀ/ nm tadpole.

**tête** /tɛt/ nf head; (visage) face; (cheveux) hair; à la ∼ de at the head of; à ∼ reposée at one's leisure; de ∼ (calculer) in one's head; faire la ∼ sulk; tenir ∼ à qn stand up to sb; il n'en fait qu'à sa ∼ he does just as he pleases; en ∼ (Sport) in the lead; faire une ∼ (au football) head the ball; une forte ∼ a rebel; la ∼ la première head first; de la ∼ aux pieds from head to toe.

**tête-à-tête** /tɛtatɛt/ nm inv tête-à-tête; en ∼ in private.

**tétée** /tete/ nf feed.

**tétine** /tetin/ nf (de biberon) teat; (sucette) dummy; (US) pacifier.

**têtu, ∼e** /tety/ adj stubborn.

**texte** /tɛkst/ nm text; (de leçon) subject; (morceau choisi) passage.

**texteur** /tɛkstœʀ/ nm (Ordinat) word-processor.

**textile** /tɛkstil/ nm & adj textile.

**texto** /tɛksto/ nm ① text message.

**TGV** abrév m (**train à grande vitesse**) TGV, high-speed train.

> **TGV** Abbreviation of Train à grande vitesse, the high-speed electric passenger train operated by the SNCF. It runs on special track and can reach speeds of up to 300 km/h (180 mph). Marseilles, for example, is now only three hours from Paris by TGV.

**thé** /te/ nm tea.

**théâtre** /teɑtʀ/ nm theatre; (d'un crime) scene; faire du ∼ act.

**théière** /tejɛʀ/ nf teapot.

**thème** /tɛm/ nm theme; (traduction: Scol) prose.

**théorie** /teɔʀi/ nf theory. **théorique** adj theoretical.

**thérapie** /teʀapi/ nf therapy.

**thermique** /tɛʀmik/ adj thermal.

**thermomètre** /tɛʀmɔmɛtʀ/ nm thermometer.

**thermos®** /tɛʀmos/ nm ou f Thermos® (flask).

**thermostat** /tɛʀmɔsta/ nm thermostat.

**thèse** /tɛz/ nf thesis.

**thon** /tɔ̃/ nm tuna.

**thym** /tɛ̃/ nm thyme.

**tibia** /tibja/ nm shinbone.

**tic** /tik/ nm (contraction) tic, twitch; (manie) habit.

**ticket** /tikɛ/ nm ticket.

**tiède** /tjɛd/ adj lukewarm; (nuit) warm.

**tiédir** /tjediʀ/ ② vt/i (faire) ∼ warm up.

**tien, ∼ne** /tjɛ̃, -ɛn/ pron le ∼, la ∼ne, les ∼(ne)s yours; à la ∼ne! cheers!

**tiens, tient** /tjɛ̃/ ➞**TENIR** 59.

**tiercé** /tjɛʀse/ nm place-betting.

**tiers, tierce** /tjɛʀ, tjɛʀs/ adj third. ●**nm** (fraction) third; (personne) third party. **tiers-monde** nm Third World.

**tige** /tiʒ/ nf (Bot) stem, stalk; (en métal) shaft, rod.

**tigre** /tigʀ/ nm tiger.

**tigresse** /tigʀɛs/ nf tigress.

**tilleul** /tijœl/ nm lime tree.

**timbre** /tɛ̃bʀ/ nm stamp; (sonnette) bell; (de voix) tone. ∼ **poste** (pl ∼s **poste**) nm postage stamp. **timbrer** ① vt stamp.

**timide** /timid/ adj shy, timid. **timidité** nf shyness.

t

**timoré,** ~e /timɔʀe/ adj timorous.

**tintement** /tɛ̃tmɑ̃/ nm (de sonnette) ringing; (de clés) jingling.

**tique** /tik/ nf tick.

**tir** /tiʀ/ nm (Sport) shooting; (action de tirer) firing; (feu, rafale) fire; ~ à l'arc archery; ~ au pigeon clay pigeon shooting.

**tirage** /tiʀaʒ/ nm (de photo) printing; (de journal) circulation; (de livre) edition; (Ordinat) hard copy; (de cheminée) draught; ~ au sort draw.

**tire-bouchon** (pl ~s) /tiʀbuʃɔ̃/ nm corkscrew.

**tirelire** /tiʀliʀ/ nf piggy bank.

**tirer** /tiʀe/ **1** vt pull; (langue) stick out; (conclusion, trait, rideaux) draw; (coup de feu) fire; (gibier) shoot; (photo) print; ~ de (sortir) take ou get out of; (extraire) extract from; (plaisir, nom) derive from; ~ parti de take advantage of; ~ profit de profit from; se faire ~ l'oreille get told off. ● vi shoot, fire (sur at); ~ sur (corde) pull at; (couleur) verge on; ~ à sa fin be drawing to a close; ~ au clair clarify; ~ au sort draw lots (for). □ se ~ vpr **1** clear off; se ~ de get out of; s'en ~ (en réchapper) pull through; (réussir **1**) cope.

**tiret** /tiʀe/ nm dash.

**tireur** /tiʀœʀ/ nm gunman; ~ d'élite marksman; ~ isolé sniper.

**tiroir** /tiʀwaʀ/ nm drawer. **tiroir-caisse** (pl tiroirs-caisses) nm till, cash register.

**tisane** /tizan/ nf herbal tea.

**tissage** /tisaʒ/ nm weaving. **tisser** **1** vt weave. **tisserand** nm weaver.

**tissu** /tisy/ nm fabric, material; (biologique) tissue; un ~ de mensonges (fig) a pack of lies. **tissu-éponge** (pl tissus-éponge)

nm towelling.

**titre** /titʀ/ nm title; (diplôme) qualification; (Comm) bond; ~s (droits) claims; (gros) ~s headlines; à ~ d'exemple as an example; à juste ~ rightly; à ~ privé in a private capacity; à ~ de on two accounts; ~ de propriété title deed.

**tituber** /titybe/ **1** vi stagger.

**titulaire** /titylɛʀ/ adj être ~ be a permanent staff member; être ~ de hold. ● nmf (de permis) holder. **titulariser** **1** vt give permanent status to.

**toast** /tost/ nm (pain) piece of toast; (canapé, allocution) toast.

**toboggan** /tɔbɔɡɑ̃/ nm (de jeu) slide; (Auto) flyover.

**toi** /twa/ pron you; (réfléchi) yourself; dépêche-~ hurry up.

**toile** /twal/ nf cloth; (tableau) canvas; ~ d'araignée cobweb; ~ de fond (fig) backdrop; la ~ (Internet) the Web.

**toilette** /twalɛt/ nf (habillement) outfit; ~s (cabinets) toilet(s); de ~ (articles, savon) toilet; faire sa ~ have a wash.

**toi-même** /twamɛm/ pron yourself.

**toit** /twa/ nm roof; ~ ouvrant (Auto) sunroof.

**toiture** /twatyʀ/ nf roof.

**tôle** /tol/ nf (plaque) iron sheet; ~ ondulée corrugated iron.

**tolérant,** ~e /tɔleʀɑ̃, -t/ adj tolerant. **tolérer** **14** vt tolerate.

**tomate** /tɔmat/ nf tomato.

**tombe** /tɔ̃b/ nf grave; (pierre) gravestone.

**tombeau** (pl ~x) /tɔ̃bo/ nm tomb.

**tomber** /tɔ̃be/ **1** vi (aux être) fall; (fièvre, vent) drop; faire ~ knock over; (gouvernement) bring down; laisser ~ (objet, amoureux) drop;

(*collègue*) let down; (*activité*) give up; **laisse ~!** 🔲 forget it!; **~ à l'eau** (*projet*) fall through; **~ bien** *ou* **à point** come at the right time; **~ en panne** break down; **~ en syncope** faint; **~ sur** (*trouver*) run across.

**tombola** /tɔ̃bɔla/ *nf* tombola; (US) lottery.

**tome** /tɔm/ *nm* volume.

**ton¹, ta** (**ton** before vowel or mute h) (*pl* **tes**) /tɔ̃, ta, tɔ̃n, te/ *adj* your.

**ton²** /tɔ̃/ *nm* (hauteur de voix) pitch; **d'un ~ sec** drily; **de bon ~** in good taste.

**tonalité** /tɔnalite/ *nf* (Mus) key; (de téléphone) dialling tone; (US) dial tone.

**tondeuse** /tɔ̃døz/ *nf* (à moutons) shears (+ *pl*); (à cheveux) clippers (+ *pl*); **~ à gazon** lawn-mower. **ton-dre** 🔳 *vt* (herbe) mow; (mouton) shear; (cheveux) cut.

**tonne** /tɔn/ *nf* tonne.

**tonneau** (*pl* **~x**) /tɔno/ *nm* barrel; (en voiture) somersault.

**tonnerre** /tɔnɛʀ/ *nm* thunder.

**tonton** /tɔ̃tɔ̃/ *nm* 🔲 uncle.

**tonus** /tɔnys/ *nm* energy.

**torche** /tɔʀʃ/ *nf* torch.

**torchon** /tɔʀʃɔ̃/ *nm* (pour la vaisselle) tea towel.

**tordre** /tɔʀdʀ/ 🔳 *vt*. □ **se ~** *vpr* **se ~ la cheville** twist one's ankle; **se ~ de douleur** writhe in pain; **se ~** (de rire) split one's sides.

**tordu, ~e** /tɔʀdy/ *adj* twisted, bent; (esprit) warped, twisted.

**torpille** /tɔʀpij/ *nf* torpedo.

**torrent** /tɔʀɑ̃/ *nm* torrent.

**torride** /tɔʀid/ *adj* torrid; (chaleur) scorching.

**torse** /tɔʀs/ *nm* chest; (Anat) torso.

**tort** /tɔʀ/ *nm* wrong; **avoir ~** be wrong (**de faire** to do); **donner ~ à** prove wrong; **être dans son ~** be in the wrong; **faire (du) ~ à** harm; **à ~** wrongly; **à ~ et à travers** without thinking.

**torticolis** /tɔʀtikɔli/ *nm* stiff neck.

**tortiller** /tɔʀtije/ 🔳 *vt* twist, twirl. □ **se ~** *vpr* wriggle.

**tortionnaire** /tɔʀsjɔnɛʀ/ *nm* torturer.

**tortue** /tɔʀty/ *nf* tortoise; (d'eau) turtle.

**tortueux, -euse** /tɔʀtyø, -z/ *adj* (chemin) twisting; (explication) tortuous.

**torture** /tɔʀtyʀ/ *nf* torture. **torturer** 🔳 *vt* torture.

**tôt** /to/ *adv* early; **au plus ~** at the earliest; **le plus ~ possible** as soon as possible; **~ ou tard** sooner or later; **ce n'est pas trop ~!** it's about time!

**total, ~e** (*mpl* **-aux**) /tɔtal, -o/ *adj* total. ● *nm* (*pl* **-aux**) total; **au ~** all in all. **totalement** *adv* totally. **totaliser** 🔳 *vt* total. **totalitaire** *adj* totalitarian.

**totalité** /tɔtalite/ *nf* **la ~ de** all of.

**touche** /tuʃ/ *nf* (de piano) key; (de peinture) touch; **(ligne de) ~** (Sport) touchline.

**toucher** /tuʃe/ 🔳 *vt* touch; (émouvoir) move, touch; (contacter) get in touch with; (cible) hit; (argent) draw; (chèque) cash; (concerner) affect. ● *vi* **~ à** touch; (question) approach; **je vais lui en ~ deux mots** I'll talk to him about it. □ **se ~** *vpr* (lignes) touch. ● *nm* (sens) touch.

**touffe** /tuf/ *nf* (de poils, d'herbe) tuft; (de plantes) clump.

**toujours** /tuʒuʀ/ *adv* always; (encore) still; (de toute façon) anyway;

pour ∼ for ever; ∼ est-il que the fact remains that.

**toupet** /tupɛ/ *nm* (culot 🅸) cheek, nerve.

**tour** /tur/ *nf* tower; (immeuble) tower block; (échecs) rook; ∼ de contrôle control tower. ● *nm* (mouvement, succession, tournure) turn; (excursion) trip; (à pied) walk; (en auto) drive; (artifice) trick; (circonférence) circumference; (Tech) lathe; ∼ (de piste) lap; à ∼ de rôle in turn; à mon ∼ when it is my turn; c'est mon ∼ de it is my turn to; faire le ∼ de go round; (question) survey; ∼ d'horizon overview; ∼ de potier potter's wheel; ∼ de taille waist measurement; (ligne) waistline.

**tourbillon** /turbijɔ̃/ *nm* whirlwind; (d'eau) whirlpool; (fig) swirl.

**tourisme** /turism/ *nm* tourism; faire du ∼ do some sightseeing.

**touriste** /turist/ *nmf* tourist. **touristique** *adj* tourist; (route) scenic.

**tourmenter** /turmɑ̃te/ *vt* torment. □ se ∼ *vpr* worry.

**tournant**, ∼e /turnɑ̃, -t/ *adj* (qui pivote) revolving. ● *nm* bend; (fig) turning-point.

**tourne-disque** (*pl* ∼s)

/turnədisk/ *nm* record-player.

**tournée** /turne/ *nf* (de facteur, au café) round; c'est ma ∼ I'll buy this round; (d'artiste) tour.

**tourner** /turne/ 🅸 *vt* turn; (film) shoot, make; ∼ le dos à turn one's back on; ∼ en dérision mock. ● *vi* turn; (toupie, tête) spin; (moteur, usine) run; ∼ autour de go round; (personne, maison) hang around; (terre) revolve round; (question) centre on; ∼ de l'œil faint; mal ∼ (affaire) turn out badly. □ se ∼ *vpr* turn.

**tournesol** /turnəsɔl/ *nm* sunflower.

**tournevis** /turnəvis/ *nm* screwdriver.

**tournoi** /turnwa/ *nm* tournament.

**tourte** /turt/ *nf* pie.

**tourterelle** /turtərɛl/ *nf* turtle dove.

**Toussaint** /tusɛ̃/ *nf* la ∼ All Saints' Day.

**tousser** /tuse/ 🅸 *vi* cough.

**tout**, ∼e (*pl* tous, toutes) /tu, tut/ *nm* (ensemble) whole; en ∼ in all; pas du ∼! not at all! ● *adj* all; (n'importe quel) any; ∼ le pays the whole country, all the country; ∼e la nuit/journée the whole night/day; ∼ un paquet a whole pack; tous les jours every day; tous les deux ans every two years; ∼ le monde everyone; tous les deux, toutes les deux both of them; tous les trois all three (of them). ● *pron* everything; all; anything; tous /tus/, toutes all; tous ensemble all together; prends ∼ take everything; ∼ ce que tu veux everything you want. ● *adv* (très) very; (entièrement) all; ∼ au bout/début right at the end/beginning; ∼ en marchant while walking; ∼ à coup all of a sudden; ∼ à fait quite, completely; ~ à l'heure in a moment; (passé) a moment ago; ~ au ou le long de throughout; ~ au plus/moins at most/least; ~ de même all the same; ~ de suite straight away; ~ entier whole; ~ neuf brand new; ~ nu stark naked. **tout-à-l'égout** nm inv main drainage.

**toutefois** /tutfwa/ adv however.

**tout(-)terrain** /tuterɛ̃/ adj inv all terrain.

**toux** /tu/ nf cough.

**toxicomane** /tɔksikɔman/ nmf drug addict.

**toxique** /tɔksik/ adj toxic.

**trac** /trak/ nm le ~ nerves; (Théât) stage fright.

**tracas** /traka/ nm worry.

**trace** /tras/ nf (traînée, piste) trail; (d'animal, de pneu) tracks; ~s de pas footprints.

**tracer** /trase/ **10** vt draw; (écrire) write; (route) open up.

**trachée-artère** /traʃeartɛr/ nf windpipe.

**tracteur** /traktœr/ nm tractor.

**tradition** /tradisjɔ̃/ nf tradition. **traditionnel, ~le** adj traditional.

**traducteur, -trice** /tradyktœr, -tris/ nm, f translator. **traduction** nf translation.

**traduire** /traduir/ **17** vt translate; ~ en justice take to court.

**trafic** /trafik/ nm (commerce, circulation) traffic.

**trafiquant, ~e** /trafikɑ̃, -t/ nm, f trafficker; (d'armes, de drogues) dealer.

**trafiquer** /trafike/ **1** vi traffic. ● vt **1** (moteur) fiddle with.

**tragédie** /traʒedi/ nf tragedy. **tragique** adj tragic.

**trahir** /trair/ **2** vt betray. **trahi-**

son nf betrayal; (Mil) treason.

**train** /trɛ̃/ nm (Rail) train; (allure) pace; aller bon ~ walk briskly; en ~ de faire (busy) doing; ~ d'atterrissage undercarriage; ~ électrique (jouet) electric train set; ~ de vie lifestyle.

**traîne** /trɛn/ nf (de robe) train; à la ~ lagging behind.

**traîneau** (pl ~x) /trɛno/ nm sleigh.

**traînée** /trɛne/ nf (trace) trail; (longue) streak; (femme: péj) slut.

**traîner** /trɛne/ **1** vt drag (along); ~ les pieds drag one's feet. ● vi (pendre) trail; (rester en arrière) trail behind; (flâner) hang about; (papiers, affaires) lie around; ~ (en longueur) drag on. □ **se ~** vpr (par terre) crawl.

**traire** /trɛr/ **29** vt milk.

**trait** /trɛ/ nm line; (en dessinant) stroke; (caractéristique) feature, trait; ~s (du visage) features; avoir ~ à relate to; d'un ~ (boire) in one gulp; ~ d'union hyphen; (fig) link.

**traite** /trɛt/ nf (de vache) milking; (Comm) draft; d'une (seule) ~ in one go, at a stretch.

**traité** /trɛte/ nm (pacte) treaty; (ouvrage) treatise.

**traitement** /trɛtmɑ̃/ nm treatment; (salaire) salary; ~ de données data processing; ~ de texte word processing.

**traiter** /trete/ **1** vt treat; (affaire) deal with; (données, produit) process; ~ qn de lâche call sb a coward. ● vi deal (avec with); ~ de (sujet) deal with.

**traiteur** /trɛtœr/ nm caterer; (boutique) delicatessen.

**traître, -esse** /trɛtr, -ɛs/ adj treacherous. ● nm, f traitor.

**trajectoire** /traʒɛktwar/ nf path.

**trajet** /tʀaʒɛ/ nm (voyage) journey; (itinéraire) route.

**trame** /tʀam/ nf (de tissu) weft.

**tramway** /tʀamwɛ/ nm tram; (US) streetcar.

**tranchant, ~e** /tʀɑ̃ʃɑ̃, -t/ adj sharp; (fig) cutting. ● nm cutting edge; à double ~ two-edged.

**tranche** /tʀɑ̃ʃ/ nf (rondelle) slice; (bord) edge; (d'âge, de revenu) bracket.

**tranchée** /tʀɑ̃ʃe/ nf trench.

**trancher** /tʀɑ̃ʃe/ [1] vt cut; (question) decide; (contraster) contrast (sur with).

**tranquille** /tʀɑ̃kil/ adj quiet; (esprit) at rest; (conscience) clear; être/laisser ~ be/leave in peace; tiens-toi ~! be quiet! **tranquillisant** nm tranquillizer. **tranquilliser** [1] vt reassure. **tranquillité** nf (peace and) quiet; (d'esprit) peace of mind.

**transcription** /tʀɑ̃skʀipsjɔ̃/ nf transcription; (copie) transcript. **transcrire** [30] vt transcribe.

**transe** /tʀɑ̃s/ nf en ~ in a trance.

**transférer** /tʀɑ̃sfeʀe/ [14] vt transfer.

**transfert** /tʀɑ̃sfɛʀ/ nm transfer; ~ d'appel (au téléphone) call diversion.

**transformation** /tʀɑ̃sfɔʀmasjɔ̃/ nf change; transformation.

**transformer** /tʀɑ̃sfɔʀme/ [1] vt change; (radicalement) transform; (vêtement) alter. □ se ~ vpr change; (radicalement) be transformed; (se) ~ en turn into.

**transgénique** /tʀɑ̃sʒenik/ adj genetically modified.

**transiger** /tʀɑ̃siʒe/ [40] vi compromise.

**transiter** /tʀɑ̃zite/ [1] vt/i ~ par pass through.

**transitif, -ive** /tʀɑ̃zitif, -v/ adj transitive.

**translucide** /tʀɑ̃slysid/ adj translucent.

**transmettre** /tʀɑ̃smɛtʀ/ [42] vt (savoir, maladie) pass on; (ondes) transmit; (à la radio) broadcast. **transmission** nf transmission; (radio) broadcasting.

**transparence** /tʀɑ̃spaʀɑ̃s/ nf transparency. **transparent, ~e** adj transparent.

**transpercer** /tʀɑ̃spɛʀse/ [10] vt pierce.

**transpiration** /tʀɑ̃spiʀasjɔ̃/ nf perspiration. **transpirer** [1] vi perspire.

**transplanter** /tʀɑ̃splɑ̃te/ [1] vt (Bot, Méd) transplant.

**transport** /tʀɑ̃spɔʀ/ nm transport(ation); durant le ~ in transit; les ~s transport (+ sg); les ~s en commun public transport (+ sg). **transporter** [1] vt transport; (à la main) carry. **transporteur** nm haulier; (US) trucker.

**transversal, ~e** (mpl -aux) /tʀɑ̃svɛʀsal, -o/ adj cross, transverse.

**trapu, ~e** /tʀapy/ adj stocky.

**traumatisant, ~e** /tʀomatizɑ̃, -t/ adj traumatic. **traumatiser** vt [1] traumatize. **traumatisme** nm trauma.

**travail** (pl -aux) /tʀavaj, -o/ nm work; (emploi, tâche) job; (façonnage) working; travaux work (+ sg); (routiers) roadworks; ~ à la chaîne production line work; travaux dirigés (Scol) practical; travaux forcés hard labour; travaux manuels handicrafts; travaux ménagers housework.

**travailler** /tʀavaje/ [1] vi work; (se déformer) warp. ● vt (façonner) work; (étudier) work at ou on.

**travailleur, -euse** /tʀavajœʀ, -øz/ nm, f worker. ● adj hardworking.

**travailliste** /tʀavajist/ adj Labour. ● nmf Labour party member.

**travers** /tʀavɛʀ/ nm (défaut) failing; à ~ through; au ~ (de) through; de ~ (chapeau, nez) crooked; (regarder) askance; j'ai avalé de ~ it went down the wrong way; en ~ (de) across.

**traversée** /tʀavɛʀse/ nf crossing.

**traverser** /tʀavɛʀse/ **1** vt cross; (transpercer) go (right) through; (période, forêt) go ou pass through.

**traversin** /tʀavɛʀsɛ̃/ nm bolster.

**travesti** /tʀavɛsti/ nm transvestite.

**trébucher** /tʀebyʃe/ **1** vi stumble, trip (over); **faire** ~ trip (up).

**trèfle** /tʀɛfl/ nm (plante) clover; (cartes) clubs.

**treillis** /tʀeji/ nm trellis; (en métal) wire mesh; (tenue militaire) combat uniform.

**treize** /tʀɛz/ adj & nm thirteen.

---

> **Treizième mois** An addition to an employee's salary, equal to his/her usual monthly payment, which some employees receive at the end of the calendar year.     *i*

---

**tréma** /tʀema/ nm diaeresis.

**tremblement** /tʀɑ̃bləmɑ̃/ nm shaking; ~ **de terre** earthquake.

**trembler** /tʀɑ̃ble/ **1** vi shake, tremble; (lumière, voix) quiver.

**tremper** /tʀɑ̃pe/ **1** vt/i soak; (plonger) dip; (acier) temper; **faire** ~ soak; ~ **dans** (fig) be mixed up. □ **se** ~ vpr (se baigner) have a dip.

**tremplin** /tʀɑ̃plɛ̃/ nm springboard.

**trente** /tʀɑ̃t/ adj & nm thirty; **se mettre sur son** ~ **et un** dress up;

**tous les** ~-**six du mois** once in a blue moon.

**trépied** /tʀepje/ nm tripod.

**très** /tʀɛ/ adv very; ~ **aimé/estimé** much liked/esteemed.

**trésor** /tʀezɔʀ/ nm treasure; **le T** ~ **public** the revenue department.

**trésorerie** /tʀezɔʀʀi/ nf (bureaux) accounts department; (du Trésor public) revenue office; (argent) funds (+ pl); (gestion) accounts (+ pl). **trésorier, -ière** nm, f treasurer.

**tressaillement** /tʀesajmɑ̃/ nm quiver; start.

**tresse** /tʀɛs/ nf braid, plait.

**trêve** /tʀɛv/ nf truce; (fig) respite; ~ **de plaisanteries** that's enough joking.

**tri** /tʀi/ nm (classement) sorting; (sélection) selection; **faire le** ~ **de** (classer) sort; (choisir) select; **centre de** ~ sorting office.

**triangle** /tʀijɑ̃gl/ nm triangle.

**tribal, -e** (mpl -aux) /tʀibal, -o/ adj tribal.

**tribord** /tʀibɔʀ/ nm starboard.

**tribu** /tʀiby/ nf tribe.

**tribunal** (mpl -aux) /tʀibynal, -o/ nm court.

**tribune** /tʀibyn/ nf (de stade) grandstand; (d'orateur) rostrum; (débat) forum; (d'église) gallery.

**tribut** /tʀiby/ nm tribute.

**tributaire** /tʀibytɛʀ/ adj ~ **de** dependent on.

**tricher** /tʀiʃe/ **1** vi cheat. **tricheur, -euse** nm, f cheat.

**tricolore** /tʀikɔlɔʀ/ adj three-coloured; (écharpe) red, white and blue; (équipe) French.

**tricot** /tʀiko/ nm (activité) knitting; (pull) sweater; **en** ~ knitted; ~ **de corps** vest; (US) undershirt. **tricoter** 🔢 *vt/i* knit.

**trier** /tʀije/ 🔢 *vt* (classer) sort; (choisir) select.

**trimestre** /tʀimɛstʀ/ *nm* quarter; (Scol) term. **trimestriel**, **~le** *adj* quarterly; (*bulletin*) end-of-term.

**tringle** /tʀɛ̃gl/ *nf* rail.

**trinquer** /tʀɛ̃ke/ 🔢 *vi* clink glasses.

**triomphant**, **~e** /tʀijɔ̃fɑ̃, -t/ *adj* triumphant. **triomphe** *nm* triumph. **triompher** 🔢 *vi* triumph (de over); (*jubiler*) be triumphant.

**tripes** /tʀip/ *nfpl* (mets) tripe (+ *sg*); (entrailles 🔢) guts.

**triple** /tʀipl/ *adj* triple, treble. ● *nm* le ~ three times as much (de as). **triplés**, **-es** *nm*, *fpl* triplets.

**tripot** /tʀipo/ *nm* gambling den.

**tripoter** /tʀipɔte/ 🔢 *vt* 🔢 (*personne*) grope; (*objet*) fiddle with.

**trisomique** /tʀizɔmik/ *adj* être ~ have Down's syndrome.

**triste** /tʀist/ *adj* sad; (*rue, temps, couleur*) dreary; (*lamentable*) dreadful. **tristesse** *nf* sadness; dreariness.

**trivial**, **~e** (*mpl* **-iaux**) /tʀivjal, -jo/ *adj* coarse.

**troc** /tʀɔk/ *nm* exchange; (Comm) barter.

**trognon** /tʀɔɲɔ̃/ *nm* (de fruit) core.

**trois** /tʀwɑ/ *adj & nm* three; hôtel ~ étoiles three-star hotel. **troisième** *adj & nmf* third.

**trombone** /tʀɔ̃bɔn/ *nm* (Mus) trombone; (*agrafe*) paperclip.

**trompe** /tʀɔ̃p/ *nf* (d'éléphant) trunk; (Mus) horn.

**tromper** /tʀɔ̃pe/ 🔢 *vt* deceive, mislead; (*déjouer*) elude. □ **se** ~ *vpr* be mistaken; **se** ~ **de** route/ d'heure take the wrong road/get the time wrong.

**trompette** /tʀɔ̃pɛt/ *nf* trumpet.

**trompeur**, **-euse** /tʀɔ̃pœʀ, -øz/ *adj* (*apparence*) deceptive.

**tronc** /tʀɔ̃/ *nm* trunk; (*boîte*) collection box.

**tronçon** /tʀɔ̃sɔ̃/ *nm* section. **tronçonneuse** /tʀɔ̃sɔnøz/ *nf* chain saw.

**trône** /tʀon/ *nm* throne. **trôner** 🔢 *vi* (*vase*) have pride of place (sur un).

**trop** /tʀo/ *adv* (*grand, loin*) too; (*boire, marcher*) too much; ~ **de** (*quantité*) too much; (*nombre*) too many; ce serait ~ beau one should be so lucky; **de** ~ **en** ~ too much; too many; il a bu un verre de ~ he's had one too many; se sentir **de** ~ feel one is in the way.

**trophée** /tʀɔfe/ *nm* trophy.

**tropical**, **~e** (*mpl* **-aux**) /tʀɔpikal, -o/ *adj* tropical. **tropique** *nm* tropic.

**trop-plein** (*pl* **~s**) /tʀoplɛ̃/ *nm* excess; (*dispositif*) overflow.

**troquer** /tʀɔke/ 🔢 *vt* exchange; (Comm) barter (contre for).

**trot** /tʀo/ *nm* trot; aller au ~ trot. **trotter** 🔢 *vi* trot.

**trotteuse** /tʀɔtøz/ *nf* (de montre) second hand.

**trottoir** /tʀɔtwaʀ/ *nm* pavement; (US) sidewalk; ~ roulant moving walkway.

**trou** /tʀu/ *nm* hole; (*moment*) gap; (*lieu*: péj) dump; ~ **de** mémoire memory lapse; ~ **de** serrure keyhole; faire son ~ carve one's niche.

**trouble** /tʀubl/ *adj* (*eau, image*) unclear; (*louche*) shady. ● *nm* (*émoi*) emotion; ~s (Pol) disturbances; (Méd) disorder (+ *sg*). **troubler** 🔢 *vt* disturb; (*eau*) make cloudy; (*inquiéter*) trouble.

□ **se** ~ vpr (*personne*) become flustered.

**trouer** /tʁue/ 🔳 vt make a hole ou holes in; **mes chaussures sont trouées** my shoes have got holes in them.

**troupe** /tʁup/ nf troop; (d'acteurs) company.

**troupeau** (*pl* ~x) /tʁupo/ nm herd; (de moutons) flock.

**trousse** /tʁus/ nf case, bag; **aux** ~**s de** hot on sb's heels; ~ **de toilette** toilet bag.

**trousseau** (*pl* ~x) /tʁuso/ nm (de clefs) bunch; (de mariée) trousseau.

**trouver** /tʁuve/ 🔳 vt find; (penser) think; **il est venu me** ~ he came to see me. □ ~ vpr (être) be; (se sentir) feel; **il se trouve que** it happens that; **si ça se trouve** maybe; **se** ~ **mal** faint.

**truand** /tʁyɑ̃/ nm gangster.

**truc** /tʁyk/ nm (moyen) way; (artifice) trick; (chose 🔢) thing. **trucage** nm (cinéma) special effect.

**truffe** /tʁyf/ nf (champignon, chocolat) truffle; (de chien) nose.

**truffer** /tʁyfe/ 🔳 vt (fig) fill, pack (de with).

**truie** /tʁui/ nf (animal) sow.

**truite** /tʁuit/ nf trout.

**truquer** /tʁyke/ 🔳 vt fix, rig; (photo) fake; (résultats) fiddle.

**tsar** /tsaʁ/ nm tsar, czar.

**tu** /ty/ pron (parent, ami, enfant) you. ➡ TAIRE 🔢.

**tuba** /tyba/ nm (Mus) tuba; (Sport) snorkel.

**tube** /tyb/ nm tube.

**tuberculose** /tybɛʁkyloz/ nf tuberculosis.

**tuer** /tɥe/ 🔳 vt kill; (d'une balle) shoot, kill; (épuiser) exhaust; ~ par

balles shoot dead. □ **se** ~ vpr kill oneself; (accident) be killed.

**tuerie** /tyʁi/ nf killing.

**tue-tête: à** ~ /atytɛt/ loc at the top of one's voice.

**tuile** /tɥil/ nf tile; (malchance 🔢) (stroke of) bad luck.

**tulipe** /tylip/ nf tulip.

**tumeur** /tymœʁ/ nf tumour.

**tumulte** /tymylt/ nm commotion; (désordre) turmoil.

**tunique** /tynik/ nf tunic.

**Tunisie** /tynizi/ nf Tunisia.

**tunnel** /tynɛl/ nm tunnel.

**turbo** /tyʁbo/ adj turbo. ●nf (voiture) turbo.

**turbulent,** ~**e** /tyʁbylɑ̃, -t/ adj boisterous, turbulent.

**turc, -que** /tyʁk/ adj Turkish. ●nm (Ling) Turkish. **T**~**, -que** Turk.

**turfiste** /tyʁfist/ nmf racegoer.

**Turquie** /tyʁki/ nf Turkey.

**tutelle** /tytɛl/ nf (Jur) guardianship; (fig) protection.

**tuteur, -trice** /tytœʁ, -tʁis/ nm, f (Jur) guardian. ●nm (bâton) stake.

**tutoiement** /tytwamɑ̃/ nm use of the 'tu' form. **tutoyer** 🔢 vt address using the 'tu' form.

**tuyau** (*pl* ~x) /tɥijo/ nm pipe; (conseil 🔢) tip; ~ **d'arrosage** hosepipe.

**TVA** *abrév f* (**taxe à la valeur ajoutée**) VAT.

**tympan** /tɛ̃pɑ̃/ nm ear-drum.

**type** /tip/ nm (genre, traits) type; (individu 🔢) bloke, guy; **le** ~ **même de** a classic example of. ● adj inv typical.

**typique** /tipik/ adj typical.

**tyran** /tiʁɑ̃/ nm tyrant. **tyrannie** nf tyranny. **tyranniser** 🔳 vt oppress, tyrannize.

# Uu

**UE** abrév f (Union européenne) European Union.

**Ukraine** /ykʀɛn/ nf Ukraine.

**ulcère** /ylsɛʀ/ nm (Méd) ulcer.

**ULM** abrév m (ultraléger motorisé) microlight.

**ultérieur**, ~e /ylteʀjœʀ/ adj later. **ultérieurement** adv later.

**ultime** /yltim/ adj final.

---

**un, une** /œ̃, yn/

● déterminant

····▸ a; (devant voyelle) an; ~ animal an animal; ~ jour one day; pas ~arbre not a single tree; il fait ~ froid! it's so cold!

● pronom

····▸ one; l'~ d'entre nous one of us; les ~s croient que... some believe...

····▸ la une the front page.

····▸ j'en veux une I want one.

● adjectif

····▸ one, a, an; j'ai ~ garçon et deux filles I have a of one boy and two girls; il est une heure it is one o'clock.

● nom masculin & féminin

····▸ par ~ one by one.

---

**unanime** /ynanim/ adj unanimous.

**unanimité** /ynanimite/ nf unanimity; à l'~ unanimously.

**uni**, ~e /yni/ adj united; (couple) close; (surface) smooth; (tissu) plain.

**unième** /ynjɛm/ adj ~first; vingt et ~ twenty-first; cent ~ one

hundred and first.

**unifier** /ynifje/ 45 vt unify.

**uniforme** /ynifɔʀm/ nm uniform.
● adj uniform. **uniformiser** 1 vt standardize. **uniformité** nf uniformity.

**unilatéral**, ~e (mpl -aux) /ynilateʀal, -o/ adj unilateral.

**union** /ynjɔ̃/ nf union; l'U~ euro- péenne the European Union.

**unique** /ynik/ adj (seul) only; (prix, voie) one; (incomparable) unique; enfant ~ only child; sens ~ one-way street. **uniquement** adv only, solely.

**unir** /yniʀ/ 2 vt unite. □ s'~ vpr unite, join.

**unité** /ynite/ nf unit; (harmonie) unity; ~ centrale (Ordinat) pro- cessor.

**univers** /ynivɛʀ/ nm universe.

**universel**, ~le /ynivɛʀsɛl/ adj universal.

**universitaire** /ynivɛʀsiteʀ/ adj (résidence) university; (niveau) aca- demic. ● nmf academic.

**université** /ynivɛʀsite/ nf uni- versity.

**uranium** /yʀanjɔm/ nm uranium.

**urbain**, ~e /yʀbɛ̃, -ɛn/ adj urban. **urbanisme** nm town planning.

**urgence** /yʀʒɑ̃s/ nf (cas) emer- gency; (de situation, tâche) ur- gency; d'~ (mesure) emergency; (transporter) urgently; les ~s casu- alty (+ sg). **urgent**, ~e adj urgent.

**urine** /yʀin/ nf urine. **urinoir** nm urinal.

**urne** /yʀn/ nf (électorale) ballot box; (vase) urn; aller aux ~s go to the polls.

**urticaire** /yʀtikɛʀ/ nf hives (+ pl), urticar.

**us** /ys/ nmpl les ~ et coutumes habits and customs.

**usage** /yzaʒ/ *nm* use; (coutume) custom; (de langage) usage; **à l'~ de** for; **d'~** (habituel) customary; **faire ~ de** make use of.

**usagé, ~e** /yzaʒe/ *adj* worn.

**usager** /yzaʒe/ *nm* user.

**usé, ~e** /yze/ *adj* worn (out); (banal) trite.

**user** /yze/ **1** *vt* wear (out). ● *vi* ~ **de** use. □ **s'~** *vpr* (tissu) wear (out).

**usine** /yzin/ *nf* factory, plant; ~ **sidérurgique** ironworks (+ *pl*).

**usité, ~e** /yzite/ *adj* common.

**ustensile** /ystɑ̃sil/ *nm* utensil.

**usuel, ~le** /yzɥɛl/ *adj* ordinary, everyday.

**usure** /yzyʀ/ *nf* (détérioration) wear (and tear).

**utérus** /yteʀys/ *nm* womb, uterus.

**utile** /ytil/ *adj* useful.

**utilisable** /ytilizabl/ *adj* usable. **utilisation** *nf* use. **utiliser** **1** *vt* use.

**utopie** /ytɔpi/ *nf* Utopia; (idée) Utopian idea. **utopique** *adj* Utopian.

**UV**[1] *abrév f* (**unité de valeur**) course unit.

**UV**[2] *abrév mpl* (**ultraviolets**) ultraviolet rays; **faire des ~** use a sunbed.

# Vv

**va** /va/ →ALLER **8**.

**vacance** /vakɑ̃s/ *nf* (poste) vacancy.

**vacances** /vakɑ̃s/ *nfpl* holiday(s); (US) vacation; **en ~** on holiday; **~ d'été, grandes ~** summer holidays. **vacancier, -ière** *nm, f* holidaymaker; (US) vacationer.

**vacant, ~e** /vakɑ̃, -t/ *adj* vacant.

**vacarme** /vakaʀm/ *nm* din.

**vaccin** /vaksɛ̃/ *nm* vaccine. **vacciner** **1** *vt* vaccinate.

**vache** /vaʃ/ *nf* cow. ● *adj* (méchant [1]) nasty.

**vaciller** /vasije/ **1** *vi* sway, wobble; (lumière) flicker; (hésiter) falter; (santé, mémoire) fail.

**vadrouiller** /vadʀuje/ **1** *vi* [1] wander about.

**va-et-vient** /vaevjɛ̃/ *nm inv* toing and froing; (de personnes) comings and goings; **faire le ~** go to and fro; (interrupteur) two-way switch.

**vagabond, ~e** /vagabɔ̃, -d/ *nm, f* vagrant.

**vagin** /vaʒɛ̃/ *nm* vagina.

**vague** /vag/ *adj* vague. ● *nm* regarder dans le ~ stare into space; il est resté dans le ~ he was vague about it. ● *nf* wave; ~ **de fond** ground swell; ~ **de froid** cold spell; ~ **de chaleur** heatwave.

**vaillant, ~e** /vajɑ̃, -t/ *adj* brave; (vigoureux) strong.

**vaille** /vaj/ →VALOIR **60**.

**vain, ~e** /vɛ̃, vɛn/ *adj* vain, futile; **en ~** in vain.

**vaincre** /vɛ̃kʀ/ **59** *vt* defeat; (surmonter) overcome. **vaincu, ~e,** *nm, f* (Sport) loser. **vainqueur** *nm* victor; (Sport) winner.

**vais** /vɛ/ →ALLER **8**.

**vaisseau** (*pl* ~x) /vɛso/ *nm* ship; (veine) vessel; ~ **spatial** spaceship.

**vaisselle** /vɛsɛl/ *nf* crockery; (à laver) dishes; **faire la ~** do the washing-up, wash the dishes; **liquide ~** washing-up liquid.

**valable** /valabl/ *adj* valid; (de qualité) worthwhile.

**valet** /valɛ/ *nm* (aux cartes) jack; (~ **de chambre**) manservant.

u
v

**valeur** /valœʀ/ nf value; (mérite) worth, value; ~s (Comm) stocks and shares; avoir de la ~ be valuable; prendre/perdre de la ~ go up/down in value; objets de ~ valuables; sans ~ worthless.

**valide** /valid/ adj (personne) fit; (billet) valid. **valider** ① vt validate.

**valise** /valiz/ nf (suit) case; faire ses ~s pack (one's bags).

**vallée** /vale/ nf valley.

**valoir** /valwaʀ/ ⑥ vi (mériter) be worth; (égaler) be as good as; (être valable) (règle) apply; faire ~ (mérite, qualité) emphasize; (terrain) cultivate; (droit) assert; se faire ~ put oneself forward; ~ cher/100 euros be worth a lot/100 euros; que vaut ce vin? what's this wine like?; ça ne me dit rien qui vaille I don't like the sound of that; ~ la peine or le coup ① be worth it; il vaut/vaudrait mieux faire it is/would be better to do. ● vt ~ qch à qn (éloges, critiques) earn sb sth; (admiration) win sb sth. □ se ~ vpr (être équivalents) be as good as each other; ça se vaut it's all the same.

**valoriser** /valɔʀize/ ① vt add value to; (produit) promote; (profession) make attractive; (région, ressources) develop.

**valse** /vals/ nf waltz.

**vandale** /vɑ̃dal/ nmf vandal.

**vanille** /vanij/ nf vanilla.

**vanité** /vanite/ nf vanity. **vaniteux, -euse** adj vain, conceited.

**vanne** /van/ nf (d'écluse) sluicegate; (propos ①) dig ①

**vantard, ~e** /vɑ̃taʀ, -d/ adj boastful. ● nm, f boaster.

**vanter** /vɑ̃te/ ① vt praise. □ se ~ vpr boast (de about); se ~ de faire pride oneself on doing.

**vapeur** /vapœʀ/ nf (eau) steam; (brume, émanation) vapour; ~s fumes; à ~ (bateau, locomotive) steam; faire cuire à la ~ steam.

**vaporisateur** /vapɔʀizatœʀ/ nm spray, atomizer. **vaporiser** ① vt spray.

**varappe** /vaʀap/ nf rock-climbing.

**variable** /vaʀjabl/ adj variable; (temps) changeable.

**varicelle** /vaʀisɛl/ nf chickenpox.

**varié, ~e** /vaʀje/ adj (non monotone, étendu) varied; (divers) various; sandwichs ~s a selection of sandwiches.

**varier** /vaʀje/ ⑮ vt/i vary.

**variété** /vaʀjete/ nf variety; spectacle de ~ variety show.

**vase** /vaz/ nm vase. ● nf silt, mud.

**vaseux, -euse** /vazø, -z/ adj (confus ①) woolly, muddy.

**vaste** /vast/ adj vast, huge.

**vaurien** /voʀjɛ̃, -ɛn/ nm, f good-for-nothing.

**vautour** /votuʀ/ nm vulture.

**vautrer (se)** /(sə)votʀe/ ① vpr sprawl; se ~ dans (vice, boue) wallow in.

**veau** (pl ~x) /vo/ nm calf; (viande) veal; (cuir) calfskin.

**vécu, ~e** /veky/ adj (réel) true, real. ⇒VIVRE ⑫.

**vedette** /vədɛt/ nf (artiste) star; en ~ (objet) in a prominent position; (personne) in the limelight; joueur ~ star player; (bateau) launch.

**végétal** (mpl -aux) /veʒetal, -o/ adj plant. ● nm (pl -aux) plant.

**végétalien, ~ne** /veʒetaljɛ̃, -ɛn/ adj & nm, f vegan.

**végétarien, ~ne** /veʒetaʀjɛ̃, -ɛn/ adj & nm, f vegetarian.

**végétation** /veʒetasjɔ̃/ nf vegetation; ~s (Méd) adenoids.

**véhicule** /veikyl/ nm vehicle.

**veille** /vɛj/ nf (état) wakefulness; (jour précédent) la ~ (de) the day before; la ~ de Noël Christmas Eve; à la ~ de on the eve of; la ~ au soir the previous evening.

**veillée** /veje/ nf evening (gathering).

**veiller** /veje/ **1** vi stay up; (monter la garde) be on watch. ● vt (malade) watch over; ~ à attend to; ~ sur watch over.

**veilleur** /vejœr/ nm ~ de nuit night-watchman.

**veilleuse** /vejøz/ nf night light; (de véhicule) sidelight; (de réchaud) pilot light; mettre qch en ~ put sth on the back burner.

**veine** /vɛn/ nf (Anat) vein; (nervure, filon) vein; (chance **1**) luck; avoir de la ~ be lucky.

**véliplanchiste** /veliplɑ̃ʃist/ nmf windsurfer.

**vélo** /velo/ nm bike; (activité) cycling; faire du ~ go cycling; ~ tout terrain mountain bike.

**vélomoteur** /velomɔtœr/ nm moped.

**velours** /v(ə)lur/ nm velvet; ~ côtelé corduroy.

**velouté**, ~e /vəlute/ adj smooth. ● nm (Culin) ~ d'asperges cream of asparagus soup.

**vendanges** /vɑ̃dɑ̃ʒ/ nfpl grape harvest.

**vendeur**, -euse /vɑ̃dœr, -øz/ nm, f shop assistant; (marchand) salesman, saleswoman; (Jur) vendor, seller.

**vendre** /vɑ̃dr/ **3** vt sell; à ~ for sale. □ se ~ vpr (être vendu) be sold; (trouver acquéreur) sell; se ~ bien sell well.

**vendredi** /vɑ̃drədi/ nm Friday; V~ saint Good Friday.

**vénéneux**, -euse /venenø, -z/ adj poisonous.

**vénérer** /venere/ **14** vt revere.

**vénérien**, ~ne /venerjɛ̃, -ɛn/ adj maladie ~ne venereal disease.

**vengeance** /vɑ̃ʒɑ̃s/ nf revenge, vengeance.

**venger** /vɑ̃ʒe/ **40** vt avenge. □ se ~ vpr take ou get one's revenge (de qn for sth; de qn on sb).

**vengeur**, -eresse /vɑ̃ʒœr, -əres/ adj vengeful. ● nm, f avenger.

**venimeux**, -euse /vənimø, -z/ adj poisonous, venomous.

**venin** /vənɛ̃/ nm venom.

**venir** /vənir/ **58** vi (aux être) come (de from); faire ~ qn send for sb, call sb; en ~ à come to; en ~ aux mains come to blows; où veut-elle en ~? what is she driving at?; il m'est venu à l'esprit or à l'idée que it occurred to me that; s'il venait à pleuvoir if it should rain; dans les jours à ~ in the next few days. ● v aux ~ de faire have just done; il vient/venait d'arriver he has/had just arrived; ~ faire come to do; viens voir come and see.

**vent** /vɑ̃/ nm wind; il fait du ~ it is windy; être dans le ~ **1** be trendy.

**vente** /vɑ̃t/ nf sale; ~ (aux enchères) auction; en ~ on ou for sale; mettre qch en ~ put sth up for sale; ~ de charité (charity) bazaar; ~ au détail/en gros retailing/wholesaling; équipe de ~ sales team.

**ventilateur** /vɑ̃tilatœr/ nm fan, ventilator. **ventiler** **1** vt ventilate.

**ventouse** /vɑ̃tuz/ nf suction pad; (pour déboucher) plunger.

**ventre** /vɑ̃tr/ nm stomach; (d'animal) belly; (utérus) womb; avoir du ~ have a paunch.

V

**venu, ~e** /vəny/ adj bien ~ (à propos) apt, timely; **mal ~** badly timed; **il serait mal ~ de faire** it wouldn't be a good idea to do. ● →VENIR 59

**venue** /vəny/ nf coming.

**ver** /vɛʀ/ nm worm; (dans la nourriture) maggot; (du bois) woodworm; **~ luisant** glow-worm; **~ à soie** silkworm; **~ solitaire** tapeworm; **~ de terre** earthworm.

**verbal, ~e** (mpl **-aux**) /vɛʀbal, -o/ adj verbal.

**verbe** /vɛʀb/ nm verb.

**verdir** /vɛʀdiʀ/ 2 vi turn green.

**véreux, -euse** /veʀø, -z/ adj wormy; (malhonnête) shady.

**verger** /vɛʀʒe/ nm orchard.

**verglas** /vɛʀɡla/ nm black ice.

**véridique** /veʀidik/ adj true.

**vérification** /veʀifikasjɔ̃/ nf check(ing), verification.

**vérifier** /veʀifje/ 45 vt check, verify; (confirmer) confirm.

**véritable** /veʀitabl/ adj true, real; (authentique) real.

**vérité** /veʀite/ nf truth; (de tableau, roman) realism; **en ~** in fact, actually.

**vermine** /vɛʀmin/ nf vermin.

**verni, ~e** /vɛʀni/ adj (chaussures) patent (leather); (chanceux ①) lucky.

**vernir** /vɛʀniʀ/ 2 vt varnish. □ **se ~** *vpr* **se ~ les ongles** apply nail polish.

**vernis** /vɛʀni/ nm varnish; (de poterie) glaze; **~ à ongles** nail polish.

**verra, verrait** /vɛʀa, vɛʀɛ/ →VOIR 64.

**verre** /vɛʀ/ nm glass; (de lunettes) lens; **~ à vin** wine glass; **prendre ou boire un ~** have a drink; **~ de contact** contact lens; **~ dépoli** frosted glass.

**verrière** /vɛʀjɛʀ/ nf (toit) glass roof; (paroi) glass wall.

**verrou** /vɛʀu/ nm bolt; **sous les ~s** behind bars.

**verrouillage** /vɛʀujaʒ/ nm **~ central** ou **centralisé** (des portes) central locking.

**verrue** /vɛʀy/ nf wart; **~ plantaire** verruca.

**vers**[1] /vɛʀ/ prép towards; (aux environs de) (temps) about; (lieu) near, around; (période) towards; **~ le soir** towards evening.

**vers**[2] /vɛʀ/ nm (poésie) line of verse.

**versatile** /vɛʀsatil/ adj unpredictable, volatile.

**verse: à ~** /avɛʀs/ loc in torrents.

**Verseau** /vɛʀso/ nm le **~** Aquarius.

**versement** /vɛʀsəmɑ̃/ nm payment; (échelonné) instalment.

**verser** /vɛʀse/ 1 vt/i pour; (larmes, sang) shed; (payer) pay. ● vi pour; (voiture) overturn; **~ dans** (fig) lapse into.

**version** /vɛʀsjɔ̃/ nf version; (traduction) translation.

**verso** /vɛʀso/ nm back (of the page); **voir au ~** see overleaf.

**vert, ~e** /vɛʀ, -t/ adj green; (vieillard) sprightly. ● nm green; **les ~s** the Greens.

**vertèbre** /vɛʀtɛbʀ/ nf vertebra; se déplacer une ∼ slip a disc.

**vertical,** ∼**e** (mpl -aux) /vɛʀtikal, -o/ adj vertical.

**vertige** /vɛʀtiʒ/ nm dizziness; ∼s dizzy spells; avoir le ∼ feel dizzy.

**vertigineux, -euse** adj dizzy; (très grand) staggering.

**vertu** /vɛʀty/ nf virtue; en ∼ de in accordance with. **vertueux, -euse** adj virtuous.

**verveine** /vɛʀvɛn/ nf verbena.

**vessie** /vesi/ nf bladder.

**veste** /vɛst/ nf jacket.

**vestiaire** /vɛstjɛʀ/ nm cloakroom; (Sport) changing-room; (US) locker-room.

**vestibule** /vɛstibyl/ nm hall; (Théât, d'hôtel) foyer.

**vestige** /vɛstiʒ/ nm (objet) relic; (trace) vestige.

**veston** /vɛstɔ̃/ nm jacket.

**vêtement** /vɛtmɑ̃/ nm article of clothing; ∼s clothes, clothing.

**vétéran** /veteʀɑ̃/ nm veteran.

**vétérinaire** /veteʀinɛʀ/ nmf vet, veterinary surgeon, (US) veterinarian.

**vêtir** /vetiʀ/ 61 vt dress. □ se ∼ vpr dress.

**veto** /veto/ nm inv veto.

**vêtu,** ∼**e** /vety/ adj dressed (de in).

**veuf, veuve** /vœf, -vœf/ adj widowed. ●nm, f widower, widow.

**veuille** /vœj/ →VOULOIR 64.

**veut, veux** /vø/ →VOULOIR 64.

**vexation** /vɛksasjɔ̃/ nf humiliation.

**vexer** /vɛkse/ 1 vt upset, hurt. □ se ∼ vpr be upset, be hurt.

**viable** /vjabl/ adj viable; (projet) feasible.

**viande** /vjɑ̃d/ nf meat.

**vibrer** /vibʀe/ 1 vi vibrate; faire ∼ (âme, foules) stir.

**vicaire** /vikɛʀ/ nm curate.

**vice** /vis/ nm (moral) vice; (physique) defect.

**vicier** /visje/ 45 vt contaminate; (air) pollute.

**vicieux, -ieuse** /visjø, -z/ adj depraved. ●nm, f pervert.

**victime** /viktim/ nf victim; (d'un accident) casualty.

**victoire** /viktwaʀ/ nf victory; (Sport) win. **victorieux, -ieuse** adj victorious; (équipe) winning.

**vidange** /vidɑ̃ʒ/ nf emptying; (Auto) oil change; (tuyau) waste pipe ou outlet.

**vide** /vid/ adj empty. ●nm (absence, manque) vacuum, void; (espace) space; (trou) gap; (sans air) vacuum; à ∼ empty; emballé sous ∼ vacuum packed; suspendu dans le ∼ dangling in space.

**vide-greniers** /vidgʀənje/ nm inv bric-a-brac sale.

**vidéo** /video/ adj inv video; jeu ∼ video game. ●nf video.

**vidéocassette** nf video (tape).

**vidéoclip** nm music video.

**vidéoconférence** nf videoconferencing; (séance) videoconference. **vidéodisque** nm videodisc. **vidéophone** nm videophone.

**vide-ordures** /vidɔʀdyʀ/ nm inv rubbish chute.

**vidéothèque** /videotɛk/ nf video library.

**vider** /vide/ 1 vt empty; (poisson) gut; (expulser 1) throw out. □ se ∼ vpr empty.

**vie** /vi/ nf life; (durée) lifetime; à ∼, pour la ∼ for life; donner la ∼ à give birth to; en ∼ alive; la ∼ est chère the cost of living is high.

**vieil** /vjɛj/ →VIEUX.

**vieillard** /vjɛjaʀ/ nm old man.

**vieille** /vjɛj/ →VIEUX.

**vieillesse** /vjɛjɛs/ nf old age.

**vieillir** /vjejiʀ/ 2 vi grow old, age; (mot, idée) become old-fashioned. ● vt age. **vieillissement** nm ageing.

**viens, vient** /vjɛ̃/ →VENIR 59.

**vierge** /vjɛʀʒ/ nf virgin; la V~ Virgo. ● adj virgin; (feuille, cassette) blank; (cahier, pellicule) unused, new.

**vieux** (vieil before vowel or mute h), **vieille** (mpl vieux) /vjø, vjɛj/ adj old. ● nm, f old man, old woman; petit ~ little old man; les ~ old people; **vieille fille** (péj) spinster; ~ garçon old bachelor. **vieux jeu** adj inv old-fashioned.

**vif, vive** /vif, viv/ adj (animé) lively; (émotion, vent) keen; (froid) biting; (lumière) bright; (douleur, contraste, parole) sharp; (souvenir, style, teint) vivid; (succès, impatience) great; brûler/enterrer ~ burn/bury alive; de vive voix personally. ● nm à ~ (plaie) open; avoir les nerfs à ~ be on edge; blessé au ~ cut to the quick.

**vigie** /viʒi/ nf lookout.

**vigilant, ~e** /viʒilɑ̃, -t/ adj vigilant.

**Vigipirate** /viʒipiʀat/ nm government public security measures.

**vigne** /viɲ/ nf (plante) vine; (vignoble) vineyard. **vigneron, ~ne** nm, f wine-grower.

**vignette** /viɲɛt/ nf (étiquette) label; (Auto) road tax disc.

**vignoble** /viɲɔbl/ nm vineyard.

**vigoureux, -euse** /viguʀø, -z/ adj vigorous, sturdy.

**vigueur** /viguʀ/ nf vigour; être/ entrer en ~ (loi) be/come into force; en ~ current.

**VIH** abrév m (virus immuno-

déficitaire humain) HIV.

**vilain, ~e** /vilɛ̃, -ɛn/ adj (mauvais) nasty; (laid) ugly. ● nm, f naughty boy, naughty girl.

**villa** /villa/ nf detached house.

**village** /vilaʒ/ nm village.

**villageois, ~e** /vilaʒwa, -z/ adj village. ● nm, f villager.

**ville** /vil/ nf town; (importante) city; ~ d'eaux spa.

**vin** /vɛ̃/ nm wine; ~ d'honneur reception.

**vinaigre** /vinɛgʀ/ nm vinegar. **vinaigrette** nf oil and vinegar dressing, vinaigrette.

**vingt** /vɛ̃/ (/vɛ̃t/ before vowel and in numbers 22-29) adj & nm twenty. **vingtaine** /vɛ̃tɛn/ nf une ~ (de) about twenty.

**vingtième** /vɛ̃tjɛm/ adj & nmf twentieth.

**vinicole** /vinikɔl/ adj wine-(producing).

**viol** /vjɔl/ nm (de femme) rape; (de lieu, loi) violation.

**violemment** /vjɔlamɑ̃/ adv violently.

**violence** /vjɔlɑ̃s/ nf violence; (acte) act of violence. **violent, ~e** adj violent.

**violer** /vjɔle/ 1 vt rape; (lieu, loi) violate.

**violet, ~te** /vjɔlɛ, -t/ adj purple. ● nm purple. **violette** nf violet.

**violon** /vjɔlɔ̃/ nm violin; ~ d'Ingres hobby.

**violoncelle** /vjɔlɔ̃sɛl/ nm cello.

**vipère** /vipɛʀ/ nf viper, adder.

**virage** /viʀaʒ/ nm bend; (en ski) turn; (changement d'attitude: fig) change of course.

**virée** /viʀe/ nf 1 trip, tour; (en voiture) drive; (à vélo) ride.

**virement** /viʀmɑ̃/ nm (Comm)

(credit) transfer; ~ **automatique** standing order.

**virer** /vire/ **1** *vi* turn; ~ **de bord** tack; (fig) do a U-turn; ~ **au rouge** turn red. ●*vt* (*argent*) transfer; (*expulser* ⊤) throw out; (*élève*) expel; (*licencier* ⊤) fire.

**virgule** /virgyl/ *nf* comma; (*dans un nombre*) (decimal) point.

**viril**, ~**e** /viril/ *adj* virile.

**virtuel**, ~**le** /virtɥɛl/ *adj* (*potentiel*) potential; (*mémoire, réalité*) virtual.

**virulent**, ~**e** /virylɑ̃, -t/ *adj* virulent.

**virus** /virys/ *nm* virus.

**vis¹** /vi/ →VIVRE 62, →VOIR 63.

**vis²** /vis/ *nf* screw.

**visa** /viza/ *nm* visa.

**visage** /vizaʒ/ *nm* face.

**vis-à-vis** /vizavi/ *prép* ~ **de** (en face de) opposite; (à l'égard de) in relation to; (comparé à) compared to, beside. ●*nm inv* (*personne*) person opposite; **en** ~ opposite each other.

**visée** /vize/ *nf* aim; **avoir des** ~**s sur** have designs on.

**viser** /vize/ **1** *vt* (*cible, centre*) aim at; (*poste, résultats*) aim for; (*concerner*) be aimed at; (*document*) stamp; ~ **à** aim at; (*mesure, propos*) be aimed at; ~ **à faire** aim to do. ●*vi* aim.

**viseur** /vizœr/ *nm* (d'arme) sights (+ *pl*); (Photo) viewfinder.

**visière** /vizjɛr/ *nf* (de casquette) peak; (de casque) visor.

**vision** /vizjɔ̃/ *nf* vision.

**visite** /vizit/ *nf* visit; (pour inspecter) inspection; (personne) visitor; **heures de** ~ visiting hours; ~ **guidée** guided tour; ~ **médicale** medical; **rendre** ~ **à**, **faire une** ~ **à** pay a visit; **être en** ~ (chez qn) be

visiting (sb); **avoir de la** ~ have visitors.

**visiter** /vizite/ **1** *vt* visit; (*appartement*) view. **visiteur**, -**euse** *nm, f* visitor.

**visser** /vise/ *vt* screw (on).

**visuel**, ~**le** /vizɥɛl/ *adj* visual. ●*nm* (Ordinat) visual display unit, VDU.

**vit** /vi/ →VIVRE 62, →VOIR 63.

**vital**, ~**e** (*mpl* -**aux**) /vital, -o/ *adj* vital.

**vitamine** /vitamin/ *nf* vitamin.

**vite** /vit/ *adv* fast, quickly; (*tôt*) soon; ~ **!** quick!; **faire** ~ be quick; **au plus** ~, **le plus** ~ **possible** as quickly as possible.

**vitesse** /vites/ *nf* speed; (*régime:* Auto) gear; **à toute** ~ at top speed; **en** ~ in a hurry, quickly; **boîte à cinq** ~**s** five-speed gearbox.

**viticole** /vitikɔl/ *adj* (*industrie*) wine; (*région*) wine-producing. **viticulteur** *nm* wine-grower.

**vitrage** /vitraʒ/ *nm* (*vitres*) windows; **double** ~ double glazing.

**vitrail** (*pl* -**aux**) /vitraj, -o/ *nm* stained-glass window.

**vitre** /vitr/ *nf* (window) pane; (de véhicule) window.

**vitrine** /vitrin/ *nf* (shop) window; (meuble) display cabinet.

**vivace** /vivas/ *adj* (*plante*) perennial; (*durable*) enduring.

**vivacité** /vivasite/ *nf* liveliness; (agilité) quickness; (d'émotion, d'intelligence) keenness; (de souvenir, style, teint) vividness.

**vivant**, ~**e** /vivɑ̃, -t/ *adj* (*example, symbole*) living; (en vie) alive, living; (*actif, vif*) lively. ●*nm* **un bon** ~ **a** bon viveur; **de son** ~ in his lifetime; **les** ~**s** the living.

**vive¹** /viv/ →VIF.

**vive²** /viv/ interj ~ le roi! long live the king!

**vivement** /vivmɑ̃/ adv (fortement) strongly; (vite, sèchement) sharply; (avec éclat) vividly; (beaucoup) greatly; ~ la fin! I'll be glad when it's the end!

**vivier** /vivje/ nm fish pond; (artificiel) fish tank.

**vivifier** /vivifje/ 45 vt invigorate.

**vivre** /vivʀ/ 69 vi live; ~ de (nourriture) live on; ~ encore be still alive; faire ~ (famille) support. ● vt (vie) live; (période, aventure) live through.

**vivres** /vivʀ/ nmpl supplies.

**VO** abrév f (version originale) en ~ in the original language.

**vocabulaire** /vɔkabylɛʀ/ nm vocabulary.

**vocal**, ~e (mpl -aux) /vɔkal, -o/ adj vocal.

**vœu** (pl ~x) /vø/ nm (souhait) wish; (promesse) vow; meilleurs ~x best wishes.

**vogue** /vɔg/ nf fashion, vogue; en ~ in fashion ou vogue.

**voguer** /vɔge/ 1 vi sail.

**voici** /vwasi/ prép here is, this is; (au pluriel) here are, these are; ~ here I am; ~ un an (temps passé) a year ago; ~ un an que it is a year since.

**voie** /vwa/ nf (route) road; (partie de route) lane; (chemin) way; (moyen) means, way; (rails) track; (quai) platform; en ~ de in the process of; en ~ de développement (pays) developing; espèce en ~ de disparition endangered species; par la ~ des airs by air; par ~ orale orally; sur la bonne/ mauvaise ~ (fig) on the right/ wrong track; montrer la ~ lead the way; ~ de dégagement slip-

road; ~ ferrée railway; (US) railroad; V ~ lactée Milky Way; ~ navigable waterway; ~ publique public highway; ~ sans issue (sur panneau) no through road; (fig) dead end.

**voilà** /vwala/ prép there is, that is; (au pluriel) there are, those are; (voici) there is, here are; le ~ there he is; ~! right!; (en offrant qch) there you are!; ~ un an (temps passé) a year ago; ~ un an que it is a year since; tu en veux? en ~ do you want some? here you are; en ~ des histoires! what a fuss!; et ~ que and then.

**voilage** /vwalaʒ/ nm net curtain.

**voile** /vwal/ nf (de bateau) sail; (Sport) sailing. ● nm veil; (tissu léger) net.

**voilé**, ~e /vwale/ adj (allusion, femme) veiled; (flou) hazy.

**voiler** /vwale/ 1 vt (dissimuler) veil; (déformer) buckle. □ se ~ vpr (devenir flou) become hazy; (se déformer) (roue) buckle.

**voilier** /vwalje/ nm sailing ship.

**voir** /vwaʀ/ 64 vt see; faire ~ qch à qn show sth to sb; laisser ~ show; avoir quelque chose à ~ avec have something to do with; ça n'a rien à ~ that's got nothing to do with it; je ne peux pas le ~ 🔲 I can't stand him. ● vi y ~ be able to see; je n'y vois rien I cannot see; ~ trouble have blurred vision; voyons let's see now; voyons, soyez sages! come on now, behave yourselves! □ se ~ vpr (dans la glace) see oneself; (être visible) show; (se produire) be seen; (se trouver) find oneself; (se fréquenter, se rencontrer) see each other; (être vu) be seen.

**voire** /vwaʀ/ adv or even, not to say.

**voirie** /vwaʀi/ *nf* (service) highway maintenance.

**voisin, ~e** /vwazɛ̃, -in/ *adj* (de voisinage) neighbouring; (proche) nearby; (adjacent) next (de to); (semblable) similar (de to). ● *nm, f* neighbour; **le ~** the man next door, the neighbour. **voisinage** *nm* neighbourhood; (proximité) proximity.

**voiture** /vwatyʀ/ *nf* (motor) car; (wagon) coach, carriage; **en ~!** all aboard!; **~ bélier** ramraiding car; **~ à cheval** horse-drawn carriage; **~ de course** racing car; **~ école** driving school car; **~ d'enfant** pram; (US) baby carriage; **~ de tourisme** saloon car.

**voix** /vwa/ *nf* voice; (suffrage) vote; **à ~ basse** in a whisper.

**vol** /vɔl/ *nm* (d'avion, d'oiseau) flight; (groupe d'oiseaux) flock, flight; (délit) theft; (hold-up) robbery; **~ à l'étalage** shoplifting; **~ à la tire** pickpocketing; **à ~ d'oiseau** as the crow flies; **de haut ~** high-ranking; **~ libre** hang-gliding; **~ à voile** gliding.

**volaille** /vɔlaj/ *nf* **la ~** (poules) poultry; **une ~** a fowl.

**volant** /vɔlɑ̃/ *nm* (steering-)wheel; (de jupe) flounce; (de badminton) shuttlecock; **donner un coup de ~** turn the wheel sharply.

**volcan** /vɔlkɑ̃/ *nm* volcano.

**volée** /vɔle/ *nf* (oiseaux) flight, flock; (de coups, d'obus, au tennis) volley; **à toute ~** hard; **à la ~** in flight, in mid-air.

**voler** /vɔle/ **1** *vi* (voiseau) fly; (dérober) steal (à from). ● *vt* steal; **~ qn** rob sb; **il ne l'a pas volé** he deserved it.

**volet** /vɔlɛ/ *nm* (de fenêtre) shutter; (de document) (folded *ou* tear-off) section; **trié sur le ~**

hand-picked.

**voleur, -euse** /vɔlœʀ, -øz/ *nm, f* thief; **au ~!** stop thief! ● *adj* thieving.

**volley-ball** /vɔlɛbol/ *nm* volleyball.

**volontaire** /vɔlɔ̃tɛʀ/ *adj* (délibéré) voluntary; (opiniâtre) determined. ● *nmf* volunteer. **volontairement** *adv* voluntarily; (exprès) intentionally.

**volonté** /vɔlɔ̃te/ *nf* (faculté, intention) will; (souhait) wish; (énergie) willpower; **à ~** (comme on veut) as required; **du vin à ~** unlimited wine; **bonne ~** goodwill; **mauvaise ~** ill will.

**volontiers** /vɔlɔ̃tje/ *adv* (de bon gré) with pleasure, willingly, gladly; (admettre) readily.

**volt** /vɔlt/ *nm* volt.

**volte-face** /vɔltafas/ *nf inv* (fig) U-turn; **faire ~** do a U-turn.

**voltige** /vɔltiʒ/ *nf* acrobatics (+ *pl*).

**volume** /vɔlym/ *nm* volume.

**volumineux, -euse** /vɔlyminø, -z/ *adj* bulky; (livre, dossier) thick.

**volupté** /vɔlypte/ *nf* voluptuousness.

**vomi** /vɔmi/ *nm* vomit.

**vomir** /vɔmiʀ/ **2** *vt* vomit; (fig) belch out. ● *vi* be sick, vomit.

**vomissement** /vɔmismɑ̃/ *nm* vomiting; **~s du matin** morning sickness.

**vont** /vɔ̃/ ➙ALLER **8**.

**vorace** /vɔʀas/ *adj* voracious.

**vos** /vo/ ➙VOTRE.

**votant, -e** /vɔtɑ̃, -t/ *nm, f* voter.

**vote** /vɔt/ *nm* (action) voting; (suffrage) vote; **~ d'une loi** passing of a bill; **~ par correspondance/procuration** postal/proxy vote.

**voter** /vɔte/ **1** *vi* vote. ● *vt* vote

**v**

for; (adopter) pass; (crédits) vote.

**votre** /vɔtʀ/ (pl **vos**) /vo/ adj your.

**vôtre** /votʀ/ pron le ou la ~, les
~s yours.

**vouer** /vwe/ **1** vt (vie, temps) dedicate (à to); **voué à l'échec** doomed
to failure.

**vouloir** /vulwaʀ/ **64** vt (exiger)
want (faire to do); (souhaiter) want;
**que veux-tu boire?** what would
you like to drink?; **je voudrais bien
y aller** I'd really like to go; **je veux
bien venir** I'm happy to come;
**comme tu voudras** as you wish;
(accepter) **veuillez vous asseoir**
please sit down; **veuillez patienter**
(au téléphone) please hold the line;
(signifier) ~ **dire** mean; **qu'est-ce
que cela veut dire?** what does that
mean?; **en** ~ **à qn** bear a grudge
against sb. □ **s'en** ~ vpr regret; **je
m'en veux de lui avoir dit** I really
regret having told her.

**voulu**, ~e /vuly/ adj (délibéré) intentional; (requis) required.

**vous** /vu/ pron (sujet, complément)
you; (indirect) (to) you; (réfléchi)
yourself; (pluriel) yourselves; (l'un
l'autre) each other. **vous-même**
pron yourself. **vous-mêmes** pron
yourselves.

**voûte** /vut/ nf (plafond) vault; (por-
che) archway.

**vouvoiement** /vuvwamã/ nm
use of the 'vous' form. **vouvoyer**
**31** vt address using the 'vous' form.

**voyage** /vwajaʒ/ nm trip; (déplacement) journey; (par mer) voyage;
~(s) (action) travelling; ~ **d'affaires** business trip; ~ **d'études** study
trip; ~ **de noces** honeymoon; ~
**organisé** (package) tour.

**voyager** /vwajaʒe/ **40** vi travel.

**voyageur**, -euse /vwajaʒœʀ, -øz/
nm, f traveller; (passager) passenger;

~ **de commerce** travelling
salesman.

**voyant**, ~e /vwajã, -t/ adj gaudy.
● nm (signal) (warning) light.

**voyelle** /vwajɛl/ nf vowel.

**voyou** /vwaju/ nm hooligan.

**vrac:** **en** ~ /ãvʀak/ loc (pêle-mêle)
haphazardly; (sans emballage)
loose; (en gros) in bulk.

**vrai**, ~e /vʀɛ/ adj true; (authentique). ● nm truth; **à** ~ **dire** to
tell the truth; **pour de** ~ for real.
**vraiment** adv really.

**vraisemblable** /vʀɛsãblabl/ adj
(probable) likely; (excuse, histoire)
plausible. **vraisemblablement** adv
probably. **vraisemblance** nf likelihood, plausibility.

**vrombir** /vʀɔ̃biʀ/ **2** vi roar.

**VRP** abrév m (**voyageur représentant placier**) rep, representative.

**VTC** abrév m (**vélo tous chemins**)
hybrid bike.

**VTT** abrév m (**vélo tout terrain**)
mountain bike.

**vu**, ~e /vy/ adj **bien** ~ well
thought of; **ce serait plutôt mal** ~
it wouldn't go down well; **bien** ~**!**
good point! ● prép in view of;
~ **que** seeing that. ● ➞ VOIR **64**.

**vue** /vy/ nf (spectacle) sight; (vision) (eye) sight; (panorama, idée,
image, photo) view; **avoir en** ~
have in mind; **à** ~ (tirer) on sight;
(payable) at sight; **de** ~ by sight;
**perdre de** ~ lose sight of; **en** ~
(proche) in sight; (célèbre) in the
public eye; **en** ~ **de faire** with a
view to doing; **à** ~ **d'œil** visibly;
**avoir des** ~**s sur** have designs on.

**vulgaire** /vylgɛʀ/ adj (grossier)
vulgar; (ordinaire) common.

**vulnérable** /vylneʀabl/ adj vulnerable.

# Ww

# Xx

**wagon** /vagɔ̃/ nm (de voyageurs) carriage; (de marchandises) wagon. **wagon-lit** (pl **wagons-lits**) nm sleeper. **wagon-restaurant** (pl **wagons-restaurants**) nm restaurant car.

**walkman®** /wokman/ nm personal stereo, walkman®.

> **Wallon** A regional Romance language spoken in southern Belgium (*Wallonie*) by approximately 600,000 *Wallons*. It belongs to the same linguistic family as the French language, and is sometimes considered a French dialect. *Wallon* should not be confused with Belgian French, which differs from the French of France in pronunciation and vocabulary only.

**waters** /watɛʀ/ nmpl toilets.
**watt** /wat/ nm watt.
**wc** /(dublə)vese/ nmpl toilet (+ sg).
**Web** /wɛb/ nm Web; un site ~ a website; une page ~ web page.
**webcam** /wɛbkam/ nf webcam.
**webmestre** /wɛbmɛstʀ/ nm webmaster.
**week-end** /wikɛnd/ nm weekend.
**whisky** (pl **-ies**) /wiski/ nm whisky.

**xénophobe** /gzenɔfɔb/ adj xenophobic. ● nmf xénophobe.
**xérès** /gzeʀɛs/ nm sherry.
**xylophone** /ksilɔfɔn/ nm xylophone.

# Yy

> **y** /i/
> ● adverbe
> ····▸ there; (dessus) on it; (pluriel) on them; (dedans) in it; (pluriel) in them; j'~ vais I'm on my way; n'~ va pas don't go; du lait? Il n'~ en a pas milk? there's none; tu n'~ arriveras jamais you'll never manage it.
> ● pronom
> ····▸ s'~ habituer get used to it.
> ····▸ s'~ attendre expect it.
> ····▸ ~ penser think about it.
> ····▸ ~ être pour qch have sth to do with it.

**yaourt** /'jauʀ(t) / nm yoghurt.
**yaourtière** nf yoghurt-maker.
**yard** /'jaʀd/ nm yard (= 91,44 cm).
**yen** /'jɛn/ nm yen.
**yeux** /jø/ ➡ ŒIL.
**yoga** /'jɔga/ nm yoga.
**yougoslave** /'jugɔslav/ adj Yugoslav. Y~ nmf Yugoslav.
**Yougoslavie** /'jugɔslavi/ nf

w
x
y

Yugoslavia.

**yo-yo®** /'jojo/ nm inv yo-yo®.

# Zz

**zapper** /zape/ **1** vi (à la télévision) channel-hop.

**zèbre** /zɛbʀ/ nm zebra.

**zèle** /zɛl/ nm zeal.

**zéro** /zeʀo/ nm nought, zero; (température) zero; (Sport) nil; (tennis) love; (personne) nonentity; **partir de ~** start from scratch; **repartir à ~** start all over again.

**zeste** /zɛst/ nm peel; **un ~ de** (fig)

a touch of.

**zézayer** /zezeje/ **31** vi lisp.

**zigzag** /zigzag/ nm zigzag; **en ~** winding.

**zinc** /zɛ̃g/ nm (métal) zinc; (comptoir **1**) bar.

**zizanie** /zizani/ nf discord; **semer la ~** put the cat among the pigeons.

**zizi** /zizi/ nm **1** willy.

**zodiaque** /zɔdjak/ nm zodiac.

**zona** /zona/ nm (Méd) shingles (+ sg).

**zone** /zon/ nf zone, area; (banlieue pauvre) slums; **~ bleue** restricted parking zone; **~ euro** eurozone; **~ de saisie** input box.

**zoo** /zo(o)/ nm zoo.

**zoom** /zum/ nm zoom lens.

**zut** /zyt/ interj **1** damn **1**.

# Phrasefinder/Phrases utiles

## Key phrases    Phrases-clés

| | |
|---|---|
| yes, please | oui, s'il vous plaît |
| no, thank you | non, merci |
| sorry! | désolé/-e! |
| you're welcome | de rien |

### Meeting people    Rencontres

| | |
|---|---|
| hello/goodbye | bonjour/au revoir |
| how are you? | comment allez-vous? |
| nice to meet you! | enchanté/-e! |

| **Asking questions** | **Poser des questions** |
|---|---|
| do you speak English/French? | parlez-vous anglais/français? |
| what's your name? | comment vous appelez-vous? |
| where are you from? | d'où venez-vous? |
| how much is it? | combien ça coûte? |
| is it far? | c'est loin d'ici? |
| where is...? | où est...? |
| can I have...? | est-ce que je peux avoir...? |
| would you like...? | voulez-vous...? |

| **About you** | **Parler de soi** |
|---|---|
| my name is... | je m'appelle... |
| I'm English/French/American | je suis anglais/-e/français/-e/américain/-e |
| I don't speak French/English very well | je ne parle pas très bien français/anglais |
| I'm here on holiday | je suis en vacances ici |
| I live near Sheffield/Bordeaux | j'habite près de Sheffield/Bordeaux |
| I'm a student | je suis étudiant/-e |

| **Emergencies** | **Urgences** |
|---|---|
| can you help me? | pouvez-vous m'aider? |
| I'm lost | je me suis perdu/-e |
| I'm ill | je suis malade |
| call an ambulance | appelez une ambulance |
| watch out! | attention! |

| **Reading signs** | **Les pancartes** |
|---|---|
| no entry | défense d'entrer |
| no smoking | défense de fumer |
| fire exit | sortie de secours |
| for sale | à vendre |
| push | pousser |
| pull | tirer |
| press | appuyer |

# Going Places/Se déplacer

## By rail and underground  En train et en métro

| | |
|---|---|
| where can I buy a ticket? | où est-ce que je peux acheter un billet? |
| what time is the next train to Paris/New York? | à quelle heure est le prochain train pour Paris/New York? |
| do I have to change? | est-ce qu'il y a un changement? |
| can I take my bike on the train? | est-ce que je peux prendre mon vélo dans le train? |
| which platform for the train to Marseilles/Bath? | de quel quai part le train pour Marseille/Bath? |
| a single/return, (Amer) round trip to Baltimore/Nice, please | un aller/aller-retour pour Baltimore/Nice, s'il vous plaît |
| I'd like an all-day ticket | je voudrais un billet valable toute la journée |
| I'd like to reserve a seat | je voudrais réserver une place |
| is there a student/senior citizen discount? | est-ce qu'il y a une réduction pour les étudiants/les personnes âgées? |
| is this the train for Lyons/Manchester? | est-ce que c'est bien le train pour Lyon/Manchester? |
| what time does the train arrive in Paris/London? | à quelle heure le train arrive-t-il à Paris/Londres? |
| have I missed the train? | est-ce que j'ai raté le train? |
| which line do I need to take for the Eiffel Tower/London Eye? | quelle ligne dois-je prendre pour aller à la tour Eiffel/au London Eye? |

| YOU WILL HEAR: | VOUS ENTENDREZ: |
|---|---|
| le train entre en gare au quai numéro 2 | the train is arriving at platform 2 |
| il y a un train pour Paris à 10 heures | there's a train to Paris at 10 o'clock |
| le train est en retard/à l'heure | the train is delayed/on time |
| prochain arrêt : ... | the next stop is... |
| votre ticket n'est pas valable | your ticket isn't valid |

| MORE USEFUL WORDS: | D'AUTRES MOTS UTILES: |
|---|---|
| underground station, (*Amer*) subway station | la station de métro |
| timetable | l'horaire |
| connection | la correspondance, le changement |
| express train | le train express |
| local train | le train régional |
| high-speed train | le TGV |

| DID YOU KNOW...? | LE SAVIEZ-VOUS...? |
|---|---|
| In a French train station, before you get on the train you must *composter* your ticket, i.e. have it stamped in the special machine positioned at the entrance of the platform to make it valid for your journey. You risk a fine if you forget to do this. | En Angleterre, l'aéroport de Londres–Heathrow est relié au centre de la capitale par le train Heathrow Express qui met moins de vingt minutes à parcourir ce trajet. |

## At the airport  En avion

| | |
|---|---|
| when's the next flight to Paris/Rome? | quand part le prochain vol pour Paris/Rome? |
| what time do I have to check in? | à quelle heure est-ce que je dois me présenter à l'enregistrement? |
| where do I check in? | où est le comptoir d'enregistrement? |
| I'd like to confirm my flight | je voudrais confirmer mon vol |
| I'd like a window seat/an aisle seat | je voudrais une place côté fenêtre/côté couloir |
| I want to change/cancel my reservation | je voudrais modifier/annuler ma réservation |
| can I carry this in my hand, (*Amer*) carry-on luggage? | puis-je prendre ce sac en bagage à main? |
| my luggage hasn't arrived | mes bagages ne sont pas arrivés |

### YOU WILL HEAR:  VOUS ENTENDREZ:

| | |
|---|---|
| le vol BA7057 est retardé/annulé | flight BA7057 is delayed/cancelled |
| veuillez vous rendre à la porte d'embarquement numéro 29 | please go to gate 29 |
| votre carte d'embarquement, s'il vous plaît | your boarding card, please |

### MORE USEFUL WORDS:  D'AUTRES MOTS UTILES:

| | |
|---|---|
| arrivals | arrivées |
| departures | départs |
| baggage claim | réception des bagages |

## Asking how to get there — Trouver son chemin

|  |  |
|---|---|
| how do I get to the airport? | comment est-ce que je fais pour aller à l'aéroport? |
| how long will it take to get there? | combien de temps est-ce qu'il faut pour y arriver? |
| how far is it from here? | combien y a-t-il d'ici? |
| which bus do I take for the cathedral? | quel bus est-ce que je dois prendre pour aller à la cathédrale? |
| where does this bus go? | où va ce bus? |
| does this bus/train go to...? | est-ce que ce bus/train va à ... ? |
| where do I get off? | pouvez-vous me dire où je dois descendre? |
| how much is it to the town centre? | quel est le prix d'un billet pour le centre-ville?...? |
| what time is the last bus? | à quelle heure est le dernier bus? |
| where's the nearest underground station, (Amer) subway station? | où est la station de métro la plus proche? |
| is this the turning for...? | est-ce que c'est là qu'il faut tourner pour aller à ... ? |
| can you call me a taxi? | pouvez-vous m'appeler un taxi, s'il vous plaît ? |

### YOU WILL HEAR: — VOUS ENTENDREZ:

| | |
|---|---|
| prenez la première rue à droite | take the first turning on the right |
| prenez à gauche aux feux/juste après l'église | turn left at the traffic lights/just past the church |

## Disabled travellers — Les voyageurs handicapés

|  |  |
|---|---|
| I'm disabled | je suis handicapé/-e |
| is there wheelchair access? | y a-t-il un accès pour les fauteuils roulants? |
| are guide dogs permitted? | les chiens d'aveugle sont-ils autorisés? |

## On the road    Par la route

| | |
|---|---|
| where's the nearest petrol station, (*Amer*) gas station? | où se trouve la station d'essence la plus proche? |
| what's the best way to get there? | quel est le meilleur chemin pour y aller? |
| I've got a puncture, (*Amer*) flat tire | j'ai crevé |
| I'd like to hire, (*Amer*) rent a bike/car | je voudrais louer un vélo/une voiture |
| where can I park around here? | où peut-on se garer par ici? |
| there's been an accident | il y a eu un accident |
| my car's broken down | ma voiture est en panne |
| the car won't start | la voiture ne démarre pas |
| where's the nearest garage? | où se trouve le garage le plus proche? |
| pump number six, please | la pompe numéro 6, s'il vous plaît |
| fill it up, please | le plein, s'il vous plaît |
| can I get my car washed here? | est-ce que je peux utiliser le lavage automatique? |
| can I park here? | puis-je me garer ici? |
| there's a problem with the brakes/lights | il y a un problème de freins/phares |
| the clutch/gearstick isn't working | l'embrayage/le levier de vitesse ne fonctionne pas |
| take the third exit off the roundabout, (*Amer*) traffic circle | prenez la troisième sortie au rond-point |
| turn right at the next junction | tournez à droite au prochain carrefour |
| slow down | ralentissez |
| I can't drink – I'm driving | je ne peux pas boire d'alcool, je conduis |
| can I buy a road map here? | est-ce que vous vendez des cartes routières? |

| YOU WILL HEAR: | VOUS ENTENDREZ: |
|---|---|
| votre permis de conduire, s'il vous plaît? | can I see your driving licence? |
| vous devez remplir un constat d'accident | you need to fill out an accident report |
| c'est un sens unique | this road is one-way |
| il est interdit de se garer ici | you can't park here |

| MORE USEFUL WORDS: | D'AUTRES MOTS UTILES: |
|---|---|
| diesel | le diesel, le gazole |
| unleaded | sans plomb |
| motorway, (*Amer*) expressway | l'autoroute |
| toll | le péage |
| satnav, (*Amer*) GPS | le GPS |
| speed camera | le radar |
| roundabout | le rond-point |
| crossroads | l'intersection, le carrefour |
| dual carriageway, (*Amer*) divided highway | la route à quatre voies |
| traffic lights | les feux de circulation |
| driver | le conducteur/la conductrice |

| DID YOU KNOW...? | LE SAVIEZ-VOUS...? |
|---|---|
| The speed limits on French roads are as follows: motorway 130 km/h (80 m/h), 110 km/h (74 m/h) when it rains, open roads 90 km/h (56 m/h), towns and villages 50 km/h (31 mph). | Pour circuler dans le centre de Londres, les motoristes doivent payer une taxe appelée *congestion charge*. |

# COMMON FRENCH ROAD SIGNS

| | |
|---|---|
| Aire de Lavallière : 2000 m | Lavallière rest area in two kilometres |
| Allumez vos feux | Switch on dipped headlights |
| Chaussée déformée | Uneven road surface |
| Circulation alternée, circulation à sens alterné | Contraflow |
| Déviation | Diverted traffic, Diversion |
| Halte péage/douanes/gendarmerie | Stop: Toll/ Customs/ Police |
| Interdiction de tourner à droite/gauche | No right/left turn |
| Interdit sauf de 19h à 9h | No entry except between 7pm and 9am |
| Prochaine sortie : gendarmerie | Next exit: Police |
| Sauf riverains | Local residents only |
| Sens interdit | No entry |
| SOS (on motorway) | Emergency stopping area |
| Travaux sur 15 kms | Roadworks for 15 kms |

# PANNEAUX DE SIGNALISATION EN PAYS ANGLOPHONES

| | |
|---|---|
| Cattle | Bétail |
| Contraflow | Circulation à sens alterné, circulation alternée |
| Ford | Passage à gué |
| Get in lane | Mettez-vous dans la bonne file |
| Give way | Cédez le passage |
| Keep clear | Arrêt et stationnement interdits |
| No overtaking, (Amer) Do not pass | Interdiction de dépasser |
| Pedestrians crossing | Passage pour piétons |
| Red route – no stopping | Axe rouge – arrêt et stationnement interdits |
| Reduce speed now | Ralentir |
| Stop | Stop |

# Keeping in touch/Rester en contact

## On the phone  Au téléphone

| | |
|---|---|
| where can I buy a phone card? | où est-ce que je peux acheter une carte de téléphone? |
| may I use your phone? | est-ce que je peux utiliser votre téléphone? |
| do you have a mobile, (Amer) cell phone? | avez-vous un portable? |
| what is your phone number? | quel est votre numéro de téléphone? |
| what is the area code for Lyons/St Albans? | quel est l'indicatif pour Lyon/St Albans? |
| I want to make a phone call | je veux téléphoner |
| I'd like to reverse the charges, (Amer) call collect | je voudrais appeler en PCV |
| the line's engaged/busy | la ligne est occupée |
| there's no answer | ça ne répond pas |
| hello, this is Natalie | allô, c'est Natalie |
| is Jean there, please? | est-ce que Jean est là, s'il vous plaît? |
| who's calling? | qui est à l'appareil? |
| sorry, wrong number | désolé/-e, vous faites erreur |
| just a moment, please | un instant, s'il vous plaît |
| would you like to hold? | vous patientez? |
| it's a business/personal call | c'est un appel professionnel/privé |
| I'll put you through to him/her | je vous le/la passe |
| s/he cannot come to the phone at the moment | il/elle n'est pas disponible pour l'instant |
| please tell him/her I called | pourriez-vous lui dire que j'ai appelé? |
| I'd like to leave a message for him/her | j'aimerais lui laisser un message |
| I'll try again later | je réessaierai plus tard |

| | |
|---|---|
| please tell him/her that Marie called | pourriez-vous lui dire que Marie a appelé, s'il vous plaît |
| can he/she ring me back? | est-ce qu'il/elle peut me rappeler? |
| my home number is... | mon numéro personnel est... |
| my business number is... | mon numéro professionnel est... |
| my fax number is... | mon numéro de télécopie est... |
| we were cut off | on a été coupé |
| I'll call you later | je vous rappelle plus tard |
| I need to top up my phone | j'ai besoin de recharger mon portable |
| the battery's run out | il n'y a plus de batterie |
| I'm running low on credit | je n'ai presque plus de crédit sur mon portable |
| send me a text | envoie-moi un texto/message |
| there's no signal here | il n'y a pas de réception ici |
| you're breaking up | la ligne est mauvaise |
| could you speak a little louder? | pouvez-vous parler un peu plus fort? |

| YOU WILL HEAR: | VOUS ENTENDREZ: |
|---|---|
| allô | hello |
| appelez-moi sur mon portable | call me on my mobile, (Amer) cell phone |
| vous voulez laisser un message? | would you like to leave a message? |

| MORE USEFUL WORDS: | D'AUTRES MOTS UTILES: |
|---|---|
| text message | le texto, le message |
| top-up card | la carte de recharge, la carte prépayée |
| phone box, (Amer) phone booth | la cabine téléphonique |
| dial 3615 | composez le 3615 |
| directory enquiries | les renseignements |

## Writing  Écrire

| | |
|---|---|
| what's your address? | quelle est votre adresse? |
| where is the nearest post office? | où est le bureau de poste le plus proche? |
| could I have a stamp for France/Italy, please? | je voudrais un timbre pour la France/l'Italie, s'il vous plaît |
| I'd like to send a parcel | je voudrais envoyer un paquet |
| where is the nearest postbox, (*Amer*) mailbox? | où se trouve la boîte aux lettres la plus proche? |
| dear Isabelle/Fred | Chère Isabelle/Cher Fred |
| dear Sir or Madam | Monsieur/Madame |
| yours sincerely | veuillez agréer, Monsieur/Madame, mes/nos sincères salutations |
| yours faithfully | veuillez agréer, Monsieur/Madame, mes/nos sincères salutations |
| best wishes | (*letter*) meilleurs vœux; (*e-mail*) bien amicalement |

### YOU WILL HEAR:  VOUS ENTENDREZ:

| | |
|---|---|
| vous voulez l'envoyer en tarif normal? | would you like to send it first class? |
| c'est un objet de valeur? | is it valuable? |

### MORE USEFUL WORDS:  D'AUTRES MOTS UTILES:

| | |
|---|---|
| letter | la lettre |
| postcode, (*Amer*) ZIP code | le code postal |
| airmail | par avion |
| fragile | fragile |
| urgent | urgent |
| registered post, (*Amer*) mail | le courrier recommandé |

## On line    En ligne

| | |
|---|---|
| are you on the Internet? | êtes-vous sur Internet? |
| what's your e-mail address? | quelle est votre adresse électronique? |
| I'll e-mail it to you on Tuesday | je vous l'enverrai par courrier électronique mardi |
| I looked it up on the Internet | j'ai vérifié sur Internet |
| the information is on their website | l'information se trouve sur leur site Internet |
| my e-mail address is jane dot smith at new99 dot com | mon adresse électronique est jane point smith arobase new99 point com |
| can I check my e-mail here? | puis-je vérifier mon courrier électronique ici? |
| I have broadband/dial-up | j'ai une connexion Internet haut-débit/par ligne téléphonique |
| do you have wireless Internet access? | avez-vous un accès sans fil à Internet? |
| I'll send you the file as an attachment | je vous enverrai le fichier en pièce jointe |

| YOU WILL SEE: | VOUS VERREZ: |
|---|---|
| rechercher | search |
| double-cliquer sur l'icône | double-click on the icon |
| ouvrir l'application | open (up) the application |
| télécharger le fichier | download file |

| MORE USEFUL WORDS: | D'AUTRES MOTS UTILES: |
|---|---|
| subject (of an email) | le sujet |
| password | le mot de passe |
| social networking site | le site de réseau social |
| search engine | le moteur de recherche |
| mouse | la souris |
| keyboard | le clavier |

13

## Meeting up | Se retrouver

| | |
|---|---|
| what shall we do this evening? | qu'est-ce qu'on fait ce soir? |
| do you want to go out tonight? | tu veux sortir ce soir? |
| where shall we meet? | où est-ce qu'on se retrouve? |
| I'll see you outside the café at 6 o'clock | on se retrouve à 6 heures devant le café |
| see you later | à tout à l'heure |
| I can't today, I'm busy | je ne peux pas aujourd'hui, je suis occupé/-e |
| I'm sorry, I've got something planned | je suis désolé/-e, j'ai déjà quelque chose de prévu |
| let's meet for a coffee in town | allons prendre un café en ville |
| would you like to see a show/film, (Amer) movie? | est-ce que tu voudrais aller voir un spectacle/un film? |
| what about next week instead? | la semaine prochaine alors? |
| shall we go for something to eat? | si on allait manger quelque part? |

| YOU WILL HEAR: | VOUS ENTENDREZ |
|---|---|
| enchanté/-e (de faire votre connaissance) | nice to meet you |
| puis-je vous offrir un verre? | can I buy you a drink? |

| MORE USEFUL WORDS: | D'AUTRES MOTS UTILES: |
|---|---|
| bar | le bar |
| bar (serving counter in a bar/pub) | le comptoir, le bar |
| meal | le repas |
| snack | le repas léger, le casse-croûte |
| date | le rendez-vous |
| cigarette | la cigarette |

# Food and Drink/Boire et manger

## Booking a table — Réserver une table

| | |
|---|---|
| can you recommend a good restaurant? | pouvez-vous me recommander un bon restaurant? |
| I'd like to reserve a table for four | je voudrais réserver une table pour quatre personnes |
| a reservation for tomorrow evening at eight o'clock | une réservation pour demain soir à huit heures |
| I booked a table for two | j'ai réservé une table pour deux |

## Ordering — Passer commande

| | |
|---|---|
| could we see the menu/wine list, please? | est-ce qu'on pourrait voir la carte/la carte des vins? |
| do you have a vegetarian/children's menu? | est-ce que vous avez un menu végétarien/enfant? |
| what would you recommend? | que (nous) conseillez-vous? |
| I'd like a white/black coffee | j'aimerais un café/un café noir |
| ... an espresso | ... un express |
| ... a decaffeinated coffee | ... un café décaféiné |
| ... a tea/a herbal tea | ... un thé/une infusion |
| the bill, (Amer) check, please | l'addition, s'il vous plaît |
| we'd like to pay separately | on voudrait payer séparément |

### YOU WILL HEAR: — ON VOUS DIRA:

| | |
|---|---|
| Désirez-vous un apéritif? | Would you like an aperitif? |
| Souhaitez-vous commander? | Are you ready to order? |
| Désirez-vous une entrée? | Would you like a starter? |
| Quel plat avez-vous choisi? | What will you have for the main course? |
| Je (vous) conseille le/la... | I can recommend the ... |
| Souhaitez-vous prendre un dessert? | Would you like a dessert? |
| Désirez-vous un café/un digestif? | Would you like coffee?/a liqueur? |
| Désirez-vous autre chose? | Anything else? |
| Bon appétit | Enjoy your meal! |

15

## The menu · Le Menu

| starters | entrées | | entrées | starters |
|---:|:---|---|---:|:---|
| hors d'oeuvres | hors d'œuvres | | hors d'œuvres | hors d'oeuvres |
| omelette | omelette | | omelette | omelette |
| soup | soupe | | soupe | soup |

| fish | poisson | | poisson | fish |
|---:|:---|---|---:|:---|
| bass | perche | | anguille | eel |
| cod | cabillaud | | cabillaud | cod |
| eel | anguille | | cal(a)mar | squid |
| hake | colin | | crevettes grises | shrimps |
| herring | hareng | | crevettes roses | prawns |
| monkfish | lotte | | colin | hake |
| mullet | mulet | | hareng | herring |
| mussels | moules | | huîtres | oysters |
| oysters | huîtres | | lotte | monkfish |
| prawns | crevettes roses | | moules | mussels |
| salmon | saumon | | mulet | mullet |
| sardines | sardines | | perche | bass |
| shrimps | crevettes grises | | sardines | sardines |
| sole | sole | | saumon | salmon |
| squid | cal(a)mar | | sole | sole |
| trout | truite | | thon | tuna |
| tuna | thon | | truite | trout |
| turbot | turbot | | turbot | turbot |

| meat | viande | | viande | meat |
|---:|:---|---|---:|:---|
| beef | bœuf | | agneau | lamb |
| chicken | poulet | | bifteck | steak |
| duck | canard | | bœuf | beef |
| goose | oie | | canard | duck |
| guinea fowl | pintade | | foie | liver |

16

| hare | lièvre | | lapin | rabbit |
|---|---|---|---|---|
| kidneys | rognons | | lièvre | hare |
| lamb | agneau | | oie | goose |
| liver | foie | | poulet | chicken |
| pork | porc | | pintade | guinea fowl |
| rabbit | lapin | | porc | pork |
| steak | bifteck | | rognons | kidneys |
| veal | veau | | sanglier | wild boar |
| wild boar | sanglier | | veau | veal |

| vegetables | légumes | | légumes | vegetables |
|---|---|---|---|---|
| artichokes | artichaut | | artichaut | artichokes |
| asparagus | asperges | | asperges | asparagus |
| aubergine | aubergine | | aubergine | aubergine |
| cabbage | chou | | carrottes | carrots |
| carrots | carrottes | | céleri | celery |
| cauliflower | chou-fleur | | champignons | mushrooms |
| celery | céleri | | chou | cabbage |
| courgettes | courgettes | | chou-fleur | cauliflower |
| endive | endives | | courgettes | courgettes |
| green beans | haricots verts | | endives | endive |
| mushrooms | champignons | | épinards | spinach |
| onions | oignons | | haricots verts | green beans |
| peas | petits pois | | oignons | onions |
| peppers | poivron | | petits pois | peas |
| potatoes | pommes de terre | | poivron | peppers |
| spinach | épinards | | pommes de terre | potatoes |

| the way it's cooked | la cuisson | | la cuisson | the way it's cooked |
|---|---|---|---|---|
| fried | poêlé | | à la vapeur | steamed |
| grilled | grillé | | à point | medium rare |

| medium rare | à point | | bien cuit | well done |
|---|---|---|---|---|
| puréed | mixé | | bleu | very rare |
| rare | saignant | | cuit à l'étouffée | stewed |
| roast | rôti | | grillé | grilled |
| steamed | à la vapeur | | mixé | puréed |
| stewed | cuit à l'étouffée | | poêlé | fried |
| very rare | bleu | | rôti | roast |
| well done | bien cuit | | saignant | rare |

| **desserts** | **fromages et desserts** | | **fromages et desserts** | **desserts** |
|---|---|---|---|---|
| cheeseboard | plateau de fromages | | fruit | fruit |
| fruit | fruit | | glace | ice cream |
| ice cream | glace | | plateau de fromages | cheeseboard |
| pie | tarte (recouverte de pâte) | | sorbet | sorbet |
| sorbet | sorbet | | tarte | tart |
| tart | tarte | | tarte (recouverte de pâte) | pie |

| **sundries** | **divers** | | **divers** | **sundries** |
|---|---|---|---|---|
| bread | pain | | assaisonnement | seasoning |
| butter | beurre | | beurre | butter |
| green salad | salade verte | | herbes | herbs |
| herbs | herbes | | huile d'olive | olive oil |
| mayonnaise | mayonnaise | | mayonnaise | mayonnaise |
| mustard | moutarde | | moutarde | mustard |
| olive oil | huile d'olive | | pain | bread |
| pepper | poivre | | poivre | pepper |
| salt | sel | | salade verte | green salad |
| sauce | sauce | | sauce | sauce |
| seasoning | assaisonnement | | sel | salt |
| vinegar | vinaigre | | vinaigre | vinegar |

| drinks | boissons | | boissons | drinks |
|---|---|---|---|---|
| beer | bière | | bière | beer |
| bottle | bouteille | | boissons non alcoolisées | soft drinks |
| carbonated | gazeux | | bouteille | bottle |
| half-bottle | demi-bouteille | | demi-bouteille | half-bottle |
| liqueur | digestif | | digestif | liqueur |
| mineral water | eau minérale | | eau minérale | mineral water |
| red wine | vin rouge | | gazeux | carbonated |
| rosé | rosé | | plat | still |
| soft drinks | boissons non alcoolisées | | rosé | rosé |
| still | plat, non gazeux | | vin | wine |
| table wine | vin de table | | vin blanc | white wine |
| white wine | vin blanc | | vin de table | table wine |
| wine | vin | | vin rouge | red wine |

# Places to stay/Où dormir

## Camping  Camper

| | |
|---|---|
| can we pitch our tent here? | est-ce qu'on peut planter notre tente ici? |
| can we park our caravan here? | est-ce qu'on peut mettre notre caravane ici? |
| what are the facilities like? | le camping est-il bien équipé? |
| how much is it per night? | c'est combien par nuit? |
| where do we park the car? | où est-ce qu'on peut garer la voiture? |
| we're looking for a campsite | on cherche un camping |
| this is a list of local campsites | c'est une liste des campings de la région |
| we go on a camping holiday every year | nous partons camper chaque année pour les vacances |

## At the hotel  À l'hôtel

| | |
|---|---|
| I'd like a double/single room with bath | je voudrais une chambre double/simple avec bain |
| we have a reservation in the name of Milne | nous avons une réservation au nom de Milne |
| we'll be staying three nights, from Friday to Sunday | nous resterons trois nuits, de vendredi à dimanche |
| how much does the room cost? | combien coûte la chambre? |
| I'd like to see the room, please | je voudrais voir la chambre, s'il vous plaît |
| what time is breakfast? | à quelle heure est le petit déjeuner? |
| bed and breakfast | chambres d'hôtes |
| we'd like to stay another night | on voudrait rester une nuit de plus |
| please call me at 7:30 | réveillez-moi à 7h30 |
| are there any messages for me? | est-ce qu'il y a des messages pour moi? |

## Hostels — Auberges de jeunesse

| | |
|---|---|
| could you tell me where the youth hostel is? | pourriez-vous me dire où se trouve l'auberge de jeunesse? |
| what time does the hostel close? | à quelle heure ferme l'auberge de jeunesse? |
| I'm staying in a hostel | je loge à l'auberge de jeunesse |
| I know a really good hostel in Dublin | je connais une très bonne auberge de jeunesse à Dublin |
| I'd like to go backpacking in Australia | j'aimerais bien aller faire de la randonnée en Australie |

## Rooms to let — Locations

| | |
|---|---|
| I'm looking for a room with a reasonable rent | je cherche une chambre à louer avec un loyer raisonnable |
| I'd like to rent an apartment for a few weeks | je voudrais louer un appartement pendant quelques semaines |
| where do I find out about rooms to let? | où est-ce que je peux me renseigner sur des chambres à louer? |
| what's the weekly rent? | quel est le montant du loyer pour la semaine? |
| I'm staying with friends at the moment | je loge chez des amis pour le moment |
| I rent an apartment on the outskirts of town | je loue un appartement en banlieue |
| the room's fine – I'll take it | la chambre est bien – je la prends |
| the deposit is one month's rent in advance | l'acompte correspond à un mois de loyer payable d'avance |

# Shopping and money/Achats et argent

## At the bank — À la banque

| | |
|---|---|
| I'd like to change some money | je voudrais changer de l'argent |
| I want to change some euros into pounds | je veux changer des euros en livres |
| do you take Eurocheques? | acceptez-vous les Eurochèques? |
| what's the exchange rate today? | quel est le taux de change aujourd'hui? |
| I prefer traveller's cheques, (*Amer*) traveler's checks to cash | je préfère les chèques de voyage à l'argent liquide |
| I'd like to transfer some money from my account | je voudrais retirer de l'argent sur mon compte |
| I'll get some money from the cash machine | je vais retirer de l'argent au distributeur |
| I usually pay by direct debit | d'habitude, je paye par prélèvement automatique |

## Finding the right shop — Trouver le bon magasin

| | |
|---|---|
| where's the main shopping district? | où se trouve le principal quartier commerçant? |
| where's a good place to buy sunglasses? | quel est le meilleur endroit pour acheter des lunettes de soleil? |
| where can I buy batteries/postcards? | où est-ce que je peux acheter des piles/cartes postales? |
| where's the nearest chemist/bookshop? | où est-ce la pharmacie/librairie la plus proche? |
| is there a good food shop around here? | est-ce qu'il y a une bonne épicerie près d'ici? |
| what time do the shops open/close? | à quelle heure ouvrent/ferment les magasins? |
| where did you get those? | où les avez-vous trouvés? |
| I'm looking for presents for my family | je cherche des cadeaux pour ma famille |
| we'll do all our shopping on Saturday | nous ferons toutes nos courses samedi |

## Are you being served? On s'occupe de vous?

| | |
|---|---|
| how much does that cost? | combien ça coûte? |
| can I try it on? | est-ce que je peux l'essayer? |
| can you keep it for me? | pouvez-vous me le/la garder? |
| do you have this in another colour, (*Amer*) color? | est-ce que vous avez ce modèle-ci dans une autre couleur? |
| I'm just looking | je regarde |
| I'll think about it | je vais réfléchir |
| I need a bigger/smaller size | il me faut une taille au-dessus/au-dessous |
| I take a size 10/a medium | je fais du 38/il me faut une taille moyenne |
| it doesn't suit me | ça ne me va pas |
| could you wrap it for me, please? | pourriez-vous l'emballer, s'il vous plaît? |
| do you take credit cards? | est-ce que vous acceptez les cartes de crédit? |
| can I pay by cheque, (*Amer*) check? | est-ce que je peux payer par chèque? |
| I'm sorry, I don't have any change | je suis désolé/-e mais je n'ai pas de monnaie |
| I'd like a receipt, please | je voudrais un reçu, s'il vous plaît |

## Changing things Faire un échange

| | |
|---|---|
| can I have a refund? | j'aimerais être remboursé/-e |
| can you mend it for me? | est-ce que vous pouvez me le/la réparer? |
| can I speak to the manager? | je voudrais parler au responsable |
| it doesn't work | ça ne marche pas |
| I'd like to change it, please | je voudrais l'échanger, s'il vous plaît |
| I bought this here yesterday | je l'ai acheté/-e ici hier |

| Currency Convertor | | Convertisseur de devises | |
|---|---|---|---|
| **€/$** | **£/$** | **£/$** | **€/$** |
| 0.25 | | 0.25 | |
| 0.50 | | 0.50 | |
| 0.75 | | 0.75 | |
| 1 | | 1 | |
| 1.5 | | 1.5 | |
| 2 | | 2 | |
| 3 | | 3 | |
| 5 | | 5 | |
| 10 | | 10 | |
| 20 | | 20 | |
| 30 | | 30 | |
| 40 | | 40 | |
| 50 | | 50 | |
| 100 | | 100 | |
| 200 | | 200 | |
| 1000 | | 1000 | |

# Sport and leisure/Sports et loisirs

## Keeping fit    Rester en bonne santé

| | |
|---|---|
| where can we play football/squash? | où est-ce qu'on peut jouer au football/squash? |
| where is the local sports centre, (*Amer*) center? | où se trouve le centre sportif? |
| what's the charge per day? | quel est le prix pour la journée? |
| is there a reduction for children/a student discount? | est-ce qu'il y a des réductions enfants/étudiants? |
| I'm looking for a swimming pool/tennis court | je cherche une piscine/un court de tennis |
| are there any yoga/pilates classes here? | est-ce qu'on donne des cours de yoga/Pilates ici? |
| I want to do aerobics | je veux faire de l'aérobic |
| is there a hotel gym? | est-ce qu'il y a une salle de gym dans l'hôtel? |
| you have to be a member | vous devez être membre |
| I would like to go fishing/riding | je voudrais aller à la pêche/monter à cheval |
| I love swimming | j'adore nager |

## Watching sport    Le sport en spectateur

| | |
|---|---|
| is there a match, (*Amer*) game on Saturday? | est-ce qu'il y a un match samedi? |
| which teams are playing? | quelles sont les équipes qui jouent? |
| where can I get tickets? | où est-ce que je peux acheter des billets? |
| I'd like to see the match, (*Amer*) game | j'aimerais voir le match |
| my favourite, (*Amer*) favorite team is... | mon équipe préférée est... |
| who's winning? | qui gagne? |
| the reds are winning 3-1 | ce sont les rouges qui gagnent 3 à 1 |

## SPORTS AND PASTIMES

| | |
|---|---|
| American football/football | le football américain/le football |
| badminton | le badminton |
| cycling | la course cycliste |
| football/soccer | le football |
| golf | le golf |
| hiking | la grande randonnée |
| horse-riding | l'équitation |
| rollerblading | le patinage en ligne |
| rugby | le rugby |
| running | la course à pied |
| sailing | la voile |
| surfing | le surf |
| swimming | la natation |

## SPORTS ET PASSE-TEMPS

| | |
|---|---|
| le basket-ball | basketball |
| la belote | belote (card game) |
| la pétanque | boules |
| les échecs | chess |
| les dames | draughts |
| le handball | handball |
| le patinage à glace | ice-skating |
| le jogging | jogging |
| la randonnée à cheval | pony-trekking |
| le ski | skiing |

## Movies/theatres/clubs | Aller au cinéma/théâtre/en boîte

| what's on? | qu'est-ce qu'il y a au programme? |
| when does the box office open/close? | à quelle heure ouvre/ferme le guichet? |
| what time does the concert/performance start? | à quelle heure commence le concert/la représentation? |
| when does it finish? | à quelle heure ça finit? |
| are there any seats left for tonight? | est-ce qu'il y a encore des places pour ce soir? |
| how much are the tickets? | combien coûtent les billets? |
| where can I get a programme, (*Amer*) program? | où est-ce que je peux me procurer un programme? |
| I want to book tickets for tonight's performance | je veux réserver des places pour la représentation de ce soir |
| I'll book seats in the circle | je vais réserver des places au balcon |
| I'd rather have seats in the stalls, (*Amer*) orchestra | je préfère avoir des places à l'orchestre |
| somewhere in the middle, but not too far back | au milieu, mais pas trop loin de la scène |
| four, please | quatre, s'il vous plaît |
| we'd like to go to a club | on voudrait aller en boîte |

## Hobbies | Passe-temps

| what do you do at, (*Amer*) on weekends? | que faites-vous les week-ends? |
| I like reading/listening to music/going out | j'aime lire/écouter de la musique/sortir |
| do you like watching TV/shopping/travelling, (*Amer*) traveling? | est-ce que tu aimes regarder la télé/faire du shopping/voyager? |
| I read a lot | je lis beaucoup |
| I collect comic books | je collectionne les bandes dessinées |

27

# Good timing/En temps et en heure

## Telling the time  Exprimer l'heure

| | |
|---|---|
| could you tell me the time? | pourriez-vous me dire l'heure? |
| what time is it? | quelle heure est-il? |
| it's 2 o'clock | il est 2 heures |
| at about 8 o'clock | vers 8 heures |
| at 9 o'clock tomorrow | à 9 heures demain |
| from 10 o'clock onwards | à partir de 10 heures |
| it starts at 8 p.m. | ça commence à 20 heures |
| at 5 o'clock in the morning/afternoon | à 5 heures du matin/de l'après-midi |
| it's five past/quarter past/half past one | il est une heure cinq/et quart/et demie |
| it's twenty-five to/quarter to/five to one | il est une heure moins vingt-cinq/le quart/cinq |
| a quarter of an hour | un quart d'heure |

## Days and dates  Jours et dates

| | |
|---|---|
| Sunday, Monday, Tuesday, Wednesday, Thursday, Friday, Saturday | dimanche, lundi, mardi, mercredi, jeudi, vendredi, samedi |
| January, February, March, April, May, June, July, August, September, October, November, December | janvier, février, mars, avril, mai, juin, juillet, août, septembre, octobre, novembre, décembre |
| what's the date today? | on est le combien aujourd'hui? |
| it's the second of June | on est le deux juin |
| what day is it? it's Monday | on est quel jour? on est lundi |
| we meet up every Monday | on se réunit tous les lundis |

| | |
|---|---|
| she comes on Tuesdays | elle vient le mardi |
| we're going away in August | nous partons en août |
| on November 8th | le 8 novembre |

## Public holidays and special days | Jours fériés

| | |
|---|---|
| Bank holiday | jour férié |
| long weekend | week-end prolongé |
| New Year's Day (1 Jan) | le Jour de l'an |
| St Valentine's Day (14 Feb) | la Saint-Valentin |
| Shrove Tuesday/Pancake Day | Mardi gras |
| Ash Wednesday | le mercredi des Cendres |
| Mother's Day | la fête des Mères |
| Palm Sunday | le dimanche des Rameaux |
| Good Friday | vendredi saint |
| Easter Day | Pâques |
| Easter Monday | le lundi de Pâques |
| Ascension Day | l'Ascension |
| Pentecost/Whitsun | la Pentecôte |
| Whit Monday | le lundi de Pentecôte |
| Father's Day | la fête des Pères |
| St John the Baptist's Day (24 Jun) | la Saint-Jean |
| Independence day (4 Jul) | la fête de l'Indépendance (aux États-Unis) |
| Bastille day (14 July) | le 14 juillet |
| Halloween (31 Oct) | Halloween (soir des fantômes et des sorcières) |
| All Saints' Day (1 Nov) | la Toussaint |
| Guy Fawkes Day/Bonfire Night (5 Nov) | fête de la Conspiration des Poudres avec feux de joie et feux d'artifice |
| Remembrance Sunday | le jour du Souvenir |
| Thanksgiving | le jour d'Action de grâces |
| Christmas Day (25 Dec) | Noël |
| Boxing Day (26 Dec) | le lendemain de Noël |
| New Year's Eve (31 Dec) | la Saint-Sylvestre |

# Health and Beauty/Santé et beauté

| At the doctor's | Chez le médecin |
|---|---|
| can I see a doctor? | est-ce que je peux voir un médecin? |
| I don't feel well | je ne me sens pas bien |
| it hurts here | j'ai mal là |
| I have a stomachache/migraine | j'ai mal au ventre/j'ai une migraine |
| are there any side effects? | est-ce qu'il y a des effets secondaires? |
| I have a sore ankle/wrist/knee | j'ai mal à la cheville/au poignet/au genou |

| YOU WILL HEAR: | VOUS ENTENDREZ: |
|---|---|
| vous devez prendre rendez-vous | you need to make an appointment |
| asseyez-vous, s'il vous plaît | please take a seat |
| est-ce que vous avez une carte européenne d'assurance-maladie (CEAM)? | do you have a European Health Insurance Card (EHIC)? |
| est-ce que vous avez une assurance-maladie? | do you have Health Insurance? |
| il faut que je prenne votre tension artérielle | I need to take your blood pressure |

| MORE USEFUL WORDS: | D'AUTRES MOTS UTILES: |
|---|---|
| nurse | l'infirmier/-ière |
| antibiotics | les antibiotiques |
| medicine | le médicament |
| infection | l'infection |
| treatment | le traitement |
| rest | le repos |

## At the pharmacy  Chez le pharmacien

| | |
|---|---|
| can I have some painkillers? | puis-je avoir quelque chose pour la douleur? |
| I have asthma/eczema/hay fever | j'ai de l'asthme/de l'eczéma/le rhume des foins |
| I've been stung by a wasp/bee | j'ai été piqué/-e par une guêpe/une abeille |
| I've got a cold/the flu | j'ai un rhume/la grippe |
| I need something for diarrhoea/stomachache | j'ai besoin de quelque chose contre la diarrhée/le mal de ventre |
| I'm pregnant | je suis enceinte |

### YOU WILL HEAR:  VOUS ENTENDREZ:

| | |
|---|---|
| avez-vous déjà pris ce médicament? | have you taken this medicine before? |
| prendre à l'heure du repas/trois fois par jour | take at mealtimes/three times a day |
| êtes-vous allergique? | are you allergic to anything? |
| est-ce que vous prenez d'autres médicaments? | are you taking any other medication? |

### MORE USEFUL WORDS:  D'AUTRES MOTS UTILES:

| | |
|---|---|
| prescription | l'ordonnance |
| plasters, (Amer) Band-Aid™ | le pansement |
| insect repellent | le produit anti-insecte |
| contraception | la contraception |
| sun cream | la crème solaire |
| aftersun | l'après-soleil |
| dosage | la posologie |

## At the hairdresser's/ beauty salon
## Chez le coiffeur/ Au salon de beauté

| | |
|---|---|
| I'd like a cut and blow dry | je voudrais une coupe et un brushing |
| just a trim, please | juste une coupe d'entretien, s'il vous plaît |
| a grade 3 back and sides | court derrière et sur les côtés |
| I'd like my hair washed first, please | je voudrais un shampooing, s'il vous plaît |
| can I have a manicure/pedicure/ facial? | puis-je avoir une manucure/un soin des pieds/un soin du visage? |
| how much is a head/back massage? | combien coûte un massage de la tête/du dos? |
| can I see a price list? | puis-je voir vos tarifs? |
| do you offer reflexology/ aromatherapy treatments? | est-ce que vous faites des séances de réflexologie/d'aromathérapie? |

| YOU WILL HEAR: | VOUS ENTENDREZ: |
|---|---|
| voulez-vous un brushing? | would you like your hair blow-dried? |
| vous avez la raie au milieu ou sur le côté? | where is your parting? |
| voulez-vous un dégradé? | would you like your hair layered? |

| MORE USEFUL WORDS: | D'AUTRES MOTS UTILES: |
|---|---|
| dry/greasy/fine/flyaway/ frizzy hair | des cheveux secs/gras/fins/ rebels/crépus |
| highlights | des mèches |
| extensions | les extensions de cheveux |
| sunbed | le lit de bronzage |
| leg/arm/bikini wax | l'épilation à la cire des jambes/des bras/du maillot |

32

## At the dentist's · Chez le dentiste

| | |
|---|---|
| I have toothache | j'ai mal aux dents |
| I'd like an emergency appointment | il me faut un rendez-vous d'urgence |
| I have cracked a tooth | je me suis cassé une dent |
| my gums are bleeding | j'ai les gencives qui saignent |

### YOU WILL HEAR: · VOUS ENTENDREZ:

| | |
|---|---|
| ouvrez la bouche | open your mouth |
| vous avez besoin d'un plombage | you need a filling |
| il faut faire une radio | we need to take an X-ray |
| rincez-vous la bouche, s'il vous plaît | please rinse |

### MORE USEFUL WORDS: · D'AUTRES MOTS UTILES:

| | |
|---|---|
| anaesthetic | l'anesthésique |
| root canal treatment | la dévitalisation |
| injection | la piqûre |
| floss | le fil dentaire |

### DID YOU KNOW...? · LE SAVIEZ-VOUS...?

In France you have to pay for healthcare, and depending on the type of care received a full or partial refund will be obtained. A doctor or dentist's surgery can often be found in a residential house or flat. A plaque at the entrance of the house or block of flats will inform the patient of the doctor's name, specialization, phone number and surgery times.

Le *National Health Service* britannique fournit un service de santé gratuit dans sa grande majorité. Ainsi les consultations généralistes et spécialistes, les hôpitaux, les urgences, la maternité, entre autres, sont gratuits. Par contre, pour la pharmacie ou d'autres soins comme la dentisterie, le patient doit payer une somme forfaitaire.

# Weights & measures/ Poids et mesures

**Length/Longueur**

| inches/pouces | 0.39 | 3.9 | 7.8 | 11.7 | 15.6 | 19.7 | 39 |
|---|---|---|---|---|---|---|---|
| cm/centimètres | 1 | 10 | 20 | 30 | 40 | 50 | 100 |

**Distance/Distance**

| miles/miles | 0.62 | 6.2 | 12.4 | 18.6 | 24.9 | 31 | 62 |
|---|---|---|---|---|---|---|---|
| km/kilomètres | 1 | 10 | 20 | 30 | 40 | 50 | 100 |

**Weight/Poids**

| pounds/livres | 2.2 | 22 | 44 | 66 | 88 | 110 | 220 |
|---|---|---|---|---|---|---|---|
| kg/kilogrammes | 1 | 10 | 20 | 30 | 40 | 50 | 100 |

**Capacity/Contenance**

| gallons/gallons | 0.22 | 2.2 | 4.4 | 6.6 | 8.8 | 11 | 22 |
|---|---|---|---|---|---|---|---|
| litres/litres | 1 | 10 | 20 | 30 | 40 | 50 | 100 |

**Temperature/Température**

| °C | 0 | 5 | 10 | 15 | 20 | 25 | 30 | 37 | 38 | 40 |
|---|---|---|---|---|---|---|---|---|---|---|
| °F | 32 | 41 | 50 | 59 | 68 | 77 | 86 | 98.4 | 100 | 104 |

**Clothing and shoe sizes/Tailles et pointures**

**Women's clothing sizes/Tailles femme**

| UK | 8 | 10 | 12 | 14 | 16 | 18 |
|---|---|---|---|---|---|---|
| US | 6 | 8 | 10 | 12 | 14 | 16 |
| Continent | 36 | 38 | 40 | 42 | 44 | 46 |

**Men's clothing sizes/Tailles homme**

| UK/US | 36 | 38 | 40 | 42 | 44 | 46 |
|---|---|---|---|---|---|---|
| Continent | 46 | 48 | 50 | 52 | 54 | 56 |

**Men's and women's shoes/Pointures homme et femme**

| UK women | 4 | 5 | 6 | 7 | 7.5 | 8 | | | |
|---|---|---|---|---|---|---|---|---|---|
| UK men | | | 6 | 7 | 8 | 9 | 10 | 11 | |
| US | 6.5 | 7.5 | 8.5 | 9.5 | 10.5 | 11.5 | 12.5 | 13.5 | 14.5 |
| Continent | 37 | 38 | 39 | 40 | 41 | 42 | 43 | 44 | 45 |

# Aa

**a** /eɪ, ə/ *determiner*

an avant voyelle ou h muet.

➡ For expressions such as make a noise, make a fortune ➡noise, fortune.

⋯▸ un/une. ~ tree un arbre; ~ chair une chaise.

⋯▸ (per) two euros ~ kilo deux euros le kilo; three times ~ day trois fois par jour.

❗ When talking about what people do or are, a is not translated into French: she's a teacher *elle est professeur*; he's a widower *il est veuf*.

**aback** /əˈbæk/ *adv* taken ~ déconcerté.

**abandon** /əˈbændən/ *vt* abandonner. ● *n* abandon *m*.

**abate** /əˈbeɪt/ *vi* (flood, fever) baisser; (storm) se calmer. ● *vt* diminuer.

**abbey** /ˈæbɪ/ *n* abbaye *f*.

**abbot** /ˈæbət/ *n* abbé *m*.

**abbreviate** /əˈbriːvɪeɪt/ *vt* abréger. **abbreviation** *n* abréviation *f*.

**abdicate** /ˈæbdɪkeɪt/ *vt/i* abdiquer.

**abdomen** /ˈæbdəmən/ *n* abdomen *m*.

**abduct** /əbˈdʌkt/ *vt* enlever. **abductor** *n* ravisseur/-euse *m/f*.

**abhor** /əbˈhɔː(r)/ *vt* (pt **abhorred**) exécrer.

**abide** /əˈbaɪd/ *vt* supporter; ~ by

respecter.

**ability** /əˈbɪlətɪ/ *n* capacité *f* (to do à faire); (talent) talent *m*.

**abject** /ˈæbdʒekt/ *adj* (state) misérable; (coward) abject.

**ablaze** /əˈbleɪz/ *adj* en feu.

**able** /ˈeɪbl/ *adj* (skilled) compétent; be ~ to do pouvoir faire; (know how to) savoir faire. **ably** *adv* avec compétence.

**abnormal** /æbˈnɔːml/ *adj* anormal. **abnormality** *n* anomalie *f*.

**aboard** /əˈbɔːd/ *adv* à bord. ● *prep* à bord de.

**abode** /əˈbəʊd/ *n* demeure *f*; of no fixed ~ sans domicile fixe.

**abolish** /əˈbɒlɪʃ/ *vt* abolir.

**Aborigine** /æbəˈrɪdʒənɪ/ *n* aborigène *m/f* (d'Australie).

**abort** /əˈbɔːt/ *vt* faire avorter; (Comput) abandonner. ● *vi* avorter.

**abortion** /əˈbɔːʃn/ *n* avortement *m*; have an ~ se faire avorter.

**abortive** /əˈbɔːtɪv/ *adj* (attempt) avorté; (coup) manqué.

**about** /əˈbaʊt/ *adv* (approximately) environ; ~ the same à peu près pareil; there was no-one ~ il n'y avait personne. ● *prep* it's ~ ... il s'agit de ...; what I like ~ her is ce que j'aime chez elle c'est; to wander ~ the streets errer dans les rues; how/what ~ some tea? et si on prenait un thé?; what ~ you? et toi? ● *adj* be ~ to do être sur le point de faire; up and ~ être debout. ~**-face**, ~**-turn** *n* (fig) volte-face *f inv*.

**above** /əˈbʌv/ *prep* au-dessus de;

**a**

he is not ~ lying il n'est pas incapable de mentir; ~ all surtout.
● adv the apartment ~ l'appartement du dessus; see ~ voir ci-dessus. ~-board adj honnête. ~-mentioned adj susmentionné.

**abrasive** /ə'breɪsɪv/ adj abrasif; (manner) mordant. ● n abrasif m.

**abreast** /ə'brest/ adv de front; keep ~ of se tenir au courant de.

**abroad** /ə'brɔːd/ adv à l'étranger.

**abrupt** /ə'brʌpt/ adj (sudden, curt) brusque; (steep) abrupt. **abruptly** adv (suddenly) brusquement; (curtly) avec brusquerie.

**abscess** /'æbses/ n abcès m.

**abseil** /'æbseɪl/ vi descendre en rappel.

**absence** /'æbsəns/ n absence f; (lack) manque m; in the ~ of faute de.

**absent** /'æbsənt/ adj absent.

**absentee** /æbsən'tiː/ n absent/-e m/f.

**absent-minded** adj distrait.

**absolute** /'æbsəluːt/ adj (monarch, majority) absolu; (chaos, idiot) véritable. **absolutely** adv absolument.

**absolve** /əb'zɒlv/ vt ~ sb of sth décharger qn de qch.

**absorb** /əb'zɔːb/ vt absorber.

**abstain** /əb'steɪn/ vi s'abstenir (from de).

**abstract¹** /'æbstrækt/ adj abstrait. ● n (summary) résumé m; in the ~ dans l'abstrait.

**abstract²** /əb'strækt/ vt tirer.

**absurd** /əb'sɜːd/ adj absurde.

**abundance** /ə'bʌndəns/ n abondance f. **abundant** adj abondant. **abundantly** adv (entirely) tout à fait.

**abuse¹** /ə'bjuːz/ vt (position) abuser de; (person) maltraiter; (insult)

injurier.

**abuse²** /ə'bjuːs/ n (misuse) abus m (of de); (cruelty) mauvais traitement m; (insults) injures fpl.

**abusive** /ə'bjuːsɪv/ adj (person) grossier; (language) injurieux.

**abysmal** /ə'bɪzml/ adj épouvantable.

**abyss** /ə'bɪs/ n abîme m.

**academic** /ækə'demɪk/ adj (career) universitaire; (year) académique; (scholarly) intellectuel; (theoretical) théorique. ● n universitaire mf.

**academy** /ə'kædəmɪ/ n (school) école f; (society) académie f.

**accelerate** /ək'seləreɪt/ vi (speed up) s'accélérer; (Auto) accélérer. **accelerator** n accélérateur m.

**accent¹** /'æksent/ n accent m.

**accent²** /æk'sent/ vt accentuer.

**accept** /ək'sept/ vt accepter. **acceptable** adj acceptable. **acceptance** n (of offer) acceptation f; (of proposal) approbation f.

**access** /'ækses/ n accès m. **accessible** adj accessible.

**accessory** /ək'sesərɪ/ adj accessoire. ● n (Jur) complice mf (to de).

**accident** /'æksɪdənt/ n accident m; (chance) hasard m; by ~ par hasard. **accidental** adj (death) accidentel; (meeting) fortuit. **accidentally** adv accidentellement; (by chance) par hasard.

**acclaim** /ə'kleɪm/ vt applaudir. ● n louanges fpl.

**acclimatize** /ə'klaɪmətaɪz/ vt/i (s')acclimater (to à).

**accommodate** /ə'kɒmədeɪt/ vt loger; (adapt to) s'adapter à; (satisfy) satisfaire. **accommodating** adj accommodant. **accommodation** n logement m.

**accompaniment** /ə'kʌmpənɪmənt/ n accompagnement

*m.* **accompany** *vt* accompagner.

**accomplice** /ə'kʌmplɪs/ *n* complice *mf* (in, to de).

**accomplish** /ə'kʌmplɪʃ/ *vt* accomplir; (*objective*) réaliser. **accomplished** *adj* très compétent. **accomplishment** *n* (feat) réussite *f*; (talent) talent *m*.

**accord** /ə'kɔːd/ *vi* concorder (with avec). ● *vt* accorder (sb sth qch à qn). ● *n* accord *m*; of my own ~ de moi-même.

**accordance** /ə'kɔːdəns/ *n* in ~ with conformément à.

**according** /ə'kɔːdɪŋ/ *adv* ~ to (*principle, law*) selon; (*person, book*) d'après. **accordingly** *adv* en conséquence.

**accordion** /ə'kɔːdɪən/ *n* accordéon *m*.

**accost** /ə'kɒst/ *vt* aborder.

**account** /ə'kaʊnt/ *n* (Comm) compte *m*; (description) compte-rendu *m*; on ~ of à cause de; on no ~ en aucun cas; take into ~ tenir compte de; it's of no ~ peu importe. □ ~ for (explain) expliquer; (represent) représenter. **accountability** *n* responsabilité *f*. **accountable** *adj* responsable (for de; to envers).

**accountancy** /ə'kaʊntənsɪ/ *n* comptabilité *f*. **accountant** *n* comptable *mf*. **accounts** *npl* comptabilité *f*, comptes *mpl*.

**accumulate** /ə'kjuːmjʊleɪt/ *vt/i* (s')accumuler.

**accuracy** /'ækjərəsɪ/ *n* (of figures) justesse *f*; (of aim) précision *f*; (of forecast) exactitude *f*. **accurate** *adj* juste, précis. **accurately** *adv* exactement, précisément.

**accusation** /ækjuː'zeɪʃn/ *n* accusation *f*.

**accuse** /ə'kjuːz/ *vt* accuser; the ~d

l'accusé/-e *m/f*.

**accustomed** /ə'kʌstəmd/ *adj* accoutumé; become ~ to s'accoutumer à.

**ace** /eɪs/ *n* (card, person) as *m*.

**ache** /eɪk/ *n* douleur *f*. ● *vi* (*person*) avoir mal; my leg ~s ma jambe me fait mal.

**achieve** /ə'tʃiːv/ *vt* (aim) atteindre; (result) obtenir; (ambition) réaliser. **achievement** *n* (feat) réussite *f*; (fulfilment) réalisation *f* (of de).

**acid** /'æsɪd/ *adj* & *n* acide (*m*). **acidity** *n* acidité *f*. ~ **rain** *n* pluies *fpl* acides.

**acknowledge** /ək'nɒlɪdʒ/ *vt* (error, authority) reconnaître. (letter) accuser réception de. **acknowledgement** *n* reconnaissance *f*.

**acne** /'æknɪ/ *n* acné *f*.

**acorn** /'eɪkɔːn/ *n* (Bot) gland *m*.

**acoustic** /ə'kuːstɪk/ *adj* acoustique. **acoustics** *npl* acoustique *f*.

**acquaint** /ə'kweɪnt/ *vt* ~ sb with sth mettre qn au courant de qch; be ~ed with (*person*) connaître. (*fact*) savoir. **acquaintance** *n* connaissance *f*.

**acquire** /ə'kwaɪə(r)/ *vt* acquérir; (habit) prendre.

**acquit** /ə'kwɪt/ *vt* (*pt* **acquitted**) (Jur) acquitter. **acquittal** *n* acquittement *m*.

**acre** /'eɪkə(r)/ *n* acre *f*, ≈ demi-hectare *m*.

**acrid** /'ækrɪd/ *adj* âcre.

**acrimonious** /ækrɪ'məʊnɪəs/ *adj* acrimonieux.

**acrobat** /'ækrəbæt/ *n* acrobate *mf*. **acrobatics** *npl* acrobaties *fpl*.

**acronym** /'ækrənɪm/ *n* acronyme *m*.

**across** /ə'krɒs/ *adv* & *prep* (side to side) d'un côté à l'autre (de); (on other side) de l'autre côté (from de); go or walk ~ traverser; lie ~ the bed se coucher en travers du lit; ~ the world partout dans le monde.

**act** /ækt/ n acte m; (Jur, Pol) loi f; (Theat) numéro m; put on an ~ jouer la comédie. ● vi agir; (Theat) jouer; ~ as servir de. ● vt (part, role) jouer.

**acting** /'æktɪŋ/ n (Theat) jeu m. ● adj (temporary) intérimaire.

**action** /'ækʃn/ n action f; (Mil) combat m; out of ~ hors service; take ~ agir.

**activate** /'æktɪveɪt/ vt (machine) faire démarrer; (alarm) déclencher.

**active** /'æktɪv/ adj actif; (volcano) en activité; take an ~ interest in s'intéresser activement à. **activist** n activiste mf. **activity** n activité f.

**actor** /'æktə(r)/ n acteur m. **actress** n actrice f.

**actual** /'æktʃʊəl/ adj réel; the ~ words les mots exacts; in the ~ house (the house itself) dans la maison elle-même. **actuality** n réalité f. **actually** adv (in fact) en fait; (really) vraiment.

**acute** /ə'kju:t/ adj (anxiety) vif; (illness) aigu; (shortage) grave; (mind) pénétrant.

**ad** /æd/ n (TV) pub 🇬🇧; small ~ petite annonce f.

**AD** abbr (Anno Domini) ap. J.-C.

**adamant** /'ædəmənt/ adj catégorique.

**adapt** /ə'dæpt/ vt/i (s')adapter (to à). **adaptability** n adaptabilité f. **adaptable** adj souple. **adaptation** n adaptation f. **adaptor** n (Electr) adaptateur m.

**add** /æd/ vt/i ajouter (to à); (in maths) additionner. □ ~ up (facts, figures) s'accorder; ~ sth up additionner qch; ~ up to s'élever à.

**adder** /'ædə(r)/ n vipère f.

**addict** /'ædɪkt/ n toxicomane mf; (fig) accro mf 🇬🇧.

**addicted** /ə'dɪktɪd/ adj be ~ avoir une dépendance f; (fig) être accro 🇬🇧 (to à). **addiction** n (Med) dépendance f (to à); passion f (for pour). **addictive** adj qui crée une dépendance.

**addition** /ə'dɪʃn/ n (item) ajout m; (in maths) addition f; in ~ en plus. **additional** adj supplémentaire.

**additive** /'ædɪtɪv/ n additif m.

**address** /ə'dres/ n adresse f; (speech) discours m. ● vt (letter) mettre l'adresse sur; (crowd) s'adresser à; ~ sth to adresser qch à. **addressee** n destinataire mf.

**adequate** /'ædɪkwət/ adj suffisant; (satisfactory) satisfaisant.

**adhere** /əd'hɪə(r)/ vi (lit, fig) adhérer (to à); ~ to (policy) observer.

**adjacent** /ə'dʒeɪsnt/ adj contigu; ~ to attenant à.

**adjective** /'ædʒɪktɪv/ n adjectif m.

**adjoin** /ə'dʒɔɪn/ vt être contigu à. **adjoining** adj (room) voisin.

**adjourn** /ə'dʒɜːn/ vt (trial) ajourner; the session was ~ed la séance a été levée. ● vi s'arrêter; (Parliament) lever la séance; ~ to passer à.

**adjust** /ə'dʒʌst/ vt (level, speed) régler; (price) ajuster; (clothes) rajuster. ● vt/i ~ (oneself) to s'adapter à. **adjustable** adj réglable. **adjustment** n (of rates) rajustement m; (of control) réglage m; (of person) adaptation f.

**ad lib** /æd 'lɪb/ vt/i (pt ad libbed) improviser.

**administer** /əd'mɪnɪstə(r)/ vt administrer.

**administration** /ədmɪnɪ'streɪʃn/ n administration f. **administrative** adj administratif. **administrator** n administrateur/-trice *m/f.*

**admiral** /ˈædmərəl/ *n* amiral *m.*

**admiration** /ædməˈreɪʃn/ *n* admiration *f.* **admire** *vt* admirer. **admirer** *n* admirateur/-trice *m/f.*

**admission** /ədˈmɪʃn/ *n* (to a place) entrée *f;* (confession) aveu *m.*

**admit** /ədˈmɪt/ *vt* (*pt* **admitted**) (acknowledge) reconnaître, admettre. (*crime*) avouer; (*new member*) admettre; ~ **to** reconnaître. **admittance** *n* entrée *f.* **admittedly** *adv* il est vrai.

**ado** /əˈduː/ *n* without more ~ sans plus de cérémonie.

**adolescence** /ædəˈlesns/ *n* adolescence *f.* **adolescent** *n* & *a* adolescent/-e *m/f.*

**adopt** /əˈdɒpt/ *vt* adopter. **adopted** *adj* (*child*) adoptif. **adoption** *n* adoption *f.* **adoptive** *adj* adoptif.

**adorable** /əˈdɔːrəbl/ *adj* adorable. **adoration** *n* adoration *f.* **adore** *vt* adorer.

**adorn** /əˈdɔːn/ *vt* orner.

**adrift** /əˈdrɪft/ *adj* & *adv* à la dérive.

**adult** /ˈædʌlt/ *adj* & *n* adulte (*mf*).

**adultery** /əˈdʌltərɪ/ *n* adultère *m.*

**adulthood** /ˈædʌlthʊd/ *n* âge *m* adulte.

**advance** /ədˈvɑːns/ *vt* (*sum*) avancer; (*tape, career*) faire avancer; (*interests*) servir. ● *vi* (*lit*) avancer; (*progress*) progresser. ● *n* avance *f;* (*progress*) progrès *m;* in ~ à l'avance. **advanced** *adj* avancé; (*studies*) supérieur.

**advantage** /ədˈvɑːntɪdʒ/ *n* avantage *m;* take ~ of profiter de; (*person*) exploiter. **advantageous** *adj* avantageux.

**adventure** /ədˈventʃə(r)/ *n* aventure *f.*

**adventurer** /ədˈventʃərə(r)/ *n* aventurier-ière *m/f.* **adventurous** *adj*

aventureux.

**adverb** /ˈædvɜːb/ *n* adverbe *m.*

**adverse** /ˈædvɜːs/ *adj* défavorable.

**advert** /ˈædvɜːt/ *n* annonce *f;* (TV) pub *f* 🎬.

**advertise** /ˈædvətaɪz/ *vt* faire de la publicité pour; (*car, house, job*) mettre une annonce pour. ● *vi* faire de la publicité; (*for staff*) passer une annonce. **advertisement** *n* publicité *f;* (in newspaper) annonce *f.* **advertiser** *n* annonceur *m.* **advertising** *n* publicité *f.*

**advice** /ədˈvaɪs/ *n* conseils *mpl;* some ~, a piece of ~ un conseil.

**advise** /ədˈvaɪz/ *vt* conseiller; (inform) aviser; ~ **against** déconseiller. **adviser** *n* conseiller/-ère *m/f.* **advisory** *adj* consultatif.

**advocate**[1] /ˈædvəkət/ *n* (Jur) avocat *m;* (supporter) partisan *m.*

**advocate**[2] /ˈædvəkeɪt/ *vt* recommander.

**aerial** /ˈeərɪəl/ *adj* aérien. ● *n* antenne *f.*

**aerobics** /eəˈrəʊbɪks/ *n* aérobic *m.*

**aeroplane** /ˈeərəpleɪn/ *n* avion *m.*

**aerosol** /ˈeərəsɒl/ *n* bombe *f* aérosol.

**aesthetic** /iːsˈθetɪk/ *adj* esthétique.

**afar** /əˈfɑː(r)/ *adv* from ~ de loin.

**affair** /əˈfeə(r)/ *n* (matter) affaire *f;* (romance) liaison *f.*

**affect** /əˈfekt/ *vt* affecter.

**affection** /əˈfekʃn/ *n* affection *f.* **affectionate** *adj* affectueux.

**affinity** /əˈfɪnətɪ/ *n* affinité *f.*

**afflict** /əˈflɪkt/ *vt* affliger.

**affluence** /ˈæfluəns/ *n* richesse *f.*

**afford** /əˈfɔːd/ *vt* avoir les moyens d'acheter; (provide) fournir; can you ~ the time? avez-vous le temps?

**afloat** /əˈfləʊt/ *adj* & *adv*

a

(boat) à flot.

**afoot** /əˈfʊt/ adv sth is ~ il se prépare qch.

**afraid** /əˈfreɪd/ adj be ~ (frightened) avoir peur (of, to de; that que); (worried) craindre (that que); I'm ~ I can't come je suis désolé mais je ne peux pas venir.

**Africa** /ˈæfrɪkə/ n Afrique f.

**African** /ˈæfrɪkən/ n Africain/-e m/f.
● adj africain.

**after** /ˈɑːftə(r)/ adv & prep après; ~ soon ~ peu après; be ~ sth rechercher qch; ~ all après tout.
● conj après que; ~ doing après avoir fait.

**aftermath** /ˈɑːftəmæθ/ n conséquences fpl (of de).

**afternoon** /ɑːftəˈnuːn/ n après-midi m or f inv; in the ~ (dans) l'après-midi.

**after:** ~ shave n après-rasage m. ~ thought n pensée f après coup.

**afterwards** /ˈɑːftəwədz/ adv après, par la suite.

**again** /əˈɡeɪn/ adv encore; ~ and ~ à plusieurs reprises; start ~ recommencer; she never saw him ~ elle ne l'a jamais revu.

**against** /əˈɡeɪnst/ prep contre; ~ the law illégal.

**age** /eɪdʒ/ n âge m; (era) ère f, époque f; I've been waiting for ~s j'attends depuis des heures. ● vt/i (pres p ageing) vieillir.

**aged**[1] /ˈeɪdʒd/ adj ~ six âgé de six ans.

**aged**[2] /ˈeɪdʒɪd/ adj âgé.

**ageism** /ˈeɪdʒɪzəm/ n discrimination f en raison de l'âge.

**agency** /ˈeɪdʒɪnsɪ/ n agence f.

**agenda** /əˈdʒendə/ n ordre m du jour; (fig) programme m.

**agent** /ˈeɪdʒənt/ n agent m.

**aggravate** /ˈæɡrəveɪt/ vt (make worse) aggraver; (annoy) exaspérer. **aggravation** n (worsening) aggravation f; (annoyance) ennuis mpl.

**aggression** /əˈɡreʃn/ n agression f. **aggressive** adj agressif. **aggressiveness** n agressivité f. **aggressor** n agresseur m.

**agitate** /ˈædʒɪteɪt/ vt agiter.

**ago** /əˈɡəʊ/ adv il y a; a month ~ il y a un mois; long ~ il y a longtemps; how long ~? il y a combien de temps?

**agonize** /ˈæɡənaɪz/ vi se tourmenter (over à propos de). **agonized** adj angoissé. **agonizing** adj déchirant. **agony** n douleur f atroce; (mental) angoisse f.

**agree** /əˈɡriː/ vi être d'accord (on sur; with avec); ~ to consentir à; ~ with (approve of) approuver.
● vt être d'accord (that sur le fait que); (admit) convenir (that que); (date, solution) se mettre d'accord sur.

**agreeable** /əˈɡriːəbl/ adj agréable; be ~ (willing) être d'accord.

**agreed** /əˈɡriːd/ adj (time, place) convenu; we're ~ nous sommes d'accord.

**agreement** /əˈɡriːmənt/ n accord m; in ~ d'accord.

**agricultural** /æɡrɪˈkʌltʃərəl/ adj agricole. **agriculture** n agriculture f.

**aground** /əˈɡraʊnd/ adv run ~ (ship) s'échouer.

**ahead** /əˈhed/ adv (in front) en avant, devant; (in advance) à l'avance; be 10 points ~ avoir 10 points d'avance; ~ of time en avance; go ~! allez-y!

**aid** /eɪd/ vt aider. ● n aide f; in ~ of au profit de.

**aide** /eɪd/ n aide mf.

**Aids** /eɪdz/ n (Med) sida m.

**aim** /eɪm/ vt (*gun*) braquer (at sur); be ~ ed at sb (*campaign, remark*) viser qn. ● vi ~ **for/at sth** viser qch; ~ **to do** avoir l'intention de faire. ● n but m; take ~ viser. **aimless** adj sans but.

**air** /eə(r)/ n air m; by ~ par avion; on the ~ à l'antenne. ● vt aérer; (*views*) exprimer. ● adj (*base, disaster*) aérien; (*pollution, pressure*) atmosphérique. ~ **bed** n matelas m pneumatique. ~ **conditioning** n climatisation f. ~**craft** n inv avion m. ~**craft carrier** n porteavions m inv. ~**field** n terrain m d'aviation. ~ **force** n armée f de l'air. ~ **freshener** n désodorisant m d'atmosphère. ~ **hostess** n hôtesse f de l'air. ~**lift** vt transporter par pont aérien. ~**line** n compagnie f aérienne. ~**liner** n avion m de ligne. ~**lock** n (in pipe) bulle f d'air; (*chamber*) sas m. ~**mail** n (by) ~**mail** par avion. ~**plane** n (US) avion m. ~**port** n aéroport m. ~ **raid** n attaque f aérienne. ~**tight** adj hermétique. ~ **traffic controller** n contrôleur/-euse m/f aérien/-ne. ~**waves** npl ondes fpl.

**airy** /ˈeərɪ/ adj (**-ier, -iest**) (*room*) clair et spacieux.

**aisle** /aɪl/ n (of church) allée f centrale; (in train) couloir m.

**ajar** /əˈdʒɑː(r)/ adv & adj entrouvert.

**akin** /əˈkɪn/ adj ~ **to** semblable à.

**alarm** /əˈlɑːm/ n alarme f; (clock) réveil m; (feeling) frayeur f. ● vt inquiéter. ~ **clock** n réveil m.

**alas** /əˈlæs/ interj hélas.

**Albania** /ælˈbeɪnɪə/ n Albanie f.

**album** /ˈælbəm/ n album m.

**alcohol** /ˈælkəhɒl/ n alcool m.

**alcoholic** /ælkəˈhɒlɪk/ adj alcoolique; (*drink*) alcoolisé. ● n alcoolique mf.

**ale** /eɪl/ n bière f.

**alert** /əˈlɜːt/ adj alerte; (watchful) vigilant. ● n alerte f; on the ~ sur le qui-vive. ● vt alerter; ~ **sb to** prévenir qn de. **alertness** n vivacité f; vigilance f.

**A-level** /ˈeɪlevl/ n ≈ baccalauréat m

**algebra** /ˈældʒɪbrə/ n algèbre f.

**Algeria** /ælˈdʒɪərɪə/ n Algérie f.

**alias** /ˈeɪlɪəs/ n (pl **-es**) faux nom m. ● prep alias.

**alibi** /ˈælɪbaɪ/ n alibi m.

**alien** /ˈeɪlɪən/ n & a étranger/-ère (m/f) (to à).

**alienate** /ˈeɪlɪəneɪt/ vt éloigner.

**alight** /əˈlaɪt/ adj en feu, allumé.

**alike** /əˈlaɪk/ adj semblable. ● adv de la même façon; look ~ se ressembler.

**alive** /əˈlaɪv/ adj vivant; ~ **to** conscient de; ~ **with** grouillant de.

---

**all** /ɔːl/

● *pronoun*

····▸ (everything) tout; **is that ~?** c'est tout?; **that was ~** (that) **he said** c'est tout ce qu'il a dit; **I ate it ~** j'ai tout mangé.

---

! Use the translation **tous** for a group of masculine or mixed gender people or objects and **toutes** for a group of feminine gender: **we were all delighted** nous étions tous ravis; '**where are the cups?**'—'**they're all in the kitchen**' 'où sont les tasses?'-'elles sont toutes dans la cuisine'.

---

● *determiner*

····▸ tout/toute/tous/toutes; ~

the time tout le temps; ~ his life toute sa vie; ~ of us nous tous; ~ (the) women toutes les femmes.

● **adverb**

····➤ (completely) tout; they were ~ alone ils étaient tout seuls; **tell me** ~ **about it** raconte-moi tout; ~ **for** tout à fait pour; **not** ~ **that** well pas si bien que ça; ~ **too** bien trop.

! When the adjective that follows is in the feminine and begins with a consonant, the translation is *toute/toutes*: she was all alone *elle était toute seule.*

**allege** /ə'ledʒ/ vt prétendre. ~**d** pp présumé; **allegedly** adv prétendument.

**allergic** /ə'lɜːdʒɪk/ adj allergique (to à). **allergy** n allergie f.

**alleviate** /ə'liːvɪeɪt/ vt alléger.

**alley** /'ælɪ/ n (street) ruelle f.

**alliance** /ə'laɪəns/ n alliance f.

**allied** /'ælaɪd/ adj allié.

**alligator** /'ælɪɡeɪtə(r)/ n alligator m.

**allocate** /'æləkeɪt/ vt (funds) affecter; (time) accorder; (task) assigner.

**allot** /ə'lɒt/ vt (pt allotted) (money) attribuer; (task) assigner. **allotment** n attribution f; (land) parcelle f de terre.

**all-out** /'ɔːlaʊt/ adj (effort) acharné; (strike) total.

**allow** /ə'laʊ/ vt (authorize) autoriser à; (let) laisser; (enable) permettre; (concede) accorder; ~ **for** tenir compte de.

**allowance** /ə'laʊəns/ n allocation f; **make** ~**s for sth** tenir compte de

qch; **make** ~**s for sb** essayer de comprendre qn.

**alloy** /'ælɔɪ/ n alliage m.

**all right** /ɔːl'raɪt/ adj (not bad) pas mal; **are you** ~? ça va?; **is it** ~ **if** ...? est-ce que ça va si ...? ● adv (see) (function) comme il faut. ● interj d'accord.

**ally**¹ /'ælaɪ/ n allié/-e m/f.

**ally**² /ə'laɪ/ vt allier; ~ **oneself with** s'allier avec.

**almighty** /ɔːl'maɪtɪ/ adj tout-puissant; (very great) formidable.

**almond** /'ɑːmənd/ n amande f. ~ **tree** n amandier m.

**almost** /'ɔːlməʊst/ adv presque; he ~ died il a failli mourir.

**alone** /ə'ləʊn/ adj & adv seul.

**along** /ə'lɒŋ/ prep le long de; walk ~ the beach marcher sur la plage. ● adv come ~ venir; walk ~ marcher; push/pull sth ~ pousser/tirer qch; all ~ (time) depuis le début; ~ with avec.

**alongside** /ə'lɒŋsaɪd/ adv à côté; come ~ (Naut) accoster. ● prep (next to) à côté de; (all along) le long de.

**aloof** /ə'luːf/ adj distant.

**aloud** /ə'laʊd/ adv à haute voix.

**alphabet** /'ælfəbet/ n alphabet m. **alphabetical** adj alphabétique.

**alpine** /'ælpaɪn/ adj (landscape) alpestre; (climate) alpin.

**already** /ɔːl'redɪ/ adv déjà.

**alright** /ɔːl'raɪt/ a & adv ➡ALL RIGHT.

**Alsatian** /æl'seɪʃn/ n (dog) berger m allemand.

**also** /'ɔːlsəʊ/ adv aussi.

**altar** /'ɔːltə(r)/ n autel m.

**alter** /'ɔːltə(r)/ vt/i changer; (building) transformer; (garment) retoucher. **alteration** n changement m;

(to building) transformation *f*; (to garment) retouche *f*.

**alternate**¹ /'ɔːltənət/ *vt/i* alterner.

**alternate**² /ɔːl'tɜːnət/ *adj* en alternance; **on** ~ **days** un jour sur deux. **alternately** *adv* alternativement.

**alternative** /ɔːl'tɜːnətɪv/ *adj* autre; (*solution*) de rechange. ● *n* (specified option) alternative *f*; (possible option) choix *m*. **alternatively** *adv* sinon.

**alternator** /'ɔːltəneɪtə(r)/ *n* alternateur *m*.

**although** /ɔːl'ðəʊ/ *conj* bien que.

**altitude** /'æltɪtjuːd/ *n* altitude *f*.

**altogether** /ɔːltə'geðə(r)/ *adv* (completely) tout à fait; (on the whole) tout compte fait.

**aluminium** /ælju'mɪnjəm/ *n* aluminium *m*.

**always** /'ɔːlweɪz/ *adv* toujours.

**am** /æm/ ➡BE.

**a.m.** /eɪem/ *adv* du matin.

**amalgamate** /ə'mælgəmeɪt/ *vt/i* (merge) fusionner; (*metals*) (s')amalgamer.

**amateur** /'æmətə(r)/ *n & adj* amateur (*m*).

**amaze** /ə'meɪz/ *vt* stupéfaire. **amazed** *adj* stupéfait. **amazement** *n* stupéfaction *f*. **amazing** *adj* stupéfiant; (great) exceptionnel.

**ambassador** /æm'bæsədə(r)/ *n* ambassadeur *m*.

**amber** /'æmbə(r)/ *n* ambre *m*; (Auto) orange *m*.

**ambiguity** /æmbɪ'gjuːətɪ/ *n* ambiguïté *f*.

**ambiguous** /æm'bɪgjʊəs/ *adj* ambigu.

**ambition** /æm'bɪʃn/ *n* ambition *f*. **ambitious** *adj* ambitieux.

**ambulance** /'æmbjʊləns/ *n* ambulance *f*.

**ambush** /'æmbʊʃ/ *n* embuscade *f*. ● *vt* tendre une embuscade à.

**amenable** /ə'miːnəbl/ *adj* obligeant; ~ **to** (responsive) sensible à.

**amend** /ə'mend/ *vt* modifier. **amendment** *n* (to rule) amendement *m*.

**amends** /ə'mendz/ *npl* **make** ~ réparer son erreur.

**amenities** /ə'miːnətɪz/ *npl* équipements *mpl*.

**America** /ə'merɪkə/ *n* Amérique *f*.

**American** /ə'merɪkən/ *n* Américain/-e *m/f*. ● *adj* américain.

**American dream** Cette expression désigne un principe américain selon lequel la réussite, en particulier financière et sociale, est accessible à quiconque travaille avec acharnement. Pour les immigrants, s'y ajoute le rêve de liberté et d'égalité.

**amiable** /'eɪmɪəbl/ *adj* aimable.

**amicable** /'æmɪkəbl/ *adj* amical.

**amid(st)** /ə'mɪd(st)/ *prep* au milieu de.

**amiss** /ə'mɪs/ *adj* there is something ~ il y a quelque chose qui ne va pas.

**ammonia** /ə'məʊnɪə/ *n* (gas) ammoniac *m*; (solution) ammoniaque *f*.

**ammunition** /æmjʊ'nɪʃn/ *n* munitions *fpl*.

**amnesty** /'æmnəstɪ/ *n* amnistie *f*.

**among(st)** /ə'mʌŋ(st)/ *prep* parmi; (affecting a group) chez; **be** ~ **the poorest** être un des plus pauvres; **be** ~ **the first** être dans les premiers.

**amorous** /'æmərəs/ *adj* amoureux.

**amount** /ə'maʊnt/ *n* quantité *f*; (total) montant *m*; (sum of money) somme f. ● vi ~ to (add up to) s'élever à; (be equivalent to) revenir à.

**amp** /æmp/ n ampère m.

**amphibian** /æmˈfɪbɪən/ n amphibie m.

**ample** /ˈæmpl/ adj (resources) largement suffisant; (proportions) généreux.

**amplifier** /ˈæmplɪfaɪə(r)/ n amplificateur m.

**amputate** /ˈæmpjʊteɪt/ vt amputer.

**amuse** /əˈmjuːz/ vt amuser.

**amusement** /əˈmjuːzmənt/ n (mirth) amusement m; (diversion) distraction f. ~ **arcade** n salle f de jeux.

**an** /æn, ən/ ▶A.

**anaemia** /əˈniːmɪə/ n anémie f.

**anaesthetic** /ænɪsˈθetɪk/ n anesthésique m.

**analyse** /ˈænəlaɪz/ vt analyser. **analysis** n (pl -yses) analyse f. **analyst** n analyste mf.

**anarchist** /ˈænəkɪst/ n anarchiste mf.

**anatomical** /ænəˈtɒmɪkl/ adj anatomique. **anatomy** n anatomie f.

**ancestor** /ˈænsestə(r)/ n ancêtre m.

**anchor** /ˈæŋkə(r)/ n ancre f. ● vt mettre à l'ancre. ● vi jeter l'ancre.

**anchovy** /ˈæntʃəvɪ/ n anchois m.

**ancient** /ˈeɪnʃənt/ adj ancien.

**ancillary** /ænˈsɪlərɪ/ adj auxiliaire.

**and** /ænd, ənd/ conj et; two hundred ~ sixty deux cent soixante; go ~ see him allez le voir; richer ~ richer de plus en plus riche.

**anew** /əˈnjuː/ adv (once more) encore, de nouveau; (in a new way) à nouveau.

**angel** /ˈeɪndʒl/ n ange m.

**anger** /ˈæŋɡə(r)/ n colère f. ● vt

mettre en colère, fâcher.

**angle** /ˈæŋgl/ n angle m. ● vi pêcher (à la ligne); ~ **for** (fig) quêter. **angler** n pêcheur/-euse mf.

**Anglo-Saxon** /æŋgləʊˈsæksn/ adj anglo-saxon. ● n Anglo-Saxon/-ne mf.

**angry** /ˈæŋgrɪ/ adj (-ier, -iest) fâché, en colère; **get** ~ se fâcher, se mettre en colère (with contre); **make sb** ~ mettre qn en colère.

**anguish** /ˈæŋgwɪʃ/ n angoisse f.

**animal** /ˈænɪml/ n & adj animal (m).

**animate¹** /ˈænɪmət/ adj (person) vivant; (object) animé.

**animate²** /ˈænɪmeɪt/ vt animer.

**aniseed** /ˈænɪsiːd/ n anis m.

**ankle** /ˈæŋkl/ n cheville f. ~ **sock** n socquette f.

**annex** /əˈneks/ vt annexer.

**anniversary** /ænɪˈvɜːsərɪ/ n anniversaire m.

**announce** /əˈnaʊns/ vt annoncer (that que). **announcement** n (spoken) annonce f; (written) avis m. **announcer** n (radio, TV) speaker/-ine mf.

**annoy** /əˈnɔɪ/ vt agacer, ennuyer. **annoyance** n contrariété f. **annoyed** adj fâché (with contre); **get** ~**ed** se fâcher. **annoying** adj ennuyeux.

**annual** /ˈænjʊəl/ adj annuel. ● n publication f annuelle. **annually** adv (earn, produce) par an; (do, inspect) tous les ans.

**annul** /əˈnʌl/ vt (pt **annulled**) annuler.

**anonymity** /ænəˈnɪmətɪ/ n anonymat m. **anonymous** adj anonyme.

**anorak** /ˈænəræk/ n anorak m.

**another** /əˈnʌðə(r)/ det & pron un/-e autre; ~ **coffee** (one more) encore un café; ~ **ten minutes** encore dix minutes, dix minutes de plus; **can I have** ~? est-ce que je peux en avoir un autre?

**answer** /ˈɑːnsə(r)/ n réponse f; (solution) solution f; (phone) **there's no** ~ ça ne répond pas. ● vt répondre à; (prayer) exaucer; ~ **the door** ouvrir la porte. ● vi répondre. □ ~ **back** répondre; ~ **for** répondre de; ~ **to** (superior) dépendre de; (description) répondre à. **answerable** adj responsable (for de; devant). **answering machine** n répondeur m.

**ant** /ænt/ n fourmi f.

**antagonism** /ænˈtæɡənɪzəm/ n antagonisme m. **antagonize** vt provoquer l'hostilité de.

**Antarctic** /ænˈtɑːktɪk/ n the ~ l'Antarctique m. ● adj antarctique.

**antenatal** /æntɪˈneɪtl/ adj prénatal.

**antenna** /ænˈtenə/ n (pl -ae) (of insect) antenne f; (pl -as; aerial: US) antenne f.

**anthem** /ˈænθəm/ n (Relig) motet m; (of country) hymne m national.

**anthrax** /ˈænθræks/ n charbon m.

**antibiotic** /æntɪbarˈɒtɪk/ n & adj antibiotique (m).

**antibody** /ˈæntɪbɒdɪ/ n anticorps m.

**anticipate** /ænˈtɪsɪpeɪt/ vt (foresee, expect) prévoir, s'attendre à.

**anticipation** /æntɪsɪˈpeɪʃn/ n attente f; **in** ~ **of** en prévision or attente de.

**anticlimax** /æntɪˈklaɪmæks/ n (let-down) déception f.

**anticlockwise** /æntɪˈklɒkwaɪz/ adv & adj dans le sens inverse des aiguilles d'une montre.

**antics** /ˈæntɪks/ npl pitreries fpl.

**antifreeze** /ˈæntɪfriːz/ n antigel m.

**antiquated** /ˈæntɪkweɪtɪd/ adj

(idea) archaïque; (building) vétuste.

**antique** /ænˈtiːk/ adj (old) ancien; (old-style) à l'ancienne. ● n objet m ancien, antiquité f. ~ **dealer** n antiquaire mf. ~ **shop** n magasin m d'antiquités.

**anti-Semitic** /æntɪsɪˈmɪtɪk/ adj antisémite.

**antiseptic** /æntɪˈseptɪk/ adj & n antiseptique (m).

**antisocial** /æntɪˈsəʊʃl/ adj asocial, antisocial; (reclusive) sauvage.

**antlers** /ˈæntləz/ npl bois mpl.

**anxiety** /æŋˈzaɪətɪ/ n (worry) anxiété f; (eagerness) impatience f.

**anxious** /ˈæŋkʃəs/ adj (troubled) anxieux; (eager) impatient (to de).

**any** /ˈenɪ/ det (some) du, de l', de la, des; (after negative) de, d'; (every) tout; (no matter which) n'importe quel; **at** ~ **moment** à tout moment; **have you** ~ **water?** avez-vous de l'eau? ● pron (no matter which one) n'importe lequel; (any amount of it or them) en; **I do not have** ~ je n'en ai pas; **did you see** ~ **of them?** en avez-vous vu? ● adv (a little) un peu; do you want ~ **more?** en avez-vous encore?; **do you have** ~ **more tea?** avez-vous encore du thé?; **I don't do it** ~ **more** je ne le fais plus.

**anybody** /ˈenɪbɒdɪ/ pron (no matter who) n'importe qui; (somebody) quelqu'un; (after negative) personne; **he did not see** ~ il n'a vu personne.

**anyhow** /ˈenɪhaʊ/ adv (anyway) de toute façon; (carelessly) n'importe comment.

**anyone** /ˈenɪwʌn/ pron ➡ANYBODY.

**anything** /ˈenɪθɪŋ/ pron (no matter what) n'importe quoi; (something) quelque chose; (after negative) rien;

he did not see ~ il n'a rien vu; ~ but nullement; ~ you do tout ce que tu fais.

**anyway** /'enɪweɪ/ adv de toute façon.

**anywhere** /'enɪweə(r)/ adv (no matter where) n'importe où; (somewhere) quelque part; (after negative) nulle part; he does not go ~ il ne va nulle part; ~ you go partout où tu vas, où que tu ailles; ~ else partout ailleurs.

**apart** /ə'pɑːt/ adv (on or to one side) à part; (separated) séparé; (into pieces) en pièces; ~ from à part, excepté; ten metres ~ à dix mètres l'un de l'autre; come ~ (break) tomber en morceaux; (machine) se démonter; legs ~ les jambes écartées; keep ~ séparer; take ~ démonter.

**apartment** /ə'pɑːtmənt/ n (US) appartement m.

**ape** /eɪp/ n singe m. ● vt singer.

**aperitif** /ə'perətɪf/ n apéritif m.

**apex** /'eɪpeks/ n sommet m.

**apologetic** /əpɒlə'dʒetɪk/ adj (tone) d'excuse; be ~ s'excuser. **apologetically** adv en s'excusant.

**apologize** /ə'pɒlədʒaɪz/ vi s'excuser (for de; to auprès de).

**apology** /ə'pɒlədʒɪ/ n excuses fpl.

**apostrophe** /ə'pɒstrəfɪ/ n apostrophe f.

**appal** /ə'pɔːl/ vt (pt appalled) horrifier. **appalling** adj épouvantable.

**apparatus** /æpə'reɪtəs/ n appareil m.

**apparent** /ə'pærənt/ adj apparent. **apparently** adv apparemment.

**appeal** /ə'piːl/ n appel m; (attractiveness) attrait m, charme m. ● vi (Jur) faire appel; ~ to sb (beg) faire appel à qn; (attract) plaire à qn; ~ to sb for sth demander qch à qn.

**appealing** adj (attractive) attirant.

**appear** /ə'pɪə(r)/ vi apparaître. (arrive) se présenter; (seem, be published) paraître. (Theat) jouer; ~ on TV passer à la télé. **appearance** n apparition f; (aspect) apparence f.

**appease** /ə'piːz/ vt apaiser.

**appendix** /ə'pendɪks/ n (pl -ices) appendice m.

**appetite** /'æpɪtaɪt/ n appétit m.

**appetizer** /'æpɪtaɪzə(r)/ n (snack) amuse-gueule m inv; (drink) apéritif m.

**appetizing** /'æpɪtaɪzɪŋ/ adj appétissant.

**applaud** /ə'plɔːd/ vt/i applaudir; (decision) applaudir à. **applause** n applaudissements mpl.

**apple** /'æpl/ n pomme f; ~-tree n pommier m.

**appliance** /ə'plaɪəns/ n appareil m.

**applicable** /'æplɪkəbl/ adj valable; if ~ le cas échéant.

**applicant** /'æplɪkənt/ n candidat/-e m/f (for à).

**application** /æplɪ'keɪʃn/ n application f; (request, form) demande f; (for job) candidature f.

**apply** /ə'plaɪ/ vt appliquer. ● vi ~ to (refer) s'appliquer à; (ask) s'adresser à; ~ for (job) postuler pour; (grant) demander; ~ oneself to s'appliquer à.

**appoint** /ə'pɔɪnt/ vt (to post) nommer; (fix) désigner; well-~ed bien équipé.

**appointment** /ə'pɔɪntmənt/ n nomination f; (meeting) rendez-vous m inv; (job) poste m; make an ~ prendre rendez-vous (with avec).

**appraisal** /ə'preɪzl/ n évaluation f. **appraise** vt évaluer.

**appreciate** /ə'priːʃɪeɪt/ vt (like) apprécier; (understand) comprendre; (be grateful for) être reconnaissant de. ● *vi* prendre de la valeur.

**appreciation** *n* appréciation *f*; (gratitude) reconnaissance *f*; (rise) augmentation *f*. **appreciative** *adj* reconnaissant; (audience) enthousiaste.

**apprehend** /æprɪ'hend/ *vt* (arrest) appréhender; (understand) comprendre. **apprehension** *n* (arrest) appréhension *f*; (fear) crainte *f*.

**apprehensive** /æprɪ'hensɪv/ *adj* inquiet; be ~ of craindre.

**apprentice** /ə'prentɪs/ *n* apprenti *m*. ● *vt* mettre en apprentissage.

**approach** /ə'prəʊtʃ/ *vt* (s')approcher de; (accost) aborder; (with request) s'adresser à. ● *vi* (s')approcher. ● *n* approche *f*; an ~ to (problem) une façon d'aborder; (person) une démarche auprès de. **approachable** *adj* abordable.

**appropriate**[1] /ə'prəʊprɪeɪt/ *vt* s'approprier.

**appropriate**[2] /ə'prəʊprɪət/ *adj* approprié, propre. **appropriately** *adv* à propos.

**approval** /ə'pruːvl/ *n* approbation *f*; on ~ à ou sous condition.

**approve** /ə'pruːv/ *vt* approuver. ● *vi* ~ of approuver. **approving** *adj* approbateur.

**approximate**[1] /ə'prɒksɪmeɪt/ *vi* ~ to se rapprocher de.

**approximate**[2] /ə'prɒksɪmət/ *adj* approximatif. **approximately** *adv* environ. **approximation** *n* approximation *f*.

**apricot** /'eɪprɪkɒt/ *n* abricot *m*.

**April** /'eɪprɪl/ *n* avril *m*. ~ **Fools Day** *n* le premier avril.

**apron** /'eɪprən/ *n* tablier *m*.

**apt** /æpt/ *adj* (suitable) approprié; be ~ to avoir tendance à.

**aptitude** /'æptɪtjuːd/ *n* aptitude *f*.

**aptly** /'æptlɪ/ *adv* à propos.

**Aquarius** /ə'kweərɪəs/ *n* Verseau *m*.

**aquatic** /ə'kwætɪk/ *adj* aquatique; (Sport) nautique.

**Arab** /'ærəb/ *n* Arabe *mf*. ● *adj* arabe.

**Arabian** /ə'reɪbɪən/ *adj* d'Arabie.

**Arabic** /'ærəbɪk/ *adj* & *n* (Ling) arabe (*m*).

**arbitrary** /'ɑːbɪtrərɪ/ *adj* arbitraire.

**arbitrate** /'ɑːbɪtreɪt/ *vi* arbitrer. **arbitration** *n* arbitrage *m*. **arbitrator** *n* médiateur/-trice *m/f*.

**arcade** /ɑː'keɪd/ *n* (shops) galerie *f*; (arches) arcades *fpl*.

**arch** /ɑːtʃ/ *n* arche *f*; (of foot) voûte *f* plantaire. ● *vt/i* (s')arquer. ● *adj* (playful) malicieux.

**archaeological** /ɑːkɪə'lɒdʒɪkl/ *adj* archéologique. **archaeologist** *n* archéologue *mf*. **archaeology** *n* archéologie *f*.

**archbishop** /ɑːtʃ'bɪʃəp/ *n* archevêque *m*.

**archery** /'ɑːtʃərɪ/ *n* tir à l'arc.

**architect** /'ɑːkɪtekt/ *n* architecte *mf*; (of plan) artisan *m*. **architectural** *adj* architectural. **architecture** *n* architecture *f*.

**archives** /'ɑːkaɪvz/ *npl* archives *fpl*.

**archway** /'ɑːtʃweɪ/ *n* voûte *f*.

**Arctic** /'ɑːktɪk/ *n* the ~ l'Arctique *m*. ● *adj* (climate) arctique; (expedition) polaire; (conditions) glacial.

**ardent** /'ɑːdnt/ *adj* ardent.

**are** /ɑː(r)/ ⇒BE.

**area** /'eərɪə/ *n* (region) région *f*; (district) quartier *m*; (fig) domaine *m*; (in geometry) aire *f*; parking/picnic ~ aire *f* de parking/de pique-nique.

**arena** /ə'riːnə/ *n* arène *f*.

**aren't** /ɑː(r)nt/ ⇒ARE NOT.

**Argentina** /ɑːdʒən'tiːnə/ *n*

Argentine f.

**arguable** /ˈɑːɡjʊəbl/ adj discutable. **arguably** adv selon certains.

**argue** /ˈɑːɡjuː/ vi (quarrel) se disputer; (reason) argumenter. ● vt (debate) discuter; ~ that alléguer que.

**argument** /ˈɑːɡjʊmənt/ n (dispute) f; (reasoning) argument m; (discussion) débat m. **argumentative** adj ergoteur.

**Aries** /ˈeəriːz/ n Bélier m.

**arise** /əˈraɪz/ vi (pt arose; pp arisen) (problem) survenir; (question) se poser; ~ from résulter de.

**aristocrat** /ˈærɪstəkræt/ n aristocrate mf.

**arithmetic** /əˈrɪθmətɪk/ n arithmétique f.

**ark** /ɑːk/ n (Relig) arche f.

**arm** /ɑːm/ n bras m; ~ in arm bras dessus bras dessous. ● vt armer; ~ed robbery vol m à main armée.

**armament** /ˈɑːməmənt/ n armement m.

**arm:** /ɑːm/ ~**band** n brassard m. ~**chair** n fauteuil m.

**armour** /ˈɑːmə(r)/ n armure f. **armoured** adj blindé. **armoury** n arsenal m.

**armpit** /ˈɑːmpɪt/ n aisselle f.

**arms** /ɑːmz/ npl (weapons) armes fpl. ~ **dealer** n trafiquant m d'armes.

**army** /ˈɑːmi/ n armée f.

**aroma** /əˈrəʊmə/ n arôme m. **aromatic** adj aromatique.

**arose** /əˈrəʊz/ ➡ARISE.

**around** /əˈraʊnd/ adv (tout) autour; (here and there) çà et là. ● prep autour de; ~ here par ici.

**arouse** /əˈraʊz/ vt (awaken, cause) éveiller; (excite) exciter.

**arrange** /əˈreɪndʒ/ vt arranger; (time, date) fixer; ~ to

s'arranger pour.

**arrangement** /əˈreɪndʒmənt/ n arrangement m; (agreement) entente f; make ~s prendre des dispositions.

**array** /əˈreɪ/ n an ~ of (display) un étalage impressionnant de.

**arrears** /əˈrɪəz/ npl arriéré m; in ~ (rent) arriéré; he is in ~ il a des retards dans ses paiements.

**arrest** /əˈrest/ vt arrêter; (attention) retenir. ● n arrestation f; under ~ en état d'arrestation.

**arrival** /əˈraɪvl/ n arrivée f; new ~ nouveau venu m, nouvelle venue f.

**arrive** /əˈraɪv/ vi arriver; ~ at (destination) arriver à; (decision) parvenir à.

**arrogance** /ˈærəɡəns/ n arrogance f.

**arrow** /ˈærəʊ/ n flèche f.

**arse** /ɑːs/ n ⊠ cul m ⊠.

**arson** /ˈɑːsn/ n incendie m criminel. **arsonist** n incendiaire mf.

**art** /ɑːt/ n art m; (fine arts) beaux-arts mpl.

**artery** /ˈɑːtəri/ n artère f.

**art gallery** n (public) musée m (d'art); (private) galerie f (d'art).

**arthritis** /ɑːˈθraɪtɪs/ n arthrite f.

**artichoke** /ˈɑːtɪtʃəʊk/ n artichaut m.

**article** /ˈɑːtɪkl/ n article m; ~ of clothing vêtement m.

**articulate** /ɑːˈtɪkjʊlət/ adj (person) capable de s'exprimer clairement; (speech) distinct.

**articulated lorry** n semiremorque m.

**artificial** /ɑːtɪˈfɪʃl/ adj artificiel.

**artist** /ˈɑːtɪst/ n artiste mf.

**arts** /ɑːts/ npl the ~ les arts mpl; (Univ) lettres fpl.

**artwork** /ˈɑːtwɜːk/ n (of book)

**as** /æz/, /əz/ *conj* comme; (while) pendant que; (over gradual period of time) au fur et à mesure que; ~ **she grew older** au fur et à mesure qu'elle vieillissait; **do ~ I say** fais ce que je dis; ~ **usual** comme d'habitude. ● *prep* ~ **a mother** en tant que mère; **a gift** en cadeau; ~ **from Monday** à partir de lundi; ~ **for**, ~ **to** quant à; ~ **if** comme si; **you look** ~ **if you're tired** vous avez l'air (d'être) fatigué. ● *adv* ~ **tall** aussi grand que; ~ **much** ~, ~ **many** autant que; ~ **soon** ~ aussitôt que; ~ **well** ~ aussi bien que; ~ **wide** ~ **possible** aussi large que possible.

**asbestos** /æz'bestɒs/ *n* amiante *f*.

**ascend** /ə'send/ *vt* gravir. ● *vi* monter.

**ascertain** /æsə'teɪn/ *vt* établir (that).

**ash** /æʃ/ *n* cendre *f*; ~(**-tree**) frêne *m*.

**ashamed** /ə'ʃeɪmd/ *adj* **be** ~ avoir honte (of de).

**ashore** /ə'ʃɔː(r)/ *adv* à terre.

**ashtray** /'æʃtreɪ/ *n* cendrier *m*.

**Asia** /'eɪʃə/ *n* Asie *f*.

**Asian** /'eɪʃn/ *n* Asiatique *mf*. ● *adj* asiatique.

**aside** /ə'saɪd/ *adv* de côté; ~ **from** à part. ● *n* aparté *m*.

**ask** /ɑːsk/ *vt/i* demander; (a question) poser; (invite) inviter; ~ **sb sth** demander qch à qn; ~ **sb to do** demander à qn de faire; ~ **about** (thing) se renseigner sur; (person) demander des nouvelles de; ~ **for** demander.

**asleep** /ə'sliːp/ *adj* endormi; (numb) engourdi. ● *adv* **fall** ~ s'endormir.

**asparagus** /ə'spærəgəs/ *n*(plant)

asperge *f*; ( Culin) asperges *fpl*.

**aspect** /'æspekt/ *n* aspect *m*; (direction) orientation *f*.

**asphyxiate** /əs'fɪksɪeɪt/ *vt/i* (s')asphyxier.

**aspire** /ə'spaɪə(r)/ *vi* aspirer (**to** à; **to do** à faire).

**aspirin** /'æspərɪn/ *n* aspirine® *f*.

**ass** /æs/ *n* âne *m*; (person 🄵) idiot/-e *mf*.

**assail** /ə'seɪl/ *vt* attaquer. **assailant** *n* agresseur *m*.

**assassin** /ə'sæsɪn/ *n* assassin *m*. **assassinate** *vt* assassiner. **assassination** *n* assassinat *m*.

**assault** /ə'sɔːlt/ *n* (Mil) assaut *m*; (Jur) agression *f*. ● *vt* (person: Jur) agresser.

**assemble** /ə'sembl/ *vt*(construct) assembler; ( gather) rassembler. ● *vi* se rassembler.

**assembly** /ə'semblɪ/ *n* assemblée *f*. ~ **line** *n* chaîne *f* de montage.

**assent** /ə'sent/ *n* assentiment *m*. ● *vi* consentir.

**assert** /ə'sɜːt/ *vt* affirmer; (rights) revendiquer. **assertion** *n* affirmation *f*. **assertive** *adj* assuré.

**assess** /ə'ses/ *vt* évaluer; ( payment) déterminer le montant de. **assessment** *n* évaluation *f*. **assessor** *n* (valuer) expert *m*.

**asset** /'æset/ *n* (advantage) atout *m*; (financial) bien *m*; ~ **s** (Comm) actif *m*.

**assign** /ə'saɪn/ *vt* (allot) assigner; ~ **sb to** (appoint) affecter qn à qn.

**assignment** /ə'saɪnmənt/ *n* (task) mission *f*; (diplomatic) poste *m*; (academic) devoir *m*.

**assist** /ə'sɪst/ *vt/i* aider. **assistance** *n* aide *f*.

**assistant** /ə'sɪstənt/ *n* aide *mf*; (in shop) vendeur/-euse *m/f*. ● *adj* (manager) adjoint.

**a**

**associate**[1] /əˈsəʊʃɪət/ n & adj associé/-e (m/f).

**associate**[2] /əˈsəʊʃɪeɪt/ vt associer. ● vi ~ with fréquenter. **association** n association f.

**assorted** /əˈsɔːtɪd/ adj divers; (foods) assorti.

**assortment** /əˈsɔːtmənt/ n assortiment m; (of people) mélange m.

**assume** /əˈsjuːm/ vt supposer; (power, attitude) prendre; (role, burden) assumer.

**assurance** /əˈʃɔːrəns/ n assurance f.

**assure** /əˈʃɔː(r)/ vt assurer.

**asterisk** /ˈæstərɪsk/ n astérisque m.

**asthma** /ˈæsmə/ n asthme m.

**astonish** /əˈstɒnɪʃ/ vt étonner.

**astound** /əˈstaʊnd/ vt stupéfier.

**astray** /əˈstreɪ/ adv go ~ s'égarer; lead ~ égarer.

**astride** /əˈstraɪd/ adv & prep à califourchon (sur).

**astrologer** /əˈstrɒlədʒə(r)/ n astrologue m. **astrology** n astrologie f.

**astronaut** /ˈæstrənɔːt/ n astronaute mf.

**astronomer** /əˈstrɒnəmə(r)/ n astronome m.

**asylum** /əˈsaɪləm/ n asile m.

**at** /æt, ət/
● preposition

➡ For expressions such as laugh at, look at ➡laugh, look.

····▸ (in position or place) à; he's ~ his desk il est à son bureau; she's ~ work/school elle est au travail/à l'école.

····▸ (at someone's house or business) chez; ~Mary's/the dentist's chez Mary/le dentiste.

····▸ (in times, ages) à; ~ four o'clock à quatre heures; ~ two years of age à l'âge de deux ans.

····▸ (in email addresses) arobase f

**ate** &/eɪt/ ➡EAT.

**atheist** /ˈeɪθɪɪst/ n athée mf.

**athlete** /ˈæθliːt/ n athlète mf. **athletic** adj athlétique. **athletics** npl athlétisme m; (US) sports mpl.

**Atlantic** /ətˈlæntɪk/ adj atlantique. ● n the ~ (Ocean) l'Atlantique m.

**atlas** /ˈætləs/ n atlas m.

**atmosphere** /ˈætməsfɪə(r)/ n (air) atmosphère f; (mood) ambiance f. **atmospheric** adj atmosphérique; d'ambiance.

**atom** /ˈætəm/ n atome m.

**atrocious** /əˈtrəʊʃəs/ adj atroce.

**atrocity** /əˈtrɒsɪtɪ/ n atrocité f.

**attach** /əˈtætʃ/ vt/i (s')attacher; (letter) joindre (to à).

**attaché** /əˈtæʃeɪ/ n (Pol) attaché/-e m/f. ~ **case** n attaché-case m.

**attached** /əˈtætʃt/ adj be ~ to (like) être attaché à; the ~ letter la lettre ci-jointe.

**attachment** /əˈtætʃmənt/ n (accessory) accessoire m; (affection) attachement m; (e-mail) pièces fpl jointes.

**attack** /əˈtæk/ n attaque f; (Med) crise f. ● vt attaquer.

**attain** /əˈteɪn/ vt atteindre (à); (gain) acquérir.

**attempt** /əˈtempt/ vt tenter. ● n tentative f; an ~ on sb's life un attentat contre qn.

**attend** /əˈtend/ vt assister à; (class) suivre; (school, church) aller à. ●vi assister; ~ (to) (look after) s'occuper de. **attendance** n présence f; (people) assistance f.

**attendant** /əˈtendənt/ n employé/-e m/f. ●adj associé.

**attention** /əˈtenʃn/ n attention f; ~! (Mil) garde-à-vous! pay ~ faire or prêter attention (to à).

**attentive** /əˈtentɪv/ adj attentif; (considerate) attentionné. **attentively** adv attentivement. **attentiveness** n attention f.

**attest** /əˈtest/ vt/i ~ (to) attester.

**attic** /ˈætɪk/ n grenier m.

**attitude** /ˈætɪtjuːd/ n attitude f.

**attorney** /əˈtɜːnɪ/ n (US) avocat/-e m/f.

**attract** /əˈtrækt/ vt attirer. **attraction** n attraction f; (charm) attrait m.

**attractive** /əˈtræktɪv/ adj attrayant, séduisant. **attractively** adv agréablement. **attractiveness** n trait m, beauté f.

**attribute**[1] /əˈtrɪbjuːt/ vt ~ to attribuer à.

**attribute**[2] /ˈætrɪbjuːt/ n attribut m.

**aubergine** /ˈəʊbəʒiːn/ n aubergine f.

**auction** /ˈɔːkʃn/ n vente f aux enchères. ●vt vendre aux enchères. **auctioneer** n commissaire priseur m.

**audacious** /ɔːˈdeɪʃəs/ adj audacieux.

**audience** /ˈɔːdɪəns/ n (theatre, radio) public m; (interview) audience f.

**audiovisual** /ɔːdɪəʊˈvɪʒʊəl/ adj audiovisuel.

**audit** /ˈɔːdɪt/ n vérification f des comptes. ●vt vérifier.

**audition** /ɔːˈdɪʃn/ n audition f. ●vt/i auditionner (for pour).

**auditor** /ˈɔːdɪtə(r)/ n commissaire m aux comptes.

**August** /ˈɔːɡəst/ n août m.

**aunt** /ɑːnt/ n tante f.

**auspicious** /ɔːˈspɪʃəs/ adj favorable.

**Australia** /ɒˈstreɪlɪə/ n Australie f.

**Australian** /ɒˈstreɪlɪən/ n Australien/-ne m/f. ●adj australien.

**Austria** /ˈɒstrɪə/ n Autriche f.

**Austrian** /ˈɒstrɪən/ n Autrichien/-ne m/f. ●adj autrichien.

**authentic** /ɔːˈθentɪk/ adj authentique.

**author** /ˈɔːθə(r)/ n auteur m.

**authoritarian** /ɔːˌθɒrɪˈteərɪən/ adj autoritaire.

**authoritative** /ɔːˈθɒrətətɪv/ adj (credible) qui fait autorité; (manner) autoritaire.

**authority** /ɔːˈθɒrɪtɪ/ n autorité f; (permission) autorisation f.

**authorization** /ɔːθəraɪˈzeɪʃn/ n autorisation f. **authorize** vt autoriser.

**autistic** /ɔːˈtɪstɪk/ adj (person) autiste; (response) autistique.

**autograph** /ˈɔːtəɡrɑːf/ n autographe m. ●vt signer, dédicacer.

**automate** /ˈɔːtəmeɪt/ vt automatiser.

**automatic** /ɔːtəˈmætɪk/ adj automatique. ●n (Auto) voiture f automatique.

**automobile** /ˈɔːtəməbiːl/ n (US) auto(mobile) f.

**autonomous** /ɔːˈtɒnəməs/ adj autonome.

**autumn** /ˈɔːtəm/ n automne m.

**auxiliary** /ɔːɡˈzɪlɪərɪ/ adj & n auxiliaire (mf); ~ (verb) auxiliaire m.

**avail** /əˈveɪl/ vt ~ oneself of profiter de. ●n of no ~ inutile; to no ~ sans résultat.

**availability** /əveɪləˈbɪlətɪ/ n dis-

**a**
**b**

ponibilité f. **available** adj disponible.

**avenge** /ə'vendʒ/ vt venger; ~ oneself se venger (**on** de).

**avenue** /'ævənjuː/ n avenue f; (line of approach:fig) voie f.

**average** /'ævərɪdʒ/ n moyenne f; **on** ~ en moyenne. ● adj moyen. ● vt faire la moyenne de; (produce, do) faire en moyenne.

**aviary** /'eɪvɪərɪ/ n volière f.

**avocado** /ævə'kɑːdəʊ/ n avocat m.

**avoid** /ə'vɔɪd/ vt éviter. **avoidance** n (of injuries) prévention f; (of responsibility) refus m.

**await** /ə'weɪt/ vt attendre.

**awake** /ə'weɪk/ vt/i (pt awoke; pp awoken) (s')éveiller. ● adj be ~ ne pas dormir, être (r)éveillé.

**award** /ə'wɔːd/ vt (grant) attribuer; (prize) décerner; (points) accorder. ● n récompense f,prix m; (scholarship) bourse f; **pay** ~ augmentation f (de salaire).

**aware** /ə'weə(r)/ adj (well-informed) averti; **be** ~ **of** (danger) être conscient de; (fact) savoir; **become** ~ **of** prendre conscience de. **awareness** n conscience f.

**away** /ə'weɪ/ adv (far) au loin; (absent) absent, parti; ~ **from** loin de; **move** ~ s'écarter; (to new home) déménager; **six kilometres** ~ à six kilomètres (de distance); **take** ~ emporter; **he was snoring** ~ il ronflait. ● adj & n ~ (match) match m à l'extérieur.

**awe** /ɔː/ n crainte f (révérencielle).

**awe-inspiring** /'ɔːɪnspaɪərɪŋ/ adj impressionnant.

**awesome** /'ɔːsəm/ adj redoutable.

**awful** /'ɔːfl/ adj affreux. **awfully** adv (badly) affreusement; (very 🔲) rudement.

**awkward** /'ɔːkwəd/ adj difficile; (inconvenient) inopportun; (clumsy)

maladroit; (embarrassing) gênant; (embarrassed) gêné. **awkwardly** adv maladroitement; avec gêne. **awkwardness** n maladresse f; (discomfort) gêne f.

**awning** /'ɔːnɪŋ/ n auvent m; (of shop) store m.

**awoke, awoken** ➡AWAKE.

**axe** /æks/ n hache f. ● vt (pres p axing) réduire; (eliminate) supprimer; (employee) renvoyer.

**axis** /'æksɪs/ n (pl axes) axe m.

**axle** /'æksl/ n essieu m.

# Bb

**BA** abbr ➡BACHELOR OF ARTS.

**babble** /'bæbl/ vi babiller; (stream) gazouiller. ● n babillage m.

**baby** /'beɪbɪ/ n bébé m. ~ **carriage** n (US) voiture f d'enfant. ~**-sit** vi faire du babysitting, garder des enfants. ~**-sitter** n baby-sitter mf.

**bachelor** /'bætʃələ(r)/ n célibataire m. **B**~ **of Arts** licencié/-e m/f ès lettres.

**back** /bæk/ n (of person, hand, page, etc.) dos m; (of house) derrière m; (of vehicle) arrière m; (of room) fond m; (of chair) dossier m; (in football) arrière m; **at the** ~ **of the book** à la fin du livre; **in** ~ **of** (US) derrière. ● adj (leg, wheel) arrière inv; (door, gate) de derrière; (taxes) arriéré. ● adv en arrière; (returned) de retour, rentré; **come** ~ revenir; **give** ~ rendre; **take** ~ reprendre; **I want it** ~ je veux le récupérer. ● vt (support) appuyer; (bet on) miser sur; (vehicle) faire reculer. ● vi (of person, vehicle) reculer. ~ **down** céder; ~**out** se désister; (Auto) sortir en marche arrière; ~ **up** (support) appuyer. ~**ache** n mal m de dos. ~**bencher** n (Pol) député m de base. ~**bone** n colonne f vertébrale. ~**date** vt antidater. ~**fire** vi (Auto) pétarader; (fig) mal tourner. ~**gammon** n trictrac m.

**background** /ˈbækgraʊnd/ n fond m, arrière-plan m; (context) contexte m; (environment) milieu m; (experience) formation f. ● adj (music, noise) de fond.

**backhand** /ˈbækhænd/ n revers m. **backhander** n (bribe) pot-de-vin m.

**backing** /ˈbækɪŋ/ n soutien m.

**back:** ~**lash** n retour m de bâton; réaction f violente (**against** contre). ~**log** n retard m. ~**number** n vieux numéro m. ~**pack** n sac m à dos. ~**side** n (buttocks ⓣ) derrière m. ~**stage** adj & adv dans les coulisses. ~**stroke** n dos m crawlé. ~**track** vi rebrousser chemin; (change one's opinion) faire marche arrière.

**backup** /ˈbækʌp/ n soutien m; (Comput) sauvegarde f. ● adj de secours; (Comput) de sauvegarde.

**backward** /ˈbækwəd/ adj (step etc.) en arrière; (retarded) arriéré.

**backwards** /ˈbækwəd/ adv en arrière; (walk) à reculons; (read) à l'envers; go ~ and forwards aller et venir.

**bacon** /ˈbeɪkən/ n lard m; (in rashers) bacon m.

**bacteria** /bækˈtɪərɪə/ npl bactéries fpl.

**bad** /bæd/ adj (worse, worst) mauvais; (wicked) méchant; (ill) malade; (accident) grave; (food) gâté; feel ~ se sentir mal; go ~ se gâter. ~ **language** gros mots mpl; too ~! tant pis!; (I'm sorry) dommage!

**badge** /bædʒ/ n badge m; (coat of arms) insigne m.

**badger** /ˈbædʒə(r)/ n blaireau m. ● vt harceler.

**badly** /ˈbædlɪ/ adv mal; (hurt) gravement; want ~ avoir grande envie de.

**badminton** /ˈbædmɪntn/ n badminton m.

**bad-tempered** adj irritable.

**baffle** /ˈbæfl/ vt déconcerter.

**bag** /bæg/ n sac m; ~ **s** (luggage) bagages mpl; (under eyes ⓣ) valises fpl; ~**s of** plein de.

**baggage** /ˈbægɪdʒ/ n bagages mpl; ~ **reclaim** réception f des bagages.

**baggy** /ˈbægɪ/ adj large.

**bagpipes** /ˈbægpaɪps/ npl cornemuse f

**bail** /beɪl/ n caution f; on ~ sous caution; (cricket) bâtonnet m. ● vt mettre en liberté provisoire.

**bailiff** /ˈbeɪlɪf/ n huissier m.

**bait** /beɪt/ n appât m. ● vt appâter; (fig) tourmenter.

**bake** /beɪk/ vt faire cuire au four; ~ **a cake** faire un gâteau. ● vi cuire; (person) faire du pain. **baked beans** npl haricots mpl blancs à la tomate. **baked potato** n pomme f de terre en robe des champs. **baker** n boulanger/-ère m/f. **bakery** n boulangerie f

**balance** /ˈbæləns/ n équilibre m; (scales) balance f; (outstanding sum: Comm) solde m; (of payments, of trade) balance f; (remainder) restant m. ● vt mettre en équilibre; (weigh up also Comm) balancer; (budget) équilibrer; (to compensate) contrebalancer. ● vi être en équilibre.

**balcony** /ˈbælkənɪ/ n balcon m.

**bald** /bɔːld/ adj chauve; (tyre) lisse; (fig) simple.

**balk** /bɔːk/ vt contrecarrer. ● vi ~

at reculer devant.

**ball** /bɔːl/ n (golf, tennis, etc.) balle f; (football) ballon m; (billiards) bille f; (of wool) pelote f; (sphere) boule f; (dance) bal m.

**ballet** /'bæleɪ/ n ballet m.

**balloon** /bə'luːn/ n ballon m.

**ballot** /'bælət/ n scrutin m. ● vt consulter par vote (sur). ~ **box** n urne f. ~ **paper** n bulletin m de vote.

**ballpoint pen** n stylo m (à) bille.

**ban** /bæn/ vt (pt banned) interdire; ~ **sb** from exclure qn de; ~ **sb** from doing interdire à qn de faire. ● n interdiction f (on de).

**banal** /bə'nɑːl/ adj banal.

**banana** /bə'nɑːnə/ n banane f.

**band** /bænd/ n (strip, group of people) bande f; (pop group) groupe m; (brass band) fanfare f. ● vi ~ together se réunir.

**bandage** /'bændɪdʒ/ n bandage m. ● vt bander.

**B and B** abbr ➡BED AND BREAKFAST.

**bandit** /'bændɪt/ n bandit m.

**bandstand** /'bændstænd/ n kiosque m à musique.

**bang** /bæŋ/ n (blow, noise) coup m; (explosion) détonation f; (of door) claquement m. ● vt/i taper; (explosion) claquer; ~ **one's head** se cogner la tête. ● interj vlan. ● adv ⚀ ~ **in the middle** en plein milieu; ~ **on time** à l'heure pile.

**banger** /'bæŋə(r)/ n (firework) pétard m; (Culin) saucisse f; (old) ~ (car ⚀) guimbarde f.

**banish** /'bænɪʃ/ vt bannir.

**banister** /'bænɪstə(r)/ n rampe f d'escalier.

**bank** /bæŋk/ n (Comm) banque f; (of river) rive f; (of sand) banc m. ● vt mettre en banque. ● vi (Aviat)

virer; ~ **with** avoir un compte à; ~ **on** compter sur. ~ **account** n compte m en banque. ~ **card** n carte f bancaire. ~ **holiday** n jour m férié.

**banking** /'bæŋkɪŋ/ n opérations fpl bancaires; (as career) la banque.

**banknote** /'bæŋknəʊt/ n billet m de banque.

**bankrupt** /'bæŋkrʌpt/ adj be ~ être en faillite; go ~ faire faillite. ● n failli/-e m/f. ● vt mettre en faillite. **bankruptcy** n faillite f.

**bank statement** n relevé m de compte.

**banner** /'bænə(r)/ n bannière f.

**baptism** /'bæptɪzəm/ n baptême m. **baptize** vt baptiser.

**bar** /bɑː(r)/ n (of metal) barre f; (on window, cage) barreau m; (of chocolate) tablette f; (pub) bar m; (counter) comptoir m; (Mus) mesure f; (fig) obstacle m; ~ **of soap** savonnette f; the ~ (Jur) le barreau. ● vt (pt barred) (obstruct) barrer; (prohibit) interdire; (exclude) exclure. ● prep sauf.

**barbecue** /'bɑːbɪkjuː/ n barbecue m. ● vt faire au barbecue.

**barbed wire** n fil m de fer barbelé.

**barber** /'bɑːbə(r)/ n coiffeur m (pour hommes).

**bar code | battle** b

**bar code** n code m (à) barres.

**bare** /beə(r)/ adj nu; (cupboard) vide. ● vt mettre à nu. ∼**foot** adj nu-pieds inv, pieds nus. **barely** adv à peine.

**bargain** /'bɑːgɪn/ n (deal) marché m; (cheap thing) occasion f. ● vi négocier; (haggle) marchander; not ∼ for ne pas s'attendre à.

**barge** /bɑːdʒ/ n péniche f. ● vi ∼ in interrompre; (into room) faire irruption.

**bark** /bɑːk/ n (of tree) écorce f; (of dog) aboiement m. ● vi aboyer.

**barley** /'bɑːlɪ/ n orge f.

**bar:** ∼**maid** n serveuse f. ∼**man** n (pl -**men**) barman m.

**barn** /bɑːn/ n grange f.

**barracks** /'bærəks/ npl caserne f.

**barrel** /'bærəl/ n tonneau m; (of oil) baril m; (of gun) canon m.

**barren** /'bærən/ adj stérile.

**barricade** /bærɪ'keɪd/ n barricade f. ● vt barricader.

**barrier** /'bærɪə(r)/ n barrière f; ticket ∼ guichet m.

**barrister** /'bærɪstə(r)/ n avocat m.

**bartender** /'bɑːtendə(r)/ n (US) barman m.

**barter** /'bɑːtə(r)/ n troc m. ● vt troquer (for contre).

**base** /beɪs/ n base f. ● vt baser (on sur; in à). ● adj ignoble. **baseball** n base-ball m.

**basement** /'beɪsmənt/ n sous-sol m.

**bash** /bæʃ/ 🔲 vt cogner; ∼**ed in** enfoncé. ● n coup m violent; have a ∼ at s'essayer à.

**basic** /'beɪsɪk/ adj fondamental, élémentaire; the ∼s l'essentiel m. **basically** adv au fond.

**basil** /'bæzl/ n basilic m.

**basin** /'beɪsn/ n (for liquids) cuvette

f; (for food) bol m; (for washing) lavabo m; (of river) bassin m.

**basis** /'beɪsɪs/ n (pl **bases**) base f.

**bask** /bɑːsk/ vi se prélasser (in à).

**basket** /'bɑːskɪt/ n corbeille f; (with handle) panier m. **basketball** n basket(- ball) m.

**Basque** /bæsk/ n (person) Basque mf; (Ling) basque m. ● adj basque.

**bass**[1] /beɪs/ adj (voice, part) de basse; (sound, note) grave. ● n (pl **basses**) basse f.

**bass**[2] /bæs/ n inv (freshwater fish) perche f; (sea) bar m.

**bassoon** /bə'suːn/ n basson m.

**bastard** /'bɑːstəd/ n (illegitimate) bâtard/-e m/f; (insult 🔲) salaud m 🔲.

**bat** /bæt/ n (cricket etc.) batte f; (table tennis) raquette f; (animal) chauvesouris f. ● vt (pt **batted**) (ball) frapper; not ∼ an eyelid ne pas sourciller.

**batch** /bætʃ/ n (of cakes, people) fournée f; (of goods, text also Comput) lot m.

**bath** /bɑːθ/ n (pl -**s**) bain m; (tub) baignoire f; have a ∼ prendre un bain; (swimming) ∼**s** piscine f. ● vt donner un bain à.

**bathe** /beɪð/ vt baigner. ● vi se baigner; (US) prendre un bain.

**bathing** /'beɪðɪŋ/ n baignade f. ∼**-costume** n maillot m de bain.

**bath:** ∼**robe** n (US) robe f de chambre. ∼**room** n salle f de bains.

**baton** /'bætn/ n (policeman's) matraque f; (Mus) baguette f.

**batter** /'bætə(r)/ vt battre. ● n (Culin) pâte f (à frire).

**battery** /'bætərɪ/ n (Mil, Auto) batterie f; (of torch, radio) pile f.

**battle** /'bætl/ n bataille f; (fig) lutte

f. ● *vi* se battre. **∼field** *n* champ *m*
de bataille.

**baulk** /bɔːk/ *vt/i* ➡**BALK.**

**bay** /beɪ/ *n* (Bot) laurier *m*; (Geog,
Archit) baie *f*; (area) aire *f*; (bark)
aboiement *m*; keep or hold at **∼**
tenir à distance. ● *vi* aboyer. **∼leaf**
*n* feuille *f* de laurier. **∼ window** *n*
fenêtre *f* en saillie.

**bazaar** /bə'zɑː(r)/ *n* (shop, market)
bazar *m*; (sale) vente *f*.

**BC** *abbr* (**before Christ**) avant J.-C.

**BBS** *abbr* (**Bulletin Board System**)
(Internet) babillard *m* électronique,
BBS *m*.

**be** /biː/

*present* am, is, are; *past* was,
were; *past participle* been.

● *intransitive verb*
····▶ être; I am tired je suis fatigué; it's me c'est moi.
····▶ (feelings) avoir; I am hot j'ai
chaud; he is hungry/thirsty il
a faim/soif; her hands are
cold elle a froid aux mains.
····▶ (age) avoir; I am 15 j'ai 15
ans.
····▶ (weather) faire; it's warm il
fait chaud; it's 25° il fait 25°.
····▶ (health) aller; how are you?
comment allez-vous or comment vas-tu?
····▶ (visit) aller; I've never been
to Italy je ne suis jamais allé
en Italie.
● *auxiliary verb*
····▶ (in tenses) I am working je
travaille; he was writing to his
mother il écrivait à sa mère;
she is to do it at once (obligation) elle doit le faire tout de
suite.

····▶ (in passives) he was killed il
a été tué; the window has
been fixed on a réparé la fenêtre.
····▶ (in tag questions) their
house is lovely, isn't it? leur
maison est très jolie, n'est-ce
pas?
····▶ (in short answers) 'I am a
painter'—'are you?' 'je suis
peintre'—'ah oui?'; 'are you a
doctor?'—'yes, I am' 'êtes-
vous médecin?'—'oui'; 'you're
not going out'—'yes I am' 'tu
ne sors pas'—'si'.

**beach** /biːtʃ/ *n* plage *f*.
**beacon** /'biːkən/ *n* (lighthouse)
phare *m*; (marker) balise *f*.
**bead** /biːd/ *n* perle *f*.
**beak** /biːk/ *n* bec *m*.
**beaker** /'biːkə(r)/ *n* gobelet *m*.
**beam** /biːm/ *n* (timber) poutre *f*;
(of light) rayon *m*; (of torch) faisceau *m*. ● *vi* rayonner. ● *vt* (broadcast) transmettre.
**bean** /biːn/ *n* haricot *m*.
**bear** /beə(r)/ *n* ours *m*. ● *vt* (*pt*
**bore**, *pp* **borne**) (carry, show, feel)
porter; (endure, sustain) supporter;
(child) mettre au monde. ● *vi* **∼**
left (go) prendre à gauche; **∼** in
mind tenir compte de. **∼ out** confirmer; **∼ up** tenir le coup. **bearable** *adj* supportable.
**beard** /bɪəd/ *n* barbe *f*.
**bearer** /'beərə(r)/ *n* porteur/-
euse *m/f*.
**bearing** /'beərɪŋ/ *n* (behaviour)
maintien *m*; (relevance) rapport *m*;
get one's **∼**s s'orienter.
**beast** /biːst/ *n* bête *f*; (person)
brute *f*.
**beat** /biːt/ *vt/i* (*pt* **beat**; *pp* **beaten**)
battre; **∼** a retreat battre en re-

traite; ∼ itl dégage! 🔲; it ∼s me 🔲 ça me dépasse. ● n (of drum, heart) battement m; (Mus) mesure f; (of policeman) ronde f. ∼ off repousser; ∼ **up** tabasser. **beating** n raclée f.

**beautiful** /ˈbjuːtɪfl/ adj beau.

**beauty** /ˈbjuːtɪ/ n beauté f. ∼**parlour** n institut m de beauté. ∼**spot** n grain m de beauté; (place) site m pittoresque.

**beaver** /ˈbiːvə(r)/ n castor m.

**became** /bɪˈkeɪm/ ➡BECOME.

**because** /bɪˈkɒz/ conj parce que; ∼ **of** à cause de.

**become** /bɪˈkʌm/ vt/i (pt **became**, pp **become**) devenir; (befit) convenir à; what has ∼ of her? qu'est-ce qu'elle est devenue?

**bed** /bed/ n lit m; (layer) couche f; (of sea) fond m; (of flowers) parterre m; **go to** ∼ (aller) se coucher. ● vi (pt **bedded**) ∼ **down** se coucher. **bed and breakfast** n chambre f avec petit déjeuner, chambre f d'hôte. ∼ **bug** n punaise f. ∼**clothes** npl couvertures fpl.

**bedding** /ˈbedɪŋ/ n literie f.

**bed:** ∼**ridden** adj cloué au lit. ∼**room** n chambre f (à coucher). ∼**side** n chevet m. ∼**sit**, ∼**sitter**, ∼**sitting-room** n chambre f meublée, studio m. ∼**spread** n dessus m de lit. ∼**time** n heure f du coucher.

**bee** /biː/ n abeille f; **make a** ∼**line for** aller tout droit vers.

**beech** /biːtʃ/ n hêtre m.

**beef** /biːf/ n bœuf m. ∼**burger** n hamburger m.

**beehive** /ˈbiːhaɪv/ n ruche f.

**been** /biːn/ ➡BE.

**beer** /bɪə(r)/ n bière f.

**beetle** /ˈbiːtl/ n scarabée m.

**beetroot** /ˈbiːtruːt/ n inv betterave f.

**before** /bɪˈfɔː(r)/ prep (time) avant; (place) devant; **the day** ∼ **yesterday** avant-hier. ● adv avant; (already) déjà; **the day** ∼ la veille. ● conj ∼ **leaving** avant de partir; ∼ **I forget** avant que j'oublie. **beforehand** adv à l'avance.

**beg** /beg/ vt (pt **begged**) (food, money, favour) demander (from à); ∼ **sb to** supplier qn de faire. ● vi mendier; **it is going** ∼**ging** personne n'en veut.

**began** /bɪˈgæn/ ➡BEGIN.

**beggar** /ˈbegə(r)/ n mendiant/-e m/f.

**begin** /bɪˈgɪn/ vt/i (pt **began**, pp **begun**, pres p **beginning**) commencer (to do à faire). **beginner** n débutant/-e m/f. **beginning** n commencement m, début m.

**begun** /bɪˈgʌn/ ➡BEGIN.

**behalf** /bɪˈhɑːf/ n **on** ∼ **of** (act, speak, campaign) pour; (phone, write) de la part de.

**behave** /bɪˈheɪv/ vi se conduire; (oneself) se conduire bien.

**behaviour** /bɪˈheɪvjə(r)/, (US) **behavior** n comportement m (towards envers).

**behead** /bɪˈhed/ vt décapiter.

**behind** /bɪˈhaɪnd/ prep derrière; (in time) en retard sur. ● adv derrière; (late) en retard; **leave** ∼ oublier. ● n (buttocks) derrière m 🔲.

**beige** /beɪʒ/ adj & n beige (m).

**being** /ˈbiːɪŋ/ n (person) être m.

**belch** /beltʃ/ vi avoir un renvoi. ● vt ∼ **out** (smoke) s'échapper. ● n renvoi m.

**Belgian** /ˈbeldʒən/ n Belge mf. ● adj belge. **Belgium** n Belgique f.

**belief** /bɪˈliːf/ n conviction f; (trust) confiance f; (faith: Relig) foi f.

**believe** /bɪˈliːv/ vt/i croire; ∼ **in** croire à; (deity) croire en.

**believer** *n* croyant/-e *m/f*.

**bell** /bel/ *n* cloche *f*; (small) clochette *f*; (on door) sonnette *f*.

**belly** /'beli/ *n* ventre *m*. ~ **button** *n* nombril *m*.

**belong** /br'lɒŋ/ *vi* ~ **to** appartenir à; (club) être membre de.

**belongings** /br'lɒŋɪŋz/ *npl* affaires *fpl*.

**beloved** /br'lʌvɪd/ *adj* & *n* bien-aimé/-e *(m/f)*.

**below** /br'ləʊ/ *prep* sous, au-dessous de; (fig) indigne de. ● *adv* en dessous; (on page) ci-dessous.

**belt** /belt/ *n* ceinture *f*; (Tech) courroie *f*; (fig) zone *f*. ● *vt* (hit ▯) rosser. ● *vi* (rush ▯) ~ **in/out** entrer/ sortir à toute vitesse.

**beltway** /'beltweɪ/ *n* (US) périphérique *m*.

**bemused** /br'mju:zd/ *adj* perplexe.

**bench** /bentʃ/ *n* banc *m*; the ~ (Jur) la magistrature (assise).

**bend** /bend/ *vt* (*pt* **bent**) (knee, arm, wire) plier; (head, back) courber. ● *vi* (road) tourner; (person) ~ **down/over** se pencher. ● *n* courbe *f*; (in road) virage *m*; (of arm, knee) pli *m*.

**beneath** /br'ni:θ/ *prep* sous, au-dessous de; (fig) indigne de. ● *adv* en dessous.

**benefactor** /'benɪfæktə(r)/ *n* bienfaiteur/-trice *m/f*.

**beneficial** /benɪ'fɪʃl/ *adj* bénéfique.

**benefit** /'benɪfɪt/ *n* avantage *m*; (allowance) allocation *f*. ● *vt* (be useful to) profiter à; (do good to) faire du bien à. ● *vi* profiter; ~ **from** tirer profit de.

**benign** /br'naɪn/ *adj* (kindly) bienveillant; (Med) bénin.

**bent** /bent/ ➡**BEND**. ● *n* (talent)

aptitude *f*; (inclination) penchant *m*. ● *adj* tordu; ▣ corrompu; ~ **on doing** décidé à faire.

**bequest** /br'kwest/ *n* legs *m*.

**bereaved** /br'ri:vd/ *adj* endeuillé; the ~ la famille endeuillée. **bereavement** *n* deuil *m*.

**berry** /'beri/ *n* baie *f*.

**berserk** /bə'sɜ:k/ *adj* fou furieux.

**berth** /bɜ:θ/ *n* (in train, ship) couchette *f*; (anchorage) mouillage *m*; give a wide ~ to éviter. ● *vi* mouiller.

**beside** /br'saɪd/ *prep* à côté de; ~ oneself hors de soi; ~ **the point** sans rapport.

**besides** /br'saɪdz/ *prep* en plus de. ● *adv* en plus.

**besiege** /br'si:dʒ/ *vt* assiéger.

**best** /best/ *adj* meilleur; the ~ book le meilleur livre; the ~ part of la plus grande partie de; the ~ thing is to le mieux est de. ● *adv* (the) ~ (behave, play) le mieux. ● *n* the ~ le meilleur, la meilleure; do one's ~ faire de son mieux; make the ~ of s'accommoder de. ~ **man** *n* témoin. ~**-seller** *n* bestseller *m*, livre *m* à succès.

**bet** /bet/ *n* pari *m*. ● *vt/i* (*pt* **bet** or **betted**, *pres p* **betting**) parier (on sur).

**betray** /br'treɪ/ *vt* trahir.

**better** /'betə(r)/ *adj* meilleur; the ~ part of la plus grande partie de; get ~ s'améliorer; (recover) se remettre. ● *adv* mieux; I had ~ go je ferais mieux de partir. ● *vt* (improve) améliorer; (do better than) surpasser. ● *n* get the ~ of l'emporter sur; so much the ~ tant mieux. ~ **off** *adj* (richer) plus riche; he is/would be ~ off at home il est/serait mieux chez lui.

**betting shop** *n* bureau *m*

du PMU.

**between** /bɪ'twiːn/ prep entre.
● adv in ~ au milieu.

**beverage** /'bevərɪdʒ/ n boisson f.

**beware** /bɪ'weə(r)/ vi prendre
garde (of à).

**bewilder** /bɪ'wɪldə(r)/ vt déconcerter.

**beyond** /bɪ'jɒnd/ prep au-delà de;
(control, reach) hors de; (besides)
excepté. ● adv au-delà; it is ~ me
ça me dépasse.

**bib** /bɪb/ n bavoir m.

**Bible** /'baɪbl/ n Bible f.

**biceps** /'baɪseps/ n biceps m.

**bicycle** /'baɪsɪkl/ n vélo m, bicyclette f. ● adj (bell, chain) de vélo;
(pump, clip) à vélo.

**bid** /bɪd/ n (at auction) enchère f;
(attempt) tentative f. ● vt/i (pt
**bade**, pp **bidden** or **bid**, pres p **bidding**) (offer) offrir, mettre une enchère (de) (for pour); ~ sb good
morning dire bonjour à qn; ~ sb
farewell faire ses adieux à qn.

**bidding** /'bɪdɪŋ/ n (at auction) enchères fpl; he did my ~ il a fait ce
que je lui ai dit.

**bifocals** /baɪ'fəʊklz/ npl verres mpl
à double foyer.

**big** /bɪg/ adj (**bigger**, **biggest**)
grand; (in bulk) gros.

**bike** /baɪk/ n vélo m.

**bikini** /bɪ'kiːnɪ/ n bikini m.

**bilberry** /'bɪlbrɪ/ n myrtille f.

**bilingual** /baɪ'lɪŋgwəl/ adj bilingue.

**bill** /bɪl/ n (invoice) facture f; (in
hotel, for gas) note f; (in restaurant)
addition f; (of sale) acte m; (Pol)

projet m de loi; (banknote: US) billet
m de banque; (Theat) on the ~ à
l'affiche; (of bird) bec m. ● vt (person: Comm) envoyer la facture à.
~**board** n panneau m d'affichage.

**billet** /'bɪlɪt/ n cantonnement m.
● vt (pt **billeted**) cantonner (on
chez).

**billiards** /'bɪljədz/ n billard m.

**billion** /'bɪlɪən/ n billion m; (US)
milliard m.

**bin** /bɪn/ n (for rubbish) poubelle f;
(for storage) casier m.

**bind** /baɪnd/ vt (pt **bound**) attacher; (book) relier; **be bound by**
être tenu par. ● n (bore) corvée f.

**binding** /'baɪndɪŋ/ n reliure f. ● adj
(agreement, contract) qui lie.

**binge** /bɪndʒ/ n (drinking) beuverie
f; (eating) gueuleton m.

**binoculars** /bɪ'nɒkjʊləz/ npl jumelles fpl.

**biochemistry** /baɪəʊ'kemɪstrɪ/ n
biochimie f.

**biodegradable** /baɪəʊdɪ
'greɪdəbl/ adj biodégradable.

**biographer** /baɪ'ɒgrəfə(r)/ n bio-
graphe mf. **biography** n biographie f.

**biological** /baɪə'lɒdʒɪkl/ adj biologique.

**biologist** /baɪ'ɒlədʒɪst/ n biolo-
giste mf.

**biology** /baɪ'ɒlədʒɪ/ n biologie f.

**bioterrorism** /baɪəʊ'terərɪzm/n
bioterrorisme m.

**birch** /bɜːtʃ/ n (tree) bouleau m;
(whip) fouet m.

**bird** /bɜːd/ n oiseau m; (girl 🔲)
nana f.

**Biro®** /'baɪrəʊ/ n stylo m à bille,
bic® m.

**birth** /bɜːθ/ n naissance f; **give** ~
accoucher. ~ **certificate** n acte m

de naissance. **~control** n contraception f. **~day** n anniversaire m. **~mark** n tache f de naissance. **~rate** n taux m de natalité.

**biscuit** /'bɪskɪt/ n biscuit m; (US) petit pain m (au lait).

**bishop** /'bɪʃəp/ n évêque m.

**bit** /bɪt/ ➡BITE. ● n morceau m; (of horse) mors m; (of tool) mèche f; **a ~** (a little) un peu; (Comput) bit m.

**bitch** /bɪtʃ/ n chienne f; (woman ▨) garce f ▨. ● vi dire du mal (about de).

**bite** /baɪt/ vt/i (pt bit; pp bitten) mordre; **~ one's nails** se ronger les ongles. ● n morsure f; (by insect) piqûre f; (mouthful) bouchée f; **have a ~** manger un morceau.

**bitter** /'bɪtə(r)/ adj amer; (weather) glacial. ● n bière f. **bitterly** adv amèrement; **it is ~ly cold** il fait un temps glacial.

**bizarre** /bɪ'zɑː(r)/ adj bizarre.

**black** /blæk/ adj noir; **~ and blue** couvert de bleus. ● n noir m; **B~** (person) Noir/-e m/f. ● vt noircir; (goods) boycotter. **~berry** n mûre f. **~bird** n merle m. **~board** n tableau m noir. **~currant** n cassis m.

**blacken** /'blækən/ vt/i noircir.

**black: ~ eye** n œil m poché. **~head** n point m noir. **~ice** n verglas m. **~leg** n jaune m.

**blacklist** /'blæklɪst/ n liste f noire. ● vt mettre à l'index.

**blackmail** /'blækmeɪl/ n chantage m. ● vt faire chanter. **blackmailer** n maître-chanteur m.

**black: ~ market** n marché m noir. **~out** n panne f de courant; (Med) syncope f; **~ pudding** n boudin m. **~ sheep** n brebis f galeuse. **~smith** n forgeron m. **~ spot** n point m noir.

**bladder** /'blædə(r)/ n vessie f.

**blade** /bleɪd/ n (of knife) lame f; (of propeller, oar) pale f; **~ of grass** brin m d'herbe.

**blame** /bleɪm/ vt accuser; **~ sb for sth** reprocher qch à qn; **he is to ~** il est responsable (for de). ● n responsabilité f (for de).

**bland** /blænd/ adj (insipid) fade.

**blank** /blæŋk/ adj (page) blanc; (screen) vide; (cheque) en blanc; **to look ~** avoir l'air ébahi. ● n blanc m; **~ (cartridge)** cartouche f à blanc.

**blanket** /'blæŋkɪt/ n couverture f; (layer) couche f.

**blasphemous** /'blæsfəməs/ adj blasphématoire; (person) blasphémateur.

**blast** /blɑːst/ n explosion f; (wave of air) souffle m; (of wind) rafale f; (noise from siren etc.) coup m. ● vt (blow up) faire sauter. **~ off** décoller. **~ furnace** n haut-fourneau m. **~ off** n lancement m.

**blatant** /'bleɪtnt/ adj (obvious) flagrant; (shameless) éhonté.

**blaze** /bleɪz/ n feu m; (accident) incendie m. ● vt **a ~ trail** faire œuvre de pionnier. ● vi (fire) brûler; (sky, eyes) flamboyer.

**bleach** /bliːtʃ/ n (for cleaning) eau f de Javel; (for hair, fabric) décolorant m. ● vt/i blanchir; (hair) décolorer.

**bleak** /bliːk/ adj (landscape) désolé; (outlook, future) sombre.

**bleed** /bliːd/ vt/i (pt bled) saigner.

**bleep** /bliːp/ n bip m.

**blemish** /'blemɪʃ/ n imperfection f; (on fruit, reputation) tache f. ● vt entacher.

**blend** /blend/ vt mélanger. ● vi se fondre ensemble; **to ~ with** se marier à. ● n mélange m. **blender** n

**bless | blunder**

mixeur *n*, mixer *n*.

**bless** /bles/ *vt* bénir; be ~ed with jouir de; ~ you! à vos souhaits! **blessed** *adj* (holy) saint; (damned 🗉) sacré. **blessing** *n* bénédiction *f*; (benefit) avantage *m*; (stroke of luck) chance *f*.

**blew** /bluː/ →BLOW.

**blight** /blaɪt/ *n* (disease: Bot) rouille *f*; (fig) plaie *f*.

**blind** /blaɪnd/ *adj* aveugle (to à); (corner, bend) sans visibilité. ● *n* aveugle. ● *n* (on window) store *m*; the ~ les aveugles *mpl*.

**blindfold** /ˈblaɪndfəʊld/ *adj* be ~ avoir les yeux bandés. ● *adv* les yeux bandés. ● *n* bandeau *m*. ● *vt* bander les yeux à.

**blindness** /ˈblaɪndnɪs/ *n* (Med) cécité *f*; (fig) aveuglement *m*.

**blind spot** *n* (Auto) angle *m* mort.

**blink** /blɪŋk/ *vi* cligner des yeux; (light) clignoter.

**bliss** /blɪs/ *n* délice *m*. **blissful** *adj* délicieux.

**blister** /ˈblɪstə(r)/ *n* ampoule *f*; (on paint) cloque *f*. ● *vi* cloquer.

**blitz** /blɪts/ *n* (Aviat) raid *m* éclair. ● *vt* bombarder.

**blob** /blɒb/ *n* (drop) (grosse) goutte *f*; (stain) tache *f*.

**block** /blɒk/ *n* bloc *m*; (buildings) pâté *m* de maisons; (in pipe) obstruction *f*; ~ (of flats) immeuble *m*; ~ letters majuscules *fpl*. ● *vt* bloquer.

**blockade** /blɒˈkeɪd/ *n* blocus *m*. ● *vt* bloquer.

**blockage** /ˈblɒkɪdʒ/ *n* obstruction *f*.

**blockbuster** *n* gros succès *m*.

**bloke** /bləʊk/ *n* 🗉 type *m*.

**blond** /blɒnd/ *adj* & *n* blond (*m*).

**blonde** /blɒnd/ *adj* & *n* blonde (*f*).

**blood** /blʌd/ *n* sang *m*. ● *adj* (donor, bath) de sang; (bank, poisoning) du sang; (group, vessel) sanguin. **~-pressure** *n* tension *f* artérielle. **~shed** *n* effusion *f* de sang. **~shot** *adj* injecté de sang. **~stream** *n* sang *m*. ~ **test** *n* prise *f* de sang.

**bloody** /ˈblʌdɪ/ *adj* (**-ier, -iest**) sanglant; 🗷 sacré. ● *adv* 🗷 vachement 🗉. **~-minded** *adj* 🗉 hargneux, obstiné.

**bloom** /bluːm/ *n* fleur *f*. ● *vi* fleurir; (person) s'épanouir.

**blossom** /ˈblɒsəm/ *n* fleur(s) *f* (*pl*). ● *vi* fleurir; (person) s'épanouir.

**blot** /blɒt/ *n* tache *f*. ● *vt* (*pt* **blotted**) tacher; (dry) sécher; ~ **out** effacer.

**blotch** /blɒtʃ/ *n* tache *f*.

**blouse** /blaʊz/ *n* chemisier *m*.

**blow** /bləʊ/ *vt/i* (*pt* **blew**; *pp* **blown**) souffler; (fuse) (faire) sauter; (squander 🗷) claquer; (opportunity) rater; ~ **one's nose** se moucher; ~ **a whistle** siffler. ● *n* coup *m*. □ ~ **away** or **off** emporter; ~ **out** souffler; ~ **over** passer; ~ **up** (faire) sauter; (tyre) gonfler; (Photo) agrandir.

**blow-dry** *n* brushing *m*. ● *vt* faire un brushing à.

**blown** /bləʊn/ →BLOW.

**bludgeon** /ˈblʌdʒən/ *n* matraque *f*. ● *vt* matraquer.

**blue** /bluː/ *adj* bleu; (movie) porno. ● *n* bleu *m*; come out of the ~ être inattendu; have the ~s avoir le cafard. **~bell** *n* jacinthe *f* des bois. **~print** *n* projet *m*.

**bluff** /blʌf/ *vt/i* bluffer. ● *n* bluff *m*; call sb's ~ dire chiche à qn. ● *adj* (person) carré.

**blunder** /ˈblʌndə(r)/ *vi* faire une bourde; (move) avancer à tâtons. ● *n* gaffe *f*.

**blunt** /blʌnt/ adj (knife) émoussé; (person) brusque. ● vt émousser. **bluntly** adv carrément.

**blur** /blɜ:(r)/ n image f floue. ● vt (pt blurred) brouiller.

**blurb** /blɜ:b/ n résumé m publicitaire.

**blush** /blʌʃ/ vi rougir. ● n rougeur f. **blusher** n fard m à joues.

**blustery** /ˈblʌstərɪ/ adj ~ wind bourrasque f.

**BMI** abbr (body mass index) IMC m.

**boar** /bɔ:(r)/ n sanglier m.

**board** /bɔ:d/ n planche f. (for notices) tableau m; (food) pension f; full ~ pension f complète; half ~ demi-pension f; (committee) conseil m; ~ of directors conseil m d'administration; go by the ~ tomber à l'eau; on ~ à bord. ● vt/i (bus, train) monter dans; (Naut) monter à bord (de); ~ with être en pension chez.

**boarding-school** n école f privée avec internat.

**boast** /bəʊst/ vi se vanter (about de). ● vt s'enorgueillir de. ● n vantardise f.

**boat** /bəʊt/ n bateau m; (small) canot m; in the same ~ logé à la même enseigne.

**bode** /bəʊd/ vi ~ well/ill être de bon/mauvais augure.

**bodily** /ˈbɒdɪlɪ/ adj (need, well-being) physique; (injury) corporel. ● adv physiquement; (in person) en personne.

**body** /ˈbɒdɪ/ n corps m; (mass) masse f; (organization) organisme m; ~ part n partie f de corps; ~(work) (Auto) carrosserie f; the main ~ le gros de. **~-building** n culturisme m. **~guard** n garde m du corps.

**bog** /bɒg/ n marais m. ● vt (pt bogged) get ~ged down s'enliser dans.

**bogus** /ˈbəʊgəs/ adj faux.

**boil** /bɔɪl/ n furoncle m; bring to the ~ porter à ébullition. ● vt/i bouillir. ~ **down to** se ramener à; ~ **over** déborder. **boiled** adj (egg) à la coque; (potatoes) à l'eau.

**boiler** /ˈbɔɪlə(r)/ n chaudière f; ~ suit bleu m (de travail).

**boisterous** /ˈbɔɪstərəs/ adj tapageur; (child) turbulent.

**bold** /bəʊld/ adj hardi; (cheeky) effronté; (type) gras.

**Bolivia** /bəˈlɪvɪə/ n Bolivie f.

**bollard** /ˈbɒlɑ:d/ n (on road) balise f

**bolt** /bəʊlt/ n (on door) verrou m; (for nut) boulon m; (lightning) éclair m. ● vt (door) verrouiller; (food) engouffrer. ● vi s'emballer.

**bomb** /bɒm/ n bombe f; ~ scare alerte f à la bombe. ● vt bombarder.

**bomber** /ˈbɒmə(r)/ n (aircraft) bombardier m; (person) plastiqueur m.

**bond** /bɒnd/ n (agreement) engagement m; (link) lien m; (Comm) obligation f; bon m; in ~ (entreposé) en douane.

**bone** /bəʊn/ n os m; (of fish) arête f. ● vt désosser. **~-dry** adj tout à fait sec.

**bonfire** /ˈbɒnfaɪə(r)/ n feu m; (for celebration) feu m de joie.

**bonnet** /ˈbɒnɪt/ n (hat) bonnet m; (of vehicle) capot m.

**bonus** /ˈbəʊnəs/ n prime f.

**bony** /ˈbəʊnɪ/ adj (-ier, -iest) (thin) osseux; (fish) plein d'arêtes.

**boo** /bu:/ interj hou. ● vt/i huer. ● n huée f.

**booby trap** /ˈbu:bɪtræp/ n mécanisme *m* piégé. ● *vt* (*pt*) **-trapped**) piéger.

**book** /bʊk/ *n* livre *m*; (*exercise*) cahier *m*; (*of* tickets etc.) carnet *m*; ~s (Comm) comptes *mpl*. ● *vt* (*reserve*) réserver; (*driver*) dresser un PV à; (*player*) prendre le nom de; (*write down*) inscrire. ● *vi* retenir des places; (*fully*) ~ed complet. ~**case** *n* bibliothèque *f.* ~**ing-office** *n* guichet *m.* ~**keeping** *n* comptabilité *f.* ~**let** *n* brochure *f.* ~**maker** *n* bookmaker *m.* ~**mark** *n* (for book, Internet) signet *m.* ~**seller** *n* libraire *mf.* ~**shop** *n* librairie *f.* ~**stall** *n* kiosque *m* (à journaux).

**boom** /buːm/ *vi* (*gun, wind, etc.*) gronder; (*trade*) prospérer. ● *n* grondement *m*; (Comm) boom *m*, prospérité *f.*

**boost** /buːst/ *vt* stimuler; (*morale*) remonter; (*price*) augmenter; (*publicize*) faire de la réclame pour.

**boot** /buːt/ *n* (knee-length) botte *f*; (anklelength) chaussure *f* (montante); (for walking) chaussure *f* de marche; (Sport) chaussure *f* de sport; (of vehicle) coffre *m*; get the ~ 🖪 se faire virer. ● *vt*/*i* ~ **up** (Comput) amorcer.

**booth** /buːð/ *n* (for telephone) cabine *f*; (at fair) baraque *f.*

**booze** /buːz/ *vi* 🖪 boire (beaucoup). ● *n* 🖪 alcool *m.*

**border** /ˈbɔːdə(r)/ *n* (edge) bord *m*; (frontier) frontière *f*; (in garden) bordure *f.* ● *vi* ~ **on** être voisin de, avoisiner.

**bore** /bɔː(r)/ *vt* ennuyer; be ~d s'ennuyer. ➡BEAR. ● *vi* (Tech) forer. ● *n* raseur-euse *m/f*; (thing) ennui *m.* **boredom** *n* ennui *m.* **boring** *adj* ennuyeux.

**born** /bɔːn/ *adj* né; be ~ naître.

**borne** /bɔːn/ ➡BEAR.

**borough** /ˈbʌrə/ *n* municipalité *f.*

**borrow** /ˈbɒrəʊ/ *vt* emprunter (from à).

**Bosnia** /ˈbɒznɪə/ *n* Bosnie *f.*

**Bosnian** /ˈbɒznɪən/ *adj* bosniaque. ● *n* Bosniaque.

**bosom** /ˈbʊzəm/ *n* poitrine *f*; ~ **friend** ami/-e *m/f* intime.

**boss** /bɒs/ *n* 🖪 patron/-ne *m/f.* ● *vt* ~ (**about**) 🖪 mener par le bout du nez.

**bossy** /ˈbɒsɪ/ *adj* autoritaire.

**botch** /bɒtʃ/ *vt* bâcler, saboter.

**both** /bəʊθ/ *det* les deux; ~ **the** books les deux livres. ● *pron* tous/ toutes (les) deux, l'un/-e et l'autre; we ~ agree nous sommes tous les deux d'accord; I bought ~ (of them) j'ai acheté les deux; I saw ~ of you je vous ai vus tous les deux; ~ Paul and Anne (et) Paul et Anne. ● *adv* à la fois.

**bother** /ˈbɒðə(r)/ *vt* (annoy, worry) ennuyer; (disturb) déranger. ● *vi* se déranger; don't ~ (*calling*) ce n'est pas la peine (d'appeler); don't ~ about us ne t'inquiète pas pour nous; I can't be ~ed j'ai la flemme 🖪. ● *n* ennui *m*; (effort) peine *f*; it's no ~ ce n'est rien.

**bottle** /ˈbɒtl/ *n* bouteille *f*; (for baby) biberon *m.* ● *vt* mettre en bouteille. ~ **up** contenir. ~ **bank** *n* collecteur *m* (de verre usagé). ~**neck** *n* (traffic jam) embouteillage *m.* ~**-opener** *n* ouvre-bouteilles *m inv.*

**bottom** /ˈbɒtəm/ *n* fond *m*; (of hill, page, etc.) bas *m*; (buttocks) derrière *m* 🖪. ● *adj* inférieur, du bas.

**bought** /bɔːt/ ➡BUY.

**bounce** /baʊns/ *vi* rebondir; (*person*) faire des bonds, bondir; (*cheques* ✗) être refusé. ● *vt* faire rebondir. ● *n* rebond *m.*

**bound** /baʊnd/ vi (leap) bondir; ~ed by limité par; ➡BIND. ● n bond m. ● adj be ~ for être en route pour, aller vers; ~ to (obliged) obligé de; (certain) sûr de.

**boundary** /ˈbaʊndrɪ/ n limite f.

**bounds** /baʊndz/ npl limites fpl; out of ~ être interdit d'accès.

**bout** /baʊt/ n période f; (Med) accès m; (boxing) combat m.

**bow¹** /bəʊ/ n (weapon) arc m; (of violin) archet m; (knot) nœud m.

**bow²** /baʊ/ n salut m; (of ship) proue f. ● vt/i (s')incliner.

**bowels** /ˈbaʊəlz/ npl intestins mpl; (fig) profondeurs fpl.

**bowl** /bəʊl/ n (for washing) cuvette f; (for food) bol m; (for soup) assiette f creuse. ● vt/i (cricket) lancer; ~ over bouleverser.

**bowler** /ˈbəʊlə(r)/ n (cricket) lanceur m; ~ (hat) (chapeau) melon m.

**bowling** /ˈbəʊlɪŋ/ n (ten-pin) bowling m; (on grass) jeu m de boules. ~-alley n bowling m.

**bow tie** n nœud m papillon.

**box** /bɒks/ n boîte f; (cardboard) carton m; (Theat) loge f; the ~ 🅃 la télé. ● vt mettre en boîte; (Sport) boxer; ~ sb's ears gifler qn; ~ in enfermer.

**boxing** /ˈbɒksɪŋ/ n boxe f. ● adj de boxe. B~ Day n le lendemain de Noël.

**box office** n guichet m.

**boy** /bɔɪ/ n garçon m; ~ band boys band m.

**boycott** /ˈbɔɪkɒt/ vt boycotter. ● n boycottage m.

**boyfriend** /ˈbɔɪfrend/ n (petit) ami m.

**bra** /brɑː/ n soutien-gorge m.

**brace** /breɪs/ n (fastener) attache f; (dental) appareil m; (tool) vilbrequin m; ~s (for trousers) bretelles fpl.

● vt soutenir; ~ oneself rassembler ses forces.

**bracket** /ˈbrækɪt/ n (for shelf etc.) tasseau m, support m; (group) tranche f; in ~s entre parenthèses f. ● vt mettre entre parenthèses or crochets.

**braid** /breɪd/ n (trimming) galon m; (of hair) tresse f.

**brain** /breɪn/ n cerveau m; ~s (fig) intelligence f. ● vt assommer. **brainless** adj stupide. ~-**wash** vt faire subir un lavage de cerveau à. ~-**wave** n idée f géniale, trouvaille f. **brainy** adj (-ier, -iest) doué.

**brake** /breɪk/ n (Auto also fig) frein m. ● vt/i freiner. ~ **light** n feu m stop.

**bran** /bræn/ n son m.

**branch** /brɑːntʃ/ n (of tree) branche f; (of road) embranchement m; (Comm) succursale f; (of bank) agence f. ● vi ~ (off) bifurquer.

**brand** /brænd/ n marque f. ● vt ~ sb as sth désigner qn comme qch.

**brand-new** /brænd'njuː/ adj tout neuf.

**brandy** /ˈbrændɪ/ n cognac m.

**brass** /brɑːs/ n cuivre m; get down to ~ tacks en venir aux choses sérieuses; the ~ (Mus) les cuivres mpl; top ~ 🅇 galonnés mpl.

**brat** /bræt/ n 🅃 môme mf 🅃.

**brave** /breɪv/ adj courageux; (smile) brave. ● n (American Indian) brave m. ● vt braver. **bravery** n courage m.

**brawl** /brɔːl/ n bagarre f. ● vi se bagarrer.

**Brazil** /brəˈzɪl/ n Brésil m.

**breach** /briːtʃ/ n (of copyright, privilege) violation f; (in relationship) rupture f; (gap) brèche f. ● vt ouvrir une brèche dans.

**bread** /bred/ n pain m; ~ and butter tartine *f* **~-bin**, (US) **~-box** *n* boîte *f* à pain. **~-crumbs** *npl* chapelure *f*.

**breadth** /bretθ/ *n* largeur *f*.

**bread-winner** /'bredwɪnə(r)/ *n* soutien *m* de famille.

**break** /breɪk/ *vt* (*pt* **broke**, *pp* **broken**) casser; (smash into pieces) briser; (vow, silence, rank, etc.) rompre; (law) violer; (a record) battre; (news) révéler; (journey) interrompre; (heart, strike, ice) briser; **~ one's arm** se casser le bras. ● *vi* (se) casser; se briser. ● *n* cassure *f*, rupture *f*; (in relationship, continuity) rupture *f*; (interval) interruption *f*; (at school) récréation *f*, récré *f*; (for coffee) pause *f*; (luck 🄸) chance *f*. **~ away from** se détacher; **~ down** *vi* (collapse) s'effondrer; (negotiations) échouer; (machine) tomber en panne; *vt* (door) enfoncer; (analyse) analyser. **~ even** rentrer dans ses frais; **~ into** cambrioler; **~ off** se détacher; (suspend) rompre; (stop talking) s'interrompre; **~ out** (fire, war, etc.) éclater; **~ up** (end) faire cesser; (couple) rompre; (marriage) se briser; (crowd) (se) disperser; (schools) être en vacances. **breakable** *adj* fragile. **breakage** *n* casse *f*.

**breakdown** /'breɪkdaʊn/ *n* (Tech) panne *f*; (Med) dépression *f*; (of figures) analyse *f*. ● *adj* (Auto) de dépannage.

**breakfast** /'brekfəst/ *n* petit déjeuner *m*.

**break** /breɪk/: **~-in** *n* cambriolage *m*. **~through** *n* percée *f*.

**breast** /brest/ *n* sein *m*; (chest) poitrine *f*. **~-feed** *vt* (*pt* **-fed**) allaiter. **~-stroke** *n* brasse *f*.

**breath** /breθ/ *n* souffle *m*, haleine *f*; **out of ~** à bout de souffle; **under one's ~** tout bas.

**breathalyser®** /'breθəlaɪzə(r)/ *n* alcootest *m*.

**breathe** /briːð/ *vt/i* respirer. **~ in** inspirer; **~ out** expirer.

**breathless** /'breθlɪs/ *adj* à bout de souffle.

**breathtaking** /'breθteɪkɪŋ/ *adj* à vous couper le souffle.

**bred** /bred/ **~BREED.**

**breed** /briːd/ *vt* (*pt* **bred**) élever; (give rise to) engendrer. ● *vi* se reproduire. ● *n* race *f*.

**breeze** /briːz/ *n* brise *f*.

**brew** /bruː/ *vt* (beer) brasser; (tea) faire infuser. ● *vi* (beer) fermenter; (tea) infuser; (fig) se préparer. ● *n* décoction *f*. **brewer** *n* brasseur *m*. **brewery** *n* brasserie *f*.

**bribe** /braɪb/ *n* pot-de-vin *m*. ● *vt* soudoyer. **bribery** *n* corruption *f*.

**brick** /brɪk/ *n* brique *f*. **~layer** *n* maçon *m*.

**bridal** /'braɪdl/ *adj* (dress) de mariée; (car, chamber) des mariés.

**bride** /braɪd/ *n* mariée *f*. **~groom** *n* marié *m*. **~smaid** *n* demoiselle *f* d'honneur.

**bridge** /brɪdʒ/ *n* pont *m*; (Naut) passerelle *f*; (of nose) arête *f*; (card game) bridge *m*. ● *vt* **~ a gap** combler une lacune.

**bridle** /'braɪdl/ *n* bride *f*. ● *vt* brider. **~-path** *n* piste *f* cavalière.

**brief** /briːf/ *adj* bref. ● *n* instructions *fpl*; (Jur) dossier *m*. ● *vt* donner des instructions à.

**briefcase** /'briːfkeɪs/ *n* serviette *f*.

**briefs** /briːfs/ *npl* slip *m*.

**bright** /braɪt/ *adj* brillant, vif; (day, room) clair; (cheerful) gai; (clever) intelligent.

**brighten** /'braɪtn/ *vt* égayer. ● *vi* (weather) s'éclaircir; (face) s'éclairer.

**brilliant** /'brɪlɪənt/ *adj* (student,

*career* brillant; (*light*) éclatant; (*very good* 🇹) super.

**brim** /brɪm/ n bord m. ●vi (pt **brimmed**) ~ **over** déborder (with de).

**bring** /brɪŋ/ vt (pt **brought**) (*thing*) apporter; (*person, vehicle*) amener; ~ **to bear** (*pressure etc.*) exercer. ~ **about** provoquer; ~ **back** (return with) rapporter; (*colour, shine*) redonner; ~ **down** faire tomber; (shoot down, knock down) abattre; ~ **forward** avancer; ~ **off** réussir; ~ **out** (take out) sortir; (show) faire ressortir; (*book*) publier; ~ **round** faire revenir à soi; ~ **up** (*child*) élever; (Med) vomir; (*question*) aborder.

**brink** /brɪŋk/ n bord m.

**brisk** /brɪsk/ adj vif.

**bristle** /'brɪsl/ n poil m. ●vi se hérisser; **bristling with** hérissé de.

**Britain** /'brɪtn/ n Grande-Bretagne f.

**British** /'brɪtɪʃ/ adj britannique; the ~ les Britanniques mpl.

**Briton** /'brɪtn/ n Britannique mf.

**Brittany** /'brɪtənɪ/ n Bretagne f.

**brittle** /'brɪtl/ adj fragile.

**broad** /brɔːd/ adj large; (*choice, range*) grand. ~ **bean** n fève f.

**broadband** /'brɔːdbænd/ adj à haut débit. ●n ADSL m haut débit m.

**broadcast** /'brɔːdkɑːst/ vt/i (pt **broadcast**) diffuser; (person) parler à la television ou à la radio. ●n émission f.

**broadly** /'brɔːdlɪ/ adv en gros.

**broad-minded** /brɔːd'maɪndɪd/ adj large d'esprit.

**broccoli** /'brɒkəlɪ/ n inv brocoli m.

**brochure** /'brəʊʃə(r)/ n brochure f.

**broke** /brəʊk/ →BREAK. ●adj (penniless 🇽) fauché.

**broken** /'brəʊkən/ →BREAK. ●adj ~ **English** mauvais anglais m.

**bronchitis** /brɒŋ'kaɪtɪs/ n bronchite f.

**bronze** /brɒnz/ n bronze m.

**brooch** /brəʊtʃ/ n broche f.

**brood** /bruːd/ n nichée f, couvée f. ●vi méditer tristement.

**broom** /bruːm/ n balai m.

**broth** /brɒθ/ n bouillon m.

**brothel** /'brɒθl/ n maison f close.

**brother** /'brʌðə(r)/ n frère m. ~**hood** n fraternité f. ~**-in-law** n (pl ~**s-in-law**) beau-frère m.

**brought** /brɔːt/ →BRING.

**brow** /braʊ/ n front m; (of hill) sommet m.

**brown** /braʊn/ adj (*object*) marron; (*hair*) brun; ~ **bread** pain m complet; ~ **sugar** sucre m roux. ●n marron m; brun m. ●vt/i brunir; (Culin) (faire) dorer.

**Brownie** /'braʊnɪ/ n jeannette f.

**browse** /braʊz/ vi flâner; (*animal*) brouter. ●vt (Comput) naviguer. **browser** n (Comput) navigateur m.

**bruise** /bruːz/ n bleu m. ●vt (*knee, arm etc.*) faire un bleu à; (*fruit*) abîmer.

**brush** /brʌʃ/ n brosse f; (skirmish) accrochage m; (bushes) broussailles fpl. ●vt brosser. ~ **against** frôler; ~ **aside** (dismiss) repousser; (move) écarter; ~ **up (on)** se remettre à.

**Brussels** /'brʌslz/ n Bruxelles. ~ **sprouts** npl choux mpl de Bruxelles.

**brutal** /'bruːtl/ adj brutal.

**brute** /bruːt/ n brute f; **by** ~ **force** par la force.

**BSE** abbr (Bovine Spongiform Encephalopathy) encephalopathie f spongiforme bovine, ESB f.

**bubble** /'bʌbl/ n bulle f; blow ~s faire des bulles. ● vi bouillonner; ~ over déborder. ~ **bath** n bain m moussant.

**buck** /bʌk/ n mâle m; (US, ▣) dollar m; pass the ~ rejeter la responsabilité (to sur). ● vi (horse) ruer; ~ up ▣ prendre courage; (hurry ▣) se grouiller ▣.

**bucket** /'bʌkɪt/ n seau m (of de).

**buckle** /'bʌkl/ n boucle f. ● vt/i (fasten) (se) boucler; (bend) voiler.

**bud** /bʌd/ n bourgeon m. ● vi (pt budded) bourgeonner.

**Buddhism** /'bʊdɪzəm/ n bouddhisme m.

**budding** /'bʌdɪŋ/ adj (talent) naissant; (athlete) en herbe.

**budge** /bʌdʒ/ vt/i (faire) bouger.

**budgerigar** /'bʌdʒərɪgɑː(r)/ n perruche f.

**budget** /'bʌdʒɪt/ n budget m. ● vi ~ for prévoir (dans son budget).

**buff** /bʌf/ n (colour) chamois m; ▣ fanatique mf.

**buffalo** /'bʌfələʊ/ n (pl -oes or -o buffle m; (US) bison m.

**buffer** /'bʌfə(r)/ n tampon m; ~ zone zone f tampon.

**buffet**[1] /'bʊfeɪ/ n (meal, counter) buffet m; ~ car buffet m.

**buffet**[2] /'bʌfɪt/ n (blow) soufflet m. ● vt (pt buffeted) souffleter.

**bug** /bʌg/ n (bedbug) punaise f; (any small insect) bestiole f; (germ) microbe m; (stomachache ▣) ennuis mpl gastriques; (device) micro m; (defect) défaut m; (Comput) bogue f, bug m. ● vt (pt bugged) mettre les micros dans; ▣ embêter.

**buggy** /'bʌgɪ/ n poussette f.

**build** /bɪld/ vt/i (pt built) bâtir, construire. ● n carrure f. ~ **up** (increase) augmenter, monter;

(accumulate) (s')accumuler. **builder** n entrepreneur m en bâtiment; (workman) ouvrier m du bâtiment.

**building** /'bɪldɪŋ/ n (structure) bâtiment m; (dwelling) immeuble m. ~ **society** n caisse f d'épargne.

**build-up** /'bɪldʌp/ n accumulation f; (fig) publicité f.

**built** /bɪlt/ ➔BUILD.

**built-in** /bɪlt'ɪn/ adj encastré.

**built-up area** n agglomération f, zone f urbanisée.

**bulb** /bʌlb/ n (Bot) bulbe m; (Electr) ampoule f.

**Bulgaria** /bʌl'geərɪə/ n Bulgarie f.

**Bulgarian** /bʌl'geərɪən/ n (person) Bulgare mf; (Ling) bulgare m. ● adj bulgare.

**bulge** /bʌldʒ/ n renflement m. ● vi se renfler, être renflé; be bulging with être gonflé or bourré de.

**bulimia** /bjuː'lɪmɪə/ n boulimie f.

**bulk** /bʌlk/ n volume f; in ~ (buy, sell) en gros; (transport) en vrac; the ~ of la majeure partie de.

**bull** /bʊl/ n taureau m. ~**dog** n bouledogue m. ~**doze** vt raser au bulldozer.

**bullet** /'bʊlɪt/ n balle f.

**bulletin** /'bʊlətɪn/ n bulletin m.

**bullet-proof** /'bʊlɪtpruːf/ adj (vest) pare-balles inv; (vehicle) blindé.

**bullfight** /'bʊlfaɪt/ n corrida f.

**bullion** /'bʊlɪən/ n or m or argent m en lingots.

**bullring** /'bʊlrɪŋ/ n arène f.

**bull's-eye** /'bʊlzaɪ/ n mille m.

**bully** /'bʊlɪ/ n (child) petite brute f; (adult) tyran m. ● vt maltraiter.

**bum** /bʌm/ n ▣ derrière m ▣; (US, ▣) vagabond/-e mf.

**bumble-bee** /'bʌmblbiː/ n bourdon m.

**bump** /bʌmp/ n (swelling) bosse f;

(on road) bosse f. ● vt/i cogner, heurter. ~ **along** cahoter; ~ **into** (hit) rentrer dans; (meet) tomber sur.

**bumper** /'bʌmpə(r)/ n pare-chocs m inv. ● adj exceptionnel.

**bumpy** /'bʌmpɪ/ adj (road) accidenté.

**bun** /bʌn/ n (cake) petit pain m; (hair) chignon m.

**bunch** /bʌntʃ/ n (of flowers) bouquet m; (of keys) trousseau m; (of people) groupe m; (of bananas) régime m; ~ **of grapes** grappe f de raisin.

**bundle** /'bʌndl/ n paquet m. ● vt mettre en paquet; (push) fourrer.

**bung** /bʌŋ/ n bouchon m. ● vt (stop up) boucher; (throw ⊠) flanquer ⊤.

**bunion** /'bʌnjən/ n (Med) oignon m.

**bunk** /bʌŋk/ n (on ship, train) couchette f. ~**-beds** npl lits mpl superposés.

**buoy** /bɔɪ/ n bouée f. ● vt ~ **up** (hearten) soutenir, encourager.

**buoyancy** /'bɔɪənsɪ/ n (of floating object) flottabilité f; (cheerfulness) gaieté f.

**burden** /'bɜːdn/ n fardeau m. ● vt ennuyer (with de).

**bureau** /'bjʊərəʊ/ n (pl -eaux) bureau m.

**bureaucracy** /bjʊə'rɒkrəsɪ/ n bureaucratie f.

**burglar** /'bɜːglə(r)/ n cambrioleur m; ~ **alarm** alarme f. **burglarize** vt (US) cambrioler. **burglary** n cambriolage m. **burgle** vt cambrioler.

**Burgundy** /'bɜːgəndɪ/ n (wine) bourgogne m.

**burial** /'berɪəl/ n enterrement m.

**burn** /bɜːn/ vt/i (pt **burned** or **burnt**) brûler. ● n brûlure f. ~

**down** être réduit en cendres. **burner** n (on cooker) brûleur m; (on computer) graveur m. **burning** adj en flammes; (fig) brûlant.

**burnt** /bɜːnt/ →**BURN.**

**burp** /bɜːp/ n ⊤ rot m. ● vi ⊤ roter.

**burrow** /'bʌrəʊ/ n terrier m. ● vt creuser.

**bursar** /'bɜːsə(r)/ n intendant/-e m/f. **bursary** n bourse f.

**burst** /bɜːst/ vt/i (pt **burst** (balloon, bubble) crever; (pipe) (faire) éclater. ● n explosion f; (of laughter) éclat m; (surge) élan m. ~ **into** (room) faire irruption dans; ~ **into tears** fondre en larmes; ~ **out laughing** éclater de rire; ~ **with** (be ~**ing with**) déborder de.

**bury** /'berɪ/ vt (person etc.) enterrer; (hide, cover) enfouir; (engross, thrust) plonger.

**bus** /bʌs/ n (pl **buses**) (auto)bus m. ● vt transporter en bus. ● vi (pt **bussed**) prendre l'autobus.

**bush** /bʊʃ/ n (shrub) buisson m; (land) brousse f.

**business** /'bɪznɪs/ n (task, concern) affaire f; (commerce) affaires fpl; (line of work) métier m; (shop) commerce m; **he has no ~ to** il n'a pas le droit de; **mean ~** être sérieux; **that's none of your ~!** ça ne vous regarde pas! ~**like** adj sérieux. ~**man** n homme m d'affaires.

**busker** /'bʌskə(r)/ n musicien/-ne m/f des rues.

**bus-stop** n arrêt m d'autobus.

**bust** /bʌst/ n (statue) buste m; (bosom) poitrine f. ● vt/i (pt **busted** or **bust**) (burst ⊠) crever; (break ⊠) se casser. ● adj (broken, finished ⊠) fichu; **go ~** ⊠ faire faillite.

**bustle** /'bʌsl/ vi s'affairer. ● n affairement *m*, remue-ménage *m*.

**busy** /'bɪzɪ/ *adj* (**-ier, -iest**) (*person*) occupé; (*street*) animé; (*day*) chargé. ● *vt* ~ **oneself** with s'occuper à.

**but** /bʌt/ *conj* mais. ● *prep* sauf; ~ **for** sans; **nobody** ~ personne d'autre que; **nothing** ~ rien que. ● *adv* (only) seulement.

**butcher** /'bʊtʃə(r)/ *n* boucher *m*. ● *vt* massacrer.

**butler** /'bʌtlə(r)/ *n* maître *m* d'hôtel.

**butt** /bʌt/ *n* (of gun) crosse *f*; (of cigarette) mégot *m*; (of joke) cible *f*; (barrel) tonneau *m*; (US, ) derrière *m* . ● *vi* ~ **in** interrompre.

**butter** /'bʌtə(r)/ *n* beurre *m*. ● *vt* beurrer. **~-bean** *n* haricot *m* blanc. **~cup** *n* bouton-d'or *m*.

**butterfly** /'bʌtəflaɪ/ *n* papillon *m*.

**buttock** /'bʌtək/ *n* fesse *f*.

**button** /'bʌtn/ *n* bouton *m*. ● *vt/i* ~ **(up)** (se) boutonner.

**buttonhole** /'bʌtnhəʊl/ *n* boutonnière *f*. ● *vt* accrocher.

**buy** /baɪ/ *vt* (*pt* **bought**) acheter (**from** à); ~ **sth for sb** acheter qch à qn, prendre qch pour qn; (believe 💥) croire, avaler.

**buzz** /bʌz/ *n* bourdonnement *m*. ● *vi* bourdonner. **buzzer** *n* sonnerie *f*.

**by** /baɪ/ *prep* par, de; (near) à côté de; (before) avant; (means) en, à, par; ~ **bike** à vélo; ~ **car** en auto; ~ **day** de jour; ~ **the kilo** au kilo; ~ **running** en courant; ~ **sea** par mer; ~ **that time** à ce moment-là; ~ **the way** à propos; ~ **oneself** tout seul. ● *adv* **close** ~ tout près; ~ **and large** dans l'ensemble.

**bye(-bye)** /'baɪbaɪ/ *interj*  au revoir, salut .

**by-election** *n* élection *f* partielle.

**Byelorussia** /bjeləʊ'rʊʃə/ *n* Biélo-

russie *f*.

**by-law** /'baɪlɔː/ *n* arrêté *m* municipal.

**bypass** /'baɪpɑːs/ *n* (Auto) rocade *f*; (Med) pontage *m*. ● *vt* contourner.

**by-product** *n* dérivé *m*; (fig) conséquence *f*.

**byte** /baɪt/ *n* octet *m*.

# Cc

**cab** /kæb/ *n* taxi *m*; (of lorry, train) cabine *f*.

**cabbage** /'kæbɪdʒ/ *n* chou *m*.

**cabin** /'kæbɪn/ *n* (hut) cabane *f*; (in ship, aircraft) cabine *f*.

**cabinet** /'kæbɪnɪt/ *n* petit placard *m*; (glassfronted) vitrine *f*; (Pol) cabinet *m*.

**cable** /'keɪbl/ *n* câble *m*. ● *vt* câbler. **~-car** *n* téléphérique *m*. **~ television** *n* télévision *f* par câble.

**cache** /kæʃ/ *n* (hoard) cache *f*; (place) cachette *f*.

**cackle** /'kækl/ *n* (of hen) caquet *m*; (laugh) ricanement *m*. ● *vi* caqueter; (laugh) ricaner.

**cactus** /'kæktəs/ *n* (*pl* **-ti** or **~es**) cactus *m*.

**cadet** /kə'det/ *n* élève *m* officier.

**Caesarean** /sɪ'zeərɪən/ *adj* ~ (section) césarienne *f*.

**café** /'kæfeɪ/ *n* café *m*, snack-bar *m*.

**caffeine** /'kæfiːn/ *n* caféine *f*.

**cage** /keɪdʒ/ *n* cage *f*. ● *vt* mettre en cage.

**cagey** /'keɪdʒɪ/ *adj* réticent.

**cagoule** /kə'guːl/ *n* K-way® *m*.

**cajole** /kə'dʒəʊl/ *vt* ~ **sb into doing sth** amener qn à faire qch par la cajolerie.

**cake** /keɪk/ n gâteau m; (of soap) pain m. ● vi former une croûte (on sur).

**calculate** /'kælkjʊleɪt/ vt calculer; (estimate) évaluer. **calculated** adj délibéré; (risk) calculé. **calculating** adj calculateur. **calculation** n calcul m. **calculator** n calculatrice f.

**calculus** /'kælkjʊləs/ n (pl -li or ~es) calcul m.

**calendar** /'kælɪndə(r)/ n calendrier m.

**calf** /kɑːf/ n (pl calves) (young cow or bull) veau m; (of leg) mollet m.

**calibre** /'kælɪbə(r)/ n calibre m.

**call** /kɔːl/ vt/i appeler; (loudly) crier; he's ~ed John il s'appelle John; ~ sb stupid traiter qn d'imbécile. ● n appel m; (of bird) cri m; (visit) visite f; make/pay a ~ on rendre visite à; be on ~ être de garde; ~ box cabine f téléphonique. ~ **centre** n centre m d'appels. ~ **back** rappeler; (visit) repasser; ~ **for** (help) appeler à; (demand) demander; (require) exiger; (collect) passer prendre; ~ **in** passer. ~ **off** annuler. ~ **on** (visit) rendre visite à; (urge) demander à (to do de faire). ~ **out** (to) appeler. ~ **round** venir. ~ **up** appeler.

**calling** /'kɔːlɪŋ/ n vocation f.

**callous** /'kæləs/ adj inhumain.

**calm** /kɑːm/ adj calme. ● n calme m. ● vt/i ~ (**down**) (se) calmer.

**calorie** /'kælərɪ/ n calorie f.

**camcorder** /'kæmkɔːdə(r)/ n caméscope® m.

**came** /keɪm/ ➡COME.

**camel** /'kæml/ n chameau m.

**camera** /'kæmərə/ n appareil(-photo) m; (TV, cinema) caméra f; in ~ à huis clos. ~**man** n (pl -men) cadreur m, cameraman m.

**camouflage** /'kæməflɑːʒ/ n camouflage m. ● vt camoufler.

**camp** /kæmp/ n camp m. ● vi camper.

**campaign** /kæm'peɪn/ n campagne f. ● vi faire campagne.

**camper** /'kæmpə(r)/ n campeur/-euse m/f. ~ (-**van**) n camping-car m.

**camping** /'kæmpɪŋ/ n camping m; go ~ faire du camping.

**campsite** /'kæmpsaɪt/ n camping m.

**campus** /'kæmpəs/ n (pl ~es) campus m.

---

**can¹** /kæn, kən/

*infinitive* be able to; *present* can; *present negative* can't, cannot (*formal*); *past* could; *past participle* been able to

● *auxiliary verb*

····▸ pouvoir; where ~ I buy stamps? où est-ce que je peux acheter des timbres?; she can't come elle ne peut pas venir.

····▸ (be allowed to) pouvoir; ~ I smoke? est-ce que je peux fumer?

····▸ (know how to) savoir; she ~ swim elle sait nager; he can't drive il ne sait pas conduire.

····▸ (with verbs of perception) I ~ hear you je t'entends; ~ they see us? est-ce qu'ils nous voient?

---

**can²** /kæn/ n (for food) boîte f; (of petrol) bidon m. ● vt (pt canned) mettre en conserve.

**Canada** /ˈkænədə/ n Canada m.

**Canadian** /kəˈneɪdɪən/ n Canadien/-ne m/f. ● adj canadien.

**canal** /kəˈnæl/ n canal m.

**canary** /kəˈneərɪ/ n canari m.

**cancel** /ˈkænsl/ vt/i (pt cancelled) (call off, revoke) annuler; (cross out) barrer; (a stamp) oblitérer; ~ out (se) neutraliser. **cancellation** n annulation f.

**cancer** /ˈkænsə(r)/ n cancer m; have ~ avoir un cancer.

**Cancer** /ˈkænsə(r)/ n Cancer m.

**cancerous** /ˈkænsərəs/ adj cancéreux.

**candid** /ˈkændɪd/ adj franc.

**candidate** /ˈkændɪdət/ n candidat/-e m/f.

**candle** /ˈkændl/ n bougie f; (in church) cierge m. **~stick** n bougeoir m.

**candy** /ˈkændɪ/ n (US) bonbon(s) m(pl). **~-floss** n barbe f à papa.

**cane** /keɪn/ n canne f; (for baskets) rotin m; (for punishment) badine f. ● vt donner des coups de badine à.

**canister** /ˈkænɪstə(r)/ n boîte f.

**cannabis** /ˈkænəbɪs/ n cannabis m.

**cannibal** /ˈkænɪbl/ n cannibale mf.

**cannon** /ˈkænən/ n (pl ~ or ~s) canon m. **~-ball** n boulet de canon.

**cannot** →CAN NOT.

**canoe** /kəˈnuː/ n canoë m. ● vi faire du canoë. **canoeist** n canoéiste mf.

**canon** /ˈkænən/ n (clergyman) chanoine m; (rule) canon m.

**can-opener** n ouvre-boîtes m inv.

**canopy** /ˈkænəpɪ/ n dais m; (for bed) baldaquin m.

**can't** →CAN NOT.

**canteen** /kænˈtiːn/ n (restaurant) cantine f; (flask) bidon m.

**canter** /ˈkæntə(r)/ n petit galop m.

● vi aller au petit galop.

**canvas** /ˈkænvəs/ n toile f.

**canvass** /ˈkænvəs/ vt/i (Comm, Pol) faire de démarchage (auprès de); ~ opinion sonder l'opinion.

**canyon** /ˈkænjən/ n cañon m.

**cap** /kæp/ n (hat) casquette f; (of bottle, tube) bouchon m; (of beer or milk bottle) capsule f; (of pen) capuchon m; (for toy gun) amorce f. ● vt (pt capped) couronner.

**capability** /keɪpəˈbɪlətɪ/ n capacité f.

**capable** /ˈkeɪpəbl/ adj (person) compétent; ~ of doing capable de faire.

**capacity** /kəˈpæsətɪ/ n capacité f; in my ~ as a doctor en ma qualité de médecin.

**cape** /keɪp/ n (cloak) cape f; (Geog) cap m.

**caper** /ˈkeɪpə(r)/ vi gambader. ● n (leap) cabriole f; (funny film) comédie f; (Culin) câpre f.

**capital** /ˈkæpɪtl/ adj (letter) majuscule; (offence) capital. ● n (town) capitale f; (money) capital m; ~ (letter) majuscule f.

**capitalism** /ˈkæpɪtəlɪzəm/ n capitalisme m.

**capitalize** /ˈkæpɪtəlaɪz/ vi ~ on tirer parti de.

---

*i*

**Capitol Hill** Ce quartier historique de Washington D.C. abrite le bâtiment du Capitole, dans lequel se réunit le Congrès depuis 1800, la cour suprême fédérale, plus haute instance judiciaire des États-Unis, et la bibliothèque du Congrès, l'une des plus grandes au monde. Par métonymie, the Capitol ou the Hill font référence au Congrès.
▷CONGRESS

**capitulate** /kə'pɪtʃʊleɪt/ vi capituler.

**Capricorn** /'kæprɪkɔːn/ n Capricorne m.

**capsize** /kæp'saɪz/ vt/i (faire) chavirer.

**capsule** /'kæpsjuːl/ n capsule f.

**captain** /'kæptɪn/ n capitaine m.

**caption** /'kæpʃn/ n (under photo) légende f; (subtitle) sous-titre m.

**captivate** /'kæptɪveɪt/ vt captiver.

**captive** /'kæptɪv/ adj & n captif/-ive (m/f.) **captivity** n captivité f.

**capture** /'kæptʃə(r)/ vt (person, animal) capturer; (moment, likeness) saisir. ● n capture f.

**car** /kɑː(r)/ n voiture f. ● adj (industry) automobile; (accident) de voiture; (journey) en voiture.

**caravan** /'kærəvæn/ n caravane f.

**carbohydrate** /kɑːbə'haɪdreɪt/ n hydrate m de carbone.

**carbon** /'kɑːbən/ n carbone m. ∼ footprint empreinte f écologique.

**carburettor** /'kɑːbərəɪtə(r)/ n carburateur m.

**card** /kɑːd/ n carte f.

**cardboard** /'kɑːdbɔːd/ n carton m.

**cardiac** /'kɑːdɪæk/ adj cardiaque; ∼ arrest arrêt m du cœur.

**cardigan** /'kɑːdɪɡən/ n cardigan m.

**carer** /'keərə(r)/ n (relative) personne ayant un parent handicapé ou un malade à charge; (professional) aide f à la domicile.

**cardinal** /'kɑːdɪnl/ adj (sin) capital; (rule) fondamental; (number) cardinal. ● n cardinal m.

**card index** n fichier m.

**care** /keə(r)/ n (attention) soin m, attention f; (worry) souci m; (looking after) soins mpl; take ∼ of (deal with) s'occuper de; (be careful with) prendre soin de; take ∼ to do sth

faire bien attention à faire qch. ● vi ∼ about s'intéresser à; ∼ for s'occuper de; (invalid) soigner; ∼ to do vouloir faire; I don't ∼ ça m'est égal.

**career** /kə'rɪə(r)/ n carrière f. ● vi ∼ in/out entrer/sortir à toute vitesse.

**carefree** /'keəfriː/ adj insouciant.

**careful** /'keəfl/ adj prudent; (research, study) méticuleux; (be) ∼! (fais) attention! **carefully** adv avec soin; (cautiously) prudemment.

**careless** /'keəlɪs/ adj négligent; (work) bâclé.

**caress** /kə'res/ n caresse f. ● vt caresser.

**caretaker** /'keəteɪkə(r)/ n concierge mf. ● adj (president) par intérim.

**car ferry** n ferry m.

**cargo** /'kɑːɡəʊ/ n (pl ∼es) chargement m; (Naut) cargaison f.

**Caribbean** /kærɪ'biːən/ adj des Caraïbes, des Antilles. ● n the ∼ (sea) la mer des Antilles; (islands) les Antilles fpl.

**caring** /'keərɪŋ/ adj affectueux.

**carnation** /kɑː'neɪʃn/ n œillet m.

**carnival** /'kɑːnɪvl/ n carnaval m.

**carol** /'kærəl/ n chant m de Noël.

**carp** /kɑːp/ n inv carpe f. ● vi maugréer.

**car-park** n parc m de stationnement, parking m.

**carpenter** /'kɑːpəntə(r)/ n (joiner) menuisier m; (builder) charpentier m. **carpentry** n menuiserie f; (structural) charpenterie f.

**carpet** /'kɑːpɪt/ n (fitted) moquette f; (loose) tapis m. ● vt (pt carpeted) mettre de la moquette dans.

**carriage** /'kærɪdʒ/ n (rail) wagon m; (ceremonial) carrosse m; (of goods) transport m; (cost) port m.

**carriageway** /ˈkærɪdʒweɪ/ n chaussée f.

**carrier** /ˈkærɪə(r)/ n transporteur m; (Med) porteur/-euse m/f; ~ (bag) sac m en plastique.

**carrot** /ˈkærət/ n carotte f.

**carry** /ˈkærɪ/ vt/i porter; (goods) transporter; (involve) comporter; (motion) voter; be carried away s'emballer. □ ~ **off** emporter; (prize) remporter; ~ **on** (continue) continuer; (business) conduire; (conversation) mener; ~ **out** (order, plan) exécuter; (duty) remplir; (experiment, operation, repair) effectuer. ~-**cot** n portebébé m.

**car sharing** n covoiturage m.

**cart** /kɑːt/ n charrette f. ● vt (heavy bag 🄣) trimballer 🄣.

**carton** /ˈkɑːtn/ n (box) boîte f; (of yoghurt, cream) pot m; (of cigarettes) cartouche f.

**cartoon** /kɑːˈtuːn/ n dessin m humoristique; (cinema) dessin m animé; (strip cartoon) bande f dessinée.

**cartridge** /ˈkɑːtrɪdʒ/ n cartouche f.

**carve** /kɑːv/ vt tailler; (meat) découper.

**car-wash** n lavage m automatique.

**cascade** /kæˈskeɪd/ n cascade f. ● vi tomber en cascade.

**case** /keɪs/ n cas m; (Jur) affaire f; (suitcase) valise f; (crate) caisse f; (for spectacles) étui m; (just) in ~ au cas où; in ~ I he comes au cas où I il viendrait; in ~ of fire en cas d'incendie; in any ~ de toute façon; the ~ for sth les arguments mpl en faveur de qch; the ~ for the defence la défense.

**cash** /kæʃ/ n espèces fpl, argent m; in ~ en espèces. ● adj (price) comptant. ● vt encaisser; ~ in (on) profiter (de). ~-**back** n retrait

d'argent à la caisse. ~ **desk** n caisse f. ~ **dispenser** n distributeur m de billets.

**cashew** /ˈkæʃuː/ n cajou m.

**cash flow** n marge f brute d'autofinancement.

**cashier** /kæˈʃɪə(r)/ n caissier/-ière m/f.

**cashmere** /kæʃˈmɪə(r)/ n cachemire m.

**cash:** ~**point** n distributeur m de billets. ~ **point card** n carte f de retrait. ~ **register** n caisse f enregistreuse.

**casino** /kəˈsiːnəʊ/ n casino m.

**casket** /ˈkɑːskɪt/ n (box) coffret m; (coffin) cercueil m.

**casserole** /ˈkæsərəʊl/ n (pan) daubière f; (food) ragoût m.

**cassette** /kəˈset/ n cassette f.

**cast** /kɑːst/ vt (pt **cast**) (object, glance) jeter; (shadow) projeter; (metal) couler; ~ **(off)** (shed) se dépouiller de; ~ **one's vote** voter; ~ **iron** fonte f. ● n (cinema, Theat, TV) distribution f; (Med) plâtre m.

**castaway** /ˈkɑːstəweɪ/ n naufragé/-e m/f.

**cast-iron** adj de fonte; (fig) en béton.

**castle** /ˈkɑːsl/ n château m; (chess) tour f.

**cast-offs** npl vieux vêtements mpl.

**castor** /ˈkɑːstə(r)/ n (wheel) roulette f.

**castrate** /kæˈstreɪt/ vt châtrer.

**casual** /ˈkæʒʊəl/ adj (informal) décontracté; (remark) désinvolte; (acquaintance) de passage; (work) temporaire. **casually** adv (remark) d'un air détaché; (dress) simplement.

**casualty** /ˈkæʒʊəltɪ/ n victime f; (part of hospital) urgences fpl.

**cat** /kæt/ n chat m; (feline) félin m.

**catalogue** /'kætəlɒg/ n catalogue m. ●vt dresser un catalogue de.

**catalyst** /'kætəlɪst/ n catalyseur m.

**catalytic** /kætə'lɪtɪk/ adj ∼ converter pot m catalytique.

**catapult** /'kætəpʌlt/ n lance-pierres m inv. ●vt projeter.

**cataract** /'kætərækt/ n (Med, Geog) cataracte f.

**catarrh** /kə'tɑː(r)/ n catarrhe m.

**catastrophe** /kə'tæstrəfɪ/ n catastrophe f.

**catch** /kætʃ/ vt (pt caught) attraper; (bus, plane) prendre; (understand) saisir; ∼ sb doing surprendre qn en train de faire; ∼ fire prendre feu; ∼ sight of apercevoir; ∼ sb's attention/eye attirer l'attention de qn. ●vi (get stuck) se prendre (in dans); (start to burn) prendre. ●n (fastening) fermeture f; (drawback) piège m; (in sport) prise f. ∼ on devenir populaire. ∼ out prendre de court. ∼ up rattraper son retard; ∼ up with sb rattraper qn.

**catching** /'kætʃɪŋ/ adj contagieux.

**catchment** /'kætʃmənt/ n ∼ area (School) secteur m.

**catch-phrase** n formule f favorite.

**catchy** /'kætʃɪ/ adj entraînant.

**category** /'kætəgərɪ/ n catégorie f.

**cater** /'keɪtə(r)/ vi organiser les réceptions; ∼ for/to (guests) accueillir; (needs) pourvoir à; (reader) s'adresser à. **caterer** n traiteur m.

**caterpillar** /'kætəpɪlə(r)/ n chenille f.

**cathedral** /kə'θiːdrəl/ n cathédrale f.

**catholic** /'kæθəlɪk/ adj éclectique. **Catholic** adj & n catholique (mf). **Catholicism** n catholicisme m.

**Catseye®** n plot m rétroréfléchissant.

**cattle** /'kætl/ npl bétail m.

**caught** /kɔːt/ ➡CATCH.

**cauliflower** /'kɒlɪflaʊə(r)/ n chou-fleur m.

**cause** /kɔːz/ n cause f; (reason) raison f, motif m. ●vt causer; ∼ sth to grow/move faire pousser/bouger qch.

**causeway** /'kɔːzweɪ/ n chaussée f.

**caution** /'kɔːʃn/ n prudence f; (warning) avertissement m. ●vt avertir. **cautious** adj prudent. **cautiously** adv prudemment.

**cave** /keɪv/ n grotte f. ●vi ∼ in s'effondrer; (agree) céder. ∼**man** n (pl **-men**) homme m des cavernes.

**cavern** /'kævən/ n caverne f.

**caviare** /'kævɪɑː(r)/ n caviar m.

**caving** /'keɪvɪŋ/ n spéléologie f.

**CCTV** abbr (closed circuit television) télévision f en circuit fermé.

**CD** abbr (compact disc) disque m compact, CD m.

**CD-ROM** /siːdiː'rɒm/ n disque m optique compact, CD-ROM m.

**cease** /siːs/ vt/i cesser. ∼**-fire** n cessez-le-feu m inv.

**cedar** /'siːdə(r)/ n cèdre m.

**cedilla** /sɪ'dɪlə/ n cédille f.

**ceiling** /'siːlɪŋ/ n plafond m.

**celebrate** /'selɪbreɪt/ vt (occasion) fêter; (Easter, mass) célébrer. ●vi faire la fête. **celebrated** adj célèbre. **celebration** n fête f.

**celebrity** /sɪ'lebrətɪ/ n célébrité f.

**celery** /'selərɪ/ n céleri m.

**cell** /sel/ n cellule f; (Electr) élément m.

**cellar** /'selə(r)/ n cave f.

**cellist** /'tʃelɪst/ n violoncelliste mf.

**cello** n violoncelle m.

**cellphone** /'selfəʊn/ n (téléphone

*m*) portable.

**Celt** /kelt/ *n* Celte *mf.*

**cement** /sɪˈment/ *n* ciment *m.* ● *vt* cimenter. ~-**mixer** *n* bétonnière *f.*

**cemetery** /ˈsemətrɪ/ *n* cimetière *m.*

**censor** /ˈsensə(r)/ *n* censeur *m.* ● *vt* censurer.

**censure** /ˈsenʃə(r)/ *n* censure *f.* ● *vt* critiquer.

**census** /ˈsensəs/ *n* recensement *m.*

**cent** /sent/ *n* cent *m.*

**centenary** /senˈtiːnərɪ/ *n* centenaire *m.*

**centigrade** /ˈsentɪɡreɪd/ *adj* centigrade.

**centilitre**, (US) **centiliter** /ˈsentɪliːtə(r)/ *n* centilitre *m.*

**centimetre**, (US) **centimeter** /ˈsentɪmiːtə(r)/ *n* centimètre *m.*

**centipede** /ˈsentɪpiːd/ *n* mille-pattes *m inv.*

**central** /ˈsentrəl/ *adj* central; ~ **heating** chauffage *m* central; ~ **locking** fermeture *f* centralisée des portes. **centralize** *vt* centraliser. **centrally** *adv* (situated) au centre.

**centre**, (US) **center** /ˈsentə(r)/ *n* centre *m.* ● *vt* (*pt* **centred**) centrer. ● *vi* ~ **on** tourner autour de.

**century** /ˈsentʃərɪ/ *n* siècle *m.*

**ceramic** /sɪˈræmɪk/ *adj* (art) céramique; (object) en céramique.

**cereal** /ˈsɪərɪəl/ *n* céréale *f.*

**ceremonial** /serɪˈməʊnɪəl/ *adj* (dress) de cérémonie. ● *n* cérémonial *m.* **ceremony** *n* cérémonie *f.*

**certain** /ˈsɜːtn/ *adj* certain; for ~ avec certitude; **make** ~ **of** s'assurer de. **certainly** *adv* certainement. **certainty** *n* certitude *f.*

**certificate** /səˈtɪfɪkət/ *n* certificat *m.*

**certify** /ˈsɜːtɪfaɪ/ *vt* certifier.

**cesspit, cesspool** /ˈsespɪt, ˈsespuːl/ *n* fosse *f* d'aisances.

**chafe** /tʃeɪf/ *vt*/*i* frotter (contre).

**chagrin** /ˈʃæɡrɪn/ *n* dépit *m.*

**chain** /tʃeɪn/ *n* chaîne *f*; ~ **reaction** réaction *f* en chaîne; ~ **store** magasin *m* à succursales multiples. ● *vt* enchaîner. ~-**smoke** *vi* fumer sans arrêt.

**chair** /tʃeə(r)/ *n* chaise *f*; (armchair) fauteuil *m*; (Univ) chaire *f*; (chairperson) président/-e *mf.* ● *vt* (preside over) présider. ~**man** *n* (*pl* -**men**) président/-e *mf.* ~**woman** *n* (*pl* -**women**) présidente *f.*

**chalk** /tʃɔːk/ *n* craie *f.*

**challenge** /ˈtʃælɪndʒ/ *n* défi *m*; (opportunity) challenge *m.* ● *vt* (summon) défier (to do de faire); (question truth of) contester. **challenger** *n* (Sport) challenger *m.* **challenging** *adj* stimulant.

**chamber** /ˈtʃeɪmbə(r)/ *n* (old use) chambre *f.* ~**maid** *n* femme *f* de chambre. ~ **music** *n* musique *f* de chambre. ~-**pot** *n* pot *m* de chambre.

**champagne** /ʃæmˈpeɪn/ *n* champagne *m.*

**champion** /ˈtʃæmpɪən/ *n* champion/-ne *mf.* ● *vt* défendre. **championship** *n* championnat *m.*

**chance** /tʃɑːns/ *n* (luck) hasard *m*; (opportunity) occasion *f*; (likelihood) chances *fpl*; (risk) risque *m*; **by** ~ par hasard; **by any** ~ par hasard; ~**s are that** it est probable que. ● *adj* fortuit. ● *vt* ~ **doing** prendre le risque de faire; ~ **it** tenter sa chance.

**chancellor** /ˈtʃɑːnsələ(r)/ *n* chancelier *m*; **C~ of the Exchequer** Chancelier de l'échiquier.

**chandelier** /ʃændəˈlɪə(r)/ *n* lustre *m.*

**change** /tʃeɪndʒ/ vt (alter) changer; (exchange) échanger (for contre). (money) changer; ~ **trains/one's dress** changer de train/de robe; ~ **one's mind** changer d'avis. ● vi changer; (money) changer; (clothes) clothes) se changer; ~ **into** se transformer en; ~ **over** passer (**to** à). ● n changement m; (money) monnaie f; **a** ~ **for the better** une amélioration; **a** ~ **for the worse** un changement en pire; **a** ~ **of clothes** des vêtements de rechange; **for a** ~ pour changer. **changeable** adj changeant. **changing room** n (in shop) cabine f d'essayage; (Sport) vestiaire m.

**channel** /tʃænl/ n (for liquid, information) canal m; (TV) chaîne f; (groove) rainure f. ● vt (pt **channelled**) canaliser. C~ n the (English) C~ la Manche; the C~ **tunnel** le tunnel sous la Manche; the C~ **Islands** les îles fpl Anglo-Normandes.

**chant** /tʃɑːnt/ n mélopée f; (of demonstrators) chant m scandé. ● vt/i scander; (Relig) psalmodier.

**chaos** /keɪɒs/ n chaos m.

**chap** /tʃæp/ n (man Ⅰ) type m Ⅰ.

**chapel** /tʃæpl/ n chapelle f.

**chaplain** /tʃæplɪn/ n aumônier m.

**chapped** /tʃæpt/ adj gercé.

**chapter** /tʃæptə(r)/ n chapitre m.

**char** /tʃɑː(r)/ vt (pt **charred**) carboniser.

**character** /kærəktə(r)/ n caractère m; (in novel, play) personnage m; **of good** ~ de bonne réputation.

**characteristic** /kærəktərɪstɪk/ adj & n caractéristique (f).

**charcoal** /tʃɑːkəʊl/ n charbon m de bois; (art) fusain m.

**charge** /tʃɑːdʒ/ n (fee) frais mpl; (Mil) charge f; (Jur) inculpation f; (task, custody) charge f; **in** ~ **of** responsable de; **take** ~ **of** prendre en charge, se charger de. ● vt (customer) faire payer; (enemy, gun) charger; (Jur) inculper (**with** de); ~ **£20 an hour** prendre 20 livres de l'heure; ~ **card** carte f d'achat. ● vi faire payer; (bull) foncer; (person) se précipiter.

**charisma** /kəˈrɪzmə/ n charisme m. **charismatic** adj charismatique.

**charitable** /tʃærɪtəbl/ adj charitable. **charity** n charité f; (organization) organisation f caritative.

**charm** /tʃɑːm/ n charme m; (trinket) amulette f. ● vt charmer. **charming** adj charmant.

**chart** /tʃɑːt/ n (graph) graphique m; (table) tableau m; (map) carte f. ● vt (route) porter sur la carte.

**charter** /tʃɑːtə(r)/ n charte f. ~ (**flight**) charter m. ● vt affréter. ~**ed accountant** n expert-comptable m.

**chase** /tʃeɪs/ vt poursuivre; ~ **away** or **off** chasser. ● vi courir (**after** après). ● n chasse f.

**chassis** /ʃæsɪ/ n châssis m.

**chastise** /tʃæˈstaɪz/ vt châtier.

**chat** /tʃæt/ n conversation f; (on Internet) causette f, bavardage m; **have a** ~ bavarder; ~ **show** talk-show m. ~**room** n salle f de causette, salle f de bavardage. ● vi (pt **chatted**) bavarder. ~ **up** Ⅰ draguer Ⅰ

**chatter** /tʃætə(r)/ n bavardage m. ● vi bavarder; **his teeth are** ~**ing** il claque des dents. ~**box** n bavard/-e m/f.

**chatty** /tʃætɪ/ adj bavard.

**chauffeur** /ʃəʊfə(r)/ n chauffeur m.

**chauvinist** /ʃəʊvɪnɪst/ n chauvin/-e m/f. **macho** m.

**cheap** /tʃiːp/ adj bon marché inv;

( *fare, rate* ) réduit; ( *joke, gimmick* ) facile; ~**er meilleur marché** *m/f*. **cheapen** *vt* déprécier. **cheaply** *adv* à bas prix.

**cheat** /tʃiːt/ *vi* tricher. ● *vt* tromper. ● *n* tricheur/-euse *m/f*.

**check** /tʃek/ *vt/i* vérifier; ( *tickets, rises, inflation* ) contrôler; ( *stop* ) arrêter; ( *tick off:* US) cocher. ● *n* contrôle *m*; ( *curb* ) frein *m*; ( *chess* ) échec *m*; ( *pattern* ) carreaux *mpl*; ( *bill:* US) addition *f*; ( *cheque:* US) chèque *m*. ~ **in** remplir la fiche; (at airport) enregistrer; ~ **out** partir; ~ **sth out** vérifier qch. ~ **up** vérifier. ~ **up on** ( *story* ) vérifier; ( *person* ) faire une enquête sur.

**check:** ~**-in** *n* enregistrement *m*. **checking account** *n* (US) compte *m* courant. ~**-list** *n* liste *f* de contrôle. ~**mate** *n* échec *m* et mat. ~**-out** *n* caisse *f*. ~**-point** *n* contrôle *m*. ~**-up** *n* examen *m* médical.

**cheek** /tʃiːk/ *n* joue *f*; (impudence) culot *m* 🗉. **cheeky** *adj* effronté.

**cheer** /tʃɪə(r)/ *n* gaieté *f*; ~**s acclamations** *fpl*; (when drinking) à la vôtre. ● *vt/i* applaudir; ~ **sb** (up) (gladden) remonter le moral à qn; ~ **up prendre courage**. **cheerful** *adj* joyeux. **cheerfulness** *n* gaieté *f*.

**cheerio** /tʃɪərɪˈəʊ/ *interj* 🗉 salut 🗉.

**cheese** /tʃiːz/ *n* fromage *m*.

**cheetah** /ˈtʃiːtə/ *n* guépard *m*.

**chef** /ʃef/ *n* chef *m*.

**chemical** /ˈkemɪkl/ *adj* chimique. ● *n* produit *m* chimique.

**chemist** /ˈkemɪst/ *n* pharmacien/-ne *m/f*; (scientist) chimiste *mf*; ~**'s (shop)** pharmacie *f*. **chemistry** *n* chimie *f*.

**cheque** /tʃek/ *n* chèque *m*. ~**-book** *n* chéquier *m*. ~ **card** *n* carte *f* bancaire.

**chequered** /ˈtʃekəd/ *adj* (pattern) à damiers; (fig) en dents de scie.

**cherish** /ˈtʃerɪʃ/ *vt* chérir; (hope) caresser.

**cherry** /ˈtʃerɪ/ *n* cerise *f*; (tree, wood) cerisier *m*.

**chess** /tʃes/ *n* échecs *mpl*. ~**-board** *n* échiquier *m*.

**chest** /tʃest/ *n* (Anat) poitrine *f*; (box) coffre *m*; ~ **of drawers** commode *f*.

**chestnut** /ˈtʃesnʌt/ *n* (nut) marron *m*, châtaigne *f*; (tree) marronnier *m*; (sweet) châtaignier *m*.

**chew** /tʃuː/ *vt* mâcher.

**chic** /ʃiːk/ *adj* chic *inv*.

**chick** /tʃɪk/ *n* poussin *m*.

**chicken** /ˈtʃɪkɪn/ *n* poulet *m*. ● *adj* 🗉 froussard. ● *vi* ~ **out** 🗉 se dégonfler. ~**-pox** *n* varicelle *f*.

**chick-pea** /ˈtʃɪkpiː/ *n* pois *m* chiche.

**chicory** /ˈtʃɪkərɪ/ *n* (for salad) endive *f*; (in coffee) chicorée *f*.

**chief** /tʃiːf/ *n* chef *m*. ● *adj* principal. **chiefly** *adv* principalement.

**chilblain** /ˈtʃɪlbleɪn/ *n* engelure *f*.

**child** /tʃaɪld/ *n* ( *pl* **children**) enfant *mf*. ~**birth** *n* accouchement *m*. **childhood** *n* enfance *f*. **childish** *adj* puéril. **childless** *adj* sans enfants. **childlike** *adj* enfantin. ~**-minder** *n* nourrice *f*.

**Chile** /ˈtʃɪlɪən/ *n* Chili *m*.

**chill** /tʃɪl/ *n* froid *m*; (Med) refroidissement *m*. ● *adj* froid. ● *vt* (person) faire frissonner; (wine) rafraîchir; ( *food* ) mettre à refroidir.

**chilli** /ˈtʃɪlɪ/ *n* ( *pl* ~**es**) piment *m*.

**chilly** /ˈtʃɪlɪ/ *adj* froid; **it's** ~ il fait froid.

**chime** /tʃaɪm/ *n* carillon *m*. ● *vt/i* carillonner.

**chimney** /ˈtʃɪmnɪ/ *n* cheminée *f*.

~-sweep n ramoneur m.

**chimpanzee** /tʃɪmpæn'ziː/ n chimpanzé m.

**chin** /tʃɪn/ n menton m.

**china** /'tʃaɪnə/ n porcelaine f.

**China** /'tʃaɪnə/ n Chine f.

**Chinese** /tʃar'niːz/ n (person) Chinois/-e m/f; (Ling) chinois m. ● adj chinois.

**chip** /tʃɪp/ n (on plate) ébréchure f; (piece) éclat m; (of wood) copeau m; (Culin) frite f; (Comput) puce f; (potato) ~s (US) chips fpl. ● vt/i (pt chipped) (s')ébrécher; ~ in 🔡 dire son mot; (with money) contribuer.

**chiropodist** /kɪ'rɒpədɪst/ n pédicure mf.

**chirp** /tʃɜːp/ n pépiement m. ● vi pépier. **chirpy** adj gai.

**chisel** /'tʃɪzl/ n ciseau m. ● vt (pt chiselled) ciseler.

**chit** /tʃɪt/ n note f; (voucher) bon m.

**chitchat** /'tʃɪttʃæt/ n 🔡 bavardage m.

**chivalrous** /'ʃɪvəlrəs/ adj galant.

**chives** /tʃaɪvz/ npl ciboulette f.

**chlorine** /'klɔːriːn/ n chlore m.

**choc ice** /'tʃɒkaɪs/ n esquimau m.

**chock-a-block** /tʃɒkə'blɒk/ adj plein à craquer.

**chocolate** /'tʃɒklət/ n chocolat m.

**choice** /tʃɔɪs/ n choix m. ● adj de choix.

**choir** /'kwaɪə(r)/ n chœur m. ~boy n jeune choriste m.

**choke** /tʃəʊk/ vt/i (s')étrangler; ~ (up) boucher. ● n starter m.

**cholesterol** /kə'lestərɒl/ n cholestérol m.

**choose** /tʃuːz/ vt/i (pt chose, pp chosen) choisir; ~ to do décider de faire. **choosy** adj difficile.

**chop** /tʃɒp/ vt/i (pt chopped) (wood) couper; (food) hacher.

chopping board planche f à découper; ~ down abattre. ● n (meat) côtelette f. **chopper** n hachoir m. 🔡 hélico m 🔡.

**choppy** /'tʃɒpɪ/ adj (sea) agité.

**chopstick** /'tʃɒpstɪk/ n baguette f (chinoise).

**chord** /kɔːd/ n (Mus) accord m.

**chore** /tʃɔː(r)/ n (routine) tâche f; (unpleasant) corvée f.

**chortle** /'tʃɔːtl/ n gloussement m. ● vi glousser.

**chorus** /'kɔːrəs/ n chœur m; (of song) refrain m.

**chose, chosen** /tʃəʊz, 'tʃəʊzən/ ⇒CHOOSE.

**Christ** /kraɪst/ n le Christ.

**christen** /'krɪsn/ vt baptiser. **christening** n baptême m.

**Christian** /'krɪstʃən/ adj & n chrétien/-ne (m/f). ~ name nom m de baptême. **Christianity** n christianisme m.

**Christmas** /'krɪsməs/ n Noël m; ~ Day/Eve le jour/la veille de Noël. ● adj (card, tree) de Noël.

**chronic** /'krɒnɪk/ adj (situation, disease) chronique; (bad 🔡) nul.

**chronicle** /'krɒnɪkl/ n chronique f.

**chronological** /krɒnə'lɒdʒɪkl/ adj chronologique.

**chrysanthemum** /krɪ'sæn θəməm/ n chrysanthème m.

**chubby** /'tʃʌbɪ/ adj (-ier, -iest) potelé.

**chuck** /tʃʌk/ vt 🔡 lancer; ~ away or out 🔡 balancer.

**chuckle** /'tʃʌkl/ n gloussement m. ● vi glousser.

**chuffed** /tʃʌft/ adj 🔡 vachement content 🔡.

**chunk** /tʃʌŋk/ n morceau m. **chunky** adj (sweater, jewellery) gros; (person) costaud.

**church** /tʃɜːtʃ/ n église f. ~ goer n pratiquant/-e m/f. ~yard n cimetière m.

**churn** /tʃɜːn/ n baratte f (milk-can) bidon m. ● vt baratter; ~ out produire en série.

**chute** /ʃuːt/ n toboggan m; (for rubbish) vide-ordures m inv.

**chutney** /'tʃʌtnɪ/ n condiment m aigredoux.

**cider** /'saɪdə(r)/ n cidre m.

**cigar** /sɪ'ɡɑː(r)/ n cigare m.

**cigarette** /sɪɡə'ret/ n cigarette f; ~ end mégot m.

**cinder** /'sɪndə(r)/ n cendre f.

**cinema** /'sɪnəmə/ n cinéma m.

**cinnamon** /'sɪnəmən/ n cannelle f.

**circle** /'sɜːkl/ n cercle m; (Theat) balcon m. ● vt (go round) tourner autour de; (word, error) encercler. ● vi tourner en rond.

**circuit** /'sɜːkɪt/ n circuit m. ~ board n carte f de circuit imprimé. ~-breaker n disjoncteur m.

**circuitous** /sɜː'kjuːɪtəs/ adj indirect.

**circular** /'sɜːkjulə(r)/ adj & n circulaire (f).

**circulate** /'sɜːkjuleɪt/ vt/i (faire) circuler. **circulation** n circulation f; (of newspaper) tirage m.

**circumcise** /'sɜːkəmsaɪz/ vt circoncire.

**circumference** /sə'kʌmfərəns/ n circonférence f.

**circumflex** /'sɜːkəmfleks/ n circonflexe m.

**circumstance** /'sɜːkəmstəns/ n circonstance f; ~s (financial) situation f; under no ~s en aucun cas.

**circus** /'sɜːkəs/ n cirque m.

**cistern** /'sɪstən/ n réservoir m.

**citizen** /'sɪtɪzn/ n citoyen/-ne m/f; (of town) habitant/-e m/f. **citizen-**

**ship** n nationalité f.

**citrus** /'sɪtrəs/ adj ~ fruit(s) agrumes mpl; ~ tree citrus m.

**city** /'sɪtɪ/ n (grande) ville f.

---

> **The City** Quartier londonien des affaires et de la finance, la *City* est le siège des grandes banques, des compagnies d'assurance et de la plupart des sociétés d'agents de change. 500 000 personnes viennent et travailler chaque jour.   *i*

---

**civic** /'sɪvɪk/ adj (official) municipal; (pride, duty) civique.

**civil** /'sɪvl/ adj civil. ~ disobedience n résistance f passive. ~ engineer n ingénieur m des travaux publics.

**civilian** /sɪ'vɪlɪən/ adj & n civil/-e (m/f).

**civilization** /sɪvəlaɪ'zeɪʃn/ n civilisation f. **civilize** vt civiliser.

**civil:** ~ law n droit m civil. ~ liberties npl libertés fpl individuelles. ~ rights npl droits mpl civils. ~ servant n fonctionnaire mf. ~ service n fonction f publique. ~ war n guerre f civile.

**claim** /kleɪm/ vt (demand) revendiquer; (assert) prétendre. ● n revendication f; (assertion) affirmation f; (for insurance) réclamation f; (right) droit m. **claimant** n (of benefits) demandeur/-euse m/f.

**clairvoyant** /kleə'vɔɪənt/ n voyant/-e m/f.

**clam** /klæm/ n palourde f.

**clamber** /'klæmbə(r)/ vi grimper.

**clammy** /'klæmɪ/ adj (-ier, -iest) moite.

**clamour** /'klæmə(r)/ n clameur f. ● vi ~ for réclamer.

**clamp** /klæmp/ n valet m; (Med)

pince f; (wheel) ~ sabot m de Denver. ● vt cramponner; ( jaw) serrer; (car) mettre un sabot de Denver à; ~ down on faire de la répression contre.

**clan** /klæn/ n clan m.

**clang** /'klæŋ/ n son m métallique.

**clap** /klæp/ vt/i ( pt **clapped**) applaudir; (put forcibly) mettre; ~ one's hands frapper dans ses mains. ● n applaudissement m; (of thunder) coup m.

**claret** /'klærət/ n bordeaux m rouge.

**clarification** /klærɪfɪ'keɪʃn/ n clarification f. **clarify** /'klærɪfaɪ/ vt/i (se) clarifier.

**clarinet** /klærə'net/ n clarinette f.

**clarity** /'klærətɪ/ n clarté f.

**clash** /klæʃ/ n choc m; (fig) conflit m. ● vi (metal objects) s'entrechoquer; (armies) s'affronter; (meetings) avoir lieu en même temps; (colours) jurer.

**clasp** /klɑːsp/ n (fastener) fermoir m. ● vt serrer.

**class** /klɑːs/ n classe f. ● vt classer; ~ sb/sth as assimiler qn/qch à.

**classic** /'klæsɪk/ adj & n classique (m). ~s (Univ) lettres fpl classiques. **classical** adj classique.

**classified** /'klæsɪfaɪd/ adj (information) secret; ~ (ad) petite annonce f.

**classroom** /'klɑːsrʊm/ n salle f de classe.

**clatter** /'klætə(r)/ n cliquetis m. ● vi cliqueter.

**clause** /klɔːz/ n clause f; (Gram) proposition f.

**claw** /klɔː/ n (of animal, small bird) griffe f; (of bird of prey) serre f; (of lobster) pince f. ● vt griffer.

**clay** /kleɪ/ n argile f.

**clean** /kliːn/ adj propre; (shape, stroke) net. ● adv complètement.

● vt nettoyer; ~ one's teeth se brosser les dents. ● vi ~ up faire le nettoyage. **cleaner** n (at home) femme f de ménage; (industrial) agent m de nettoyage; (of clothes) teinturier/-ière m/f. **cleanliness** n propreté f. **cleanly** adv proprement; (sharply) nettement.

**cleanse** /klenz/ vt nettoyer; (fig) purifier.

**clean-shaven** adj glabre.

**clear** /klɪə(r)/ adj (explanation) clair; (need, sign) évident; (glass) transparent; (profit) net; (road) dégagé; make sth ~ être très clair sur qch; ~ of (away from) à l'écart de.
● adv complètement; **stand** ~ s'éloigner de. ● vt (free) dégager (of de). (table) débarrasser; (building) évacuer; (cheque) compenser; (jump over) franchir; (debt) liquider; (Jur) disculper. ● vi ( fog) se dissiper; (cheque) être compensé. ~ **away** or **off** (remove) enlever. ~ **off** or **out** ⏻ décamper. ~ **out** (clean) nettoyer. ~ **up** (tidy) ranger; (weather) s'éclaircir.

**clearance** /'klɪərəns/ n (permission) autorisation f; (space) espace m; ~ **sale** liquidation f.

**clear-cut** adj net.

**clearing** /'klɪərɪŋ/ n clairière f.

**clearly** /'klɪəlɪ/ adv clairement.

**clef** /klef/ n (Mus) clé f.

**cleft** /kleft/ n fissure f.

**clench** /klentʃ/ vt serrer.

**clergy** /'klɜːdʒɪ/ n clergé m. ~**man** n ( pl **-men**) ecclésiastique m.

**cleric** /'klerɪk/ n clerc m. **clerical** adj (Relig) clérical; (staff, work) de bureau.

**clerk** /klɑːk/ n employé/-e m/f de bureau; (US) **(sales)** ~ vendeur/-euse m/f.

**clever** /'klevə(r)/ adj intelligent; (skilful) habile.

**click** /klɪk/ n déclic m; (Comput) clic m. ● vi faire un déclic; (people 🔟) sympathiser; (Comput) cliquer (on sur.) ● vt (heels, tongue) faire claquer.

**client** /'klaɪənt/ n client-e m/f.

**clientele** /kliːɑ̃'tel/ n clientèle f.

**cliff** /klɪf/ n falaise f.

**climate** /'klaɪmɪt/ n climat m. ~ change changement m climatique.

**climax** /'klaɪmæks/ n (of story, contest) point m culminant; (sexual) orgasme m.

**climb** /klaɪm/ vt grimper; (steps) monter; (tree, ladder) grimper à; (mountain) faire l'ascension de. ● vi grimper; ~ into (car) monter dans; ~ into bed se mettre au lit. ● n (of mountain) escalade f; (steep hill, rise) montée f. ~ down (fig) reculer. **climber** n (Sport) alpiniste mf.

**clinch** /klɪntʃ/ vt (deal) conclure; (victory, order) décrocher.

**cling** /klɪŋ/ vi (pt **clung**) se cramponner (to à); (stick) coller. ~-**film** n scellofrais® m.

**clinic** /'klɪnɪk/ n centre m médical; (private) clinique f. **clinical** adj clinique.

**clink** /klɪŋk/ n tintement m. ● vt/i (faire) tinter.

**clip** /klɪp/ n (for paper) trombone m; (for hair) barrette f; (for tube) collier m; (of film) extrait m. ● vt (pt **clipped**) (fasten) attacher (to à). cut) couper.

**clippers** /'klɪpəz/ npl tondeuse f; (for nails) coupe-ongles m inv.

**clipping** /'klɪpɪŋ/ n (from press) coupure f de presse.

**cloak** /kləʊk/ n cape f; (man's) houppelande f. ~**room** n vestiaire m; (toilet) toilettes fpl.

**clobber** /'klɒbə(r)/ n 🔟 attirail m. ● vt (hit 🔟) tabasser 🔟.

**clock** /klɒk/ n pendule f; (large) horloge f. ● vi on/in ou off ou out pointer; ~ **up** (miles) faire. ~-**tower** n beffroi m. ~**wise** adj & adv dans le sens des aiguilles d'une montre.

**clockwork** /'klɒkwɜːk/ n mécanisme m. ● adj mécanique.

**clog** /klɒg/ n sabot m. ● vt/i (pt **clogged**) (se) boucher.

**cloister** /'klɔɪstə(r)/ n cloître m.

**clone** /kləʊn/ n clone m. ● vt cloner.

**close¹** /kləʊs/ adj (friend) proche (to de). (link) étroit; (examination) minutieux; (match) serré; (weather) lourd; (together (crowded) serrés; ~ **by**, ~ **at hand** tout près; have a ~ shave l'échapper belle; keep a ~ watch on surveiller de près. ● adv près. ● n (street) impasse f.

**close²** /kləʊz/ vt fermer; (meeting, case) mettre fin à. ● vi se fermer; (shop) fermer; (meeting, play) prendre fin. ● n fin f.

**closely** /'kləʊslɪ/ adv (follow) de près. **closeness** n proximité f.

**closet** /'klɒzɪt/ n (US) placard m.

**close-up** n gros plan m.

**closure** /'kləʊʒə(r)/ n fermeture f.

**clot** /klɒt/ n (of blood) caillot m; (in sauce) grumeau m. ● vt/i (pt **clotted**) (se) coaguler.

**cloth** /klɒθ/ n (fabric) tissu m; (duster) chiffon m; (table-cloth) nappe f.

**clothe** /kləʊð/ vt vêtir.

**clothes** /kləʊðz/ npl vêtements mpl. ~-**hanger** n cintre m. ~-**line** n corde f à linge.

**clothing** /'kləʊðɪŋ/ n vêtements mpl.

**cloud** /klaʊd/ n nuage m. ● vi ~

over se couvrir (de nuages); (face) s'assombrir. **cloudy** adj (sky) couvert; (liquid) trouble.

**clout** /klaʊt/ n (blow) coup m de poing; (power) influence f. ● vt frapper.

**clove** /kləʊv/ n clou m de girofle; ∼ of garlic gousse f d'ail.

**clover** /'kləʊvə(r)/ n trèfle m.

**clown** /klaʊn/ n clown m. ● vi faire le clown.

**club** /klʌb/ n (group) club m; (weapon) massue f; (golf) ∼ club m (de golf); ∼s (cards) trèfle m. ● vt/i (pt clubbed) matraquer. ∼ together cotiser.

**cluck** /klʌk/ vi glousser.

**clue** /kluː/ n indice m; (in crossword) définition f; I haven't a ∼ 🛈 je n'en ai pas la moindre idée.

**clump** /klʌmp/ n massif m.

**clumsy** /'klʌmzɪ/ adj (-ier, -iest) maladroit; (tool) peu commode.

**clung** /klʌŋ/ ⇒CLING.

**cluster** /'klʌstə(r)/ n (of people, islands) groupe m; (of flowers, berries) grappe f. ● vi se grouper.

**clutch** /klʌtʃ/ vt (hold) serrer fort; (grasp) saisir. ● vi ∼ at (try to grasp) essayer de saisir. ● n (Auto) embrayage m; (of eggs) couvée f; (of people) groupe m.

**clutter** /'klʌtə(r)/ n désordre m. ● vt ∼ (up) encombrer.

**coach** /kəʊtʃ/ n autocar m; (of train) wagon m; (horse-drawn) carrosse m; (Sport) entraîneur/-euse m/f. ● vt (team) entraîner; (pupil) donner des leçons particulières à.

**coal** /kəʊl/ n charbon m. ∼field n bassin m houiller. ∼-mine n mine f de charbon.

**coarse** /kɔːs/ adj grossier.

**coast** /kəʊst/ n côte f. ● vi (car, bicycle) descendre en roue libre.

**coastal** adj côtier.

**coast:** ∼guard n (person) gardecôte m; (organization) gendarmerie f maritime. ∼line n littoral m.

**coat** /kəʊt/ n manteau m; (of animal) pelage m; (of paint) couche f; ∼ of arms armoiries fpl. ● vt enduire, couvrir; (with chocolate) enrober (with de). **coating** n couche f.

**coax** /kəʊks/ vt cajoler.

**cob** /kɒb/ n (of corn) épi m.

**cobbler** /'kɒblə(r)/ n cordonnier m.

**cobblestones** /'kɒblstəʊnz/ npl pavés mpl.

**cobweb** /'kɒbweb/ n toile f d'araignée.

**cocaine** /kəʊ'keɪn/ n cocaïne f.

**cock** /kɒk/ n (rooster) coq m. (oiseau) mâle m. ● vt (gun) armer; (ears) dresser.

**cockerel** /'kɒkrəl/ n jeune coq m.

**cockle** /'kɒkl/ n (Culin) coque f.

**cock:** ∼pit n poste m de pilotage. ∼roach n cafard m. ∼tail n cocktail m.

**cocky** /'kɒkɪ/ adj (-ier, -iest) trop sûr de soi.

**cocoa** /'kəʊkəʊ/ n cacao m.

**coconut** /'kəʊkənʌt/ n noix f de coco.

**COD** abbr (cash on delivery) envoi m contre remboursement.

**cod** /kɒd/ n inv morue f. ∼-liver oil huile f de foie de morue.

**code** /kəʊd/ n code m. ● vt coder.

**coerce** /kəʊ'ɜːs/ vt contraindre.

**coexist** /kəʊɪg'zɪst/ vi coexister.

**coffee** /'kɒfɪ/ n café m. ∼ bar n café-bar m. ∼ bean n grain m de café. ∼-pot n cafetière f. ∼-table n table f basse.

**coffin** /'kɒfɪn/ n cercueil m.

**cog** /kɒg/ n pignon m; (fig) rouage m.

**cognac** /'kɒnjæk/ n cognac m.

**coil** /kɔɪl/ vt/i (s')enrouler. ● n (of rope) rouleau m; (of snake) anneau m; (contraceptive) stérilet m.

**coin** /kɔɪn/ n pièce f (de monnaie). ● vt (word) inventer.

**coincide** /kəʊɪn'saɪd/ vi coïncider. **coincidence** n coïncidence f. **coincidental** adj dû à une coïncidence.

**colander** /'kʌləndə(r)/ n passoire f.

**cold** /kəʊld/ adj froid; (person) be or feel ~ avoir froid; it is ~ il fait froid; get ~ feet avoir les jetons ▯; ~-blooded (lit) à sang froid; (fig) sans pitié. ● n froid m; (Med) rhume m; ~ sore bouton m de fièvre. **coldness** n froideur f.

**coleslaw** /'kəʊlslɔ:/ n salade f de chou cru.

**colic** /'kɒlɪk/ n coliques fpl.

**collaborate** /kə'læbəreɪt/ vi collaborer.

**collapse** /kə'læps/ vi s'effondrer; (person) s'écrouler; (fold) se plier. ● n effondrement m.

**collar** /'kɒlə(r)/ n col m; (of dog) collier m. ~-bone n clavicule f.

**collateral** /kə'lætərəl/ n nantissement m.

**colleague** /'kɒli:g/ n collègue mf.

**collect** /kə'lekt/ vt rassembler; (pick up) ramasser; (call for) passer prendre; (money, fare) encaisser; (taxes, rent) percevoir; (as hobby) collectionner. ● vi se rassembler; (dust) s'amasser. ● adv call ~ (US) appeler en PCV. **collection** n collection f; (of money) collecte f; (in church) quête f; (of mail) levée f.

**collective** /kə'lektɪv/ adj collectif.

**collector** /kə'lektə(r)/ n (as hobby) collectionneur/-euse m/f; (of taxes) percepteur m; (of rent, debt) encaisseur m.

**college** /'kɒlɪdʒ/ n (for higher edu-

cation) établissement m d'enseignement supérieur; (within university) collège m; be at ~ faire des études supérieures.

**collide** /kə'laɪd/ vi entrer en collision (with avec).

**colliery** /'kɒlɪərɪ/ n houillère f.

**collision** /kə'lɪʒn/ n collision f.

**colloquial** /kə'ləʊkwɪəl/ adj familier. **colloquialism** n expression f familière.

**Colombia** /kə'lɒmbɪə/ n Colombie f.

**colon** /'kəʊlən/ n (Gram) deux-points m inv; (Anat) côlon m.

**colonel** /'kɜ:nl/ n colonel m.

**colonial** /kə'ləʊnɪəl/ adj & n colonial/-e (m/f).

**colour**, (US) **color** /'kʌlə(r)/ n couleur f; ~-blind daltonien. ● adj (photo) en couleur; (TV set) couleur inv. ● vt colorer; (with crayon) colorier. **coloured** adj de couleur. **colourful** adj aux couleurs vives; (fig) haut en couleur. **colouring** n (of skin) teint m; (in food) colorant m.

**colt** /kəʊlt/ n poulain m.

**column** /'kɒləm/ n colonne f.

**coma** /'kəʊmə/ n coma m.

**comb** /kəʊm/ n peigne m. ● vt peigner; ~ one's hair se peigner; ~ a place passer un lieu au peigne fin.

**combat** /'kɒmbæt/ n combat m. ● vt (pt combated) combattre.

**combination** /kɒmbɪ'neɪʃn/ n combinaison f.

**combine**[1] /kəm'baɪn/ vt/i (se) combiner, (s')unir.

**combine**[2] /'kɒmbaɪn/ n (Comm) groupe m; ~ harvester moissonneuse-batteuse f.

**come** /kʌm/ vi (pt came. pp come) venir; (bus, letter) arriver; (postman) passer; ~ and look! viens voir!; ~

in (*size, colour*) exister en; **when it ~s to** lorsqu'il s'agit de. ~ **about** survenir. ~ **across** (*meaning*) passer; ~ **across sth** tomber sur qch. ~ **away** (*leave*) partir; (*come off*) se détacher. ~ **back** revenir. ~ **by** obtenir. ~ **down** descendre; (*price*) baisser; ~ **forward** se présenter. ~ **in** entrer; in useful être utile. ~ **in for** recevoir. ~ **into** (*money*) hériter de. ~ **off** (*succeed*) réussir; (*fare*) s'en tirer; (*detach*) se détacher. ~ **on** (*actor*) entrer en scène; (*light*) s'allumer; (*improve*) faire des progrès; ~ **on!** allez!. ~ **out** sortir. ~ **round** reprendre connaissance; (*change mind*) changer d'avis; ~ **through** s'en tirer. ~ **to** reprendre connaissance; ~ **to sth** (*amount*) revenir à qch. ~ **to** (*decision, conclusion*) arriver à qch. ~ **up** (*problem*) être soulevé; (*opportunity*) se présenter; (*sun*) se lever; ~ **up against** se heurter à. ~ **up with** trouver.

**comedian** /kə'miːdɪən/ *n* comique *m*.

**comedy** /'kɒmədɪ/ *n* comédie *f*.

**comfort** /'kʌmfət/ *n* confort *m*; (*consolation*) réconfort *m*. ●*vt* consoler. **comfortable** (*chair, car*) confortable; (*person*) à l'aise; (*wealthy*) aisé.

**comfortably** /'kʌmftəblɪ/ *adv* confortablement; ~ **off** aisé.

**comfy** /'kʌmfɪ/ *adj* 🄸 ➡COMFORTABLE.

**comic** /'kɒmɪk/ *adj* comique. ●*n* (*person*) comique *m*; ~ (*book*), ~ **strip** bande *f* dessinée.

**coming** /'kʌmɪŋ/ *n* arrivée *f*; ~**s and goings** allées et venues *fpl*. ●*adj* à venir.

**comma** /'kɒmə/ *n* virgule *f*.

**command** /kə'mɑːnd/ *n* (*authority*) commandement *m*; (*order*) ordre *m*; (*mastery*) maîtrise *f*. ●*vt*

ordonner à (**to do** de faire); (*be able to use*) disposer de; (*respect*) inspirer. **commandeer** *vt* réquisitionner. **commander** *n* commandant *m*. **commanding** *adj* imposant. **commandment** *n* commandement *m*.

**commando** /kə'mɑːndəʊ/ *n* commando *m*.

**commemorate** /kə'meməreɪt/ *vt* commémorer.

**commence** /kə'mens/ *vt*/*i* commencer.

**commend** /kə'mend/ *vt* (*praise*) louer; (*entrust*) confier.

**commensurate** /kə'menʃərət/ *adj* proportionné.

**comment** /'kɒment/ *n* commentaire *m*. ●*vi* faire des commentaires; ~ **on** commenter. **commentary** *n* commentaire *m*; (*radio, TV*) reportage *m*. **commentate** *vi* faire un reportage. **commentator** *n* commentateur/-trice *m*/*f*.

**commerce** /'kɒmɜːs/ *n* commerce *m*.

**commercial** /kə'mɜːʃl/ *adj* commercial; (*traveller*) de commerce. ●*n* publicité *f*.

**commiserate** /kə'mɪzəreɪt/ *vi* compatir (**with** avec).

**commission** /kə'mɪʃn/ *n* commission *f*; (*order for work*) commande *f*; **out of** ~ hors service. ●*vt* (*order*) commander; (*Mil*) nommer officier; ~ **to do** charger de faire. **commissioner** *n* préfet *m* (de police); (in EU) membre *m* de la Commission européenne.

**commit** /kə'mɪt/ *vt* (*pt* **committed**) commettre; (*entrust*) confier; ~ **oneself** s'engager; ~ **perjury** se parjurer; ~ **suicide** se suicider; ~ **to memory** apprendre par cœur. **commitment** *n* engagement *m*.

**committee** /kə'mɪtɪ/ n comité m.

**commodity** /kə'mɒdətɪ/ n article m.

**common** /'kɒmən/ adj (shared by all) commun (to à); (usual) courant; (vulgar) vulgaire, commun; **in ~** en commun; **~ people** le peuple; **~ sense** bon sens m. ●n terrain m communal; **the C~s** Chambre f des Communes.

**commoner** /'kɒmənə(r)/ n roturier/-ière m/f.

**common law** n droit m coutumier.

**commonly** /'kɒmənlɪ/ adv communément.

**commonplace** /'kɒmənpleɪs/ adj banal. ●n banalité f.

**common-room** n salle f de détente.

**Commonwealth** /'kɒmənwelθ/ n **the ~** le Commonwealth m.

> **Commonwealth of Nations** *i* Association de nations ayant pour la plupart fait partie de l'empire britannique et qui maintiennent une coopération avec la Grande-Bretagne en matière d'économie, de culture et d'éducation. Des championnats d'athlétisme, les *Commonwealth Games* ont lieu tous les quatre ans. Le mot *Commonwealth* figure dans le nom officiel de quelques États américains (*Kentucky, Virginia, Pennsylvania, Massachusetts*).

**commotion** /kə'məʊʃn/ n (noise) vacarme m; (disturbance) agitation f.

**communal** /'kɒmjʊnl/ adj (shared) commun; (life) collectif.

**commune** /'kɒmjuːn/ n (group) communauté f.

**communicate** /kə'mjuːnɪkeɪt/ vt/i communiquer. **communication**

n communication f. **communicative** adj communicatif.

**communion** /kə'mjuːnɪən/ n communion f.

**Communism** /'kɒmjʊnɪzəm/ n communisme m. **Communist** adj & n communiste (mf).

**community** /kə'mjuːnətɪ/ n communauté f.

**commute** /kə'mjuːt/ vi faire la navette. ●vt (Jur) commuer. **commuter** n navetteur/-euse m/f.

**compact** /kəm'pækt/ adj compact; (lady's case) poudrier m.

**compact disc** n disque m compact. **~ player** n platine f laser.

**companion** /kəm'pænɪən/ n compagnon/-agne m/f. **companionship** n camaraderie f.

**company** /'kʌmpənɪ/ n (companionship, firm) compagnie f; (guests) invités/-es m/fpl.

**comparative** /kəm'pærətɪv/ adj (study, form) comparatif; (comfort) relatif.

**compare** /kəm'peə(r)/ vt comparer (with, to à). **~d with** par rapport à. ●vi être comparable. **comparison** n comparaison f.

**compartment** /kəm'pɑːtmənt/ n compartiment m.

**compass** /'kʌmpəs/ n (for direction) boussole f; (scope) portée f; a pair of **~es** un compas.

**compassionate** /kəm'pæʃənət/ adj compatissant.

**compatible** /kəm'pætəbl/ adj compatible.

**compel** /kəm'pel/ vt (pt **compelled**) contraindre. **compelling** adj irrésistible.

**compensate** /'kɒmpenseɪt/ vt/i (financially) dédommager (for de). **~ for sth** compenser qch. **compensation** n compensation f; (financial) dédommagement *m.*

**compete** /kəm'piːt/ *vi* concourir; ~ **with** rivaliser avec.

**competent** /'kɒmpɪtənt/ *adj* compétent.

**competition** /kɒmpə'tɪʃn/ *n* (contest) concours *m;* (Sport) compétition *f;* (Comm) concurrence *f.*

**competitive** /kəm'petɪtɪv/ *adj* (*prices*) compétitif; (*person*) qui a l'esprit de compétition.

**competitor** /kəm'petɪtə(r)/ *n* concurrent/-e *m/f.*

**compile** /kəm'paɪl/ *vt* (list) dresser; (book) rédiger.

**complacency** /kəm'pleɪsnsɪ/ *n* suffisance *f.*

**complain** /kəm'pleɪn/ *vi* se plaindre (about, of de). **complaint** *n* plainte *f;* (official) réclamation *f;* (illness) maladie *f.*

**complement** /'kɒmplɪmənt/ *n* complément *m.* ● *vt* compléter. **complementary** *adj* complémentaire.

**complete** /kəm'pliːt/ *adj* complet; (finished) achevé; (downright) parfait. ● *vt* achever; (a form) remplir. **completely** *adv* complètement. **completion** *n* achèvement *m.*

**complex** /'kɒmpleks/ *adj* complexe. ● *n* (Psych) complexe *m.*

**complexion** /kəm'plekʃn/ *n* (of face) teint *m;* (fig) caractère *m.*

**compliance** /kəm'plaɪəns/ *n* (agreement) conformité *f.*

**complicate** /'kɒmplɪkeɪt/ *vt* compliquer. **complicated** *adj* compliqué. **complication** *n* complication *f.*

**compliment** /'kɒmplɪmənt/ *n* compliment *m.* ● *vt* complimenter. **complimentary** *adj* (offert) à titre gracieux; (praising) flatteur.

**comply** /kəm'plaɪ/ *vi* ~ **with** se conformer à, obéir à.

**component** /kəm'pəʊnənt/ *n* (of machine) pièce *f;* (chemical substance) composant *m;* (element: fig) composante *f.* ● *adj* constituant.

**compose** /kəm'pəʊz/ *vt* composer; ~ **oneself** se calmer. **composed** *adj* calme. **composer** *n* (Mus) compositeur *m.* **composition** *n* composition *f.*

**composure** /kəm'pəʊʒə(r)/ *n* calme *m.*

**compound** /'kɒmpaʊnd/ *n* (substance, word) composé *m;* (enclosure) enclos *m.* ● *adj* composé.

**comprehend** /kɒmprɪ'hend/ *vt* comprendre. **comprehension** *n* compréhension *f.*

**comprehensive** /kɒmprɪ'hensɪv/ *adj* étendu, complet; (*insurance*) tous risques *inv.* ~ **school** *n* collège *m* d'enseignement secondaire.

**compress** /kəm'pres/ *vt* comprimer.

**comprise** /kəm'praɪz/ *vt* comprendre, inclure.

**compromise** /'kɒmprəmaɪz/ *n* compromis *m.* ● *vt* compromettre. ● *vi* transiger, arriver à un compromis.

**compulsive** /kəm'pʌlsɪv/ *adj* (Psych) compulsif; (*liar, smoker*) invétéré.

**compulsory** /kəm'pʌlsərɪ/ *adj* obligatoire.

**compute** /kəm'pjuːt/ *vt* calculer.

**computer** /kəm'pjuːt/ *n* ordinateur *m;* ~ **science** informatique *f.* **computerize** *vt* informatiser.

**comrade** /'kɒmreɪd/ *n* camarade *mf.*

**con**¹ /kɒn/ *vt* (*pt* **conned**) 🔲 rouler 🔲, escroquer (out of de.) ● *n* 🔲 escroquerie *f.*

**con**² /kɒn/ →**PRO.**

**conceal** /kən'siːl/ *vt*

dissimuler (from à.)

**concede** /kən'si:d/ vt concéder.
● vi céder.

**conceited** /kən'si:tɪd/ adj vaniteux.

**conceive** /kən'si:v/ vt/i concevoir;
~ of concevoir.

**concentrate** /'kɒnsntreɪt/ vt/i
(se) concentrer. **concentration** n
concentration f.

**concept** /'kɒnsept/ n concept m.

**conception** /kən'sepʃn/ n conception f.

**concern** /kən'sɜ:n/ n (interest,
business) affaire f; (worry) inquiétude f; (firm: Comm) entreprise f, affaire f. ● vt concerner; ~ oneself
with, be ~ed with s'occuper de.
**concerned** adj inquiet. **concerning**
prep en ce qui concerne.

**concert** /'kɒnsət/ n concert m.

**concession** /kən'seʃn/ n concession f.

**conciliation** /kənsɪlɪ'eɪʃn/ n conciliation f.

**concise** /kən'saɪs/ adj concis.

**conclude** /kən'klu:d/ vt conclure.
● vi se terminer. **conclusion** n conclusion f. **conclusive** adj concluant.

**concoct** /kən'kɒkt/ vt confectionner; (invent: fig) fabriquer. **concoction** n mélange m.

**concourse** /'kɒŋkɔ:s/ n (Rail)
hall m.

**concrete** /'kɒŋkri:t/ n béton m.
● adj de béton; (fig) concret. ● vt
bétonner.

**concur** /kən'kɜ:(r)/ vi (pt concurred) être d'accord.

**concurrently** /kən'kʌrəntlɪ/ adv
simultanément.

**concussion** /kən'kʌʃn/ n commotion f (cérébrale).

**condemn** /kən'dem/ vt

condamner.

**condensation** /kɒndən'seɪʃn/ n
(on walls) condensation f; (on windows) buée f. **condense** vt/i (se)
condenser.

**condition** /kən'dɪʃn/ n condition f;
on ~ that à condition que. ● vt
conditionner. **conditional** adj conditionnel.

**conditioner** /kən'dɪʃənə(r)/ n
après-shampooing m.

**condolences** /kən'dəʊlənsɪz/ npl
condoléances fpl.

**condom** /'kɒndɒm/ n préservatif m.

**condone** /kən'dəʊn/ vt pardonner,
fermer les yeux sur.

**conducive** /kən'dju:sɪv/ adj ~ to
favorable à.

**conduct**[1] /'kɒndʌkt/ n conduite f.

**conduct**[2] /kən'dʌkt/ vt conduire;
(orchestra) diriger. **conductor** n
chef m d'orchestre; (of bus) receveur m; (on train: US) chef m de
train; (Electr) conducteur m. **conductress** n receveuse f.

**cone** /kəʊn/ n cône m. (of icecream) cornet m.

**confectioner** /kən'fekʃənə(r)/ n
confiseur/-euse m/f. **confectionery**
n confiserie f.

**confer** /kən'fɜ:(r)/ vt/i (pt conferred) conférer.

**conference** /'kɒnfərəns/ n conférence f.

**confess** /kən'fes/ vt/i avouer;
(Relig) (se) confesser. **confession** n
confession f; (of crime) aveu m.

**confide** /kən'faɪd/ vt confier. ● vi
~ in se confier à.

**confidence** /'kɒnfɪdəns/ n (trust)
confiance f. (boldness) confiance f
en soi; (secret) confidence f; in ~
en confidence. **confident** adj sûr.

**confidential** /kɒnfɪˈdenʃl/ adj confidentiel.

**configuration** /kənfɪgəˈreɪʃn/ n configuration f. ● **configure** vt configurer.

**confine** /kənˈfaɪn/ vt enfermer; (limit) limiter; ~d space espace m réduit; ~d to limité à.

**confirm** /kənˈfɜːm/ vt confirmer. **confirmed** adj (bachelor) endurci; (smoker) invétéré.

**confiscate** /ˈkɒnfɪskeɪt/ vt confisquer.

**conflict¹** /ˈkɒnflɪkt/ n conflit m.

**conflict²** /kənˈflɪkt/ vi (statements, views) être en contradiction (with avec.) (appointments) tomber en même temps (with que). **conflicting** adj contradictoire.

**conform** /kənˈfɔːm/ vt/i (se) conformer.

**confound** /kənˈfaʊnd/ vt confondre.

**confront** /kənˈfrʌnt/ vt affronter; ~ with confronter avec.

**confuse** /kənˈfjuːz/ vt (bewilder) troubler; (mistake, confound) confondre; become ~d s'embrouiller; I am ~d je m'y perds. **confusing** adj déroutant. **confusion** n confusion f.

**congeal** /kənˈdʒiːl/ vt/i (se) figer.

**congested** /kənˈdʒestɪd/ adj (road) embouteillé; (passage) encombré; (Med) congestionné. **congestion** n (traffic) encombrement(s) m(pl); (Med) congestion f.

**congratulate** /kənˈgrætʃʊleɪt/ vt féliciter (on de). **congratulations** npl félicitations fpl.

**congregate** /ˈkɒngrɪgeɪt/ vi se rassembler. **congregation** n assemblée f.

**congress** /ˈkɒngres/ n congrès m. C ~ (US) le Congrès.

**conjugate** /ˈkɒndʒʊgeɪt/ vt conjuguer. **conjugation** n conjugaison f.

**conjunction** /kənˈdʒʌŋkʃn/ n (Ling) conjonction f. in ~with conjointement avec.

**conjunctivitis** /kəndʒʌŋktɪ ˈvaɪtɪs/ n conjonctivite f.

**conjure** /ˈkʌndʒə(r)/ vi faire des tours de passe-passe. ● vt ~ up faire apparaître. **conjuror** n prestidigitateur/-trice m/f.

**con man** n ⊠ escroc m.

**connect** /kəˈnekt/ vt/i (se) relier; (in mind) faire le rapport entre; (install, wire up to mains) brancher; ~ with (of train) assurer la correspondance avec; ~ed (idea, event) lié; be ~ed with avoir rapport à.

**connection** /kəˈnekʃn/ n rapport m. (Rail) correspondance f; (phone call) communication f; (Electr) contact m; (joining piece) raccord m; ~s (Comm) relations fpl.

**connive** /kəˈnaɪv/ vi ~ at se faire le complice de.

**conquer** /ˈkɒŋkə(r)/ vt vaincre; (country) conquérir. **conqueror** n conquérant m.

**conquest** /ˈkɒŋkwest/ n conquête f.

**conscience** /ˈkɒnʃəns/ n conscience f. **conscientious** adj consciencieux.

**conscious** /'kɒnʃəs/ adj conscient; (deliberate) voulu. **consciously** adv consciemment. **consciousness** n conscience f; (Med) connaissance f.

**conscript** /'kɒnskrɪpt/ n appelé m.

**consecutive** /kən'sekjʊtɪv/ adj consécutif.

**consensus** /kən'sensəs/ n consensus m.

**consent** /kən'sent/ vi consentir (to à). ● n consentement m.

**consequence** /'kɒnsɪkwəns/ n conséquence f. **consequently** adv par conséquent.

**conservation** /kɒnsə'veɪʃn/ n préservation f. ~ area zone f protégée. **conservationist** n défenseur m de l'environnement.

**conservative** /kən'sɜːvətɪv/ adj conservateur; (estimate) minimal.

**Conservative Party** n parti m conservateur.

**conservatory** /kən'sɜːvətrɪ/ n (greenhouse) serre f; (room) véranda f.

**conserve** /kən'sɜːv/ vt conserver; (energy) économiser.

**consider** /kən'sɪdə(r)/ vt considérer; (allow for) tenir compte de; (possibility) envisager (doing de faire).

**considerable** /kən'sɪdərəbl/ adj considérable; (much) beaucoup de.

**considerate** /kən'sɪdərət/ adj prévenant, attentionné. **consideration** n considération f. (respect) égard(s) m(pl)

**considering** /kən'sɪdərɪŋ/ prep compte tenu de.

**consignment** /kən'saɪnmənt/ n envoi m.

**consist** /kən'sɪst/ vi consister (of en; in doing à faire).

**consistency** /kən'sɪstənsɪ/ n (of liquids) consistance f. (of argument)

coherence f.

**consistent** /kən'sɪstənt/ adj cohérent. ~ with conforme à.

**consolation** /kɒnsə'leɪʃn/ n consolation f.

**consolidate** /kən'sɒlɪdeɪt/ vt/i (se) consolider.

**consonant** /'kɒnsənənt/ n consonne f.

**conspicuous** /kən'spɪkjʊəs/ adj (easily seen) en évidence; (showy) voyant; (noteworthy) remarquable.

**conspiracy** /kən'spɪrəsɪ/ n conspiration f.

**constable** /'kʌnstəbl/ n agent m de police, gendarme m.

**constant** /'kɒnstənt/ adj (questions) incessant; (unchanging) constant; (friend) fidèle. ● n constante f. **constantly** adv constamment.

**constellation** /kɒnstə'leɪʃn/ n constellation f.

**constipation** /kɒnstɪ'peɪʃn/ n constipation f.

**constituency** /kən'stɪtjʊənsɪ/ n circonscription f électorale.

**constituent** /kən'stɪtjʊənt/ adj constitutif. ● n élément m constitutif; (Pol) électeur/-trice m/f.

**constitution** /kɒnstɪ'tjuːʃn/ n constitution f.

**constrain** /kən'streɪn/ vt contraindre. **constraint** n contrainte f.

**constrict** /kən'strɪkt/ vt (flow) comprimer; (movement) gêner.

**construct** /kən'strʌkt/ vt construire. **construction** n construction f. **constructive** adj constructif.

**consulate** /'kɒnsjʊlət/ n consulat m.

**consult** /kən'sʌlt/ vt consulter. ● vi ~ with conférer avec. **consultant** n conseiller/-ère m/f. (Med) spécialiste m/f. **consultation** n consultation f.

**consume** /kən'sjuːm/ vt consommer; (destroy) consumer. **consumer** n consommateur/-trice m/f.

**consummate** /'kɒnsəmeɪt/ vt consommer.

**consumption** /kən'sʌmpʃn/ n consommation f; (Med) phtisie f.

**contact** /'kɒntækt/ n contact m; (person) relation f. ● vt contacter. ~ **lenses** npl lentilles fpl (de contact).

**contagious** /kən'teɪdʒəs/ adj contagieux.

**contain** /kən'teɪn/ vt contenir; ~ oneself se contenir. **container** n récipient m; (for transport) container m.

**contaminate** /kən'tæmɪneɪt/ vt contaminer.

**contemplate** /'kɒntəmpleɪt/ vt (gaze at) contempler; (think about) envisager.

**contemporary** /kən'temprərɪ/ adj & n contemporain/-e (m/f).

**contempt** /kən'tempt/ n mépris m. **contemptible** adj méprisable. **contemptuous** adj méprisant.

**contend** /kən'tend/ vt soutenir. ● vi ~ with (compete) rivaliser avec; (face) faire face à. **contender** n adversaire m/f.

**content**[1] /'kɒntent/ n (of letter) contenu m; (amount) teneur f; ~s contenu m.

**content**[2] /kən'tent/ adj satisfait. ● vt contenter. **contented** adj satisfait. **contentment** n contentement m.

**contest**[1] /'kɒntest/ n (competition) concours m; (struggle) lutte f.

**contest**[2] /kən'test/ vt contester; (compete for or in) disputer. **contestant** n concurrent/-e m/f.

**context** /'kɒntekst/ n contexte m.

**continent** /'kɒntɪnənt/ n continent m; the C ~ l'Europe f (conti-

nentale). **continental** adj continental, européen. **continental quilt** n couette f.

**contingency** /kən'tɪndʒənsɪ/ n éventualité f. ~ **plan** plan m d'urgence.

**continual** /kən'tɪnjʊəl/ adj continuel.

**continuation** /kəntɪnjʊ'eɪʃn/ n continuation f. (after interruption) reprise f; (new episode) suite f.

**continue** /kən'tɪnjuː/ vt/i continuer; (resume) reprendre. **continued** adj continu.

**continuous** /kən'tɪnjʊəs/ adj continu. **continuously** adv (without a break) sans interruption; (repeatedly) continuellement.

**contort** /kən'tɔːt/ vt tordre; ~ oneself se contorsionner.

**contour** /'kɒntʊə(r)/ n contour m.

**contraband** /'kɒntrəbænd/ n contrebande f.

**contraception** /kɒntrə'sepʃn/ n contraception f. **contraceptive** adj & n contraceptif (m).

**contract**[1] /'kɒntrækt/ n contrat m.

**contract**[2] /kən'trækt/ vt/i (se) contracter. **contraction** n contraction f.

**contractor** /kən'træktə(r)/ n entrepreneur/-euse m/f.

**contradict** /kɒntrə'dɪkt/ vt contredire. **contradictory** adj contradictoire.

**contrary**[1] /'kɒntrərɪ/ adj contraire (to à). ● n contraire m. on the ~ au contraire. ● adv ~ to contrairement à.

**contrary**[2] /kən'treərɪ/ adj entêté.

**contrast**[1] /'kɒntrɑːst/ n contraste m.

**contrast**[2] /kən'trɑːst/ vt/i contraster.

**contravention** /kɒntrə'venʃn/ n

infraction f.

**contribute** /kənˈtrɪbjuːt/ vt donner. ● vi ~ to contribuer à; (take part) participer à; (newspaper) collaborer à. **contribution** n contribution f. **contributor** n collaborateur/-trice m/f.

**contrive** /kənˈtraɪv/ vt imaginer; ~ to do trouver moyen de faire.

**control** /kənˈtrəʊl/ vt (pt controlled) (firm) diriger; (check) contrôler; (restrain) maîtriser. ● n contrôle m. (mastery) maîtrise f. ~s commandes fpl. (knobs) boutons mpl; have under ~ (event) avoir en main; in ~ of maître de. ~ tower n tour f de contrôle.

**controversial** /kɒntrəˈvɜːʃl/ adj discutable, discuté. **controversy** n controverse f.

**conurbation** /kɒnɜːˈbeɪʃn/ n agglomération f. conurbation f.

**convalesce** /kɒnvəˈles/ vi être en convalescence.

**convene** /kənˈviːn/ vt convoquer. ● vi se réunir.

**convenience** /kənˈviːnɪəns/ n commodité f. ~s toilettes fpl. all modern ~s tout le confort moderne; at your ~ quand cela vous conviendra, à votre convenance. ~ foods npl plats mpl tout préparés.

**convenient** /kənˈviːnɪənt/ adj commode, pratique; (time) bien choisi; be ~ for convenir à.

**convent** /ˈkɒnvənt/ n couvent m.

**convention** /kənˈvenʃn/ n (assembly, agreement) convention f. (custom) usage m. **conventional** adj conventionnel.

**conversation** /kɒnvəˈseɪʃn/ n conversation f. **conversational** adj (tone) de la conversation; (French) de tous les jours.

**converse¹** /kənˈvɜːs/ vi s'entretenir, converser (with avec).

**converse²** /ˈkɒnvɜːs/ adj & n inverse (m). **conversely** adv inversement.

**conversion** /kənˈvɜːʃn/ n conversion f.

**convert¹** /kənˈvɜːt/ vt convertir; (house) aménager. ● vi ~ into se transformer en.

**convert²** /ˈkɒnvɜːt/ n converti/-e m/f.

**convertible** /kənˈvɜːtəbl/ adj convertible. ● n (car) décapotable f.

**convey** /kənˈveɪ/ vt (wishes, order) transmettre; (goods, people) transporter; (idea, feeling) communiquer. **conveyor belt** n tapis m roulant.

**convict¹** /kənˈvɪkt/ vt déclarer coupable.

**convict²** /ˈkɒnvɪkt/ n prisonnier/-ière m/f.

**conviction** /kənˈvɪkʃn/ n (Jur) condamnation f. (opinion) conviction f.

**convince** /kənˈvɪns/ vt convaincre.

**convoke** /kənˈvəʊk/ vt convoquer.

**convoy** /ˈkɒnvɔɪ/ n convoi m.

**convulse** /kənˈvʌls/ vt convulser; (fig) bouleverser; be ~d with laughter se tordre de rire.

**cook** /kʊk/ vt/i (faire) cuire; (of person) faire la cuisine; ~ up 🗓 fabriquer. ● n cuisinier/-ière m/f. **cooker** n (stove) cuisinière f. **cookery** n cuisine f.

**cookie** /ˈkʊkɪ/ n (US) biscuit m.

**cooking** /ˈkʊkɪŋ/ n cuisine f. ● adj de cuisine.

**cool** /kuːl/ adj frais; (calm) calme; (unfriendly) froid. ● n fraîcheur f. (calmness 🗷) sang-froid m; in the ~ au frais. ● vt/i rafraîchir. ~ box n glacière f.

**coolly** /ˈkuːllɪ/ adv calmement, froidement.

**coop** /kuːp/ n poulailler m. ● vt ~ up enfermer.

**cooperate** /kəʊˈɒpəreɪt/ vi coopérer. **co-operation** n coopération f.

**cooperative** /kəʊˈɒpərətɪv/ adj coopératif. ● n coopérative f.

**coordinate** /kəʊˈɔːdɪnət/ vt coordonner.

**cop** /kɒp/ vt (pt copped) 🅰 piquer. ● n (policeman) 🅰 flic m. ~ out 🅰 se dérober.

**cope** /kəʊp/ vi s'en sortir; se débrouiller; ~ with (problem) faire face à.

**copper** /ˈkɒpə(r)/ n cuivre m. (coin) sou m; 🅰 flic m. ● adj de cuivre.

**copulate** /ˈkɒpjʊleɪt/ vi s'accoupler.

**copy** /ˈkɒpɪ/ n copie f. (of book, newspaper) exemplaire m; (print: Photo) épreuve f. ● vt/i copier.

**copyright** /ˈkɒpɪraɪt/ n droit m d'auteur, copyright m.

**copy-writer** n rédacteur-concepteur m, rédactrice-conceptrice f.

**cord** /kɔːd/ n (petite) corde f; (of curtain, pyjamas) cordon m; (Electr) cordon m électrique; (fabric) velours m côtelé.

**cordial** /ˈkɔːdɪəl/ adj cordial. ● n (drink) sirop m.

**corduroy** /ˈkɔːdərɔɪ/ n velours m côtelé.

**core** /kɔː(r)/ n (of apple) trognon m; (of problem) cœur m; (Tech) noyau m. ● vt (apple) évider.

**cork** /kɔːk/ n liège m. (for bottle) bouchon m. ● vt boucher. **cork-screw** n tire-bouchon m.

**corn** /kɔːn/ n blé m. (maize: US) maïs m; (seed) grain m; (hard skin) cor m.

**cornea** /ˈkɔːnɪə/ n cornée f.

**corner** /ˈkɔːnə(r)/ n coin m; (bend in road) virage m; (football) corner m. ● vt coincer, acculer; (market) accaparer. ● vi prendre un virage.

**cornflour** /ˈkɔːnflaʊə(r)/ n farine f de maïs.

**cornice** /ˈkɔːnɪs/ n corniche f.

**corny** /ˈkɔːnɪ/ adj (-ier, -iest) (joke) éculé.

**corollary** /kəˈrɒlərɪ/ n corollaire m.

**coronary** /ˈkɒrənrɪ/ n infarctus m.

**coronation** /kɒrəˈneɪʃn/ n couronnement m.

**corporal** /ˈkɔːpərəl/ n caporal m. ~**punishment** n châtiment m corporel.

**corporate** /ˈkɔːpərət/ adj (ownership) en commun; (body) constitué.

**corporation** /kɔːpəˈreɪʃn/ n (Comm) société f.

**corpse** /kɔːps/ n cadavre m.

**corpuscle** /ˈkɔːpʌsl/ n globule m.

**correct** /kəˈrekt/ adj (right) exact, juste, correct; (proper) correct; you are ~ vous avez raison. ● vt corriger.

**correction** /kəˈrekʃn/ n correction f.

**correlate** /ˈkɒrəleɪt/ vt/i (faire) correspondre.

**correspond** /kɒrɪˈspɒnd/ vi correspondre. **correspondence** n correspondance f.

**corridor** /ˈkɒrɪdɔː(r)/ n couloir m.

**corrode** /kəˈrəʊd/ vt/i (se) corroder.

**corrugated** /ˈkɒrəgeɪtɪd/ adj ondulé; ~ **iron** tôle f ondulée.

**corrupt** /kəˈrʌpt/ adj corrompu. ● vt corrompre. **corruption** n corruption f.

**Corsica** /ˈkɔːsɪkə/ n Corse f.

**cosh** /kɒʃ/ n matraque f. ● vt matraquer.

**cosmetic** /kɒz'metɪk/ n produit m de beauté. ● adj cosmétique; (fig, pej) superficiel. ~ **surgery** n chirurgie f esthétique

**cosmopolitan** /kɒzmə'pɒlɪtn/ adj & n cosmopolite (mf).

**cosmos** /'kɒzmɒs/ n cosmos m.

**cost** /kɒst/ vt (pt cost) coûter. (pt costed) établir le prix de. ● n coût m. ~s (Jur) dépens mpl. **at all** ~s à tout prix; **to one's** ~ à ses dépens; ~ **price** prix m de revient; ~ **of living** coût m de la vie. ~-**effective** adj rentable.

**costly** /'kɒstlɪ/ adj (-ier, -iest) coûteux; (valuable) précieux.

**costume** /'kɒstjuːm/ n costume m. (for swimming) maillot m. ~ **jewellery** npl bijoux mpl de fantaisie.

**cosy** /'kəʊzɪ/ adj (-ier, -iest) confortable, intime.

**cot** /kɒt/ n lit m d'enfant; (campbed: US) lit m de camp.

**cottage** /'kɒtɪdʒ/ n petite maison f de campagne; (thatched) chaumière f. ~ **pie** n hachis m Parmentier.

**cotton** /'kɒtn/ n coton m. (for sewing) fil m (à coudre). ● vi — **on** 🔲 piger. ~ **wool** n coton m hydrophile.

**couch** /kaʊtʃ/ n canapé m. ● vt (express) formuler.

**cough** /kɒf/ vi tousser. ● n toux f. ~ **up** 🔲 cracher, payer.

**could** /kʊd/ →CAN¹.

**couldn't** →COULD NOT.

**council** /'kaʊnsl/ n conseil m. ~ **house** n maison f louée par la municipalité, ≈ H.L.M. m or f.

**councillor** /'kaʊnsələ(r)/ n conseiller/-ère mf/f municipal/-e.

**counsel** /'kaʊnsl/ n conseil m. ● n inv (Jur) avocat/-e m/f. **counsellor** n conseiller/-ère m/f.

**count** /kaʊnt/ vt/i compter. ● n (numerical record) décompte m. (nobleman) comte m. ~ **on** compter sur.

**counter** /'kaʊntə(r)/ n comptoir m. (in bank) guichet m; (token) jeton m. ● adv ~ **to** à l'encontre de. ● adj opposé. ● vt opposer; (blow) parer. ● vi riposter.

**counteract** /kaʊntə'rækt/ vt neutraliser.

**counterbalance** /'kaʊntəbæləns/ n contrepoids m. ● vt contrebalancer.

**counterfeit** /'kaʊntəfɪt/ adj & n faux (m). ● vt contrefaire.

**counterfoil** /'kaʊntəfɔɪl/ n souche f.

**counter-productive** /kaʊntəprə'dʌktɪv/ adj qui produit l'effet contraire.

**countess** /'kaʊntɪs/ n comtesse f.

**countless** /'kaʊntlɪs/ adj innombrable.

**country** /'kʌntrɪ/ n (land, region) pays m. (homeland) patrie f; (countryside) campagne f.

**countryman** /'kʌntrɪmən/ n (pl -men) campagnard m; (fellow citizen) compatriote m.

**countryside** /'kʌntrɪsaɪd/ n campagne f.

**county** /'kaʊntɪ/ n comté m.

**coup** /kuː/ n (achievement) joli coup m. (Pol) coup m d'état.

**couple** /'kʌpl/ n (people, animals) couple m. **a** ~ **of** (two or three) deux ou trois. ● vt/i (s')accoupler.

**coupon** /'kuːpɒn/ n coupon m; (for shopping) bon m or coupon m de réduction.

**courage** /'kʌrɪdʒ/ n courage m.

**courgette** /kʊə'ʒet/ n courgette f.

**courier** /'kʊrɪə(r)/ n messager/-ère m/f; (for tourists) guide m.

**course** /kɔːs/ n cours m; (for training) stage m; (series) série f; (Culin) plat m; (for golf) terrain m; (at sea) itinéraire m; ~ change → changer de cap; ~ (of action) façon f de faire; during the ~ of pendant; in due ~ en temps utile; of ~ bien sûr.

**court** /kɔːt/ n cour f; (tennis) court m; go to ~ aller devant les tribunaux. ● vt faire la cour à; (danger) rechercher.

**courteous** /ˈkɜːtɪəs/ adj courtois.

**courtesy** /ˈkɜːtəsɪ/ n courtoisie f; by ~ of avec la permission de.

**courthouse** /ˈkɔːthaʊs/ n (US) palais m de justice.

**court-martial** vt (pt -martialled) faire passer en conseil de guerre. ● n cour f martiale.

**court:** ~room n salle f de tribunal. ~shoe n escarpin m. ~yard n cour f.

**cousin** /ˈkʌzn/ n cousin/-e m/f. first ~ cousin/-e m/f germain/-e.

**cove** /kəʊv/ n anse f, crique f.

**covenant** /ˈkʌvənənt/ n convention f.

**cover** /ˈkʌvə(r)/ vt couvrir. ● n (for bed, book) couverture f; (lid) couvercle m; (for furniture) housse f; (shelter) abri m; take ~ se mettre à l'abri. ~ cacher; (crime) couvrir; ~up for couvrir.

**coverage** /ˈkʌvərɪdʒ/ n reportage m.

**covering** /ˈkʌvərɪŋ/ n enveloppe f. ~ letter lettre f d'accompagnement.

**covert** /ˈkʌvət/ adj (activity) secret; (threat) voilé; (look) dérobé.

**cover-up** n opération f de camouflage.

**cow** /kaʊ/ n vache f.

**coward** /ˈkaʊəd/ n lâche mf.

**cowboy** /ˈkaʊbɔɪ/ n cow-boy m.

**cowshed** /ˈkaʊʃed/ n étable f.

**coy** /kɔɪ/ adj (faussement) timide, qui fait le or la timide.

**cozy** US →**cosy**.

**crab** /kræb/ n crabe m. ~-apple n pomme f sauvage.

**crack** /kræk/ n fente f; (in glass) fêlure f; (noise) craquement m; (joke 🗨) plaisanterie f. ● adj 🗨 d'élite. ● vt/i (break partially) (se) fêler; (split) (se) fendre; (nut) casser; (joke) raconter; (problem) résoudre; get ~ing 🗨 s'y mettre. ~ down on 🗨 sévir contre. ~ up 🗨 craquer.

**cracker** /ˈkrækə(r)/ n (Culin) biscuit m (salé); (for Christmas) diablotin f.

**crackle** /ˈkrækl/ vi crépiter. ● n crépitement m.

**cradle** /ˈkreɪdl/ n berceau m. ● vt bercer.

**craft** /krɑːft/ n métier m artisanal; (technique) art m; (boat) bateau m.

**craftsman** /n (pl -men) artisan m.

**craftsmanship** n art m.

**crafty** /ˈkrɑːftɪ/ adj (-ier, -iest) rusé.

**crag** /kræg/ n rocher m à pic.

**cram** /kræm/ vt/i (pt crammed) (for an exam) bachoter (for pour;) ~ into (pack) (s')entasser dans; ~ with (fill) bourrer de.

**cramp** /kræmp/ n crampe f.

**cramped** /kræmpt/ adj à l'étroit.

**cranberry** /ˈkrænbərɪ/ n canneberge f.

**crane** /kreɪn/ n grue f. ● vt (neck) tendre.

**crank** /kræŋk/ n excentrique mf. (Tech) manivelle f.

**crap** /kræp/ n (nonsense 🗨) conneries fpl 🗨; (faeces 🗨) merde f 🗨.

**crash** /kræʃ/ n accident m; (noise) fracas m; (of thunder) coup m; (of firm) faillite f. ● vt/i avoir un accident (avec); (of plane) s'écraser; (two vehicles) se percuter; ~ into rentrer dans. ~ course n cours m intensif. ~-helmet n casque m (anti-choc). ~-land vt atterrir en catastrophe.

**crate** /kreɪt/ n cageot m.

**cravat** /krə'væt/ n foulard m.

**crave** /kreɪv/ vt/i ~ for désirer ardemment. **craving** n envie f irrésistible.

**crawl** /krɔːl/ vi (insect) ramper; (vehicle) se traîner; be ~ing with grouiller de. ● n (pace) pas m. (swimming) crawl m.

**crayfish** /kreɪfɪʃ/ n inv écrevisse f.

**crayon** /'kreɪən/ n craie f grasse.

**craze** /kreɪz/ n engouement m.

**crazy** /'kreɪzɪ/ adj (-ier, -iest) fou; ~ about (person) fou de; (thing) fana ou fou de.

**creak** /kriːk/ n grincement m. ● vi grincer.

**cream** /kriːm/ n crème f. ● adj crème inv. ● vt écrémer.

**crease** /kriːs/ n pli m. ● vt/i (se) froisser.

**create** /kriː'eɪt/ vt créer. **creation** n création f. **creative** adj (person) créatif; (process) créateur. **creator** n créateur/-trice m/f.

**creature** /'kriːtʃə(r)/ n créature f.

**crèche** /kreʃ/ n garderie f.

**credentials** /krɪ'denʃlz/ npl (identity) pièces fpl d'identité; (competence) références fpl.

**credibility** /kredə'bɪlətɪ/ n crédibilité f.

**credit** /'kredɪt/ n (credence) crédit m. (honour) honneur m; in ~ créditeur; ~s (cinema) générique m. ● adj (balance) créditeur. ● vt croire; (Comm) créditer; ~ sb with attribuer à qn. ~ **card** n carte f de cré-

dit. ~ **note** n avoir m.

**creditor** /'kredɪtə(r)/ n créancier/-ière m/f.

**creditworthy** /'kredɪtwɜːðɪ/ adj solvable.

**creed** /kriːd/ n credo m.

**creek** /kriːk/ n (US) ruisseau m. up the ~ 𝔪 dans le pétrin 𝔪.

**creep** /kriːp/ vi (pt crept) (insect, cat) ramper; (fig) se glisser. ● n (person 𝔪) pauvre type m 𝟙. give sb the ~s faire frissonner qn. **creeper** n liane f.

**cremate** /krɪ'meɪt/ vt incinérer. **cremation** n incinération f. **crematorium** n (pl -ia) crématorium m.

**crêpe** /kreɪp/ n crêpe m. ~ **paper** n papier m crêpon.

**crept** /krept/ →CREEP.

**crescent** /'kresnt/ n croissant m; (of houses) rue f en demi-lune.

**cress** /kres/ n cresson m.

**crest** /krest/ n crête f. (coat of arms) armoiries fpl.

**cretin** /'kretɪn/ n crétin/-e m/f.

**crevice** /'krevɪs/ n fente f.

**crew** /kruː/ n (of plane, ship) équipage m; (gang) équipe f. ~ **cut** n coupe f en brosse. ~ **neck** n (col) ras du cou m.

**crib** /krɪb/ n lit m d'enfant. ● vt/i (pt cribbed) copier.

**cricket** /'krɪkɪt/ n (Sport) cricket m. (insect) grillon m.

**crime** /kraɪm/ n crime m; (minor) délit m; (acts) criminalité f.

**criminal** /'krɪmɪnl/ adj & n criminel/-le (m/f).

**crimson** /'krɪmzn/ adj & n cramoisi (m).

**cringe** /krɪndʒ/ vi reculer; (fig) s'humilier.

**crinkle** /'krɪŋkl/ vt/i (cloth) (se)

froisser. ● *n* pli *m.*

**cripple** /'krɪpl/ *n* infirme *mf.* ● *vt* estropier; (fig) paralyser.

**crisis** /'kraɪsɪs/ *n* (*pl* **crises**) crise *f.*

**crisp** /krɪsp/ *adj* (Culin) croquant; (air, reply) vif. **crisps** *npl* chips *fpl.*

**criss-cross** /'krɪskrɒs/ *adj* entrecroisé. ● *vt/i* (s')entrecroiser.

**criterion** /kraɪˈtɪərɪən/ *n* (*pl* **-ia**) critère *m.*

**critic** /'krɪtɪk/ *n* critique *m.* **critical** *adj* critique. **critically** *adv* d'une manière critique; (ill) gravement.

**criticism** /'krɪtɪsɪzəm/ *n* critique *f.*

**criticize** /'krɪtɪsaɪz/ *vt/i* critiquer.

**croak** /krəʊk/ *n* (bird) croassement *m;* (frog) coassement *m.* ● *vi* croasser; coasser.

**Croatia** /krəʊˈeɪʃə/ *n* Croatie *f.*

**Croatian** /krəʊˈeɪʃn/ *n* Croate *mf.* ● *adj* Croate.

**crochet** /'krəʊʃeɪ/ *n* crochet *m.* ● *vt* faire du crochet.

**crockery** /'krɒkərɪ/ *n* vaisselle *f.*

**crocodile** /'krɒkədaɪl/ *n* crocodile *m.*

**crook** /krʊk/ *n* (criminal 🔢) escroc *m;* (stick) houlette *f.*

**crooked** /'krʊkɪd/ *adj* tordu; (winding) tortueux; (askew) de travers; (dishonest: fig) malhonnête.

**crop** /krɒp/ *n* récolte *f;* (fig) quantité *f.* ● *vt* (*pt* **cropped**) couper. ● *vi* ~ **up** se présenter.

**cross** /krɒs/ *n* croix *f;* (hybrid) hybride *m.* ● *vt/i* traverser; (legs, animals) croiser; (cheque) barrer; (paths) se croiser; ~ **sb's mind** venir à l'esprit de qn. ● *adj* en colère, fâché (with contre). talk at ~ purposes parler sans se comprendre. ▢ ~ **off** or **out** rayer. ~-**check** *vt* vérifier (pour confirmer).

~-**country (running)** *n* cross *m.*

~-**examine** *vt* faire subir un contre-interrogatoire à. ~-**eyed** *adj* be ~-**eyed** loucher. ~-**fire** *n* feux *mpl* croisés.

**crossing** /'krɒsɪŋ/ *n* (by boat) traversée *f;* (on road) passage *m* clouté.

**crossly** /'krɒslɪ/ *adv* avec colère.

**cross:** ~-**reference** *n* renvoi *m.* ~**roads** *n* carrefour *m.* ~**word** *n* mots *mpl* croisés.

**crotch** /krɒtʃ/ *n* (of garment) entrejambes *m inv.*

**crouch** /kraʊtʃ/ *vi* s'accroupir.

**crow** /krəʊ/ *n* corbeau *m;* as the ~ **flies** à vol d'oiseau. ● *vi* (of cock) chanter; (fig) jubiler. ~**bar** *n* pied-de-biche *m.*

**crowd** /kraʊd/ *n* foule *f.* **crowded** *adj* plein.

**crown** /kraʊn/ *n* couronne *f;* (top part) sommet *m.* ● *vt* couronner.

**Crown Court** *n* Cour *f* d'assises.

**crucial** /'kru:ʃl/ *adj* crucial.

**crucifix** /'kru:sɪfɪks/ *n* crucifix *m.*

**crucify** /'kru:sɪfaɪ/ *vt* crucifier.

**crude** /kru:d/ *adj* (raw) brut; (rough, vulgar) grossier.

**cruel** /krʊəl/ *adj* (**crueller, cruellest**) cruel.

**cruise** /kru:z/ *n* croisière *f.* ● *vi* (ship) croiser; (tourists) faire une croisière; (vehicle) rouler; **cruising speed** vitesse *f* de croisière.

**crumb** /krʌm/ *n* miette *f.*

**crumble** /'krʌmbl/ *vt/i* (s')effriter; (bread) (s')émietter; (collapse) s'écrouler.

**crumple** /'krʌmpl/ *vt/i* (se) froisser.

**crunch** /krʌntʃ/ *vt* croquer. ● *n* (event) moment *m* critique; **when it comes to the** ~ quand ça devient sérieux.

**crusade** /kru:'seɪd/ n croisade f.
**crusader** n (knight) croisé m; (fig)
militant/-e m/f.

**crush** /krʌʃ/ vt écraser; (clothes)
froisser. ● n (crowd) presse f; a ~
on ≋ le béguin pour.

**crust** /krʌst/ n croûte f. **crusty** adj
croustillant.

**crutch** /krʌtʃ/ n béquille f; (crotch)
entrejambes m inv.

**crux** /krʌks/ n the ~ of (problem)
le point crucial de.

**cry** /kraɪ/ n cri m. ● vi (weep) pleurer; (call out) crier. □ ~ off se décommander.

**crying** /kraɪɪŋ/ adj (need) urgent;
a ~ shame une vraie honte. ● n
pleurs mpl.

**cryptic** /krɪptɪk/ adj énigmatique.

**crystal** /krɪstl/ n cristal m.
~-clear adj parfaitement clair.

**cub** /kʌb/ n petit m; Cub (Scout)
louveteau m.

**Cuba** /kju:bə/ n Cuba f.

**cube** /kju:b/ n cube m. **cubic** adj
cubique; (metre) cube.

**cubicle** /kju:bɪkl/ n (in room, hospital) box m; (at swimming-pool) cabine f.

**cuckoo** /kʊku:/ n coucou m.

**cucumber** /kju:kʌmbə(r)/ n concombre m.

**cuddle** /kʌdl/ vt câliner. ● vi (kiss
and) ~ s'embrasser. ● n caresse f.
**cuddly** adj câlin; **cuddly toy** peluche f.

**cue** /kju:/ n signal m; (Theat) réplique f; (billiards) queue f.

**cuff** /kʌf/ n manchette f; (US: on
trousers) revers m; off the ~ im-
promptu. ● vt gifler. ~-link n bouton m de manchette.

**cul-de-sac** /kʌldəsæk/ n (pl **culs-**

**de-sac**) impasse f.

**cull** /kʌl/ vt (select) choisir; (kill)
massacrer.

**culminate** /kʌlmɪneɪt/ vi ~ in se
terminer par. **culmination** n point
m culminant.

**culprit** /kʌlprɪt/ n coupable mf.

**cult** /kʌlt/ n culte m.

**cultivate** /kʌltɪveɪt/ vt cultiver.
**cultivation** n culture f.

**cultural** /kʌltʃərəl/ adj culturel.

**culture** /kʌltʃə(r)/ n culture f. **cul-
tured** adj cultivé.

**cumbersome** /kʌmbəsəm/ adj
encombrant.

**cunning** /kʌnɪŋ/ adj rusé. ● n astuce f, ruse f.

**cup** /kʌp/ n tasse f; (prize) coupe f;
**Cup final** finale f de la coupe.

**cupboard** /kʌbəd/ n placard m.

**cup-tie** n match m de coupe.

**curate** /kjʊərət/ n vicaire m.

**curator** /kjʊə'reɪtə(r)/ n (of museum) conservateur m.

**curb** /kɜ:b/ n (restraint) frein m; (of
path) (US) bord m du trottoir. ● vt
(desires) refréner; (price increase)
freiner.

**cure** /kjʊə(r)/ vt guérir; (fig) éliminer; (Culin) fumer; (in brine) saler.
● n (recovery) guérison f; (remedy)
remède m.

**curfew** /kɜ:fju:/ n couvre-feu m.

**curiosity** /kjʊərɪ'ɒsətɪ/ n curiosité
f. **curious** adj curieux.

**curl** /kɜ:l/ vt/i (hair) boucler. ● n
boucle f. □ ~up se pelotonner;
(shrivel) se racornir.

**curler** /kɜ:lə(r)/ n bigoudi m.

**curly** /kɜ:lɪ/ adj (-ier, -iest) bouclé.

**currant** /kʌrənt/ n raisin m de Co-
rinthe.

**currency** /kʌrənsɪ/ n (money)

monnaie f; (of word) fréquence f;
foreign ~ devises fpl étrangères.

**current** /'kʌrənt/ adj (term, word)
usité; (topical) actuel; (year) en
cours. ● n courant m. ~ **account** n
compte m courant. ~ **events** npl
l'actualité f.

**currently** /'kʌrəntlɪ/ adv actuelle-
ment.

**curriculum** /kə'rɪkjʊləm/ n (pl
-la) programme m scolaire. ~ **vitae**
n curriculum vitae m.

**curry** /'kʌrɪ/ n curry m. ● vt ~ favour with chercher les bonnes grâces de.

**curse** /kɜːs/ n (spell) malédiction f;
(swearword) juron m. ● vt maudire.
● vi (swear) jurer.

**cursor** /'kɜːsə(r)/ n curseur m.

**curt** /kɜːt/ adj brusque.

**curtain** /'kɜːtn/ n rideau m.

**curve** /kɜːv/ n courbe f. ● vi (line)
s'incurver; (edge) se recourber;
(road) faire une courbe. ● vt
courber.

**cushion** /'kʊʃn/ n coussin m. ● vt
(a blow) amortir; (fig) protéger.

**custard** /'kʌstəd/ n crème f anglaise; (set) flan m.

**custody** /'kʌstədɪ/ n (of child)
garde f; (Jur) détention f préventive.

**custom** /'kʌstəm/ n coutume f;
(patronage: Comm) clientèle f. **customary** adj habituel.

**customer** /'kʌstəmə(r)/ n client/-e
m/f; (person 🖵) type m.

**customize** /'kʌstəmaɪz/ vt person-
naliser.

**custom-made** adj fait sur
mesure.

**customs** /'kʌstəmz/ npl douane f.
● adj douanier. ~ **officer** n douanier m.

**cut** /kʌt/ vt/i (pt cut. pres p cutting)

vt couper; (hedge) tailler; (prices) réduire. ● vi couper. ● n (wound)
coupure f; (of clothes) coupe f; (in surgery) incision f; (share) part f; (in
prices) réduction f. ▫ ~ **back** vi
faire des économies. vt réduire.
~ **down (on)** réduire. ~ **in** (in conversation) intervenir. ~ **off** couper;
(tide, army) isoler; ~ **out** (in découper; (leave out) supprimer; vi (engine) s'arrêter. ~ **short** (visit)
écourter. ~ **up** couper; (carve) découper.

**cutback** /'kʌtbæk/ n réduction f.

**cute** /kjuːt/ adj 🖵 mignon.

**cutlery** /'kʌtlərɪ/ n couverts mpl.

**cutlet** /'kʌtlɪt/ n côtelette f.

**cut-price** adj à prix réduit.

**cutting** /'kʌtɪŋ/ adj cinglant. ● n
(from newspaper) coupure f; (plant)
bouture f.

**CV** abbr ➡ CURRICULUM VITAE.

**cyanide** /'saɪənaɪd/ n cyanure m.

**cyberspace** /'saɪbəspeɪs/ n cyberspace m.

**cycle** /'saɪbəspeɪs/ n cycle m; (bicycle) vélo m. ● vi aller à vélo.

**cycling** /'saɪklɪŋ/ n cyclisme m. ~
**shorts** npl cycliste m.

**cyclist** /'saɪklɪst/ n cycliste mf.

**cylinder** /'sɪlɪndə(r)/ n cylindre m.

**cymbal** /'sɪmbl/ n cymbale f.

**cynic** /'sɪnɪk/ n cynique mf. **cynical**
adj cynique. **cynicism** n cynisme m.

**cypress** /'saɪprəs/ n cyprès m.

**Cypriot** /'sɪprɪət/ n Cypriote mf.
● adj cypriote.

**Cyprus** /'saɪprəs/ n Chypre f.

**cyst** /sɪst/ n kyste m.

**czar** /zɑː(r)/ n tsar m.

**Czech** /tʃek/ n (person) Tchèque mf;
(Ling) tchèque m. ~ **Republic** n République f tchèque.

# Dd

**dab** /dæb/ vt (pt dabbed) tamponner; ~ sth on appliquer qch par petites touches. ● n touche f.

**dabble** /'dæbl/ vi ~ in sth faire qch en amateur.

**dad** /dæd/ n 🔢 papa m. **daddy** n 🔢 papa m.

**daffodil** /'dæfədɪl/ n jonquille f.

**daft** /dɑ:ft/ adj bête.

**dagger** /'dægə(r)/ n poignard m.

---

**Dáil Éireann** Ces mots de gaélique irlandais, que l'on prononce /dɔɪl 'ɛ:r(ə)n/ désignent la Chambre des représentants au parlement de la République d'Irlande. Les 166 députés qui la composent représentent 42 circomscriptions électorales et sont élus par un système de scrutin à la représentation proportionnelle pour cinq ans.

---

**daily** /'deɪlɪ/ adj quotidien. ● adv tous les jours. ● n (newspaper) quotidien m.

**dainty** /'deɪntɪ/ adj (-ier, -iest) (lace, food) délicat; (shoe, hand) mignon.

**dairy** /'deərɪ/ n (on farm) laiterie f; (shop) crémerie f. ● adj (farm, cow, product) laitier; (butter) fermier.

**daisy** /'deɪzɪ/ n pâquerette f.

**dam** /dæm/ n barrage m.

**damage** /'dæmɪdʒ/ n (to property) dégâts mpl; (Med) lésions fpl; to do sth ~ (cause, trade) porter atteinte à; ~s (Jur) dommages-intérêts mpl. ● vt (property) endommager; (health) nuire à; (reputation) porter atteinte à. **damaging** adj (to health) nuisible; (to reputation) préjudiciable.

**damn** /dæm/ vt (Relig) damner; (condemn: fig) condamner. ● interj 🔢 zut 🔢, merde 🔣. ● n not give/care a ~ about se ficher de 🔢. ● adj fichu 🔢. ● adv franchement.

**damp** /dæmp/ n humidité f. ● adj humide. **dampen** vt (lit) humecter; (fig) refroidir. **dampness** n humidité f.

**dance** /dɑ:ns/ vt/i danser. ● n danse f; (gathering) bal m; ~ hall dancing m. **dancer** n danseur/-euse m/f.

**dandelion** /'dændɪlaɪən/ n pissenlit m.

**dandruff** /'dændrʌf/ n pellicules fpl.

**Dane** /deɪn/ n Danois/-e m/f.

**danger** /'deɪndʒə(r)/ n danger m; (risk) risque m; be in ~ of risquer de. **dangerous** adj dangereux.

**dangle** /'dæŋgl/ vt (object) balancer; (legs) laisser pendre. ● vi (object) se balancer (from à).

**Danish** /'deɪnɪʃ/ n (Ling) danois m. ● adj danois.

**dare** /deə(r)/ vt oser (s'obscurcir. ~ sth to do faire); ~ sb to do défier qn de faire. ● n défi m. **daring** adj audacieux.

**dark** /dɑ:k/ adj (day, colour, suit, mood, warning) sombre; (hair, eyes, skin) brun; (secret, thought) noir. ● n noir m; (nightfall) tombée f de la nuit; in the ~ (fig) dans le noir. **darken** vt/i (sky) (s')obscurcir; (mood) (s')assombrir. **darkness** n obscurité f. ~-room n chambre f noire.

**darling** /'dɑ:lɪŋ/ adj & n chéri/-e (m/f).

**dart** /dɑ:t/ n fléchette f; ~s (game) fléchettes fpl. ● vi ~ in/away entrer/filer comme une flèche.

**dash** /dæʃ/ vi se sauver. ● vt (hope) anéantir; ~ **off** se sauver. ● vt (hope) anéantir; ~ **sth against** projeter qch contre. ● n course f folle; (of liquid) goutte f; (of colour) touche f; (in punctuation) tiret m.

**dashboard** /'dæʃbɔ:d/ n tableau m de bord.

**data** /'deɪtə/ npl données fpl. ~**base** n base f de données. ~ **capture** n saisie f de données. ~ **processing** n traitement m des données. ~ **protection** n protection f de l'information.

**date** /deɪt/ n date f; (meeting) rendezvous m; (fruit) datte f; out of ~ (old-fashioned) démodé; (passport) périmé; to ~ à ce jour; up to ~ (modern) moderne; (list) à jour. ● vt/i dater; (go out with) sortir avec; ~ **from** dater de. **dated** adj démodé.

**daughter** /'dɔ:tə(r)/ n fille f. ~-**in-law** n (pl ~**s-in-law**) belle-fille f.

**daunt** /dɔ:nt/ vt décourager.

**dawdle** /'dɔ:dl/ vi flâner, traînasser ⏍.

**dawn** /dɔ:n/ n aube f. ● vi (day) se lever; it ~ed on me that je me suis rendu compte que.

**day** /deɪ/ n jour m; (whole day) journée f; (period) époque f; the ~ before la veille; the following or next ~ le lendemain. ~**break** n aube f.

**daydream** /'deɪdri:m/ n rêves mpl. ● vi rêvasser (about de).

**day:** ~**light** n jour m. ~**time** n journée f. ~ **trader** spéculateur m à la journée, scalpeur m.

**daze** /deɪz/ n in a ~ (from blow) étourdi; (from drug) hébété. **dazed** adj (by blow) abasourdi; (by news) ahuri.

**dazzle** /'dæzl/ vt éblouir.

**dead** /ded/ adj mort; (numb) engourdi. ● adv complètement; in ~ centre au beau milieu; **stop** ~ s'arrêter net. ● n in the ~ of au cœur de; the ~ les morts. **deaden** vt (sound, blow) amortir; (pain) calmer. ~ **end** n impasse f. ~**line** n date f limite. ~**lock** n impasse f.

**deadly** /'dedlɪ/ adj (-**ier**, -**iest**) mortel; (weapon) meurtrier.

**deaf** /def/ adj sourd. **deafen** vt assourdir. **deafness** n surdité f.

**deal** /di:l/ vt (pt **dealt**) donner; (blow) porter. ● vi (trade) être en activité; ~ **in** être dans le commerce de. ● n affaire f; (cards) donne f; **a great** or **good** ~ beaucoup (of de). ▫ ~ **with** (handle, manage) s'occuper de; (be about) traiter de. **dealer** n marchand/-e m/f; (agent) concessionaire m/f. **dealings** npl relations fpl.

**dear** /dɪə(r)/ adj cher; ~ **Sir/ Madam** Monsieur/Madame. ● n (my) ~ mon chéri/ma chérie m/f. ● adv cher. ● interj oh ~! oh mon Dieu!

**death** /deθ/ n mort f; ~ **penalty** peine f de mort.

**debatable** /dɪ'beɪtəbl/ adj discutable.

**debate** /dɪ'beɪt/ n (formal) débat m; (informal) discussion f. ● vt (formally) débattre de; (informally) discuter.

**debit** /'debɪt/ n débit m. ● adj (balance) débiteur. ● vt (pt **debited**) débiter.

**debris** /'debri:/ n débris mpl; (rubbish) déchets mpl.

**debt** /det/ n dette f; **be in** ~ avoir des dettes.

**debug** /di:'bʌg/ vt (Comput) déboguer.

**decade** /'dekeɪd/ n décennie f.

**decadent** /'dekədənt/ adj décadent.

**decaffeinated** /di:'kæfɪneɪtɪd/ adj décaféiné.

**decay** /dɪ'keɪ/ vi (vegetation) pourrir; (tooth) se carier; (fig) décliner. ● n pourriture f; (of tooth) carie f; (fig) déclin m.

**deceased** /dɪ'si:st/ adj décédé. ● n défunt/-e m/f.

**deceit** /dɪ'si:t/ n tromperie f. **deceitful** adj trompeur.

**deceive** /dɪ'si:v/ vt tromper.

**December** /dɪ'sembə(r)/ n décembre m.

**decent** /'di:snt/ adj (respectable) comme il faut; (adequate) convenable; (good) bon; (kind) gentil; (not indecent) décent. **decently** adv convenablement.

**deception** /dɪ'sepʃn/ n tromperie f. **deceptive** adj trompeur.

**decide** /dɪ'saɪd/ vt/i décider (to do de faire); (question) régler; ~ on se décider pour. **decided** adj (firm) résolu; (clear) net. **decidedly** adv nettement.

**decimal** /'desɪml/ adj décimal. ● n décimale f; ~ point virgule f.

**decipher** /dɪ'saɪfə(r)/ vt déchiffrer.

**decision** /dɪ'sɪʒn/ n décision f.

**decisive** /dɪ'saɪsɪv/ adj (conclusive) décisif; (firm) décidé.

**deck** /dek/ n pont m; (of cards: US) jeu m; (of bus) étage m. ~-chair n chaise f longue.

**declaration** /deklə'reɪʃn/ n déclaration f. **declare** vt déclarer.

**decline** /dɪ'klaɪn/ vt/i refuser; (fall) baisser. ● n (waning) déclin m; (drop) baisse f; **in ~** sur le déclin.

**decode** /di:'kəʊd/ vt décoder.

**decommission** /di:kə'mɪʃn/vt (arms) mettre hors service; (reactor) démanteler.

**decompose** /di:kəm'pəʊz/ vt/i (se) décomposer.

**decor** /'deɪkɔ:(r)/ n décor m.

**decorate** /'dekəreɪt/ vt décorer; (room) refaire, peindre. **decoration** n décoration f. **decorative** adj décoratif.

**decorator** /'dekəreɪtə(r)/ n peintre m; (interior) ~ décorateur/-trice m/f.

**decoy** /'di:kɔɪ/ n (person, vehicle) leurre m; (for hunting) appeau m.

**decrease¹** /dɪ'kri:s/ vt/i diminuer.

**decrease²** /'di:kri:s/ n diminution f.

**decree** /dɪ'kri:/ n (Pol, Relig) décret m; (Jur) jugement m. ● vt (pt **decreed**) décréter.

**decrepit** /dɪ'krepɪt/ adj (building) délabré; (person) décrépit.

**dedicate** /'dedɪkeɪt/ vt dédier; ~ oneself to se consacrer à. **dedicated** /'dedɪkeɪtɪd/ adj dévoué; ~ **line** (Internet) ligne f spécialisée.

**dedication** /dedɪ'keɪʃn/ n dévouement m; (in book) dédicace f.

**deduce** /dɪ'dju:s/ vt déduire.

**deduct** /dɪ'dʌkt/ vt déduire; (from wages) retenir.

**deed** /di:d/ n acte m.

**deem** /di:m/ vt considérer.

**deep** /di:p/ adj (water, mud, carpet) épais. ● adv profondément; ~ **in thought** absorbé dans ses pensées. **deepen** vt/i (admiration, concern) augmenter.

**deep-freeze** n congélateur m. ● vt congeler.

**deep vein thrombosis** n thrombose f veineuse profonde.

**deer** /dɪə(r)/ n inv cerf m; (doe) biche f.

**deface** /dɪ'feɪs/ vt dégrader.

d

**default** /dɪˈfɔːlt/ vi (Jur) ~ (on payments) ne pas régler ses échéances. ● n (on payments) non-remboursement m; by ~ par défaut; win by ~ gagner par forfait. ● adj (Comput) par défaut.

**defeat** /dɪˈfiːt/ vt vaincre; (thwart) faire échouer. ● n défaite f.

**defect¹** /ˈdiːfekt/ n défaut m.

**defect²** /dɪˈfekt/ vi faire défection; ~ to passer à.

**defective** /dɪˈfektɪv/ adj défectueux.

**defector** /dɪˈfektə(r)/ n transfuge mf.

**defence** /dɪˈfens/ n défense f.

**defend** /dɪˈfend/ vt défendre. **defendant** n (Jur) accusé/-e m/f. **defender** défenseur m.

**defensive** /dɪˈfensɪv/ adj défensif. ● n défensive f.

**defer** /dɪˈfɜː(r)/ vt (pt deferred) (postpone) reporter; (judgement) suspendre; (payment) différer.

**deference** /ˈdefərəns/ n déférence f. **deferential** adj déférent.

**defiance** /dɪˈfaɪəns/ n défi m; in ~ of contre. **defiant** adj rebelle. **defiantly** adv avec défi.

**deficiency** /dɪˈfɪʃənsɪ/ n insuffisance f; (fault) défaut m.

**deficient** /dɪˈfɪʃnt/ adj insuffisant; be ~ in manquer de.

**deficit** /ˈdefɪsɪt/ n déficit m.

**define** /dɪˈfaɪn/ vt définir.

**definite** /ˈdefɪnɪt/ adj (exact) précis; (obvious) net; (firm) ferme; (certain) certain. **definitely** adv certainement; (clearly) nettement.

**definition** /defɪˈnɪʃn/ n définition f.

**deflate** /dɪˈfleɪt/ vt dégonfler.

**deflect** /dɪˈflekt/ vt (missile) dévier; (criticism) détourner.

**deforestation** /diːfɒrɪˈsteɪʃn/ n déforestation f.

**deform** /dɪˈfɔːm/ vt déformer.

**defraud** /dɪˈfrɔːd/ vt (client, employer) escroquer; (state, customs) frauder; ~ sb of sth escroquer qch à qn.

**defrost** /diːˈfrɒst/ vt dégivrer.

**deft** /deft/ adj adroit.

**defunct** /dɪˈfʌŋkt/ adj défunt.

**defuse** /diːˈfjuːz/ vt désamorcer.

**defy** /dɪˈfaɪ/ vt défier; (attempts) résister à.

**degenerate¹** /dɪˈdʒenəreɪt/ vi dégénérer (into en).

**degenerate²** /dɪˈdʒenərət/ adj & n dégénéré/-e (m/f).

**degrade** /dɪˈɡreɪd/ vt (humiliate) humilier; (damage) dégrader.

**degree** /dɪˈɡriː/ n degré m; (Univ) diplôme m universitaire; (Bachelor's degree) licence f; to such a ~ that à tel point que.

**dehydrate** /diːˈhaɪdreɪt/ vt/i (se) déshydrater.

**deign** /deɪn/ vt ~ to do daigner faire.

**dejected** /dɪˈdʒektɪd/ adj découragé.

**delay** /dɪˈleɪ/ vt (flight) retarder; (decision) différer; ~ doing attendre pour faire. ● n of plane, post) retard m; (time lapse) délai m.

**delegate¹** /ˈdelɪɡət/ n délégué /-e m/f.

**delegate²** /ˈdelɪɡeɪt/ vt déléguer. **delegation** n délégation f.

**delete** /dɪˈliːt/ vt supprimer; (Comput) effacer; (with pen) barrer. **deletion** n suppression f; (with line) rature f.

**deliberate¹** /dɪˈlɪbəreɪt/ vi délibérer.

**deliberate²** /dɪˈlɪbərət/ adj délibéré; (*steps, manner*) mesuré. **deliberately** *adv* (*do, say*) exprès; (*sarcastically, provocatively*) délibérément.

**delicacy** /ˈdelɪkəsɪ/ *n* délicatesse *f*; (*food*) mets *m* raffiné.

**delicate** /ˈdelɪkət/ *adj* délicat.

**delicatessen** /delɪkəˈtesn/ *n* épicerie *f* fine.

**delicious** /dɪˈlɪʃəs/ *adj* délicieux.

**delight** /dɪˈlaɪt/ *n* joie *f*, plaisir *m*. ● *vt* ravir. *vi* ~ **in** prendre plaisir à. **delighted** *adj* ravi. **delightful** *adj* charmant/-e.

**delinquent** /dɪˈlɪŋkwənt/ *adj* & *n* délinquant/-e (*m/f*).

**delirious** /dɪˈlɪrɪəs/ *adj* délirant.

**deliver** /dɪˈlɪvə(r)/ *vt* (*message*) remettre; (*goods*) livrer; (*speech*) faire; (*baby*) mettre au monde; (*rescue*) délivrer. **delivery** *n* (*of goods*) livraison *f*; (*of mail*) distribution *f*; (*of baby*) accouchement *m*.

**delude** /dɪˈluːd/ *vt* tromper; ~ oneself se faire des illusions.

**deluge** /ˈdeljuːdʒ/ *n* déluge *m*. ● *vt* submerger (**with** de).

**delusion** /dɪˈluːʒn/ *n* illusion *f*.

**delve** /delv/ *vi* fouiller.

**demand** /dɪˈmɑːnd/ *vt* (*request, require*) demander; (*forcefully*) exiger. ● *n* (*request*) demande *f*; (*pressure*) exigence *f*; **in** ~ très demandé; **on** ~ à la demande. **demanding** *adj* exigeant.

**demean** /dɪˈmiːn/ *vt* ~ oneself s'abaisser.

**demeanour**, (US)**demeanor** /dɪˈmiːnə(r)/ *n* comportement *m*.

**demented** /dɪˈmentɪd/ *adj* fou.

**demise** /dɪˈmaɪz/ *n* disparition *f*.

**demo** /ˈdeməʊ/ *n* (demonstration Ⅱ) manif *f* Ⅱ.

**democracy** /dɪˈmɒkrəsɪ/ *n* démocratie *f*.

**democrat** /ˈdeməkræt/ *n* démocrate *mf*. **democratic** *adj* démocratique.

**demolish** /dɪˈmɒlɪʃ/ *vt* démolir.

**demon** /ˈdiːmən/ *n* démon *m*.

**demonstrate** /ˈdemənstreɪt/ *vt* démontrer; (*concern, skill*) manifester. ● *vi* (Pol) manifester. **demonstration** *n* démonstration *f*; (Pol) manifestation *f*. **demonstrative** *adj* démonstratif. **demonstrator** *n* manifestant/-e *m/f*.

**demoralize** /dɪˈmɒrəlaɪz/ *vt* démoraliser.

**demote** /diːˈməʊt/ *vt* rétrograder.

**den** /den/ *n* (of lion) antre *m*; (room) tanière *f*.

**denial** /dɪˈnaɪəl/ *n* (of rumour) démenti *m*; (of rights) négation *f*; (of request) rejet *m*.

**denim** /ˈdenɪm/ *n* jean *m*; ~**s** (jeans) jean *m*.

**Denmark** /ˈdenmɑːk/ *n* Danemark *m*.

**denomination** /dɪnɒmɪˈneɪʃn/ *n* (Relig) confession *f*; (money) valeur *f*.

**denounce** /dɪˈnaʊns/ *vt* dénoncer.

**dense** /dens/ *adj* dense. **densely** *adv* (*packed*) très. **density** *n* densité *f*.

**dent** /dent/ *n* bosse *f*. ● *vt* cabosser.

**dental** /ˈdentl/ *adj* dentaire; ~ floss fil *m* dentaire; ~ surgeon chirurgien-dentiste *m*.

**dentist** /ˈdentɪst/ *n* dentiste *mf*. **dentistry** *n* médecine *f* dentaire.

**dentures** /ˈdentʃəz/ *npl* dentier *m*.

**deny** /dɪˈnaɪ/ *vt* nier (**that** que); (rumour) démentir; ~ **sb sth** refuser qch à qn.

**deodorant** /diːˈəʊdərənt/ *n* déodorant *m*.

**depart** /dɪˈpɑːt/ *vi* partir; ~ **from**

(deviate) s'éloigner de.

**department** /dɪ'pɑːtmənt/ n (in shop) rayon m; (in hospital, office) service m; (Univ) département m; D~ of Health ministère m de la Santé; ~ store grand magasin m.

**departure** /dɪ'pɑːtʃə(r)/ n départ m; a ~ from (custom, truth) une entorse à.

**depend** /dɪ'pend/ vi dépendre (on de). ~ on (rely on) compter sur; **it (all)** ~s ça dépend; ~ing on the season suivant la saison. **dependable** adj (person) digne de confiance. **dependant** n personne f à charge. **dependence** n dépendance f.

**dependent** /dɪ'pendənt/ adj dépendant; **be** ~ en dépendre de.

**depict** /dɪ'pɪkt/ vt (describe) dépeindre; (in picture) représenter.

**deplete** /dɪ'pliːt/ vt réduire.

**deport** /dɪ'pɔːt/ vt expulser.

**depose** /dɪ'pəʊz/ vt déposer.

**deposit** /dɪ'pɒzɪt/ vt (pt **deposited**) déposer. ● n (in bank) dépôt m; (on house) versement m initial; (on holiday) acompte m; (against damage) caution f; (on bottle) consigne f; (of mineral) gisement m; ~ account compte m de dépôt. **depositor** n (Comm) déposant/-e m/f.

**depot** /'depəʊ/ n dépôt m; (US) gare f.

**depreciate** /dɪ'priːʃɪeɪt/ vt/i (se) déprécier.

**depress** /dɪ'pres/ vt déprimer. **depressing** adj déprimant. **depression** n dépression f; (Econ) récession f.

**deprivation** /deprɪ'veɪʃn/ n privation f.

**deprive** /dɪ'praɪv/ vt ~ of priver de. **deprived** adj démuni.

**depth** /depθ/ n profondeur f; (of knowledge, ignorance) étendue f; (of colour, emotion) intensité f.

**deputize** /'depjʊtaɪz/ vi ~ for remplacer.

**deputy** /'depjʊtɪ/ n adjoint/-e m/f. ● adj adjoint; ~ chairman vice-président m.

**derail** /dɪ'reɪl/ vt faire dérailler. **derailment** n déraillement m.

**deranged** /dɪ'reɪndʒd/ adj dérangé.

**derelict** /'derəlɪkt/ adj abandonné.

**deride** /dɪ'raɪd/ vt ridiculiser. **derision** n moqueries fpl. **derisory** adj dérisoire.

**derivative** /də'rɪvətɪv/ adj & n dérivé (m).

**derive** /dɪ'raɪv/ vt ~ sth from tirer qch de. ● vi ~ from découler de.

**derogatory** /dɪ'rɒgətrɪ/ adj (word) péjoratif; (remark) désobligeant.

**descend** /dɪ'send/ vt/i descendre; **be** ~ed from descendre de. **descendant** n descendant/-e m/f. **descent** n descente f; (lineage) origine f.

**describe** /dɪ'skraɪb/ vt décrire; ~ sb as sth qualifier qn de qch. **description** n description f. **descriptive** adj descriptif.

**desert¹** /'dezət/ n désert m.

**desert²** /dɪ'zɜːt/ vt/i abandonner; (cause) déserter. **deserted** adj désert. **deserter** n déserteur m.

**deserts** /dɪ'zɜːts/ npl get one's ~ avoir ce qu'on mérite.

**deserve** /dɪ'zɜːv/ vt mériter (to de). **deservedly** adv à juste titre. **deserving** adj (person) méritant; (action) louable.

**design** /dɪ'zaɪn/ n (sketch) plan m; (idea) conception f; (pattern) motif m; (art of designing) design m; (aim) dessein m. ● vt (sketch) dessiner;

(devise, intend) concevoir.

**designate** /'dezɪgneɪt/ vt désigner.

**designer** /dɪ'zaɪnə(r)/ n concepteur/-trice m/f; (of fashion, furniture) créateur/-trice m/f. ●adj (clothes) de haute couture; (sunglasses, drink) de dernière mode.

**desirable** /dɪ'zaɪərəbl/ adj (outcome) souhaitable; (person) désirable.

**desire** /dɪ'zaɪə(r)/ n désir m. ●vt désirer.

**desk** /desk/ n bureau m; (of pupil) pupitre m; (in hotel) réception f; (in bank) caisse f.

**desolate** /'desələt/ adj (place) désolé; (person) affligé.

**despair** /dɪ'speə(r)/ n désespoir m. ●vi désespérer (of de).

**desperate** /'despərət/ adj désespéré; (criminal) prêt à tout; be ~ for avoir désespérément besoin de. **desperately** adv désespérément; (worried) terriblement; (ill) gravement.

**desperation** /despə'reɪʃn/ n désespoir m; in ~ en désespoir de cause.

**despicable** /dɪ'spɪkəbl/ adj méprisable.

**despise** /dɪ'spaɪz/ vt mépriser.

**despite** /dɪ'spaɪt/ prep malgré.

**despondent** /dɪ'spɒndənt/ adj découragé.

**dessert** /dɪ'zɜːt/ n dessert m. **~spoon** n cuillère f à dessert.

**destination** /destɪ'neɪʃn/ n destination f.

**destiny** /'destɪnɪ/ n destin m.

**destitute** /'destɪtjuːt/ adj sans ressources.

**destroy** /dɪ'strɔɪ/ vt détruire; (animal) abattre. **destroyer** n (warship) contre-torpilleur m.

**destruction** /dɪ'strʌkʃn/ n destruction f. **destructive** adj destructeur.

**detach** /dɪ'tætʃ/ vt détacher; ~ed house maison f (individuelle).

**detail** /'diːteɪl/ n détail m; go into ~ entrer dans les détails. ●vt (plans) exposer en détail.

**detain** /dɪ'teɪn/ vt retenir; (in prison) placer en détention. **detainee** n détenu/-e m/f.

**detect** /dɪ'tekt/ vt (error, trace) déceler; (crime, mine, sound) détecter. **detection** n détection f. **detective** n inspecteur/-trice m/f; (private) détective m.

**detention** /dɪ'tenʃn/ n détention f; (School) retenue f.

**deter** /dɪ'tɜː(r)/ vt (pt **deterred**) dissuader (from de).

**detergent** /dɪ'tɜːdʒənt/ adj & n détergent (m).

**deteriorate** /dɪ'tɪərɪəreɪt/ vi se détériorer.

**determine** /dɪ'tɜːmɪn/ vt déterminer; ~ to do résoudre de faire. **determined** adj (person) décidé; (air) résolu.

**deterrent** /dɪ'terənt/ n moyen m de dissuasion. ●adj (effect) dissuasif.

**detest** /dɪ'test/ vt détester.

**detonate** /'detəneɪt/ vt/i (faire) détoner. **detonation** n détonation f. **detonator** n détonateur m.

**detour** /'diːtʊə(r)/ n détour m.

**detract** /dɪ'trækt/ vi ~ from (success, value) porter atteinte à; (pleasure) diminuer.

**detriment** /'detrɪmənt/ n to the ~ of au détriment de. **detrimental** adj nuisible (to à).

**devalue** /diː'væljuː/ vt dévaluer.

**devastate** /'devəsteɪt/ vt (place) ravager; (person) accabler.

**develop** /dɪ'veləp/ vt (plan) élaborer; (mind, body) développer; (land) mettre en valeur; (illness) attraper; (habit) prendre. ● vi (child, country, plot, business) se développer; (hole, crack) se former.

**development** /dɪ'veləpmənt/ n développement m; (housing) ~ lotissement m; (new) ~ fait m nouveau.

**deviate** /'diːvɪeɪt/ vi dévier; ~ from (norm) s'écarter de.

**device** /dɪ'vaɪs/ n appareil m; (means) moyen m; (bomb) engin m explosif.

**devil** /'devl/ n diable m.

**devious** /'diːvɪəs/ adj (person) retors.

**devise** /dɪ'vaɪz/ vt (scheme) concevoir; (product) inventer.

**devoid** /dɪ'vɔɪd/ adj ~ of dépourvu de.

**devolution** /diːvə'luːʃn/ n (Pol) régionalisation f.

**devote** /dɪ'vəʊt/ vt consacrer (to à). **devoted** adj dévoué. **devotion** n dévouement m; (Relig) dévotion f.

**devour** /dɪ'vaʊə(r)/ vt dévorer.

**devout** /dɪ'vaʊt/ adj fervent.

**dew** /djuː/ n rosée f.

**diabetes** /daɪə'biːtiːz/ n diabète m. **diabetic** /daɪə'betɪk/ adj & n diabétique (mf).

**diabolical** /daɪə'bɒlɪkl/ adj diabolique; (bad Ⅱ) atroce.

**diagnose** /'daɪəgnəʊz/ vt diagnostiquer. **diagnosis** n (pl -oses) diagnostic m.

**diagonal** /daɪ'ægənl/ adj diagonal. ● n diagonale f.

**diagram** /'daɪəgræm/ n schéma m.

**dial** /'daɪəl/ n cadran m. ● vt (pt dialled) (number) faire; (person) appeler; **dialling code** indicatif m; **dialling tone** tonalité f.

**dialect** /'daɪəlekt/ n dialecte m.

**dialogue** /'daɪəlɒg/ n dialogue m.

**diameter** /daɪ'æmɪtə(r)/ n diamètre m.

**diamond** /'daɪəmənd/ n diamant m; (shape) losange m; (baseball) terrain m; ~s (cards) carreau m.

**diaper** /'daɪəpə(r)/ n (US) couche f.

**diaphragm** /'daɪəfræm/ n diaphragme m.

**diarrhoea**, (US) **diarrhea** /daɪə'rɪə/ n diarrhée f.

**diary** /'daɪərɪ/ n (for appointments) agenda m; (journal) journal m intime.

**dice** /daɪs/ n inv dé m. ● vt (food) couper en dés.

**dictate** /dɪk'teɪt/ vt/i dicter.

**dictation** /dɪk'teɪʃn/ n dictée f.

**dictator** /dɪk'teɪtə(r)/ n dictateur m. **dictatorship** n dictature f.

**dictionary** /'dɪkʃənrɪ/ n dictionnaire m.

**did** /dɪd/ ➙DO.

**didn't** ➙DID NOT.

**die** /daɪ/ vi (pres p **dying**) mourir; (plant) crever; be dying to do mourir d'envie de faire. □ ~ **down** diminuer. ~ **out** disparaître.

**diesel** /'diːzl/ n gazole m; ~ **engine** moteur m diesel.

**diet** /'daɪət/ n (usual food) alimentation f; (restricted) régime m. ● vi être au régime. **dietary** adj alimentaire. **dietician** /daɪə'tɪʃn/ n diététicien/-ne m/f.

**differ** /'dɪfə(r)/ vi différer (from de).

**difference** /'dɪfrəns/ n différence f; (disagreement) différend m. **different** adj différent (from, to de).

**differentiate** /dɪfə'renʃɪeɪt/ vt différencier. ● vi faire la différence (between entre).

**differently** /'dɪfrəntlɪ/ adv différemment (from de).

**difficult** /'dɪfɪkəlt/ adj difficile.

**difficulty** n difficulté f.

**diffuse**¹ /dɪˈfjuːs/ adj diffus.

**diffuse**² /dɪˈfjuːz/ vt diffuser.

**dig** /dɪg/ vt/i (pt **dug**; pres p **digging**) (excavate) creuser; (in garden) bêcher. ● n (poke) coup m de coude; (remark) pique f ☐; (Archeol) fouilles fpl. □ ~ **up** déterrer.

**digest** /daɪˈdʒest/ vt/i digérer. **digestible** adj digestible. **digestion** n digestion f.

**digger** /ˈdɪgə(r)/ n excavateur m.

**digit** /ˈdɪdʒɪt/ n chiffre m. ● **digitize** vt numériser.

**digital** /ˈdɪdʒɪtl/ adj (clock) à affichage numérique; (display, recording) numérique. □ ~ **audio tape** n cassette f audionumérique. ~ **camera** n appareil m photo numérique.

**dignified** /ˈdɪgnɪfaɪd/ adj digne.

**dignitary** /ˈdɪgnɪtərɪ/ n dignitaire m.

**dignity** /ˈdɪgnətɪ/ n dignité f.

**digress** /daɪˈgres/ vi faire une digression.

**dilapidated** /dɪˈlæpɪdeɪtɪd/ adj délabré.

**dilate** /daɪˈleɪt/ vt/i (se) dilater.

**dilemma** /daɪˈlemə/ n dilemme m.

**diligent** /ˈdɪlɪdʒənt/ adj appliqué.

**dilute** /daɪˈljuːt/ vt diluer.

**dim** /dɪm/ adj (dimmer, dimmest) (weak) faible; (dark) sombre; (indistinct) vague; ☐ stupide. ● vt/i (pt **dimmed**) (light) baisser.

**dime** /daɪm/ n (US) (pièce f de) dix cents.

**dimension** /dɪˈmenʃn/ n dimension f.

**diminish** /dɪˈmɪnɪʃ/ vt/i diminuer.

**dimple** /ˈdɪmpl/ n fossette f.

**din** /dɪn/ n vacarme m.

**dine** /daɪn/ vi dîner. **diner** n dîneur/-euse m/f; (US) restaurant m

à service rapide.

**dinghy** /ˈdɪŋɡɪ/ n dériveur m.

**dingy** /ˈdɪndʒɪ/ adj (-ier, -iest) minable.

**dining room** /ˈdaɪnɪŋrʊm/n salle f à manger.

**dinner** /ˈdɪnə(r)/ n (evening meal) dîner m; (lunch) déjeuner m; have ~ dîner. ~**-jacket** n smoking m. ~ **party** n dîner m.

**dinosaur** /ˈdaɪnəsɔː(r)/ n dinosaure m.

**dip** /dɪp/ vt/i (pt **dipped**) plonger; ~ **into** (book) feuilleter; (savings) puiser dans; ~ **one's headlights** se mettre en code. ● n (slope) déclivité f; (in sea) bain m rapide.

**diploma** /dɪˈpləʊmə/ n diplôme m (in en).

**diplomacy** /dɪˈpləʊməsɪ/ n diplomatie f. **diplomat** n diplomate mf. **diplomatic** adj (Pol) diplomatique; (tactful) diplomate.

**dire** /ˈdaɪə(r)/ adj affreux; (need, poverty) extrême.

**direct** /daɪˈrekt/ adj direct. ● adv directement. ● vt diriger; (letter, remark) adresser; (a play) mettre en scène; ~ **sb** to indiquer à qn le chemin de; (order) signifier à qn de.

**direction** /daɪˈrekʃn/ n direction f; (Theat) mise f en scène; ~**s** indications fpl; ask ~**s** demander le chemin; ~**s for use** mode m d'emploi.

**directly** /daɪˈrektlɪ/ adv directement; (at once) tout de suite. ● conj dès que.

**director** /daɪˈrektə(r)/ n directeur/-trice m/f; (Theat) metteur m en scène.

**directory** /daɪˈrektərɪ/ n (phone book) annuaire m. ~ **enquiries** npl renseignements mpl téléphoniques.

**dirt** /dɜːt/ n saleté f; (earth) terre f; ~ **cheap** ☒ très bon marché inv.

~-**track** n (Sport) cendrée f.

**dirty** /'dɜːtɪ/ adj (-**ier**, -**iest**) sale; (word) grossier; **get** ~ se salir. ● vt/i (se) salir.

**disability** /dɪsə'bɪlətɪ/ n handicap m.

**disable** /dɪs'eɪbl/ vt rendre infirme. **disabled** adj handicapé.

**disadvantage** /dɪsəd'vɑːntɪdʒ/ n désavantage m. **disadvantaged** adj défavorisé.

**disagree** /dɪsə'griː/ vi ne pas être d'accord (**with** avec.); ~ **with** sb (food, climate) ne pas convenir à qn. **disagreement** n désaccord m; (quarrel) différend m.

**disappear** /dɪsə'pɪə(r)/ vi disparaître. **disappearance** n disparition f (**of** de).

**disappoint** /dɪsə'pɔɪnt/ vt décevoir. **disappointment** n déception f.

**disapproval** /dɪsə'pruːvl/ n désapprobation f (**of** de).

**disapprove** /dɪsə'pruːv/ vi ~ (**of**) désapprouver.

**disarm** /dɪs'ɑːm/ vt/i désarmer. **disarmament** n désarmement m.

**disarray** /dɪsə'reɪ/ n désordre m.

**disaster** /dɪ'zɑːstə(r)/ n désastre m. **disastrous** adj désastreux.

**disband** /dɪs'bænd/ vt disperser. ● vt dissoudre.

**disbelief** /dɪsbɪ'liːf/ n incrédulité f.

**disc** /dɪsk/ n disque m; (Comput) ⇒**DISK**.

**discard** /dɪs'kɑːd/ vt se débarrasser de; (beliefs) abandonner.

**discharge** /dɪs'tʃɑːdʒ/ vt (unload) décharger; (liquid) déverser; (duty) remplir; (dismiss) renvoyer; (prisoner) libérer. ● vi (of pus) s'écouler.

**disciple** /dɪ'saɪpl/ n disciple m.

**disciplinary** /'dɪsɪplɪmərɪ/ adj disciplinaire.

**discipline** /'dɪsɪplɪn/ n discipline f.

● vt discipliner; (punish) punir.

**disc jockey** n disc-jockey m, animateur m.

**disclaimer** /dɪs'kleɪmə(r)/ n démenti m.

**disclose** /dɪs'kləʊz/ vt révéler. **disclosure** n révélation f (**of** de).

**disco** /'dɪskəʊ/ n (club [T]) discothèque f; (event) soirée f disco.

**discolour** /dɪs'kʌlə(r)/ vt/i (se) décolorer.

**discomfort** /dɪs'kʌmfət/ n gêne f.

**disconcert** /dɪskən'sɜːt/ vt déconcerter.

**disconnect** /dɪskə'nekt/ vt détacher; (unplug) débrancher; (cut off) couper.

**discontent** /dɪskən'tent/ n mécontentement m.

**discontinue** /dɪskən'tɪnjuː/ vt (service) supprimer; (production) arrêter.

**discord** /'dɪskɔːd/ n discorde f; (Mus) discordance f.

**discount**[1] /'dɪskaʊnt/ n remise f; (on minor purchase) rabais m.

**discount**[2] /dɪs'kaʊnt/ vt (advice) ne pas tenir compte de; (possibility) écarter.

**discourage** /dɪs'kʌrɪdʒ/ vt décourager.

**discourse** /'dɪskɔːs/ n discours m.

**discourteous** /dɪs'kɜːtɪəs/ adj peu courtois.

**discover** /dɪs'kʌvə(r)/ vt découvrir. **discovery** n découverte f.

**discreet** /dɪs'kriːt/ adj discret.

**discrepancy** /dɪs'krepənsɪ/ n divergence f.

**discretion** /dɪs'kreʃn/ n discrétion f.

**discriminate** /dɪs'krɪmɪneɪt/ vt/i distinguer; ~ **against** faire de la discrimination contre. **discriminat-**

**ing** adj qui a du discernement. **discrimination** n discernement m; (bias) discrimination f.

**discus** /'dɪskəs/ n disque m.

**discuss** /dɪˈskʌs/ vt (talk about) discuter de; (in writing) examiner. **discussion** n discussion f.

**disdain** /dɪsˈdeɪn/ n dédain m.

**disease** /dɪˈziːz/ n maladie f.

**disembark** /dɪsɪmˈbɑːk/ vt/i débarquer.

**disenchanted** /dɪsɪnˈtʃɑːntɪd/ adj désabusé.

**disentangle** /dɪsɪnˈtæŋgl/ vt démêler.

**disfigure** /dɪsˈfɪgə(r)/ vt défigurer.

**disgrace** /dɪsˈgreɪs/ n (shame) honte f; (disfavour) disgrâce f. ● vt déshonorer. **disgraced** adj (in disfavour) disgracié. **disgraceful** adj honteux.

**disgruntled** /dɪsˈgrʌntld/ adj mécontent.

**disguise** /dɪsˈgaɪz/ vt déguiser. ● n déguisement m; **in** ~ déguisé.

**disgust** /dɪsˈgʌst/ n dégoût m. ● vt dégoûter.

**dish** /dɪʃ/ n plat m; the ~es (crockery) la vaisselle. □ ~ **out** ⚹ distribuer; ~ **up** servir.

**dishcloth** /ˈdɪʃklɒθ/ n lavette f; (for drying) torchon m.

**dishearten** /dɪsˈhɑːtn/ vt décourager.

**dishevelled** /dɪˈʃevld/ adj échevelé.

**dishonest** /dɪsˈɒnɪst/ adj malhonnête.

**dishonour**, (US) **dishonor** /dɪsˈɒnə(r)/ n déshonneur f.

**dishwasher** /ˈdɪʃwɒʃə(r)/ n lave-vaisselle m inv.

**disillusion** /dɪsɪˈluːʒn/ vt désabuser. **disillusionment** n désillusion f.

**disincentive** /dɪsɪnˈsentɪv/ n be

a ~ to décourager.

**disinclined** /dɪsɪnˈklaɪnd/ adj ~ **to** peu disposé à.

**disinfect** /dɪsɪnˈfekt/ vt désinfecter. **disinfectant** n désinfectant m.

**disintegrate** /dɪsˈɪntɪgreɪt/ vt/i (se) désintégrer.

**disinterested** /dɪsˈɪntrəstɪd/ adj désintéressé.

**disjointed** /dɪsˈdʒɔɪntɪd/ adj (talk) décousu.

**disk** /dɪsk/ n (US) ➡DISC; (Comput) disque m. ~ **drive** n drive m, lecteur m de disquettes.

**diskette** /dɪˈsket/ n disquette f.

**dislike** /dɪsˈlaɪk/ n aversion f. ● vt ne pas aimer.

**dislocate** /ˈdɪsləkeɪt/ vt (limb) disloquer.

**dislodge** /dɪsˈlɒdʒ/ vt (move) déplacer; (drive out) déloger.

**disloyal** /dɪsˈlɔɪəl/ adj déloyal (**to** envers).

**dismal** /ˈdɪzməl/ adj morne, triste.

**dismantle** /dɪsˈmæntl/ vt démonter, défaire.

**dismay** /dɪsˈmeɪ/ n consternation f (**at** devant). ● vt consterner.

**dismiss** /dɪsˈmɪs/ vt renvoyer; (appeal) rejeter; (from mind) écarter. **dismissal** n renvoi m.

**dismount** /dɪsˈmaʊnt/ vi descendre, mettre pied à terre.

**disobedient** /dɪsəˈbiːdɪənt/ adj désobéissant.

**disobey** /dɪsəˈbeɪ/ vt désobéir à. ● vi désobéir.

**disorder** /dɪsˈɔːdə(r)/ n désordre m; (ailment) trouble(s) m(pl). **disorderly** adj désordonné.

**disorganized** /dɪsˈɔːgənaɪzd/ adj désorganisé.

**disown** /dɪsˈəʊn/ vt renier.

**disparaging** /dɪˈspærɪdʒɪŋ/ adj

désobligeant.

**dispassionate** /dɪˈspæʃənət/ *adj* impartial; (*unemotional*) calme.

**dispatch** /dɪˈspætʃ/ *vt* (send, complete) expédier; (*troops*) envoyer. ● *n* expédition *f*, envoi *m*; (*report*) dépêche *f*.

**dispel** /dɪˈspel/ *vt* (*pt* **dispelled**) dissiper.

**dispensary** /dɪˈspensərɪ/ *n* (in hospital) pharmacie *f*; (in pharmacy) officine *f*.

**dispense** /dɪˈspens/ *vt* distribuer; (*medicine*) préparer. ● *vi* ∼ with se passer de. **dispenser** *n* (container) distributeur *m*.

**disperse** /dɪˈspɜːs/ *vt/i* (se) disperser.

**display** /dɪˈspleɪ/ *vt* montrer, exposer; (*feelings*) manifester. ● *n* exposition *f*; manifestation *f*; (Comm) étalage *m*; (of computer) visuel *m*.

**displeased** /dɪsˈpliːzd/ *adj* mécontent (with de).

**disposable** /dɪˈspəʊzəbl/ *adj* jetable.

**disposal** /dɪˈspəʊzl/ *n* (of waste) évacuation *f*; at sb's ∼ à la disposition de qn.

**dispose** /dɪˈspəʊz/ *vt* disposer. ● *vi* ∼ of se débarrasser de; well ∼d to bien disposé envers.

**disposition** /dɪspəˈzɪʃn/ *n* disposition *f*; (*character*) naturel *m*.

**disprove** /dɪsˈpruːv/ *vt* réfuter.

**dispute** /dɪˈspjuːt/ *vt* contester. ● *n* discussion *f*; (Pol) conflit *m*; in ∼ contesté.

**disqualify** /dɪsˈkwɒlɪfaɪ/ *vt* rendre inapte; (Sport) disqualifier; ∼ from driving retirer le permis à.

**disquiet** /dɪsˈkwaɪət/ *n* inquiétude *f*. **disquieting** *adj* inquiétant.

**disregard** /dɪsrɪˈgɑːd/ *vt* ne pas tenir compte de. ● *n*

indifférence *f* (for à).

**disrepair** /dɪsrɪˈpeə(r)/ *n* délabrement *m*.

**disreputable** /dɪsˈrepjʊtəbl/ *adj* peu recommandable.

**disrepute** /dɪsrɪˈpjuːt/ *n* discrédit *m*.

**disrespect** /dɪsrɪˈspekt/ *n* manque *m* de respect. **disrespectful** *adj* irrespectueux.

**disrupt** /dɪsˈrʌpt/ *vt* (disturb, break up) perturber; (*plans*) déranger. **disruption** *n* perturbation *f*. **disruptive** *adj* perturbateur.

**dissatisfied** /dɪˈsætɪsfaɪd/ *adj* mécontent.

**dissect** /dɪˈsekt/ *vt* disséquer.

**disseminate** /dɪˈsemɪneɪt/ *vt* diffuser.

**dissent** /dɪˈsent/ *vi* différer (from de). ● *n* dissentiment *m*.

**dissertation** /dɪsəˈteɪʃn/ *n* mémoire *m*.

**disservice** /dɪsˈsɜːvɪs/ *n* do a ∼ to sb rendre un mauvais service à qn.

**dissident** /ˈdɪsɪdənt/ *adj* & *n* dissident/-e (*m/f*).

**dissimilar** /dɪˈsɪmɪlə(r)/ *adj* dissemblable, différent.

**dissipate** /ˈdɪsɪpeɪt/ *vt/i* (se) dissiper. **dissipated** *adj* (person) dissolu.

**dissolve** /dɪˈzɒlv/ *vt/i* (se) dissoudre.

**dissuade** /dɪˈsweɪd/ *vt* dissuader.

**distance** /ˈdɪstəns/ *n* distance *f*; from a ∼ de loin; in the ∼ au loin. **distant** *adj* éloigné, lointain; (*relative*) éloigné; (*aloof*) distant.

**distaste** /dɪsˈteɪst/ *n* dégoût *m*. **distasteful** *adj* désagréable.

**distil** /dɪsˈtɪl/ *vt* (*pt* **distilled**) distiller.

**distinct** /dɪsˈtɪŋkt/ *adj* distinct; (definite) net; as ∼ from par oppo-

sition à. **distinction** n distinction f;
(in exam) mention f très bien. **distinctive** adj distinctif.

**distinguish** /dɪˈstɪŋgwɪʃ/ vt/i distinguer.

**distort** /dɪˈstɔːt/ vt déformer. **distortion** n distorsion f; (of facts) déformation f.

**distract** /dɪˈstrækt/ vt distraire.
**distracted** adj (distraught) éperdu.
**distracting** adj gênant. **distraction**
n (lack of attention, entertainment)
distraction f.

**distraught** /dɪˈstrɔːt/ adj éperdu.

**distress** /dɪˈstres/ n douleur f;
(poverty, danger) détresse f. ● vt
peiner. **distressing** adj pénible.

**distribute** /dɪˈstrɪbjuːt/ vt distribuer.

**district** /ˈdɪstrɪkt/ n région f; (of
town) quartier m.

**distrust** /dɪsˈtrʌst/ n méfiance f.
● vt se méfier de.

**disturb** /dɪˈstɜːb/ vt déranger;
(alarm, worry) troubler. **disturbance** n dérangement m (de de);
(noise) tapage m. **disturbances** npl
(Pol) troubles mpl. **disturbed** adj
troublé; (psychologically) perturbé.
**disturbing** adj troublant.

**disused** /dɪsˈjuːzd/ adj désaffecté.

**ditch** /dɪtʃ/ n fossé m. ● vt ⊠ abandonner.

**ditto** /ˈdɪtəʊ/ adv idem.

**dive** /daɪv/ vi plonger; (rush) se
précipiter. ● n plongeon m; (of
plane) piqué m; (place ⊠) bouge m.
**diver** n plongeur/-euse m/f.

**diverge** /daɪˈvɜːdʒ/ vi diverger. **divergent** adj divergent.

**diverse** /daɪˈvɜːs/ adj divers.

**diversion** /daɪˈvɜːʃn/ n détournement m; (distraction) diversion f; (of
traffic) déviation f **divert** vt détourner; (traffic) dévier.

**divide** /dɪˈvaɪd/ vt/i (se) diviser.

**dividend** /ˈdɪvɪdend/ n dividende m.

**divine** /dɪˈvaɪn/ adj divin.

**diving:** ∼-board n plongeoir m.
∼-suit n scaphandre m.

**division** /dɪˈvɪʒn/ n division f.

**divorce** /dɪˈvɔːs/ n divorce m (from
avec). ● vt/i divorcer (d'avec).

**divulge** /daɪˈvʌldʒ/ vt divulguer.

**DIY** abbr ▶DO-IT-YOURSELF.

**dizziness** /ˈdɪzɪnɪs/ n vertige m.

**dizzy** /ˈdɪzɪ/ adj (-ier, -iest) vertigineux; be or feel ∼ avoir le vertige.

---

### do /duː/

present do, does; present negative
don't, do not; past did; past participle done

● transitive and intransitive verb
···▸ faire; she is doing her
homework elle fait ses
devoirs.
···▸ (progress, be suitable) aller;
how are you doing? comment
ça va?
···▸ (be enough) suffire; will
five dollars ∼? cinq dollars, ça
suffira?

● auxiliary verb
···▸ (in questions) ∼ you like
Mozart? aimes-tu Mozart?,
est-ce que tu aimes Mozart?;
did your sister phone? est-ce
que ta sœur a téléphoné?, ta
sœur a-t-elle téléphoné?
···▸ (in negatives) I don't like
Mozart je n'aime pas Mozart.
···▸ (emphatic uses) I ∼ like
your dress j'aime beaucoup ta

robe; I ∼ think you should go je pense vraiment que tu devrais y aller.

••••▶ (referring back to another verb) **I live in Orford and so do Lily** j'habite à Orford et Lily aussi; **she gets paid more than I** ∼ elle est payée plus que moi; **'I don't like carrots'—'neither** ∼ **I'** 'je n'aime pas les carottes'—'moi non plus'.

••••▶ (imperatives) **don't shut the door** ne ferme pas la porte; ∼ **be quiet** tais-toi!

••••▶ (short questions and answers) **you like fish, don't you?** tu aimes le poisson, n'est-ce pas?; **Lola didn't phone, did she?** Lola n'a pas téléphoné par hasard?; **'does he play tennis?'—'no he doesn't/yes he does'** 'est-ce qu'il joue au tennis?'—'non/oui'; **'Marion didn't say that'—'yes she did'** 'Marion n'a pas dit ça'—'si'.

◻ **do away with** supprimer. **do up** (fasten) fermer; (house) refaire; **do with** it's ∼ with c'est à propos de; **it's nothing to** ∼ **with** ça n'a rien à voir avec. **do without** se passer de.

**docile** /'dəʊsaɪl/ adj docile.

**dock** /dɒk/ n (Jur) banc m des accusés; dock m. ● vi arriver au port. ● vt mettre à quai; (wages) faire une retenue sur.

**doctor** /'dɒktə(r)/ n médecin m, docteur m; (Univ) docteur m. ● vt (cat) châtrer; (fig) altérer.

**doctorate** /'dɒktərət/ n doctorat m.

**document** /'dɒkjʊmənt/ n docu-

ment m. **documentary** adj & n documentaire (m). **documentation** n documentation f.

**dodge** /dɒdʒ/ vt esquiver. ● vi faire un saut de côté. ● n mouvement m de côté.

**dodgems** /'dɒdʒəmz/ npl autos fpl tamponneuses.

**dodgy** /'dɒdʒɪ/ adj (-ier, -iest) (🄣: difficult) épineux, délicat; (untrustworthy) louche 🄣.

**doe** /dəʊ/ n (deer) biche f.

**does** /dʌz/ ➡DO.

**doesn't** ➡DOES NOT.

**dog** /dɒɡ/ n chien m. ● vt (pt dogged) poursuivre. ∼-collar n col romain. ∼-eared adj écorné.

**dogged** /'dɒɡɪd/ adj obstiné.

**dogma** /'dɒɡmə/ n dogme m. **dogmatic** adj dogmatique.

**dogsbody** /'dɒɡzbɒdɪ/ n bonne f à tout faire.

**do-it-yourself** /duːɪtjɔːˈself/ n bricolage m.

**doldrums** /'dɒldrəmz/ npl be in the ∼ (person) avoir le cafard.

**dole** /dəʊl/ vt ∼ **out** distribuer. ● n 🄣 indemnité f de chômage; **on the** ∼ 🄣 au chômage.

**doll** /dɒl/ n poupée f. ● vt ∼ **up** 🄣 bichonner.

**dollar** /'dɒlə(r)/ n dollar m.

**dollop** /'dɒləp/ n (of food 🄣) gros morceau m.

**dolphin** /'dɒlfɪn/ n dauphin m.

**domain** /dəʊˈmeɪn/ n domaine m.

**dome** /dəʊm/ n dôme m.

**domestic** /dəˈmestɪk/ adj familial, (trade, flights) intérieur; (animal) domestique. **domesticated** adj (animal) domestiqué.

**domestic science** n arts mpl ménagers.

**dominant** /'dɒmɪnənt/ adj

dominant.

**dominate** /'dɒmɪneɪt/ vt/i dominer. **domination** n domination f.

**domineering** /dɒmɪ'nɪərɪŋ/ adj dominateur.

**domino** /'dɒmɪnəʊ/ n (pl ~es) domino m; ~es (game) dominos mpl.

**donate** /dəʊ'neɪt/ vt faire don de. **donation** n don m.

**done** /dʌn/ ➞DO.

**donkey** /'dɒŋkɪ/ n âne m. ~ work n travail m pénible.

**donor** /'dəʊnə(r)/ n donateur/-trice m/f; (of blood) donneur/-euse m/f.

**don't** ➞DO NOT.

**doodle** /'duːdl/ vi griffonner.

**doom** /duːm/ n (ruin) ruine f; (fate) destin m. ● vt be ~ed to être destiné ou condamné à; ~ed (to failure) voué à l'échec.

**door** /dɔː(r)/ n porte f; (of vehicle) portière f, porte f. ~bell n sonnette f. ~man n (pl ~men) portier m. ~mat n paillasson m. ~step n pas m de (la) porte, seuil m. ~way n porte f.

**dope** /dəʊp/ n ① cannabis m; (idiot ①) imbécile mf. ● vt doper. **dopey** adj (foolish) imbécile.

**dormant** /'dɔːmənt/ adj en sommeil.

**dormitory** /'dɔːmɪtrɪ/ n dortoir m; (Univ, US) résidence f.

**dosage** /'dəʊsɪdʒ/ n dose f; (on label) posologie f.

**dose** /dəʊs/ n dose f.

**dot** /dɒt/ n point m; on the ~ ① à l'heure pile.

**dot-com** /dɒt'kɒm/ n (société) point com f; ~ **millionaire** n millionaire mf de l'Internet. ~ **shares** npl actions fpl des sociétés point com.

**dote** /dəʊt/ vi ~ on adorer.

**dotted** /'dɒtɪd/ adj (fabric) à pois;

~ **line** pointillé m; ~ **with** parsemé de.

**double** /'dʌbl/ adj double; (room, bed) pour deux personnes; ~ the size deux fois plus grand. ● adv deux fois; pay ~ payer le double. ● n double m; (stuntman) doublure f; ~s (tennis) double m; at or on the ~ au pas de course. ● vt/i doubler; (fold) plier en deux. ~**bass** n (Mus) contrebasse f. ~**check** vt revérifier. ~**chin** n double menton m. ~**cross** vt tromper. ~**decker** n autobus m à impériale.

**doubt** /daʊt/ n doute m. ● vt douter de; ~ **if** or **that** douter que. **doubtful** adj incertain, douteux; (person) qui a des doutes. **doubtless** adv sans doute.

**dough** /dəʊ/ n pâte f; (money ⊠) fric m ①.

**doughnut** /'dəʊnʌt/ n beignet m.

**douse** /daʊs/ vt arroser; (light, fire) éteindre.

**dove** /dʌv/ n colombe f.

**Dover** /'dəʊvə(r)/ n Douvres.

**dowdy** /'daʊdɪ/ adj (-ier, -iest) (clothes) sans chic, monotone; (person) sans élégance.

**down** /daʊn/ adv en bas; (of sun) couché; (lower) plus bas; come or go ~ descendre; go ~ to the post office aller à la poste; ~ **under** aux antipodes; ~ **with** à bas. ● prep en bas de; (along) le long de. ● vt (knock down, shoot down) abattre; (drink) vider. ● n (fluff) duvet m.

**down:** ~-**and-out** n clochard/-e m/f. ~**cast** adj démoralisé. ~**fall** n chute f. ~**grade** vt déclasser. ~-**hearted** adj découragé.

**downhill** /daʊn'hɪl/ adv go ~ descendre; (pej) baisser.

**down:** ~**load** n (Comput) télécharger. ~-**market** adj bas de

d

gamme. ~ **payment** n acompte m. ~**pour** n grosse averse f.

**downright** /'daʊnraɪt/ adj (utter) véritable; (honest) franc. ● adv carrément.

**downstairs** /daʊn'steəz/ adv en bas. ● adj d'en bas.

**down:** ~**stream** adv en aval. ~**-to-earth** adj pratique.

**downtown** /'daʊntaʊn/ adj (US) du centre-ville; ~ **Boston** le centre de Boston.

**downward** /'daʊnwəd/ adj & adv, **downwards** adv vers le bas.

**doze** /dəʊz/ vi somnoler; ~ **off** s'assoupir. ● n somme m.

**dozen** /'dʌzn/ n douzaine f; a ~ **eggs** une douzaine d'œufs; ~s of 🔢 des dizaines de.

**Dr** abbr (**Doctor**) Docteur.

**drab** /dræb/ adj terne.

**draft** /drɑːft/ n (outline) brouillon m; (Comm) traite f; **the** ~ (Mil, US) la conscription; **a** ~ **treaty** un projet de traité; (US) ➡**DRAUGHT**. ● vt faire le brouillon de; (draw up) rédiger.

**drag** /dræɡ/ vt/i (pt dragged) traîner; (river) draguer; (pull away) arracher; ~ **on** s'éterniser. ● n (task 🔢) corvée f; (person 🔢) raseur/-euse m/f; **in** ~ en travesti.

**dragon** /'dræɡən/ n dragon m.

**drain** /dreɪn/ vt (land) drainer; (ve-

getables) égoutter; (tank, glass) vider; (use up) épuiser; ~ **(off)** (liquid) faire écouler. ● vi ~ **(off)** (of liquid) s'écouler. ● n (sewer) égout m; ~**(-pipe)** tuyau m d'écoulement; **a** ~ **on** une ponction sur.

**draining-board** n égouttoir m.

**drama** /'drɑːmə/ n art m dramatique, théâtre m; (play, event) drame m. **dramatic** /-'mætɪk/ adj (situation) dramatique; (increase) spectaculaire.

**dramatist** n dramaturge m. **dramatize** vt adapter pour la scène; (fig) dramatiser.

**drank** /dræŋk/ ➡**DRINK**.

**drape** /dreɪp/ vt draper. **drapes** npl (US) rideaux mpl.

**drastic** /'dræstɪk/ adj sévère.

**draught** /drɑːft/ n courant m d'air. ~**s** (game) dames fpl. ~ **beer** n bière f pression.

**draughty** /'drɑːftɪ/ adj plein de courants d'air.

**draw** /drɔː/ vt (pt drew; pp drawn) (picture) dessiner; (line) tracer; (pull) tirer; (attract) attirer. ● vi dessiner; (Sport) faire match nul; (come, move) venir. ● n (Sport) match m nul; (in lottery) tirage m au sort. □ ~ **back** reculer. ~ **near** (s')approcher (to de). ~ **out** (money) retirer. ~ **up** vi (stop) s'arrêter; vt (document) dresser; (chair) approcher.

**drawback** /'drɔːbæk/ n inconvénient m.

**drawbridge** /'drɔːbrɪdʒ/ n pont-levis m.

**drawer** /'drɔː(r)/ n tiroir m.

**drawing** /'drɔːɪŋ/ n dessin m. ~**-board** n planche f à dessin. ~**-pin** n punaise f. ~**-room** n salon m.

**drawl** /drɔːl/ n voix f traînante.

**drawn** /drɔːn/ ➡**DRAW**. ● adj (features) tiré; (*match*) nul.

**dread** /drɛd/ n terreur f, crainte f.
● vt redouter. **dreadful** adj épouvantable, affreux. **dreadfully** adv terriblement.

**dream** /driːm/ n rêve m. ● vt/i (pt **dreamed** or **dreamt**) rêver; ~ up imaginer. ● adj (ideal) de ses rêves.

**dreary** /ˈdrɪərɪ/ adj (-ier, -iest) triste; (boring) monotone.

**dredge** /drɛdʒ/ vt (river) draguer; ~ sth up (fig) exhumer.

**dregs** /drɛgz/ npl lie f.

**drench** /drɛntʃ/ vt tremper.

**dress** /drɛs/ n robe f. (clothing) tenue f. ● vt/i (s')habiller; (food) assaisonner; (wound) panser; ~ up se déguiser en; get ~ed s'habiller. ~ **circle** n premier balcon m.

**dresser** /ˈdrɛsə(r)/ n (furniture) buffet m; be a stylish ~ s'habiller avec chic.

**dressing** /ˈdrɛsɪŋ/ n (sauce) assaisonnement m; (bandage) pansement m. ~**gown** n robe f de chambre. ~**room** n (Sport) vestiaire m; (Theat) loge f. ~**table** n coiffeuse f.

**dressmaker** /ˈdrɛsmeɪkə(r)/ n couturière f. **dressmaking** n couture f.

**dress rehearsal** n répétition f générale.

**dressy** /ˈdrɛsɪ/ adj (-ier, -iest) chic inv.

**drew** /druː/ ➝DRAW.

**dribble** /ˈdrɪbl/ vi (liquid) dégouliner; (person) baver; (football) dribbler.

**dried** /draɪd/ adj (fruit) sec.

**drier** /ˈdraɪə(r)/ n séchoir m.

**drift** /drɪft/ vi aller à la dérive; (pile up) s'amonceler; ~ **towards** glisser vers. ● n dérive f; amoncellement m; (of events) tournure f; (meaning)

sens m; (snow) ~ congère f. **driftwood** n bois m flotté.

**drill** /drɪl/ n (tool) perceuse f; (for teeth) roulette f; (training) exercice m; (procedure ⊤) marche f à suivre; (pneumatic) ~ marteau m piqueur. ● vt percer; (train) entraîner. ● vi être à l'exercice.

**drink** /drɪŋk/ vt/i (pt **drank**; pp **drunk**) boire. ● n (liquid) boisson f; (glass of alcohol) verre m; a ~ of water un verre d'eau. **drinking water** n eau f potable.

**drip** /drɪp/ vi (pt **dripped**) (é)goutter; (washing) s'égoutter. ● n goutte f; (person ⊠) lavette f.

**drip-dry** vt laisser égoutter. ● adj sans essorage.

**drive** /draɪv/ vt (pt **drove**; pp **driven**) (vehicle) conduire; (sb somewhere) chasser, pousser; (machine) actionner; ~ **mad** rendre fou. ● vi conduire. ● n promenade f en voiture; (private road) allée f; (fig) énergie f; (Psych) instinct m; (Pol) campagne f; (Auto) traction f; (golf, Comput) drive m; it's a two-hour ~ il y a deux heures de route; lefthand ~ conduite f à gauche. □ ~ **at** en venir à.

**drivel** /ˈdrɪvl/ n bêtises fpl.

**driver** /ˈdraɪvə(r)/ n conducteur/-trice m/f, chauffeur m. ~**'s license** n (US) permis m de conduire.

**driving** /ˈdraɪvɪŋ/ n conduite f; **take one's** ~ **test** passer son permis. ● adj (rain) battant; (wind) cinglant. ~ **licence** n permis m de conduire. ~ **school** n auto-école f.

**drizzle** /ˈdrɪzl/ n bruine f. ● vi bruiner.

**drone** /drəʊn/ n (of engine) ronronnement m; (of insects) bourdonnement m. ● vi ronronner; bourdonner.

**drool** /druːl/ vi baver (over sur).

**droop** /druːp/ vi pencher, tomber.

**drop** /drɒp/ n goutte f; (fall, lowering) chute f. ● vt/i (pt **dropped**) (laisser) tomber; (decrease, lower) baisser; ~ (**off**) (person from car) déposer; ~ **a line** écrire un mot (**to** à). □ ~ **in** passer (**on** chez). ~ **off** (doze) s'assoupir. ~ **out** se retirer (**of** de); (of friend) abandonner.

**dropout** /ˈdrɒpaʊt/ n marginal/-e m/f; raté/-e m/f.

**droppings** /ˈdrɒpɪŋz/ npl crottes fpl.

**drought** /draʊt/ n sécheresse f.

**drove** /drəʊv/ ⟶DRIVE.

**droves** /drəʊvz/ npl foules fpl.

**drown** /draʊn/ vt/i (se) noyer.

**drowsy** /ˈdraʊzɪ/ adj somnolent; be or feel ~ avoir envie de dormir.

**drug** /drʌɡ/ n drogue f; (Med) médicament m. ● vt (pt **drugged**) droguer. ~ **addict** n drogué/-e m/f. **drugstore** n (US) drugstore m.

**drum** /drʌm/ n tambour m; (for oil) bidon m; ~**s** batterie f. ● vi (pt **drummed**) tambouriner. ● vt ~ **into sb** répéter sans cesse à qn; ~ **up** (support) susciter; (business) créer. **drummer** n tambour m; (in pop group) batteur m.

**drumstick** /ˈdrʌmstɪk/ n baguette f de tambour; (of chicken) pilon m.

**drunk** /drʌŋk/ ⟶DRINK. ● adj ivre; get ~ s'enivrer. ● n ivrogne/-esse m/f. **drunkard** n ivrogne/-esse m/f. **drunken** adj ivre. **drunkenness** n ivresse f.

**dry** /draɪ/ adj (**drier, driest**) sec; (day) sans pluie; be or feel ~ avoir soif. ● vt/i (faire) sécher; ~ **up** (dry dishes) essuyer la vaisselle; (of supplies) (se) tarir; (be silent 🄏) se taire. ~**-clean** vt nettoyer à sec. ~**-cleaner** n teinturier m. ~ **run** n galop m d'essai.

**DTD** abbr (Document Type Definition) DTD f.

**dual** /ˈdjuːəl/ adj double. ~ **carriageway** n route f à quatre voies. ~**-purpose** adj qui fait double emploi.

**dub** /dʌb/ vt (pt **dubbed**) (film) doubler (**into** en); (nickname) surnommer.

**dubious** /ˈdjuːbɪəs/ adj (pej) douteux; be ~ **about** avoir des doutes sur.

**duck** /dʌk/ n canard m. ● vi se baisser subitement. ● vt (head) baisser; (person) plonger dans l'eau.

**duct** /dʌkt/ n conduit m.

**dud** /dʌd/ adj (tool 🄏) mal fichu; (coin 🄏) faux; (cheque 🄏) sans provision. ● n be a ~ (not work 🄏) ne pas marcher.

**due** /djuː/ adj (owing) dû; (expected) attendu; (proper) qui convient; ~ **to** à cause de; (caused by) ~ dû à; she's ~ **to leave now** il est prévu qu'elle parte maintenant; in ~ **course** (at the right time) en temps voulu; (later) plus tard. ● adv ~ **east** droit vers l'est. ● n dû m; ~**s** droits mpl; (of club) cotisation f.

**duel** /ˈdjuːəl/ n duel m.

**duet** /djuːˈet/ n duo m.

**dug** /dʌɡ/ ⟶DIG.

**duke** /djuːk/ n duc m.

**dull** /dʌl/ adj ennuyeux; (colour) terne; (weather) maussade; (sound) sourd. ● vt (pain) atténuer; (shine) ternir.

**duly** /ˈdjuːlɪ/ adv comme il convient; (as expected) comme prévu.

**dumb** /dʌm/ adj muet; (stupid 🄏) bête. □ ~ **down** (course, TV coverage) baisser le niveau intellectuel de.

**dumbfound** /dʌmˈfaʊnd/ vt sidérer, ahurir.

**dummy** /'dʌmɪ/ n (of tailor) mannequin m; (of baby) sucette f. ● adj factice. ~ **run** n galop m d'essai.

**dump** /dʌmp/ vt déposer; (get rid of 🄓) se débarrasser de. ● n tas m d'ordures; (refuse tip) décharge f; (Mil) dépôt m; (dull place) trou m 🄓; be in the ~s 🄓 avoir le cafard.

**dune** /dju:n/ n dune f.

**dung** /dʌŋ/ n (excrement) bouse f, crotte f; (manure) fumier m.

**dungarees** /dʌŋɡə'ri:z/ npl salopette f.

**dungeon** /'dʌndʒən/ n cachot m.

**duplicate**¹ /'dju:plɪkət/ n double m. ● adj identique.

**duplicate**² /'dju:plɪkeɪt/ vt faire un double de; (on machine) polycopier.

**durable** /'djʊərəbl/ adj (tough) résistant; (enduring) durable.

**duration** /djʊ'reɪʃn/ n durée f.

**during** /'djʊərɪŋ/ prep pendant.

**dusk** /dʌsk/ n crépuscule m.

**dusky** /'dʌskɪ/ adj (-ier, -iest) foncé.

**dust** /dʌst/ n poussière f. ● vt/i épousseter; (sprinkle) saupoudrer (with de). ~**bin** n poubelle f.

**duster** /'dʌstə(r)/ n chiffon m.

**dust**: ~**man** n (pl -men) éboueur m. ~**pan** n pelle f (à poussière).

**dusty** /'dʌstɪ/ adj (-ier, -iest) poussiéreux.

**Dutch** /dʌtʃ/ adj néerlandais; go ~ partager les frais. ● n (Ling) néerlandais m. ~**man** n Néerlandais m. ~**woman** n Néerlandaise f.

**dutiful** /'dju:tɪfl/ adj obéissant.

**duty** /'dju:tɪ/ n devoir m; (tax) droit m; (of official) fonction f; on ~ de service. ~-**free** adj hors-taxe.

**duvet** /'du:veɪ/ n couette f.

**DVD** abbr (**digital versatile disc**) DVD m.

**dwarf** /dwɔ:f/ n nain/-e m/f. ● vt rapetisser.

**dwell** /dwel/ vi (pt **dwelt**) demeurer; ~ **on** s'étendre sur. **dweller** n habitant/-e m/f. **dwelling** n habitation f.

**dwindle** /'dwɪndl/ vi diminuer.

**dye** /daɪ/ vt teindre. ● n teinture f.

**dying** /'daɪɪŋ/ adj mourant; (art) qui se perd.

**dynamic** /daɪ'næmɪk/ adj dynamique.

**dynamite** /'daɪnəmaɪt/ n dynamite f.

**dynasty** /'dɪnəstɪ/ n dynastie f. *(not visible)*

**dysentery** /'dɪsəntrɪ/ n dysenterie f.

**dyslexia** /dɪs'leksɪə/ n dyslexie f. **dyslexic** adj & n dyslexique (mf).

d
e

# Ee

**each** /i:tʃ/ det chaque inv; ~ **one** chacun/-e m/f. ● pron chacun/-e m/f; oranges at 30p ~ des oranges à 30 pence pièce.

**each other** pron l'un/l'une l'autre, les uns/les unes les autres; **know** ~ se connaître; **love** ~ s'aimer.

**eager** /'i:ɡə(r)/ adj impatient (to de); (person, acceptance) enthousiaste; ~ **for** avide de.

**eagle** /'i:ɡl/ n aigle m.

**ear** /ɪə(r)/ n oreille f; (of corn) épi m. ~**ache** n mal m à l'oreille. ~**drum** n tympan m.

**earl** /ɜ:l/ n comte m.

**early** /'ɜ:lɪ/ (-ier, -iest) adv tôt, de bonne heure; (ahead of time) en avance; **as I said earlier** comme je l'ai déjà dit. ● adj (attempt, years) premier; (hour) matinal; (fruit) précoce; *(retirement)* anticipé; have an ~ dinner dîner tôt; in ~ summer au début de l'été; at the earliest au plus tôt.

**earmark** /'ɪəmɑ:k/ vt désigner (for pour).

**earn** /ɜ:n/ vt gagner; *(interest:* Comm) rapporter.

**earnest** /'ɜ:nɪst/ adj sérieux; in ~ sérieusement.

**earnings** /'ɜ:nɪŋz/ npl salaire m; *(profits)* gains mpl.

**ear:** ~**phones** npl casque m. ~**ring** n boucle f d'oreille. ~**shot** n within/in ~shot à portée de voix.

**earth** /ɜ:θ/ n terre f; why/how/where on ...? pourquoi/comment/où diable...? ● vt *(Electr)* mettre à la terre. **earthenware** n faïence f. ~**quake** n tremblement m de terre.

**ease** /i:z/ n facilité f; *(comfort)* bien-être m; at ~ à l'aise; *(Mil)* au repos; with ~ facilement. ● vt *(pain, pressure)* atténuer; *(congestion)* réduire; *(transition)* faciliter. ● vi *(pain, pressure)* s'atténuer; *(congestion, rain)* diminuer.

**easel** /'i:zl/ n chevalet m.

**east** /i:st/ n est m; the E~ *(Orient)* l'Orient m. ● adj *(side, coast)* est; *(wind)* d'est. ● adv à l'est.

**Easter** /'i:stə(r)/ n Pâques m; ~ egg œuf m de Pâques.

**easterly** /'i:stəlɪ/ adj *(wind)* d'est; *(direction)* de l'est.

**eastern** de l'est; ~ France l'est de la France.

**eastward** /'i:stwəd/ adj *(side)* est inv; *(journey)* vers l'est.

**easy** /'i:zɪ/ adj *(-ier, -iest)* facile; go ~ with ⬛ y aller doucement avec; take it ~ ne te fatigue pas. ~**going** adj accommodant.

**eat** /i:t/ vt/i *(pt ate; pp eaten)* manger; ~ into ronger.

**eavesdrop** /'i:vzdrɒp/ vi *(pt -dropped)* écouter aux portes.

**ebb** /eb/ n reflux m. ● vi descendre; *(fig)* décliner.

**EC** abbr **(European Commission)** CE f.

**eccentric** /ɪk'sentrɪk/ adj & n excentrique *(mf)*.

**echo** /'ekəʊ/ n *(pl -oes)* écho m. ● vt répercuter; *(idea, opinion)* reprendre. ● vi retentir, résonner (to, with de).

**eclipse** /ɪ'klɪps/ n éclipse f. ● vt éclipser.

**ecological** /i:kə'lɒdʒɪkl/ adj écologique.

**ecology** /ɪ'kɒlədʒɪ/ n écologie f.

**e-commerce** /'i:kɒmɜ:s/ n commerce m électronique, commerce m en ligne.

**economic** /i:kə'nɒmɪk/ adj économique; *(profitable)* rentable; ~ refugee réfugié/-e m/f économique. **economical** adj économique; *(person)* économe. **economics** n économie f, sciences fpl économiques. **economist** n économiste mf.

**economize** /ɪ'kɒnəmaɪz/ vi ~ (on) économiser.

**economy** /ɪ'kɒnəmɪ/ n économie f. ~**class syndrome** n syndrome m de la classe économique.

**ecosystem** /'i:kəʊsɪstəm/ n écosystème m.

**ecstasy** /'ekstəsɪ/ n extase f; *(drug)* ecstasy m.

**edge** /edʒ/ n bord m; *(of town)* abords mpl; *(of knife)* tranchant m; have the ~ on ⬛ l'emporter sur; on ~ énervé. ● vt *(trim)* border. ● vi ~ forward avancer doucement.

**edgeways** /'edʒweɪz/ adv I can't

**get a word in** ~ je n'arrive pas à placer un mot.

**edible** /'edɪbl/ adj comestible.

> **Edinburgh Festival** Festival international des Arts qui se déroule tous les étés à Édimbourg (Écosse) depuis 1947. Pendant trois semaines, au programme du festival institutionnel et du festival parallèle (*Fringe festival*), se côtoient les plus grands noms de la musique, de la danse, du théâtre, les artistes d'avant-garde et les nouveaux talents.

**edit** /'edɪt/ vt (pt **edited**) (*newspaper, page*) être le rédacteur/la rédactrice de; (*check*) réviser; (*cut*) couper; (*TV, cinema*) monter.

**edition** /ɪ'dɪʃn/ n édition f.

**editor** /'edɪtə(r)/ n (*writer*) rédacteur/-trice m/f; (*of works, anthology*) éditeur/-trice m/f; (*TV, cinema*) monteur/-teuse m/f; **the** ~ (*in chief*) le rédacteur en chef.

**editorial** /edɪ'tɔːrɪəl/ adj de la rédaction. ● n éditorial m.

**educate** /'edʒʊkeɪt/ vt instruire; (*mind*) éduquer. **educated** adj instruit. **education** /-'keɪʃn/ n (*schooling*) études fpl. **educational** adj éducatif; (*method*) d'enseignement.

**eel** /iːl/ n anguille f.

**eerie** /'ɪərɪ/ adj (**-ier, -iest**) sinistre.

**effect** /ɪ'fekt/ n effet m; **come into** ~ entrer en vigueur; **in** ~ effectivement; **take** ~ agir. ● vt effectuer.

**effective** /ɪ'fektɪv/ adj efficace; (*actual*) effectif. **effectively** adv efficacement; (*in effect*) en réalité. **effectiveness** n efficacité f.

**effeminate** /ɪ'femɪnət/ adj efféminé.

**effervescent** /efə'vesnt/ adj effervescent.

**efficiency** /ɪ'fɪʃnsɪ/ n efficacité f; (*of machine*) rendement m. **efficient** adj efficace. **efficiently** adv efficacement.

**effort** /'efət/ n efforts mpl; **make an** ~ faire un effort; **be worth the** ~ en valoir la peine. **effortless** adj facile.

**effusive** /ɪ'fjuːsɪv/ adj expansif.

**e.g.** /iː'dʒiː/ abbr par ex.

**egg** /eg/ n œuf m. ● vt ~ **on** pousser. ~**cup** n coquetier m. ~**plant** n (US) aubergine f. ~**shell** n coquille f d'œuf.

**ego** /'iːgəʊ/ n amour-propre m; (*Psych*) moi m. **egotism** n égotisme m. **egotist** n égotiste mf.

**Egypt** /'iːdʒɪpt/ n Égypte f.

**EHIC** abbr (**European Health Insurance Card**) CEAM f.

**eiderdown** /'aɪdədaʊn/ n édredon m.

**eight** /eɪt/ adj & n huit (m). **eighteen** adj & n dix-huit (m). **eighth** adj & n huitième (mf). **eighty** adj & n quatre-vingts (m).

**either** /'aɪðə/ det & pron l'un/une ou l'autre; (*with negative*) ni l'un/une ni l'autre; **you can take** ~ tu peux prendre n'importe lequel/laquelle. ● adv non plus. ● conj ~...or ou (bien)...ou (bien); (*with negative*) ni...ni.

**eject** /ɪ'dʒekt/ vt (*troublemaker*) expulser; (*waste*) rejeter.

**elaborate**[1] /ɪ'læbərət/ adj compliqué.

**elaborate**[2] /ɪ'læbəreɪt/ vt élaborer. ● vi préciser; ~ **on** s'étendre sur.

**elastic** /ɪ'læstɪk/ adj & n élastique (m); ~ **band** élastique m. **elasticity** n élasticité f.

**elated** /ɪ'leɪtɪd/ adj transporté de joie.

**elbow** /'elbəʊ/ n coude m; ~ **room** espace m vital.

**elder** /'eldə(r)/ adj & n aîné/-e (m/f); (tree) sureau m.

**elderly** /'eldəlɪ/ adj âgé; the ~ les personnes fpl âgées.

**eldest** /'eldɪst/ adj & n aîné/-e (m/f).

**elect** /ɪ'lekt/ vt élire; ~ **to do** choisir de faire. ● adj (president etc.) futur. **election** n élection f. **elector** n électeur/-trice m/f. **electoral** adj électoral. **electorate** n électorat m.

**electric** /ɪ'lektrɪk/ adj électrique; ~ **blanket** couverture f chauffante. **electrical** adj électrique. **electrician** /-ɪʃn/ n électricien/-ne m/f. **electricity** n électricité f. **electrify** vt électrifier; (excite) électriser. **electrocute** vt électrocuter.

**electronic** /ɪlek'trɒnɪk/ adj électronique. ~ **publishing** n édutique f. **electronics** n électronique f.

**elegance** /'elɪɡəns/ n élégance f.

**element** /'elɪmənt/ n élément m; (of heater etc.) résistance f. **elementary** adj élémentaire.

**elephant** /'elɪfənt/ n éléphant m.

**elevate** /'elɪveɪt/ vt élever. **elevation** n élévation f. **elevator** n (US) ascenseur m.

**eleven** /ɪ'levn/ adj & n onze (m). **eleventh** adj & n onzième (mf).

**elicit** /ɪ'lɪsɪt/ vt obtenir (from de).

**eligible** /'elɪdʒəbl/ adj admissible (for à); be ~ **for** (entitled to) avoir droit à.

**eliminate** /ɪ'lɪmɪneɪt/ vt éliminer.

**elm** /elm/ n orme m.

**elongate** /'iːlɒŋɡeɪt/ vt allonger.

**elope** /ɪ'ləʊp/ vi s'enfuir (with avec). **elopement** n fugue f (amoureuse).

**eloquence** /'eləkwəns/ n éloquence f.

**else** /els/ adv d'autre; **somebody/nothing** ~ quelqu'un/rien d'autre; **everybody** ~ tous les autres; **somewhere/something** ~ autre part/chose; **or** ~ ou bien. **elsewhere** adv ailleurs.

**elude** /ɪ'luːd/ vt échapper à.

**elusive** /ɪ'luːsɪv/ adj insaisissable.

**email** /'iːmeɪl/ n (medium) courrier m électronique; (item) e-mail m, mél m; ~ **sb** envoyer un e-mail à qn; ~ **sth** envoyer qch par courrier électronique.

**emancipate** /ɪ'mænsɪpeɪt/ vt émanciper.

**embankment** /ɪm'bæŋkmənt/ n (of river) quai m; (of railway) remblai m.

**embark** /ɪm'bɑːk/ vt embarquer. ● vi (Naut) embarquer; ~ **on** (journey) entreprendre; (campaign, career) se lancer dans.

**embarrass** /ɪm'bærəs/ vt plonger dans l'embarras; be/feel ~ed être; se sentir gêné. **embarrassment** n confusion f, gêne f.

**embassy** /'embəsɪ/ n ambassade f.

**embed** /ɪm'bed/ vt (pt **embedded**) enfoncer (in dans).

**embellish** /ɪm'belɪʃ/ vt embellir.

**embers** /'embəz/ npl braises fpl.

**embezzle** /ɪm'bezl/ vt détourner (from de). **embezzlement** n détournement m de fonds.

**emblem** /'embləm/ n emblème m.

**embodiment** /ɪm'bɒdɪmənt/ n incarnation f. **embody** vt incarner; (legally) incorporer.

**emboss** /ɪm'bɒs/ vt (metal) repousser; (paper) gaufrer.

**embrace** /ɪm'breɪs/ vt (person) étreindre; (religion) embrasser; (include) comprendre. ● n étreinte f.

**embroider** /ɪm'brɔɪdə(r)/ vt broder. **embroidery** n broderie f.

**embryo** /'embriəu/ n embryon m.

**emerald** /'emərəld/ n émeraude f.

**emerge** /ɪ'mɜːdʒ/ vi (person) sortir (from de); it ~d that il est apparu que. **emergence** n apparition f.

**emergency** /ɪ'mɜːdʒənsɪ/ n (crisis) crise f; (urgent case: Med) urgence f; in an ~ en cas d'urgence. ●adj d'urgence. ~ exit n sortie f de secours; ~ landing n atterrissage m forcé. ~ room n (US) salle f des urgences.

**emigrant** /'emɪgrənt/ n émigrant/-e m/f. **emigrate** vi émigrer.

**eminence** /'emɪnəns/ n éminence f. **eminent** adj éminent.

**emission** /ɪ'mɪʃn/ n émission f.

**emit** /ɪ'mɪt/ vt (pt emitted) émettre.

**emotion** /ɪ'məʊʃn/ n émotion f. **emotional** adj (development) émotif; (reaction) émotionel; (film, scene) émouvant.

**emotive** /ɪ'məʊtɪv/ adj qui soulève les passions.

**emperor** /'empərə(r)/ n empereur m.

**emphasis** /'emfəsɪs/ n accent m; lay ~ on mettre l'accent sur. **emphasize** vt mettre l'accent sur. **emphatic** adj catégorique; (manner) énergique.

**empire** /'empaɪə(r)/ n empire m.

**employ** /ɪm'plɔɪ/ vt employer. **employee** n employé/-e m/f. **employer** n employeur/-euse m/f.

**employment** /ɪm'plɔɪmənt/ n emploi m; find ~ trouver du travail.

**empower** /ɪm'paʊə(r)/ vt autoriser (to do à faire).

**empty** /'emptɪ/ adj (-ier, -iest) vide; (street) désert; (promise) vain; on an ~ stomach à jeun. ●vt/i (se) vider. ~-handed adj les mains vides.

**emulate** /'emjʊleɪt/ vt imiter.

**enable** /ɪ'neɪbl/ vt ~ sb to permettre à qn de.

**enamel** /ɪ'næml/ n émail m. ●vt (pt enamelled) émailler.

**encase** /ɪn'keɪs/ vt revêtir, recouvrir (in de).

**enchant** /ɪn'tʃɑːnt/ vt enchanter.

**enclose** /ɪn'kləʊz/ vt entourer; (land) clôturer; (with letter) joindre. **enclosed** (space) clos; (with letter) ci-joint. **enclosure** n enceinte f; (with letter) pièce f jointe.

**encompass** /ɪn'kʌmpəs/ vt inclure.

**encore** /'ɒŋkɔː(r)/ interj & n bis (m).

**encounter** /ɪn'kaʊntə(r)/ vt rencontrer. ●n rencontre f.

**encourage** /ɪn'kʌrɪdʒ/ vt encourager.

**encroach** /ɪn'krəʊtʃ/ vi ~ upon empiéter sur.

**encyclopedia** /ɪnsaɪklə'piːdɪə/ n encyclopédie f. **encyclopaedic** adj encyclopédique.

**end** /end/ n fin f; (farthest part) bout m; come to an ~ prendre fin; ~-product produit m fini; in the ~ finalement; no ~ of 🛈 énormément de; on ~ (upright) debout; (in a row) de suite; put an ~to mettre fin à; ~ one's days finir ses jours. ●vi se terminer; ~ up doing finir par faire.

**endanger** /ɪn'deɪndʒə(r)/ vt mettre en danger.

**endearing** /ɪn'dɪərɪŋ/ adj attachant.

**endeavour**, (US) **endeavor** /ɪn'devə(r)/ n (attempt) tentative f; (hard work) effort m. ●vi faire tout son possible (to do pour faire).

**ending** /'endɪŋ/ n fin f.

**endive** /ˈendɪv/ n chicorée f.

**endless** /ˈendlɪs/ adj interminable; (supply) inépuisable; (patience) infini.

**endorse** /ɪnˈdɔːs/ vt (candidate, decision) appuyer; (product, claim) approuver; (cheque) endosser.

**endurance** /ɪnˈdjʊərəns/ n endurance f.

**endure** /ɪnˈdjʊə(r)/ vt supporter. ● vi durer. **enduring** adj durable.

**enemy** /ˈenəmɪ/ n & adj ennemi/-e (m/f).

**energetic** /enəˈdʒetɪk/ adj énergique. **energy** n énergie f.

**enforce** /ɪnˈfɔːs/ vt (rule, law) appliquer, faire respecter; (silence, discipline) imposer (on à); ~d forcé.

**engage** /ɪnˈɡeɪdʒ/ vt (staff) engager; (attention) retenir; be ~d in se livrer à. ● vi ~ in se livrer à. **engaged** adj fiancé; (busy) occupé; **get** ~d se fiancer. **engagement** n fiançailles fpl; (meeting) rendezvous m; (undertaking) engagement m.

**engaging** /ɪnˈɡeɪdʒɪŋ/ adj attachant, engageant.

**engine** /ˈendʒɪn/ n moteur m; (of train) locomotive f; (of ship) machines fpl. ~**-driver** n mécanicien m.

**engineer** /endʒɪˈnɪə(r)/ n ingénieur m; (repairman) technicien m; (on ship) mécanicien m. ● vt (contrive) manigancer.

**engineering** /endʒɪˈnɪərɪŋ/ n ingénierie f; (industry) mécanique f; **civil** ~ génie m civil.

**England** /ˈɪŋɡlənd/ n Angleterre f.

**English** /ˈɪŋɡlɪʃ/ adj anglais. ● n (Ling) anglais m; the ~ les Anglais mpl. ~**man** n Anglais m. ~**-speaking** adj anglophone. ~**woman** n Anglaise f.

**engrave** /ɪnˈɡreɪv/ vt graver.

**engrossed** /ɪnˈɡrəʊst/ adj

absorbé (**in** dans).

**engulf** /ɪnˈɡʌlf/ vt engouffrer.

**enhance** /ɪnˈhɑːns/ vt (prospects, status) améliorer; (price, value) augmenter.

**enjoy** /ɪnˈdʒɔɪ/ vt aimer (doing faire); (benefit from) jouir de; ~ **oneself** s'amuser; ~ **your meal!** bon appétit! **enjoyable** adj agréable. **enjoyment** n plaisir m.

**enlarge** /ɪnˈlɑːdʒ/ vt agrandir. ● vi s'agrandir; (pupil) se dilater; ~ **on** s'étendre sur. **enlargement** n agrandissement m.

**enlighten** /ɪnˈlaɪtn/ vt éclairer (on sur). **enlightenment** n instruction f; (information) éclaircissement m.

**enlist** /ɪnˈlɪst/ vt (person) recruter; (fig) obtenir. ● vi s'engager.

**enmity** /ˈenmətɪ/ n inimitié f.

**enormous** /ɪˈnɔːməs/ adj énorme. **enormously** adv énormément.

**enough** /ɪˈnʌf/ adv & n assez; have ~ **of** en avoir assez de. ● det assez de; ~ **glasses/time** assez de verres/de temps.

**enquire** →INQUIRE.

**enquiry** →INQUIRY.

**enrage** /ɪnˈreɪdʒ/ vt mettre en rage, rendre furieux.

**enrol** /ɪnˈrəʊl/ vt/i (pt enrolled) (s')inscrire. **enrolment** n inscription f.

**ensure** /ɪnˈʃɔː(r)/ vt garantir; ~ **that** (ascertain) s'assurer que.

**entail** /ɪnˈteɪl/ vt entraîner.

**entangle** /ɪnˈtæŋɡl/ vt emmêler.

**enter** /ˈentə(r)/ vt (room, club, phase) entrer dans; (note down, register) inscrire; (data, name) saisir. ● vi entrer (**into** dans); ~ **for** s'inscrire à.

**enterprise** /ˈentəpraɪz/ n entreprise f; (boldness) initiative f. **enterprising** adj entreprenant.

**entertain** /entə'teɪn/ vt amuser, divertir; (guests) recevoir; (ideas) considérer. **entertainer** n artiste mf. **entertaining** adj divertissant. **entertainment** n divertissement m; (performance) spectacle m.

**enthral** /ɪn'θrɔːl/ vt (pt **enthralled**) captiver.

**enthusiasm** /ɪn'θjuːzɪæzəm/ n enthousiasme m (for pour).

**enthusiast** /ɪn'θjuːzɪæst/ n passionné/-e m/f (for de). **enthusiastic** adj (supporter) enthousiaste; be ~ic about être enthousiasmé par. **enthusiastically** adv avec enthousiasme.

**entice** /ɪn'taɪs/ vt attirer; ~ sb to do entraîner qn à faire.

**entire** /ɪn'taɪə(r)/ adj entier. **entirely** adv entièrement. **entirety** n in its ~ty en entier.

**entitle** /ɪn'taɪtl/ vt donner droit à (to sth à qch; to do de faire); ~d (book) intitulé; be ~d to sth avoir droit à qch.

**entrance**[1] /'entrəns/ n (entering, way in) entrée f (to de); (right to enter) admission f. ● adj (charge, exam) d'entrée.

**entrance**[2] /ɪn'trɑːns/ vt transporter.

**entrant** /'entrənt/ n (Sport) concurrent/-e m/f; (in exam) candidat/-e m/f.

**entrenched** /ɪn'trentʃt/ adj (opinion) inébranlable; (Mil) retranché.

**entrepreneur** /ɒntrəprə'nɜː(r)/ n entrepreneur/-euse m/f.

**entrust** /ɪn'trʌst/ vt confier; ~ sb with sth confier qch à qn.

**entry** /'entrɪ/ n entrée f; ~ form fiche f d'inscription.

**envelop** /ɪn'veləp/ vt (pt **enveloped**) envelopper.

**envelope** /'envələʊp/ n

enveloppe f.

**envious** /'envɪəs/ adj envieux (of de).

**environment** /ɪn'vaɪərənmənt/ n (ecological) environnement m; (social) milieu m. **environmental** adj du milieu, de l'environnement. **environmentalist** n écologiste mf.

**envisage** /ɪn'vɪzɪdʒ/ vt prévoir (doing de faire).

**envoy** /'envɔɪ/ n envoyé/-e m/f.

**envy** /'envɪ/ n envie f. ● vt envier; ~ sb sth envier qch à qn.

**epic** /'epɪk/ n épopée f. ● adj épique.

**epidemic** /epɪ'demɪk/ n épidémie f.

**epilepsy** /'epɪlepsɪ/ n épilepsie f.

**episode** /'epɪsəʊd/ n épisode m.

**epitome** /ɪ'pɪtəmɪ/ n modèle m. **epitomize** vt incarner.

**equal** /'iːkwəl/ adj & n égal/-e (m/f); ~ opportunities/rights égalité f des chances/droits; ~ to (task) à la hauteur de. ● vt (pt **equalled**) égaler. **equality** n égalité f. **equalize** vt/i égaliser. **equalizer** n (goal) but m égalisateur. **equally** adv (divide) en parts égales; (just as) tout aussi.

**equanimity** /ekwə'nɪmətɪ/ n sérénité f.

**equate** /ɪ'kweɪt/ vt assimiler (with à). **equation** n équation f.

**equator** /ɪ'kweɪtə(r)/ n équateur m.

**equilibrium** /iːkwɪ'lɪbrɪəm/ n équilibre m.

**equip** /ɪ'kwɪp/ vt (pt **equipped**) équiper (with de). **equipment** n équipement m.

**equity** /'ekwɪtɪ/ n équité f.

**equivalence** /ɪ'kwɪvələns/ n équivalence f.

**era** /'ɪərə/ n ère f, époque f.

**eradicate** /ɪˈrædɪkeɪt/ vt éliminer; (*disease*) éradiquer.

**erase** /ɪˈreɪz/ vt effacer. **eraser** n (rubber) gomme f.

**erect** /ɪˈrekt/ adj droit. ● vt ériger. **erection** n érection f.

**erode** /ɪˈrəʊd/ vt éroder; (fig) saper. **erosion** n érosion f.

**erotic** /ɪˈrɒtɪk/ adj érotique.

**errand** /ˈerənd/ n commission f, course f.

**erratic** /ɪˈrætɪk/ adj (*behaviour, person*) imprévisible; (*performance*) inégal.

**error** /ˈerə(r)/ n erreur f.

**erupt** /ɪˈrʌpt/ vi (volcano) entrer en éruption; (fig) éclater.

**escalate** /ˈeskəleɪt/ vt intensifier. ● vi (*conflict*) s'intensifier. **escalation** n intensification f. **escalator** n escalier m mécanique, escalator® m.

**escapade** /ˈeskəpeɪd/ n frasque f.

**escape** /ɪˈskeɪp/ vt échapper à. ● vi s'enfuir, s'évader; (gas) fuir. ● n fuite f, évasion f; (of gas etc.) fuite f; **have a lucky** ~ **narrow** ~ l'échapper belle.

**escapism** /ɪˈskeɪpɪzəm/ n évasion f (du réel).

**escort**¹ /ˈeskɔːt/ n (guard) escorte f; (companion) compagnon / compagne m/f.

**escort**² /ɪˈskɔːt/ vt escorter.

**Eskimo** /ˈeskɪməʊ/ n Esquimau/-de m/f.

**especially** /ɪˈspeʃəlɪ/ adv en particulier.

**espionage** /ˈespɪənɑːʒ/ n espionnage m.

**espresso** /eˈspresəʊ/ n (café) express m.

**essay** /ˈeseɪ/ n (in literature) essai m; (School) rédaction f; (Univ) dissertation f.

**essence** /ˈesns/ n essence f.

**essential** /ɪˈsenʃl/ adj essentiel; **the** ~**s** l'essentiel m. **essentially** adv essentiellement.

**establish** /ɪˈstæblɪʃ/ vt établir; (business) fonder.

**establishment** /ɪˈstæblɪʃmənt/ n (process) instauration f; (institution) établissement m; **the E**~ l'ordre m établi.

**estate** /ɪˈsteɪt/ n (house and land) domaine m; (possessions) biens mpl; (housing estate) cité f; ~ **agent** n agent m immobilier. ~ **car** n break m.

**esteem** /ɪˈstiːm/ n estime f.

**esthetic** /esˈθetɪk/ adj (US) ➞**AESTHETIC**.

**estimate**¹ /ˈestɪmət/ n (calculation) estimation f; (Comm) devis m.

**estimate**² /ˈestɪmeɪt/ vt évaluer; ~ **that** estimer que. **estimation** n (esteem) estime f; (judgment) opinion f.

**Estonia** /ɪˈstəʊnɪə/ n Estonie f.

**estuary** /ˈestʃʊərɪ/ n estuaire m.

**eternal** /ɪˈtɜːnl/ adj éternel.

**eternity** /ɪˈtɜːnətɪ/ n éternité f.

**ethic** /ˈeθɪk/ n éthique f; ~**s** moralité f. **ethical** adj éthique.

**ethnic** /ˈeθnɪk/ adj ethnique. ~ **cleansing** nettoyage m ethnique.

**EU** abbr **European Union** UE f, Union f européenne.

**euphoria** /juːˈfɔːrɪə/ n euphorie f.

**euro** /ˈjʊərəʊ/ n euro m. ~ **zone** zone f euro.

**Europe** /ˈjʊərəp/ n Europe f.

**European** /jʊərəˈpɪən/ adj & n européen/-ne (m/f); ~ **Community** Communauté f européenne.

**eurosceptic** /ˈjʊərəʊskeptɪk/ n eurosceptique mf.

**euthanasia** /ˈjuːθəˈneɪziə/ n euthanasie f.

**evacuate** /ɪˈvækjʊeɪt/ vt évacuer.

**evade** /ɪˈveɪd/ vt (blow) esquiver; (question) éluder.

**evaluation** /ɪvæljʊˈeɪʃn/ n évaluation f.

**evaporate** /ɪˈvæpjʊˈeɪʃn/ vi s'évaporer; ~d milk lait m condensé.

**evasion** /ɪˈveɪʒn/ n fuite f (of de-vant); (excuse) faux-fuyant m; tax ~ évasion f fiscale. **evasive** adj évasif.

**eve** /iːv/ n veille f (of de).

**even** /ˈiːvn/ adj (surface, voice, con-test) égal; (teeth, hem) régulier; (number) pair; **get** ~**with** se ven-ger de. ● adv même; ~ **better**/etc. (still) encore mieux/etc.; ~ **so** quand même. □ ~ **out** (differences) s'atténuer; ~ **sth out** (inequalities) réduire qch; ~ **up** équilibrer.

**evening** /ˈiːvnɪŋ/ n soir m; (whole evening, event) soirée f.

**evenly** /ˈiːvnlɪ/ adv (spread, apply) uniformément; (breathe) régulière-ment; (equally) en parts égales.

**event** /ɪˈvent/ n événement m; (Sport) épreuve f; **in the** ~ **of** en cas de. **eventful** adj mouvementé.

**eventual** /ɪˈventʃʊəl/ adj (outcome, decision) final; (aim) à long terme. **eventuality** n éventualité f. **eventu-ally** adv finalement; (in future) un jour ou l'autre.

**ever** /ˈevə(r)/ adv jamais; (at all times) toujours.

**evergreen** /ˈevəgriːn/ n arbre m à feuilles persistantes.

**everlasting** /evəˈlɑːstɪŋ/ adj éternel.

**ever since** prep & adv depuis.

**every** /ˈevrɪ/ adj ~ **house/window** toutes les maisons/les fenêtres; ~ **time/minute** chaque fois/minute; ~ **day** tous les jours; ~ **other day**

tous les deux jours. **everybody** pron tout le monde. **everyday** adj quoti-dien. **everyone** pron tout le monde. **everything** pron tout. **everywhere** adv partout; ~**where he goes** par-tout où il va.

**evict** /ɪˈvɪkt/ vt expulser (from de).

**evidence** /ˈevɪdəns/ n (proof) preuves fpl (that que; of, for de); (testimony) témoignage m; (traces) trace f (of de); **give** ~ témoigner; **be in** ~ être visible. **evident** adj manifeste. **evidently** adv (appar-ently) apparemment; (obviously) manifestement.

**evil** /ˈiːvl/ adj malfaisant. ● n mal m.

**evoke** /ɪˈvəʊk/ vt évoquer.

**evolution** /iːvəˈluːʃn/ n évolu-tion f.

**evolve** /ɪˈvɒlv/ vi évoluer. ● vt élaborer.

**ewe** /juː/ n brebis f.

**ex-** /eks/ pref ex-, ancien.

**exact** /ɪɡˈzækt/ adj exact; **the** ~ **opposite** exactement le contraire. ● vt exiger (from de). **exactly** adv exactement.

**exaggerate** /ɪɡˈzædʒəreɪt/ vt/i exagérer.

**exalted** /ɪɡˈzɔːltɪd/ adj élevé.

**exam** /ɪɡˈzæm/ n ⊠ examen m.

**examination** /ɪɡzæmɪˈneɪʃn/ n examen m.

**examine** /ɪɡˈzæmɪn/ vt examiner; (witness) interroger. **examiner** n examinateur/-trice m/f.

**example** /ɪɡˈzɑːmpl/ n exemple m; **for** ~ par exemple; **make an** ~ **of** punir pour l'exemple.

**exasperate** /ɪɡˈzæspəreɪt/ vt exaspérer.

**excavate** /ˈekskəveɪt/ vt fouiller. **excavations** npl fouilles fpl.

**exceed** /ɪkˈsiːd/ vt dépasser. **ex-ceedingly** adv extrêmement.

**excel** /ɪk'sel/ vi (pt **excelled**) exceller (at, in en; at doing à faire). ● vt surpasser.

**excellence** /'eksələns/ n excellence f. **excellent** adj excellent.

**except** /ɪk'sept/ prep sauf, excepté; ~ for à part. ● vt excepter. **excepting** prep sauf, excepté.

**exception** /ɪk'sepʃn/ n exception f; take ~ to s'offusquer de. **exceptional** adj exceptionnel.

**excerpt** /'eksɜːpt/ n extrait m.

**excess**[1] /ɪk'ses/ n excès m.

**excess**[2] /'ekses/ adj ~ weight excès m de poids; ~ baggage excédent m de bagages.

**excessive** /ɪk'sesɪv/ adj excessif.

**exchange** /ɪks'tʃeɪndʒ/ vt échanger (for contre). ● n échange m; (between currencies) change m; ~ rate taux m de change; telephone ~ central m téléphonique.

**Exchequer** /ɪks'tʃekə(r)/ n (Pol) ministère m britannique des finances.

**excise** /'eksaɪz/ n excise f, taxe f.

**excite** /ɪk'saɪt/ vt exciter; (enthuse) enthousiasmer. **excited** adj excité; get ~d s'exciter. **excitement** n excitation f. **exciting** adj passionnant.

**exclaim** /ɪk'kleɪm/ vt s'exclamer.

**exclamation** /ekskləˈmeɪʃn/ n exclamation f; ~ mark or point (US) point m d'exclamation.

**exclude** /ɪk'skluːd/ vt exclure.

**exclusive** /ɪk'skluːsɪv/ adj (club) fermé; (rights) exclusif; (news item) en exclusivité; ~ of meals repas non compris. **exclusively** adv exclusivement.

**excruciating** /ɪk'skruːʃɪeɪtɪŋ/ adj atroce.

**excursion** /ɪk'skɜːʃn/ n excursion f.

**excuse**[1] /ɪk'skjuːz/ vt excuser; ~

from (exempt) dispenser de; ~ me! excusez-moi, pardon!

**excuse**[2] /ɪk'skjuːs/ n (reason) excuse f; (pretext) prétexte m (for sth à qch; for doing pour faire).

**ex-directory** /eksdaɪˈrektərɪ/ adj sur liste rouge.

**execute** /'eksɪkjuːt/ vt exécuter. **executioner** n bourreau m.

**executive** /ɪg'zekjutɪv/ n (person) cadre m; (committee) exécutif m. ● adj exécutif.

**exemplary** /ɪg'zemplərɪ/ adj exemplaire.

**exemplify** /ɪg'zemplɪfaɪ/ vt illustrer.

**exempt** /ɪg'zempt/ adj exempt (from de). ● vt exempter.

**exercise** /'eksəsaɪz/ n exercice m; ~ book cahier m. ● vt exercer; (restraint, patience) faire preuve de. ● vi faire de l'exercice.

**exert** /ɪg'zɜːt/ vt exercer; ~ oneself se fatiguer. **exertion** n effort m.

**exhaust** /ɪg'zɔːst/ vt épuiser. ● n (Auto) pot m d'échappement.

**exhaustive** /ɪg'zɔːstɪv/ adj exhaustif.

**exhibit** /ɪg'zɪbɪt/ vt exposer; (fig) manifester. ● n objet m exposé.

**exhibition** /eksɪˈbɪʃn/ n exposition f; (of skill) démonstration f. **exhibitionist** n exhibitionniste mf.

**exhibitor** /ɪg'zɪbɪtə(r)/ n exposant/-e m/f.

**exhilarate** /ɪg'zɪləreɪt/ vt griser.

**exile** /'eksaɪl/ n exil m; (person) exilé/-e m/f. ● vt exiler.

**exist** /ɪg'zɪst/ vi exister. **existence** n existence f; be in ~ence exister. **existing** adj actuel.

**exit** /'eksɪt/ n sortie f. ● vt/i (also Comput) sortir (de).

**exodus** /'eksədəs/ n exode m.

**exonerate** /ɪgˈzɒnəreɪt/ vt disculper.

**exotic** /ɪgˈzɒtɪk/ adj exotique.

**expand** /ɪkˈspænd/ vt développer; (workforce) accroître. ● vi se développer; (population) s'accroître; (metal) se dilater.

**expanse** /ɪkˈspæns/ n étendue f.

**expansion** /ɪkˈspænʃn/ n développement m; (Pol, Comm) expansion f.

**expatriate** /eksˈpætrɪət/ adj & n expatrié/-e (m/f).

**expect** /ɪkˈspekt/ vt s'attendre à; (suppose) supposer; (demand) exiger; (baby) attendre.

**expectancy** /ɪkˈspektənsɪ/ n attente f.

**expectant** /ɪkˈspektənt/ adj ~ mother future maman f.

**expectation** /ekspekˈteɪʃn/ n (assumption) prévision f; (hope) aspiration f; (demand) exigence f.

**expedient** /ɪkˈspiːdɪənt/ adj opportun. ● n expédient m.

**expedition** /ekspɪˈdɪʃn/ n expédition f.

**expel** /ɪkˈspel/ vt (pt expelled) expulser; (pupil) renvoyer.

**expend** /ɪkˈspend/ vt consacrer.

**expenditure** /ɪkˈspendɪtʃə(r)/ n dépenses fpl.

**expense** /ɪkˈspens/ n frais mpl; at sb's ~ aux frais de qn; ~ account frais mpl de représentation. **expensive** adj cher; (tastes) de luxe. **expensively** adv luxueusement.

**experience** /ɪkˈspɪərɪəns/ n expérience f. ● vt (undergo) connaître; (feel) éprouver; ~d expérimenté.

**experiment** /ɪkˈsperɪmənt/ n expérience f. ● vi expérimenter, faire des essais.

**expert** /ˈekspɜːt/ n spécialiste mf. ● adj spécialisé, expert. **expertise** n compétence f. **expertly** adv de

manière experte.

**expire** /ɪkˈspaɪə(r)/ vi expirer; ~d périmé. **expiry** n expiration f.

**explain** /ɪkˈspleɪn/ vt expliquer. **explanation** n explication f. **explanatory** adj explicatif.

**explicit** /ɪkˈsplɪsɪt/ adj explicite.

**explode** /ɪkˈspləʊd/ vt/i (faire) exploser.

**exploit**[1] /ˈeksplɔɪt/ n exploit m.

**exploit**[2] /ɪkˈsplɔɪt/ vt exploiter.

**exploration** /eksplərˈeɪʃn/ n exploration f. **exploratory** adj (talks) exploratoire. **explore** vt explorer; (fig) étudier. **explorer** n explorateur/-trice m/f.

**explosion** /ɪkˈspləʊʒn/ n explosion f. **explosive** adj & n explosif (m).

**exponent** /ɪkˈspəʊnənt/ n avocat/-e m/f (of de).

**export**[1] /ɪkˈspɔːt/ vt exporter.

**export**[2] /ˈekspɔːt/ n (process) exportation f; (product) produit m d'exportation.

**expose** /ɪkˈspəʊz/ vt exposer; (disclose) révéler.

**exposure** /ɪkˈspəʊʒə(r)/ n révélation f; (Photo) pose f; die of ~ mourir de froid.

**express** /ɪkˈspres/ vt exprimer. ● adj exprès. ● adv send sth ~ envoyer qch en exprès. ● n (train) rapide m. **expression** n expression f. **expressive** adj expressif. **expressly** adv expressément.

**exquisite** /ˈekskwɪzɪt/ adj exquis.

**extend** /ɪkˈstend/ vt (visit) prolonger; (house) agrandir; (range) élargir; (arm, leg) étendre. ● vi (stretch) s'étendre; (in time) se prolonger. **extension** n (of line, road) prolongement m; (of visa, loan) prorogation f; (building) addition f; (phone number) poste m; (cable) rallonge f.

**extensive** /ɪkˈstensɪv/ adj vaste;

(study) approfondi; (damage) considérable. **extensively** adv (much) beaucoup; (very) très.

**extent** /ɪkˈstent/ n (size, scope) étendue f; (degree) mesure f; to some ~ dans une certaine mesure; to such an ~ that à tel point que.

**extenuating** /ɪkˈstenjʊeɪtɪŋ/ adj atténuant.

**exterior** /ɪkˈstɪərɪə(r)/ adj & n extérieur (m).

**exterminate** /ɪkˈstɜːmɪneɪt/ vt exterminer.

**external** /ɪkˈstɜːnl/ adj extérieur; (cause, medical use) externe.

**extinct** /ɪkˈstɪŋkt/ adj (species) disparu; (volcano, passion) éteint.

**extinguish** /ɪkˈstɪŋgwɪʃ/ vt éteindre. **extinguisher** n extincteur m.

**extol** /ɪkˈstəʊl/ vt (pt **extolled**) louer, chanter les louanges de.

**extort** /ɪkˈstɔːt/ vt extorquer (from à). **extortion** n (Jur) extorsion f. **extortionate** adj exorbitant.

**extra** /ˈekstrə/ adj supplémentaire; ~ charge supplément m; ~ time (football) prolongation f. ● **strong** extrafort. ● adv encore; plus. ● n supplément m; (cinema) figurant/-e m/f.

**extract¹** /ɪkˈstrækt/ vt sortir (from de); (tooth) extraire; (promise) arracher.

**extract²** /ˈekstrækt/ n extrait m.

**extra-curricular** /ekstrəkəˈrɪkjʊlə(r)/ adj parascolaire.

**extradite** /ˈekstrədaɪt/ vt extrader.

**extramarital** /ekstrəˈmærɪtl/ adj extraconjugal.

**extramural** /ekstrəˈmjʊərəl/ adj (Univ) hors faculté.

**extraordinary** /ɪkˈstrɔːdnrɪ/ adj extraordinaire.

**extravagance** /ɪkˈstrævəgəns/ n prodigalité f. **extravagant** adj (person) dépensier; (claim) extravagant.

**extreme** /ɪkˈstriːm/ adj & n extrême (m). **extremely** adv extrêmement. **extremist** n extrémiste mf. **extremity** n extrémité f.

**extricate** /ˈekstrɪkeɪt/ vt dégager.

**extrovert** /ˈekstrəvɜːt/ n extraverti/-e m/f.

**exuberance** /ɪgˈzjuːbərəns/ n exubérance f.

**exude** /ɪgˈzjuːd/ vt (charm) respirer; (smell) exhaler.

**eye** /aɪ/ n œil m (pl yeux); keep an ~ on surveiller. ● vt (pt **eyed**; pres p **eyeing**) regarder. **~ball** n globe m oculaire. **~brow** n sourcil m. **~-catching** adj attrayant. **~lash** n cil m. **~lid** n paupière f. **~-opener** n révélation f. **~-shadow** n ombre f à paupières. **~sight** n vue f. **~sore** n horreur f. **~witness** n témoin m oculaire.

# Ff

**fable** /ˈfeɪbl/ n fable f.

**fabric** /ˈfæbrɪk/ n (cloth) tissu m.

**fabulous** /ˈfæbjʊləs/ adj fabuleux; (marvellous 🗓) formidable.

**face** /feɪs/ n visage m, figure f; (expression) air m; (appearance, dignity) face f; (of clock) cadran m; (Geol) face f; (of rock) paroi f; in the ~ of face à; make a (funny) ~ faire la grimace; ~ to ~ face à face. ● vt être en face de; (risk) devoir affronter; (confront) faire face à; (situation) I can't ~ him je n'ai pas le courage de le voir. ● vi (person) regarder; (chair) être tourné vers; (window) donner sur; ~ up to faire face à; **~d with** face à.

**facelift** /'feıslıft/ n lifting m; give a ~ to donner un coup de neuf à.

**face value** n valeur f nominale; take sth at~ prendre qch au pied de la lettre.

**facial** /'feıʃl/ adj (hair) du visage; (injury) au visage. ● n soin m du visage.

**facility** /fə'sılətı/ n (building) complexe m; (feature) fonction f; facilities (equipment) équipements mpl.

**facsimile** /fæk'sımılı/ n facsimilé m.

**fact** /fækt/ n fait m; as a matter of ~, in ~ en fait; know for a ~ that savoir de source sûre que; owing/due to the ~ that étant donné que.

**factor** /'fæktə(r)/ n facteur m.

**factory** /'fæktərı/ n usine f.

**factual** /'fæktʃʊəl/ adj (account, description) basé sur les faits; (evidence) factuel.

**faculty** /'fæklti/ n faculté f.

**fade** /feıd/ vi (sound) s'affaiblir; (memory) s'effacer; (flower) se faner; (material) se décolorer; (colour) passer.

**fail** /feıl/ vi échouer; (grow weak) (s'af)faiblir; (run short) manquer; (engine) tomber en panne. ● vt (exam) échouer à; ~ to (not do) ne pas faire; (not be able) ne pas réussir à faire; **without ~** à coup sûr.

**failing** /'feılıŋ/ n défaut m; ~ that/ this sinon.

**failure** /'feıljə(r)/ n échec m; (person) raté/-e m/f; (breakdown) panne f; ~ to do (inability) incapacité f de faire.

**faint** /feınt/ adj léger, faible; feel ~ (ill) se sentir mal; I haven't the ~est idea je n'en ai pas la moindre

idée. ● vi s'évanouir. ● n évanouissement m; ~-hearted adj timide.

**fair** /feə(r)/ n foire f. ● adj (hair) blond; (skin) clair; (weather) beau; (amount) raisonnable; (just) juste, équitable. ● adv (play) loyalement. ~ **trade** commerce m équitable.

**fairground** n champ m de foire.

**fairly** /'feəlı/ adv (justly) équitablement; (rather) assez.

**fairness** /'feənıs/ n justice f.

**fairy** /'feərı/ n fée f. ~ **story**, ~-**tale** n conte m de fées.

**faith** /feıθ/ n (belief) foi f; (confidence) confiance f.

**faithful** /'feıθfl/ adj fidèle.

**fake** /feık/ n (forgery) faux m; (person) imposteur m; **it is a** ~ c'est un faux. ● adj faux, fausse. ● vt (signature) contrefaire; (results) falsifier; (illness) feindre.

**falcon** /'fɔːlkən/ n faucon m.

**fall** /fɔːl/ vi (pt fell; pp fallen) tomber; ~ **short** être insuffisant. ● n chute f; (autumn: US) automne m; Niagara F~s chutes fpl du Niagara. □ ~ **back on** se rabattre sur. ~ **behind** prendre du retard. ~ **down** or **off** tomber. ~ **for** (person 🗓) tomber amoureux de; (a trick 🗓) se laisser prendre à. ~ **in** (Mil) se mettre en rangs. ~ **off** (decrease) diminuer. ~ **out** se brouiller (with avec). ~ **over** tomber (par terre). ~ **through** (plans) tomber à l'eau.

**fallacy** /'fæləsı/ n erreur f.

**false** /fɔːls/ adj faux. ~ **teeth** npl dentier m.

**falter** /'fɔːltə(r)/ vi (courage) faiblir; (when speaking) bafouiller 🗓.

**fame** /feım/ n renommée f; **famed** adj célèbre (for pour).

**familiar** /fə'mılıə(r)/ adj familier; **be** ~ **with** connaître.

**family** /'fæməlɪ/ n famille f.

**famine** /'fæmɪn/ n famine f.

**famished** /'fæmɪʃt/ adj affamé.

**famous** /'feɪməs/ adj célèbre (for pour).

**fan** /fæn/ n (mechanical) ventilateur m; (hand-held) éventail m; (of person) fan m f◻; admirateur/-trice m/f; (enthusiast) fervent/-e m/f, passionné/-e m/f. ● vt (pt **fanned**) (face) éventer; (fig) attiser. ● vi ~ out se déployer en éventail.

**fanatic** /fə'nætɪk/ n fanatique mf.

**fan belt** n courroie f de ventilateur.

**fancy** /'fænsɪ/ n (whim, fantasy) fantaisie f; take a ~to sb se prendre d'affection pour qn; it took my ~ ça m'a plu. ● adj (buttons etc.) fantaisie inv; (prices) extravagant; (impressive) impressionnant. ● vt s'imaginer; (want ◻) avoir envie de; (like ◻) aimer. ~ **dress** n déguisement m.

**fang** /fæŋ/ n (of dog) croc m; (of snake) crochet m.

**fantasize** /'fæntəsaɪz/ vi fantasmer.

**fantastic** /fæn'tæstɪk/ adj fantastique.

**fantasy** /'fæntəsɪ/ n fantaisie f; (daydream) fantasme m.

**fanzine** /'fænziːn/ n magazine n des fans, fanzine m.

**FAQ** abbr (**Frequently Asked Questions**) (Internet) FAQ f, foire f aux questions.

**far** /fɑː(r)/ adv loin; (much) beaucoup; (very) très; ~ **away**, ~ **off** au loin; as ~ as (up to) jusqu'à; as ~ as I know autant que je sache; by ~ de loin; ~ **from** loin de. ● adj lointain; (end, side) autre. ~**away** adj lointain.

**farce** /fɑːs/ n farce f.

**fare** /feə(r)/ n (prix du) billet m;

(food) nourriture f. ● vi (progress) aller; (manage) se débrouiller.

**Far East** n Extrême-Orient m.

**farewell** /feə'wel/ interj & n adieu m.

**farm** /fɑːm/ n ferme f. ● vt cultiver; ~ **out** céder en sous-traitance. ● vi être fermier. **farmer** n fermier m. ~**house** n ferme f. **farming** n agriculture f. ~**yard** n basse-cour f.

**fart** /fɑːt/ ◻ vi péter ◻. ● n pet m ◻.

**farther** /'fɑːðə(r)/ adv plus loin. ● adj plus éloigné.

**farthest** /'fɑːðɪst/ adv le plus loin. ● adj le plus éloigné.

**fascinate** /'fæsɪneɪt/ vt fasciner.

**Fascism** /'fæʃɪzəm/ n fascisme m.

**fashion** /'fæʃn/ n (current style) mode f; (manner) façon f; in ~ à la mode; out of ~ démodé. ● vt façonner. **fashionable** adj à la mode.

**fast** /fɑːst/ adj rapide; (colour) grand teint inv; (firm) fixe, solide; be ~ (of a clock) avancer. ● adv vite; (firmly) ferme; be ~ **asleep** dormir d'un sommeil profond. ● vi jeûner. ● n jeûne m.

**fasten** /'fɑːsn/ vt/i (s')attacher. **fastener, fastening** n attache f, fermeture f.

**fast food** n fast-food m, restauration f rapide.

**fat** /fæt/ n graisse f; (on meat) gras m. ● adj (**fatter, fattest**) gros, gros; (meat) gras; (profit) gros; a ~ **lot** ◻ bien peu (of de).

**fatal** /'feɪtl/ adj mortel; (fateful, disastrous) fatal. **fatality** n mort m. **fatally** adv mortellement.

**fate** /feɪt/ n sort m. **fateful** adj fatidique.

**father** /'fɑːðə(r)/ n père m. ~**hood** n paternité f. ~**-in-law** n (pl ~**s-inlaw**) beau-père m.

**fathom** /'fæðəm/ n brasse f (= 1.8 m). ● vt ~(out) comprendre.

**fatigue** /fə'ti:g/ n épuisement m; (Tech) fatigue f. ● vt fatiguer.

**fatten** /'fætn/ vt/i engraisser. **fattening** adj qui fait grossir.

**fatty** /'fætɪ/ adj (food) gras; (tissue) adipeux.

**faucet** /'fɔ:sɪt/ n (US) robinet m.

**fault** /fɔ:lt/ n (defect, failing) défaut m; (blame) faute f; (Geol) faille f; at ~ fautif; find ~ with critiquer. ● vt ~ sth/sb prendre en défaut qn/qch. **faulty** adj défectueux.

**favour**, (US) **favor** /'feɪvə(r)/ n faveur f; do sb a ~ rendre service à qn; in ~ of pour. ● vt favoriser; (support) être en faveur de; (prefer) préférer. **favourable** adj favorable.

**favourite** /'feɪvərɪt/ adj & n favori/-te (m/f).

**fawn** /fɔ:n/ n (animal) faon m; (colour) beige m foncé. ● vi ~ on flagorner.

**fax** /fæks/ n fax m, télécopie f. ● vt faxer, envoyer par télécopie. ~ **machine** n fax m, télécopieur m; (for public use) Publifax® m.

**FBI** abbr (**Federal Bureau of Investigation**) (US) Police f judiciaire fédérale.

**fear** /fɪə(r)/ n crainte f, peur f; (fig) risque m; for ~ of/that de peur de/que. ● vt craindre.

**feasible** /'fi:zəbl/ adj faisable; (likely) plausible.

**feast** /fi:st/ n festin m; (Relig) fête f. ● vi festoyer. ● vt régaler (on de).

**feat** /fi:t/ n exploit m.

**feather** /'feðə(r)/ n plume f. ● vt ~ one's nest s'enrichir.

**feature** /'fi:tʃə(r)/ n caractéristique f; (of person, face) trait m; (film) long métrage m; (article) article m de fond. ● vt (advert) représenter;

(give prominence to) mettre en vedette. ● vi figurer (**in** dans).

**February** /'februərɪ/ n février m.

**fed** /fed/ ➡**FEED**. ● adj be ~ **up** ⊞ en avoir marre ⊞ (**with** de).

**federal** /'fedərəl/ adj fédéral.

**fee** /fi:/ n (for entrance) prix m; ~(**s**) (of doctor) honoraires mpl; (of actor, artist) cachet m; (for tuition) frais mpl; (for enrolment) droits mpl.

**feeble** /'fi:bl/ adj faible.

**feed** /fi:d/ vt (pt fed) nourrir, donner à manger à; (suckle) allaiter; (supply) alimenter. ● vi se nourrir (**on** de). ~ **in information** rentrer des données. ● n nourriture f; (of baby) tétée f.

**feedback** /'fi:dbæk/ n réaction (s f) pl; (Med, Tech) feed-back m.

**feel** /fi:l/ vt (pt felt) (touch) tâter; (be conscious of) sentir; (emotion) ressentir; (experience) éprouver; (think) estimer. ● vi (tired, lonely) se sentir; ~ **hot/thirsty** avoir chaud/ soif; ~ **as if** avoir l'impression que; ~ **awful** (ill) se sentir malade; ~ **like** (want ⊞) avoir envie de.

**feeler** /'fi:lə(r)/ n antenne f; **put** out ~ **s** tâter le terrain.

**feeling** /'fi:lɪŋ/ n (emotion) sentiment m; (physical) sensation f; (impression) impression f.

**feet** /fi:t/ ➡**FOOT.**

**feign** /feɪn/ vt feindre.

**fell** /fel/ ➡**FALL.** ● vt (cut down) abattre.

**fellow** /'feləʊ/ n compagnon m, camarade m; (of society) membre m; (man ⊞) type m ⊞.

~**-countryman** n compatriote m.
~**-passenger** n compagnon m de voyage.

**fellowship** /'feləʊʃɪp/ n camaraderie f; (group) association f.

**felony** /'felənɪ/ n crime m.

**felt** /felt/ ➤FEEL. • n feutre m. ~-**tip** n feutre m.

**female** /'fiːmeɪl/ adj (animal) femelle; (voice, sex) féminin. • n femme f; (animal) femelle f.

**feminine** /'femənɪn/ adj & n féminin (m). **femininity** n féminité f.

**feminist** n féministe mf.

**fence** /fens/ n barrière f; **sit on the** ~ ne pas prendre position. • vt (in) clôturer. • vi (Sport) faire de l'escrime. **fencing** n escrime f.

**fend** /fend/ vi ~ **for oneself** se débrouiller tout seul. • vt ~ **off** (blow, attack) parer.

**fender** /'fendə(r)/ n (for fireplace) garde-cendre m; (mudguard: US) garde-boue m inv.

**ferment¹** /'fɜːment/ n ferment m; (excitement: fig) agitation f.

**ferment²** /fə'ment/ vt/i (faire) fermenter.

**fern** /fɜːn/ n fougère f.

**ferocious** /fə'rəʊʃəs/ adj féroce.

**ferret** /'ferɪt/ n (animal) furet m. • vi ~ **about** fureter. • vt ~ **out** dénicher.

**ferry** /'ferɪ/ n (long-distance) ferry m; (short-distance) bac m. • vt transporter.

**fertile** /'fɜːtaɪl/ adj fertile; (person, animal) fécond. **fertilizer** n engrais m.

**festival** /'festɪvl/ n festival m; (Relig) fête f.

**festive** /'festɪv/ adj de fête, gai; ~ **season** période f des fêtes. **festivity** n réjouissances fpl.

**fetch** /fetʃ/ vt (go for) aller chercher; (bring person) amener; (bring thing) apporter; (be sold for) rapporter.

**fête** /feɪt/ n fête f; (church) kermesse f. • vt fêter.

**fetish** /'fetɪʃ/ n (object) fétiche m;

(Psych) obsession f.

**feud** /fjuːd/ n querelle f.

**fever** /'fiːvə(r)/ n fièvre f. **feverish** adj fiévreux.

**few** /fjuː/ det peu de; a ~ **houses** quelques maisons; quite a ~ **people** un bon nombre de personnes. • pron quelques-uns/quelques-unes.

**fewer** /'fjuːə(r)/ det moins de; be ~ être moins nombreux (than que). **fewest** det le moins de.

**fiancé** /fɪ'ɒseɪ/ n fiancé m. **fiancée** n fiancée f.

**fibre**, (US) **fiber** /'faɪbə(r)/ n fibre f. ~**glass** n fibre f de verre.

**fiction** /'fɪkʃn/ n fiction f; (works of) ~ romans mpl. **fictional** adj fictif.

**fiddle** /'fɪdl/ n ① violon m; (swindle ①) combine f. • vi ① frauder. • vt ① falsifier; ~ **with** ① tripoter ①.

**fidget** /'fɪdʒɪt/ vi gigoter sans cesse.

**field** /fiːld/ n champ m; (Sport) terrain m; (fig) domaine m. • vt (ball: cricket) bloquer.

**fierce** /fɪəs/ adj féroce; (storm, attack) violent.

**fiery** /'faɪərɪ/ adj (-ier, -iest) (hot) ardent; (spirited) fougueux.

**fifteen** /fɪf'tiːn/ adj & n quinze (m).

**fifth** /fɪfθ/ adj & n cinquième (mf).

**fifty** /'fɪftɪ/ adj & n cinquante (m).

**fig** /fɪg/ n figue f.

**fight** /faɪt/ vi (pt fought) se battre; (struggle: fig) lutter; (quarrel) se disputer. • vt se battre avec; (evil: fig) lutter contre. • n (struggle) lutte f; (quarrel) dispute f; (brawl) bagarre f; (Mil) combat m. □ ~ **back** se défendre (against contre). ~**off** surmonter. ~**over** se disputer qch. **fighter** n (determined person) lutteur/-euse m/f; (plane) avion m de chasse. **fighting** n combats mpl.

**figment** /'fɪgmənt/ n a ~ of the imagination un produit de l'imagination.

**figure** /'fɪgə(r)/ n (number) chiffre m; (diagram) figure f; (shape) forme f; (body) ligne f; ~s arithmétique f. ● vt s'imaginer. ● vi (appear) figurer; that ~s (US, ①) c'est logique; ~ out comprendre; ~ of speech n façon f de parler.

**file** /faɪl/ n (tool) lime f; dossier m, classeur m; (Comput) fichier m; (row) file f. ● vt limer; ( papers) classer; (Jur) déposer. □ ~ in entrer en file. ~ past défiler devant.

**filing cabinet** n classeur m.

**fill** /fɪl/ vt/i (se) remplir. ● n have had one's ~ en avoir assez. □ ~ in ( form) remplir. ~ out prendre du poids. ~ up (Auto) faire le plein (de carburant); (bath, theatre) (se) remplir.

**fillet** /'fɪlɪt/ n filet m. ● vt découper en filets.

**filling** /'fɪlɪŋ/ n (of tooth) plombage m; (of sandwich) garniture f. ~ **station** n station-service f.

**film** /fɪlm/ n film m; (Photo) pellicule f. ● vt filmer. ~-goer n cinéphile mf. ~star n vedette f de cinéma.

**filter** /'fɪltə(r)/ n filtre m; (traffic signal) flèche f. ● vt/i filtrer; (of traffic) suivre la flèche. ~ coffee n café m filtre.

**filth** /fɪlθ/ n crasse f. **filthy** adj crasseux.

**fin** /fɪn/ n (of fish, seal) nageoire f; (of shark) aileron m.

**final** /'faɪnl/ adj dernier; (conclusive) définitif. ● n (Sport) finale f.

**finale** /fɪ'nɑːlɪ/ n (Mus) finale m.

**finalize** /'faɪnəlaɪz/ vt mettre au point, fixer.

**finally** /'faɪnəlɪ/ adv (lastly, at last) enfin, finalement; (once and for all) définitivement.

**finance** /'faɪnæns/ n finance f. ● adj financier. ● vt financer. **financial** adj financier.

**find** /faɪnd/ vt ( pt found) trouver; (sth lost) retrouver. ● n trouvaille f; ~ out découvrir; vi se renseigner (about sur). **findings** npl conclusions fpl.

**fine** /faɪn/ adj fin; (excellent) beau; ~ arts beaux-arts mpl. ● n amende f. ● vt condamner à une amende.

**finger** /'fɪŋgə(r)/ n doigt m. ● vt palper. ~**nail** n ongle m. ~**print** n empreinte f digitale. ~**tip** n bout m du doigt.

**finish** /'fɪnɪʃ/ vt/i finir; ~ doing finir de faire; ~ up doing finir par faire; ~ up se retrouver à. ● n fin f; (of race) arrivée f; (appearance) finition f.

**finite** /'faɪnaɪt/ adj fini.

**Finland** /'fɪnlənd/ n Finlande f. **Finn** n Finlandais/-e mf.

**Finnish** /'fɪnɪʃ/ adj finlandais. ● n (Ling) finnois m.

**fir** /fɜː(r)/ n sapin m.

**fire** /'faɪə(r)/ n (element) feu m; (blaze) incendie m; (heater) radiateur m; **set** ~ **to** mettre le feu à. ● vt (bullet) tirer; (dismiss) renvoyer; (fig) enflammer. ● vi tirer (at sur). ~ **a gun** tirer un coup de revolver/de fusil. ~ **alarm** n alarme f incendie. ~**arm** n arme f à feu. ~ **brigade** n pompiers mpl. ~ **engine** n voiture f de pompiers. ~ **escape** n escalier m de secours. ~ **extinguisher** n extincteur m. ~ **man** n ( pl -**men**) pompier m. ~**place** n cheminée f. ~ **station** n caserne f de pompiers. ~**wall** n mur m coupe-feu; (Internet) pare-feu m inv. ~**wood** n bois m de chauffage.

∼**work** n feu m d'artifice.

**firing squad** n peloton m d'exécution.

**firm** /fɜːm/ n entreprise f, société f. ● adj ferme; (belief) solide.

**first** /fɜːst/ adj premier; at ∼ hand de première main; at ∼ sight à première vue; ∼ of all tout d'abord. ● n premier/-ière m/f. ● adv d'abord, premièrement; (arrive) le premier, la première; at ∼ d'abord. ∼ **aid** n premiers soins mpl. ∼-**class** adj de première classe. ∼ **floor** n premier étage m; (US) rez-de-chaussée m inv. ∼ **gear** n première (vitesse) f. ∼ **Lady** n (US) épouse f du Président.

**firstly** /ˈfɜːstlɪ/ adv premièrement.

**first name** n prénom m.

**fish** /fɪʃ/ n poisson m; ∼ **shop** poissonnerie f. ● vi pêcher; ∼ **for** (cod) pêcher; ∼ **out** (from water) repêcher; (take out 🆃) sortir. **fisherman** n (pl -**men**) n pêcheur m.

**fishing** /ˈfɪʃɪŋ/ n pêche f; go ∼ aller à la pêche. ∼ **rod** n canne f à pêche.

**fishmonger** /ˈfɪʃmʌŋgə(r)/ n poissonnier/-ière m/f.

**fist** /fɪst/ n poing m.

**fit** /fɪt/ n accès m, crise f; be a good ∼ (dress) être à la bonne taille. ● adj (**fitter, fittest**) en bonne santé; (proper) convenable; (good enough) bon; (able) capable; in no ∼ **state to do** pas en état de faire. ● vt/i (pt **fitted**) (into space) aller; (install) poser. ∼ **in** vt caser; vi (newcomer) s'intégrer. ∼ **out**, ∼ **up** équiper.

**fitness** /ˈfɪtnɪs/ n forme f; (of remark) justesse f.

**fitted** /ˈfɪtɪd/ adj (wardrobe) encastré. ∼ **carpet** n moquette f.

**fitting** /ˈfɪtɪŋ/ adj approprié. ● n essayage m. ∼ **room** n cabine f d'essayage.

**five** /faɪv/ adj & n cinq (m).

**fix** /fɪks/ vt (make firm, attach, decide) fixer; (mend) réparer; (deal with) arranger; ∼ **sb up with sth** trouver qch à qn.

**fixture** /ˈfɪkstʃə(r)/ n (Sport) match m; ∼**s** (in house) installations fpl.

**fizz** /fɪz/ vi pétiller. ● n pétillement m. **fizzy** adj gazeux.

**flabbergast** /ˈflæbəgɑːst/ vt sidérer.

**flabby** /ˈflæbɪ/ adj flasque.

**flag** /flæg/ n drapeau m; (Naut) pavillon m. ● vt (pt **flagged**) ∼ (**down**) faire signe de s'arrêter à. ● vi (weaken) faiblir; (sick person) s'affaiblir. ∼**pole** n mât m. ∼**stone** n dalle f.

**flake** /fleɪk/ n flocon m; (of paint, metal) écaille f. ● vi s'écailler.

**flamboyant** /flæmˈbɔɪənt/ adj (colour) éclatant; (manner) extravagant.

**flame** /fleɪm/ n flamme f; burst into ∼s exploser; go up in ∼s brûler. ● vi flamber.

**flamingo** /fləˈmɪŋgəʊ/ n flamant m (rose).

**flammable** /ˈflæməbl/ adj inflammable.

**flan** /flæn/ n tarte f; (custard tart) flan m.

**flank** /flæŋk/ n flanc m. ● vt flanquer.

**flannel** /ˈflænl/ n (material) flannelle f; (for face) gant m de toilette.

**flap** /flæp/ vi (pt **flapped**) battre. ● vt ∼ **its wings** battre des ailes. ● n (of pocket) rabat m; (of table) abattant m.

**flare** /fleə(r)/ vi ∼ **up** (fighting) éclater. ● n flamboiement m; (Mil) fusée f éclairante; (in skirt) évasement m. **flared** adj évasé.

**flash** /flæʃ/ vi briller; (on and off) clignoter; ~ **past** passer à toute vitesse. ● vt faire briller; (aim torch) diriger (at sur); (flaunt) étaler; ~ **one's headlights** faire un appel de phares. ● n (of news, camera) flash m; **in a** ~ en un éclair. ~**back** n retour m en arrière. ~**light** n lampe f de poche.

**flask** /flɑːsk/ n (for chemicals) flacon m; (for drinks) thermos® m or f inv.

**flat** /flæt/ adj (**flatter, flattest**) plat; (tyre) à plat; (refusal) catégorique. ● (fare, rate) fixe. ● adv (say) carrément. ● n (rooms) appartement m; (tyre 𝄫) crevaison f; (Mus) bémol m.

**flat out** adv (drive) à toute vitesse; (work) d'arrache-pied.

**flatten** /ˈflætn/ vt/i (s')aplatir.

**flatter** /ˈflætə(r)/ vt flatter.

**flaunt** /flɔːnt/ vt étaler, afficher.

**flavour**, (US) **flavor** /ˈfleɪvə(r)/ n goût m; (of ice-cream) parfum m. ● vt parfumer (with à), assaisonner (with de). **flavouring** n arôme m artificiel.

**flaw** /flɔː/ n défaut m.

**flea** /fliː/ n puce f. ~ **market** n marché m aux puces.

**fleck** /flek/ n petite tache f.

**fled** /fled/ ⇒FLEE.

**flee** /fliː/ vt/i (pt **fled**) fuir.

**fleece** /fliːs/ n toison f; (garment) polaire f. ● vt plumer.

**fleet** /fliːt/ n (Naut, Aviat) flotte f; **a** ~ **of vehicles** (in reserve) parc m; (on road) convoi m.

**fleeting** /ˈfliːtɪŋ/ adj très bref.

**Flemish** /ˈflemɪʃ/ adj flamand. ● n (Ling) flamand m.

**flesh** /fleʃ/ n chair f; **one's (own)**

~ **and blood** la chair de sa chair.

**flew** /fluː/ ⇒FLY.

**flex** /fleks/ vt (knee) fléchir; (muscle) faire jouer. ● n (Electr) fil m.

**flexible** /ˈfleksəbl/ adj flexible.

**flexitime** /ˈfleksɪtaɪm/ n horaire m variable.

**flick** /flɪk/ n petit coup m. ● vt donner un petit coup à; ~ **through** feuilleter.

**flight** /flaɪt/ n (of bird, plane) vol m; ~ **of stairs** escalier m; (fleeing) fuite f; **take** ~ prendre la fuite. ~**deck** n poste m de pilotage.

**flimsy** /ˈflɪmzɪ/ adj (**-ier, -iest**) (pej) mince, peu solide.

**flinch** /flɪntʃ/ vi (wince) broncher; (draw back) reculer.

**fling** /flɪŋ/ vt (pt **flung**) jeter.

**flint** /flɪnt/ n (rock) silex m.

**flip** /flɪp/ vt (pt **flipped**) donner un petit coup à; ~ **through** feuilleter. ● n chiquenaude f.

**flippant** /ˈflɪpənt/ adj désinvolte.

**flipper** /ˈflɪpə(r)/ n (of seal) nageoire f; (of swimmer) palme f.

**flirt** /flɜːt/ vi flirter. ● n flirteur/-euse m/f.

**float** /fləʊt/ vt/i (faire) flotter. ● n flotteur m; (cart) char m.

**flock** /flɒk/ n (of sheep) troupeau m; (of people) foule f. ● vi affluer.

**flog** /flɒg/ vt (pt **flogged**) (beat) fouetter; (sell 𝄫) vendre.

**flood** /flʌd/ n inondation f; (fig) flot m. ● vt inonder. ● vi (building) être inondé; (river) déborder; (people: fig) affluer.

**floodlight** /ˈflʌdlaɪt/ n projecteur m. ● vt (pt **floodlit**) illuminer.

**floor** /flɔː(r)/ n sol m, plancher m; (for dancing) piste f; (storey) étage m. ● vt (knock down) terrasser; (baffle) stupéfier. ~**board** n planche f

**flop** /flɒp/ vi (pt **flopped**) (drop) s'affaler; (fail 🄵) échouer; (head) tomber. ● n 🄵 échec m, fiasco m.

**floppy** /'flɒpɪ/ adj lâche, flasque. ~ **(disk)** n disquette f.

**florist** /'flɒrɪst/ n fleuriste mf.

**flounder** /'flaʊndə(r)/ vi (animal, person) se débattre (in dans); (economy) stagner. ● n flet m; (US) poisson m plat.

**flour** /'flaʊə(r)/ n farine f.

**flourish** /'flʌrɪʃ/ vi prospérer. ● vt brandir. ● n geste m élégant.

**flout** /flaʊt/ vt se moquer de.

**flow** /fləʊ/ vi (circulate) circuler; (traffic) s'écouler; (hang loosely) flotter; ~ in affluer; ~ into (of river) se jeter dans. ● n (of liquid, traffic) écoulement m; (of tide) flux m; (of orders, words: fig) flot m. ~ **chart** n organigramme m.

**flower** /'flaʊə(r)/ n fleur f. ● vi fleurir.

**flown** /fləʊn/ ⇒FLY.

**flu** /fluː/ n grippe f.

**fluctuate** /'flʌktjʊeɪt/ vi varier.

**fluent** /'fluːənt/ adj (style) aisé; be ~ (in a language) parler (une langue) couramment.

**fluff** /flʌf/ n peluche(s) f(pl). (down) duvet m.

**fluid** /'fluːɪd/ adj & n fluide (m).

**fluke** /fluːk/ n coup m de chance.

**flung** /flʌŋ/ ⇒FLING.

**fluoride** /'flɔːraɪd/ n fluor m.

**flush** /flʌʃ/ vi rougir. ● vt nettoyer à grande eau; ~ **the toilet** tirer la chasse d'eau. ● n (blush) rougeur f; (fig) excitation f. ● adj ~ **with** (level with) au ras de. □ ~ **out** chasser.

**fluster** /'flʌstə(r)/ vt énerver.

**flute** /fluːt/ n flûte f.

**flutter** /'flʌtə(r)/ vi voleter; (of wings) battre. ● n (wings) batte-

ment m; (fig) agitation f; (bet 🄵) pari m.

**flux** /flʌks/ n changement m continuel.

**fly** /flaɪ/ n mouche f; (of trousers) braguette f. ● vi (pt **flew**; pp **flown**) voler; (passengers) voyager en avion; (flag) flotter; (rush) filer. ● vt (aircraft) piloter; (passengers, goods) transporter par avion; (flag) arborer. □ ~ **off** s'envoler.

**flyer** /'flaɪə(r)/ n (person) aviateur m; (circular) prospectus m.

**flying** /'flaɪɪŋ/ adj (saucer) volant; **with** ~ **colours** haut la main; ~ **start** excellent départ m; ~ **visit** f éclair (adj inv). ● n (activity) aviation f.

**flyover** /'flaɪəʊvə(r)/ n pont m (routier).

**foal** /fəʊl/ n poulain m.

**foam** /fəʊm/ n écume f, mousse f; ~ **(rubber)** caoutchouc m mousse. ● vi écumer, mousser.

**focus** /'fəʊkəs/ n (pl ~**es** or **-ci**) foyer m; (fig) centre m; **be in/out of** ~ être/ne pas être au point. ● vt/i (faire) converger; (instrument) mettre au point; (with camera) faire la mise au point (on sur); (fig) (se) concentrer. ~ **group** groupe m de discussion.

**fodder** /'fɒdə(r)/ n fourrage m.

**foe** /fəʊ/ n ennemi/-e m/f.

**foetus** /'fiːtəs/ n fœtus m.

**fog** /fɒg/ n brouillard m. ● vt/i (pt **fogged**) (window) (s')embuer.

**foggy** /'fɒgɪ/ adj brumeux; **it is** ~ il fait du brouillard.

**foil** /fɔɪl/ n (tin foil) papier m d'aluminium; (deterrent) repoussoir m. ● vt (thwart) déjouer.

**fold** /fəʊld/ vt/i (paper, clothes) (se) plier; (arms) croiser; (fail) s'effondrer. ● n pli m; (for sheep) parc m à moutons; (Relig) bercail m. **folder** n (file) chemise f; (leaflet) dépliant m. **folding** adj pliant.

**foliage** /'fəʊlɪʤ/ n feuillage m.

**folk** /fəʊk/ n gens mpl; ~s parents mpl. ● adj (dance) folklorique; (music) folk.

**folklore** /'fəʊklɔː(r)/ n folklore m.

**follow** /'fɒləʊ/ vt/i suivre; it ~s that it s'ensuit que; ~ suit en faire autant; ~ up (letter) donner suite à. **follower** n partisan m.

**following** /'fɒləʊɪŋ/ n partisans mpl. ● adj suivant; ~ day lendemain. ● prep à la suite de.

**fond** /fɒnd/ adj (loving) affectueux; (hope) cher; be ~ of aimer.

**fondle** /'fɒndl/ vt caresser.

**fondness** /'fɒndnɪs/ n affection f; (for things) attachement m.

**food** /fuːd/ n nourriture f; French ~ la cuisine française. ● adj alimentaire. ~ processor n robot m (ménager).

**fool** /fuːl/ n idiot/-e m/f. ● vt duper. ● vi ~ around faire l'idiot; **foolish** adj idiot.

**foot** /fʊt/ n (pl **feet**) pied m; (measure) pied m (=30.48 cm); (of stairs, page) bas m; on ~ à pied; on or to one's feet debout; under sb's feet dans les jambes de qn. ● vt (bill) payer.

**foot-and-mouth disease** n fièvre f aphteuse.

**football** /'fʊtbɔːl/ n (ball) ballon m; (game) football m. **footballer** n footballeur m.

**foot**: ~-bridge n passerelle f; ~hold n prise f.

**footing** /'fʊtɪŋ/ n on an equal ~ sur un pied d'égalité; be on a friendly ~ with sb avoir des rapports amicaux avec qn; lose one's ~ perdre pied.

**foot**: ~note n note f (en bas de la page). ~path n (in countryside) sentier m; (in town) chemin m. ~print n empreinte f (de pied). ~step n pas m. ~wear n chaussures fpl.

**for** /fɔː(r)/

● preposition

····▸ pour; ~ me pour moi; music ~ dancing de la musique pour danser; what is it ~? ça sert à quoi?

····▸ (with a time period that is still continuing) depuis; I've been waiting ~ two hours j'attends depuis deux heures; I haven't seen him ~ ten years je ne l'ai pas vu depuis dix ans.

····▸ (with a time period that has ended) pendant; I waited ~ two hours j'ai attendu pendant deux heures.

····▸ (with a future time period) pour; I'm going to Paris ~ six weeks je vais à Paris pour six semaines.

····▸ (with distances) pendant; I drove ~ 50 kilometres j'ai roulé pendant 50 kilomètres.

**forbid** /fə'bɪd/ vt (pt **forbade**. pp **forbidden**) interdire, défendre (sb to do à qn de faire); ~ sb to interdire or défendre qch à qn; you are forbidden to leave il vous est interdit de partir. **forbidding** adj menaçant.

**force** /fɔːs/ n force f; come into ~ entrer en vigueur; the ~s les forces fpl armées. ● vt forcer. ~ into faire entrer de force. □ ~ on imposer à. **forced** adj forcé. ~ **on** imposer à. **forced** adj forcé.

**force-feed** vt (pt **-fed**) (person)

nourrir de force; (animal) gaver.

**forceful** /'fɔːsfl/ adj énergique.

**ford** /fɔːd/ n gué m. ● vt passer à gué.

**forearm** /'fɔːrɑːm/ n avant-bras m inv.

**forecast** /'fɔːkɑːst/ vt (pt forecast) prévoir. ● n weather ~ météo f.

**forecourt** /'fɔːkɔːt/ n (of garage) devant m; (of station) cour f.

**forefinger** /'fɔːfɪŋgə(r)/ n index m.

**forefront** /'fɔːfrʌnt/ n at/in the ~ of à la pointe de.

**foregone** /'fɔːgɒn/ adj it's a ~ conclusion c'est couru d'avance.

**foreground** /'fɔːgraʊnd/ n premier plan m.

**forehead** /'fɒrɪd/ n front m.

**foreign** /'fɒrən/ adj étranger; (trade) extérieur; (travel) à l'étranger. **foreigner** n étranger/-ère m/f.

**foreman** /'fɔːmən/ n (pl -men) contremaître m.

**foremost** /'fɔːməʊst/ adj le plus éminent. ● adv first and ~ tout d'abord.

**forensic** /fə'rensɪk/ adj médico-légal; ~ medicine médecine f légale.

**foresee** /fɔː'siː/ vt (pt -saw, pp -seen) prévoir.

**forest** /'fɒrɪst/ n forêt f. **forestry** n sylviculture f.

**foretaste** /'fɔːteɪst/ n avant-goût m.

**forever** /fə'gevə(r)/ adv toujours.

**foreword** /'fɔːwɜːd/ n avant-propos m inv.

**forfeit** /'fɔːfɪt/ n (penalty) peine f; (in game) gage m. ● vt perdre.

**forgave** /fə'geɪv/ ⇒FORGIVE.

**forge** /fɔːdʒ/ n forge f. ● vt (metal, friendship) forger; (copy) contrefaire, falsifier. ● vi ~ ahead aller de l'a-

vant, avancer. **forger** n faussaire m. **forgery** n faux m, contrefaçon f.

**forget** /fə'get/ vt/i (pt forgot, pp forgotten) oublier; ~ oneself s'oublier. **forgetful** adj distrait. ~-me-not n myosotis m.

**forgive** /fə'gɪv/ vt (pt forgave, pp forgiven) pardonner (sb for sth qch à qn).

**fork** /fɔːk/ n fourchette f; (for digging) fourche f; (in road) bifurcation f. ● vi (road) bifurquer; ~ out ⓣ payer. **forked** adj fourchu. ~-lift truck n chariot m élévateur.

**form** /fɔːm/ n forme f; (document) formulaire m; (School) classe f; on ~ en forme. ● vt/i (se) former.

**formal** /'fɔːml/ adj officiel, en bonne et due forme; (person) compassé, cérémonieux; (dress) de cérémonie; (denial, grammar) formel; (language) soutenu. **formality** n cérémonial m; (requirement) formalité f.

**format** /'fɔːmæt/ n format m. ● vt (pt formatted) (disk) formater.

**former** /'fɔːmə(r)/ adj ancien; (first of two) premier. ● n the ~ celui-là, celle-là. **formerly** adv autrefois.

**formula** /'fɔːmjʊlə/ n (pl -ae or -as) formule f. **formulate** vt formuler.

**fort** /fɔːt/ n (Mil) fort m; to hold the ~ s'occuper de tout.

**forth** /fɔːθ/ adv from this day ~ à partir d'aujourd'hui; and so ~ et ainsi de suite; go back and ~ aller et venir.

**forthcoming** /fɔːθ'kʌmɪŋ/ adj à venir, prochain; (sociable ⓣ) communicatif.

**forthright** /'fɔːθraɪt/ adj direct.

**forthwith** /fɔːθ'wɪθ/ adv sur-le-champ.

**fortnight** /'fɔːtnaɪt/ n quinze jours

mpl, quinzaine f.

**fortnightly** /ˈfɔːtnaɪtlɪ/ adj bimensuel. • adv tous les quinze jours.

**fortunate** /ˈfɔːtʃənət/ adj heureux; be ~ avoir de la chance. **fortunately** adv heureusement.

**fortune** /ˈfɔːtʃuːn/ n fortune f; make a ~ faire fortune; have the good ~ to avoir la chance de. ~-**teller** n diseur/-euse m/f de bonne aventure.

**forty** /ˈfɔːtɪ/ adj & n quarante (m). ~ winks un petit somme.

**forward** /ˈfɔːwəd/ adj en avant; (advanced) précoce; (bold) effronté. • n (Sport) avant m. • adv en avant; come ~ se présenter; go ~ avancer. • vt (letter, e-mail) faire suivre; (goods) expédier; (fig) favoriser. **forwardness** n précocité f. **forwards** adv en avant.

**fossil** /ˈfɒsl/ adj & n fossile m.

**foster** /ˈfɒstə(r)/ vt (promote) encourager; (child) élever. • adj (child, parent) adoptif; (family, home) de placement.

**fought** /fɔːt/ ➡ **FIGHT**.

**foul** /faʊl/ adj (smell, weather) infect; (place, action) immonde; (language) ordurier. • n (football) faute f. • vt souiller, encrasser; ~ up 🔲 gâcher. ~-**mouthed** adj grossier.

**found** /faʊnd/ ➡ **FIND**. • vt fonder. **foundation** n fondation f; (basis) fondement m; (make-up) fond m de teint. **founder** n fondateur/-trice m/f.

**fountain** /ˈfaʊntɪn/ n fontaine f; ~-**pen** n stylo m à encre.

**four** /fɔː(r)/ adj & n quatre (m).

**fourteen** /fɔːˈtiːn/ adj & n quatorze (m).

**fourth** /fɔːθ/ adj & n quatrième (mf).

**four-wheel drive** n (car)

quatre-quatre m.

**fowl** /faʊl/ n (one bird) poulet m; (group) volaille f.

**fox** /fɒks/ n renard m. • vt (baffle) mystifier; (deceive) tromper.

**fraction** /ˈfrækʃn/ n fraction f.

**fracture** /ˈfræktʃə(r)/ n fracture f. • vt/i (se) fracturer.

**fragile** /ˈfrædʒaɪl/ adj fragile.

**fragment** /ˈfrægmənt/ n fragment m.

**fragrance** /ˈfreɪɡrəns/ n parfum m.

**frail** /freɪl/ adj frêle.

**frame** /freɪm/ n (of building, boat) charpente f; (of picture) cadre m; (of window) châssis m; (of spectacles) monture f; ~ **of mind** humeur f. • vt encadrer; (fig) formuler; (Jur, 🔲) monter un coup contre. ~**work** n structure f; (context) cadre m.

**France** /frɑːns/ n France f.

**franchise** /ˈfræntʃaɪz/ n (Pol) droit m de vote; (Comm) franchise f.

**frank** /fræŋk/ adj franc. • vt affranchir. **frankly** adv franchement.

**frantic** /ˈfræntɪk/ adj frénétique. ~ **with** fou de.

**fraternity** /frəˈtɜːnətɪ/ n (bond) fraternité f; (group, club) confrérie f.

**fraud** /frɔːd/ n (deception) fraude f; (person) imposteur m. **fraudulent** adj frauduleux.

**fray** /freɪ/ n the ~ la bataille. • vt/i (s')effilocher.

**freckle** /ˈfrekl/ n tache f de rousseur.

**free** /friː/ adj libre; (gratis) gratuit; (lavish) généreux; ~ (of charge) gratuit(ement); a ~ hand carte f blanche. • vt (pt freed) libérer; (clear) dégager.

**freedom** /ˈfriːdəm/ n liberté f.

**free:** ~ **enterprise** n la libre entre-prise. ~ **kick** n coup m franc. ~**lance** adj & n free-lance (mf), indépendant/-e (m/f).

**freely** /'fri:li/ adv librement.

**Freemason** /'fri:meɪsn/ n franc-maçon m.

**Freenet** /'fri:net/ n (Comput) Li-bertel m.

**free:** ~**phone**, ~ **number** n nu-méro m vert. ~**range** adj (eggs) de ferme.

**Freeware** /'fri:weə(r)/ n (Comput) Gratuiciel m.

**freeway** /'fri:weɪ/ n (US) auto-route f.

**freeze** /fri:z/ vt/i (pt **froze**. pp **frozen**) geler; (Culin) (se) congeler; (wages) bloquer. ●n gel m. blocage m; ~**dried** adj lyophilisé.

**freezer** /'fri:zə(r)/ n congélateur m.

**freezing** /'fri:zɪŋ/ adj glacial; below ~ au-dessous de zéro.

**freight** /freɪt/ n fret m.

**French** /frentʃ/ adj français. ●n (Ling) français m; the ~ les Français mpl; ~ **bean** n haricot m vert; ~ **fries** npl frites fpl; ~**man** n Français m; ~**speaking** adj francophone; ~ **window** n porte-fenêtre f; ~**wo-man** n Française f.

**frenzied** /'frenzɪd/ adj frénétique. **frenzy** n frénésie f.

**frequent**[1] /'fri:kwənt/ adj fréquent.

**frequent**[2] /frɪ'kwent/ vt fré-quenter.

**fresco** /'freskəʊ/ n fresque f.

**fresh** /freʃ/ adj frais; (different, add-itional) nouveau; (cheeky [I]) culotté.

**freshen** /'freʃn/ vi (weather) fraî-chir. ~ **up** (person) se rafraîchir.

**freshly** /'freʃlɪ/ adv nouvellement.

**freshness** /'freʃnɪs/ n fraîcheur f.

**freshwater** /'freʃwɔːtə(r)/ adj d'eau douce.

**friction** /'frɪkʃn/ n friction f.

**Friday** /'fraɪdɪ/ n vendredi m.

**fridge** /frɪdʒ/ n frigo m.

**fried** /fraɪd/ ➡**FRY**. ●adj frit; ~ **eggs** œufs mpl sur le plat.

**friend** /frend/ n ami/-e m/f. **friendly** adj (-ier, -iest) amical, gentil. **friendship** n amitié f.

**frieze** /fri:z/ n frise f.

**fright** /fraɪt/ n peur f; (person, thing) horreur f.

**frighten** /'fraɪtn/ vt effrayer; ~ **off** faire fuir. **frightened** adj effrayé; be ~**ed** avoir peur (of de). **frighten-ing** adj effrayant.

**frill** /frɪl/ n (trimming) fanfreluche f; with no ~s très simple.

**fringe** /frɪndʒ/ n (edging, hair) frange f; (of area) bordure f; (of so-ciety) marge f. ~ **benefits** npl avan-tages mpl sociaux.

**frisk** /frɪsk/ vt (search) fouiller.

**fritter** /'frɪtə(r)/ n beignet m. ●vt ~ **away** gaspiller.

**frivolity** /frɪ'vɒlətɪ/ n frivolité f.

**frizzy** /'frɪzɪ/ adj crépu.

**fro** ➡**TO AND FRO**.

**frog** /frɒg/ n grenouille f; a ~ in one's throat un chat dans la gorge.

**frolic** /'frɒlɪk/ vi (pt **frolicked**) s'é-battre. ●n ébats mpl.

**from** /frɒm/ prep de; (with time, prices) à partir de, de; (habit, con-viction) par; (according to) d'après; take ~ sb prendre à qn; take ~ one's pocket prendre dans sa poche.

**front** /frʌnt/ n (of car, train) avant m; (of garment, building) devant m; (Mil, Pol) front m; (of book, pamph-let) début m; (appearance: fig) facade f. ● adj de devant, avant inv; (first) premier; ~ **door** porte f d'entrée; in ~ (of) devant. **frontage** n façade f.

**frontier** /'frʌntɪə(r)/ n frontière f.

**frost** /frɒst/ n gel m, gelée f; (on glass) givre m. ● vt/i (se) givrer. ~**-bite** n gelure f.

**frosty** /'frɒstɪ/ adj (weather, welcome) glacial; (window) givré.

**froth** /frɒθ/ n (on beer) mousse f; (on water) écume f. ● vi mousser, écumer.

**frown** /fraʊn/ vi froncer les sourcils; ~ **on** désapprouver. ● n froncement m de sourcils.

**froze** /frəʊz/ →FREEZE.

**frozen** /'frəʊzn/ →FREEZE. ● adj congelé.

**fruit** /fruːt/ n fruit m; (collectively) fruits mpl. **fruitful** adj (discussions) fructueux. ~ **machine** n machine f à sous.

**frustrate** /frʌ'streɪt/ vt (plan) faire échouer; (person: Psych) frustrer; (upset 🔢) exaspérer. **frustration** n (Psych) frustration f; (disappointment) déception f.

**fry** /fraɪ/ vt/i (pt **fried**) (faire) frire. **frying-pan** n poêle f (à frire).

**FTP** abbr (**File Transfer Protocol**) (Internet) protocole m FTP.

**fudge** /fʌdʒ/ n caramel m mou. ● vt (issue) esquiver.

**fuel** /'fjuːəl/ n combustible m; (for car engine) carburant m. ● vt (pt **fuelled**) alimenter en combustible.

**fugitive** /'fjuːdʒətɪv/ n & a fugitif/-ive (m/f).

**fulfil** /fʊl'fɪl/ vt (pt **fulfilled**) accomplir, réaliser; (condition) remplir; ~ **oneself** s'épanouir. **fulfilling** adj satisfaisant. **fulfilment** n réalisation f; épanouissement m.

**full** /fʊl/ adj plein (de); (bus,

hotel) complet; (programme) chargé; (skirt) ample; **be** ~ **(up)** n'avoir plus faim; **at** ~ **speed** à toute vitesse. ● n in ~ intégralement; **to the** ~ complètement. ~ **back** n (Sport) arrière m. ~ **moon** n pleine lune f. ~ **name** n nom m et prénom m. ~**-scale** adj (drawing etc.) grandeur nature m; (fig) de grande envergure. ~ **stop** n point m. ~**-time** adj & adv à plein temps.

**fully** /'fʊlɪ/ adv complètement; ~ **fledged** (member, citizen) à part entière.

**fume** /fjuːm/ vi rager. **fumes** npl émanations fpl, vapeurs fpl.

**fun** /fʌn/ n amusement m; **be** ~ être chouette; **for** ~ pour rire; **make** ~ **of** se moquer de.

**function** /'fʌŋkʃn/ n (purpose, duty) fonction f; (event) réception f. ● vi fonctionner.

**fund** /fʌnd/ n fonds m. ● vt fournir les fonds pour.

**fundamental** /fʌndə'mentl/ adj fondamental. **fundamentalist** n intégriste mf.

**funeral** /'fjuːnərəl/ n enterrement m. ● adj funèbre.

**funfair** /'fʌnfeə(r)/ n fête f foraine.

**fungus** /'fʌŋɡəs/ n (pl **-gi**) (plant) champignon m; (mould) moisissure f.

**funnel** /'fʌnl/ n (for pouring) entonnoir m; (of ship) cheminée f.

**funny** /'fʌnɪ/ adj (**-ier, -iest**) drôle; (odd) bizarre.

**fur** /fɜː(r)/ n (for garment) fourrure f; (on animal) poils mpl; (in kettle) tartre m.

**furious** /'fjʊərɪəs/ adj furieux.

**furnace** /'fɜːnɪs/ n fourneau m.

**furnish** /'fɜːnɪʃ/ vt (room) meubler; (supply) fournir. **furnishings** npl ameublement m.

F

**furniture** /ˈfɜːnɪtʃə(r)/ n meubles mpl, mobilier m.

**furry** /ˈfɜːrɪ/ adj (animal) à fourrure; (toy) en peluche.

**further** /ˈfɜːðə(r)/ adj plus éloigné; (additional) supplémentaire. ● adv plus loin; (more) davantage. ● vt avancer. ~ education n formation f continue.

**furthermore** /ˌfɜːðəˈmɔː(r)/ adv en outre, de plus.

**furthest** /ˈfɜːðɪst/ adj le plus éloigné. ● adv le plus loin.

**fury** /ˈfjʊərɪ/ n fureur f.

**fuse** /fjuːz/ vt/i (melt) fondre; (unite: fig) fusionner; ~ the lights faire sauter les plombs. ● n (of plug) fusible m; (of bomb) amorce f.

**fuss** /fʌs/ n (when upset) histoire(s) f(pl); (when excited) agitation f; make a ~ faire des histoires, s'agiter; (about food) faire des chichis; make a ~ of faire grand cas de. ● vi s'agiter. **fussy** /ˈfʌsɪ/ (finicky) tatillon; (hard to please) difficile.

**future** /ˈfjuːtʃə(r)/ adj futur. ● n avenir m; Gram futur m; in ~ à l'avenir.

**fuzzy** /ˈfʌzɪ/ adj (hair) crépu; (photograph) flou; (person 🅸) à l'esprit confus.

# Gg

**Gaelic** /ˈɡeɪlɪk/ n gaélique m.

**gag** /ɡæɡ/ n (on mouth) bâillon m; (joke) blague f. ● vt (pt **gagged**) bâillonner.

**gain** /ɡeɪn/ vt (respect, support) gagner; (speed, weight) prendre. ● vi (of clock) avancer. ● n (increase) augmentation f (in de); (profit) gain m.

**galaxy** /ˈɡæləksɪ/ n galaxie f.

**gale** /ɡeɪl/ n tempête f.

**gallery** /ˈɡælərɪ/ n galerie f; (art) ~ musée m.

**Gallic** /ˈɡælɪk/ adj français.

**gallon** /ˈɡælən/ n gallon m (imperial = 4.546 litres; Amer. = 3.785 litres).

**gallop** /ˈɡæləp/ n galop m. ● vi (pt **galloped**) galoper.

**galore** /ɡəˈlɔː(r)/ adv (prizes, bargains) en abondance; (drinks, sandwiches) à gogo 🅸.

**gamble** /ˈɡæmbl/ vt/i jouer. ~ on miser sur. ● n (venture) entreprise f risquée; (bet) pari m; (risk) risque m. **gambling** n jeu m.

**game** /ɡeɪm/ n jeu m; (football) match m; (tennis) partie f; (animals, birds) gibier m. ● adj (brave) courageux. ~ for prêt à. ~**keeper** n gardechasse m.

**gammon** /ˈɡæmən/ n jambon m.

**gang** /ɡæŋ/ n (of youths) bande f; (of workmen) équipe f. ● vi ~ up se liguer (on, against contre).

**gangmaster** n gangmaster m, chef m d'équipe (d'ouvriers saisonniers).

**gangway** /ˈɡæŋweɪ/ n passage m; (aisle) allée f; (of ship) passerelle f.

**gaol** /dʒeɪl/ n & vt ⇒**JAIL**.

---

🅸 **Gap Year** La prise d'une année sabbatique est une pratique répandue chez les jeunes britanniques avant d'entrer à l'université. Certains trouvent un stage dans une entreprise et en profitent pour mettre de côté de l'argent pour leurs études, mais beaucoup partent travailler ou étudier à l'étranger ou faire le tour du monde.

**gap** /gæp/ n trou m, vide m; (in time) intervalle m; (in education) lacune f; (difference) écart m.

**gape** /geɪp/ vi rester bouche bée. **gaping** adj béant.

**garage** /'gærɑːʒ/ n garage m. ● vt mettre au garage.

**garbage** /'gɑːbɪdʒ/ n (US) ordures fpl.

**garden** /'gɑːdn/ n jardin m. ● vi jardiner. **gardener** n jardinier/-ière m/f. **gardening** n jardinage m.

**gargle** /'gɑːgl/ vi se gargariser.

**garish** /'geərɪʃ/ adj (clothes) tape-à-l'œil.

**garland** /'gɑːlənd/ n guirlande f.

**garlic** /'gɑːlɪk/ n ail m.

**garment** /'gɑːmənt/ n vêtement m.

**garnish** /'gɑːnɪʃ/ vt garnir (with de). ● n garniture f.

**garter** /'gɑːtə(r)/ n jarretière f.

**gas** /gæs/ n (pl -es) gaz m; (Med) anesthésie m; (petrol: US) essence f. ● adj (mask, pipe) à gaz. ● vt asphyxier; (Mil) gazer.

**gash** /gæʃ/ n entaille f. ● vt entailler.

**gasoline** /'gæsəliːn/ n (petrol: US) essence f.

**gasp** /gɑːsp/ vi haleter; (in surprise: fig) avoir le souffle coupé. ● n halètement m.

**gate** /geɪt/ n (in garden, airport) porte f; (of field, level crossing) barrière f. ~**way** n porte f; (Internet) passerelle f.

**gather** /'gæðə(r)/ vt (people, objects) rassembler; (pick up) ramasser; (flowers) cueillir; (fig) comprendre; ~ **speed** prendre de la vitesse; (sewing) froncer. ● vi (people) se rassembler; (pile up) s'accumuler. **gathering** n réunion f.

**gauge** /geɪdʒ/ n jauge f, indicateur m. ● vt (speed, distance) jauger; (reaction, mood) évaluer.

**gaunt** /gɔːnt/ adj décharné.

**gauze** /gɔːz/ n gaze f.

**gave** /geɪv/ ➡GIVE.

**gay** /geɪ/ adj (joyful) gai; (homosexual) gay inv. ● n gay m/f.

**gaze** /geɪz/ vi ~ (at) regarder (fixement). ● n regard m (fixe).

**GB** abbr ➡GREAT BRITAIN.

**gear** /gɪə(r)/ n (equipment) matériel m; (Tech) engrenage m; (Auto) vitesse f; **in** ~ en prise. **out of** ~ au point mort. ● vt **to be geared to** s'adresser à. ~**box** f vitesses. ~**lever**, (US) ~**shift** n levier m de vitesse.

**geese** /giːs/ ➡GOOSE.

**gel** /dʒel/ n (for hair) gel m.

**gem** /dʒem/ n pierre f précieuse.

**Gemini** /'dʒemɪnaɪ/ n Gémeaux mpl.

**gender** /'dʒendə(r)/ n (Ling) genre m; (of person) sexe m.

**gene** /dʒiːn/ n gène m. ~ **library** n génothèque f.

**general** /'dʒenrəl/ adj général. ● n général m; **in** ~ en général.

**general election** n élections fpl législatives.

**generalization** /dʒenrəlaɪˈzeɪʃn/ n généralisation f. **generalize** vt/i généraliser.

**general practitioner** n (Med) généraliste m.

**generate** /'dʒenəreɪt/ vt produire.

**generation** /dʒenəˈreɪʃn/ n génération f.

**generator** /'dʒenəreɪtə(r)/ n (Electr) groupe m électrogène.

**generosity** /dʒenəˈrɒsɪtɪ/ n générosité f. **generous** adj généreux; (plentiful) copieux.

**genetics** /dʒɪˈnetɪks/ n génétique f.

**Geneva** /dʒɪˈniːvə/ n Genève.

**genial** /ˈdʒiːnɪəl/ adj affable, sympathique.

**genitals** /ˈdʒenɪtlz/ npl organes mpl génitaux.

**genius** /ˈdʒiːnɪəs/ n (pl ~es) génie m.

**genome** /ˈdʒiːnəʊm/ n génome m.

**gentle** /ˈdʒentl/ adj (mild, kind) doux; (pressure, breeze) léger; (reminder, hint) discret.

**gentleman** /ˈdʒentlmən/ n (pl -men) (man) monsieur m; (well-bred) gentleman m.

**gently** /ˈdʒentlɪ/ adv doucement.

**gents** /dʒents/ npl (toilets) toilettes fpl; (on sign) 'Messieurs'.

**genuine** /ˈdʒenjʊɪn/ adj (reason, motive) vrai; (jewel, substance) véritable; (person, belief) sincère.

**geography** /dʒɪˈɒɡrəfɪ/ n géographie f.

**geology** /dʒɪˈɒlədʒɪ/ n géologie f.

**geometry** /dʒɪˈɒmɪtrɪ/ n géométrie f.

**geriatric** /dʒerɪˈætrɪk/ adj gériatrique.

**germ** /dʒɜːm/ n (Med) microbe m.

**German** /ˈdʒɜːmən/ n (person) Allemand/-e m/f; (Ling) allemand m. ● adj allemand.

**German measles** n rubéole f.

**Germany** /ˈdʒɜːmənɪ/ n Allemagne f.

**gesture** /ˈdʒestʃə(r)/ n geste m.

**get** /ɡet/

past got; past participle got, gotten (US); present participle getting

● transitive verb

····▸ recevoir. we got a letter

nous avons reçu une lettre.

····▸ (obtain) I got a job in Paris j'ai trouvé un travail à Paris. I'll ~ sth to eat at the airport je mangerai qch à l'aéroport.

····▸ (buy) acheter. ~ sb a present acheter un cadeau à qn.

····▸ (achieve) obtenir. he got it right il a obtenu le bon résultat. ~ good grades avoir de bonnes notes.

····▸ (fetch) chercher. go and ~ a chair va chercher une chaise.

····▸ (transport) prendre. we can ~ the bus on peut prendre le bus.

····▸ (understand 🄸) comprendre. now let me ~ this right alors si je comprends bien...

····▸ (experience) ~ a surprise être surpris. ~ a shock avoir un choc.

····▸ (illness) ~ measles attraper la rougeole. ~ a cold s'enrhumer.

····▸ (ask or persuade) ~ him to call me dis-lui de m'appeler. I'll ~ her to help me je lui demanderai de m'aider.

····▸ (cause to be done) ~ a TV repaired faire réparer une télévision. ~ one's hair cut se faire couper les cheveux.

● intransitive verb

····▸ devenir. he's getting old il vieillit; it's getting late il se fait tard.

····▸ (in passives) ~ married se marier. ~ hurt se blesser.

····▸ (arrive) arriver. ~ to the airport arriver à l'aéroport. □ ~ about (person) se déplacer. ~ along (manage) se

**débrouiller;** (progress) avancer. **~ along with** s'entendre avec. **~ at** (reach) atteindre; (imply) vouloir dire. **~ away** partir; (escape) s'échapper. **~ back** revenir. ● vt récupérer. **~ by** vi (manage) se débrouiller. ● vt (pass) passer. **~ down** vt/i descendre. ● vt (depress) déprimer. **~ in** entrer. **~ into** (car) monter dans; (dress) mettre. **~ off** vt (bus) descendre; (remove) enlever. ● vi (from bus) descendre; (leave) partir; (Jur) être acquitté. **~ on** vi (to bus) monter; (succeed) réussir. ● vt (bus) monter. **~ on with** (person) s'entendre avec; (job) attaquer. **~ out** sortir. **~ out of** (fig) se soustraire. **~ over** (illness) se remettre de. **~ round** (rule) contourner; (person) entortiller. **~ through** vi passer; (on phone) **~ through to sb** avoir qn. ● vt traverser. **~ up** se lever. **~ up to** faire.

**getaway** /'ɡetəweɪ/ n fuite f.

**ghastly** /'ɡɑːstlɪ/ adj (-ier, -iest) affreux.

**gherkin** /'ɡɜːkɪn/ n cornichon m.

**ghetto** /'ɡetəʊ/ n ghetto m.

**ghost** /ɡəʊst/ n fantôme m.

**giant** /'dʒaɪənt/ n & adj géant (m).

**gibberish** /'dʒɪbərɪʃ/ n baragouin m, charabia m.

**giblets** /'dʒɪblɪts/ npl abats mpl.

**giddy** /'ɡɪdɪ/ adj (-ier, -iest) vertigineux. **be** or **feel ~** avoir le vertige.

**gift** /ɡɪft/ n (present) cadeau m; (ability) don m.

**gifted** /'ɡɪftɪd/ adj doué.

**gift wrap** n papier m cadeau.

**gigantic** /dʒaɪˈɡæntɪk/ adj gigantesque.

**giggle** /'ɡɪɡl/ vi ricaner (sottement), glousser. ● n ricanement m; **the ~s** le fou rire.

**gimmick** /'ɡɪmɪk/ n truc m.

**gin** /dʒɪn/ n gin m.

**ginger** /'dʒɪndʒə(r)/ n gingembre m. ● adj (hair) roux. **~ beer** n boisson f gazeuse au gingembre. **~bread** n pain m d'épices.

**gingerly** /'dʒɪndʒəlɪ/ adv avec précaution.

**giraffe** /dʒɪˈrɑːf/ n girafe f.

**girl** /ɡɜːl/ n (child) (petite) fille f; (young woman) (jeune) fille f. **~ band** n girls band m. **~friend** n amie f; (of boy) petite amie f.

**giro** /'dʒaɪrəʊ/ n virement m bancaire; (cheque) mandat m.

**gist** /dʒɪst/ n essentiel m.

**give** /ɡɪv/ vt (pt **gave**; pp **given**) donner; (gesture) faire; (laugh, sigh) pousser; **~ sb sth** donner qch à qn. ● vi donner; (yield) céder; (stretch) se détendre. ● n élasticité f. □ **~ away** donner; (secret) trahir; **~ back** rendre. **~ in** (yield) céder (to à). **~ off** (heat, fumes) dégager; (signal, scent) émettre. **~ out** distribuer. **~ over** (devote) consacrer; (stop 🔢) cesser; **~ up** vt/i (renounce) renoncer (à); (yield) céder. **~ oneself up** se rendre. **~ way** céder; (collapse) s'effondrer.

**given** /'ɡɪvn/ ➡GIVE. ● adj donné. **~ name** n prénom m.

**glad** /ɡlæd/ adj content. **gladly** adv avec plaisir.

**glamorous** /'ɡlæmərəs/ adj séduisant, ensorcelant.

**glamour**, (US) **glamor** /'ɡlæmə(r)/ n enchantement m, séduction f.

g

**glance** /glɑːns/ n coup m d'œil. ● vi ~ at jeter un coup d'œil à.

**gland** /glænd/ n glande f.

**glare** /gleə(r)/ vi briller très fort. ~ at regarder d'un air furieux. ● n (of lights) éclat m (aveuglant); (stare: fig) regard m furieux. **glaring** adj (dazzling) éblouissant; (obvious) flagrant.

**glass** /glɑːs/ n verre m. **glasses** npl (spectacles) lunettes fpl.

**glaze** /gleɪz/ vt (door) vitrer; (pottery) vernisser. ● n vernis m.

**gleam** /gliːm/ n lueur f. ● vi luire.

**glide** /glaɪd/ vi glisser; (of plane) planer. **glider** n planeur m.

**glimpse** /glɪmps/ n (insight) aperçu m; catch a ~ of entrevoir.

**glitter** /ˈglɪtə(r)/ vi scintiller. ● n scintillement m.

**global** /ˈgləʊbl/ adj (world-wide) mondial; (allembracing) global. ~ **warming** n réchauffement m de la planète.

**globalization** /gləʊbəlaɪˈzeɪʃən/ n globalisation f.

**globe** /gləʊbəlaɪˈzeɪʃən/ n globe m.

**gloom** /gluːm/ n obscurité f; (sadness: fig) tristesse f. **gloomy** adj triste; (pessimisty) pessimiste.

**glorious** /ˈglɔːrɪəs/ adj splendide; (deed, hero) glorieux.

**glory** /ˈglɔːrɪ/ n gloire f; (beauty) splendeur f. ● vi ~ in être très fier de.

**gloss** /glɒs/ n lustre m, brillant m. ● adj brillant. ● vi ~ over (make light of) glisser sur; (cover up) dissimuler.

**glossary** /ˈglɒsərɪ/ n glossaire m.

**glossy** /ˈglɒsɪ/ adj brillant.

**glove** /glʌv/ n gant m. ~ **compartment** n (Auto) boîte f à gants.

**glow** /gləʊ/ vi (fire) rougeoyer;

(person, eyes) rayonner. ● n rougeoiement m, éclat m. **glowing** adj (report) enthousiaste.

**glucose** /ˈgluːkəʊs/ n glucose m.

**glue** /gluː/ n colle f ● vt (pres p gluing) coller.

**GM** abbr (genetically modified) transgénique.

**gnaw** /nɔː/ vt/i ronger.

**GNP** abbr (**Gross National Product**) produit m national brut, PNB m.

---

**go** /gəʊ/

present **go**, **goes**; past **went**; past participle **gone**

● intransitive verb

····▸ aller. ~ **to school/town/ market** aller à l'école/en ville/ au marché. ~ **for a swim/ walk** aller nager/se promener.

····▸ (leave) s'en aller. **I must be ~ing** il faut que je m'en aille.

····▸ (vanish) **the money's gone** il n'y a plus d'argent. **my bike's gone** mon vélo n'est plus là.

····▸ (work, function) marcher. **is the car ~ing?** est-ce que la voiture marche?

····▸ (become) devenir. ~ **blind** devenir aveugle. ~ **pale/red** pâlir/rougir.

····▸ (turn out, progress) aller. **how's it going?** comment ça va? **how did the exam ~?** comment s'est passé l'examen?

····▸ (in future tenses) be ~ing **to do** aller faire.

● noun

····▸ (turn) tour m; (try) essai m;

have a ~! essaie!; full of ~ ☐ dynamique.
☐ **go across** traverser. **go after** poursuivre. **go away** partir. ~ away! va-t'en!, allez-vous-en! **go back** retourner. ~ back in rentrer. ~ back to work reprendre le travail. **go down** (quality, price) baisser; (person) descendre; (sun) se coucher. **go in** entrer. **go in for** (exam) se présenter à. **go off** (leave) partir; (bomb) exploser; (alarm clock) sonner; (milk) tourner; (light) s'éteindre. **go on** (continue) continuer; (light) s'allumer; ~ on doing continuer à faire. what's ~ing on? qu'est-ce qui se passe? **go out** sortir; (light, fire) s'éteindre. **go over** vérifier. **go round** (be enough) être assez. ~ round to see sb passer voir qn. **go through** (check) examiner; (search) fouiller; ~ through a difficult time traverser une période difficile. **go together** aller ensemble. **go under** (sink) couler; (fail) échouer. **go up** (person) monter; (price, salary) augmenter. **go without** se passer de.

**go-ahead** /'gəʊəhed/ n feu m vert. ● adj dynamique.

**goal** /gəʊl/ n but m. ~**keeper** n gardien m de but. ~**post** n poteau m de but.

**goat** /gəʊt/ n chèvre f.

**gobble** /'gɒbl/ vt engouffrer.

**go-between** /'gəʊbɪtwiːn/ n intermédiaire mf.

**god** /gɒd/ n dieu m. ~**child** n (pl -children) filleul/-e m/f. ~**daughter** n filleule f.

**goddess** /'gɒdɪs/ n déesse f.

**god:** ~**father** n parrain m.

~**mother** n marraine f. ~**send** n aubaine f. ~**son** n filleul m.

**goggles** /'gɒglz/ npl lunettes fpl (protectrices).

**going** /'gəʊɪŋ/ n it is slow/hard ~ c'est lent/difficile. ● adj (price, rate) actuel.

**go-kart** /'gəʊkɑːt/ n kart m.

**gold** /gəʊld/ n or m. ● adj en or, d'or.

**golden** /'gəʊldən/ adj en or, d'or; (in colour) doré; (opportunity) unique.

**gold:** ~**fish** n poisson m rouge. ~**-plated** adj plaqué or. ~**smith** n orfèvre m.

**golf** /gɒlf/ n golf m. ~**-course** n terrain m de golf.

**gone** /gɒn/ ⇒GO. ● adj parti. ~ six o'clock six heures passées. the butter's all ~ il n'y a plus de beurre.

**good** /gʊd/ adj (**better, best**) bon; (weather) beau; (well-behaved) sage; as ~ as (almost) pratiquement. that's ~ of you c'est gentil (de ta part). be ~ with savoir s'y prendre avec. feel ~ se sentir bien. it is ~ for you ça vous fait du bien. ● n bien m; do ~ faire du bien. is it any ~? est-ce que c'est bon? it's no ~ ça ne vaut rien. it is no ~ shouting ça ne sert à rien de crier. for ~ pour toujours. ~ afternoon interj bonjour. ~bye interj & n au revoir (m inv). ~ evening interj bonsoir. G~ Friday n Vendredi m saint. ~-looking adj beau. ~ morning interj bonjour. ~-natured adj gentil.

**goodness** /'gʊdnɪs/ n bonté f; my ~! mon Dieu!

**goodnight** interj bonsoir, bonne nuit.

**goods** /gʊdz/ npl marchandises fpl.

**goodwill** /gʊd'wɪl/ n bonne volonté f.

**google®** /'gu:gl/vt/i chercher sur (le moteur de recherche) Google®, googler.

**goose** /gu:s/ n (pl **geese**) oie f.
**gooseberry** n groseille f à maquereau. **~-pimples** npl chair f de poule.

**gorge** /gɔ:dʒ/ n (Geog) gorge f. ● vt ~ oneself se gaver (on de).

**gorgeous** /'gɔ:dʒəs/ adj magnifique, splendide, formidable.

**gorilla** /gə'rɪlə/ n gorille m.

**gory** /'gɔ:rɪ/ adj (-ier, -iest) sanglant; (horrific: fig) horrible.

**gospel** /'gɒspl/ n évangile m; the G~ l'Évangile m.

**gossip** /'gɒsɪp/ n bavardages mpl, commérages mpl; (person) bavard/-e m/f. ● vi bavarder.

**got** /gɒt/ ➡GET. ● have ~ avoir. have ~ to do devoir faire.

**govern** /'gʌvn/ vt/i gouverner. **governess** n gouvernante f. **government** n gouvernement m. **governor** n gouverneur m.

**gown** /gaʊn/ n robe f; (of judge, teacher) toge f.

**GP** abbr ➡GENERAL PRACTITIONER.

**GPS** abbr (Global Positioning System) GPS m.

**grab** /græb/ vt (pt **grabbed**) saisir.

**grace** /greɪs/ n grâce f. ● vt (honour) honorer; (adorn) orner. **graceful** adj gracieux.

**gracious** /'greɪʃəs/ adj (kind) bienveillant; (elegant) élégant.

**grade** /greɪd/ n catégorie f; (of goods) qualité f; (on scale) grade m; (school mark) note f; (class: US) classe f. ● vt classer; (school work) noter. ~ **school** n (US) école f primaire.

**gradual** /'grædʒʊəl/ adj progressif, graduel. **gradually** adv progressivement, peu à peu.

**graduate¹** /'grædʒʊət/ n (Univ) diplômé/-e m/f.

**graduate²** /'grædʒʊeɪt/ vi obtenir son diplôme. ● vt graduer. **graduation** n remise f des diplômes.

**graffiti** /grə'fi:tɪ/ npl graffiti mpl.

**graft** /grɑ:ft/ n (Med, Bot) greffe f; (work) boulot m. ● vt greffer (on to sur); (work) trimer.

**grain** /greɪn/ n (seed, quantity, texture) grain m; (in wood) fibre f.

**gram** /græm/ n gramme m.

**grammar** /'græmə(r)/ n grammaire f.

**grand** /grænd/ adj magnifique; (duke, chorus) grand.

**grandad** /'grændæd/ n 🆃 papy m.

**grand:** ~**child** n (girl) petite-fille f; (boy) petit-fils m; her ~**children** see petits-enfants mpl. ~**daughter** n petite-fille f. ~**father** n grand-père m. ~**ma** n ➡GRANNY. ~**mother** n grand-mère f. ~**parents** npl grands-parents mpl. ~**piano** n piano m à queue. ~**son** n petit-fils m. ~**stand** n tribune f.

**granny** /'grænɪ/ n 🆃mémé f, mamie f.

**grant** /grɑ:nt/ vt (permission) accorder; (request) accéder à; (admit) admettre (that que); **take sth for** ~**ed** considérer qch comme une chose acquise. ● n subvention f; (Univ) bourse f.

**granule** /'grænju:l/ n (of sugar, salt) grain m; (of coffee) granulé m.

**grape** /greɪp/ n grain m de raisin. ~**s** raisin(s) m (pl).

**grapefruit** /'greɪpfru:t/ n inv pamplemousse m.

**graph** /grɑ:f/ n graphique m.

**graphic** /'græfɪk/ adj (arts) graphique; (fig) vivant, explicite. **graphics** npl (Comput) graphiques mpl.

**grasp** /grɑ:sp/ vt saisir. ● n (hold)

prise *f*; (strength of hand) poigne *f*; (reach) portée *f*; (fig) compréhension *f*.

**grass** /grɑːs/ *n* herbe *f*. **~hopper** *n* sauterelle *f*. **~land** *n* prairie *f*.

**grass roots** *npl* peuple *m*. ● *adj* (movement) populaire; (support) de base.

**grate** /greɪt/ *n* (hearth) âtre *m*; (fire basket) grille *f*. ● *vt* râper. ● *vi* grincer.

**grateful** /ˈgreɪtfl/ *adj* reconnaissant.

**grater** /ˈgreɪtə(r)/ *n* râpe *f*.

**gratified** /ˈgrætɪfaɪd/ *adj* très heureux. **gratify** *vt* faire plaisir à.

**grating** /ˈgreɪtɪŋ/ *n* (bars) grille *f*; (noise) grincement *m*.

**gratitude** /ˈgrætɪtjuːd/ *n* reconnaissance *f*.

**gratuity** /grəˈtjuːətɪ/ *n* (tip) pourboire *m*; (bounty: Mil) prime *f*.

**grave**[1] /greɪv/ *n* tombe *f*. ● *adj* (serious) grave.

**grave**[2] /grɑːv/ *adj* ~ accent accent *m* grave.

**gravel** /ˈgrævl/ *n* graviers *mpl*.

**grave:** ~**stone** *n* pierre *f* tombale. ~**yard** *n* cimetière *m*.

**gravity** /ˈgrævətɪ/ *n* (seriousness) gravité *f*; (force) pesanteur *f*.

**gravy** /ˈgreɪvɪ/ *n* jus *m* (de viande).

**gray** /greɪ/ *adj* & *n* ➞**GREY**.

**graze** /greɪz/ *vi* (eat) paître. ● *vt* (touch) frôler; (scrape) écorcher. ● *n* écorchure *f*.

**grease** /griːs/ *n* graisse *f*. ● *vt* graisser. **greasy** *adj* graisseux.

**great** /greɪt/ *adj* grand; (very good ⚠) génial ⚠, formidable ⚠, (grandfather, grandmother) arrière.

**Great Britain** *n* Grande-Bretagne *f*.

**greatly** /ˈgreɪtlɪ/ *adv* (very) très;

(much) beaucoup.

**Greece** /griːs/ *n* Grèce *f*.

**greed** /griːd/ *n* avidité *f*; (for food) gourmandise *f*. **greedy** *adj* avide; gourmand.

**Greek** /griːk/ *n* (person) Grec/-que *m/f*; (Ling) grec *m*. ● *adj* grec.

**green** /griːn/ *adj* vert; (fig) naïf. ● *n* vert *m*; (grass) pelouse *f*; (golf) green *m*; ~s légumes *mpl* verts. ~**grocer** *n* marchand/-e *m/f* de fruits et légumes.

**Green Card** Document qui permet à un étranger de vivre et de travailler aux États-Unis, et qui lui donne les mêmes droits que ceux d'un citoyen américain, à l'exception du droit de vote. Les services de l'immigration américains distribuent 50 000 *green cards* par an au moyen d'une loterie à laquelle participent des millions de candidats.

**greenhouse** *n* serre *f*. ~ **effect** effet *m* de serre.

**greet** /griːt/ *vt* (welcome) accueillir; (address politely) saluer. **greeting** *n* accueil *m*.

**greetings** /ˈgriːtɪŋz/ *interj* salutations ⚠ ● *npl* (Christmas) vœux *mpl*. ~ **card** *n* carte *f* de vœux.

**grew** /gruː/ ➞**GROW**.

**grey** /greɪ/ *adj* gris; (fig) triste; go ~ (hair, person) grisonner. ● *n* gris *m*. ~**hound** *n* lévrier *m*.

**grid** /grɪd/ *n* grille *f*; (network: Electr) réseau *m*.

**grief** /griːf/ *n* chagrin *m*; come to ~ (person) avoir un malheur; (fail) tourner mal.

**grievance** /ˈgriːvns/ *n* griefs *mpl*.

**grieve** /griːv/ *vt/i* (s')affliger; ~ for pleurer.

**grill** /grɪl/ n (cooking device) gril m; (food) grillade f; (Auto) calandre f. • vt/i (faire) griller; (interrogate) mettre sur la sellette.

**grim** /grɪm/ adj sinistre.

**grimace** /grɪˈmeɪs/ n grimace f. • vi grimacer.

**grime** /graɪm/ n crasse f.

**grin** /grɪn/ vi (pt **grinned**) sourire. • n (large) sourire m.

**grind** /graɪnd/ vt (pt **ground**) (grain) écraser; (coffee) moudre; (sharpen) aiguiser; ~ one's teeth grincer des dents. • vi ~ to a halt s'immobiliser. • n corvée f.

**grip** /grɪp/ vt (pt **gripped**) saisir; (interest) passionner. • n prise f; (strength of hand) poigne f; (of tyre) adhérence f; come to ~s with en venir aux prises avec.

**grisly** /ˈgrɪzlɪ/ adj (**-ier, -iest**) (remains) macabre; (sight) horrible.

**gristle** /ˈgrɪsl/ n cartilage m.

**grit** /grɪt/ n (for roads) sable m; (fig) courage m. • vt (pt **gritted**) (road) sabler; (teeth) serrer.

**groan** /grəʊn/ vi gémir. • n gémissement m.

**grocer** /ˈgrəʊsə(r)/ n (person) épicier/-ière m/f; (shop) épicerie f. **groceries** npl (shopping) courses fpl; (goods) épicerie f. **grocery** n (shop) épicerie f.

**groin** /grɔɪn/ n aine f.

**groom** /gruːm/ n marié m; (for horses) palefrenier/-ière m/f. • vt (horse) panser; (fig) préparer.

**groove** /gruːv/ n (for door etc.) rainure f; (in record) sillon m.

**grope** /grəʊp/ vi tâtonner. ~ for chercher à tâtons.

**gross** /grəʊs/ adj (behaviour) vulgaire; (Comm) brut. • n inv grosse f.

**grotto** /ˈgrɒtəʊ/ n (pl **~es**) grotte f.

**grouch** /graʊtʃ/ vi (grumble 🔲) rouspéter, râler.

**ground¹** /graʊnd/ n terre f, sol m; (area) terrain m; (reason) raison f; (Electr, US) masse f; ~s terres fpl, parc m; (of coffee) marc m; on the ~ par terre. lose ~ perdre du terrain. • vt/i (Naut) échouer; (aircraft) retenir au sol.

**ground²** /graʊnd/ ➡GRIND. • adj ~ beef (US) bifteck m haché.

**ground:** ~**floor** n rez-de-chaussée m inv. ~**work** n travail m préparatoire.

**group** /gruːp/ n groupe m. • vt/i (se) grouper. ~**ware** n (Comput) logiciel m de groupe.

**grovel** /ˈgrɒvl/ vi (pt **grovelled**) ramper.

**grow** /grəʊ/ vi (pt **grew**; pp **grown**) (person) grandir; (plant) pousser; (become) devenir; (crime) augmenter. • vt cultiver. ~ up devenir adulte, grandir. **grower** n cultivateur/-trice m/f.

**growl** /graʊl/ vi (dog) gronder; (person) grogner. • n grognement m.

**grown** /grəʊn/ ➡GROW. • adj adulte. ~-**up** adj & n adulte (mf).

**growth** /grəʊθ/ n (of person, plant) croissance f; (in numbers) accroissement m; (of hair, tooth) pousse f; (Med) grosseur f, tumeur f.

**grudge** /grʌdʒ/ vt ~ doing faire à contrecœur. ~ sb sth (success, wealth) en vouloir à qn de qch. • n rancune f; have a ~ against en vouloir à.

**grumble** /ˈgrʌmbl/ vi ronchonner, grogner (at après).

**grumpy** /ˈgrʌmpɪ/ adj (**-ier, -iest**) grincheux, grognon.

**grunt** /grʌnt/ vi grogner. • n grognement m.

**guarantee** /gærən'tiː/ n garantie f.
● vt garantir.

**guard** /gɑːd/ vt protéger; (watch) surveiller. ● vi ~ against se protéger contre. ● n (Mil) garde f; (person) garde m; (on train) chef m de train.

**guardian** /'gɑːdɪən/ n gardien·ne m/f; (of orphan) tuteur·trice m/f.

**guess** /ges/ vt/i deviner; (suppose) penser. ● n conjecture f.

**guest** /gest/ n invité·e m/f; (in hotel) client·e m/f. ~house n pension f. ~room n chambre f d'amis.

**guidance** /'gaɪdns/ n (advice) conseils mpl; (information) information f.

**guide** /gaɪd/ n (person, book) guide m; (girl) guide f. ● vt guider. ~book n guide m. ~dog n chien m d'aveugle. ~line n indication f; (advice) conseils mpl.

**guillotine** /'gɪlətiːn/ n (for execution) guillotine f; (for paper) massicot m.

**guilt** /gɪlt/ n culpabilité f. **guilty** adj coupable.

**guinea-pig** /'gɪnɪpɪg/ n (animal) cochon m d'Inde; (fig) cobaye m.

**guitar** /gɪ'tɑː(r)/ n guitare f.

**gulf** /gʌlf/ n (part of sea) golfe m; (hollow) gouffre m.

**gull** /gʌl/ n mouette f, (larger) goéland m.

**gullible** /'gʌləbl/ adj crédule.

**gully** /'gʌlɪ/ n (ravine) ravin m; (drain) rigole f.

**gulp** /gʌlp/ vt ~ (down) avaler en vitesse. ● vi (from fear etc.) avoir la gorge serrée. ● n gorgée f.

**gum** /gʌm/ n (Anat) gencive f; (glue) colle f; (for chewing) chewing-gum m. ● vt (pt gummed) gommer.

**gun** /gʌn/ n (pistol) revolver m; (rifle) fusil m; (large) canon m. ● vt (pt gunned) ~ down abattre. ~fire n fusillade f. ~powder n poudre f à canon. ~shot n coup m de feu.

**gurgle** /'gɜːgl/ n (of water) gargouillement m; (of baby) gazouillis m. ● vi (water) gargouiller; (baby) gazouiller.

**gush** /gʌʃ/ vi ~ (out) jaillir. ● n jaillissement m.

**gust** /gʌst/ n rafale f; (of smoke) bouffée f.

**gut** /gʌt/ n (belly 🔲) ventre m. ● vt (pt gutted) (fish) vider; (of fire) dévaster. **gutted** adj 🔲 abattu.

**guts** /gʌts/ npl 🔲 (insides of human) tripes fpl 🔲; (insides of animal, building) entrailles fpl; (courage) cran m 🔲.

**gutter** /'gʌtə(r)/ n (on roof) gouttière f; (in street) caniveau m.

**guy** /gaɪ/ n (man 🔲) type m.

**gym** /dʒɪm/ n (place) gymnase m; (activity) gym(nastique) f.

**gymnasium** /dʒɪm'neɪzɪəm/ n gymnase m.

**gymnastics** /dʒɪm'næstɪks/ npl gymnastique f.

**gynaecologist** /gaɪnə'kɒlədʒɪst/ n gynécologue mf.

**gypsy** /'dʒɪpsɪ/ n bohémien·ne m/f.

● ● ● ● ● ● ● ● ● ● ● ● ● ● ● ● ● ●

# Hh

● ● ● ● ● ● ● ● ● ● ● ● ● ● ● ● ● ●

**habit** /'hæbɪt/ n habitude f; (costume: Relig) habit m; be in/get into the ~ of avoir/prendre l'habitude de.

**habitual** /hə'bɪtʃʊəl/ adj (usual) habituel; (smoker, liar) invétéré.

**hack** /hæk/ n (writer) écrivaillon m.

● vi (Comput) pirater; ~ **into** s'introduire dans. ● vt tailler. **hacker** n (Comput) pirate m informatique.

**hackneyed** /'hæknɪd/ adj rebattu.

**had** /hæd/ ⇒HAVE.

**haddock** /'hædək/ n inv églefin m.

**haemorrhage** /'hemərɪdʒ/ n hémorragie f.

**haggard** /'hægəd/ adj (person) exténué; (face, look) défait.

**haggle** /'hægl/ vi marchander; ~ **over** sth discuter du prix de qch.

**hail** /heɪl/ n grêle f. ● vt (greet) saluer; (taxi) héler. ● vi grêler; ~ **from** vanc n grêlon m.

**hair** /heə(r)/ n (on head) cheveux mpl; (on body, of animal) poils mpl; (single strand on head) cheveu m; (on body) poil m. ~**brush** n brosse f à cheveux. ~**cut** n coupe f de cheveux. ~**do** n Ⓣ coiffure f. ~**dresser** n coiffeur/-euse m/f. ~**drier** n séchoir m (à cheveux). ~**pin** n épingle f à cheveux. ~**remover** n dépilatoire m. ~**style** n coiffure f.

**hairy** /'heərɪ/ adj (-ier, -iest) poilu; (terrifying) Ⓣ horrifiant.

**half** /hɑːf/ n (pl **halves**) (part) moitié f; (fraction) demi m; ~ **a dozen** une demi-douzaine; ~ **an hour** une demi-heure; **four and a** ~ quatre et demi; **an hour and a** ~ une heure et demie; ~ **and half** moitié moitié; **in** ~ en deux. ● adj demi; ~ **price** à moitié prix. ● adv à moitié. ~**-back** n (Sport) demi m. ~**-hearted** adj tiède. ~**-mast** n at ~**-mast** en berne. ~**-term** n vacances fpl de demi-trimestre. ~**-time** n mi-temps f. ~**-way** adv à mi-chemin. ~**wit** n imbécile m/f.

**hall** /hɔːl/ n (in house) entrée f; (corridor) couloir m; (in airport) hall m; (for events) salle f; ~ **of residence** résidence f universitaire.

**hallmark** /'hɔːlmɑːk/ n (on gold) poinçon m; (fig) caractéristique f.

**hallo** ⇒HELLO.

**Hallowe'en** /hæləʊ'iːn/ n la veille de la Toussaint.

**halt** /hɔːlt/ n arrêt m; (temporary) suspension f; (Mil) halte f. ● vt (proceedings) interrompre; (arms sales, experiments) mettre fin à. ● vi (vehicle) s'arrêter; (army) faire halte.

**halve** /hɑːv/ vt (time) réduire de moitié; (fruit) couper en deux.

**ham** /hæm/ n jambon m.

**hamburger** /'hæmbɜːgə(r)/ n hamburger m.

**hammer** /'hæmə(r)/ n marteau m. ● vt/i marteler; ~ **sth into** sth enfoncer qch dans qch; ~ **sth out** (agreement) parvenir à qch.

**hammock** /'hæmək/ n hamac m.

**hamper** /'hæmpə(r)/ n panier m. ● vt gêner.

**hamster** /'hæmstə(r)/ n hamster m.

**hand** /hænd/ n main f; (of clock) aiguille f; (writing) écriture f; (worker) ouvrier/-ière m/f; (cards) jeu m; **give sb a** ~ donner un coup de main à qn; **at** ~ proche; **on** ~ disponible; **on the one** ~...**on the other** ~ d'une part...d'autre part; **to** ~ à portée de la main. ● vt ~ **sb sth**, ~ **sth to sb** donner qch à qn. □ ~**in** or **over** remettre; ~ **out** distribuer. ~**bag** n sac m à main. ~**baggage** n bagages mpl à main. ~**book** n manuel m. ~**brake** n frein m à main. ~**cuffs** npl menottes fpl.

**handicap** /'hændɪkæp/ n handicap m. ● vt (pt **handicapped**) handicaper.

**handkerchief** /'hæŋkətʃɪf/ n (pl ~s) mouchoir m.

**handle** /'hændl/ n (of door, bag) poignée f; (of implement) manche m; (of cup, bucket) anse f; (of frying pan) queue f. ● vt (manage) manier; (deal with) traiter; (touch) manipuler.

**handout** /'hændaʊt/ n document m; (leaflet) prospectus m; (money) aumône f.

**hands-free kit** n kit m mains libres conducteur.

**handshake** /'hændʃeɪk/ n poignée f de main.

**handsome** /'hænsəm/ adj (good looking) beau; (generous) généreux.

**handwriting** /'hændraɪtɪŋ/ n écriture f.

**handy** /'hændɪ/ adj (-ier, -iest) (book, skill) utile; (size, shape, tool) pratique; (person) doué. ~**man** n (pl -**men**) bricoleur m.

**hang** /hæŋ/ vt (pt hung) (from hook, hanger) accrocher; (from rope) suspendre; (pt hanged) (person) pendre. ● vi (from hook) être accroché; (from rope) être suspendu; (person) être pendu. ● n get the ~ of doing 🔲 piger comment faire 🔲. □ ~ **about** traîner; ~ **on** 🔲 hold out) tenir; (wait) attendre; ~ **on to sth** s'agripper à qch; ~ **out** vi 🔲 (live) crécher 🔲; (spend time) passer son temps; vt (washing) étendre; ~ **up** (telephone) raccrocher.

**hanger** /'hæŋə(r)/ n (for clothes) cintre m.

**hang-gliding** /'hæŋglaɪdɪŋ/ n vol m libre.

**hangover** /'hæŋəʊvə(r)/ n gueule f de bois 🔲.

**hang-up** /'hæŋʌp/ n 🔲 complexe m.

**haphazard** /hæp'hæzəd/ adj peu méthodique.

**happen** /'hæpən/ vi arriver, se passer; ~ **to sb** arriver à qn; it so ~s that il se trouve que.

**happily** /'hæpɪlɪ/ adv joyeusement; (fortunately) heureusement.

**happiness** /'hæpɪnɪs/ n bonheur m.

**happy** /'hæpɪ/ adj (-ier, -iest) heureux; i'm not ~ about it je ne suis pas content; ~ **with sth** satisfait de qch; ~ **medium** juste milieu m.

**harass** /'hærəs/ vt harceler. **harassment** n harcèlement m.

**harbour**, (US) **harbor** /'hɑːbə(r)/ n port m. ● vt (shelter) héberger.

**hard** /hɑːd/ adj dur; (difficult) difficile, dur; (evidence, fact) solide; find it ~**to do** avoir du mal à faire; ~ **on sb** dur envers qn. ● adv (work) dur; (pull, hit, cry) fort; (think, study) sérieusement. ~**board** n aggloméré m. ~ **copy** n (Comput) tirage m. ~ **disk** n disque m dur.

**hardly** /'hɑːdlɪ/ adv à peine; (expect, hope) difficilement; ~ **ever** presque jamais.

**hardship** /'hɑːdʃɪp/ n (poverty) privations fpl; (ordeal) épreuve f.

**hard:** ~ **shoulder** n bande f d'arrêt d'urgence. ~ **up** adj 🔲 fauché 🔲. ~**ware** n (Comput) matériel m, hardware m; (goods) quincaillerie f. ~**working** adj travailleur.

**hardy** /'hɑːdɪ/ adj (-ier, -iest) résistant.

**hare** /heə(r)/ n lièvre m.

**harm** /hɑːm/ n mal m; there is no ~ in it il n'y a pas de mal à. ● vt (person) faire du mal à; (object) endommager. **harmful** adj nuisible. **harmless** adj inoffensif.

**harmony** /'hɑːmənɪ/ n harmonie f.

**harness** /'hɑːnɪs/ n harnais m. ● vt (horse) harnacher; (use) exploiter.

**harp** /hɑːp/ n harpe f. ● vi ~ **on** (about) rabâcher.

**harrowing** /'hærəʊɪŋ/ adj (experience) atroce; (story) déchirant.

**harsh** /hɑːʃ/ adj (punishment) sé-

h

vère; (*person*) dur; (*light*) cru; (*voice*) rude; (*chemical*) corrosif. **harshness** *n* dureté *f*.

**harvest** /'haːvɪst/ *n* récolte *f*; the wine ~ les vendanges *fpl*. ● *vt* (*corn*) moissonner; (*vegetables*) récolter.

**has** /hæz/ →HAVE.

**hassle** /'hæsl/ *n* complications *fpl*. ● *vt* ① talonner (*about* à propos de); (*worry*) stresser.

**haste** /heɪst/ *n* hâte *f*; in ~ à la hâte; make ~ se dépêcher.

**hasty** /'heɪstɪ/ *adj* (*-ier*, *-iest*) précipité.

**hat** /hæt/ *n* chapeau *m*.

**hatch** /hætʃ/ *n* (*Aviat*) panneau *m* mobile; (*Naut*) écoutille *f*; (*for food*) passeplats *m inv*. ● *vt/i* (*eggs*) (faire) éclore.

**hate** /heɪt/ *n* haine *f*. ● *vt* détester; (*violently*) haïr; (*sport, food*) avoir horreur de.

**hatred** /'heɪtrɪd/ *n* haine *f*.

**haughty** /'hɔːtɪ/ *adj* (*-ier*, *-iest*) hautain.

**haul** /hɔːl/ *vt* tirer. ● *n* (*by thieves*) butin *m*; (*by customs*) saisie *f*; it will be a long ~ l'étape sera longue; long/short ~ (*transport*) long/court courrier *m*. **haulage** *n* transport *m* routier. **haulier** *n* (*firm*) société *f* de transports routiers.

**haunt** /hɔːnt/ *vt* hanter. ● *n* lieu *m* de prédilection.

### have /hæv/

● *present* have, has;
● *past* had;
● *past participle* had

● *transitive verb*

····▸ (*possess*) avoir; I ~ (*got*) a car j'ai une voiture; they ~ (got) problems ils ont des problèmes.

····▸ (*do sth*) ~ a try essayer; ~ a bath prendre un bain.

····▸ ~ sth done faire faire qch; ~ your hair cut se faire couper les cheveux.

● *auxiliary verb*

····▸ (*in perfect tenses*) avoir; être; I ~ seen him je l'ai vu; she had fallen elle était tombée.

····▸ (*in tag questions*) you've seen her, haven't you? tu l'as vue, n'est-ce pas?; you haven't seen her, ~you? tu ne l'as pas vue, par hasard?

····▸ (*in short answers*) 'you've never met him'—'yes I ~' 'tu ne l'as jamais rencontré'—'mais si!'

····▸ (*must*) ~ to devoir; I ~ to go je dois partir; you don't ~ to do it tu n'es pas obligé de le faire.

➡ For expressions such as have a walk, have dinner →walk, dinner.

**haven** /'heɪvn/ *n* refuge *m*; (*fig*) havre *m*.

**havoc** /'hævək/ *n* dévastation *f*.

**hawk** /hɔːk/ *n* faucon *m*.

**hay** /heɪ/ *n* foin *m*; ~ fever rhume *m* des foins.

**haywire** /'heɪwaɪə(r)/ *adj* go ~ (*plans*) dérailler; (*machine*) se détraquer.

**hazard** /'hæzəd/ *n* risque *m*; ~ (*warning*) lights feux *mpl* de détresse. ● *vt* hasarder.

**haze** /heɪz/ *n* brume *f*.

**hazel** /'heɪzl/ *n* (*bush*) noisetier *m*.

~**nut** n noisette f.

**hazy** /'heɪzɪ/ adj (**-ier, -iest**) (misty) brumeux; (fig) vague.

**he** /hiː/ pron il; (emphatic) lui; **here ~ is** le voici.

**head** /hed/ n tête f; (leader) chef m; (of beer) mousse f; ~**s or tails?** pile ou face? ● vt (list) être en tête de; (team) être à la tête de; (chapter) intituler; **the ball** faire une tête. ● vi ~ **for** se diriger vers.

**headache** /'hedeɪk/ n mal m de tête; **have a** ~ avoir mal à la tête.

**heading** /'hedɪŋ/ n titre m; (subject category) rubrique f.

**head:** ~**lamp,** ~**light** n phare m. ~**line** n gros titre m. ~**master** n directeur m. ~**mistress** n directrice f. ~ **office** n siège m social. ~**on** adj & adv de front. ~**phones** npl casque m. ~**quarters** npl siège m social; (Mil) quartier m général. ~ **rest** n (Auto) repose-tête m inv. ~**strong** adj têtu.

**heal** /hiːl/ vt/i guérir.

**health** /helθ/ n santé f; ~ **centre** n centre m médico-social. ~ **food** n produits mpl diététiques. ~ **insurance** n assurance f maladie.

**healthy** /'helθɪ/ adj (person, plant, skin, diet) sain; (air) salutaire.

**heap** /hiːp/ n tas m; ~**s of** 🔢 un tas de. ● vt ~ (**up**) entasser.

**hear** /hɪə(r)/ vt (pt **heard**) entendre; (news, rumour) apprendre; (lecture, broadcast) écouter. ● vi entendre; ~ **from** recevoir des nouvelles de; ~ **of** or **about** entendre parler de.

**hearing** /'hɪərɪŋ/ n ouïe f; (of case) audience f; **give sb a** ~ écouter qn. ~**-aid** n prothèse f auditive.

**hearse** /hɜːs/ n corbillard m.

**heart** /hɑːt/ n cœur m; ~**s** (cards) cœur m; **at** ~ au fond; **by** ~ par

cœur; **be** ~**-broken** avoir le cœur brisé; **lose** ~ perdre courage. ~ **attack** n crise f cardiaque. ~**burn** n brûlures fpl d'estomac. ~**felt** adj sincère.

**hearth** /hɑːθ/ n foyer m.

**heartily** /'hɑːtɪlɪ/ adv (greet) chaleureusement; (laugh, eat) de bon cœur.

**hearty** /'hɑːtɪ/ adj (**-ier, -iest**) (sincere) chaleureux; (meal) solide.

**heat** /hiːt/ n chaleur f; (contest) épreuve f éliminatoire. ● vt (house) chauffer; ~ (**up**) (food) faire chauffer; (reheat) réchauffer. **heated** adj (fig) passionné; (lit) (pool) chauffé. **heater** n appareil m de chauffage.

**heather** /'heðə(r)/ n bruyère f.

**heating** /'hiːtɪŋ/ n chauffage m.

**heave** /hiːv/ vt (lift) hisser; (pull) traîner péniblement; ~ **a sigh** pousser un soupir. ● vi (pull) tirer de toutes ses forces; (retch) avoir un haut-le-cœur.

**heaven** /'hevn/ n ciel m.

**heavily** /'hevɪlɪ/ adv lourdement; (smoke, drink) beaucoup.

**heavy** /'hevɪ/ adj (**-ier, -iest**) lourd; (cold, work) gros; (traffic) dense. ~ **goods vehicle** n poids m lourd. ~**-handed** adj maladroit. ~**weight** n poids m lourd.

**Hebrew** /'hiːbruː/ n (person) Hébreu m; (Ling) hébreu m. ● adj hébreu; (Ling) hébraïque.

**hectic** /'hektɪk/ adj (activity) intense; (period, day) mouvementé.

**hedge** /hedʒ/ n haie f. ● vi (in answering) se dérober.

**hedgehog** /'hedʒhɒg/ n hérisson m.

**heel** /hiːl/ n talon m.

**hefty** /'heftɪ/ adj (**-ier, -iest**) (person) costaud 🔢; (object) pesant.

**height** /haɪt/ n hauteur f; (of person) taille *f*; (of plane, mountain) altitude *f*; (of fame, glory) apogée *m*; (of joy, folly, pain) comble *m*.

**heir** /eə(r)/ *n* héritier/-ière *m/f*. **heiress** *n* héritière *f*. **heirloom** *n* objet *m* de famille.

**held** /held/ ⟶HOLD.

**helicopter** /ˈhelɪkɒptə(r)/ *n* hélicoptère *m*.

**hell** /hel/ *n* enfer *m*.

**hello** /həˈləʊ/ *interj* bonjour!; (on phone) allô!

**helmet** /ˈhelmɪt/ *n* casque *m*.

**help** /help/ *vt/i* aider (to do à faire); ~ (sb) with a bag/the housework aider qn à porter un sac/à faire le ménage; ~ oneself se servir; he can't ~ it ce n'est pas de sa faute. ● *n* aide *f*. ● *interj* au secours! **helper** *n* aide *mf*. **helpful** *adj* utile; (*person*) serviable. **helping** *n* portion *f*. **helpless** *adj* impuissant.

**hem** /hem/ *n* ourlet *m*. ● *vt* (*pt* **hemmed**) faire un ourlet à; ~ **in** cerner.

**hen** /hen/ *n* poule *f*.

**hence** /hens/ *adv* (for this reason) d'où; (from now) d'ici. **henceforth** *adv* désormais.

**hepatitis** /hepəˈtaɪtɪs/ *n* hépatite *f*.

**her** /hɜː(r)/ *pron* la, l'; (indirect object) lui; **it's** ~ c'est elle; for ~ pour elle. ● *adj* son, sa; *pl* ses.

**herb** /hɜːb/ *n* herbe *f*; ~**s** (Culin) fines herbes *fpl*.

**herd** /hɜːd/ *n* troupeau *m*.

**here** /hɪə(r)/ *adv* ici; ~! (take this) tiens!; tenez!; ~ **is**, ~ **are** voici; I'm ~ je suis là. **hereabouts** *adv* par ici. **hereafter** *adv* après; (in book) ci-après. **hereby** *adv* par le présent acte; (in letter) par la présente.

**herewith** /hɪəˈwɪð/ *adv* ci-joint.

**heritage** /ˈherɪtɪdʒ/ *n* patrimoine

*m*. ~ **tourism** *n* tourisme *m* culturel.

**hernia** /ˈhɜːnɪə/ *n* hernie *f*.

**hero** /ˈhɪərəʊ/ *n* (*pl* ~**es**) héros *m*. **heroic** /hɪˈrəʊɪk/ *adj* héroïque.

**heroin** /ˈherəʊɪn/ *n* héroïne *f*.

**heroine** /ˈherəʊɪn/ *n* héroïne *f*.

**heron** /ˈherən/ *n* héron *m*.

**herring** /ˈherɪŋ/ *n* hareng *m*.

**hers** /hɜːz/ *pron* le sien, la sienne, les sien(ne)s; **it is** ~ c'est à elle ou le sien ou la sienne.

**herself** /hɜːˈself/ *pron* (emphatic) elle-même; (reflexive) se; **proud of** ~ fière d'elle; **by** ~ toute seule.

**hesitate** /ˈhezɪteɪt/ *vi* hésiter. **hesitation** *n* hésitation *f*.

**heterosexual** /hetərəˈsekʃʊəl/ *adj* & *n* hétérosexuel/-le (*m/f*).

**hexagon** /ˈheksəgən/ *n* hexagone *m*.

**heyday** /ˈheɪdeɪ/ *n* apogée *m*.

**HGV** *abbr* ⟶HEAVY GOODS VEHICLE.

**hi** /haɪ/ *interj* Ⓣ salut! Ⓣ.

**hiccup** /ˈhɪkʌp/ *n* hoquet *m*; **(the)** ~**s** le hoquet. ● *vi* hoqueter.

**hide** /haɪd/ *vt* (*pt* **hid**; *pp* **hidden**) cacher (from à). ● *vi* se cacher (from de); **go into hiding** se cacher. ● *n* (skin) peau *f*.

**hideous** /ˈhɪdɪəs/ *adj* (*monster*, *object*) hideux; (*noise*) affreux.

**hiding** /ˈhaɪdɪŋ/ *n* **go into** ~ se cacher; **give sb a** ~ administrer une correction à qn.

**hierarchy** /ˈhaɪərɑːkɪ/ *n* hiérarchie *f*.

**hi-fi** /ˈhaɪfaɪ/ *n* (chaîne *f*) hi-fi *f* *inv*.

**high** /haɪ/ *adj* haut; (*price*, *number*) élevé; (*priest*, *speed*) grand; (*voice*) aigu; **in the** ~ **season** en pleine saison. ● *n* **a (new)** ~ un niveau record. ● *adv* haut. ⟶**brow** *n* intellectuel/-le (*m/f*). ~ **chair** *n* chaise f haute. **~ court** n cour f suprême. **higher education** n enseignement m supérieur. **~jump** n saut m en hauteur. **~-level** adj à haut niveau.

**highlight** /'haɪlaɪt/ n (best moment) point m fort; **~s** (in hair) reflet m; (artificial) mèches fpl; (Sport) résumé m. ● vt (emphasize) souligner.

**highly** /'haɪlɪ/ adv extrêmement; (paid) très bien; **speak/think ~ of** dire/penser beaucoup de bien de.

**Highness** /'haɪnɪs/ n Altesse f.

**high:** **~-rise (building)** n tour f. **~ school** n lycée m. **~-speed** adj (train) à grande vitesse; (film) ultra-rapide. **~ street** n rue f principale. **~-tech** adj de pointe.

> **High School** Établissement d'enseignement secondaire aux États-Unis, souvent subdivisé en *Junior high school* (12-14 ans) et *Senior high school* (15-17 ans) où les élèves passent un examen pour être admis dans un *College* (établissement d'enseignement supérieur).
>

**highway** /'haɪweɪ/ n route f nationale; (US) autoroute f; **~ code** code m de la route.

**hijack** /'haɪdʒæk/ vt détourner. ● n détournement m. **hijacker** n pirate m (de l'air).

**hike** /haɪk/ n randonnée f; **price ~** hausse f de prix. ● vi faire de la randonnée.

**hilarious** /hɪ'leərɪəs/ adj désopilant.

**hill** /hɪl/ n colline f; (slope) côte f. **hilly** adj vallonné.

**him** /hɪm/ pron le, l'; (indirect object) lui; **it's ~** c'est lui; **for ~** pour lui.

**himself** /hɪm'self/ pron (emphatic) lui-même; (reflexive) se; **proud of ~** fier de lui; **by ~** tout seul.

**hind** /haɪnd/ adj de derrière.

**hinder** /'hɪndə(r)/ vt (hamper) gêner; (prevent) empêcher. **hindrance** n obstacle m, gêne f.

**hindsight** /'haɪndsaɪt/ n **with ~** rétrospectivement.

**Hindu** /hɪn'du:/ n Hindou/-e m/f. ● adj hindou.

**hinge** /hɪndʒ/ n charnière f. ● vi **on** dépendre de.

**hint** /hɪnt/ n allusion f; (of spice, accent) pointe f; (of colour) touche f; (advice) conseil m. ● vt laisser entendre. ● vi **~ at** faire allusion à.

**hip** /hɪp/ n hanche f.

**hippopotamus** /hɪpə'pɒtəməs/ n (pl **~es**) hippopotame m.

**hire** /'haɪə(r)/ vt (thing) louer; (person) engager. ● n location f. **~-car** n voiture f de location. **~-purchase** n achat m à crédit.

**his** /hɪz/ adj son, sa, pl ses. ● pron le sien, la sienne, les sien(ne)s; **it is ~** c'est à lui or le sien or à elle or la sienne.

**hiss** /hɪs/ n sifflement m. ● vt/i siffler.

**history** /'hɪstrɪ/ n histoire f; **make ~** entrer dans l'histoire.

**hit** /hɪt/ vt (pt **hit**; pres p **hitting**) frapper; (collide with) heurter; (find) trouver; (affect, reach) toucher. ● vi **~ on** (find) tomber sur; **~ it off** s'entendre bien (with avec). ● n (blow) coup m; (fig) succès m; (song) tube m 🔟; (on Internet) (visit) visite f; accès m; (result) page f trouvée, résultat m.

**hitch** /hɪtʃ/ vt (fasten) accrocher; **~ up** remonter. ● n (snag) anicroche f. **~-hike** vi faire du stop 🔟. **~-hiker** n auto-stoppeur/-euse m/f.

**hi-tech** /'hɪtʃaɪk/ adj

de pointe.

**HIV** abbr (**human immunodefi-
ciency virus**) VIH m.

**hive** /haɪv/ n ruche f. ● vt ~ **off** séparer; (industry) céder.

**HIV-positive** adj séropositif.

**hoard** /hɔːd/ vt amasser; (supplies)
stocker. ● n trésor m; (of provisions)
provisions fpl.

**hoarse** /hɔːs/ adj enroué.

**hoax** /həʊks/ n canular m.

**hobby** /'hɒbɪ/ n passe-temps m inv.

**hockey** /'hɒkɪ/ n hockey m.

**hog** /hɒg/ n cochon m. ● vt (pt
**hogged**) □ monopoliser.

**hold** /həʊld/ vt (pt **held**) tenir;
(contain) contenir; (conversation,
opinion) avoir; (shares, record, person) détenir; ~ (**the line**), please
ne quittez pas. ● vi (rope, weather)
tenir. ● n prise f; get ~ of attraper;
(ticket) se procurer; (person) (by
phone) joindre; on ~ en attente.
□ ~ **back** (contain) retenir; (hide)
cacher; ~ **down** (job) garder; (person) tenir; (costs) limiter; ~ **on**
(stand firm) tenir bon; (wait) attendre; ~ **on to** (keep) garder; (cling
to) se cramponner à; ~ **out** vt
(offer) offrir; vi (resist) tenir le coup;
~ **up** (support) soutenir; (delay) retarder; (rob) attaquer.

**holder** /'həʊldə(r)/ n détenteur/-
trice m/f; (of passport, post) titulaire
mf; (for object) support m.

**holding** /'həʊldɪŋ/ n participation f.

**hold-up** /'həʊldʌp/ n retard m; (of
traffic) embouteillage m; (robbery)
hold-up m inv.

**hole** /həʊl/ n trou m.

**holiday** /'hɒlədeɪ/ n vacances fpl;
(public) jour m férié; (time off)
congé m. ● vi passer ses vacances.
● adj de vacances. ~-**maker** n

vacancier/-ière m/f.

**Holland** /'hɒlənd/ n Hollande f.

**hollow** /'hɒləʊ/ adj creux; (fig)
faux. ● n creux m. ● vt creuser.

**holly** /'hɒlɪ/ n houx m.

**holy** /'həʊlɪ/ adj (**-ier, -iest**) saint;
(water) bénit; H~ **Ghost**, H~
**Spirit** Saint-Esprit m.

**homage** /'hɒmɪdʒ/ n hommage m.

**home** /həʊm/ n (place to live) logement m; maison f; (institution) maison f; (family base) foyer m; (country) pays m. ● adj de la maison, du
foyer; (of family) de famille; (Pol) intérieur; (match, visit) à domicile.
● adv (at) ~ à la maison, chez soi;
come or go ~ rentrer; (from
abroad) rentrer dans son pays; feel
at ~ with être à l'aise avec. ~
**computer** n ordinateur m, PC m.

**homeland** /'həʊmlænd/ n patrie f;
~ **security** n sécurité f des frontières.

**homeless** /'həʊmlɪs/ adj sans abri.
● n the ~ les sans-abri mpl.

**homely** /'həʊmlɪ/ adj (**-ier, -iest**)
(cosy) accueillant; (simple) sans prétention; (person: US) sans attraits.

**home:** ~-**made** adj (fait) maison.
H~ **Office** n ministère m de l'Intérieur. ~ **page** n (Internet) page f
d'accueil. H~ **Secretary** n Ministre
m de l'Intérieur. ~**sick** adj be ~**sick**
avoir le mal du pays. ~**work** n devoirs mpl.

**homosexual** /hɒmə'sekʃʊəl/ adj
& n homosexuel/-le (m/f).

**honest** /'ɒnɪst/ adj (truthful) intègre; (trustworthy) honnête; (sincere) franc. **honestly** adv honnête-
ment; franchement. **honesty** n
honnêteté f.

**honey** /'hʌnɪ/ n miel m; (person □)
chéri/-e m/f. ~**moon** n voyage m de
noces; (fig) lune f de miel.

**honk** /hɒŋk/ vi klaxonner.

**honorary** /ˈɒnərərɪ/ adj (person) honoraire; (degree) honorifique.

**honour**, (US) **honor** /ˈɒnə(r)/ n honneur m. ● vt honorer.

**hood** /hʊd/ n capuchon m; (on car, pram) capote f; (car engine cover: US) capot m.

**hoof** /huːf/ n (pl ~s) sabot m.

**hook** /hʊk/ n crochet m; (on garment) agrafe f; (for fishing) hameçon m; off the ~ tiré d'affaire; (phone) décroché. ● vt accrocher.

**hoot** /huːt/ n (of owl) (h)ululement m; (of car) coup m de klaxon. ● vi (owl) (h)ululer; (car) klaxonner; (jeer) huer.

**hoover** /ˈhuːvə(r)/ vt ~ a room passer l'aspirateur dans une pièce.

**Hoover®** /ˈhuːvə(r)/ n aspirateur m.

**hop** /hɒp/ vi (pt **hopped**) sauter (à cloche-pied); ~ in! ⊤ vas-y, monte! ● n bond m; ~s houblon m.

**hope** /həʊp/ n espoir m. ● vt/i espérer; ~ for espérer avoir; I ~ so je l'espère.

**hopeful** /ˈhəʊpfl/ adj (news, sign) encourageant; (person) plein d'espoir; (mood) optimiste. **hopefully** adv (with luck) avec un peu de chance; (with hope) avec optimisme.

**hopeless** /ˈhəʊplɪs/ adj désespéré; (useless: fig) nul ⊤.

**horizon** /həˈraɪzn/ n horizon m.

**horizontal** /hɒrɪˈzɒntl/ adj horizontal.

**hormone** /ˈhɔːməʊnl/ n hormone f.

**horn** /hɔːn/ n corne f; (of car) klaxon® m; (Mus) cor m.

**horoscope** /ˈhɒrəskəʊp/ n horoscope m.

**horrible** /ˈhɒrɪbl/ adj horrible.

**horrid** /ˈhɒrɪd/ adj horrible.

**horrific** /həˈrɪfɪk/ adj horrifiant.

**horrify** /ˈhɒrɪfaɪ/ vt horrifier.

**horror** /ˈhɒrə(r)/ n horreur f. ● adj (film, story) d'épouvante.

**horse** /hɔːs/ n cheval m. ~**back** n on ~back à cheval. ~**chestnut** n marron m (d'Inde). ~**man** n (pl -men) cavalier m. ~**power** n puissance f (en chevaux). ~**race** n course f de chevaux. ~**radish** n raifort m. ~**shoe** n fer m à cheval. ~ **show** n concours m hippique.

**hose** /həʊz/ n tuyau m. ● vt arroser. ~**pipe** n tuyau m.

**hospitable** /hɒˈspɪtəbl/ adj hospitalier.

**hospital** /ˈhɒspɪtl/ n hôpital m.

**host** /həʊst/ n (to guests) hôte m; (on TV) animateur m; (Internet) ordinateur m hôte; a ~ of une foule de; (Relig) hostie f.

**hostage** /ˈhɒstɪdʒ/ n otage m; hold sb ~ garder qn en otage.

**hostel** /ˈhɒstl/ n foyer m; (youth) ~ auberge f (de jeunesse).

**hostess** /ˈhəʊstɪs/ n hôtesse f.

**hostile** /ˈhɒstaɪl/ adj hostile.

**hot** /hɒt/ adj (**hotter**, **hottest**) chaud; (Culin) épicé; be or feel ~ avoir chaud; it is ~ il fait chaud; in ~ water ⊤ dans le pétrin. ● vt/i (pt **hotted**) ~ up ⊤ chauffer. ~ **air balloon** n montgolfière f. ~ **dog** n hot-dog m.

**hotel** /həʊˈtel/ n hôtel m.

**hot:** ~**headed** adj impétueux. ~**list** n (Internet) signets mpl favoris. ~**plate** n plaque f chauffante. ~ **water bottle** n bouillotte f.

**hound** /haʊnd/ n chien m de chasse. ● vt poursuivre.

**hour** /aʊə(r)/ n heure f.

**hourly** /ˈaʊəlɪ/ adj horaire; on an ~ basis à l'heure. ● adv toutes les heures.

**house¹** /haʊs/ n maison f; (Pol) Chambre f; on the ~ aux frais de la maison.

**house²** /haʊz/ vt loger; (of building) abriter.

**household** /'haʊshəʊld/ n (house, family) ménage m. ● adj ménager.

**house:** ~keeper n gouvernante f. ~-proud adj méticuleux. ~-warming n pendaison f de crémaillère. ~wife n (pl -wives) ménagère f. ~work n travaux mpl ménagers.

**housing** /'haʊzɪŋ/ n logement m; ~ association service m de logement; ~ development cité f; (smaller) lotissement m.

**hover** /'hɒvə(r)/ vi (bird) voleter; (vacillate) vaciller. **hovercraft** n aéroglisseur m.

**how** /haʊ/ adv comment; ~ are you? comment allez-vous?; ~ long/tall is...? quelle est la longueur/hauteur de...?; ~ many?, ~ much? combien?; ~ pretty! comme or que c'est joli!; ~ about a walk? si on faisait une promenade?; ~ do you do? (greeting) enchanté.

**however** /haʊ'evə(r)/ adv (nevertheless) cependant; ~ hard I try j'ai beau essayer; ~ much it costs quel que soit le prix; ~ young/poor he is si jeune/pauvre soit-il; ~ you like comme tu veux.

**howl** /haʊl/ n hurlement m. ● vi hurler.

**HP** abbr ➙HIRE-PURCHASE.

**hp** abbr ➙HORSEPOWER.

**HQ** abbr ➙HEADQUARTERS.

**hub** /hʌb/ n moyeu m; (fig) centre m.

**hug** /hʌg/ vt (pt hugged) serrer dans ses bras. ● n étreinte f; give

sb a ~ serrer qn dans ses bras.

**huge** /hjuːdʒ/ adj énorme.

**hull** /hʌl/ n (of ship) coque f.

**hum** /hʌm/ vt/i (pt hummed) (person) fredonner; (insect) bourdonner; (engine) ronronner. ● n bourdonnement m; ronronnement m.

**human** /'hjuːmən/ adj humain. ● n humain m. ~ being n être m humain.

**humane** /hjuː'meɪn/ adj (person) humain; (act) d'humanité; (killing) sans cruauté.

**humanitarian** /hjuːmænɪ'teərɪən/ adj humanitaire.

**humanity** /hjuː'mænətɪ/ n humanité f.

**humble** /'hʌmbl/ adj humble.

**humid** /'hjuːmɪd/ adj humide.

**humiliate** /hjuː'mɪlɪeɪt/ vt humilier.

**humorous** /'hjuːmərəs/ adj humoristique; (person) plein d'humour.

**humour**, (US) **humor** /'hjuːmə(r)/ n humour m; (mood) humeur f. ● vt amadouer.

**hump** /hʌmp/ n bosse f. ● vt 🔟 porter.

**hunchback** /'hʌntʃbæk/ n bossu/-e m/f.

**hundred** /'hʌndrəd/ adj & n cent (m); two ~ and one deux cent un; ~s of des centaines de. **hundredth** adj & n centième (mf).

**hung** /hʌŋ/ ➙HANG.

**Hungarian** /hʌŋ'geərɪən/ n (person) Hongrois/-e m/f; (Ling) hongrois m. ● adj hongrois. **Hungary** n Hongrie f.

**hunger** /'hʌŋgə(r)/ n faim f. ● vi ~ for avoir faim de.

**hungry** /'hʌŋgrɪ/ adj (-ier, -iest) affamé; be ~ avoir faim.

**hunt** /hʌnt/ vt/i chasser; ~ for chercher. ● n chasse f. **hunter** n chasseur m. **hunting** n chasse f.

**hurdle** /ˈhɜːdl/ n (Sport) haie f; (fig) obstacle m.

**hurricane** /ˈhʌrɪkən/ n ouragan m.

**hurry** /ˈhʌrɪ/ vi se dépêcher; ~ out sortir précipitamment. ● vt (work) terminer à la hâte; (person) bousculer. ● n hâte f; in a ~ pressé.

**hurt** /hɜːt/ vt/i (pt **hurt**) faire mal (à); (injure, offend) blesser. ● adj blessé. ● n blessure f.

**hurtle** /ˈhɜːtl/ vi ~ down dévaler; ~ along a road foncer sur une route.

**husband** /ˈhʌzbənd/ n mari m.

**hush** /hʌʃ/ vt faire taire; ~ up (news) étouffer. ● n silence m. ● interj chut!

**husky** /ˈhʌskɪ/ adj (-ier, -iest) enroué. ● n husky m.

**hustle** /ˈhʌsl/ vt (push, rush) bousculer. ● vi (hurry) se dépêcher; (work: US) se démener. ● n ~ and **bustle** agitation f.

**hut** /hʌt/ n cabane f.

**hyacinth** /ˈhaɪəsɪnθ/ n jacinthe f.

**hydrant** /ˈhaɪdrənt/ n (fire) ~ bouche f d'incendie.

**hydraulic** /haɪˈdrɔːlɪk/ adj hydraulique.

**hydroelectric** /haɪdrəʊɪˈlektrɪk/ adj hydroélectrique.

**hydrogen** /ˈhaɪdrədʒən/ n hydrogène m; ~ **bomb** bombe f à hydrogène.

**hyena** /haɪˈiːnə/ n hyène f.

**hygiene** /ˈhaɪdʒiːn/ n hygiène f. **hygienic** adj hygiénique.

**hymn** /hɪm/ n cantique m; (fig) hymne m.

**hype** /haɪp/ n [T] battage m publicitaire. ● vt ~ (up) (film, book) faire

du battage pour.

**hyperactive** /haɪpərˈæktɪv/ adj hyperactif.

**hyperlink** /ˈhaɪpəlɪŋk/ n hyperlien m.

**hypermarket** /ˈhaɪpəmɑːkɪt/ n hypermarché m.

**hypertext** /ˈhaɪpətekst/ n hypertexte m.

**hyphen** /ˈhaɪfn/ n trait m d'union.

**hypnosis** /hɪpˈnəʊsɪs/ n hypnose f.

**hypocrisy** /hɪˈpɒkrəsɪ/ n hypocrisie f. **hypocrite** n hypocrite mf. **hypocritical** adj hypocrite.

**hypothesis** /haɪˈpɒθəsɪs/ n (pl **-ses**) hypothèse f.

**hysteria** /hɪˈstɪərɪə/ n hystérie f. **hysterical** adj hystérique. **hysterics** /hɪˈsterɪks/ npl crise f de nerfs; be in ~ rire aux larmes.

# I i

**I** /aɪ/ pron je, j'; (stressed) moi.

**ice** /aɪs/ n glace f; (on road) verglas m. ● vt (cake) glacer. ● vi ~ (up) (window) se givrer; (river) geler. ~**box** n (US) réfrigérateur m. ~**-cream** n glace f. ~**-cube** n glaçon m. ~ **hockey** n hockey m sur glace.

**Iceland** /ˈaɪslənd/ n Islande f. **Icelander** n Islandais/-e m/f. **Icelandic** adj à n islandais (m).

**ice:** ~ **lolly** n glace f (sur bâtonnet). ~ **rink** n patinoire f. ~ **skate** n patin m à glace.

**icicle** /ˈaɪsɪkl/ n stalactite f (de glace).

**icing** /'aɪsɪŋ/ n (sugar) glaçage m.

**icy** /'aɪsɪ/ adj (-ier, -iest) (hands, wind) glacé; (road) verglacé; (manner, welcome) glacial.

**ID** /ɪd/ n pièce f d'identité; ~ **card** carte f d'identité.

**idea** /aɪ'dɪə/ n idée f.

**ideal** /aɪ'dɪːəl/ adj idéal. ● n idéal m.

**identical** /aɪ'dentɪkl/ adj identique.

**identification** /aɪdentɪfɪ'keɪʃn/ n identification f; (papers) pièce f d'identité.

**identify** /aɪ'dentɪfaɪ/ vt identifier. ● vi ~ **with** s'identifier à.

**identikit** /aɪ'dentɪkɪt/ n ~ **picture** portraitrobot m.

**identity** /aɪ'dentɪtɪ/ n identité f; ~ **theft** vol m d'identité.

**ideological** /aɪdɪə'lɒdʒɪkl/ adj idéologique.

**idiom** /'ɪdɪəm/ n (phrase) idiome m; (language) parler m, langue f. **idiomatic** adj idiomatique.

**idiosyncrasy** /ɪdɪə'sɪŋkrəsɪ/ n particularité f.

**idiot** /'ɪdɪət/ n idiot/-e m/f. **idiotic** adj idiot.

**idle** /'aɪdl/ adj (lazy) paresseux; (doing nothing) oisif; (boast, threat) vain. ● vi (engine) tourner au ralenti. ● vt ~ **away** gaspiller.

**idol** /'aɪdl/ n idole f. **idolize** vt idolâtrer.

**idyllic** /ɪ'dɪlɪk/ adj idyllique.

**i.e.** abbr c-à-d, c'est-à-dire.

**if** /ɪf/ conj si.

**ignite** /ɪg'naɪt/ vt/i (s')enflammer.

**ignition** /ɪg'nɪʃn/ n (Auto) allumage m; ~ (switch) contact m; ~ **key** clé f de contact.

**ignorance** /'ɪgnərəns/ n ignorance f. **ignorant** adj ignorant (of de). **ignorantly** adv par ignorance.

**ignore** /ɪg'nɔː(r)/ vt (person) igno-

rer; (mistake, remark) ne pas relever; (feeling, fact) ne pas tenir compte de.

**ill** /ɪl/ adj malade. ● adv mal. ● n mal m. ~-**advised** adj malavisé. ~ **at ease** adj mal à l'aise. ~-**bred** adj mal élevé.

**illegal** /ɪ'liːgl/ adj illégal.

**illegible** /ɪ'ledʒəbl/ adj illisible.

**illegitimate** /ɪlɪ'dʒɪtɪmət/ adj illégitime.

**ill:** ~-**fated** adj malheureux. ~ **feeling** n ressentiment m.

**illiterate** /ɪ'lɪtərət/ adj & n analphabète (mf).

**illness** /'ɪlnɪs/ n maladie f.

**ill-treat** vt maltraiter.

**illuminate** /ɪ'luːmɪneɪt/ vt éclairer; (decorate with lights) illuminer. **illumination** n éclairage m. illumination f.

**illusion** /ɪ'luːʒn/ n illusion f.

**illustrate** /'ɪləstreɪt/ vt illustrer. **illustration** n illustration f. **illustrative** adj qui illustre.

**image** /'ɪmɪdʒ/ n image f; (of firm, person) image f de marque. **imagery** n images fpl.

**imaginable** /ɪ'mædʒɪnəbl/ adj imaginable. **imaginary** adj imaginaire. **imagination** n imagination f. **imaginative** adj plein d'imagination.

**imagine** /ɪ'mædʒɪn/ vt (s')imaginer (that que); ~ **being rich** s'imaginer riche.

**imbalance** /ɪm'bæləns/ n déséquilibre m.

**imitate** /'ɪmɪteɪt/ vt imiter.

**immaculate** /ɪ'mækjʊlət/ adj impeccable.

**immaterial** /ɪmə'tɪərɪəl/ adj sans importance (to pour; that que).

**immature** /ɪmə'tjʊə(r)/ adj (person) immature; (*plant*) qui n'est pas arrivé à maturité.

**immediate** /ɪˈmiːdɪət/ *adj* immédiat.

**immediately** /ɪˈmiːdɪətlɪ/ *adv* immédiatement. ● *conj* dès que.

**immense** /ɪˈmens/ *adj* immense. **immensely** *adv* extrêmement, immensément. **immensity** *n* immensité *f.*

**immerse** /ɪˈmɜːs/ *vt* plonger (in dans). **immersion** *n* immersion *f;* **immersion heater** chauffe-eau *m inv* électrique.

**immigrant** /ˈɪmɪɡrənt/ *n & adj* immigré/-e (*m/f*). (newly-arrived) immigrant/-e (*m/f*). **immigrate** *vi* immigrer. **immigration** *n* immigration *f.*

**imminent** /ˈɪmɪnənt/ *adj* imminent.

**immobilizer** /ɪˈməʊbɪlaɪzə(r)/ *n* système *m* antidémarrage.

**immoral** /ɪˈmɒrəl/ *adj* immoral.

**immortal** /ɪˈmɔːtl/ *adj* immortel.

**immune** /ɪˈmjuːn/ *adj* immunisé (from, to contre); (*reaction, system*) immunitaire. **immunity** *n* immunité *f.* **immunization** *n* immunisation *f.* **immunize** *vt* immuniser.

**impact** /ˈɪmpækt/ *n* impact *m.*

**impair** /ɪmˈpeə(r)/ *vt* (*performance*) affecter; (*ability*) affaiblir.

**impart** /ɪmˈpɑːt/ *vt* communiquer, transmettre.

**impartial** /ɪmˈpɑːʃl/ *adj* impartial.

**impassable** /ɪmˈpɑːsəbl/ *adj* (*barrier*) infranchissable; (*road*) impraticable.

**impassive** /ɪmˈpæsɪv/ *adj* impassible.

**impatience** /ɪmˈpeɪʃns/ *n* impatience *f.* **impatient** *adj* impatient; **get impatient** s'impatienter. impa-

tiently *adv* impatiemment.

**impeccable** /ɪmˈpekəbl/ *adj* impeccable.

**impede** /ɪmˈpiːd/ *vt* entraver.

**impediment** /ɪmˈpedɪmənt/ *n* entrave *f;* **speech ~** défaut *m* d'élocution.

**impending** /ɪmˈpendɪŋ/ *adj* imminent.

**imperative** /ɪmˈperətɪv/ *adj* urgent. ● *n* impératif *m.*

**imperfect** /ɪmˈpɜːfɪkt/ *adj* incomplet; (faulty) défectueux. ● *n* (Gram) imparfait *m.* **imperfection** *n* imperfection *f.*

**imperial** /ɪmˈpɪərɪəl/ *adj* impérial; (measure) conforme aux normes britanniques. **imperialism** *n* impérialisme *m.*

**impersonal** /ɪmˈpɜːsənl/ *adj* impersonnel.

**impersonate** /ɪmˈpɜːsəneɪt/ *vt* se faire passer pour; (mimic) imiter.

**impertinent** /ɪmˈpɜːtɪnənt/ *adj* impertinent.

**impervious** /ɪmˈpɜːvɪəs/ *adj* imperméable (to à).

**impetuous** /ɪmˈpetʃʊəs/ *adj* impétueux.

**impetus** /ˈɪmpɪtəs/ *n* impulsion *f.*

**impinge** /ɪmˈpɪndʒ/ *vi* ~ on altérer; (encroach) empiéter sur.

**implement** /ˈɪmplɪmənt/ *n* instrument *m;* (tool) outil *m.* ● *vt* exécuter, mettre en application; (*software*) implanter. **implementation** *n* mise *f* en application.

**implicit** /ɪmˈplɪsɪt/ *adj* (implied) implicite (in dans); (unquestioning) absolu.

**imply** /ɪmˈplaɪ/ *vt* (assume, mean) impliquer; (insinuate) laisser entendre.

**impolite** /ɪmpəˈlaɪt/ *adj* impoli.

**import**[1] /ɪm'pɔ:t/ vt importer.

**import**[2] /'ɪmpɔ:t/ n (article) importation f; (meaning) signification f.

**importance** /ɪm'pɔ:tns/ n importance f. **important** adj important.

**impose** /ɪm'pəʊz/ vt imposer (on sb à qn; on sth sur qch). ● vi s'imposer; ~ on sb abuser de la bienveillance de qn. **imposing** adj imposant.

**impossible** /ɪm'pɒsəbl/ adj impossible. ● n the ~ l'impossible m.

**impotent** /'ɪmpətənt/ adj impuissant.

**impound** /ɪm'paʊnd/ vt confisquer, saisir.

**impoverish** /ɪm'pɒvərɪʃ/ vt appauvrir.

**impractical** /ɪm'præktɪkl/ adj peu réaliste.

**impregnable** /ɪm'pregnəbl/ adj imprenable.

**impress** /ɪm'pres/ vt impressionner; ~ sth on sb faire bien comprendre qch à qn. **impression** n impression f. **impressionable** adj impressionnable. **impressive** adj impressionnant.

**imprint**[1] /'ɪmprɪnt/ n empreinte f.

**imprint**[2] /ɪm'prɪnt/ vt (fix) graver (on dans); (print) imprimer.

**imprison** /ɪm'prɪzn/ vt emprisonner.

**improbable** /ɪm'prɒbəbl/ adj (not likely) improbable; (incredible) invraisemblable.

**improper** /ɪm'prɒpə(r)/ adj (unseemly) malséant; (dishonest) irrégulier.

**improve** /ɪm'pru:v/ vt/i (s')améliorer. **improvement** n amélioration f.

**improvise** /'ɪmprəvaɪz/ vt/i improviser.

**impudent** /'ɪmpjʊdənt/ adj impudent.

**impulse** /'ɪmpʌls/ n impulsion f; on ~ sur un coup de tête. **impulsive** adj impulsif. **impulsively** adv par impulsion.

**impurity** /ɪm'pjʊərətɪ/ n impureté f.

**in** /ɪn/ prep (inside, within) dans; (expressing place, position) à, en; (expressing time) en, dans; ~ the box/garden dans la boîte/le jardin; ~ Paris/school à Paris/l'école; ~ town en ville; ~ the country à la campagne; ~ English en anglais; ~ India en Inde; ~ Japan au Japon; ~ winter en hiver; ~ spring au printemps; ~ an hour (at end of) au bout d'une heure; ~ an hour('s time) dans une heure; ~ (the space of) an hour en une heure; ~ doing en faisant; ~ the evening le soir; one ~ ten un sur dix; ~ between entre les deux; (time) entretemps; ~ a firm voice d'une voix ferme; ~ blue en bleu; ~ ink à l'encre; ~ uniform en uniforme; ~ a skirt en jupe; ~ a whisper en chuchotant; ~ a loud voice d'une voix forte; the best ~ le meilleur de; we are ~ for on va avoir; have it ~ for sb 🅸 avoir qn dans le collimateur. ● adv (inside) dedans; (at home) là, à la maison; (in fashion) à la mode; come ~ entrer; run ~ entrer en courant.

**inability** /ɪnə'bɪlətɪ/ n incapacité f (to do de faire).

**inaccessible** /ɪnæk'sesəbl/ adj inaccessible.

**inaccurate** /ɪn'ækjʊrət/ adj inexact.

**inactive** /ɪn'æktɪv/ adj inactif. **inactivity** n inaction f.

**inadequate** /ɪn'ædɪkwət/ adj insuffisant.

**inadvertently** /ɪnəd'vɜ:təntlɪ/ adv par mégarde.

**inadvisable** /ˌɪnədˈvaɪzəbl/ *adj* inopportun, à déconseiller.

**inane** /ɪˈneɪn/ *adj* idiot, débile.

**inanimate** /ɪnˈænɪmət/ *adj* inanimé.

**inappropriate** /ɪnəˈprəʊprɪət/ *adj* inopportun; (*term*) inapproprié.

**inarticulate** /ˌɪnɑːˈtɪkjʊlət/ *adj* qui a du mal à s'exprimer.

**inasmuch as** /ˌɪnəzˈmʌtʃəz/ *adv* dans la mesure où; (*because*) vu que.

**inaugurate** /ɪˈnɔːgjʊreɪt/ *vt* (open, begin) inaugurer; (*person*) investir.

**inborn** /ɪnˈbɔːn/ *adj* inné.

**inbred** /ɪnˈbred/ *adj* (inborn) inné.

**Inc.** *abbr* (**incorporated**) S.A.

**incapable** /ɪnˈkeɪpəbl/ *adj* incapable (of doing de faire).

**incapacitate** /ɪnkəˈpæsɪteɪt/ *vt* immobiliser.

**incense¹** /ˈɪnsens/ *n* encens *m*.

**incense²** /ɪnˈsens/ *vt* mettre en fureur.

**incentive** /ɪnˈsentɪv/ *n* motivation *f*; (payment) prime *f*.

**incessant** /ɪnˈsesnt/ *adj* incessant. **incessantly** *adv* sans cesse.

**incest** /ˈɪnsest/ *n* inceste *m*. **incestuous** *adj* incestueux.

**inch** /ɪntʃ/ *n* pouce *m* (=2.54 cm.). ●*vi* ~ towards se diriger petit à petit vers.

**incidence** /ˈɪnsɪdəns/ *n* fréquence *f*.

**incident** /ˈɪnsɪdənt/ *n* incident *m*. **incidental** *adj* secondaire. **incidentally** *adv* à propos; (by chance) par la même occasion.

**incinerate** /ɪnˈsɪnəreɪt/ *vt* incinérer. **incinerator** *n* incinérateur *m*.

**incite** /ɪnˈsaɪt/ *vt* inciter, pousser.

**inclination** /ɪŋklɪˈneɪʃn/ *n* (tendency) tendance *f*; (desire) envie *f*.

**incline¹** /ɪnˈklaɪn/ *vt/i* (s')incliner; be ~d to avoir tendance à.

**incline²** /ɪnˈklaɪn/ *n* pente *f*.

**include** /ɪnˈkluːd/ *vt* comprendre, inclure. **including** *prep* (y) compris. **inclusion** *n* inclusion *f*.

**inclusive** /ɪnˈkluːsɪv/ *adj* & *adv* inclus; ~ of delivery livraison comprise.

**income** /ˈɪnkʌm/ *n* revenus *mpl*; ~ tax impôt *m* sur le revenu.

**incoming** /ˈɪnkʌmɪŋ/ *adj* (tide) montant; (tenant, government) nouveau; (call) qui vient de l'extérieur.

**incompatible** /ɪnkəmˈpætɪbl/ *adj* incompatible.

**incompetent** /ɪnˈkɒmpɪtənt/ *adj* incompétent.

**incomplete** /ɪnkəmˈpliːt/ *adj* incomplet.

**incomprehensible** /ɪnkɒmprɪˈhensəbl/ *adj* incompréhensible.

**inconceivable** /ɪnkənˈsiːvəbl/ *adj* inconcevable.

**inconclusive** /ɪnkənˈkluːsɪv/ *adj* peu concluant.

**incongruous** /ɪnˈkɒŋgrʊəs/ *adj* déconcertant, surprenant.

**inconsiderate** /ɪnkənˈsɪdərət/ *adj* (person) peu attentif à autrui; (act) maladroit.

**inconsistent** /ɪnkənˈsɪstənt/ *adj* (argument) incohérent; (performance) inégal; (behaviour) changeant; ~ with en contradiction avec.

**inconspicuous** /ɪnkənˈspɪkjʊəs/ *adj* qui passe inaperçu.

**incontinent** /ɪnˈkɒntɪnənt/ *adj* incontinent.

**inconvenience** /ɪnkənˈviːnɪəns/ *n* dérangement *m*; (drawback) inconvénient *m*. ●*vt* déranger. **inconvenient** *adj* incommode; if it's not inconvenient for you si cela ne vous dérange pas.

**incorporate** /ɪnˈkɔːpəreɪt/ vt incorporer (into dans); (contain) comporter.

**incorrect** /ɪnkəˈrekt/ adj incorrect.

**increase¹** /ˈɪnkriːs/ n augmentation f (in, of de). be on the ~ être en progression.

**increase²** /ɪnˈkriːs/ vt/i augmenter. **increasing** adj croissant. **increasingly** adv de plus en plus.

**incredible** /ɪnˈkredəbl/ adj incroyable.

**incriminate** /ɪnˈkrɪmɪneɪt/ vt incriminer. **incriminating** adj compromettant.

**incubate** /ˈɪŋkjʊbeɪt/ vt (eggs) couver. **incubation** n incubation f. **incubator** n couveuse f.

**incur** /ɪnˈkɜː(r)/ vt ( pl incurred ) ( penalty, anger) encourir; (debts) contracter.

**indebted** /ɪnˈdetɪd/ adj ~ to sb redevable à qn (for de); (grateful) reconnaissant à qn.

**indecent** /ɪnˈdiːsnt/ adj indécent.

**indecisive** /ɪndɪˈsaɪsɪv/ adj indécis; (ending) peu concluant.

**indeed** /ɪnˈdiːd/ adv en effet; (emphatic) vraiment.

**indefinite** /ɪnˈdefɪnət/ adj vague; (period, delay) illimité. **indefinitely** adv indéfiniment.

**indelible** /ɪnˈdeləbl/ adj indélébile.

**indemnity** /ɪnˈdemnəti/ n (protection) assurance f; (payment) indemnité f.

**indent** /ɪnˈdent/ vt (text) renforcer. **indentation** n (dent) marque f.

**independence** /ɪndɪˈpendəns/ n indépendance f. **independent** adj indépendant. **independently** adv de façon indépendante; independently of indépendamment de.

**index** /ˈɪndeks/ n (pl ~es) (in

book) index m; (in library) catalogue m; (in economy) indice m; ~ card fiche f; ~ (finger) index m. ● vt classer. ~-**linked** adj indexé.

**India** /ˈɪndɪə/ n Inde f.

**Indian** /ˈɪndɪən/ n Indien/-ne m/f. ● adj indien.

**indicate** /ˈɪndɪkeɪt/ vt indiquer. **indication** n indication f.

**indicative** /ɪnˈdɪkətɪv/ adj & n indicatif (m).

**indicator** /ˈɪndɪkeɪtə(r)/ n (pointer) aiguille f; (on vehicle) clignotant m; (board) tableau m.

**indict** /ɪnˈdaɪt/ vt inculper. **indictment** n accusation f.

**indifferent** /ɪnˈdɪfrənt/ adj indifférent; (not good) médiocre.

**indigenous** /ɪnˈdɪdʒɪnəs/ adj indigène.

**indigestible** /ɪndɪˈdʒestəbl/ adj indigeste. **indigestion** n indigestion f.

**indignant** /ɪnˈdɪɡnənt/ adj indigné.

**indirect** /ɪndɪˈrekt/ adj indirect. **indirectly** adv indirectement.

**indiscreet** /ɪndɪˈskriːt/ adj indiscret. **indiscretion** n indiscrétion f.

**indiscriminate** /ɪndɪˈskrɪmɪnət/ adj sans distinction. **indiscriminately** adv sans distinction.

**indisputable** /ɪndɪˈspjuːtəbl/ adj indiscutable.

**individual** /ɪndɪˈvɪdʒʊəl/ adj individuel; (tuition) particulier. ● n individu m. **individualist** n individualiste m/f. **individuality** n individualité f. **individually** adv individuellement.

**indoctrinate** /ɪnˈdɒktrɪneɪt/ vt endoctriner. **indoctrination** n endoctrinement m.

**indolent** /ˈɪndələnt/ adj indolent.

**Indonesia** /ɪndəʊˈniːzjə/ n Indonésie f.

**indoor** /ˈɪndɔː(r)/ adj (clothes) d'intérieur; (pool, court) couvert. **indoors** adv à l'intérieur.

**induce** /ɪnˈdjuːs/ vt (influence) persuader; (stronger) inciter (to do à faire). **inducement** n (financial) récompense f; (incentive) motivation f.

**induction** /ɪnˈdʌkʃn/ n (Electr) induction f; (inauguration) installation f.

**indulge** /ɪnˈdʌldʒ/ vt (person, whim) céder à; (child) gâter. ● vi ~ in se livrer à. **indulgence** n indulgence f; (treat) plaisir m. **indulgent** adj indulgent.

**industrial** /ɪnˈdʌstriəl/ adj industriel; (accident) du travail; ~ action grève f; ~ dispute conflit m social. **industrialist** n industriel/-le m/f. **industrialized** adj industrialisé.

**industrious** /ɪnˈdʌstriəs/ adj diligent.

**industry** /ˈɪndəstri/ n industrie f; (zeal) zèle m.

**inebriated** /ɪˈniːbrieɪtɪd/ adj ivre.

**inedible** /ɪnˈedɪbl/ adj immangeable.

**ineffective** /ɪnɪˈfektɪv/ adj inefficace.

**inefficient** /ɪnɪˈfɪʃnt/ adj inefficace; (person) incompétent.

**ineligible** /ɪnˈelɪdʒəbl/ adj inéligible; be ~ for ne pas avoir droit à.

**inept** /ɪˈnept/ adj incompétent; (tactless) maladroit.

**inequality** /ɪnɪˈkwɒlətɪ/ n inégalité f.

**inescapable** /ɪnɪˈskeɪpəbl/ adj indéniable.

**inevitable** /ɪnˈevɪtəbl/ adj inévitable.

**inexcusable** /ɪnɪkˈskjuːzəbl/ adj inexcusable.

**inexhaustible** /ɪnɪgˈzɔːstəbl/ adj inépuisable.

**inexpensive** /ɪnɪkˈspensɪv/ adj pas cher.

**inexperience** /ɪnɪkˈspɪərɪəns/ n inexpérience f. **inexperienced** adj inexpérimenté.

**infallible** /ɪnˈfæləbl/ adj infaillible.

**infamous** /ˈɪnfəməs/ adj (person) tristement célèbre; (deed) infâme.

**infancy** /ˈɪnfənsɪ/ n petite enfance f; in its ~ (fig) à ses débuts mpl. **infant** n (baby) bébé m; (at school) enfant m. **infantile** adj infantile.

**infatuated** /ɪnˈfætʃʊeɪtɪd/ adj ~ with entiché de. **infatuation** n engouement m.

**infect** /ɪnˈfekt/ vt contaminer; ~ sb with sth transmettre qch à qn. **infection** n infection f. **infectious** adj contagieux.

**infer** /ɪnˈfɜː(r)/ vt (pt inferred) (deduce) déduire.

**inferior** /ɪnˈfɪərɪə(r)/ adj inférieur (to à). (work, product) de qualité inférieure. ● n inférieur/-e m/f. **inferiority** n infériorité f.

**inferno** /ɪnˈfɜːnəʊ/ n (hell) enfer m; (blaze) brasier m.

**infertile** /ɪnˈfɜːtaɪl/ adj infertile.

**infest** /ɪnˈfest/ vt infester (with de).

**infidelity** /ɪnfɪˈdelətɪ/ n infidélité f.

**infighting** /ˈɪnfaɪtɪŋ/ n conflits mpl internes.

**infinite** /ˈɪnfɪnət/ adj infini. **infinitely** adv infiniment. **infinitive** n infinitif m. **infinity** n infinité f.

**infirm** /ɪnˈfɜːm/ adj infirme. **infirmary** n hôpital m; (sick-bay) infirmerie f. **infirmity** n infirmité f.

**inflame** /ɪnˈfleɪm/ vt enflammer. **inflammable** adj inflammable. **inflammation** n inflammation f. **inflammatory** adj incendiaire.

**inflatable** /ɪnˈfleɪtəbl/ adj gonflable. **inflate** vt (lit, fig) gonfler.

**inflation** /ɪnˈfleɪʃn/ n inflation f.

**inflection** /ɪnˈflekʃn/ n (of word root) flexion f; (of vowel, voice) inflexion f.

**inflict** /ɪnˈflɪkt/ vt infliger (on à).

**influence** /ˈɪnfluəns/ n influence f; under the ~ (drunk 🆃) éméché. ● vt (person) influencer; (choice) influer sur. **influential** adj (powerful) influent; (theory, artist) très suivi.

**influenza** /ɪnfluˈenzə/ n grippe f.

**influx** /ˈɪnflʌks/ n afflux m.

**inform** /ɪnˈfɔːm/ vt informer (of de). keep ~ed tenir au courant.

**informal** /ɪnˈfɔːml/ adj (simple) simple, sans façons; (unofficial) officieux; (colloquial) familier. **informality** n simplicité f. **informally** adv (dress) en tenue décontractée; (speak) en toute simplicité.

**informant** /ɪnˈfɔːmənt/ n indicateur-trice m/f.

**information** /ɪnfəˈmeɪʃn/ n renseignements mpl, informations fpl; some ~ un renseignement. ~ **superhighway** n autoroute f de l'information. ~ **technology** n informatique f.

**informative** /ɪnˈfɔːmətɪv/ adj (book) riche en renseignements; (visit) instructif.

**informer** /ɪnˈfɔːmə(r)/ n indicateur-trice m/f.

**infrequent** /ɪnˈfriːkwənt/ adj rare.

**infringe** /ɪnˈfrɪndʒ/ vt (rule) enfreindre; (rights) ne pas respecter. **infringement** n infraction f.

**infuriate** /ɪnˈfjʊərɪeɪt/ vt exaspérer.

**ingenuity** /ɪndʒɪˈnjuːətɪ/ n ingéniosité f.

**ingot** /ˈɪŋgət/ n lingot m.

**ingrained** /ɪnˈɡreɪnd/ adj (hatred) enraciné; (dirt) bien incrusté.

**ingratiate** /ɪnˈɡreɪʃɪeɪt/ vt ~ one-self with se faire bien voir de.

**ingredient** /ɪnˈɡriːdɪənt/ n ingrédient m.

**inhabit** /ɪnˈhæbɪt/ vt habiter. **inhabitable** adj habitable. **inhabitant** n habitant-e m/f.

**inhale** /ɪnˈheɪl/ vt inhaler; (smoke) avaler. **inhaler** n inhalateur m.

**inherent** /ɪnˈhɪərənt/ adj inhérent (in à). **inherently** adv en soi, par sa nature.

**inherit** /ɪnˈherɪt/ vt hériter de; ~ sth from sb hériter qch de qn. **inheritance** n héritage m.

**inhibit** /ɪnˈhɪbɪt/ vt (restrain) inhiber; (prevent) empêcher, entraver.

**inhospitable** /ɪnhɒˈspɪtəbl/ adj inhospitalier.

**inhuman** /ɪnˈhjuːmən/ adj inhumain.

**initial** /ɪˈnɪʃl/ n initiale f. ● vt (pt **initialled**) parapher. ● adj initial.

**initiate** /ɪˈnɪʃɪeɪt/ vt (project) mettre en œuvre; (talks) amorcer; (person) initier (into à). **initiation** n initiation f; (start) amorce f.

**initiative** /ɪˈnɪʃɪətɪv/ n initiative f.

**inject** /ɪnˈdʒekt/ vt injecter (into dans). (new element) insuffler (into à). **injection** n injection f, piqûre f.

**injure** /ˈɪndʒə(r)/ vt blesser; (damage) nuire à. **injury** n blessure f.

**injustice** /ɪnˈdʒʌstɪs/ n injustice f.

**ink** /ɪŋk/ n encre f.

**inkling** /ˈɪŋklɪŋ/ n petite idée f.

**inland** /ˈɪnlənd/ adj intérieur; I~ Revenue service m des impôts britannique.

**in-laws** /ˈɪnlɔːz/ npl (parents) beaux-parents mpl; (family) belle-famille f.

**inlay**[1] /ɪnˈleɪ/ vt (pt **inlaid**) incruster (with de); (on wood) marqueter.

**inlay**[2] /ˈɪnleɪ/ n incrustation f; (on

wood) marqueterie f.

**inlet** /'ɪnlet/ n bras m de mer; (Tech) arrivée f.

**inmate** /'ɪnmeɪt/ n (of asylum) interné/-e m/f; (of prison) détenu /-e m/f.

**inn** /ɪn/ n auberge f.

**innate** /ɪ'neɪt/ adj inné.

**inner** /'ɪnə(r)/ adj intérieur; ~ city quartiers mpl déshérités; ~ tube chambre f à air.

**innocent** /'ɪnəsnt/ adj & n innocent/-e (m/f).

**innocuous** /ɪ'nɒkjʊəs/ adj inoffensif.

**innovate** /'ɪnəveɪt/ vi innover.

**innuendo** /ɪnjuː'endəʊ/ n (pl ~es) insinuations fpl; (sexual) allusions fpl grivoises.

**innumerable** /ɪ'njuːmərəbl/ adj innombrable.

**inoculate** /ɪ'nɒkjʊleɪt/ vt vacciner (against contre).

**inopportune** /ɪn'ɒpətjuːn/ adj inopportun.

**in-patient** /'ɪnpeɪʃnt/ n malade mf hospitalisé/-e.

**input** /'ɪnpʊt/ n (of energy) alimentation f (of en); (contribution) contribution f; (data) données fpl; (computer process) saisie f des données. • vt (data) saisir.

**inquest** /'ɪnkwest/ n enquête f.

**inquire** /ɪn'kwaɪə(r)/ vi se renseigner (about, into sur). • vt demander.

**inquiry** /ɪn'kwaɪərɪ/ n demande f de renseignements; (inquest) enquête f.

**inquisitive** /ɪn'kwɪzətɪv/ adj curieux.

**inroad** /'ɪnrəʊd/ n make ~s into faire une avancée sur.

**insane** /ɪn'seɪn/ adj fou; (Jur)

aliéné. **insanity** n folie f; (Jur) aliénation f mentale.

**inscribe** /ɪn'skraɪb/ vt inscrire. **inscription** n inscription f.

**inscrutable** /ɪn'skruːtəbl/ adj énigmatique.

**insect** /'ɪnsekt/ n insecte m. **insecticide** n insecticide m.

**insecure** /ɪnsɪ'kjʊə(r)/ adj (person) qui manque d'assurance; (job) précaire; (lock, property) peu sûr. **insecurity** n (of person) manque m d'assurance; (of situation) insécurité f.

**insensitive** /ɪn'sensətɪv/ adj insensible; (remark) indélicat.

**inseparable** /ɪn'seprəbl/ adj inséparable (from de).

**insert** /ɪn'sɜːt/ vt insérer (in dans).

**in-service** /ɪnsɜː'rvɪs/ adj (training) continu.

**inshore** /ɪn'ʃɔː(r)/ adj côtier.

**inside** /ɪn'saɪd/ n intérieur m; ~s 🔲 entrailles fpl. • adj intérieur. • adv à l'intérieur; go ~ entrer. • prep à l'intérieur de; (of time) en moins de; ~ out à l'envers; (thoroughly) à fond.

**insight** /'ɪnsaɪt/ n (perception) perspicacité f; (idea) aperçu m.

**insignia** /ɪn'sɪgnɪə/ npl insigne m.

**insignificant** /ɪnsɪg'nɪfɪkənt/ adj (cost, difference) négligeable; (person) insignifiant.

**insincere** /ɪnsɪn'sɪə(r)/ adj peu sincère.

**insinuate** /ɪn'sɪnjʊeɪt/ vt insinuer.

**insist** /ɪn'sɪst/ vi/i insister (that pour que). ~ on exiger; ~ on doing vouloir à tout prix faire. **insistence** n insistance f. **insistent** adj insistant. **insistently** adv avec insistance.

**insofar as** /ɪnsəʊ'fɑːəz/ adv dans la mesure où.

**insolent** /ˈɪnsələnt/ adj insolent.

**insolvent** /ɪnˈsɒlvənt/ adj insolvable.

**insomnia** /ɪnˈsɒmnɪə/ n insomnie f. **insomniac** n insomniaque mf.

**inspect** /ɪnˈspekt/ vt (school, machinery) inspecter; (tickets) contrôler. **inspection** n inspection f; (of passport, ticket) contrôle m. **inspector** n inspecteur-trice m/f; (on bus) contrôleur-euse m/f.

**inspiration** /ɪnspəˈreɪʃn/ n inspiration f. **inspire** vt inspirer.

**install** /ɪnˈstɔːl/ vt installer.

**instalment** /ɪnˈstɔːlmənt/ n (payment) versement m; (of serial) épisode m.

**instance** /ˈɪnstəns/ n exemple m; (case) cas m; for ∼ par exemple; in the first ∼ en premier lieu.

**instant** /ˈɪnstənt/ adj immédiat; (food) instantané. ● n instant m. **instantaneous** adj instantané. **instantly** adv immédiatement.

**instead** /ɪnˈsted/ adv plutôt; ∼ of doing au lieu de faire; ∼ of sb à la place de qn.

**instep** /ˈɪnstep/ n cou-de-pied m.

**instigate** /ˈɪnstɪgeɪt/ vt (attack) lancer; (proceedings) engager.

**instil** /ɪnˈstɪl/ vt (pt instilled) inculquer; (fear) insuffler.

**instinct** /ˈɪnstɪŋkt/ n instinct m. **instinctive** adj instinctif.

**institute** /ˈɪnstɪtjuːt/ n institut m. ● vt instituer; (proceedings) engager. **institution** n institution f; (school, hospital) établissement m.

**instruct** /ɪnˈstrʌkt/ vt (teach) instruire; (order) ordonner; ∼ sb in sth enseigner qch à qn; ∼ sb to do donner l'ordre à qn de faire. **instruction** n instruction f. **instructions** npl (for use) mode m d'emploi. **instructive** adj instructif.

**instructor** n (skiing, driving) moniteur-trice m/f.

**instrument** /ˈɪnstrəmənt/ n instrument m.

**instrumental** /ɪnstrəˈmentl/ adj instrumental; be ∼ in contribuer à. **instrumentalist** n instrumentaliste mf.

**insubordinate** /ɪnsəˈbɔːdɪnət/ adj insubordonné.

**insufficient** /ɪnsəˈfɪʃnt/ adj insuffisant.

**insular** /ˈɪnsjʊlə(r)/ adj (Geog) insulaire; (mind, person: fig) borné.

**insulate** /ˈɪnsjʊleɪt/ vt (room, wire) isoler.

**insulin** /ˈɪnsjʊlɪn/ n insuline f.

**insult¹** /ɪnˈsʌlt/ vt insulter.

**insult²** /ˈɪnsʌlt/ n insulte f.

**insurance** /ɪnˈʃɔːrəns/ n assurance f (against contre).

**insure** /ɪnˈʃɔː(r)/ vt assurer; ∼ that (US) s'assurer que.

**intact** /ɪnˈtækt/ adj intact.

**intake** /ˈɪnteɪk/ n (of food) consommation f; (School, Univ) admissions fpl.

**integral** /ˈɪntɪgrəl/ adj intégral (to à).

**integrate** /ˈɪntɪgreɪt/ vt/i (s')intégrer (with à; into dans).

**integrity** /ɪnˈtegrətɪ/ n intégrité f.

**intellect** /ˈɪntəlekt/ n intelligence f. **intellectual** adj & n intellectuel-le (m/f).

**intelligence** /ɪnˈtelɪdʒəns/ n intelligence f; (Mil) renseignements mpl. **intelligent** adj intelligent. **intelligently** adv intelligemment.

**intend** /ɪnˈtend/ vt (outcome) vouloir; ∼ to do avoir l'intention de faire. **intended** adj (result) voulu; (visit) projeté.

**intense** /ɪnˈtens/ adj intense; (person) sérieux. **intensely** adv (very) extrêmement.

**intensify** /ɪnˈtensɪfaɪ/ vt/i (s')intensifier.

**intensive** /ɪnˈtensɪv/ adj intensif; in ~ care en réanimation.

**intent** /ɪnˈtent/ n intention f. ● adj absorbé; ~ on doing résolu à faire.

**intention** /ɪnˈtenʃn/ n intention f. **intentional** adj intentionnel.

**intently** /ɪnˈtentlɪ/ adv attentivement.

**interact** /ɪntərˈækt/ vi (factors) agir l'un sur l'autre; (people) communiquer. **interactive** adj (TV, video) interactif.

**intercept** /ɪntəˈsept/ vt intercepter.

**interchange** /ˈɪntətʃeɪndʒ/ n (road junction) échangeur m. (exchange) échange m.

**interchangeable** /ɪntəˈtʃeɪndʒəbl/ adj interchangeable.

**intercom** /ˈɪntəkɒm/ n interphone® m.

**interconnected** /ɪntəkəˈnektɪd/ adj (parts) raccordé; (problems) lié.

**intercourse** /ˈɪntəkɔːs/ n rapports mpl.

**interest** /ˈɪntrəst/ n intérêt m; ~ rate taux m d'intérêt. ● vt intéresser (in à). **interested** adj intéressé; be ~ed in s'intéresser à. **interesting** adj intéressant.

**interface** /ˈɪntəfeɪs/ n interface f.

**interfere** /ɪntəˈfɪə(r)/ vi se mêler des affaires des autres; ~ in se mêler de; ~ with (freedom) empiéter sur; (tamper with) toucher. **interference** n ingérence f; (sound, light waves) brouillage m; (radio) parasites mpl.

**interim** /ˈɪntərɪm/ n in the ~ entre-temps. ● adj (government) provisoire; (payment) intermédiaire.

**interior** /ɪnˈtɪərɪə(r)/ n intérieur m.

● adj intérieur.

**interjection** /ɪntəˈdʒekʃn/ n interjection f.

**interlock** /ɪntəˈlɒk/ vt/i (Tech) (s')emboîter, (s')enclencher.

**interlude** /ˈɪntəluːd/ n intervalle m; (Theat, Mus) intermède m.

**intermediary** /ɪntəˈmiːdɪərɪ/ adj & n intermédiaire (mf).

**intermediate** /ɪntəˈmiːdɪət/ adj intermédiaire; (exam, level) moyen.

**intermission** /ɪntəˈmɪʃn/ n (Theat) entracte m.

**intermittent** /ɪntəˈmɪtənt/ adj intermittent.

**intern¹** /ɪnˈtɜːn/ vt interner.

**intern²** /ˈɪntɜːn/ n (US) stagiaire mf; (Med) interne mf.

**internal** /ɪnˈtɜːnl/ adj interne; (domestic: Pol) intérieur; I~ Revenue (US) service m des impôts américain.

**international** /ɪntəˈnæʃnəl/ adj international.

**Internet** /ˈɪntənet/ n Internet m; on the ~ sur Internet; ~ access accès à Internet; ~ service provider fournisseur m d'accès Internet.

**interpret** /ɪnˈtɜːprɪt/ vt interpréter (as comme). ● vi faire l'interprète. **interpretation** n interprétation f. **interpreter** n interprète mf.

**interrelated** /ɪntərɪˈleɪtɪd/ adj interdépendant, lié.

**interrogate** /ɪnˈterəgeɪt/ vt interroger. **interrogative** adj & n (Ling) interrogatif (m).

**interrupt** /ɪntəˈrʌpt/ vt/i interrompre. **interruption** n interruption f.

**intersect** /ɪntəˈsekt/ vt/i (lines, roads) (se) croiser. **intersection** n intersection f.

**interspersed** /ɪntəˈspɜːst/ adj parsemé (with de).

i

**intertwine** /ɪntə'twaɪn/ vt/i (s')entrelacer.

**interval** /'ɪntəvl/ n intervalle m; (Theat) entracte m.

**intervene** /ɪntə'vi:n/ vi intervenir; (of time) s'écouler (**between** entre); (happen) arriver.

**interview** /'ɪntəvju:/ n (for job) entretien m; (by a journalist) interview f. ●vt (candidate) faire passer un entretien à; (celebrity) interviewer.

**intestine** /ɪn'testɪn/ n intestin m.

**intimacy** /'ɪntɪməsɪ/ n intimité f.

**intimate¹** /'ɪntɪmeɪt/ vt (state) annoncer; (hint) laisser entendre.

**intimate²** /'ɪntɪmət/ adj intime. **intimately** adv intimement.

**intimidate** /ɪn'tɪmɪdeɪt/ vt intimider.

**into** /'ɪntu:/, /'ɪntə/ prep (put, go, fall) dans; (divide, translate, change) en; **be** ~ **jazz** être fana du jazz ▣; 8 ~ 24 **is** 3 24 divisé par 8 égale 3.

**intolerant** /ɪn'tɒlərənt/ adj intolérant.

**intonation** /ɪntə'neɪʃn/ n intonation f.

**intoxicate** /ɪn'tɒksɪkeɪt/ vt enivrer. **intoxicated** adj ivre. **intoxication** n ivresse f.

**intractable** /ɪn'træktəbl/ adj (person) intraitable; (problem) rebelle.

**intranet** /'ɪntrənet/ n (Comput) intranet m.

**intransitive** /ɪn'trænsətɪv/ adj intransitif.

**intravenous** /ɪntrə'vi:nəs/ adj (Med) intraveineux.

**intricate** /'ɪntrɪkət/ adj complexe.

**intrigue** /ɪn'tri:g/ vt intriguer. ●n intrigue f. **intriguing** adj fascinant; (curious) curieux.

**intrinsic** /ɪn'trɪnzɪk/ adj

**intrinsèque** (**to** à).

**introduce** /ɪntrə'dju:s/ vt (person, idea, programme) présenter; (object, law) introduire (**into** dans). **introduction** n introduction f; (of person) présentation f. **introductory** adj (words) préliminaires.

**introvert** /'ɪntrəvɜ:t/ n introverti-e m/f.

**intrude** /ɪn'tru:d/ vi (person) s'imposer (**on sb** à qn), déranger. **intruder** n intrus/-e m/f. **intrusion** n intrusion f.

**intuition** /ɪntju:'ɪʃn/ n intuition f. **intuitive** adj intuitif.

**inundate** /'ɪnʌndeɪt/ vt inonder (**with** de).

**invade** /ɪn'veɪd/ vt envahir.

**invalid¹** /'ɪnvəlɪːd/ n malade mf; (disabled) infirme mf.

**invalid²** /ɪn'vælɪd/ adj (passport) pas valable; (claim) sans fondement. **invalidate** vt (argument) infirmer; (claim) annuler.

**invaluable** /ɪn'væljʊəbl/ adj inestimable.

**invariable** /ɪn'veərɪəbl/ adj invariable. **invariably** adv invariablement.

**invasion** /ɪn'veɪʒn/ n invasion f.

**invent** /ɪn'vent/ vt inventer. **invention** n invention f. **inventive** adj inventif. **inventor** n inventeur/-trice m/f.

**inventory** /'ɪnvəntrɪ/ n inventaire m.

**invert** /ɪn'vɜ:t/ vt (order) intervertir; (image, values) renverser; ~**ed commas** guillemets mpl.

**invest** /ɪn'vest/ vt investir; (time, effort) consacrer. ●vi faire un investissement; ~ **in** (buy) s'acheter.

**investigate** /ɪn'vestɪgeɪt/ vt examiner; (crime) enquêter sur. **investigation** n investigation f. **investi-**

**gator** n (police) enquêteur/-euse m/f.

**investment** /ɪnˈvestmənt/ n investissement m; emotional ~ engagement m personnel. **investor** n investisseur/-euse m/f; (in shares) actionnaire m/f.

**invigilate** /ɪnˈvɪdʒɪleɪt/ vi (exam) surveiller. **invigilator** n surveillant/-e m/f.

**invigorate** /ɪnˈvɪgəreɪt/ vt revigorer.

**invisible** /ɪnˈvɪzəbl/ adj invisible.

**invitation** /ɪnvɪˈteɪʃn/ n invitation f. **invite** vt inviter; (ask for) demander. **inviting** adj engageant.

**invoice** /ˈɪnvɔɪs/ n facture f. ● vt facturer.

**involuntary** /ɪnˈvɒləntrɪ/ adj involontaire.

**involve** /ɪnˈvɒlv/ vt impliquer; (person) faire participer (in à). **involved** adj (complex) compliqué; (at stake) en jeu; **be** ~d **in** (work) participer à; (crime) être mêlé à. **involvement** n participation f (in à).

**inward** /ˈɪnwəd/ adj (feeling) intérieur. **inwardly** adv intérieurement. **inwards** adv vers l'intérieur.

**iodine** /ˈaɪədiːn/ n iode m; (antiseptic) teinture f d'iode.

**iota** /aɪˈəʊtə/ n iota m; not one ~ of pas un grain de.

**IOU** abbr (**I owe you**) reconnaissance f de dette.

**IQ** abbr (**intelligence quotient**) QI m.

**Iran** /ɪˈrɑːn/ n Iran m.

**Iraq** /ɪˈrɑːk/ n Irak m.

**irate** /aɪˈreɪt/ adj furieux.

**IRC** abbr (**Internet Relay Chat**) (Internet) conversation f IRC.

**Ireland** /ˈaɪələnd/ n Irlande f.

**Irish** /ˈaɪərɪʃ/ n & adj irlandais (m).

~**man** n Irlandais m. ~**woman** n Irlandaise f.

**iron** /ˈaɪən/ n fer m; (appliance) fer (à repasser). ● adj (will) de fer; (bar) en fer. ● vt repasser.

**ironic** /aɪˈrɒnɪk/ adj ironique.

**iron:** ironing-board n planche f à repasser. ~**monger** n quincaillier m.

**irony** /ˈaɪrənɪ/ n ironie f.

**irrational** /ɪˈræʃənl/ adj irrationnel; (person) pas raisonnable.

**irregular** /ɪˈregjʊlə(r)/ adj irrégulier.

**irrelevant** /ɪˈreləvnt/ adj hors de propos.

**irreplaceable** /ɪrɪˈpleɪsəbl/ adj irremplaçable.

**irresistible** /ɪrɪˈzɪstəbl/ adj irrésistible.

**irrespective** /ɪrɪˈspektɪv/ adj ~ **of** sans tenir compte de.

**irresponsible** /ɪrɪˈspɒnsəbl/ adj irresponsable.

**irreverent** /ɪˈrevərənt/ adj irrévérencieux.

**irrigate** /ˈɪrɪgeɪt/ vt irriguer.

**irritable** /ˈɪrɪtəbl/ adj irritable.

**irritate** /ˈɪrɪteɪt/ vt irriter. **irritating** adj irritant.

**is** /ɪz/ ➞BE.

**ISDN** abbr (integrated services digital network) RNIS n, réseau m numérique à intégration de services.

**Islam** /ˈɪzlɑːm/ n (faith) islam m; (Muslims) Islam m. **Islamic** adj islamique.

**island** /ˈaɪlənd/ n île f.

**isle** /aɪl/ n île f.

**isolate** /ˈaɪsəleɪt/ vt isoler. **isolation** n isolement m.

**Israel** /ˈɪzreɪl/ n Israël m.

**Israeli** /ɪzˈreɪlɪ/ n Israélien/-ne m/f. ● adj israélien.

**issue** /'ɪʃuː/ n question f; (outcome) résultat m; (of magazine) numéro m; (of stamps) émission f; (offspring) descendance f; at ~ in cause. • vt distribuer; (stamps) émettre; (book) publier; (order) délivrer. • vi ~ from provenir de.

---

**it**
/ɪt/
*pronoun*
····▸ (subject) il, elle; 'where's the book/chair?'— 'it's in the kitchen' 'où est le livre/la chaise?'—'il/elle est dans la cuisine'.

····▸ (object) le, la, l'; ~'s my book and I want ~ c'est mon livre et je le veux; I liked his shirt, did you notice ~? sa chemise m'a plu, l'as-tu remarquée?; give ~ to me donne-le-moi.

····▸ (with preposition) we talked a lot about ~ on en a beaucoup parlé; Elliott went to ~ Elliott y est allé.

····▸ (impersonal) il; ~'s raining il pleut; ~ will snow il va neiger.

---

**IT** *abbr* ▸ INFORMATION TECHNOLOGY.
**Italian** /ɪ'tæljən/ n (person) Italien/-ne m/f; (Ling) italien m. • adj italien.
**italics** /ɪ'tælɪks/ npl italique m.
**Italy** /'ɪtəlɪ/ n Italie f.
**itch** /ɪtʃ/ n démangeaison f. • vi démanger; my arm ~es j'ai le bras qui me démange; be ~ing to do mourir d'envie de faire.
**item** /'aɪtəm/ n article m; (on agenda) point m.
**itemize** /'aɪtəmaɪz/ vt détailler; ~d bill facture f détaillée.

**itinerary** /aɪ'tɪnərərɪ/ n itinéraire m.
**its** /ɪts/ det son, sa; pl ses.
**it's** ▸ IT IS, IT HAS.
**itself** /ɪt'self/ pron lui-même, elle-même; (reflexive) se.

**ivory** /'aɪvərɪ/ n ivoire m; ~ tower tour f d'ivoire.
**ivy** /'aɪvɪ/ n lierre m.

---

**The Ivy League** Ce terme *i* désigne les huit universités les plus prestigieuses de la côte des États-Unis (Harvard, Yale, Columbia, Cornell, Dartmouth, Brown, Princeton, Pennsylvania). Elles doivent ce nom au lierre qui pousse sur les bâtiments des plus anciennes d'entre elles. Ces universités sont réputées tant dans les domaines académiques que sportifs.

---

# Jj

**jab** /dʒæb/ vt (pt jabbed) ~ sth into sth planter qch dans qch. • n coup m; (injection) piqûre f.
**jack** /dʒæk/ n (Auto) cric m; (cards) valet m; (Electr) jack m. • vt ~ up soulever avec un cric.
**jacket** /'dʒækɪt/ n veste f, veston m; (of book) jaquette f.
**jackknife** /'dʒæknaɪf/ n couteau m pliant. • vi (lorry) se mettre en portefeuille.
**jackpot** /'dʒækpɒt/ n gros lot m; hit the ~ gagner le gros lot.
**jade** /dʒeɪd/ n (stone) jade m.
**jaded** /'dʒeɪdɪd/ adj (tired) fatigué.

(bored) blasé.

**jagged** /'dʒægɪd/ adj (rock) déchiqueté; (knife) dentelé.

**jail** /dʒeɪl/ n prison f. ● vt mettre en prison.

**jam** /dʒæm/ n confiture f; (traffic) ~ embouteillage m. ● vt/i (pt **jammed**) (wedge) (se) coincer; (cram) (s')entasser; (street) encombrer; (radio) brouiller.

**Jamaica** /dʒə'meɪkə/ n Jamaïque f.

**jam-packed** adj 🔲 bondé; ~ with bourré de.

**jangle** /'dʒæŋgl/ n tintement m. ● vt/i (faire) tinter.

**janitor** /'dʒænɪtə(r)/ n (US) gardien m.

**January** /'dʒænjʊərɪ/ n janvier m.

**Japan** /dʒə'pæn/ n Japon m.

**Japanese** /dʒæpə'niːz/ n (person) Japonais-e m/f; (Ling) japonais m. ● adj japonais.

**jar** /dʒɑː(r)/ n pot m, bocal m. ● vi (pt **jarred**) rendre un son discordant; (colours) détonner. ● vt ébranler.

**jargon** /'dʒɑːgən/ n jargon m.

**jaundice** /'dʒɔːndɪs/ n jaunisse f.

**javelin** /'dʒævlɪn/ n javelot m.

**jaw** /dʒɔː/ n mâchoire f.

**jay** /dʒeɪ/ n geai m.

**jazz** /dʒæz/ n jazz m. ● vt ~ up (dress) rajeunir; (event) animer.

**jealous** /'dʒeləs/ adj jaloux. **jealousy** n jalousie f.

**jeans** /dʒiːnz/ npl jean m.

**jeer** /dʒɪə(r)/ vt/i ~ (at) huer. ● n huée f.

**jelly** /'dʒelɪ/ n gelée f. ~**fish** n méduse f.

**jeopardize** /'dʒepədaɪz/ vt (career, chance) compromettre; (lives) mettre en péril.

**jerk** /dʒɜːk/ n secousse f; (fool 🔲)

crétin m 🔲. ● vt tirer brusquement. **jerky** adj saccadé.

**jersey** /'dʒɜːzɪ/ n (garment) pullover m; (fabric) jersey m.

**jet** /dʒet/ n (plane, stream) jet m; (mineral) jais m; ~ **lag** décalage m horaire.

**jettison** /'dʒetɪsn/ vt jeter pardessus bord; (Aviat) larguer; (fig) rejeter.

**jetty** /'dʒetɪ/ n jetée f.

**Jew** /dʒuː/ n juif/juive m/f.

**jewel** /'dʒuːəl/ n bijou m. **jeweller** n bijoutier-ière m/f. **jeweller('s)** n (shop) bijouterie f. **jewellery** n bijoux mpl.

**Jewish** /'dʒuːɪʃ/ adj juif.

**jibe** /dʒaɪb/ n moquerie f.

**jigsaw** /'dʒɪgsɔː/ n puzzle m.

**jingle** /'dʒɪŋgl/ vt/i (faire) tinter. ● n tintement m; (advertising) refrain m publicitaire, sonal m.

**jinx** /dʒɪŋks/ n (person) portemalheur m inv; (curse) sort m.

**jitters** /'dʒɪtəz/ npl have the ~ 🔲 être nerveux. **jittery** adj nerveux.

**job** /dʒɒb/ n emploi m; (post) poste m; out of a ~ sans emploi; it is a good ~ that heureusement que; just the ~ tout à fait ce qu'il faut. ~ **centre** n bureau m des services nationaux de l'emploi. **jobless** adj sans emploi.

**jockey** /'dʒɒkɪ/ n jockey m.

**jog** /dʒɒg/ n go for a ~ aller faire un jogging. ● vt (pt **jogged**) heurter; (memory) rafraîchir. ● vi faire du jogging. **jogging** n jogging m.

**join** /dʒɔɪn/ vt (attach) réunir, joindre; (club) devenir membre de; (company) entrer dans; (army) s'engager dans; (queue) se mettre dans; ~ **sb** (in activity) se joindre à qn; (meet) rejoindre qn. ● vi (become member) adhérer; (pieces) se joint-dre; (roads) se rejoindre. ● n raccord m. □ ~ in participer; ~ in sth participer à qch; ~ up (Mil) s'engager; ~ up relier qch. joiner n menuisier/-ière m/f.

joint /dʒɔɪnt/ adj (action) collectif; (measures, venture) commun; (winner) ex aequo inv; (account) joint; ~ author coauteur m. ● n (join) joint m; (Anat) articulation f; (Culin) rôti m; out of ~ déboîté.

joke /dʒəʊk/ n plaisanterie f; (trick) farce f; it's no ~ ce n'est pas drôle. ● vi plaisanter. joker n blagueur/-euse m/f; (cards) joker m.

jolly /'dʒɒlɪ/ adj (-ier, -iest) (person) enjoué; (tune) joyeux. ● adv 🄯 drôlement.

jolt /dʒəʊlt/ vt secouer. ● vi cahoter. ● n secousse f; (shock) choc m.

jostle /'dʒɒsl/ vt/i (se) bousculer.

jot /dʒɒt/ vt (pt jotted) ~ (down) noter.

journal /'dʒɜːnl/ n journal m. journalism n journalisme m. journalist n journaliste mf.

journey /'dʒɜːnɪ/ n (trip) voyage m; (short or habitual) trajet m. ● vi voyager.

joy /dʒɔɪ/ n joie f. joyful adj joyeux.

joy: ~riding n rodéo m à la voiture volée. ~stick n (Comput) manette f; (Aviat) manche m à balai.

jubilant /'dʒuːbɪlənt/ adj (person) exultant; (mood) réjoui.

Judaism /'dʒuːdeɪɪzəm/ n judaïsme m.

judge /dʒʌdʒ/ n juge m. ● vt juger; (distance) estimer; judging by/from à en juger par. judg(e)ment n jugement m.

judicial /dʒuː'dɪʃl/ adj judiciaire. judiciary n magistrature f.

judo /'dʒuːdəʊ/ n judo m.

jug /dʒʌg/ n (glass) carafe f; (pot-

tery) pichet m.

juggernaut /'dʒʌgənɔːt/ n (lorry) poids m lourd.

juggle /'dʒʌgl/ vt/i jongler (avec). juggler n jongleur/-euse m/f.

juice /dʒuːs/ n jus m. juicy adj juteux; (details 🄯) croustillant.

jukebox /'dʒuːkbɒks/ n jukebox m.

July /dʒu'laɪ/ n juillet m.

jumble /'dʒʌmbl/ vt mélanger. ● n (of objects) tas m; (of ideas) fouillis m; ~ sale vente f de charité.

jumbo /'dʒʌmbəʊ/ n (also ~ jet) gros-porteur m.

jump /dʒʌmp/ vt sauter; ~ the lights passer au feu rouge; ~ the queue passer devant tout le monde. ● vi sauter; (in surprise) sursauter; (price) monter en flèche; ~ at (opportunity) sauter sur. ● n saut m, bond m; (increase) bond m.

jumper /'dʒʌmpə(r)/ n pull-(over) m; (dress; US) robe f chasuble.

jump-leads npl câbles mpl de démarrage.

jumpy /'dʒʌmpɪ/ adj nerveux.

junction /'dʒʌŋkʃn/ n (of roads) carrefour m; (on motorway) échangeur m.

June /dʒuːn/ n juin m.

jungle /'dʒʌŋgl/ n jungle f.

junior /'dʒuːnɪə(r)/ adj (young) jeune; (in rank) subalterne; (school) primaire. ● n cadet/-te m/f; (School) élève mf du primaire.

junk /dʒʌŋk/ n bric-à-brac m inv; (poor quality) camelote f; ~ food nourriture f industrielle.

junkie /'dʒʌŋkɪ/ n 🄯 drogué/ -e m/f.

junk: ~ mail n prospectus mpl. ~-shop n boutique f de bric-à-brac.

jurisdiction /dʒʊərɪs'dɪkʃn/ n

compétence f; (Jur) juridiction f.

**juror** /ˈdʒʊərə(r)/ n juré m.

**jury** /ˈdʒʊərɪ/ n jury m.

**just** /dʒʌst/ adj (fair) juste. ● adv (immediately, slightly) juste; (simply) tout simplement; (exactly) exactement; **he has/had ~ left** il vient/venait de partir; **have ~ missed** avoir manqué de peu; **I'm ~ leaving** je suis sur le point de partir; **it's ~ a cold** ce n'est qu'un rhume; **~ as tall/well** aussi grand/bien que; **~ listen!** écoutez donc!; **it's ~ ridiculous** c'est vraiment ridicule.

**justice** /ˈdʒʌstɪs/ n justice f; **J~ of the Peace** juge m de paix.

**justification** /dʒʌstɪfɪˈkeɪʃn/ n justification f. **justify** vt justifier.

**jut** /dʒʌt/ vi (pt jutted) **~ (out)** s'avancer en saillie.

**juvenile** /ˈdʒuːvənaɪl/ adj (childish) puéril; (offender) mineur; (delinquent) jeune. ● n jeune mf; (Jur) mineur/-e m/f.

**juxtapose** /dʒʌkstəˈpəʊz/ vt juxtaposer.

••••••••••••••••••••••••••••

# Kk

••••••••••••••••••••••••••••

**kangaroo** /kæŋɡəˈruː/ n kangourou m.

**karate** /kəˈrɑːtɪ/ n karaté m.

**kebab** /kɪˈbæb/ n brochette f.

**keel** /kiːl/ n (of ship) quille f. ● vi **~ over** (bateau) chavirer; (person) s'écrouler.

**keen** /kiːn/ adj (interest, wind, feeling) vif; (mind, analysis) pénétrant; (edge, appetite) aiguisé; (eager) en-

thousiaste; **be ~ on** être passionné de; **be ~ to do** or **on doing** tenir beaucoup à faire. **keenly** adv vivement. **keenness** n enthousiasme m.

**keep** /kiːp/ vt (pt kept) garder; (promise, shop, diary) tenir; (family) faire vivre; (animals) élever; (rule) respecter; (celebrate) célébrer; (delay) retenir; **~ sth clean/warm** garder qch propre/au chaud; **~ sb in/out** empêcher qn de sortir/d'entrer; **~ sb from doing** empêcher qn de faire. ● vi (food) se conserver; **~ to do** or **on doing** (continue doing f) faire. ● n pension f; (of castle) donjon m. □ **~ down** rester allongé; **~ sth down** limiter qch; **~ your voice down** baisse la voix!; **~ to** (road) ne pas s'écarter de; (rules) respecter; **~ up** (car, runner) suivre; (rain) continuer; **~ up with sb** (in speed) aller aussi vite que; (class, inflation, fashion, news) suivre.

**keeper** /ˈkiːpə(r)/ n gardien/-ne m/f.

**keepsake** /ˈkiːpseɪk/ n souvenir m.

**kennel** /ˈkenl/ n niche f.

**kept** /kept/ →KEEP.

**kerb** /kɜːb/ n bord m du trottoir.

**kernel** /ˈkɜːnl/ n amande f; **~ of truth** fond m de vérité.

**kettle** /ˈketl/ n bouilloire f.

**key** /kiː/ n clé f; (of computer, piano) touche f. ● adj (industry, figure) clé (inv). ● vt **~ (in)** saisir. **~board** n clavier m. **~hole** n trou m de serrure. **~pad** n (of telephone) clavier m numérique. **~ring** n porte-clés m inv. **~stroke** n (Comput) frappe f.

**khaki** /ˈkɑːkɪ/ n adj kaki inv.

**kick** /kɪk/ vt/i donner un coup de pied (à); (horse) botter. ● n coup m de pied; (of gun) recul m; **get a ~ out of doing** Ⅰ prendre plaisir à faire. □ **~ out** Ⅰ virer Ⅰ.

**kick-off** n coup m d'envoi.

**kid** /kɪd/ n (goat, leather) chevreau m; (child 🔲) gosse mf 🔲. ● vt/i (pt **kidded**) blaguer.

**kidnap** /ˈkɪdnæp/ vt (pt **kidnapped**) enlever. **kidnapping** n enlèvement m.

**kidney** /ˈkɪdnɪ/ n rein m; (Culin) rognon m.

**kill** /kɪl/ vt tuer; (rumour: fig) arrêter. ● n mise f à mort. **killer** n tueur/-euse m/f. **killing** n meurtre m.

**kiln** /kɪln/ n four m.

**kilo** /ˈkiːləʊ/ n kilo m.

**kilobyte** /ˈkɪləbaɪt/ n kilo-octet m.

**kilogram** /ˈkɪləɡræm/ n kilogramme m.

**kilometre**, (US) **kilometer** /ˈkɪləmiːtə(r)/ n kilomètre m.

**kilowatt** /ˈkɪləwɒt/ n kilowatt m.

**kin** /kɪn/ n parents mpl.

**kind** /kaɪnd/ n genre m, sorte f; in ~ en nature; ~ of (somewhat 🔲) assez. ● adj gentil, bon.

**kindergarten** /ˈkɪndəɡɑːtn/ n jardin m d'enfants.

**kindle** /ˈkɪndl/ vt/i (s')allumer.

**kindly** /ˈkaɪndlɪ/ adj (-ier, -iest) (person) gentil; (interest) bienveillant. ● adv avec gentillesse; would you ~ do auriez-vous l'amabilité de faire.

**kindness** /ˈkaɪndnɪs/ n bonté f.

**king** /kɪŋ/ n roi m. **kingdom** n royaume m; (Bot) règne m. **kingfisher** n martin-pêcheur m. ~**-size(d)** adj géant.

**kiosk** /ˈkiːɒsk/ n kiosque m; telephone ~ cabine f téléphonique; (Internet) borne f interactive, kiosque m.

**kiss** /kɪs/ n baiser m. ● vt/i (s')embrasser.

**kit** /kɪt/ n (clothing) affaires fpl; (set of tools) trousse f; (for assembly) kit m. ● vt (pt **kitted**) ~ out équiper.

**kitchen** /ˈkɪtʃɪn/ n cuisine f.

**kite** /kaɪt/ n (toy) cerf-volant m; (bird) milan m.

**kitten** /ˈkɪtn/ n chaton m.

**kitty** /ˈkɪtɪ/ n (fund) cagnotte f.

**knack** /næk/ n tour m de main (of doing pour faire).

**knead** /niːd/ vt pétrir.

**knee** /niː/ n genou m. ~**cap** n rotule f.

**kneel** /niːl/ vi (pt **knelt**) ~ (down) se mettre à genoux; (in prayer) s'agenouiller.

**knew** /njuː/ ➡**KNOW**.

**knickers** /ˈnɪkəz/ npl petite culotte f, slip m.

**knife** /naɪf/ n (pl **knives**) couteau m. ● vt poignarder.

**knight** /naɪt/ n chevalier m; (chess) cavalier m. ● vt anoblir. ~**hood** n titre m de chevalier.

**knit** /nɪt/ vt/i (pt **knitted** or **knit**) tricoter; (bones) (se) souder. **knitting** n tricot m. **knitwear** n tricots mpl.

**knob** /nɒb/ n bouton m.

**knock** /nɒk/ vt/i cogner; (criticize 🔲) critiquer; ~ sth off/out faire tomber qch. ● n coup m. □ ~ **down** (chair, pedestrian) renverser; (demolish) abattre; (reduce) baisser; ~ **off** (stop work 🔲) arrêter de travailler; ~ £ 10 off faire une réduction de 10 livres; ~ **it off** 🔲 ça suffit!; ~ **out** assommer; ~ **over** renverser; ~ **up** (meal) préparer en vitesse.

**knockout** /ˈnɒkaʊt/ n (boxing) knock-out m.

**knot** /nɒt/ n nœud m. ● vt (pt **knotted**) nouer.

**know** /nəʊ/ vt/i (pt **knew**; pp

453 | **knowingly | land**

**known**) (*answer, reason, language*)
savoir (that que); (*person, place,
name, rule, situation*) connaître; (recognize) reconnaître; ~ how to do
savoir faire; ~ about (*event*) être au
courant de; (*subject*) s'y connaître
en; ~ of (from experience) connaître; (from information) avoir entendu parler de. **~-how** n savoir-
faire m inv.

**knowingly** /ˈnəʊɪŋlɪ/ adv (intentionally) délibérément; (meaningfully) d'un air entendu.

**knowledge** /ˈnɒlɪdʒ/ n connaissance f; (learning) connaissances fpl.
**knowledgeable** adj savant.

**knuckle** /ˈnʌkl/ n jointure f, articulation f.

**Koran** /kəˈrɑːn/ n Coran m.

**Korea** /kəˈrɪə/ n Corée f.

**kosher** /ˈkəʊʃə(r)/ adj casher inv.

# L l

**lab** /læb/ n 🄸 labo m.

**label** /ˈleɪbl/ n étiquette f. ● vt (pt
**labelled**) étiqueter.

**laboratory** /ləˈbɒrətrɪ/ n laboratoire m.

**laborious** /ləˈbɔːrɪəs/ adj laborieux.

**labour**, (US) **labor** /ˈleɪbə(r)/ n travail m; (workers) main-d'œuvre f; in
~ en train d'accoucher. ● vi peiner
(to do à faire). ● vt trop insister sur.

**Labour** /ˈleɪbə(r)/ n le parti travailliste. ● adj travailliste.

**laboured** /ˈleɪbəd/ adj laborieux.

**labourer** /ˈleɪbərə(r)/ n ouvrier/-
ière m/f; (on farm) ouvrier/-ière m/f

agricole.

**lace** /leɪs/ n dentelle f; (of shoe)
lacet m. ● vt (shoe) lacer; (drink)
arroser.

**lacerate** /ˈlæsəreɪt/ vt lacérer.

**lack** /læk/ n manque m; for ~ of
faute de. ● vt manquer de; be
~ing manquer (in de).

**lad** /læd/ n garçon m, gars m.

**ladder** /ˈlædə(r)/ n échelle f; (in
stocking) maille f filée. ● vt/i (stocking) filer.

**laden** /ˈleɪdn/ adj chargé (with de).

**ladle** /ˈleɪdl/ n louche f.

**lady** /ˈleɪdɪ/ n (pl **ladies**) dame f; ladies and gentlemen mesdames et
messieurs; young ~ jeune femme
or fille f. **~bird** n coccinelle f.

**ladylike** /ˈleɪdɪlaɪk/ adj distingué.

**lag** /læg/ vi (pt **lagged**) traîner. ● n
(pipes) calorifuger. ● n (interval) décalage m.

**lager** /ˈlɑːɡə(r)/ n bière f blonde.

**lagoon** /ləˈɡuːn/ n lagune f.

**laid** /leɪd/ →LAY¹. ~ back adj décontracté.

**lain** /leɪn/ →LIE².

**lake** /leɪk/ n lac m.

**lamb** /læm/ n agneau m; leg of ~
gigot m d'agneau.

**lame** /leɪm/ adj boiteux.

**lament** /ləˈment/ n lamentation f.
● vt/i se lamenter (sur).

**laminated** /ˈlæmɪneɪtɪd/ adj
laminé.

**lamp** /læmp/ n lampe f. **~post** n
réverbère m. **~shade** n abat-jour
m inv.

**lance** /lɑːns/ vt (Med) inciser.

**land** /lænd/ n terre f; (plot) terrain
m; (country) pays m. ● adj terrestre;
(policy, reform) agraire. ● vt/i débarquer; (aircraft) (se) poser, (faire) atterrir; (fall) tomber; (obtain) décro-

cher; (*a blow*) porter; ∼ **up** se retrouver.

**landing** /'lændɪŋ/ *n* débarquement *m*; (Aviat) atterrissage *m*; (top of stairs) palier *m*. ∼**-stage** *n* débarcadère *m*.

**land:** ∼**lady** *n* propriétaire *f*; (of pub) patronne *f*. ∼**lord** *n* propriétaire *m*; (of pub) patron *m*. ∼**mark** *n* (point de) repère *m*. ∼**mine** *f* terrestre.

**landscape** /'lænskeɪp/ *n* paysage *m*. ● *vt* aménager.

**landslide** /'lændslaɪd/ *n* glissement de terrain; (Pol) raz-de-marée *m inv* (électoral).

**lane** /leɪn/ *n* (path, road) chemin *m*; (strip of road) voie *f*; (of traffic) file *f*; (Aviat) couloir *m*.

**language** /'læŋgwɪdʒ/ *n* langue *f*; (speech, style) langage *m*. ∼ **engineering** *n* ingénierie *f* des langues. ∼ **laboratory** *n* laboratoire *m* de langue.

**lank** /læŋk/ *adj* (hair) plat.

**lanky** /'læŋkɪ/ *adj* (**-ier, -iest**) grand et maigre.

**lantern** /'læntən/ *n* lanterne *f*.

**lap** /læp/ *n* genoux *mpl*; (Sport) tour *m* (de piste). ● *vi* (*pt* **lapped**) (*waves*) clapoter. □ ∼ **up** laper.

**lapel** /lə'pel/ *n* revers *m*.

**lapse** /læps/ *vi* (decline) se dégrader; (expire) se périmer; ∼ **into** retomber dans. ● *n* défaillance *f*, erreur *f*; (of time) intervalle *m*.

**laptop** /'læptɒp/ *n* (Comput) portable *m*.

**lard** /lɑːd/ *n* saindoux *m*.

**larder** /'lɑːdə(r)/ *n* garde-manger *m inv*.

**large** /lɑːdʒ/ *adj* grand, gros; at ∼ en liberté; by and ∼ en général.
**largely** *adv* en grande mesure.

**lark** /lɑːk/ *n* (bird) alouette *f*; (bit of

fun 🔟) rigolade *f*. ● *vi* 🔟 rigoler.

**larva** /'lɑːvə/ *n* (*pl* **-vae**) larve *f*.

**laryngitis** /lærɪn'dʒaɪtɪs/ *n* laryngite *f*.

**laser** /'leɪzə(r)/ *n* laser *m*. ∼ **printer** *n* imprimante *f* laser. ∼ **treatment** *n* (Med) laserothérapie *f*.

**lash** /læʃ/ *vt* fouetter. ● *n* coup *m* de fouet; (eyelash) cil *m*. □ ∼ **out** (spend) dépenser follement; ∼ **out against** attaquer.

**lass** /læs/ *n* jeune fille *f*.

**lasso** /læ'suː/ *n* lasso *m*.

**last** /lɑːst/ *adj* dernier; the ∼ **straw** le comble; the ∼ **word** le mot de la fin; on its ∼ **legs** sur le point de rendre l'âme; ∼ **night** hier soir. ● *adv* en dernier; (most recently) la dernière fois. ● *n* dernier/-ière *m/f*; (remainder) reste *m*; at (long) ∼ enfin. ● *vi* durer. ∼**-ditch** *adj* ultime. **lasting** *adj* durable. **lastly** *adv* en dernier lieu. ∼**-minute** *adj* de dernière minute.

**latch** /lætʃ/ *n* loquet *m*.

**late** /leɪt/ *adj* (not on time) en retard; (former) ancien; (hour, fruit) tardif; the ∼ **Mrs X** feu Mme X. ● *adv* (not early) tard; (not on time) en retard; in ∼ **July** fin juillet; of ∼ dernièrement. **lately** *adv* dernièrement. **latest** *adj* ➜**LATE**; (last) dernier.

**lathe** /leɪð/ *n* tour *m*.

**lather** /'lɑːðə(r)/ *n* mousse *f*. ● *vt* savonner. ● *vi* mousser.

**Latin** /'lætɪn/ *n* (Ling) latin *m*. ● *adj* latin. ∼ **America** *n* Amérique *f* latine.

**latitude** /'lætɪtjuːd/ *n* latitude *f*.

**latter** /'lætə(r)/ *adj* dernier. ● *the* ∼ celui-ci, celle-ci.

**Latvia** /'lætvɪə/ *n* Lettonie *f*.

**laudable** /'lɔːdəbl/ *adj* louable.

**laugh** /lɑːf/ *vi* rire (at de). ● *n* rire

m. **laughable** adj ridicule.

**laughing stock** n risée f.

**laughter** /ˈlɑːftə(r)/ n (act) rire m; (sound of laughs) rires mpl.

**launch** /lɔːntʃ/ vt (rocket) lancer; (boat) mettre à l'eau; ~ (out) into se lancer dans. ● n lancement m; (boat) vedette f. **launching pad** n aire f de lancement.

**launderette** /ˈlɔːndrəmæt/ n laverie f automatique.

**laundry** /ˈlɔːndrɪ/ n (place) blanchisserie f; (clothes) linge m.

**laurel** /ˈlɒrəl/ n laurier m.

**lava** /ˈlɑːvə/ n lave f.

**lavatory** /ˈlævətrɪ/ n toilettes fpl.

**lavender** /ˈlævəndə(r)/ n lavande f.

**lavish** /ˈlævɪʃ/ adj (person) généreux; (lush) somptueux. ● vt prodiguer (on à). **lavishly** adv luxueusement.

**law** /lɔː/ n loi f; (profession, subject of study) droit m; ~ and order l'ordre public. ~**-abiding** adj respectueux des lois. ~**-court** n tribunal m.

**lawful** /ˈlɔːfl/ adj légal.

**lawn** /lɔːn/ n pelouse f, gazon m. ~**-mower** n tondeuse f à gazon.

**lawsuit** /ˈlɔːsuːt/ n procès m.

**lawyer** /ˈlɔːjə(r)/ n avocat m.

**lax** /læks/ adj (government) laxiste; (security) relâché.

**laxative** /ˈlæksətɪv/ n laxatif m.

**lay**¹ /leɪ/ adj (non-clerical) laïque; (worker) non-initié. ● vt (pt **laid**) poser, mettre; (trap) tendre; (table) mettre; (plan) former; (eggs) pondre. ● vi pondre; ~ **waste** ravager. □ ~ **aside** mettre de côté; ~ **down** (dé)poser; (condition) (im-)poser; ~ **off** vt (worker) licencier; vi ⓣ arrêter; ~ **on** (provide) fournir; ~ **out** (design) dessiner; (display) disposer; (money) dépenser.

**lay**² /leɪ/ →**LIE**².

**lay-by** /ˈleɪbaɪ/ n (pl ~**s**) aire f de repos.

**layer** /ˈleɪə(r)/ n couche f.

**layman** /ˈleɪmən/ n (pl -**men**) profane m.

**layout** /ˈleɪaʊt/ n disposition f.

**laze** /leɪz/ vi paresser. **laziness** n paresse f. **lazy** adj (-ier, -iest) paresseux.

**lead**¹ /liːd/ vt/i (pt **led**) mener; (team) diriger; (life) mener; (induce) amener; ~ **to** conduire à, mener à. ● n avance f; (clue) indice m; (leash) laisse f; (Theat) premier rôle m; (wire) fil m; **in the** ~ en tête. □ ~ **away** entraîner; ~ **up to** (come to) en venir à; (precede) précéder.

**lead**² /led/ n plomb m; (of pencil) mine f.

**leader** /ˈliːdə(r)/ n chef m; (of country, club) dirigeant/-e mf; (leading article) éditorial m. **leadership** n direction f.

**lead-free** adj (petrol) sans plomb.

**leading** /ˈliːdɪŋ/ adj principal.

**leaf** /liːf/ n (pl **leaves**) feuille f; (of table) rallonge f. ● vi ~ **through** feuilleter.

**leaflet** /ˈliːflɪt/ n prospectus m.

**leafy** /ˈliːfɪ/ adj feuillu.

**league** /liːɡ/ n ligue f; (Sport) championnat m; **in** ~ **with** de mèche avec.

**leak** /liːk/ n fuite f. ● vi fuir; (news: fig) s'ébruiter. ● vt répandre; (fig) divulguer.

**lean**¹ /liːn/ adj maigre. ● n (of meat) maigre m.

**lean**² /liːn/ vt/i (pt **leaned** or **leant**) (rest) (s')appuyer; (slope) pencher. □ ~ **out** se pencher à l'extérieur; ~ **over** (of person) se pencher.

**leaning** /ˈliːnɪŋ/ adj penché. ● n tendance f.

**leap** /liːp/ vi (pt leaped or leapt) bondir. ● n bond m. ~ year n année f bissextile.

**learn** /lɜːn/ vt/i (pt learned or learnt) apprendre (to do à faire). **learned** adj érudit. **learner** n débutant/-e m/f; **learning curve** n courbe f d'apprentissage.

**lease** /liːs/ n bail m. ● vt louer à bail.

**leash** /liːʃ/ n laisse f.

**least** /liːst/ adj the ~ (smallest amount of) le moins de; (slightest) le or la moindre. ● n le moins. ● adv le moins; (with adjective) le or la moins; at ~ au moins.

**leather** /ˈleðə(r)/ n cuir m.

**leave** /liːv/ vt (pt left) laisser; (depart from) quitter; (consent) laisser tranquille; be left (over) rester. ● n (holiday) congé m; (consent) permission f; take one's ~ prendre congé (of de); on ~ (Mil) en permission. □ ~ alone (thing) ne pas toucher; (person) laisser tranquille; ~ behind laisser; ~ out omettre.

**Lebanon** /ˈlebənən/ n Liban m.

**lecture** /ˈlektʃə(r)/ n cours m, conférence f; (rebuke) réprimande f. ● vt/i faire un cours ou une conférence (à); (rebuke) réprimander. **lecturer** n conférencier/-ière m/f; (Univ) enseignant/-e m/f.

**led** /led/ ➡LEAD[1].

**ledge** /ledʒ/ n (window) rebord m; (rock) saillie f.

**ledger** /ˈledʒə(r)/ n grand livre m.

**leech** /liːtʃ/ n sangsue f.

**leek** /liːk/ n poireau m.

**leer** /lɪə(r)/ vi ~ (at) lorgner. ● n regard m sournois.

**leeway** /ˈliːweɪ/ n (fig) liberté f d'action; (Naut) dérive f.

**left** /left/ ➡LEAVE. ● adj gauche. ● adv à gauche. ● n gauche f.

~-**hand** adj à or de gauche.

~-**handed** adj gaucher.

**left luggage (office)** n consigne f.

**left-overs** npl restes mpl.

**left-wing** adj de gauche.

**leg** /leg/ n jambe f; (of animal) patte f; (of table) pied m; (of chicken) cuisse f; (of lamb) gigot m; (of journey) étape f.

**legacy** /ˈlegəsɪ/ n legs m.

**legal** /ˈliːgl/ adj légal; (affairs) juridique.

**legend** /ˈledʒənd/ n légende f.

**leggings** /ˈlegɪŋz/ npl (for woman) caleçon m.

**legible** /ˈledʒəbl/ adj lisible.

**legionnaire** /liːdʒəˈneə(r)/ n légionnaire m.

**legislation** /ledʒɪsˈleɪʃn/ n (body of laws) législation f; (law) loi f. **legislature** n corps m législatif.

**legitimate** /lɪˈdʒɪtɪmət/ adj légitime.

**leisure** /ˈleʒə(r)/ n loisirs mpl; at one's ~ à tête reposée. ● adj (centre) de loisirs.

**leisurely** /ˈleʒəlɪ/ adj lent. ● adv sans se presser.

**lemon** /ˈlemən/ n citron m.

**lemonade** /leməˈneɪd/ n (fizzy) limonade f; (still) citronnade f.

**lend** /lend/ vt (pt lent) prêter; (credibility) conférer; ~ itself to se prêter à.

**length** /leŋθ/ n longueur f; (in time) durée f; (section) morceau m; at ~ (at last) enfin; at (great) ~ longuement.

**lengthen** /ˈleŋθən/ vt/i (s')allonger.

**lengthways** /ˈleŋθweɪz/ adv dans le sens de la longueur.

**lengthy** /ˈleŋθɪ/ adj long.

**lenient** /ˈliːnɪənt/ adj indulgent.

**lens** /lenz/ n lentille f; (of spectacles) verre m; (Photo) objectif m.

**lent** /lent/ →LEND.

**Lent** /lent/ n Carême m.

**lentil** /'lentl/ n lentille f.

**Leo** /'li:əʊ/ n Lion m.

**leopard** /'lepəd/ n léopard m.

**leotard** /'li:əta:d/ n body m.

**leprosy** /'leprəsɪ/ n lèpre f.

**lesbian** /'lezbɪən/ n lesbienne f. ● adj lesbien.

**less** /les/ adj (in quantity) moins de (than que). ● adv, n & prep moins; ~ than (with numbers) moins de; ~ work ~ than travailler moins que; ten pounds ~ dix livres de moins; ~ and ~ de moins en moins.

**lessen** vt/i diminuer. **lesser** adj moindre.

**lesson** /'lesn/ n leçon f.

**let** /let/ vt (pt **let**; pres p **letting**) laisser; (lease) louer. ● v aux ~ us do, ~'s do faisons; ~ him do qu'il fasse; ~ me know the results informe-moi des résultats. ● n location f. □ ~ **down** baisser; (deflate) dégonfler; (fig) décevoir; ~ **go** vt lâcher; vi lâcher prise; ~ **sb in/out** laisser or faire entrer/sortir qn; ~ a dress out élargir une robe; ~ **oneself in for** (task) s'engager à; (trouble) s'attirer; ~ **off** (explode, fire) faire éclater or partir; (excuse) dispenser; (not punish) ne pas punir; ~ **up** 🔲 s'arrêter.

**let-down** n déception f.

**lethal** /'li:θl/ adj mortel; (weapon) meurtrier.

**letter** /'letə(r)/ n lettre f. ~**-bomb** n lettre f piégée. ~**-box** n boîte f à or aux lettres.

**lettering** /'letərɪŋ/ n (letters) caractères mpl.

**lettuce** /'letɪs/ n laitue f, salade f.

**let-up** /'letʌp/ n répit m.

**leukaemia** /lu:'ki:mɪə/ n leucémie f.

**level** /'levl/ adj plat, uni; (on surface) horizontal; (in height) au même niveau (with que); (in score) à égalité. ● n niveau m; (spirit) ~ niveau m à bulle; be on the 🔲 être franc. ● vt (pt **levelled**) niveler; (aim) diriger. ~ **crossing** n passage m à niveau. ~**-headed** adj équilibré.

**lever** /'li:və(r)/ n levier m. ● vt soulever au moyen d'un levier.

**leverage** /'li:vərɪdʒ/ n influence f.

**levy** /'levɪ/ vt (tax) prélever. ● n impôt m.

**lexicon** /'leksɪkən/ n lexique m.

**liability** /laɪə'bɪlətɪ/ n responsabilité f; 🔲 handicap m; **liabilities** (debts) dettes fpl.

**liable** /'laɪəbl/ adj be ~ to do avoir tendance à faire, pouvoir faire; ~ to (illness) sujet à; (fine) passible de; ~ for responsable de.

**liaise** /lɪ'eɪz/ vi 🔲 faire la liaison. **liaison** n liaison f.

**liar** /'laɪə(r)/ n menteur/-euse m/f.

**libel** /'laɪbl/ n diffamation f. ● vt (pt **libelled**) diffamer.

**liberal** /'lɪbərəl/ adj libéral; (generous) généreux, libéral.

**Liberal** /'lɪbərəl/ adj & n (Pol) libéral/-e (m/f).

**liberate** /'lɪbəreɪt/ vt libérer.

**liberty** /'lɪbətɪ/ n liberté f; at ~ to libre de; take liberties prendre des libertés.

**Libra** /'li:brə/ n Balance f.

**librarian** /laɪ'breərɪən/ n bibliothécaire mf.

**library** /'laɪbrərɪ/ n bibliothèque f.

**libretto** /lɪ'bretəʊ/ n livret m.

**lice** /laɪs/ →LOUSE.

**licence**, (US) **license** /'laɪsns/ n permis m; (for television) redevance *f;* (Comm) licence *f;* (liberty: fig) licence *f.* ~ **plate** *n* plaque *f* minéralogique.

**license** /'laɪsns/ *vt* accorder un permis à, autoriser.

**lick** /lɪk/ *vt* lécher; (defeat 🔲) rosser; (fig) a ~ of paint un petit coup de peinture. ● *n* coup de langue.

**lid** /lɪd/ *n* couvercle *m.*

**lie**[1] /laɪ/ *n* mensonge *m.* ● *vi* (*pt* lied; *pres p* lying) (tell lies) mentir.

**lie**[2] /laɪ/ *vi* (*pt* lay; *pp* lain; *pres p* lying) s'allonger; (remain) rester; (be) se trouver, être; (in grave) reposer; be lying être allongé. □ ~ **down** s'allonger; ~ **in** faire la grasse matinée; ~ **low** se cacher.

**lieutenant** /lef'tenant/ *n* lieutenant *m.*

**life** /laɪf/ *n* (*pl* lives) vie *f.* ~-**belt** *n* bouée *f* de sauvetage. ~**boat** *n* canot *m* de sauvetage. ~**buoy** *n* bouée *f* de sauvetage. ~ **coach** *n* conseiller/-ère *m/f* en développement personnel. ~ **cycle** *n* cycle *m* de vie. ~-**guard** *n* sauveteur *m.* ~ **insurance** *n* assurance-vie *f.* ~-**jacket** *n* gilet *m* de sauvetage.

**lifeless** /'laɪflɪs/ *adj* inanimé.

**lifelike** /'laɪflaɪk/ *adj* très ressemblant.

**life:** ~**long** *adj* de toute la vie. ~ **sentence** *n* condamnation *f* à perpétuité. ~-**size(d)** *adj* grandeur nature *inv.* ~ **story** *n* vie *f.* ~-**style** *n* style *m* de vie. ~ **support machine** *n* appareil *m* de respiration artificielle.

**lifetime** /'laɪftaɪm/ *n* vie *f;* in one's ~ de son vivant.

**lift** /lɪft/ *vt* lever; (steal 🔲) voler. ● *vi* (of fog) se lever. ● *n* (in building) ascenseur *m;* give a ~ to emmener (en voiture). ~-**off** *n* (Aviat)

décollage *m.*

**light** /laɪt/ *n* lumière *f;* (lamp) lampe *f;* (for fire, on vehicle) feu *m;* (headlight) phare *m;* **bring to** ~ révéler; **come to** ~ être révélé; **have you got a** ~? vous avez du feu? ● *adj* (not dark) clair; (not heavy) léger. ● *vt* (*pt* lit *or* lighted) allumer; (room) éclairer; (match) frotter. □ ~ **up** s'allumer; *vt* (room) éclairer. ~ **bulb** *n* ampoule *f.*

**lighten** /'laɪtn/ *vt* (give light to) éclairer; (make brighter) éclaircir; (make less heavy) alléger.

**lighter** /'laɪtə(r)/ *n* briquet *m;* (for stove) allume-gaz *m inv.*

**light:** ~-**headed** *adj* (dizzy) qui a un vertige; (frivolous) étourdi. ~-**hearted** *adj* gai. ~**house** *n* phare *m.*

**lighting** /'laɪtɪŋ/ *n* éclairage *m.*

**lightly** /'laɪtlɪ/ *adv* légèrement.

**lightning** /'laɪtnɪŋ/ *n* éclair *m,* foudre *f.* ● *adj* (visit) éclair *inv.*

**lightweight** /'laɪtweɪt/ *adj* léger. ● *n* (boxing) poids *m* léger.

**light year** *n* année *f* lumière.

**like**[1] /laɪk/ *adj* semblable, pareil; ~-**minded** avoir les mêmes sentiments. ● *prep* comme. ● *conj* 🔲 comme. ● *n* pareil *m;* the ~s of you les gens comme vous.

**like**[2] /laɪk/ *vt* aimer (bien); I should ~ je voudrais, j'aimerais; would you ~? voudriez-vous?, voudrais-tu?; ~s goûts *mpl.* **likeable** *adj* sympathique.

**likelihood** /'laɪklɪhʊd/ *n* probabilité *f.*

**likely** /'laɪklɪ/ *adj* (-ier, -iest) probable. ● *adv* probablement; he is ~ to do it fera probablement; not ~! 🔲 pas question!

**likeness** /'laɪknɪs/ *n* ressemblance *f.*

**likewise** /ˈlaɪkwaɪz/ *adv* également.

**liking** /ˈlaɪkɪŋ/ *n* (for thing) penchant *m*; (for person) affection *f*.

**lilac** /ˈlaɪlək/ *n* lilas *m*. ●*adj* lilas *inv*.

**Lilo®** /ˈlaɪləʊ/ *n* matelas *m* pneumatique.

**lily** /ˈlɪlɪ/ *n* lis *m*, lys *m*.

**limb** /lɪm/ *n* membre *m*.

**limber** /ˈlɪmbə(r)/ *vi* ~ up faire des exercices d'assouplissement.

**limbo** /ˈlɪmbəʊ/ *n* be in ~ (forgotten) être tombé dans l'oubli.

**lime** /laɪm/ *n* (fruit) citron *m* vert; ~(-tree) tilleul *m*.

**limelight** /ˈlaɪmlaɪt/ *n* in the ~ en vedette.

**limestone** /ˈlaɪmstəʊn/ *n* calcaire *m*.

**limit** /ˈlɪmɪt/ *n* limite *f*. ●*vt* limiter.

**limited company** *n* société *f* anonyme.

**limp** /lɪmp/ *vi* boiter. ●*n* have a ~ boiter. ●*adj* mou.

**line** /laɪn/ *n* ligne *f*; (track) voie *f*; (wrinkle) ride *f*; (row) rangée *f*, file *f*; (of poem) vers *m*; (rope) corde *f*; (of goods) gamme *f*; (queue: US) queue *f*; be in ~ for avoir de bonnes chances de; hold the ~ ne quittez pas; in ~ with en accord avec; stand in ~ faire la queue. ●*vt* (paper) régler; (streets) border; (garment) doubler; (fill) remplir, garnir. □ ~ up (s')aligner; (in queue) faire la queue; ~ sth up prévoir qch. ~ **dancing** danse *f* en ligne.

**linen** /ˈlɪnɪn/ *n* (sheets) linge *m*; (material) lin *m*.

**liner** /ˈlaɪnə(r)/ *n* paquebot *m*.

**linesman** /ˈlaɪnzmən/ *n* (football) juge *m* de touche; (tennis) juge *m* de ligne.

**linger** /ˈlɪŋɡə(r)/ *vi* s'attarder; (smells) persister.

**linguist** /ˈlɪŋɡwɪst/ *n* linguiste *mf*. **linguistics** *n* linguistique *f*.

**lining** /ˈlaɪnɪŋ/ *n* doublure *f*.

**link** /lɪŋk/ *n* lien *m*; (of chain) maillon *m*. ●*vt* relier; (relate) (re)lier; ~ up (of roads) se rejoindre. **linkage** *n* lien *m*. **links** *n inv* terrain *m* de golf. ~-**up** *n* liaison *f*.

**lino** /ˈlaɪnəʊ/ *n* lino *m*.

**lion** /ˈlaɪən/ *n* lion *m*. **lioness** *n* lionne *f*.

**lip** /lɪp/ *n* lèvre *f*; (edge) rebord *m*; pay ~-**service** to n'approuver que pour la forme. ~-**read** *vt*/*i* lire sur les lèvres. ~-**salve** *n* baume *m* pour les lèvres. ~-**stick** *n* rouge *m* (à lèvres).

**liquid** /ˈlɪkwɪd/ *n* & *adj* liquide (*m*).

**liquidation** /lɪkwɪˈdeɪʃn/ *n* liquidation *f*; go into ~ déposer son bilan.

**liquidize** /ˈlɪkwɪdaɪz/ *vt* passer au mixeur. **liquidizer** *n* mixeur *m*.

**liquor** /ˈlɪkə(r)/ *n* alcool *m*.

**liquorice** /ˈlɪkərɪs/ *n* réglisse *f*.

**lisp** /lɪsp/ *n* zézaiement *m*; with a ~ en zézayant. ●*vi* zézayer.

**list** /lɪst/ *n* liste *f*. ●*vt* dresser la liste de. ●*vi* (ship) gîter.

**listen** /ˈlɪsn/ *vi* écouter; ~ to, ~ in (to) écouter. **listener** *n* auditeur/-trice *m*/*f*.

**listless** /ˈlɪstlɪs/ *adj* apathique.

**lit** /lɪt/ ⇒LIGHT.

**liter** ⇒LITRE.

**literal** /ˈlɪtərəl/ *adj* (meaning) littéral; (translation) mot à mot. **literally** *adv* littéralement; mot à mot.

**literary** /ˈlɪtərərɪ/ *adj* littéraire.

**literate** /ˈlɪtərət/ *adj* qui sait lire et écrire.

**literature** /ˈlɪtrətʃə(r)/ *n* littérature *f*; (brochures) documentation *f*.

**Lithuania** /lɪθjuˈeɪnɪə/ *n*

Lituanie f.

**litigation** /lɪtɪˈɡeɪʃn/ n litiges mpl.

**litre**, (US) **liter** /ˈliːtə(r)/ n litre m.

**litter** /ˈlɪtə(r)/ n (rubbish) détritus mpl, papiers mpl; (animals) portée f. ● vt éparpiller; (make untidy) laisser des détritus dans; ~ed with jonché de. ~bin n poubelle f.

**little** /ˈlɪtl/ adj petit; (not much) peu de. ● n peu m; a ~ un peu (de). ● adv peu.

**live**[1] /laɪv/ adj vivant; (wire) sous tension; (broadcast) en direct; be a ~ wire être très dynamique.

**live**[2] /lɪv/ vi vivre; (reside) habiter, vivre; ~ it up mener la belle vie. □ ~ down faire oublier; ~ on (feed oneself on) vivre de; (continue) survivre; ~ up to se montrer à la hauteur de.

**livelihood** /ˈlaɪvlɪhʊd/ n moyens mpl d'existence.

**lively** /ˈlaɪvlɪ/ adj (-ier, -iest) vif, vivant.

**liven** /ˈlaɪvn/ vt/i ~ up (s')animer; (cheer up) (s')égayer.

**liver** /ˈlɪvə(r)/ n foie m.

**livestock** /ˈlaɪvstɒk/ n bétail m.

**livid** /ˈlɪvɪd/ adj livide; (angry) furieux.

**living** /ˈlɪvɪŋ/ adj vivant. ● n vie f; make a ~ gagner sa vie; ~ conditions fpl de vie; ~room n salle f de séjour.

**lizard** /ˈlɪzəd/ n lézard m.

**load** /ləʊd/ n charge f; (loaded goods) chargement m, charge f; (weight, strain) poids m; ~s of 🔢 des tas de 🔢. ● vt charger.

**loaf** /ləʊf/ n (pl **loaves**) pain m. ● vi ~ (about) fainéanter.

**loan** /ləʊn/ n prêt m; (money borrowed) emprunt m. ● vt prêter.

**loathe** /ləʊð/ vt détester (doing faire). **loathing** n dégoût m.

**lobby** /ˈlɒbɪ/ n entrée f, vestibule m; (Pol) lobby m, groupe m de pression. ● vt faire pression sur.

**lobster** /ˈlɒbstə(r)/ n homard m.

**local** /ˈləʊkl/ adj local; (shops) du quartier; ~ **government** administration f locale. ● n personne f du coin; (pub 🔢) pub m du coin.

**localization** /ləʊkəlaɪˈzeɪʃn/ n localisation f.

**locally** /ˈləʊklɪ/ adv localement; (nearby) dans les environs.

**locate** /ləʊˈkeɪt/ vt (situate) situer; (find) repérer.

**location** /ləʊˈkeɪʃn/ n emplacement m; on ~ (cinema) en extérieur.

**lock** /lɒk/ n (of door) serrure f; (on canal) écluse f; (of hair) mèche f. ● vt/i fermer à clef; (wheels) bloquer; (se) bloquer. □ ~ **in** or **up** (person) enfermer; ~ **out** (by mistake) enfermer dehors.

**locker** /ˈlɒkə(r)/ n casier m.

**locket** /ˈlɒkɪt/ n médaillon m.

**locksmith** /ˈlɒksmɪθ/ n serrurier m.

**locum** /ˈləʊkəm/ n (doctor) remplaçant·e m/f.

**lodge** /lɒdʒ/ n (house) pavillon m (de gardien or de chasse); (of porter) loge f. ● vt (accommodate) loger; (money, complaint) déposer. ● vi être logé (with chez); (become fixed) se loger. **lodger** n locataire mf, pensionnaire mf. **lodgings** n logement m.

**loft** /lɒft/ n grenier m.

**lofty** /ˈlɒftɪ/ adj (-ier, -iest) (tall, noble) élevé; (haughty) hautain.

**log** /lɒɡ/ n (of wood) bûche f; ~ (~book) (Naut) journal m de bord; (Auto) ~ carte f grise. ● vt (pt **logged**) noter; (distance) parcourir. □ ~ **on** (Comput) se connecter; ~

off (Comput) se déconnecter.

**logic** /ˈlɒdʒɪk/ adj logique. **logical** adj logique.

**logistics** /ləˈdʒɪstɪks/ n logistique f.

**loin** /lɔɪn/ n (Culin) filet m; ~s reins mpl.

**loiter** /ˈlɔɪtə(r)/ vi traîner.

**loll** /lɒl/ vi se prélasser.

**lollipop** /ˈlɒlɪpɒp/ n sucette f.

**London** /ˈlʌndən/ n Londres. **Londoner** n Londonien/-ne m/f.

**lone** /ləʊn/ adj solitaire.

**lonely** (-ier, -iest) solitaire; (person) seul, solitaire.

**long** /lɒŋ/ adj long; how ~ is? quelle en est la longueur de?; (in time) quelle est la durée de?; how ~? combien de temps?; a ~ time longtemps. ● adv longtemps; he will not be ~ il n'en a pas pour longtemps; as or so ~ as pourvu que; before ~ avant peu; I no longer do je ne fais plus. ● vi avoir bien or très envie (for, to de); ~ for sb se languir de qn.
~-distance adj (flight) sur long parcours; (phone call) interurbain; (runner) de fond. ~ face grimace f. ~hand n écriture f courante.

**longing** /ˈlɒŋɪŋ/ n envie f (for de); (nostalgia) nostalgie f (for de).

**longitude** /ˈlɒŋdʒɪtjuːd/ n longitude f.

**long:** ~ jump n saut m en longueur. ~-range adj (missile) à longue portée; (forecast) à long terme. ~-sighted adj presbyte. ~-standing adj de longue date. ~-term adj à long terme. ~ wave n grandes ondes fpl. ~-winded adj verbeux.

**loo** /luː/ n 🔲 toilettes fpl.

**look** /lʊk/ vi regarder; (seem) avoir l'air; ~ like ressembler à, avoir l'air de. ● n regard m; (appearance) air

m, aspect m; (good) ~s beauté f.
□ ~ after s'occuper de, soigner; ~ at regarder; ~ back repenser à; ~ down on mépriser; ~ for chercher; ~ forward to attendre avec impatience; ~ in on passer voir; ~ into examiner; ~ out faire attention; ~ out for (person) guetter; (symptoms) guetter l'apparition de; ~ round se retourner; ~ up (word) chercher; (visit) passer voir; ~ up to respecter.

**lookout** /ˈlʊkaʊt/ n (Mil) poste m de guet; (person) guetteur m; be on the ~ for rechercher.

**loom** /luːm/ vi surgir; (war) menacer; (interview) être imminent. ● n métier m à tisser.

**loony** /ˈluːnɪ/ n & adj 🔲 fou, folle (mf).

**loop** /luːp/ n boucle f. ● vt boucler.
~hole n lacune f.

**loose** /luːs/ adj (knot) desserré; (page) détaché; (clothes) ample, lâche; (tooth) qui bouge; (lax) relâché; (not packed) en vrac; (inexact) vague; (pej) immoral; at a ~ end désœuvré; come ~ bouger.
**loosely** adv sans serrer; (roughly) vaguement. **loosen** vt (slacken) desserrer; (untie) défaire.

**loot** /luːt/ n butin m. ● vt piller.

**lord** /lɔːd/ n seigneur m; (British title) lord m; the L~ le Seigneur; (good) L~! mon Dieu!

**lorry** /ˈlɒrɪ/ n camion m.

**lose** /luːz/ vt/i (pt lost) perdre; get lost se perdre. **loser** n perdant/-e m/f.

**loss** /lɒs/ n perte f; be at a ~ être perplexe; be at a ~ to être incapable de; heat ~ déperdition f de chaleur.

**lost** /lɒst/ ⇒**LOSE**. ● adj perdu. ~ **property** n objets mpl trouvés.

**lot** /lɒt/ n the ~ (le) tout m; (people) tous mpl, toutes fpl; a ~ (of), ~s (of) beaucoup (de); quite a ~ (of) [T] pas mal (de); (fate) sort m; (at auction) lot m; (land) lotissement m.

**lotion** /ˈləʊʃn/ n lotion f.

**lottery** /ˈlɒtərɪ/ n loterie f.

**loud** /laʊd/ adj bruyant, fort. ● adv fort; out ~ tout haut. **loudly** adv fort. ~**speaker** n haut-parleur m.

**lounge** /laʊndʒ/ vi paresser. ● n salon m.

**louse** /laʊs/ n (pl lice) pou m.

**lousy** /ˈlaʊzɪ/ adj (-ier, -iest) [T] infect.

**lout** /laʊt/ n rustre m.

**lovable** /ˈlʌvəbl/ adj adorable.

**love** /lʌv/ n amour m; (tennis) zéro m; in ~ amoureux (with de); make ~ faire l'amour. ● vt (person) aimer; (like greatly) aimer bien (to do faire). ~ **affair** n liaison f amoureuse. ~ **life** n vie f amoureuse.

**lovely** /ˈlʌvlɪ/ adj (-ier, -iest) joli; (delightful to us) très agréable.

**lover** /ˈlʌvə(r)/ n (male) amant m; (female) maîtresse f; (devotee) amateur m (of de).

**loving** /ˈlʌvɪŋ/ adj affectueux.

**low** /ləʊ/ adj & adv bas; ~ in faible teneur en qch. ● n (low pressure) dépression f; reach a (new) ~ atteindre son niveau le plus bas. ● vi meugler. ~-**calorie** adj basses-calories. ~-**cut** adj décolleté.

**lower** /ˈləʊə(r)/ adj & adv →LOW. ● vt baisser; ~ oneself s'abaisser.

**low**: ~-**fat** adj (diet) sans matières grasses; (cheese) allégé. ~**key** adj modéré; (discreet) discret. ~**lands** npl plaine(s) f(pl). ~**lying** adj à faible altitude.

**loyal** /ˈlɔɪəl/ adj loyal (to envers).

**loyalty** /ˈlɔɪəltɪ/ n fidélité f. ~**card** n carte f de fidélité.

**lozenge** /ˈlɒzəndʒ/ n (shape) losange m; (tablet) pastille f.

**LP** n (disque m) 33 tours m.

**Ltd.** abbr (Limited) SA.

**lubricant** /ˈluːbrɪkənt/ n lubrifiant m. **lubricate** vt lubrifier.

**luck** /lʌk/ n chance f; bad ~ malchance f; good ~! bonne chance!

**luckily** /ˈlʌkɪlɪ/ adv heureusement.

**lucky** /ˈlʌkɪ/ adj (-ier, -iest) qui a de la chance, heureux; (event) heureux; (number) qui porte bonheur; it's ~ that heureusement que.

**ludicrous** /ˈluːdɪkrəs/ adj ridicule.

**lug** /lʌg/ vt (p lugged) traîner.

**luggage** /ˈlʌgɪdʒ/ n bagages mpl. ~-**rack** n porte-bagages m inv.

**lukewarm** /luːkˈwɔːm/ adj tiède.

**lull** /lʌl/ vt he ~ed them into thinking that il leur a fait croire que. ● n accalmie f.

**lullaby** /ˈlʌləbaɪ/ n berceuse f.

**lumber** /ˈlʌmbə(r)/ n bois m de charpente. ● vt [T] ~ sb with (chore) coller à qn [T]. ~**jack** n bûcheron m.

**luminous** /ˈluːmɪnəs/ adj lumineux.

**lump** /lʌmp/ n morceau m; (swelling on body) grosseur f; (in liquid) grumeau m. ● vt ~ **together** réunir. ~ **sum** n somme f globale.

**lunacy** /ˈluːnəsɪ/ n folie f.

**lunar** /ˈluːnə(r)/ adj lunaire.

**lunatic** /ˈluːnətɪk/ n fou/folle m/f.

**lunch** /lʌntʃ/ n déjeuner m. ● vi déjeuner.

**luncheon** /ˈlʌntʃən/ n déjeuner m. ~ **voucher** n chèque-repas m.

**lung** /lʌŋ/ n poumon m.

**lunge** /lʌndʒ/ vi bondir (at sur; forward en avant).

**lurch** /lɜːtʃ/ n leave in the ~ planter là, laisser en plan. ● vi (person) tituber.

**lure** /lʊə(r)/ vt appâter, attirer. ● n (attraction) attrait m, appât m.

**lurid** /'lʊərɪd/ adj choquant, affreux; (gaudy) voyant.

**lurk** /lɜːk/ vi se cacher; (in ambush) s'embusquer; (prowl) rôder; (suspicion, danger) menacer.

**luscious** /'lʌʃəs/ adj appétissant.

**lush** /lʌʃ/ adj luxuriant.

**lust** /lʌst/ n luxure f.

**Luxemburg** /'lʌksəmbɜːg/ n Luxembourg m.

**luxurious** /lʌg'zjʊərɪəs/ adj luxueux.

**luxury** /'lʌkʃərɪ/ n luxe m. ● adj de luxe.

**lying** /'laɪɪŋ/ →LIE¹, →LIE². ● n mensonges mpl.

**lyric** /'lɪrɪk/ adj lyrique. **lyrical** adj lyrique. **lyrics** npl paroles fpl.

---

# Mm

---

**MA** abbr →MASTER OF ARTS.

**mac** /mæk/ n 🔲 imper m.

**machine** /mə'ʃiːn/ n machine f. ● vt (sew) coudre à la machine; (Tech) usiner. ~-gun n mitrailleuse f.

**mackerel** /'mækrəl/ n inv maquereau m.

**mackintosh** /'mækɪntɒʃ/ n imperméable m.

**mad** /mæd/ adj (madder, maddest) fou; (foolish) insensé; (dog) enragé; (angry 🔲) furieux; be ~ about se passionner pour; (person)

être fou de; drive sb ~ exaspérer qn; like ~ comme un fou. ~ **cow disease** n maladie f de la vache folle.

**madam** /'mædəm/ n madame f; (unmarried) mademoiselle f.

**made** /meɪd/ →MAKE.

**madly** /'mædlɪ/ adv (interested, in love) follement; (frantically) comme un fou.

**madman** /'mædmən/ n (pl -men) fou m.

**madness** /'mædnɪs/ n folie f.

**magazine** /mægə'ziːn/ n revue f, magazine m; (of gun) magasin m.

**maggot** /'mægət/ n (in fruit) ver m, (for fishing) asticot m.

**magic** /'mædʒɪk/ n magie f. ● adj magique.

**magician** /mə'dʒɪʃn/ n magicien/-ne m/f.

**magistrate** /'mædʒɪstreɪt/ n magistrat m.

**magnet** /'mægnɪt/ n aimant m. **magnetic** adj magnétique.

**magnificent** /mæg'nɪfɪsnt/ adj magnifique.

**magnify** /'mægnɪfaɪ/ vt grossir; (sound) amplifier; (fig) exagérer. **magnifying glass** n loupe f.

**magpie** /'mægpaɪ/ n pie f.

**mahogany** /mə'hɒgənɪ/ n acajou m.

**maid** /meɪd/ n (servant) bonne f; (in hotel) femme f de chambre.

**maiden** /'meɪdn/ n (old use) jeune fille f. ● adj (aunt) célibataire; (voyage) premier. ~ **name** n nom m de jeune fille.

**mail** /meɪl/ n (postal service) poste f; (letters) courrier m; (armour) cotte f de mailles. ● adj (bag, van) postal. ● vt envoyer par la poste. ~ **box** n boîte f aux lettres; (Comput) boîte f aux lettres électronique. **mailing**

list *n* liste *f* d'adresses. ∼**man** *n* (*pl* -**men**) (US) facteur *m*. ∼**order** *n* vente *f* par correspondance. ∼ **shot** *n* publipostage *m*.

**main** /meɪn/ *adj* principal; a ∼ road une grande route. ∼**s** *n* (*water*/ *gas*) ∼ conduite *f* d'eau/de gaz; the ∼**s** (Electr) le secteur; in the ∼ en général. ∼ **land** *n* continent *m*. ∼**land** *n* continent *m*. ∼**stream** *n* tendance *f* principale, ligne *f*.

**maintain** /meɪn'teɪn/ *vt* (continue, keep, assert) maintenir; (*house, machine, family*) entretenir; (*rights*) soutenir.

**maintenance** /'meɪntənəns/ *n* (care) entretien *m*; (continuation) maintien *m*; (allowance) pension *f* alimentaire.

**maisonette** /meɪzə'net/ *n* duplex *m*.

**maize** /meɪz/ *n* maïs *m*.

**majestic** /mə'dʒestɪk/ *adj* majestueux.

**majesty** /'mædʒəstɪ/ *n* majesté *f*.

**major** /'meɪdʒə(r)/ *adj* majeur. ● *n* commandant *m*. ● *vi* ∼ **in** (Univ, US) se spécialiser en.

**majority** /mə'dʒɒrətɪ/ *n* majorité *f*; the ∼ of people la plupart des gens. ● *adj* majoritaire.

**make** /meɪk/ *vt/i* (*pt* made) faire; (manufacture) fabriquer; (*friends*) se faire; (*money*) gagner; (decision) prendre; (*place, position*) arriver à; (cause to be) rendre; ∼ **sb do sth** faire faire qch à qn; (force) obliger qn à faire qch; **be made of** être fait de; ∼ **oneself at home** se mettre à l'aise; ∼ **sb happy** rendre qn heureux; ∼ **it** arriver; (succeed) réussir; **I** ∼ **it 9 o'clock** j'ai dans mon idée qu'il est neuf heures; **I** ∼ **it 150** d'après moi, ça fait 150; **I cannot** ∼ **anything of it** je n'y comprends rien; **can you** ∼ **Friday?**

vendredi, c'est possible?; ∼ **as if to** faire mine de. ∼ (brand) marque *f* □ ∼ **do** (manage) se débrouiller (**with** avec); (cause) tendre à créer; (satisfy) ∼ **good** *vi* réussir; *vt* compenser; (repair) réparer; ∼ **for** se diriger vers; ∼ **off** filer (with avec); ∼ **out** distinguer; (understand) comprendre; (draw up) faire; (assert) prétendre; ∼ **up** *vt* faire, former; (story) inventer; (deficit) combler; *vi* se réconcilier; ∼ **up for** compenser; (time) rattraper; ∼ **up one's mind** se décider.

**make-believe** *adj* feint, illusoire. ● *n* fantaisie *f*.

**maker** /'meɪkə(r)/ *n* fabricant *m*.

**makeshift** /'meɪkʃɪft/ *adj* improvisé.

**make-up** /'meɪkʌp/ *n* maquillage *m*; (of object) constitution *f*; (Psych) caractère *m*.

**malaria** /mə'leərɪə/ *n* paludisme *m*.

**Malaysia** /mə'leɪzɪə/ *n* Malaisie *f*.

**male** /meɪl/ *adj* (voice, sex) masculin; (Bot, Tech) mâle. ● *n* mâle *m*.

**malfunction** /mæl'fʌŋkʃn/ *n* mauvais fonctionnement *m*. ● *vi* mal fonctionner.

**malice** /'mælɪs/ *n* méchanceté *f*.

**malicious** *adj* méchant.

**malignant** /mə'lɪgnənt/ *adj* malveillant; (tumour) malin.

**mall** /mɔːl/ *n* (shopping) ∼ (in suburbs) centre *m* commercial; (in town) galerie *f* marchande.

**malnutrition** /mælnjuː'trɪʃn/ *n* sousalimentation *f*.

**Malta** /'mɔːltə/ *n* Malte *f*.

**mammal** /'mæml/ *n* mammifère *m*.

**mammoth** /'mæməθ/ *n* mammouth *m*. ● *adj* (task) gigantesque; (organization) géant.

m

**man** /mæn/ n (pl **men**) homme m; (in sports team) joueur m; (chess) pièce f; ~ to man d'homme à homme. ● vt (pt **manned**) (desk) tenir; (ship) armer; (guns) servir; (be on duty at) être de service à.

**manage** /'mænɪdʒ/ vt (project, organization) diriger; (shop, affairs) gérer; (handle) manier; I could ~ another drink 🄸 je prendrais bien encore un verre; can you ~ Friday? vendredi, c'est possible? ● vi se débrouiller; ~ to do réussir à faire. **manageable** adj (tool, size, person) maniable; (job) faisable.

**management** /'mænɪdʒmənt/ n (managers) direction f; (of shop) gestion f.

**manager** /'mænɪdʒə(r)/ n directeur/-trice m/f; (of shop) gérant/-e m/f; (of actor) impresario m.

**mandate** /'mændeɪt/ n mandat m.

**mandatory** /'mændətərɪ/ adj obligatoire.

**mane** /meɪn/ n crinière f.

**mango** /'mæŋɡəʊ/ n (pl ~es) mangue f.

**manhandle** /'mænhændl/ vt maltraiter, malmener.

**man:** ~hole n regard m. ~hood n âge m d'homme; (quality) virilité f.

**maniac** /'meɪnɪæk/ n maniaque mf, fou m, folle f.

**manicure** /'mænɪkjʊə(r)/ n manucure f. ● vt soigner, manucurer.

**manifest** /'mænɪfest/ adj manifeste. ● vt manifester.

**manipulate** /mə'nɪpjʊleɪt/ vt (tool, person) manipuler.

**mankind** /mæn'kaɪnd/ n genre m humain.

**manly** /'mænlɪ/ adj viril.

**man-made** adj (fibre) synthétique; (pond) artificiel; (disaster)

d'origine humaine.

**manned** // adj (spacecraft) habité.

**manner** /'mænə(r)/ n manière f; (attitude) attitude f; (kind) sorte f; ~s (social behaviour) manières fpl.

**mannerism** /'mænərɪzəm/ n particularité f; (quirk) manie f.

**manoeuvre** /mə'nuːvə(r)/ n manœuvre f. ● vt/i manœuvrer.

**manor** /'mænə(r)/ n manoir m.

**manpower** /'mænpaʊə(r)/ n main-d'œuvre f.

**mansion** /'mænʃn/ n (in countryside) demeure f; (in town) hôtel m particulier.

**manslaughter** /'mænslɔːtə(r)/ n homicide m involontaire.

**mantelpiece** /'mæntlself/ n (manteau m de) cheminée f.

**manual** /'mænjʊəl/ adj (labour) manuel; (typewriter) mécanique. ● n (handbook) manuel m.

**manufacture** /mænjʊ'fæktʃə(r)/ vt fabriquer. ● n fabrication f.

**manure** /mə'njʊə(r)/ n fumier m.

**many** /'menɪ/ adj & n beaucoup (de); a great or good ~ un grand nombre (de); ~ a bien des.

**map** /mæp/ n carte f; (of streets) plan m. ● vt (pt **mapped**) faire la carte de; ~ out (route) tracer; (arrange) organiser.

**mar** /mɑː(r)/ vt (pt **marred**) gâcher.

**marble** /'mɑːbl/ n marbre m; (for game) bille f.

**March** /mɑːtʃ/ n mars m.

**march** /mɑːtʃ/ vi (Mil) marcher (au pas). ● n ~ off (lead away) emmener. ● n marche f.

**margin** /'mɑːdʒɪn/ n marge f.

**marginal** /'mɑːdʒɪnl/ adj marginal; (increase) léger, faible; (seat: Pol) disputé.

**marinate** /'mærɪneɪt/ vt faire

# marine | match

466

mariner (in dans).

**marine** /məˈriːn/ adj marin. ●n (shipping) marine f; (sailor) fusilier m marin.

**marital** /ˈmærɪtl/ adj conjugal. ~ **status** n situation f de famille.

**mark** /mɑːk/ n (currency) mark m; (stain) tache f; (trace) marque f; (School) note f; (target) but m. ●vt marquer; (exam) corriger; ~ out délimiter; (person) désigner; ~ time marquer le pas.

**marker** /ˈmɑːkə(r)/ n (pen) marqueur m; (tag) repère m; (School, Univ) examinateur/-trice m/f.

**market** /ˈmɑːkɪt/ n marché m; on the ~ en vente. ●vt (sell) vendre; (launch) commercialiser. ● re**search** n étude f de marché.

**marmalade** /ˈmɑːməleɪd/ n confiture f d'oranges.

**maroon** /məˈruːn/ n bordeaux m inv. ●adj bordeaux inv.

**marooned** /məˈruːnd/ adj abandonné; (snowbound) bloqué.

**marquee** /mɑːˈkiː/ n grande tente f; (of circus) chapiteau m; (awning; US) auvent m.

**marriage** /ˈmærɪdʒ/ n mariage m (to avec).

**married** /ˈmærɪd/ adj marié (to à); (life) conjugal; get ~ se marier (to avec).

**marrow** /ˈmærəʊ/ n (of bone) moelle f; (vegetable) courge f.

**marry** /ˈmærɪ/ vt épouser; (give or unite in marriage) marier. ●vi se marier.

**marsh** /mɑːʃ/ n marais m.

**marshal** /ˈmɑːʃl/ n maréchal m; (at event) membre m du service d'ordre. ●vt (pt marshalled) rassembler.

**martyr** /ˈmɑːtə(r)/ n martyr/-e m/f. ●vt martyriser.

**marvel** /ˈmɑːvl/ n merveille f. ●vi (pt marvelled) s'émerveiller (at de).

**marvellous** /ˈmɑːvələs/ adj merveilleux.

**marzipan** /ˈmɑːzɪpæn/ n pâte f d'amandes.

**masculine** /ˈmæskjʊlɪn/ adj & n masculin (m).

**mash** /mæʃ/ n (potatoes 🗊) purée f. ●vt écraser. **mashed potatoes** npl purée f (de pommes de terre).

**mask** /mɑːsk/ n masque m. ●vt masquer.

**Mason** /ˈmeɪsn/ n franc-maçon m.

**masonry** /ˈmeɪsənrɪ/ n maçonnerie f.

**mass** /mæs/ n (Relig) messe f; masse f; the ~es les masses fpl. ●vt/i (se) masser.

**massacre** /ˈmæsəkə(r)/ n massacre m. ●vt massacrer.

**massage** /ˈmæsɑːʒ/ n massage m. ●vt masser.

**massive** /ˈmæsɪv/ adj (large) énorme; (heavy) massif.

**mass media** n médias mpl.

**mass-produce** vt fabriquer en série.

**mast** /mɑːst/ n (on ship) mât m; (for radio, TV) pylône m.

**master** /ˈmɑːstə(r)/ n maître m; (in secondary school) professeur m; M~ of Arts titulaire mf d'une maîtrise ès lettres. ●vt maîtriser.

**masterpiece** /ˈmɑːstəpiːs/ n chef-d'œuvre m.

**mastery** /ˈmɑːstərɪ/ n maîtrise f.

**mat** /mæt/ n (petit) tapis m; (at door) paillasson m.

**match** /mætʃ/ n (for lighting fire) allumette f; (Sport) match m; (equal) égal/-e m/f; (marriage) mariage m; (sb to marry) parti m; be a

~ for pouvoir tenir tête à. ● vt opposer; (go with) aller avec; (cups) assortir; (equal) égaler. ● vi (be alike) être assorti. **matchbox** n boîte f à allumettes.

**matching** /'mætʃɪŋ/ adj assorti.

**mate** /meɪt/ n camarade mf; (of animal) compagnon m, compagne f; (assistant) aide mf; (chess) mat m. ● vt/i (s')accoupler (with avec).

**material** /mə'tɪərɪəl/ n matière f; (fabric) tissu m; (documents, for building) matériau(x) m(pl); ~s (equipment) matériel m. ● adj matériel; (fig) important. **materialistic** adj matérialiste.

**materialize** /mə'tɪərɪəlaɪz/ vi se matérialiser, se réaliser.

**maternal** /mə'tɜːnl/ adj maternel.

**maternity** /mə'tɜːnəti/ n maternité f. ● adj (clothes) de grossesse. ~ **hospital** n maternité f. ~ **leave** n congé m maternité.

**mathematics** /mæθə'mætɪks/ n & npl mathématiques fpl.

**maths**, (US) **math** /mæθs/ n maths fpl.

**mating** /'meɪtɪŋ/ n accouplement m.

**matrimony** /'mætrɪmənɪ/ n mariage m.

**matron** /'meɪtrən/ n (married, elderly) dame f âgée; (in hospital) infirmière f en chef.

**matt** /mæt/ adj mat.

**matter** /'mætə(r)/ n (substance) matière f; (affair) affaire f; as a ~ of fact en fait; what is the ~? qu'est-ce qu'il y a? ● vi importer; it does not ~ ça ne fait rien; no ~ what happens quoi qu'il arrive.

**mattress** /'mætrɪs/ n matelas m.

**mature** /mə'tjʊə(r)/ adj (psychologically) mûr; (plant) adulte. ● vt/i (se) mûrir. **maturity** n maturité f.

**mauve** /məʊv/ adj & n mauve (m).

**maverick** /'mævərɪk/ n non-conformiste mf.

**maximize** /'mæksɪmaɪz/ vt porter au maximum.

**maximum** /'mæksɪməm/ adj & n (pl **-ima**) maximum (m).

---

### may /meɪ/

*past* **might**

● *auxiliary verb*

····▶ (possibility) they ~ be able to come ils pourront peut-être venir; she ~ not have seen him elle ne l'a peut-être pas vu; it ~ rain il risque de pleuvoir; 'will you come?'—'I **might**' 'tu viendras?' —'peut-être'.

····▶ (permission) you ~ leave vous pouvez partir; ~ I smoke? puis-je fumer?

····▶ (wish) ~ he be happy qu'il soit heureux.

---

**May** /meɪ/ n mai m.

**maybe** /'meɪbiː/ adv peut-être.

**mayhem** /'meɪhem/ n (havoc) ravages mpl.

**mayonnaise** /meɪə'neɪz/ n mayonnaise f.

**mayor** /meə(r)/ n maire m.

**maze** /meɪz/ n labyrinthe m.

**Mb** abbr (**megabyte**) (Comput) Mo.

**me** /miː/ pron me, m'; (after prep.) moi; (indirect object) me, m'; he knows ~ il me connaît.

**meadow** /'medəʊ/ n pré m.

**meagre** /'miːgə(r)/ adj maigre.

**meal** /miːl/ n repas m; (grain) farine f.

**mean** /miːn/ adj (poor) misérable; (miserly) avare; (unkind) méchant; (average) moyen. ● n milieu m; (average) moyenne f; in the ∼-time en attendant. ● vt (pt meant) vouloir dire, signifier; (involve) entraîner; I ∼ that! je suis sérieux; be meant for être destiné à; ∼ to do avoir l'intention de faire.

**meaning** /ˈmiːnɪŋ/ n sens m, signification f. **meaningful** adj significatif. **meaningless** adj dénué de sens.

**means** /miːnz/ n moyen(s) m (pl); by ∼ of sth au moyen de qch. ● npl (wealth) moyens mpl financiers; by all ∼ certainement; by no ∼ nullement.

**meant** /ment/ →MEAN.

**meantime** /ˈmiːntaɪm/, meanwhile adv en attendant.

**measles** /ˈmiːzlz/ n rougeole f.

**measure** /ˈmeʒə(r)/ n mesure f; (ruler) règle f. ● vt/i mesurer; ∼up to être à la hauteur de qch. **measurement** n mesures fpl.

**meat** /miːt/ n viande f. **meaty** adj de viande; (fig) substantiel.

**mechanic** /mɪˈkænɪk/ n mécanicien/-ne m/f.

**mechanical** /mɪˈkænɪkl/ adj mécanique.

**mechanism** /ˈmekənɪzəm/ n mécanisme m.

**medal** /ˈmedl/ n médaille f.

**meddle** /ˈmedl/ vi (interfere) se mêler (in de); (tinker) toucher (with à).

**media** /ˈmiːdɪə/ n →MEDIUM. ● npl the∼ les média mpl; talk to the ∼ parler à la presse.

**median** /ˈmiːdɪən/ adj médian. ● n médiane f.

**mediate** /ˈmiːdɪeɪt/ vi servir d'intermédiaire.

**medical** /ˈmedɪkl/ adj médical; (student) en médecine. ● n visite f médicale.

**medication** /medɪˈkeɪʃn/ n médicaments mpl.

**medicine** /ˈmedsn/ n (science) médecine f; (substance) médicament m.

**medieval** /medɪˈiːvl/ adj médiéval.

**mediocre** /miːdɪˈəʊkə(r)/ adj médiocre.

**meditate** /ˈmedɪteɪt/ vt/i méditer.

**Mediterranean** /medɪtəˈreɪnɪən/ adj méditerranéen. ● n the ∼ la Méditerranée f.

**medium** /ˈmiːdɪəm/ n (pl media) (mid-point) milieu m; (for transmitting data) support m; (pl mediums) (person) médium m. ● adj moyen.

**medley** /ˈmedlɪ/ n mélange m; (Mus) potpourri m.

**meet** /miːt/ vt (pt met) rencontrer; (see again) retrouver; (be introduced to) faire la connaissance de; (face) faire face à; (requirement) satisfaire. ● vi se rencontrer; (see each other again) se retrouver; (see in session) se réunir.

**meeting** /ˈmiːtɪŋ/ n réunion f; (between two people) rencontre f.

**megabyte** /ˈmegəbaɪt/ n (Comput) mégaoctet m.

**melancholy** /ˈmelənkəlɪ/ n mélancolie f. ● adj mélancolique.

**mellow** /ˈmeləʊ/ adj (fruit) mûr; (sound, colour) moelleux, doux; (person) mûri. ● vt/i (mature) mûrir; (soften) (s')adoucir.

**melody** /ˈmelədɪ/ n mélodie f.

**melon** /ˈmelən/ n melon m.

**melt** /melt/ vt/i (faire) fondre.

**member** /ˈmembə(r)/ n membre m. M∼ of Parliament n député m. **membership** n adhésion f; (members) membres mpl; (fee) cotisation f.

**memento** /mɪˈmentəʊ/ n (pl ~es) (object) souvenir m.

**memo** /ˈmeməʊ/ n note f.

**memoir** /ˈmemwɑː(r)/ n (record, essay) mémoire m.

**memorandum** /meməˈrændəm/ n note f.

**memorial** /məˈmɔːrɪəl/ n monument m. ● adj commémoratif.

**memorize** /ˈmeməraɪz/ vt apprendre par cœur.

**memory** /ˈmeməri/ n (mind, in computer) mémoire f; (thing remembered) souvenir m; from ~ de mémoire; in ~ of à la mémoire de.

**men** /men/ →MAN.

**menace** /ˈmenəs/ n menace f; (nuisance) peste f. ● vt menacer.

**mend** /mend/ vt réparer; (darn) raccommoder; ~ one's ways s'amender. ● n raccommodage m; on the ~ en voie de guérison.

**meningitis** /menɪnˈdʒaɪtɪs/ n méningite f.

**menopause** /ˈmenəpɔːz/ n ménopause f.

**mental** /ˈmentl/ adj mental; (hospital) psychiatrique.

**mentality** /menˈtælətɪ/ n mentalité f.

**mention** /ˈmenʃn/ vt mentionner; don't ~it! il n'y a pas de quoi, je vous en prie! ● n mention f.

**menu** /ˈmenjuː/ n (food, on computer) menu m; (list) carte f.

**MEP** abbr (Member of the European Parliament) député m au Parlement européen.

**mercenary** /ˈmɜːsɪnərɪ/ adj & n mercenaire (m.)

**merchandise** /ˈmɜːtʃəndaɪz/ n marchandises fpl.

**merchant** /ˈmɜːtʃənt/ n marchand m. ● adj (ship, navy) marchand. ~

**bank** n banque f de commerce.

**merciful** /ˈmɜːsɪfl/ adj miséricordieux.

**mercury** /ˈmɜːkjʊrɪ/ n mercure m.

**mercy** /ˈmɜːsɪ/ n pitié f; at the ~ of à la merci de.

**mere** /mɪə(r)/ adj simple. **merest** adj moindre.

**merge** /mɜːdʒ/ vt/i (se) mêler (with à); (companies: Comm) fusionner. **merger** n fusion f.

**mermaid** /ˈmɜːmeɪd/ n sirène f.

**merrily** /ˈmerɪlɪ/ adv (happily) joyeusement; (unconcernedly) avec insouciance.

**merry** /ˈmerɪ/ adj (-ier, -iest) gai; make ~ faire la fête. ~-go-round n manège m.

**mesh** /meʃ/ n maille f; (fabric) tissu m à mailles; (network) réseau m.

**mesmerize** /ˈmezməraɪz/ vt hypnotiser.

**mess** /mes/ n désordre m, gâchis m; (dirt) saleté f; (Mil) mess m; make a ~ of gâcher. ● vt ~ up gâcher.; vi ~ about s'amuser; (dawdle) traîner; ~ with (tinker with) tripoter.

**message** /ˈmesɪdʒ/ n message m.

**messenger** /ˈmesɪndʒə(r)/ n messager/-ère m/f.

**messy** /ˈmesɪ/ adj (-ier, -iest) en désordre; (dirty) sale.

**met** /met/ →MEET.

**metal** /ˈmetl/ n métal m. ● adj de métal. **metallic** /mɪˈtælɪk/ adj métallique; (paint, colour) métallisé.

**metallurgy** /mɪˈtælədʒɪ/ n métallurgie f.

**metaphor** /ˈmetəfɔː(r)/ n métaphore f.

**meteor** /ˈmiːtɪə(r)/ n météore m.

**meteorite** /ˈmiːtɪəraɪt/ n météorite m.

**meteorology** /miːtɪəˈrɒlədʒɪ/

m

météorologie f.

**meter** /'mi:tə(r)/ n compteur m; (US) ➞METRE.

**method** /'meθəd/ n méthode f.

**methylated spirit(s)** /'meθəleitid 'spirit(s)/ n alcool m à brûler.

**meticulous** /mɪ'tɪkjʊləs/ adj méticuleux.

**metre**, (US) **meter** /'mi:tə(r)/ n mètre m.

**metric** /'metrɪk/ adj métrique.

**metropolis** /mə'trɒpəlɪs/ n métropole f. **metropolitan** adj métropolitain.

**mew** /mju:/ n miaulement m. ● vi miauler.

**mews** /mju:z/ npl appartements mpl chic aménagés dans d'anciennes écuries.

**Mexico** /'meksɪkəʊ/ n Mexique m.

**miaow** /mi:'aʊ/ n & vi ➞MEW.

**mice** /maɪs/ ➞MOUSE.

**mickey** /'mɪki/ n take the ~ out of ⊞ se moquer de.

**microchip** /'maɪkrəʊtʃɪp/ n puce f; circuit m intégré.

**microlight** /'maɪkrəʊlaɪt/ n ULM m.

**microprocessor** /'maɪkrəʊ prəʊsesə(r)/ n microprocesseur m.

**microscope** /'maɪkrəskəʊp/ n microscope m.

**microwave** /'maɪkrəwerv/ n micro-onde f; ~ (oven) four m à micro-ondes. ● vt passer au four à micro-ondes.

**mid** /mɪd/ adj in ~ air en plein ciel; in ~ March à la mi-mars; in ~ afternoon milieu m de l'après-midi; he's in his ~ twenties il a environ vingt-cinq ans.

**midday** /mɪd'deɪ/ n midi m.

**middle** /'mɪdl/ adj (door, shelf) du

milieu; (size) moyen. ● n milieu m; in the ~ of au milieu de. **~-aged** adj d'âge mûr. **M~ Ages** n Moyen âge m. ~ **class** n classe f moyenne. **M~ East** n Moyen-Orient m.

**midge** /mɪdʒ/ n moucheron m.

**midget** /'mɪdʒɪt/ n nain/-e m/f. ● adj minuscule.

**midnight** /'mɪdnaɪt/ n minuit f; it's ~ il est minuit.

**midst** /mɪdst/ n in the ~ of au beau milieu de; in our ~ parmi nous.

**midsummer** /mɪd'sʌmə(r)/ n milieu m de l'été; (solstice) solstice m d'été.

**midway** /mɪd'weɪ/ adv ~ between/along à mi-chemin entre/le long de.

**midwife** /'mɪdwaɪf/ n (pl -wives) sagefemme f.

**might**[1] /maɪt/ v aux I ~ have been killed j'aurais pu être tué; you ~ try doing sth vous pourriez faire qch; ~ ➞MAY.

**might**[2] /maɪt/ n puissance f.

**mighty** /'maɪti/ adj puissant; (huge ⊞) énorme. ● adv ⊞ vachement f.

**migrant** /'maɪgrənt/ adj & n (bird) migrateur (m); (worker) migrant/-e (m/f).

**migrate** /maɪ'greɪt/ vi émigrer. **migration** n migration f.

**mild** /maɪld/ adj (surprise, taste, tobacco, advice) léger; (weather, cheese, soap, person) doux; (case, infection) bénin.

**mile** /maɪl/ n mile m (= 1,6 km); walk for ~s marcher pendant des kilomètres; ~ better ⊞ bien meilleur. **mileage** n nombre m de miles, kilométrage m.

**milestone** /'maɪlstəʊn/ n (lit) borne f; (fig) étape f importante.

**military** /ˈmɪlɪtrɪ/ *adj* militaire.

**militia** /mɪˈlɪʃə/ *n* milice *f*.

**milk** /mɪlk/ *n* lait *m*. ● *vt* (*cow*) traire; (*fig*) pomper.

**milkman** /ˈmɪlkmən/ *n* (*pl* -men) laitier *m*.

**milky** /ˈmɪlkɪ/ *adj* (*skin, colour*) laiteux; (*tea*) au lait; M~ Way Voie *f* lactée.

**mill** /mɪl/ *n* moulin *m*; (*factory*) usine *f*. ● *vt* moudre. ● *vi* ~ around grouiller.

**millennium** /mɪˈlenɪəm/ *n* (*pl* ~s) millénaire *m*.

**millimetre**, (US) **millimeter** /ˈmɪlɪmiːtə(r)/ *n* millimètre *m*.

**million** /ˈmɪljən/ *n* million *m*; a ~ pounds un million de livres. **millionaire** *n* millionnaire *m*.

**millstone** /ˈmɪlstəʊn/ *n* meule *f*; (*fig*) boulet *m*.

**mime** /maɪm/ *n* (*actor*) mime *mf*; (*art*) mime *m*. ● *vt/i* mimer.

**mimic** /ˈmɪmɪk/ *vt* (*pt* mimicked) imiter. ● *n* imitateur/-trice *m/f*.

**mince** /mɪns/ *vt* hacher; not to ~ matters ne pas mâcher ses mots. ● *n* viande *f* hachée.

**mind** /maɪnd/ *n* esprit *m*; (*sanity*) raison *f*; (*opinion*) avis *m*; be on sb's ~ préoccuper qn; bear that in ~ ne l'oubliez pas; change one's ~ changer d'avis; make up one's ~ se décider (to à). ● *vt* (*have charge of*) s'occuper de; (*heed*) faire attention à; I do not ~ the noise le bruit ne me dérange pas; I don't ~ ça m'est égal; would you ~ checking? je peux vous demander de vérifier?

**minder** /ˈmaɪndə(r)/ *n* (*bodyguard*) garde *m* de corps; (*child*) ~ nourrice *f*.

**mindless** /ˈmaɪndlɪs/ *adj* (*programme*) bête; (*work*) abrutissant;

(*vandalism*) gratuit.

**mine** /maɪn/ *n* mine *f*. ● *vt* extraire; (Mil) miner. ● *pron* le mien, la mienne, les mien(ne)s; the blue car is ~ la voiture bleue est la mienne or à moi.

**minefield** /ˈmaɪnfiːld/ *n* (*lit*) champ *m* de mines; (*fig*) terrain *m* miné.

**miner** /ˈmaɪnə(r)/ *n* mineur *m*.

**mineral** /ˈmɪnərəl/ *n* & *adj* minéral (*m*); ~ water eau *f* minérale.

**minesweeper** /ˈmaɪnswiːpə(r)/ *n* (*ship*) dragueur *m* de mines.

**mingle** /ˈmɪŋgl/ *vt/i* (se) mêler (with à).

**minibus** /ˈmɪnɪbʌs/ *n* minibus *m*.

**minicab** /ˈmɪnɪkæb/ *n* taxi *m* (*non agréé*).

**minimal** /ˈmɪnɪml/ *adj* minimal.

**minimize** /ˈmɪnɪmaɪz/ *vt* minimiser; (Comput) réduire.

**minimum** /ˈmɪnɪməm/ *adj* & *n* (*pl* -ima minimum *m*.

**minister** /ˈmɪnɪstə(r)/ *n* ministre *m*. **ministerial** *adj* ministériel. **ministry** *n* ministère *m*.

**mink** /mɪŋk/ *n* vison *m*.

**minor** /ˈmaɪnə(r)/ *adj* (*change, surgery*) mineur; (*injury, burn*) léger; (*road*) secondaire. ● *n* (Jur) mineur/-e *m/f*.

**minority** /maɪˈnɒrətɪ/ *n* minorité *f*; in the ~ en minorité. ● *adj* minoritaire.

**mint** /mɪnt/ *n* (Bot, Culin) menthe *f*; (*sweet*) bonbon *m* à la menthe; (*fortune* 🔢) fortune *f*. ● *vt* frapper; in ~ condition à l'état neuf.

**minus** /ˈmaɪnəs/ *prep* moins; (*without* 🔢) sans. ● *n* moins *m*; (*drawback*) inconvénient *m*.

**minute**[1] /ˈmɪnɪt/ *n* minute *f*; ~s (*of meeting*) compte-rendu *m*.

m

**minute** /maɪˈnjuːt/ *adj* (*object*) minuscule; (*risk, variation*) minime.

**miracle** /ˈmɪrəkl/ *n* miracle *m*.

**mirror** /ˈmɪrə(r)/ *n* miroir *m*, glace *f*; (Auto) rétroviseur *m*. ● *vt* refléter.

**misbehave** /mɪsbɪˈheɪv/ *vi* se conduire mal.

**miscalculation** /mɪskælkjʊˈleɪʃn/ *n* (lit) erreur *f* de calcul; (fig) mauvais calcul *m*.

**miscarriage** /ˈmɪskærɪdʒ/ *n* fausse couche *f*; ~ **of justice** erreur *f* judiciaire.

**miscellaneous** /mɪsəˈleɪnɪəs/ *adj* divers.

**mischief** /ˈmɪstʃɪf/ *n* (playfulness) espièglerie *f*; (by children) bêtises *fpl*. **mischievous** *adj* espiègle; (malicious) méchant.

**misconduct** /mɪsˈkɒndʌkt/ *n* mauvaise conduite *f*.

**misconstrue** /mɪskənˈstruː/ *vt* mal interpréter.

**misdemeanour**, (US) **misdemeanor** /mɪsdɪˈmiːnə(r)/ *n* (Jur) délit *m*.

**miser** /ˈmaɪzə(r)/ *n* avare *mf*.

**miserable** /ˈmɪzrəbl/ *adj* (sad) malheureux; (wretched) misérable; (performance, result) lamentable.

**misery** /ˈmɪzərɪ/ *n* (unhappiness) souffrance *f*; (misfortune) misère *f*; (person 🔲) rabat-joie *mf inv*.

**misfit** /ˈmɪsfɪt/ *n* inadapté/-e *m/f*.

**misfortune** /mɪsˈfɔːtʃuːn/ *n* malheur *m*.

**misgiving** /mɪsˈɡɪvɪŋ/ *n* (doubt) doute *m*; (apprehension) crainte *f*.

**misguided** /mɪsˈɡaɪdɪd/ *adj* (foolish) imprudent; (mistaken) erroné; **be** ~ (person) se tromper.

**mishap** /ˈmɪshæp/ *n* incident *m*.

**misjudge** /mɪsˈdʒʌdʒ/ *vt* (distance, speed) mal évaluer; (person)

mal juger.

**mislay** /mɪsˈleɪ/ *vt* (*pt* mislaid) égarer.

**mislead** /mɪsˈliːd/ *vt* (*pt* misled) tromper. **misleading** *adj* trompeur.

**misplace** /mɪsˈpleɪs/ *vt* mal ranger; (lose) égarer. **misplaced** *adj* (fear, criticism) déplacé.

**misprint** /ˈmɪsprɪnt/ *n* coquille *f*, faute *f* typographique.

**misread** /mɪsˈriːd/ *vt* (*pt* misread) mal lire; (intentions) mal interpréter.

**miss** /mɪs/ *vt/i* manquer; (bus) rater; **he** ~**es her**/Paris elle/Paris lui manque; **you're** ~**ing the point** tu n'as rien compris; ~ **sth out** omettre qch; ~ **out on** sth laisser passer qch. ● *n* coup *m* manqué; **it was a near** ~ on l'a échappé belle.

**Miss** /mɪs/ *n* Mademoiselle *f*; ~ **Smith** (written) Mlle Smith.

**misshapen** /mɪsˈʃeɪpən/ *adj* difforme.

**missile** /ˈmɪsaɪl/ *n* (Mil) missile *m*; (thrown) projectile *m*.

**mission** /ˈmɪʃn/ *n* mission *f*. **missionary** *n* missionnaire *mf*.

**misspell** /mɪsˈspel/ *vt* (*pt* misspelt or misspelled) mal écrire.

**mist** /mɪst/ *n* brume *f*; (on window) buée *f*. ● *vt/i* (s')embuer.

**mistake** /mɪˈsteɪk/ *n* erreur *f*; **by** ~ par erreur; **make a** ~ faire une erreur. ● *vt* (*pt* mistook; *pp* mistaken) (meaning) mal interpréter; ~ **for** prendre pour.

**mistaken** /mɪˈsteɪkən/ *adj* (enthusiasm) mal placé; **be** ~ avoir tort.

**mistletoe** /ˈmɪsltəʊ/ *n* gui *m*.

**mistreat** /mɪsˈtriːt/ *vt* maltraiter.

**mistress** /ˈmɪstrɪs/ *n* maîtresse *f*.

**misty** /ˈmɪstɪ/ *adj* (-ier, -iest) brumeux; (window) embué.

**misunderstanding** /mɪsʌndə-

'stændɪŋ/ n malentendu m.

**misuse** /mɪs'ju:z/ vt (word) mal employer; (power) abuser de; (equipment) faire mauvais usage de.

**mitten** /'mɪtn/ n moufle f.

**mix** /mɪks/ n mélange m. ● vt mélanger; (drink) préparer; (cement) malaxer. ● vi se mélanger (with avec, à); (socially) être sociable; ~ with sb fréquenter qn. □ ~ up (confuse) confondre; (jumble up) mélanger; get ~ed up in se trouver mêlé à.

**mixed** /mɪkst/ adj (school) mixte; (collection, diet) varié; (nuts, sweets) assorti.

**mixer** /'mɪksə(r)/ n (Culin) batteur m électrique; be a good ~ être sociable; ~ tap mélangeur m.

**mixture** /'mɪkstʃə(r)/ n mélange m.

**mix-up** /'mɪksʌp/ n confusion f (over sur).

**moan** /məʊn/ n gémissement m. ● vi gémir; (complain ⊞) râler ⊞.

**mob** /mɒb/ n (crowd) foule f; (gang) gang m; the M~ la Mafia. ● vt (pt mobbed) assaillir.

**mobile** /'məʊbaɪl/ adj mobile; ~ phone téléphone m portable. ● n mobile m.

**mobilize** /'məʊbɪlaɪz/ vt/i mobiliser.

**mock** /mɒk/ vt/i se moquer (de). ● adj faux.

**mockery** /'mɒkəri/ n moquerie f; a ~ of une parodie de.

**mock-up** n maquette f.

**mode** /məʊd/ n mode m.

**model** /'mɒdl/ n (Comput, Auto) modèle m; (scale representation) maquette f; (person showing clothes) mannequin m. ● adj modèle; (car) modèle réduit inv; (railway) miniature. ● vt (pt modelled)

modeler; (clothes) présenter. ● vi être mannequin; (pose) poser.

**modelling** n métier m de mannequin.

**modem** /'məʊdem/ n modem m.

**moderate** /'mɒdərət/ adj & n modéré/-e (m/f).

**moderation** /mɒdə'reɪʃn/ n modération f; in ~ avec modération.

**modern** /'mɒdn/ adj moderne; ~ languages langues fpl vivantes. **modernize** vt moderniser.

**modest** /'mɒdɪst/ adj modeste. **modesty** n modestie f.

**modification** /mɒdɪfɪ'keɪʃn/ n modification f. **modify** vt modifier.

**module** /'mɒdju:l/ n module m.

**moist** /mɔɪst/ adj (soil) humide; (skin, palms) moite; (cake) moelleux. **moisten** vt humecter. **moisture** n humidité f. **moisturizer** n crème f hydratante.

**molar** /'məʊlə(r)/ n molaire f.

**mold** (US) →MOULD.

**mole** /məʊl/ n grain m de beauté; (animal) taupe f.

**molecule** /'mɒlɪkju:l/ n molécule f.

**molest** /mə'lest/ vt (pester) importuner; (sexually) agresser sexuellement.

**moment** /'məʊmənt/ n (short time) instant m; (point in time) moment m. **momentarily** adv momentanément; (soon: US) très bientôt. **momentary** adj momentané.

**momentum** /mə'mentəm/ n élan m.

**monarch** /'mɒnək/ n monarque m. **monarchy** n monarchie f.

**Monday** /'mʌndeɪ/ n lundi m.

**monetary** /'mʌnɪtrɪ/ adj monétaire.

**money** /'mʌnɪ/ n argent m; make

m

~ (person) gagner de l'argent; (business) rapporter de l'argent. ~-**box** n tirelire f. ~ **order** n mandat m postal.

**monitor** /'mɒnɪtə(r)/ n dispositif m de surveillance; (Comput) moniteur m. ● vt surveiller; (broadcast) être à l'écoute de.

**monk** /mʌŋk/ n moine m.

**monkey** /'mʌŋkɪ/ n singe m.

**monopolize** /mə'nɒpəlaɪz/ vt monopoliser. **monopoly** n monopole m.

**monotonous** /mə'nɒtənəs/ adj monotone. **monotony** n monotonie f.

**monsoon** /mɒn'suːn/ n mousson f.

**monster** /'mɒnstə(r)/ n monstre m. **monstrous** adj monstrueux.

**month** /mʌnθ/ n mois m.

**monthly** /'mʌnθlɪ/ adj mensuel. ● adv (pay) au mois; (publish) tous les mois. ● n (periodical) mensuel m.

**monument** /'mɒnjʊmənt/ n monument m.

**moo** /muː/ vi meugler.

**mood** /muːd/ n humeur f; in a good/bad ~ de bonne/mauvaise humeur. **moody** adj d'humeur changeante.

**moon** /muːn/ n lune f.

**moonlight** /'muːnlaɪt/ n clair m de lune. **moonlighting** n travail m au noir.

**moor** /mɔː(r)/ n lande f. ● vt amarrer.

**mop** /mɒp/ n balai m à franges; ~ of hair crinière f 🔲. ● vt (pt mopped) ~ (up) éponger.

**moped** /'məʊped/ n vélomoteur m.

**moral** /'mɒrəl/ adj moral. ● n morale f; ~s moralité f.

**morale** /mə'rɑːl/ n moral m.

**morbid** /'mɔːbɪd/ adj morbide.

**more** /mɔː(r)/ adv plus; ~ **serious** plus sérieux; **work** ~ travailler plus; **sleep** ~ **and** ~ dormir de plus en plus; **once** ~ une fois de plus; **I don't go there any** ~ je n'y vais plus; ~ **or less** plus ou moins. ● det plus de; **a little** ~ **wine** un peu plus de vin; ~ **bread** encore un peu de pain; **there's no** ~ **bread** il n'y a plus de pain; **nothing** ~ rien de plus. ● pron plus; **cost** ~ **than** coûter plus cher que; **I need** ~ **of it** il m'en faut davantage.

**moreover** /mɔː'rəʊvə(r)/ adv de plus.

**morning** /'mɔːnɪŋ/ n matin m; (whole morning) matinée f.

**Morocco** /mə'rɒkəʊ/ n Maroc m.

**morsel** /'mɔːsl/ n morceau m.

**mortal** /'mɔːtl/ adj & n mortel-le (m/f).

**mortgage** /'mɔːɡɪdʒ/ n emprunt-logement m. ● vt hypothéquer.

**mortuary** /'mɔːtʃərɪ/ n morgue f.

**mosaic** /məʊ'zeɪɪk/ n mosaïque f.

**mosque** /mɒsk/ n mosquée f.

**mosquito** /məs'kiːtəʊ/ n (pl ~es) moustique m.

**moss** /mɒs/ n mousse f.

**most** /məʊst/ det (nearly all) la plupart de; ~ **people** la plupart des gens; **the** ~ **votes/money** le plus de voix/d'argent. ● n le plus. ● pron la plupart; ~ **of us** la plupart d'entre nous; ~ **of the money** la plus grande partie de l'argent; **the** ~ **I can do is** ... tout ce que je peux faire c'est ... ● adv **the** ~ **beautiful house/hotel in Oxford** la maison la plus belle/l'hôtel le plus beau d'Oxford; ~ **interesting** très intéressant; **what I like** ~ (of all) is ce que j'aime le plus c'est. **mostly** adv surtout.

**moth** /mɒθ/ n papillon m de nuit; (in cloth) mite f.

**mother** /'mʌðə(r)/ n mère f. ● vt (lit) materner; (fig) dorloter. **motherhood** n maternité f. ~-**in-law** n (pl ~**s-in-law**) belle-mère f. ~-**of-pearl** n nacre f. **M~'s Day** n la fête des mères. ~-**to-be** n future maman f. ~ **tongue** n langue f maternelle.

**motion** /'məʊʃn/ n mouvement m; (proposal) motion f. ● ~ **picture** (US) film m. ● vt/i ~ (**to**) sb to faire signe à qn. **motionless** adj immobile.

**motivate** /'məʊtɪveɪt/ vt motiver.

**motive** /'məʊtɪv/ n motif m; (Jur) mobile m.

**motor** /'məʊtə(r)/ n moteur m; (car) auto f. ● adj (industry, insurance, vehicle) automobile; (activity, disorder; Med) moteur. ~**bike** n moto f. ~ **car** n auto f. ~-**cyclist** n motocycliste mf. ~ **home** n autocaravane f.

**motorist** /'məʊtərɪst/ n automobiliste mf.

**motorway** /'məʊtəweɪ/ n autoroute f.

**mottled** /'mɒtld/ adj tacheté.

**motto** /'mɒtəʊ/ n (pl ~**es**) devise f.

**mould** /məʊld/ n (shape) moule m; (fungus) moisissure f. ● vt mouler; (influence) former. **moulding** n moulure f. **mouldy** adj moisi.

**mount** /maʊnt/ n (hill) mont m; (horse) monture f. ● vt (stairs) gravir; (platform, horse, bike) monter sur; (jewel, picture, campaign, exhibit) monter. ● vi monter; (number, toll) augmenter; (concern) grandir.

**mountain** /'maʊntɪn/ n montagne f. ~ **bike** (vélo) tout terrain m, VTT m. **mountaineer** n alpiniste mf.

**mourn** /mɔːn/ vt/i ~ (**for**) pleurer.

**mournful** adj mélancolique.

**mourning** n deuil m.

**mouse** /maʊs/ n (pl **mice**) souris f. ~**trap** n souricière f.

**mouth** /maʊθ/ n bouche f; (of dog, cat) gueule f; (of cave, tunnel) entrée f. **mouthful** n bouchée f. ~**wash** n eau f dentifrice. ~**watering** adj appétissant.

**move** /muːv/ vt (object) déplacer; (limb, head) bouger; (emotionally) émouvoir; ~ **house** déménager. ● vi bouger; (vehicle) rouler; (change address) déménager; (act) agir. ● n mouvement m; (in game) coup m; (player's turn) tour m; (step, act) manœuvre f; (house change) déménagement m; **on the** ~ en mouvement. □ ~ **back** reculer; ~ **in** emménager; ~ **in with** s'installer avec; ~ **on** (person) se mettre en route; (vehicle) repartir; (time) passer; ~ **sth on** faire avancer qch; ~ **sb on** faire circuler qn; ~ **over** or **up** se pousser.

**movement** /'muːvmənt/ n mouvement m.

**movie** /'muːvɪ/ n (US) film m; **the** ~**s** le cinéma.

**moving** /'muːvɪŋ/ adj (vehicle) en marche; (part, target) mobile; (staircase) roulant; (touching) émouvant.

**mow** /məʊ/ vt (pp **mowed** or **mown**) (lawn) tondre; (hay) couper; ~ **down** faucher. **mower** n tondeuse f.

**MP** abbr ➞ MEMBER OF PARLIAMENT.

**Mr** /'mɪstə(r)/ n (pl **Messrs**) ~ Smith Monsieur or M. Smith; ~ **President** Monsieur le Président.

**Mrs** /'mɪsɪz/ n (pl **Mrs**) ~ Smith Madame or Mme Smith.

**Ms** /məz/ n Mme.

**much** /mʌtʃ/ adv beaucoup; **too** ~ trop; **very** ~ beaucoup; **I like them**

m

as ~ as you (do) je les aime autant que toi. ● *pron* beaucoup; not ~ pas grand-chose; he didn't say ~ il n'a pas dit grand-chose; I ate so ~ that j'ai tellement mangé que. ● *det* beaucoup de; too ~ money trop d'argent; how ~ time is left? combien de temps reste-t-il?

**muck** /mʌk/ *n* saletés *fpl*; (manure) fumier *m*. □ ~ about 🗍 faire l'imbécile. **mucky** *adj* sale.

**mud** /mʌd/ *n* boue *f*.

**muddle** /'mʌdl/ *n* (mix-up) malentendu *m*; (mess) pagaille *f* 🗍; get into a ~ s'embrouiller. □ ~ through se débrouiller; ~ up embrouiller.

**muddy** /'mʌdɪ/ *adj* couvert de boue.

**muffle** /'mʌfl/ *vt* emmitoufler; (bell) assourdir; (voice) étouffer.

**mug** /mʌg/ *n* grande tasse *f*; (for beer) chope *f*; (face 🗷) gueule *f* 🗷; (fool 🗍) poire *f* 🗍. ● *vt* (*pt* mugged) agresser. **mugger** *n* agresseur *m*.

**muggy** /'mʌgɪ/ *adj* lourd.

**mule** /mjuːl/ *n* mulet *m*.

**multicoloured** /ˈmʌltɪˈkʌləd/ *adj* multicolore.

**multiple** /'mʌltɪpl/ *adj & n* multiple (*m*); ~ sclerosis sclérose *f* en plaques.

**multiplication** /ˌmʌltɪplɪˈkeɪʃn/ *n* multiplication *f*. **multiply** *vt/i* (se) multiplier.

**multistorey** /mʌltɪˈstɔːrɪ/ *adj* (car park) à niveaux multiples.

**mum** /mʌm/ *n* 🗍 maman *f*.

**mumble** /'mʌmbl/ *vt/i* marmonner.

**mummy** /'mʌmɪ/ *n* (mother 🗍) maman *f*; (embalmed body) momie *f*.

**mumps** /mʌmps/ *n* oreillons *mpl*.

**munch** /mʌntʃ/ *vt* mâcher.

**mundane** /mʌnˈdeɪn/ *adj* terre-à-terre.

**municipal** /mjuːˈnɪsɪpl/ *adj* municipal.

**mural** /'mjʊərəl/ *adj* mural. ● *n* peinture *f* murale.

**murder** /'mɜːdə(r)/ *n* meurtre *m*. ● *vt* assassiner. **murderer** *n* meurtrier *m*, assassin *m*.

**murky** /'mɜːkɪ/ *adj* (-ier, -iest) (water) glauque; (past) trouble.

**murmur** /'mɜːmə(r)/ *n* murmure *m*. ● *vt/i* murmurer.

**muscle** /'mʌsl/ *n* muscle *m*. ● *vi* ~ in 🗍 s'imposer (on dans).

**muscular** /'mʌskjʊlə(r)/ *adj* (tissue, disease) musculaire; (body, person) musclé.

**museum** /mjuːˈzɪəm/ *n* musée *m*.

**mushroom** /'mʌʃrʊm/ *n* champignon *m*. ● *vi* (town) proliférer; (demand) s'accroître rapidement.

**music** /'mjuːzɪk/ *n* musique *f*.

**musical** /'mjuːzɪkl/ *adj* (person) musicien; (voice) mélodieux; (accompaniment) musical; (instrument) de musique. ● *n* comédie *f* musicale.

**musician** /mjuːˈzɪʃn/ *n* musicien-ne *m/f*.

**Muslim** /'mʊzlɪm/ *n* Musulman-e *m/f*. ● *adj* musulman.

**mussel** /'mʌsl/ *n* moule *f*.

**must** /mʌst/ *v aux* devoir; you ~ go vous devez partir, il faut que vous partiez; she ~ be consulted il faut la consulter; he ~ be old il doit être vieux; I ~ have done it j'ai dû le faire. ● *n* be a ~ 🗍 être indispensable.

**mustard** /'mʌstəd/ *n* moutarde *f*.

**musty** /'mʌstɪ/ *adj* (-ier, -iest) (room) qui sent le renfermé.

(smell) de moisi.

**mute** /mjuːt/ adj & n muet/-te (m/f). **muted** adj (colour) sourd; (response) tiède; (celebration) mitigé.

**mutilate** /ˈmjuːtɪleɪt/ vt mutiler.

**mutter** /ˈmʌtə(r)/ vt/i marmonner.

**mutton** /ˈmʌtn/ n mouton m.

**mutual** /ˈmjuːtʃuəl/ adj (reciprocal) réciproque; (common) commun; (consent) mutuel. **mutually** adv mutuellement.

**muzzle** /ˈmʌzl/ n (snout) museau m; (device) muselière f; (of gun) canon m. ● vt museler.

**my** /maɪ/ adj mon, ma, pl mes.

**myself** /maɪˈself/ pron (reflexive) me, m'; I've hurt ~ je me suis fait mal; (emphatic) moi-même; I did it ~ je l'ai fait moi-même; (after preposition) moi, moi-même; I am proud of ~ je suis fier de moi.

**mysterious** /mɪˈstɪərɪəs/ adj mystérieux.

**mystery** /ˈmɪstərɪ/ n mystère m.

**mystic** /ˈmɪstɪk/ adj & n mystique (m/f). **mystical** adj mystique.

**myth** /mɪθ/ n mythe m. **mythical** adj mythique. **mythology** n mythologie f.

............................................

# Nn

**nag** /næg/ vt/i (pt nagged) critiquer; (pester) harceler. **nagging** adj persistant.

**nail** /neɪl/ n clou m; (of finger, toe) ongle m; on the ~ sans tarder, tout de suite. ● vt clouer. ~ **polish** n vernis m à ongles.

**naïve** /naɪˈiːv/ adj naïf.

**naked** /ˈneɪkɪd/ adj nu; to the ~

eye à l'œil nu.

**name** /neɪm/ n nom m; (fig) réputation f. ● vt nommer; (terms) fixer; be ~d after porter le nom de.

**namely** /ˈneɪmlɪ/ adv à savoir.

**nanny** /ˈnænɪ/ n nurse f.

**nap** /næp/ n somme m.

**nape** /neɪp/ n nuque f.

**napkin** /ˈnæpkɪn/ n serviette f.

**nappy** /ˈnæpɪ/ n couche f.

**narcotic** /nɑːˈkɒtɪk/ adj & n narcotique (m).

**narrative** /ˈnærətɪv/ n récit m. **narrator** n narrateur/-trice m/f.

**narrow** /ˈnærəʊ/ adj étroit. ● vt/i (se) rétrécir; (limit) (se) limiter; ~ down the choices limiter les choix. ~-**minded** adj à l'esprit étroit; (ideas) étroit.

**nasal** /ˈneɪzl/ adj nasal.

**nasty** /ˈnɑːstɪ/ adj (-ier, -iest) mauvais, désagréable; (malicious) méchant.

**nation** /ˈneɪʃn/ n nation f.

**national** /ˈnæʃənl/ adj national. ● n ressortissant/-e m/f.

**nationality** /næʃəˈnælətɪ/ n nationalité f.

**nationalize** /ˈnæʃnəlaɪz/ vt nationaliser.

**nationally** /ˈnæʃnəlɪ/ adv à l'échelle nationale.

............................................

**National Trust** Association   *i*   caritative britannique fondée en 1895 pour assurer la protection de certains édifices ou parties de littoral menacés par l'industrialisation. Cette association est aujourd'hui le premier propriétaire foncier britannique car elle a acquis ou reçu en dons depuis sa création de nombreux sites et bâtiments; la plupart sont ouverts au public.

m
n

**native** /'neɪtɪv/ n (local inhabitant) autochtone mf; (non-European) indigène mf; be a ~ of être originaire de. ● adj indigène; (country) natal; (inborn) inné; ~ **language** langue f maternelle; ~ **speaker of French** personne f de langue maternelle française.

**natural** /'nætʃrəl/ adj naturel.

**naturally** /'nætʃrəlɪ/ adv (normally, of course) naturellement; (by nature) de nature.

**nature** /'neɪtʃə(r)/ n nature f.

**naughty** /'nɔːtɪ/ adj (-ier, -iest) vilain, méchant; (indecent) grivois.

**nausea** /'nɔːsɪə/ n nausée f. **nauseous** adj (smell) écœurant.

**nautical** /'nɔːtɪkl/ adj nautique.

**naval** /'neɪvl/ adj (battle) naval; (officer) de marine.

**navel** /'neɪvl/ n nombril m.

**navigate** /'nævɪgeɪt/ vt (sea) naviguer sur; (ship) piloter. ● vi naviguer. **navigation** n navigation f.

**navy** /'neɪvɪ/ n marine f. ● adj ~ (blue) bleu inv marine.

**near** /nɪə(r)/ adv près; draw ~ (s')approcher (to de). ● prep près de. ● adj proche; ~ **to** près de. ● vt approcher de.

**nearby** /nɪə'baɪ/ adj proche. ● adv à proximité.

**nearly** /'nɪəlɪ/ adv presque; I ~ forgot j'ai failli oublier; not ~ as pretty as loin d'être aussi joli que.

**nearness** /'nɪənɪs/ n proximité f.

**nearside** /'nɪəsaɪd/ adj (Auto) du côté du passager.

**neat** /niːt/ adj soigné, net; (room) bien rangé; (clever) habile; (drink) sec. **neatly** adv avec soin; habilement.

**necessarily** /nesə'serəlɪ/ adv nécessairement.

**necessary** /'nesəsərɪ/ adj nécessaire.

**necessitate** /nɪ'sesɪteɪt/ vt nécessiter.

**necessity** /nɪ'sesətɪ/ n nécessité f; (thing) chose f indispensable.

**neck** /nek/ n cou m; (of dress) encolure f. ~ **and neck** adj à égalité. ~**lace** n collier m. ~**line** n encolure f. ~**tie** n cravate f.

**nectarine** /'nektərɪn/ n brugnon m, nectarine f.

**need** /niːd/ n besoin m. ● vt avoir besoin de; (demand) demander; you ~ **not come** vous n'êtes pas obligé de venir.

**needle** /'niːdl/ n aiguille f.

**needless** /'niːdlɪs/ adj inutile.

**needlework** /'niːdlwɜːk/ n couture f; (object) ouvrage m (à l'aiguille).

**needy** /'niːdɪ/ adj (-ier, -iest) nécessiteux. ● n the ~ les indigents.

**negative** /'negətɪv/ adj négatif. ● n (of photograph) négatif m; (word: Gram) négation f; in the ~ (answer) par la négative; (Gram) à la forme négative.

**neglect** /nɪ'glekt/ vt négliger, laisser à l'abandon; ~ **to do** négliger de faire. ● n manque m de soins; (state of) ~ abandon m.

**negligent** /'neglɪdʒənt/ adj négligent.

**negotiate** /nɪ'gəʊʃɪeɪt/ vt/i négocier. **negotiation** n négociation f.

**neigh** /neɪ/ n hennissement m. ● vi hennir.

**neighbour**, (US) **neighbor** /'neɪbə(r)/ n voisin/-e m/f. **neighbourhood** n voisinage m, quartier m; in the ~**hood of** aux alentours de. **neighbouring** adj voisin. **neighbourly** adj amical.

**neither** /'naɪðə(r)/ adj & pron

aucun/-e des deux, ni l'un/-e ni l'autre. ● adv ni; ~ **big nor small** ni grand ni petit. ● conj (ne) non plus; ~ **am I coming** je ne viendrai pas non plus.

**nephew** /ˈnefju:/ n neveu m.

**nerve** /nɜːv/ n nerf m; (courage) courage m; (calm) sang-froid m; (impudence 🗉) culot m; ~s (before exams) trac m. **~-racking** adj éprouvant.

**nervous** /ˈnɜːvəs/ adj nerveux; **be** or **feel** ~ (afraid) avoir peur; ~ **breakdown** dépression f nerveuse. **nervousness** n nervosité f; (fear) crainte f.

**nest** /nest/ n nid m. ● vi nicher. **~-egg** n pécule m.

**nestle** /ˈnesl/ vi se blottir.

**net** /net/ n filet m; (Comput) net m, Internet m. ● vt (pt **netted**) prendre au filet. ● adj (weight) net. **~ball** n netball m.

**Netherlands** /ˈneðələndz/ n the ~ les Pays-Bas mpl.

**netiquette** /ˈnetɪket/ n nétiquette f.

**Netsurfer** /ˈnetsɜːfə(r)/ n Internaute mf.

**nettle** /ˈnetl/ n ortie f.

**network** /ˈnetwɜːk/ n réseau m.

**neurotic** /njʊˈrɒtɪk/ adj & n névrosé/-e (m/f).

**neuter** /ˈnjuːtə(r)/ adj & n neutre (m). ● vt (castrate) castrer.

**neutral** /ˈnjuːtrəl/ adj neutre; ~ (gear) (Auto) point m mort.

**never** /ˈnevə(r)/ adv (ne) jamais; he ~ refuses il ne refuse jamais; I ~ saw him 🗉 je ne l'ai pas vu; ~ again plus jamais; ~ **mind** (don't worry) ne vous en faites pas; (it doesn't matter) peu importe.

**nevertheless** /nevəðəˈles/ adv néanmoins, toutefois.

**new** /njuː/ adj nouveau; (brand-new) neuf. **~-born** adj nouveau-né. **~comer** n nouveau venu m, nouvelle venue f.

**newly** /ˈnjuːlɪ/ adv nouvellement. **~-weds** npl jeunes mariés mpl.

**news** /njuːz/ n nouvelle(s) f(pl); (radio, press) informations fpl; (TV) actualités fpl, informations fpl. ~ **agency** n agence f de presse. **~agent** n marchand/-e m/f de journaux. **~caster** n présentateur/-trice m/f. **~group** n (Internet) forum m de discussion. **~letter** n bulletin m. **~paper** n journal m.

**new year** n nouvel an m. **New Year's Day** n le jour de l'an. **New Year's Eve** n la Saint-Sylvestre.

**New Zealand** /njuːˈziːlənd/ n Nouvelle-Zélande f.

**next** /nekst/ adj prochain; (adjoining) voisin; (following) suivant; ~ **to** à côté de; ~ **door** à côté (de). ● adv la prochaine fois; (afterwards) ensuite. ● n suivant/-e m/f; (e-mail) message m suivant. **~-door** adj d'à côté. ~ **of kin** parent m le plus proche.

**nib** /nɪb/ n plume f.

**nibble** /ˈnɪbl/ vt/i grignoter.

**nice** /naɪs/ adj agréable, bon; (kind) gentil; (pretty) joli; (respectable) bien inv; (subtle) délicat. **nicely** adv agréablement; gentiment; (well) bien.

**nicety** /ˈnaɪsətɪ/ n subtilité f.

**niche** /niːʃ/ n (recess) niche f; (fig) place f, situation f.

**nick** /nɪk/ n petite entaille f; **be in good/bad** ~ 🗉 être en bon/mauvais état. ● vt (steal, arrest 🗉) piquer.

**nickel** /ˈnɪkl/ n (metal) nickel m; (US) pièce f de cinq cents.

**nickname** /ˈnɪkneɪm/ n surnom m. ● vt surnommer.

n

**nicotine** /'nɪkəti:n/ n nicotine f.

**niece** /ni:s/ n nièce f.

**niggling** /'nɪɡlɪŋ/ adj (person) tatillon; (detail) insignifiant.

**night** /naɪt/ n nuit f; (evening) soir m. ● adj de nuit. ~**-cap** n boisson f (avant d'aller se coucher). ~**-club** n boîte f de nuit. ~**-dress** n chemise f de nuit. ~**-fall** n tombée f de la nuit. **nightie** n chemise f de nuit.

**nightingale** /'naɪtɪŋɡeɪl/ n rossignol m.

**nightly** /'naɪtlɪ/ adj & adv (de) chaque nuit or soir.

**night** /naɪt/: ~**mare** n cauchemar m. ~**-time** n nuit f.

**nil** /nɪl/ n (Sport) zéro m. ● adj (chances, risk) nul.

**nimble** /'nɪmbl/ adj agile.

**nine** /naɪn/ adj & n neuf (m).

**nineteen** /naɪn'ti:n/ adj & n dix-neuf (m).

**ninety** /'naɪntɪ/ adj & n quatre-vingt-dix (m).

**ninth** /naɪnθ/ adj & n neuvième (mf).

**nip** /nɪp/ vt/i (pt **nipped**) (pinch) pincer; (rush ⒯) courir; ~ **out/back** sortir/rentrer rapidement. ● n pincement m.

**nipple** /'nɪpl/ n mamelon m; (of baby's bottle) tétine f.

**nippy** /'nɪpɪ/ adj (-ier, -iest) (air) piquant; (car) rapide.

**nitrogen** /'naɪtrədʒən/ n azote m.

**no** /nəʊ/ det aucun/-e; pas de; ~ **man** aucun homme; ~ **money** no **time** pas d'argent/de temps; ~ **one** →NOBODY; ~ **smoking/entry** défense de fumer/d'entrer; ~ **way!** ⒯ pas question! ● adv non. ● n (pl **noes**) non m inv.

**nobility** /nəʊ'bɪlətɪ/ n noblesse f.

**noble** /'nəʊbl/ adj noble. ~**man** n

(pl **-men**) noble m.

**nobody** /'nəʊbədɪ/ pron (ne) personne; he knows ~ il ne connaît personne. ● n nullité f.

**nocturnal** /nɒk'tɜ:nl/ adj nocturne.

**nod** /nɒd/ vt/i (pt **nodded**); ~ (one's head) faire un signe de tête; ~ **off** s'endormir. ● n signe m de tête.

**noise** /nɔɪz/ n bruit m; make a ~ faire du bruit. **noisily** adv bruyamment. **noisy** adj (-ier, -iest) bruyant.

**no man's land** n no man's land m.

**nominal** /'nɒmɪnl/ adj symbolique, nominal; (value) nominal.

**nominate** /'nɒmɪneɪt/ vt nommer; (put forward) proposer.

**none** /nʌn/ pron aucun/-e; ~ **of us** aucun/-e de nous; I have ~ je n'en ai pas.

**non-existent** /nɒnɪɡ'zɪstənt/ adj inexistant.

**nonplussed** /nɒn'plʌst/ adj perplexe.

**nonsense** /'nɒnsns/ n absurdités fpl.

**non-smoker** /nɒn'sməʊkə(r)/ n non-fumeur m.

**non-stick** /nɒn'stɪk/ adj antiadhésif.

**non-stop** /nɒn'stɒp/ adj (train, flight) direct. ● adv sans arrêt.

**noodles** /'nu:dlz/ npl nouilles fpl.

**noon** /nu:n/ n midi m.

**nor** /nɔ:(r)/ adv ni. ● conj (ne) non plus; ~ **shall I come** je ne viendrai pas non plus.

**norm** /nɔ:m/ n norme f.

**normal** /'nɔ:ml/ adj normal.

**Norman** /'nɔ:mən/ n Normand/-e m/f. ● adj (village) normand; (arch) roman.

**north** /nɔːθ/ n nord m. ● adj nord inv, du nord. ● adv vers le nord.

**North America** n Amérique f du Nord.

**north-east** /nɔːθˈiːst/ n nord-est m.

**northerly** /ˈnɔːðəlɪ/ adj (wind, area) du nord; (point) au nord.

**northern** /ˈnɔːðən/ adj (accent) du nord; (coast) nord. **northerner** n habitant/-e m/f du nord.

**northward** /ˈnɔːθwəd/ adj (side) nord inv; (journey) vers le nord.

**north-west** /nɔːθˈwest/ n nord-ouest m.

**Norway** /ˈnɔːweɪ/ n Norvège f.

**Norwegian** /nɔːˈwiːdʒən/ n (person) Norvégien/-ne m/f; (language) norvégien m. ● adj norvégien.

**nose** /nəʊz/ n nez m. ● vi ~ about fouiner.

**nosedive** /ˈnəʊzdaɪv/ n piqué m. ● vi descendre en piqué.

**nostalgia** /nɒˈstældʒə/ n nostalgie f.

**nostril** /ˈnɒstrɪl/ n narine f; (of horse) naseau m.

**nosy** /ˈnəʊzɪ/ adj (-ier, -iest) ⚀ curieux, indiscret.

**not** /nɒt/ adv (ne) pas; I do ~ know je ne sais pas; ~ at all pas du tout; ~ yet pas encore; I suppose ~ je suppose que non.

**notably** /ˈnəʊtəblɪ/ adv notamment.

**notch** /nɒtʃ/ n entaille f. ● vt ~ up (score) marquer.

**note** /nəʊt/ n note f; (banknote) billet m; (short letter) mot m. ● vt noter; (notice) remarquer. ~book n carnet m.

rien m; (person) nullité f. ● adv nullement.

**notice** /ˈnəʊtɪs/ n avis m, annonce f; (poster) affiche f; (advance) ~ préavis m; at short ~ dans des délais très brefs; give in one's ~ donner sa démission; take ~ faire attention (of à). ● vt remarquer, observer. **noticeable** adj visible. ~-board n tableau m d'affichage.

**notify** /ˈnəʊtɪfaɪ/ vt (inform) aviser; (make known) notifier.

**notion** /ˈnəʊʃn/ n idée f, notion f.

**notorious** /nəʊˈtɔːrɪəs/ adj (criminal) notoire; (district) mal famé; (case) tristement célèbre.

**notwithstanding** /nɒtwɪθˈstændɪŋ/ prep malgré. ● adv néanmoins.

**nought** /nɔːt/ n zéro m.

**noun** /naʊn/ n nom m.

**nourish** /ˈnʌrɪʃ/ vt nourrir. **nourishing** adj nourrissant. **nourishment** n nourriture f.

**novel** /ˈnɒvl/ n roman m. ● adj nouveau. **novelist** n romancier/-ière m/f; **novelty** n nouveauté f.

**November** /nəˈvembə(r)/ n novembre m.

**now** /naʊ/ adv maintenant. ● conj maintenant que; just ~ maintenant; (a moment ago) tout à l'heure; ~ and again, ~ and then de temps à autre.

**nowadays** /ˈnaʊədeɪz/ adv de nos jours.

**nowhere** /ˈnəʊweə(r)/ adv nulle part.

**nozzle** /ˈnɒzl/ n (tip) embout m; (of hose) jet m.

**nuclear** /ˈnjuːklɪə(r)/ adj nucléaire.

**nude** /njuːd/ adj nu. ● n nu/-e m/f; in the ~ tout nu.

**nudge** /nʌdʒ/ vt pousser du coude. ● n coup m de coude.

**nudism** /'nju:dɪzəm/ n nudisme m.
**nudity** n nudité f.

**nuisance** /'nju:sns/ n (thing, event) ennui m; (person) peste f; be a ~ être embêtant.

**null** /nʌl/ adj nul.

**numb** /nʌm/ adj engourdi (with par). ● vt engourdir.

**number** /'nʌmbə(r)/ n nombre m; (of ticket, house, page) numéro m; (written figure) chiffre m; a ~ of people plusieurs. ● vt numéroter; (count, include) compter. ~-**plate** n plaque f d'immatriculation.

**numeral** /'nju:mərəl/ n chiffre m.

**numerate** /'nju:mərət/ adj qui sait compter.

**numerical** /nju:'merɪkl/ adj numérique.

**numerous** /'nju:mərəs/ adj nombreux.

**nun** /nʌn/ n religieuse f.

**nurse** /nɜ:s/ n infirmier/-ière m/f; (nanny) nurse f. ● vt soigner; (hope) nourrir.

**nursery** /'nɜ:səri/ n (room) chambre f d'enfants; (for plants) pépinière f; (day) ~ crèche f. ~ **rhyme** n comptine f. ~ **school** n (école) maternelle f.

**nursing home** n maison f de retraite.

**nut** /nʌt/ n (walnut, Brazil nut) noix f; (hazelnut) noisette f; (peanut) cacahuète f; (Tech) écrou m. ~**crackers** npl casse-noix m inv.

**nutmeg** /'nʌtmeg/ n muscade f.

**nutrient** /'nju:trɪənt/ n substance f nutritive.

**nutritious** /nju:'trɪʃəs/ adj nutritif.

**nuts** /nʌts/ adj (crazy 🄴) cinglé.

**nutshell** /'nʌtʃel/ n coquille f de noix; in a ~ en un mot.

**nylon** /'naɪlɒn/ n nylon m.

# Oo

**oak** /əʊk/ n chêne m.

**OAP** abbr **old-age pensioner** retraité/-e m/f.

**oar** /ɔ:(r)/ n rame f.

**oath** /əʊθ/ n (promise) serment m; (swearword) juron m.

**oats** /əʊts/ npl avoine f.

**obedience** /ə'bi:dɪəns/ n obéissance f. **obedient** adj obéissant. **obediently** adv docilement.

**obese** /əʊ'bi:s/ adj obèse.

**obey** /ə'beɪ/ vt/i obéir (à).

**object¹** /'ɒbdʒɪkt/ n (thing) objet m; (aim) but m; (Gram) complément m d'objet; money is no ~ l'argent n'est pas un problème.

**object²** /əb'dʒekt/ vi protester. ● vt ~ that objecter que; ~ to (behaviour) désapprouver; (plan) protester contre. **objection** n objection f; (drawback) inconvénient m.

**objective** /əb'dʒektɪv/ adj & n objectif (m).

**obligation** /ɒblɪ'geɪʃn/ n devoir m.

**obligatory** /ə'blɪgətrɪ/ adj obligatoire.

**oblige** /ə'blaɪdʒ/ vt obliger (to do à faire).

**oblivion** /ə'blɪvɪən/ n oubli m. **oblivious** adj inconscient (to, of de).

**oblong** /'ɒblɒŋ/ adj oblong. ● n rectangle m.

**obnoxious** /əb'nɒkʃəs/ adj odieux.

**oboe** /'əʊbəʊ/ n hautbois m.

**obscene** /əb'si:n/ adj obscène.

**obscure** /əbˈskjʊə(r)/ adj obscur.
● vt obscurcir; (conceal) cacher.

**observance** /əbˈzɜːvəns/ n (of law) respect m; (of sabbath) observance f. **observant** adj observateur.

**observation** /ɒbzəˈveɪʃn/ n observation f.

**observe** /əbˈzɜːv/ vt observer; (remark) remarquer.

**obsess** /əbˈses/ vt obséder. **obsession** n obsession f. **obsessive** adj (person) maniaque; (thought) obsédant; (illness) obsessionnel.

**obsolete** /ˈɒbsəliːt/ adj dépassé.

**obstacle** /ˈɒbstəkl/ n obstacle m.

**obstinate** /ˈɒbstənət/ adj obstiné.

**obstruct** /əbˈstrʌkt/ vt (road) bloquer; (view) cacher; (progress) gêner. **obstruction** n (act) obstruction f; (thing) obstacle m; (in traffic) encombrement m.

**obtain** /əbˈteɪn/ vt obtenir. ● vi avoir cours. **obtainable** adj disponible.

**obvious** /ˈɒbvɪəs/ adj évident. **obviously** adv manifestement.

**occasion** /əˈkeɪʒn/ n occasion f; (big event) événement m; on ~ à l'occasion.

**occasional** /əˈkeɪʒənl/ adj (event) qui a lieu de temps en temps; the ~ letter une lettre de temps en temps. **occasionally** adv de temps à autre.

**occupation** /ɒkjʊˈpeɪʃn/ n (activity) occupation f; (job) métier m, profession f. **occupational therapy** n ergothérapie f.

**occupier** /ˈɒkjʊpaɪə(r)/ n occupant/-e m/f.

**occupy** /ˈɒkjʊpaɪ/ vt occuper.

**occur** /əˈkɜː(r)/ vi (pt **occurred**) se produire; (arise) se présenter; ~ to sb venir à l'esprit de qn.

**occurrence** /əˈkʌrəns/ n (event)

fait m; (instance) occurrence f.

**ocean** /ˈəʊʃn/ n océan m.

**Oceania** /əʊʃiˈeɪniə/ n Océanie f.

**o'clock** /əˈklɒk/ adv it is six ~ il est six heures; at one ~ à une heure.

**October** /ɒkˈtəʊbə(r)/ n octobre m.

**octopus** /ˈɒktəpəs/ n (pl) ~es pieuvre f.

**odd** /ɒd/ adj bizarre; (number) impair; (left over) qui reste; (sock) dépareillé; write the ~ article écrire un article de temps en temps; ~ jobs menus travaux mpl; twenty ~ vingt et quelques. **oddity** n bizarrerie f.

**odds** /ɒdz/ npl chances fpl; (in betting) cote f (on de); at ~ en désaccord; it makes no ~ ça ne fait rien; ~ and ends de petites choses.

**odour**, (US) **odor** /ˈəʊdə(r)/ n odeur f. **odourless** adj inodore.

---

**of** /ɒv/        o

➡️ For expressions such as of course, consist of ➡course, consist.

● preposition
····▸ de; a photo ~ the dog une photo du chien; the king ~ the beasts le roi des animaux; (made) ~ gold en or; it's kind ~ you c'est très gentil de votre part; some ~ us quelques-uns d'entre nous; ~ it/them en; have you heard ~ it? est-ce que tu en as entendu parler?

**off** /ɒf/ adv be ~ partir, s'en aller; I'm ~ je m'en vais; 30 metres ~ à 30 mètres; a month ~ dans un mois. ● adj (gas, water) coupé; (tap) fermé; (light, TV) éteint; (party, match) annulé; (bad) (food) avarié; (milk) tourné; **Friday is my day ~** je ne travaille pas le vendredi; 25% **~** 25% de remise. ● prep 3 metres **~ the ground** 3 mètres (au-dessus) du sol; **just ~ the kitchen** juste à côté de la cuisine; **that is ~ the point** là est la question.

**offal** /'ɒfl/ n abats mpl.

**offence** /ə'fens/ n (Jur) infraction f; **give ~ to** offenser; **take ~** s'offenser (at de).

**offend** /ə'fend/ vt offenser; **be ~ed** s'offenser (at de). ● vi (Jur) commettre une infraction. **offender** n délinquant/-e m/f.

**offensive** /ə'fensɪv/ adj (remark) injurieux; (language) grossier; (smell) repoussant; (weapon) offensif. ● n offensive f.

**offer** /'ɒfə(r)/ vt ( pt offered) offrir. ● n offre f; **on ~** en promotion.

**offhand** /ɒf'hænd/ adj désinvolte. ● adv à l'improviste.

**office** /'ɒfɪs/ n bureau m; (duty) fonction f; **in ~** au pouvoir. ● adj de bureau.

**officer** /'ɒfɪsə(r)/ n (army) officier m; (police) policier m; (government **~**) fonctionnaire mf.

**official** /ə'fɪʃl/ adj officiel. ● n (civil servant) fonctionnaire mf; (of party, union) officiel/-le m/f; (of police, customs) agent m.

**off**: **~-licence** n magasin m de vins et spiritueux. **~-line** adj autonome; (switched off) déconnecté; (Comput) hors connexion. **~-load** vt (stock) écouler; (Comput) décharger. **~-peak** adj (call) au tarif réduit; (travel) en période creuse. **~-putting** adj rebutant. **~-set** ( pt -set. pres p-setting) compenser. **~-shore** adj (out to sea) au large, en mer; (towards the shore) de terre; an

**~ breeze** une brise de terre. ● adv ( funds) hors-lieu inv. **~-side** adj (Sport) hors jeu inv; (Auto) du côté du conducteur. **~-spring** n inv progéniture f.

**often** /'ɒfn/ adv souvent; **how ~ do you meet?** vous vous voyez tous les combien?; **every so ~** de temps en temps.

**oil** /ɔɪl/ n (for lubrication, cooking) huile f; (for fuel) pétrole m; (for heating) mazout m. ● vt huiler. **~ field** n gisement m pétrolifère. **~-painting** n peinture f à l'huile. **~ skins** npl ciré m. **~-tanker** n pétrolier m.

**oily** /'ɔɪlɪ/ adj graisseux.

**ointment** /'ɔɪntmənt/ n pommade f.

**OK, okay** /əʊ'keɪ/ adj d'accord; **is it ~ if…?** ça va si…?; **feel ~** aller bien.

**old** /əʊld/ adj vieux; (person) vieux, âgé; (former) ancien; **how ~ is he?** quel âge a-t-il?; **he is eight years ~** il a huit ans; **~er, ~est** aîné. **~ age** n vieillesse f. **~-age pensioner** n retraité/-e m/f. **~-fashioned** adj démodé; (person) vieux jeu inv. **~ man** n vieillard m, vieux m. **~ woman** n vieille f.

**olive** /'ɒlɪv/ n olive f; **~ oil** huile f d'olive. ● adj olive inv.

**Olympic** /ə'lɪmpɪk/ adj olympique.

∼ **Games** *npl* Jeux *mpl* olympiques.

**omelette** /ˈɒmlɪt/ *n* omelette *f.*

**omen** /ˈəʊmən/ *n* augure *m.*

**ominous** /ˈɒmɪnəs/ *adj* (*presence, cloud*) menaçant; (*sign*) de mauvais augure.

**omission** /əˈmɪʃn/ *n* omission *f.*

**omit** *vt* (*pt* **omitted**) omettre.

**on** /ɒn/ *prep sur;* ∼ the table sur la table; put the key ∼ it mets la clé dessus; ∼ 22 March le 22 mars; ∼ Monday lundi; ∼ TV à la télé; ∼ video en vidéo; be ∼ steroids prendre des stéroïdes; ∼ arriving en arrivant. ● *adj* (*TV, oven, light*) allumé; (*dishwasher, radio*) en marche; (*tap*) ouvert; (*lid*) mis; the match is still ∼ le match aura lieu quand même; the news is ∼ in 10 minutes les informations sont dans 10 minutes. ● *adv* have sth ∼ porter qch; 20 years ∼ 20 ans plus tard; from that day ∼ à partir de ce jour-là; further ∼ plus loin; ∼ and off (*occasionally*) de temps en temps; go ∼ and ∼ (*person*) parler pendant des heures.

**once** /wʌns/ *adv* une fois; (*formerly*) autrefois. ● *conj* une fois que; all at ∼ tout à coup.

**oncoming** /ˈɒnkʌmɪŋ/ *adj* (*vehicle*) qui approche.

**one** /wʌn/ *det* & *n un/-e* (*m/f*). ● *pron* un/-e *m/f;* (*impersonal*) on; ∼ (and only) seul (et unique); a big ∼ un grand/une grande; this/that ∼ celui-ci/-là, celle-ci/-là; an∼ other l'un/-e l'autre. ∼ off *adj* 🎅 unique, exceptionnel. ∼**self** *pron* soi-même; (*reflexive*) se. ∼-**way** *adj* (*street*) à sens unique; (*ticket*) simple.

**ongoing** /ˈɒnɡəʊɪŋ/ *adj* (*process*) continu; be ∼ être en cours.

**onion** /ˈʌnɪən/ *n* oignon *m.*

**on-line** /ɒnˈlaɪn/ *adj* & *adv* en ligne.

**onlooker** /ˈɒnlʊkə(r)/ *n* spectateur/-trice *m/f.*

**only** /ˈəʊnlɪ/ *adj* seul; ∼ son fils unique. ● *adv* & *conj* seulement; he is ∼ six il n'a que six ans.

**onset** /ˈɒnset/ *n* début *m.*

**onward(s)** /ˈɒnwəd(z)/ *adv* en avant.

**open** /ˈəʊpən/ *adj* ouvert; (*view*) dégagé; (*free to all*) public; (*undisguised*) manifeste; (*question*) en attente; in the ∼ air en plein air. ● *vt/i* (*door*) (s')ouvrir; (*shop, play*) ouvrir; ∼ out *or* up (s')ouvrir. ∼-**ended** *adj* (*stay*) de durée indéterminée; (*debate, question*) ouvert. ∼-**heart** *adj* (*surgery*) à cœur ouvert.

**opening** /ˈəʊpnɪŋ/ *n* (*of book*) début *m;* (*of exhibition, shop*) ouverture *f;* (*of film*) première *f;* (*in market*) débouché *m;* (*job*) poste *m* (disponible).

**open:** ∼-**minded** *adj* be ∼-minded avoir l'esprit ouvert. ∼-**plan** *adj* paysagé.

---

**Open University** Organisme britannique d'enseignement universitaire à distance. Les étudiants de tous âges travaillent chez eux et suivent les cours à la télévision ou sur Internet; ils envoient leurs travaux à leur directeur d'études (*tutor*) qu'ils peuvent rencontrer lors de stages en été. Les diplômes obtenus ont la même valeur que ceux délivrés par les universités traditionnelles.

---

**opera** /ˈɒprə/ *n* opéra *m.*

**operate** /ˈɒpəreɪt/ *vt/i* opérer; (*Tech*) (faire) fonctionner; ∼ on (*Med*) opérer; operating theatre salle *f* d'opération.

**operation** /ɒpəˈreɪʃn/ n opération f; have an ~ se faire opérer; in ~ (plan) en vigueur; (mine) en service.

**operative** /ˈɒpərətɪv/ n employé, -e m/f. ● adj (law) en vigueur.

**operator** /ˈɒpəreɪtə(r)/ n opérateur/-trice m/f; (telephonist) standardiste m/f.

**opinion** /əˈpɪnɪən/ n opinion f, avis m. **opinionated** adj qui a des avis sur tout.

**opponent** /əˈpəʊnənt/ n adversaire m/f.

**opportunity** /ɒpəˈtjuːnɪtɪ/ n occasion f (to do de faire).

**oppose** /əˈpəʊz/ vt s'opposer à; as ~d to par opposition à. **opposing** adj opposé.

**opposite** /ˈɒpəzɪt/ adj (direction, side) opposé; (building) d'en face. ● n contraire m. ● adv en face. ● prep ~ (to) en face de.

**opposition** /ɒpəˈzɪʃn/ n opposition f.

**oppress** /əˈpres/ vt opprimer. **oppressive** adj (cruel) oppressif; (heat) oppressant.

**opt** /ɒpt/ vi ~ for opter pour; ~ out refuser de participer (of à); ~ to do choisir de faire.

**optical** /ˈɒptɪkl/ adj optique. ~ **illusion** n illusion f d'optique. ~ **scanner** n lecteur m optique.

**optician** /ɒpˈtɪʃn/ n opticien/-ne m/f.

**optimism** /ˈɒptɪmɪzəm/ n optimisme m. **optimist** n optimiste m/f. **optimistic** adj optimiste.

**option** /ˈɒpʃn/ n option f; (choice) choix m.

**optional** /ˈɒpʃənl/ adj facultatif; ~ extras accessoires mpl en option.

**oral** /ˈɔːrəl/ n & adj oral (m).

**orange** /ˈɒrɪndʒ/ n (fruit) orange f; (colour) orange m. ● adj (colour) orange inv.

**orbit** /ˈɔːbɪt/ n orbite f. ● vt décrire une orbite autour de.

**orchard** /ˈɔːtʃəd/ n verger m.

**orchestra** /ˈɔːkɪstrə/ n orchestre m.

**orchid** /ˈɔːkɪd/ n orchidée f.

**ordeal** /ɔːˈdiːl/ n épreuve f.

**order** /ˈɔːdə(r)/ n ordre m; (Comm) commande f; in ~ (tidy) en ordre; (document) en règle; in ~ that pour que; in ~ to pour. ● vt ordonner; (goods) commander; ~ sb to ordonner à qn de.

**orderly** /ˈɔːdəlɪ/ adj (tidy) ordonné; (not unruly) discipliné. ● n (Mil) planton m; (Med) aide-soignant, -e m/f.

**ordinary** /ˈɔːdənrɪ/ adj (usual) ordinaire; (average) moyen.

**ore** /ɔː(r)/ n minerai m.

**organ** /ˈɔːgən/ n organe m; (Mus) orgue m.

**organic** /ɔːˈgænɪk/ adj organique; (produce) biologique.

**organization** /ɔːgənaɪˈzeɪʃn/ n organisation f.

**organize** /ˈɔːgənaɪz/ vt organiser.

**organizer** /ˈɔːgənaɪzə(r)/ n organisateur/-trice m/f; electronic ~ agenda m électronique.

**orgasm** /ˈɔːgæzəm/ n orgasme m.

**Orient** /ˈɔːrɪənt/ n the ~ l'Orient m. **oriental** adj oriental.

**origin** /ˈɒrɪdʒɪn/ n origine f.

**original** /əˈrɪdʒənl/ adj original; (inhabitant) premier; (member) originaire. **originality** n originalité f. **originally** adv (at the outset) à l'origine.

**originate** /əˈrɪdʒɪneɪt/ vi (plan) prendre naissance; ~ from provenir de; (person) venir de. ● vt être l'auteur de. **originator** n (of idea) auteur m; (of invention) créateur/-trice m/f.

**ornament** /'ɔ:nəmənt/ n (decoration) ornement m; (object) objet m décoratif.

**orphan** /'ɔ:fn/ n orphelin/-e m/f. ● vt rendre orphelin. **orphanage** n orphelinat m.

**orthopaedic** /ɔ:θə'pi:dɪk/ adj orthopédique.

**ostentatious** /ɒsten'teɪʃəs/ adj tape-à-l'œil inv.

**osteopath** /'ɒstɪəpæθ/ n ostéopathe mf.

**ostrich** /'ɒstrɪtʃ/ n autruche f.

**other** /'ʌðə(r)/ adj autre; the ~ one l'autre mf. ● n & pron autre mf; (some) ~s d'autres. ● adv ~ than (apart from) à part; (otherwise than) autrement que. **otherwise** adv autrement.

**otter** /'ɒtə(r)/ n loutre f.

**ouch** /aʊtʃ/ interj aïe!

**ought** /ɔ:t/ v aux devoir; you ~ to stay vous devriez rester; he ~ to succeed il devrait réussir; I ~ to have done it j'aurais dû le faire.

**ounce** /aʊns/ n once f (= 28.35 g).

**our** /'aʊə(r)/ adj notre, pl nos.

**ours** /'aʊəz/ poss le or la nôtre, les nôtres.

**ourselves** /aʊə'selvz/ pron (reflexive) nous; (emphatic) nous-mêmes; (after preposition) for ~ pour nous, pour nous-mêmes.

**out** /aʊt/ adv dehors; he's ~ il est sorti; further ~ plus loin; be ~ (book) être publié; (light) être éteint; (sun) briller; (flower) être épanoui; (tide) être bas; (player) être éliminé; ~ of hors de; go/walk/get ~ of sortir de; ~ of pity par pitié; made ~ of fait de; 5

~ of 6 5 sur 6. ~**break** n (of war) déclenchement m; (of violence, boils) éruption f. ~**burst** n explosion f. ~**cast** n paria m. ~**class** vt surclasser. ~**come** n résultat m. ~**cry** n tollé m. ~**dated** adj démodé. ~**door** adj (activity) de plein air; (pool) en plein air. ~**doors** adv dehors.

**outer** /'aʊtə(r)/ adj extérieur; ~ space espace m extra-atmosphérique.

**outfit** /'aʊtfɪt/ n (clothes) tenue f.

**outgoing** /'aʊtgəʊɪŋ/ adj (minister, tenant) sortant; (sociable) ouvert. **outgoings** npl dépenses fpl.

**outgrow** /aʊt'grəʊ/ vt (pt -grew, pp -grown) (clothes) devenir trop grand pour; (habit) dépasser.

**outing** /'aʊtɪŋ/ n sortie f.

**outlaw** /'aʊtlɔ:/ n hors-la-loi m inv. ● vt déclarer illégal.

**outlet** /'aʊtlet/ n (for water, gas) tuyau m de sortie; (for goods) débouché m; (for feelings) exutoire m.

**outline** /'aʊtlaɪn/ n contour m; (of plan) grandes lignes fpl; (of essay) plan m. ● vt tracer le contour de; (summarize) exposer brièvement.

**out:** ~**live** vt survivre à. ~**look** n perspective f. ~**number** vt surpasser en nombre. ~ **of date** adj démodé; (expired) périmé. ~ **of hand** adj incontrôlable. ~ **of order** adj en panne. ~ **of work** adj sans travail. ~**patient** n malade mf externe.

**output** /'aʊtpʊt/ n rendement m; (Comput) sortie f. ● vt/i (Comput) sortir.

**outrage** /'aʊtreɪdʒ/ n (anger) indignation f; (atrocity) attentat m; (scandal) outrage m. ● vt (morals) outrager; (person) scandaliser. **outrageous** adj scandaleux.

**outright** /'aʊtraɪt/ adv (com-

o

pletely) catégoriquement; (killed) sur le coup. ● adj (majority) absolu; (ban) catégorique; (hostility) pur et simple.

**outset** /'aʊtset/ n début m.

**outside** /aʊt'saɪd/ n extérieur m. ● adv dehors. ● prep en dehors de; (in front of) devant. ● adj extérieur.

**outsider** n étranger/-ère m/f; (Sport) outsider m.

**out:** ~ skirts npl périphérie f. ~spoken adj franc. ~standing adj exceptionnel; (not settled) en suspens.

**outward** /'aʊtwəd/ adj & adv vers l'extérieur; (sign) extérieur. (journey) d'aller. **outwards** adv vers l'extérieur.

**oval** /'əʊvl/ n & adj ovale (m).

**Oval Office** Symbole même de la présidence américaine, le bureau ovale du président des États-Unis est situé dans l'aile ouest de la Maison-Blanche et a été inauguré en 1909. Le goût des pièces de forme ovale remonte à la présidence de George Washington (1789-1797) qui donnait des réceptions à son domicile de Philadelphie dans un salon ovale.

**ovary** /'əʊvərɪ/ n ovaire m.

**oven** /'ʌvn/ n four m.

**over** /'əʊvə(r)/ prep (across) par-dessus; (above) au-dessus de; (covering) sur; (more than) plus de; it's ~ the road c'est de l'autre côté de la rue; ~ here/there par ici/là; children ~ six les enfants de plus de six ans; ~ the weekend pendant le weekend; all ~ the house partout dans la maison.
● adj, adv (term) terminé; (war) fini; get sth ~ with en finir avec qch.

ask sb ~ inviter qn; ~ and ~ (again) à plusieurs reprises; five times ~ cinq fois de suite.

**overall** /əʊvər'ɔːl/ adj global, d'ensemble; (length) total. ● adv globalement.

**overalls** /'əʊvərɔːls/npl combinaison f.

**over** /'əʊvə(r)/ ~board adv par-dessus bord. ~cast adj couvert. ~charge vt faire payer trop cher à. ~coat n pardessus m.

**overcome** /əʊvə'kʌm/ vt (pt -came. pp -come) (enemy) vaincre; (difficulty, fear) surmonter; ~by accablé de.

**overcrowded** /əʊvə'kraʊdɪd/ adj bondé; (country) surpeuplé.

**overdo** /əʊvə'duː/ vt (pt -did. pp -done) (Culin) trop cuire; ~ it (overwork) en faire trop.

**over:** ~ dose n surdose f, overdose f. ~ draft n découvert m. ~ draw vt (pt -drew. pp -drawn) faire un découvert sur. ~ due adj en retard; (bill) impayé.

**overflow¹** /əʊvə'fləʊ/ vi déborder.

**overflow²** /'əʊvəfləʊ/ n (outlet) trop-plein m. ~ car park n parking m de délestage.

**overhaul** /əʊvə'hɔːl/ vt réviser.

**overhead¹** /əʊvə'hed/ adv au-dessus; (in sky) dans le ciel.

**overhead²** /'əʊvəhed/ adj aérien; ~ projector n rétroprojecteur m. **overheads** npl frais mpl généraux.

**over:** ~hear vt (pt overheard) entendre par hasard. ~lap vt/i (pt -lapped) se chevaucher. ~leaf adv au verso. ~load vt surcharger. ~look vt (window) donner sur; (miss) ne pas voir.

**overnight¹** /əʊvə'naɪt/ adv dans la nuit; (instantly: fig) du jour au lendemain.

**overnight²** /ˈəʊvənaɪt/ adj (train) de nuit; (stay) d'une nuit; (fig) soudain.

**over:** ~**power** vt (thief) maîtriser; (army) vaincre; (fig) accabler. ~**priced** adj trop cher. ~**rate** vt surestimer. ~**react** vi réagir de façon excessive. ~**riding** adj (consideration) numéro un; (importance) primordial. ~**rule** vt (decision) annuler.

**overrun** /əʊvəˈrʌn/ vt (pt **-ran**. pp **-run**. pres p **-running**) (country) envahir; (budget) dépasser. ● vi (meeting) durer plus longtemps que prévu.

**overseas** /əʊvəˈsiːz/ adj étranger. ● adv outre-mer, à l'étranger.

**over:** ~**see** vt (pt **-saw**. pp **-seen**) surveiller. ~**sight** n omission f. ~**sleep** vi (pt **-slept**) se réveiller trop tard. ~**take** vt/i (pt **-took**. pp **-taken**) dépasser; (fig) frapper. ~**time** n heures fpl supplémentaires. ~**turn** vt/i (se) renverser. ~**weight** adj trop gros.

**overwhelm** /əʊvəˈwelm/ vt (enemy) écraser; (shame) accabler. **overwhelmed** adj (with offers, calls) submergé (with, by de); (with shame, work) accablé; (by sight) ébloui. **overwhelming** adj (heat, grief) accablant; (defeat, victory) écrasant; (urge) irrésistible.

**overwork** /əʊvəˈwɜːk/ vt/i (se) surmener. ● n surmenage m.

**owe** /əʊ/ vt devoir. **owing** adj dû; owing to en raison de.

**owl** /aʊl/ n hibou m.

**own** /əʊn/ adj propre. ● pron my ~ le mien, la mienne; a house of one's ~ sa propre maison; on one's ~ tout seul. ● vt posséder; ~ up (to) ● avouer. **owner** n propriétaire mf. **ownership** n propriété f; (of land) possession f.

---

**Oxbridge** Formé de la combinaison de Oxford et Cambridge, ce mot-valise est fréquemment employé pour désigner les universités de ces deux villes, en particulier quand on veut les distinguer des autres universités britanniques, car ce sont les plus prestigieuses.

**oxygen** /ˈɒksɪdʒən/ n oxygène m.

**oyster** /ˈɔɪstə(r)/ n huître f.

**ozone** /ˈəʊzəʊn/ n ozone m; ~ layer couche f d'ozone.

# Pp

**PA** abbr ➤**PERSONAL ASSISTANT**.

**pace** /peɪs/ n pas m; (speed) allure f; keep ~ with suivre. ● vt (room) arpenter. ~ **(up and down)** faire les cent pas.

**Pacific** /pəˈsɪfɪk/ n ~ (Ocean) océan m Pacifique.

**pack** /pæk/ n paquet m; (Mil) sac m; (of hounds) meute f; (of thieves) bande f; (of lies) tissu m. ● vt (into case) mettre dans une valise; (into box, crate) emballer; (for sale) conditionner; (crowd) remplir complètement; ~ one's suitcase faire sa valise. ● vi faire ses valises; ~ **into** (cram) s'entasser dans; ~ **off** expédier; send ~**ing** envoyer promener.

**package** /ˈpækɪdʒ/ n paquet m; (Comput) progiciel m; ~ **deal** offre f globale; ~ **holiday** voyage m organisé. ● vt empaqueter.

**packed** /pækt/ adj (crowded) bondé; ~ **lunch** repas m froid.

**packet** /ˈpækɪt/ n paquet m.

**packing** /'pækɪŋ/ n (action, material) emballage m.

**pad** /pæd/ n (of paper) bloc m; (to protect) protection f; (for ink) tampon m; (launch) ~ rampe f de lancement. ~ vt (pt **padded**) rembourrer; (text: fig) délayer. ● vi (pt **padded**) (walk) marcher à pas feutrés. **padding** n rembourrage m.

**paddle** /'pædl/ n pagaie f. ● vt ~ a canoe pagayer. ● vi patauger.

**padlock** /'pædlɒk/ n cadenas m. ● vt cadenasser.

**paediatrician** /ˌpiːdjə'trɪʃən/ n pédiatre mf.

**pagan** /'peɪgən/ adj & n païen-ne (m/f).

**page** /peɪdʒ/ n (of book) page f. ● vt (on pager) rechercher; (over speaker) faire appeler. **pager** n radiomessageur m.

**pain** /peɪn/ n douleur f; ~s efforts mpl; be in ~ souffrir; take ~s to se donner du mal pour. ● vt (grieve) peiner. **painful** adj douloureux; (laborious) pénible. ~**killer** n analgésique m. **painless** adj (operation) indolore; (death) sans souffrance; (trouble-free) sans peine. **painstaking** adj minutieux.

**paint** /peɪnt/ n peinture f. ~s (in tube, box) couleurs fpl. ● vt/i peindre. ~ **brush** n pinceau m. **painter** n peintre m. **painting** n peinture f. ~**work** n peintures fpl.

**pair** /peə(r)/ n paire f; (of people) couple m; a ~ of trousers un pantalon. ● vi ~ off former un couple.

**pajamas** /pə'dʒɑːməz/ npl (US) ➞PYJAMAS.

**Pakistan** /ˌpɑːkɪ'stɑːn/ n Pakistan m.

**palace** /'pælɪs/ n palais m.

**palatable** /'pælətəbl/ adj (food) savoureux; (solution) acceptable.

**palate** n palais m.

**pale** /peɪl/ adj pâle. ● vi pâlir.

**Palestine** /'pæləstaɪn/ n Palestine f.

**pallid** /'pælɪd/ adj pâle.

**palm** /pɑːm/ n (of hand) paume f; (tree) palmier m; (symbol) palme f. □ ~ **off** 🔒 ~ sth off as faire passer qch pour; ~ sth off on sb refiler qch à qn 🔒.

**palpitate** /'pælpɪteɪt/ vi palpiter.

**paltry** /'pɔːltrɪ/ adj (-ier, -iest) dérisoire, piètre.

**pamper** /'pæmpə(r)/ vt choyer.

**pamphlet** /'pæmflɪt/ n brochure f.

**pan** /pæn/ n casserole f; (for frying) poêle f.

**pancake** /'pænkeɪk/ n crêpe f.

**pandemonium** /ˌpændɪ'məʊnɪəm/ n tohu-bohu m.

**pander** /'pændə(r)/ vi ~ to (person, taste) flatter bassement.

**pane** /peɪn/ n carreau m, vitre f.

**panel** /'pænl/ n (of door) panneau m; (of experts, judges) commission f; (on discussion programme) invités mpl; (instrument) ~ tableau m de bord.

**pang** /pæŋ/ n serrement m au cœur; ~s of conscience remords mpl.

**panic** /'pænɪk/ n panique f. ● vt/i (pt **panicked**) s'affoler. ~**stricken** adj pris de panique, affolé.

**pansy** /'pænzɪ/ n (Bot) pensée f.

**pant** /pænt/ vi haleter.

**panther** /'pænθə(r)/ n panthère f.

**pantomime** /'pæntəmaɪm/ n (show) spectacle m de Noël; (mime) mime m.

**pantry** /'pæntrɪ/ n garde-manger m inv.

**pants** /pænts/ npl (underwear) slip

*m*; (trousers: US) pantalon *m*.

**paper** /ˈpeɪpə(r)/ *n* papier *m*; (newspaper) journal *m*; (exam) épreuve *f*; (essay) exposé *m*; (wallpaper) papier *m* peint; (identity) ~s papiers *mpl* (d'identité); on ~ par écrit. ● *vt* (room) tapisser. ~**back** *n* livre *m* de poche. ~**clip** *n* trombone *m*. ~ **feed tray** *n* (Comput) bac *m* d'alimentation en papier. ~ **work** *n* (work) travail *m* administratif; (documentation) documents *mpl*.

**par** /pɑː(r)/ *n* be below ~ ne pas être en forme; on a ~ with ~ (performance) comparable à; (person) l'égal de; (golf) par *m*.

**parachute** /ˈpærəʃuːt/ *n* parachute *m*. ● *vi* descendre en parachute.

**parade** /pəˈreɪd/ *n* (procession) parade *f*; (Mil) défilé *m*. ● *vi* défiler. ● *vt* faire étalage de.

**paradise** /ˈpærədaɪs/ *n* paradis *m*.

**paradox** /ˈpærədɒks/ *n* paradoxe *m*.

**paraffin** /ˈpærəfɪn/ *n* pétrole *m* (lampant); (wax) paraffine *f*.

**paragliding** /ˈpærəɡlaɪdɪŋ/ *n* parapente *m*.

**paragon** /ˈpærəɡən/ *n* modèle *m*.

**paragraph** /ˈpærəɡrɑːf/ *n* paragraphe *m*.

**parallel** /ˈpærəlel/ *adj* parallèle. ● *n* parallèle *m*; (maths) parallèle *f*.

**Paralympics** /ˌpærəˈlɪmpɪks/ *npl* the ~ les jeux paralympiques.

**paralyse** /ˈpærəlaɪz/ *vt* paralyser. **paralysis** *n* paralysie *f*.

**paramedic** /ˌpærəˈmedɪk/ *n* auxiliaire *mf* médical/-e.

**parameter** /pəˈræmɪtə(r)/ *n* paramètre *m*.

**paramount** /ˈpærəmaʊnt/ *adj* suprême.

**paranoia** /ˌpærəˈnɔɪə/ *n* paranoïa *f*.

**paranoid** *adj* paranoïaque; (Psych) paranoïde.

**paraphernalia** /ˌpærəfəˈneɪlɪə/ *n* attirail *m*.

**parasol** /ˈpærəsɒl/ *n* ombrelle *f*; (on table, at beach) parasol *m*.

**paratrooper** /ˈpærətruːpə(r)/ *n* (Mil) parachutiste *mf*.

**parcel** /ˈpɑːsl/ *n* paquet *m*.

**parchment** /ˈpɑːtʃmənt/ *n* parchemin *m*.

**pardon** /ˈpɑːdn/ *n* pardon *m*; (Jur) grâce *f*; I beg your ~ je vous demande pardon. ● *vt* (*pt* pardoned) pardonner (sb for sth qch à qn); (Jur) gracier.

**parent** /ˈpeərənt/ *n* parent *m*.

**parenthesis** /pəˈrenθəsɪs/ *n* (*pl* -theses) parenthèse *f*.

**parenthood** /ˈpeərənthʊd/ *n* (fatherhood) paternité *f*; (motherhood) maternité *f*.

**Paris** /ˈpærɪs/ *n* Paris.

**parish** /ˈpærɪʃ/ *n* (Relig) paroisse *f*; (municipal) commune *f*.

**park** /pɑːk/ *n* parc *m*. ● *vt/i* (se) garer; (remain parked) stationner. ~ **and ride** *n* parc *m* relais.

**parking** /ˈpɑːkɪŋ/ *n* stationnement *m*; no ~ stationnement interdit. ~ **lot** *n* (US) parking *m*. ~ **meter** *n* parcmètre *m*. ~ **ticket** *n* (fine) contravention *f*, PV *m* ▣.

**parliament** /ˈpɑːləmənt/ *n* parlement *m*. **parliamentary** *adj* parlementaire.

> **Parliament** Corps législatif britannique composé de la Chambre des communes (*House of Commons*) et de la Chambre des Lords (*House of Lords*) qui siègent au Palais de Westminster. Le souverain convoque et dissout le Parlement, ouvre chaque

session parlementaire et signe les textes de lois. ▸SCOTTISH PARLIAMENT, ▸WELSH ASSEMBLY, ▸DÁIL

**parlour**, (US) **parlor** /'pɑːlə(r)/ n salon m.

**parody** /'pærədɪ/ n parodie f. ● vt parodier.

**parole** /pə'rəʊl/ n on ~ en liberté conditionnelle.

**parrot** /'pærət/ n perroquet m.

**parry** /'pærɪ/ vt (Sport) parer; (question) éluder. ● n parade f.

**parsley** /'pɑːslɪ/ n persil m.

**parsnip** /'pɑːsnɪp/ n panais m.

**part** /pɑːt/ n partie f; (of serial) épisode m; (of machine) pièce f; (Theat) rôle m; (in dispute) parti m; **in ~** en partie; **on the ~ of** de la part de; **take ~ in** participer à. ● adj partiel. ● adv en partie. ● vt/i (separate) (se) séparer; **~ with** se séparer de.

**part-exchange** n reprise f; **take sth in ~** reprendre qch.

**partial** /'pɑːʃl/ adj partiel; (biased) partial; **be ~ to** avoir un faible pour.

**participant** /pɑː'tɪsɪpənt/ n participant/-e m/f. **participate** vi participer (in à). **participation** n participation f.

**participle** /'pɑːtɪsɪpl/ n participe m.

**particular** /pə'tɪkjʊlə(r)/ n détail m; ~s détails mpl; **in ~** en particulier. ● adj particulier; (fussy) difficile; (careful) méticuleux; **that ~ man** cet homme-là. **particularly** adv particulièrement.

**parting** /'pɑːtɪŋ/ n séparation f; (in hair) raie f. ● adj d'adieu.

**partition** /pɑː'tɪʃn/ n (of room) cloison f; (Pol) partition f. ● vt (room) cloisonner; (country)

partager.

**partly** /'pɑːtlɪ/ adv en partie.

**partner** /'pɑːtnə(r)/ n (professional) associé/-e m/f; (economic, sporting) partenaire mf; (spouse) époux/-se m/f; (unmarried) partenaire mf. **partnership** n association f.

**partridge** /'pɑːtrɪdʒ/ n perdrix f.

**part-time** adj & adv à temps partiel.

**party** /'pɑːtɪ/ n fête f; (formal) réception f; (group) groupe m; (Pol) parti m; (Jur) partie f.

**pass** /pɑːs/ vt/i (pt passed) passer; (overtake) dépasser; (in exam) réussir; (approve) (candidate) admettre; (invoice) approuver; (remark) faire; (judgement) prononcer; (law, bill) adopter; ~ (by) (building) passer devant; (person) croiser. ● n (permit) laisser-passer m inv; (ticket) carte f d'abonnement; (Geog) col m; (Sport) passe f; ~ (mark) (in exam) moyenne f. □ ~ away mourir; ~ out (faint) s'évanouir; ~ sth out distribuer qch; ~ over (overlook) délaisser; ~ up (forego) laisser passer.

**passage** /'pæsɪdʒ/ n (way through, text) passage m; (voyage) traversée f; (corridor) couloir m.

**passenger** /'pæsɪndʒə(r)/ n (in car, plane, ship) passager/-ère m/f; (in train, bus, tube) voyageur/-euse m/f.

**passer-by** /pɑːsə'baɪ/ n (pl passers-by) passant/-e m/f.

**passing** /'pɑːsɪŋ/ adj (motorist) qui passe; (whim) passager; (reference) en passant.

**passion** /'pæʃn/ n passion f. **passionate** adj passionné.

**passive** /'pæsɪv/ adj passif.

**passport** /'pɑːspɔːt/ n passeport m.

**password** /'pɑːswɜːd/ n mot m

de passe.

**past** /pɑːst/ adj (times, problems) passé; (president) ancien; the ~ months ces derniers mois. ● n passé m. ● prep (beyond) après; walk/go ~ sth passer devant qch; 10 ~ 6 six heures dix; it's ~ 11 il est 11 heures passées. ● adv go/walk ~ passer.

**pasta** /ˈpæstə/ n pâtes fpl (alimentaires).

**paste** /peɪst/ n (glue) colle f; (dough) pâte f; (of fish, meat) pâté m; (jewellery) strass m. ● vt coller.

**pasteurize** /ˈpɑːstʃəraɪz/ vt pasteuriser.

**pastime** /ˈpɑːstaɪm/ n passe-temps m inv.

**pastry** /ˈpeɪstrɪ/ n (dough) pâte f; (tart) pâtisserie f.

**pat** /pæt/ vt (pt patted) tapoter. ● n petite tape f.

**patch** /pætʃ/ n pièce f; (over eye) bandeau m; (spot) tache f; (of snow, ice) plaque f; (of vegetables) carré m; bad ~ période f difficile. □ ~ up (trousers) rapiécer; (quarrel) résoudre.

**patent** /ˈpeɪtnt/ adj (obvious) manifeste; (patented) breveté. ~ leather cuir m verni. ● n brevet m. ● vt faire breveter.

**path** /pɑːθ/ n (pl -s) sentier m, chemin m; (in park) allée f; (of rocket) trajectoire f.

**pathetic** /pəˈθetɪk/ adj misérable; (bad) lamentable.

**patience** /ˈpeɪʃns/ n patience f.

**patient** /ˈpeɪʃnt/ adj patient. ● n patient/-e m/f. **patiently** adv patiemment.

**patriotic** /pætrɪˈɒtɪk/ adj patriotique; (person) patriote.

**patrol** /pəˈtrəʊl/ n patrouille f; ~ car voiture f de police. ● vt/i pa-

trouiller (dans).

**patron** /ˈpeɪtrən/ n (of the arts) mécène m; (customer) client/-e m/f. **patronage** n clientèle f; (support) patronage m. **patronize** vt (person) traiter avec condescendance; (establishment) fréquenter.

**patter** /ˈpætə(r)/ n (of steps) bruit m; (of rain) crépitement m.

**pattern** /ˈpætn/ n motif m, dessin m; (for sewing) patron m; (for knitting) modèle m.

**paunch** /pɔːntʃ/ n ventre m.

**pause** /pɔːz/ n pause f. ● vi faire une pause; (hesitate) hésiter.

**pave** /peɪv/ vt paver; ~ the way ouvrir la voie (for à).

**pavement** /ˈpeɪvmənt/ n trottoir m; (US) chaussée f.

**paving stone** n pavé m.

**paw** /pɔː/ n patte f. ● vt (animal) donner des coups de patte à; (touch 🆒) peloter 🆒.

**pawn** /pɔːn/ n pion m. ● vt mettre en gage. **~broker** n prêteur/-euse m/f sur gages. **~-shop** n mont-de-piété m.

**pay** /peɪ/ vt (pt paid) payer; (interest) rapporter; (compliment, attention) faire; (visit, homage) rendre. ● vi payer; (business) rapporter; ~ for sth payer qch. ● n salaire m; ~ rise augmentation f (de salaire). ~ back (loan) rembourser; ~ in déposer; ~ off (loan) rembourser; (worker) congédier; (succeed) être payant; ~ out payer, débourser.

**payable** /ˈpeɪəbl/ adj payable; ~ to (cheque) à l'ordre de.

**payment** /ˈpeɪmənt/ n paiement m; (regular) versement m; (reward) récompense f.

**payroll** /ˈpeɪrəʊl/ n fichier m des salaires; be on the ~ of être employé par.

p

**PC** abbr →PERSONAL COMPUTER.

**PDA** abbr (personal digital assistant) assistant m personnel numérique.

**PE** abbr (**physical education**) éducation f physique, EPS f.

**pea** /piː/ n (petit) pois m.

**peace** /piːs/ n paix f; ~ of mind tranquillité f d'esprit. **peaceful** adj (tranquil) paisible; (peaceable) pacifique.

**peach** /piːtʃ/ n pêche f.

**peacock** /ˈpiːkɒk/ n paon m.

**peak** /piːk/ n (of mountain) pic m; (of cap) visière f; (maximum) maximum m; (on graph) sommet m; (of career) apogée m; (of fitness) meilleur m; ~ hours heures fpl de pointe.

**peal** /piːl/ n (of bells) carillon m; (of laughter) éclat m.

**peanut** /ˈpiːnʌt/ n cacahuète f; ~s (money) 🅸 clopinettes fpl 🅸.

**pear** /peə(r)/ n poire f.

**pearl** /pɜːl/ n perle f.

**peasant** /ˈpeznt/ n paysan/-ne m/f.

**peat** /piːt/ n tourbe f.

**pebble** /ˈpebl/ n caillou m; (on beach) galet m.

**peck** /pek/ vt/i (food) picorer; (attack) donner des coups de bec (à). ● n coup m de bec; a ~ on the cheek une bise.

**peckish** /ˈpekɪʃ/ adj be ~ 🅸 avoir faim.

**peculiar** /pɪˈkjuːlɪə(r)/ adj (odd) bizarre; (special) particulier (to à). **peculiarity** n bizarrerie f.

**pedal** /ˈpedl/ n pédale f. ● vi pédaler.

**pedantic** /pɪˈdæntɪk/ adj pédant.

**peddle** /ˈpedl/ vt colporter; (drugs) faire du trafic de.

**pedestrian** /pɪˈdestrɪən/ n piéton m. ● adj (precinct, street) piétonnier;

( fig) prosaïque; ~ crossing passage m pour piétons.

**pedigree** /ˈpedɪgriː/ n (of animal) pedigree m; (of person) ascendance f. ● adj (dog) de pure race.

**pee** /piː/ vi 🅸 faire pipi 🅸.

**peek** /piːk/ vi & n →PEEP.

**peel** /piːl/ n (on fruit) peau m f; (removed) épluchures fpl. ● vt (fruit, vegetables) éplucher; (prawn) décortiquer. ● vi (of skin) peler; (of paint) s'écailler.

**peep** /piːp/ vi jeter un coup d'œil (furtif) (at à). ● n coup m d'œil (furtif). ~hole n judas m.

**peer** /pɪə(r)/ vi ~ (at) regarder fixement. ● n (equal, noble) pair m. **peerage** n pairie f.

**peg** /peg/ n ( for clothes) pince f à linge; (to hang coats) patère f; ( for tent) piquet m. ● vt (pt **pegged**) (clothes) accrocher avec des pinces; (prices) indexer.

**pejorative** /pɪˈdʒɒrətɪv/ adj péjoratif.

**pelican** /ˈpelɪkən/ n pélican m; ~ crossing passage m pour piétons.

**pellet** /ˈpelɪt/ n (round mass) boulette f; ( for gun) plomb m.

**pelt** /pelt/ vt bombarder (with de). ● n (skin) peau f.

**pelvis** /ˈpelvɪs/ n (Anat) bassin m.

**pen** /pen/ n stylo m; ( for sheep) enclos m; ( for baby, cattle) parc m.

**penal** /ˈpiːnl/ adj pénal. **penalize** vt pénaliser.

**penalty** /ˈpenltɪ/ n peine f; ( fine) amende f; (in football) penalty m.

**penance** /ˈpenəns/ n pénitence f.

**pence** /pens/ →PENNY.

**pencil** /ˈpensl/ n crayon m. ● vt ( pt **pencilled**) crayonner; ~ in noter provisoirement. ~-**sharpener** n taille-crayons m inv.

**pending** /'pendɪŋ/ adj (matter) en souffrance; (Jur) in instance. ● prep (until) en attendant.

**penetrate** /'penɪtreɪt/ vt pénétrer; (silence, defences) percer; (organization) infiltrer. ● vi pénétrer. **penetrating** adj pénétran☒

**pen-friend** /'penfrend/ n correspondant/ -e m/f.

**penguin** /'peŋgwɪn/ n manchot m, pingouin m.

**pen:** ~knife n (pl ~knives) canif m. ~-name n pseudonyme m.

**penniless** /'penɪlɪs/ adj sans le sou.

**penny** /'penɪ/ n (pl **pennies** or **pence**) (unit of currency) penny m; (small amount) centime m.

**pension** /'penʃn/ n (from state) pension f; (from employer) retraite f; ~ scheme plan m de retraite. ● vt ~ off mettre à la retraite. **pensioner** n retraité/-e m/f.

**pensive** /'pensɪv/ adj songeur.

**penthouse** /'penthaʊs/ n appartement m de luxe (au dernier étage).

**penultimate** /pen'ʌltɪmət/ adj avant-dernier.

**people** /'piːpl/ npl gens mpl, personnes fpl; English ~ les Anglais mpl; ~ say on dit. ● vt peupler. ~ **carrier** n monospace m.

**pepper** /'pepə(r)/ n poivre m; (vegetable) poivron m. ● vt (Culin) poivrer.

**peppermint** /'pepəmɪnt/ n (plant) menthe f poivrée; (sweet) bonbon m à la menthe.

**per** /pɜː(r)/ prep par; ~ annum par an; ~ cent pour cent; ~ kilo le kilo; ten km ~ hour dix km à l'heure.

**percentage** /pə'sentɪdʒ/ n pourcentage n.

**perception** /pə'sepʃn/ n perception f. **perceptive** adj perspicace.

**perch** /pɜːtʃ/ n (of bird) perchoir m. ● vi (se) percher.

**perennial** /pə'renɪəl/ adj perpétuel; (plant) vivace.

**perfect**[1] /pə'fekt/ vt perfectionner.

**perfect**[2] /'pɜːfɪkt/ adj parfait. ● n (Ling) parfait m. **perfectly** adv parfaitement.

**perfection** /pə'fekʃn/ n perfection f; to ~ à la perfection.

**perforate** /'pɜːfəreɪt/ vt perforer.

**perform** /pə'fɔːm/ vt (task) exécuter; (function) remplir; (operation) procéder à; (play) jouer; (song) chanter. ● vi (actor, musician, band) jouer; ~ **well/badly** (candidate, business) avoir de bons/de mauvais résultats. **performance** n interprétation f; (of car, team) performance f; (show) représentation f; (fuss) histoire f. **performer** n artiste mf.

**perfume** /'pɜːfjuːm/ n parfum m.

**perhaps** /pə'hæps/ adv peut-être.

**peril** /'perəl/ n péril m. **perilous** adj périlleux.

**perimeter** /pə'rɪmɪtə(r)/ n périmètre m.

**period** /'pɪərɪəd/ n période f; (era) époque f; (lesson) cours m; (Gram) point m; (Med) règles fpl; ● adj d'époque. **periodical** n périodique m.

**peripheral** /pə'rɪfərəl/ adj (vision, suburb) périphérique; (issue) annexe. ● n (Comput) périphérique m.

**perish** /'perɪʃ/ vi périr; (rubber) se détériorer.

**perjury** /'pɜːdʒərɪ/ n faux témoignage m.

**perk** /pɜːk/ n ① avantage m. ● vt/i ~ **up** ① (se) remonter. **perky** adj ① gai.

**perm** /pɜːm/ n permanente f. ● vt **have one's hair** ~ed se faire faire une permanente.

**permanent** /'pɜːmənənt/ adj permanent. **permanently** adv (happy) en permanence; (employed) de façon permanente.

**permissible** /pə'mɪsɪbl/ adj permis.

**permission** /pə'mɪʃn/ n permission f.

**permissive** /pə'mɪsɪv/ adj libéral; (pej) permissif.

**permit¹** /pə'mɪt/ vt (pt permitted) permettre (sb to à qn de), autoriser (sb to qn à).

**permit²** /'pɜːmɪt/ n permis m.

**perpendicular** /pɜːpən'dɪkjʊlə(r)/ adj perpendiculaire.

**perpetrator** /'pɜːpɪtreɪtə(r)/ n auteur m.

**perpetuate** /pə'petjueɪt/ vt perpétuer.

**perplexed** /pə'plekst/ adj perplexe.

**persecute** /'pɜːsɪkjuːt/ vt persécuter.

**perseverance** /pɜːsɪ'vɪərəns/ n persévérance f. **persevere** vi persévérer.

**persist** /pə'sɪst/ vi persister (in doing à faire). **persistence** n persistance f. **persistent** adj (cough, snow) persistant; (obstinate) obstiné; (noise, pressure) continuel.

**person** /'pɜːsn/ n personne f; in ~ en personne.

**personal** /'pɜːsənl/ adj (life, problem, opinion) personnel; (safety, freedom, insurance) individuel. ~ ad n petite annonce f. ~ **assistant** n secrétaire mf de direction. ~ **computer** n ordinateur m (personnel), microordinateur m.

**personality** /pɜːsə'næləti/ n personnalité f; (star) vedette f.

**personal:** ~ **organizer** n agenda

m. ~ **stereo** n baladeur m.

**personnel** /pɜːsə'nel/ n personnel m.

**perspiration** /pɜːspɪ'reɪʃn/ n (sweat) sueur f; (sweating) transpiration f. **perspire** vi transpirer.

**persuade** /pə'sweɪd/ vt persuader (to de). **persuasion** n persuasion f. **persuasive** adj persuasif.

**pertinent** /'pɜːtɪnənt/ adj pertinent.

**perturb** /pə'tɜːb/ vt troubler.

**Peru** /pə'ruː/ n Pérou m.

**pervasive** /pə'veɪsɪv/ adj (smell) pénétrant; (feeling) envahissant.

**perverse** /pə'vɜːs/ adj (desire) pervers; (refusal, attitude) illogique. **perversion** n perversion f.

**pervert¹** /pə'vɜːt/ vt (truth) travestir; (values) fausser; (justice) entraver.

**pervert²** /'pɜːvɜːt/ n pervers-e m/f.

**pessimist** /'pesɪmɪst/ n pessimiste mf. **pessimistic** adj pessimiste.

**pest** /pest/ n (insect) insecte m nuisible; (animal) animal m nuisible; (person ⊞) enquiquineur-euse m/f ⊞.

**pester** /'pestə(r)/ vt harceler.

**pet** /pet/ n animal m de compagnie; (favourite) chouchou-te m/f. ● adj (theory, charity) favori; ~ **hate** bête f noire; ~ **name** petit nom m. ● vt (pt petted) caresser; (spoil) chouchouter ⊞.

**petal** /'petl/ n pétale m.

**peter** /'piːtə(r)/ vi ~ **out** (conversation) tarir; (supplies) s'épuiser.

**petite** /pə'tiːt/ adj (woman) menue.

**petition** /pə'tɪʃn/ n pétition f. ● vt adresser une pétition à.

**petrol** /'petrəl/ n essence f. ~ **bomb** n cocktail m molotov. ~ **station** n station-service f. ~ **tank** n réservoir m d'essence.

**petticoat** /'petɪkəʊt/ n jupon m.

**petty** /'petɪ/ adj (-ier, -iest) (minor) petit; (mean) mesquin; ~ cash petite caisse f.

**pew** /pju:/ n banc m (d'église).

**pharmacist** /'fɑ:məsɪst/ n pharmacien/-ne m/f. **pharmacy** n pharmacie f.

**phase** /feɪz/ n phase f. ● vt ~ in/out introduire/supprimer peu à peu.

**PhD** abbr (**Doctor of Philosophy**) doctorat m.

**pheasant** /'feznt/ n faisan/-e m/f.

**phenomenon** /fə'nɒmɪnən/ n (pl -ena) phénomène m.

**phew** /fju:/ interj ouf.

**philosopher** /fɪ'lɒsəfə(r)/ n philosophe mf. **philosophical** adj philosophique; (resigned) philosophe. **philosophy** n philosophie f.

**phlegm** /flem/ n (Med) mucosité f.

**phobia** /'fəʊbɪə/ n phobie f.

**phone** /fəʊn/ n téléphone m; on the ~ au téléphone. ● vt (person) téléphoner à; to ~ England téléphoner en Angleterre. ● vi téléphoner; ~ back rappeler. ~-book n annuaire m. ~ booth, ~ box n cabine f téléphonique. ~ call n coup m de fil [T]. ~-card n télécarte f. ~-in n émission f à ligne ouverte. ~ number n numéro m de téléphone.

**phonetic** /fə'netɪk/ adj phonétique.

**phoney** /'fəʊnɪ/ adj (-ier, -iest) [T] faux. ● n (person) charlatan m; it's a ~ c'est un faux.

**photocopier** /'fəʊtəʊkɒpɪə(r)/ n photocopieuse f.

**photocopy** /'fəʊtəʊkɒpɪ/ n photocopie f. ● vt photocopier.

**photograph** /'fəʊtəgrɑ:f/ n pho-

tographie f. ● vt photographier.
**photographer** n photographe mf.

**phrase** /freɪz/ n expression f; (idiom) locution f. ● vt exprimer, formuler. ~-**book** n guide m de conversation.

**physical** /'fɪzɪkl/ adj physique.

**physicist** /'fɪzɪsɪst/ n physicien/-ne m/f.

**physics** /'fɪzɪks/ n physique f.

**physiotherapist** /fɪzɪəʊ'θerəpɪst/ n kinésithérapeute mf.
**physiotherapy** n kinésithérapie f.

**physique** /fɪ'zi:k/ n physique m.

**piano** /pɪ'ænəʊ/ n piano m.

**pick** /pɪk/ n choix m; (best) meilleur/-e m/f; (tool) pioche f. ● vt choisir; (flower) cueillir; (lock) crocheter; ~ a quarrel with chercher querelle à; ~ one's nose se curer le nez. □ ~ **on** harceler; ~ **out** choisir; (identify) distinguer; ~ **up** ramasser; (sth fallen) relever; (weight) soulever; (habit, passenger, speed) prendre; (learn) apprendre; vi s'améliorer.

**pickaxe** /'pɪkæks/ n pioche f.

**picket** /'pɪkɪt/ n (striker) gréviste mf; (stake) piquet m; ~ (**line**) piquet m de grève. ● vt (pt **picketed**) installer un piquet de grève devant.

**pickle** /'pɪkl/ n conserves fpl au vinaigre; (gherkin) cornichon m. ● vt conserver dans du vinaigre.

**pick-up** /'pɪkʌp/ n (stylus-holder) lecteur m; (on guitar) capteur m; (collection) ramassage m; (improvement) reprise f.

**picnic** /'pɪknɪk/ n pique-nique m. ● vi (pt **picnicked**) pique-niquer.

**pictorial** /pɪk'tɔ:rɪəl/ adj (magazine) illustré; (record) graphique.

**picture** /'pɪktʃə(r)/ n image f; (painting) tableau m; (photograph) photo f; (drawing) dessin m; (film)

film *m*; (fig) description *f*; the ~s le cinéma. ● *vt* s'imaginer; be ~d (shown) être représenté.

**picturesque** /pɪktʃəˈresk/ *adj* pittoresque.

**pie** /paɪ/ *n* (sweet) tarte *f*; (savoury) tourte *f*.

**piece** /piːs/ *n* morceau *m*; (of string, ribbon) bout *m*; (of currency, machine) pièce *f*; a ~ of advice/furniture un conseil/meuble; go to ~s (fig) s'effondrer; take to ~s démonter.

**pier** /pɪə(r)/ *n* jetée *f*.

**pierce** /pɪəs/ *vt* percer.

**pig** /pɪg/ *n* porc *m*, cochon *m*.

**pigeon** /ˈpɪdʒɪn/ *n* pigeon *m*. ~-hole *n* casier *m*.

**pig-headed** *adj* entêté.

**pigsty** /ˈpɪgstaɪ/ *n* porcherie *f*.

**pigtail** /ˈpɪgteɪl/ *n* natte *f*.

**pike** /paɪk/ *n inv* (fish) brochet *m*.

**pile** /paɪl/ *n* (heap) tas *m*; (stack) pile *f*; (of carpet) poil *m*; ~s of [T] un tas de [T]. ● *vt* ~ (up) entasser. ● *vi* ~ into s'engouffrer dans; ~ up (snow, leaves) s'entasser; (debts, work) s'accumuler. ~-up *n* (Auto) carambolage *m*.

**pilgrim** /ˈpɪlgrɪm/ *n* pèlerin *m*. **pilgrimage** *n* pèlerinage *m*.

**pill** /pɪl/ *n* pilule *f*.

**pillar** /ˈpɪlə(r)/ *n* pilier *m*. ~-box *n* boîte *f* aux lettres.

**pillion** /ˈpɪlɪən/ *n* siège *m* de passager; ride ~ monter en croupe.

**pillow** /ˈpɪləʊ/ *n* oreiller *m*. ~case *n* taie *f* d'oreiller.

**pilot** /ˈpaɪlət/ *n* pilote *m*. ● *adj* pilote. ● *vt* (*pt* **piloted**) piloter. ~-light *n* veilleuse *f*.

**pimple** /ˈpɪmpl/ *n* bouton *m*.

**pin** /pɪn/ *n* épingle *f*; (of plug) fiche *f*; (for wood, metal) goujon *m*; (in

surgery) broche *f*; have ~s and needles avoir des fourmis. ● *vt* (*pt* **pinned**) épingler, attacher; (trap) coincer; ~ sb down (fig) forcer qn à se décider; ~ up accrocher.

**pinafore** /ˈpɪnəfɔː(r)/ *n* tablier *m*.

**pincers** /ˈpɪnsəz/ *npl* tenailles *fpl*.

**pinch** /pɪntʃ/ *vt* pincer; (steal [T]) piquer. ● *vi* (be too tight) serrer. ● *n* (mark) pinçon *m*; (of salt) pincée *f*; at a ~ à la rigueur.

**pine** /paɪn/ *n* (tree) pin *m*. ● *vi* (away) dépérir; ~ for languir après.

**pineapple** /ˈpaɪnæpl/ *n* ananas *m*.

**pinecone** /ˈpaɪnkəʊn/ *n* pomme *f* de pin.

**pink** /pɪŋk/ *adj* & *n* rose (*m*).

**pinpoint** /ˈpɪnpɔɪnt/ *vt* (*problem, cause, location*) indiquer; (*time*) déterminer.

**pint** /paɪnt/ *n* pinte *f* (GB = 0.57 litre; US = 0.47 litre).

**pin-up** /ˈpɪnʌp/ *n* [T] pin-up *f inv*. [T]

**pioneer** /paɪəˈnɪə(r)/ *n* pionnier *m*. ● *vt* ~ the use of être le premier à utiliser.

**pious** /ˈpaɪəs/ *adj* pieux.

**pip** /pɪp/ *n* (seed) pépin *m*; (sound) top *m*.

**pipe** /paɪp/ *n* tuyau *m*; (to smoke) pipe *f*; (Mus) chalumeau *m*; ~s cornemuse *f*. ● *vt* transporter par tuyau. □ ~ **down** se taire.

**pipeline** /ˈpaɪplaɪn/ *n* oléoduc *m*; in the ~ en cours.

**piping** /ˈpaɪpɪŋ/ *n* tuyauterie *f*; ~ hot fumant.

**pirate** /ˈpaɪərət/ *n* pirate *m*. ● *vt* pirater.

**Pisces** /ˈpaɪsiːz/ *n* Poissons *mpl*.

**pistol** /ˈpɪstl/ *n* pistolet *m*.

**pit** /pɪt/ *n* fosse *f*; (mine) puits *m*; (quarry) carrière *f*; (for orchestra)

# pitch | play

fosse *f*; (of stomach) creux *m*; (of cherry: US) noyau *m*. ● *vt* (*pt* **pitted**) marquer; (fig) opposer; ~ oneself against se mesurer à.

**pitch** /pɪtʃ/ *n* (Sport) terrain *m*; (of voice, note) hauteur *f*; (degree) degré *m*; (Mus) ton *m*; (tar) brai *m*. ● *vt* jeter; (tent) planter. ● *vi* (ship) tanguer. □ ~ **in** ▣ contribuer.

**pitfall** /ˈpɪtfɔːl/ *n* écueil *m*.

**pitiful** /ˈpɪtɪfl/ *adj* pitoyable. **pitiless** *adj* impitoyable.

**pit stop** *n* arrêt *m* mécanique.

**pittance** /ˈpɪtns/ *n* earn a ~ gagner trois fois rien.

**pity** /ˈpɪtɪ/ *n* pitié *f*; (regrettable fact) dommage *m*; take ~ on avoir pitié de; what a ~! quel dommage! ● *vt* avoir pitié de.

**pivot** /ˈpɪvət/ *n* pivot *m*. ● *vi* (*pt* **pivoted**) pivoter.

**placard** /ˈplækɑːd/ *n* affiche *f*.

**place** /pleɪs/ *n* endroit *m*, lieu *m*; (house) maison *f*; (seat, rank) place *f*; at or to my ~ chez moi; change ~s change de place; in the first ~ d'abord; out of ~ déplacé; take ~ avoir lieu. ● *vt* placer; (order) passer; (remember) situer; be ~d (in race) se placer. ~**-mat** *n* set *m*.

**placid** /ˈplæsɪd/ *adj* placide.

**plagiarism** /ˈpleɪdʒərɪzəm/ *n* plagiat *m*. **plagiarize** *vt/i* plagier.

**plague** /pleɪɡ/ *n* (bubonic) peste *f*; (epidemic) épidémie *f*; (of ants, locusts) invasion *f*. ● *vt* harceler.

**plaice** /pleɪs/ *n inv* carrelet *m*.

**plain** /pleɪn/ *adj* (obvious) clair; (candid) franc; (simple) simple; (not pretty) sans beauté; (not patterned) uni; ~ chocolate chocolat *m* noir; in ~ clothes en civil. ● *adv* franchement. ● *n* plaine *f*. **plainly** *adv* clairement; franchement; simplement.

**plaintiff** /ˈpleɪntɪf/ *n* (Jur)

plaignant/-e *m/f*.

**plaintive** /ˈpleɪntɪv/ *adj* plaintif.

**plait** /plæt/ *vt* tresser. ● *n* natte *f*.

**plan** /plæn/ *n* projet *m*, plan *m*; (diagram) plan *m*. ● *vt* (*pt* **planned**) projeter (to do de faire); (timetable, day) organiser; (economy, work) planifier. ● *vi* prévoir; ~ on s'attendre à.

**plane** /pleɪn/ *n* (level) plan *m*; (aeroplane) avion *m*; (tool) rabot *m*. ● *adj* plan. ● *vt* raboter.

**planet** /ˈplænɪt/ *n* planète *f*.

**plank** /plæŋk/ *n* planche *f*.

**planning** /ˈplænɪŋ/ *n* (of economy, work) planification *f*; (of holiday, party) organisation *f*; (of town) urbanisme *m*; family ~ planning *m* familial; ~ permission permis *m* de construire.

**plant** /plɑːnt/ *n* plante *f*; (Tech) matériel *m*; (factory) usine *f*. ● *vt* planter; (bomb) placer.

**plaster** /ˈplɑːstə(r)/ *n* plâtre *m*; (adhesive) sparadrap *m*. ● *vt* plâtrer; (cover) couvrir (with de).

**plastic** /ˈplæstɪk/ *adj* en plastique; (art, substance) plastique; ~ surgery chirurgie *f* esthétique. ● *n* plastique *m*.

**plate** /pleɪt/ *n* assiette *f*; (of metal) plaque *f*; (silverware) argenterie *f*; (in book) gravure *f*. ● *vt* (metal) plaquer.

**plateau** /ˈplætəʊ/ *n* (*pl* ~**x**) plateau *m*; (fig) palier *m*.

**platform** /ˈplætfɔːm/ *n* (stage) estrade *f*; (for speaking) tribune *f*; (Rail) quai *m*; (Pol) plate-forme *f*.

**platoon** /pləˈtuːn/ *n* (Mil) section *f*.

**play** /pleɪ/ *vt/i* jouer; (instrument) jouer de; (record) mettre; (game) jouer à; (opponent) jouer contre; (match) disputer; ~ safe ne pas prendre de risques. ● *n* jeu *m*;

**P**

(Theat) pièce f. □ ~ **down** minimiser; ~**on** (*fears*) exploiter; ~ **up** 🇮 commencer à faire des siennes 🇮; ~ **up** sth mettre l'accent sur qch.

**playful** /ˈpleɪfl/ adj (*remark*) taquin; (*child*) joueur.

**play**: ~**ground** n cour f de récréation. ~**group**, ~**school** n garderie f

**playing** /ˈpleɪɪŋ/ n (Sport) jeu m; (Theat) interprétation f. ~**card** n carte f à jouer. ~**field** n terrain m de sport.

**play**: ~**pen** n parc m (pour bébé). ~**wright** n auteur m dramatique.

**plc** abbr (**public limited company**) SA.

**plea** /pliː/ n (for mercy, tolerance) appel m; (for food, money) demande f; (reason) excuse f; make a ~ of guilty plaider coupable.

**plead** /pliːd/ vt/i supplier; (Jur) plaider.

**pleasant** /ˈpleznt/ adj agréable.

**please** /pliːz/ vt/i plaire (à), faire plaisir (à); ~ oneself, do as one ~s faire ce qu'on veut. ● adv s'il vous ou te plaît. **pleased** adj content (with de). **pleasing** adj agréable.

**pleasure** /ˈpleʒə(r)/ n plaisir m; with ~ avec plaisir; my ~ je vous en prie.

**pleat** /pliːt/ n pli m. ● vt plisser.

**pledge** /pledʒ/ n (token) gage m; (promise) promesse f. ● vt promettre; (pawn) mettre en gage.

**plentiful** /ˈplentɪfl/ adj abondant.

**plenty** /ˈplentɪ/ n abondance f; ~ (of) (a great deal) beaucoup (de); (enough) assez (de).

**pliers** /ˈplaɪəz/ npl pinces fpl.

**plight** /plaɪt/ n détresse f.

**plinth** /plɪnθ/ n socle m.

**plod** /plɒd/ vi (pt **plodded**) avancer péniblement.

**plonk** /plɒŋk/ n 🇮 pinard m 🇮.

**plot** /plɒt/ n (conspiracy) complot m; (of novel) intrigue f; ~ **(of land)** terrain m. ● vt/i (pt **plotted**) (plan) comploter; (mark out) tracer.

**plough** /plaʊ/ n charrue f. ● vt/i labourer. □ ~ **back** réinvestir; ~ **through** avancer péniblement dans.

**plow** /plaʊ/ n & vt/i (US) ➡**PLOUGH**.

**ploy** /plɔɪ/ n stratagème m.

**pluck** /plʌk/ vt (flower, fruit) cueillir; (bird) plumer; (eyebrows) épiler; (strings: Mus) pincer; ~ **up** courage prendre son courage à deux mains. **plucky** adj courageux.

**plug** /plʌg/ n (for sink) bonde f; (Electr) fiche f, prise f. ● vt (pt **plugged**) (hole) boucher; (publicize 🇮) faire du battage autour de. □ ~ **in** brancher. ~**hole** n bonde f.

**plum** /plʌm/ n prune f; ~ **pudding** (plum-)pudding m.

**plumber** /ˈplʌmə(r)/ n plombier m.

**plume** /pluːm/ n (of feathers) panache m.

**plummet** /ˈplʌmɪt/ vi tomber, plonger.

**plump** /plʌmp/ adj potelé, dodu.

**plunge** /plʌndʒ/ vt/i (dive, thrust) plonger; (fall) tomber. ● n plongeon m; (fall) chute f; take the ~ se jeter à l'eau. **plunger** n (for sink) ventouse f.

**plural** /ˈplʊərəl/ adj pluriel; (noun) au pluriel; (ending) du pluriel. ● n pluriel m.

**plus** /plʌs/ prep plus; ten ~ plus de dix. ● adj (Electr & fig) positif. ● n signe m plus; (fig) atout m.

**ply** /plaɪ/ vt (tool) manier; (trade) exercer. ● vi faire la navette; ~ **sb** **with drink** offrir continuellement à boire à qn.

**plywood** /ˈplaɪwʊd/ n contreplaqué m.

**p.m.** /piːˈem/ adv de l'après-midi or du soir.

**pneumatic drill** /njuːˈmætɪk drɪl/ n marteaupiqueur m.

**pneumonia** /njuːˈməʊnɪə/ n pneumonie f.

**PO** abbr ⇒POST OFFICE.

**poach** /pəʊtʃ/ vt/i (game) braconner; (staff) débaucher; (Culin) pocher.

**PO Box** n boîte f postale.

**pocket** /ˈpɒkɪt/ n poche f; be out of ~ avoir perdu de l'argent. ● adj de poche. ● vt empocher. ~-book n (notebook) carnet m; (wallet: US) portefeuille m; (handbag: US) sac m à main. ~-money n argent m de poche.

**pod** /pɒd/ n (peas) cosse f; (vanilla) gousse f.

**podgy** /ˈpɒdʒɪ/ adj (-ier, -iest) dodu.

**poem** /ˈpəʊɪm/ n poème m. **poet** n poète m. **poetic** adj poétique. **poetry** n poésie f.

**point** /pɔɪnt/ n (position) point m; (tip) pointe f; (decimal point) virgule f; (remark) remarque f; good ~s qualités fpl; on the ~ of sur le point de; ~ in time moment m; ~ of view point m de vue; to the ~ pertinent; what is the ~? à quoi bon? ● vt (aim) braquer; (show) indiquer. ● out signaler. ● vi indiquer du doigt; ~ out that, make the ~ that faire remarquer que. ~-blank adj & adv point blanc.

**pointed** /ˈpɔɪntɪd/ adj (sharp) pointu; (window) en pointe; (remark) lourd de sens.

**pointless** /ˈpɔɪntlɪs/ adj inutile.

**poise** /pɔɪz/ n (confidence) assurance f; (physical elegance) aisance f.

**poison** /ˈpɔɪzn/ n poison m. ● vt empoisonner. **poisonous** adj (substance) toxique; (plant) vénéneux; (snake) venimeux.

**poke** /pəʊk/ vt/i (push) pousser; (fire) tisonner; (thrust) fourrer; ~ fun at se moquer de. ● (petit) coup m. ● out (head) sortir.

**poker** /ˈpəʊkə(r)/ n (for fire) tisonnier m; (cards) poker m.

**Poland** /ˈpəʊlənd/ n Pologne f.

**polar** /ˈpəʊlə(r)/ adj polaire.

**pole** /pəʊl/ n (stick) perche f; (for flag) mât m; (Geog) pôle m.

**Pole** /pəʊl/ n Polonais-e m/f.

**pole-vault** n saut m à la perche.

**police** /pəˈliːs/ n police f. ● vt faire la police dans. ~ constable n agent m de police. ~-man (pl -men) agent m de police. ~ station n commissariat m de police. ~-woman n (pl -women) femme-agent f.

**policy** /ˈpɒlɪsɪ/ n politique f; (insurance) police f (d'assurance).

**polish** /ˈpɒlɪʃ/ vt polir; (shoes, floor) cirer. ● n (for shoes) cirage m; (for floor) encaustique f; (for nails) vernis m; (shine) poli m; (fig) raffinement m. ● off finir en vitesse; ● up (language) perfectionner.

**Polish** /ˈpəʊlɪʃ/ adj polonais. ● n (Ling) polonais m.

**polished** /ˈpɒlɪʃt/ adj raffiné.

**polite** /pəˈlaɪt/ adj poli.

**political** /pəˈlɪtɪkl/ adj politique.

**politician** /pɒlɪˈtɪʃn/ n homme m politique, femme f politique.

**politics** /ˈpɒlətɪks/ n politique f.

**poll** /pəʊl/ n (vote casting) scrutin m; (survey) sondage m; go to the ~s aller aux urnes. ● vt (votes) obtenir.

**pollen** /'pɒlən/ n pollen m.

**polling booth** n isoloir m.

**polling station** n bureau m de vote.

**pollution** /pə'luːʃn/ n pollution f.

**polo** /'pəʊləʊ/ n polo m. ~ **neck** n col m roulé.

**pomegranate** /'pɒmɪgrænɪt/ n grenade f.

**pomp** /pɒmp/ n pompe f.

**pompous** /'pɒmpəs/ adj pompeux.

**pond** /pɒnd/ n étang m; (artificial) bassin m; (stagnant) mare f.

**ponder** /'pɒndə(r)/ vt/i réfléchir (à), méditer (sur).

**pong** /pɒŋ/ n (stink 🔢) puanteur f. • vi 🔢 puer.

**pony** /'pəʊnɪ/ n poney m. ~**tail** n queue f de cheval.

**poodle** /'puːdl/ n caniche m.

**pool** /puːl/ n (puddle) flaque f; (pond) étang m; (of blood) mare f; (for swimming) piscine f; (fund) fonds m commun; (of ideas) réservoir m; (snooker) billard m américain; ~s pari m mutuel sur le football. • vt mettre en commun.

**poor** /pɔː(r)/ adj (not wealthy) pauvre; (not good) médiocre, mauvais.

**poorly** /'pɔːlɪ/ adj malade. • adv mal.

**pop** /pɒp/ n (noise) pan m; (music) pop m. • adj pop inv. • vt/i (pt popped) (burst) crever; (put) mettre; ~ in/out/off entrer/sortir/partir. □ ~ up surgir. ~-up fenêtre f pop-up.

**pope** /pəʊp/ n pape m.

**poppy** /'pɒpɪ/ n pavot m; (wild) coquelicot m.

**popular** /'pɒpjʊlə(r)/ adj populaire; (in fashion) en vogue; be ~ with plaire à.

**population** /pɒpjʊ'leɪʃn/ n population f.

**porcelain** /'pɔːsəlɪn/ n porcelaine f.

**porcupine** /'pɔːkjʊpaɪn/ n porc-épic m.

**pork** /pɔːk/ n porc m.

**pornography** /pɔː'nɒgrəfɪ/ n pornographie f.

**port** /pɔːt/ n (harbour) port m; (left: Naut) bâbord m; ~ **of call** escale f; (wine) porto m.

**portable** /'pɔːtəbl/ adj portable.

**porter** /'pɔːtə(r)/ n (carrier) porteur m; (doorkeeper) portier m.

**portfolio** /pɔːt'fəʊlɪəʊ/ n (Pol, Comm) portefeuille m.

**portion** /'pɔːʃn/ n (at meal) portion f; (part) partie f.

**portrait** /'pɔːtreɪt/ n portrait m.

**portray** /pɔː'treɪ/ vt représenter.

**Portugal** /'pɔːtʃʊgl/ n Portugal m.

**Portuguese** /pɔːtʃʊ'giːz/ n (Ling) portugais m; (person) Portugais/-e m/f. • adj portugais.

**pose** /pəʊz/ vt/i poser; ~ **as** (expert) se poser en. • n pose f.

**poser** /'pəʊzə(r)/ n (person) frimeur/-euse m/f; (puzzle) colle f.

**posh** /pɒʃ/ adj 🔢 chic inv.

**position** /pə'zɪʃn/ n position f; (job, state) situation f. • vt placer.

**positive** /'pɒzətɪv/ adj positif; (sure) sûr, certain; (real) réel, vrai.

**possess** /pə'zes/ vt posséder.

**possession** /pə'zeʃn/ n possession f; take ~ of prendre possession de.

**possessive** /pə'zesɪv/ adj possessif.

**possible** /'pɒsəbl/ adj possible.

**possibly** /'pɒsəblɪ/ adv peut-être; if I ~ can si cela m'est possible; I cannot ~ leave il m'est impossible de partir.

**post** /pəʊst/ n (pole) poteau m;

(station, job) poste *m*; (mail service) poste *f*; (letters) courrier *m*. ● *adj* postal. ● *vt* (letter) poster; keep ~ed tenir au courant; ~ (**up**) (a notice) afficher; (appoint) affecter.

**postage** /ˈpəʊstɪdʒ/ *n* affranchissement *m*; tarif *m* postal.

**postal** /ˈpəʊstl/ *adj* postal. ~ **order** *n* mandat *m*.

**post**: ~**box** *n* boîte *f* aux lettres. ~**card** *n* carte *f* postale. ~ **code** *n* code *m* postal.

**poster** /ˈpəʊstə(r)/ *n* (for information) affiche *f*; (for decoration) poster *m*.

**postgraduate** /pəʊstˈɡrædʒʊət/ *n* étudiant/-e *m/f* de troisième cycle.

**posthumous** /ˈpɒstjʊməs/ *adj* posthume.

**post**: ~**man** *n* (*pl* -**men**) facteur *m*. ~**mark** *n* cachet *m* de la poste.

**post-mortem** /pəʊstˈmɔːtəm/ *n* autopsie *f*.

**post office** *n* poste *f*.

**postpone** /pəˈspəʊn/ *vt* remettre.

**postscript** /ˈpəʊskrɪpt/ *n* (to letter) postscriptum *m* inv.

**posture** /ˈpɒstʃə(r)/ *n* posture *f*. ● *vi* prendre des poses.

**pot** /pɒt/ *n* pot *m*; (drug 🆇) hasch *m*; **go to** ~ 🆇 aller à la ruine; **take** ~ **luck** tenter sa chance. ● *vt* (plants) mettre en pot.

**potato** /pəˈteɪtəʊ/ *n* (*pl* -**es**) pomme *f* de terre.

**pot-belly** *n* bedaine *f*.

**potential** /pəˈtenʃl/ *adj* & *n* potentiel (*m*).

**pothole** /ˈpɒthəʊl/ *n* (in rock) caverne *f*; (in road) nid *m* de poule.

**pot-holing** *n* spéléologie *f*.

**potter** /ˈpɒtə(r)/ *n* potier *m*. ● *vi* bricoler. **pottery** *n* (art) poterie *f*; (objects) poteries *fpl*.

**potty** /ˈpɒtɪ/ *adj* (-**ier**, -**iest**) (crazy 🆇) toqué. ● *n* pot *m*.

**pouch** /paʊtʃ/ *n* poche *f*; (for tobacco) blague *f*.

**poultry** /ˈpəʊltrɪ/ *n* volailles *fpl*.

**pounce** /paʊns/ *vi* bondir (on sur). ● *n* bond *m*.

**pound** /paʊnd/ *n* (weight) livre *f* (= 454 g); (money) livre *f*; (for dogs, cars) fourrière *f*. ● *vt* (crush) piler; (bombard) pilonner. ● *vi* frapper fort; (of heart) battre fort; (walk) marcher à pas lourds.

**pour** /pɔː(r)/ *vt* verser. ● *vi* couler, ruisseler (from de); (rain) pleuvoir à torrents. □ ~ **in/out** (people) arriver/sortir en masse; ~ **off** or **out** vider. **pouring rain** *n* pluie *f* torrentielle.

**pout** /paʊt/ *vi* faire la moue.

**poverty** /ˈpɒvətɪ/ *n* misère *f*, pauvreté *f*.

**powder** /ˈpaʊdə(r)/ *n* poudre *f*. ● *vt* poudrer.

**power** /ˈpaʊə(r)/ *n* (strength) puissance *f*; (control) pouvoir *m*; (energy) énergie *f*; (Electr) courant *m*. ● *vt* (engine) faire marcher; (plane) propulser; ~**ed by** (engine) propulsé par; (generator) alimenté par. ~ **cut** *n* coupure *f* de courant.

**powerful** /ˈpaʊəfl/ *adj* puissant.

**powerless** /ˈpaʊəlɪs/ *adj* impuissant.

**power**: ~**point** *n* prise *f* de courant. ~-**station** *n* centrale *f* électrique.

**practical** /ˈpræktɪkl/ *adj* pratique. ~ **joke** *n* farce *f*.

**practice** /ˈpræktɪs/ *n* (procedure) pratique *f*; (of profession) exercice *m*; (Sport) entraînement *m*; **in** ~ (in fact) en pratique; (well-trained) en forme; **out of** ~ rouillé; **put into** ~ mettre en pratique.

**practise** /'præktɪs/ vt/i (musician, typist) s'exercer (à); (Sport) s'entraîner (à); (put into practice) pratiquer; (profession) exercer.

**practitioner** /præk'tɪʃənə(r)/ n praticien/-ienne m/f; dental ~ dentiste mf.

**praise** /preɪz/ vt faire l'éloge de; (God) louer. ● n éloges mpl, louanges fpl.

**pram** /præm/ n landau m.

**prance** /prɑːns/ vi caracoler.

**prawn** /prɔːn/ n crevette f rose.

**pray** /preɪ/ vi prier. **prayer** n prière f.

**preach** /priːtʃ/ vt/i prêcher; ~ at or to prêcher.

**precarious** /prɪ'keərɪəs/ adj précaire.

**precaution** /prɪ'kɔːʃn/ n précaution f.

**precede** /prɪ'siːd/ vt précéder.

**precedence** /'presɪdəns/ n (in importance) priorité f; (in rank) préséance f.

**precedent** /'presɪdənt/ n précédent m.

**precinct** /'priːsɪŋkt/ n quartier m commerçant; (pedestrian area) zone f piétonne; (district: US) circonscription f.

**precious** /'preʃəs/ adj précieux.

**precipitate** /prɪ'sɪpɪteɪt/ vt (person, event, chemical) précipiter.

**précis** /'preɪsiː/ n résumé m.

**precise** /prɪ'saɪs/ adj précis; (careful) méticuleux. **precision** n précision f.

**precocious** /prɪ'kəʊʃəs/ adj précoce.

**preconceived** /priːkən'siːvd/ adj préconçu.

**predator** /'predətə(r)/ n prédateur m.

**predicament** /prɪ'dɪkəmənt/ n situation f difficile.

**predict** /prɪ'dɪkt/ vt prédire. **predictable** adj prévisible. **prediction** n prédiction f.

**predispose** /priːdɪ'spəʊz/ vt prédisposer to do à faire).

**predominant** /prɪ'dɒmɪnənt/ adj prédominant.

**pre-empt** /priː'empt/ vt (anticipate) anticiper; (person) devancer.

**preface** /'prefɪs/ n (to book) préface f; (to speech) préambule m.

**prefect** /'priːfekt/ n (pupil) élève m/f chargé/-e de la discipline; (official) préfet m.

**prefer** /prɪ'fɜː(r)/ vt (pt preferred) préférer (to do faire). **preferably** adv de préférence. **preference** n préférence f. **preferential** adj préférentiel.

**prefix** /'priːfɪks/ n préfixe m.

**pregnancy** /'pregnənsɪ/ n grossesse f. **pregnant** adj (woman) enceinte; (animal) pleine; (pause) éloquent.

**prehistoric** /priːhɪ'stɒrɪk/ adj préhistorique.

**prejudge** /priː'dʒʌdʒ/ vt (issue) préjuger de; (person) juger d'avance.

**prejudice** /'predʒʊdɪs/ n préjugé(s) m(pl); (harm) préjudice m. ● vt (claim) porter préjudice à; (person) léser. **prejudiced** adj partial; (person) qui a des préjugés.

**premature** /'premətjʊə(r)/ adj prématuré.

**premeditated** /priː'medɪteɪtɪd/ adj prémédité.

**premises** /'premɪsɪz/ npl locaux mpl; on the ~ sur les lieux.

**premium** /'priːmɪəm/ n (insurance) prime f; be at a ~ être précieux.

**preoccupied** /priˈɒkjʊpaɪd/ adj préoccupé.

**preparation** /prepəˈreɪʃn/ n préparation f; ~s préparatifs mpl.

**preparatory** /prɪˈpærətrɪ/ adj préparatoire. ~ **school** n école f primaire privée; (US) école f secondaire privée.

**prepare** /prɪˈpeə(r)/ vt/i (se) préparer (for à); be ~d for (expect) s'attendre à; ~d to prêt à.

**preposition** /prepəˈzɪʃn/ n préposition f.

**preposterous** /prɪˈpɒstərəs/ adj absurde, ridicule.

**prep school** n →PREPARATORY SCHOOL.

**prerequisite** /priːˈrekwɪzɪt/ n condition f préalable.

**prescribe** /prɪˈskraɪb/ vt prescrire.

**prescription** /prɪˈskrɪpʃn/ n (Med) ordonnance f.

**presence** /ˈprezns/ n présence f; ~ of mind présence f d'esprit.

**present**[1] /ˈpreznt/ adj présent. ● n présent m; (gift) cadeau m; at ~ à présent; for the ~ pour le moment.

**present**[2] /prɪˈzent/ vt présenter; (film, concert) donner; ~ sb with offrir à qn. **presentation** n présentation f. **presenter** n présentateur/-trice m/f.

**preservation** /prezəˈveɪʃn/ n (of food) conservation f; (of wildlife) préservation f.

**preservative** /prɪˈzɜːvətɪv/ n (Culin) agent m de conservation.

**preserve** /prɪˈzɜːv/ vt préserver; (Culin) conserver. ● n réserve f; (fig) domaine m; (jam) confiture f.

**presidency** /ˈprezɪdənsɪ/ n présidence f.

**president** /ˈprezɪdənt/ n président/-e m/f.

**press** /pres/ vt/i (button) appuyer (sur); (squeeze) presser; (iron) repasser; (pursue) poursuivre; be ~ed for (time) manquer de; ~ for sth faire pression pour avoir qch; ~ sb to do sth pousser qn à faire qch; ~ on continuer (with sth qch). ● n (newspapers, machine) presse f; (for wine) pressoir m. ~ **cutting** n coupure f de presse.

**pressing** /ˈpresɪŋ/ adj pressant.

**press:** ~ **release** n communiqué m de presse. ~**stud** n boutonpression m. ~**-up** n pompe f.

**pressure** /ˈpreʃə(r)/ n pression f. ● vt faire pression sur. ~**cooker** n cocotte-minute f. ~ **group** n groupe m de pression.

**pressurize** /ˈpreʃəraɪz/ vt (cabin) pressuriser; (person) faire pression sur.

**prestige** /preˈstiːʒ/ n prestige m.

**presumably** /prɪˈzjuːməblɪ/ adv vraisemblablement.

**presume** /prɪˈzjuːm/ vt (suppose) présumer.

**pretence**, (US) **pretense** /prɪˈtens/ n feinte f, simulation f; (claim) prétention f; (pretext) prétexte m.

**pretend** /prɪˈtend/ vt/i faire semblant (to do de faire); ~ to (lay claim to) prétendre à.

**pretentious** /prɪˈtenʃəs/ adj prétentieux.

**pretext** /ˈpriːtekst/ n prétexte m.

**pretty** /ˈprɪtɪ/ adj (-ier, -iest) joli. ● adv assez; ~ **much** presque.

**prevail** /prɪˈveɪl/ vi (be usual) dominer; (win) prévaloir; ~ on persuader (to do de faire). **prevailing** adj actuel; (wind) dominant.

**prevalent** /ˈprevələnt/ adj répandu.

**prevent** /prɪˈvent/ vt empêcher (from doing de faire). **prevention**

P

*n* prévention *f* **preventive** *adj* préventif.

**preview** /'priːvjuː/ *n* avant-première *f*; (fig) aperçu *m*.

**previous** /'priːvɪəs/ *adj* précédent, antérieur; ~ **to** avant. **previously** *adv* auparavant.

**prey** /preɪ/ *n* proie *f*; **bird of ~** rapace *m*. ● *vi* ~ **on** faire sa proie de; (worry) préoccuper.

**price** /praɪs/ *n* prix *m*. ● *vt* fixer le prix de. **priceless** *adj* inestimable; (amusing 🔢) impayable 🔢.

**prick** /prɪk/ *vt* (with pin) piquer; ~ **up one's ears** dresser l'oreille. ● *n* piqûre *f*.

**prickle** /'prɪkl/ *n* piquant *m*.

**pride** /praɪd/ *n* orgueil *m*; (satisfaction) fierté *f*; ~ **of place** place *f* d'honneur. ● *vpr* ~ **oneself on** s'enorgueillir de.

**priest** /priːst/ *n* prêtre *m*.

**prim** /prɪm/ *adj* (**primmer, primmest**) guindé, méticuleux.

**primarily** /'praɪmərəlɪ/ *adv* essentiellement.

**primary** /'praɪmərɪ/ *adj* (school, elections) primaire; (chief, basic) premier, fondamental. ● *n* (Pol: US) primaire *f*.

**prime** /praɪm/ *adj* principal, premier; (first-rate) excellent. ● *vt* (pump, gun) amorcer; (surface) apprêter. **P~ Minister** *n* Premier Ministre *m*.

**primitive** /'prɪmɪtɪv/ *adj* primitif.

**primrose** /'prɪmrəʊz/ *n* primevère *f* (jaune).

**prince** /prɪns/ *n* prince *m*. **princess** *n* princesse *f*.

**principal** /'prɪnsəpl/ *adj* principal. ● *n* (of school) directeur/-trice *m/f*.

**principle** /'prɪnsəpl/ *n* principe *m*; **in/on ~** en/par principe.

**print** /prɪnt/ *vt* imprimer; (write in capitals) écrire en majuscules; **~ed matter** imprimés *mpl*. ● *n* (of foot) empreinte *f*; (letters) caractères *mpl*; (photograph) épreuve *f*; (engraving) gravure *f*; **in ~** disponible; **out of ~** épuisé. **printer** *n* (person) imprimeur *m*; (Comput) imprimante *f*.

**prion** /'priːɒn/ *n* prion *m*.

**prior** /praɪə(r)/ *adj* précédent. ● *n* (Relig) prieur *m*. ~ **to** *prep* avant (de).

**priority** /praɪ'ɒrɪtɪ/ *n* priorité *f*; **take ~** avoir la priorité (over sur).

**prise** /praɪz/ *vt* forcer; ~ **open** ouvrir en forçant.

**prison** /'prɪzn/ *n* prison *f*. **prisoner** *n* prisonnier/-ière *m/f*. ~ **officer** *n* gardien/-ne *m/f* de prison.

**pristine** /'prɪstiːn/ *adj* **be in ~ condition** être comme neuf.

**privacy** /'prɪvəsɪ/ *n* intimité *f*, solitude *f*.

**private** /'praɪvɪt/ *adj* privé; (confidential) personnel; (lessons, house) particulier; (ceremony) intime; **in ~** en privé; (of ceremony) dans l'intimité. ● *n* (soldier) simple soldat *m*. **privately** *adv* en privé; dans l'intimité; (inwardly) intérieurement.

**privilege** /'prɪvəlɪdʒ/ *n* privilège *m*. **privileged** *adj* privilégié; **be ~d to** avoir le privilège de.

**prize** /praɪz/ *n* prix *m*. ● *vt* (value) priser.

**pro** /prəʊ/ *n* **the ~s and cons** le pour et le contre.

**probable** /'prɒbəbl/ *adj* probable. **probably** *adv* probablement.

**probation** /prə'beɪʃn/ *n* (testing) essai *m*; (Jur) liberté *f* surveillée.

**probe** /prəʊb/ *n* (device) sonde *f*; (fig) enquête *f*. ● *vt* sonder. ● *vi* ~ **into** sonder.

**problem** /'prɒbləm/ *n* problème *m*. ● *adj* difficile. **problematic** *adj* problématique.

**procedure** /prə'siːdʒə(r)/ n procédure f; (way of doing sth) démarche f à suivre.

**proceed** /prə'siːd/ vi (go) aller, avancer; (pass) passer (to à); (act) procéder; ~ (with) continuer; ~ to do se mettre à faire.

**proceedings** /prə'siːdɪŋz/ npl (discussions) débats mpl; (meeting) réunion f; (report) actes mpl; (Jur) poursuites fpl.

**proceeds** /'prəʊsiːdz/ npl (profits) produit m, bénéfices mpl.

**process** /'prəʊses/ n processus m; (method) procédé m; in ~ en cours; in the ~ of doing en train de faire. ~or n (Culin) robot m (ménager); (Comput) unité f centrale. ● vt (material, data) traiter.

**procession** /prə'seʃn/ n défilé m.

**procrastinate** /prəʊ'kræstɪneɪt/ vi différer, tergiverser.

**procure** /prə'kjʊə(r)/ vt obtenir.

**prod** /prɒd/ vt/i (pt **prodded**) pousser doucement. ● n petit coup m.

**prodigy** /'prɒdɪdʒɪ/ n prodige m.

**produce**[1] /'prɒdjuːs/ n produits mpl.

**produce**[2] /prə'djuːs/ vt/i produire; (bring out) sortir; (show) présenter; (cause) provoquer; (Theat, TV) mettre en scène; (radio) réaliser; (cinema) produire. **producer** n metteur m en scène; réalisateur m; producteur m.

**product** /'prɒdʌkt/ n produit m.

**production** /prə'dʌkʃn/ n production f; (Theat, TV) mise f en scène; (radio) réalisation f.

**productive** /prə'dʌktɪv/ adj productif. **productivity** n productivité f.

**profession** /prə'feʃn/ n profession f.

**professional** /prə'feʃənl/ adj professionnel; (of high quality) de professionnel; (person) qui exerce une profession libérale. ● n professionnel/-le m/f.

**professor** /prə'fesə(r)/ n professeur m (titulaire d'une chaire).

**proficient** /prə'fɪʃnt/ adj compétent.

**profile** /'prəʊfaɪl/ n (of face) profil m; (of body, mountain) silhouette f; (by journalist) portrait m.

**profit** /'prɒfɪt/ n profit m, bénéfice m. ● vi ~ by tirer profit de. **profitable** adj rentable.

**profound** /prə'faʊnd/ adj profond.

**profusely** /prə'fjuːslɪ/ adv (bleed) abondamment; (apologize) avec effusion. **profusion** n profusion f.

**program** /'prəʊgræm/ n (US) ➡PROGRAMME; (computer) ~ programme m. ● vt (pt **programmed**) programmer.

**programme** /'prəʊgræm/ n programme m; (broadcast) émission f.

**programmer** /'prəʊgræmə(r)/ n programmeur/-euse m/f.

**programming** /'prəʊgræmɪŋ/ n (Comput) programmation f.

**progress**[1] /'prəʊgres/ n progrès m (pl) (in ~) en cours; make ~ faire des progrès; ~ report compte-rendu m.

**progress**[2] /prə'gres/ vi (advance, improve) progresser.

**progressive** /prə'gresɪv/ adj progressif; (reforming) progressiste.

**prohibit** /prə'hɪbɪt/ vt interdire (sb from doing à qn de faire).

**project**[1] /prə'dʒekt/ vt projeter. ● vi (jut out) être en saillie.

**project**[2] /'prɒdʒekt/ n (plan) projet m; (undertaking) entreprise f; (School) dossier m.

**projection** /prə'dʒekʃn/ n projection f.; saillie f.; (estimate) prévision f.

**projector** /prə'dʒektə(r)/ n projecteur m.

**proliferate** /prə'lɪfəreɪt/ vi proliférer.

**prolong** /prə'lɒŋ/ vt prolonger.

**prominent** /'prɒmɪnənt/ adj (projecting) proéminent; (conspicuous) bien en vue; (fig) important.

**promiscuous** /prə'mɪskjʊəs/ adj de mœurs faciles.

**promise** /'prɒmɪs/ n promesse f. ● vt/i promettre. **promising** adj prometteur; (person) qui promet.

**promote** /prə'məʊt/ vt promouvoir; (advertise) faire la promotion de. **promotion** n promotion f.

**prompt** /prɒmpt/ adj rapide; (punctual) à l'heure, ponctuel. ● adv (on the dot) pile. ● vt inciter; (cause) provoquer; (Theat) souffler à. ● n (Comput) message m guide-opérateur. **prompter** n souffleur/-euse m/f. **promptly** adv rapidement; ponctuellement.

**prone** /prəʊn/ adj ~ sujet à.

**pronoun** /'prəʊnaʊn/ n pronom m.

**pronounce** /prə'naʊns/ vt prononcer. **pronunciation** n prononciation f.

**proof** /pruːf/ n (evidence) preuve f.; (test, trial copy) épreuve f.; (of alcohol) teneur f en alcool. ● adj ~ against à l'épreuve de.

**prop** /prɒp/ n support m; (Theat) accessoire m. ● vt (pt propped) ~ (up) (support) étayer; (lean) appuyer.

**propaganda** /prɒpə'gændə/ n propagande f.

**propel** /prə'pel/ vt (pt propelled) (vehicle, ship) propulser; (person) pousser.

**propeller** /prə'pelə(r)/ n hélice f.

**proper** /'prɒpə(r)/ adj correct, bon; (adequate) convenable; (real) vrai; (thorough 🔢) parfait. **properly** adv correctement, comme il faut; (adequately) convenablement.

**proper noun** n nom m propre.

**property** /'prɒpətɪ/ n (house) propriété f.; (things owned) biens mpl, propriété f. ● adj immobilier, foncier.

**prophecy** /'prɒfəsɪ/ n prophétie f.

**prophet** /'prɒfɪt/ n prophète m.

**proportion** /prə'pɔːʃn/ n (ratio, dimension) proportion f.; (amount) partie f.

**proposal** /prə'pəʊzl/ n proposition f.; (of marriage) demande f en mariage.

**propose** /prə'pəʊz/ vt proposer. ● vi faire une demande en mariage; ~ to do se proposer de faire.

**proposition** /prɒpə'zɪʃn/ n proposition f.; (matter 🔢) affaire f. ● vt 🔢 faire des propositions malhonnêtes à.

**proprietor** /prə'praɪətə(r)/ n propriétaire mf.

**propriety** /prə'praɪətɪ/ n (correct behaviour) bienséance f.

**prose** /prəʊz/ n prose f.; (translation) thème m.

**prosecute** /'prɒsɪkjuːt/ vt poursuivre en justice.

**prosecution** n poursuites fpl. **prosecutor** n procureur m.

**prospect¹** /ˈprɒspekt/ n (outlook) perspective f; (chance) espoir m.

**prospect²** /prəˈspekt/ vt/i prospecter.

**prospective** /prəˈspektɪv/ adj (future) futur; (possible) éventuel.

**prospectus** /prəˈspektəs/ n brochure f; (Univ) livret m de l'étudiant.

**prosperity** /prɒˈsperɪtɪ/ n prospérité f. **prosperous** adj prospère.

**prostitute** /ˈprɒstɪtjuːt/ n prostituée f.

**prostrate** /ˈprɒstreɪt/ adj (prone) à plat ventre; (exhausted) prostré.

**protect** /prəˈtekt/ vt protéger. **protection** n protection f. **protective** adj protecteur; (clothes) de protection.

**protein** /ˈprəʊtiːn/ n protéine f.

**protest¹** /ˈprəʊtest/ n protestation f; under~ en protestant.

**protest²** /prəˈtest/ vt/i protester.

**Protestant** /ˈprɒtɪstənt/ adj & n protestant/-e m/f.

**protester** /prəˈtestə(r)/ n manifestant/-e m/f.

**protocol** /ˈprəʊtəkɒl/ n protocole m.

**protrude** /prəˈtruːd/ vi dépasser.

**proud** /praʊd/ adj fier, orgueilleux.

**prove** /pruːv/ vt prouver. ● vi (~ to be) easy se révéler facile; ~ oneself faire ses preuves. **proven** adj éprouvé.

**proverb** /ˈprɒvɜːb/ n proverbe m.

**provide** /prəˈvaɪd/ vt fournir (sb with sth qch à qn). ● vi ~ for (allow for) prévoir; (guard against) parer à; (person) pourvoir aux besoins de.

**provided** /prəˈvaɪdɪd/ conj ~ that

à condition que.

**providing** /prəˈvaɪdɪŋ/ conj ➡PROVIDED.

**province** /ˈprɒvɪns/ n province f; (fig) compétence f.

**provision** /prəˈvɪʒn/ n (stock) provision f; (supplying) fourniture f; (stipulation) dispositions fpl; ~s (food) provisions fpl.

**provisional** /prəˈvɪʒənl/ adj provisoire.

**provocative** /prəˈvɒkətɪv/ adj provocant.

**provoke** /prəˈvəʊk/ vt provoquer.

**prow** /praʊ/ n proue f.

**prowess** /ˈpraʊɪs/ n prouesses fpl.

**prowl** /praʊl/ vi rôder.

**proxy** /ˈprɒksɪ/ n by ~ par procuration.

**prudish** /ˈpruːdɪʃ/ adj pudibond, prude.

**prune** /pruːn/ n pruneau m. ● vt (cut) tailler.

**pry** /praɪ/ vi ~ into mettre son nez dans.

**psalm** /sɑːm/ n psaume m.

**pseudonym** /ˈsjuːdənɪm/ n pseudonyme m.

**psychiatric** /saɪkɪˈætrɪk/ adj psychiatrique. **psychiatrist** n psychiatre mf. **psychiatry** n psychiatrie f.

**psychic** /ˈsaɪkɪk/ adj (phenomenon) métapsychique; (person) doué de télépathie.

**psychoanalyse** /saɪkəʊˈænəlaɪz/ vt psychanalyser.

**psychological** /saɪkəˈlɒdʒɪkl/ adj psychologique. **psychologist** n psychologue mf. **psychology** n psychologie f.

**PTO** abbr (please turn over) TSVP.

**pub** /pʌb/ n pub m.

**Pub** Au Royaume-Uni, établissement où l'on sert des boissons (alcoolisées ou non) et parfois des repas légers. Certains appartiennent à une marque de bière alors que les *free houses* sont indépendants. C'est un lieu convivial où l'on vient passer un bon moment (fléchettes, billard, jeux de groupes). Aujourd'hui, la loi leur permet d'ouvrir de 11h à 23h.

**puberty** /'pjuːbəti/ *n* puberté *f.*

**public** /'pʌblɪk/ *adj* public; (*library*) municipal; **in ~** en public.

**publican** /'pʌblɪkən/ *n* patron/-ne *m/f* de pub.

**publication** /pʌblɪ'keɪʃn/ *n* publication *f.*

**public house** *n* pub *m.*

**publicity** /pʌb'lɪsəti/ *n* publicité *f.*

**publicize** /'pʌblɪsaɪz/ *vt* faire connaître au public.

**public:** **~ relations** *n* relations *fpl* publiques. **~ school** *n* école *f* privée; (US) école *f* publique. **~ transport** *n* transports *mpl* en commun.

**Public schools** Mis à part l'Écosse où ce terme désigne souvent une école publique, les *public schools* britanniques sont en réalité des écoles privées qui fonctionnent souvent sur le mode de l'internat et dont les frais de scolarité sont très élevés. Ces écoles accordent cependant des bourses aux élèves brillants mais peu fortunés. Les *public schools* américaines sont des écoles publiques et la scolarité y est gratuite. ▸STATE SCHOOL

**publish** /'pʌblɪʃ/ *vt* publier. **publisher** *n* éditeur *m.* **publishing** *n*

édition *f.*

**pudding** /'pʊdɪŋ/ *n* dessert *m*; (steamed) pudding *m.*

**puddle** /'pʌdl/ *n* flaque *f* d'eau.

**puff** /pʌf/ *n* (of smoke) bouffée *f*; (of breath) souffle *m.* ● *vt/i* souffler. **~ at** (*cigar*) tirer sur. **~ out** (swell) (se) gonfler.

**pull** /pʊl/ *vt/i* tirer; (*muscle*) se froisser; **~ a face** faire une grimace; **~ one's weight** faire sa part du travail; **~ sb's leg** faire marcher qn. ● *n* traction *f*; (fig) attraction *f*; (influence) influence *f*; **give a ~** tirer. **~ away** (Auto) démarrer; **~ back** or **out** (withdraw) (se) retirer; **~ down** (building) démolir; **~ in** (enter) entrer; (stop) s'arrêter; **~ off** enlever; (fig) réussir; **~ out** (from bag) sortir; (extract) arracher; (Auto) déboîter; **~ over** (Auto) se ranger (sur le côté); **~ through** s'en tirer; **~ oneself together** se ressaisir.

**pull-down menu** *n* (Comput) menu *m* déroulant.

**pulley** /'pʊli/ *n* poulie *f.*

**pullover** /'pʊləʊvə(r)/ *n* pull (-over) *m.*

**pulp** /pʌlp/ *n* (of fruit) pulpe *f*; (for paper) pâte *f* à papier.

**pulpit** /'pʊlpɪt/ *n* chaire *f.*

**pulsate** /pʌl'seɪt/ *vi* battre.

**pulse** /pʌls/ *n* (Med) pouls *m.*

**pump** /pʌmp/ *n* pompe *f*; (plimsoll) chaussure *f* de sport. ● *vt/i* pomper; (*person*) soutirer des renseignements à; **~ up** gonfler.

**pumpkin** /'pʌmpkɪn/ *n* citrouille *f.*

**pun** /pʌn/ *n* jeu *m* de mots.

**punch** /pʌntʃ/ *vt* donner un coup de poing à; (*ticket*) poinçonner. ● *n* coup *m* de poing; (vigour 🆃) punch *m*; (device) poinçonneuse *f*; (drink) punch *m.* **~-line** *n* chute *f.*

**punctual** /'pʌŋktʃʊəl/ *adj* à l'heure; (habitually) ponctuel.

**punctuation** /pʌŋktʃʊ'eɪʃn/ *n* ponctuation *f.*

**puncture** /'pʌŋktʃə(r)/ *n* crevaison *f.* ● *vt/i* crever.

**pungent** /'pʌndʒənt/ *adj* âcre.

**punish** /'pʌnɪʃ/ *vt* punir (**for** sth de qch). **punishment** *n* punition *f.*

**punk** /pʌŋk/ *n* (music, fan) punk *m;* (US: ⓣ) voyou *m.*

**punt** /pʌnt/ *n* (boat) barque *f.* (Hist) (Irish pound) livre *f* irlandaise.

**puny** /'pjuːnɪ/ *adj* **-ier, -iest** chétif.

**pupil** /'pjuːpl/ *n* (person) élève *mf;* (of eye) pupille *f.*

**puppet** /'pʌpɪt/ *n* marionnette *f.*

**puppy** /'pʌpɪ/ *n* chiot *m.*

**purchase** /'pɜːtʃəs/ *vt* acheter (**from** sb à qn). ● *n* achat *m.*

**pure** /pjʊə(r)/ *adj* pur.

**purgatory** /'pɜːgətrɪ/ *n* purgatoire *m.*

**purge** /pɜːdʒ/ *vt* purger (**of** de). ● *n* purge *f.*

**purification** /pjʊərɪfɪ'keɪʃn/ *n* (of water, air) épuration *f;* (Relig) purification *f.* **purify** *vt* épurer, purifier.

**puritan** /'pjʊərɪtən/ *n* puritain *m.* **puritanical** /-'tænɪkl/ *adj* puritain/-e *m/f.*

**purity** /'pjʊərətɪ/ *n* pureté *f.*

**purple** /'pɜːpl/ *adj & n* violet (*m*).

**purpose** /'pɜːpəs/ *n* but *m;* (determination) résolution *f;* **on** ~ exprès; **to no** ~ sans résultat.

**purr** /pɜː(r)/ *n* ronronnement *m.* ● *vi* ronronner.

**purse** /pɜːs/ *n* porte-monnaie *m inv;* (handbag: US) sac *m* à main. ● *vt* (lips) pincer.

**pursue** /pə'sjuː/ *vt* poursuivre.

**pursuit** /pə'sjuːt/ *n* poursuite *f;* (hobby) activité *f,* occupation *f.*

**pus** /pʌs/ *n* pus *m.*

**push** /pʊʃ/ *vt/i* pousser; (button) appuyer sur; (thrust) enfoncer; (recommend ⓣ) proposer avec insistance; **be ~ed for** (time) manquer de; **be ~ing thirty** ~ friser la trentaine; ~ **sb around** bousculer qn. ● *n* poussée *f;* (effort) gros effort *m;* (drive) dynamisme *m;* **give the** ~ **to** ⓣ flanquer à la porte ⓣ. □ ~ **in** resquiller; ~ **on** continuer; ~ **up** (lift) relever; (prices) faire monter.

**pushchair** /'pʊʃtʃeə(r)/ *n* poussette *f.*

**pusher** /'pʊʃə(r)/ *n* revendeur/-euse *m/f* (de drogue).

**push-up** *n* pompe *f.*

**put** /pʊt/ *vt/i* (*pt* **put;** *pres p* **putting**) mettre, placer, poser; (question) poser; ~ **the damage at a million** estimer les dégâts à un million; ~ **sth tactfully** dire qch avec tact. □ ~ **across** communiquer; ~ **away** ranger; (in hospital, prison) enfermer; ~ **back** (postpone) remettre; (delay) retarder; ~ **down** (dé)poser; (write) inscrire; (pay) verser; (suppress) réprimer; ~ **forward** (plan) soumettre; ~ **in** (insert) introduire; (fix) installer; (submit) soumettre; ~ **in for** faire une demande de; ~ **off** (postpone) renvoyer à plus tard; (disconcert) déconcerter; (displease) rebuter; ~ **sb off sth** dégoûter qn de qch; ~ **on** (clothes, radio) mettre; (light) allumer; (accent, weight) prendre; ~ **out** sortir; (stretch) (é)tendre; (extinguish) éteindre; (disconcert) déconcerter; (inconvenience) déranger; ~ **up** lever, remonter; (building) construire; (notice) mettre; (price) augmenter; (guest) héberger; (offer) offrir; ~ **up with** supporter.

**putt** /pʌt/ *vi* putter. ● *n* putt *m.*

**putty** /'pʌtɪ/ *n* mastic *m.*

P

**puzzle** /'pʌzl/ n énigme f; (game) casse-tête m inv; (jigsaw) puzzle m. ● vt rendre perplexe. ● vi se creuser la tête.

**pyjamas** /pə'dʒɑːməz/ npl pyjama m.

**pylon** /'paɪlən/ n pylône m.

# Qq

**quack** /kwæk/ n (of duck) coin-coin m inv; (doctor) charlatan m.

**quadrangle** /'kwɒdræŋgl/ (of college) n cour f.

**quadruple** /'kwɒdrʊpl/ adj & n quadruple (m). ● vt/i quadrupler.

**quail** /kweɪl/ n (bird) caille f.

**quaint** /kweɪnt/ adj pittoresque; (old) vieillot; (odd) bizarre.

**qualification** /kwɒlɪfɪ'keɪʃn/ n diplôme m; (ability) compétence f; (fig) réserve f, restriction f.

**qualified** /'kwɒlɪfaɪd/ adj diplômé; (able) qualifié (to do pour faire); (fig) conditionnel.

**qualify** /'kwɒlɪfaɪ/ vt qualifier; (modify) mettre des réserves à; (statement) nuancer. ● vi obtenir son diplôme (as de); (Sport) se qualifier; ~ for remplir les conditions requises pour.

**quality** /'kwɒlətɪ/ n qualité f.

**qualm** /kwɑːm/ n scrupule m.

**quantity** /'kwɒntətɪ/ n quantité f.

**quarantine** /'kwɒrəntiːn/ n quarantaine f.

**quarrel** /'kwɒrəl/ n dispute f, querelle f ● vi (pt **quarrelled**) se disputer.

**quarry** /'kwɒrɪ/ n (excavation) carrière f; (prey) proie f. ● vt extraire.

**quart** /kwɔːt/ n ≈ litre m.

**quarter** /'kwɔːtə(r)/ n quart m; (of year) trimestre m; (25 cents: US) quart m de dollar; (district) quartier m; ~s logement m; from all ~s de toutes parts. ● vt diviser en quatre; (troops) cantonner.

**quarterly** /'kwɔːtəlɪ/ adj trimestriel. ● adv tous les trois mois.

**quartet** /kwɔː'tet/ n quatuor m.

**quartz** /kwɔːts/ n quartz m. ● adj (watch) à quartz.

**quash** /kwɒʃ/ vt (suppress) étouffer; (Jur) annuler.

**quaver** /'kweɪvə(r)/ vi trembler, chevroter. ● n (Mus) croche f.

**quay** /kiː/ n (Naut) quai m.

**queasy** /'kwiːzɪ/ adj feel ~ avoir mal au cœur.

**queen** /kwiːn/ n reine f; (cards) dame f.

**queer** /kwɪə(r)/ adj étrange; (dubious) louche; ✗ homosexuel.

**quench** /kwentʃ/ vt éteindre; (thirst) étancher; (desire) étouffer.

**query** /'kwɪərɪ/ n question f. ● vt mettre en question.

**quest** /kwest/ n recherche f.

**question** /'kwestʃən/ n question f; in ~ en question; out of the ~ hors de question. ● vt interroger; (doubt) mettre en question, douter de. ~ mark n point m d'interrogation.

**questionnaire** /kwestʃə'neə(r)/ n questionnaire m.

**queue** /kjuː/ n queue f. ● vi (pres p queuing) faire la queue.

**quibble** /'kwɪbl/ vi ergoter.

**quick** /kwɪk/ adj rapide; (clever) vif/vive; be ~ (hurry) se dépêcher. ● adv vite. cut to the ~ piquer au vif. **quicken** vt/i (s')accélérer. **quickly** adv rapidement, vite. ~**sand** n sables mpl mouvants.

**quid** /kwɪd/ n inv 🄸 livre f sterling.

**quiet** /'kwaɪət/ adj (calm, still) tranquille; (silent) silencieux; (gentle) doux; (discreet) discret; keep ~ se taire. ● n tranquillité f; on the ~ en cachette. ~**course** n vt/i calmer.

**quieten** /'kwaɪətn/ vt/i (soften) doucement; (sit) en silence.

**quietly** adv (speak) doucement; (sit) en silence.

**quilt** /kwɪlt/ n édredon m; (continental) ~ couette f.

**quirk** /kwɜːk/ n bizarrerie f.

**quit** /kwɪt/ vt (pt quitted) quitter; (smoking) arrêter de. ● vi abandonner; (resign) démissionner; ~ doing (US) cesser de faire.

**quite** /kwaɪt/ adv tout à fait, vraiment; (rather) assez; ~ a few un bon nombre de.

**quits** /kwɪts/ adj quitte (with envers); call it ~ en rester là.

**quiver** /'kwɪvə(r)/ vi trembler.

**quiz** /kwɪz/ n (pl quizzes) test m; (game) jeu-concours m. ● vt (pt quizzed) questionner.

**quotation** /kwəʊ'teɪʃn/ n citation f; (price) devis m; (stock exchange) cotation f. ~ **marks** guillemets mpl.

**quote** /kwəʊt/ vt citer; (reference, number) rappeler; (price) indiquer; (share price) coter. ● vi ~ for faire un devis pour; ~ from citer. ● n (quotation) citation f; (estimate) devis m; in ~s 🄸 entre guillemets.

· · · · · · · · · · · · · · · · · · · · · · · · · · · ·

# Rr

· · · · · · · · · · · · · · · · · · · · · · · · · · · ·

**rabbi** /'ræbaɪ/ n rabbin m.

**rabbit** /'ræbɪt/ n lapin m.

**rabies** /'reɪbiːz/ n (disease) rage f.

**race** /reɪs/ n (contest) course f; (group) race f. ● adj racial; ~ re-

tions relations fpl inter-raciales. ● vt (compete with) faire la course avec; (horse) faire courir. ● vi courir; (pulse) battre précipitamment; (engine) s'emballer. ~**course** n champ m de courses. ~**horse** n cheval m de course. ~**track** n piste f; (for horses) champ m de course.

**racing** /'reɪsɪŋ/ n courses fpl; ~ **car** voiture f de course.

**racism** /'reɪsɪzəm/ n racisme m. **racist** adj & n raciste (mf).

**rack** /ræk/ n (shelf) étagère f; (for clothes) portant m; (for luggage) compartiment m à bagages; (for dishes) égouttoir m. ● vt ~ one's brains se creuser la cervelle.

**racket** /'rækɪt/ n (Sport) raquette f; (noise) vacarme m; (swindle) escroquerie f; (crime) trafic m.

**radar** /'reɪdɑː(r)/ n & adj radar (m).

**radial** /'reɪdɪəl/ n (tyre) pneu m radial.

**radiate** /'reɪdɪeɪt/ vt (happiness) rayonner de; (heat) émettre. ● vi rayonner (from de). **radiation** n (radioactivity) radiation f. **radiator** n radiateur m.

**radical** /'rædɪkl/ n & a radical/-e (m/f).

**radio** /'reɪdɪəʊ/ n radio f; on the ~ à la radio. ● vt (message) envoyer par radio; (person) appeler par radio.

**radioactive** /reɪdɪəʊ'æktɪv/ adj radioactif.

**radiographer** /reɪdɪ'ɒgrəfə(r)/ n manipulateur/-trice m/f radiographe.

**radish** /'rædɪʃ/ n radis m.

**radius** /'reɪdɪəs/ n (pl -dii) rayon m.

**raffle** /'ræfl/ n tombola f.

**rag** /ræg/ n chiffon m; ~s loques fpl.

**rage** /reɪdʒ/ n rage f, colère f; be all the ~ faire fureur. ● vi (person)

tempêter; (*storm, battle*) faire rage.
**ragged** /ˈrægɪd/ *adj* (*clothes*) en loques; (*person*) dépenaillé.
**raid** /reɪd/ *n* (Mil, on stock market) raid *m*; (by police) rafle *f*; (by criminals) hold-up *m inv*. ● *vt* faire un raid or une rafle or un hold-up dans.
**raider** *n* (thief) pillard *m*; (Mil) commando *m*; (corporate) raider *m*.
**rail** /reɪl/ *n* (on balcony) balustrade *f*; (stairs) rampe *f*; (for train) rail *m*; (for curtain) tringle *f*; by ~ par chemin de fer.
**railing** /ˈreɪlɪŋ/ *n* (*also* ~s) grille *f*.
**railway**, (US) **railroad** *n* chemin *m* de fer. ~ **line** *n* voie *f* ferrée. ~ **station** *n* gare *f*.
**rain** /reɪn/ *n* pluie *f*. ● *vi* pleuvoir. ~**bow** *n* arc-en-ciel *m*. ~**coat** *n* imperméable *m*. ~**fall** *n* précipitation *f*. ~ **forest** *n* forêt *f* tropicale.
**rainy** /ˈreɪnɪ/ *adj* (-**ier**, -**iest**) pluvieux; (*season*) des pluies.
**raise** /reɪz/ *vt* (barrier, curtain) lever; (child, cattle) élever; (question) soulever; (price, salary) augmenter. ● *n* (US) augmentation *f*.
**raisin** /ˈreɪzn/ *n* raisin *m* sec.
**rake** /reɪk/ *n* râteau *m*. ● *vt* (garden) ratisser; (search) fouiller dans. □ ~ **in** (money) amasser; ~ **up** (past) remuer.
**rally** /ˈrælɪ/ *vt/i* (se) rallier; (strength) reprendre; (after illness) aller mieux; ~ **round** venir en aide. ● *n* rassemblement *m*; (Auto) rallye *m*; (tennis) échange *m*.
**ram** /ræm/ *n* bélier *m*. ● *vt* (*pt* **rammed**) (thrust) enfoncer; (crash into) rentrer dans.
**RAM** *abbr* (**random access memory**) RAM *f*.
**ramble** /ˈræmbl/ *n* randonnée *f*. ● *vi* faire une randonnée. □ ~ **on** discourir.

**ramp** /ræmp/ *n* (slope) rampe *f*; (in garage) pont *m* de graissage.
**rampage**[1] /ˈræmpeɪdʒ/ *vi* se déchaîner (through places).
**rampage**[2] /ˈræmpeɪdʒ/ *n* go on the ~ tout saccager.
**ran** /ræn/ ➤**RUN**.
**rancid** /ˈrænsɪd/ *adj* rance.
**random** /ˈrændəm/ *adj* (fait) au hasard. ● *n* at ~ au hasard.
**rang** /ræŋ/ ➤**RING**[2].
**range** /reɪndʒ/ *n* (of prices, products) gamme *f*; (of people, beliefs) variété *f*; (of radar, weapon) portée *f*; (of aircraft) autonomie *f*; (of mountains) chaîne *f*. ● *vi* aller; (vary) varier.
**rank** /ræŋk/ *n* rang *m*; (Mil) grade *m*. ● *vt/i* ~ **among** (se) classer parmi.
**ransack** /ˈrænsæk/ *vt* (search) fouiller; (pillage) mettre à sac.
**ransom** /ˈrænsəm/ *n* rançon *f*.
**rap** /ræp/ *n* coup *m* sec; (Mus) rap *m*. ● *vi* (*pt* **rapped**) donner des coups secs (on sur).
**rape** /reɪp/ *vt* violer. ● *n* viol *m*.
**rapid** /ˈræpɪd/ *adj* rapide.
**rapist** /ˈreɪpɪst/ *n* violeur *m*.
**rapturous** /ˈræptʃərəs/ *adj* (delight) extasié; (welcome) enthousiaste.
**rare** /reə(r)/ *adj* rare; (Culin) saignant. **rarely** *adv* rarement.
**rascal** /ˈrɑːskl/ *n* coquin/-e *m/f*.
**rash** /ræʃ/ *n* (Med) rougeurs *fpl*. ● *adj* irréfléchi.
**raspberry** /ˈrɑːzbrɪ/ *n* framboise *f*.
**rat** /ræt/ *n* rat *m*. ● *vi* (*pt* **ratted**) ~ **on** (desert) lâcher; (inform on) dénoncer.
**rate** /reɪt/ *n* (ratio, level) taux *m*; (speed) rythme *m*; (price) tarif *m*; (of exchange) taux *m*; at any ~ en

tout cas. ● vt (value) estimer; (deserve) mériter; ~ sth highly admirer beaucoup qch. ● vi ~ as être considéré comme.

**rather** /'rɑːðə(r)/ adv (by preference) plutôt; (fairly) assez, plutôt; (a little) un peu; I would ~ go j'aimerais mieux partir; ~ than go plutôt que de partir.

**rating** /'reɪtɪŋ/ n (score, value) cote f; the ~s (TV) l'indice m d'écoute, l'audimat® m.

**ratio** /'reɪʃɪəʊ/ n proportion f.

**ration** /'ræʃn/ n ration f. ● vt rationner.

**rational** /'ræʃənl/ adj rationnel; (person) sensé.

**rationalize** /'ræʃnəlaɪz/ vt justifier; (organize) rationaliser.

**rattle** /'rætl/ vi (bottles, chains) s'entrechoquer; (window) vibrer. ● vt (bottles, chains) faire s'entrechoquer; (fig, 🔤) énerver. ● n (cltoy) hochet m. ~snake n serpent m à sonnette, crotale m.

**rave** /reɪv/ vi (enthuse) s'emballer; (in fever) délirer; (in anger) tempêter.

**raven** /'reɪvn/ n corbeau m.

**ravenous** /'rævənəs/ adj be ~ avoir une faim de loup.

**ravine** /rə'viːn/ n ravin m.

**raving** /'reɪvɪŋ/ adj ~ lunatic fou m furieux, folle f furieuse.

**ravishing** /'rævɪʃɪŋ/ adj ravissant.

**raw** /rɔː/ adj cru; (not processed) brut; (wound) à vif; (immature) inexpérimenté; get a ~ deal être mal traité; ~ material matière f première.

**ray** /reɪ/ n (of light) rayon m; ~ of hope lueur f d'espoir.

**razor** /'reɪzə(r)/ n rasoir m. ~blade n lame f de rasoir.

**re** /riː/ prep au sujet de; (at top of letter) objet.

**reach** /riːtʃ/ vt (place, level) atteindre; (decision) arriver à; (contact) joindre; (audience, market) toucher. ● vi ~ up/down lever/baisser le bras; ~ across étendre le bras. ● n portée f; within ~ of à portée de; (close to) à proximité de.

**react** /rɪ'ækt/ vi réagir. **reaction** n réaction f. **reactor** n réacteur m.

**read** /riːd/ vt/i (pt **read**) lire; (study) étudier; (instrument) indiquer; ~ about sb lire quelque chose sur qn; ~ out lire à haute voix. **reader** n lecteur/-trice m/f. **reading** n lecture f; (measurement) indication f; (interpretation) interprétation f.

**readjust** /riːə'dʒʌst/ vt rajuster. ● vi se réadapter (to à).

**read-only memory, ROM** n mémoire f morte.

**ready** /'redɪ/ adj (-ier, -iest) prêt; (quick) prompt. ~-made adj tout fait. ~-to-wear adj prêt-à-porter.

**real** /rɪəl/ adj (not imaginary) véritable, réel; (not artificial) vrai; it's a ~ shame c'est vraiment dommage. ~ **estate** n biens mpl immobiliers.

**realism** /'riːəlɪzm/ n réalisme m. **realistic** adj réaliste.

**reality** /rɪ'ælətɪ/ n réalité f. ~ TV n télé-réalité f.

**reasonable** /'riːznəbl/ adj raisonnable.

**realize** /'rɪəlaɪz/ vt se rendre compte de, comprendre; (fulfil, turn into cash) réaliser; (price) atteindre.

**really** /'rɪəlɪ/ adv vraiment.

**reap** /riːp/ vt (crop) recueillir; (benefits) récolter.

**reappear** /riːə'pɪə(r)/ vi reparaître.

**rear** /rɪə(r)/ n arrière m; (of person) derrière m. 🔤 ● adj (seat) arrière f

(*entrance*) de derrière. ● *vt* élever.
● *vi* (*horse*) se cabrer. ~-**view mirror** *n* rétroviseur *m*.

**reason** /'ri:zn/ *n* raison *f* (to do, for doing de faire); within ~ dans la limite du raisonnable.

**reassurance** /ri:ə'ʃɔ:rəns/ *n* réconfort *m*. **reassure** *vt* rassurer.

**rebate** /'ri:beɪt/ *n* (refund) remboursement *m*; (discount) remise *f*.

**rebel**[1] /'rebl/ *n* & *adj* rebelle (*mf*).

**rebel**[2] /rɪ'bel/ *vi* (*pt* rebelled) se rebeller. **rebellion** *n* rébellion *f*.

**rebound**[1] /rɪ'baʊnd/ *vi* rebondir; ~ on (backfire) se retourner contre.

**rebound**[2] /'ri:baʊnd/ *n* rebond *m*.

**rebuke** /rɪ'bju:k/ *vt* réprimander. ● *n* réprimande *f*.

**recall** /rɪ'kɔ:l/ *vt* (remember) se souvenir de; (call back) rappeler. ● *n* (memory) mémoire *f*; (Comput, Mil) rappel *m*.

**recap** /rɪ'kæp/ *vt/i* (*pt* recapped) récapituler. ● *n* récapitulation *f*.

**recede** /rɪ'si:d/ *vi* s'éloigner; his hair is receding son front se dégarnit.

**receipt** /rɪ'si:t/ *n* (written) reçu *m*; (of letter) réception *f*; ~s (Comm) recettes *fpl*.

**receive** /rɪ'si:v/ *vt* recevoir; (stolen goods) receler. **receiver** *n* (telephone) combiné *m*; (TV) récepteur *m*.

**recent** /'ri:snt/ *adj* récent. **recently** *adv* récemment.

**receptacle** /rɪ'septəkl/ *n* récipient *m*.

**reception** /rɪ'sepʃn/ *n* réception *f*; give sb a warm ~ donner un accueil chaleureux à qn.

**recess** /rɪ'ses/ *n* (alcove) alcôve *m*; (for door) embrasure *f*; (jur, Pol) vacances *fpl*; (School, US) récréation *f*.

**recession** /rɪ'seʃn/ *n* récession *f*.

**recharge** /ri:'tʃɑ:dʒ/ *vt* recharger.

**recipe** /'resəpɪ/ *n* recette *f*.

**recipient** /rɪ'sɪpɪənt/ *n* (of honour) récipiendaire *mf*; (of letter) destinataire *mf*.

**reciprocate** /rɪ'sɪprəkeɪt/ *vt* (compliment) retourner; (kindness) payer de retour. ● *vi* en faire autant.

**recite** /rɪ'saɪt/ *vi* réciter.

**reckless** /'reklɪs/ *adj* imprudent.

**reckon** /'rekən/ *vt/i* calculer; (judge) considérer; (think) penser; ~ on/with compter sur/avec. **reckoning** *n* (guess) estimation *f*; (calculation) calculs *mpl*.

**reclaim** /rɪ'kleɪm/ *vt* récupérer; (flooded land) assécher.

**recline** /rɪ'klaɪn/ *vi* s'allonger; (seat) s'incliner.

**recluse** /rɪ'klu:s/ *n* reclus/-e *m/f*.

**recognition** /rekəg'nɪʃn/ *n* reconnaissance *f*; beyond ~ méconnaissable; gain ~ être reconnu.

**recognize** /'rekəgnaɪz/ *vt* reconnaître.

**recollect** /rekə'lekt/ *vt* se souvenir de, se rappeler. **recollection** *n* souvenir *m*.

**recommend** /rekə'mend/ *vt* recommander. **recommendation** *n* recommandation *f*.

**reconcile** /'rekənsaɪl/ *vt* (people) réconcilier; (facts) concilier; ~ oneself to se résigner à.

**recondition** /ri:kən'dɪʃn/ *vt* remettre à neuf.

**reconsider** /ri:kən'sɪdə(r)/ *vt* réexaminer. ● *vi* réfléchir.

**reconstruct** /ri:kən'strʌkt/ *vt* reconstruire; (crime) faire une reconstitution de.

**record**[1] /rɪ'kɔ:d/ *vt/i* (in register, on tape) enregistrer; (in diary) noter; ~**that** rapporter que.

**record²** /ˈrekɔːd/ n (of events) compte-rendu m; (official) procès-verbal m; (personal, administrative) dossier m; (historical) archives fpl; (past history) réputation f; (Mus) disque m; (Sport) record m; (criminal) ~ casier m judiciaire; **off the** ~ officieusement. ● adj record inv.

**recorder** /rɪˈkɔːdə(r)/ n (Mus) flûte f à bec.

**recording** /rɪˈkɔːdɪŋ/ n enregistrement m.

**record-player** n tourne-disque m.

**recover** /rɪˈkʌvə(r)/ vt recouvrer. ● vi se remettre; (economy) se redresser. **recovery** n (Med) rétablissement m; (of economy) relance f.

**recreation** /rekrɪˈeɪʃn/ n récréation f.

**recruit** /rɪˈkruːt/ n recrue f. ● vt recruter. **recruitment** n recrutement m.

**rectangle** /ˈrektæŋɡl/ n rectangle m.

**rectify** /ˈrektɪfaɪ/ vt rectifier.

**recuperate** /rɪˈkuːpəreɪt/ vt récupérer. ● vi se rétablir.

**recur** /rɪˈkɜː(r)/ vi (pt **recurred**) se reproduire.

**recycle** /riːˈsaɪkl/ vt recycler.

**red** /red/ adj (**redder, reddest**) rouge; (hair) roux. ● n rouge m; **in the** ~ en déficit. **R~ Cross** n Croix-Rouge f. ~**currant** n groseille f.

**redecorate** /riːˈdekəreɪt/ vt repeindre, refaire.

**redeploy** /riːdɪˈplɔɪ/ vt réorganiser; (troops) répartir.

**red:** ~-**handed** adj en flagrant délit. ~-**hot** adj brûlant.

**redirect** /riːdɪˈrekt/ vt (traffic) dévier; (letter) faire suivre.

**redness** /ˈrednɪs/ n rougeur f.

**redo** /riːˈduː/ vt (pt -**did**; pp -**done**) refaire.

**redress** /rɪˈdres/ vt (wrong) redresser; (balance) rétablir. ● n réparation f.

**reduce** /rɪˈdjuːs/ vt réduire; (temperature) faire baisser. **reduction** n réduction f.

**redundancy** /rɪˈdʌndənsɪ/ n licenciement m.

**redundant** /rɪˈdʌndənt/ adj superflu; (worker) licencié; **make** ~ licencier.

**reed** /riːd/ n (plant) roseau m.

**reef** /riːf/ n récif m, écueil m.

**reel** /riːl/ n (of thread) bobine f; (of film) bande f; (winding device) dévidoir m. ● vi chanceler. ● vt ~ **off** réciter.

**refectory** /rɪˈfektrɪ/ n réfectoire m.

**refer** /rɪˈfɜː(r)/ vt/i (pt **referred**) ~ **to** (allude to) faire allusion à; (concern) s'appliquer à; (consult) consulter; (direct) renvoyer à.

**referee** /refəˈriː/ n (Sport) arbitre m. ● vt (pt **refereed**) arbitrer.

**reference** /ˈrefərəns/ n référence f; (mention) allusion f; (person) personne f pouvant fournir des références; **in** or **with** ~ **to** en ce qui concerne; (Comm) suite à.

**referendum** /refəˈrendəm/ n (pl ~**s**) référendum m.

**refill¹** /riːˈfɪl/ vt (glass) remplir à nouveau; (pen) recharger.

**refill²** /ˈriːfɪl/ n recharge f.

**refine** /rɪˈfaɪn/ vt raffiner.

**reflect** /rɪˈflekt/ vt refléter; (heat, light) renvoyer. ● vi réfléchir (on à); ~ **well/badly on sb** faire honneur/du tort à qn.

**reflection** /rɪˈflekʃn/ n réflexion f; (image) reflet m; **on** ~ à la réflexion.

**reflective** /rɪˈflektɪv/ adj (surface) réfléchissant; (person) réfléchi.

**reflector** /rɪˈflektə(r)/ n (on car) catadioptre m.

**reflex** /ˈriːfleks/ adj & n réflexe (m).

**reflexive** /rɪˈfleksɪv/ adj (Gram) réfléchi.

**reform** /rɪˈfɔːm/ vt réformer. ● vi (person) s'amender. ● n réforme f.

**refrain** /rɪˈfreɪn/ n refrain m. ● vi s'abstenir (from de).

**refresh** /rɪˈfreʃ/ vt (drink) rafraîchir; (rest) reposer. **refreshments** npl rafraîchissements mpl.

**refrigerate** /rɪˈfrɪdʒəreɪt/ vt réfrigérer. **refrigerator** n réfrigérateur m.

**refuel** /riːˈfjʊəl/ vt/i (pt refuelled) (se) ravitailler.

**refuge** /ˈrefjuːdʒ/ n refuge m; take ~ se réfugier. **refugee** n réfugié/-e m/f.

**refund¹** /riːˈfʌnd/ vt rembourser.

**refund²** /ˈriːfʌnd/ n remboursement m.

**refurbish** /riːˈfɜːbɪʃ/ vt remettre à neuf.

**refuse¹** /rɪˈfjuːz/ vt/i refuser.

**refuse²** /ˈrefjuːs/ n ordures fpl.

**regain** /rɪˈgeɪn/ vt retrouver; (lost ground) regagner.

**regard** /rɪˈgɑːd/ vt considérer; as ~s en ce qui concerne. ● n regard m, estime f; in this ~ à cet égard; ~s amitiés fpl. **regarding** prep en ce qui concerne.

**regardless** /rɪˈgɑːdlɪs/ adv malgré tout; ~ of sans tenir compte de.

**regime** /reɪˈʒiːm/ n régime m.

**regiment** /ˈredʒɪmənt/ n régiment m.

**region** /ˈriːdʒən/ n région f; in the ~ of environ.

**register** /ˈredʒɪstə(r)/ n registre m.

● vt (record) enregistrer; (vehicle) faire immatriculer; (birth) déclarer; (letter) recommander; (indicate) indiquer; (express) exprimer. ● vi (enrol) s'inscrire; (at hotel) se présenter; (fig) être compris.

**registrar** /redʒɪˈstrɑː(r)/ n officier m de l'état civil; (Univ) responsable m du bureau de la scolarité.

**registration** /redʒɪˈstreɪʃn/ n (of voter, student) inscription f; (of birth) déclaration f; ~ (number) (Auto) numéro m d'immatriculation.

**registry office** n bureau m de l'état civil.

**regret** /rɪˈgret/ n regret m. ● vt (pt regretted) regretter (to do de faire). **regretfully** adv à regret.

**regular** /ˈregjʊlə(r)/ adj régulier; (usual) habituel. ● n habitué/-e m/f. **regularity** n régularité f. **regularly** adv régulièrement.

**regulate** /ˈregjʊleɪt/ vt régler. **regulation** n (rule) règlement m; (process) réglementation f.

**rehabilitate** /riːəˈbɪlɪteɪt/ vt (in public esteem) réhabiliter; (prisoner) réinsérer.

**rehearsal** /rɪˈhɜːsl/ n répétition f. **rehearse** vt/i répéter.

**reign** /reɪn/ n règne m. ● vi régner (over us).

**reimburse** /riːɪmˈbɜːs/ vt rembourser.

**reindeer** /ˈreɪndɪə(r)/ n inv renne m.

**reinforce** /riːɪnˈfɔːs/ vt renforcer. **reinforcement** n renforcement m; ~s renforts mpl.

**reinstate** /riːɪnˈsteɪt/ vt (person) réintégrer; (law) rétablir.

**reject¹** /ˈriːdʒekt/ n marchandise f de deuxième choix.

**reject²** /rɪˈdʒekt/ vt (offer, plea) rejeter; (goods) refuser. **rejection** n (personal) rejet *m*; (of candidate, work) refus *m*.

**rejoice** /rɪ'dʒɔɪs/ *vi* se réjouir.

**relapse** /'riːlæps/ *n* rechute *f*. ● *vi* rechuter; ~ **into** retomber dans.

**relate** /rɪ'leɪt/ *vt* raconter; (associate) associer. ● *vi* ~ **to** se rapporter à; (get on with) s'entendre avec. **related** *adj* (ideas) lié; **we are** ~**d** nous sommes parents.

**relation** /rɪ'leɪʃn/ *n* rapport *m*; (person) parent/-e *m/f*. **relationship** *n* relations *fpl*; (link) rapport *m*.

**relative** /'relətɪv/ *n* parent/-e *m/f*. ● *adj* relatif; (respective) respectif.

**relax** /rɪ'læks/ *vt* (grip) relâcher; (muscle) décontracter; (discipline) assouplir. ● *vi* (person) se détendre; (grip) se relâcher. **relaxation** *n* détente *f*. **relaxing** *adj* délassant.

**relay**[1] /'riːleɪ/ *n* (also ~ **race**) course *f* de relais.

**relay**[2] /rɪ'leɪ/ *vt* relayer.

**release** /rɪ'liːs/ *vt* (prisoner) libérer; (fastening) lâcher; (object, hand) lâcher; (film) faire sortir; (news) publier. ● *n* libération *f*; (of film) sortie *f*; (new record, film) nouveauté *f*.

**relevance** /'reləvəns/ *n* pertinence *f*, intérêt *m*.

**relevant** /'reləvənt/ *adj* pertinent; **be** ~ **to** avoir rapport à.

**reliability** /rɪlaɪə'bɪlɪtɪ/ *n* (of firm) sérieux *m*; (of car) fiabilité *f*; (of person) honnêteté *f*. **reliable** *adj* (firm) sérieux; (person, machine) fiable.

**reliance** /rɪ'laɪəns/ *n* dépendance *f*.

**relic** /'relɪk/ *n* vestige *m*; (object) relique *f*.

**relief** /rɪ'liːf/ *n* soulagement *m* (from à); (assistance) secours *m*; (outline) relief *m*; ~ **road** route *f* de délestage.

**relieve** /rɪ'liːv/ *vt* soulager; (help) secourir; (take over from) relayer.

**religion** /rɪ'lɪdʒən/ *n* religion *f*. **religious** *adj* religieux.

**relish** /'relɪʃ/ *n* plaisir *m*; (Culin) condiment *m*. ● *vt* (food) savourer; (idea) se réjouir de.

**relocate** /riːləʊ'keɪt/ *vt* muter. ● *vi* (company) déménager; (worker) être muté. **relocation** *n* délocalisation *f*.

**reluctance** /rɪ'lʌktəns/ *n* répugnance *f*.

**reluctant** /rɪ'lʌktənt/ *adj* (person) peu enthousiaste; (consent) accordé à contrecœur; ~ **to** peu disposé à. **reluctantly** *adv* à contrecœur.

**rely** /rɪ'laɪ/ *vi* ~ **on** (count) compter sur; (be dependent) dépendre de.

**remain** /rɪ'meɪn/ *vi* rester. **remainder** *n* reste *m*.

**remand** /rɪ'mɑːnd/ *vt* mettre en détention provisoire. ● *n* **on** ~ en détention provisoire.

**remark** /rɪ'mɑːk/ *n* remarque *f*. ● *vt* remarquer. ● *vi* ~ **on** faire des remarques sur. **remarkable** *adj* remarquable.

**remedy** /'remədɪ/ *n* remède *m*. ● *vt* remédier à.

**remember** /rɪ'membə(r)/ *vt* se souvenir de, se rappeler; ~ **to do** ne pas oublier de faire. **remembrance** *n* souvenir *m*.

**remind** /rɪ'maɪnd/ *vt* rappeler (sb of sth qch à qn); ~ **sb to do** rappeler à qn de faire. **reminder** *n* rappel *m*.

**reminisce** /remɪ'nɪs/ *vi* évoquer ses souvenirs.

**remission** /rɪ'mɪʃn/ *n* (Med) rémission *f*; (Jur) remise *f*.

**remnant** /'remnənt/ *n* reste *m*; (trace) vestige *m*; (of cloth) coupon *m*.

**remodel** /ˌriːˈmɒdl/ *vt* (*pt* remodelled) remodeler.

**remorse** /rɪˈmɔːs/ *n* remords *m*.

**remote** /rɪˈməʊt/ *adj* (*place, time*) lointain; (*person*) distant; (*slight*) vague; ~ **control** télécommande *f*.

**removable** /rɪˈmuːvəbl/ *adj* amovible.

**removal** /rɪˈmuːvl/ *n* (of employee) renvoi *m*; (of threat) suppression *f*; (of troops) retrait *m*; (of stain) détachage *m*; (from house) déménagement *m*; ~ **men** déménageurs *mpl*.

**remove** /rɪˈmuːv/ *vt* enlever; (dismiss) renvoyer; (do away with) supprimer; (Comput) effacer.

**remunerate** /rɪˈmjuːnəreɪt/ *vt* rémunérer. **remuneration** *n* rémunération *f*.

**render** /ˈrendə(r)/ *vt* rendre.

**renegade** /ˈrenɪɡeɪd/ *n* renégat/-e *m/f*.

**renew** /rɪˈnjuː/ *vt* renouveler; (resume) reprendre. **renewable** *adj* renouvelable.

**renounce** /rɪˈnaʊns/ *vt* renoncer à; (disown) renier.

**renovate** /ˈrenəveɪt/ *vt* rénover.

**renown** /rɪˈnaʊn/ *n* renommée *f*.

**rent** /rent/ *n* loyer *m*. ● *vt* louer; for ~ à louer. **rental** *n* prix *m* de location.

**reopen** /riːˈəʊpən/ *vt/i* rouvrir.

**reorganize** /riːˈɔːɡənaɪz/ *vt* réorganiser.

**rep** /rep/ *n* (Comm) représentant/-e *m/f*.

**repair** /rɪˈpeə(r)/ *vt* réparer. ● *n* réparation *f*; in good/bad ~ en bon/mauvais état.

**repatriate** /riːˈpætrieɪt/ *vt* rapatrier. **repatriation** *n* rapatrie-

ment *m*.

**repay** /riːˈpeɪ/ *vt* (*pt* repaid) rembourser; (reward) récompenser. **repayment** *n* remboursement *m*.

**repeal** /rɪˈpiːl/ *vt* abroger. ● *n* abrogation *f*.

**repeat** /rɪˈpiːt/ *vt/i* répéter; (renew) renouveler; ~ itself, ~ oneself se répéter. ● *n* répétition *f*; (broadcast) reprise *f*.

**repel** /rɪˈpel/ *vt* (*pt* repelled) repousser.

**repent** /rɪˈpent/ *vi* se repentir (of de).

**repercussion** /riːpəˈkʌʃn/ *n* répercussion *f*.

**repetition** /repɪˈtɪʃn/ *n* répétition *f*.

**replace** /rɪˈpleɪs/ *vt* (put back) remettre; (take the place of) remplacer. **replacement** *n* remplacement *m* (of de); (person) remplaçant/-e *m/f*; (new part) pièce *f* de rechange.

**replay** /ˈriːpleɪ/ *n* (Sport) match *m* rejoué; (recording) répétition *f* immédiate.

**replenish** /rɪˈplenɪʃ/ *vt* (refill) remplir; (renew) renouveler.

**replica** /ˈreplɪkə/ *n* copie *f* exacte.

**reply** /rɪˈplaɪ/ *vt/i* répondre. ● *n* réponse *f*.

**report** /rɪˈpɔːt/ *vt* rapporter, annoncer (that que); (notify) signaler; (denounce) dénoncer. ● *vi* faire un rapport; ~ (on) (news item) faire un reportage sur; ~ to (go) se présenter chez. ● *n* rapport *m*; (in press) reportage *m*; (School) bulletin *m*. **reporter** *n* reporter *m*.

**repossess** /riːpəˈzes/ *vt* reprendre.

**represent** /reprɪˈzent/ *vt* représenter.

**representation** /reprɪzenˈteɪʃn/ *n* représentation *f*; make ~s to protester auprès de.

**representative** /reprɪˈzentətɪv/ adj représentatif, typique (of de). ● n représentant/-e m/f.

**repress** /rɪˈpres/ vt réprimer.

**reprieve** /rɪˈpriːv/ n (delay) sursis m; (pardon) grâce f. ● vt accorder un sursis à; gracier.

**reprimand** /ˈreprɪmɑːnd/ vt réprimander. ● n réprimande f.

**reprisals** /rɪˈpraɪzlz/ npl représailles fpl.

**reproach** /rɪˈprəʊtʃ/ vt reprocher (sb for sth qch à qn). ● n reproche m.

**reproduce** /riːprəˈdjuːs/ vt/i (se) reproduire. **reproduction** n reproduction f. **reproductive** adj reproducteur.

**reptile** /ˈreptaɪl/ n reptile m.

**republic** /rɪˈpʌblɪk/ n république f. **republican** adj & n républicain/-e (m/f).

**repudiate** /rɪˈpjuːdɪeɪt/ vt répudier; (contract) refuser d'honorer.

**reputable** /ˈrepjʊtəbl/ adj honorable, de bonne réputation.

**reputation** /repjʊˈteɪʃn/ n réputation f.

**repute** /rɪˈpjuːt/ n réputation f.

**request** /rɪˈkwest/ n demande f. ● vt demander (of, from à).

**require** /rɪˈkwaɪə(r)/ vt (of thing) demander; (of person) avoir besoin de; (demand, order) exiger. **required** adj requis. **requirement** n exigence f; (condition) condition f (requise).

**rescue** /ˈreskjuː/ vt sauver. ● n sauvetage m (of de); (help) secours m.

**research** /rɪˈsɜːtʃ/ n recherche(s) f(pl). ● vt/i faire des recherches (sur). **researcher** n chercheur/-euse m/f.

**resemblance** /rɪˈzembləns/ n ressemblance f. **resemble** vt

ressembler à.

**resent** /rɪˈzent/ vt être indigné de, s'offenser de. **resentment** n ressentiment m.

**reservation** /rezəˈveɪʃn/ n (doubt) réserve f; (booking) réservation f; (US) réserve f (indienne); make a ~ réserver.

**reserve** /rɪˈzɜːv/ vt réserver. ● n (stock, land) réserve f; (Sport) remplaçant/-e m/f; in ~ en réserve; the ~s (Mil) les réserves fpl. **reserved** adj (person, room) réservé.

**reshuffle** /riːˈʃʌfl/ n (Pol) remanier. ● n (Pol) remaniement m (ministériel).

**residence** /ˈrezɪdəns/ n résidence f; (of students) foyer m; in ~ (doctor) résidant.

**resident** /ˈrezɪdənt/ adj résidant; be ~ résider. ● n habitant/-e m/f; (foreigner) résident/-e m/f; (in hotel) pensionnaire mf. **residential** adj résidentiel.

**resign** /rɪˈzaɪn/ vt abandonner; (job) démissionner de. ● vi démissionner; ~ oneself to se résigner à. **resignation** n résignation f; (from job) démission f. **resigned** adj résigné.

**resilience** /rɪˈzɪliəns/ n élasticité f; ressort m.

**resin** /ˈrezɪn/ n résine f.

**resist** /rɪˈzɪst/ vt/i résister (à). **resistance** n résistance f. **resistant** adj (Med) rebelle; (metal) résistant.

**resolution** /rezəˈluːʃn/ n résolution f.

**resolve** /rɪˈzɒlv/ vt résoudre (to do de faire). ● n résolution f.

**resort** /rɪˈzɔːt/ vi ~ to avoir recours à. ● n (recourse) recours m; (place) station f; in the last ~ en dernier ressort.

**resource** /rɪˈsɔːs/ n ressource f;

# respect | return

∼s (wealth) ressources *fpl.* **resourceful** *adj* ingénieux.

**respect** /rɪˈspekt/ *n* respect *m*; (aspect) égard *m*; **with** ∼ **to** à l'égard de, relativement à. ● *vt* respecter.

**respectability** /rɪspektəˈbɪlətɪ/ *n* respectabilité *f.* **respectable** *adj* respectable.

**respectful** /rɪˈspektfl/ *adj* respectueux.

**respective** /rɪˈspektɪv/ *adj* respectif.

**respite** /ˈrespaɪt/ *n* répit *m.*

**respond** /rɪˈspɒnd/ *vi* répondre (**to** à); ∼ (react) to) réagir à. **response** *n* réponse *f.*

**responsibility** /rɪspɒnsəˈbɪlətɪ/ *n* responsabilité *f.* **responsible** *adj* responsable; (*job*) qui comporte des responsabilités.

**responsive** /rɪˈspɒnsɪv/ *adj* réceptif.

**rest** /rest/ *vt/i* (se) reposer; (lean) (s')appuyer (on sur); (be buried, lie) reposer; (remain) demeurer. ● *n* repos *m*; (support) support *m*; **have a** ∼ se reposer; **the** ∼ (remainder) le reste (**of** de); (other people) les autres.

**restaurant** /ˈrestrɒnt/ *n* restaurant *m.*

**restless** /ˈrestlɪs/ *adj* agité.

**restoration** /restəˈreɪʃn/ *n* rétablissement *m*; restauration *f.*

**restore** /rɪˈstɔː(r)/ *vt* rétablir; (*building*) restaurer; ∼ **sth to sb** restituer qch à qn.

**restrain** /rɪˈstreɪn/ *vt* contenir; ∼ **sb from** retenir qn de. **restrained** *adj* (moderate) mesuré; (in control of self) maître de soi.

**restrict** /rɪˈstrɪkt/ *vt* restreindre. **restriction** *n* restriction *f.*

**rest room** *n* (US) toilettes *fpl.*

**result** /rɪˈzʌlt/ *n* résultat *m.* ● *vi*

résulter; ∼ **in** aboutir à.

**resume** /rɪˈzjuːm/ *vt/i* reprendre.

**résumé** /ˈrezjuːmeɪ/ *n* résumé *m*; (of career: US) CV *m*, curriculum vitae *m.*

**resurrect** /rezəˈrekt/ *vt* ressusciter.

**resuscitate** /rɪˈsʌsɪteɪt/ *vt* réanimer.

**retail** /ˈriːteɪl/ *n* détail *m.* ● *adj* & *adv* au détail. ● *vt/i* (se) vendre (au détail). **retailer** *n* détaillant/-e *mf.*

**retain** /rɪˈteɪn/ *vt* (hold back, remember) retenir; (keep) conserver.

**retaliate** /rɪˈtælɪeɪt/ *vi* riposter. **retaliation** *n* représailles *fpl.*

**retch** /retʃ/ *vi* avoir un haut-le-cœur.

**retire** /rɪˈtaɪə(r)/ *vi* (from work) prendre sa retraite; (withdraw) se retirer; (go to bed) se coucher. **retired** *adj* retraité. **retirement** *n* retraite *f.*

**retort** /rɪˈtɔːt/ *vt/i* répliquer. ● *n* réplique *f.*

**retrace** /riːˈtreɪs/ *vt* ∼ **one's steps** revenir sur ses pas.

**retract** /rɪˈtrækt/ *vt/i* (se) rétracter.

**retrain** /riːˈtreɪn/ *vt/i* (se) recycler.

**retreat** /rɪˈtriːt/ *vi* (Mil) battre en retraite. ● *n* retraite *f.*

**retrieval** /rɪˈtriːvl/ *n* (Comput) extraction *f.* **retrieve** *vt* (*object*) récupérer; (*situation*) redresser; (*data*) extraire.

**retrospect** /ˈretrəʊspekt/ *n* **in** ∼ rétrospectivement.

**return** /rɪˈtɜːn/ *vi* (come back) revenir; (go back) retourner; (go home) rentrer. ● *vt* (give back) rendre; (bring back) rapporter; (send back) renvoyer; (put back) remettre. ● *n* retour *m*; (yield) rapport *m*; ∼**s** (Comm) bénéfices *mpl*; **in** ∼ **for** en

**reunion | ride**

échange de. ~ **ticket** n aller-retour m.

**reunion** /riː'juːnɪən/ n réunion f.

**reunite** /riːjuː'naɪt/ vt réunir.

**rev** /rev/ n (Auto 🔢) tour m. • vt/i (pt **revved**) ~ **(up)** (engine 🔢) (s')emballer.

**reveal** /rɪ'viːl/ vt révéler; (allow to appear) laisser voir.

**revelation** /revə'leɪʃn/ n révélation f.

**revenge** /rɪ'vendʒ/ n vengeance f. • vt venger.

**revenue** /'revənjuː/ n revenu m.

**reverberate** /rɪ'vɜːbəreɪt/ vi (sound, light) se répercuter.

**reverend** /'revərənd/ adj révérend.

**reversal** /rɪ'vɜːsl/ n renversement m; (of view) revirement m.

**reverse** • adj contraire, inverse. • n contraire m; (back) revers m, envers m; (gear) marche f arrière. • vt (situation, bracket) renverser; (order) inverser; (decision) annuler; ~ **the charges** appeler en PCV. • vi (Auto) faire marche arrière.

**review** /rɪ'vjuː/ n (inspection, magazine) revue f; (of book) critique f. • vt passer en revue; (situation) réexaminer; faire la critique de. **reviewer** n critique m.

**revise** /rɪ'vaɪz/ vt réviser; (text) revoir. **revision** n révision f.

**revival** /rɪ'vaɪvl/ n (of economy) reprise f; (of interest) regain m.

**revive** /rɪ'vaɪv/ vt (person, hopes) ranimer; (custom) rétablir. • vi se ranimer.

**revoke** /rɪ'vəʊk/ vt révoquer.

**revolt** /rɪ'vəʊlt/ vt/i (se) révolter. • n révolte f. **revolting** adj dégoûtant.

**revolution** /revə'luːʃn/ n révolution f.

**revolve** /rɪ'vɒlv/ vi tourner.

**revolver** /rɪ'vɒlvə(r)/ n revolver m.

**revolving door** n porte f à tambour.

**reward** /rɪ'wɔːd/ n récompense f. • vt récompenser (for de). **rewarding** adj rémunérateur; (worthwhile) qui (en) vaut la peine.

**rewind** /riː'waɪnd/ vt (pt **rewound**) rembobiner.

**rewire** /riː'waɪə(r)/ vt refaire l'installation électrique de.

**rhetorical** /rɪ'tɒrɪkl/ adj (de) rhétorique; (question) de pure forme.

**rheumatism** /'ruːmətɪzəm/ n rhumatisme m.

**rhinoceros** /raɪ'nɒsərəs/ n (pl ~es) rhinocéros m.

**rhubarb** /'ruːbɑːb/ n rhubarbe f.

**rhyme** /raɪm/ n rime f; (poem) vers mpl. • vt/i (faire) rimer.

**rhythm** /'rɪðəm/ n rythme m. **rhythmic(-al)** adj rythmique.

**rib** /rɪb/ n côte f.

**ribbon** /'rɪbən/ n ruban m; **in** ~**s** en lambeaux.

**rice** /raɪs/ n riz m. ~ **pudding** n riz au lait.

**rich** /rɪtʃ/ adj riche.

**r**

**rid** /rɪd/ vt (pt **rid**; pres p **ridding**) débarrasser (of de); **get** ~ **of** se débarrasser de.

**ridden** /'rɪdn/ →**RIDE**.

**riddle** /'rɪdl/ n énigme f. • vt ~ **with** (bullets) cribler de; (mistakes) bourrer de.

**ride** /raɪd/ vi (pt **rode**; pp **ridden**) aller (à bicyclette, à cheval); (in car) rouler; (on a horse as sport) monter à cheval. • vt (a particular horse) monter; (distance) parcourir. • n promenade f, tour m; (distance) trajet m; **give sb a** ~ (US) prendre qn en voiture; **go for a** ~ aller faire un tour (à bicyclette, à cheval). **rider** n cavalier/-ière m/f; (in horse race) jockey m; (cyclist) cycliste mf; (motorcyclist) motocycliste mf.

**ridge** /rɪdʒ/ n arête f; crête f.

**ridiculous** /rɪ'dɪkjʊləs/ adj ridicule.

**riding** /'raɪdɪŋ/ n équitation f.

**rifle** /'raɪfl/ n fusil m. ● vt (rob) dévaliser.

**rift** /rɪft/ n (crack) fissure f; (between people) désaccord m.

**rig** /rɪg/ vt (pt **rigged**) (equip) équiper; (election, match) truquer. ● n (for oil) derrick m. □ ~ **out** habiller; ~ **up** (arrange) arranger.

**right** /raɪt/ adj (morally) bon; (fair) juste; (best) bon, qu'il faut; (not left) droit; be ~ (person) avoir raison (to do); (calculation, watch) être exact; put ~ arranger, rectifier. ● n (entitlement) droit m; (not left) droite f; (not evil) le bien; be in the ~ avoir raison; on the ~ à droite. ● vt (a wrong, sth fallen) redresser. ● adv (not left) à droite; (directly) tout droit; (exactly) bien, juste; (completely) tout à fait; ~ away tout de suite; ~ now (at once) tout de suite; (at present) en ce moment.

**righteous** /'raɪtʃəs/ adj vertueux.

**rightful** /'raɪtfl/ adj légitime.

**right-handed** adj droitier.

**rightly** /'raɪtlɪ/ adv correctement; (with reason) à juste titre.

**right of way** n (Auto) priorité f.

**right wing** adj de droite.

**rigid** /'rɪdʒɪd/ adj rigide.

**rigorous** /'rɪgərəs/ adj rigoureux.

**rim** /rɪm/ n bord m.

**rind** /raɪnd/ n (on cheese) croûte f; (on bacon) couenne f; (on fruit) écorce f.

**ring**¹ /rɪŋ/ n (hoop) anneau m;

(jewellery) bague f; (circle) cercle m; (boxing) ring m; (wedding) ~ alliance f. ● vt entourer; (word in text) entourer d'un cercle.

**ring**² /rɪŋ/ vt/i (pt **rang**; pp **rung**) sonner; (of words) retentir; ~ the bell sonner. ● n sonnerie f; give sb a ~ donner un coup de fil à qn. □ ~ **back** rappeler; ~ **off** raccrocher; ~ **up** téléphoner (à). ~**tone** sonnerie f.

**ring road** n périphérique m.

**rink** /rɪŋk/ n patinoire f.

**rinse** /rɪns/ vt rincer; ~ **out** rincer. ● n rinçage f.

**riot** /'raɪət/ n émeute f; (of colours) profusion f; run ~ se déchaîner. ● vi faire une émeute.

**rip** /rɪp/ vt/i (pt **ripped**) (se) déchirer; let ~ (not check) laisser courir; ~ **off** ⊠ rouler. ● n déchirure f.

**ripe** /raɪp/ adj mûr. **ripen** vt/i mûrir.

**rip-off** n 🗉 vol m; arnaque f 🗉.

**ripple** /'rɪpl/ n ride f; ondulation f. ● vt/i (water) (se) rider.

**rise** /raɪz/ vi (pt **rose**; pp **risen**) (increase) monter, s'élever; (stand up, get up) se lever; (rebel) se soulever; (sun) se lever; (water) monter; ~ **up** se soulever. ● n (slope) pente f; (increase) hausse f; (in pay) augmentation f; (progress, boom) essor m; give ~ **to** donner lieu à.

**risk** /rɪsk/ n risque m; at ~ menacé. ● vt risquer; ~ **doing** (venture) se risquer à faire. **risky** adj risqué.

**rite** /raɪt/ n rite m; last ~s derniers sacrements mpl.

**rival** /'raɪvl/ n rival/-e m/f. ● adj rival; (claim) opposé. ● vt (pt **rivalled**) rivaliser avec.

**river** /'rɪvə(r)/ n rivière f; (flowing into sea) fleuve m. ● adj (fishing, traffic) fluvial.

**rivet** /ˈrɪvɪt/ n (bolt) rivet m. ● vt (pt **riveted**) riveter.

**Riviera** /rɪvɪˈeərə/ n (the French) ~ la Côte d'Azur.

**road** /rəʊd/ n route f; (in town) rue f; (small) chemin m; the ~ to (glory: fig) le chemin de. ● adj (sign, safety) routier. ~-**map** n carte f routière. ~ **rage** n violence f au volant. ~**worthy** adj en état de marche.

**roam** /rəʊm/ vi errer. ● vt (streets, seas) parcourir.

**roar** /rɔː(r)/ n hurlement m; (of lion, wind) rugissement m; (of lorry, thunder) grondement m. ● vi/t hurler; (lion, wind) rugir; (lorry, thunder) gronder; ~ **with laughter** rire aux éclats.

**roast** /rəʊst/ vt/i rôtir. ● n (meat) rôti m. ● adj rôti. ~-**beef** n rôti m de bœuf.

**rob** /rɒb/ vt (pt **robbed**) voler (sb of sth qch à qn); (bank, house) dévaliser; (deprive) priver (of de). **robber** n voleur/-euse m/f. **robbery** n vol m.

**robe** /rəʊb/ n (of judge) robe f; (dressinggown) peignoir m.

**robin** /ˈrɒbɪn/ n rouge-gorge m.

**robot** /ˈrəʊbɒt/ n robot m.

**robust** /rəʊˈbʌst/ adj robuste.

**rock** /rɒk/ n roche f; (rock face, boulder) rocher m; (hurled stone) pierre f; (sweet) sucre m d'orge; (Mus) rock m; on the ~s (drink) avec des glaçons; (marriage) en crise. ● vt/i (se) balancer; (shake) (faire) trembler; (child) bercer. ~-**climbing** n varappe f.

**rocket** /ˈrɒkɪt/ n fusée f.

**rocking-chair** n fauteuil m à bascule.

**rocky** /ˈrɒkɪ/ adj (-ier, -iest) (ground) rocailleux; (hill) rocheux;

(shaky: fig) branlant.

**rod** /rɒd/ n (metal) tige f; (wooden) baguette f; (for fishing) canne f à pêche.

**rode** /rəʊd/ →RIDE.

**roe** /rəʊ/ n œufs mpl de poisson.

**rogue** /rəʊg/ n (dishonest) bandit m; (mischievous) coquin/-e m/f.

**role** /rəʊl/ n rôle m.

**roll** /rəʊl/ vt/i rouler; ~ (about) (child, dog) se rouler; be ~ing (in money) □ rouler sur l'or. ● n rouleau m; (list) liste f; (bread) petit pain m; (of drum, thunder) roulement m; (of ship) roulis m. □ ~ **out** étendre; ~ **over** se retourner; ~ **up** (sleeves) retrousser.

**roll-call** n appel m.

**roller** /ˈrəʊlə(r)/ n rouleau m. ~ **blade** n patin m en ligne, roller m. ~-**coaster** n montagnes fpl russes. ~-**skate** n patin m à roulettes.

**ROM** abbr (**read-only memory**) mémoire f morte.

**Roman** /ˈrəʊmən/ adj & n romain/-e (m/f). ~ **Catholic** adj & n catholique (mf).

**romance** /rəʊˈmæns/ n (novel) roman m d'amour; (love) amour m; (affair) idylle f; (fig) poésie f.

**Romania** /rəʊˈmeɪnɪə/ n Roumanie f.

**Romanian** /rəʊˈmeɪnɪən/ adj roumain. ● n (person) Roumain/-e m/f; (language) roumain m.

**romantic** /rəʊˈmæntɪk/ adj (love) romantique; (of the imagination) romanesque.

**roof** /ruːf/ n toit m; (of mouth) palais m. ● vt recouvrir. ~-**rack** n galerie f. ~-**top** n toit m.

**room** /ruːm/ n pièce f; (bedroom) chambre f; (large hall) salle f; (space) place f; ~ **for manoeuvre** marge f de manœuvre. ~-**mate** n camarade *mf* de chambre.

**roomy** /'ru:mɪ/ *adj* spacieux; (*clothes*) ample.

**root** /ru:t/ *n* racine *f*; (*source*) origine *f*; take ∼ prendre racine. ●*vt/i* (s')enraciner. □ ∼ **about** fouiller; ∼ **for** (US ⊤) encourager; ∼ **out** extirper.

**rope** /rəʊp/ *n* corde *f*; know the ∼s être au courant. ●*vt* attacher; ∼ **in** (*person*) enrôler.

**rose** /rəʊz/ *n* rose *f*. ●**➡RISE**.

**rosé** /'rəʊzeɪ/ *n* rosé *m*.

**rosy** /'rəʊzɪ/ *adj* (**-ier, -iest**) rose; (*hopeful*) plein d'espoir.

**rot** /rɒt/ *vt/i* (*pt* **rotted**) pourrir.

**rota** /'rəʊtə/ *n* liste *f* (de service).

**rotary** /'rəʊtərɪ/ *adj* rotatif.

**rotate** /rəʊ'teɪt/ *vt/i* (faire) tourner; (*change round*) alterner.

**rotten** /'rɒtn/ *adj* pourri; (*tooth*) gâté; (*bad* ⊤) mauvais, sale.

**rough** /rʌf/ *adj* (*manners*) rude; (*to touch*) rugueux; (*ground*) accidenté; (*violent*) brutal; (*bad*) mauvais; (*estimate*) approximatif. ●*adv* (*live*) à la dure.

**roughage** /'rʌfɪdʒ/ *n* fibres *fpl*.

**roughly** /'rʌflɪ/ *adv* rudement; (*approximately*) à peu près.

r

**round** /raʊnd/ *adj* rond. ●*n* (*circle*) rond *m*; (*slice*) tranche *f*; (*of visits, drinks*) tournée *f*; (*competition*) partie *f*; manche *f*; (*boxing*) round *m*; (*of talks*) série *f*; ∼ **of applause** applaudissements *mpl*; go the ∼s circuler. ●*prep* autour de; she lives ∼ here elle habite par ici; ∼ the clock vingt-quatre heures sur vingt-quatre. ●*adv* autour; ∼ about (*nearby*) par ici; (*fig*) à peu près; go or come ∼ to a (*friend*) passer chez; enough to go ∼ assez pour tout le monde. ●*vt* (*object*) arrondir; (*corner*) tourner. □ ∼ **off** termi-

ner; ∼ **up** rassembler

**roundabout** /'raʊndəbaʊt/ *n* (in fairground) manège *m*; (for traffic) rond-point *m* (à sens giratoire). ●*adj* indirect.

**round trip** *n* voyage *m* aller-retour.

**round-up** *n* rassemblement *m*; (of suspects) rafle *f*.

**route** /ru:t/ *n* itinéraire *m*, parcours *m*; (Naut, Aviat) route *f*.

**routine** /ru:'ti:n/ *n* routine *f*. ●*adj* de routine.

**row**[1] /rəʊ/ *n* rangée *f*, rang *m*; in a ∼ (consecutive) consécutif. ●*vi* ramer; (Sport) faire de l'aviron. ∼ **a boat up the river** remonter la rivière à la rame.

**row**[2] /raʊ/ *n* (noise ⊤) tapage *m*; (quarrel ⊤) dispute *f*. ●*vi* ⊤ se disputer.

**rowdy** /'raʊdɪ/ *adj* (**-ier, -iest**) tapageur.

**rowing** /'rəʊɪŋ/ *n* aviron *m*. ∼**-boat** *n* bateau *m* à rames.

**royal** /'rɔɪəl/ *adj* royal. **royalty** *n* famille *f* royale; **royalties** droits *mpl* d'auteur.

**RSI** *abbr* (repetitive strain injury) TMS *m*, trouble *m* musculo-squelettique.

**rub** /rʌb/ *vt/i* (*pt* **rubbed**) frotter; ∼ **it in** insister, en rajouter. ●*n* friction *f*. □ ∼ **out** (s')effacer.

**rubber** /'rʌbə(r)/ *n* caoutchouc *m*; (eraser) gomme *f*. ∼ **band** *n* élastique *m*. ∼ **stamp** *n* tampon *m*.

**rubbish** /'rʌbɪʃ/ *n* (refuse) ordures *fpl*; (junk) saletés *fpl*; (fig) bêtises *fpl*.

**rubble** /'rʌbl/ *n* décombres *mpl*.

**ruby** /'ru:bɪ/ *n* rubis *m*.

**rucksack** /'rʌksæk/ *n* sac *m* à dos.

**rude** /ru:d/ *adj* impoli, grossier; (improper) indécent; (blow) brutal.

**ruffle** /'rʌfl/ *vt* (hair) ébouriffer;

(*clothes*) froisser; (*person*) contrarier. ● *n* (frill) ruche *f*.

**rug** /rʌg/ *n* petit tapis *m*.

**rugby** /'rʌgbɪ/ *n* rugby *m*.

**rugged** /'rʌgɪd/ *adj* (*surface*) rude, rugueux; (*ground*) accidenté; (*character*, *features*) rude.

**ruin** /'ruːɪn/ *n* ruine *f*. ● *vt* (destroy) ruiner; (*damage*) abîmer; (*spoil*) gâter.

**rule** /ruːl/ *n* règle *f*; (regulation) règlement *m*; (Pol) gouvernement *m*; as a ~ en règle générale. ● *vt* gouverner; (master) dominer; (decide) décider; ~ out exclure. ● *vi* régner. **ruler** *n* dirigeant/-e *m/f*, gouvernant *m*; (measure) règle *f*.

**ruling** /'ruːlɪŋ/ *adj* (*class*) dirigeant; (*party*) au pouvoir. ● *n* décision *f*.

**rum** /rʌm/ *n* rhum *m*.

**rumble** /'rʌmbl/ *vi* gronder; (*stomach*) gargouiller. ● *n* grondement *m*; gargouillement *m*.

**rumour**, (US) **rumor** /'ruːmə(r)/ *n* bruit *m*, rumeur *f*; there's a ~ that le bruit court que.

**rump** /rʌmp/ *n* (of animal) croupe *f*; (of bird) croupion *m*; (steak) romsteck *m*.

**run** /rʌn/ *vi* (*pt* ran; *pp* run; *pres p* running) courir; (flow) couler; (pass) passer; (function) marcher; (melt) fondre; (extend) s'étendre; (of bus) circuler; (of play) se jouer; (last) durer; (of colour in washing) déteindre; (in election) être candidat. ● *vt* manage diriger; (event) organiser; (risk, race) courir; (house) tenir; (temperature, errand) faire; (Comput) exécuter. ● *n* course *f*; (journey) parcours *m*; (outing) promenade *f*; (rush) ruée *f*; (series) série *f*; (for chickens) enclos *m*; (in cricket) point *m*; in the long ~ avec le temps; on the ~ en fuite.

□ ~ **across** rencontrer par hasard; ~ **away** s'enfuir; (of vehicle) descendre en courant; (of vehicle) renverser; (production) réduire progressivement; (belittle) dénigrer; ~ **into** (hit) heurter; ~ **off** (copies) tirer; ~ **out** (be used up) s'épuiser; (of lease) expirer; ~ **out of** manquer de; ~ **over** (of vehicle) écraser; (*details*) revoir; ~ **through** regarder qch rapidement; ~ **sth through** sth passer qch à travers qch; ~ **up** (bill) accumuler.

**runaway** /'rʌnəweɪ/ *n* fugitif/-ive *m/f*. ● *adj* fugitif; (horse, vehicle) fou; (inflation) galopant.

**rung** /rʌŋ/ ➡**RING²**. ● *n* (of ladder) barreau *m*.

**runner** /'rʌnə(r)/ *n* coureur/-euse *m/f*. ~ **bean** *n* haricot *m* d'Espagne. **~-up** *n* second/-e *m/f*.

**running** /'rʌnɪŋ/ *n* course *f* à pied; (of business) gestion *f*; (of machine) marche *f*; **be in the** ~ être sur les rangs pour. ● *adj* (commentary) suivi; (water) courant; **four days** ~ quatre jours de suite.

**runway** /'rʌnweɪ/ *n* piste *f*.

**rural** /'rʊərəl/ *adj* rural.

**rush** /rʌʃ/ *vi* (move) se précipiter; (be in a hurry) se dépêcher. ● *vt* (person) bousculer; (Mil) prendre d'assaut; ~ **to** envoyer d'urgence à. ● *n* ruée *f*; (haste) bousculade *f*; (plant) jonc *m*; in a ~ pressé. **~-hour** *n* heure *f* de pointe.

**Russia** /'rʌʃə/ *n* Russie *f*.

**Russian** /'rʌʃn/ *adj* russe. ● *n* (person) Russe *mf*; (language) russe.

**rust** /rʌst/ *n* rouille *f*. ● *vt/i* rouiller.

**rustle** /'rʌsl/ *vt/i* (papers) froisser.

**rusty** /'rʌstɪ/ *adj* rouillé.

**ruthless** /'ruːθlɪs/ *adj* impitoyable.

**rye** /raɪ/ *n* seigle *m*.

# Ss

**sabbath** /'sæbəθ/ n (Jewish) sabbat m; (Christian) jour m du seigneur.

**sabbatical** /sə'bætɪkl/ adj (Univ) sabbatique.

**sabotage** /'sæbətɑːʒ/ n sabotage m. ● vt saboter.

**saccharin** /'sækərɪn/ n saccharine f.

**sack** /sæk/ n (bag) sac m; get the ~ ⟨🔢⟩ être renvoyé. ● vt ⟨🔢⟩ renvoyer; (plunder) saccager. **sacking** n (cloth) toile f à sac; (dismissal 🔢) renvoi m.

**sacrament** /'sækrəmənt/ n sacrement m.

**sacred** /'seɪkrɪd/ adj sacré.

**sacrifice** /'sækrɪfaɪs/ n sacrifice m. ● vt sacrifier.

**sad** /sæd/ adj (**sadder, saddest**) triste.

**saddle** /'sædl/ n selle f. ● vt (horse) seller.

**sadist** /'seɪdɪst/ n sadique mf. **sadistic** adj sadique.

**sadly** /'sædlɪ/ adv tristement; (unfortunately) malheureusement.

**sadness** /'sædnɪs/ n tristesse f.

**safe** /seɪf/ adj (not dangerous) sans danger; (reliable) sûr; (out of danger) en sécurité; (after accident) sain et sauf; ~ from à l'abri de. ● n coffre-fort m.

**safeguard** /'seɪfɡɑːd/ n sauvegarde f. ● vt sauvegarder.

**safely** /'seɪflɪ/ adv sans danger; (in safe place) en sûreté.

**safety** /'seɪftɪ/ n sécurité f. ~-belt n ceinture f de sécurité. ~-pin n épingle f de sûreté. ~-valve n sou-

pape f de sûreté.

**saffron** /'sæfrən/ n safran m.

**sag** /sæg/ vi (pt **sagged**) (beam, mattress) s'affaisser; (flesh) être flasque.

**sage** /seɪdʒ/ n (herb) sauge f.

**Sagittarius** /sædʒɪ'teərɪəs/ n Sagittaire m.

**said** /sed/ ⇒SAY.

**sail** /seɪl/ n voile f; (journey) tour m en bateau. ● vi (person) voyager en bateau; (as sport) faire de la voile; (set off) prendre la mer; ~ across traverser. ● vt (boat) piloter; (sea) traverser. **sailing-boat, sailing-ship** n voilier m.

**sailor** /'seɪlə(r)/ n marin m.

**saint** /seɪnt/ n saint/-e mf.

**sake** /seɪk/ n for the ~ of pour.

**salad** /'sæləd/ n salade f.

**salaried** /'sælərɪd/ adj salarié.

**salary** /'sælərɪ/ n salaire m.

**sale** /seɪl/ n vente f; for ~ à vendre; on ~ en vente; (reduced) en solde; ~s (reductions) soldes mpl; ~s assistant, (US) ~s clerk vendeur/-euse mf.

**salesman** /'seɪlzmən/ n (pl -men) (in shop) vendeur m; (traveller) représentant m.

**saline** /'seɪlaɪn/ adj salin. ● n sérum m physiologique.

**saliva** /sə'laɪvə/ n salive f.

**salmon** /'sæmən/ n inv saumon m.

**salon** /'sælɒn/ n salon m.

**saloon** /sə'luːn/ n (on ship) salon m; ~ (car) berline f.

**salt** /sɔːlt/ n sel m. ● vt saler. **salty** adj salé.

**salutary** /'sæljʊtrɪ/ adj salutaire.

**salute** /sə'luːt/ n salut m. ● vt saluer. ● vi faire un salut.

**salvage** /'sælvɪdʒ/ n sauvetage m; (of waste) récupération f. ● vt sau-

529

same | savour

ver; (for re-use) récupérer.

**same** /seɪm/ adj même (as que).
● pron the ~ le même, la même, les mêmes; at the ~ time en même temps; the ~ (thing) la même chose.

**sample** /'sɑːmpl/ n échantillon m; (of blood) prélèvement m. ● vt essayer; (food) goûter.

**sanctimonious** /sæŋktɪ 'məʊnɪəs/ adj (pej) supérieur.

**sanction** /'sæŋkʃn/ n sanction f. ● vt sanctionner.

**sanctity** /'sæŋktɪtɪ/ n sainteté f.

**sanctuary** /'sæŋktʃʊərɪ/ n (safe place) refuge m; (Relig) sanctuaire m; (for animals) réserve f.

**sand** /sænd/ n sable m; ~s (beach) plage f.

**sandal** /'sændl/ n sandale f.

**sandpaper** /'sændpeɪpə(r)/ n papier m de verre. ● vt poncer.

**sandpit** /'sændpɪt/ n bac m à sable.

**sandwich** /'sænwɪdʒ/ n sandwich m; ~ course cours m avec stage pratique.

**sandy** /'sændɪ/ adj (beach) de sable; (soil) sablonneux; (hair) blond roux m.

**sane** /seɪn/ adj (view) sensé; (person) sain d'esprit.

**sang** /sæŋ/ ⇒SING.

**sanitary** /'sænɪtrɪ/ adj (clean) hygiénique; (system) sanitaire; ~ towel serviette f hygiénique.

**sanitation** /sænɪ'teɪʃn/ n installations fpl sanitaires.

**sanity** /'sænɪtɪ/ n équilibre m mental; (sense) bon sens m.

**sank** /sæŋk/ ⇒SINK.

**Santa (Claus)** /'sæntə (klɔːz)/ n le père Noël.

**sapphire** /'sæfaɪə(r)/ n saphir m.

**sarcasm** /'sɑːkæzəm/ n sarcasme m. **sarcastic** adj sarcastique.

**sash** /sæʃ/ n (on uniform) écharpe f; (on dress) ceinture f.

**sat** /sæt/ ⇒SIT.

**satchel** /'sætʃəl/ n cartable m.

**satellite** /'sætəlaɪt/ n & adj satellite (m); ~ dish antenne f parabolique.

**satire** /'sætaɪə(r)/ n satire f. **satirical** adj satirique.

**satisfaction** /sætɪs'fækʃn/ n satisfaction f.

**satisfactory** /sætɪs'fæktərɪ/ adj satisfaisant.

**satisfy** /'sætɪsfaɪ/ vt satisfaire; (convince) convaincre.

**satphone** /'sætfəʊn/ n téléphone m satellite.

**saturate** /'sætʃəreɪt/ vt saturer. **saturated** adj (wet) trempé.

**Saturday** /'sætədeɪ/ n samedi m.

**sauce** /sɔːs/ n sauce f.

**saucepan** /'sɔːspæn/ n casserole f.

**saucer** /'sɔːsə(r)/ n soucoupe f.

**Saudi Arabia** /saʊdɪ ə'reɪbɪə/ n Arabie f saoudite.

**sausage** /'sɒsɪdʒ/ n (for cooking) saucisse f; (ready to eat) saucisson m.

**savage** /'sævɪdʒ/ adj (blow, temper) violent; (attack) sauvage. ● n sauvage mf. ● vt attaquer sauvagement.

**save** /seɪv/ vt sauver; (money) économiser; (time) gagner; (keep) garder; ~ (sb) doing sth éviter (à qn) de faire qch. ● n (football) arrêt m. **saver** n épargnant/-e m/f. **saving** n économie f. **savings** npl économies fpl.

**saviour**, (US) **savior** /'seɪvɪə(r)/ n sauveur m.

**savour**, (US) **savor** /'seɪvə(r)/ n saveur f. ● vt savourer. **savoury** adj (tasty) savoureux; (Culin) salé.

**saw** /sɔ:/ → SEE. ● n scie f. ● vt (pt sawed; pp sawn or sawed) scier.

**sawdust** /'sɔ:dʌst/ n sciure f.

**saxophone** /'sæksəfəʊn/ n saxophone m.

**say** /seɪ/ vt/i (pt said) dire; (prayer) faire. ● n have a ~ dire son mot; (in decision) avoir voix au chapitre. **saying** n proverbe m.

**scab** /skæb/ n croûte f.

**scaffolding** /'skæfəldɪŋ/ n échafaudage m.

**scald** /skɔ:ld/ vt (injure, cleanse) ébouillanter. ● n brûlure f.

**scale** /skeɪl/ n (for measuring) échelle f; (extent) étendue f; (Mus) gamme f; (on fish) écaille f; on a small ~ sur une petite échelle; ~ model maquette f. ● vt (climb) escalader; ~ down réduire. **scales** npl (for weighing) balance f.

**scallop** /'skɒləp/ n coquille f Saint-Jacques.

**scalp** /skælp/ n cuir m chevelu.

**scampi** /'skæmpɪ/ npl (fresh) langoustines fpl; (breaded) scampi mpl.

**scan** /skæn/ vt (pt scanned) scruter; (quickly) parcourir. ● n (ultrasound) échographie f; (CAT) scanner m.

**scandal** /'skændl/ n scandale m; (gossip) potins mpl T.

**Scandinavia** /skændɪ'neɪvɪə/ n Scandinavie f.

**scanty** /'skæntɪ/ adj (-ier, -iest) maigre; (clothing) minuscule.

**scapegoat** /'skeɪpgəʊt/ n bouc m émissaire.

**scar** /skɑ:(r)/ n cicatrice f. ● vt (pt scarred) marquer.

**scarce** /skeəs/ adj rare. **scarcely** adv à peine.

**scare** /skeə(r)/ vt faire peur à; be ~d avoir peur. ● n peur f; bomb ~ alerte f à la bombe. **scarecrow** n

épouvantail m.

**scarf** /skɑ:f/ n (pl **scarves**) écharpe f; (over head) foulard m.

**scarlet** /'skɑ:lət/ adj écarlate; ~ fever scarlatine f.

**scary** /'skeərɪ/ adj (-ier, -iest) T qui fait peur.

**scathing** /'skeɪðɪŋ/ adj cinglant.

**scatter** /'skætə(r)/ vt (throw) éparpiller, répandre; (disperse) disperser. ● vi se disperser.

**scavenge** /'skævɪndʒ/ vi fouiller (dans les ordures). **scavenger** n (animal) charognard m.

**scene** /si:n/ n scène f; (of accident, crime) lieu m; (sight) spectacle m; behind the ~s en coulisse. **scenery** n paysage m; (Theat) décors mpl. **scenic** adj panoramique.

**scent** /sent/ n (perfume) parfum m; (trail) piste f. ● vt flairer; (make fragrant) parfumer.

**sceptic** /'skeptɪk/ n sceptique mf. **sceptical** adj sceptique. **scepticism** n scepticisme m.

**schedule** /'ʃedjuːl/, /'skedʒʊl/ n horaire m; (for job) planning m; behind ~ en retard; on ~ dans les temps. ● vt prévoir; ~d flight vol m régulier.

**scheme** /skiːm/ n projet m; (dishonest) combine f; pension ~ plan m de retraite. ● vi comploter.

**schizophrenic** /skɪtsəʊ'frenɪk/ adj & n schizophrène (mf).

**scholar** /'skɒlə(r)/ n érudit/-e m/f. **school** /skuːl/ n école f; go to ~ aller à l'école. ● adj (age, year, holidays) scolaire. ~**boy** n élève m. ~**girl** n élève f. **schooling** n scolarité f. ~**teacher** n (primary) instituteur/-trice m/f; (secondary) professeur m.

**science** /'saɪəns/ n science f; teach ~ enseigner les sciences. **scientific**

*adj* scientifique. **scientist** *n* scientifique *mf*.

**scissors** /ˈsɪzəz/ *npl* ciseaux *mpl*.

**scold** /skəʊld/ *vt* gronder.

**scoop** /skuːp/ *n* (shovel) pelle *f*; (measure) mesure *f*; (for ice cream) cuillère *f* à glace; (news) exclusivité *f*.

**scooter** /ˈskuːtə(r)/ *n* (child's) trottinette *f*; (motor cycle) scooter *m*.

**scope** /skəʊp/ *n* étendue *f*; (competence) compétence *f*; (opportunity) possibilité *f*.

**scorch** /skɔːtʃ/ *vt* brûler; (iron) roussir.

**score** /skɔː(r)/ *n* score *m*; (Mus) partition *f*; on that ∼ à cet égard. ● *vt* marquer; (success) remporter. ● *vi* marquer un point; (football) marquer un but; (keep score) marquer les points. **scorer** *n* (Sport) marqueur *m*.

**scorn** /skɔːn/ *n* mépris *m*. ● *vt* mépriser.

**Scorpio** /ˈskɔːpɪəʊ/ *n* Scorpion *m*.

**Scot** /skɒt/ *n* écossais/-e *m/f*.

**Scotland** /ˈskɒtlənd/ *n* écosse *f*.

**Scottish** /ˈskɒtɪʃ/ *adj* écossais.

> **Scottish Parliament** En 1997, les Écossais se prononcèrent par référendum pour le rétablissement de leur parlement. Celui-ci siège depuis 1999 à Édimbourg et comprend 129 membres. Ses compétences s'étendent aux affaires internes à l'Écosse (santé, éducation, environnement, etc.), mais il dispose d'un pouvoir fiscal limité et la défense, les affaires étrangères et les finances restent contrôlées par Londres.

**scoundrel** /ˈskaʊndrəl/ *n* gredin *m*.

**scour** /ˈskaʊə(r)/ *vt* (pan) récurer; (search) parcourir. **scourer** *n* tampon *m* à récurer.

**scourge** /skɜːdʒ/ *n* fléau *m*.

**scout** /skaʊt/ *n* éclaireur *m*. ● *vi* ∼ around for rechercher.

**scowl** /skaʊl/ *n* air *m* renfrogné. ● *vi* prendre un air renfrogné.

**scramble** /ˈskræmbl/ *vi* (clamber) grimper. ● *vt* (eggs) brouiller. ● *n* (rush) course *f*.

**scrap** /skræp/ *n* petit morceau *m*; ∼s (of metal, fabric) déchets *mpl*; (of food) restes *mpl*; (fight 🔢) bagarre *f*. ● *vt* (*pt* scrapped) abandonner; (car) détruire.

**scrape** /skreɪp/ *vt* gratter; (damage) érafler. ● *vi* ∼ against érafler. □ ∼ through réussir de justesse.

**scrap:** ∼-**paper** *n* papier *m* brouillon. ∼**yard** *n* casse *f*.

**scratch** /skrætʃ/ *vt/i* (se) gratter; (with claw, nail) griffer; (graze) érafler; (mark) rayer. ● *n* (on body) égratignure *f*; (on surface) éraflure *f*; start from ∼ partir de zéro; up to ∼ à la hauteur. ∼ **card** *n* jeu *m* de grattage.

**scrawl** /skrɔːl/ *n* gribouillage *m*. ● *vt/i* gribouiller.

**scrawny** /ˈskrɔːnɪ/ *adj* (-**ier**, -**iest**) décharné.

**scream** /skriːm/ *vt/i* crier. ● *n* cri *m* (perçant).

**screech** /skriːtʃ/ *vi* (scream) hurler; (tyres) crisser. ● *n* cri *m* strident; (of tyres) crissement *m*.

**screen** /skriːn/ *n* écran *m*; (folding) paravent *m*. ● *vt* masquer; (protect) protéger; (film) projeter; (candidates) filtrer; (Med) faire subir un test de dépistage. **screening** *n* (cinema) projection *f*; (Med) dépistage *m*.

**screen:** ∼**play** *n* scénario *m*. ∼

saver n protecteur m d'écran.

**screw** /skru:/ n vis f. ● vt visser; ~ up (eyes) plisser; (ruin 🆘) cafouiller 🆘. □ ~**driver** n tournevis m.

**scribble** /ˈskrɪbl/ vt/i griffonner. ● n griffonnage m.

**script** /skrɪpt/ n script m; (of play) texte m.

**scroll** /skrəʊl/ n rouleau m. ● vt/i (Comput) (faire) défiler. ~ **bar** n barre f de défilement.

**scrounge** /skraʊndʒ/ 🆘 vt (favour) quémander; (cigarette) piquer 🆘; ~ money from sb taper de l'argent à qn. ● vi ~ off sb vivre sur le dos de qn.

**scrub** /skrʌb/ n (land) broussailles fpl. ● vt/i (pt scrubbed) nettoyer (à la brosse), frotter.

**scruffy** /ˈskrʌfi/ adj (-ier, -iest) 🆘 dépenaillé.

**scrum** /skrʌm/ n (rugby) mêlée f.

**scruple** /ˈskru:pl/ n scrupule m.

**scrutinize** /ˈskru:tɪnaɪz/ vt scruter. **scrutiny** n examen m minutieux.

**scuba-diving** /ˈsku:bədaɪvɪŋ/ n plongée f sous-marine.

**scuffle** /ˈskʌfl/ n bagarre f.

**sculpt** /skʌlpt/ vt/i sculpter. **sculptor** n sculpteur m.

**sculpture** /ˈskʌlptʃə(r)/ n sculpture f.

**scum** /skʌm/ n (on liquid) mousse f; (people: pej) racaille f.

**scurry** /ˈskʌri/ vi se précipiter, courir (for pour chercher); ~ off se sauver.

**sea** /si:/ n mer f; at ~ en mer; by ~ par mer. ● adj (air) marin; (bird) de mer; (voyage) par mer. ~**food** n fruits mpl de mer. ~**gull** n mouette f.

**seal** /si:l/ n (animal) phoque m; (insignia) sceau m; (with wax) cachet m. ● vt sceller; cacheter; (stick

down) coller. □ ~ **off** (area) boucler.

**seam** /si:m/ n (in cloth) couture f; (of coal) veine f.

**search** /sɜ:tʃ/ vt/i (examine) fouiller; (seek) chercher; (study) examiner; (Comput) rechercher. ● n fouille f; (quest) recherches fpl; (Comput) recherche f; in ~ of à la recherche de. ~ **engine** n (Internet) moteur m de recherche. ~**light** n projecteur m. ~-**warrant** n mandat m de perquisition.

**sea**: ~**shell** n coquillage m. ~**shore** n (coast) littoral m; (beach) plage f.

**seasick** /ˈsi:sɪk/ adj be ~ avoir le mal de mer.

**seaside** /ˈsi:saɪd/ n bord m de la mer.

**season** /ˈsi:zn/ n saison f; ~ **ticket** carte f d'abonnement. ● vt assaisonner. **seasonal** adj saisonnier. **seasoning** n assaisonnement m.

**seat** /si:t/ n siège m; (place) place f; (of trousers) fond m; take a ~ asseyez-vous. ● vt (put) placer; the room ~s 30 la salle peut accueillir 30 personnes. ~-**belt** n ceinture f (de sécurité).

**seaweed** /ˈsi:wi:d/ n algue f marine.

**secluded** /sɪˈklu:dɪd/ adj retiré.

**seclusion** /sɪˈklu:ʒn/ n isolement m.

**second**[1] /ˈsekənd/ adj deuxième, second; a ~ chance une nouvelle chance; have ~ thoughts avoir des doutes. ● n deuxième mf, second/-e m/f; (unit of time) seconde f; ~ s (food) rab m. 🆘 ● adv (in race) deuxième; (secondly) deuxièmement. ● vt (proposal) appuyer.

**second**[2] /sɪˈkɒnd/ vt (transfer) détacher (to à).

**secondary** /'sekəndrɪ/ adj secondaire; ~**school** lycée m, école f secondaire.

**second-best** n pis-aller m.

**second-class** adj (Rail) de deuxième classe; (post) au tarif lent.

**second hand** n (on clock) trotteuse f.

**second-hand** adj & adv (article) d'occasion; (information) de seconde main.

**secondly** /'sekəndlɪ/ adv deuxièmement.

**second-rate** adj médiocre.

**secrecy** /'si:krəsɪ/ n secret m.

**secret** /'si:krɪt/ adj secret. ● n secret m; **in** ~ en secret.

**secretarial** /sekrə'teərɪəl/ adj (work) de secrétaire.

**secretary** /'sekrɪtrɪ/ n secrétaire mf; S~ **of State** ministre m; (US) ministre m des Affaires étrangères.

**secrete** /sɪ'kri:t/ vt (Med) sécréter; (hide) cacher.

**secretive** /'si:krətɪv/ adj secret. **secretly** adv secrètement.

**sect** /sekt/ n secte f. **sectarian** adj sectaire.

**section** /'sekʃn/ n partie f; (in store) rayon m; (of newspaper) rubrique f; (of book) passage m.

**sector** /'sektə(r)/ n secteur m.

**secular** /'sekjʊlə(r)/ adj (school) laïque; (art, music) profane.

**secure** /sɪ'kjʊə(r)/ adj (safe) sûr; (job, marriage) stable; (knot, lock) solide; (window) bien fermé; (feeling) de sécurité; (person) sécurisé. ● vt attacher; (obtain) s'assurer; (ensure) assurer.

**security** /sɪ'kjʊərətɪ/ n (safety) sécurité f; (for loan) caution f; ~ **guard** vigile m.

**sedate** /sɪ'deɪt/ adj calme. ● vt don-

ner un sédatif à. **sedative** n sédatif m.

**seduce** /sɪ'dju:s/ vt séduire. **seducer** n séducteur/-trice m/f. **seduction** n séduction f. **seductive** adj séduisant.

**see** /si:/ vt/i (pt) saw; pp seen voir; **see you (soon)!** à bientôt!; ~**ing that** vu que. □ ~ **out** (person) raccompagner à la porte; ~ **through** (deception) déceler; (person) percer à jour; ~ **sth through** mener qch à bonne fin; ~ **to** s'occuper de; ~ **to it that** veiller à ce que.

**seed** /si:d/ n graine f; (collectively) graines f pl; (origin: fig) germe m; (tennis) tête f de série. **seedling** n plant m.

**seek** /si:k/ vt (pt) **sought** chercher.

**seem** /si:m/ vi sembler; he ~s to think it a pity he had to décide.

**seen** /si:n/ ⇒**SEE**.

**seep** /si:p/ vi suinter; ~ **into** s'infiltrer dans.

**see-saw** /'si:sɔ:/ n tapecul m. ● vt osciller.

**seethe** /si:ð/ vi ~ **with** (anger) bouillir de; (people) grouiller de.

**segment** /'segmənt/ n segment m; (of orange) quartier m.

**segregate** /'segrɪgeɪt/ vt séparer.

**seize** /si:z/ vt saisir; (territory, prisoner) s'emparer de. ● vi ~ **on** (chance) saisir; ~ **up** (engine) se gripper.

**seizure** /'si:ʒə(r)/ n (Med) crise f.

**seldom** /'seldəm/ adv rarement.

**select** /sɪ'lekt/ vt sélectionner. ● adj privilégié. **selection** n sélection f. **selective** adj sélectif.

**self** /self/ n (pl **selves**) moi m; (on cheque) moi-même. ~**-assured** adj plein d'assurance. ~**-catering** (holiday) en location. ~**-centred**, (US) ~**-centered** adj égocentrique.

~**-confident** adj sûr de soi.
~**-conscious** adj timide.
~**-contained** adj (flat) indépendant.
~**-control** n sangfroid m.
~**-defence** n autodéfense f; (Jur) légitime défense f. ~**-employed** adj qui travaille à son compte.
~**-esteem** n amour-propre m.
~**-governing** adj autonome.
~**-indulgent** adj complaisant.
~**-interest** n intérêt m personnel.

**selfish** /ˈselfɪʃ/ adj égoïste.

**selfless** /ˈselflɪs/ adj désintéressé.

**self:** ~**-portrait** n autoportrait m.
~**-reliant** adj autosuffisant.
~**-respect** n respect m de soi.
~**-righteous** adj satisfait de soi.
~**-sacrifice** n abnégation f.
~**-satisfied** adj satisfait de soi.
~**-seeking** adj égoïste. ~**-service** n & adj libre-service (m).

**sell** /sel/ vt/i (pt **sold**) vendre; ~ well se vendre bien. □ ~ **off** liquider; ~ **out** (items) se vendre; **have sold out** avoir tout vendu.

**Sellotape®** /ˈseləuteɪp/ n scotch m.

**sell-out** n (betrayal) 🇬🇧 revirement m; **be a** ~ (show) afficher complet.

**semester** /sɪˈmestə(r)/ n (Univ) semestre m.

**semicircle** /ˈsemɪsɜːkl/ n demi-cercle m.

**semicolon** /semɪˈkəʊlən/ n point-virgule m.

**semi-detached** /semɪdɪˈtætʃt/ adj ~ **house** maison f jumelée.

**semifinal** /semɪˈfaɪnl/ n demi-finale f.

**seminar** /ˈsemɪnɑː(r)/ n séminaire m.

**semolina** /seməˈliːnə/ n semoule f.

**senate** /ˈsenɪt/ n sénat m. **senator** n sénateur m.

**send** /send/ vt/i (pt **sent**) envoyer.

□ ~ **away** (dismiss) renvoyer; ~ (**away** or **off**) **for** commander (par la poste); ~ **back** renvoyer; ~ **for** (person, help) envoyer chercher; ~ **up** 🇬🇧 parodier.

**senile** /ˈsiːnaɪl/ adj sénile.

**senior** /ˈsiːnɪə(r)/ adj plus âgé (**to** que); (in rank) haut placé; **be** ~ **to sb** être le supérieur de qn. ● n aîné/-e m/f. ~ **citizen** n personne f âgée. ~ **school** n lycée m.

**sensation** /senˈseɪʃn/ n sensation f. **sensational** adj sensationnel.

**sense** /sens/ n sens m; (mental impression) sentiment m; (common sense) bon sens m; ~**s** (mind) raison f; **there's no** ~ **in doing** cela ne sert à rien de faire; **make** ~ avoir un sens; **make** ~ **of** comprendre. ● vt (pres)sentir. **senseless** adj insensé; (Med) sans connaissance.

**sensible** /ˈsensəbl/ adj raisonnable; (clothing) pratique.

**sensitive** /ˈsensətɪv/ adj sensible (**to** à); (issue) difficile.

**sensory** /ˈsensərɪ/ adj sensoriel.

**sensual** /ˈsenʃʊəl/ adj sensuel. **sensuality** n sensualité f.

**sensuous** /ˈsenʃʊəs/ adj sensuel.

**sent** /sent/ →**SEND.**

**sentence** /ˈsentəns/ n phrase f; (punishment: Jur) peine f. ● vt ~ **to** condamner à.

**sentiment** /ˈsentɪmənt/ n sentiment m. **sentimental** adj sentimental.

**sentry** /ˈsentrɪ/ n sentinelle f.

**separate**¹ /ˈsepərət/ adj (piece) à part; (issue) autre; (sections) différent; (organizations) distinct.

**separate**² /ˈsepəreɪt/ vt/i (se) séparer.

**separately** /ˈsepərətlɪ/ adv séparément.

**separation** /sepə'reɪʃn/ n séparation f.

**September** /sep'tembə(r)/ n septembre m.

**septic** /'septɪk/ adj (wound) infecté; ~ **tank** fosse f septique.

**sequel** /'si:kwəl/ n suite f.

**sequence** /'si:kwəns/ n (order) ordre m; (series) suite f; (in film) séquence f.

**Serb** /sɜ:b/ adj serbe. ● n (person) Serbe mf; (Ling) serbe m.

**Serbia** /'sɜ:bɪə/ n Serbie f.

**sergeant** /'sɑ:dʒənt/ n (Mil) sergent m; (policeman) brigadier m.

**serial** /'sɪərɪəl/ n feuilleton m. ● adj (Comput) série inv.

**series** /'sɪəri:z/ n inv série f.

**serious** /'sɪərɪəs/ adj sérieux; (accident, crime) grave.

**seriously** /'sɪərɪəslɪ/ adv sérieusement; (ill) gravement; **take** ~ prendre au sérieux.

**sermon** /'sɜ:mən/ n sermon m.

**serpent** /'sɜ:pənt/ n serpent m.

**serrated** /sɪ'reɪtɪd/ adj dentelé.

**serum** /'sɪərəm/ n sérum m.

**servant** /'sɜ:vənt/ n domestique mf.

**serve** /sɜ:v/ vt/i servir; faire; (transport, hospital) desservir; ~ as/to servir de/à; ~ a purpose être utile; ~ a sentence (Jur) purger une peine. ● n (tennis) service m.

**server** /'sɜ:və(r)/ n serveur m; remote ~ téléserveur m.

**service** /'sɜ:vɪs/ n service m; (maintenance) révision f; (Relig) office m; ~s (Mil) forces fpl armées. ● vt (car) réviser. ~**area** n (Auto) aire f de services. ~ **charge** n service m. ~ **station** n station-service f.

**session** /'seʃn/ n séance f; be in ~ (Jur) tenir séance.

**set** /set/ vt (pt) set; pres p setting placer; (table) mettre; (limit) fixer; (clock) mettre à l'heure; (example, task) donner; (TV), (cinema) situer; ~ **fire to** mettre le feu à; ~ **free** libérer; ~ **to music** mettre en musique. ● vi (sun) se coucher; (jelly) prendre; ~ **sail** partir. ● n (of chairs, stamps) série f; (of knives, keys) jeu m; (of people) groupe m; (TV), (radio) poste m; (Theat) décor m; (tennis) set m; (mathematics) ensemble m. ● adj (time, price) fixe; (procedure) bien determiné; (meal) à prix fixe; (book) au programme; ~ **against** opposé à; **be** ~ **on doing** tenir absolument à faire. □~ **about** se mettre à; ~ **back** (delay) retarder; (cost $) coûter; ~ **in** (take hold) s'installer, commencer; ~ **off** or **out** partir; ~ **off** (panic, riot) déclencher; (bomb) faire exploser; ~ **out** (state) présenter; ~ **out to do sth** chercher à faire qch; ~ **up** (stall) monter; (equipment) assembler; (experiment) préparer; (company) créer; (meeting) organiser. ~**back** n revers m.

**settee** /se'ti:/ n canapé m.

**setting** /'setɪŋ/ n cadre m; (on dial) position f.

**settle** /'setl/ vt (arrange, pay) régler; (date) fixer; (nerves) calmer. ● vi (come to rest) (bird) se poser; (dust) se déposer; (live) s'installer. □~ **down** se calmer; (marry etc.) se ranger; ~ **for** accepter; ~ **in** s'installer; ~ **up (with)** régler.

**settlement** /'setlmənt/ n règlement m (of de); (agreement) accord m; (place) colonie f.

**settler** /'setlə(r)/ n colon m.

**seven** /'sevn/ adj & n sept (m).

**seventeen** /sevn'ti:n/ adj & n dix-sept (m).

**seventh** /'sevnθ/ adj & n septième (mf).

**seventy** /'sevntɪ/ adj & n soixante-dix (m).

**sever** /'sevə(r)/ vt (cut) couper; (relations) rompre.

**several** /'sevrəl/ adj & pron plusieurs; ~ of us plusieurs d'entre nous.

**severe** /sɪ'vɪə(r)/ adj (harsh) sévère; (serious) grave.

**sew** /səʊ/ vt/i (pt sewed; pp sewn or sewed) coudre.

**sewage** /'suːɪdʒ/ n eaux fpl usées.

**sewer** /'suːə(r)/ n égout m.

**sewing** /'səʊɪŋ/ n couture f. ~-machine n machine f à coudre.

**sewn** /səʊn/ ⇒SEW.

**sex** /seks/ n sexe m; have ~ avoir des rapports (sexuels). ● adj sexuel. **sexist** adj & n sexiste (mf). **sexual** adj sexuel.

**shabby** /'ʃæbɪ/ adj (-ier, -iest) (place, object) miteux; (person) habillé de façon miteuse; (treatment) mesquin.

**shack** /ʃæk/ n cabane f.

**shade** /ʃeɪd/ n ombre f; (of colour, opinion) nuance f; (for lamp) abat-jour m inv; a ~ bigger légèrement plus grand. ● vt (tree) ombrager; (hat) projeter une ombre sur.

**shadow** /'ʃædəʊ/ n ombre f. ● vt (follow) filer. **S~ Cabinet** n cabinet m fantôme.

**shady** /'ʃeɪdɪ/ adj (-ier, -iest) ombragé; (dubious) véreux.

**shaft** /ʃɑːft/ n (of tool) manche m; (of arrow) tige f; (in machine) axe m; (of mine) puits m; (of light) rayon m.

**shake** /ʃeɪk/ vt (pt shook; pp shaken) secouer; (bottle) agiter; (belief) ébranler; ~ hands with serrer la main à; ~ one's head dire

non de la tête. ● vi trembler. ● n secousse f; give sth a ~ secouer qch. □ ~ off se débarrasser de. ~-up n (Pol) remaniement m.

**shaky** /'ʃeɪkɪ/ adj (-ier, -iest) (hand, voice) tremblant; (ladder) branlant; (weak: fig) instable.

**shall** /ʃæl/ v aux I ~ do je ferai; we ~ see nous verrons; ~ we go. . . ? si on allait . . . ?

**shallow** /'ʃæləʊ/ adj peu profond; (fig) superficiel.

**shame** /ʃeɪm/ n honte f; it's a ~ c'est dommage. ● vt faire honte à.

**shampoo** /ʃæm'puː/ n shampooing m. ● vt faire un shampooing à.

**shandy** /'ʃændɪgæf/ n panaché m.

**shan't** /ʃɑːnt/ ⇒SHALL NOT.

**shanty** /'ʃæntɪ/ n (shack) baraque f; ~ town bidonville m.

**shape** /ʃeɪp/ n forme f. ● vt (clay) modeler; (rock) façonner; (future: fig) déterminer; ~ sth into balls faire des boules avec qch. ● vi ~ up (plan) prendre tournure; (person) faire des progrès.

**share** /ʃeə(r)/ n part f; (Comm) action f. ● vt/i partager; (feature) avoir en commun. ~holder n actionnaire mf. ~ware n (Comput) logiciel m contributif.

**shark** /ʃɑːk/ n requin m.

**sharp** /ʃɑːp/ adj (knife) tranchant; (pin) pointu; (point, angle, cry) aigu; (person, mind) vif; (tone) acerbe. ● adv (stop) net; (sing, play) trop haut; six o'clock ~ six heures pile. ● n (Mus) dièse m.

**sharpen** /'ʃɑːpən/ vt aiguiser; (pencil) tailler.

**shatter** /'ʃætə(r)/ vt (glass) fracasser; (hope) briser. ● vi (glass) voler en éclats.

**shave** /ʃeɪv/ vt/i (se) raser. ● n have a ~ se raser. **shaver** n rasoir *m* électrique.

**shaving** /ˈʃeɪvɪŋ/ *n* (of wood) copeau *m*. ● *adj* (*cream, foam, gel*) à raser.

**shawl** /ʃɔːl/ *n* châle *m*.

**she** /ʃiː/ *pron* elle. ● *n* (*animal*) femelle *f*.

**shear** /ʃɪə(r)/ *vt* (*pp* **shorn** or **sheared**) (*sheep*) tondre; ~ **off** se détacher.

**shears** /ʃɪəz/ *npl* cisaille *f*.

**shed** /ʃed/ *n* remise *f*. ● *vt* (*pt* **shed**; *pres p* **shedding**) perdre; (*light, tears*) répandre.

**sheen** /ʃiːn/ *n* lustre *m*.

**sheep** /ʃiːp/ *n inv* mouton *m*. ~**-dog** *n* chien *m* de berger.

**sheepish** /ˈʃiːpɪʃ/ *adj* penaud.

**sheepskin** /ˈʃiːpskɪn/ *n* peau *f* de mouton.

**sheer** /ʃɪə(r)/ *adj* pur; (*steep*) à pic; (*fabric*) très fin. ● *adv* à pic.

**sheet** /ʃiːt/ *n* drap *m*; (of paper) feuille *f*; (of glass, ice) plaque *f*.

**shelf** /ʃelf/ *n* (*pl* **shelves**) étagère *f*; (in shop, fridge) rayon *m*; (in oven) plaque *f*.

**shell** /ʃel/ *n* coquille *f*; (on beach) coquillage *m*; (of building) carcasse *f*; (explosive) obus *m*. ● *vt* (*nut*) décortiquer; (*peas*) écosser; (Mil) bombarder.

**shellfish** /ˈʃelfɪʃ/ *n* (lobster etc.) crustacés *mpl*; (mollusc) coquillages *mpl*.

**shelter** /ˈʃeltə(r)/ *n* abri *m*. ● *vt/i* (s')abriter; (give lodging to) donner asile à.

**shelve** /ʃelv/ *vt* (*plan*) mettre en suspens.

**shepherd** /ˈʃepəd/ *n* berger *m*; ~'s pie hachis *m* Parmentier. ● *vt* (*people*) guider.

**sherry** /ˈʃerɪ/ *n* xérès *m*.

**shield** /ʃiːld/ *n* bouclier *m*; (screen) écran *m*. ● *vt* protéger.

**shift** /ʃɪft/ *vt/i* (se) déplacer, bouger; (exchange, alter) changer de. ● *n* changement *m*; (workers) équipe *f*; (work) poste *m*; ~ **work** travail *m* posté, travail *m* par roulement.

**shifty** /ˈʃɪftɪ/ *adj* (**-ier, -iest**) louche.

**shimmer** /ˈʃɪmə(r)/ *vi* chatoyer. ● *n* chatoiement *m*.

**shin** /ʃɪn/ *n* tibia *m*.

**shine** /ʃaɪn/ *vt* (*pt* **shone**) (torch) braquer (sur sur). ● *vi* (light, sun, hair) briller; (brass) reluire. ● *n* lustre *m*.

**shingle** /ˈʃɪŋgl/ *n* (pebbles) galets *mpl*; (on roof) bardeau *m*.

**shingles** /ˈʃɪŋglz/ *npl* (Med) zona *m*.

**shiny** /ˈʃaɪnɪ/ *adj* (**-ier, -iest**) brillant.

**ship** /ʃɪp/ *n* bateau *m*, navire *m*. ● *vt* (*pt* **shipped**) transporter. **shipment** *n* (by sea) cargaison *f*; (by air, land) chargement *m*. **shipping** *n* (ships) navigation *f*. ~**wreck** *n* épave *f*; (event) naufrage *m*.

**shirt** /ʃɜːt/ *n* chemise *f*; (woman's) chemisier *m*.

**shiver** /ˈʃɪvə(r)/ *vi* frissonner. ● *n* frisson *m*.

**shock** /ʃɒk/ *n* choc *m*; (Electr) décharge *f*; in ~ en état de choc; ~ **absorber** amortisseur *m*. ● *adj* (result) choc *inv*; (tactics) de choc. ● *vt* choquer.

**shoddy** /ˈʃɒdɪ/ *adj* (**-ier, -iest**) mal fait; (behaviour) mesquin.

**shoe** /ʃuː/ *n* chaussure *f*; (of horse) fer *m*; (brake) ~ sabot *m* (de frein). ● *vt* (*pt* **shod**; *pres p* **shoeing**) (horse) ferrer. ~**lace** *n* lacet *m*. ~ **size** *n* pointure *f*.

s

**shone** /ʃɒn/ →SHINE.

**shook** /ʃʊk/ →SHAKE.

**shoot** /ʃuːt/ vt (pt **shot**) (gun) tirer un coup de; (bullet) tirer; (missile, glance) lancer; (person) tirer sur; (kill) abattre; (execute) fusiller; (film) tourner. ● vi tirer (at sur). ● n (Bot) pousse f. □ ~ **down** abattre; ~ **out** (rush) sortir en vitesse; ~ **up** (spurt) jaillir; (grow) pousser vite.

**shooting** /ʃuːtɪŋ/ n (killing) meurtre m (par arme à feu) hear ~ entendre des coups de feu.

**shop** /ʃɒp/ n magasin m; (small) boutique f; (workshop) atelier m. ● vi (pt **shopped**) faire ses courses; ~ **around** comparer les prix. □ ~ **assistant** n vendeur/-euse m/f. ~-**floor** n (workers) ouvriers mpl. ~**keeper** n commerçant/-e m/f. ~**lifter** n voleur/-euse m/f à l'étalage.

**shopper** /ʃɒpə(r)/ n acheteur/-euse m/f.

**shopping** /ʃɒpɪŋ/ n (goods) achats mpl; go ~ (for food) faire les courses; (for clothes etc.) faire les magasins. ~ **bag** n sac m à provisions. ~ **centre**, (US) ~ **center** n centre m commercial.

**shop window** n vitrine f.

**shore** /ʃɔː(r)/ n côte f, rivage m; on ~ à terre.

**short** /ʃɔːt/ adj court; (person) petit; (brief) court, bref; (curt) brusque; be ~ (of) manquer (de); everything ~ of tout sauf; nothing ~ of rien de moins que; cut ~ écourter; cut sb ~ interrompre qn; fall ~ of ne pas arriver à; he is called Tom for ~ son diminutif est Tom; in ~ en bref. ● adv (stop) net. ● n (Electr) court-circuit m; (film) courtmétrage m; ~s (trousers) short m.

**shortage** /ʃɔːtɪdʒ/ n manque m.

**short:** ~**bread** n sablé m. ~-**change** vt (cheat) rouler 🗊. ~ **circuit** n court-circuit m. ~-**coming** n défaut m. ~ **cut** n raccourci m.

**shorten** /ʃɔːtn/ vt raccourcir.

**shortfall** /ʃɔːtfɔːl/ n déficit m.

**shorthand** /ʃɔːthænd/ n sténographie f; ~ **typist** sténodactylo f.

**short:** ~ **list** n liste f des candidats choisis. ~-**lived** adj de courte durée.

**shortly** /ʃɔːtlɪ/ adv bientôt.

**short:** ~-**sighted** adj myope. ~-**staffed** adj à court de personnel; ~ **story** nouvelle f. ~-**term** adj à court terme.

**shot** /ʃɒt/ →SHOOT. ● n (firing, attempt) coup m de feu; (person) tireur m; (bullet) balle f; (photograph) photo f; (injection) piqûre f; like a ~ sans hésiter. ~**gun** n fusil m de chasse.

**should** /ʃʊd/ v aux devoir; you ~ help me vous devriez m'aider; I ~ have stayed j'aurais dû rester; I ~ like to j'aimerais bien; if he ~ come s'il venait.

**shoulder** /ʃəʊldə(r)/ n épaule f. ● vt (responsibility) endosser; (burden) se charger de. ~ **bag** n sac m à bandoulière. ~ **blade** n omoplate f.

**shout** /ʃaʊt/ n cri m. ● vt/i crier (at après). □ ~ **sth out** lancer qch à haute voix.

**shove** /ʃʌv/ n give sth a ~ pousser qch. ● vt/i pousser; ~ **off!** 🗊 tire-toi! 🗊.

**shovel** /ʃʌvl/ n pelle f. ● vt (pt **shovelled**) pelleter.

**show** /ʃəʊ/ vt (pt **showed**; pp **shown**) montrer; (dial, needle) indiquer; (put on display) exposer; (film) donner; (conduct) conduire;

~ **sb in/out** faire entrer/sortir qn. ● **vi** (be visible) se voir. ● **n** (exhibition) exposition f; salon m; (Theat) spectacle m; (cinema) séance f; (of strength) démonstration f; **for** ~ pour l'effet; **on** ~ exposé. □ ~ **off** faire le fier/la fière; (exhibit) exhiber qch/qn; ~ **up** se voir; (appear) se montrer; ~ **sb up** ⊞ faire honte à qn.

**shower** /'ʃaʊə(r)/ n douche f; (of rain) averse f. ● **vt** ~ **with** couvrir de. ● **vi** se doucher.

**showing** /'ʃəʊɪŋ/ n performance f; (cinema) séance f.

**show-jumping** n concours m hippique.

**shown** /ʃəʊn/ ⇒**SHOW**.

**show:** ~**-off** n m'as-tu-vu mf inv ⊞. ~**room** n salle f d'exposition.

**shrank** /ʃræŋk/ ⇒**SHRINK**.

**shrapnel** /'ʃræpnl/ n éclats mpl d'obus.

**shred** /ʃred/ n lambeau m; (least amount: fig) parcelle f. ● **vt** (pt) **shredded** déchiqueter; (Culin) râper.

**shrewd** /ʃruːd/ adj (person) habile; (move) astucieux.

**shriek** /ʃriːk/ n hurlement m. ● **vt/i** hurler.

**shrill** /ʃrɪl/ adj (voice) perçant; (tone) strident.

**shrimp** /ʃrɪmp/ n crevette f.

**shrine** /ʃraɪn/ n (place) lieu m de pèlerinage.

**shrink** /ʃrɪŋk/ vt/i (pt **shrank**; pp **shrunk** rétrécir; (lessen) diminuer; ~ **from** reculer devant.

**shrivel** /'ʃrɪvl/ vt/i (pt **shrivelled**) (se) ratatiner.

**shroud** /ʃraʊd/ n linceul m. ● **vt** (veil) envelopper.

**Shrove Tuesday** n mardi m gras.

**shrub** /ʃrʌb/ n arbuste m.

**shrug** /ʃrʌg/ vt (pt) **shrugged** ~ one's shoulders hausser les épaules; ~ **sth off** ignorer qch.

**shrunk** /ʃrʌŋk/ ⇒**SHRINK**.

**shudder** /'ʃʌdə(r)/ vi frémir. ● **n** frémissement m.

**shuffle** /'ʃʌfl/ vt ( feet) traîner; (cards) battre. ● **vi** traîner les pieds.

**shun** /ʃʌn/ vt (pt **shunned**) fuir.

**shut** /ʃʌt/ vt (pt **shut**; pres p **shutting**) fermer. ● **vi** (door) se fermer; (shop) fermer. □ ~ **in** or **up** enfermer; ~ **up** ⊞ se taire; ~ **sb up** ⊞ faire taire qn.

**shutter** /'ʃʌtə(r)/ n volet m; (Photo) obturateur m.

**shuttle** /'ʃʌtl/ n (bus) navette f; ~ service service m de navette. ● **vi** faire la navette. ● **vt** transporter.

**shuttlecock** /'ʃʌtlkɒk/ n (badminton) volant m.

**shy** /ʃaɪ/ adj timide. ● **vi** ~ **away from** se tenir à l'écart de.

**sibling** /'sɪblɪŋ/ n frère/sœur m/f.

**sick** /sɪk/ adj malade; (humour) macabre; (mind) malsain; **be** ~ (vomit) vomir; **be** ~ **of** ⊞ en avoir assez or marre de ⊞; **feel** ~ avoir mal au cœur. ~**-leave** n congé m de maladie.

**sickly** /'sɪklɪ/ adj (-ier, -iest) (person) maladif; (taste, smell) écœurant.

**sickness** /'sɪknɪs/ n maladie f.

**sick-pay** n indemnité f de maladie.

**side** /saɪd/ n côté m; (of road, river) bord m; (of hill, body) flanc m; (Sport) équipe f; (TV ⊞) chaîne f; ~ **by** ~ côte à côte. ● adj latéral. ● **vi** ~ **with** se ranger du côté de. ~**board** n buffet m. ~**effect** n effet m secondaire. ~**light** n (Auto) feu m de position. ~**line** n activité f secondaire. ~**show** n attraction f. ~**step** vt (pt) -**stepped** éviter.

**~street** n rue f latérale. **~track** vt fourvoyer. **~ walk** n (US) trottoir m.

**sideways** /ˈsaɪdweɪz/ adj (look) de travers. ● adv (move) latéralement; (look at) de travers.

**siding** /ˈsaɪdɪŋ/ n voie f de garage.

**sidle** /ˈsaɪdl/ vi s'avancer furtivement (**up to** vers).

**siege** /siːdʒ/ n siège m.

**siesta** /sɪˈestə/ n sieste f.

**sieve** /sɪv/ n tamis m; (for liquids) passoire f. ● vt tamiser.

**sift** /sɪft/ vt tamiser. ● vi ~ **through** examiner.

**sigh** /saɪ/ n soupir m. ● vt/i soupirer.

**sight** /saɪt/ n vue f; (scene) spectacle m; (on gun) mire f; at or on ~ à vue; **catch** ~ **of** apercevoir; **in** ~ visible; **lose** ~ **of** perdre de vue. ● vt apercevoir.

**sightseeing** /ˈsaɪtsiːɪŋ/ n tourisme m.

**sign** /saɪn/ n signe m; (notice) panneau m. ● vt/i signer. □ ~ **on** (as unemployed) pointer au chômage; ~ **up** (s')engager.

**signal** /ˈsɪɡnl/ n signal m. ● vt (pt **signalled**) (gesture) faire signe (**that** que); (indicate) indiquer.

**signatory** /ˈsɪɡnətrɪ/ n signataire mf.

**signature** /ˈsɪɡnətʃə(r)/ n signature f; ~ **tune** indicatif m.

**significance** /sɪɡˈnɪfɪkəns/ n importance f; (meaning) signification f. **significant** adj important; (meaningful) significatif. **significantly** adv (much) sensiblement.

**signify** /ˈsɪɡnɪfaɪ/ vt signifier.

**signpost** /ˈsaɪnpəʊst/ n panneau m indicateur.

**silence** /ˈsaɪləns/ n silence m. ● vt faire taire.

**silent** /ˈsaɪlənt/ adj silencieux; (film) muet. **silently** adv silencieusement.

**silhouette** /sɪluːˈet/ n silhouette f. ● vt **be ~d against** se profiler contre.

**silicon** /ˈsɪlɪkən/ n silicium m; ~ **chip** puce f électronique.

**silk** /sɪlk/ n soie f.

**silly** /ˈsɪlɪ/ adj (**-ier, -iest**) bête.

**silver** /ˈsɪlvə(r)/ n argent m; (silverware) argenterie f. ● adj en argent.

**SIM card** /ˈsɪmkɑːd/ n carte f SIM.

**similar** /ˈsɪmɪlə(r)/ adj semblable (**to** à). **similarity** n ressemblance f. **similarly** adv de même.

**simile** /ˈsɪmɪlɪ/ n comparaison f.

**simmer** /ˈsɪmə(r)/ vt/i (soup) mijoter; (water) (laisser) frémir.

**simple** /ˈsɪmpl/ adj simple.

**simplicity** /sɪmˈplɪsətɪ/ n simplicité f.

**simplify** /ˈsɪmplɪfaɪ/ vt simplifier.

**simplistic** /sɪmˈplɪstɪk/ adj simpliste.

**simply** /ˈsɪmplɪ/ adv simplement; (absolutely) absolument.

**simulate** /ˈsɪmjʊleɪt/ vt simuler.

**simultaneous** /ˌsɪmlˈteɪnɪəs/ adj simultané.

**sin** /sɪn/ n péché m. ● vi (pt **sinned**) pécher.

---

**since** /sɪns/

● **preposition**

‣ depuis; **I haven't seen him ~ Monday** je ne l'ai pas vu depuis lundi; **I've been waiting ~ yesterday** j'attends depuis hier; **she had been living in Paris ~ 1985** elle habitait Paris depuis 1985.

● *conjunction*

····▸ (in time expressions) depuis que; ~ she's been working here depuis qu'elle travaille ici; ~ she left depuis qu'elle est partie or depuis son départ.

····▸ (because) comme; ~ he was ill, he couldn't go comme il était malade, il ne pouvait pas y aller.

● *adverb*

····▸ depuis; he hasn't been seen ~ on ne l'a pas vu depuis.

**sincere** /sɪnˈsɪə(r)/ *adj* sincère. **sincerely** *adv* sincèrement. **sincerity** *n* sincérité *f*.

**sinful** /ˈsɪnfl/ *adj* immoral; ~ man pécheur *m*.

**sing** /sɪŋ/ *vt/i* (*pt* sang; *pp* sung) chanter.

**singe** /sɪndʒ/ *vt* (*pres p* singeing) brûler légèrement; (with iron) roussir.

**singer** /ˈsɪŋə(r)/ *n* chanteur/ -euse *m/f*.

**single** /ˈsɪŋgl/ *adj* seul; (not double) simple; (unmarried) célibataire; (room, bed) pour une personne; (ticket) simple; **in ~ file** en file indienne. ● *n* (ticket) aller simple *m*; (record) 45 tours *m inv*; ~s (tennis) simple *m*. ● *vt* ~ **out** choisir. **~-handed** *adj* tout seul. **~-minded** *adj* tenace. ~ **parent** *n* parent *m* isolé.

**singular** /ˈsɪŋgjʊlə(r)/ *n* singulier *m*. ● *adj* (strange) singulier; (noun) au singulier.

**sinister** /ˈsɪnɪstə(r)/ *adj* sinistre.

**sink** /sɪŋk/ *vt* (*pt* sank; *pp* sunk) (boat) couler; (well) forer; (post) enfoncer. ● *vi* (boat) couler; (sun, level) baisser; (wall) s'effondrer. ● *n* (in kitchen) évier *m*; (wash-basin) lavabo *m*. □ ~ **in** (news) faire son chemin.

**sinner** /ˈsɪnə(r)/ *n* pécheur/ -eresse *m/f*.

**sip** /sɪp/ *n* petite gorgée *f*. ● *vt* (*pt* sipped) boire à petites gorgées.

**siphon** /ˈsaɪfn/ *n* siphon *m*. ● *vt* ~ **off** siphonner.

**sir** /sɜː(r)/ *n* Monsieur *m*; **Sir** (title) Sir *m*.

**siren** /ˈsaɪərən/ *n* sirène *f*.

**sirloin** /ˈsɜːlɔɪn/ *n* aloyau *m*.

**sister** /ˈsɪstə(r)/ *n* sœur *f*; (nurse) infirmière *f* en chef. **~-in-law** *n* (*pl* **~s-in-law**) belle-sœur *f*.

**sit** /sɪt/ *vt/i* (*pt* sat; *pres p* sitting) (s')asseoir; (committee) siéger; ~ (for) (exam) se présenter à; be ~ting être assis. □ ~ **around** ne rien faire; ~ **down** s'asseoir.

**site** /saɪt/ *n* emplacement *m*; (building) ~ chantier *m*. ● *vt* construire.

**sitting** /ˈsɪtɪŋ/ *n* séance *f*; (in restaurant) service *m*. **~-room** *n* salon *m*.

**situate** /ˈsɪtjʊeɪt/ *vt* situer; be ~d être situé. **situation** *n* situation *f*.

**six** /sɪks/ *adj* & *n* six (*m*).

**sixteen** /sɪkˈstiːn/ *adj* & *n* seize (*m*).

**sixth** /sɪksθ/ *adj* & *n* sixième (*mf*).

**sixty** /ˈsɪkstɪ/ *adj* & *n* soixante (*m*).

**size** /saɪz/ *n* dimension *f*; (of person, garment) taille *f*; (of shoes) pointure *f*; (of sugar) montant *m*; (extent) ampleur *f*. □ ~ **up** (person) se faire une opinion de; (situation) évaluer. **sizeable** *adj* assez grand.

**skate** /skeɪt/ *n* patin *m*; (fish) raie *f*. ● *vi* patiner.

**skateboard** /ˈskeɪtbɔːd/ *n* skateboard *m*, planche *f* à roulettes. ● *vi* faire du skateboard.

**skating** /'skeɪtɪd/ n patinage m.

**skeleton** /'skelɪtn/ n squelette m; ~ staff effectifs mpl minimums.

**sketch** /sketʃ/ n esquisse f; (hasty) croquis m; (Theat) sketch m. ● vt faire une esquisse or un croquis de. ● vi faire des esquisses.

**sketchy** /'sketʃɪ/ adj (-ier, -iest) (details) insuffisant; (memory) vague.

**skewer** /'skjuːə(r)/ n brochette f.

**ski** /skiː/ n ski m. ● adj de ski. ● vi (pt ski'd or skied; pres p skiing) skier; (go skiing) faire du ski.

**skid** /skɪd/ vi (pt skidded) déraper. ● n dérapage m.

**skier** /'skiːə(r)/ n skieur/-euse m/f.

**skiing** /'skiːɪŋ/ n ski m.

**ski jump** n saut m à ski.

**skilful** /'skɪlfl/ adj habile.

**ski lift** n remontée f mécanique.

**skill** /skɪl/ n habileté f; (craft) compétence f; ~s connaissances fpl.

**skilled** adj (worker) qualifié; (talented) consommé.

**skim** /skɪm/ vt (pt skimmed) écumer; (milk) écrémer; (pass over) effleurer. ● vi ~ through parcourir.

**skimpy** /'skɪmpɪ/ adj (clothes) étriqué.

**skin** /skɪn/ n peau f. ● vt (pt skinned) (animal) écorcher; (fruit) éplucher.

**skinny** /'skɪnɪ/ adj (-ier, -iest) ▣ maigre.

**skip** /skɪp/ vi (pt skipped) sautiller; (with rope) sauter à la corde. ● vt (page, class) sauter. ● n petit saut m; (container) benne f.

**skipper** /'skɪpə(r)/ n capitaine m.

**skirmish** /'skɜːmɪʃ/ n escarmouche f.

**skirt** /skɜːt/ n jupe f. ● vt contourner. **skirting-board** n plinthe f.

**skittle** /'skɪtl/ n quille f.

**skull** /skʌl/ n crâne m.

**sky** /skaɪ/ n ciel m. ~-blue adj & n bleu ciel m inv. ~ marshal n garde m armé (à bord d'un avion.) ~scraper n gratte-ciel m inv.

**slab** /slæb/ n (of stone) dalle f.

**slack** /slæk/ adj (not tight) détendu; (person) négligent; (period) creux. ● n (in rope) mou m. ● vi se relâcher.

**slacken** /'slækən/ vt (rope) donner du mou à; (grip) relâcher; (pace) réduire. ● vi (grip, rope) se relâcher; (activity) ralentir; (rain) se calmer.

**slam** /slæm/ vt/i (door) claquer; (throw) flanquer; (criticize ▣) critiquer. ● n (noise) claquement m.

**slander** /'slɑːndə(r)/ n (offence) diffamation f; (statement) calomnie f. ● vt calomnier; (Jur) diffamer. **slanderous** adj diffamatoire.

**slang** /slæŋ/ n argot m.

**slant** /slɑːnt/ vt/i (faire) pencher; (news) présenter sous un certain jour. ● n inclinaison f; (bias) angle m. **slanted** adj (biased) orienté; (sloping) en pente.

**slap** /slæp/ vt (pt slapped) (strike) donner une tape à; (face) gifler; (put) flanquer ▣. ● n claque f; (on face) gifle f. ● adv tout droit.

**slapdash** /'slæpdæʃ/ adj (person) brouillon ▣; (work) bâclé ▣.

**slash** /slæʃ/ vt (picture, tyre) taillader; (throat) balafrer; (throat) couper; (fig) réduire (radicalement). ● n lacération f.

**slat** /slæt/ n (in blind) lamelle f; (on bed) latte f.

**slate** /sleɪt/ n ardoise f. ● vt ▣ taper sur ▣.

**slaughter** /'slɔːtə(r)/ vt massacrer; (animal) abattre. ● n massacre m; abattage m.

**slave** /sleɪv/ n esclave mf. ● vi trimer 🔲. **slavery** n esclavage m.

**sleazy** /'sliːzɪ/ adj (**-ier, -iest**) 🔲 (story) scabreux; (club) louche.

**sledge** /sledʒ/ n luge f (horse-drawn) traîneau m.

**sleek** /sliːk/ adj (hair) lisse, brillant; (shape) élégant.

**sleep** /sliːp/ n sommeil m; go to ∼ s'endormir. ● vi (pt **slept**) dormir; (spend the night) coucher; ∼ **in** faire la grasse matinée. ● vt loger.

**sleeper** /'sliːpə(r)/ n (Rail) (berth) couchette f; (on track) traverse f.

**sleeping-bag** n sac m de couchage.

**sleeping-pill** n somnifère m.

**sleep-walker** n somnambule mf.

**sleepy** /'sliːpɪ/ adj (**-ier, -iest**) somnolent; be ∼ avoir sommeil.

**sleet** /sliːt/ n neige f fondue.

**sleeve** /sliːv/ n manche f; (of record) pochette f; up one's ∼ en réserve.

**sleigh** /sleɪ/ n traîneau m.

**slender** /'slendə(r)/ adj (person) mince; (majority) faible.

**slept** /slept/ ⇒SLEEP.

**slice** /slaɪs/ n tranche f. ● vt couper (en tranches).

**slick** /slɪk/ adj (adept) habile; (insincere) roublard 🔲. ● n (oil) ∼ marée f noire.

**slide** /slaɪd/ vt/i (pt **slid**) glisser; ∼ **into** (go silently) se glisser dans. ● n glissade f; (fall: fig) baisse f; (in playground) toboggan m; (for hair) barrette f; (Photo) diapositive f.

**sliding** /'slaɪdɪŋ/ adj (door) coulissant; ∼ **scale** échelle f mobile.

**slight** /slaɪt/ adj petit, léger; (slender) mince; (frail) frêle. ● vt (insult) offenser. ● n affront m. **slightest** adj moindre. **slightly** adv légèrement.

**slim** /slɪm/ adj (**slimmer, slimmest**) mince. ● vi (pt **slimmed**) maigrir.

**slime** /slaɪm/ n dépôt m gluant; (on riverbed) vase f. **slimy** adj visqueux; (fig) servile.

**sling** /slɪŋ/ n (weapon, toy) fronde f; (bandage) écharpe f. ● vt (pt **slung**) jeter, lancer.

**slip** /slɪp/ vt/i (pt **slipped**) glisser; ∼**ped disc** hernie f discale; ∼ sb's mind échapper à qn. ● n (mistake) erreur f; (petticoat) combinaison f; (paper) bout m de papier; ∼ **of the tongue** lapsus m; ∼ **away** s'esquiver; ☐ **into** (go) se glisser dans; (clothes) mettre; ☐ **up** 🔲 faire une gaffe 🔲.

**slipper** /'slɪpə(r)/ n pantoufle f.

**slippery** /'slɪpərɪ/ adj glissant.

**slip road** n bretelle f.

**slit** /slɪt/ n fente f. ● vt (pt **slit**; pres p **slitting**) déchirer; ∼ **sth open** ouvrir qch; ∼ **sb's throat** égorger qn.

**slither** /'slɪðə(r)/ vi glisser.

**sliver** /'slɪvə(r)/ n (of glass) éclat m; (of soap) reste m.

**slobber** /'slɒbə(r)/ vi baver.

**slog** /slɒg/ 🔲 vt (pt **slogged**) (hit) frapper dur; (work) bosser 🔲. ● n (work) travail m dur.

**slogan** /'sləʊgən/ n slogan m.

**slope** /sləʊp/ vi être en pente; (handwriting) pencher. ● n pente f; (of mountain) flanc m.

**sloppy** /'slɒpɪ/ adj (**-ier, -iest**) (food) liquide; (work) négligé; (person) négligent.

**slosh** /slɒʃ/ vt 🔲 répandre; (hit 🔲) frapper. ● vi clapoter.

**slot** /slɒt/ n fente f. ● vt/i (pt **slotted**) (s')insérer.

**sloth** /sləʊθ/ n paresse f.

**slot-machine** n distributeur m automatique; (for gambling) machine f à sous.

**slouch** /slaʊtʃ/ vi être avachi.

**Slovakia** /sləˈvækɪə/ n Slovaquie f.

**Slovenia** /sləˈviːnɪə/ n Slovénie f.

**slovenly** /ˈslʌvnlɪ/ adj débraillé.

**slow** /sləʊ/ adj lent; be ~ (clock) retarder; in ~ motion au ralenti. ● adv lentement. ● vt/i ralentir. **slowly** adv lentement. **slowness** n lenteur f.

**sludge** /slʌdʒ/ n vase f.

**slug** /slʌg/ n (mollusc) limace f; (bullet 🗵) balle f; (blow 🗵) coup m.

**sluggish** /ˈslʌgɪʃ/ adj (person) léthargique; (circulation) lent.

**slum** /slʌm/ n taudis m.

**slump** /slʌmp/ n (Econ) effondrement m; (in support) baisse f. ● vi (demand, trade) chuter; (economy) s'effondrer; (person) s'affaler.

**slung** slʌŋ/ ⇒SLING.

**slur** /slɜː(r)/ vt/i (pt slurred) (words) mal articuler. ● n calomnie f (on sur).

**slush** /slʌʃ/ n (snow) neige f fondue. ~ fund n caisse f noire.

**sly** /slaɪ/ adj (crafty) rusé; (secretive) sournois. ● n on the ~ en cachette.

**smack** /smæk/ n tape f; (on face) gifle f. ● vt donner une tape à; (face) gifler. ● vi ~ of sth sentir qch. ● adv 🗵 tout droit.

**small** /smɔːl/ adj petit. ● n ~ of the back creux m des reins. ● adv (cut) menu. ~ ad n petite annonce f. ~ business n petite entreprise f. ~ change n petite monnaie f. ~-pox n variole f. ~ print n petits caractères mpl. ~ talk n banalités fpl.

**smart** /smɑːt/ adj élégant; (clever)

malin, habile; (restaurant) chic inv; (Comput) intelligent. ● vi (wound) brûler.

**smarten** /ˈsmɑːtn/ vt/i ~ (up) embellir; ~ (oneself) up s'arranger.

**smash** /smæʃ/ vt/i (se) briser, (se) fracasser; (opponent, record) pulvériser. ● n (noise) fracas m; (blow) coup m; (car crash) collision f; (hit record 🗵) tube m. 🗵

**smashing** /ˈsmæʃɪŋ/ adj 🗵 épatant.

**SME** abbr (small and medium enterprises) PME.

**smear** /smɪə(r)/ vt (stain) tacher; (coat) enduire; (discredit: fig) diffamer. ● n tache f; (effort to discredit) propos m diffamatoire; ~ (test) frottis m.

**smell** /smel/ n odeur f; (sense) odorat m. ● vt/i (pt smelt or smelled) sentir; ~ of sentir. **smelly** adj qui sent mauvais.

**smelt** /smelt/ ⇒SMELL.

**smile** /smaɪl/ n sourire m. ● vi sourire.

**smiley** /ˈsmaɪlɪ/ n (Internet) binette f.

**smirk** /smɜːk/ n petit sourire m satisfait.

**smitten** /ˈsmɪtn/ adj (in love) fou d'amour.

**smog** /smɒg/ n smog m.

**smoke** /sməʊk/ n fumée f; have a ~ fumer. ● vt/i fumer. **smoked** adj fumé. **smokeless** adj (fuel) non polluant. **smoker** n fumeur/-euse m/f. **smoky** adj (air) enfumé.

**smooth** /smuːð/ adj (surface) lisse; (movement) aisé; (manners) onctueux; (flight) sans heurts. ● vt lisser; (process) faciliter.

**smoothly** /ˈsmuːðlɪ/ adv (move, flow) doucement; (brake, start) en douceur; go ~ marcher bien.

**smother** /ˈsmʌðə(r)/ vt (stifle) étouffer; (cover) couvrir.

**smoulder** /ˈsmǝʊldǝ(r)/ vi (lit) se consumer; (fig) couver.

**smudge** /smʌdʒ/ n trace f. ● vt/i (ink) (s')étaler.

**smug** /smʌg/ adj (**smugger**, **smuggest**) suffisant.

**smuggle** /ˈsmʌgl/ vt passer (en contrebande). **smuggler** n contrebandier/-ière m/f. **smuggling** n contrebande f.

**smutty** /ˈsmʌtɪ/ adj grivois.

**snack** /snæk/ n casse-croûte m inv.

**snag** /snæg/ n inconvénient m; (in cloth) accroc m.

**snail** /sneɪl/ n escargot m.

**snake** /sneɪk/ n serpent m.

**snap** /snæp/ vt/i (pt **snapped**) (whip, fingers) (faire) claquer; (break) (se) casser net; (say) dire sèchement. ● n claquement m; (Photo) photo f. ● adj soudain. □ ～ **up** (buy) sauter sur.

**snapshot** /ˈsnæpʃɒt/ n photo f.

**snare** /sneǝ(r)/ n piège m.

**snarl** /snɑːl/ vi gronder (en montrant les dents). ● n grondement m. **～-up** n embouteillage m.

**snatch** /snætʃ/ vt (grab) attraper; (steal) voler; (opportunity) saisir; ～ sth from sb arracher qch à qn. ● n (theft) vol m; (short part) fragment m.

**sneak** /sniːk/ vi aller furtivement. ● n 🔟 rapporteur/-euse m/f.

**sneer** /snɪǝ(r)/ n sourire m méprisant. ● vi sourire avec mépris.

**sneeze** /sniːz/ n éternuement m. ● vi éternuer.

**snide** /snaɪd/ adj narquois.

**sniff** /snɪf/ vt/i renifler. ● n reniflement m.

**snigger** /ˈsnɪgǝ(r)/ n ricanement m. ● vi ricaner.

**snip** /snɪp/ vt (pt **snipped**) couper.

**sniper** /ˈsnaɪpǝ(r)/ n tireur m embusqué.

**snippet** /ˈsnɪpɪt/ n bribe f.

**snivel** /ˈsnɪvl/ vi (pt **snivelled**) pleurnicher.

**snob** /snɒb/ n snob mf.

**snooker** /ˈsnuːkǝ(r)/ n snooker m.

**snoop** /snuːp/ vi 🔟 fourrer son nez partout.

**snooty** /ˈsnuːtɪ/ adj (**-ier**, **-iest**) 🔟 snob inv, hautain.

**snooze** /snuːz/ n petit somme m. ● vi sommeiller.

**snore** /snɔː(r)/ n ronflement m. ● vi ronfler.

**snorkel** /ˈsnɔːkl/ n tuba m.

**snort** /snɔːt/ n grognement m. ● vi (person) grogner; (horse) s'ébrouer.

**snout** /snaʊt/ n museau m.

**snow** /snǝʊ/ n neige f. ● vi neiger; be ～ed under with être submergé m.

**snowball** /ˈsnǝʊbɔːl/ n boule f de neige. ● vi faire boule de neige.

**snow:** ～**board** n snowboard m. ～**boarding** n surf m des neiges. ～**bound** adj bloqué par la neige. ～**drift** n congère f. ～**drop** n perceneige m or f inv. ～**flake** n flocon m de neige. ～**man** n (pl **-men**) bonhomme m de neige. ～**plough** n chasse-neige m inv.

**snub** /snʌb/ vt (pt **snubbed**) rembarrer. ● n rebuffade f.

**snuffle** /ˈsnʌfl/ vi renifler.

**snug** /snʌg/ adj (**snugger**, **snuggest**) (cosy) confortable; (tight) bien ajusté.

**snuggle** /ˈsnʌgl/ vi se pelotonner.

**so** /sǝʊ/ adv si, tellement; (thus) ainsi; ～ **good as** aussi bon que; **that is** ～ c'est ça; **I think** ～ je pense que oui; **five or** ～ environ cinq; ～ **as to** de ma-

nière à; ~ far jusqu'ici; ~ long! 🔲
à bientôt!; ~ many, ~ much tant
(de); ~ that pour que. ● *conj* donc,
alors.

**soak** /səʊk/ *vt/i* (faire) tremper (in
dans). □ ~ **in** pénétrer; ~ **up** absorber. **soaking** *adj* trempé.

**soap** /səʊp/ *n* savon *m*. ● *vt* savonner. ~ **opera** *n* feuilleton *m*. ~
**powder** *n* lessive *f*.

**soar** /sɔː(r)/ *vi* monter (en flèche).

**sob** /sɒb/ *n* sanglot *m*. ● *vi* (*pt*
**sobbed**) sangloter.

**sober** /ˈsəʊbə(r)/ *adj* qui n'a pas bu
d'alcool; (serious) sérieux. ● *vi* ~
**up** dessoûler.

**soccer** /ˈsɒkə(r)/ *n* football *m*.

**sociable** /ˈsəʊʃəbl/ *adj* sociable.

**social** /ˈsəʊʃl/ *adj* social. ● *n* réunion *f* (amicale), fête *f*.

**socialism** /ˈsəʊʃəlɪzəm/ *n* socialisme *m*. **socialist** *adj* & *n* socialiste (*mf*).

**socialize** /ˈsəʊʃəlaɪz/ *vi* se mêler
aux autres; ~ **with** fréquenter.

**socially** /ˈsəʊʃəlɪ/ *adv* socialement;
(meet) en société.

**social:** ~ **security** *n* aide *f* sociale.
~ **worker** *n* travailleur/-euse *m/f*
social/-e.

**society** /səˈsaɪətɪ/ *n* société *f*.

**sociological** /səʊsɪəˈlɒdʒɪkl/ *adj*
sociologique. **sociologist** *n* sociolo-
gue *mf*. **sociology** *n* sociologie *f*.

**sock** /sɒk/ *n* chaussette *f*. ● *vt* (hit
🔲) flanquer un coup (de poing) à.

**socket** /ˈsɒkɪt/ *n* (for lamp) douille
*f*; (Electr) prise *f* (de courant); (of
eye) orbite *f*.

**soda** /ˈsəʊdə/ *n* soude *f*; ~(-water)
eau *f* de Seltz.

**sodden** /ˈsɒdn/ *adj* détrempé.

**sofa** /ˈsəʊfə/ *n* canapé *m*. ~ **bed** *n*
canapé-lit *m*.

**soft** /sɒft/ *adj* (gentle, lenient) doux;
(not hard) doux, mou; (heart, wood)
tendre; (silly) ramolli. ~ **drink** *n*
boisson *f* non alcoolisée.

**soften** /ˈsɒfn/ *vt/i* (se) ramollir;
(tone down, lessen) (s')adoucir.

**soft spot** *n* to have a ~ **for sb**
avoir un faible pour qn.

**software** /ˈsɒftweə(r)/ *n* logiciel *m*.

**soggy** /ˈsɒgɪ/ *adj* (-ier, -iest)
(ground) détrempé; (food) ramolli.

**soil** /sɔɪl/ *n* sol *m*, terre *f*. ● *vt/i* (se)
salir.

**sold** /səʊld/ →SELL. ● *adj* ~ **out**
épuisé.

**solder** /ˈsəʊldə(r)/ *n* soudure *f*. ● *vt*
souder.

**soldier** /ˈsəʊldʒə(r)/ *n* soldat *m*.
● *vi* ~ **on** 🔲 persévérer.

**sole** /səʊl/ *n* (of foot) plante *f*; (of
shoe) semelle *f*; (fish) sole *f*. ● *adj*
unique, seul. **solely** *adv* uniquement.

**solemn** /ˈsɒləm/ *adj* solennel.

**solicitor** /səˈlɪsɪtə(r)/ *n* notaire *m*;
(for court and police work) ≈
avocat/-e *m/f*.

**solid** /ˈsɒlɪd/ *adj* solide; (not hollow)
plein; (gold) massif; (mass) compact; (meal) substantiel. ● *n* solide
*m*; ~s (food) aliments *mpl* solides.

**solidarity** /sɒlɪˈdærətɪ/ *n* solidarité *f*.

**solidify** /səˈlɪdɪfaɪ/ *vt/i* (se) solidifier.

**solitary** /ˈsɒlɪtrɪ/ *adj* (alone) solitaire; (only) seul.

**solo** /ˈsəʊləʊ/ *n* solo *m*. ● *adj* (Mus)
solo *inv*; (flight) en solitaire.

**soluble** /ˈsɒljʊbl/ *adj* soluble.

**solution** /səˈluːʃn/ *n* solution *f*.

**solve** /sɒlv/ *vt* résoudre.

**solvent** /ˈsɒlvənt/ *adj* (Comm)

solvable. ● n (dis)solvant m.

**some** /sʌm, səm/

● *determiner*

••••▸ (unspecified amount) du/de l'/de la/des; **I have to buy ~ bread** je dois acheter du pain; **have ~ water** prenez de l'eau; **~ sweets** des bonbons.

••••▸ (certain) certains/certaines; **~ people say that** certains disent que.

••••▸ (unknown) un/une; **~ man came to the house** un homme est venu à la maison.

••••▸ (considerable amount) **we stayed there for ~ time** nous sommes restés là assez longtemps; **it will take ~ doing** ça ne va pas être facile à faire.

➡ In front of a plural adjective *des* changes to *de*: **some pretty dresses** *de jolies robes*.

● *pronoun*

••••▸ en; **he wants ~** il en veut; **have ~** reprenez-en.

••••▸ (certain) certains/certaines; **~ are expensive** certains sont chers.

● *adverb*

••••▸ environ; **~ 20 people** environ 20 personnes.

**somebody** /'sʌmbədɪ/ *pron* quelqu'un. ● n **be a ~** être quelqu'un.

**somehow** /'sʌmhaʊ/ *adv* d'une manière ou d'une autre; (for some reason) je ne sais pas pourquoi.

**someone** /'sʌmwʌn/ *pron* & n →SOMEBODY.

**someplace** /'sʌmpleɪs/ *adv* (US)

→SOMEWHERE.

**somersault** /'sʌməsɔːlt/ n roulade f. ● vi faire une roulade.

**something** /'sʌmθɪŋ/ *pron* & n quelque chose; **~ good** quelque chose de bon; **~ like** un peu comme.

**sometime** /'sʌmtaɪm/ *adv* un jour; **~ in June** en juin. ● *adj* (former) ancien.

**sometimes** /'sʌmtaɪmz/ *adv* quelquefois, parfois.

**somewhat** /'sʌmwɒt/ *adv* quelque peu, un peu.

**somewhere** /'sʌmweə(r)/ *adv* quelque part.

**son** /sʌn/ n fils m.

**song** /sɒŋ/ n chanson f; (of bird) chant m.

**son-in-law** /'sʌnɪnlɔː/ n (*pl* **sons-in-law**) gendre m.

**soon** /suːn/ *adv* bientôt; (early) tôt; **I would ~er stay** j'aimerais mieux rester; **~ after** peu après; **~er or later** tôt ou tard.

**soot** /sʊt/ n suie f.

**soothe** /suːð/ vt calmer.

**sophisticated** /sə'fɪstɪkeɪtɪd/ *adj* raffiné; (machine) sophistiqué.

**sopping** /'sɒpɪŋ/ *adj* trempé.

**soppy** /'sɒpɪ/ *adj* (**-ier, -iest**) 🆃 sentimental.

**sorcerer** /'sɔːsərə(r)/ n sorcier m.

**sordid** /'sɔːdɪd/ *adj* sordide.

**sore** /sɔː(r)/ *adj* douloureux; (vexed) en rogne (**at, with** contre). ● n plaie f.

**sorely** /'sɔːlɪ/ *adv* fortement.

**sorrow** /'sɒrəʊ/ n chagrin m.

**sorry** /'sɒrɪ/ *adj* (**-ier, -iest**) (regretful) désolé (**to** de; **that** que); (wretched) triste; **feel ~ for** plaindre; **~!** pardon!

**sort** /sɔːt/ n genre m, sorte f, espèce

*f;* (person ⚠) type *m;* what ∼ of? quel genre d'?; **be out of** ∼s ne pas être dans son assiette. ● *vt* ∼ **(out)** (classify) trier; ∼ **out** (tidy) ranger; (arrange) arranger; (problem) régler.

**so-so** /sәʊ'sәʊ/ adj & adv comme ci comme ça.

**sought** /sɔ:t/ ⇒SEEK.

**soul** /sәʊl/ *n* âme *f.*

**sound** /saʊnd/ *n* son *m,* bruit *m.* ● adj solide; (healthy) sain; (sensible) sensé. ● *vt/i* sonner; (seem) sembler (as if que); (test) sonder; ∼ **out** sonder; ∼ **a horn** klaxonner; ∼ **like** sembler être. ∼ **asleep** adj profondément endormi. ∼ **barrier** *n* mur *m* du son.

**soundly** /'saʊndlɪ/ adv (sleep) à poings fermés; (built) solidement.

**sound-proof** /'saʊndpru:f/ adj insonorisé. ● *vt* insonoriser.

**sound-track** /'saʊndtræk/ *n* bande *f* sonore.

**soup** /su:p/ *n* soupe *f,* potage *m.*

**sour** /'saʊә(r)/ adj aigre. ● *vt/i* (s')aigrir.

**source** /sɔ:s/ *n* source *f.*

**south** /saʊθ/ *n* sud *m.* ● adj sud inv, du sud. ● adv vers le sud.

**South Africa** *n* Afrique *f* du Sud.

**South America** *n* Amérique *f* du Sud.

**south-east** *n* sud-est *m.*

**southern** /'sʌðәn/ adj du sud. **southerner** *n* habitant/-e *m/f* du sud.

**southward** /'saʊθwәd/ adj (side) sud inv; (journey) vers le sud.

**south-west** *n* sud-ouest *m.*

**souvenir** /su:vә'nɪә(r)/ *n* souvenir *m.*

**sovereign** /'sɒvrɪn/ *n & adj* souverain/-e (*m/f*).

**sow**¹ /sәʊ/ *vt* (*pt* sowed or sown) (seed) semer; (land) ensemencer.

**sow**² /saʊ/ *n* (pig) truie *f.*

**soya** /'sɔɪә/ *n* soja *m.* ∼ **sauce** *n* sauce *f* soja.

**spa** /spɑ:/ *n* station *f* thermale.

**space** /speɪs/ *n* espace *m;* (room) place *f;* (period) période *f.* ● adj (research) spatial. ● *n* ∼ **(out)** espacer. ∼**craft** *n* inv, ∼**ship** *n* engin *m* spatial. ∼**suit** *n* combinaison *f* spatiale.

**spacious** /'speɪʃәs/ adj spacieux.

**spade** /speɪd/ *n* (for garden) bêche *f;* (child's) pelle *f;* (cards) pique *m.* ∼**work** *n* (fig) travail *m* préparatoire.

**spaghetti** /spә'getɪ/ *n* spaghetti *mpl.*

**spam** /spæm/ *n* (Comput) multipostage *m* abusif.

**Spain** /speɪn/ *n* Espagne *f.*

**span** /spæn/ *n* (of arch) portée *f;* (of wings) envergure *f;* (of time) durée *f.* ● *vt* (*pt* spanned) enjamber; (in time) embrasser.

**Spaniard** /'spænjәd/ *n* Espagnol/ -e *m/f.*

**spaniel** /'spænjәl/ *n* épagneul *m.*

**Spanish** /'spænɪʃ/ adj espagnol. ● *n* (Ling) espagnol *m.*

**spank** /spæŋk/ *vt* donner une fessée à.

**spanner** /'spænә(r)/ *n* (tool) clé *f* (plate); (adjustable) clé *f* à molette.

**spare** /speә(r)/ *vt* (treat leniently) épargner; (do without) se passer de; (afford to give) donner, accorder. ● adj en réserve; (surplus) de trop; (tyre, shoes) de rechange; (room, bed) d'ami; **are there any** ∼ **tickets?** y a-t-il encore des places? ● *n* ∼ **(part)** pièce *f* de rechange. ∼ **time** *n* loisirs *mpl.*

**sparing** /ˈspeərɪŋ/ adj frugal. **sparingly** adv en petite quantité.

**spark** /spɑːk/ n étincelle f. ● vt ~ off (initiate) provoquer.

**sparkle** /ˈspɑːkl/ vi étinceler. ● n étincellement m. **sparkling** adj (wine) mousseux; (eyes) brillant.

**spark-plug** n bougie f.

**sparrow** /ˈspærəʊ/ n moineau m.

**sparse** /spɑːs/ adj clairsemé. **sparsely** adv (furnished) peu.

**spasm** /ˈspæzəm/ n (of muscle) spasme m; (of coughing, anger) accès m.

**spat** /spæt/ ⇒SPIT.

**spate** /speɪt/ n a ~ of (letters) une avalanche de.

**spatter** /ˈspætə(r)/ vt éclabousser (with de).

**spawn** /spɔːn/ n frai m, œufs mpl. ● vt pondre. ● vi frayer.

**speak** /spiːk/ vi (pt **spoke**; pp **spoken**) parler. ● vt (say) dire; (language) parler. □ ~ up parler plus fort.

**speaker** /ˈspiːkə(r)/ n (in public) orateur m; (Pol) président m; (loudspeaker) baffle m; be a French/a good ~ parler français/bien.

**spear** /spɪə(r)/ n lance f.

**spearmint** /ˈspɪəmɪnt/ n menthe f verte.

**special** /ˈspeʃl/ adj spécial; (exceptional) exceptionnel.

**specialist** /ˈspeʃəlɪst/ n spécialiste mf.

**speciality**, **specialty** /speʃrˈælətɪ/ n spécialité f.

**specialize** /ˈspeʃəlaɪz/ vi se spécialiser (in en).

**specially** /ˈspeʃəlɪ/ adv spécialement.

**species** /ˈspiːʃiːz/ n inv espèce f.

**specific** /spəˈsɪfɪk/ adj précis, explicite.

**specification** /spesɪfɪˈkeɪʃn/ n (of design) spécification f; (of car equipment) caractéristiques fpl. **specify** vt spécifier.

**specimen** /ˈspesɪmən/ n spécimen m, échantillon m.

**speck** /spek/ n (stain) (petite) tache f; (particle) grain m.

**specs** /speks/ npl 🔲 lunettes fpl.

**spectacle** /ˈspektəkl/ n spectacle m. **spectacles** n lunettes fpl. **spectacular** adj spectaculaire.

**spectator** /spekˈteɪtə(r)/ n spectateur -trice m/f.

**spectrum** /ˈspektrəm/ n (pl **-tra**) spectre m; (of ideas) gamme f.

**speculate** /ˈspekjʊleɪt/ vi s'interroger (about sur); (Comm) spéculer. **speculation** n conjectures fpl; (Comm) spéculation f. **speculator** n spéculateur -trice m/f.

**speech** /spiːtʃ/ n (faculty) parole f; (diction) élocution f; (dialect) langage m; (address) discours m. **speechless** adj muet (with de).

**speed** /spiːd/ n (of movement) vitesse f; (swiftness) rapidité f. **speed camera** n radar m. **speed dating⊘** n rencontres fpl rapides, speed dating m. ● vi (pt **sped**) (drive too fast) aller trop vite; (pt **speeded**) (drive too fast) aller trop vite. □ ~ up accélérer; (of pace) s'accélérer.

**speedboat** /ˈspiːdbəʊt/ n vedette f.

**speeding** /ˈspiːdɪŋ/ n excès m de vitesse.

**speed limit** n limitation f de vitesse.

**speedometer** /spɪˈdɒmɪtə(r)/ n compteur m (de vitesse).

**spell** /spel/ n (magic) charme m, sortilège m; (curse) sort m; (of time) (courte) période f. ● vt/i (pt **spelled**

or **spelt**) écrire; (mean) signifier; ~
out épeler; (explain) expliquer.
**~checker** n correcteur m orthogra-
phique.

**spelling** /'spelɪŋ/ n orthographe f.
● adj (mistake) d'orthographe.

**spend** /spend/ vt (pt **spent**)
(money) dépenser (on pour); (time,
holiday) passer; (energy) consacrer
(on à). ● vi dépenser.

**spent** /spent/ ➡**SPEND**. ● adj
(used) utilisé; (person) épuisé.

**sperm** /spɜːm/ n (pl **sperms** or
**sperm**) sperme m.

**sphere** /sfɪə(r)/ n sphère f.

**spice** /spaɪs/ n épice f; (fig) piquant m.

**spick-and-span** adj impeccable.

**spicy** /'spaɪsɪ/ adj épicé; piquant.

**spider** /'spaɪdə(r)/ n araignée f.

**spike** /spaɪk/ n pointe f.

**spill** /spɪl/ vt (pt **spilled** or **spilt**)
renverser, répandre. ● vi se répan-
dre; ~ over déborder.

**spin** /spɪn/ vt/i (pt **spun**; pres p
**spinning**) (wool, web) filer; (turn)
(faire) tourner; (story) débiter; ~
out faire durer. ● n (movement, excursion) tour m.

**spinach** /'spɪnɪdʒ/ n épinards mpl.

**spinal** /'spaɪnl/ adj vertébral. ~
**cord** n moelle f épinière.

**spin-drier** n essoreuse f.

**spine** /spaɪn/ n colonne f vertébrale; (prickle) piquant m.

**spin-off** /'spɪnɒf/ n avantage m accessoire;
(by-product) dérivé m.

**spinster** /'spɪnstə(r)/ n célibataire
f; (pej) vieille fille f.

**spiral** /'spaɪərəl/ adj en spirale;
(staircase) en colimaçon. ● n spirale
f. ● vi (pt **spiralled**) (prices) monter
(en flèche).

**spire** /'spaɪə(r)/ n flèche f.

**spirit** /'spɪrɪt/ n esprit m; (boldness)
courage m; ~s (morale) moral m;
(drink) spiritueux mpl. ● vt ~ away
faire disparaître. **spirited** adj fougueux. **~-level** n niveau m à bulle.

**spiritual** /'spɪrɪtʃʊəl/ adj spirituel.

**spit** /spɪt/ vt/i (pt **spat** or **spit**; pres
p **spitting**) cracher; (of rain) crachi-
ner; ~ out cracher; the ~ting
image of le portrait craché ou vivant de. ● n crachat s m(pl); (for
meat) broche f.

**spite** /spaɪt/ n rancune f; in ~ of
malgré. ● vt contrarier.

**splash** /splæʃ/ vt éclabousser. ● vi
faire des éclaboussures; ~ (about)
patauger. ● n (act, mark) éclabous-
sure f; (sound) plouf m; (of colour)
tache f.

**spleen** /spliːn/ n (Anat) rate f.

**splendid** /'splendɪd/ adj magnifique, splendide.

**splint** /splɪnt/ n (Med) attelle f.

**splinter** /'splɪntə(r)/ n éclat m; (in
finger) écharde f. ~ **group** n
groupe m dissident.

**split** /splɪt/ vt/i (pt **split**; pres p
**splitting**) (se) fendre; (tear) (se)
déchirer; (divide) (se) diviser;
(share) partager; ~ **one's sides** se
tordre (de rire). ● n fente f; déchirure f; (share ▯) part f, partage m;
(quarrel) rupture f; (Pol) scission f
□ ~ **up** (couple) rompre. ~ **second**
n fraction f de seconde.

**splutter** /'splʌtə(r)/ vi cracher;
(stammer) bafouiller; (engine)
tousser.

**spoil** /spɔɪl/ vt (pt **spoilt** or
**spoiled**) (pamper) gâter; (ruin) abîmer; (mar) gâcher, gâter. ● n ~(s)
butin m. ~**-sport** n trouble-fête
mf inv.

**spoke**[1] /spəʊk/ n rayon m.

**spoke**[2], **spoken** ➡**SPEAK**.

# spokesman | sprout

**spokesman** /ˈspəʊksmən/ n (pl **-men**) porteparole m inv.

**sponge** /spʌndʒ/ n éponge f. ● vt éponger. ● vi ~ on vivre aux crochets de. ~**bag** n trousse f de toilette. ~**cake** n génoise f.

**sponsor** /ˈspɒnsə(r)/ n (of concert) parrain m, sponsor m; (surety) garant m; (for membership) parrain m, marraine f; (member) parrainer, sponsoriser; (member) parrainer. **sponsorship** n patronage m; parrainage m.

**spontaneous** /spɒnˈteɪnɪəs/ adj spontané.

**spoof** /spuːf/ n [T] parodie f.

**spoon** /spuːn/ n cuiller f, cuillère f.

**spoonful** /ˈspuːnfʊl/ n (pl ~s) cuillerée f.

**sport** /spɔːt/ n sport m; (good) ~ (person [T]) chic type m; ~ car/coat voiture/veste f de sport. ● vt (display) exhiber, arborer.

**sporting** /ˈspɔːtɪŋ/ adj sportif; a ~ chance une assez bonne chance.

**sportsman** /ˈspɔːtsmən/ n (pl **-men**) sportif m.

**sporty** /ˈspɔːtɪ/ adj [T] sportif.

**spot** /spɒt/ n (mark, stain) tache f; (dot) point m; (in pattern) pois m; (drop) goutte f; (place) endroit m; (pimple) bouton m; a ~ of [T] un peu de; on the ~ sur place; (without delay) sur le coup. ● vt (pt **spotted**) [T] apercevoir. ~ **check** n contrôle m surprise.

**spotless** /ˈspɒtlɪs/ adj impeccable.

**spotlight** /ˈspɒtlaɪt/ n (lamp) projecteur m, spot m.

**spotty** /ˈspɒtɪ/ adj (skin) boutonneux.

**spouse** /spaʊz/ n époux m, épouse f.

**spout** /spaʊt/ n (of teapot) bec m; (of liquid) jet m; **up the** ~ (ruined) [T] fichu. ● vi jaillir.

**sprain** /spreɪn/ n entorse f, foulure f. ● vt ~ one's wrist se fouler le poignet.

**sprang** /spræŋ/ ➡SPRING.

**sprawl** /sprɔːl/ vi (town, person) s'étaler. ● n étalement m.

**spray** /spreɪ/ n (of flowers) gerbe f; (water) gerbe f d'eau; (from sea) embruns mpl; (device) bombe f, atomiseur m. ● vt (surface, insecticide, plant) vaporiser; (person) asperger; (crops) traiter.

**spread** /spred/ vt/i (pt **spread**) (stretch, extend) (s')étendre; (news, fear) (se) répandre; (illness) (se) propager; (butter) (s')étaler. ● n propagation f; (of population) distribution f; (paste) pâte f à tartiner; (food) belle table f. ~**-eagled** adj bras et jambes écartés. ~**sheet** n tableur m.

**spree** /spriː/ n go on a ~ (have fun [T]) faire la noce.

**sprig** /sprɪg/ n petite branche f.

**sprightly** /ˈspraɪtlɪ/ adj (**-ier, -iest**) alerte, vif.

**spring** /sprɪŋ/ vi (pt **sprang**; pp **sprung**) bondir. ● vt ~ sth on sb annoncer qch de but en blanc à qn. ● n bond m; (device) ressort m; (season) printemps m; (of water) source f. ~ **from** provenir de; ~ **up** surgir. ~**board** n tremplin m. ~ **onion** n oignon m blanc.

**springy** /ˈsprɪŋɪ/ adj (**-ier, -iest**) élastique.

**sprinkle** /ˈsprɪŋkl/ vt (with liquid) arroser (with de); (with salt, flour) saupoudrer (with de); (sand) répandre. **sprinkler** n (in garden) arroseur m; (for fires) extincteur m (à déclenchement automatique).

**sprint** /sprɪnt/ vi (Sport) sprinter. ● n sprint m.

**sprout** /spraʊt/ vt/i pousser. ● n

**s**

**spruce** (on plant) pousse *f*; (Brussels) ~s choux *mpl* de Bruxelles.

**spruce** /spruːs/ *adj* pimpant. ● *vt* ~ oneself up se faire beau. ● *n* (tree) épicéa *m*.

**sprung** /sprʌŋ/ ➡SPRING.

**spud** /spʌd/ *n* Ⅱ patate *f*.

**spun** /spʌn/ ➡SPIN.

**spur** /spɜː(r)/ *n* (of rider) éperon *m*; (stimulus) aiguillon *m*; on the ~ of the moment sous l'impulsion du moment. ● *vt* (*pt* **spurred**) éperonner.

**spurious** /ˈspjʊərɪəs/ *adj* faux.

**spurn** /spɜːn/ *vt* repousser.

**spurt** /spɜːt/ *vi* jaillir; (fig) accélérer. ● *n* jet *m*; (of energy) sursaut *m*.

**spy** /spaɪ/ *n* espion/-ne *m/f*. ● *vi* espionner. ● *vt* apercevoir.

**squabble** /ˈskwɒbl/ *vi* se chamailler. ● *n* chamaillerie *f*.

**squad** /skwɒd/ *n* (of soldiers) escouade *f*; (Sport) équipe *f*.

**squadron** /ˈskwɒdrən/ *n* (Mil) escadron *m*; (Aviat) escadrille *f*.

**squalid** /ˈskwɒlɪd/ *adj* sordide.

**squander** /ˈskwɒndə(r)/ *vt* (money, time) gaspiller.

**square** /skweə(r)/ *n* carré *m*; (open space in town) place *f*. ● *adj* carré; (honest) honnête; (meal) solide; (boring Ⅱ) ringard; (all) ~ (quits) quitte; ~ metre mètre *m* carré. ● *vt* (settle) régler; ~ up to faire face à.

**squash** /skwɒʃ/ *vt* écraser; (crowd) serrer. ● *n* (game) squash *m*; (marrow: US) courge *f*; lemon ~ citronnade *f*; orange ~ orangeade *f*.

**squat** /skwɒt/ *vi* (*pt* **squatted**) s'accroupir; ~ in a house squatteriser une maison. ● *adj* (dumpy) trapu. **squatter** *n* squatter *m*.

**squawk** /skwɔːk/ *n* cri rauque. ● *vi* pousser un cri rauque.

**squeak** /skwiːk/ *n* petit cri *m*; (of door) grincement *m*. ● *vi* crier; grincer.

**squeal** /skwiːl/ *n* cri aigu. ● *vi* pousser un cri aigu; ~ on (inform on Ⅱ) dénoncer.

**squeamish** /ˈskwiːmɪʃ/ *adj* (trop) délicat.

**squeeze** /skwiːz/ *vt* presser; (hand, arm) serrer; (extract) exprimer (from de); (extort) soutirer (from à). ● *vi* (force one's way) se glisser. ● *n* pression *f*; (Comm) restrictions *fpl* de crédit.

**squid** /skwɪd/ *n* calmar *m*.

**squint** /skwɪnt/ *vi* loucher; (with half-shut eyes) plisser les yeux. ● *n* (Med) strabisme *m*.

**squirm** /skwɜːm/ *vi* se tortiller.

**squirrel** /ˈskwɪrəl/ *n* écureuil *m*.

**squirt** /skwɜːt/ *vt/i* (faire) jaillir. ● *n* jet *m*.

**stab** /stæb/ *vt* (*pt* **stabbed**) (with knife) poignarder. ● *n* coup *m* (de couteau); have a ~ at sth essayer de faire qch.

**stability** /stəˈbɪlətɪ/ *n* stabilité *f*. **stabilize** *vt* stabiliser.

**stable** /ˈsteɪbl/ *adj* stable. ● *n* écurie *f*; ~-**boy** *n* lad *m*.

**stack** /stæk/ *n* tas *m*. ● *vt* (~ up) entasser, empiler.

**stadium** /ˈsteɪdɪəm/ *n* stade *m*.

**staff** /stɑːf/ *n* personnel *m*; (in school) professeurs *mpl*; (Mil) état-major *m*; (stick) bâton *m*. ● *vt* pourvoir en personnel.

**stag** /stæg/ *n* cerf *m*.

**stage** /steɪdʒ/ *n* (Theat) scène *f*; (phase) stade *m*, étape *f*; (platform in hall) estrade *f*; go on the ~ faire du théâtre. ● *vt* mettre en scène; (fig) organiser. ~ **door** *n* entrée *f* des artistes. ~ **fright** *n* trac *m*.

**stagger** /ˈstægə(r)/ *vi* chanceler.

● vt (shock) stupéfier; ( payments) échelonner. **staggering** adj stupéfiant.

**stagnate** /stæg'neɪt/ vi stagner.

**stag night** n soirée f pour enterrer une vie de garçon.

**staid** /steɪd/ adj sérieux.

**stain** /steɪn/ vt tacher; (wood) colorer. ● n tache f; (colouring) colorant m. **stained glass window** n vitrail m.

**stainless steel** n acier m inoxydable.

**stain remover** n détachant m.

**stair** /steə(r)/ n marche f; the ~s l'escalier m. **~case**, **~way** n escalier m.

**stake** /steɪk/ n (post) pieu m; (wager) enjeu m; at ~ en jeu. ● vt (area) jalonner; (wager) jouer; ~ a claim to revendiquer.

**stale** /steɪl/ adj pas frais; (bread) rassis; (smell) de renfermé.

**stalk** /stɔːk/ n (of plant) tige f. ● vi marcher de façon guindée. ● vt (hunter) chasser; (murderer) suivre.

**stall** /stɔːl/ n (in stable) stalle f; (in market) éventaire m; (Theat) orchestre m. ● vt/i (Auto) caler; ~ (for time) temporiser.

**stallion** /'stælɪən/ n étalon m.

**stamina** /'stæmɪnə/ n résistance f.

**stammer** /'stæmə(r)/ vt/i bégayer. ● n bégaiement m.

**stamp** /stæmp/ vt/i ~ (one's foot) taper du pied. ● vt (letter) timbrer. ● n (for postage, marking) timbre m; (mark: fig) sceau m. ~ **out** supprimer. **~-collecting** n philatélie f.

**stampede** /stæm'piːd/ n fuite f désordonnée; (rush: fig) ruée f. ● vi s'enfuir en désordre; se ruer.

**stand** /stænd/ vi (pt **stood**) être or se tenir (debout); (rise) se lever; (be situated) se trouver; (Pol) être can-

didat (for à); ~ **in line** (US) faire la queue; ~ **to reason** être logique. ● vt mettre (debout); (tolerate) supporter; ~ **a chance** avoir une chance. ● n (stance) position f; (Mil) résistance f; (for lamp) support m; (at fair) stand m; (in street) kiosque m; (for spectators) tribune f; (Jur, US) barre f; **make a** ~ prendre position. ~ **back** reculer; ~ **by** or **around** ne rien faire; ~ **by** (be ready) se tenir prêt; ( promise, person) rester fidèle à; ~ **down** se désister; ~ **for** représenter; ⟨⟩ supporter; ~ **in for** remplacer; ~ **out** ressortir; ~ **up** se lever; ~ **up for** défendre; ~ **up to** résister à.

**standard** /'stændəd/ n norme f; (level) niveau m (voulu); (flag) étendard m; ~ **of living** niveau m de vie; ~s (morals) principes mpl. ● adj ordinaire.

**standard of living** n niveau m de vie.

**standby** /'stændbaɪ/ adj de réserve. ● n be a ~ être de réserve.

**stand-in** /'stændɪn/ n remplaçant/- e m/f.

**standing** /'stændɪŋ/ adj debout inv. ● n réputation f; (duration) durée f. ~ **order** n prélèvement m bancaire.

**standpoint** /'stændpɔɪnt/ n point m de vue.

**standstill** /'stændstɪl/ n at a ~ immobile; **bring/come to a** ~ (s')immobiliser.

**stank** /stæŋk/ ➙STINK.

**staple** /'steɪpl/ n agrafe f. ● vt agrafer. ● adj principal, de base. **stapler** n agrafeuse f.

**star** /stɑː(r)/ n étoile f; (person) vedette f. ● vt (pt **starred**) ( film) avoir pour vedette. ● vi ~ **in** être la vedette de.

**starch** /stɑːtʃ/ n amidon m; (in food) fécule f. ● vt amidonner.

**s**

**stardom** /'stɑːdəm/ n célébrité f.

**stare** /steə(r)/ vi ~ **at** regarder fixement. ● n regard m fixe.

**starfish** /'stɑːfɪʃ/ n étoile f de mer.

**stark** /stɑːk/ adj (desolate) désolé; (severe) austère; (utter) complet; ( fact) brutal. ● adv complètement.

**starling** /'stɑːlɪŋ/ n étourneau m.

**start** /stɑːt/ vt/i commencer; (machine) (se) mettre en marche; (fashion) lancer; (cause) provoquer; (jump) sursauter; ~ **to do** commencer se mettre à faire; ~**ing tomorrow** à partir de demain. ● n commencement m, début m; (of race) départ m; (lead) avance f; (jump) sursaut m. □ ~ **off** commencer (doing par faire); ~ **out** partir; ~ **up** (business) lancer. **starter** n (Auto) démarreur m; (runner) partant m; (Culin) entrée f.

**starting point** n point m de départ.

**startle** /'stɑːtl/ vt (make jump) faire tressaillir; (shock) alarmer.

**starvation** /stɑːˈveɪʃn/ n faim f.

**starve** /stɑːv/ vi mourir de faim. ● vt affamer; (deprive) priver.

**stash** /stæʃ/ vt cacher.

**state** /steɪt/ n état m; (pomp) apparat m; S~ état m; the S~s les États-Unis; **get into a** ~ s'affoler. ● adj d'état, de l'état; (school) public. ● vt affirmer (that que); (views) exprimer; (fix) fixer.

intègrent normalement une comprehensive school, ou, à l'issue d'un examen d'entrée, une grammar school. ▷**PUBLIC SCHOOLS.**

**stately** /'steɪtlɪ/ adj (-ier, -iest) majestueux. ~ **home** n château m.

**statement** /'steɪtmənt/ n déclaration f; (of account) relevé m.

**statesman** /'steɪtsmən/ n (pl -men) homme m d'état.

**static** /'stætɪk/ adj statique. ● n (radio, TV) parasites mpl.

**station** /'steɪʃn/ n (Rail) gare f; (TV) chaîne f; (Mil) poste m; (rank) condition f. ● vt poster, placer; ~**ed at** or **in** (Mil) en garnison à.

**stationary** /'steɪʃənrɪ/ adj immobile, stationnaire; (vehicle) à l'arrêt.

**stationery** /'steɪʃənrɪ/ n papeterie f.

**station wagon** n (US) break m.

**statistic** /stəˈtɪstɪk/ n statistique f; ~**s** statistique f.

**statue** /'stætjuː/ n statue f.

**status** /'steɪtəs/ n (pl ~**es**) situation f, statut m; (prestige) standing m.

**statute** /'stætʃuːt/ n loi f; ~**s** (rules) statuts mpl. **statutory** adj statutaire; (holiday) légal.

**staunch** /stɔːntʃ/ adj (friend) loyal, fidèle.

**stave** /steɪv/ n (Mus) portée f. ● vt ~ **off** éviter, conjurer.

**stay** /steɪ/ vi rester; (spend time) séjourner; (reside) loger. ● vt (hunger) tromper. ● n séjour m. □ ~ **away from** (school) ne pas aller à; ~ **behind** or ~ **on** rester; ~ **in** rester à la maison; ~ **up** veiller, se coucher tard.

**stead** /sted/ n **stand sb in good** ~ être utile à qn.

**steadfast** /'stedfɑːst/ adj ferme.

**steady** /'stedɪ/ adj (-ier, -iest) stable; (hand, voice) ferme; (regular) régulier; (staid) sérieux. ● vt maintenir, assurer; (calm) calmer.

**steak** /steɪk/ n steak m, bifteck m; (of fish) darne f.

**steal** /stiːl/ vt/i (pt **stole**; pp **stolen**) voler (**from sb** à qn).

**steam** /stiːm/ n vapeur f; (on glass) buée f. ● vt (cook) cuire à la vapeur. ● vi fumer. **~-engine** n locomotive f à vapeur

**steamer** /'stiːmə(r)/ n (Culin) cuit-vapeur m; (boat) (bateau à) vapeur m.

**steel** /stiːl/ n acier m; ~ industry sidérurgie f; ● vpr ~ oneself s'endurcir, se cuirasser.

**steep** /stiːp/ adj raide, rapide; (price: 🆑) excessif. ● vt (soak) tremper; **~ed in** (fig) imprégné de.

**steeple** /'stiːpl/ n clocher m.

**steer** /stɪə(r)/ vt diriger; (ship) gouverner; (fig) guider. ● vi (in ship) gouverner; ~ **clear of** éviter.

**steering-wheel** n volant m.

**stem** /stem/ n tige f; (of glass) pied m. ● vi (pt **stemmed**) ~ **from** provenir de. ● vt (pt **stemmed**) (check, stop) endiguer, contenir. ~ **cell** n cellule f souche.

**stench** /stentʃ/ n puanteur f.

**stencil** /'stensɪl/ n pochoir m. ● vt (pt **stencilled**) décorer au pochoir.

**step** /step/ vt (pt **stepped**) marcher, aller. ● n pas m; (stair) marche f; (of train) marchepied m; (action) mesure f; ~**s** (ladder) escabeau m; **in** ~ au pas; (fig) conforme (**with** à). **~ down** (fig) démissionner; (from ladder) descendre; ~ **forward** faire un pas en avant; ~ **in** (intervene) intervenir; ~ **up** (pressure) augmenter. **~brother** n demi-frère m. **~daughter** n belle-fille f.

**~father** n beau-père m. **~ladder** n escabeau m. **~mother** n belle-mère f. **stepping-stone** n (fig) tremplin m. **~sister** n demi-sœur f. **~son** n beau-fils m.

**stereo** /'sterɪəʊ/ n stéréo f; (record-player) chaîne f stéréo. ● adj stéréo inv.

**stereotype** /'sterɪətaɪp/ n stéréotype m.

**sterile** /'steraɪl/ adj stérile. **sterility** n stérilité f.

**sterilize** /'sterɪlaɪz/ vt stériliser.

**sterling** /'stɜːlɪŋ/ n livre(s) f (pl) sterling. ● adj sterling inv; (silver) fin; (fig) excellent.

**stern** /stɜːn/ adj sévère. ● n (of ship) arrière m.

**steroid** /'stɪərɔɪd/ n stéroïde m.

**stew** /stjuː/ vt/i cuire à la casserole; **~ed fruit** compote f; **~ed tea** thé m trop infusé. ● n ragoût m.

**steward** /stjʊəd/ n (of club) intendant m; (on ship) steward m. **stewardess** n hôtesse f.

**stick** /stɪk/ vt (pt **stuck**) (glue) coller; (put 🆑) mettre; (endure 🆑) supporter. ● vi (adhere) coller, adhérer; (to pan) attacher; (remain 🆑) rester; (be jammed) être coincé; **be stuck with sb** se farcir qn. ● n bâton m; (for walking) canne f. ~ **at** persévérer dans; ~ **out** (head) sortir; (tongue) tirer; vi (protrude) dépasser; ~ **to** (promise) rester fidèle à; ~ **up for** 🆑 défendre.

**sticker** /'stɪkə(r)/ n autocollant m.

**sticky** /'stɪkɪ/ adj **-ier, -iest** poisseux; (label, tape) adhésif.

**stiff** /stɪf/ adj raide; (limb, joint) ankylosé; (tough) dur; (drink) fort; (price) élevé; (manner) guindé; ~ **neck** torticolis m.

**stifle** /'staɪfl/ vt/i étouffer.

**stiletto** /stɪˈletəʊ/ adj & n ~s, ~ heels talons mpl aiguille.

**still** /stɪl/ adj immobile; (quiet) calme, tranquille; keep ~! arrête de bouger! ● n silence m. ● adv encore, toujours; (even) encore; (nevertheless) malgré tout.

**stillborn** /ˈstɪlbɔːn/ adj mort-né.

**still life** n nature f morte.

**stimulate** /ˈstɪmjʊleɪt/ vt stimuler. **stimulation** n stimulation f.

**stimulus** /ˈstɪmjʊləs/ n (pl -li) (spur) stimulant m.

**sting** /stɪŋ/ n piqûre f; (of insect) aiguillon m. ● vt/i (pt **stung**) piquer.

**stingy** /ˈstɪndʒɪ/ adj (-ier, -iest) avare (with de).

**stink** /stɪŋk/ n puanteur f. ● vi (pt **stank** or **stunk**; pp **stunk**) ~ (of) puer.

**stipulate** /ˈstɪpjʊleɪt/ vt stipuler.

**stir** /stɜː(r)/ vt (pt **stirred**) remuer; (excite) exciter; ~ up (trouble) provoquer. ● n agitation f.

**stirrup** /ˈstɪrəp/ n étrier m.

**stitch** /stɪtʃ/ n point m; (in knitting) maille f; (Med) point m de suture; (muscle pain) point m de côté; be in ~es 🄸 avoir le fou rire. ● vt coudre.

**stock** /stɒk/ n réserve f; (Comm) stock m; (financial) valeurs fpl; (family) souche f; (soup) bouillon m; **we're out of ~** il n'y en a plus; **take ~** (fig) faire le point; **in ~** en stock. ● adj (goods) courant. ● vt (shop) approvisionner; (sell) vendre. ● vi ~ up s'approvisionner (with de). ~**-broker** n agent m de change. ~ **cube** n bouillon-cube m. **S~ Exchange** n Bourse f.

**stocking** /ˈstɒkɪŋ/ n bas m.

**stock market** n Bourse f.

**stockpile** /ˈstɒkpaɪl/ n stock m. ● vt stocker; (arms) amasser.

**stock-taking** n (Comm) inventaire m.

**stocky** /ˈstɒkɪ/ adj (-ier, -iest) trapu.

**stodgy** /ˈstɒdʒɪ/ adj lourd.

**stole, stolen** ⇒**STEAL**.

**stomach** /ˈstʌmək/ n estomac m; (abdomen) ventre m. ● vt (put up with) supporter. ~**-ache** n mal m à l'estomac or au ventre.

**stone** /stəʊn/ n pierre f; (pebble) caillou m; (in fruit) noyau m; (weight) 6,350 kg. ● adj de pierre; ~**-cold**/**-deaf** complètement froid/sourd. ● vt (throw stones) lapider; (fruit) dénoyauter.

**stony** /ˈstəʊnɪ/ adj pierreux.

**stood** /stʊd/ ⇒**STAND**.

**stool** /stuːl/ n tabouret m.

**stoop** /stuːp/ vi (bend) se baisser; (condescend) s'abaisser. ● n **have a ~** être voûté.

**stop** /stɒp/ vt/i (pt **stopped**) arrêter (doing de faire); (moving, talking) s'arrêter; (prevent) empêcher (from de); (hole, leak) boucher; (pain, noise) cesser; (stay) 🄸 rester. ● n arrêt m; (full stop) point m ~ (-over) halte f; (port of call) escale f ~ **off** s'arrêter; ~ **up** boucher.

**stopgap** /ˈstɒpgæp/ n bouche-trou m. ● adj intérimaire.

**stoppage** /ˈstɒpɪdʒ/ n arrêt m; (of work) arrêt m de travail; (of pay) retenue f.

**stopper** /ˈstɒpə(r)/ n bouchon m.

**stop-watch** n chronomètre m.

**storage** /ˈstɔːrɪdʒ/ n (of goods, food) emmagasinage m. ~ **heater** n radiateur m électrique à accumulation.

**store** /stɔː(r)/ n réserve f; (warehouse) entrepôt m; (shop) grand magasin m; (US) magasin m; **have in ~ for** réserver à; **set ~ by** attacher du prix à. ● vt (for future) mettre en réserve; (in warehouse, mind) emmagasiner. ~-room n réserve f.

**storey** /'stɔːrɪ/ n étage m.

**stork** /stɔːk/ n cigogne f.

**storm** /stɔːm/ n tempête f, orage m. ● vt prendre d'assaut. ● vi (rage) tempêter.

**story** /'stɔːrɪ/ n histoire f, (in press) article m; (storey: US) étage m. ~-teller n conteur/-euse m/f.

**stout** /staut/ adj corpulent; (strong) solide. ● n bière f brune.

**stove** /stəuv/ n cuisinière f.

**stow** /stəu/ vt ~ away (put away) ranger; (hide) cacher. ● vi voyager clandestinement.

**straddle** /'strædl/ vt être à cheval sur, enjamber.

**straggler** /'stræglə(r)/ n traînard/-e m/f.

**straight** /streit/ adj droit; (tidy) en ordre; (frank) franc; ~ face visage m sérieux; get sth ~ mettre qch au clair. ● adv (in straight line) droit; (direct) tout droit; ~ ahead or on tout droit; ~ away tout de suite; ~ off ⊡ sans hésiter. ● n (Sport) ligne f droite.

**straighten** /'streitn/ vt (nail, situation) redresser; (tidy) arranger.

**straightforward** /streit'fɔːwəd/ adj honnête; (easy) simple.

**straight off** adj ⊡ sans hésiter.

**strain** /strein/ vt (rope, ears) tendre; (limb) fouler; (eyes) fatiguer; (muscle) froisser; (filter) passer; (vegetables) égoutter; (fig) mettre à l'épreuve. ● vi fournir des efforts. ● n tension f; (fig) effort m; (breed) race f; (of virus) variété f; ~s (tune: Mus) accents mpl. **strained** adj forcé; (relations) tendu. **strainer** n passoire f.

**strait** /streit/ n détroit m; ~s dé-

troit m; be in dire ~s être aux abois. ~-jacket n camisole f de force.

**strand** /strænd/ n (thread) fil m, brin m; (of hair) mèche f.

**stranded** /'strændɪd/ adj (person) en rade; (ship) échoué.

**strange** /streindʒ/ adj étrange; (unknown) inconnu. **stranger** n inconnu-e m/f.

**strangle** /'stræŋgl/ vt étrangler.

**stranglehold** /'stræŋglhəuld/ n have a ~ on tenir à la gorge.

**strap** /stræp/ n (of leather) courroie f; (of dress) bretelle f; (of watch) bracelet m. ● vt (pt **strapped**) attacher.

**strategic** /strə'tiːdʒɪk/ adj stratégique. **strategy** n stratégie f.

**straw** /strɔː/ n paille f; the last ~ le comble.

**strawberry** /'strɔːbrɪ/ n fraise f.

**stray** /strei/ vi s'égarer; (deviate) s'écarter. ● adj perdu; (isolated) isolé. ● n animal m perdu.

**streak** /striːk/ n raie f, bande f; (trace) trace f; (period) période f; (tendency) tendance f. ● vt (mark) strier. ● vi filer à toute allure.

**stream** /striːm/ n ruisseau m; (current) courant m; (flow) flot m; (in school) classe f (de niveau). ● vi ruisseler (with de); (eyes, nose) couler.

**streamline** /'striːmlaɪn/ vt rationaliser. **streamlined** adj (shape) aérodynamique.

**street** /striːt/ n rue f. ~-car n (US) tramway m. ~ lamp n réverbère m. ~ map n indicateur m des rues.

**strength** /streŋθ/ n force f; (of wall, fabric) solidité f; on the ~ of en vertu de. **strengthen** vt renforcer, fortifier.

**strenuous** /'strenjʊəs/ adj (exer-

*cise)* énergique; *(work)* ardu.

**stress** /stres/ *n* (emphasis) accent *m*; (pressure) pression *f*; (Med) stress *m*. ● *vt* souligner, insister sur.

**stretch** /stretʃ/ *vt* (pull taut) tendre; *(arm, leg)* étendre; *(neck)* tendre; *(clothes)* étirer; *(truth)* forcer; ~ one's legs se dégourdir les jambes. ● *vi* s'étirer; *(person)* s'étirer; *(clothes)* se déformer. ● *n* étendue *f*; *(period)* période *f*; *(of road)* tronçon *m*; at a ~ d'affilée. ● *adj* (fabric) extensible.

**stretcher** /stretʃə(r)/ *n* brancard *m*.

**strew** /struː/ *vt* (*pt* **strewed**;*pp* **strewed** or **strewn**) *(scatter)* répandre; *(cover)* joncher.

**strict** /strɪkt/ *adj* strict.

**stride** /straɪd/ *vi* (*pt* **strode**; *pp* **stridden**) faire de grands pas. ● *n* grand pas *m*.

**strife** /straɪf/ *n* conflit(s) *m(pl)*.

**strike** /straɪk/ *vt* (*pt* **struck**) frapper; *(blow)* donner; *(match)* frotter; *(gold)* trouver. ● *vi* faire grève; (attack) attaquer; *(clock)* sonner. ● *n* (of workers) grève *f*; (Mil) attaque *f*; (find) découverte *f*; ~ off ou ~ out rayer; ~ up (a friendship) lier amitié (with avec).

**striker** *n* gréviste *mf*; (football) attaquant/-e *m/f*. **striking** *adj* frappant.

**string** /strɪŋ/ *n* ficelle *f*; (of violin, racket) corde *f*; (of pearls) collier *m*; (of lies) chapelet *m*; the ~s (Mus) les cordes; **pull ~s** faire jouer ses relations. ● *vt pt* **strung** (thread) enfiler. **stringed** *adj* (instrument) à cordes.

**stringent** /strɪndʒənt/ *adj* rigoureux, strict.

**stringy** /strɪŋi/ *adj* filandreux.

**strip** /strɪp/ *vt/i* (*pt* **stripped**) (un-

dress) (se) déshabiller; (deprive) dépouiller. ● *n* bande *f*.

**stripe** /straɪp/ *n* rayure *f*, raie *f*. **striped** *adj* rayé.

**strip light** *n* néon *m*.

**stripper** /strɪpə(r)/ *n* strip-teaseur/-euse *m/f*; (solvent) décapant.

**strip-tease** *n* strip-tease *m*.

**strive** /straɪv/ *vi* (*pt* **strove**; *pp* **striven**) s'efforcer (to).

**strode** /strəʊd/ ➡STRIDE.

**stroke** /strəʊk/ *vt* (with hand) caresser. ● *n* coup *m*; (of pen) trait *m*; (swimming) nage *f*; (Med) attaque *f*, congestion *f*; at a ~ d'un seul coup.

**stroll** /strəʊl/ *vi* flâner; ~ in entrer tranquillement. ● *n* petit tour *m*. **stroller** *n* (US) poussette *f*.

**strong** /strɒŋ/ *adj* fort; *(shoes, fabric)* solide; **be fifty** ~ être fort de cinquante personnes. **~hold** *n* bastion *m*.

**strongly** /strɒŋli/ *adv* (greatly) fortement; (with energy) avec force; (deeply) profondément.

**strove** /strəʊv/ ➡STRIVE.

**struck** /strʌk/ ➡STRIKE.

**structure** /strʌktʃə(r)/ *n* (of cell, poem) structure *f*; (building) construction *f*.

**struggle** /strʌgl/ *vi* lutter, se battre. ● *n* lutte *f*; (effort) effort *m*; **have a ~ to** avoir du mal à.

**strum** /strʌm/ *vt* (*pt* **strummed**) gratter de.

**strung** /strʌŋ/ ➡STRING. ● *adj* ~ **up** (tense) nerveux.

**strut** /strʌt/ *n* (support) étai *m*. ● *vi* (*pt* **strutted**) se pavaner.

**stub** /stʌb/ *n* bout *m*; (counterfoil) talon *m*. ● *vt* (*pt* **stubbed**) ~ one's toe se cogner le doigt de pied.
□ ~ **out** écraser.

**stubble** /'stʌbl/ n (on chin) barbe f de plusieurs jours; (remains of wheat) chaume m.

**stubborn** /'stʌbən/ adj obstiné.

**stuck** /stʌk/ ➡STICK. ● adj (jammed) coincé; **I'm ~** (for answer) je sèche. **~-up** adj 🗵 prétentieux.

**stud** /stʌd/ n (on jacket) clou m; (for collar) bouton m; (stallion) étalon m; (horse farm) haras m. ● vt (pt **studded**) clouter.

**student** /'stjuːdnt/ n (Univ) étudiant/-e m/f; (School) élève mf. ● adj (restaurant, life) universitaire.

**studio** /'stjuːdɪəʊ/ n studio m.

**studious** /'stjuːdɪəs/ adj (person) studieux; (deliberate) étudié.

**study** /'stʌdɪ/ n étude f; (office) bureau m. ● vt/i étudier.

**stuff** /stʌf/ n substance f; 🗵 (things) (s) f (pl). ● vt rembourrer; (animal) empailler; (cram) bourrer; (Culin) farcir; (block up) boucher; (put) fourrer. **stuffing** n bourre f; (Culin) farce f.

**stuffy** /'stʌfɪ/ adj (-ier, -iest) mal aéré; (dull) 🗵 vieux jeu inv.

**stumble** /'stʌmbl/ vi trébucher; **~ across** or **on** tomber sur. **stumbling block** n obstacle m.

**stump** /stʌmp/ n (of tree) souche f; (of limb) moignon m; (of pencil) bout m.

**stumped** /stʌmpt/ adj embarrassé.

**stun** /stʌn/ vt (pt **stunned** étourdir; (bewilder) stupéfier.

**stung** /stʌŋ/ ➡STING.

**stunk** /stʌŋk/ ➡STINK.

**stunning** /'stʌnɪŋ/ adj (delightful 🗵) sensationnel.

**stunt** /stʌnt/ vt (growth) retarder. ● n (feat 🗵) tour m de force; (trick 🗵) truc m; (dangerous) cascade f.

**stupid** /'stjuːpɪd/ adj stupide, bête.

**stupidity** n stupidité f.

**sturdy** /'stɜːdɪ/ adj (-ier, -iest) robuste.

**stutter** /'stʌtə(r)/ vi bégayer. ● n bégaiement m.

**sty** /staɪ/ n (pigsty) porcherie f; (on eye) orgelet m.

**style** /staɪl/ n style m; (fashion) mode f; (sort) genre m; (pattern) modèle m; **do sth in ~** faire qch avec classe. ● vt (design) créer; **~ sb's hair** coiffer qn.

**stylish** /'staɪlɪʃ/ adj élégant.

**stylist** /'staɪlɪst/ n (of hair) coiffeur/-euse m/f.

**suave** /swɑːv/ adj (urbane) courtois; (smooth: pej) doucereux.

**subconscious** /sʌb'kɒnʃəs/ adj & n inconscient (m), subconscient (m.).

**subcontract** /sʌbkən'trækt/ vt sous-traiter.

**subdue** /səb'djuː/ vt (feeling) maîtriser; (country) subjuguer. **subdued** adj (person, mood) morose; (light) tamisé; (criticism) contenu.

**subject¹** /'sʌbdʒɪkt/ adj (state) soumis; **~ to** soumis à; (liable to, dependent on) sujet à. ● n sujet m; (focus) objet m; (School,Univ) matière f; (citizen) ressortissant/-e m/f, sujet/-te m/f.

**subject²** /səb'dʒekt/ vt soumettre.

**subjective** /səb'dʒektɪv/ adj subjectif.

**subject-matter** n contenu m.

**subjunctive** /səb'dʒʌŋktɪv/ adj & n subjonctif (m).

**sublet** /sʌb'let/ vt sous-louer.

**submarine** /sʌbmə'riːn/ n sous-marin m.

**submerge** /səb'mɜːdʒ/ vt submerger. ● vi plonger.

**submissive** /səb'mɪsɪv/ adj soumis.

**submit** /səbˈmɪt/ vt/i (pt **submit-ted**) (se) soumettre (to à).

**subordinate** /səˈbɔːdɪnət/ adj subalterne; (Gram) subordonné. ● n subordonné-e f.

**subpoena** /səˈpiːnə/ n (Jur) citation f, assignation f.

**subscribe** /səbˈskraɪb/ vt/i verser (de l'argent) (to à); ~ to (loan, theory) souscrire à; (newspaper) s'abonner à, être abonné à. **subscriber** n abonné-e f. **subscription** n abonnement m; (membership dues) cotisation f.

**subsequent** /ˈsʌbsɪkwənt/ adj (later) ultérieur; (next) suivant. **subsequently** adv par la suite.

**subside** /səbˈsaɪd/ vi (land) s'affaisser; (flood, wind) baisser.

**subsidiary** /səbˈsɪdɪərɪ/ adj accessoire. ● n (Comm) filiale f.

**subsidize** /ˈsʌbsɪdaɪz/ vt subventionner. **subsidy** n subvention f.

**substance** /ˈsʌbstəns/ n substance f.

**substandard** /sʌbˈstændəd/ adj de qualité inférieure.

**substantial** /səbˈstænʃl/ adj considérable; (meal) substantiel.

**substitute** /ˈsʌbstɪtjuːt/ n succédané m; (person) remplaçant-e m/f. ● vt substituer (for à).

**subtitle** /ˈsʌbtaɪtl/ n sous-titre m.

**subtle** /ˈsʌtl/ adj subtil.

**subtract** /səbˈtrækt/ vt soustraire.

**suburb** /ˈsʌbɜːb/ n faubourg m, banlieue f; ~s banlieue f. **suburban** adj de banlieue. **suburbia** n la banlieue.

**subway** /ˈsʌbweɪ/ n passage m souterrain; (US) métro m.

**succeed** /səkˈsiːd/ vi réussir (in doing à faire). ● vt (follow) succéder à.

**success** /səkˈses/ n succès m,

réussite f.

**successful** /səkˈsesfl/ adj réussi, couronné de succès; (favourable) heureux; (in exam) reçu; be ~ in doing réussir à faire.

**succession** /səkˈseʃn/ n succession f; in ~ de suite.

**successive** /səkˈsesɪv/ adj successif; six ~ days six jours consécutifs.

**successor** /səkˈsesə(r)/ n successeur m.

**such** /sʌtʃ/ det & pron tel(le), tel(le)s; (so much) tant(de). ● adv si; ~ a book un tel livre; ~ books de tels livres; ~ courage tant de courage; ~ a big house une si grande maison; ~ as comme, tel que; as ~ en tant que tel; there's no ~ thing ça n'existe pas. ~-**and**-~ adj tel ou tel.

**suck** /sʌk/ vt sucer. □ ~ **in** or **up** aspirer. **sucker** n (rubber pad) ventouse f; (person ⒤) dupe f.

**suction** /ˈsʌkʃn/ n succion f.

**sudden** /ˈsʌdn/ adj soudain, subit; all of a ~ tout à coup. **suddenly** adv subitement, brusquement.

**sue** /suː/ vt (pres p) **suing** poursuivre (en justice).

**suede** /sweɪd/ n daim m.

**suffer** /ˈsʌfə(r)/ vt/i souffrir; (loss, attack) subir. **sufferer** n victime f, malade m/f. **suffering** n souffrance(s) f(pl).

**sufficient** /səˈfɪʃnt/ adj (enough) suffisamment de; (big enough) suffisant.

**suffix** /ˈsʌfɪks/ n suffixe m.

**suffocate** /ˈsʌfəkeɪt/ vt/i suffoquer.

**sugar** /ˈʃʊgə(r)/ n sucre m. ● vt sucrer.

**suggest** /səˈdʒest/ vt suggérer. **suggestion** n suggestion f.

**suicidal** /suːɪˈsaɪdl/ adj suicidaire.

**suicide** /ˈsuːɪsaɪd/ n suicide m;

561

# suit | superimpose

commit ~ se suicider.

**suit** /suːt/ n (man's) costume m; (woman's) tailleur m; (cards) couleur f ● vt convenir à; (garment, style) aller à; (adapt) adapter.

**suitable** /'suːtəbl/ adj qui convient (for à), convenable. **suitably** adv convenablement.

**suitcase** /'suːtkeɪs/ n valise f.

**suite** /swiːt/ n (rooms) suite f; (furniture) mobilier m.

**suited** /'suːtɪd/ adj (well) ~ (matched) bien assorti; ~ to fait pour, apte à.

**sulk** /sʌlk/ vi bouder.

**sullen** /'sʌlən/ adj maussade.

**sultana** /sʌl'tɑːnə/ n raisin m de Smyrne, raisin m sec.

**sultry** /'sʌltrɪ/ adj (-ier, -iest) étouffant, lourd; (fig) sensuel.

**sum** /sʌm/ n somme f; (in arithmetic) calcul m ● vt/i (pt summed) ~ up résumer, récapituler; (assess) évaluer.

**summarize** /'sʌməraɪz/ vt résumer.

**summary** /'sʌmərɪ/ n résumé m. ● adj sommaire.

**summer** /'sʌmə(r)/ n été m. ● adj d'été. ~time n (season) été m.

**summery** /'sʌmərɪ/ adj estival.

**summit** /'sʌmɪt/ n sommet m; ~ (conference) (Pol) conférence f au sommet m.

**summon** /'sʌmən/ vt appeler; ~ sb to a meeting convoquer qn à une réunion; ~ up (strength, courage) rassembler.

**summons** /'sʌmənz/ n (Jur) assignation f. ● vt assigner.

**sun** /sʌn/ n soleil m. ● vt (pt sunned) ~ oneself se chauffer au soleil. ~burn n coup m de soleil.

**Sunday** /'sʌndeɪ/ n dimanche m. ~ school n catéchisme m.

**sundry** /'sʌndrɪ/ adj divers; sundries articles mpl divers; all and ~ tout le monde.

**sunflower** /'sʌnflaʊə(r)/ n tournesol m.

**sung** /sʌŋ/ →SING.

**sun-glasses** npl lunettes fpl de soleil.

**sunk** /sʌŋk/ →SINK.

**sunken** /'sʌŋkən/ adj (ship) submergé; (eyes) creux.

**sunlight** /'sʌnlaɪt/ n soleil m.

**sunny** /'sʌnɪ/ adj (-ier, -iest) ensoleillé.

**sun:** ~rise n lever m du soleil. ~roof n toit m ouvrant. ~ screen n filtre m solaire. ~set n coucher m du soleil. ~shine n soleil m. ~stroke n insolation f.

**sun-tan** /'sʌntæn/ n bronzage m. ~ lotion n lotion f solaire. ~ oil n huile f solaire.

**super** /'suːpə(r)/ adj 🔢 formidable.

**superb** /suː'pɜːb/ adj superbe.

**superficial** /suːpə'fɪʃl/ adj superficiel.

**superfluous** /suː'pɜːfluəs/ adj superflu.

**superimpose** /suːpərɪm'pəʊz/ vt

s

superposer (on à).

**superintendent** /su:pərɪn
'tendənt/ n directeur/-trice m/f; (of
police) commissaire m.

**superior** /su:'pɪərɪə(r)/ adj & n
supérieur/-e m (f).

**superlative** /su:'pɜ:lətɪv/ adj suprême. ● n (Gram) superlatif m.

**supermarket** /'su:pəma:kɪt/ n
supermarché m.

**supersede** /su:pə'si:d/ vt remplacer, supplanter.

**superstition** /su:pə'stɪʃn/ n superstition f. **superstitious** adj superstitieux.

**superstore** /'su:pəstɔ:(r)/ n hypermarché m.

**supervise** /'su:pəvaɪz/ vt surveiller,
diriger. **supervision** n surveillance f.
**supervisor** n surveillant/-e m/f;
(shop) chef m de rayon; (firm) chef
m de service.

**supper** /'sʌpə(r)/ n dîner m; (late at
night) souper m.

**supple** /'sʌpl/ adj souple.

**supplement¹** /'sʌplɪmənt/ n supplément m. **supplementary** adj
supplémentaire.

**supplement²** /'sʌplɪmənt/ vt
compléter.

**supplier** /sə'plaɪə(r)/ n fournisseur m.

**supply** /sə'plaɪ/ vt fournir; (equip)
pourvoir; (feed) alimenter (with
en). ● n provision f; (of gas) alimentation f; **supplies** (food) vivres mpl;
(material) fournitures fpl.

**support** /sə'pɔ:t/ vt soutenir; (family) assurer la subsistance de. ● n
soutien m, appui m; (Tech) support
m. **supporter** n partisan/-e m/f;
(Sport) supporter m. **supportive** adj
qui soutient et encourage.

**suppose** /sə'pəʊz/ vt/i supposer;
be ~d to do être censé faire, de-

voir faire; **supposing he comes**
supposons qu'il vienne. **supposedly**
adv soi-disant, prétendument.

**suppress** /sə'pres/ vt (put an end
to) supprimer; (restrain) réprimer;
(stifle) étouffer.

**supreme** /su:'pri:m/ adj suprême.

**surcharge** /'sɜ:tʃɑ:dʒ/ n supplément m; (tax) surtaxe f.

**sure** /ʃɔ:(r)/ adj sûr; **make ~ of**
s'assurer de; **make ~ that** vérifier
que. ● adv (US 🔢) pour sûr. **surely**
adv sûrement.

**surf** /sɜ:f/ n ressac m. ● vi faire du
surf; (Internet) surfer.

**surface** /'sɜ:fɪs/ n surface f. ● adj
superficiel. ● vt revêtir. ● vi faire
surface; (fig) réapparaître.

**surfer** /'sɜ:fə(r)/ n surfeur/-euse
m/f; (Internet) internaute m/f.

**surge** /sɜ:dʒ/ vi (waves, crowd) déferler; (increase) monter. ● n (wave)
vague f; (rise) montée f.

**surgeon** /'sɜ:dʒən/ n chirurgien m.

**surgery** /'sɜ:dʒərɪ/ n chirurgie f;
(office) cabinet m; (session) consultation f; **need ~** devoir être opéré.

**surgical** /'sɜ:dʒɪkl/ adj chirurgical.
**~ spirit** n alcool m à 90 degrés.

**surly** /'sɜ:lɪ/ adj (-ier, -iest) bourru.

**surname** /'sɜ:neɪm/ n nom m de
famille.

**surplus** /'sɜ:pləs/ n surplus m. ● adj
en surplus.

**surprise** /sə'praɪz/ n surprise f. ● vt
surprendre. **surprised** adj surpris (at
de). **surprising** adj surprenant.

**surrender** /sə'rendə(r)/ vi se rendre. ● vt (hand over) remettre; (Mil)
rendre. ● n (Mil) reddition f; (of
passport) remise f.

**surround** /sə'raʊnd/ vt entourer;
(Mil) encercler. **surrounding** adj environnant. **surroundings** npl envi-

rons *mpl*; (setting) cadre *m*.

**surveillance** /sɜːˈveɪləns/ *n* surveillance *f*.

**survey**[1] /səˈveɪ/ *vt* (review) passer en revue; (inquire into) enquêter sur; (building) inspecter.

**survey**[2] /ˈsɜːveɪ/ *n* (inquiry) enquête *f*; inspection *f*; (general view) vue *f* d'ensemble.

**surveyor** /səˈveɪə(r)/ *n* expert *m* (géomètre).

**survival** /səˈvaɪvl/ *n* survie *f*.

**survive** /səˈvaɪv/ *vt/i* survivre (à). **survivor** *n* survivant/-e *m/f*.

**susceptible** /səˈseptəbl/ *adj* sensible (to à); **~ to** (prone to) prédisposé à.

**suspect**[1] /səˈspekt/ *vt* soupçonner; (doubt) douter de.

**suspect**[2] /ˈsʌspekt/ *n & adj* suspect/-e (*m/f*).

**suspend** /səˈspend/ *vt* (hang, stop) suspendre; (licence) retirer provisoirement. **suspended sentence** *n* condamnation *f* avec sursis.

**suspender** /səˈspendə(r)/ *n* jarretelle *f*; **~s** (braces: US) bretelles *fpl*. **~ belt** *n* porte-jarretelles *m*.

**suspension** /səˈspenʃn/ *n* suspension *f*; retrait *m* provisoire.

**suspicion** /səˈspɪʃn/ *n* soupçon *m*; (distrust) méfiance *f*.

**suspicious** /səˈspɪʃəs/ *adj* soupçonneux; (causing suspicion) suspect; **be ~ of** se méfier de. **suspiciously** *adv* de façon suspecte.

**sustain** /səˈsteɪn/ *vt* supporter; (effort) soutenir; (suffer) subir.

**sustenance** /ˈsʌstɪnəns/ *n* (food) nourriture *f*; (nourishment) valeur *f* nutritive.

**swallow** /ˈswɒləʊ/ *vt/i* avaler; **~ up** (absorb, engulf) engloutir. ● *n* hirondelle *f*.

**swam** /swæm/ ➡SWIM.

**swamp** /swɒmp/ *n* marais *m*. ● *vt* (flood, overwhelm) submerger.

**swan** /swɒn/ *n* cygne *m*.

**swap** /swɒp/ *vt/i* (*pt* **swapped**) ⚁ échanger. ● *n* échange *m*.

**swarm** /swɔːm/ *n* essaim *m*. ● *vi* fourmiller; **~ into or round** (crowd) envahir.

**swat** /swɒt/ *vt* (*pt* **swatted**) (fly) écraser.

**sway** /sweɪ/ *vt/i* (se) balancer; (influence) influencer. ● *n* balancement *m*; (rule) empire *m*.

**swear** /sweə(r)/ *vt/i* (*pt* **swore**; *pp* **sworn**) jurer (to de, that qch); **~ at** injurier; **~ by sth** ⚁ ne jurer que par qch. **~-word** *n* juron *m*.

**sweat** /swet/ *n* sueur *f*. ● *vi* suer.

**sweater** /ˈswetə(r)/ *n* pull-over *m*.

**sweat-shirt** *n* sweat-shirt *m*.

**swede** /swiːd/ *n* rutabaga *m*. **Swede** /swiːd/ *n* Suédois/-e *m/f*. **Sweden** *n* Suède *f*.

**Swedish** /ˈswiːdɪʃ/ *adj* suédois. ● *n* (Ling) suédois *m*.

**sweep** /swiːp/ *vt/i* (*pt* **swept**) (floor) balayer; (carry away) emporter, entraîner; (chimney) ramoner. ● *n* coup *m* de balai; (curve) courbe *f*; (movement) geste *m*, mouvement *m*; (for chimneys) ramoneur *m*. **~ by** passer rapidement or majestueusement. **sweeper** *n* (for carpet) balai *m* mécanique; (football) libero *m*.

**sweet** /swiːt/ *adj* (not sour, pleasant) doux; (not savoury) sucré; (charming ⚁) gentil; **have a ~ tooth** aimer les sucreries. ● *n* bonbon *m*; (dish) dessert *m*. **~corn** *n* maïs *m*.

**sweeten** /ˈswiːtn/ *vt* sucrer; (fig) adoucir. **sweetener** *n* édulcorant *m*.

**sweetheart** /ˈswiːthɑːt/ *n* petit/-e ami/-e *m/f*; (term of endearment) chéri/-e m/f.

**sweetly** /'swiːtlɪ/ adv gentiment.

**sweetness** /'swiːtnɪs/ n douceur f; goût m sucré.

**sweet pea** n pois m de senteur.

**swell** /swel/ vt/i (pt swelled; pp swollen or swelled) (increase) grossir; (expand) (se) gonfler; (hand, face) enfler. ● n (of sea) houle f. **swelling** n (Med) enflure f.

**sweltering** /'sweltərɪŋ/ adj étouffant.

**swept** /swept/ ⟶SWEEP.

**swerve** /swɜːv/ vi faire un écart.

**swift** /swɪft/ adj rapide. ● n (bird) martinet m.

**swim** /swɪm/ vt/i (pt swam; pp swum; pres p swimming) nager; (be dizzy) tourner. ● vt traverser à la nage; (distance) nager. ● n baignade f; go for a ~ aller se baigner. **swimmer** n nageur/-euse m/f.

**swimming** n natation f.

**swimming pool** n piscine f.

**swimsuit** /'swɪmsuːt/ n maillot m (de bain).

**swindle** /'swɪndl/ vt escroquer. ● n escroquerie f.

**swine** /swaɪn/ npl (pigs) pourceaux mpl. ● n inv (person 🎓) salaud m.

**swing** /swɪŋ/ vt/i (pt swung) (se) balancer; (turn round) tourner; (pendulum) osciller. ● n balancement m; (seat) balançoire f; (of opinion) revirement m (towards en faveur de); (Mus) rythme m; be in full ~ battre son plein. □ ~ round (person) se retourner.

**swipe** /swaɪp/ vt (hit 🎓) frapper; (steal 🎓) piquer. ● ~ card n carte f magnétique, badge m.

**swirl** /swɜːl/ vi tourbillonner. ● n tourbillon m.

**Swiss** /swɪs/ adj suisse. ● n inv Suisse m/f.

**switch** /swɪtʃ/ n bouton m (électrique), interrupteur m; (shift) changement m, revirement m. ● vt (transfer) transférer; (exchange) échanger (for contre); (reverse positions of) changer de place; ~ trains (change) changer de train. ● vi changer. □ ~ off éteindre; ~ on mettre, allumer.

**switchboard** /'swɪtʃbɔːd/ n standard m.

**Switzerland** /'swɪtsələnd/ n Suisse f.

**swivel** /'swɪvl/ vt/i (pt swivelled) (faire) pivoter.

**swollen** /'swəʊlən/ ⟶SWELL.

**swoop** /swuːp/ vi (bird) fondre; (police) faire une descente, foncer. ● n (police raid) descente f.

**sword** /sɔːd/ n épée f.

**swore** /swɔː(r)/ ⟶SWEAR.

**sworn** /swɔːn/ ⟶SWEAR. ● adj (enemy) juré; (ally) dévoué.

**swot** /swɒt/ vt/i (pt swotted) (study 🎓) bûcher 🎓. ● n 🎓 bûcheur/-euse m/f🎓.

**swum** /swʌm/ ⟶SWIM.

**swung** /swʌŋ/ ⟶SWING.

**syllabus** /'sɪləbəs/ n (pl ~es) (School, Univ) programme m.

**symbol** /'sɪmbl/ n symbole m. **symbolic (al)** adj symbolique. **symbolize** vt symboliser.

**symmetrical** /sɪ'metrɪkəl/ adj symétrique.

**sympathetic** /sɪmpə'θetɪk/ adj compatissant; (fig) compréhensif.

**sympathize** /'sɪmpəθaɪz/ vi ~ with (pity) plaindre; (fig) comprendre les sentiments de. **sympathizer** n sympathisant/-e m/f.

**sympathy** /'sɪmpəθɪ/ n (pity) compassion f; (fig) compréhension f; (solidarity) solidarité f; (condolences) condoléances fpl; (affinity) affinité *f*; be in ∼ with comprendre, être en accord avec.

**symptom** /'sɪmptəm/ *n* symptôme *m*.

**synagogue** /'sɪnəgɒg/ *n* synagogue *f*.

**synonym** /'sɪnənɪm/ *n* synonyme *m*.

**synopsis** /sɪ'nɒpsɪs/ *n* (*pl* **-opses**) résumé *m*.

**syntax** /'sɪntæks/ *n* syntaxe *f*.

**synthesis** /'sɪnθəsɪs/ *n* (*pl* **-theses**) synthèse *f*.

**synthetic** /sɪn'θetɪk/ *adj* synthétique.

**syringe** /sɪ'rɪndʒ/ *n* seringue *f*.

**syrup** /'sɪrəp/ *n* (liquid) sirop *m*; (treacle) mélasse *f* raffinée.

**system** /'sɪstəm/ *n* système *m*; (body) organisme *m*; (order) méthode *f*. **systematic** *adj* systématique.

**systems analyst** *n* analyste-programmeur/- euse *m*/*f*.

• • • • • • • • • • • • • • • • • • • •

# Tt

**tab** /tæb/ *n* (on can) languette *f*; (on garment) patte *f*; (label) étiquette *f*; (US Ⓣ) addition *f*; (Comput) tabulatrice *f*; (setting) tabulation *f*.

**table** /'teɪbl/ *n* table *f*; at (the) ∼ à table; **lay** *or* **set** the ∼ mettre la table. • *vt* (motion) présenter. ∼-**cloth** *n* nappe *f*. ∼-**mat** *n* set *m* de table. ∼**spoon** *n* cuillère *f* de service.

**tablet** /'tæblɪt/ *n* (of stone) plaque *f*; (drug) comprimé *m*.

**table tennis** *n* tennis *m* de table.

ping-pong® *m*.

**taboo** /tə'buː/ *n* & *a* tabou (*m*).

**tacit** /'tæsɪt/ *adj* tacite.

**tack** /tæk/ *n* (nail) clou *m*; (stitch) point *m* de bâti; (course of action) voie *f*. • *vt* (nail) clouer; (stitch) bâtir; (add) ajouter. • *vi* (Naut) louvoyer.

**tackle** /'tækl/ *n* équipement *m*; (in soccer) tacle *m*; (in rugby) plaquage *m*. • *vt* (problem) s'attaquer à; (player) tacler, plaquer.

**tact** /tækt/ *n* tact *m*. **tactful** *adj* plein de tact.

**tactics** /'tæktɪks/ *npl* tactique *f*.

**tadpole** /'tædpəʊl/ *n* têtard *m*.

**tag** /tæg/ *n* (label) étiquette *f*. • *vt* (*pt* **tagged**) (label) étiqueter. • *vi* ∼ **along** Ⓣ suivre.

**tail** /teɪl/ *n* queue *f*; ∼**s** (coat) habit *m*; ∼**s!** (on coin) pile! • *vt* (follow) filer. • *vi* ∼ **away** *or* **off** diminuer. ∼-**back** *n* bouchon *m*. ∼-**gate** *n* hayon *m*.

**tailor** /'teɪlə(r)/ *n* tailleur *m*. • *vt* (garment) façonner; (fig) adapter. ∼-**made** *adj* fait sur mesure.

**take** /teɪk/ *vt*/*i* (*pt* **took**; *pp* **taken**) prendre (**from sb** à qn); (carry) emporter, porter (**to** à); (escort) emmener; (contain) contenir; (tolerate) supporter; (accept) accepter; (prize) remporter; (exam) passer; (precedence) avoir; (view) adopter; ∼ **sb home** ramener qn chez lui; **be taken by** *or* **with** être impressionné par; **be taken ill** tomber malade; it ∼**s time** il faut du temps pour. □ ∼ **after** tenir de; ∼ **apart** démonter; (fig) descendre en flammes Ⓣ; ∼ **away** (object) enlever; (person) emmener; (pain) supprimer; ∼ **back** reprendre; (return) rendre; (accompany) raccompagner; (statement) retirer; ∼ **down** (object) descendre; (notes) prendre; ∼ **in** (ob-

*ject*) rentrer; (*include*) inclure; (*cheat*) tromper; ~ **off** (Aviat) décoller; ~ **sth off** enlever qch; ~ **sb off** imiter qn; ~ **on** (*task, staff, passenger*) prendre; (*challenger*) relever le défi de; ~ **out** sortir; (*stain*) enlever; ~ **over** *vt* (*country, firm*) prendre le contrôle de; *vi* prendre le pouvoir; ~ **over from** remplacer; ~ **part** participer (in à); ~ **place** avoir lieu; ~ **to** se prendre d'amitié pour; (*activity*) prendre goût à; ~ **to doing** se mettre à faire; ~ **up** (*object*) monter; (*hobby*) se mettre à; (*occupy*) prendre; (*resume*) reprendre; ~ **up with** se lier avec. ~**away** *n* (*meal*) repas *m* à emporter. ~**off** *n* (Aviat) décollage *m*. ~**over** *n* (Pol) prise *f* de pouvoir; (Comm) rachat *m*.

**tale** /teɪl/ *n* conte *m*; (*report*) récit *m*; (*lie*) histoire *f*.

**talent** /ˈtælənt/ *n* talent *m*. **talented** *adj* doué.

**talk** /tɔːk/ *vt/i* parler; (*chat*) bavarder; ~ **sb into doing** persuader qn de faire; ~ **sth over** discuter de qch. ● *n* (*talking*) propos *mpl*; (*conversation*) conversation *f*; (*lecture*) exposé *m*.

**talkative** /ˈtɔːkətɪv/ *adj* bavard.

**tall** /tɔːl/ *adj* (*high*) haut; (*person*) grand.

**tame** /teɪm/ *adj* apprivoisé; (*dull*) insipide. ● *vt* apprivoiser; (*lion*) dompter.

**tamper** /ˈtæmpə(r)/ *vi* ~ **with** (*lock, machine*) tripoter; (*accounts, evidence*) trafiquer.

**tan** /tæn/ *vt/i* (*pt* **tanned**) bronzer; (*hide*) tanner. ● *n* bronzage *m*.

**tangerine** /tændʒəˈriːn/ *n* mandarine *f*.

**tangle** /ˈtæŋgl/ *vt/i* ~ **(up)** s'emmêler. ● *n* enchevêtrement *m*.

**tank** /tæŋk/ *n* réservoir *m*; (*vat*)

cuve *f*; (for fish) aquarium *m*; (Mil) char *m* (de combat).

**tanker** /ˈtæŋkə(r)/ *n* (lorry) camion-citerne *m*; (ship) navire-citerne *m*; **oil/petrol** ~ pétrolier *m*.

**tantrum** /ˈtæntrəm/ *n* crise *f* (de colère).

**tap** /tæp/ *n* (for water) robinet *m*; (knock) petit coup *m*; **on** ~ disponible. ● *vt* (*pt* **tapped**) (knock) taper (document); (resources) exploiter; (phone) mettre sur écoute.

**tape** /teɪp/ *n* bande *f* (magnétique); (cassette) cassette *f*; (video) cassette *f* vidéo; (fabric) ruban *m*; (sticky) scotch (r) *m*. ● *vt* (record) enregistrer; ~ **sth to sth** coller qch à qch. ~**measure** *n* mètre *m* ruban. ~ **recorder** *n* magnétophone *m*.

**tapestry** /ˈtæpəstri/ *n* tapisserie *f*.

**tar** /tɑː(r)/ *n* goudron *m*. ● *vt* (*pt* **tarred**) goudronner.

**target** /ˈtɑːgɪt/ *n* cible *f*; (objective) objectif *m*. ● *vt* (city) prendre pour cible; (weapon) diriger; (in marketing) viser.

**tariff** /ˈtærɪf/ *n* (price list) tarif *m*; (on imports) droit *m* de douane.

**tarmac**® /ˈtɑːmæk/ *n* macadam *m*; (runway) piste *f*.

**tarpaulin** /tɑːˈpɔːlɪn/ *n* bâche *f*.

**tarragon** /ˈtærəgən/ *n* estragon *m*.

**tart** /tɑːt/ *n* tarte *f*. ● *adj* aigrelet.

**task** /tɑːsk/ *n* tâche *f*.

**taste** /teɪst/ *n* goût *m*; (experience) aperçu *m*. ● *vt* (eat, enjoy) goûter à; (try) goûter; (perceive taste of) sentir (le goût de). ● *vi* ~ **of** or **like** avoir un goût de. **tasteful** *adj* de bon goût.

**tattoo** /təˈtuː/ *vt* tatouer. ● *n* tatouage *m*.

**tatty** /ˈtæti/ *adj* (**-ier, -iest**) [▪] miteux.

**taught** /tɔːt/ ➡TEACH.

**taunt** /tɔːnt/ vt railler. ● n raillerie f.

**Taurus** /'tɔːrəs/ n Taureau m.

**tax** /tæks/ n (on goods, services) taxe f; (on income) impôt m. ● vt imposer; (put to test: fig) mettre à l'épreuve. **taxable** adj imposable.
**taxation** n imposition f; (taxes) impôts mpl.

**tax:** ~ **collector** n percepteur m. ~**-deductible** adj déductible des impôts. ● **disc** n vignette f. ~**-free** adj exempt d'impôts. ~ **haven** n paradis m fiscal.

**taxi** /'tæksɪ/ n taxi m. ~ **rank** n station f de taxi.

**tax:** ~**payer** n contribuable mf. ~ **relief** n dégrèvement m fiscal. ~ **return** n déclaration f d'impôts.

**tea** /tiː/ n (drink, meal) thé m; (children's snack) goûter m; ~ **bag** sachet m de thé.

**teach** /tiːtʃ/ vt (pt **taught**) apprendre (sb sth qch à qn); (in school) enseigner (sb sth qch à qn). ● vi enseigner. **teacher** n enseignant/-e m/f; (secondary) professeur m; (primary) instituteur/-trice m/f.

**team** /tiːm/ n équipe f; (of animals) attelage m. ● vi ~ **up** faire équipe (with avec).

**teapot** /'tiːpɒt/ n théière f.

**tear¹** /teə(r)/ vt/i (pt **tore**; pp **torn**) (se) déchirer; (snatch) arracher (from à); (rush) aller à toute vitesse. ● n déchirure f.

**tear²** /tɪə(r)/ n larme f; in ~s en larmes. ~**-gas** n gaz m lacrymogène.

**tease** /tiːz/ vt taquiner. ● n taquin/-e m/f.

**tea:** ~ **shop** n salon m de thé. ~**spoon** n petite cuillère f.

**teat** /tiːt/ n tétine f.

**tea-towel** n torchon m.

**technical** /'teknɪkl/ adj technique.

**technician** /tek'nɪʃn/ n technicien/-ne m/f.

**technique** /tek'niːk/ n technique f.

**techno** /'teknəʊ/ n (Mus) techno f.

**technology** /tek'nɒlədʒɪ/ n technologie f.

**technophobe** /'teknəʊfəʊb/ n technophobe mf.

**teddy** /'tedɪ/ adj ~ **bear** ours m en peluche.

**tedious** /'tiːdɪəs/ adj ennuyeux.

**tee** /tiː/ n (golf) tee m.

**teenage** /'tiːneɪdʒ/ adj (girl, boy) adolescent; (fashion) des adolescents. **teenager** n jeune mf, adolescent/-e m/f.

**teens** /tiːnz/ npl in one's ~ adolescent.

**teeth** /tiːθ/ ➡TOOTH.

**teethe** /tiːð/ vi faire ses dents.

**teetotaller** /tiː'təʊtələ(r)/ n personne f qui ne boit pas d'alcool.

**telecommunications** /telɪkəmjuːnɪ'keɪʃnz/ npl télécommunications fpl.

**telecommuting** /telɪkə'mjuːtɪŋ/ n télétravail m.

**teleconferencing** /telɪ'kɒnfərənsɪŋ/ n téléconférence f.

**telegram** /'telɪgræm/ n télégramme m.

**telegraph** /'telɪgrɑːf/ n télégraphe m. ● adj télégraphique.

**telephone** /'telɪfəʊn/ n téléphone m. ● vt (person) téléphoner à; (message) téléphoner. ● vi téléphoner. ~ **book** n annuaire m. ~ **booth**, ~ **box** n cabine f téléphonique. ~ **call** n coup m de téléphone. ~ **number** n numéro m de téléphone.

**telephoto** /telɪ'fəʊtəʊ/ adj ~ **lens** téléobjectif m.

**telescope** /'telɪskəʊp/ n télescope m.

*m*. ● *vt/i* (se) télescoper.

**teletext** /'telitekst/ *n* télétexte *m*.

**televise** /'telivaiz/ *vt* téléviser.

**television** /'telivi3n/ *n* télévision *f*; **~ set** poste *m* de télévision, téléviseur *m*.

**teleworking** /'teliwɜːkɪŋ/ *n* télétravail *m*.

**telex** /'teleks/ *n* télex *m*. ● *vt* envoyer par télex.

**tell** /tel/ *vt* (*pt* **told**) dire (sb sth qch à qn); (story) raconter; (distinguish) distinguer; ~ **sb to do sth** dire à qn de faire qch; ~ **sth from sth** voir la différence entre qch et qch. ● *vt* (show) avoir un effet; (know) savoir. □ ~ **off** 🔲 gronder.

**temp** /temp/ *n* intérimaire *mf*. ● *vi* faire de l'intérim.

**temper** /'tempə(r)/ *n* humeur *f*; (anger) colère *f*; **lose one's ~** se mettre en colère.

**temperament** /'tempramant/ *n* tempérament *m*. **temperamental** *adj* capricieux.

**temperature** /'temprətʃə(r)/ *n* température *f*; **have a ~** avoir de la fièvre *or* de la température.

**temple** /'templ/ *n* temple *m*; (of head) tempe *f*.

**temporary** /'temprəri/ *adj* temporaire, provisoire.

**tempt** /tempt/ *vt* tenter; ~ **sb to do** donner envie à qn de faire.

**ten** /ten/ *adj* & *n* dix (*m*).

**tenacious** /tɪ'neɪʃəs/ *adj* tenace.

**tenancy** /'tenənsi/ *n* location *f*; **tenant** *n* locataire *mf*.

**tend** /tend/ *vt* s'occuper de. ● *vi* ~ **to** (be apt to) avoir tendance à; (look after) s'occuper de. **tendency** *n* tendance *f*.

**tender** /'tendə(r)/ *adj* tendre; (sore, painful) sensible. ● *vt* offrir, donner. ● *vi* faire une soumission. ● *n*

(Comm) soumission *f*; **be legal ~** (money) avoir cours.

**tendon** /'tendən/ *n* tendon *m*.

**tennis** /'tenis/ *n* tennis *m*. ● *adj* (court, match) de tennis.

**tenor** /'tenə(r)/ *n* (meaning) sens *m* général; (Mus) ténor *m*.

**tense** /tens/ *n* (Gram) temps *m*. ● *adj* tendu. ● *vt* (muscles) tendre, raidir. ● *vi* (face) se crisper.

**tension** /'tenʃn/ *n* tension *f*.

**tent** /tent/ *n* tente *f*.

**tentative** /'tentətɪv/ *adj* provisoire; (hesitant) timide.

**tenth** /tenθ/ *adj* & *n* dixième (*mf*).

**tepid** /'tepɪd/ *adj* tiède.

**term** /tɜːm/ *n* (word, limit) terme *m*; (of imprisonment) temps *m*; (School) trimestre *m*; ~**s** conditions *fpl*; **on good/bad ~s** en bons/ mauvais termes; **in the short/long ~** à court/long terme; **come to ~s with sth** accepter qch; ~ **of office** (Pol) mandat *m*. ● *vt* appeler.

**terminal** /'tɜːmɪnl/ *adj* (point) terminal; (illness) incurable. ● *n* (oil, computer) terminal *m*; (Rail) terminus *m*; (Electr) borne *f*; **air ~** aérogare *f*.

**terminate** /'tɜːmɪneɪt/ *vt* mettre fin à. ● *vi* prendre fin.

**terminus** /'tɜːmɪnəs/ *n* (*pl* **-ni**) (station) terminus *m*.

**terrace** /'terəs/ *n* terrasse *f*; (houses) rangée *f* de maisons contiguës; **the ~s** (Sport) les gradins *mpl*.

**terracotta** /terə'kɒtə/ *n* terre *f* cuite.

**terrible** /'terəbl/ *adj* affreux, atroce.

**terrific** /tə'rɪfɪk/ *adj* (huge) énorme; (great 🔲) formidable.

**terrify** /'terɪfaɪ/ *vt* terrifier; **be terrified of** avoir très peur de.

**t**

**territory** /ˈterətrɪ/ n territoire m.

**terror** /ˈterə(r)/ n terreur f.

**terrorism** /ˈterərɪzəm/ n terrorisme m. **terrorist** n terroriste mf.

**test** /test/ n épreuve f; (written exam) contrôle m; (of machine, product) essai m; (of sample) analyse f; driving ~ examen m du permis de conduire. • vt évaluer; (School) contrôler; (machine, product) essayer; (sample) analyser; (patience, strength) mettre à l'épreuve. • vi ~ for faire une recherche de.

**testament** /ˈtestəmənt/ n testament m; Old/New T~ Ancien/ Nouveau Testament m.

**testicle** /ˈtestɪkl/ n testicule m.

**testify** /ˈtestɪfaɪ/ vt/i témoigner (to de; that que).

**testimony** /ˈtestɪmənɪ/ n témoignage m.

**test tube** n éprouvette f.

**tetanus** /ˈtetənəs/ n tétanos m.

**text** /tekst/ n texte m. • vt ~ sb envoyer un texto à qn. ~book n manuel m. ~ message n texto m.

**texture** /ˈtekstʃə(r)/ n (of paper) grain m; (of fabric) texture f.

**than** /ðæn/, /ðən/ conj que, qu'; (with numbers) de; more/less ~ ten plus/moins de dix.

**thank** /θæŋk/ vt remercier; ~ you!, ~s! merci! **thankful** adj reconnaissant. **thanks** npl remerciements mpl; ~s to grâce à. **Thanksgiving (Day)** n (US) jour m d'Action de Grâces.

---

**that** /ðæt/ pl **those**

● determiner

····▸ ce, cet, cette, ces; ~ dog ce chien; ~ man cet homme; ~ woman cette femme; those

books ces livres; at ~ moment à ce moment-là.

❗ To distinguish that/those from this/these, you add -là to the noun: I prefer that car je préfère cette voiture-là.

● pronoun

····▸ cela, ça, ce; what's ~?, what are those? qu'est-ce que c'est (que ça)?; who's ~? qui est-ce?; ~ is my brother c'est or voilà mon frère; those are my parents ce sont mes parents.

····▸ (emphatic) celui-là, celle-là, ceux-là, celles-là; all the dresses are nice but I like ~/those best toutes les robes sont jolies mais je préfère celle-là/celles-là.

● relative pronoun

····▸ (for subject) qui; the man ~ stole the car l'homme qui a volé la voiture.

····▸ (for object) que; the girl ~ I met la fille que j'ai rencontrée.

❗ With a preposition, use lequel/laquelle/lesquels/ lesquelles: the chair ~ I was sitting on la chaise sur laquelle j'étais assis.
With a preposition that translates as à, use auquel/à laquelle/ auxquels/auxquelles: the girls ~ I was talking to les filles auxquelles je parlais.
With a preposition that translates as de, use dont: the people ~ I've talked about les personnes dont j'ai parlé.

● conjunction que; she said ~ she would do it elle a dit qu'elle le ferait.

t

**thatched** /'θætʃd/ adj de chaume; ~ **cottage** chaumière f.

**thaw** /θɔː/ vt/i (faire) dégeler; (snow) (faire) fondre. ● n dégel m.

---

**the** /ðə, ðiː/ determiner

····▸ le, l', la, les; ~ **dog** le chien; ~ **tree** l'arbre; ~ **chair** la chaise; to ~ **shops** aux magasins.

! With a preposition that translates as à: à + le = au and à + les = aux.

---

**theatre** /'θɪətə(r)/ n théâtre m.

**theft** /θeft/ n vol m.

**their** /ðeə(r)/ adj leur, pl leurs.

**theirs** /ðeəz/ pron le or la leur, les leurs.

**them** /ðem/, /ðəm/ pron les; (after preposition) eux, elles; (to) ~ leur; phone ~! téléphone-leur!; I know ~ je les connais; both of ~ tous/toutes les deux.

**theme** /θiːm/ n thème m. ~ **park** n parc m de loisirs (à thème).

**themselves** /ðəm'selvz/ pron eux-mêmes, elles-mêmes; (reflexive) se; (after preposition) eux, elles.

**then** /ðen/ adv alors; (next) ensuite, puis; (therefore) alors, donc. ● adj d'alors; from ~ on dès lors.

**theology** /θɪ'ɒlədʒɪ/ n théologie f.

**theory** /'θɪərɪ/ n théorie f.

**therapy** /'θerəpɪ/ n thérapie f.

**there** /ðeə/ adv là; (with verb) y; (over there) là-bas; he goes ~ il y va; on ~ là-dessus; ~ is, ~ are il y a; (pointing) voilà. ● interj; ~, ~ are il y a; ~, allons, allons!

**therefore** /'ðeəfɔː(r)/ adv donc.

**thermal** /'θɜːml/ adj thermique.

**thermometer** /θə'mɒmɪtə(r)/ n thermomètre m.

**Thermos®** /'θɜːməs/ n thermos ® m or f inv.

**thermostat** /'θɜːməstæt/ n thermostat m.

**thesaurus** /θɪ'sɔːrəs/ n (pl -ri) dictionnaire m de synonymes.

**these** /ðiːz/ ➡THIS.

**thesis** /'θiːsɪs/ n (pl theses) thèse f.

**they** /ðeɪ/ pron ils, elles; (emphatic) eux, elles; (people in general) on.

**thick** /θɪk/ adj épais; (stupid) bête; be 6 cm ~ avoir 6 cm d'épaisseur.

**thief** /θiːf/ n (pl thieves) voleur/-euse m/f.

**thigh** /θaɪ/ n cuisse f.

**thin** /θɪn/ adj (thinner, thinnest) mince; (person) maigre, mince; (sparse) clairsemé; (fine) fin. ● vt/i (pt thinned) ~ (down) (paint) diluer; (soup) allonger.

**thing** /θɪŋ/ n chose f; ~s (belongings) affaires fpl; the best ~ is to le mieux est de; the (right) ~ ce qu'il faut (for sb à qn).

**think** /θɪŋk/ vt/i (pt thought) penser (about, of à); (carefully) réfléchir (about, of à); (believe) croire; I ~ so je crois que oui; ~ of doing envisager de faire. □ ~ **over** bien réfléchir à; □ ~ **up** inventer.

**third** /θɜːd/ adj troisième. ● n troisième mf; (fraction) tiers m. **T~ World** n tiers-monde m.

**thirst** /θɜːst/ n soif f.

**thirsty** /'θɜːstɪ/ adj be ~ avoir soif; make ~ donner soif à.

**thirteen** /θɜː'tiːn/ adj & n treize (m).

**thirty** /'θɜːtɪ/ adj & n trente (m).

**this** /ðɪs/*pl* **these**

● *determiner*
····▸ ce/cet/cette/ces; ~ **dog** ce chien; ~ **man** cet homme; ~ **woman** cette femme; these **books** ces livres.

**!** To distinguish from that and those, you need to add *-ci* after the noun: **I prefer this car** je préfère cette voiture-ci.

● *pronoun*
····▸ ce; **what's** ~?, **what are these?** qu'est-ce que c'est?; **who is** ~? qui est-ce?; ~ **is the kitchen** voici la cuisine; ~ **is Sophie** je te *or* vous présente Sophie; **these are your things** ce sont tes affaires.
····▸ (*emphatic*) celui-ci/celle-ci/ceux-ci/celles-ci; **all the dresses are nice but I like** ~/**these** toutes ces robes sont jolies mais je préfère celle-ci/celles-ci.

**thistle** /ˈθɪsl/ *n* chardon *m*.

**thorn** /θɔːn/ *n* épine *f*.

**thorough** /ˈθʌrə/ *adj* (detailed) approfondi; (meticulous) minutieux. **thoroughly** *adv* (clean, study) à fond; (very) tout à fait.

**those** /ðəʊz/ ➡ **THAT**.

**though** /ðəʊ/ *conj* bien que. ● *adv* quand même.

**thought** /θɔːt/ ➡ **THINK**. ● *n* pensée *f*, idée *f*. **thoughtful** *adj* pensif; (kind) prévenant.

**thousand** /ˈθaʊznd/ *adj* & *n* mille (*m inv*); ~**s of** des milliers de. **thousandth** *adj* & *n* millième (*mf*).

**thread** /θred/ *n* (yarn & fig) fil *m*; (of screw) pas *m*. ● *vt* enfiler; ~ **one's way** se faufiler.

**threat** /θret/ *n* menace *f*. **threaten**

*vt/i* menacer (with de).

**three** /θriː/ *adj* & *n* trois (*m*).

**threw** /θruː/ ➡ **THROW**.

**thrill** /θrɪl/ *n* frisson *m*; (pleasure) plaisir *m*. ● *vt* transporter (de joie); **be** ~**ed** être ravi. ● *vi* frissonner (de joie).

**thrive** /θraɪv/ *vi* (*pt* **thrived** *or* **throve**,*pp* **thrived** *or* **thriven**) prospérer; **he** ~**s on** it cela lui réussit.

**throat** /θrəʊt/ *n* gorge *f*; **have a sore** ~ avoir mal à la gorge.

**throb** /θrɒb/ *vi* (*pt* **throbbed**) (heart) battre; (engine) vibrer. ● *n* (pain) élancement *m*; (of engine) vibration *f*. **throbbing** *adj* (pain) lancinant.

**throne** /θrəʊn/ *n* trône *m*.

**through** /θruː/ *prep* à travers; (during) pendant; (by means of) par, (out of) par; (by reason of) grâce à, à cause de. ● *adv* à travers; (entirely) jusqu'au bout. ● *adj* (train) direct; **be** ~ (finished) avoir fini; **come** *or* **go** ~ (cross, pierce) traverser; **I'm putting you** ~ je vous passe votre correspondant.

**throughout** /θruːˈaʊt/ *prep* ~ **the country** dans tout le pays; ~ **the day** pendant toute la journée. ● *adv* (place) partout; (time) tout le temps.

**throw** /θrəʊ/ *vt* (*pt* **threw**; *pp* **thrown**) jeter, lancer; (baffle) déconcerter; ~ **a party** faire une fête. ● *n* jet *m*; (of dice) coup *m*. □ **away** jeter; (get rid of) se débarrasser de; ~ **out** jeter; (person) expulser; (reject) rejeter; ~ **up** (arms) lever; (vomit 🛈) vomir.

**thrust** /θrʌst/ *vt* (*pt* **thrust**) pousser. ● *n* poussée *f*.

**thud** /θʌd/ *n* bruit *m* sourd.

**thug** /θʌg/ *n* voyou *m*.

**thumb** /θʌm/ *n* pouce *m*. ● *vt*

*t*

# thump | tingle

572

(book) feuilleter; ~ **a lift** faire de l'autostop. **~-index** n répertoire m à onglets.

**thump** /θʌmp/ vt/i cogner (sur); (heart) battre fort. ● n coup m.

**thunder** /'θʌndə(r)/ n tonnerre m. ● vi (weather, person) tonner. **~storm** n orage m.

**Thursday** /'θɜːzdeɪ/ n jeudi m.

**thus** /ðʌs/ adv ainsi.

**thwart** /θwɔːt/ vt contrecarrer.

**thyme** /taɪm/ n thym m.

**tick** /tɪk/ n (sound) tic-tac m; (mark) coche f; (moment 🄸) instant m; (insect) tique f. ● vt faire tic-tac. ● vt (~ off) cocher. ▫ ~ **over** tourner au ralenti.

**ticket** /'tɪkɪt/ n billet m; (for bus, cloakroom) ticket m; (label) étiquette f. ● **~-collector** n contrôleur/-euse m/f. **~-office** n guichet m.

**tickle** /'tɪkl/ vt chatouiller; (amuse: fig) amuser. ● n chatouillement m.

**tidal** /'taɪdl/ adj (river) à marées. ● **wave** n raz-de-marée m inv.

**tide** /taɪd/ n marée f. (of events)

**tidy** /'taɪdɪ/ adj (-ier,-iest) (room) bien rangé; (appearance, work) soigné; (methodical) ordonné; (amount 🄸) joli. ● vt/i (~ up) faire du rangement; ~ **sth** ranger qch; ~ **oneself up** s'arranger.

**tie** /taɪ/ vt (pres p tying) attacher; (knot) faire; (scarf) nouer; (link) lier. ● vi (in football) faire match nul; (in race) être ex aequo. ● n (necktie) cravate f; (fastener) attache f; (link) lien m; (draw) match m nul. ~ **down** attacher; ~ **in with** être lié à; ~ **up** attacher; (money) immobiliser; (occupy) occuper.

**tier** /tɪə(r)/ n étage m, niveau m; (in stadium) gradin m.

**tiger** /'taɪgə(r)/ n tigre m.

**tight** /taɪt/ adj (clothes, budget) serré; (grip) ferme; (rope) tendu; (security) strict; (angle) aigu. ● adv (hold, sleep) bien; (squeeze) fort.

**tighten** /'taɪtn/ vt/i (se) tendre; (bolt) (se) resserrer; (control) renforcer.

**tights** /taɪts/ npl collant m.

**tile** /taɪl/ n (on wall, floor) carreau m; (on roof) tuile f. ● vt carreler; couvrir de tuiles.

**till** /tɪl/ n caisse f (enregistreuse). ● vt (land) cultiver. ● prep & conj ►UNTIL.

**timber** /'tɪmbə(r)/ n bois m (de construction); (trees) arbres mpl.

**time** /taɪm/ n temps m; (moment) moment m; (epoch) époque f; (by clock) heure f; (occasion) fois f; (rhythm) mesure f; ~**s** (multiplying) fois fpl; **any** ~ n'importe quand; **for the** ~ being pour le moment; **from** ~ **to** ~ de temps en temps; **have a good** ~ s'amuser; **in no** ~ en un rien de temps; **in** ~ à temps; (eventually) avec le temps; **a long** ~ longtemps; **on** ~ à l'heure; **what's the** ~? quelle heure est-il?; ~ **off** du temps libre. ● vt choisir le moment de; (measure) minuter; (Sport) chronométrer. ~ **limit** n délai m.

**timer** /'taɪmə(r)/ n minuterie f; (for cooker) minuteur m.

**time:** **~-scale** n délais mpl. **~-table** n horaire m. ~ **zone** n fuseau m horaire.

**timid** /'tɪmɪd/ adj timide; (fearful) peureux.

**tin** /tɪn/ n étain m; (container) boîte f. **~(-plate)** n fer-blanc m. ● vt (pt **tinned**) mettre en boîte. **~-foil** n papier m d'aluminium.

**tingle** /'tɪŋgl/ vi picoter. ● n picotement m.

573

# tin-opener | together

**tin-opener** n ouvre-boîtes m inv.

**tint** /tɪnt/ n teinte f; (for hair) shampooing m colorant. ● vt teinter.

**tiny** /ˈtaɪni/ adj (-ier, -iest) tout petit.

**tip** /tɪp/ n (of stick, pen, shoe, ski) pointe f; (of nose, finger, wing) bout m; (gratuity) pourboire m; (advice) tuyau m; (for rubbish) décharge f. ● vt/i (pt tipped) (tilt) pencher; (overturn) (faire) basculer; (pour) verser; (empty) déverser; (give money) donner un pourboire à. □ ~ off prévenir.

**tiptoe** /ˈtɪptəʊ/ n on ~ sur la pointe des pieds.

**tire** /ˈtaɪə(r)/ vt/i (se) fatiguer; ~ of se lasser de. ● n (US) pneu m.

**tired** /ˈtaɪəd/ adj fatigué; be ~ of en avoir assez de.

**tiring** /ˈtaɪərɪŋ/ adj fatigant.

**tissue** /ˈtɪʃuː/ n tissu m; (handkerchief) mouchoir m en papier; ~ (paper) papier m de soie.

**tit** /tɪt/ n (bird) mésange f; give ~ for tat rendre coup pour coup.

**title** /ˈtaɪtl/ n titre m. □ ~ **deed** n titre m de propriété.

---

**to** /tuː, tə/
● preposition

⋯▸ à; ~ Paris à Paris; give the book ~ Jane donne le livre à Jane; ~ the office au bureau; ~ the shops aux magasins.

⋯▸ (with feminine countries) en; ~ France en France.

⋯▸ (to + personal pronoun) me/te/lui/nous/vous/leur; she gave it ~ them elle le leur a donné; I'll say it ~ her je vais

le lui dire.

!  à + le = au
   à + les = aux.

● in an infinitive
to is not translated (to go aller; to sing chanter)

⋯▸ (in order to) pour; he's gone into town ~ buy a shirt il est parti en ville pour acheter une chemise.

⋯▸ (after adjectives) à; de; be easy/difficult ~ read être facile/difficile à lire; it's easy/difficult to read her writing c'est facile/difficile de lire son écriture.

➡ For verbal expressions using the infinitive 'to' such as to tell sb to do sth, to help sb to do sth ➡tell, help.

**toad** /təʊd/ n crapaud m.

**toast** /təʊst/ n pain m grillé, toast m; (drink) toast m. ● vt (bread) faire griller; (drink to) porter un toast à. **toaster** n grille-pain m inv.

**tobacco** /təˈbækəʊ/ n tabac m.

**tobacconist** /təˈbækənɪst/ n marchand/-e m/f de tabac; ~'s (shop) tabac m.

**toboggan** /təˈbɒɡən/ n toboggan m, luge f.

**today** /təˈdeɪ/ n & adv aujourd'hui (m).

**toddler** /ˈtɒdlə(r)/ n bébé m (qui fait ses premiers pas).

**toe** /təʊ/ n orteil m; (of shoe) bout m; on one's ~s vigilant. ● vt ~ the line se conformer.

**together** /təˈɡeðə(r)/ adv ensemble; (at same time) à la fois; ~ with avec.

# toilet | touch

**toilet** /'tɔɪlɪt/ n toilettes fpl.

**toiletries** /'tɔɪlɪtrɪz/ npl articles mpl de toilette.

**token** /'təʊkən/ n (symbol) témoignage m; (voucher) bon m; (coin) jeton m. ● adj symbolique.

**told** /təʊld/ →TELL.

**tolerance** /'tɒlərəns/ n tolérance f.

**tolerate** /'tɒləreɪt/ vt tolérer.

**toll** /təʊl/ n péage m; death ~ nombre m de morts; take its ~ faire des ravages. ● vi (bell) sonner.

**tomato** /tə'mɑːtəʊ/ n (pl ~es) tomate f.

**tomb** /tuːm/ n tombeau m.

**tomorrow** /tə'mɒrəʊ/ n & adv demain (m); ~ morning/night demain matin/soir; the day after ~ après-demain.

**ton** /tʌn/ n tonne f (= 1016 kg); (metric) tonne f (= 1000 kg); ~s of 🆃 des masses de.

**tone** /təʊn/ n ton m; (of radio, telephone) tonalité f. ● vt ~ down atténuer. ● vi ~ (in) s'harmoniser (with avec).

**tongs** /tɒŋz/ npl (for coal) pincettes fpl; (for sugar) pince f; (for hair) fer m.

**tongue** /tʌŋ/ n langue f.

**tonic** /'tɒnɪk/ n (Med) tonique m. ● adj (effect, accent) tonique; ~ (water) tonic m, Schweppes® m.

**tonight** /tə'naɪt/ n & adv (evening) ce soir; (night) cette nuit.

**tonsil** /'tɒnsl/ n amygdale f.

**too** /tuː/ adv trop; (also) aussi; ~ many people trop de gens; I've got ~much/many j'en ai trop; me ~ moi aussi.

**took** →TAKE.

**tool** /tuːl/ n outil m. ~bar n barre f d'outils. ~box n boîte f à outils.

**toot** /tuːt/ n coup m de klaxon®.

● vt/i ~ (the horn) klaxonner.

**tooth** /tuːθ/ n (pl teeth) dent f. ~ache n mal m de dents. ~brush n brosse f à dents. ~paste n dentifrice m. ~pick n cure-dents m inv.

**top** /tɒp/ n (highest point) sommet m; (upper part) haut m; (upper surface) dessus m; (lid) couvercle m; (of bottle, tube) bouchon m; (of beer bottle) capsule f; (of list) tête f; on ~ of sur; (fig) en plus de. ● adj (shelf) du haut; (step, floor) dernier; (in rank) premier; (best) meilleur; (distinguished) éminent; (maximum) maximum. ● vt (pt topped) (exceed) dépasser; (list) venir en tête de; ~ up remplir; ~ped with (dome) surmonté de; (cream) recouvert de.

**topic** /'tɒpɪk/ n sujet m.

**topless** /'tɒplɪs/ adj aux seins nus.

**torch** /tɔːtʃ/ n (electric) lampe f de poche; (flaming) torche f.

**tore** /tɔː(r)/ →TEAR¹.

**torment** /tɔː'ment/ vt tourmenter.

**torn** /tɔːn/ →TEAR¹.

**torrent** /'tɒrənt/ n torrent m.

**tortoise** /'tɔːtəs/ n tortue f. ~shell n écaille f.

**torture** /'tɔːtʃə(r)/ n torture f; (fig) supplice m. ● vt torturer.

**Tory** /'tɔːrɪ/ n & a tory (mf), conservateur/-trice (m/f).

**toss** /tɒs/ vt lancer; (salad) tourner; (pancake) faire sauter. ● vi se retourner; ~ a coin, ~ up tirer à pile ou face (for pour).

**tot** /tɒt/ n petit/-e enfant m/f; (drink) petit verre m.

**total** /'təʊtl/ n & a total (m). ● vt (pt totalled) (add up) additionner; (amount to) se monter à.

**touch** /tʌtʃ/ vt toucher; (tamper with) toucher à. ● vi se toucher. ● n (sense) toucher m; (contact) contact *m*; (of artist, writer) touche *f*; a ~of (small amount) un petit peu de; get in ~ with se mettre en contact avec; □ ~ off (Aviat) atterrir; ~ up retoucher. ~**down** n atterrissage *m* (Aviat). ~ **line** n ligne *f* de touche. ~-**tone** adj (phone) à touches.

**tough** /tʌf/ adj (negotiator) coriace; (law) sévère; (time) difficile; (robust) robuste.

**tour** /tʊə(r)/ n voyage *m*; (visit) visite *f*; (by team) tournée *f*; on ~ en tournée. ● vt visiter.

**tourist** /ˈtʊərɪst/ n touriste *mf*. ● adj touristique. ~ **office** n syndicat *m* d'initiative.

**tournament** /ˈtɔːnəmənt/ n tournoi *m*.

**tout** /taʊt/ vi ~ (for) racoler ⚀. ● vt (sell) revendre. ● n racoleur/-euse *m/f*; revendeur/-euse *m/f*.

**tow** /təʊ/ vt remorquer. ● n remorque *f*; on ~ en remorque.

**toward(s)** /təˈwɔːd(z)/ prep vers; (of attitude) envers.

**towel** /ˈtaʊəl/ n serviette *f*.

**tower** /ˈtaʊə(r)/ n tour *f*. ● vi ~ above dominer.

**town** /taʊn/ n ville *f*; in ~ en ville. ~ **council** n conseil *m* municipal. ~ **hall** n mairie *f*.

**tow:** ~ **path** n chemin *m* de halage. ~ **truck** n dépanneuse *f*.

**toxic** /ˈtɒksɪk/ adj toxique.

**toy** /tɔɪ/ n jouet *m*. ● vi ~ with (object) jouer avec; (idea) caresser.

**trace** /treɪs/ n trace *f*. ● vt (person) retrouver; (cause) déterminer; (life) retracer; (draw) tracer; (with tracing paper) décalquer.

**track** /træk/ n (of person, car) traces *fpl*; (of missile) trajectoire *f*; (path) sentier *m*; (Sport) piste *f*;

(Rail) voie *f*; (on disc) morceau *m*; keep ~ of suivre. ● vt suivre la trace or la trajectoire de. □ ~ **down** retrouver. ~ **suit** n survêtement *m*.

**tractor** /ˈtræktə(r)/ n tracteur *m*.

**trade** /treɪd/ n commerce *m*; (job) métier *m*; (swap) échange *m*. ● vi faire du commerce; ~ on exploiter. ● vt échanger. ● adj commercial. ~-**in** n reprise *f*. ~ **mark** n marque *f* (de fabrique); (registered) marque *f* déposée.

**trader** /ˈtreɪdə(r)/ n commerçant/-e *m/f*; (on stockmarket) opérateur/-trice *m/f*.

**trade union** n syndicat *m*.

**trading** /ˈtreɪdɪŋ/ n commerce *m*; (on stockmarket) transactions *fpl* (boursières).

**tradition** /trəˈdɪʃn/ n tradition *f*.

**traffic** /ˈtræfɪk/ n trafic *m*; (on road) circulation *f*. ● vi (pt **trafficked**) faire du trafic (in de). ~ **jam** n embouteillage *m*. ~-**lights** *npl* feux *mpl* (de circulation). ~ **warden** n contractuel/-le *m/f*.

**trail** /treɪl/ vt/i traîner; (plant) ramper; (track) suivre; ~ **behind** traîner. ● n (of powder) traînée *f*; (track) piste *f*; (path) sentier *m*.

**trailer** /ˈtreɪlə(r)/ n remorque *f*; (caravan) caravane *f*; (film) bande-annonce *f*.

**train** /treɪn/ n (Rail) train *m*; (underground) rame *f*; (procession) file *f*; (of dress) traîne *f*. ● vt (instruct, develop) former; (sportsman) entraîner; (animal) dresser; (ear) exercer; (aim) braquer. ● vi être formé, étudier; (Sport) s'entraîner. **trained** adj (skilled) qualifié; (doctor) diplômé. **trainee** n stagiaire *m*. **trainer** n (Sport) entraîneur/-euse *m/f*. **trainers** *npl* (shoes) chaussures *fpl* de sport. **training** n formation *f*.

t

(Sport) entraînement *m*.

**tram** /træm/ *n* tram(way) *m*.

**tramp** /træmp/ *vi* marcher (d'un pas lourd). ● *vt* parcourir. ● *n* (vagrant) clochard/-e *m/f*; (sound) bruit *m*.

**trample** /'træmpl/ *vt/i* ~ (on) piétiner; (fig) fouler aux pieds.

**tranquil** /'træŋkwɪl/ *adj* tranquille. **tranquillizer** *n* tranquillisant *m*.

**transact** /træn'zækt/ *vt* négocier. **transaction** *n* transaction *f*.

**transcript** /'trænskrɪpt/ *n* transcription *f*.

**transfer**[1] /træns'fɜː(r)/ *vt* (*pt* **transferred**) transférer; (*power*) céder; (*employee*) muter. ● *vi* être transféré; (*employee*) être muté.

**transfer**[2] /'trænsfɜː(r)/ *n* transfert *m*; (of employee) mutation *f*; (image) décalcomanie *f*.

**transform** /træns'fɔːm/ *vt* transformer.

**transitive** /'trænzɪtɪv/ *adj* transitif.

**translate** /trænz'leɪt/ *vt* traduire. **translation** *n* traduction *f*. **translator** *n* traducteur-trice *m/f*.

**transmit** /trænz'mɪt/ *vt* (*pt* **transmitted**) transmettre. **transmitter** *n* émetteur *m*.

**transparency** /træns'pærənsɪ/ *n* transparence *f*; (Photo) diapositive *f*.

**transplant** /træns'plɑːnt/ *vt* transplanter. ● /'trænsplɑːnt/ *n* transplantation *f*; (Med) greffe *f*.

**transport**[1] /træns'pɔːt/ *vt* transporter.

**transport**[2] /'trænspɔːt/ *n* transport *m*.

**trap** /træp/ *n* piège *m*. ● *vt* *pt* **trapped** (jam, pin down) coincer; (cut off) bloquer; (snare) prendre au piège.

**trash** /træʃ/ *n* (refuse) ordures *fpl*; (nonsense) idioties *fpl*. **~-can** *n* (US)

poubelle *f*.

**trauma** /'trɔːmə/ *n* traumatisme *m*. **traumatic** *adj* traumatisant.

**travel** /'trævl/ *vi* (*pt* **travelled**, US **traveled**) voyager; (*vehicle, bullet*) aller. ● *vt* parcourir. ● *n* voyages *mpl*. **~ agency** *n* agence *f* de voyages.

**traveller**, (US) **traveler** /'trævlə(r)/ *n* voyageur/-euse *m/f*; **~'s cheque** chèque *m* de voyage.

**trawler** /'trɔːlə(r)/ *n* chalutier *m*.

**tray** /treɪ/ *n* plateau *m*; (on office desk) corbeille *f*.

**treacle** /'triːkl/ *n* mélasse *f*.

**tread** /tred/ *vi* (*pt* **trod**, *pp* **trodden**) marcher (on sur). ● *vt* fouler. ● *n* (sound) pas *m*; (of tyre) chape *f*.

**treasure** /'treʒə(r)/ *n* trésor *m*. ● *vt* (*gift, memory*) chérir; (*friendship, possession*) tenir beaucoup à.

**treasury** /'treʒərɪ/ *n* trésorerie *f*; the T~ le ministère des Finances.

**treat** /triːt/ *vt* traiter; ~ sb to sth offrir qch à qn. ● *n* (pleasure) plaisir *m*; (food) gâterie *f*. **treatment** *n* traitement *m*.

**treaty** /'triːtɪ/ *n* traité *m*.

**treble** /'trebl/ *adj* triple; ~ clef clé *f* de sol. ● *vt/i* tripler. ● *n* (voice) soprano *m*.

**tree** /triː/ *n* arbre *m*.

**trek** /trek/ *n* randonnée *f*. ● *vi* (*pt* **trekked**) ~ across/through traverser péniblement; go ~king faire de la randonnée.

**tremble** /'trembl/ *vi* trembler.

**tremendous** /trɪ'mendəs/ *adj* énorme; (excellent) formidable.

**tremor** /'tremə(r)/ *n* tremblement *m*; (earth) ~ secousse *f*.

**trench** /trentʃ/ *n* tranchée *f*.

**trend** /trend/ *n* tendance *f*; (fashion) mode *f* **trendy** *adj* ▯ branché ▯.

**trespass** /ˈtrespəs/ vi s'introduire illégalement (on dans). **trespasser** n intrus/-e m/f.

**trial** /ˈtraɪəl/ n (Jur) procès m; (test) essai m; (ordeal) épreuve f; go on ~ passer en jugement; by ~ and error par expérience.

**triangle** /ˈtraɪæŋgl/ n triangle m.

**tribe** /traɪb/ n tribu f.

**tribunal** /traɪˈbjuːnl/ n tribunal m.

**tributary** /ˈtrɪbjʊtərɪ/ n affluent m.

**tribute** /ˈtrɪbjuːt/ n tribut m; pay ~ to rendre hommage à.

**trick** /trɪk/ n tour m; (dishonest) combine f; (knack) astuce f; do the ~ [] faire l'affaire. ● vt tromper. **trickery** n ruse f.

**trickle** /ˈtrɪkl/ vi dégouliner; ~ in/out arriver ou partir en petit nombre. ● n filet m; (fig) petit nombre m.

**tricky** /ˈtrɪkɪ/ adj (task) difficile; (question) épineux; (person) malin.

**trifle** /ˈtraɪfl/ n bagatelle f; (cake) diplomate m; a ~ (small amount) un peu. ● vi ~ with jouer avec.

**trigger** /ˈtrɪgə(r)/ n (of gun) gâchette f; (of machine) manette f. ● vt ~ (off) (initiate) déclencher.

**trim** /trɪm/ adj (trimmer, trimmest) soigné; (figure) svelte. ● vt (pt trimmed) (hair, grass) couper; (budget) réduire; (decorate) décorer. ● n (cut) coupe f d'entretien; (decoration) garniture f; in ~ en forme.

**trinket** /ˈtrɪŋkɪt/ n babiole f.

**trip** /trɪp/ vt/i (pt tripped) (faire) trébucher. ● n (journey) voyage m; (outing) excursion f.

**triple** /ˈtrɪpl/ adj triple. ● vt/i tripler. **triplets** npl triplés/-es m/fpl.

**tripod** /ˈtraɪpɒd/ n trépied m.

**trite** /traɪt/ adj banal.

**triumph** /ˈtraɪʌmf/ n triomphe m. ● vi triompher (over de).

**trivial** /ˈtrɪvɪəl/ adj insignifiant.

**trod, trodden** /trɒd(ən)/ →TREAD.

**trolley** /ˈtrɒlɪ/ n chariot m.

**trombone** /trɒmˈbəʊn/ n (Mus) trombone m.

**troop** /truːp/ n bande f; ~s (Mil) troupes fpl. ● vi ~ in/out entrer/sortir en bande.

**trophy** /ˈtrəʊfɪ/ n trophée m.

**tropic** /ˈtrɒpɪk/ n tropique m; ~s tropiques mpl.

**trot** /trɒt/ n trot m; on the ~ [] coup sur coup. ● vi (pt trotted) trotter.

**trouble** /ˈtrʌbl/ n problèmes mpl; ennuis mpl; (pains, effort) peine f; be in ~ avoir des ennuis; go to a lot of ~ se donner du mal; what's the ~? quel est le problème? ● vt (bother) déranger; (worry) tracasser. ● vi ~ (oneself) to do se donner la peine de faire. **~maker** n provocateur/-trice m/f. **~shooter** n conciliateur/-trice m/f. (Tech) expert m.

**troublesome** /ˈtrʌbləsəm/ adj ennuyeux.

**trousers** /ˈtraʊzəz/ npl pantalon m; short ~ short m.

**trout** /traʊt/ n inv truite f.

**trowel** /ˈtraʊəl/ n (garden) déplantoir m; (for mortar) truelle f.

**truant** /ˈtruːənt/ n (School) élève m/f qui fait l'école buissonnière; play ~ sécher les cours.

**truce** /truːs/ n trève f.

**truck** /trʌk/ n (lorry) camion m; (cart) chariot m; (Rail) wagon m de marchandises. **~driver** n routier m.

**true** /truː/ adj vrai; (accurate) exact; (faithful) fidèle.

**truffle** /ˈtrʌfl/ n truffe f.

**truly** /'truːlɪ/ adv vraiment; (faithfully) fidèlement; (truthfully) sincèrement.

**trumpet** /'trʌmpɪt/ n trompette f.

**trunk** /trʌŋk/ n (of tree, body) tronc m; (of elephant) trompe f; (box) malle f; (Auto, US) coffre m; ∼s (for swimming) slip m de bain.

**trust** /trʌst/ n confiance f; (association) trust m; **in** ∼ en dépôt. ● vt avoir confiance en; **to** ∼ **sb with** confier à qn. ● vi ∼ **in** or **to** s'en remettre à. **trustee** n administrateur/-trice m/f. **trustworthy** adj digne de confiance.

**truth** /truːθ/ n (pl ∼**s**) vérité f. **truthful** adj (account) véridique; (person) qui dit la vérité.

**try** /traɪ/ vt/i (pt **tried**) essayer; (be a strain on) éprouver; (Jur) juger; ∼ **on** or **out** essayer; ∼ **to** essayer de faire. ● n (attempt) essai m; (rugby) essai m.

**T-shirt** /'tiːʃɜːt/ n tee-shirt m.

**tub** /tʌb/ n (for flowers) bac m; (of ice cream) pot m; (bath) baignoire f.

**tube** /tjuːb/ n tube m; **the** ∼ 🇬🇧 le métro.

**tuberculosis** /tjuːbɜːkjʊ'ləʊsɪs/ n tuberculose f.

**tuck** /tʌk/ n pli m. ● vt (put away, place) ranger; (hide) cacher. ● vi ∼ **in** or **into** 🇬🇧 attaquer; ∼ **in** (shirt) rentrer; (blanket, person) border.

**Tuesday** /'tjuːzdeɪ/ n mardi m.

**tug** /tʌg/ vt (pt **tugged**) tirer. ● vi ∼ **at/on** tirer sur. ● n (boat) remorqueur m.

**tuition** /tjuː'ɪʃn/ n cours mpl; (fee) frais mpl pédagogiques.

**tulip** /'tjuːlɪp/ n tulipe f.

**tumble** /'tʌmbl/ vi (fall) dégringoler. ● n chute f. ∼-**drier** n sèche-linge m inv.

**tumbler** /'tʌmblə(r)/ n verre m

droit.

**tummy** /'tʌmɪ/ n 🇬🇧 ventre m.

**tumour** /'tjuːmə(r)/ n tumeur f.

**tuna** /'tjuːnə/ n thon m.

**tune** /tjuːn/ n air m; **be in** ∼/**out of** ∼ (instrument) être/ne pas être en accord; (singer) chanter juste/faux. ● vt (engine) régler; (Mus) accorder. ● vi ∼ **in** (**to**) (radio),TV écouter. □ ∼ **up** s'accorder.

**Tunisia** /tjuː'nɪzɪə/ n Tunisie f.

**tunnel** /'tʌnl/ n tunnel m; (in mine) galerie f. ● vi (pt **tunnelled**) creuser un tunnel (**into** dans).

**turf** /tɜːf/ n (pl **turf** or **turves**) gazon m; **the** ∼ (racing) le turf. ● vt ∼ **out** 🇬🇧 jeter dehors.

**Turk** /tɜːk/ n Turc m, Turque f. **Turkey** /tɜːkɪ/ n Turquie f.

**turkey** /tɜːkɪ/ n dinde f.

**Turkish** /'tɜːkɪʃ/ adj turc. ● n (Ling) turc m.

**turn** /tɜːn/ vt/i tourner; (person) se tourner; (to other side) retourner; (change) se transformer (**into** en); (become) devenir; (deflect) détourner; (milk) tourner. ● n tour m; (in road) tournant m; (of mind, events) tournure f; **do a good** ∼ rendre service; **in** ∼ à tour de rôle; **take** ∼**s** se relayer. □ ∼ **against** se retourner contre; ∼ **away** vi se détourner; vt (avert) détourner; (refuse) refuser; (send back) renvoyer; ∼ **back** vi (return) retourner; (vehicle) faire demi-tour; vt (fold) rabattre; ∼ **down** refuser; (fold) rabattre; (reduce) baisser; ∼ **off** (light) éteindre; (engine) arrêter; (tap) fermer; (of driver) tourner; ∼ **on** (light) allumer; (engine) allumer; (tap) ouvrir; ∼ **out** (light) éteindre; (empty) vider; (produce) produire; **it** ∼**s out that** il se trouve que; ∼ **out well/badly** bien/mal se terminer; ∼ **over** (se) retourner;

**round** (person) se retourner; ~ **up** vi arriver; (be found) se retrouver; vt (find) déterrer; (collar) remonter.

**turning** /'tɜːnɪŋ/ n rue f; (bend) virage m.

**turnip** /'tɜːnɪp/ n navet m.

**turn:** ~**out** n assistance f; ~**over** n (pie) chausson m; (money) chiffre m d'affaires. ~**table** n (for record) platine f.

**turquoise** /'tɜːkwɔɪz/ adj turquoise inv.

**turtle** /'tɜːtl/ n tortue f (de mer). ~**neck** n col m montant.

**tutor** /'tjuːtə(r)/ n (private) professeur m particulier; (Univ) (GB) chargé-e m/f de travaux dirigés.

**tutorial** /tjuː'tɔːrɪəl/ n (Univ) classe f de travaux dirigés.

**tuxedo** /tʌk'siːdəʊ/ n (US) smoking m.

**TV** /tiː'viː/ n télé f.

**tweezers** /'twiːzəz/ npl pince f (à épiler).

**twelfth** /twelfθ/ adj & n douzième (mf).

**twelve** /twelv/ adj & n douze (m); ~ (o'clock) midi m or minuit m.

**twentieth** /'twentɪəθ/ adj & n vingtième (mf).

**twenty** /'twentɪ/ adj & n vingt (m).

**twice** /twaɪs/ adv deux fois.

**twig** /twɪg/ n brindille f.

**twilight** /'twaɪlaɪt/ n crépuscule m. ● adj crépusculaire.

**twin** /twɪn/ n & a jumeau-elle (m/f). ● vt (pt twinned) jumeler.

**twinge** /twɪndʒ/ n (of pain) élancement m; (of conscience, doubt) accès m.

**twinkle** /'twɪŋkl/ vi (star) scintiller; (eye) pétiller. ● n scintillement m; pétillement m.

**twinning** /'twɪnɪŋ/ n jumelage m.

**twist** /twɪst/ vt tordre; (weave together) entortiller; (roll) enrouler; (distort) déformer. ● vi (rope) s'entortiller; (road) zigzaguer. ● n torsion f; (in rope) tortillon m; (in road) tournant m; (in play, story) coup m de théâtre.

**twitch** /twɪtʃ/ vi (person) trembloter; (mouth) trembler; (string) vibrer. ● n (tic) tic m; (jerk) secousse f.

**two** /tuː/ adj & n deux (m); in ~s par deux; break in ~ casser en deux.

**tycoon** /taɪ'kuːn/ n magnat m.

**type** /taɪp/ n type m, genre m; (print) caractères mpl. ● vt (write) taper (à la machine). ~**face** n police f (de caractères). ~**writer** n machine f à écrire.

**typical** /'tɪpɪkl/ adj typique.

**typist** /'taɪpɪst/ n dactylo mf.

**tyrant** /'taɪərənt/ n tyran m.

**tyre** /'taɪə(r)/ n pneu m.

# Uu

**udder** /'ʌdə(r)/ n pis m, mamelle f.

**UFO** /'juːfəʊ/ n OVNI m.

**UHT** abbr ultra heat treated ~ milk lait m longue conservation.

**ugly** /'ʌglɪ/ adj (-ier, -iest) laid.

**UK** abbr =UNITED KINGDOM.

**Ukraine** /juː'kreɪn/ n Ukraine f.

**ulcer** /'ʌlsə(r)/ n ulcère m.

**ulterior** /ʌl'tɪərɪə(r)/ adj ultérieur; ~ motive arrière-pensée f.

**ultimate** /'ʌltɪmət/ adj dernier, ultime; (definitive) définitif; (basic) fondamental.

**ultrasound** /'ʌltrəsaʊnd/ n

ultrason m.

**umbilical cord** /ʌmˈbɪlɪkl kɔːd/ n cordon m ombilical.

**umbrella** /ʌmˈbrelə/ n parapluie m.

**umpire** /ˈʌmpaɪə(r)/ n arbitre m. ● vt arbitrer.

**umpteenth** /ʌmpˈtiːnθ/ adj 🄸 énième.

**UN** abbr (**United Nations**) ONU f.

**unable** /ʌnˈeɪbl/ adj incapable; (through circumstances) dans l'impossibilité (to do de faire).

**unacceptable** /ʌnəkˈseptəbl/ adj (suggestion) inacceptable; (behaviour) inadmissible.

**unanimous** /juːˈnænɪməs/ adj unanime. **unanimously** adv à l'unanimité.

**unattended** /ʌnəˈtendɪd/ adj sans surveillance.

**unattractive** /ʌnəˈtræktɪv/ adj (idea) peu attrayant; (person) peu attirant.

**unauthorized** /ʌnˈɔːθəraɪzd/ adj non autorisé.

**unavoidable** /ʌnəˈvɔɪdəbl/ adj inévitable.

**unbearable** /ʌnˈbeərəbl/ adj insupportable.

**unbelievable** /ʌnbɪˈliːvəbl/ adj incroyable.

**unbiased** /ʌnˈbaɪəst/ adj impartial.

**unblock** /ʌnˈblɒk/ vt déboucher.

**unborn** /ʌnˈbɔːn/ adj (child) à naître; (generation) à venir.

**uncalled-for** /ʌnˈkɔːldfɔː(r)/ adj injustifié, déplacé.

**uncanny** /ʌnˈkænɪ/ adj (-ier, -iest) étrange, troublant.

**uncivilized** /ʌnˈsɪvɪlaɪzd/ adj barbare.

**uncle** /ˈʌŋkl/ n oncle m.

**Uncle Sam** Interprétation plaisante des initiales U.S.Am. (United States of America). Personnification du gouvernement ou du peuple des États-Unis représentés par un grand homme maigre avec une barbiche, habillé aux couleurs du drapeau américain. C'est à lui que l'on a recours pour faire appel au patriotisme de la population, mais aussi pour caricaturer les États-Unis.

**uncomfortable** /ʌnˈkʌmftəbl/ adj (chair) inconfortable; (feeling) pénible; feel or be ~ (person) être mal à l'aise.

**uncommon** /ʌnˈkɒmən/ adj rare.

**unconscious** /ʌnˈkɒnʃəs/ adj sans connaissance, inanimé; (not aware) inconscient (of de). ● n inconscient m.

**unconventional** /ʌnkənˈvenʃənl/ adj peu conventionnel.

**uncouth** /ʌnˈkuːθ/ adj grossier.

**uncover** /ʌnˈkʌvə(r)/ vt découvrir.

**undecided** /ʌndɪˈsaɪdɪd/ adj indécis.

**under** /ˈʌndə(r)/ prep sous; (less than) moins de; (according to) selon. ● adv au-dessous; ~ it/there là-dessous. ~age adj mineur. ~cover adj secret. ~cut vt (pt -cut; pres p -cutting) (Comm) vendre moins cher que. ~dog n (Pol) opprimé-e m/f; (socially) déshérité-e m/f. ~done adj pas assez cuit. ~estimate vt sous-estimer. ~fed adj sous-alimenté. ~go vt (pt -went; pp -gone) subir. ~graduate n étudiant/-e m/f (qui prépare la licence).

**underground** /ˈʌndəɡraʊnd/ adj souterrain; (secret) clandestin. ● adv sous terre. ● n (rail) métro m.

**under:** ∼**line** vt souligner. ∼**mine** vt saper.

**underneath** /ʌndə'niːθ/ prep sous. ● adv (en) dessous.

**under:** ∼**pants** npl slip m. ∼**rate** vt sous-estimer.

**understand** /ʌndə'stænd/ vt/i (pt **-stood**) comprendre.

**understanding** /ʌndə'stændɪŋ/ adj compréhensif. ● n compréhension f; (agreement) entente f.

**undertake** /ʌndə'teɪk/ vt/i (pt **-took**; pp **-taken**) entreprendre. ∼**taker** n entrepreneur m de pompes funèbres. ∼**taking** n (task) entreprise f; (promise) promesse f.

**underwater** /ʌndə'wɔːtə(r)/ adj sous-marin. ● adv sous l'eau.

**under:** ∼**wear** n sous-vêtements mpl. ∼**world** n (of crime) milieu m, pègre f.

**undo** /ʌn'duː/ vt (pt **-did**; pp **-done**) défaire, détacher; (wrong) réparer; (Comput) annuler.

**undress** /ʌn'dres/ vt/i (se) déshabiller; get ∼ed se déshabiller.

**undue** /ʌn'djuː/ adj excessif.

**unearth** /ʌn'ɜːθ/ vt déterrer.

**uneasy** /ʌn'iːzɪ/ adj (ill at ease) mal à l'aise; (worried) inquiet; (situation) difficile.

**uneducated** /ʌn'edʒʊkeɪtɪd/ adj (person) inculte; (speech) populaire.

**unemployed** /ʌnɪm'plɔɪd/ adj en chômage. ● npl the ∼ les chômeurs mpl.

**unemployment** /ʌnɪm 'plɔɪmənt/ n chômage m; ∼ benefit allocations fpl de chômage.

**uneven** /ʌn'iːvn/ adj inégal.

**unexpected** /ʌnɪk'spektɪd/ adj inattendu, imprévu. **unexpectedly** adv (arrive) à l'improviste; (small, fast) étonnamment.

**unfair** /ʌn'feə(r)/ adj injuste.

**unfaithful** /ʌn'feɪθfl/ adj infidèle.

**unfit** /ʌn'fɪt/ adj (Med) pas en forme; (ill) malade; (unsuitable) impropre (for à); ∼ to (unable) pas en état de.

**unfold** /ʌn'fəʊld/ vt déplier; (expose) exposer. ● vi se dérouler.

**unforeseen** /ʌnfɔː'siːn/ adj imprévu.

**unforgettable** /ʌnfə'getəbl/ adj inoubliable.

**unfortunate** /ʌn'fɔːtʃənət/ adj malheureux; (event) fâcheux.

**ungrateful** /ʌn'greɪtfl/ adj ingrat.

**unhappy** /ʌn'hæpɪ/ adj (**-ier, -iest**) (person) malheureux; (face) triste; (not pleased) mécontent (with de).

**unharmed** /ʌn'hɑːmd/ adj indemne, sain et sauf.

**unhealthy** /ʌn'helθɪ/ adj (**-ier, -iest**) (climate) malsain; (person) en mauvaise santé.

**unheard-of** /ʌn'hɜːdɒv/ adj inouï.

**unhurt** /ʌn'hɜːt/ adj indemne.

**uniform** /'juːnɪfɔːm/ n uniforme m. ● adj uniforme.

**unify** /'juːnɪfaɪ/ vt unifier.

**unintentional** /ʌnɪn'tenʃənl/ adj involontaire.

**uninterested** /ʌn'ɪntrəstɪd/ adj indifférent (in à).

**union** /'juːnɪən/ n union f; (trade union) syndicat m; U∼ Jack drapeau m du Royaume-Uni.

**unique** /juː'niːk/ adj unique.

**unit** /'juːnɪt/ n unité f; (of furniture) élément m; ∼ trust ≈ SICAV f.

**unite** /juː'naɪt/ vt/i (s')unir.

**United Kingdom** n Royaume-Uni m.

**United Nations** npl Nations fpl Unies.

**United States (of America)**

u

*n pl* états-Unis *mpl* (d'Amérique).

**unity** /ˈjuːnətɪ/ *n* unité *f*.

**universal** /juːnɪˈvɜːsl/ *adj* universel.

**universe** /ˈjuːnɪvɜːs/ *n* univers *m*.

**university** /juːnɪˈvɜːsətɪ/ *n* université *f*. ● *adj* universitaire; *(student, teacher)* d'université.

**unkind** /ʌnˈkaɪnd/ *adj* pas gentil, méchant.

**unknown** /ʌnˈnəʊn/ *adj* inconnu. ● *n* the ∼ l'inconnu *m*.

**unleaded** /ʌnˈledɪd/ *adj* sans plomb.

**unless** /ənˈles/ *conj* à moins que.

**unlike** /ʌnˈlaɪk/ *adj* différent. ● *prep* contrairement à; *(different from)* différent de.

**unlikely** /ʌnˈlaɪklɪ/ *adj* improbable.

**unload** /ʌnˈləʊd/ *vt* décharger.

**unlock** /ʌnˈlɒk/ *vt* ouvrir.

**unlucky** /ʌnˈlʌkɪ/ *adj* -ier, -iest malheureux; *(number)* qui porte malheur.

**unmarried** /ʌnˈmærɪd/ *adj* célibataire.

**unnatural** /ʌnˈnætʃrəl/ *adj* pas naturel, anormal.

**unnecessary** /ʌnˈnesəsrɪ/ *adj* inutile.

**unnoticed** /ʌnˈnəʊtɪst/ *adj* inaperçu.

**unofficial** /ʌnəˈfɪʃl/ *adj* officieux.

**unpack** /ʌnˈpæk/ *vt* (suitcase) défaire; *(contents)* déballer. ● *vi* défaire sa valise.

**unpleasant** /ʌnˈpleznt/ *adj* désagréable (to avec).

**unplug** /ʌnˈplʌg/ *vt* débrancher.

**unpopular** /ʌnˈpɒpjʊlə(r)/ *adj* impopulaire; ∼ with mal vu de.

**unprofessional** /ʌnprəˈfeʃənl/ *adj* peu professionnel.

**unqualified** /ʌnˈkwɒlɪfaɪd/ *adj*

non diplômé; *(success)* total; be ∼ to ne pas être qualifié pour.

**unravel** /ʌnˈrævl/ *vt* (pt unravelled) démêler.

**unreasonable** /ʌnˈriːznəbl/ *adj* irréaliste.

**unrelated** /ʌnrɪˈleɪtɪd/ *adj* sans rapport (to avec).

**unreliable** /ʌnrɪˈlaɪəbl/ *adj* peu sérieux; *(machine)* peu fiable.

**unrest** /ʌnˈrest/ *n* troubles *mpl*.

**unroll** /ʌnˈrəʊl/ *vt* dérouler.

**unruly** /ʌnˈruːlɪ/ *adj* indiscipliné.

**unsafe** /ʌnˈseɪf/ *adj* (dangerous) dangereux; *(person)* en danger.

**unscheduled** /ʌnˈʃedjuːld/ *adj* pas prévu.

**unscrupulous** /ʌnˈskruːpjʊləs/ *adj* sans scrupules, malhonnête.

**unsettled** /ʌnˈsetld/ *adj* instable.

**unsightly** /ʌnˈsaɪtlɪ/ *adj* laid.

**unskilled** /ʌnˈskɪld/ *adj* (worker) non qualifié.

**unsound** /ʌnˈsaʊnd/ *adj* (roof) en mauvais état; *(investment)* douteux.

**unsteady** /ʌnˈstedɪ/ *adj* (step) chancelant; *(ladder)* instable; *(hand)* mal assuré.

**unsuccessful** /ʌnsəkˈsesfl/ *adj* (result, candidate) malheureux; *(attempt)* infructueux; be ∼ ne pas réussir (in doing à faire).

**unsuitable** /ʌnˈsuːtəbl/ *adj* inapproprié; be ∼ ne pas convenir.

**unsure** /ʌnˈʃɔː(r)/ *adj* incertain.

**untidy** /ʌnˈtaɪdɪ/ *adj* (-ier, -iest) *(person)* désordonné; *(room)* en désordre; *(work)* mal soigné.

**untie** /ʌnˈtaɪ/ *vt* (knot, parcel) défaire; *(person)* détacher.

**until** /ʌnˈtɪl/ *prep* jusqu'à; not ∼ pas avant. ● *conj* jusqu'à ce que; not ∼ pas avant que.

**untrue** /ʌnˈtruː/ *adj* faux.

**unused** /ʌnˈjuːst/ adj (new) neuf; (not in use) inutilisé.

**unusual** /ʌnˈjuːʒl/ adj exceptionnel; (strange) insolite, étrange.

**unwanted** /ʌnˈwɒntɪd/ adj (useless) superflu; (child) non désiré.

**unwelcome** /ʌnˈwelkəm/ adj fâcheux; (guest) importun.

**unwell** /ʌnˈwel/ adj souffrant.

**unwilling** /ʌnˈwɪlɪŋ/ adj peu disposé (to à); (accomplice) malgré soi.

**unwind** /ʌnˈwaɪnd/ vt/i (pt **unwound**) (se) dérouler; (relax 🗊) se détendre.

**unwise** /ʌnˈwaɪz/ adj imprudent.

**unwrap** /ʌnˈræp/ vt déballer.

**up** /ʌp/ adv en haut, en l'air; (out of bed) levé; (out of bed) levé, debout; (finished) fini; be ~ (level, price) avoir monté. ● prep (a hill) en haut de; (a tree) dans; (a ladder) sur; **come** or **go** ~ monter; ~ **in the bedroom** là-haut dans la chambre; ~ **there** là-haut; ~ **to** jusqu'à; (task) à la hauteur de; **it is** ~ **to you** ça dépend de vous (to de); be ~ **to sth** (able) être capable de qch; (plot) préparer qch; be ~ **to** (in book) en être à; be ~ **against** faire face à; ~ **to date** moderne; (news) récent. ● n ~s and downs les hauts et les bas mpl.

**up-and-coming** adj prometteur.

**upbringing** /ˈʌpbrɪŋɪŋ/ n éducation f.

**update** /ʌpˈdeɪt/ vt mettre à jour.

**upgrade** /ʌpˈɡreɪd/ vt améliorer; (person) promouvoir.

**upheaval** /ʌpˈhiːvl/ n bouleversement m.

**uphill** /ʌpˈhɪl/ adj qui monte; (fig) difficile. ● adv /ʌpˈhɪl/ **go** ~ monter.

**upholstery** /ʌpˈhəʊlstərɪ/ n rembourrage m; (in vehicle) garniture f.

**upkeep** /ˈʌpkiːp/ n entretien m.

**up-market** adj haut-de-gamme.

**upon** /əˈpɒn/ prep sur.

**upper** /ˈʌpə(r)/ adj supérieur; **have the** ~ **hand** avoir le dessus. ● n (of shoe) empeigne f. ~ **class** n aristocratie f. ~**most** adj (highest) le plus haut.

**upright** /ˈʌpraɪt/ adj droit. ● n (post) montant m.

**uprising** /ˈʌpraɪzɪŋ/ n soulèvement m.

**uproar** /ˈʌprɔː(r)/ n tumulte m.

**uproot** /ʌpˈruːt/ vt déraciner.

**upset¹** /ʌpˈset/ vt (pt **upset**; pres p **upsetting**) (overturn) renverser; (plan, stomach) déranger; (person) contrarier, affliger. ● adj peiné.

**upset²** /ˈʌpset/ n dérangement m; (distress) chagrin m.

**upside-down** /ʌpsaɪd ˈdaʊn/ adv (lit) à l'envers; (fig) sens dessus dessous.

**upstairs** /ʌpˈsteəz/ adv en haut. ● adj (flat) du haut.

**uptight** /ʌpˈtaɪt/ adj 🗊 tendu, coincé 🗊.

**up-to-date** adj à la mode; (records) à jour.

**upward** /ˈʌpwəd/ adj & adv, **upwards** adv vers le haut.

**urban** /ˈɜːbən/ adj urbain.

**urge** /ɜːdʒ/ vt conseiller vivement (to do de conseiller); ~ **on** encourager. ● n forte envie f.

**urgency** /ˈɜːdʒənsɪ/ n urgence f; (of request, tone) insistance f. **urgent** adj urgent; (request) pressant.

**urinal** /jʊəˈraɪnl/ n urinoir m.

**urine** /ˈjʊərɪn/ n urine f.

**us** /ʌs, əs/ pron nous; (to) ~ nous; **both of** ~ nous/toutes les deux.

**US** abbr ➡ **UNITED STATES**.

**USA** abbr ➡ **UNITED STATES OF AMERICA**.

**use**¹ /juːz/ vt se servir de, utiliser. (consume) consommer; ~ up épuiser.

**use**² /juːs/ n usage m, emploi m; in ~ en usage; it is no ~ doing ça ne sert à rien de faire; make ~ of se servir de; of ~ utile.

**used**¹ /juːzd/ adj (car) d'occasion.

**used**² /juːst/ v aux he ~ to smoke il fumait (autrefois). ● adj ~ to habitué à.

**useful** /ˈjuːsfl/ adj utile.

**useless** /ˈjuːslɪs/ adj inutile; (person) incompétent.

**user** /ˈjuːzə(r)/ n (of road, service) usager m; (of product) utilisateur/-trice m/f. ~-friendly adj facile d'emploi; (Comput) convivial. ~name nom m d'utilisateur.

**usual** /ˈjuːʒl/ adj habituel, normal; as ~ comme d'habitude. **usually** adv d'habitude.

**utility** /juːˈtɪlətɪ/ n utilité f; (public) ~ service m public.

**utmost** /ˈʌtməʊst/ adj (furthest, most intense) extrême; the ~ care le plus grand soin. ● n do one's ~ faire tout son possible.

**utter** /ˈʌtə(r)/ adj complet, absolu. ● vt prononcer.

**U-turn** /ˈjuːtɜːn/ n demi-tour m; (fig) volteface f inv.

••••••••••••••••••••••••••••••

# Vᴠ

**u**
**v**

••••••••••••••••••••••••••••••

**vacancy** /ˈveɪkənsɪ/ n (post) poste m vacant; (room) chambre f disponible.

**vacant** /ˈveɪkənt/ adj (post) vacant; (seat) libre; (look) vague.

**vacate** /vəˈkeɪt/ vt quitter.

**vacation** /vəˈkeɪʃn/ n vacances fpl.

**vaccinate** /ˈvæksɪneɪt/ vt vacciner.

**vacuum** /ˈvækjʊəm/ n vide m. ~ cleaner n aspirateur m. ~-packed adj emballé sous vide.

**vagina** /vəˈdʒaɪnə/ n vagin m.

**vagrant** /ˈveɪɡrənt/ n vagabond/-e m/f.

**vague** /veɪɡ/ adj vague; (outline) flou; be ~ about ne pas préciser.

**vain** /veɪn/ adj (conceited) vaniteux; (useless) vain; in ~ en vain.

**valentine** /ˈvæləntaɪn/ n ~ (card) carte f de la Saint-Valentin.

**valid** /ˈvælɪd/ adj (argument, ticket) valable; (passport) valide.

**valley** /ˈvælɪ/ n vallée f.

**valuable** /ˈvæljʊəbl/ adj (object) de valeur; (help) précieux. **valuables** npl objets mpl de valeur.

**valuation** /væljʊˈeɪʃn/ n (of painting) expertise f; (of house) évaluation f.

**value** /ˈvæljuː/ n valeur f; ~ added tax taxe f à la valeur ajoutée, TVA f. ● vt (appraise) évaluer; (cherish) attacher de la valeur à.

**valve** /vælv/ n (Tech) soupape f; (of tyre) valve f; (Med) valvule f.

**van** /væn/ n camionnette f.

**vandal** /ˈvændl/ n vandale mf.

**vanguard** /ˈvænɡɑːd/ n in the ~ of à l'avantgarde f de.

**vanilla** /vəˈnɪlə/ n vanille f.

**vanish** /ˈvænɪʃ/ vi disparaître.

**vapour** /ˈveɪpə(r)/ n vapeur f.

**variable** /ˈveərɪəbl/ adj variable.

**varicose** /ˈværɪkəʊs/ adj ~ veins varices fpl.

**varied** /ˈveərɪd/ adj varié.

**variety** /vəˈraɪətɪ/ n variété f; (entertainment) variétés fpl.

**various** /ˈveərɪəs/ adj divers.

**varnish** /ˈvɑːnɪʃ/ n vernis m. ● vt

vernir.

**vary** /'veəri/ vt/i varier.

**vase** /va:z/ n vase m.

**vast** /va:st/ adj (space) vaste; (in quantity) énorme.

**vat** /væt/ n cuve f.

**VAT** abbr (value added tax) TVA f.

**vault** /vɔ:lt/ n (roof) voûte f; (in bank) chambre f forte; (tomb) caveau m; (jump) saut m. ● vt/i sauter.

**VCR** abbr → VIDEO CASSETTE RECORDER.

**VDU** abbr → VISUAL DISPLAY UNIT.

**veal** /vi:l/ n veau m.

**vegan** /'vi:gən/ adj & n végétalien/-ne (m/f).

**vegetable** /'vedʒtəbl/ n légume m. ● adj végétal.

**vegetarian** /vedʒɪ'teərɪən/ adj & n végétarien/-ne (m/f).

**vehicle** /'vi:əkl/ n véhicule m.

**veil** /veɪl/ n voile m.

**vein** /veɪn/ n (in body, rock) veine f; (on leaf) nervure f.

**velvet** /'velvɪt/ n velours m.

**vending-machine** /'vendɪŋ mə 'ʃi:n/ n distributeur m automatique.

**veneer** /vɪ'nɪə(r)/ n (on wood) placage m; (fig) vernis m.

**venereal** /və'nɪərɪəl/ adj vénérien.

**venetian** /və'ni:ʃn/ adj ~ blind jalousie f.

**vengeance** /'vendʒəns/ n vengeance f; with a ~ de plus belle.

**venison** /'venɪsn/ n venaison f.

**venom** /'venəm/ n venin m.

**vent** /vent/ n bouche f, conduit m; (in coat) fente f. ● vt (anger) décharger (on sur).

**ventilate** /'ventɪleɪt/ vt ventiler.

**ventilator** n ventilateur m.

**venture** /'ventʃə(r)/ n entreprise f.

● vt/i (se) risquer.

**venue** /'venju:/ n lieu m.

**verb** /vɜ:b/ n verbe m.

**verbal** /'vɜ:bl/ adj verbal.

**verdict** /'vɜ:dɪkt/ n verdict m.

**verge** /vɜ:dʒ/ n bord m; on the ~ of doing sur le point de faire. ● vi ~ on friser, frôler.

**verify** /'verɪfaɪ/ vt vérifier.

**vermin** /'vɜ:mɪn/ n vermine f.

**versatile** /'vɜ:sətaɪl/ adj (person) aux talents variés; (mind) souple.

**verse** /vɜ:s/ n strophe f, (of Bible) verset m; (poetry) vers mpl.

**version** /'vɜ:ʃn/ n version f.

**versus** /'vɜ:səs/ prep contre.

**vertebra** /'vɜ:tɪbrə/ n (pl -brae) vertèbre f.

**vertical** /'vɜ:tɪkl/ adj vertical.

**vertigo** /'vɜ:tɪgəʊ/ n vertige m.

**very** /'veri/ adv très. ● adj (actual) même; the ~ day le jour même; at the ~ end tout à la fin; the ~ first le tout premier; ~ much beaucoup.

**vessel** /'vesl/ n vaisseau m.

**vest** /vest/ n maillot m de corps; (waistcoat: US) gilet m.

**vet** /vet/ n vétérinaire mf. ● vt (pt vetted) (candidate) examiner (de près).

**veteran** /'vetərən/ n vétéran m. ● war ~ ancien combattant m.

**veterinary** /'vetrɪnrɪ/ adj vétérinaire; ~ surgeon vétérinaire mf.

**veto** /'vi:təʊ/ n (pl ~es) veto m; (right) droit m de veto. ● vt mettre son veto à.

**vibrate** /vaɪ'breɪt/ vt/i (faire) vibrer.

**vicar** /'vɪkə(r)/ n pasteur m.

**vice** /vaɪs/ n (depravity) vice m; (Tech) étau m.

**v**

**vicinity** /vɪˈsɪnətɪ/ n environs mpl; in the ∼ of à proximité de.

**vicious** /ˈvɪʃəs/ adj (spiteful) méchant; (violent) brutal; ∼ circle cercle m vicieux.

**victim** /ˈvɪktɪm/ n victime f.

**victor** /ˈvɪktə(r)/ n vainqueur m. **victory** n victoire f.

**video** /ˈvɪdɪəʊ/ adj (game, camera) vidéo inv. ● n (recorder) magnétoscope m; (film) vidéo f; ∼ (cassette) cassette f vidéo. ∼ game n jeu m vidéo. ∼phone n vidéophone m. ● vt enregistrer.

**videotape** /ˈvɪdɪəʊteɪp/ n bande f vidéo. ● vt (programme) enregistrer; (wedding) filmer avec une caméra vidéo.

**view** /vjuː/ n vue f; in my ∼ à mon avis; in ∼ of compte tenu de; on ∼ exposé; with a ∼ to dans le but de. ● vt (watch) regarder; (consider) considérer (as comme); (house) visiter. **viewer** n (TV) téléspectateur/-trice m/f.

**view:** ∼finder n viseur m. ∼point n point m de vue.

**vigilant** /ˈvɪdʒɪlənt/ adj vigilant.

**vigour,** (US) **vigor** /ˈvɪgə(r)/ n vigueur f.

**vile** /vaɪl/ adj (base) vil; (bad) abominable.

**villa** /ˈvɪlə/ n pavillon m; (for holiday) villa f.

**village** /ˈvɪlɪdʒ/ n village m.

**villain** /ˈvɪlən/ n scélérat m, bandit m; (in story) méchant m.

**vindictive** /vɪnˈdɪktɪv/ adj vindicatif.

**vine** /vaɪn/ n vigne f.

**vinegar** /ˈvɪnɪgə(r)/ n vinaigre m.

**vineyard** /ˈvɪnjəd/ n vignoble m.

**vintage** /ˈvɪntɪdʒ/ n (year) année f, millésime m. ● adj (wine) de grand

cru; (car) d'époque.

**viola** /vɪˈəʊlə/ n (Mus) alto m.

**violate** /ˈvaɪəleɪt/ vt violer.

**violence** /ˈvaɪələns/ n violence f. **violent** adj violent.

**violet** /ˈvaɪələt/ n (Bot) violette f; (colour) violet m.

**violin** /vaɪəˈlɪn/ n violon m.

**VIP** abbr (**very important person**) personnalité f, VIP m.

**virgin** /ˈvɜːdʒɪn/ n (woman) vierge f.

**Virgo** /ˈvɜːgəʊ/ n Vierge f.

**virtual** /ˈvɜːtʃʊəl/ adj quasi-total; (Comput) virtuel. **virtually** adv pratiquement.

**virtue** /ˈvɜːtʃuː/ n vertu f; (advantage) mérite m; by ∼ of en raison de.

**virus** /ˈvaɪərəs/ n virus m.

**visa** /ˈviːzə/ n visa m.

**visibility** /vɪzəˈbɪlətɪ/ n visibilité f. **visible** adj visible.

**vision** /ˈvɪʒn/ n vision f.

**visit** /ˈvɪzɪt/ vt (pt **visited**) (person) rendre visite à; (place) visiter. ● vi être en visite. ● n (tour, call) visite f; (stay) séjour m. **visitor** n visiteur/-euse m/f; (guest) invité/-e m/f.

**visual** /ˈvɪʒʊəl/ adj visuel. ∼ display unit n visuel m, console f de visualisation.

**visualize** /ˈvɪʒʊəlaɪz/ vt se représenter; (foresee) envisager.

**vital** /ˈvaɪtl/ adj vital.

**vitamin** /ˈvɪtəmɪn/ n vitamine f.

**vivacious** /vɪˈveɪʃəs/ adj plein de vivacité.

**vivid** /ˈvɪvɪd/ adj (colour, imagination) vif; (description, dream) frappant.

**vivisection** /vɪvɪˈsekʃn/ n vivisection f

# Ww

**vocabulary** /vəˈkæbjʊlərɪ/ n vocabulaire m.

**vocal** /ˈvəʊkl/ adj vocal; (person) qui s'exprime franchement. ~ **cords** npl cordes fpl vocales.

**vocation** /vəʊˈkeɪʃn/ n vocation f. **vocational** adj professionnel.

**voice** /vɔɪs/ n voix f. ● vt (express) formuler. ~ **mail** n messagerie f vocale.

**void** /vɔɪd/ adj vide (of de); (not valid) nul. ● n vide m.

**volatile** /ˈvɒlətaɪl/ adj (person) versatile; (situation) explosif.

**volcano** /vɒlˈkeɪnəʊ/ n (pl **-es**) volcan m.

**volley** /ˈvɒlɪ/ n (of blows, in tennis) volée f; (of gunfire) salve f.

**volt** /vəʊlt/ n (Electr) volt m. **voltage** n tension f.

**volume** /ˈvɒljuːm/ n volume m.

**voluntary** /ˈvɒləntrɪ/ adj volontaire; (unpaid) bénévole.

**volunteer** /vɒlənˈtɪə(r)/ n volontaire mf. ● vi s'offrir (**to do** pour faire); (Mil) s'engager comme volontaire. ● vt offrir.

**vomit** /ˈvɒmɪt/ vt/i (pt **vomited**) vomir. ● n vomi m.

**vote** /vəʊt/ n vote m; (right) droit m de vote. ● vt/i voter; ~ **sb in** élire qn. **voter** n électeur/-trice m/f. **voting** n vote m (of de); (poll) scrutin m.

**vouch** /vaʊtʃ/ vi ~ **for** se porter garant de.

**voucher** /ˈvaʊtʃə(r)/ n bon m.

**vowel** /ˈvaʊəl/ n voyelle f.

**voyage** /ˈvɔɪdʒ/ n voyage m (en mer).

**vulgar** /ˈvʌlɡə(r)/ adj vulgaire.

**vulnerable** /ˈvʌlnərəbl/ adj vulnérable.

**wad** /wɒd/ n (pad) tampon m; (bundle) liasse f.

**wade** /weɪd/ vi ~ **through** (mud) patauger dans. (book: fig) avancer péniblement dans.

**wafer** /ˈweɪfə(r)/ n (biscuit) gaufrette f.

**waffle** /ˈwɒfl/ n (talk 🗊) verbiage m; (cake) gaufre f. ● vi 🗊 divaguer.

**wag** /wæɡ/ vt/i (pt **wagged**) (tail) remuer.

**wage** /weɪdʒ/ vt (campaign) mener; ~ **war** faire la guerre. ● n (weekly, daily) salaire m; ~s salaire m. **~-earner** n salarié/-e m/f.

**wagon** /ˈwæɡən/ n (horse-drawn) chariot m; (Rail) wagon m (de marchandises).

**wail** /weɪl/ vi gémir. ● n gémissement m.

**waist** /weɪst/ n taille f. **~coat** n gilet m.

**wait** /weɪt/ vt/i attendre; I can't ~ **to start** j'ai hâte de commencer; let's ~ **and see** attendons voir; ~ **for** attendre; ~ **on** servir. ● n attente f.

**waiter** /ˈweɪtə(r)/ n garçon m, serveur m.

**waiting-list** n liste f d'attente.

**waiting-room** n salle f d'attente.

**waitress** /ˈweɪtrɪs/ n serveuse f.

**waive** /weɪv/ vt renoncer à.

**wake** /weɪk/ vt/i (pt **woke**; pp **woken**) ~ **(up)** (se) réveiller. ● n (track) sillage m; **in the** ~ **of** (after) à la suite de. ~ **up call** n réveil m téléphoné.

**Wales** /weɪlz/ n pays m de Galles.

**walk** /wɔːk/ vi marcher; (not ride) aller à pied; (stroll) se promener. ● vt (streets) parcourir; (distance) faire à pied; (dog) promener. ● n promenade f, tour m; (gait) démarche f; (pace) marche f, pas m; (path) allée f; have a ~ faire une promenade. □~ out (go away) partir; (worker) faire grève; ~ out on abandonner.

**walkie-talkie** /wɔːkɪˈtɔːkɪ/ n talkie-walkie m.

**walking** /ˈwɔːkɪŋ/ n marche f (à pied). ● adj (corpse, dictionary: fig) ambulant.

**walkman®** /ˈwɔːkmən/ n walkman® m, baladeur m.

**walk:** ~**out** n grève f surprise. ~**over** n victoire f facile.

**wall** /wɔːl/ n mur m; (of tunnel, stomach) paroi f. ● adj mural. **walled** adj (city) fortifié.

| |
|---|
| **Wall Street** Cette petite rue new yorkaise est le centre de la finance et des affaires aux États-Unis. *Wall Street* est souvent employé pour désigner la Bourse de New York, également située dans cette rue. |

**wallet** /ˈwɒlɪt/ n portefeuille m.

**wallpaper** /ˈwɔːlpeɪpə(r)/ n papier m peint. ● vt tapisser.

**walnut** /ˈwɔːlnʌt/ n (nut) noix f; (tree) noyer m.

**waltz** /wɔːls/ n valse f ● vi valser.

**wander** /ˈwɒndə(r)/ vi errer; (stroll) flâner; (digress) s'écarter du sujet; (in mind) divaguer.

**wane** /weɪn/ vi décroître.

**want** /wɒnt/ vt vouloir (to do faire); (need) avoir besoin de (doing d'être fait); (ask for) demander; I ~ you to do it je veux que vous le fassiez. ● vi ~ for manquer de. ● n (need, poverty) besoin m; (desire) désir m; (lack) manque m; for ~ of faute de. **wanted** adj (criminal) recherché par la police.

**war** /wɔː(r)/ n guerre f; at ~ en guerre; on the ~path sur le sentier de la guerre.

**ward** /wɔːd/ n (in hospital) salle f; (minor: Jur) pupille mf; (Pol) division f électorale. ● vt ~ off (danger) prévenir.

**warden** /ˈwɔːdn/ n directeur/-trice m/f; (of park) gardien/-ne m/f; (traffic ~) contractuel/-le m/f.

**wardrobe** /ˈwɔːdrəʊb/ n (furniture) armoire f; (clothes) garde-robe f.

**warehouse** /ˈweəhaʊs/ n entrepôt m.

**wares** /weəz/ npl marchandises fpl.

**warfare** /ˈwɔːfeə(r)/ n guerre f.

**warm** /wɔːm/ adj chaud; (hearty) chaleureux; be or feel ~ avoir chaud; it is ~ il fait chaud. ● vt/i ~ (up) (se) réchauffer; (food) chauffer; (liven up) (s')animer; (exercise) s'échauffer.

**warmth** /wɔːmθ/ n chaleur f.

**warn** /wɔːn/ vt avertir, prévenir; ~ sb off sth (advise against) mettre qn en garde contre qch; (forbid) interdire qch à qn.

**warning** /ˈwɔːnɪŋ/ n avertissement m; (notice) avis m; without ~ sans prévenir. ~ **light** n voyant m. ~ **triangle** n triangle m de sécurité.

**warp** /wɔːp/ vt/i (wood) (se) voiler; (pervert) pervertir; (judgment) fausser.

**warrant** /ˈwɒrənt/ n (for arrest) mandat m f; (Comm) autorisation f ● vt justifier.

**warranty** /ˈwɒrəntɪ/ n garantie f.

**wart** /wɔːt/ n verrue f.

**wartime** /ˈwɔːtaɪm/ n in ~ en

temps de guerre.

**wary** /'weəri/ adj (**-ier, -iest**) prudent.

**was** /wɒz, wəz/ ➡BE.

**wash** /wɒʃ/ vt/i (se) laver. (flow over) baigner; ~ one's hands of se laver les mains de • n lavage m; (clothes) lessive f; **have a** ~ se laver. ~ **up** faire la vaisselle; (US) se laver. ~**basin** n lavabo m.

**washer** /'wɒʃə(r)/ n rondelle f.

**washing** /'wɒʃɪŋ/ n lessive f. ~**-machine** n machine f à laver. ~**-powder** n lessive f.

**washing-up** n vaisselle f. □ ~ **liquid** n liquide m vaisselle.

**wash:** ~**-out** n fiasco m. ~**-room** n (US) toilettes fpl.

**wasp** /wɒsp/ n guêpe f.

**wastage** /'weɪstɪdʒ/ n gaspillage m.

**waste** /weɪst/ vt gaspiller; (time) perdre. • vi ~ away dépérir. • adj superflu; ~ **products** or **matter** déchets mpl. • n gaspillage m; (of time) perte f; (rubbish) déchets mpl; **lay** ~ dévaster. **wasteful** adj peu économique; (person) gaspilleur.

**waste:** ~**land** n (desolate) terre f désolée; (unused) terrain m vague. ~ **paper** n vieux papiers mpl. ~**-paper basket** n corbeille f (à papier).

**watch** /wɒtʃ/ vt/i (television) regarder; observer; (guard, spy on) surveiller; (be careful about) faire attention à. • n (for telling time) montre f; (Naut) quart m; **be on the** ~ guetter; **keep** ~ surveiller. ~ **out** (take care) faire attention (for à). ~ **out for** (keep watch) guetter.

**water** /'wɔːtə(r)/ n eau f; **by** ~ en bateau. • vt arroser. • vi (eyes) larmoyer; **my/his mouth** ~s l'eau

me/lui vient à la bouche. □ ~ **down** couper (d'eau); (tone down) édulcorer. ~**-colour** n (painting) aquarelle f. ~**-cress** n cresson m (de fontaine). ~**fall** n chute f d'eau, cascade f. ~ **heater** n chauffe-eau m. **watering-can** n arrosoir m. ~**-lily** n nénuphar m. ~**-melon** n pastèque f. ~**proof** adj (material) imperméable. ~ **shed** n (in affairs) tournant m décisif. ~**-skiing** n ski m nautique. ~**tight** adj étanche. ~**-way** n voie f navigable.

**watery** /'wɔːtəri/ adj (colour) délavé; (eyes) humide; (soup) trop liquide.

**wave** /weɪv/ n vague f; (in hair) ondulation f; (radio) onde f; (sign) signe m. • vt agiter. • vi faire signe (de la main); (move in wind) flotter.

**waver** /'weɪvə(r)/ vi vaciller.

**wavy** /'weɪvi/ adj (line) onduleux; (hair) ondulé.

**wax** /wæks/ n cire f; (for skis) fart m. • vt cirer; farter; (car) lustrer.

**way** /weɪ/ n (road, path) chemin m (**to** de); (distance) distance f; (direction) direction f; (manner) façon f; (means) moyen m; ~**s** (habits) habitudes fpl; **be in the** ~ bloquer le passage; (hindrance: fig) gêner (qn); **be on one's** or **the** ~ être sur son or le chemin; **by the** ~ à propos; **by the** ~**side** au bord de la route; **by** ~ **of** comme; (via) par; **get out of one's** ~ se donner du mal; **go out of one's** ~ dans un sens; **make one's** ~ **somewhere** se rendre quelque part; **push one's** ~ **through** se frayer un passage; **that** ~ par là; **this** ~ par ici; **in** ~ entrée f; ~ **out** sortie f. • adv 🄸 loin.

**we** /wiː/ pron nous.

**weak** /wiːk/ adj faible; (delicate) fragile.

**weakness** /'wiːknɪs/ n faiblesse f;

(fault) point *m* faible; a ~ for (liking) un faible pour.

**wealth** /welθ/ *n* richesse *f*; (riches, resources) richesses *fpl*; (quantity) profusion *f*.

**wealthy** /'welθɪ/ *adj* (**-ier, -iest**) riche. ● the ~ les riches *mpl*.

**weapon** /'wepən/ *n* arme *f*; ~s of mass destruction armes *fpl* de destruction massive.

**wear** /weə(r)/ *vt* (*pt* **wore**; *pp* **worn**) porter; (put on) mettre; (expression) avoir. ● *vi* (last) durer; ~ (out) (s')user. ● *n* (use) usage *m*; (damage) usure *f* ~ **down** user; ~ **off** (colour, pain) passer; ~ **out** (exhaust) épuiser.

**weary** /'wɪərɪ/ *adj* (**-ier, -iest**) fatigué, las. ● *vi* ~ of se lasser de.

**weather** /'weðə(r)/ *n* temps *m*; under the ~ patraque. ● *adj* météorologique. ● *vt* (survive) réchapper de or à. ~ **forecast** *n* météo *f*.

**weave** /wiːv/ *vt/i* (*pt* **wove**; *pp* **woven**) tisser; (basket) tresser; (move) se faufiler. ● *n* (style) tissage *m*.

**web** /web/ *n* (of spider) toile *f*; (on foot) palmure *f*.

**Web** /web/ *n* (Comput) Web *m*. ~**cam** *n* webcam *f*. ~**master** *n* administrateur *m* de site Internet. ~**page** *n* page *f* Web. ~**search** *n* recherche *f* sur le Web. ~**site** *n* site *m* Internet.

**wedding** /'wedɪŋ/ *n* mariage *m*. ~**ring** *n* alliance *f*.

**wedge** /wedʒ/ *n* (of wood) coin *m*; (under wheel) cale *f*. ● *vt* caler; (push) enfoncer; (crowd) coincer.

**Wednesday** /'wenzdɪ/ *n* mercredi *m*.

**weed** /wiːd/ *n* mauvaise herbe *f*. ● *vt/i* désherber; ~ **out** extirper.

**week** /wiːk/ *n* semaine *f*; a ~

today/tomorrow aujourd'hui/demain en huit. ~**day** *n* jour *m* de semaine. ~**end** *n* week-end *m*, fin *f* de semaine.

**weekly** /'wiːklɪ/ *adv* toutes les semaines. ● *adj & n* (periodical) hebdomadaire (*m*).

**weep** /wiːp/ *vt/i* (*pt* **wept**) pleurer (for sb qn).

**weigh** /weɪ/ *vt/i* peser; ~ **anchor** lever l'ancre. ~ **down** lester (avec un poids); (bend) faire plier; (fig) accabler; ~ **up** calculer.

**weight** /weɪt/ *n* poids *m*; lose/put on ~ perdre/prendre du poids. ~**lifting** *n* haltérophilie *f*. ~**training** *n* musculation *f* en salle.

**weird** /wɪəd/ *adj* bizarre.

**welcome** /'welkəm/ *adj* agréable; (timely) opportun; be ~ être le or la bienvenu(e), être les bienvenu(e)s; you're ~! il n'y a pas de quoi; ~ **to do** libre de faire. ● *interj* soyez le or la bienvenu(e), soyez les bienvenu(e)s. ● *n* accueil *m*. ● *vt* accueillir; (as greeting) souhaiter la bienvenue à; (fig) se réjouir de.

**weld** /weld/ *vt* souder. ● *n* soudure *f*.

**welfare** /'welfeə(r)/ *n* bien-être *m*; (aid) aide *f* sociale. **W**~ **State** *n* état-providence *m*.

**well**[1] /wel/ *n* puits *m*.

**well**[2] /wel/ *adv* (**better, best**) bien; do ~ (succeed) réussir; ~! bravo! ● *adj* bien *inv*; as ~ aussi; be ~ (healthy) aller bien. ● *interj* eh bien; (surprise) tiens.

**well:** ~**behaved** *adj* sage. ~**being** *n* bien-être *m inv*.

**wellington** /'welɪŋtən/ *n* (boot) botte *f* de caoutchouc.

**well:** ~**known** *adj* (bien) connu. ~**meaning** *adj* bien intentionné. ~ **off** aisé, riche. ~**read** *adj* instruit. **~-to-do** adj riche. **~-wisher** n admirateur/-trice m/f.

**Welsh** /welʃ/ adj gallois. ● n (Ling) gallois m.

> **i**
> **Welsh Assembly** L'Assemblée du Pays de Galles a été établie à Cardiff en 1999, à l'issue d'un référendum auprès de la population galloise. À la différence du parlement écossais, elle n'a pas de réel pouvoir législatif, mais ses 60 membres peuvent aménager les lois nationales en fonction des besoins spécifiques des Gallois. ▸SCOTTISH PARLIAMENT.

**went** /went/ ➡GO.

**wept** /wept/ ➡WEEP.

**were** /wɜː(r)/ ➡BE.

**west** /west/ n ouest m; the W~ (Pol) l'Occident m. ● adj d'ouest. ● adv vers l'ouest.

**western** /ˈwestən/ adj de l'ouest; (Pol) occidental. ● n (film) western m. **westerner** n occidental/-e m/f.

**West Indies** /west ˈɪndiːz/ n Antilles fpl.

**westward** /ˈwestwəd/ adj (side) ouest inv; (journey) vers l'ouest.

**wet** /wet/ adj (wetter, wettest) mouillé; (damp, rainy) humide; (paint) frais; get ~ se mouiller. ● vt (pt wetted) mouiller. ● n the ~ l'humidité f; (rain) la pluie f. **~suit** n combinaison f de plongée.

**whale** /weɪl/ n baleine f.

**wharf** /wɔːf/ n quai m.

**what** /wɒt/
● pronoun
····➤ (in questions as object pronoun) qu'est-ce que?; ~ are

we going to do? qu'est-ce que nous allons faire?
····➤ (in questions as subject pronoun) qu'est-ce qui; ~ happened? qu'est-ce qui s'est passé?
····➤ (introducing clause as object) ce que; I don't know ~ he wants je ne sais pas ce qu'il veut.
····➤ (introducing clause as subject) ce qui; tell me ~ happened raconte moi ce qui s'est passé.
····➤ (with prepositions) quoi; ~ are you thinking about? à quoi penses-tu?

● determiner
····➤ quel/quelle/quels/quelles; ~ train did you catch? quel train as-tu pris?; ~ time is it? quelle heure est-il?

**whatever** /wɒtˈevə(r)/ adj ~ book quel que soit le livre. ● pron (no matter what) quoi que, quoi qu'; (anything that) tout ce qui; (object) tout ce que or qui; ~ happens quoi qu'il arrive; ~ happened? qu'est-ce qui est arrivé?; ~ the problems quels que soient les problèmes; ~ you want tout ce que vous voulez; nothing ~ rien du tout.

**whatsoever** /wɒtsəʊˈevə(r)/ adj & pron ▸WHATEVER.

**wheat** /wiːt/ n blé m, froment m.

**wheel** /wiːl/ n roue f; at the ~ (of vehicle) au volant; (helm) au gouvernail. ● vt pousser. ● vi tourner; ~ and deal faire des combines. **~barrow** n brouette f. **~chair** n fauteuil m roulant.

**when** /wen/ adv & pron quand. ● conj quand, lorsque; the day/mo-

w

ment ~ le jour/moment où.

**whenever** /wen'evə(r)/ *conj & adv* (at whatever time) quand; (every time that) chaque fois que.

**where** /weə(r)/ *adv, conj & pron* où; (whereas) alors que; (the place that) là où.

**whereabouts** /weərə'baʊts/ *adv* (à peu près) où. ● *n* sb's ~ l'endroit où se trouve qn.

**whereas** /weər'æz/ *conj* alors que.

**wherever** /weər'evə(r)/ *conj & adv* où que; (everywhere) partout où; (anywhere) (là) où; (emphatic where) où donc.

**whether** /'weðə(r)/ *conj* si; not know ~ ne pas savoir si; ~ I go or not que j'aille ou non.

---

**which** /wɪtʃ/

● *pronoun*

····▸ (in questions) lequel/ laquelle/lesquels/lesquelles; there are three peaches, ~ do you want? il y a trois pêches, laquelle veux-tu?

····▸ (in questions with superlative adjective) quel/quelle/ quels/quelles; ~ (apple) is the biggest? quelle est la plus grosse?

····▸ (in relative clauses as subject) qui; the book ~ is on the table le livre qui est sur la table.

····▸ (in relative clauses as object) que; the book ~ Tina is reading le livre que lit Tina.

● *determiner*

····▸ quel/quelle/quels/quelles; ~ car did you choose? quelle voiture as-tu choisie?

---

**whichever** /wɪtʃ'evə(r)/ *adj* ~ book quel que soit le livre que or qui; take ~ book you wish prenez le livre que vous voulez. ● *pron* celui/celle/ceux/celles qui or que.

**while** /waɪl/ *n* moment m. ● *conj* (when) pendant que; (although) bien que; (as long as) tant que. ● *vt* ~ away (time) passer.

**whilst** /waɪlst/ *conj* ▶WHILE.

**whim** /wɪm/ *n* caprice m.

**whine** /waɪn/ *vi* gémir, se plaindre. ● *n* gémissement m.

**whip** /wɪp/ *n* fouet m. ● *vt* (*pt* **whipped**) fouetter; (Culin) fouetter, battre; (seize) enlever brusquement. ● *vi* (move) aller en vitesse. □ ~ **up** exciter; (cause) provoquer; (meal ▯) préparer.

**whirl** /wɜːl/ *vt/i* (faire) tourbillonner. ● *n* tourbillon m. **~pool** *n* tourbillon m. **~wind** *n* tourbillon m (de vent).

**whisk** /wɪsk/ *vt* (snatch) enlever or emmener brusquement; (Culin) fouetter. ● *n* (Culin) fouet m.

**whiskers** /'wɪskə(r)z/ *npl* (of animal) moustaches *fpl*; (of man) favoris *mpl*.

**whisper** /'wɪspə(r)/ *vt/i* chuchoter. ● *n* chuchotement m; (rumour: fig) rumeur f, bruit m.

**whistle** /'wɪsl/ *n* sifflement m; (instrument) sifflet m. ● *vt/i* siffler; ~ at or for siffler.

**white** /waɪt/ *adj* blanc. ● *n* blanc m; (person) blanc/-che m/f. ~ **coffee** *n* café m au lait. **~-collar worker** *n* employé/-e m/f de bureau. ~ **elephant** *n* projet m coûteux et peu rentable. ~ **lie** *n* pieux mensonge m. W~ **Paper** *n* livre m blanc.

**whitewash** /'waɪtwɒʃ/ *n* blanc m de chaux. ● *vt* blanchir à la chaux; (person: fig) blanchir.

**w**

**Whitsun | will**

**Whitsun** /'wɪtsn/ n la Pentecôte.

**whiz** /wɪz/ vi (pt **whizzed**) (through air) fendre l'air; (hiss) siffler; (rush) aller à toute vitesse. ~**-kid** n jeune prodige m.

**who** /huː/ pron qui.

**whoever** /huː'evə(r)/ pron (no matter who) qui que ce soit qui or que; (the one who) quiconque; tell ~ you want dites-le à qui vous voulez.

**whole** /həʊl/ adj entier; (intact) intact; the ~ house toute la maison. ● n totalité f; (unit) tout m; on the ~ dans l'ensemble. ~**foods** npl aliments npl naturels et diététiques. ~**-hearted** adj sans réserve. ~**meal** adj complet.

**wholesale** /'həʊlseɪl/ adj (firm) de gros; (fig) systématique. ● adv (in large quantities) en gros; (fig) en masse.

**wholesome** /'həʊlsəm/ adj sain.

**wholly** /'həʊllɪ/ adv entièrement.

**whom** /huːm/ pron (that) que, qu'; (after prepositions & in questions) qui; qu'~ dont; with ~ avec qui.

**whooping cough** /'huːpɪŋ kɒf/ n coqueluche f.

**whose** /huːz/ pron & a à qui, de qui; ~ hat is this?, ~ is this hat? à qui est ce chapeau?; ~ son are you? de qui êtes-vous le fils?; the man ~ hat I see l'homme dont je vois le chapeau.

**why** /waɪ/ adv pourquoi; the reason ~ la raison pour laquelle.

**wicked** /'wɪkɪd/ adj méchant, mauvais, vilain.

**wide** /waɪd/ adj large; (ocean) vaste. ● adv (fall) loin du but; open ~ ouvrir tout grand; ~ open grand ouvert; ~ awake éveillé. **widely** adv (spread, spaced) largement; (travel) beaucoup; (generally) généralement; (extremely) extrêmement.

**widespread** /'waɪdspred/ adj très répandu.

**widow** /'wɪdəʊ/ n veuve f. **widowed** adj (man) veuf; (woman) veuve. **widower** n veuf m.

**width** /wɪdθ/ n largeur f.

**wield** /wiːld/ vt (axe) manier; (power: fig) exercer.

**wife** /waɪf/ n (pl **wives**) femme f, épouse f.

**wig** /wɪg/ n perruque f.

**wiggle** /'wɪgl/ vt/i remuer; (hips) tortiller; (worm) se tortiller.

**wild** /waɪld/ adj sauvage; (sea, enthusiasm) déchaîné; (mad) fou; (angry) furieux. ● adv (grow) à l'état sauvage.

**wildlife** /'waɪldlaɪf/ n faune f.

---

**will¹** /wɪl/

present **will**; present negative **won't, will not**; past **would**

● auxiliary verb

····▸ (in future tense) he'll come il viendra; it ~ be sunny tomorrow il va faire du soleil demain.

····▸ (inviting and requesting) ~ you have some coffee? est-ce que vous voulez du café?

····▸ (making assumptions) they won't know what's happened ils ne doivent pas savoir ce qui s'est passé.

····▸ (in short questions and answers) you'll come again, won't you? tu reviendras, n'est-ce pas?; 'they won't forget'—'yes they ~' 'ils n'oublieront pas'—'si'.

w

·····➤ (capacity) the lift ~ hold 12 l'ascenseur peut transporter 12 personnes.

·····➤ (ability) the car won't start la voiture ne veut pas démarrer.

● *transitive verb* ~ sb's death souhaiter ardemment la mort de qn.

**will²** /wɪl/ n volonté f; (document) testament m; **at** ~ quand or comme on veut.

**willing** /'wɪlɪŋ/ adj (help, offer) spontané; (helper) bien disposé; **to** ~ disposé à. **willingly** adv (with pleasure) volontiers; (not forced) volontairement. **willingness** n empressement m (to do à faire).

**willow** /'wɪləʊ/ n saule m.

**will-power** /'wɪlpaʊə(r)/ n volonté f.

**win** /wɪn/ vt/i (pt **won**; pres p **winning**) gagner; (prize) remporter; (fame) acquérir, trouver; ~ **round** convaincre. ● n victoire f.

**winch** /wɪntʃ/ n treuil m. ● vt hisser au treuil.

**wind¹** /wɪnd/ n vent m; (breath) souffle m; **get** ~ **of** avoir vent de; **in the** ~ dans l'air. ● vt essouffler. ~ **farm** n ferme f d'éoliennes. ~ **turbine** moteur m éolien.

**wind²** /waɪnd/ vt/i (pt **wound**) (s')enrouler; (of path, river) serpenter; ~ (**up**) (clock) remonter; ~ (end) (se) terminer; ~ **up in hospital** finir à l'hôpital.

**windmill** /'wɪndmɪl/ n moulin m à vent.

**window** /'wɪndəʊ/ n fenêtre f; (glass pane) vitre f; (in vehicle, train) vitre f; (in shop) vitrine f; (counter) guichet m; (Comput) fenêtre f. ~-**box** n jardinière f. ~-**cleaner** n laveur m de carreaux.

~-**dresser** n étalagiste mf. ~-**ledge** n rebord m de (la) fenêtre. ~-**shopping** n lèche-vitrines m. ~-**sill** n (inside) appui m de la fenêtre; (outside) rebord m de (la) fenêtre.

**windscreen** /'wɪndskriːn/ n pare-brise m inv. ~ **wiper** n essuie-glace m.

**windshield** /'wɪndʃiːld/ n (US) ➥WINDSCREEN.

**windsurfing** /'wɪndsɜːfɪŋ/ n planche f à voile.

**windy** /'wɪndɪ/ adj (-**ier**, -**iest**) venteux; **it is** ~ il y a du vent.

**wine** /waɪn/ n vin m. ~-**cellar** n cave f (à vin). ~-**glass** n verre m à vin. ~-**grower** n viticulteur m. ~-**list** n carte f des vins. ~-**tasting** n dégustation f de vins.

**wing** /wɪŋ/ n aile f; ~**s** (Theat) coulisses fpl; **under one's** ~ sous son aile. ~ **mirror** n rétroviseur m extérieur.

**wink** /wɪŋk/ vi faire un clin d'œil; (light, star) clignoter. ● n clin m d'œil; clignotement m.

**winner** /'wɪnə(r)/ n (of game) gagnant/-e m/f; (of fight) vainqueur m.

**winning** /'wɪnɪŋ/ ➥WIN. ● adj (number, horse) gagnant; (team) victorieux; (smile) engageant. **winnings** npl gains mpl.

**winter** /'wɪntə(r)/ n hiver m.

**wipe** /waɪp/ vt essuyer. ~ **up** essuyer la vaisselle. ● vi ~ **up** essuyer la vaisselle. ● n coup m de torchon or d'éponge. □ ~ **out** (destroy) anéantir; (remove) effacer.

**wire** /waɪə(r)/ n fil m; (US) télégramme m.

**wiring** /'waɪərɪŋ/ n (Electr) installation f électrique.

**wisdom** /'wɪzdəm/ n sagesse f.

**wise** /waɪz/ adj prudent, sage;

w

(look) averti.

**wish** /wɪʃ/ n (specific) souhait m, vœu m; (general) désir m; best ~es (in letter) amitiés fpl; (on greeting card) meilleurs vœux mpl. • vt souhaiter, vouloir, désirer (to do sth); (bid) souhaiter. • vi ~ for souhaiter; I ~ he'd leave je voudrais bien qu'il parte.

**wishful** /ˈwɪʃfl/ adj it's ~ thinking c'est prendre ses désirs pour des réalités.

**wistful** /ˈwɪstfl/ adj mélancolique.

**wit** /wɪt/ n intelligence f; (humour) esprit m; (person) homme m d'esprit, femme f d'esprit.

**witch** /wɪtʃ/ n sorcière f.

**with** /wɪð/ prep avec; (having) à; (because of) de; (at the house of) chez; the man ~ the beard l'homme à la barbe; fill ~ remplir de; pleased/shaking ~ content/frémissant de.

**withdraw** /wɪðˈdrɔː/ vt/i (pt withdrew; pp withdrawn) (se) retirer. **withdrawal** n retrait m.

**wither** /ˈwɪðə(r)/ vt/i (se) flétrir.

**withhold** /wɪðˈhəʊld/ vt (pt withheld) refuser (de donner); (retain) retenir; (conceal) cacher (from à).

**within** /wɪˈðɪn/ prep & adv à l'intérieur (de); (in distances) à moins de; ~ a month (before) avant un mois; ~ sight en vue.

**without** /wɪˈðaʊt/ prep sans; ~ my knowing sans que je sache.

**withstand** /wɪðˈstænd/ vt (pt withstood) résister à.

**witness** /ˈwɪtnɪs/ n témoin m; (evidence) témoignage m; bear ~ to témoigner de. • vt être le témoin de, voir. ~ box, ~ stand n barre f des témoins.

**witty** /ˈwɪtɪ/ adj (-ier, -iest) spirituel.

**wives** /waɪvz/ ➡**WIFE.**

**wizard** /ˈwɪzəd/ n magicien m; (genius: fig) génie m.

**WMD** abbr (weapon of mass destruction) ADM f.

**woke, woken** ➡**WAKE.**

**wolf** /wʊlf/ n (pl wolves) loup m. • vt (food) engloutir.

**woman** /ˈwʊmən/ n (pl women) femme f; ~ doctor femme f médecin; ~ driver femme f au volant.

**women** /ˈwɪmɪn/ ➡**WOMAN.**

**won** /wʌn/ ➡**WIN.**

**wonder** /ˈwʌndə(r)/ n émerveillement m; (thing) merveille f; it is no ~ ce n'est pas étonnant (that que). • vi s'étonner (at de); (reflect) songer (about à).

**wonderful** /ˈwʌndəfl/ adj merveilleux.

**won't** /wəʊnt/ ➡**WILL NOT.**

**wood** /wʊd/ n bois m.

**wooden** /ˈwʊdn/ adj en or de bois. (stiff: fig) raide, comme du bois.

**wood:** ~wind n (Mus) bois mpl. ~work n (craft, objects) menuiserie f

**wool** /wʊl/ n laine f. **woollen** adj de laine. **woollens** npl lainages mpl.

**woolly** /ˈwʊlɪ/ adj laineux; (vague) nébuleux. • n (garment 🄙) lainage m

**word** /wɜːd/ n mot m; (spoken) parole f, mot m; (promise) parole f; (news) nouvelles fpl; by ~ of mouth de vive voix; give/keep one's ~ donner/tenir sa parole; have a ~ with parler à; in other ~s autrement dit. • vt rédiger. **wording** n termes mpl.

**word processing** n traitement m de texte. **word processor** n machine f à traitement de texte.

**wore** /wɔː(r)/ ➡**WEAR.**

**work** /wɜːk/ n travail m; (product,

book) œuvre f, ouvrage m; (building work) travaux mpl; ~s (Tech) mécanisme m; (factory) usine f. ● vi (person) travailler; (drug) agir; (Tech) fonctionner, marcher. ● vt (Tech) faire fonctionner, faire marcher; (land, mine) exploiter; (shape, hammer) travailler; ~ **sb** (make work) faire travailler qn. □ ~ **out** vt (solve) résoudre; (calculate) calculer; (elaborate) élaborer; vi (succeed) marcher; (Sport) s'entraîner; ~ **up** vt développer; vi (to climax) monter vers; ~**ed up** (person) énervé.

**workaholic** /wɜːkəˈhɒlɪk/ n Ⓘ bourreau m de travail.

**worker** /ˈwɜːkə(r)/ n travailleur/-euse m/f; (manual) ouvrier/-ière m/f.

**work-force** n main-d'œuvre f.

**working** /ˈwɜːkɪŋ/ adj (day, lunch) de travail; ~s mécanisme m; in ~ order en état de marche.

**working class** n classe f ouvrière. ● adj ouvrier.

**workman** /ˈwɜːkmən/ n (pl -men) ouvrier m.

**work:** ~**out** n séance f de mise en forme. ~**shop** n atelier m. ~**-station** n poste m de travail.

**world** /wɜːld/ n monde m; best in the ~ meilleur au monde. ● adj (power) mondial; (record) du monde.

**world-wide** adj universel.

**World Wide Web, WWW** n World Wide Web m, réseau m des réseaux.

**w**    **worm** /wɜːm/ n ver m. ● vt ~ one's way into s'insinuer dans.

**worn** /wɔːn/ ⇒WEAR. ● adj usé. ~**-out** adj (thing) complètement usé; (person) épuisé.

**worried** /ˈwʌrɪd/ adj inquiet.

**worry** /ˈwʌrɪ/ vt/i (s')inquiéter. ● n

souci m.

**worse** /wɜːs/ adj pire, plus mauvais; be ~ off perdre. ● adv plus mal. ● n pire m. **worsen** vt/i empirer.

**worship** /ˈwɜːʃɪp/ n (adoration) culte m. ● vt (pt worshipped) adorer. ● vi faire ses dévotions.

**worst** /wɜːst/ adj pire, plus mauvais. ● adv (the) ~ (sing) le plus mal. ● n the ~ (one) (person, object) le or la pire; the ~ (thing) le pire.

**worth** /wɜːθ/ adj be ~ valoir; it is ~ waiting ça vaut la peine d'attendre; it is ~ (one's) while ça (en) vaut la peine. ● n valeur f; ten pence ~ of (pour) dix pence de. **worthless** adj qui ne vaut rien. **worthwhile** adj qui (en) vaut la peine.

**worthy** /ˈwɜːðɪ/ adj (-ier, -iest) digne (of de); (laudable) louable.

**would** /wʊd/ v aux he ~ do/you ~ sing (conditional tense) il ferait/ tu chanterais; he ~ have done il aurait fait; I ~ come every day (used to) je venais chaque jour; I ~ like some tea je voudrais du thé; ~ **you come here?** voulez-vous venir ici?; he wouldn't come il a refusé de venir. ~**be** adj soidisant.

**wound**[1] /wuːnd/ n blessure f. ● vt blesser; the ~**ed** les blessés mpl.

**wound**[2] /waʊnd/ ⇒WIND[2].

**wove, woven** /wəʊv, ˈwəʊvn/ ⇒WEAVE.

**wrap** /ræp/ vt (pt wrapped) ● ~ (up) envelopper. ● vi ~ up (dress warmly) se couvrir; ~**ped up in** (engrossed) absorbé dans.

**wrapping** /ˈræpɪŋ/ n emballage m.

**wreak** /riːk/ vt ~ havoc faire des ravages.

**wreath** /riːθ/ n (of flowers, leaves) couronne f.

**wreck** /rek/ n (sinking) naufrage m; (ship, remains, person) épave f; (vehicle) voiture f accidentaée or délabrée. ● vt détruire; (ship) provoquer le naufrage de. **wreckage** n (pieces) débris mpl; (wrecked building) décombres mpl.

**wrestle** /ˈresl/ vi lutter, se débattre (**with** contre).

**wrestling** /ˈreslɪŋ/ n lutte f; (all-in) ~ catch m.

**wriggle** /ˈrɪgl/ vt/i (se) tortiller.

**wring** /rɪŋ/ vt (pt **wrung**) (twist) tordre; (clothes) essorer; ~ **out of** (obtain from) arracher à.

**wrinkle** /ˈrɪŋkl/ n (crease) pli m; (on skin) ride f ● vt/i (se) rider.

**wrist** /rɪst/ n poignet m.

**write** /raɪt/ vt/i (pt **wrote**; pp **written**) écrire. □ ~ **back** répondre; ~ **down** noter; ~ **off** (debt) passer aux profits et pertes; (vehicle) considérer bon pour la casse; ~ **up** (from notes) rédiger.

**write-off** /ˈraɪtɒf/ n perte f totale.

**writer** /ˈraɪtə(r)/ n auteur m, écrivain m; ~ **of** auteur de.

**write-up** /ˈraɪtʌp/ n compte-rendu m.

**writing** /ˈraɪtɪŋ/ n écriture f; ~(s) (works) écrits mpl; **in** ~ par écrit. ~-**paper** n papier m à lettres.

**written** /ˈrɪtn/ →WRITE.

**wrong** /rɒŋ/ adj (incorrect, mistaken) faux, mauvais. (unfair) injuste; (amiss) qui ne va pas; (clock) pas à l'heure; **be** ~ (person) avoir tort (**to** de); (be mistaken) se tromper; **go** ~ (err) se tromper; (turn out badly) mal tourner; **it is** ~ **to** (morally) c'est mal de; **what's** ~? qu'est-ce qui ne va pas?; **what is** ~ **with you?** qu'est-ce que vous avez?

● adv mal. ● n injustice f; (evil) mal m; **be in the** ~ avoir tort. ● vt faire (du) tort à. **wrongful** adj injustifié, injuste. **wrongfully** adv à tort. **wrongly** adv mal; (blame) à tort.

**wrote** /rəʊt/ →WRITE.

**wrought iron** /rɔːt ˈaɪən/ n fer m forgé.

**wrung** /rʌŋ/ →WRING.

**Xmas** /ˈkrɪsməs/ n Noël m.

**X-ray** /ˈeksreɪ/ n rayon m X; (photograph) radio (graphie) f. ● vt radiographier.

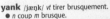

**yank** /jæŋk/ vt tirer brusquement. ● n coup m brusque.

**yard** /jɑːd/ n (measure) yard m (= 0.9144 metre); (of house) cour f; (garden: US) jardin m; (for storage) chantier m, dépôt m. ~**stick** n mesure f.

**yawn** /jɔːn/ vi bâiller. ● n bâillement m.

**yeah** /jeə/ adv 🄸 ouais.

**year** /jɪə(r)/ n an m, année f; **school/tax** ~ année scolaire/fiscale; **be ten** ~**s old** avoir dix ans. **yearly** /ˈjɪəlɪ/ adj annuel. ● adv annuellement.

**yearn** /jɜːn/ vi avoir bien or très envie (**for**, **to** de).

**yeast** /ji:st/ n levure f.

**yell** /jel/ vt/i hurler. ● n hurlement m.

**yellow** /'jeləʊ/ adj jaune; (cowardly 🗏) froussard. ● n jaune m.

**yes** /jes/ adv oui; (as answer to negative question) si. ● n oui m inv.

**yesterday** /'jestədeɪ/ n & adv hier (m).

**yet** /jet/ adv encore; (already) déjà. ● conj pourtant, néanmoins.

**yew** /ju:/ n if m.

**yield** /ji:ld/ vt (produce) produire, rendre; (profit) rapporter; (surrender) céder. ● n rendement m.

**yoga** /'jəʊɡə/ n yoga m.

**yoghurt** /'jɒɡət/ n yaourt m.

**yolk** /jəʊk/ n jaune m (d'œuf).

**you** /ju:/ pron (familiar form) tu, pl vous; (polite form) vous; (object) te, t', pl vous; (polite) vous; (after prep.) toi, pl vous; (polite) vous; (indefinite) on; (object) vous; (polite) vous; **to** ~ te, t', pl vous; (polite) vous; **I gave** ~ **a pen** je vous ai donné un stylo; **I know** ~ je te connais or je vous connais.

**young** /jʌŋ/ adj jeune. ● n (people) jeunes mpl; (of animals) petits mpl.

**your** /jɔ:(r)/ adj (familiar form) ton, ta, pl tes; (polite form, & familiar form pl.) votre, pl vos.

**yours** /jɔ:z/ pron (familiar form) le tien, la tienne, les tien(ne)s; (polite form, & familiar form pl.) le or la vôtre, les vôtres; ~ **faithfully/sincerely** je vous prie d'agréer mes salutations les meilleures.

**yourself** /jɔ:'self/ pron (familiar form) toimême; (polite form) vous-même; (reflexive & after pre-

positions) te, t'; vous; **proud of** ~ fier de toi. **yourselves** pron vous-mêmes; (reflexive) vous.

**youth** /ju:θ/ n jeunesse f; (young man) jeune m. ~ **hostel** n auberge f de jeunesse.

**Yugoslav** /'ju:ɡəʊslɑːv/ adj yougoslave. ● n Yougoslave mf.

**Yugoslavia** /ju:ɡəʊ'slɑːvɪə/ n Yougoslavie f.

# Zz

**zap** /zæp/ vt 🗏 (kill) descendre; (Comput) enlever.

**zeal** /zi:l/ n zèle m.

**zebra** /'zebrə/ n zèbre m. ~ **crossing** n passage m pour piétons.

**zero** /'zɪərəʊ/ n zéro m.

**zest** /zest/ n (gusto) entrain m; (spice: fig) piment m; (of orange or lemon peel) zeste m.

**zip** /zɪp/ n (vigour) allant m; ~(**-fastener**) fermeture f éclair(r). ● vt (pt **zipped**) fermer avec une fermeture éclair(r); (Comput) compresser. **Zip code** (US) n code m postal.

**zodiac** /'zəʊdɪæk/ n zodiaque m.

**zone** /zəʊn/ n zone f.

**zoo** /zu:/ n zoo m.

**zoom** /zu:m/ vi (rush) se précipiter. □ ~ **off** or **past** filer (comme une flèche). ~ **lens** n zoom m.

**zucchini** /zu:'ki:nɪ/ n inv (US) courgette f.

# French Verbs

## 1 chanter

### Present indicative

| je | chante |
|---|---|
| tu | chantes |
| il | chante |
| nous | chantons |
| vous | chantez |
| ils | chantent |

### Future indicative

| je | chanterai |
|---|---|
| tu | chanteras |
| il | chantera |
| nous | chanterons |
| vous | chanterez |
| ils | chanteront |

### Imperfect indicative

| je | chantais |
|---|---|
| tu | chantais |
| il | chantait |
| nous | chantions |
| vous | chantiez |
| ils | chantaient |

### Perfect indicative

| j' | ai | chanté |
|---|---|---|
| tu | as | chanté |
| il | a | chanté |
| elle | a | chanté |
| nous | avons | chanté |
| vous | avez | chanté |
| ils | ont | chanté |
| elles | ont | chanté |

### Present subjunctive

| (que) | je | chante |
|---|---|---|
| (que) | tu | chantes |
| (qu') | il | chante |
| (que) | nous | chantions |
| (que) | vous | chantiez |
| (qu') | ils | chantent |

### Present conditional

| je | chanterais |
|---|---|
| tu | chanterais |
| il | chanterait |
| nous | chanterions |
| vous | chanteriez |
| ils | chanteraient |

### Past participle

chanté/chantée

### Pluperfect indicative

| j' | avais | chanté |
|---|---|---|
| tu | avais | chanté |
| il | avait | chanté |
| elle | avait | chanté |
| nous | avions | chanté |
| vous | aviez | chanté |
| ils | avaient | chanté |
| elles | avaient | chanté |

## 2 finir

### Present indicative

| je | finis |
| tu | finis |
| il | finit |
| nous | finissons |
| vous | finissez |
| ils | finissent |

### Present subjunctive

| (que) | je | finisse |
| (que) | tu | finisses |
| (qu') | il | finisse |
| (que) | nous | finissions |
| (que) | vous | finissiez |
| (qu') | ils | finissent |

### Future indicative

| je | finirai |
| tu | finiras |
| il | finira |
| nous | finirons |
| vous | finirez |
| ils | finiront |

### Present conditional

| je | finirais |
| tu | finirais |
| il | finirait |
| nous | finirions |
| vous | finiriez |
| ils | finiraient |

### Imperfect indicative

| je | finissais |
| tu | finissais |
| il | finissait |
| nous | finissions |
| vous | finissiez |
| ils | finissaient |

### Past participle

| | fini/finie |

### Pluperfect indicative

| j' | avais | fini |
| tu | avais | fini |
| il | avait | fini |
| elle | avait | fini |
| nous | avions | fini |
| vous | aviez | fini |
| ils | avaient | fini |
| elles | avaient | fini |

### Perfect indicative

| j' | ai | fini |
| tu | as | fini |
| il | a | fini |
| elles | a | fini |
| nous | avons | fini |
| vous | avez | fini |
| ils | ont | fini |
| elles | ont | fini |

## 3 attendre

### Present indicative

| | |
|---|---|
| j' | attends |
| tu | attends |
| il | attend |
| nous | attendons |
| vous | attendez |
| ils | attendent |

### Present subjunctive

| | | |
|---|---|---|
| (que) | j' | attende |
| (que) | tu | attendes |
| (qu') | il | attende |
| (que) | nous | attendions |
| (que) | vous | attendiez |
| (qu') | ils | attendent |

### Future indicative

| | |
|---|---|
| j' | attendrai |
| tu | attendras |
| il | attendra |
| nous | attendrons |
| vous | attendrez |
| ils | attendront |

### Present conditional

| | |
|---|---|
| j' | attendrais |
| tu | attendrais |
| il | attendrait |
| nous | attendrions |
| vous | attendriez |
| ils | attendraient |

### Imperfect indicative

| | |
|---|---|
| j' | attendais |
| tu | attendais |
| il | attendait |
| nous | attendions |
| vous | attendiez |
| ils | attendaient |

### Past participle

attendu/attendue

### Pluperfect indicative

| | | |
|---|---|---|
| j' | avais | attendu |
| tu | avais | attendu |
| il | avait | attendu |
| elle | avait | attendu |
| nous | avions | attendu |
| vous | aviez | attendu |
| ils | avaient | attendu |
| elles | avaient | attendu |

### Perfect indicative

| | | |
|---|---|---|
| j' | ai | attendu |
| tu | as | attendu |
| il | a | attendu |
| elle | a | attendu |
| nous | avons | attendu |
| vous | avez | attendu |
| ils | ont | attendu |
| elles | ont | attendu |

## 4 être

### Present indicative

| je | suis |
|----|------|
| tu | es |
| il | est |
| nous | sommes |
| vous | êtes |
| ils | sont |

### Present subjunctive

| (que) | je | sois |
|-------|-----|------|
| (que) | tu | sois |
| (qu') | il | soit |
| (que) | nous | soyons |
| (que) | vous | soyez |
| (qu') | ils | soient |

### Future indicative

| je | serai |
|----|-------|
| tu | seras |
| il | sera |
| nous | serons |
| vous | serez |
| ils | seront |

### Present conditional

| je | serais |
|----|--------|
| tu | serais |
| il | serait |
| nous | serions |
| vous | seriez |
| ils | seraient |

### Imperfect indicative

| j' | étais |
|----|-------|
| tu | étais |
| il | était |
| nous | étions |
| vous | étiez |
| ils | étaient |

### Past participle

été (*invariable*)

### Pluperfect indicative

| j' | avais | été |
|----|-------|-----|
| tu | avais | été |
| il | avait | été |
| elle | avait | été |
| nous | avions | été |
| vous | aviez | été |
| ils | avaient | été |
| elles | avaient | été |

### Perfect indicative

| j' | ai | été |
|----|-----|-----|
| tu | as | été |
| il | a | été |
| elle | a | été |
| nous | avons | été |
| vous | avez | été |
| ils | ont | été |
| elles | ont | été |

# 5 avoir

## Present indicative

| | |
|---|---|
| j' | ai |
| tu | as |
| il | a |
| nous | avons |
| vous | avez |
| ils | ont |

## Present subjunctive

| | | |
|---|---|---|
| (que) | j' | aie |
| (que) | tu | aies |
| (qu') | il | ait |
| (que) | nous | ayons |
| (que) | vous | ayez |
| (qu') | ils | aient |

## Future indicative

| | |
|---|---|
| j' | aurai |
| tu | auras |
| il | aura |
| nous | aurons |
| vous | aurez |
| ils | auront |

## Present conditional

| | |
|---|---|
| j' | aurais |
| tu | aurais |
| il | aurait |
| nous | aurions |
| vous | auriez |
| ils | auraient |

## Imperfect indicative

| | |
|---|---|
| j' | avais |
| tu | avais |
| il | avait |
| nous | avions |
| vous | aviez |
| ils | avaient |

## Past participle

eu/eue

## Pluperfect indicative

| | | |
|---|---|---|
| j' | avais | eu |
| tu | avais | eu |
| il | avait | eu |
| elle | avait | eu |
| nous | avions | eu |
| vous | aviez | eu |
| ils | avaient | eu |
| elles | avaient | eu |

## Perfect indicative

| | | |
|---|---|---|
| j' | ai | eu |
| tu | as | eu |
| il | a | eu |
| elle | a | eu |
| nous | avons | eu |
| vous | avez | eu |
| ils | ont | eu |
| elles | ont | eu |

### [6] acheter

**1** j'achète **2** j'achèterai **3** j'achetais
**4** que j'achète **5** acheté

### [7] acquérir

**1** j'acquiers, nous acquérons,
ils acquièrent **2** j'acquerrai
**3** j'acquérais **4** que j'acquière
**5** acquis

### [8] aller

**1** je vais, tu vas, il va, nous allons,
vous allez, ils vont **2** j'irai **3** j'allais
**4** que j'aille, que nous allions, qu'ils
aillent **5** allé

### [9] asseoir

**1** j'assois, tu assois, il assoit, nous
assoyons, vous assoyez, ils assoient
**2** j'assoirai **3** j'assoyais **4** que
j'assoie, que nous assoyions, qu'ils
assoient **5** assis

### [10] avancer

**1** nous avançons **3** j'avançais

### [11] battre

**1** je bats, il bat, nous battons
**2** je battrai **3** je battais **4** que je
batte **5** battu

### [12] boire

**1** je bois, il boit, nous buvons,
ils boivent **2** je boirai **3** je buvais
**4** que je boive **5** bu

### [13] bouillir

**1** je bous, il bout, nous bouillons,
ils bouillent **2** je bouillirai **3** je bouillais **4** que je bouille
**5** bouilli

### [14] céder

**1** je cède, nous cédons, ils cèdent
**2** je céderai **3** je cédais **4** que je
cède **5** cédé

### [15] créer

**1** je crée, nous créons **2** je créerai
**3** je créais **4** que je crée **5** créé

### [16] conclure

**1** je conclus, il conclut, nous
concluons, ils concluent **2** je
conclurai **3** je concluais **4** que je
conclue **5** conclu (*but* inclus)

### [17] conduire

**1** je conduis, nous conduisons,
**2** je conduirai **3** je conduisais
**4** que je conduise **5** conduit (*but*
lui, nui)

### [18] connaître

**1** je connais, il connaît, nous
connaissons **2** je connaîtrai
**3** je connaissais **4** que je connaisse
**5** connu

### [19] coudre

**1** je couds, il coud, nous cousons,
ils cousent **2** je coudrai **3** je cousais
**4** que je couse **5** cousu

### [20] courir

**1** je cours, il court, nous courons,
ils courent **2** je courrai **3** je courais
**4** que je coure **5** couru

---

**1** Present Indicative  **2** Future Indicative  **3** Imperfect Indicative
**4** Present Subjunctive  **5** Past Participle

## [21] couvrir

**1** je couvre **2** je couvrirai **3** je couvrais **4** que je couvre **5** couvert

## [22] craindre

**1** je crains, il craint, nous craignons, ils craignent **2** je craindrai **3** je craignais **4** que je craigne **5** craint

## [23] croire

**1** je crois, il croit, nous croyons, ils croient **2** je croirai **3** je croyais, nous croyions **4** que je croie, que nous croyions **5** cru

## [24] croître1

**1** je croîs, il croît, nous croissons **2** je croîtrai **3** je croissais **4** que je croisse **5** crû/crue (*but* accru, décru)

## [25] cueillir

**1** je cueille **2** je cueillerai **3** je cueillais **4** que je cueille **5** cueilli

## [26] devoir

**1** je dois, il doit, nous devons, ils doivent **2** je devrai **3** je devais **4** que je doive, que nous devions **5** dû/due

## [27] dire

**1** je dis, il dit, nous disons, vous dites, ils disent **2** je dirai **3** je disais **4** que je dise **5** dit

## [28] dissoudre

**1** je dissous, il dissout, nous dissolvons, ils dissolvent **2** je dissoudrai **3** je dissolvais **4** que je dissolve **5** dissous/dissoute

## [29] distraire

**1** je distrais, il distrait, nous distrayons **2** je distrairai **3** je distrayais **4** que je distraie **5** distrait

## [30] écrire

**1** j'écris, il écrit, nous écrivons **2** j'écrirai **3** j'écrivais **4** que j'écrive **5** écrit

## [31] employer

**1** j'emploie, nous employons, ils emploient **2** j'emploierai **3** j'employais, nous employions **4** que j'emploie, que nous employions **5** employé

## [32] envoyer

**1** j'envoie, nous envoyons, ils envoient **2** j'enverrai **3** j'envoyais, nous envoyions **4** que j'envoie, que nous envoyions **5** envoyé

## [33] faire

**1** je fais, nous faisons (*say* /fəzɔ̃/), vous faites, ils font **2** je ferai **3** je faisais (*say* /fəze/) **4** que je fasse, que nous fassions **5** fait

## [34] falloir (*impersonal*)

**1** il faut **2** il faudra **3** il fallait **4** qu'il faille **5** fallu

## [35] fuir

**1** je fuis, nous fuyons **2** je fuirai **3** je fuyais, nous fuyions **4** que je fuie, que nous fuyions **5** fui

**1** Present Indicative **2** Future Indicative **3** Imperfect Indicative
**4** Present Subjunctive **5** Past Participle

## [36] haïr
**1** je hais, il hait, nous haïssons, ils haïssent **2** je haïrai **3** je haïssais **4** que je haïsse **5** haï

## [37] interdire
**1** j'interdis, vous interdisez **2** j'interdirai **3** j'interdisais **4** que j'interdise **5** interdit

## [38] jeter
**1** je jette, nous jetons, ils jettent **2** je jetterai **3** je jetais **4** que je jette **5** jeté

## [39] lire
**1** je lis, il lit, nous lisons **2** je lirai **3** je lisais **4** que je lise **5** lu

## [40] manger
**1** je mange, nous mangeons **2** je mangerai **3** je mangeais **4** que je mange, que nous mangions **5** mangé

## [41] maudire
**1** je maudis, il maudit, nous maudissons **2** je maudirai **3** je maudissais **4** que je maudisse **5** maudit

## [42] mettre
**1** je mets, tu mets, nous mettons **2** je mettrai **3** je mettais **4** que je mette **5** mis

## [43] mourir
**1** je meurs, il meurt, nous mourons **2** je mourrai **3** je mourais **4** que je meure **5** mort

## [44] naître
**1** je nais, il naît, nous naissons **2** je naîtrai **3** je naissais **4** que je naisse **5** né

## [45] oublier
**1** j'oublie, nous oublions, ils oublient **2** j'oublierai **3** j'oubliais, nous oubliions, vous oubliiez **4** que nous oubliions, que vous oubliiez **5** oublié

## [46] partir
**1** je pars, nous partons **2** je partirai **3** je partais **4** que je parte **5** parti

## [47] plaire
**1** je plais, il plaît (but il tait), nous plaisons **2** je plairai **3** je plaisais **4** que je plaise **5** plu

## [48] pleuvoir *(impersonal)*
**1** il pleut **2** il pleuvra **3** il pleuvait **4** qu'il pleuve **5** plu

## [49] pouvoir
**1** je peux, il peut, nous pouvons, ils peuvent **2** je pourrai **3** je pouvais **4** que je puisse, que nous puissions **5** pu

## [50] prendre
**1** je prends, il prend, nous prenons **2** je prendrai **3** je prenais **4** que je prenne **5** pris

---

**1** Present Indicative    **2** Future Indicative    **3** Imperfect Indicative
**4** Present Subjunctive    **5** Past Participle

## [51] prévoir

1 je prévois, il prévoit, nous prévoyons, ils prévoient 2 je prévoirai 3 je prévoyais, nous prévoyions 4 que je prévoie, que nous prévoyions 5 prévu

## [52] recevoir

1 je reçois, il reçoit, nous recevons, ils reçoivent 2 je recevrai 3 je recevais 4 que je reçoive, que nous recevions 5 reçu

## [53] résoudre

1 je résous, il résout, nous résolvons, ils résolvent 2 je résoudrai 3 je résolvais 4 que je résolve 5 résolu

## [54] rire

1 je ris, nous rions, ils rient 2 je rirai 3 je riais, nous riions 4 que je rie, que nous riions 5 ri

## [55] savoir

1 je sais, il sait, nous savons, ils savent 2 je saurai 3 je savais 4 que je sache, que nous sachions 5 su

## [56] suffire

1 il suffit, ils suffisent 2 il suffira 3 il suffisait 4 qu'il suffise 5 suffi (*but* frit)

## [57] suivre

1 je suis, il suit, nous suivons 2 je suivrai 3 je suivais 4 que je suive 5 suivi

## [58] tenir

1 je tiens, il tient, nous tenons, ils tiennent 2 je tiendrai 3 je tenais 4 que je tienne, que nous tenions 5 tenu

## [59] vaincre

1 je vaincs, il vainc, nous vainquons, ils vainquent 2 je vaincrai 3 je vainquais 4 que je vainque 5 vaincu

## [60] valoir

1 je vaux, il vaut, nous valons 2 je vaudrai 3 je valais 4 que je vaille, que nous valions 5 valu

## [61] vêtir

1 je vêts, il vêt, nous vêtons 2 je vêtirai 3 je vêtais 4 que je vête 5 vêtu

## [62] vivre

1 je vis, il vit, nous vivons, ils vivent 2 je vivrai 3 je vivais 4 que je vive 5 vécu

## [63] voir

1 je vois, nous voyons, ils voient 2 je verrai 3 je voyais, nous voyions 4 que je voie, que nous voyions 5 vu

## [64] vouloir

1 je veux, il veut, nous voulons, ils veulent 2 je voudrai 3 je voulais 4 que je veuille, que nous voulions 5 voulu

---

1 Present Indicative  2 Future Indicative  3 Imperfect Indicative
4 Present Subjunctive  5 Past Participle

## What are the equivalent tenses in English

**Present indicative**
je chante = I sing, I'm singing
**Future indicative**
je chanterai = I will sing
**Imperfect indicative**
je chantais = I was singing
**Perfect indicative**
j'ai chanté = I sang, I have sung
**Pluperfect indicative**
j'avais chanté = I had sung
**Present subjunctive**
bien que je chante = although I sing

**Present conditional**
si je pouvais, je chanterais
= if I could, I would sing
**Past participle**
chanté/chantée = sung

## How to conjugate a reflexive verb

**Present indicative and other simple tenses**
je me lave
tu te laves
il se lave
elle se lave
nous nous lavons
vous vous lavez
ils se lavent
elles se lavent
**in the negative form**
je ne me lave pas
tu ne te laves pas
il ne se lave pas
elle ne se lave pas
nous ne nous lavons pas
vous ne vous lavez pas
ils ne se lavent pas
elles ne se lavent pas

**Perfect indicative and other compound tenses**
*(always with auxiliary être)*
je me suis lavé
tu t'es lavé
il s'est lavé
elle s'est lavée
nous nous sommes lavés
vous vous êtes lavés
ils se sont lavés
elles se sont lavées
**in the negative form**
je ne me suis pas lavé
tu ne t'es pas lavé
il ne s'est pas lavé
elle ne s'est pas lavée
nous ne nous sommes pas lavés
vous ne vous êtes pas lavés
ils ne se sont pas lavés
elles ne se sont pas lavées

# Verbes irréguliers anglais

| Infinitif | Prétérit | Participe passé | Infinitif | Prétérit | Participe passé |
|---|---|---|---|---|---|
| **be** | was | been | **drive** | drove | driven |
| **bear** | bore | borne | **eat** | ate | eaten |
| **beat** | beat | beaten | **fall** | fell | fallen |
| **become** | became | become | **feed** | fed | fed |
| **begin** | began | begun | **feel** | felt | felt |
| **bend** | bent | bent | **fight** | fought | fought |
| **bet** | bet, | bet, | **find** | found | found |
| | betted | betted | **flee** | fled | fled |
| **bid** | bade, bid | bidden, bid | **fly** | flew | flown |
| **bind** | bound | bound | **freeze** | froze | frozen |
| **bite** | bit | bitten | **get** | got | got, gotten US |
| **bleed** | bled | bled | **give** | gave | given |
| **blow** | blew | blown | **go** | went | gone |
| **break** | broke | broken | **grow** | grew | grown |
| **breed** | bred | bred | **hang** | hung, | hung, |
| **bring** | brought | brought | | hanged | hanged |
| **build** | built | built | **have** | had | had |
| **burn** | burnt, | burnt, | **hear** | heard | heard |
| | burned | burned | **hide** | hid | hidden |
| **burst** | burst | burst | **hit** | hit | hit |
| **buy** | bought | bought | **hold** | held | held |
| **catch** | caught | caught | **hurt** | hurt | hurt |
| **choose** | chose | chosen | **keep** | kept | kept |
| **cling** | clung | clung | **kneel** | knelt | knelt |
| **come** | came | come | **know** | knew | known |
| **cost** | cost, | cost, | **lay** | laid | laid |
| | costed (vt) | costed | **lead** | led | led |
| **cut** | cut | cut | **lean** | leaned, | leaned, |
| **deal** | dealt | dealt | | leant | leant |
| **dig** | dug | dug | | | |
| **do** | did | done | **learn** | learnt, | learnt, |
| **draw** | drew | drawn | | learned | learned |
| **dream** | dreamt, | dreamt, | **leave** | left | left |
| | dreamed | dreamed | **lend** | lent | lent |
| **drink** | drank | drunk | **let** | let | let |
| | | | **lie** | lay | lain |

| Infinitif | Prétérit | Participe passé | Infinitif | Prétérit | Participe passé |
|---|---|---|---|---|---|
| **lose** | lost | lost | **spend** | spent | spent |
| **make** | made | made | **spit** | spat | spat |
| **mean** | meant | meant | **spoil** | spoilt, spoiled | spoilt, spoiled |
| **meet** | met | met | | | |
| **pay** | paid | paid | **spread** | spread | spread |
| **put** | put | put | **spring** | sprang | sprung |
| **read** | read | read | **stand** | stood | stood |
| **ride** | rode | ridden | **steal** | stole | stolen |
| **ring** | rang | rung | **stick** | stuck | stuck |
| **rise** | rose | risen | **sting** | stung | stung |
| **run** | ran | run | **stride** | strode | stridden |
| **say** | said | said | **strike** | struck | struck |
| **see** | saw | seen | **swear** | swore | sworn |
| **seek** | sought | sought | **sweep** | swept | swept |
| **sell** | sold | sold | **swell** | swelled | swollen, swelled |
| **send** | sent | sent | | | |
| **set** | set | set | **swim** | swam | swum |
| **sew** | sewed | sewn, sewed | **swing** | swung | swung |
| **shake** | shook | shaken | **take** | took | taken |
| **shine** | shone | shone | **teach** | taught | taught |
| **shoe** | shod | shod | **tear** | tore | torn |
| **shoot** | shot | shot | **tell** | told | told |
| **show** | showed | shown | **think** | thought | thought |
| **shut** | shut | shut | **throw** | threw | thrown |
| **sing** | sang | sung | **thrust** | thrust | thrust |
| **sink** | sank | sunk | **tread** | trod | trodden |
| **sit** | sat | sat | **under-stand** | under-stood | understood |
| **sleep** | slept | slept | | | |
| **sling** | slung | slung | **wake** | woke | woken |
| **smell** | smelt, smelled | smelt, smelled | **wear** | wore | worn |
| | | | **win** | won | won |
| **speak** | spoke | spoken | **write** | wrote | written |
| **spell** | spelled, spelt | spelled, spelt | | | |

# Numbers/Les nombres

## cardinal numbers/ les nombres cardinaux

| | |
|---|---|
| 0 | zero **zéro** |
| 1 | one **un** |
| 2 | two **deux** |
| 3 | three **trois** |
| 4 | four **quatre** |
| 5 | five **cinq** |
| 6 | six **six** |
| 7 | seven **sept** |
| 8 | eight **huit** |
| 9 | nine **neuf** |
| 10 | ten **dix** |
| 11 | eleven **onze** |
| 12 | twelve **douze** |
| 13 | thirteen **treize** |
| 14 | fourteen **quatorze** |
| 15 | fifteen **quinze** |
| 16 | sixteen **seize** |
| 17 | seventeen **dix-sept** |
| 18 | eighteen **dix-huit** |
| 19 | nineteen **dix-neuf** |
| 20 | twenty **vingt** |
| 21 | twenty-one **vingt et un** |
| 22 | twenty-two **vingt-deux** |
| 30 | thirty **trente** |
| 40 | forty **quarante** |
| 50 | fifty **cinquante** |
| 60 | sixty **soixante** |
| 70 | seventy **soixante-dix** |
| 80 | eighty **quatre-vingt** |
| 90 | ninety **quatre-vingt-dix** |

| | |
|---|---|
| 100 | a hundred **cent** |
| 101 | a hundred and one **cent un** |
| 110 | a hundred and ten **cent dix** |
| 200 | two hundred **deux cents** |
| 250 | two hundred and fifty **deux cent cinquante** |
| 1,000 | one thousand **mille** |
| 1,001 | one thousand and one **mille un** |
| 2,000 | two thousand **deux mille** |
| 10,000 | ten thousand **dix mille** |
| 100,000 | a hundred thousand **cent mille** |
| 1,000,000 | a million **un million** |

## Ordinal numbers/ Les nombres ordinaux

| | | |
|---|---|---|
| 1st | first | **premier** |
| 2nd | second | **deuxième** |
| 3rd | third | **troisième** |
| 4th | fourth | **quatrième** |
| 5th | fifth | **cinquième** |
| 6th | sixth | **sixième** |
| 7th | seventh | **septième** |
| 8th | eighth | **huitième** |
| 9th | ninth | **neuvième** |
| 10th | tenth | **dixième** |
| 11th | eleventh | **onzième** |
| 12th | twelfth | **douzième** |
| 13th | thirteenth | **treizième** |
| 14th | fourteenth | **quatorzième** |
| 15th | fifteenth | **quinzième** |

| | | |
|---|---|---|
| 16th | sixteenth **seizième** | |
| 17th | seventeenth **dix-septième** | |
| 18th | eighteenth **dix-huitième** | |
| 19th | nineteenth **dix-neuvième** | |
| 20th | twentieth **vingtième** | |
| 21st | twenty-first **vingt et unième** | |
| 22nd | twenty-second **vingt-deuxième** | |
| 30th | thirtieth **trentième** | |
| 40th | fortieth **quarantième** | |
| 50th | fiftieth **cinquantième** | |
| 60th | sixtieth **soixantième** | |
| 70th | seventieth **soixante-dixième** | |
| 80th | eightieth **quatre-vingtième** | |
| 90th | ninetieth **quatre-vingt-dixième** | |
| 100th | hundredth **centième** | |
| 101st | hundred and first **cent unième** | |
| 110th | hundred and tenth **cent dixième** | |
| 200th | two hundredth **deux centième** | |
| 250th | two hundred and fiftieth **deux cent cinquantième** | |
| 1,000th | thousandth **millième** | |
| 1,001st | thousand and first **mille et unième** | |
| 2,000th | two thousandth **deux millième** | |
| 10,000th | ten thousandth **dix millième** | |
| 100,000th | hundred thousandth **cent millième** | |
| 1,000,000th | millionth **millionième** | |

## Fractions/Les fractions

| | | |
|---|---|---|
| ½ | a half **un demi** | |
| ⅓ | a third **un tiers** | |
| ¼ | a quarter **un quart** | |
| ⅒ | a tenth **un dixième** | |
| ⅔ | two-thirds **deux tiers** | |
| ⅝ | five-eighths **cinq huitième** | |
| ¹⁄₁₀₀ | one hundredth **un centième** | |
| 1½ | one and a half **un et demi** | |
| 2¼ | two and a quarter **deux et un quart** | |

## Decimals/Les décimaux

| | | |
|---|---|---|
| 0.1 | point one **zéro virgule un** | |
| 0.25 | point two five **zéro virgule vingt-cinq** | |
| 1.2 | one point two **un virgule deux** | |
| 1.46 | one point four six **un virgule quarante-six** | |

## Percentages/Pourcentages

| | | |
|---|---|---|
| 25% | twenty-five per cent **vingt-cinq pour cent** | |
| 50% | fifty per cent **cinquante pour cent** | |
| 100% | a hundred per cent **cent pour cent** | |
| 365% | three hundred and sixty-five per cent **trois cent soixante-cinq pour cent** | |
| 4.25% | four point two five per cent **quatre virgule vingt-cinq pour cent** | |